The **Rough Gui**

Greec

written and researched by

Lance Chilton, Marc Dubin, Nick Edwards, Mark Ellingham, John Fisher, Geoff Garvey and Natania Jansz

with additional contributions by

Michael Haag and George Pissalides

NEW YORK • LONDON • DELHI

www.roughguides.com

Contents

◀◀ Taverna, Amorgós ◀ Shipwreck Bay, Zákynthos

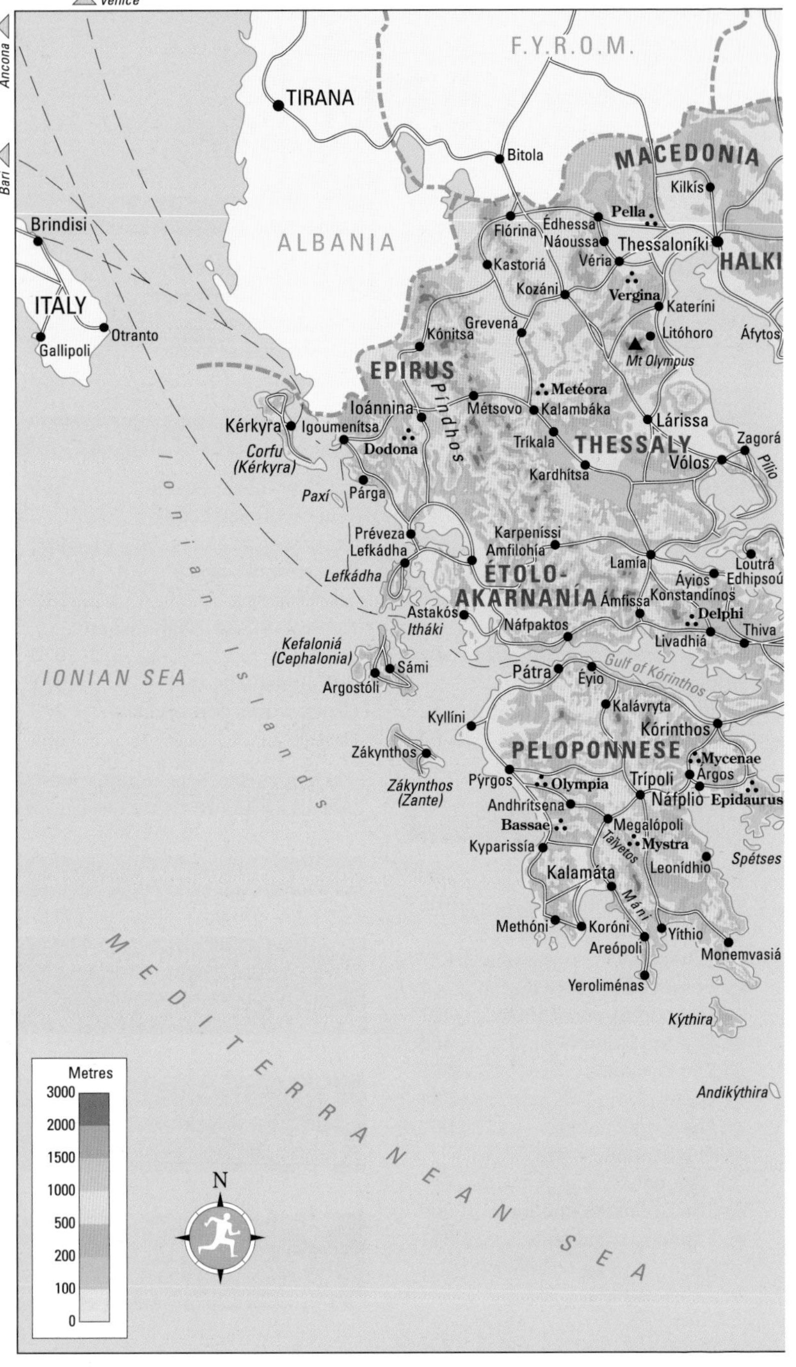
Venice
Ancona
Bari
F.Y.R.O.M.
TIRANA
Bitola
MACEDONIA
Kilkís
ALBANIA
Brindisi
ITALY
Otranto
Gallipoli
Pella
Flórina
Édhessa
Náoussa
Thessaloníki
HALKI
Kastoriá
Véria
Kozáni
Vergina
Kateríni
Grevená
Kónitsa
Litóhoro
Áfytos
Mt Olympus
EPIRUS
Píndhos
Metéora
Ioánnina
Métsovo
Kalambáka
Kérkyra
Igoumenítsa
Dodona
Lárissa
Corfu (Kérkyra)
Tríkala
THESSALY
Zagorá
Vólos
Pílio
Kardhítsa
Paxí
Párga
Ionian Islands
Préveza
Lefkádha
Karpeníssi
Amfilohía
Lamía
Loutrá Edhipsoú
Lefkádha
ÉTOLO-AKARNANÍA
Áyios Konstandínos
Ámfissa
Delphi
Astakós
Itháki
Náfpaktos
Thiva
Livadhiá
Kefaloniá (Cephalonia)
Sámi
Gulf of Kórinthos
IONIAN SEA
Argostóli
Pátra
Éyio
Kalávryta
Kyllíni
Kórinthos
Zákynthos
PELOPONNESE
Mycenae
Pýrgos
Olympia
Trípoli
Argos
Zákynthos (Zante)
Náfplio
Epidaurus
Andhrítsena
Megalópoli
Bassae
Mystra
Kyparissía
Taïyetos
Leonídhio
Spétses
Kalamáta
Máni
Methóni
Koróni
Yíthio
Areópoli
Monemvasiá
Yeroliménas
Kýthira
Andikýthira
MEDITERRANEAN SEA
Metres
3000
2000
1500
1000
500
200
100
0
N

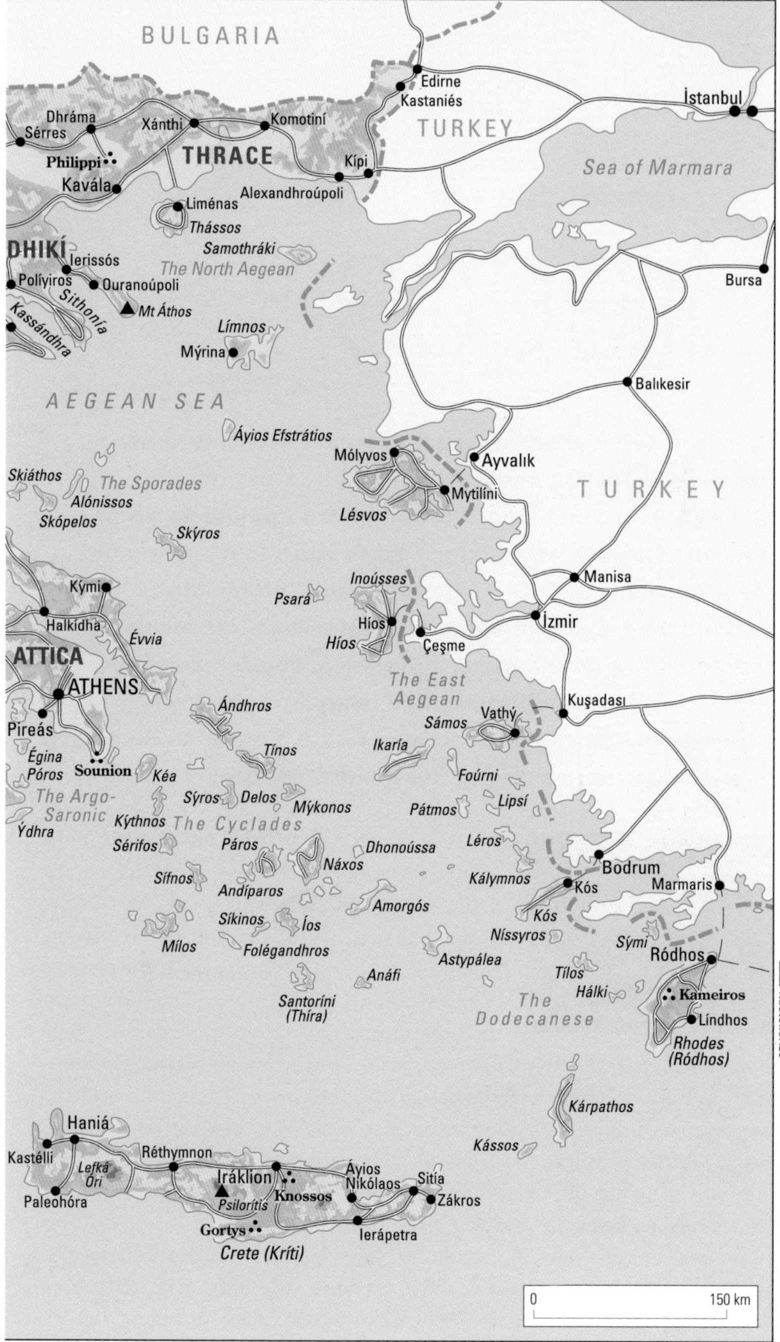
BULGARIA
Edirne
Kastaniés
İstanbul
TURKEY
Dhráma
Sérres
Xánthi
Komotiní
Philippi
THRACE
Kípi
Sea of Marmara
Kavála
Alexandhroúpoli
Liménas
Thássos
Samothráki
DHIKÍ
Ierissós
The North Aegean
Bursa
Políyiros
Ouranoúpoli
Sithonía
Mt Áthos
Kassándhra
Límnos
Mýrina
Balıkesir
AEGEAN SEA
Áyios Efstrátios
Mólyvos
Ayvalık
Skiáthos
The Sporades
Mytilíni
TURKEY
Alónissos
Lésvos
Skópelos
Skýros
Manisa
Inoússes
Kými
Psará
İzmir
Halkídha
Híos
Évvia
Híos
Çeşme
ATTICA
The East Aegean
ATHENS
Kuşadası
Ándhros
Vathý
Pireás
Sámos
Tínos
Ikaría
Égina
Póros
Sounion
Kéa
Foúrni
The Argo-Saronic
Sýros
Delos
Mýkonos
Pátmos
Lipsí
Ýdhra
Kýthnos
The Cyclades
Sérifos
Páros
Dhonoússa
Léros
Bodrum
Náxos
Sífnos
Kálymnos
Kós
Marmaris
Andíparos
Amorgós
Kós
Síkinos
Íos
Níssyros
Sými
Mílos
Folégandhros
Ródhos
Astypálea
Anáfi
Tílos
Kastellórizo
Santoríni (Thíra)
The Dodecanese
Hálki
Kameiros
Líndhos
Rhodes (Ródhos)
Kárpathos
Haniá
Kássos
Kastélli
Réthymnon
Lefká Óri
Áyios Nikólaos
Sitía
Iráklion
Knossos
Zákros
Psiloritis
Paleohóra
Gortys
Ierápetra
Crete (Kríti)
0
150 km

Introduction to Greece

With over sixty inhabited islands and a territory that stretches from the south Aegean Sea to the middle of the Balkan peninsula, Greece offers enough to fill months of travel. The historic sites span four millennia, encompassing both the legendary and the obscure, where a visit can still seem like a personal discovery. Beaches are parcelled out along a convoluted coastline equal to France's in length, and islands range from backwaters where the boat calls twice a week to resorts as cosmopolitan as any in the Mediterranean.

Modern Greece is the result of extraordinarily diverse **influences**. Romans, Arabs, Latin Crusaders, Venetians, Slavs, Albanians, Turks, Italians, not to mention the Byzantine Empire, have been and gone since the time of Alexander the Great. All have left their mark: the Byzantines in countless churches and monasteries; the Venetians in impregnable fortifications in the Peloponnese; and other Latin powers, such as the Knights of Saint John and the Genoese, in imposing castles across the northern and eastern Aegean. Equally obvious is the heritage of four centuries of Ottoman Turkish rule which, while universally derided, contributed substantially to Greek music, cuisine, language and the way of life. Significant, and still-existing, minorities – Vlachs, Muslims, Catholics, Jews, Gypsies – have also helped to forge the hard-to-define but resilient **Hellenic identity**, which has kept alive the people's sense of themselves throughout their turbulent history.

With no indigenous ruling class or formal Renaissance period to impose superior models of taste or patronize the arts, medieval Greek peasants, fishermen and shepherds created a vigorous and truly **folk culture**, which found expression in the songs and dances, costumes, embroidery, carved furniture and the white cubist houses of popular imagination. Since the 1960s much of this has disappeared under the impact of Western consumer values, relegated to folklore museums at best, but recently the country's architectural and musical heritage in particular have undergone a renaissance, with buildings rescued from dereliction and performers reviving half-forgotten musical traditions.

Not to be missed are Greece's great ancient sites and medieval castles

Of course there are also formal cultural activities: **museums** that shouldn't be missed, magnificent medieval mansions and **castles**, as well as the great **ancient sites** dating from the Neolithic,

▲ Ancient olive tree

Fact file

- Greece is one of the EU's 27 members, its **surface area** of 131,957 square kilometres (50,949 square miles) divided into 51 provinces. No other country, except Indonesia, Denmark and the Philippines, has so much territory in the form of islands. The **population** is overwhelmingly **Greek-speaking** and 95 percent are **Greek Orthodox** in faith, though there are Catholic, Sunni Muslim, Jewish, Armenian and evangelical Christian minorities, plus pockets of Turkish-, Romany- and Macedonian-speakers. Well over half the population live in urban areas.
- Per "native" population of 10.4 million, Greece has Europe's highest proportion of **immigrants** – officially 800,000, but effectively 1.4 million, two-thirds of these Albanian.
- Greece is a **parliamentary republic**, with the president as head of state, and a 300-seat parliament led by the prime minister. PASOK, the (ostensibly) social-democratic party, governed for 19 of 23 years after 1981, finally being ousted in 2004 by the centre-right Néa Dhimokratía party, returned to power by a narrower margin in 2007. There are also two small communist parties which between them typically pick up eight to ten percent of the vote, and a far-right nationalist party, LAOS, at four percent.
- **Tourism** is the country's main foreign-currency earner. **Shipping** ranks second, with banking, services and light industry gaining on **agricultural products** such as olive oil and olives, citrus and wine.

▲ Rhodes Old Town

Mycenean, Minoan, Classical, Hellenistic, Roman and Byzantine eras. Greece hosts some excellent summer **festivals** too, bringing international theatre, dance and musical groups to perform at ancient theatres, as well as castle courtyards and more contemporary venues in coastal and island resorts.

But the call to cultural duty will never be too overwhelming on a Greek holiday. The **hedonistic pleasures** of languor and warmth – going lightly dressed, swimming in balmy seas at dusk, talking and drinking under the stars – are just as appealing. Despite recent improvements to the tourism "product", Greece is still essentially a land for easy-going sybarites, not for those who crave orthopaedic mattresses, faultless plumbing, cordon bleu cuisine and obsequious service. Except at the growing number of luxury facilities in new or restored buildings, hotel and pension rooms can be box-like; Greek food at its best is fresh, abundant and uncomplicated.

The Greek people

To attempt an understanding of the Greek people, it's useful to realize just how recent and traumatic were the events that created the modern state and **national character** – the latter a complex blend of extroversion and pessimism, which cannot be accounted for merely by Greece's position as a natural bridge between Europe and the Middle East. Until the early decades of the twentieth century many parts of Greece were under Ottoman (or in the case of the Dodecanese, Italian) rule. Meanwhile, numerous Greek Orthodox lived in Asia Minor, Egypt, western Europe and in the northern Balkans. The Balkan Wars of 1912–13, Greece's 1917–18 World War I involvement fighting Bulgaria, the Greco–Turkish war of 1919–22 and the organized **population exchanges** – essentially regulated ethnic cleansing – which followed each of these conflicts had sudden, profound effects. Worse was to come during World War II, and its aftermath of **civil war** between the Communists and the UK- and US-backed Nationalist government forces. The viciousness of this period found a later echo in nearly seven years of **military dictatorship** under the colonels' junta between 1967 and 1974.

Such memories of misrule, diaspora and catastrophe (including frequent, devastating earthquakes) remain uncomfortably close for many Greeks, despite three-plus decades of democratic stability and the country's absorption into the EU. The poverty and enduring lack of opportunity long frustrated talented and resourceful Greeks, many of whom **emigrated**. Those who stayed were lulled, until the late 1980s, by a civil-service-driven full-employment policy which resulted in the lowest jobless rate in western Europe. The downside of this was a staggering lack of worker initiative and a burgeoning public deficit, but official attempts to impose a more austere economic line are still often met by strikes. Since the early 1990s, Greece has become fully integrated into the Western economy, privatization and competition have demolished state monopolies, and inevitably growing disparities in wealth have appeared.

The Evil Eye

Belief in the Evil Eye (in Greek, simply *to máti* or "the Eye") is pan-Mediterranean and goes at least as far back as Roman times, but nowhere has it hung on so tenaciously as in Greece (and neighbouring coastal Turkey). In a nutshell, whenever something attractive, valuable or unusual – an infant, a new car, a prized animal – becomes suddenly, inexplicably indisposed, it is assumed to be *matiasméno* or "eyed". Blue-eyed individuals are thought most capable of casting this spell, always unintentionally or at least unconsciously (unlike *máyia* or wilful black magic). The diagnosis is confirmed by discreet referral to a "wise woman", who is also versed in the proper counter-spell. But prevention is always better than cure, and this involves two main strategies. When admiring something or someone, the admirer – blue-eyed or otherwise – must mock-spit ("*phtoo, phtoo, phtoo*!") to counteract any stirrings of envy which, according to anthropologists, are the root-cause of the Eye. And the proud owners or parents will protect the object of admiration in advance with a blue amulet, hung about the baby's/animal's neck or the car's rear-view mirror, or even painted directly onto a boat-bow.

Wayside shrines

Throughout Greece you'll see, by the side of the road, small shrines or *proskynitária* which usually hold a saint's icon, an oil lamp, a few floatable wicks and a box of matches. Unlike in Latin America, they don't necessarily mark the spot where someone met their end in a motoring accident (though increasingly they do); typically they were erected by a family or even one individual in fulfilment of a vow or *támma* to a specific saint in thanks for favours granted, in particular being spared de ath in a road mishap. *Proskynitária* come in various sizes and designs, from spindly, derrick-like metal constructions to sumptuous, gaily painted models of small cathedrals in marble and plaster which you can practically walk into. Often they indicate the presence of a larger but less convenient (and often locked) church off in the countryside nearby, dedicated to the same saint, and act as a substitute shrine where the devout wayfarer can pay reverence to the icon it contains.

The meticulousness of traditional Greek craftworkers was legendary, even if their values and skills took a back seat to the demands of crisis and profiteering when the evacuation of Asia Minor and the rapid 1950s depopulation of rural villages prompted the graceless **urbanization** of Athens and other cities. Amidst the often superficial sophistication that resulted, it's easy to forget the nearness of the village past and stubbornly lingering Third World attributes. Buses operate with Teutonic efficiency, but ferries sail with an unpredictability little changed since the time of Odysseus; privately run banks are state-of-the-art, but health care provision is woeful.

Social attitudes, too, underwent a sea change as Greece adapted to mass tourism and modern life. The encounter was painful and at times destructive, as the values of a rural, conservative society have been irrevocably lost. Though younger Greeks are flexible as they rake the proceeds into the till, at least in tourist areas, visitors still need to be sensitive in their behaviour towards the older generation. The mind boggles imagining the reaction of black-clad elders to nudism, or even scanty clothing, in a country where the **Orthodox church** was, until the 1990s, an all-but-established faith and the self-appointed guardian of national identity. Orthodoxy is still seen by many as synonymous with Greekness – as in the huge 2000 row surrounding the EU-mandated removal of religious affiliation from identity cards. Although senior clerics have since then almost completely

▲ Helmos Ski Centre, Kalávryta, Peloponnese

depleted a huge reservoir of respect with regressive stances on a number of social issues, and a string of literally ungodly scandals throughout 2004–05, even the most cynical, worldly young Greeks – who never otherwise set foot in a church – are still likely to be married, buried and have their children baptized with Orthodox rites.

Where to go

Sprawling, polluted **Athens** is an obligatory, almost unavoidable introduction to Greece. Home to over a third of the population, on first acquaintance the city is a nightmare for many, but also – as Greeks themselves often joke – *tó megálo horió*: the largest "village" in the country. It also offers the widest range of cultural diversions, from museums to concerts; the best-stocked shops; some of the most accomplished restaurants and stimulating clubs, plus – due to its hosting of the 2004 summer Olympics – a noticeably improved infrastructure. **Thessaloníki**, the metropolis of the North, after years of playing provincial second fiddle to the capital, has emerged in its own right as a stimulating, cutting-edge place with restaurants and nightlife to match Athens', Byzantine monuments compensating for a lack of "ancient" ones, and – among the inhabitants – a tremendous capacity for enjoying life. In all honesty, there are no other "world class" cities in Greece. The mainland shows its best side in the well-preserved ruins of **Corinth**, **Olympia** and **Delphi** (plus the Athenian **Parthenon**), the frescoed and mosaic-ed Byzantine churches and monasteries at **Mount**

Áthos, **Metéora**, **Ósios Loukás**, **Kastoriá**, **Árta** and **Mystra**, the massive fortified towns of **Monemvasiá**, **Náfplio**, **Koróni** and **Methóni**, the distinctive architecture of **Zagóri**, **Pílio** and the **Máni**, and the long, sandy **beaches** on the Peloponnesian, Pílio and Epirot coast. Perhaps more surprisingly, the mainland mountains offer some of the best and least-exploited hiking, rafting, canyoning and skiing in southeastern Europe.

Out in the Aegean or Ionian seas, you're even more spoilt for choice. Perhaps the best strategy for initial visits is to sample assorted **islands** from neighbouring archipelagos – Crete, the Dodecanese, the Cyclades and the northeast Aegean are all reasonably well connected with each other, though the Sporades, Argo-Saronic and Ionian groups offer limited (or no) possibilities for island-hopping. If time and money are short, the best place to head for is well-preserved **Ýdhra** in the Argo-Saronic Gulf, just a short ride from Pireás (the main port of Athens), but an utterly different place once the day-cruises have gone. Similarly, **Skýros**, remotest and most unspoilt of the Sporades, is a good choice within modest reach of Athens or Thessaloníki. Among the Cyclades, cataclysmically volcanic **Santoríni (Thíra)** and **Mýkonos** with its perfectly preserved harbour-town rank as must-see spectacles, but fertile, mountainous **Náxos**, dramatically cliff-girt **Amorgós** or gently rolling **Sífnos** have life more independent of cruise-ship tourism and seem more amenable to long stays. **Crete** could (and does) fill an entire Rough Guide to itself, but the highlights here are **Knossos** and the nearby **archeological museum** in

The mainland mountains offer some of the best hiking, rafting and skiing in southeastern Europe

▼ Hadrian's Arch, Athens

The períptero

The *períptero* or pavement kiosk is a quintessentially Greek institution. They originally began as a government-sponsored employment scheme for wounded veterans of the Balkan Wars and World War I; the concessions are jealously guarded by their descendants or sold on for tidy sums. Positioned on platíes and strategic thoroughfares all over Greece, they keep long hours and contribute considerably to the air of public street-safety after dark. If you are lost, the *períptero* is the first place to go for directions, and they usually know what you're looking for. Their stock in trade is predictable: sweets, bagged nuts, tissues, newspapers, magazines, bus tickets, shaving needs, key-rings with football-team logos, cigarettes, pens and pencils, (often heat-damaged) photo film, plus cold drinks. Most of them used to have at least one telephone, with a queue of customers waiting their turn to shout down a crackly line, either across town or across the globe. Now, few kiosks sport even a card-phone, but they're still one of the best places to buy a top-up card for your Greek pay-as-you-go mobile, or discount calling card for fixed phones.

Iráklion, the other Minoan palaces at **Phaestos** and **Ayía Triádha**, and the west in general – the proud city of **Haniá**, with its hinterland extending to the relatively unspoilt southwest coast, reachable via the fabled **Samariá Gorge**. **Rhodes**, with its unique old town, is capital of the Dodecanese, but picturesque, Neoclassical **Sými** opposite, and austere, volcanic **Pátmos**, the island of Revelations, are far more manageable. It's easy to continue north via **Híos**, with its striking medieval architecture, to balmy, olive-cloaked **Lésvos**, perhaps the most traditional island in its way of life. The Ionian islands are – probably more than any other spots except Crete, Skiáthos, Kós and Rhodes – package-holiday territory, but if you're leaving Greece towards Italy by all means stop off at **Corfu** to at least savour the Venetian-style main town, which along with neighbouring **Paxí** islet avoided severe 1953 earthquake damage.

When to go

Most places and people are far more agreeable, and resolutely Greek, outside the mid-July-to-end-August **peak season**, when soaring temperatures, plus crowds of foreigners and locals alike, can be overpowering. You won't miss out on **warm weather** if you come in **June or September**, excellent times almost everywhere but particularly in the islands. An exception to this pattern, however, is the north-mainland coast – notably the Halkidhikí peninsula – and the islands of Samothráki and Thássos, which only really cater to visitors during **July and August**. In mid-**October** you will almost certainly hit a stormy spell, especially in western Greece or in the mountains, but for most of that month the "little summer of Áyios Dhimítrios" (the Greek equivalent of **Indian summer**) prevails, and the southerly Dodecanese and Crete are extremely pleasant. Autumn in general is beautiful; the light is softer, the sea often balmier than the air and the colours subtler.

December to March are the coldest and least reliably sunny months, though even then there are many crystal-clear, fine days, and the glorious lowland flowers begin to bloom very early in spring. The more northerly latitudes and high altitudes endure far colder and wetter conditions, with the mountains themselves under snow from November to May. The **mildest winter** climate is found on Rhodes, or in the southeastern parts of Crete. As spring slowly warms up, **April** is still uncertain, though superb for wild flowers, green landscapes and photography; by **May** the weather is more settled and predictable, and Crete, the Peloponnese, the Ionian islands and the Cyclades are perhaps at their best, even if the sea is still a little cool for swimming. However, thanks to global climate change, recent years have seen erratic weather, with unusually cold Mays, often warm Octobers, severe downpours and flooding in odd months, unpredictable summer heat levels and usually wet (though not always cold) winters, plus much earlier spring flowering.

Other factors that affect ideal timing for Greek travels have to do with the level of tourism and the amenities provided. Late May, especially half-term week in the UK, can be surprisingly busy. Service standards, particularly in tavernas, slip under high-season pressure, and room rates top out from

▲ Tour boats, Spinalónga, Crete

mid-July to about September 10 (as well as during Easter or Christmas week). If you can only visit during midsummer, reserve a package well in advance, or plan your itinerary off the beaten track: you might for example explore the less obvious parts of the Peloponnese and the northern mainland, or island-hop with an eye for the remoter places.

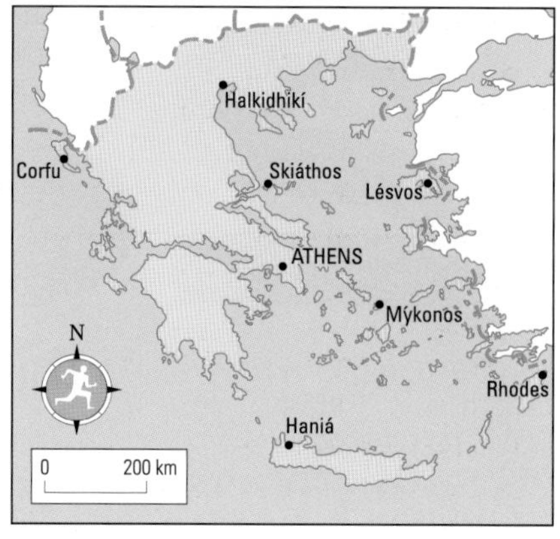

Out of season, especially between late October and late April, you have to contend with reduced ferry and plane services (and nonexistent hydrofoil or catamaran departures), plus fairly skeletal facilities when you arrive. You will, however, find reasonable service on main routes and at least one hotel and taverna open in the port or main town of all but the tiniest isles. On the mainland, winter travel poses no special difficulties except, of course, in mountain villages either cut off by snow or (at weekends especially) monopolized by avid Greek skiers.

Average temperatures (°F) and rainfall

	Jan			Mar			May			July			Sept			Nov		
	°F		Rain	°F		Rain	°F		Rain	°F		Rain	°F		Rain	°F		Rain
	Max	Min	Days	Max	Min	Days	Max	Min	Days	Max	Min	Days	Max	Min	Days	Max	Min	Days
Athens																		
	54	44	13	60	46	10	76	60	9	90	72	2	84	66	4	65	52	12
Crete (Haniá)																		
	60	46	17	64	48	11	76	56	5	86	68	0	82	64	3	70	54	10
Cyclades (Mýkonos)																		
	58	50	14	62	52	8	72	62	5	82	72	0.5	78	68	1	66	58	9
North Greece (Halkidhikí)																		
	50	36	7	59	44	9	77	58	10	90	70	4	83	64	5	60	47	9
Ionians (Corfu)																		
	56	44	13	62	46	10	74	58	6	88	70	2	82	64	5	66	52	12
Dodecanese (Rhodes)																		
	58	50	15	62	48	7	74	58	2	86	70	0	82	72	1	68	60	7
Sporades (Skiáthos)																		
	55	45	12	58	47	10	71	58	3	82	71	0	75	64	8	62	53	12
East Aegean (Lésvos)																		
	54	42	11	60	46	7	76	60	6	88	70	2	82	66	2	64	50	9

28 things not to miss

It's not possible to see everything that Greece has to offer in one trip – and we don't suggest you try. What follows is a selective taste of the country's highlights: outstanding buildings and ancient sites, natural wonders and colourful festivals. They're arranged in five colour-coded categories, which you can browse through to find the very best things to see and experience. All highlights have a page reference to take you straight into the guide, where you can find out more.

01 Hozoviótissa Monastery Page **567** • Wedged into a sheer cliff-face with only its facade showing, this monastery is the pride and joy of rugged, friendly Amorgós, hikers' mecca of the Cyclades.

02 Sámos Page **743** • Despite recent fires, Sámos remains arguably the most verdant and beautiful of the east Aegean islands.

03 Ósios Loukás Page **285** • Decorated with vivid mosaics, Ósios Loukás monastery ranks as one of Greece's finest Byzantine buildings.

04 Monemvasiá Page **202** • The heavily fortified medieval town of Monemvasiá shelters on the south flank of its island-like rock.

05 Samariá Gorge Crete's Page **647** • The magnificent Samariá Gorge is the longest in Europe.

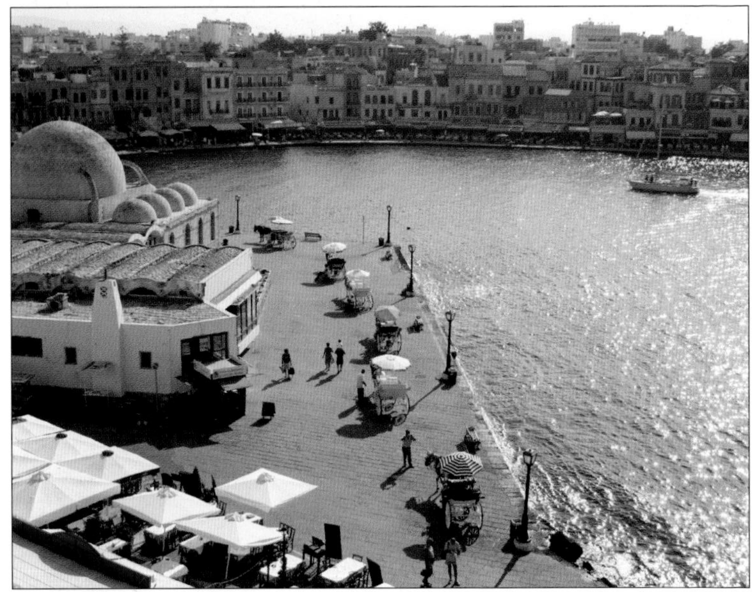

06 Haniá Old Town waterfront Page **642** • Haniá, Crete's most lively town, displays intriguing vestiges of its Venetian and Ottoman past.

07 Yialós harbour Page 693 • The mansions of Sými's picturesque harbour, built with wealth from the sponge trade, are part of an architecturally protected area.

08 Mount Pílio Page 314 • Mount Pílio peninsula has it all: lush countryside, excellent beaches, characterful villages and some superb hiking trails.

09 Knossos palace, Crete Page 602 • The most restored, vividly coloured and ultimately the most exciting of Crete's Minoan palaces.

10 Lindos acropolis, Rhodes Page **680** • The Hellenistic acropolis of Lindos, high above modern Líndhos village, offers magnificent views along the length of Rhodes island.

12 The Metéora Page **338** • The exquisite Byzantine monasteries of the Metéora, perched atop pinnacles of rock, are mainland Greece's most extraordinary sight.

11 Mystra Page **231** • The Byzantine town of Mystra is the best-preserved and most dramatic site in the Peloponnese.

13 Beaches and watersports Page **61** • Greece's extensive coast provides numerous opportunities for getting into the water, or just lying next to it.

14 Loggerhead sea turtle Page **385** • The Ionian islands harbour one of the Mediterranean's main concentrations of the endangered loggerhead sea turtle.

15 Kérkyra (Corfu) old town Page **845** • With its elegant Venetian architecture and fine museums, Corfu's capital is the cultural heart of the Ionians.

16 Delphi's Tholos Page **292** • Delphi, site of the famous oracle, was believed by the ancient Greeks to be the centre of the earth.

17 Mount Olympus Page **429** • Believed by the ancient Greeks to be the home of the gods, Mount Olympus is Greece's highest and most magical mountain.

18 Préspa lakes Page **443** • The eerily beautiful Préspa lakes are a haven for birds and other wildlife.

19 Monastery of Ayíou Ioánnou Theológou, Pátmos Page **732** • Built in honour of St John the Divine, this huge monastery is a warren of interconnecting courtyards, chapels, stairways, arcades, galleries and roof terraces.

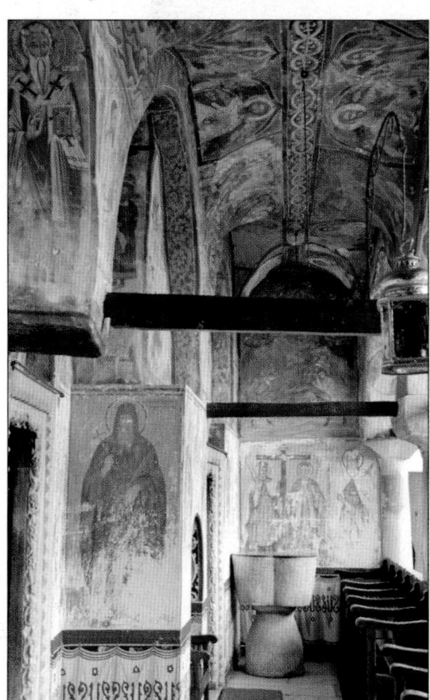

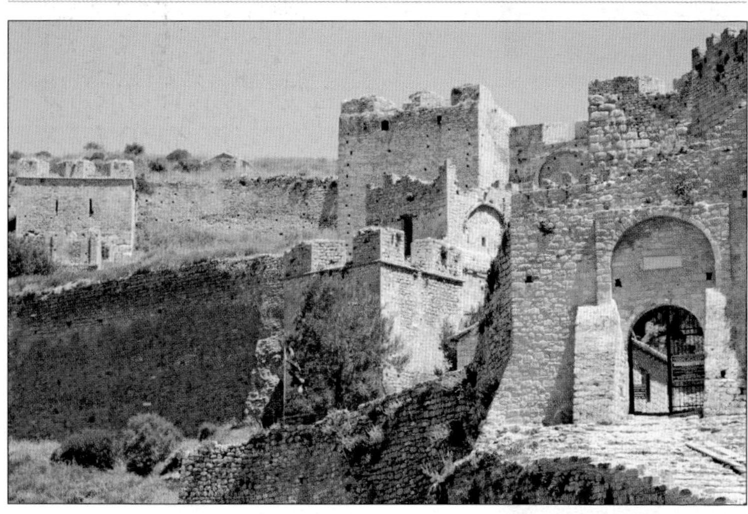

20 Fortifications of Acrocorinth Page **173** • Acrocorinth is a huge, barren rock crowned by a great medieval fortress.

21 Skýros Town Page **825** • Topped with a castle, the old town of Skýros is an architectural showcase, and hosts Greece's liveliest pre-Lenten carnival.

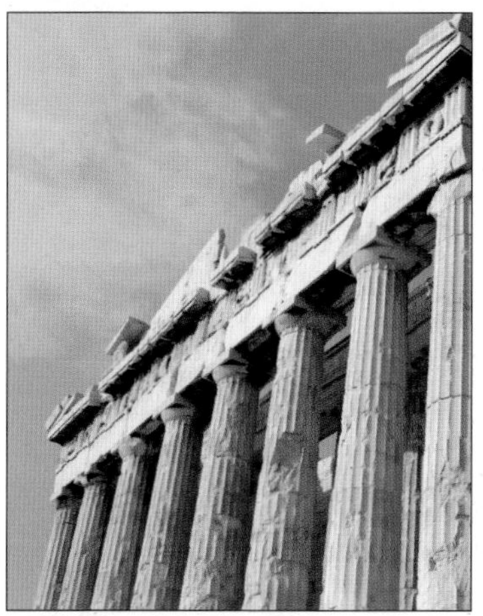

22 The Acropolis Page **100** • Dominating Athens, the Acropolis is as fascinating as it is famous.

23 Osíou Grigoríou monastery, Mount Áthos Page **463** • Almost protruding into the sea, Osíou Grigoríou is one of twenty monasteries in the "monks' republic" of Mount Áthos.

24 Náfplio Page **185** • Elegant, Venetian-flavoured Náfplio covers a peninsula in the Argolid Gulf, culminating in the massive Palamídhi fortress.

25 Nightlife Page **147** • The after-dark scene in Athens (shown here) and the most popular island resorts is lively, varied and long.

27 Víkos Gorge Page **369** • A hike through or around the Víkos Gorge is likely to be one of the highlights of a visit to the Zagóri region.

26 Lion Gate, Mycenae Page **180** • Imposing relief lions guard the main entrance to the Citadel of Mycenae.

28 Windsurfing off Vassilikí, Lefkádha Page **866** • Located in a vast, cliff-flanked bay, Vassilikí is one of Europe's biggest windsurfing centres.

Basics

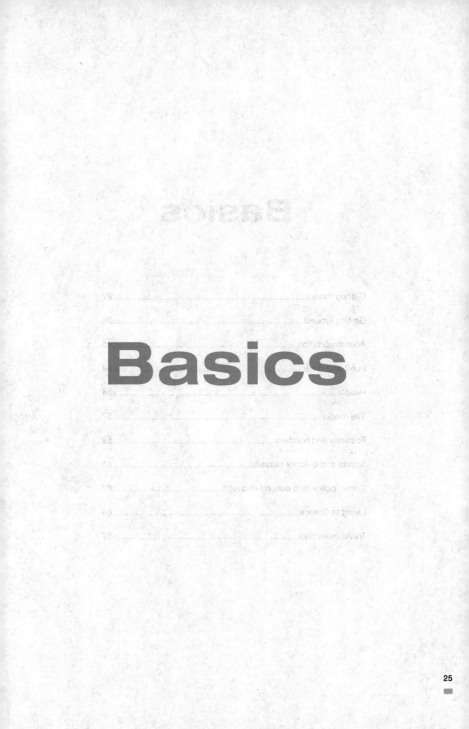

Basics

Getting there

Whatever your starting point, by far the easiest way to get to Greece is to fly. It's two thousand miles or so from the UK and Ireland to Athens and there are direct flights to a variety of Greek destinations from all major British airports. Even if your starting point is North America, Australia, New Zealand or South Africa, the most cost-effective way to Greece may well be to get to London – or Amsterdam or one of many other Northern European cities – and pick up an onward flight from there.

Airfares depend on the season, with the highest in July, August and during Easter week. But May, June and September are also popular, and since far fewer flights operate through the winter, bargains are rare at any time.

When buying flights it always pays to **shop around**; check out a few of the general travel websites listed on p.30 (as well as the airlines' own) to get an idea of the going rates, but bear in mind that many such websites don't include charters or budget airlines (such as easyJet) in their searches. Be aware too that a **package deal**, with accommodation included, can sometimes be as cheap as, or even cheaper than, a flight alone: there's no rule that says you have to use your accommodation every night, or even at all. If you are under 26, or a full-time student, or over 60, you may well be eligible for special **student/youth or senior fares**, so it's worth asking about these. Remember that all cheap tickets will be restricted in some way – usually with stiff charges if you need to make any changes – so double-check details before buying.

Overland alternatives from the UK or Northern Europe involve at least three days of non-stop travel. If you want to take your time over the journey, then **driving** or travelling **by train** can be enjoyable, although invariably more expensive than flying. We've included only brief details of these routes here.

If you want the organizational work done for you, every mainstream **tour operator** includes Greece in its portfolio. You'll find far more interesting alternatives, however, through the small **specialist agencies** listed on p.32. As well as traditional village-based accommodation and less-known islands, many also offer **walking** or **nature holidays** and other special interests such as **yoga**, **photography** and above all **sailing**, with options ranging from shore-based clubs with dinghy tuition, through organized yacht flotillas to bareboat charters.

Flights from the UK and Ireland

Unless you book far in advance, there are few bargain **fares** to Greece. EasyJet can fly you from Gatwick or Luton to Athens and back for as little as £50, but you'll have to move very fast to find fares this cheap. Realistically their prices are little different from those of the **scheduled** operators, and you can expect to pay £150–200 at most times of the year: British Airways have frequent flights from Heathrow, Olympic from Heathrow and Manchester (via Heathrow). All three also have direct flights to Thessaloníki, while easyJet has taken over GB Airways, and is expected to continue their direct flights from Gatwick to Iráklion (Crete). Olympic has the advantage of direct connections to its own domestic flights, but is notorious for long delays, and in permanent financial difficulty. From **Dublin**, Aer Lingus have four direct flights a week from April to October, on which you should hope to find a seat for between €220 and €320. At other times of year, or from any other **regional airport** in the UK or Ireland, you'll have to make at least one stop en route to Athens, in London or elsewhere. It can pay to think laterally here: one of the best routings from Dublin, for example, is on Malev Hungarian airlines via Budapest – with good prices (from around

€200) and convenient connections. With any flight to Athens, you can buy a **domestic connecting flight** on Olympic or Aegean to one of almost three dozen additional Greek mainland and island airports.

Charter flights offer considerably more possibilities, with direct services from many regional airports to **Thessaloníki**, **Kalamáta**, **Kavála** (for Thássos), **Vólos** (for Mount Pílio) and **Préveza (Áktio)** on the Greek mainland, and to the islands of **Crete**, **Rhodes**, **Kós**, **Corfu**, **Mýkonos**, **Zákynthos**, **Kefaloniá**, **Skiáthos**, **Sámos**, **Santoríni**, **Lésvos** and **Límnos**. On the whole these operate from early May to late October, and again there are few bargains, with prices starting at around £200 return from the London airports, more than that from the regional airports (rarely less than €400 from Dublin). Most of the operators now offer flight-only deals, often allowing you to book one way only, either through their own websites or through package and specialist operators; thus you could fly into Athens with one operator, leave from an island with another. Remember that packages may cost little more, and if you're booking at the last minute can even cost less than the flight alone; also that it may cost less to travel via Athens with a connecting flight.

Fly less – stay longer! Travel and climate change

Climate change is the single biggest issue facing our planet. It is caused by a build-up in the atmosphere of carbon dioxide and other greenhouse gases, which are emitted by many sources – including planes. Already, flights account for around 3–4 percent of human-induced global warming: that figure may sound small, but it is rising year on year and threatens to counteract the progress made by reducing greenhouse emissions in other areas.

Rough Guides regard travel, overall, as a global benefit, and feel strongly that the advantages to developing economies are important, as are the opportunities for greater contact and awareness among peoples. But we all have a responsibility to limit our personal "carbon footprint". That means giving thought to how often we fly and what we can do to redress the harm that our trips create.

Flying and climate change

Pretty much every form of motorized travel generates CO_2, but planes are particularly bad offenders, releasing large volumes of greenhouse gases at altitudes where their impact is far more harmful. Flying also allows us to travel much further than we would contemplate doing by road or rail, so the emissions attributable to each passenger become truly shocking. For example, one person taking a return flight between Europe and California produces the equivalent impact of 2.5 tonnes of CO_2 – similar to the yearly output of the average UK car.

Less harmful planes may evolve but it will be decades before they replace the current fleet – which could be too late for avoiding climate chaos. In the meantime, there are limited options for concerned travellers: to reduce the amount we travel by air (take fewer trips, stay longer!), to avoid night flights (when plane contrails trap heat from Earth but can't reflect sunlight back to space), and to make the trips we do take "climate neutral" via a carbon offset scheme.

Carbon offset schemes

Offset schemes run by **climatecare.org**, **carbonneutral.com** and others allow you to "neutralize" the greenhouse gases that you are responsible for releasing. Their websites have simple calculators that let you work out the impact of any flight. Once that's done, you can pay to fund projects that will reduce future carbon emissions by an equivalent amount (such as the distribution of low-energy light bulbs and cooking stoves in developing countries). Please take the time to visit our website and make your trip climate neutral.

@www.roughguides.com/climatechange

Flights from the US and Canada

Direct **nonstop** flights from New York to Athens – daily for much of the year – are operated by Olympic Airlines, Delta (both from JFK) and Continental (from Newark). Between May and October, US Airways also flies daily from Philadelphia to Athens. Olympic and its domestic competitor Aegean offer reasonably priced add-on flights within Greece, especially to the Greek islands. Code-sharing airlines can quote through fares with one of the above, or a European partner, from virtually every major US city, connecting either at New York or a European hub such as London or Frankfurt.

Fares vary greatly, so it's worth putting in a little time on the Internet, or using a good travel agent; book as far ahead as possible to get the best price. The lowest starting point is around US$600 for a restricted, off-season flight from the east coast, rising to about $1200 for a similar deal in summer; from the west coast, expect to pay ten to twenty percent more. The lower fares are rarely on the most direct flights, so check the routing to avoid lengthy delays or stopovers. Remember too that you may be better off getting a domestic flight to New York or Philadelphia and heading directly to Athens from there, or buying a cheap flight to London (beware of changing airports) or another European city, and onward travel from there.

As with the US, airfares **from Canada** vary depending on where you start your journey, and whether you take a direct service. Olympic flies to Athens out of Toronto, with a stop in Montreal, from one to four times weekly depending on the time of year; they're rarely the cheapest option, though. Air Transat also have seasonal weekly flights from Toronto and Montreal to Athens. Otherwise you'll have to choose among one- or two-stop itineraries on a variety of European carriers, or perhaps Delta via New York; costs run from Can$800 in low season from Toronto to more than double that from Vancouver in high season.

Flights from Australia and New Zealand

There are **no direct flights** from Australia or New Zealand to Greece; you'll have to change planes in Southeast Asia or Europe. Tickets purchased direct from the airlines tend to be expensive; travel agents or Australia-based websites generally offer much better deals on fares and have the latest information on limited specials and stopovers. For a simple return fare, you may also have to buy an add-on internal flight to get you to the international departure point.

Fares **from Australia** start from around Aus$1500, rising to around Aus$2500 depending on season, routing, validity, number of stopovers, etc. The shortest flights and best fares are generally with airlines like Thai, Singapore and Emirates that can fly you directly to Athens from their Asian hubs, though you'll also find offers on Swiss, KLM and other European carriers. **From New Zealand**, prices are significantly higher: rarely less than NZ$2000, rising to over NZ$3000 for a more flexible high-season flight.

If Greece is only one stop on a longer journey, you might consider buying a **Round-the-World** (RTW) fare, although Greece never seems to be included in any of the cheaper deals, which means you might have to stump up around Aus$3400/NZ$3800 for one of the fully flexible multi-stop fares from One World or the Star Alliance. At that price, you may be better off with a cheaper deal and a separate ticket to Greece once you get to Europe.

Flights from South Africa

From South Africa, Olympic have three direct flights a week between Johannesburg and Athens: the most convenient, though rarely the least expensive option. Alternative routes include EgyptAir via Cairo, Emirates via Dubai, or just about any of the major European airlines through their domestic hub. Prices start at R6000–7000 for a good low-season deal, to easily double that in high season or if the cheaper seats have gone.

By train

Travelling **by train from the UK or Ireland** takes two-and-a-half to three-and-a-half days and will almost always work out more expensive than flying. It also takes a fair bit of planning, since there's no through train and tickets have to be bought from several separate operators. However, you do have the chance to stop over on the way, while with an InterRail (for European residents only) or Eurail (for all others) pass you can take in Greece as part of a wider rail trip around Europe. The most practical **route** from Britain crosses France and Italy before embarking on the ferry from Bari or Brindisi to Pátra (Patras); alternatively, the much longer all-overland route goes via Vienna and Budapest. Booking well in advance (essential in summer) and going for the cheapest seats on each leg, you can do this for less than £200, not including the incidental expenses along the way. Using rail passes will cost you more, but give far more flexibility. For full details of all the alternatives, check out the Man in Seat 61 website (see p.35).

By car and ferry

Driving to Greece can be a pleasant proposition if you have plenty of time to dawdle along the way. It's only worth considering if you do want to explore en route, though, or are going to stay for an extended period. The most popular **route** is again down through France and Italy to catch one of the Adriatic ferries (see box below); this is much the best way to get to western and southern Greece, the Ionian islands, and to Athens and most of the islands except those in the northeast Aegean. The much longer alternative through Eastern Europe (Hungary, Romania and Bulgaria) is fraught with visa problems, and only makes sense if you want to explore northern Greece on the way.

Departure tax is levied on all international ferries – currently €10 per person and per car or motorbike, usually (but not always) included within the quoted price of the ticket. To non-EU states it's €19 per person, sometimes levied twice (on entry and exit).

Online booking

www.charterflights.co.uk (UK & Ireland). Excellent listings of charter flights from airports throughout the UK and Ireland.

www.cheapflights.co.uk (UK & Ireland).

Italy–Greece ferries

Sailing from **Italy to Greece**, you've a choice of five ports. Regular car and passenger ferries link Ancona, Bari and Brindisi with Igoumenítsa (the port of Epirus in western Greece) and/or Pátra (at the northwest tip of the Peloponnese). Generally, these ferries run year-round, but services are reduced December to April. Ferries also sail less regularly from Venice and Trieste to Pátra via Igoumenítsa/Corfu. The longer routes are more expensive, but the extra cost almost exactly matches what you'll pay in Italian motorway tolls and fuel to get to Brindisi. On most ferries you can stop over in Corfu for no extra charge. For direct access to Athens and the Aegean islands head for Pátra, from where you can cut across country to Pireás.

In summer (especially July–Aug) it's essential to book tickets a few weeks ahead. During the winter you can usually just turn up at the main ports (Brindisi and Ancona have the most reliable departures at that time of year), but it's still wise to book a few days in advance if you're taking a car or want a cabin.

The following companies operate ferries; their websites have full route, fare and booking details. Viamare Travel Ltd (0870/410 6040, www.viamare.com) is the UK agent for most of these companies, and there are also links and booking for all of them at www.openseas.gr and www.ferries.gr.

Agoudimos Bari and Brindisi: www.agoudimos-lines.com.

ANEK Ancona and Venice: www.anek.gr.

Endeavor Lines Brindisi: www.endeavor-lines.com.

Minoan Lines Ancona and Venice: www.minoan.gr.

Superfast Ferries Ancona and Bari: www.superfast.com.

Ventouris Bari: www.ventouris.gr.

www.cheapflights.com (US), www.cheapflights.ca (Canada), www.cheapflights.com.au (Australia & New Zealand). No direct booking, but lists flights and offers from dozens of operators, with web links to most.
www.cheaptickets.com (US). Discount flight specialists.
www.ebookers.com (UK), www.ebookers.ie (Ireland). Efficient, easy-to-use flight finder; scheduled flights only.
www.expedia.co.uk (UK & Ireland), www.expedia.com (US), www.expedia.ca (Canada). Discount airfares, all-airline search engine and daily deals.
www.lastminute.com (UK), www.us.lastminute.com (US), www.lastminute.ie (Ireland), www.lastminute.com.au (Australia). Package holiday and flight-only deals available at very short notice.
www.opodo.co.uk Owned by, and run in conjunction with, nine major European airlines, a reliable source of scheduled fares anywhere in the world.
www.orbitz.com (US). Comprehensive web travel source, with the usual flight, car rental and hotel deals but also great follow-up customer service.
www.priceline.com (US). Name-your-own-price auction website that has deals at around forty percent off standard fares, as well as a regular flight-finder. Be sure to check the terms before bidding.
www.travelocity.co.uk (UK & Ireland), www.travelocity.com (US), www.travelocity.ca (Canada). Destination guides, hot web fares and deals for car rental, accommodation and lodging.
www.travelonline.co.za (SA). Discount flights and information from South Africa.
www.zuji.com.au (Australia), www.zuji.co.nz (NZ). Destination guides, hot fares and great deals for car rental, accommodation and lodging.

Airlines

Aegean Airways www.aegeanair.com. Domestic flights from Athens.
Aer Lingus UK 0870/876 5000, Republic of Ireland 0818/365 000, www.aerlingus.com.
Aeroflot Australia 02/9262 2233, www.aeroflot.com.au.
Air Canada Canada/US 1-888/247–2262, www.aircanada.com.
Air France US 1-800/237-2747, Canada 1-800/667-2747, SA 0861/340 340, www.airfrance.com.
Air New Zealand Australia 13 24 76, www.airnz.com.au, New Zealand 0800/737 000, www.airnz.co.nz.
Air Transat Canada 1-866/847-1112, www.airtransat.com.
American Airlines US 1-800/433-7300, www.aa.com.
British Airways UK 0870/850 9850, Republic of Ireland 1890 626 747, US 1-800/AIRWAYS, Australia 1300/767 177, New Zealand 09/966 9777, SA 27/11441 8400, www.ba.com.
Continental Airlines US 1-800/523-3273, international 1-800/231-0856, www.continental.com.
Delta Air Lines US 1-800/221-1212, international 1-800/241-4141, www.delta.com.
easyJet UK 0905/821 0905, www.easyjet.com.
EgyptAir SA 27/214217 503, www.egyptair.com.eg.
Emirates Australia 03/9940 7807 or 02/9290 9700, New Zealand 05/0836 4728, SA 27/0861 364728, www.emirates.com.
Gulf Air Australia 1300/366 337, SA www.gulfairco.com.
KLM Australia 1300/392 192, New Zealand 09/921 6040, www.klm.com.
Lufthansa US 1-800/399-5838, Canada 1-800/563-5954, SA 086127/0861 842538, www.lufthansa.com.
Malev Republic of Ireland 01/844 4303, www.malev.hu.
Northwest/KLM US 1-800/225-2525, international 1-800/447-4747, www.nwa.com, www.klm.com.
Olympic Airlines UK 0870/606 0460, US 1-800/223-1226 or 718/896-7393, SA 27/2141 92502 www.olympicairlines.com.
Qantas Australia 13 13 13, New Zealand 0800/808 767, www.qantas.com.
Royal Jordanian Australia 02/9244 2701, New Zealand 03/365 3910, www.rja.com.jo.
Singapore Airlines Australia 13 10 11, New Zealand 0800/808 909, www.singaporeair.com.
South African Airways 27/21936 2111, www.flysaa.com.
Swiss US 1-877/FLY-SWISS, Australia 1300/724 666, New Zealand 09/977 2238, www.swiss.com.
Thai Airways Australia 1300/651 960, New Zealand 09/377 3886, www.thaiair.com.
United Airlines US 1-800/UNITED-1, international 1-800/538-2929, www.united.com.
US Airways US 1-800/428-4322, www.usair.com.
Virgin Atlantic US 1-800/862-8621, www.virgin-atlantic.com.

Charter airlines and package companies

Avro UK ⓣ0871/622 4476, ⓦwww.avro.co.uk. Flights from Gatwick, Birmingham, Manchester and more.
Excel Airways UK ⓣ0870/320 7777, Republic of Ireland ⓣ0818/220 220, ⓦwww.excelairways.com or ⓦwww.freedomflights.co.uk. Frequent flights from numerous UK regional airports and Dublin, plus some packages.
First Choice UK ⓣ0871/200 7799, ⓦwww.firstchoice.co.uk. Package holidays and frequent flights from numerous UK regional airports.
Thomas Cook UK ⓣ0870/750 5711, ⓦwww.thomascook.com, ⓦwww.flythomascook.com. Frequent flights and packages from UK regional airports.
Thomson UK ⓣ0870/165 0079, ⓦwww.thomson.co.uk, ⓦwww.thomsonfly.com. The biggest charter and package operator from the UK, serving numerous regional airports.

Flights and travel agents

Air Brokers International US ⓣ1-800/883-3273, ⓦwww.airbrokers.com. Consolidator and specialist in RTW tickets.
Airtech US ⓣ212/219-7000, ⓦwww.airtech.com. Last-minute and standby flight deals.
Aran Travel International Republic of Ireland ⓣ091/562 595. Good-value flights and holidays.
Argo UK ⓣ0870/066 7070, ⓦwww.argo-holidays.com. Long-established Greek specialist for upmarket holidays and good flight-only deals.
BestFlights Australia ⓣ1300/767 757, ⓦwww.bestflights.com.au. Cheap flights and RTW deals from Australia and New Zealand.
BootsnAll US ⓣ1-866/549-7614, ⓦwww.bootsnall.com. General agent for independent travel with flights, hotel reservations and online advice.
Educational Travel Center US ⓣ1-800/747-5551 or 608/256-5551, ⓦwww.edtrav.com. Low-cost fares worldwide, student/youth discount offers, Eurail passes.
Flight Centre US ⓣ1-866/WORLD-51, ⓦwww.flightcentre.us, Canada ⓣ1-888/WORLD-02, ⓦwww.flightcentre.ca, Australia ⓣ13 3133, ⓦwww.flightcentre.com.au, New Zealand ⓣ0800/243 544, ⓦwww.flightcentre.co.nz, South Africa ⓣ0860/400 727, ⓦwww.flightcentre.co.za. Rock-bottom fares worldwide.
North South Travel UK ⓣ01245/608291, ⓦwww.northsouthtravel.co.uk. Friendly, competitive flight agency, offering discounted fares worldwide. Profits are used to support projects in the developing world, especially the promotion of sustainable tourism.
Rosetta Travel Northern Ireland ⓣ028/9064 4996, ⓦwww.rosettatravel.com. Flight and holiday agent, specializing in deals direct from Belfast.
STA Travel UK ⓣ0870/ 160 0599, ⓦwww.statravel.co.uk, US ⓣ1-800/781-4040, ⓦwww.statravel.com, Australia ⓣ134 STA, ⓦwww.statravel.com.au, New Zealand ⓣ0800/474 400, ⓦwww.statravel.co.nz, South Africa ⓣ0861/781 781, ⓦwww.statravel.co.za. Worldwide specialists in low-cost flights and tours for students and under-26s.
Student Flights US ⓣ1-800 255-8000 ⓦwww.isecard.com/studentflights. Student/youth fares, plus student IDs and European rail and bus passes.
Trailfinders UK ⓣ0845/058 5858, ⓦwww.trailfinders.com, Republic of Ireland ⓣ01/677 7888, ⓦwww.trailfinders.ie, Australia ⓣ1300/780 212, ⓦwww.trailfinders.com.au. One of the best-informed and most efficient agents for independent travellers; branches in all the UK's largest cities, plus Dublin.
Travel Cuts US ⓣ1-800/592-CUTS, Canada ⓣ1-888 246-9762, ⓦwww.travelcuts.com. Popular, long-established student-travel organization, with good worldwide offers; not only for students.
Travelers Advantage US ⓣ1-877/259-2691, ⓦwww.travelersadvantage.com. Discount travel club, with low airfares, cashback deals and discounted car rental. Membership required ($1 for 2-month trial).
Travelosophy US ⓣ1-800/332-2687, ⓦwww.itravelosophy.com. Good range of discounted and student fares worldwide.

Specialist agents and operators

Astra US ⓣ303/321-5403, ⓦwww.astragreece.com. Very personal, idiosyncratic, two-week tours led by veteran Hellenophile Thordis Simonsen, during spring and autumn. Itineraries include Crete, Epirus and Thessaly, the Peloponnese and the immediate environs of her adopted Lakonian village.
Cachet Travel UK ⓣ020/8847 8700, ⓦwww.cachet-travel.co.uk. Attractive range of villas and apartments in the more unspoilt south and west of Crete, plus Kárpathos and remote corners of Sámos.
CV Travel UK ⓣ0870/606 0013, ⓦwww.cvtravel.co.uk. Quality villas on Corfu, Kefaloniá, Paxí, Spétses, Lefkádha and Crete.
Direct Greece UK ⓣ0870/191 9244, ⓦwww.direct-greece.co.uk. Moderately priced villas, apartments and restored houses on Rhodes, Hálki, Zákynthos, Kefaloniá, Lésvos, Corfu, Lefkádha and Crete, plus (on the mainland) Párga and the outer Máni.

Freedom of Greece UK ⓣ0870/220 1200, ⓦwww.freedomofgreece.com. Wide range of apartments and villas on the mainland or smaller islands, including plenty of budget options.

Grecian Tours Australia ⓣ03/9663 3711, ⓦwww.greciantours.com.au. A variety of accommodation and sightseeing tours, plus flights.

Greek Islands Club UK ⓣ020/8232 9780, ⓦwww.greekislandsclub.com. Part of Sunvil (see opposite), specializing in upmarket villas with private pools, especially in the Ionian islands.

Greek Sun Holidays UK ⓣ01732/740317, ⓦwww.greeksun.co.uk. Good-value package holidays mainly in the Dodecanese, northeast Aegean and Cyclades; also tailor-made island-hopping itineraries.

Hellenic Adventures US ⓣ1-800/851-6349 or 612/827-0937, ⓦwww.hellenicadventures.com. Small-group escorted tours led by enthusiastic expert guides, as well as itineraries for independent travellers, cruises and other travel services.

Hidden Greece UK ⓣ020/8758 4707, ⓦwww.hidden-greece.co.uk. Specialist agent putting together tailor-made packages to smaller destinations at reasonable prices.

Homeric Tours US ⓣ1-800/223-5570, ⓦwww.homerictours.com. Hotel packages, individual tours, escorted group tours and fly/drive deals. Good source of inexpensive flights.

Houses of Pelion UK ⓣ0870/199 9191, ⓦwww.pelion.co.uk. Local specialist offering an excellent collection of inland cottages, houses and apartments on the Pílio peninsula.

Inntravel UK ⓣ01653/617755, ⓦwww.inntravel.co.uk. High-quality packages and tailor-made itineraries and fly-drives to unspoilt areas of the mainland, Crete and smaller islands; also walking and other special-interest holidays.

Island Wandering UK ⓣ0870/777 9944, ⓦwww.islandwandering.com. Tailor-made island-hopping itineraries between most Greek archipelagos.

Pure Crete UK ⓣ020/8760 0879, ⓦwww.pure-crete.com. Characterful, converted cottages and farmhouses in western Crete, plus walking, wildlife and other special-interest trips.

Simply Travel UK ⓣ0870/166 4979, ⓦwww.simplytravel.co.uk. Although now part of the vast TUI organisation, Simply still manages a personal touch, and has plenty of excellent, upmarket accommodation in Crete and the Ionian islands as well as the mainland.

Simpson Travel UK ⓣ0845/811 6502, ⓦwww.simpsontravel.com. Classy villas, upmarket hotels and village hideaways on Crete, Corfu, Paxí and Meganíssi.

Sun Island Tours Australia ⓣ1300/665 673, ⓦwww.sunislandtours.com.au. An assortment of island-hopping, fly-drives, cruises and guided land-tour options, as well as upscale accommodation on big-name islands such as Rhodes, Kós and Sámos.

Sunvil Holidays UK ⓣ020/8758 4758, ⓦwww.sunvil.co.uk/greece. High-quality outfit specializing in upmarket hotels and villas in the Ionian islands, the Sporades, western Crete, Lésvos, Límnos, Sámos, Ikaría, Pátmos, the Peloponnese, the Pílio, Párga and Sývota. Also mainland fly-drives and walking holidays on Amorgós.

Tourlite Zeus US ⓣ1-800/272-7600, ⓦwww.tourlite.com. Specialists in Greek travel, can arrange tailor-made or package vacations.

Travel à la Carte UK ⓣ01635/33800, ⓦwww.travelalacarte.co.uk. Established Corfu specialist, now diversified into beach and rural villas on Skiáthos, Hálki, Paxí and Sými as well.

Walking, nature and special-interest holidays

ATG Oxford UK ⓣ01865/315678, ⓦwww.atg-oxford.co.uk. Somewhat pricey but high-standard guided walks on Crete and select Cyclades and Dodecanese islands, plus the Máni and Zagóri on the mainland.

Classic Adventures US ⓣ1-800/777-8090, ⓦwww.classicadventures.com. Spring or autumn rural cycling tours of "classical Greece", crossing the north Peloponnese to Zákynthos, or Crete.

Exodus UK ⓣ0870/240 5550, ⓦwww.exodus.co.uk. One-week treks across Évvia or the White Mountains of Crete.

Explore Worldwide UK ⓣ01252/760 000, ⓦwww.exploreworldwide.com. A variety of tours, many combining hiking with sailing between the islands.

Free Spirit Travel UK ⓣ01273/564230, ⓦwww.freespirituk.com. Yoga and meditation in western Crete, Zákynthos or the Peloponnese, plus family and walking holidays (or a combination of them).

Jonathan's Tours ⓣ33/561046447, ⓦwww.jonathanstours.com. Family-run walking holidays on Crete, Lésvos, Lefkádha and Zagóri; spring and autumn departures.

Marengo Guided Walks UK ⓣ01485/532710, ⓦwww.marengowalks.com. Annually changing programme of easy walks guided by ace botanist Lance Chilton; typical one-week offerings may include Sámos, Sými, central Pílio, northern Lésvos, Crete, the Párga area, southern Peloponnese and Thássos.

Naturetrek UK ⓣ01962/733051, ⓦwww.naturetrek.co.uk. Fairly pricey but expertly led one- or two-week natural history tours; offerings include butterflies of the southern mainland, springtime birds and flora on Sámos, and wildlife of Crete.

Northwest Passage US ⓣ1-800/RECREATE, ⓦwww.nwpassage.com. Excellent sea-kayaking and hiking "inn-to-inn" tours, plus yoga and art experiences, as well as combinations thereof; mostly in Crete.

Ramblers Holidays UK ⓣ01707/331133, ⓦwww.ramblersholidays.co.uk. Spring hiking in Crete, Easter on Sámos, "Classical" (mainland) walks and many more.

Sherpa Expeditions UK ⓣ020/8577 2717, ⓦwww.sherpa-walking-holidays.co.uk. Self-guided and escorted 8-day outings on Crete or Zagóri; more challenging escorted tours of the peaks around Mt Olympus.

Skyros Holidays UK ⓣ01983/865566, ⓦwww.skyros.co.uk. Holistic health, fitness, crafts and "personal growth" holidays on the island of Skýros, as well as well-regarded writers' workshops.

Swim Trek UK ⓣ020/8696 6220, ⓦwww.swimtrek.com. Week-long tours of Náxos and the small islands around it, swimming between the islands: the brainchild of Aussie cross-channel swimmer Simon Murie.

The Travelling Naturalist UK ⓣ01305/267994, ⓦwww.naturalist.co.uk. Wildlife holiday company that runs excellent bird-watching and wild-flower-spotting trips to Crete, Kós, Lesvós and the mainland.

Walking Plus UK ⓣ020/8835 8303, ⓦwww.walkingplus.co.uk. Enthusiastic Gilly and Robin Cameron Cooper offer guided and self-guided off-season walks in the Cyclades and around Athens.

Walks Worldwide UK ⓣ01524/242000, ⓦwww.walksworldwide.com. Escorted and self-guided treks on Corfu, Mount Pílio, Náxos and the Máni, plus unusual routes on Mt Olympus.

Yoga Plus UK ⓣ01273/276175, ⓦwww.yogaplus.co.uk. Astanga yoga courses in a remote part of southern Crete. Accommodation is included, but transport is not.

Sailing holidays

Nautilus Yachting UK ⓣ01732/867445, ⓦwww.nautilus-yachting.co.uk. Bareboat yacht charter, flotillas and sailing courses from a wide variety of marinas.

Neilson UK ⓣ0870/333 3356, ⓦwww.neilson.co.uk. Half a dozen excellent beach activity clubs, plus flotillas and bareboat charter in the Ionians.

Seafarer Cruising & Sailing UK ⓣ0870/442 2447, ⓦwww.seafarercruises.com. Ionian and Argo-Saronic flotillas, beach club, bareboat charter, courses and small-boat island cruises.

Setsail Holidays UK ⓣ01787/310445, ⓦwww.setsail.co.uk. Bareboat charters across the country, flotillas from Skiáthos, and a sail-and-stay programme based on Póros.

Sportif UK ⓣ01273/844919, ⓦwww.sportif-uk.com. Windsurfing packages and instruction on Kós, Rhodes, Sámos and Kárpathos.

Sunsail UK ⓣ0870/112 8612, ⓦwww.sunsail.com. Worldwide company with mainland beach club, plus flotillas and bareboat mainly in the Ionians and Sporades.

Templecraft ⓣ01732/867445, ⓦwww.templecraft.com. Bareboat charters and flotilla holidays in the Ionian archipelago.
Valef Yachts US ⓣ1-800/223-3845, ⓦwww.valefyachts.com. Small-boat cruises around the islands and luxury crewed yacht or motor boat charter.

Rail contacts

The Man in Seat 61 ⓦwww.seat61.com. Named after British rail buff Mark Smith's favourite seat on the Eurostar, this brilliant site has full details of all the possible ways of getting to Greece by train and ferry, plus links to all the necessary train, ferry and ticket websites. Also has a rail shop feature, where many tickets and passes can be purchased.
BootsnAll US ⓣ1-866/549-7614, ⓦwww.bootsnall.com. Eurail passes and other tickets, plus rail blogs and phone helpline.
CIT World Travel Australia ⓣ02/9267 1255 or 03/9650 5510, ⓦwww.cittravel.com.au. Eurail passes and other tickets.
Europrail International Canada ⓣ1-888/667-9734, ⓦwww.europrail.net. Eurail passes and other tickets.
Eurostar UK ⓣ0870/518 6186, outside UK ⓣ0044/12336 17575, ⓦwww.eurostar.com.
Rail Europe US ⓣ1-877/257-2887, Canada ⓣ1-800/361-RAIL, UK ⓣ0870/837 1371, ⓦwww.raileurope.com/us, ⓦwww.raileurope.co.uk. Discounted rail fares for under-26s on a variety of European routes; also agents for most tickets including Eurail, InterRail and Eurostar.
Rail Plus Australia ⓣ1300/555 003 or 03/9642 8644, New Zealand ⓣ09/377 5415, ⓦwww.railplus.com.au, ⓦwww.railplus.co.nz. Eurail and other passes.

Ferry contacts

Brittany Ferries UK ⓣ0870/366 5333, Republic of Ireland ⓣ021/427 7801, ⓦwww.brittanyferries.co.uk, ⓦwww.brittanyferries.ie. Portsmouth to Caen, St Malo or Cherbourg; Poole to Cherbourg; Plymouth to Roscoff; Cork to Roscoff.
Eurotunnel UK ⓣ0870/535 3535, ⓦwww.eurotunnel.com.
Irish Ferries Britain ⓣ0870/517 1717, Northern Ireland ⓣ353/818 300 400, Republic of Ireland ⓣ0818/300 400, ⓦwww.irishferries.com. Dublin to Holyhead; Rosslare to Pembroke, Cherbourg and Roscoff.
Norfolkline UK ⓣ0870/870 1020, Republic of Ireland ⓣ01/819 2999, ⓦwww.norfolkline.com. Dublin and Belfast to Liverpool; Dover to Dunkirk.
P&O Ferries UK ⓣ0870/598 0333, ⓦwww.poferries.com. Dover to Calais; Hull to Rotterdam and Zeebrugge.
P&O Irish Sea UK ⓣ0870/242 4777, Republic of Ireland ⓣ01/407 3434, ⓦwww.poirishsea.com. Dublin to Liverpool.
Sea France UK ⓣ0870/443 1653, ⓦwww.seafrance.com. Dover to Calais.
SpeedFerries UK ⓣ0871/222 7456, ⓦwww.speedferries.com. Dover to Boulogne.
Stena Line UK ⓣ0870/570 7070, Northern Ireland ⓣ0870/520 4204, Republic of Ireland ⓣ01/204 7777, ⓦwww.stenaline.co.uk. Rosslare to Fishguard; Dun Laoghaire or Dublin to Holyhead; Belfast to Stranraer; Harwich to Hook of Holland.
Superfast Ferries UK ⓣ0870/234 0870, ⓦwww.superfast.com. Rosyth to Zeebrugge.
Transmanche UK ⓣ0800/917 1201, ⓦwww.transmancheferries.com. Newhaven to Dieppe.

Getting around

The standard overland public transport in Greece is the bus. Train networks are limited, though the service on the Athens–Pátra and Athens–Thessaloníki lines is excellent. Buses cover most primary routes on the mainland and provide basic connections on the islands. The best way to supplement buses is to rent a scooter, motorbike or car, especially on the islands where – in any substantial town or resort – you will find at least one rental outlet. Inter-island travel means taking ferries, catamarans or hydrofoils, which will eventually get you to any of the sixty-plus inhabited isles. Internal flights are relatively expensive, but can save literally days of travel: Athens–Rhodes is just two hours return, versus 28 hours by boat.

Buses

Bus services on **major routes** are efficient and frequent, departing promptly at scheduled departure times. On **secondary roads** they're less regular, with long gaps, but even the remotest villages will be connected a couple of days weekly to the provincial capital. These buses often depart shortly before dawn, returning to the village between 1.30 and 3pm. On islands there are usually buses to connect the port and main town (if different) for ferry arrivals or departures. The network is nationally run by a single syndicate known as the **KTEL** (*Kratikó Tamío Ellinikón Leoforíon*). In medium-sized or large towns there may be several scattered terminals for services in different directions, so make sure you have the right station for your departure.

Traditional two-toned cream-and-green **coaches** are being slowly replaced by hi-tech, navy-and-green models. For major intercity lines such as Athens–Pátra, **ticketing** is computerized, with assigned seating, and such buses often get fully booked at the *ekdhotíria* (ticket-issuing office). On secondary rural/island routes, it's first-come, first-served, with some standing allowed, and tickets dispensed on the spot by an *ispráktoras* or conductor.

Trains

The Greek mainland's railway network is run by **OSE** (*Organismós Sidherodhrómon Elládhos*; ⓣ1110 or ⓦwww.ose.gr,); with a few exceptions, trains are slower than equivalent buses. However, they can be much cheaper – fifty percent less on non-express services (but much the same on express), even more if you buy a return ticket – and some lines are intrinsically enjoyable, none more than the rack-and-pinion service between Dhiakoftó and Kalávryta in the **Peloponnese** (see p.271).

Timetables are available annually as small, Greek-only booklets; the best places to obtain them are the OSE offices in Athens at Sína 6, in Thessaloníki at Aristotélous 18, or main train stations in these cities as well as Lárissa, Vólos and Pátra. Always check station schedule boards or their information counters for photocopied addenda sheets, which are more current than the booklet. Trains leave promptly at the outset, with good timekeeping en route.

If you're starting a journey at a station with computerized facilities you can (at no extra cost) **reserve a seat**; a carriage and seat number will be printed on your ticket.

There are two basic **classes of wagon**: first and second, the former almost double the cost of the latter. An express category of train, **Intercity** (IC or ICE on timetables), exists for departures between Alexandroúpoli, Thessaloníki, Vólos, Kalambáka, Athens, Pátra and Kalamáta. German-made rolling stock is relatively sleek, and usually much faster than a bus; stiff supplements are charged depending on distance travelled. There is one nightly **sleeper** in each direction between Athens and Thessaloníki, with first-class compartments costing €31–45 depending on the number of bunks (1–3).

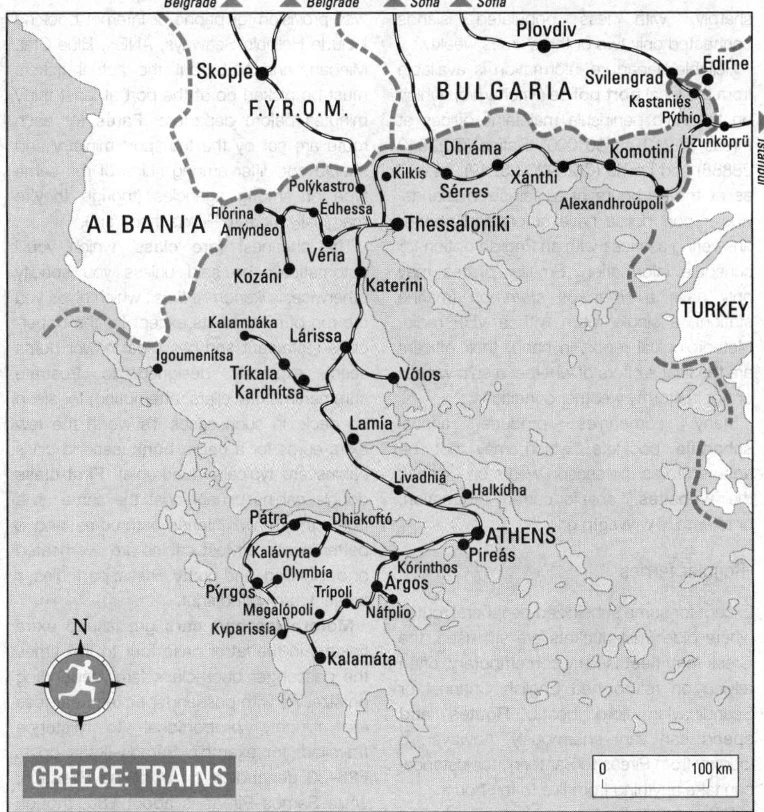

Tickets issued on board carry a fifty-percent penalty charge; by contrast, under-26s and over-60s get 25 percent **discounts** at off-peak seasons for non-express trains.

Credit cards are theoretically accepted as payment at the midtown OSE offices of Athens, Lárissa, Vólos and Thessaloníki, as well as Athens, Vólos, Thessaloníki, Alexandhroúpoli and Pátra stations; however, some readers have experienced difficulty in this respect, so check first. **InterRail** and **Eurail pass holders** must secure reservations, and pay express supplements, like everyone else.

Sea transport

There are several varieties of sea-going vessels: **roll-on-roll-off** short-haul barges, nicknamed *pandófles* ("slippers"), designed to shuttle mostly vehicles short distances; larger **ordinary ferries**, which never exceed 17 knots in velocity; the new generation of **"high-speed"** boats (*tahyplóö*) and catamarans, which usually carry cars, and capable of attaining 27 knots; **hydrofoils**, similarly quick but which carry only passengers; and local **kaïkia**, small boats which do short hops and excursions in season.

Ferry, high-speed, catamaran and hydrofoil connections are indicated both on the route **map** (see p.39) and in the "Travel details" at the end of relevant chapters. Schedules are notoriously erratic, however, and must be verified seasonally; details given are for departures between late June and early September. When sailing in season from **Pireás** to the Cyclades or Dodecanese, you should have a choice of at least two, sometimes three, daily departures. **Out-of-season** departure frequencies drop sharply, with less populated islands connected only two or three times weekly.

Reliable departure information is available from the local **port police** (*limenarhío*), which on the Attic peninsula maintains offices at Pireás (☎210 45 50 000), Rafína (☎22940 28888) and Lávrio (☎22920 25249), as well as at the harbours of all fair-sized islands. Busier port police have automated phone-answering services with an English option for schedule information. Smaller places may only have a *limenikós stathmós* (marine station), a single room with a VHF radio. Meteorological report in hand, their officers are the final arbiters of whether a ship will sail or not in stormy weather conditions.

Many companies produce annual **schedule** booklets, which may not be adhered to as the season wears on – check their **websites** (if any) for current information, or refer to ⓦwww.gtp.gr.

Regular ferries

Except for some subsidized peripheral routes where older rust-buckets are still used, the Greek ferry **fleet** is fairly contemporary, often relying on refurbished English Channel or Scandinavian fjord boats. **Routes and speed** can vary enormously, however; a journey from Pireás to Santoríni, for instance, can take anything from five to ten hours.

Tickets are best bought a day before departure, unless you need to reserve a cabin berth or space for a car. If a boat fails to sail for mechanical or bad-weather reasons, your money is refunded; changes to departure date at your own initiative may incur a small penalty charge. During holiday periods – Christmas/New Year, the week before and after Easter, late July to early September – and around the dates of elections, ferries need to be booked at least ten days in advance.

You cannot **buy** your ticket on board (though you can usually upgrade your class of travel); sometimes there may not even be a last-minute sales booth at the quayside. Staff at the gangway will prevent you embarking if you don't have a ticket (the only exceptions may be short-haul services, for example from Igoumenítsa to Corfu, or the central mainland to Évvia). All other ticket sales are now **computerized**. Companies with provision for phone or Internet booking include Hellenic Seaways, ANEK, Blue Star, Minoan, and NEL, but the actual tickets must be picked up at the port at least thirty minutes before departure. **Fares** for each route are set by the transport ministry and should not differ among ships of the same type or among agencies (though they're marginally more to Pireás than from).

The cheapest **fare class**, which you'll automatically be sold unless you specify otherwise, is *ikonomikí thési*, which gives you the run of most boats except for the upper-class restaurant and bar. Most newer boats seem expressly designed to frustrate summertime travellers attempting to sleep on deck. In such cases it's worth the few extra euros for a **cabin bunk** (second-class cabins are typically quadruple). **First-class** double cabins usually cost the same as a flight; they have interior bathrooms and a better location. Most cabins are overheated or overchilled, and pretty airless; portholes, if present, are bolted shut.

Motorbikes and cars get issued extra tickets, in the latter case four to five times the passenger deck-class fare, depending on size. As with passenger tickets, car fees are roughly proportional to distance travelled: for example Sámos–Ikaría costs €26–30 depending on port and direction, while Sámos–Pireás is about €80, though short hops like Rafína–Marmári (1hr) at €29 car and driver are a rip-off. It's really only worth dragging a car to the larger islands like Crete, Rhodes, Híos, Lésvos, Sámos, Corfu or Kefaloniá, and even then for a stay of more than four days. Elsewhere, you may find it cheaper to leave your car on the mainland and rent another on arrival. Technically, written permission is required to take rental motorbikes and cars on ferries, though in practice nobody ever quizzes you on this.

Ferries sell a limited range (biscuits, greasy pizzas) of overpriced, mediocre **food on board**; honourable exceptions are the meals served on overnight sailings to Crete.

Hydrofoils, catamarans and tahyplóa (high-speed boats)

Hydrofoils – commonly known as *dhelfínia* or "Flying Dolphins" – are at least twice as

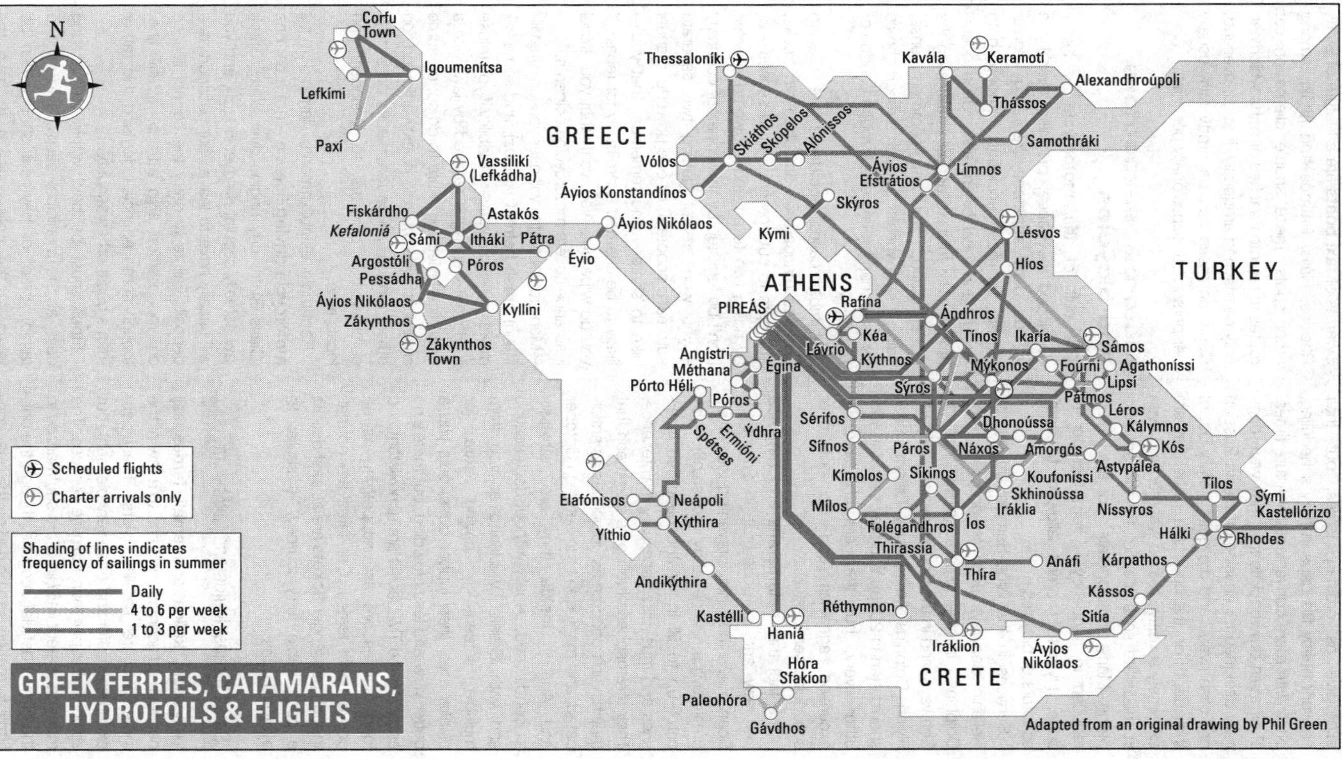

GREEK FERRIES, CATAMARANS, HYDROFOILS & FLIGHTS
N
Scheduled flights
Charter arrivals only
Shading of lines indicates frequency of sailings in summer
Daily
4 to 6 per week
1 to 3 per week
GREECE
TURKEY
ATHENS
CRETE
Corfu Town
Lefkími
Igoumenítsa
Paxí
Vassilikí (Lefkádha)
Fiskárdho
Kefaloniá
Sámi
Ithháki
Astakós
Pátra
Argostóli
Pessádha
Póros
Áyios Nikólaos
Zákynthos
Zákynthos Town
Kyllíni
Éyio
Áyios Nikólaos
Áyios Konstandínos
Vólos
Thessaloníki
Skiáthos
Skópelos
Alónissos
Kými
Skýros
Kavála
Keramotí
Thássos
Alexandhroúpoli
Samothráki
Límnos
Áyios Efstrátios
Lésvos
Híos
PIREÁS
Rafína
Lávrio
Kéa
Kýthnos
Ándhros
Tínos
Ikaría
Sámos
Agathoníssi
Foúrni
Lipsí
Pátmos
Léros
Kálymnos
Kós
Mýkonos
Sýros
Angístri
Méthana
Égina
Pórto Héli
Póros
Ýdhra
Ermióni
Spétses
Sérifos
Sífnos
Kímolos
Mílos
Páros
Náxos
Dhonoússa
Amorgós
Koufoníssi
Skhinoússa
Iráklia
Síkinos
Folégandhros
Íos
Thirassía
Thíra
Anáfi
Astypálea
Nissyros
Tílos
Sými
Kastellórizo
Hálki
Rhodes
Kárpathos
Kássos
Sitía
Áyios Nikólaos
Iráklion
Réthymnon
Haniá
Kastélli
Hóra Sfakíon
Paleohóra
Gávdhos
Elafónisos
Neápoli
Kýthira
Ýíthio
Andikýthira
Adapted from an original drawing by Phil Green

expensive as ordinary ferries, but their network neatly fills gaps in ferry scheduling, often with more convenient departure times. Their main drawback is that they were originally designed for cruising on placid Russian or Polish rivers, and are quite literally out of their depth on the open sea. Thus they are extremely sensitive to bad weather, and even in moderate seas are not for the seasick-prone. Many don't operate – or are heavily reduced in frequency – from October to June. Hydrofoils aren't allowed to carry scooters or bicycles.

Services in the Argo-Saronic are run by Hellenic Seaways and Vasilopoulos Flying Dolphins, in the Sporades by Hellenic Seaways, and in the Dodecanese by Aegean Flying Dolphins (Kós-based Dinoris Lines should start in 2008). You may see craft with other livery, but they are chartered by excursion agencies and do not offer scheduled services.

The fact that **catamarans and tahyplóa** are new and purpose-built in France or Scandinavia has not prevented numerous breakdowns, since they constantly play catch-up to fill in weather-cancelled itineraries and thus miss necessary maintenance. Their stratospheric fuel costs also mean that they haven't become as ubiquitous as anticipated, and many don't run between October and April. **Inside** they are ruthlessly air-conditioned, usually without deck seating and with Greek TV blaring at you from multiple screens – paying extra for *dhiakikriméni thési* (upper class) gets you a better view and less crowding, but there's no escaping the TV. Cabins are nonexistent and food facilities are as unappetizing as on conventional ferries. Car fares are normal, though passenger **tickets** are at least double a comparable ferry journey, ie similar to hydrofoil rates.

Small ferries, kaïkia and taxi boats

In season, **kaïkia** and **small ferries** sail between adjacent islands and to a few of the more obscure satellite islets. These are extremely useful and often very pleasant, but seldom cheaper than mainline services. The more consistent *kaïki* links are summarized in the "Travel details" sections, though the only firm information is to be had on the quayside.

Swarms of **taxi boats** are a feature of Sými, Rhodes, Hálki, Pátmos and Itháki, among other spots; these shuttle clients on set routes to remote beaches or ports which can only be reached arduously, if at all, overland. Costs on these can be pretty stiff, usually per person but occasionally per boat.

Motorbikes, scooters and bicycles

The cult of the **motorcycle** is highly developed in Greece, presided over by a jealous deity apparently requiring regular human sacrifice; accidents among both foreign and local bikers are routine occurrences, with multiple annual fatalities on the busier islands. But with common sense, riding a two-wheeler through a resort should be safer than piloting one through London or New York.

In most cases **accidents** are due to unskilled manoeuvres on rutted dirt tracks, attempts to cut corners – in all senses – or by riding two to an underpowered scooter. Don't be tempted by this apparent economy – you won't regret getting two separate automatic scooters, or one powerful manual bike to share – and remember that you're likely to be charged exorbitantly for repairs if you do wipe out. Also, verify that your travel insurance covers motorcycle accidents.

Many rental outfits will offer you (an often ill-fitting) **crash helmet** (*krános*), and some will make you sign a waiver of liability if you refuse it. Helmet-wearing is required by law, with a €185 fine levied for failure to do so; on some smaller islands the rule is laxly enforced, on others random police roadblocks do a brisk commerce in citations, to foreigners and locals alike.

Reputable establishments demand a full **motorcycle driving licence** – not a car one (Class B) for any engine over 80cc (Greek law actually stipulates "over 50cc"), and you will usually have to leave your passport as a deposit. Failure to carry the correct licence on your person also attracts a stiff fine, though some agencies demand this rather than a passport as security.

Fines must be paid within ten working days at the municipal cashier's (*dhimotikó tamío*); proof of payment should then be taken to the police station to have the citation cancelled. Non-payment will mean a court date being set, and the Greek authorities – so dilatory in other respects – are amazingly efficient at translating summons into foreign languages and serving them at your overseas address. No-shows are automatically convicted, and a conviction will make re-entry to Greece awkward.

Small **motor scooters** with automatic transmission, known in Greek as *papákia* (little ducks) after their characteristic noise, are good transport for all but the hilliest terrain. They're available for rent on many islands and in a few of the popular mainland resorts for €8–18 per day. Prices can be bargained down out of peak season, or for a longer rental period.

Before riding off, always check the bike's **mechanical state**. Bad brakes, non-functioning electrics and worn or oil-fouled spark plugs are the most common defects; dealers often keep the front brakes far too loose, with the commendable intention of preventing you going over the handlebars. If you break down, you're responsible for returning the machine; better outlets offer a free retrieval service.

Scooters are practical enough, but thirsty on fuel; make sure there's a kick-start as backups to the battery, since ignition switches commonly fail. Only models of 90cc and above are powerful enough for two riders. Bungee cords for tying down bundles are supplied on request, while capacious baskets are also often attached. Ultra-trendy, low-slung models with fat, small-radius tyres are unstable on anything other than the smoothest, flattest island roads. If you intend to go off-road, always choose more traditionally designed bikes with large-radius, nobbly, narrow tyres, if available. Again, if you're going to spend your vacation astride a scooter, consider bringing or buying cyclists' or motorcyclists' **gloves**; they may look stupid during summer, but if you lose all the skin off your hands when you go for a spill, the wounds take months to heal, and leave huge scars.

True **motorbikes** with manual transmissions (*mihanákia*) and safer tyres (as above) are less common than they ought to be. For two riders, the least powerful safe model is the Honda Cub 90 or Yamaha 80 Townmate. Better is the Honda Astrea 100 and its off-brand clones (eg Kawasaki Kaze), very powerful but scarcely bigger than 50cc models. With the proper licence, bikes of 125cc and up are available in many resorts. **Quads** are also increasingly offered – without doubt the most stupid-looking and impractical conveyance yet devised, and very unstable on turns (thus helmets are supplied).

Cycling

Cycling in Greece is not such hard going as you might imagine (except in summer), especially on one of the mountain bikes that are now the rule at rental outfits; they rarely cost more than €7 a day. You do, however, need steady nerves, as roads are generally narrow with no verges or bike lanes (except on Kós, Lefkádha and in Tríkala, Édhessa or Mesolóngi); many Greek drivers consider cyclists a lower form of life, on a par with the snakes regularly found run over.

If you have your own mountain or touring bike (the latter not rented in Greece), consider taking it along by **train** or **plane** (it's free if within your 20–23kg international air allowance, but arrange it in writing with the airline beforehand to avoid huge charges at check-in). Once in Greece you can take a bike for free on most ferries, in the guard's van on most trains (for a small fee), and in the luggage bays of buses. Any small spare parts you might need are best brought along, since specialist shops are only found in the provincial capitals and main cities.

Driving and car rental

If you intend to **drive your own car to and within Greece**, remember that insurance contracted in any EU state is valid in any other, but in many cases this is only third-party cover – the statutory legal minimum. Competition in the industry is intense, however, so many UK insurers will throw in full, pan-European cover for free or for a nominal sum, for up to sixty days.

EU citizens bringing their own cars are free to circulate in the country for six months, or until their home-based road tax or insurance expires, whichever happens first; see p.65 for details on keeping a car in

Greece for longer. **Non-EU nationals** will get a car entered in their passport; the carnet normally allows you to keep a vehicle in Greece for up to six months, exempt from road tax.

Car rental

Car rental in Greece starts at around €300 a week in high season for the smallest vehicle from a one-off outlet or local chain, including unlimited mileage, tax and insurance. Overseas tour operator and international chain brochures threaten rates of nearly €400 but, except in August, no rental company fetches that price. Outside peak season, at smaller local outfits, you can get terms of €30 per day, all inclusive, with even better **rates** for three days or more – or prebooked on the Internet. Rates for open **jeeps** vary from €65 to €100 per day.

Brochure prices in Greece almost never include VAT at 19 percent, **collision damage waiver** (CDW) and personal insurance. The CDW typically has a deductible of €400–600, some or all of which can be levied for even the tiniest scratch or missing mudguard. To avoid this, it is strongly recommended that you pay the €5–7 extra per day for Super Collision Damage Waiver, Franchise Waiver or Liability Waiver Surcharge, as it is variously called. Even better, frequent travellers should take out **annual excess insurance** through Insurance 4 Car Hire (ⓦwww.insurance-4carhire.com), which will cover all UK- and North America-based drivers.

All agencies will require a blank **credit card** slip as a deposit (destroyed when you return the vehicle safely); minimum **age requirements** vary from 21 to 23. **Driving licences** issued by any European Economic Area state are honoured, but an International Driving Permit is required by all other drivers, including Australians, New Zealanders and North Americans. This must be arranged before departure in your home country. Some unscrupulous agencies still rent to these nationals on production of just a home licence, but you can be arrested and charged if caught by the traffic police without an IDP if you require one.

In peak season, you may get a better price through one of the **overseas booking companies** that deal with local firms than if you negotiate for rental in Greece itself. One of the most competitive companies in Britain is Skycars (ⓣ0870/789 7789, ⓦwww.skycars.com); ⓦwww.rentacar-uk.com also comes recommended. Autorent, Antena, Auto Union, Budget, Payless, Kosmos, National/Alamo, Reliable, Tomaso, and Eurodollar are dependable Greek, or smaller international, chains with branches in many towns; all are cheaper than Hertz, Sixt or Avis. Still it's worth visiting the biggest operators' websites; with a Frequent Flyer discount code you occasionally match quotes of the discount booking companies noted above. Specific local recommendations are given in the guide.

In terms of **models**, Greek outlets typically offer the Citroën Saxo, Kia Pikanto, Daewoo Matiz or Fiat Cinquecento/Seisento as A-group cars, and Opel (Vauxhall) Corsa 1.2, Fiat Uno/Punto, Peugeot 106, Hyundai Atos/Getz, Renault Clio/Twingo, or Nissan Micra in the B group, in which the Atos and the Clio are most robust. In the C or D categories, suitable for two adults and two kids, Renault Mègane or Peugeot 307 are preferable to the Seat Cordoba/Ibiza. The standard four-wheel-drive option is a Suzuki jeep (1.3- or 1.6-litre), mostly open – great for bashing down steep, rutted tracks.

Driving in Greece

As in all of continental Europe, you **drive on the right** in Greece. The country has one of the highest (fatal) **accident rates** in Europe, and on mainland motorways or the larger tourist islands it's obvious why. Local driving habits can be atrocious; overtaking is erratic, tailgating and barging out from side roads are preferred pastimes, lane lines go unheeded, turn signals go unused and motorbikes hog the road or weave from side to side. **Drunk driving** is also a major issue; Sunday afternoons in rural areas are particularly bad, and you should be extra vigilant driving late at night at weekends or on holidays. Well-publicized police **breathalyzing** campaigns are confronting the problem – the legal limit of .025 mcgm blood alcohol is half of that in most countries – with radar guns deployed against speeders as well.

Matters are made worse by **poor road conditions**: signposting is absent or badly placed, pavement markings are faded, curves are invariably banked the wrong way and slick with olive-blossom drop in May, asphalt can turn into a one-lane surface or a dirt track without warning, railway crossings are rarely guarded, and you're heavily dependent on magnifying mirrors at blind intersections in congested villages. Uphill drivers demand their **right of way**, as do those first to approach a one-lane bridge; **flashed headlights** usually mean the opposite of what they do in the UK or North America, here signifying that the other driver insists on coming through or overtaking. (However, this gesture rapidly repeated from someone approaching means they're warning you of a police control-point ahead.) **Parking** in almost every mainland town, plus the biggest island centres, is uniformly a nightmare owing to oversubscription. **Pay-and-display** systems (plus residents-only schemes) are common, and it's rarely clear where you obtain tickets (sometimes from a kiosk, sometimes from a machine).

There are a limited number of **motorways** between Pátra, Athens and Thessaloníki, on which tolls (€2–3) are levied at often densely placed gates. They're nearly twice as quick as the old roads, and good for novices to Greek conditions. But even on these, there may be no proper far-right lane for slower traffic, which is expected to straddle the solid white line at the verge and allow speeders to pass.

Seatbelt use is compulsory – you may be fined for non-observance at the many check-points – as is keeping a first-aid kit in the boot (many rental companies skimp on this), and children under the age of 10 are not allowed to sit in the front seats. It's illegal to drive away from any kind of **accident** – or to move the vehicles before the police appear – and where serious injury has resulted to the other party you can be held at a police station for up to 24 hours. For any substantial property damage, you wait for the police to arrive; they will take down the details of (and probably breathalyze) all drivers, help you fill out the accident report (*filikí dhílosi*, completed by both parties), give a copy to everyone for insurance purposes (or forward one to the rental company if your car is rented), and finally give you permission to leave if the car hasn't been crippled. Though forensics aren't their long suit, they're generally more civil and calm than the Greek drivers actually involved in the accident.

Tourists with proof of AA/RAC/AAA membership are given free road assistance from ELPA, the Greek equivalent, which runs **breakdown services** on several of the larger islands; in an emergency ring ⓣ10400. Many car rental companies have an agreement with ELPA's competitors Hellas Service (ⓣ1057), Interamerican (ⓣ1168) and Express Service (ⓣ1154). You will get a faster response if you dial the local number for the province or island you're in (ask for these in advance).

Fuel, whether regular unleaded (*amólyvdhi*), super or diesel, is currently over €1.10 per litre across the country, often €1.30-plus in remoter areas. Lead-replacement fuel for older cars without catalytic converters is called "Neo Super" or "Super LRP". Most scooters and motorbikes run better on super, even if they nominally take regular.

It is possible to run short of fuel **after dark or at weekends** anywhere in Greece; most stations close at 7 or 8pm, and nearly as many are shut all day Sunday. This is not much of an issue along major highways, but applies everywhere else. One pump per district will always remain open, but interpreting the Greek-only pharmacy-type-rota lists posted at shut stations is another matter. Stations which claim to be open around the clock are in fact **automated-only at night** – you have to use bill-taking machines, which don't give change. If you fill your tank without having exhausted your credit, punch the button for a receipt and get change during attended hours. Petrol stations run by multinational companies are more likely to take **credit cards** than Greek chains, but this rule is not infallible, especially in tourist areas or along main highways – always ask (broken card machines or down phone lines are common).

Taxis

Greek **taxis** are among the cheapest in the Mediterranean – so long as you get an honest driver who switches the meter on (see the caveats about Athens on p.94) and doesn't use high-tech devices to doctor the reading. Use of the meter is mandatory within city or town limits, where Tariff 1 applies, while in rural areas or between midnight and 5am Tariff 2 is in effect. On certain islands, set rates apply on specific fixed routes – these might only depart when full. Otherwise, throughout Greece the meter starts at €0.85, though the minimum **fare** is €1.75; baggage in the boot is charged at €0.35 per piece. Additionally, there are surcharges of €2 for leaving or entering an airport (€3 for Athens), and €0.80 for leaving a harbour area. If you summon a taxi by phone on spec, there's a €1.50 charge, while a prearranged rendezvous is €2.10 extra; the meter starts running from the moment the driver begins heading towards you. All categories of supplemental charges must be set out on a card affixed to the dashboard. For a week or so before and after Orthodox Easter, and Christmas, a *filodhórima* or gratuity of about ten percent is levied. Any or all of these extras will legitimately bump up the basic rate of about €9 per ten rural kilometres.

Domestic flights

Scheduled Greek **domestic flights** are operated by national carrier Olympic Airlines (including its subsidiary Olympic Aviation; Ⓣ801 11 44 444, Ⓦwww.olympicairlines.com), Aegean Airlines (Ⓣ801 11 20 000, Ⓦwww.aegeanair.com) and Sky Express (Ⓣ281 02/23 500, Ⓦwww.skyexpress.gr). They cover a broad network of island and mainland destinations, though most routes are to and from Athens or Thessaloníki. Aegean often undercuts Olympic fare-wise, and surpasses it service-wise, though services are less frequent; Sky Express, established 2007, is pricey and restricted to various routes between Iráklio (Crete) and nearby islands. Olympic and Aegean publish schedule booklets at least twice yearly (spring and autumn); they are easiest obtained from major airport counters.

All three airlines are geared to web and call-centre **e-ticket sales**; Olympic has closed most of its town-centre sales offices, except for Athens, Thessaloníki, Iráklion, Kós, Rhodes and Haniá, while Aegean and Sky Express never had many to begin with. Tickets bought through travel agencies attract a minimum €10 commission charge.

Fares to/between the islands cost at least double the cost of a deck-class ferry journey, but on inter-island routes poorly served by boat (Rhodes–Sámos or Corfu–Kefaloniá, for example), consider this time well bought, and indeed some subsidized peripheral routes cost less than a hydrofoil/catamaran journey. The cheapest web fares on Aegean are non-changeable and non-refundable, but with Olympic you can **change** your flight date, space permitting, without penalty up to 24 hours before your original departure.

Island flights are often full in peak season; if they're an essential part of your plans, make **reservations** at least a month in advance. If a flight you want is full, waiting lists exist – and worth signing on to; there are almost always cancellations. Many Olympic flights use small 46- or 74-seat ATR turbo-prop planes or "Dash 8" (De Havilland) 37-seaters, which won't fly in strong winds or (depending on the airport) after dark; Aegean uses more robust Avro or Airbus jets, Sky Express BAe Jetstream ones. A 15-kilo baggage **weight limit** can be strictly enforced; if, however, you've just arrived from overseas or purchased your ticket outside Greece, you're allowed the standard international limits (20–23 kilos).

Additionally, AirSea Lines (Ⓣ801 11 800 600, Ⓦwww.airsealines.com) theoretically operate **hydro-planes** between Pátra and Ioánnina, via all intervening Ionian islands except Zákynthos. They have, however, been subject to shutdown orders instigated by interested parties; check the current state of play on their website.

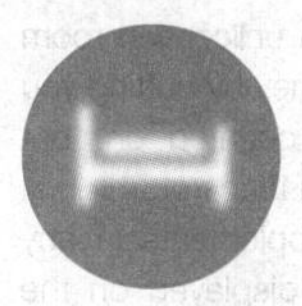

Accommodation

There are huge numbers of tourist beds in Greece, so for much of the season you can turn up almost anywhere and find a room – if not in a hotel, then in a block of rooms (the standard island accommodation) or a private house. Only from late July to early September, and around Easter, the country's high seasons, are you likely to experience problems. At these times, if you don't have accommodation reserved well in advance, you'd be wise to avoid the main tourist trails, turn up at new places early in the day and take whatever is available – you may be able to exchange it for something better later on.

Out of season, most private rooms and campsites operate only from April or May to October, leaving hotels as your only option. During winter you may have to stay in the main towns or ports. There will often be very little life outside these places anyway, with all seasonal beach bars and restaurants closed. On many smaller islands, there may be just one hotel and perhaps one taverna staying open year-round. Be warned also that resort or harbour hotels which do operate through the winter are likely to have a certain number of prostitutes as long-term guests; licensed prostitution is legal in Greece, and the management may consider this the most painless way to keep the bills paid.

Hotels

Hotels and self-catering complexes in larger resorts are often contracted out on a seasonal basis by foreign package-holiday companies, though there are often vacancies available (especially in spring or autumn) for walk-in trade. The tourist police set official **categories** for hotels, which range from L (Luxury) down to the rarely encountered E class; all except the top category have to keep within set price limits. The letter system is being slowly replaced with a star grading system; L is five-star, E is no-star, etc. Letter ratings were supposed to correspond to **facilities** available, though in practice there are E-class hotels which are smarter than nearby C-class outfits.

Mainland town hotels with a predominantly business clientele tend to charge the same over-inflated rates all year. In ski resorts and other places with significant October-to-April leisure tourism, such as Galaxídhi, Náfplio, Pílion and Mount Ménalo, rates can be markedly higher at weekends and holidays, and are generally so during winter to cover heating bills; the only exceptions are lowland Peloponnese (which has enough foreign tourism to generate some healthy competition), and to a certain extent Athens.

C-class hotels and below have only to provide the most rudimentary of continental breakfasts – sometimes optional for an extra charge – while B-class and above will usually offer a buffet breakfast including cheese, cold meats, eggs and cereals.

Private rooms

The most common island and mainland-resort accommodation consists of **privately let rooms** (*dhomátia*): many newer ones are studios (*garsoniéra*) or apartments (*dhiamérismata*), with at least a rudimentary kitchenette (sink, fridge and heating rings). Like hotels, these are regulated and officially divided into three classes (A to C), according to facilities. The bulk of them are in newer, purpose-built blocks, but a few are still inside people's houses, where you may be treated to disarming hospitality.

Licensed rooms are mostly reasonably clean, however limited their other amenities. Many are modern, fully furnished places with en-suite bathroom, TV, air-conditioning (sometimes at an extra charge), and a fridge. There may be a choice of rooms at various prices – owners usually show you the most expensive first. Price and quality are not necessarily directly linked, so always see a room before agreeing to take it.

Areas to **look for rooms**, along with recommendations of the best places, are included in the Guide. However, the rooms may find you: owners descend on ferry or bus arrivals to fill any space they have, sometimes with photos of the premises. Many island municipalities have outlawed this practice, owing to widespread bait-and-switch tactics and the pitching of unlicensed rooms. Rooms can often be much further than you had expected. In smaller places you'll often see rooms advertised, sometimes in German (*Zimmer*); the Greek signs to look out for are "ENIKIAZÓMENA DHOMÁTIA" or "ENIKIÁZONTEH DHOMÁTIA". In the more developed island resorts, where package holiday-makers predominate, room owners may require you to stay for at least three days, or even a week.

Some room proprietors ask to keep your **passport** – ostensibly for the tourist police, but in reality to prevent you skipping out with an unpaid bill. Most owners will be satisfied with just noting down your details, as is done in most hotels, and they'll almost always return the documents once you get to know them, or if you need them for another purpose.

If you are **stranded**, or arrive very late in a remote mountain or island village, you may well find someone with an unlicensed room prepared to earn extra money by putting you up. This should not be counted on, but things work out more often than not.

By law, **prices** and supplements in any establishment should be displayed on the back of the door of your room, or over the reception desk. If you feel you're being overcharged at a place that is officially registered, threaten to report it to the tourist office or police, who will generally take your side in such cases – it's an offence to charge over the permitted price for the **current season**. Small amounts over the posted price may be legitimately explained by municipal tax or out-of-date forms, but usually you will pay less than the maximum. Depending on location, there are often three seasons: typically October to May (low), June to mid-July, and September (mid) and mid-July through August (high). In **winter**, officially from November 1 until early April, private rooms – except in Ródhos Old Town and the biggest towns of Crete – are mostly closed to keep the few open hotels in business.

Some proprietors only check their email at infrequent intervals, if at all, and **phoning** may be essential for advance booking.

Accommodation price codes

Throughout the book accommodation is categorized according to the following **price codes**, which denote the **cheapest available double room in high season**. Prices are for the room only, except where otherwise indicated. Many hotels, especially those in category ❹ and over, include breakfast in the price; we indicate this by including "B&B" in the listing, but check when booking. During low season, rates can drop by more than fifty percent, especially for stays of three or more nights – exceptions are during the Christmas and Greek Easter weeks. Single rooms, if available, cost around seventy percent of the price of a double.

Old-fashioned rooms in remoter places, sometimes with a shared bathroom, tend to fall into the ❶ price category. Basic en-suite rooms without cooking facilities weigh in at ❷; newer, well-equipped rooms, self-catering studios, and modest C-class hotels occupy the top end of the ❸ niche, the better ones edging into ❹. Category ❺ corresponds to the better-value B-class hotels and the humbler designer inns in trendier centres, while ❻ tallies with most of B-class and the state-of-the-art restoration projects. ❼–❽ means A- and L-class, and the sky's the limit here – €500 is by no means unheard of these days.

❶ Up to €30
❷ €31–40
❸ €41–60
❹ €61–85
❺ €86–110
❻ €111–150
❼ €151–200
❽ Over €200

Youth hostels and **mountain refuges** typically charge €7–9 for a dorm bed.

Villas and long-term rentals

The easiest – and usually cheapest – way to arrange a **villa rental** is through one of the package-holiday companies detailed on p.32. They represent some superb places, from fairly simple to luxurious, and costs can be very reasonable, especially if shared between a few people. Several of the companies listed will arrange **twin-centre** stays on two islands over two weeks.

On the islands, a few local travel agents arrange villa rentals, though they are often villas the overseas companies turned down or could not fill. **Out of season**, you can sometimes get a good deal on villa or apartment rental for a month or more by asking around locally, though with the increasing desirability of the islands as year-round residences, "good deal" means anything under €600 per month for a large studio (*garsoniéra*) or €800 for a small one-bedroom flat.

Youth hostels

Greece has few **youth hostels**, and they tend, with a few exceptions, to be pretty run-down. Competition from inexpensive rooms and unofficial "student hostels", open to all, means they are simply not as cost-effective as elsewhere in Europe. It's best to have a valid IYHF card, but you can often buy one on the spot, or maybe just pay a little extra for your bed. Extra payment for sheets and towels can bump up the price. Dorms tend to have four to six beds; most hostels have a curfew of 11pm or midnight, and many places only open in spring and summer. The only surviving hostels on the **mainland** are in Athens, Olymbía, Pátra and Thessaloníki. On the **islands** you'll find them on Thíra, Corfu, Rhodes and Crete. Few of these are officially recognized by the IYHF.

Monasteries

Greek **monasteries** and **convents** have a tradition of putting up travellers (of the appropriate sex). On the mainland, this is still a customary – if steadily decreasing – practice, used mostly by villagers on pilgrimage; on the islands, monastic hospitality is not common, so check locally before heading out to a monastery for the night. Also, dress modestly – no shorts or short skirts – and try to arrive early in the evening, not later than 8pm or sunset (whichever is earlier). For men, the most exciting monastic experience is a visit to the "Monks' Republic" of Mount Athos (see p.457), on the Halkidhikí peninsula, near Thessaloníki. This is, however, a far from casual travel option, involving a fair amount of advance planning and the securing of a permit.

Camping

Officially recognized campsites range from ramshackle compounds on the islands to highly organized and rather soulless complexes, formerly run by EOT prior to privatization. Most places cost about €5–7 a night per person, slightly less per tent, and €6–8 per camper van, but at the fanciest sites rates for two people plus a tent can almost equal the price of a basic room. The Panhellenic Camping Association regularly publishes a booklet, available from many EOT offices, listing most officially recognized Greek campsites.

Freelance camping (outside a campsite, with or without a tent), as the EOT calls it, was forbidden under a law originally enacted to harass gypsies, but is increasingly enforced against tourists. A further drawback is the increased prevalence of theft in rural areas. You will feel less vulnerable inside a tent, camper van or even a rock-cave, with some protection from wind, sun, insects and stray animals raiding your food. You will always need at least a light sleeping bag, since even summer nights can get cool and damp; a foam pad is also recommended for pitching on harder ground.

If you do camp rough, exercise sensitivity and discretion. Police will crack down on people camping (and especially littering) around popular tourist beaches, particularly when a large community of campers develops. Off the beaten track, however, nobody is very bothered, though it is always best to ask permission in the local taverna or café. During high season, when everything – even authorized campsites – may be full, attitudes towards freelance camping are more relaxed, even in the more touristy places. At such times the best strategy is to find a sympathetic taverna, which in exchange for regular patronage will probably be willing to guard small valuables and let you use their facilities.

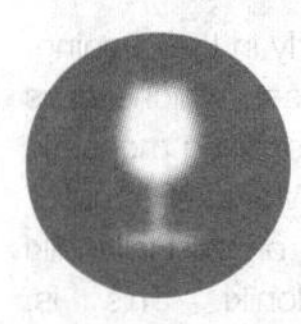

Food and drink

Despite depressed wages and an economic crunch for most Greeks, they still socialize outside their homes fairly frequently, sharing a meal with friends or family on average once a week. The atmosphere is always relaxed and informal, with pretensions rare outside of the more chi-chi parts of Athens and certain major resorts. Drinking is traditionally meant to accompany food, though a range of bars and clubs exists.

Breakfast

Greeks don't generally eat **breakfast**, something reflected in the abysmal quality of most hotel "continental" offerings; the choice of juice tends to be orange and orange, with fresh fruit rare and processed cheese/mortadella the rule at any place below "B" category – make that "A" category in low season, when skimping on ingredients prevails. *Méli me voútyro* is syrupy, commercial honey and prepacked pats of butter (or margarine) to slather on bread or *friganiés* (melba-toast slivers). Confusingly, jam is called *marmeládha* in Greek; proper marmalade is rare. Tea means obscure Sri Lankan brands of bag, often left to stew in a metal pot. The only egg-and-bacon kinds of places are in resorts where foreigners congregate, or where there are returned North American- or Australian-Greeks. Such outlets can sometimes be good value (€5.50–8 for the works, including coffee), especially if there's competition.

Picnics and snacks

Picnic fare is easily available at bakeries and *manávika* (fruit-and-veg stalls). **Bread** is often of minimal nutritional value and inedible within a day of purchase. It's worth paying extra at the bakery (*foúrnos*) for *olikís* (wholemeal), *sikalísio* (rye bread) or *oktásporo* (multi-grain). The fat Kalamáta or Ámfissa **olives** are more expensive, but tastier. However, locally gathered olives – especially the slightly shrivelled *throúmbes* or fully ripe, ground-gathered olives (*hamádhes*) – have a distinctive nutty taste. The best **honey** comes from the less forested islands (eg Límnos, Náxos, Kálymnos and Astypálea) or areas of the mainland. Adulteration scams abound, however, and much that is touted as thyme (*thymarísio*) honey isn't – always taste first if possible.

Honey is the ideal topping for the famous local **yoghurt**. All larger towns have at least one dairy shop where locally produced yoghurts are sold in plastic or clay containers of various sizes. Sheep-milk yoghurt (*próvio*) is richer and sweeter, scarcely requiring honey; cow's-milk yoghurt is tarter but more widely available. **Feta cheese** is ubiquitous, often with a dozen varieties to choose from, made from goat's, sheep's or cow's milk in varying proportions. You're allowed to taste before buying; this sampling advice goes for other indigenous cheeses as well, the most palatable of which are the various *graviéra*.

Greece imports very little produce from abroad, aside from bananas, the odd pineapple and a few mangoes. **Fruit** is relatively expensive and available mainly by season, though in more cosmopolitan spots one can find such things as avocados (the light-green Fuerte variety from Crete is excellent) for much of the year. Reliable picnic fruits include cherries (June–July); *yiarmádhes*, a giant peach available from August to mid-September (after which they go mealy and should be avoided); *krystália*, small, heavenly green pears that appear a month or two later, until November; *vaniliés*, orange- or red-fleshed plums (July to early Oct); and the *himoniátiko* melon (called casava in North America; Sept–Nov), in a yellow, puckered skin with green flecks. Greece also has a burgeoning kiwi industry, and while the first crop in October coincides with the end of the tourist season, availability continues into the following May. Less portable, but succulent, are figs; there's a crop of small fruits in May, followed by larger ones in August and September. Salad **vegetables** are more reasonably priced; besides the famous, enormous tomatoes (June–Sept), there's a bewildering variety of cool-season greens, including rocket, dill, enormous spring onions and lettuces.

Traditional **snacks** can be another sort of culinary delight, though they are being elbowed aside by Western fast food at nationwide chains such as *Goody's* (burgers, pasta and salad bar), *Everest* and *Grigoris Mikroyevmata* (turnovers and baguette sandwiches), *Roma Pizza* and *Theios Vanias* (baked pastries) – somewhat less insipid for being home-grown. However, independently produced kebabs (*souvlákia*) are widely available, and in most larger centres you'll find *yíros* – doner kebab with garnish in pítta bread – purveyed at *souvladzídhika* and *yirádhika* respectively. Other snacks include *tyrópites* (cheese pies – the best are the *striftés* or *kouroú* if available) and *spanokópites* (spinach pies), found at the baker's, as are *voutímata* (dark biscuits with molasses, cinnamon and butter). Pizza can be very good as well, sold *al metro* (by the piece).

Restaurants

Greek cuisine and **restaurants** are usually straightforward, and with care it remains affordable – typically €12–16 per person for a substantial (non-seafood) meal with a measure of house wine. But even when preparation is basic, raw materials should be wholesome – Greeks are fussy about freshness and provenance, shunning pre-fried chips and frozen New Zealand chops. That said, there's a lot of lazy cooking in resorts, where menus are dominated by badly done pizza, spaghetti bolognese, chops and "tourist moussaká": a dish stuffed with cheap potato slices, and nary a forkful of mince. There are, moreover, growing numbers of **"koultouriárika"** restaurants, often pretentious attempts at Greek nouvelle (or fusion) cuisine with speciality wine lists, which tend to be long on airs and graces, and (at €25–50 a head) short on value. The exceptions have been singled out in the text.

In the absence of recommendations, the best strategy is to **go where Greeks go**. And, despite EU regulations increasingly limiting staff hours, they go late: 2 to 3.30pm for **lunch**, 9 to 11pm (10pm–midnight Fri/Sat) for **dinner**. You can eat earlier, but you'll probably get indifferent service and food if you frequent touristy establishments. One good omen is the waiter bringing a carafe of refrigerated water, unbidden, rather than pushing you to order bottled stuff.

Waiters often urge you into ordering more than you want, then bring things you haven't ordered. Although cash-register receipts are required everywhere, these are often only for the grand total, and itemized **bills** will be in Greek script. Bill-padding has, alas, become endemic, as a few unwarranted euros extra per party adds up over time; even without reading Greek, ensure that the number and cost of items tally with what you ordered. Though menu prices are supposedly inclusive of all taxes and service, an extra **tip** of 5–10 percent directly to the waiter is in order if they've done well.

Bread is generally counted as part of the "cover" charge (€0.50–1 per person), so you have to pay for it even if (as so often) it's barely edible. **Children** are always welcome, day or night, at family tavernas; kids are expected to be kids – playing tag around the tables – but they are not allowed to cramp adults' style.

Estiatória

The two most common types of restaurant are the **estiatório** and the taverna. Distinctions are slight, though the former is more commonly found in large towns and emphasize the more complicated, oven-baked casserole dishes termed **mayireftá** (literally, "cooked"). With their long hours and tiny profit margins, *estiatória* (sometimes known as *inomayiría*, "wine-and-cook-houses") are, alas, a vanishing breed. An *estiatório* will generally feature a variety of *mayireftá* such as moussaka, macaroni pie, meat or game stews, stuffed tomatoes or peppers, the oily vegetable casseroles called *ladherá,* and oven-baked meat and fish. Usually you point at the steam trays to choose these dishes.

Batches are cooked in the morning and then left to stand, which is why *mayireftá* food is often **lukewarm**. Greeks don't mind this (many believe that hot food is bad for you), and most such dishes are enhanced by being allowed to steep in their own juice. **Desserts** (*epidhórpia*) of the pudding-and-pie variety don't exist at *estiatória*, though yoghurt is occasionally served. **Fruit**, however, is always available in season; watermelon (often on the house), melon and grapes are the summer standards. Autumn treats worth asking after include *kydhóni stó foúrno*, or *mílo psitó*, baked quince or apple with honey, cinnamon, or nut topping. At tavernas in the northern mainland you may be offered a complementary slice of sweet semolina halva (*simigdhalísios halvás*).

Tavernas and psistariés

Tavernas range from the glitzy and fashionable to rough-and-ready beachside ones with seating under a reed canopy,. Really primitive ones have a very limited (often unwritten) menu, but the more elaborate will offer some of the main *mayireftá* dishes mentioned above, as well as standard taverna fare: **mezédhes** (hors d'oeuvres) or **orektiká** (appetizers) and **tís óras** (meat and fish, fried or grilled to order). On the mainland where there are rivers, trout, frogs' legs, eel and freshwater crayfish are sometimes found. **Psistariés** (grill-houses) serve spit-roasted lamb, pork, goat, chicken or *kokorétsi* (grilled offal roulade). They will usually have a limited selection of *mezédhes* and salads (*salátes*), but no *mayireftá*. In rural areas, roadside *psistariés* are often called *exohiká kéndra*.

Since the idea of **courses** is foreign to Greek cuisine, starters, main dishes and salads often arrive together unless you request otherwise. The best strategy is to order a selection of *mezédhes* and salads to share, in local fashion. Waiters encourage you to take *horiátiki saláta* – the so-called Greek **salad**, including feta cheese – because it is the most expensive. If you only want tomato and cucumber, ask for *angourodomáta. Láhano-karóto* (cabbage-carrot) and *maroúli* (lettuce) are the typical cool-season salads.

The most common **mezédhes** are *tzatzíki* (yoghurt, garlic and cucumber dip), *melitzanosaláta* (aubergine/eggplant dip), fried courgette/zucchini or aubergine/eggplant slices, *yígandes* (white haricot beans in hot tomato sauce), *tyropitákia* or *spanakópites* (small cheese and spinach pies), *revythókeftedhes* or *pittaroúdhia* (chickpea patties similar to falafel), octopus salad and *mavromátika* (black-eyed peas).

Among **meats**, *souvláki* and chops are reliable choices, often locally produced, sold by the kilo or the platter. Pork is usually better and cheaper than veal, especially as *pansétta* (spare ribs). The best *souvláki*, not always available, is lamb; more commonly encountered are rib chops (*païdhákia*); roast lamb (*arní psitó*) is considered *estiatório* fare. *Keftédhes* (breadcrumbed meatballs), *biftékia* (pure-meat patties) and the spicy, coarse-grain sausages called *loukánika* are cheap and good. Chicken is widely available but typically battery-farmed. Other dishes worth trying are stewed goat (*gídha vrastí*) or baked goat (*katsíki stó foúrno*) – goat in general is a wonderfully healthy meat, typically free-range and undosed with antibiotics or hormones.

Fish and seafood

For the inexperienced, ordering **fish** and **seafood** can be fraught with peril. Summer visitors get a poor choice, most of it frozen, farmed or imported from Egypt, Bangladesh or Morocco. Trawling is prohibited from late May until early October, when only lamp-lure, trident, "doughnut" trap and multihook line methods are allowed. The few fish caught in these months tend to be smaller and drier, and served with *ladholémono* (oil and lemon) sauce. Taverna owners often comply only minimally with the requirement to indicate when seafood is **frozen** (look for the abbreviation "kat", "k" or just an asterisk on the Greek-language side of the menu).

Thus it's best to set your sights on the humbler, seasonally migrating or perennially local species. The cheapest consistently available fish are *gópes* (bogue) and *marídhes* (picarel), the latter eaten head and all. In the Dodecanese, *yermanós* is a good frying fish which appears in spring; a more widespread, inexpensive May–June treat is fresh, grilled or fried *bakaliáros* (hake), the classic UK fish-and-chip shop species. *Gávros* (anchovy), *atherína* (sand smelts) and *sardhélles* (sardines) are late-summer fixtures, at their best in the northeast Aegean. *Koliós* (mackerel) is excellent either grilled or baked in sauce. Especially in autumn you may find *psarósoupa* (fish soup) or *kakaviá* (bouillabaisse).

Less esteemed species tend to **cost** €18–35 per kilo; choicer varieties of fish, such as red mullet, *tsipoúra* (gilt-head bream), *sykiós/pandelís* (corvina), seabass or *fangrí* (common bream), will be expensive if wild – €40–60 per kilo, depending on what the market will bear. If the price seems too good to be true, it's almost certainly **farmed**. Prices are usually quoted by the kilo (less often by the portion); standard procedure is to go to the glass cooler and pick your specimen, then have it weighed (uncleaned) in your presence. Overcharging, especially where a printed menu is absent, is not uncommon; have weight and price confirmed orally or on a slip of paper at the scales.

Cheaper **seafood** (*thalassiná*) such as fried baby squid (usually frozen); *thrápsalo* (large, grillable deep-water squid) and octopus are summer staples; often mussels, cockles and small prawns will also be offered at reasonable sums (€20–26 per kilo).

Wines

All eateries will offer you a choice of bottled **wines**, and many still have their own house variety: kept in barrels, sold in bulk (*varelísio* or *hýma)* by the quarter-, half- or full litre, and served in glass flagons or (more usually) the brightly coloured tin "monkey-cups" called *kantária*. Per-litre prices depend on locale and quality, ranging from €4 (Thessaly, Skýros) to €10–11 (Corfu, Rhodes). Non-resinated wine is almost always more than decent; if in doubt, order some soda water, which can render even the roughest wine drinkable when added. **Retsina** – pine-resinated wine, often an acquired taste – is also available straight from the barrel, though the bottled brands Yeoryiadhi from Thessaloníki, Liokri from Ahaïa and Malamatina from central Greece are all quaffable and more consistent in quality.

Among **bottled wines** available nationwide, Cambas Attikos, Zítsa and Rhodian CAIR products (especially the Moulin and 2400 range) are good, inexpensive whites, while Boutari Naoussa and Kourtakis Apelia are decent, mid-range reds. For a better but still moderately priced red, choose either Boutari or Tsantali Merlot, or Averof Katoï from Epirus.

Travelling around **wine-producing islands**, however, you may as well sample local bottlings. Almost anything produced on Límnos is decent; Alexandrine muscat is used for whites, the local *límnio* grape for reds and rosés. Thíra, another volcanic island, has premium **white wines** such as Ktima Arghyrou and Boutari Nykhteri, and the Gentilini Robola white of Kefaloniá is justly esteemed. Páros (Moraïtis), Náxos and Ikaría (Ktima Karimali Ikariotikos) all have acceptable local vintages, while Crete has labels superior to the mass-market Logado, such as Economou (Sitía) and Lyrarakis (Iráklion). On Rhodes, Alexandhris products from Émbonas are well thought of, as is the Emery label (Villaré white), and products of the Triandafyllou winery near Ialyssós, especially their Taxidheftis white.

Curiously, island **red wines** are almost uniformly mediocre, except for Methymneos on Lésvos, Karimali on Ikaría and Hatziemmanouil from Kós; you're better off choosing reds from the mainland. Carras on Halkidhikí does the excellent Porto Carras, while Ktima Tselepou offers a very palatable Cabernet-Merlot blend. Andonopoulou (Pátra, including an organic line), Ktima Papaïoannou Nemea (Peloponnese), and Tsantali Rapsani (Thessaly) are all superb, velvety reds – and

Vegetarians

If you are **vegetarian**, you may experience difficulty, and will often have to assemble a meal from various *mezédhes*. Yoghurt with honey, *tzatzíki* and Greek salad in rotation begin to pall after a while, and many supposed "vegetable" dishes are cooked in stock or have pieces of meat added to liven them up. Wholly or largely vegetarian restaurants, however, are on the increase in touristy areas, and highlighted throughout the Guide where appropriate.

likely to be found only in better tavernas or *káves* (bottle shops). Andonopoulou, Tselepos (Mantinía domaine), Spyropoulos (again Mantinía) and Papaïoannou also do excellent **mainland whites**, especially the Spyropoulos Orino Mantinia, sometimes organically produced.

Other **premium microwineries** on the mainland whose products have long been fashionable, in both red and white, include the vastly overrated Hatzimihali (central Greece), the outstanding Dhiamandakou (near Náoussa, red and white), Athanasiadhi (central Greece), Skouras (Argolid) and the two rival Lazaridhi vintners (Dhráma, east Macedonia), especially their superb Merlots. For any of these you can expect to pay €9–15 per bottle in a shop, double that at a taverna. The best available current **guide** to the emerging Greek domaines and vintners is Konstantinos Lazarakis' *The Wines of Greece*.

Finally, CAIR on Rhodes makes **"champagne"** ("naturally sparkling wine fermented en bouteille", says the label), in both brut and demi-sec versions. It's not Moët & Chandon quality by any means, but at about €6 per bottle, nobody's complaining.

Cafés, cake shops and bars

A venerable institution, likely to survive the onslaught of mass global culture, is the **kafenío**, found in every Greek town, village and hamlet. In addition, you'll encounter **zaharoplastía** (sweet shops), **frappádhika** and **barákia**.

Kafenía, frappádhika and coffee

The **kafenío** (plural *kafenía*) is the traditional Greek coffee-house or café. Although its main business is "Greek" (Middle Eastern) **coffee** – prepared *skéto* or *pikró* (unsweetened), *métrio* (medium) or (*var*ý) *glykó* ([very] sweet) – it also serves instant coffee, spirits such as ouzo, brandy (usually Metaxa or Botrys brand, in three grades), beer, the sage-based tea known variously as *alisfakiá* (islands) or *tsái vounoú* (mainland), soft drinks and juices. One quality fizzy soft-drink brand to single out is Vólos-based Epsa, with its nine-pin-shaped bottles and high juice content. A refreshing curiosity – confined to Corfu and Paxí – is *tsitsibýra* (ginger beer), a legacy of the nineteenth-century British occupation of the Ionian islands; cloudy, greyish-white and fizzy, it tastes vaguely of lemon and the beginnings of fermentation.

Another refreshing drink is *kafés frappé*, iced instant coffee with sugar and (optionally) condensed milk – uniquely Greek despite its French name. Like Greek coffee, it is always accompanied by a glass of water. *Freddoccino* is a newer, cappuccino-based alternative to the traditional cold frappé. An entire class of venue, the **frappádhiko**, is devoted to it: the haunt of those nursing a single (expensive) such concoction for hours,. As they're all much of a muchness, we've just indicated where these establishments cluster in a given town.

"Nes"(café) has become the generic term for all instant **coffee**, regardless of brand; it's pretty vile, and since the 1990s there's been a reaction against it. Even the smallest provincial capital or resort will have at least one *frappádhiko* which also does a range of foreign-style coffees – filter, dubbed *fíltros* or *gallikós* (French); cappuccino; and espresso – at overseas prices. Outside of the largest towns, properly made premium coffees will be harder to find.

Like tavernas, *kafenía* and *frappádhika* range from the chrome and cutting-edge to the old-fashioned, spit-on-the-floor or mock-retro variety, with marble or brightly painted metal tables and cane-bottomed chairs. *Kafenía* still form the pivot of life in remoter villages, and many men spend most of their waking hours there, especially in winter. Greek women are rarely seen in more traditional *kafenía*; even in resorts, there is invariably one coffee house that the local men have reserved for themselves.

Some *kafenía* close at siesta time, but many remain open from early in the morning until late at night. The chief summer socializing time is 6–8pm, immediately after the afternoon nap, when one takes a pre-dinner ouzo.

Ouzo, tsípouro, mezédhes, ouzerís and mezedhopolía

Ouzo and the similar **tsípouro** (north mainland) and **tsikoudhiá** (Crete) are simple spirits of up to 48 percent alcohol, distilled from the grape-mash residue of wine-making, and then usually flavoured with anise, cinnamon, pear essence or fennel. There are nearly thirty brands of ouzo or *tsípouro*, with the best reckoned to be from Lésvos and Sámos islands, or Zítsa and Týrnavos on the mainland.

You will be served two glasses: one with the ouzo, and one full of water to be tipped into your ouzo just until it turns a milky white. Drunk straight, the strong, burning taste is hardly refreshing. It is also common to add **ice cubes**, a bowl of which will be provided upon request. The next measure up from a glass is a *karafáki* – a 200-millilitre vial, and the favourite means of delivery for *tsípouro* – which will very rapidly render you legless if you don't alternate tippling with snacks. A much smoother, unflavoured variant of ouzo is **soúma**, found chiefly on Rhodes and Sámos, but in theory anywhere grapes are grown. The smoothness is deceptive – as with *tsípouro*, two or three glasses of it and you had better not have any other plans for the afternoon.

Once, every ouzo was automatically accompanied by a small plate of **mezédhes** on the house: cheese, cucumber, tomato, a few olives, sometimes octopus or a couple of small fish. Nowadays "*ouzomezés*" is a separate, pricier option. Often, however, this is "off-menu", but if you order a *karafáki* you will automatically be served a selection of snacks.

Ouzerís (called **tsipourádhika** in Vólos, Thessaloníki and other major centres of the north mainland), found in the better resorts and select neighbourhoods of larger islands and towns, specialize in ouzo and *mezédhes*. In some places you also find *mezedhopolía*, a bigger, more elaborate kind of *ouzerí*. *Ouzerís* and *mezedhopolía* are well worth trying for the marvellous variety of *mezédhes* they serve (though some mediocre tavernas have counterfeited the name). At the genuine article, several plates of *mezédhes* plus drinks will effectively substitute for a more involved meal at a taverna (though it works out more expensive if you have a healthy appetite). Faced with an often bewilderingly varied menu, you might opt for a *pikilía* (assortment) available in several sizes, the most expensive one usually emphasizing seafood. At some *ouzerís* or *tsipourádhika* waiters wield an enormous tray laden with cold offerings – you pick the ones you like.

Sweets and desserts

The **zaharoplastío**, a cross between café and patisserie, serves coffee, a limited range of alcohol, yoghurt with honey and sticky cakes. The better establishments offer an amazing variety of pastries, cream-and-chocolate confections, honey-soaked Greco–Turkish sweets like *baklavás*, *kataïfi* (honey-drenched "shredded wheat"), *loukoumádhes* (deep-fried batter puffs dusted with cinnamon and dipped in syrup), *galaktoboúreko* (custard pie) and so on. If you want a slant towards dairy products and away from pure sugar, seek out a **galaktopolío**, where you'll often find *ryzógalo* (rice pudding), *kréma* (custard) and locally made *yiaoúrti* (yoghurt). Both *zaharoplastía* and *galaktopolía* are more family-oriented places than a *kafenío*. **Traditional specialities** include "spoon sweets" or *glyká koutalioú* (syrupy preserves of quince, grape, fig, citrus fruit or cherry) and the now-rare *ipovrýhio* ("submarine"), a piece of mastic submerged in a glass of water.

Ice cream, sold principally at the parlours which have swept across Greece (Dhodhoni is the posh home-grown chain, Haägen-Dazs the competition), can be very good and almost indistinguishable from Italian prototypes. A scoop (*baláki*) costs €1.10–1.50; you'll be asked if you want it in a cup (*kypelláki*) or a cone (*konáki*), and whether you want toppings like *santí* (whipped cream) or nuts.

Bars, beer and mineral water

Bars (*barákia*) are ubiquitous across Greece, ranging from clones of Spanish bodegas to musical beachside bars more active by day than at night. At their most sophisticated, however, they are well-executed theme venues in ex-industrial premises or Neoclassical houses, with both Greek and international soundtracks. Although recommendations are given in the Guide, most Greek bars have a half-life of about a year; the best way to find current hot spots, especially if they're more club than bar, is to look out for posters advertising bar-hosted events in the neighbourhood.

Shots and **cocktails** are invariably expensive: €5–8; beer in a bar will run €3.50–5, up to €11 for imports in trendier parts of Athens – beware. **Beers** are mostly foreign labels made locally under licence at just a handful of breweries on the central mainland. **Local brands** include Alfa, a hoppy lager brewed in Athens that's the best and most consistent mainstream label; Mythos, a mild lager in a green bottle, originally made by Boutari vintners but now wholly owned by Scottish and Newcastle; Veryina, brewed in Komotiní and common in the northeastern mainland and isles; and Zorbas, a lager worth sampling for the hokey label alone. Athens also has a **micro-brewery**, Craft: they produce lager in three grades (blonde, "smoked" and black), as well as a red ale, but distribution is limited.

Kronenberg 1664 and Kaiser, a sharp (light and dark) pilsner, are two of the more common quality **foreign-licence varieties**. Most of the market, however, is cornered by bland, inoffensive Amstel – the standard cheapie, also available as a very palatable, strong (seven percent) **bock** – and by Heineken, too sharp for many, still referred to as a *prássini* ("green") by bar and taverna staff after its bottle colour, despite the advent of identically-hued Mythos. Genuinely **imported** German beers, such as Bitburger, Fisher and Warsteiner (plus a few British and Irish ones), are found in Athens and at busier resorts.

The ubiquitous Loutraki **mineral water** is not esteemed by the Greeks themselves, who prefer various brands from Crete and Epirus. In many tavernas there has been a backlash against plastic bottles, and you can now get mineral water in glass bottles. Souroti, Epsa and Sariza are the principal labels of naturally **sparkling** (*aerioúho* in Greek) water, in small bottles; Tuborg club soda is also widespread.

Health

All European Economic Area (EEA) countries and Swiss nationals are entitled to free medical care in Greece upon presentation of the European Health Insurance Card (EHIC), obtainable in the UK from the post office, by phone or online (☎0845/606 2030, ⓦwww.dh.gov.uk/travellers). "Free", however, means admittance only to the lowest grade of state hospital (krátiko nosokomío), and does not include nursing care, special tests or medication. If you need prolonged medical care, rely on private treatment, slightly less expensive than in western Europe – this is where your travel insurance policy (see p.69) comes in handy. The US, Canada, Australia and New Zealand have no formal healthcare agreements with Greece (other than free emergency trauma treatment).

There are no required **inoculations** for Greece, though ensure that your tetanus jab is current. **Drinking water** is safe almost everywhere (unless signposted otherwise), though you will encounter brackish supplies on many islands, and nitrate levels exceed advised limits in some agricultural areas. Bottled water is universally available if you're feeling cautious.

Doctors and hospitals

You'll find English-speaking **doctors** in any of the larger centres. For an **ambulance**, phone ☎166. In **emergencies**, treatment is given free in state **hospitals** (ask for the *epígonda peristatiká* – casualty ward). As an inpatient, you'll get only the most basic care, and food and changes of bedding are not provided (it's assumed your family will do this). Better are the free state-run **outpatient clinics** (*yiatría*) attached to most public hospitals (where there may be a small appointment fee) and also found stand-alone in rural locales. These operate on a first-come, first-served basis, so go early; usual hours are 8am to 1pm, though sometimes in the afternoon too.

Pharmacies, drugs and contraception

A **pharmacy** (*farmakío*) will suffice for most minor complaints. Greek pharmacists dispense medicines which elsewhere could only be prescribed by a doctor; in the larger towns and resorts there'll be one who speaks good English. Pharmacies are usually closed evenings and Saturday mornings, but all have a **schedule** (in both English and Greek) on their door showing the complete roster of night and weekend duty pharmacists locally.

Greeks are famously hypochondriac, so pharmacies are veritable Aladdin's caves of arcane drugs and formulas – just about everything available in North America and northern Europe is here, and then some. **Homeopathic** and **herbal remedies** are sold in most of the larger pharmacies alongside more conventional products.

If you use any form of **prescription drug**, bring along a copy of the prescription, together with the drug's generic name; this will help should you need to replace it, and also avoids possible problems with customs officials. For example, in theory all codeine-containing compounds are illegal in Greece, but in practice as long as you have a prescription nobody is going to make trouble for you.

Hayfever sufferers should be prepared for the early Greek pollen season from April to June. Pollen from Aleppo and Calabrian pine in April/May can be particularly noxious. Pharmacies do stock appropriate tablets, but it's best to come supplied.

Don't count on getting **contraceptive pills** or spermicidal jelly/foam outside of the largest towns, over-the-counter at the larger pharmacies. **Condoms**, however, are inexpensive and ubiquitous – just ask for *profylaktiká* (less formally, *plastiká* or *kapótes*) at any pharmacy, sundries store or corner *períptero* (kiosk). Sanitary towels are most often sold in supermarkets; **tampons** can be trickier to find in remoter spots.

Specific health problems

The main visitor health problems relate to **overexposure to the sun**. So don't spend too long out in it, cover up, wear a hat, and drink plenty of fluids in the hot months to avoid any danger of **sunstroke.** To avoid hazards by the sea, goggles or a dive mask for swimming and footwear for walking over wet or rough rocks are useful.

Hazards of the sea

You may meet an armada of **jellyfish** (*tsoúkhtres*), especially in late summer; they come in various colours and sizes ranging from purple "pizzas" – *médhouses* – to invisible, minute creatures. Fenistil ointment is one recommended over-the-counter remedy for jellyfish (and other) stings; welts usually subside of their own accord within a few hours.

Less vicious but more common are black, spiky **sea urchins** (*ahiní*), which infest rocky shorelines year-round; if you step on one, a sterilized sewing needle and olive oil are effective for removing spines; if you don't extract them they'll fester, and walking on the wound pushes them in further.

Stingrays and skates (Greek names include *platý*, *seláhi*, *vátos* or *trígona*) can injure with their barbed tails: they frequent bays with sandy bottoms where they camouflage themselves, so shuffle your feet getting in. Take care also not to tread on a *dhrákena* (**weever fish**) which also buries itself in shallow-water sand with just its poisonous dorsal and gill spines protruding. If you do, the pain is excruciating, and the exceptionally potent venom can cause permanent paralysis of the affected area. Imperative first aid is immersing your foot in water as hot as you can stand, which degrades the toxin and relieves the swelling and pain, but you should still head straight to the nearest clinic for an antidote injection.

When snorkelling in deeper water, you may spot a brightly coloured **moray eel** (*sméma*) sliding back and forth out of its rocky lair. Keep a respectful distance – their slightly comical air and clown-colours belie an irritable temper and the ability to inflict nasty bites or even sever fingers.

Sandflies, mosquitoes, wasps and ticks

Mosquitoes (*kounóupia*) in Greece carry nothing worse than their bite, but are infuriating. The most widespread solution are small plug-in electrical devices that vaporize a semi-odourless insecticide tablet; many accommodation proprietors supply them routinely. Liquid insect repellents are available from most shops and pharmacies. Small electronic ultrasound generators have been proven ineffective and are a waste of money.

If you are sleeping on a **beach**, use insect repellent, either lotion or wrist/ankle bands, and/or a tent with a screen to deter **sandflies**. Their bites potentially spread two forms of leishmaniasis, difficult-to-diagnose parasitic infections characterized in one form by ulcerating skin lesions, in the other (visceral or kala-azar) by chronic fever, anaemia, weight loss, and death if untreated by long courses of medication.

Wasps (*sfigónes, sfíkes*) are ubiquitous during the wine-making season (Aug–Oct) when they're attracted by fermenting grape-mess. Some mind their own business, others are very aggressive, even dive-bombing swimmers out at sea. If a big one gets trapped under your helmet while you're on a scooter, the pain of the sting can make you lose control of the bike – get a helmet with a visor and keep it down. One good repellent measure while dining is coffee grounds set alight. Domestic **bees** (*mélisses*) can be aggressive near their hives; scrape the embedded sting from your skin with a fingernail to prevent injection of more venom. Alternatively, invest in an Aspivenin suction kit from a big-town pharmacy – light-weight and suitable for removing venom from various stings.

Ticks mostly feed on sheep, but wait on vegetation for new hosts. Check your legs after walking through long grass near flocks. If it has started to feed, you should detach it carefully by rocking or twisting, rather than pulling it off (which leaves the head embedded); do not use traditional tricks such as solvents or a lighted match. Ticks carry Lyme disease, which is now endemic in Europe.

Snakes, scorpions and insects

Adders (*ohiés*) and **scorpions** (*skorpií*) occur throughout Greece; both creatures are shy – scorpions are nocturnal – but take care when climbing over dry-stone walls where snakes like to sun themselves, and don't put hands or feet in places where you haven't looked first. Wiggly, fast-moving, six-inch **centipedes** (*skolópendres*) which look like a rubber toy should also be avoided, as they bite – hard.

Snakes, venomous or not, may bite if threatened; if a snake injects venom, swelling will occur within thirty minutes. If this happens, keep the bitten part still, and all body movements as gentle as possible. If medical attention is not nearby, bind the limb firmly to slow the blood circulation, but not so tightly as to stop the blood flow.

In addition to munching its way through a fair fraction of Greece's surviving pine forests, the **processionary caterpillar** –named for the long, nose-to-tail convoys which individuals form at certain points in their life cycle – sports highly irritating hairs. If you touch one, or even a tree trunk they've been on recently, you'll know all about it, and the welts may require antihistamine lotion or pills to heal.

Plants

If you snap a **wild-fig shoot** while walking, avoid contact with the highly irritant **sap**. The immediate antidote to the active alkaloid is a mild acid – lemon juice or vinegar; left unneutralized, fig "milk" raises welts which take a month to heal. Severe allergic reactions have to be treated with strong steroids, either topical cream (available from pharmacies) or intravenously in hospital casualty wards.

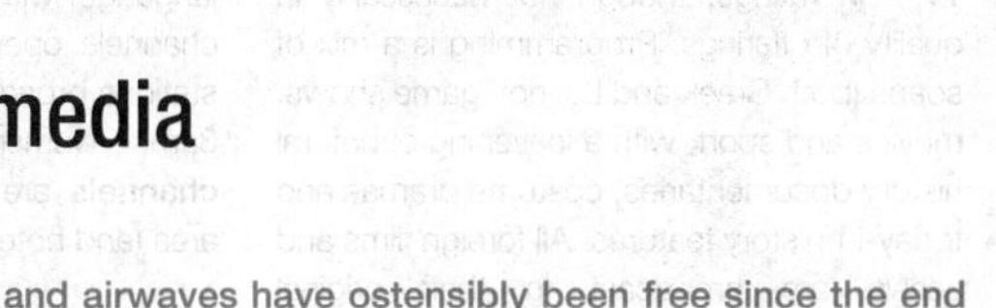

The media

Although the Greek press and airwaves have ostensibly been free since the end of the colonels' dictatorship in 1974, few would propose the Greek mass media as a paradigm of objective journalism. Many papers are sensational, state-run radio and TV often biased in favour of the ruling party, and private channels imitative of the worst American programming.

British newspapers are available at a cost of €2–2.75 for dailies, or €4.50 for Sunday editions. You'll find day-old copies (same day by noon in Athens) of *The Times*, *The Daily Telegraph*, *The Independent* and *The Guardian*'s European edition, plus a few of the tabloids, in all resorts as well as in major towns and airports. **American/international** alternatives include *USA Today* and the *International Herald Tribune*, the latter including a free, abridged English translation of the respected Greek daily *Kathimerini* (online at Ⓦwww.ekathimerini.com; Among **foreign magazines**, *Time* and *Newsweek* are commonly sold.

There are few surviving **locally produced** English-language magazines or papers. Glossy *Odyssey* (€6) magazine is published every other month by and for wealthy diaspora Greeks, with a range of features and reviews. The main English-language newspaper, available in most resorts, is the *Athens News* (weekly every Friday, online at Ⓦwww.athensnews.gr; €2.50), in colour with good features and Balkan news, plus entertainment and arts listings.

Greek publications

Most **newspapers** have an overt **political slant**, including funding from parliamentary parties. Only a handful of quality dailies have paper-of-record status; these include **centre-right** *Kathimerini* – whose former proprietress Helen Vlahos attained heroic status for defying the junta – and centre-left *Eleftherotypia*, especially its weekend editions. Indeed, most titles do a brisk trade in CDs, DVDs and books bundled with their Saturday/Sunday issues. *To Vima* (with its excellent *Vimagazino* supplement), *Avriani*, and *Ta Nea* stake out pro-PASOK territory, the latter esteemed for its Saturday magazine, *Takhydhromos*. On the far Left, *Avyi* is the Syriza forum, while *Rizospastis* acts as the organ of the KKE. On the **Right**, *Apoyevmatini* supports Néa Dhimokratía, while *Estia's* no-photo format and reactionary politics are both stuck somewhere in the early 1900s.

Among **magazines** not merely translations of overseas titles, *To Pondiki* (The Mouse) is a satirical weekly revue similar to Britain's *Private Eye*; its covers are spot-on and accessible to anyone with minimal Greek. *Andi*, an intelligent analytical fortnightly going since 1974 (its first issue confiscated by the junta), has reviews, political analysis and cultural critiques, in the mould of Britain's *New Statesman*.

Radio

Greek **radio** music programmes vary in quality, and since deregulation, the airways are positively cluttered as every island town sets up its own studio and transmitter. The two state-run networks are ER1 (a mix of news, talk and pop music) and ER2 (pop music).

On heavily touristed islands like Rhodes, Corfu and Crete, there will usually be at least one FM station trying its luck at **English programming** by and for foreigners. The Turkish state radio's Third Channel is also widely (if unpatriotically) listened to on east Aegean islands for its classical, jazz and blues programmes. Nearer Athens, check out the world music broadcast, Odhiki Voithia, Mondays at 23.59hr, on Sto Kokkino Radio 105.5FM.

Television

Greece's state-funded **TV stations**, ET1, NET and ET3, lag behind private channels – Antenna, Star, Alpha, Alter and Makedonia

TV – in ratings, though not necessarily in quality of offerings. Programming is a mix of soaps (both Greek and Latino), game shows, movies and sport, with a leavening of natural history documentaries, costume dramas and today-in-history features. All foreign films and serials are broadcast in their original language, with Greek subtitles. Most private channels operate around the clock; public stations broadcast from around 5.30am until 3am. Numerous **cable and satellite channels** are available, depending on the area (and hotel) you're in.

Festivals and holidays

Religious ceremonies punctuate the Greek year, mostly celebrations of one or other of a multitude of saints. With some kind of saint listed literally every day, there are scores of local festivals, or paniyíria, honouring the patron of the local parish church. You're unlikely to travel around Greece for long without stumbling on some sort of observance – sometimes spreading right across the town or island, sometimes tiny and local. They are celebrated with gusto and always with respect to local tradition. In addition, a major wedding or baptism will bring out a vast extended family, all of whom will expect lavish hospitality. No significant event, in fact, is allowed to go by without some kind of party to mark it – and especially in smaller villages and islands away from the tourist trail, visitors will very likely be invited to join in.

Saints' days are also celebrated as **name days**. If you learn that it's an acquaintance's name day, you wish them *Khrónia Pollá* ("many years", as in "many happy returns").

Some of the more important nationwide festivals and holidays are listed below; **public holidays** are marked with **PH**.The *paramoní*, or **eve of the festival,** is often as significant as the day itself, and many of the events are actually celebrated on the night before. If you show up on the morning of the date given you may find that you have missed most of the music, dancing and drinking. Remember too that religious dates will follow the Orthodox calendar. This is broadly similar to the Catholic year, except for **Easter**, which can fall as many as four (but usually one or two) weeks to either side of the Western festival.

For more on Easter and name days, see the *An Orthodox nation* colour insert.

Festival and holiday calendar

January 1: New Year's Day (*Protokhroniá*) in Greece is the feast day of Áyios Vassílios (St Basil). The traditional New Year greeting is "*Kalí Khroniá*". **PH**

January 6: Epiphany (*Theofánia*, or *Tón Fóton*) marks the baptism of Jesus as well as the end of the twelve days of Christmas. Baptismal fonts, lakes, rivers and seas are blessed, especially harbours (such as Pireás), where the priest traditionally casts a crucifix into the water, with local youths competing for the privilege of recovering it. **PH**

February/March

Carnival festivities – known in Greek as **Apokriátika** – span three weeks, climaxing during the seventh weekend before Easter. **Pátra Carnival**, with a chariot parade and costume parties, is one of the largest and most outrageous in the Mediterranean. Interesting, too, are the *boúles* or **masked revels** which take place around Macedonia (particularly at Náoussa), Thrace (Xánthi), and the outrageous **Goat Dance** on Skýros in the Sporades. The Ionian islands, especially Kefaloniá, are also good for carnival, as is Ayiássos on Lésvos, while Athenians celebrate by going around hitting each other on the head with plastic hammers.

Clean Monday (*Katharí Dheftéra*), the day after Carnival ends and the first day of Lent, 48 days before Easter, marks the start of fasting and is traditionally spent picnicking and flying kites. **PH**

March 25: Independence Day and the feast of the **Annunciation** (*Evangelismós* in Greek) is both a religious and a national holiday, with, on the one hand, military parades and dancing to celebrate the beginning of the revolt against Ottoman rule in 1821, and, on the other, church services to honour the news given to Mary that she was to become the Mother of Christ. There are major festivities on Tínos, Ýdhra and any locality with a monastery or church named Evangelístria or Evangelismós. **PH**

March/April
Easter (April 19, 2009; April 4, 2010; April 24, 2011) is by far the most important festival of the Greek year – infinitely more so than Christmas. The festival is an excellent time to be in Greece, both for its beautiful religious ceremonies and for the days of feasting and celebration that follow, though you'll need to book accommodation months in advance. The mountainous island of Ýdhra, with its alleged 360 churches and monasteries, is the prime Easter resort; other famous Easter celebrations are held at Corfu, Pyrgí on Híos, Ólymbos on Kárpathos and St John's monastery on Pátmos, where on Holy Thursday the abbot washes the feet of twelve monks in the village square, in imitation of Christ doing the same for his disciples. Good Friday and Easter Monday are also public holidays. **PH**

April 23: The feast of **Áyios Yeóryios** (St George), the patron of shepherds, is a big rural celebration, with much feasting and dancing at associated shrines and towns. If it falls during Lent, festivities are postponed until the Monday after Easter.

May 1: May Day (*Protomayiá*) is the great urban holiday when townspeople traditionally make for the countryside to picnic and fly kites, returning with bunches of wild flowers. Wreaths are hung on their doorways or balconies until they are burnt in bonfires on St John's eve (June 23). There are also large demonstrations by the Left for Labour Day. **PH**

May 21: The feast of **Áyios Konstandínos** (St Constantine) and his mother, **Ayía Eléni** (St Helen): the former, as emperor, championed Christianity in the Byzantine Empire. There are firewalking ceremonies in certain Macedonian villages; elsewhere celebrated rather more conventionally as the name day for two of the more popular Christian names in Greece.

May/June
Áyio Pnévma (Whit Monday), fifty days after Easter, sees services to commemorate the descent of the Holy Spirit to the assembled disciples. Many young Greeks take advantage of the long weekend, marking the start of summer, to head for the islands. **PH**

June 29 & 30: The joint feast of **Áyios Pétros** and **Áyios Pávlos** (SS Peter and Paul), two of the more widely celebrated name days, is on June 29. Celebrations often run together with those for the Holy **Apostles** (Áyii Apóstoli), the following day.

July 17: The feast of **Ayía Marína**: a big event in rural areas, as she's an important protector of crops.

July 20: The feast of **Profítis Ilías** (the Prophet Elijah) is widely celebrated at the countless hill- or mountaintop shrines of Profítis Ilías. The most famous is on Mount Taïyetos, near Spárti, with an overnight vigil.

July 26: Ayía Paraskeví is celebrated in parishes or villages bearing that name, especially in Epirus.

August 6: Metamórfosis toú Sotíros (Transfiguration of the Saviour) provides another excuse for celebrations, particularly at Khristós Ráhon village on Ikaría, and at Plátanos on Léros. On Hálki the date is marked by messy food fights with flour, eggs and squid ink.

August 15: Apokímisis tís Panayías (Assumption of the Blessed Virgin Mary). This is the day when people traditionally return to their home village, and the heart of the holiday season, so in many places there will be no accommodation available on any terms. Even some Greeks will resort to sleeping in the streets at the great pilgrimage to Tínos; also major festivities at Páros, at Ayiássos on Lésvos, and at Ólymbos on Kárpathos. **PH**

August 29: Apokefálisis toú Prodhrómou (Beheading of John the Baptist). Popular pilgrimages and celebrations at Vrykoúnda on Kárpathos.

September 8: Yénnisis tís Panayías (Birth of the Virgin Mary) sees special services in churches dedicated to the event, and a double cause for rejoicing on Spétses where they also celebrate the anniversary of the battle of the straits of Spétses. Elsewhere, there's a pilgrimage of childless women to the monastery at Tsambíka, Rhodes.

September 14: A last major summer festival, the **Ípsosis toú Stavroú** (Exaltation of the Cross), keenly observed on Hálki.
September 24: The feast of **Áyios Ioánnis Theológos** (St John the Divine), observed on Níssyros and Pátmos, where at the saint's monastery there are

Cultural festivals

Throughout the summer you'll find **festivals** of music, dance and theatre at venues across Greece, with many of the events taking place at atmospheric outdoor venues. Some, in the resorts and islands, are unashamedly aimed at drawing tourists, others more seriously artistic. The granddaddy of them all is Athens' **Hellenic Festival** (see p.147), which has been running every summer (late May to late Sept) for over fifty years, and now incorporates both a **jazz** festival and the **Epidaurus Festival** (July & Aug), with open-air performances of Classical drama in the ancient theatre. Others include:

Astypálea Municipal Festival July–Aug.
Itháki Music Festival July.
Ioánnina Folk Festival Mid-July–mid-Aug.
Ippokrateia Festival Kós; July–Aug.
Iráklion Festival Early Aug.
Kalamáta Dance Festival July–Aug.
Kassándhra Festival Svíri and Áfytos July–Aug.
Lefkádha Arts Jamboree Aug.
Manolis Kalomiris Festival Sámos; mid-July to early Sept.
Ólymbos Festival Mid-July to early Sept.
Pátra International Festival July–Sept.
Philippi/Thássos Festival Early July to early Sept.
Réthymnon Renaissance Festival July–Aug.
Rhodes Festival Aug–Oct.
Sáni Festival Kassándhra Halkidhikí; early July to early Sept.
Sými Festival Late June–early Sept).
Thessaloníki: Dhimitría Cultural Festival Oct, and a prestigious **film festival** Nov.
Thíra Music Festival Aug–Sept.
Vólos Festival Aug.

solemn, beautiful liturgies the night before and early in the morning.

October 26: The feast of **Áyios Dhimítrios** (St Demetrios), another popular name day, particularly celebrated in Thessaloníki, of which he is the patron saint. In rural areas the new wine is traditionally broached on this day, a good excuse for general inebriation.

October 28: Óhi Day is a national holiday with parades, folk dancing and speeches to commemorate prime minister Metaxas' one-word reply to Mussolini's 1940 ultimatum: *Ohi!* ("No!"). **PH**

November 8: Another popular name day, the feast of the **Archangels Michael and Gabriel** (Mihaïl and Gavriïl, or *tón Taxiárhon*), marked by rites at the numerous churches named after them, particularly at the rural monastery of Taxiárhis on Sými, and the big monastery of Mandamádhos, Lésvos.

December 6: The feast of **Áyios Nikólaos** (St Nicholas), the patron of seafarers, who has many chapels dedicated to him.

December 25 & 26: If less all-encompassing than Greek Easter, **Christmas** (*Khristoúyenna*) is still an important religious feast, and increasingly with all the usual commercial trappings: decorations, gifts and alarming outbreaks of plastic Santas on house-eaves. **PH**

December 31: New Year's Eve (*Paramoní Protohroniá*), when, as on the other twelve days of Christmas, a few children still go door-to-door singing the traditional *kálanda* (carols), receiving money in return. Adults tend to sit around playing cards, often for money. A special baked loaf, the *vassilópitta*, in which a coin is concealed to bring its finder good luck throughout the year, is cut at midnight.

Sports and outdoor pursuits

The Greek seashore offers endless scope for watersports, with windsurfing boards for rent in most resorts and, increasingly, parasailing facilities. On land, the greatest attraction lies in hiking, through what is one of Europe's more impressive mountain terrains. Winter also sees possibilities for skiing at a number of underrated centres.

In terms of spectating, the twin Greek obsessions are **football** (soccer) and **basketball**, with **volleyball** a close third in popularity. Many facilities, mostly in or near the capital, were improved for the **2004 Athens Olympics**, which has undoubtedly left its mark on the national sports scene for years to come.

Watersports

Windsurfing is very popular around Greece: the country's bays and coves are ideal for beginners. Particularly good areas, with established schools, include Vassilikí on Lefkádha island, Kéfalos on Kós, Zákynthos, western Náxos, Kokkári on Sámos, several spots on Lésvos and Páros, Corfu's west coast, numerous locales on Crete, and Karathónas, Mavrovoúni and Methóni in the Peloponnese. Board rental rates are very reasonable – about €10–15 an hour, with good discounts for longer periods – and instruction is generally also available. **Water-skiing** is now a rarity, but at many resorts, **parasailing** (*parapént* in Greek) is also possible – rates start at €30 a go.

A combination of steady winds, appealing seascapes and numerous natural harbours has long made Greece a tremendous place for **sailing**. Holiday companies offer all sorts of packaged and tailor-made cruises (see "Sailing holidays" p.34), and small boats and motorized dinghies are rented out by the day at many resorts. Spring and autumn are the most pleasant and cheapest seasons; *meltémi* winds can make for nauseous sailing between late June and early September, and summer rates can be three times shoulder-season prices.

Because of the potential for pilfering submerged antiquities, **scuba diving** is still fairly restricted, though the government has relaxed its controls of late and there are now over one hundred dive centres spread throughout parts of the mainland, the Dodecanese, the Ionians, the Cyclades and Crete. Single dives start around €40 and various courses are available. For more information and an update on new, approved sites, contact the Hellenic Federation of Underwater Activities (☎210 98 19 961).

In the Peloponnese, central mainland and Epirus, there's much potential for **rafting** and **kayaking**.

Skiing

Skiing is a comparative newcomer to Greece, beginning on Mount Parnassós in the 1950s. With global warming, snow conditions are unpredictable at the southernmost resorts, and runs remain generally short. However, there are now eighteen ski centres scattered about the mountains, and what they may lack in professionalism is often made up for by an easy-going, unpretentious après-ski scene. Costs are, however, on a par with those of northern Europe, at around €20 a day for rental of skis and boots, plus €12–27 a day for a lift pass. The season generally lasts from the beginning of January to the beginning of April, with a few extra weeks possible at either end, depending on snow conditions. No foreign package operators currently feature Greece among their offerings – it's very much a local, weekender scene.

The most developed of the resorts is Kelária-Fterólakkas on **Parnassós**, the legendary mountain near Delphi, though high winds often close the lifts. Other major ski centres include **Vórras** (Mount Kaïmaktsalán), near Édhessa; **Veloúhi** (Mount

Tymfristós), near Karpeníssi in central Greece; **Helmós**, near Kalávryta on the Peloponnese; and **Vérmion**, near Náoussa in Macedonia.

Walking

If you have the time and stamina, **walking** is probably the single best way to see the remoter backcountry. This guide includes some of the more accessible mountain hikes, as well as suggestions for more casual walking on the mainland and islands.

In addition, you may want to acquire one or more of the countrywide or regional **hiking guidebooks**; see Contexts p.962. See also p.72 for details of hiking maps available, and p.34 for details of companies offering walking holidays in the mountains.

Football and basketball

Football (soccer) is far and away the most popular sport in Greece – both in terms of participating and watching, its status strengthened still further by Greece's unexpected emergence as Euro 2004 champions. The most important teams are Panathanaïkós and AEK of Athens, Olympiakós of Pireás and PAOK of Thessaloníki. Matches – usually Wednesday nights and Sunday afternoons – take place between September to May. In mid-autumn you could catch one of the Greek teams playing European competition.

The national **basketball** team is one of the continent's strongest, while at club level, many of the football teams maintain basketball squads – Panathanaïkós are the most consistently successful.

Crime, police and cultural etiquette

Greece is one of Europe's safest countries, with a low crime rate and a deserved reputation for honesty. It is also a deeply traditional country, and it's more likely that you'll (inadvertently or otherwise) give offence than receive it; it pays to be aware of the most common misdemeanors, along with some positive cultural etiquette to observe.

Though undeniably safer than much of Europe – if you leave a bag or wallet at a café, you'll probably find it scrupulously looked after, pending your return – **theft** and **muggings** at archeological sites, in towns, remote villages and resorts have increased recently. With this in mind, it's best to lock rooms and cars securely. There has also been a huge rise in pickpocketing on the old section of the **Athens metro** (not the heavily policed new extension). See p.75 for **emergency phone numbers**.

Police and potential offences

There is a single, nationwide **police force**, the *Ellinikí Astynomía*, rather than the division into urban corps and rural gendarmerie as in most of Europe. Greek police are prone to be gruff and monolingual, and some have little regard for foreigners. Police practice often falls short of northern European norms, with fit-ups or beatings in custody not unknown.

You are required to **carry suitable ID** on you at all times – either a passport, national ID card or a driving licence. Otherwise, the most common causes of a brush with authority are beach nudity, camping outside authorized sites, public inebriation or lewd behaviour, and taking photos in forbidden areas.

Nude (sun)bathing is explicitly legal on very few beaches (most famously on Mýkonos), and is deeply offensive to more traditional Greeks – exercise sensitivity to where you are. It is, for example, bad etiquette to swim or sunbathe nude within sight of a church, of which there are many along the Greek coast. Generally, if a beach has become fairly well established as naturist, or is secluded, laws go unenforced. Police will only appear if nudity is getting too overt on mainstream stretches. Usually, there will only be a warning, but you can officially be arrested straight off – facing up to three days in jail and a stiff fine. **Topless (sun)bathing** for women is technically legal nationwide, but specific locales – eg, in front of "family" tavernas – often opt out by posting signs. Similar guidelines apply to **camping rough**; though ostensibly illegal, you're still unlikely to incur anything more than a warning to move on.

The **hours between 3 and 5pm**, the midday *mikró ýpno* (siesta), are sacrosanct – it's not acceptable to make phone calls to strangers or any sort of noise (especially with motorcycles) at this time. **Quiet** is also legally mandated **between midnight and 8am** in residential areas, though Greek construction crews frequently violate this by starting up at 7.30am or so.

The well-publicized ordeal of twelve British plane-spotters who processed through Greek jails and courts in 2001–02 on espionage charges (they had, however, received warnings on prior occasions) should be ample warning to **take no pictures** at all in and around airports or military installations. The latter are well festooned with signs of a bellows camera with a red "X" through it.

Any sort of **disrespect** towards the Greek state or Orthodox Church in general, or Greek civil servants in particular, may be actionable, so best keep your comments to yourself. This is a culture where verbal injuries matter, where libel laws greatly favour plaintiffs, and the alleged public utterance of *malákas* (wanker) can result in a court case.

Drunkenness has always been held in contempt in Greece, where the inability to hold one's liquor is considered unmanly and shameful. Inebriation will be considered an aggravating factor if you're busted for something else, not an excuse.

Drug offences are considered major crimes; the maximum penalty for "causing the use of drugs by someone under 18", for example, is life imprisonment and an astronomical fine. Theory is not always practice, but foreigners caught possessing even small amounts of cannabis or harder stuff get long jail sentences if there's evidence that they've been supplying to others. Moreover, you could be inside on remand for over a year awaiting a trial date, with little chance of bail being granted.

If you get arrested for any offence, you have a right to **contact your consulate**, which will arrange a lawyer for your defence. Beyond this, there is little they can, or in most cases will, do. Details of consulates in Athens and Thessaloníki appear in their respective "Listings" sections. There are honorary British consuls on Rhodes, Crete and Corfu as well.

Women and lone travellers

Thousands of **women** travel independently in Greece without being **harassed** or feeling intimidated. With the westernisation of relationships between unmarried Greek men and women, almost all of the traditional Mediterranean macho impetus for trying one's luck with foreign girls has faded. Any hassle is from the nearly extinct professionally single Greek men, known as *kamákia* (fish harpoons), who haunt beach bars and dance clubs. Foreign women are more at risk of **sexual assault** at certain notorious resorts (Kávos in Corfu; Laganás in Zákynthos; Faliráki in Rhodes) by northern European men than by ill-intentioned locals. It is sensible not to bar-crawl alone or to accept late-night rides from strangers (**hitching** at any time is not advisable for lone female travellers). In more remote areas intensely traditional villagers may wonder why women travelling alone are unaccompanied, and may not welcome their presence in exclusively male *kafenía*. Travelling with a man, you're more likely to be treated as a *xéni*, a word meaning both (female) stranger and guest.

Lone men need to be wary of being invited into bars in the largest mainland towns and island ports, in particular near Sýndagma in Athens; these bars are invariably staffed with hostesses (who may also be prostitutes) persuading you to treat them to drinks. At the end of the night you'll be landed with an outrageous bill, some of which goes towards the hostess's commission; physical threats are brought to bear on reluctant payers.

Cultural hints

Bargaining isn't a regular feature of tourist life, though possible with private rooms and some hotels out of season. You may also be able to negotiate better prices for vehicle rental, especially for longer periods. Restaurant bills incorporate a service charge and with the increasing cost of food, drink and services in Greece, generous **tipping** has decreased; if you want to tip, rounding up the bill is usually sufficient. If you receive particular hospitality, avoid reciprocating with excessive cash as this can cause offence.

Slovenly dress can be considered offensive (though amongst Greek men there's a style lately for untucked-in shirt-tails); Greek fashion-victim-hood – certainly in annual expenditure on clothing – is at near-Italian levels. Poverty is an uncomfortably close memory for many, who will consider grunge attire to be making light of hard times.

Most monasteries impose a fairly strict **dress code** for visitors: no shorts, with women expected to cover their arms and wear skirts (though most Greek women visitors will be in trousers); the necessary wraps are sometimes provided on the spot.

Living in Greece

Many habitual visitors fall in love with Greece to the extent that they take up part- or full-time residence there, more likely buying property than renting it, and most probably retired or self-employed rather than working at the prevailing low Greek pay scales. Beyond the first, easy hurdle of obtaining a residence certificate, there are other issues to consider: working, keeping a vehicle, Internet connection and animal welfare. For the full scoop on real estate, consult Buying a Property: Greece (Navigator Guides, UK).

Residence and voting

EU (and EEA) nationals are allowed to stay indefinitely in any EU state, but to ensure avoidance of any problems – eg, in setting up a bank account – you should, after the third month of stay, get a **certificate of registration** (*vevéosi engrafís*). This does not need to be renewed and, according to a presidential decree of June 2007, replaces the previously issued five-year **residence permit** (*ádhia dhiamonís*). However, there has been a countrywide delay in dispensing the required application forms to provincial aliens' bureaux and police stations so don't expect a smooth transition until late 2008.

EU nationals with a registration certificate become eligible to **vote** in municipal elections (every four years, next in Oct 2010) and Euro elections (next in 2009), though in the latter case they must choose a country – you can't vote in both the UK and Greece. Bring your passport and certificate to the nearest town hall and you will be entered onto the computerized voter registration rolls in a matter of minutes.

Residence/work permits for **non-EU/non-EEA nationals** can only be obtained on application to a Greek embassy or consulate outside of Greece; you have a much better chance of securing one if you are married to a Greek, are of Greek background by birth (an *omoyenís*), or have permanent-resident status in another EU state, but even then expect complications.

Many non-EU nationals working illegally in Greece still resort to the pre-Schengen ploy

Greek-language courses

The longest established outlet is The Athens Centre, Arhimídhous 48, 116 36 Athens (Ⓣ210 70 12 268, Ⓦwww.athenscentre.gr). One to try on Crete is Lexis, 48 Dhaskaloyiánni, 73100 Haniá (Ⓣ28210 55673, Ⓦwww.lexis.edu.gr). There are always advertisements in the *Athens News* for other, more transient schools.

of heading off to Turkey for a few days every three months and re-entering at a different border post for a new passport stamp; this usually works, but if not, penalties as described on p.69 potentially apply.

Working

EU membership notwithstanding, **short-term unskilled work** in Greece is usually badly paid and undocumented, with employers notoriously skimping on the requirement to pay IKA (social insurance contributions) for their employees. The influx, since 1990, of 1.3 million immigrants from various countries – chiefly Albania, south Asia and central Europe – has resulted in a surplus of unskilled labour and severely depressed wages. Undocumented, **non-EU/non-EEA nationals** working in Greece do so surreptitiously, with chronic risk of denunciation to the police and instant deportation as Greek immigration authorities are cracking down hard on any suitable target, whether Albanian, Senegalese, South African or North American. That old foreigners' standby, **teaching English**, is now available only to TEFL certificate-holders – preferably Greeks, non-EU nationals of Greek descent and EU/EEA nationals in that order. If you are a foreign national of Greek descent you are an *omoyenís* as defined above, and have tremendous employment, taxation and residence privileges.

Others may prefer **tourism-related work**. Most women working casually in Greece find waiting jobs in bars or restaurants around the main resorts; men, unless they are trained chefs, will find it harder to secure any position, even washing up. Corfu, with its British slant, is an obvious choice for bar work; Rhodes, Kós, Crete, Skiáthos, Páros, Íos and Santoríni are also promising. Start looking around April or May; you'll get a better salary if you're taken on for a full season. You might also staff one of the **windsurfing** schools or **scuba** operations that have sprung up on several islands.

The most common tourism-related work is serving as a **rep for a package holiday company**. All you need is EU nationality and the appropriate language, though knowledge of Greek is a big plus. English-only speakers are largely restricted to places with a big British package trade: Crete, Rhodes, Kós, Skiáthos, Sámos, Lésvos and the Ionian islands. Many such staff are recruited from Britain, but it's common to be hired through local affiliates in April or May. A major advantage, however you're taken on, is that you're guaranteed about six months of steady work, often with use of a car thrown in.

Keeping a car or motorcycle

Both tourist visitors and residents, of any nationality, are only allowed to **keep a vehicle in Greece** with foreign number plates for six months, or until the current road-tax sticker and/or insurance from your home country expires, whichever happens first. After that you face inconvenient choices: re-exporting the car, storing it for six months, or obtaining local registration. Many holiday home-owners long used the six-on, six-off system, storing their EU-plated car off-road under customs seal, but this has become difficult now that most Greek insurers will no longer cover foreign-registered cars. Especially on isolated islands, many foreigners just drive along for years on foreign plates with no current road tax, but if you're caught – either by ordinary traffic police or plainclothes customs inspectors stationed at busy ferry docks –both are empowered to impound the vehicle immediately, and the "ransom" (basically a fine plus arbitrary import duty) is prohibitive. If circulating with foreign plates, you must always be able to prove that your car has been in

Greece for less than six months (the dated ticket for any ferry you may have arrived on from Turkey or Italy is considered sufficient evidence).

The easiest car models to have serviced and buy **parts** for in Greece are VWs (including old microbuses and Transporter vans), Mercedes, BMWs, Audis, Opels, Ladas, Skodas and virtually all French, Italian, Korean and Japanese makes. British models are trickier, but you should be fine if you haven't brought anything too esoteric – the Mini is, for example, still a cult vehicle in Greece, Fords are represented, and the Opel is the continental brand of Vauxhall.

Should you decide to import your beloved buggy, **duties** run anywhere from 30 to 120 percent of the value of the car, depending on its age and engine size; the nearest Greek embassy overseas can provide a current table of fees. Take your car or motorcycle to the nearest customs compound, where personnel will inspect it and make a written application to headquarters in Piréas; within ten working days you (or rather your designated *ektelonistís* or **customs agent**) will receive an assessment of duty, against which there is no appeal, and which must be paid immediately. For EU-plated cars this is blatantly illegal – their owners should get Greek plates at little or no cost on demand – but despite being referred to the European Court several times on this (and always losing), the Greek state shows no sign of stopping this lucrative practice. The only way out is to make a declaration at your nearest Greek embassy or consulate that you intend to take up full-time residence in Greece (ie are not just a holiday-home owner); such an official document should satisfy the most exigent Greek official and get you a pair of Greek plates in a few weeks. In any case, you will immediately begin to save massive amounts of money by paying insurance at local rates rather than the inflated rates levied on all foreign-registered cars.

You will also need to get a **kárta kavsaeríon** – exhaust emissions compliance card – and visit either a state-run or private **KTEO** (equivalent to a UK MOT check) to certify that the vehicle is roadworthy.

If this all sounds too much hassle, the **price of cars and scooters** has plunged in Greece and many models costs less than in Britain – a Korean compact runabout starts at around €6000, plus tax, while a new scooter can be had for €1200–1500. But given the stiff fines for being caught driving even an 80cc scooter on a car licence (see p.40), budget €450–500 for a **licence course**, and enough facility in reading Greek to pass the written test.

Internet connection

There are currently several fixed-telephony providers besides OTE and a myriad of Internet providers, among which Otenet, Forthnet and HOL are the biggest players. Much of Greece still hasn't access to broadband (or ADSL as it's universally known); **dial-up** subscriptions cost from €10 per month if you pre-pay a year, plus modest hourly charges. The Yermanos electronic-widgets chain is one of the most impartial outlets for all providers, though once you're signed on with a particular company it's best to renew direct with them. **ADSL** is overpriced by north European standards – around €35 a month at the lowest speeds – but EU pressure is pushing rates down in some cases to €18 per month if you pre-pay for a year; free connection and router box deals are also frequent.

Pets and animal welfare

No single issue potentially pits foreign residents (especially English ones) in Greece against their locally born neighbours more than the status of **pets** and **animal welfare** in general. Abuse, especially in rural areas, is rife: hunting dogs are kept chained to outdoor stakes in all weathers, without enough water or food, while surplus kittens are routinely drowned in a weighted sack. Strychnine-bait poisoning of "extra" or annoying animals is the rule (especially in winter when there are no soft-hearted foreigners around to leave food out for strays) – so never, ever let your dog run loose. There is also a stubborn resistance at all social levels to neutering, or to spending money on an animal beyond a handful of pet food. Most Greek animal-lovers are urban and/or foreign-educated, as are vets and pet-shop owners, who have made little headway against deeply ingrained attitudes.

Beasts are seen as part of the rural economy, with a job to do; when their usefulness is over, they are disposed of without sentimentality. It is also deeply offensive to many Greeks (especially taverna owners) for foreigners to feed the under-table cats running in mendicant packs, as signs often warn you.

Under both European and Greek law it's an offence to poison, torture or abandon an animal, but in the countryside you are just wasting your breath by proselytizing to change opinions. If you feel strongly about the foregoing, support an **animal welfare organization**, found anywhere with large numbers of foreign residents. Useful UK-run organizations include the Greek Animal Welfare Fund (Ⓦ www.gawf.org.uk) and Greek Animal Rescue (Ⓦ www.greekanimalrescue.com). Both organize mass neuterings by visiting vets, maintain feeding stations and organize the adoption of strays overseas.

Travel essentials

Travelling with children

Children are worshipped and indulged, demonstrably to excess, and present few problems when travelling. They are not segregated from adults at meal times, and early on in life are inducted into the typical late-night routine – kids at tavernas are expected to eat (and up to their capabilities, talk) like adults. Outside of certain all-inclusive resorts with childrens' programmes, however, there are very few amusements specifically for them – certainly nothing like Disney World Paris. Luxury hotels are more likely to offer some kind of **babysitting or crèche service**.

Most domestic ferry-boat companies and airlines offer child **discounts**, ranging from fifty to one hundred percent depending on their age; hotels and rooms won't charge extra for infants, and levy a modest supplement for "third" beds which the child occupies by him/herself.

Costs

The **cost of living** in Greece has increased astronomically since it joined the EU, particularly after the adoption of the euro, and raising of the VAT rate in early 2005. Prices in shops and cafés now match or exceed those of many other EU member countries (including the UK). However, outside the established resorts, travel remains affordable, with the aggregate cost of restaurant meals, short-term accommodation and public transport falling somewhere in between that of cheaper Spain or France and pricier Italy.

Prices depend on where and when you go. Mainland cities, larger tourist resorts and the trendier small islands (such as Sými, Ýdhra, Mýkonos, Paxí and Pátmos) are more expensive, and costs everywhere increase sharply during July–August, Christmas, New Year and Easter.

On most islands a daily per-person **budget** of £35/US$70/€50 will get you basic accommodation and meals, plus a short ferry or bus ride, as one of a couple. Camping would cut costs marginally. On £63/US$126/€90 a day you could be living quite well, plus sharing the cost of renting a large motorbike or small car. See p.46 for accommodation costs.

Inter-island **ferry fares**, a mainly unavoidable expense, are subsidized by the government in an effort to preserve remote island communities. Local ferries in the Cyclades are a bit pricier for the sea miles travelled.

A basic taverna **meal** with bulk wine or a beer costs around €11–15 per person. Add a better bottle of wine, seafood or more careful cooking, and it could be up to €18–30 a head; you'll rarely pay more than that. Even in the most developed of resorts, with inflated "international" menus, there is often a basic but decent taverna where the locals eat.

Travellers with disabilities

Unfortunately, many of the delights of Greece like stepped alleys and ancient monuments are inaccessible or hazardous for anyone with mobility impairments. Access to all but the newest public buildings and hotels can also be difficult. In general the **disabled**, except notably on Kós, are not especially well catered to in Greece. Few street corners have wheelchair ramps, beeps for the sight-impaired are rare at pedestrian crossings, and outside Athens few buses are of the "kneeling" type. Only Athens airport, its metro and airline staff in general (who are used to handling wheelchairs), are disabled-friendly. However, as relevant EU-wide legislation is implemented, the situation should improve.

Some advance planning will make a trauma-free holiday in Greece more likely. The Greek National Tourist Office is helpful as long as you have specific questions; they also publish a useful questionnaire that you might send to hotels or self-catering accommodation. Before purchasing **travel insurance**, ensure that pre-existing medical conditions are not excluded. A **medical certificate** of your fitness to travel is also extremely useful; some airlines or insurance companies may insist on it.

Electricity

Voltage is 220 volts AC. Round, two-pin plugs are used; adapters should be purchased beforehand in the UK, as they can be difficult to find locally; standard 5-, 6- or 7.5-amp models permit operation of a hair dryer or travel iron. Unless they're dual voltage, North American appliances will require both a step-down transformer and a plug adapter (the latter easy to find in Greece).

Entry requirements

UK and all other EU nationals need only a valid **passport** to enter Greece, and are no longer stamped in on arrival or out upon departure. US, Australian, New Zealand, Canadian and most non-EU Europeans receive mandatory entry and exit stamps in their passports and can stay, as tourists, for ninety days (cumulative) in any six-month period. Such nationals arriving by flight or boat from another EU state not party to the Schengen Agreement may not be stamped in routinely at minor Greek ports, so make sure this is done in order to avoid unpleasantness on exit. Your passport must be valid for three months after your arrival date.

Unless of Greek descent, or married to an EU national, visitors from **non-EU** countries

Discounts

Various official and quasi-official **youth, student and teacher ID cards** soon pay for themselves in savings; they all cost around £9/US$22 (or local equivalent) for a year. Full-time students are eligible for the **International Student ID Card** (ISIC; ⓦwww.isiccard.com), which entitles the bearer to cut-price transport and discounts at museums, theatres and other attractions, though often not accepted as valid proof of age. If you're not a student but aged under 26, you can qualify for the **International Youth Travel Card**, which provides similar benefits to the ISIC. Teachers qualify for the **International Teacher Identity Card** (ITIC), offering insurance benefits but limited travel discounts. Consult the website of the International Student Travel Confederation (ⓦwww.isic.org) for the nearest retail outlet for any of these cards.

Seniors are entitled to a discount on bus passes in the major cities; Olympic Airways also offer discounts on full fares on domestic flights. Proof of age is necessary.

are currently not, in practice, being given extensions to tourist visas by the various Aliens' Bureaux in Greece. You must leave not just Greece but the entire Schengen Group – essentially the entire EU as it was before May 2004, minus Britain and Eire, plus Norway and Iceland – and stay out until the maximum 90-days-in-180 rule, as set forth above, is satisfied. If you overstay your time and then leave under your own power – ie are not deported – you'll be hit with a huge fine upon departure, and possibly be banned from re-entering for a period of time; no excuses will be entertained except (just maybe) a doctor's certificate stating you were immobilized in hospital. It cannot be overemphasized just how exigent Greek immigration officials have become on this issue.

Greek embassies abroad

Australia 9 Turrana St, Yarralumla, Canberra, ACT 2600 ☎02/6273 3011.
Britain 1A Holland Park, London W11 3TP ☎020/7221 6467, ⓦwww.greekembassy.org.uk.
Canada 80 Maclaren St, Ottawa, ON K2P 0K6 ☎613/238-6271.
Ireland 1 Upper Pembroke St, Dublin 2 ☎01/676 7254.
New Zealand 5–7 Willeston St, Wellington ☎04/473 7775.
USA 2217 Massachusetts Ave NW, Washington, DC 20008 ☎202/939-1300, ⓦwww.greekembassy.org.

Gay and lesbian travellers

Greece is deeply ambivalent about **homosexuality**: ghettoized as "to be expected" in the arts, theatre and music scenes, but apt to be closeted elsewhere – though the rampant 2004–05 sex scandals amongst the Orthodox clergy blew the door wide open on the prevalent hypocrisy. The age of consent for same-sex acts is 17, and (male) bisexual behaviour common but rarely admitted; the legal code itself, however, still contains pejorative references to passive partners. Greek men are terrible flirts, but cruising them is a semiotic minefield and definitely at your own risk – references in (often obsolete) gay guides to "known" male cruising grounds should be treated sceptically. "Out" gay Greeks are rare, and "out" local lesbians rarer still; foreign same-sex couples will be regarded in the provinces with some bemusement but accorded the standard courtesy as foreigners – as long as they refrain from public displays of affection, taboo in rural areas. There is a sizeable gay contingent in Athens, Thessaloníki and Pátra, plus a fairly obvious scene at resorts like Ýdhra, Rhodes and Mýkonos. Skála Eressoü on Lésvos, the birthplace of Sappho, is (appropriately) an international mecca for lesbians. Even in Athens, however, most gay nightlife is underground (often literally so in the siting of clubs), with no visible signage for nondescript premises.

Insurance

Even though EU healthcare privileges apply in Greece (see p.54 for details), you should consider taking out an **insurance policy** before travelling to cover against theft, loss, illness or injury. Before paying for a whole new policy, however, it's worth checking whether you are already covered: some all-risks homeowners' or renters' insurance policies may cover your possessions when overseas, and many private medical schemes (such as BUPA or WPA in the UK) offer coverage extensions for abroad.

In Canada, provincial health plans usually provide partial cover for medical mishaps overseas, while holders of official student/teacher/youth cards in Canada and the US are entitled to meagre accident coverage and hospital inpatient benefits. **Students** will often find that their student health coverage extends during the vacations and for one term beyond the date of last enrolment. Most **credit-card issuers** also offer some sort of basic vacation insurance, if you pay for the holiday with their card – however, it's vital to check what these policies cover.

After exhausting the possibilities above, you might want to contact a **specialist travel insurance** company, or consider the travel insurance deal we offer (see box, p.70). A typical travel insurance policy usually provides cover for the **loss** of baggage, tickets and – up to a certain limit – cash, cards or cheques, as well as **cancellation** or curtailment of your journey.

Rough Guides travel insurance

Rough Guides has teamed up with Columbus Direct to offer you **travel insurance** that can be tailored to suit your needs. Products include a low-cost **backpacker** option for long stays; a **short break** option for city getaways; a typical **holiday package** option; and others. There are also annual **multi-trip** policies for those who travel regularly. Different sports and activities (trekking, skiing, etc) can usually be covered, if required.

See our website (ⓦwww.roughguides.com/website/shop) for eligibility and purchasing options. Alternatively, UK residents should call ⓣ0870/033 9988; Australians should call ⓣ1300/669 999 and New Zealanders should call ⓣ0800/55 9911. All other nationalities should call ⓣ+44 870/890 2843.

Unless an extra premium is paid, most exclude "**dangerous sports**": in the Greek islands this means motorbiking, windsurfing and possibly sailing, and on the mainland this could mean rafting, skiing or trekking. Some policies can be chopped and changed to exclude coverage you don't need – for example, sickness and accident benefits can often be excluded or included. They never pay out for medical treatment relating to injuries incurred whilst under the influence of alcohol or drugs. If you take medical coverage, ascertain whether benefits are paid as treatment proceeds or only after return home, whether there is a **24-hour medical emergency number**, and how much the deductible excess is. With baggage cover, make sure that the **per-article limit** will cover your most valuable possession. UK travel agents and tour operators are likely to **require travel insurance** when you book a package holiday, though it does not have to be their own.

Make any claim as soon as possible. If you have medical treatment, keep all receipts for medicines and treatment. If you have anything stolen or lost, you must obtain an **official statement** from the police or the airline which lost your bags – with numerous claims being fraudulent, most insurers won't even consider one unless you have a police report.

Internet

Rates at **Internet cafés** tend to be about €2–4 per hour. If you are travelling with your own **laptop**, you may well be able to roam in Greece depending on what agreement your home ISP has with any Greek partners. Check with your ISP, and get the local dial-up number, before you leave. Charges tend to be fairly high, but for a few minutes per day, still work out less than going to an Internet café. Alternatively, you can take out a temporary **Internet account** with one of the half-dozen Greek ISPs (minimum one month, cost €10–14/month). Some hotels and cafés offer Wi-Fi Internet access, sometimes free to customers.

Laundries

Plindíria, as they're known in Greek, are available in the main resort towns; sometimes an attended service wash is available for little or no extra charge over the basic cost of €8–10 per wash and dry. Self-catering villas will usually be furnished with a drying line and a selection of plastic wash-tubs or a bucket. In hotels, laundering should be done in a more circumspect manner, particularly if the hotel offers laundry as a payable service.

Mail

Post offices are open Monday to Friday from 7.30am to 2pm, though certain main branches are also open evenings and Saturday mornings. **Airmail letters** take 3–7 days to reach the rest of Europe, 5–12 days to North America, a little longer for Australia and New Zealand. Generally, the larger the island (and the busier its airport), the quicker the service. Postal rates for up to 20g are a uniform €0.65 to all overseas destinations. For a modest fee (about €3) you can shave a day or two off delivery time to any destination by using the express service (*katepígonda*). **Registered** (*systiméno*) delivery is also available for a similar amount, but proves quite slow unless coupled with express service. For a simple letter or card, a stamp (*grammatósimo*) can also be purchased at authorized postal agencies (usually stationers or postcard shops).

Parcels should (and often can) only be handled in the main provincial or county capitals; this way, your bundle will be in Athens, and on an international flight, within a day or so. For non-EU/EEA destinations, always present your box open for inspection, and come prepared with tape and scissors – most post offices will sell cardboard boxes, but nothing to close the package. An array of services is available: air parcel (fast and expensive), surface-air lift (a couple of weeks slower but much cheaper), insured, and proof of delivery among others.

Ordinary **post boxes** are bright yellow, express boxes dark red, but it's best to use those adjacent to an actual post office, since days may pass between collections at boxes elsewhere. If there are two slots, "ESOTERIKÓ" is for domestic mail, "EXOTERIKÓ" for overseas. Often there are more: one box or slot for mail into Athens and suburbs, one for your local province, one for "other" parts of Greece, and one for overseas; if in doubt, ask someone.

The **poste restante** system is reasonably efficient, especially at the post offices of larger towns. Mail should be clearly addressed and marked "poste restante", with your surname underlined, to the main post office of whichever town you choose. It will be held for a month and you'll need your passport to collect it.

Maps

Maps in Greece are an endless source of confusion and often outright misinformation. Each cartographic company seems to have its own peculiar system of transcribing Greek letters into the Roman alphabet – and these, as often as not, do not match the transliterations on road signs.

The most reliable **general touring maps** of Greece are those published by Athens-based Anavasi (Ⓦwww.anavasi.gr), Road Editions (Ⓦwww.road.gr) and newcomer Orama (Ⓦwww.nakas-maps.gr). Anavasi and Road Editions products are widely available in Greece at selected bookstores, as well as at petrol stations and general tourist shops country-wide. In Britain they are found at Stanfords (Ⓣ020/7836 1321, Ⓦwww.stanfords.co.uk) and the Hellenic Book Service (Ⓣ020/7267 9499, Ⓦwww.hellenicbookservice.com); in the US, they're sold through Omni Resources (Ⓣ910/227-8300, Ⓦwww.omnimap.com). Anavasi is probably the best of the three, for detail of paths and unsurfaced roads: all are based on large-scale military maps, and where they duplicate coverage you may want to buy both.

Touring maps of **individual islands** are more easily available on the spot, and while most local ones are wildly inaccurate or obsolete, the following are reasonably reliable and up to date. These include the Anavasi and Road products for **Crete**, plus nearly forty more Road titles for other islands at scales of 1:25000–1:70000, including the Ionians, east Aegean, Sporades and most Cyclades and Dodecanese. Anavasi cover the Cyclades, Sporades, Hios and Kalymnos well at scales of 1:25000–1:60000.

The most useful foreign-produced map of **Athens** is the *Rough Guide City Map*; it is full-colour, non-tearable, weatherproof and pocket-sized, detailing attractions, places to shop, eat, drink and sleep as well as the city streets. If you can read Greek, and plan to stay for some time in the city, the *Athina-Pireás Proastia Hartis-Odhigos* street atlas, published by the Fotis brothers, is invaluable, though pricey. It has a complete index, down to the tiniest alley, and also shows cinemas and most hotels, as well as all the metro stations. The only comparable product for **Thessaloníki** is Emvelia's offering, which also includes Halkidhikí and the immediate surroundings; they also do a folding map of Thessaloníki if you don't want the indexed atlas.

Money

Greece's currency is the **euro** (€). Up-to-date **exchange rates** can be found on Ⓦwww.oanda.com. Greek shopkeepers do not

Hiking/topographical maps

Hiking/topographical maps are gradually improving in quality and availability. **Road Editions**, in addition to their touring maps, produce 1:50,000, GPS-compatible topographical maps for mainland mountain ranges, including Áthos, Pílio, Parnassós, Ólymbos, Taiyettos, Ágrafa and Íti, usually with rudimentary route directions in English.

Anavasi (Ⓣ210 72 93 541, Ⓦwww.mountains.gr/anavasi) publishes a GPS-compatible, CD-ROM-available series covering the mountains of central Greece (including Ólymbos) and Epirus, some on the Peloponnese, the White Mountains and Psiloritis on Crete and Mt Dhýrfis on Évvia. Anavasi products use the same military source maps as Road, but are frequently more accurate. They are sold in the better Athens bookstores, as well as their own shopfront at Stoá Arsakíou 6A in central Athens, but do not have much international distribution.

Finally, for hiking in particular areas of Crete, Corfu, Kálymnos, Lésvos, Messinía, Párga, Pílio, Sámos, Sými, and Thássos, map-and-guide booklets published by **Marengo Publications** in England also prove very useful. Stanfords (see p.71) keeps a good stock of these, or order from Marengo direct on Ⓣ01485/532710, Ⓦwww.marengowalks.com.

bother much with shortfalls of 10 cents or less, whether in their favour (especially) or yours.

Euro notes exist in denominations of 5, 10, 20, 50, 100, 200 and 500 euros, and coins in denominations of 1, 2, 5, 10, 20 and 50 cents and 1 and 2 euros. Avoid getting stuck with **counterfeit euro notes** (€100 and €200 ones abound). The best tests are done by the naked eye: genuine notes all have a hologram strip or (if over €50) patch at one end, there's a watermark at the other, plus a security thread embedded in the middle. If you end up with such a note, you'll have no recourse to a refund.

Banks and exchange

Greek **banks** normally open Monday to Thursday 8.30am–2.30pm and Friday 8.30am–2pm. Always take your passport with you as proof of identity and expect long queues. Large hotels and some travel agencies also provide an exchange service, though with hefty commissions. On small islands with no full-service bank, "authorized" bank agents will charge an additional fee for posting a travellers' cheque to a proper branch.

A number of authorized brokers for exchanging foreign cash have emerged in Athens and other major tourist centres. When changing small amounts, choose those bureaux that charge a flat percentage commission (usually 1 percent) rather than a high minimum. There is a small number of 24-hour automatic **foreign-note-changing machines**, but a high minimum commission tends to be deducted. There is no need to **purchase euros** beforehand unless you're arriving at some ungodly hour to one of the remoter frontier posts. All major airports have an ATM or banking booth for incoming international flights.

Traveller's cheques, credit cards and ATMs

The safest way to carry money is as **traveller's cheques** (ideally in euros), which can be cashed at most banks, though rarely elsewhere. Cashing the cheques will incur a minimum charge of €1.20–2.40 depending on the bank; for larger amounts, a set percentage will apply.

Credit/debit cards are also likely to be your main source of funds while travelling, by withdrawing money (using your usual PIN) from the vast network of Greek **ATMs**. Larger airports have at least one ATM in the arrivals hall, and any town or island with a population larger than a few thousand (or substantial tourist traffic) also has them. Most accept Visa, MasterCard, Visa Electron, Plus and Cirrus cards; American Express holders are restricted to the ATMs of Alpha and National Bank.

ATM transactions with **debit cards** linked to a current account attract **charges** of 2.25 percent on the sterling/dollar transaction value, plus a commission fee of a similar amount; the tourist rate rather than the more favourable interbank rate will be applied. A few banks or building societies (such as Nationwide) waive some or all of these fees. Using **credit cards** at an ATM costs roughly the same, however inflated interest accrues from the moment of use.

Major credit cards are not usually accepted by cheaper tavernas or hotels, but they can be essential for renting cars. Major travel agents may also accept them, though a **three-percent surcharge** is often levied on the purchase of ferry tickets.

In an emergency you can arrange to have substantial amounts of **money wired** from your home bank to a bank in Greece. Receiving funds by SWIFT transfer takes anywhere from two to ten working days. From the UK, a bank charge of 0.03 percent, with a minimum of £17, maximum £35, is typically levied for two-day service; some building societies charge a £20 flat fee irrespective of the amount. If you choose this method, your home bank will need the IBAN (international bank account number) for the account to which funds are being sent or, failing that, the bank name and branch code. It's unwise to transfer more than the equivalent of €10,000; above that limit, as part of measures to combat money-laundering, the receiving Greek bank will begin asking awkward questions and imposing punitive commissions.

Having money wired from home is less convenient and even more expensive than using a bank; local affiliate offices are thin on the ground in Greece, although you may find that main post offices are the designated receiving points for Western Union. However, the funds should be available for collection at Amex's or Western Union's local representative office within hours – sometimes minutes – of being sent.

Movies

Greek cinemas show the regular major release movies, which in the case of English-language titles will almost always be in English with Greek subtitles. In summer open-air screens operate in all the major towns and some of the resorts, and these are absolutely wonderful. You may not hear much thanks to crackly speakers and locals chatting away throughout, but watching a movie under the stars on a warm night is simply a great experience. There are usually two screenings, at about 9pm and 11pm, with the sound at the latter turned down to avoid complaints of noise from neighbours.

Opening hours and entrance fees

It's difficult to generalize about Greek **opening hours**, especially museum and site schedules, which change constantly. The traditional timetable starts with shops opening 8.30/9am and closing for a long break at lunchtime. Most places, except banks, reopen in the mid to late afternoon. Tourist areas tend to adopt a more northern European timetable, with shops, travel agencies and offices, as well as the most important archeological sites and museums, usually open throughout the day.

Private businesses, or anyone providing a service, frequently operate a straight 9am to 5/6pm schedule. If someone is actually selling something, then they are more likely to follow a split shift as detailed below.

Shopping hours during the hottest months are theoretically Monday, Wednesday and Saturday from 9am to 2.30pm, and Tuesday, Thursday and Friday from 8.30am to 2pm and 6 to 9pm. During the cooler months the morning schedule shifts slightly forward, the evening session a half or even a full hour back. In Athens many places keep a continuous schedule (*synehés orário*) during the winter, but this is not yet universally observed, even with EU pressure, and the threat of its legal enforcement. There are so many exceptions to rules by virtue of holidays and professional idiosyncrasy that you can't count on getting anything done except from Monday to Friday, between 9.30am and 1pm. **Delis** and **butchers** are not allowed to sell fresh meat during summer afternoons (though some flout this rule); similarly, **fishmongers**

are only open in the morning until they sell out (usually by noon). **Pharmacies** only open Monday to Friday, with a duty pharmacist open on Saturdays). **Travel agencies** at the busiest resorts are open from about 9am to 10pm Monday to Saturday, with some Sunday hours as well.

Most **government agencies** are open to the public on weekdays from 8am to 2pm. In general, however, you'd be optimistic to show up after 1pm expecting to be served the same day, as queues can be long, and many services cease at that hour.

Monasteries are generally open from approximately 9am to 1pm and 5 to 8pm (3.30 to 6.30pm in winter) for limited visits.

Opening hours of **ancient sites** and **museums** vary; as far as possible, times are quoted in the text, but these change with exasperating frequency, and at smaller sites may be subject to the availability of a local site guard. Unless specified, the times quoted are generally summer hours, in effect from around late May to the end of September. Reckon on later opening and earlier closing in winter. Hours will be reduced on the numerous public holidays and festivals – or the equally numerous strikes. The most important holidays, when almost everything will be closed, are listed on p.58.

All the major **ancient sites**, like most **museums**, charge **entrance fees** ranging from €2 to €12, with an average fee of around €3. Entrance to all state-run sites and museums is **free** on Sundays and public holidays from November to March, although they will be shut on public holidays (see p.58).

Phones

All Greek phone numbers require dialling of all ten digits, including the area code. Land lines begin with 2; mobiles begin with 6. All land-line exchanges are digital, and you should have few problems reaching any number from either overseas or within Greece. Mobile phone users are well looked after, with a signal even in the Athens metro.

Call boxes, poorly maintained and sited at the noisiest street corners, usually work only with phonecards (*tilekártes*), available in denominations starting at €4, from kiosks and newsagents, though call box payphones are now appearing. Call boxes cannot be rung back; however, the green **countertop cardphones** kept by some hotels can. Other options for local calls include **counter coin-op phones** in bars, *kafenía* and hotel lobbies; these take small coins and can usually be rung back.

Local or intercity calls to land lines are cheap on OTE *tilekártes*, but if you plan on making lots of international calls, you'll want a **calling card**, all of which involve calling a free access number from either certain phone boxes or a fixed line (not a mobile) and then entering a twelve-digit code. OTE has its own scheme, but competitors generally prove cheaper. Always tell the card vendor where you intend to call, to get the card best suited for you (Altec's Talk Talk for the UK). Avoid making calls **from hotel rooms**, as a large surcharge will be applied. It is worth bringing a Skype phone for your laptop, for cheap calls to a land line overseas via Wi-Fi.

Three **mobile phone networks** operate in Greece: Vodafone-Panafon, Cosmote and Q-Telecom/WIND Hellas. Calling any of their numbers from Britain, you will find that costs are exactly the same as calling a fixed phone, though of course such numbers are pricey when rung locally. **Coverage** countrywide is good, though there are a few "dead" zones in the mountains, or on really remote islets. Contract-free plans are heavily promoted in Greece, and if you're here for more than a week or so, buying a **pay-as-you-go** SIM card (for €15–20) from any of the mobile phone outlets will pay for itself very quickly, and you can reuse the same number on your next visit. Top-up cards – starting from €8–10 – are available at all *períptera* (kiosks). UK providers may tell you that another SIM can't be fitted without a hefty surcharge to unlock your phone, but you are legally entitled to the unblock code from the manufacturer after (usually) six months of use. Otherwise, have a mobile shop in Greece unblock the phone for a small charge. North American users will only be able to use tri-band phones in Greece. Roaming with your UK provider within the EU will now land you with charges capped at €0.51 equivalent per minute (or €0.26 to receive calls).

Phone codes and numbers

Phoning Greece from abroad

Dial ⓣ0030 + the full number

Phoning abroad from Greece

Dial the country code (below) + area code (minus any initial 0) + number

Australia	ⓣ0061	UK	ⓣ0044
New Zealand	ⓣ0064	Ireland	ⓣ00353
Canada	ⓣ001	USA	ⓣ001
South Africa	ⓣ0027		

Greek phone prefixes

Local call rate	ⓣ0801	Toll-free/Freefone	ⓣ0800

Useful Greek telephone numbers

Ambulance	ⓣ166	Police/Emergency	ⓣ100
Fire brigade, urban	ⓣ199	Speaking clock	ⓣ141
Forest fire reporting	ⓣ191	Tourist police	ⓣ171 (Athens);
Operator	ⓣ132 (Domestic)	ⓣ210 171 (elsewhere)	
Operator	ⓣ139 (International)		

Photography

Fuji and Kodak **print films** are reasonably priced and easy to have processed. APS film is also widely sold and processed. Kodak and Fuji slide films can be purchased, again at UK prices or better, in larger centres, but often cannot be processed there. Memory media for digital cameras are widely available.

It's free to **take photos** of open-air sites, though museum photography and the use of videos or tripods anywhere requires an extra fee and written permit. This usually has to be arranged in writing from the nearest Department of Antiquities (*Eforía Arheotíton*).

Time

Greek summer time begins at 2am on the last Sunday in March, when the clocks go forward one hour, and ends at 2am the last Sunday in October when they go back. This change is not well publicized locally, and visitors miss planes and ferries every year. Greek time is always two hours ahead of Britain. For North America, the difference is seven hours for Eastern Standard Time, ten hours for Pacific Standard Time, with daylight saving starting 2–3 weeks earlier and ending a week later than Europe.

Toilets

Public toilets are usually in parks or squares, often subterranean; otherwise try a bus station. Except in tourist areas, public toilets tend to be filthy – it's best to use those in restaurants and bars. Remember that throughout Greece, you drop paper in the adjacent wastebins, not the toilet bowl.

Tourist Information

The **National Tourist Organization of Greece** (Ellinikós Organismós Tourismoú, or EOT; GNTO abroad, ⓦwww.gnto.gr) maintains offices in most European capitals, plus major cities in North America and Australia (see p.76). It publishes an array of free, glossy, regional pamphlets, invariably several years out of date, fine for getting a picture of where you want to go, though low on useful facts.

In Greece, you will find official **EOT offices** in many of the larger towns and resorts where, in addition to the usual leaflets, you can find weekly **schedules** for the inter-island **ferries** – rarely entirely accurate, but useful as a guideline. EOT staff may be able to advise on **bus** and **train** departures as well as current opening hours for local sites and museums, and occasionally can assist with accommodation.

Where there is no EOT office, you can get information from municipally-run tourist offices – these can be more highly motivated and helpful than EOT branches. In the absence of any of these, you can visit the **Tourist Police**, essentially a division (often just a single room) of the local police. They can sometimes provide you with lists of rooms to let, which they regulate, but they're really the place to go if you have a **serious complaint** about a taxi, or an accommodation or eating establishment.

Greek national tourist offices abroad

Australia & New Zealand 51 Pitt St, Sydney, NSW 2000 ⓣ02/9241 1663, ⓔhto@tpg.com.au.
Canada 91 Scollard St, 2nd Floor, Toronto, ON M5R 1GR ⓣ416/968-2220, ⓔgrnto.tor@sympatico.ca.
UK 4 Conduit St, London W1R 0DJ ⓣ020/7495 4300, ⓔEOT-greektouristoffice@btinternet.com.
USA 645 5th Ave, New York, NY 10022 ⓣ212/421-5777, ⓔinfo@greektourism.com.

Guide

Guide

1

Athens and around

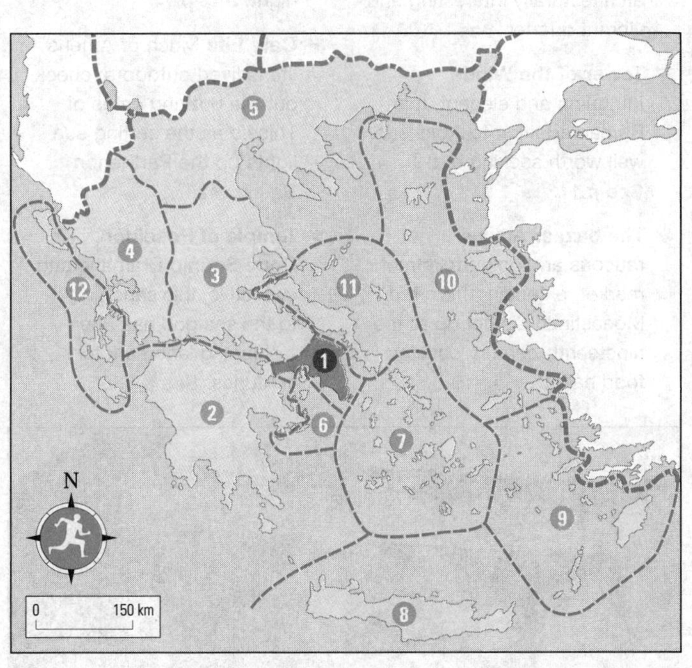

CHAPTER 1 Highlights

* **The Acropolis** Rising above the city, the great rock of the Acropolis symbolizes not just Athens, but the birth of European civilization. See p.100

* **Pláka** Wander the narrow alleys and steep steps of this architecturally interesting and vibrant quarter. See p.108

* **Tower of the Winds** Intriguing and elegant, this Roman addition to Athens is well worth seeking out. See p.113

* **The bazaar** Athens' raucous and colourful street market, extending from the Monastiráki district up to the nineteenth-century covered food hall. See p.119

* **National Archeological Museum** The world's finest collection of ancient Greek art and sculpture. See p.120

* **Psyrrí** The heart of Athens' new nightlife, packed with bars, cafés and restaurants that are buzzing till late at night. See p.141

* **Café Life** Much of Athens' life is lived outdoors; check out the buzzing cafés of Thissío as the setting sun lights up the Parthenon. See p.142

* **Temple of Poseidon, Cape Soúnio** Dramatic and evocative, this sanctuary to the sea god has been a shipping landmark for centuries. See p.158

▲ The Erechtheion

Athens and around

For all too many people, **ATHENS** is a city that happened two-and-a-half thousand years ago. It's true that even now the past looms large – literally, in the shape of the mighty Acropolis that dominates almost every view, as well as on every visitor's itinerary. Yet the modern conurbation is home to over four million people – more than a third of the Greek nation's population – and has undergone a transformation in the twenty-first century. The stimulus of the 2004 Olympics made it far more than a repository of antiquities, lifting it above the clichés of pollution and impossible traffic that have blighted its reputation in recent years.

Even now it is far from a beautiful city – the scramble for growth in the decades after World War II, when the population grew from around 700,000 to close to its present level, was an architectural disaster. But for the first time, Athens is starting to make the most of what it has, while massive investment in new roads, rail and metro, along with extensive pedestrianization in the centre, has resolved some of the worst traffic and smog problems. The views for which Athens was once famous are reappearing and, despite inevitable globalization and the appearance of all the usual high-street and fast-food chains, the city retains its character to a remarkable degree. Hectic modernity is always tempered with an air of intimacy and hominess; as any Greek will tell you, Athens is merely the largest village in the country.

However often you've visited, the vestiges of the ancient Classical Greek city, most famously represented by the **Parthenon** and other remains that top the **Acropolis**, are an inevitable focus; along with the refurbished **National Archeological Museum**, the finest collection of Greek antiquities anywhere in the world, they should certainly be a priority. The majority of the several million visitors who pass through each year do no more, perhaps managing an evening or two dining in the romantic, touristy tavernas of Pláka. In so doing, they never manage to escape the crowds and so see little of the Athens Athenians know. Even on a brief visit, it does not do Athens justice to see it purely as a collection of ancient sites and museum pieces. It's worth taking the time to explore some of the city's neighbourhoods. For all its tourists, the nineteenth-century quarter of **Pláka**, with its mix of Turkish, Neoclassical and Greek-island architecture, and its intriguing little museums devoted to traditional arts, from ceramics to music, is perhaps the most easily appreciated. Just to its north, the **bazaar** area retains an almost Middle Eastern atmosphere in its life and trade, with the added bonus of some of the centre's best nightlife in neighbouring **Psyrrí** and up-and-coming **Gázi**. More traditional Athenian escapes are also nearby, in the form of the shady **National Gardens** and the elegant, upmarket quarter of **Kolonáki**. There are also startling **views** to be enjoyed from the

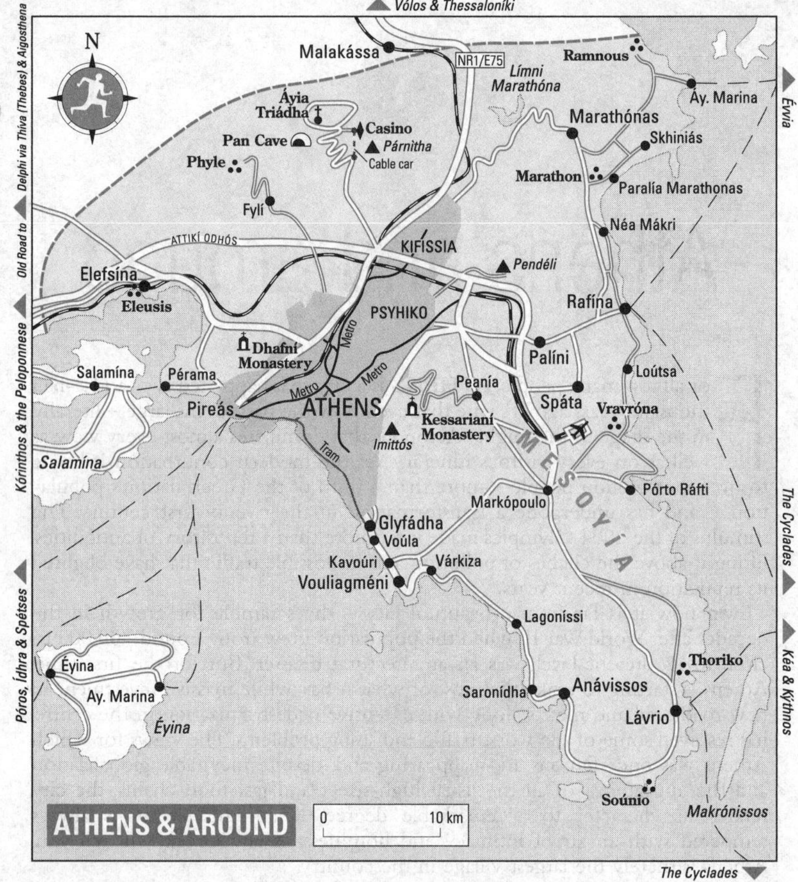

many hills – Lykavitós and Filopáppou above all – while in summer, the **beach** is just a tram ride away.

The biggest surprise in Athens for most people, however, is the vibrant life of the city itself. **Cafés** are packed day and night and the streets stay lively until 3 or 4am, with some of the best **bars and clubs** in the country. **Eating out** is great, with establishments ranging from traditional tavernas to gourmet restaurants. In summer, much of the action takes place outdoors, from dining on the street, to clubbing on the beach, to **open-air cinema**, **concerts** and **classical drama**. There's a diverse **shopping** scene, too, ranging from colourful bazaars and lively street markets to chic suburban malls crammed with the latest designer goods. And with a good-value, extensive public transportation system allied to inexpensive cabs, you'll have no difficulty getting around.

Outside Athens, in the rest of the state of Attica, the emphasis shifts more exclusively to ancient sites. The Temple of Poseidon at Soúnio is the most popular trip and rightly so, with its dramatic clifftop position above the cape. Lesser known and less visited are the sanctuaries at **Ramnous** and **Eleusis** (Elefsína), or the burial mound from the great victory at **Marathon**. There are also easily accessible **beaches** all around the coast. Moving on is quick and easy, with scores of **ferries** and hydrofoils leaving daily from the port at **Pireás** (Piraeus) and, somewhat less frequently, from the two other Attic ferry terminals at **Rafína** and **Lávrio**.

Some history

Athens has been inhabited continuously for over seven thousand years. Its acropolis, supplied with spring water, commanding views of all seaward approaches and encircled by protective mountains on its landward side, was a natural choice for prehistoric settlement and for the **Mycenaeans**, who established a palace-fortress on the rock. Unlike other Mycenaean centres, Athens was not sacked and abandoned during the Doric invasion of about 1200 BC, and so the Athenians always maintained that they were "pure" Ionians with no Doric element. Gradually, Athens emerged as a city-state that dominated the region, ruled by kings who stood at the head of a land-owning aristocracy known as the *Eupatridae* (the "well-born"), who governed through a Council which met on the Areopagus – the Hill of Ares. Though significant, Athens at this stage was overshadowed by larger, more powerful city-states such as Corinth and Sparta.

Increasing wealth, however, led to unrest, with a large class of farmers and the like excluded from political life but forced to pay rent or taxes to the nobility. Among the reforms aimed at addressing this were new, fairer laws drawn up by **Draco** (whose "draconian" lawcode was published in 621 BC), and the appointment of **Solon** as ruler (594 BC), with a mandate to introduce sweeping economic and political reform and reduce the power of the *Eupatridae.* Although Solon's reforms greatly increased the franchise, and indeed laid the foundations of what eventually became Athenian democracy, they failed to stop internal unrest, and eventually **Peisistratos**, his cousin, seized power in the middle of the sixth century BC. Peisistratos is usually called a tyrant, but this simply means he seized power by force: thanks to his populist policies he was in fact a well-liked and successful ruler who greatly expanded Athens' power, wealth and influence.

His sons **Hippias and Hipparchus** were less successful: Hipparchus was assassinated in 514 BC and Hippias overthrown in 510 BC. A new leader, **Kleisthenes**, took the opportunity for more radical change: he introduced ten classes or tribes based on place of residence, each of which elected fifty members to the *Boule* or Council of State, an administrative body which decided on issues to be discussed by the full Assembly. The Assembly was open to all citizens and was both a legislature and a supreme court. This system was

The Olympic legacy

The **2004 Olympics** can take much of the credit for getting Athens back on the map and regenerating the city's infrastructure, with a greatly enhanced metro and an entirely new tram, as well as an extensive network of pedestrian streets in the city centre. Successful as they were in many ways, however, the legacy of the Games is not an entirely happy one. In the rush to be ready on time many of the works went disastrously over budget – a price that Athenians will be paying for decades to come – while inadequate planning means that few of the costly stadia have found any purpose in life since the Games finished. Many of the smaller venues are already starting to deteriorate, and seem likely eventually to be demolished, to be replaced by yet more shopping malls.

The rise and fall of Classical Athens

Perhaps the most startling aspect of ancient, Classical Athens is how suddenly it emerged to the glory for which we remember it – and how short its heyday proved to be. In the middle of the **fifth century BC**, Athens was little more than a country town in its street layout and buildings – a scattered jumble of single-storey houses or wattle huts, intersected by narrow lanes. Sanitary conditions were notoriously lax: human waste and rubbish were dumped outside the town with an almost suicidal disregard for plague and disease. And on the rock of the Acropolis, a site reserved for the city's most sacred monuments, stood blackened ruins – temples and sanctuaries razed by the Persians in 480 BC.

There was little to suggest that the city was entering a unique phase of its history in terms of power, prestige and creativity. But following the victory over the Persians at Salamis, Athens stood unchallenged for a generation. It grew rich on the export of olive oil and silver from the mines of Attica, but above all it benefited from its control of the **Delian League**, an alliance of Greek city-states formed as insurance against Persian resurgence. The Athenians relocated the League's treasury from the island of Delos to their own acropolis, ostensibly on the grounds of safety, and with its revenues their leader **Pericles** (see p.903) was able to create the so-called **Golden Age** of the city. Great endowments were made for monumental construction, arts in all spheres were promoted, and – most significantly – it was all achieved under stable, **democratic rule**. The Delian League's wealth enabled office-holders to be properly paid, thereby making it possible for the poor to play a part in government. Pericles's constitution ensured that all policies of the state were to be decided by a general assembly of Athenian male citizens – six thousand constituted a quorum.

In line with this system of democratic participation, a new and exalted notion of the Athenian citizen emerged. This was a man who could shoulder political responsibility, take public office and play a part in the **cultural** and **religious events** of the time. The latter assumed ever-increasing importance. The city's Panathenaic festival, honouring its protectress deity Athena, was upgraded along the lines of the Olympic Games to include drama, music and athletic contests. The next five decades were to witness the great dramatic works of **Aeschylus**, **Sophocles** and **Euripides**, and the comedies of **Aristophanes**. Foreigners such as **Herodotus**, considered the inventor of history, and **Anaxagoras**, the philosopher, were drawn to live in the city. And they, in turn, were surpassed by native Athenians. **Thucydides** wrote *The Peloponnesian War*, a pioneering work of documentation and analysis, while **Socrates** posed the

the basis of **Athenian democracy** and remained in place, little changed, right through to Roman times.

Around 500 BC Athens sent troops to aid the Ionian Greeks of Asia Minor, who were rebelling against the Persian Empire; this in turn provoked a Persian invasion of Greece. In 490 BC the Athenians and their allies defeated a far larger Persian force at the **Battle of Marathon**. In 480 BC the Persians returned, capturing and sacking Athens, and leaving much of the city burned to the ground. That same year, however, a naval victory at **Salamis** sealed victory over the Persians, and also secured Athens' position as Greece's leading city-state, enabling it to bring much of the Aegean and central Greece together in the **Delian League**. This was the birth of the **Classical period** (see box), Athens' Golden Age. When the **Romans** took control of the city in the second century BC, they revered it as the source of much of their own heritage but did relatively little to add to its architectural splendour. (Athens' Roman history is outlined in the box on p.113.)

problems of philosophy that were to exercise his follower **Plato** and to shape the discipline to the present day.

But it was the great civic **building programme** that became the most visible and powerful symbol of the age. Under the patronage of Pericles and with vast public funds made available from the Delian treasury, the architects **Iktinos**, **Mnesikles** and **Kallikrates**, and the sculptor **Fidias**, transformed the city. Their buildings included the Parthenon and Erechtheion on the Acropolis; the Hephaisteion and several *stoas* (arcades) around the Agora; a new *odeion* (theatre) on the South Slope of the Acropolis hill; and, outside the city, the temples at Soúnio and Ramnous.

Athenian culture flourished under democracy, but the system was not without its contradictions and failures. Only one in seven inhabitants of the city was an actual citizen; the political status and civil rights that they enjoyed were denied to the many thousands of women, foreigners and slaves. The fatal mistake of the Athenian democracy, however, was allowing itself to be drawn into the **Peloponnesian War** against Sparta, its persistent rival, in 431 BC. Pericles, having roused the assembly to a pitch of patriotic fervour, died of the plague two years after war began, leaving Athens at the mercy of a series of far less capable leaders. In 415 BC a disastrous campaign in Sicily saw a third of the navy lost; in 405 BC defeat was finally accepted after the rest of the fleet was destroyed by Sparta in the Dardanelles. Demoralized, Athens succumbed to a brief period of oligarchy.

Through succeeding decades Athens was overshadowed by Thebes, though it recovered sufficiently to enter a new phase of democracy, the **age of Plato**. However, in 338 BC, nearly one-and-a-half centuries after the original defeat of the Persians, Athens was again called to defend the Greek city-states, this time against the incursions of **Philip of Macedon**. Demosthenes, said to be as powerful an orator as Pericles, spurred the Athenians to fight, in alliance with the Thebans, at Chaironeia. There they were routed, in large part by the cavalry commanded by Philip's son, Alexander (later to become known as Alexander the Great), and Athens fell under the control of the Macedonian empire.

The city continued to be favoured, particularly by **Alexander the Great**, a former pupil of Aristotle, who respected both Athenian culture and its democratic institutions. Following his death, however, came a more uncertain era, which saw periods of independence and Macedonian rule, until 146 BC when the **Romans** swept through southern Greece and it was incorporated into the Roman province of Macedonia.

Christians and Turks

The emergence of **Christianity** was perhaps the most significant step in Athens' long decline from the glories of its Classical heyday. Having survived with little change through years of Roman rule, the city lost its pivotal role in the Roman-Greek world after the division of the Roman Empire into Eastern and Western halves, and the establishment of Byzantium (Constantinople) as capital of the Eastern – **Byzantine** – empire. There, a new Christian sensibility soon outshone the prevailing ethic of Athens, where schools of philosophy continued to teach a pagan Neoplatonism. In 529 AD these schools were finally closed by Justinian I, and the city's temples, including the Parthenon, were reconsecrated as churches.

Athens rarely featured in the chronicles of the Middle Ages, passing through the hands of various foreign powers before the arrival in 1456 of **Sultan Mehmet II**, the Turkish conqueror of Constantinople. **Turkish Athens** was never much more than a garrison town, occasionally (and much to the detriment of its Classical buildings) on the front line of battles with the Venetians and other

Western powers. The links with the West, which had preserved a sense of continuity with the Classical and Roman city, were severed, and the flood of visitors was reduced to a trickle of French and Italian ambassadors to the Turkish court, and the occasional traveller or painter. The city does not seem to have been oppressed by Ottoman rule, however: the Greeks enjoyed some autonomy, and both Jesuit and Capuchin monasteries continued to thrive. Although the Acropolis became the home of the Turkish governor and the Parthenon was used as a mosque, life in the village-like quarters around the Acropolis drifted back to a semi-rural existence.

Four centuries of Ottoman occupation followed until, in 1821, the Greeks of Athens rose and joined the **rebellion sweeping the country**. They occupied the Turkish quarters of the lower town – the current Pláka – and laid siege to the Acropolis. The Turks withdrew, but five years later were back to reoccupy the Acropolis fortifications, while the Greeks evacuated to the countryside. When the Ottoman garrison finally left in 1834, and the Bavarian architects of the new German-born monarchy moved in, Athens, with a population of only 5000, was at its nadir.

Modern Athens

Athens was not the first-choice capital of modern Greece: that honour went instead to Náfplio in the Peloponnese. In 1834, though, the new king Otto transferred the capital and court to Athens. The reasoning was almost purely symbolic and sentimental: Athens was not only insignificant in terms of population and physical extent but was then at the edge of the territories of the new Greek state. Soon, while the archeologists stripped away all the Turkish and Frankish embellishments from the Acropolis, a city began to take shape: the grand Neoclassical plan was for processional avenues radiating out from great squares, a plan that can still be made out on maps but has long ago been subverted by the realities of daily life. **Pireás**, meanwhile, grew into a port again, though until the nineteenth century its activities continued to be dwarfed by the main Greek shipping centres on the islands of Sýros and Ýdhra.

The first mass expansion of both municipalities came suddenly, in 1923, as the result of the tragic Greek–Turkish war in **Asia Minor**. The peace treaty that resolved the war entailed the exchange of Greek and Turkish ethnic populations. A million and a half "Greek" Christians, mostly from age-old settlements along the Asia Minor coast, but also many Turkish-speaking peoples from the communities of inland Anatolia, arrived in Greece as refugees. Over half of them settled in Athens, Pireás and the neighbouring villages, changing at a stroke the whole make-up of the capital. Their integration and survival is one of the great events of the city's history.

Athens was hit hard by German occupation in World War II: during the winter of 1941–42 there were an estimated two thousand deaths from starvation each day. In late 1944, when the Germans finally left, the capital saw the first skirmishes of **civil war**, and from 1946 to 1949 Athens was a virtual island, with road approaches to the Peloponnese and the north only tenuously kept open.

During the 1950s, with the civil war over, the city again started to expand rapidly. A massive **industrial investment** programme – financed largely by the Americans, who had won Greece for their sphere of influence – took place, and the capital saw huge **immigration** from the war-torn, impoverished countryside. The open spaces between the old refugee suburbs began to fill and, by the late 1960s, Greater Athens covered a continuous area from the slopes of mounts Pendéli and Párnitha down to Pireás and Elefsína. Much of this development is unremittingly ugly, since old buildings were demolished wholesale in the name of a quick buck, particularly during the colonels' junta of 1967–74 (see p.920). Financial incentives encouraged homeowners to demolish their houses and replace them with apartment blocks up to six storeys high; almost everyone took advantage, and as a result most central streets seem like narrow canyons between these ugly, concrete blocks. Unrestrained industrial development on the outskirts was equally rampant, and the combined result was an appallingly polluted city, frequently choking under a noxious brown cloud known as the *néfos*.

Growth in recent decades has been much slower, but it's only since the 1990s – and more recently with a huge boost from the Olympics – that much effort has gone in to improving the city's environment. Although Athens still lags far behind Paris or London in terms of open space, the evidence of recent efforts is apparent. What's left of the city's architectural heritage has been extensively restored; there's clean public transportation; new building is controlled and there's some interesting, radical modern architecture (some of the Olympic facilities or the new Acropolis Museum, for example). Pollution is far less severe than it once was. Hopefully, it is a trend that will continue.

Arrival

There are numerous ways that you could find yourself **arriving** in Athens.

By plane

Athens' **Eleftheríos Venizélos** airport (Ⓦwww.aia.gr) is at Spáta, 33km southeast of the city. It's a slick operation, with excellent access to Athens and to major roads bypassing the city. Facilities include **ATMs** and banks with **money-changing** facilities on all levels and **luggage storage** with Pacific (Ⓣ210 35 30 160) on the Arrivals level. There's also the usual array of travel agencies and car rental places, plus a very handy official **EOT tourist office** (Mon–Sat 9am–7pm, Sun 10am–4pm; Ⓣ210 35 30 445) on the Arrivals level. Finally, there's a one-room **museum** displaying artefacts discovered in the area – mainly during construction of the airport – which is much more interesting than you might expect.

Public transportation from the airport is excellent. The metro and suburban trains share a station. The **Metro** (line 3; €6 single, €10 return, discounts for multiple tickets) is usually more convenient, taking you straight into the heart of the city where you can change to the other metro lines at either Monastiráki or Sýndagma: trains run every half-hour from 6.30am to 11.30pm, and take around 45 minutes. The **suburban train** runs to Laríssis station (see p.90), not quite so handy for the centre of town; it is, though, more comfortable and runs longer hours (5.50am–1.20am) for identical fares. Some continue all the way to Pireás (approx hourly; 1hr 5min), and there are also direct trains to Kórinthos (two-hourly; 7.05am–11.05pm; 1hr 30min) if you're heading for the Peloponnese.

Buses can be slower, especially at rush hours, but they're also much cheaper, more frequent, run all night and offer direct links to other parts of the city, including Pireás. The most useful are the #X95 to Sýndagma square (at least three an hour, day and night), and #X96 to the port at Pireás via Glyfádha and the beach suburbs (at least two an hour, day and night); others include the #X93 to the bus stations and #X92 to the northern suburb of Kifissiá. **Tickets** cost €3.20 from a booth beside the stops – be sure to validate your ticket on the bus. There are also limited **regional bus services** to the ports of Rafína (15 daily;

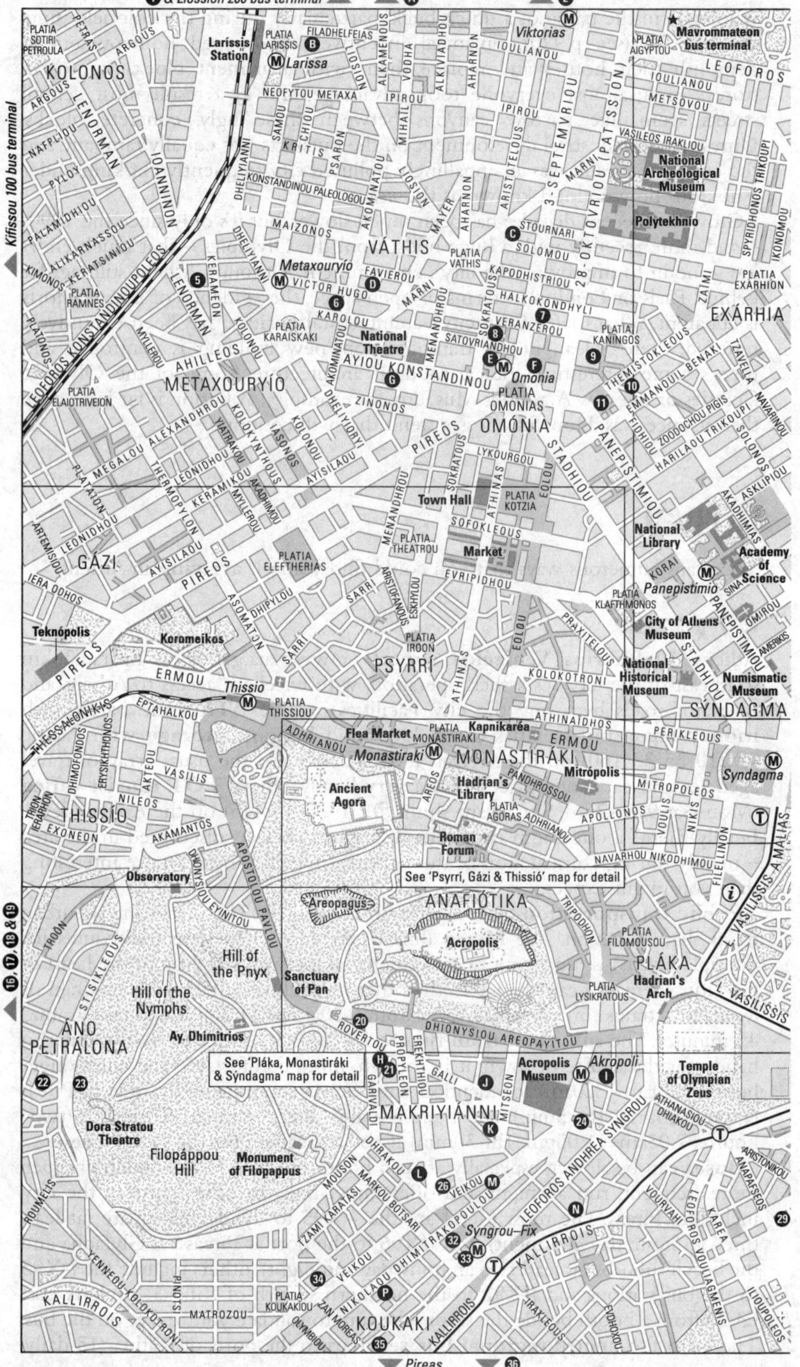
1 & Liossion 260 bus terminal
A
2
Kifissou 100 bus terminal
16, 17, 18 & 19
Pireas
36
KOLONOS
PLATIA SOTIRI PETROULA
PETRAS
ARGOUS
LENORMAN
NAFPLIOU
PYLOY
PALAMIDHIOU
ALIKARNASSOU
KERATSINIOU
KIMONOS
PLATIA RAMNES
IOANNINON
Laríssis Station
PLATIA LARISSIS
Larissa
FILADHELFEIAS
NEOFYTOU METAXA
SAMOU
CHIOU
KRITIS
PSARON
KONSTANDINOU PALEOLOGOU
DHELIYIANNI
NIOVIS
ALKAMENOUS
VODHA
MIHAIL
ALKIVIADHOU
AHARNON
IPIROU
LIOSION
AKOMINATOU
Viktorias
IOULIANOU
ARISTOTELOUS
3-SEPTEMVRIOU
28-OKTOVRIOU (PATISSION)
MARNI
Mavrommateon bus terminal
PLATIA AIGYPTOU
LEOFOROS
METSOVOU
VASILEOS IRAKLIOU
National Archeological Museum
Polytekhnío
SPYRIDHONOS TRIKOUPI
IKONOMOU
ZAÏMI
PLATIA EXARHION
EXÁRHIA
MAIZONOS
VÁTHIS
MAYER
PLATIA VATHIS
STOURNARI
SOLOMOU
KAPODHISTRIOU
HALKOKONDHYLI
VERANZEROU
SATOVRIANDHOU
Metaxouryío
VICTOR HUGO
FAVIEROU
KAROLOU
PLATIA KARAISKAKI
National Theatre
AYIOU KONSTANDINOU
MENANDHROU
SOKRATOUS
Omonia
PLATIA OMONIAS
OMÓNIA
PLATIA KANINGOS
THEMISTOKLEOUS
EMMANOUIL BENAKI
TZAVELLA
NAVARINOU
ZOODOCHOU PIGIS
HARILAOU TRIKOUPI
SOLONOS
FIDHIOU
PANEPISTIMIOU
STADHIOU
LYKOURGOU
EOLOU
ATHINAS
LEOFOROS KONSTANDINOUPOLEOS
PLATONOS
MYLLEROU
AHILLEOS
METAXOURYÍO
PLATIA ELAIOTRIVEION
ALEXANDHROU
MEGALOU
LEONIDHOU
KOLOKYNTHOUS
IASONOS
KOLONOU
ZINONOS
PIREOS
THERMOPYLON
KERAMIKOU
AKADHIMOU
AYISILAOU
Town Hall
PLATIA KOTZIA
SOFOKLEOUS
PLATIA THEATROU
Market
EVRIPIDHOU
ASKLIPIOU
AKADHIMIAS
National Library
Academy of Science
KORAI
Panepistimio
SINA
PLATIA KLAFTHMONOS
City of Athens Museum
OMIROU
AMERIKIS
ARTEMISIOU
GÁZI
IERA ODHOS
PLATIA ELEFTHERIAS
ASOMATON
DHIPYLOU
SARRI
ARISTOFANOUS
ESKHYLOU
PRAXITELOUS
Teknópolis
Kerameikos
PLATIA IROON
PSYRRÍ
KOLOKOTRONI
National Historical Museum
Numismatic Museum
ERMOU
Thissio
PLATIA THISSIOU
EPTAHALKOU
THESSALONIKIS
ATHINAIDHOS
SÝNDAGMA
Flea Market
PLATIA MONASTIRAKI
Kapnikaréa
PERIKLEOUS
ADHRIANOU
Monastiraki
MONASTIRÁKI
Mitrópolis
Syndagma
DHIMOFONDOS
ERYSIKHTHONOS
AKTEOU
VASILIS
Ancient Agora
AREOS
Hadrian's Library
PANDHROSSOU
MITROPOLEOS
NILEOS
THISSÍO
PLATIA AGORAS
APOLLONOS
VOULIS
NIKIS
EXONEON
AKAMANTOS
Roman Forum
NAVARHOU NIKODHIMOU
Observatory
DHIONYSIOU EVINITOU
APOSTOLOU PAVLOU
See 'Psyrrí, Gázi & Thissió' map for detail
FILELLINON
Areopagus
ANAFIÓTIKA
TRIPODHON
VASILISSIS AMALIAS
Acropolis
PLATIA FILOMOUSOU
PLÁKA
Hill of the Pnyx
Sanctuary of Pan
Hill of the Nymphs
PLATIA LYSIKRATOUS
Hadrian's Arch
L. VASILISSIS
STISIKLEOUS
ÁNO PETRÁLONA
Ay. Dhimitrios
ROVERTOU
DHIONYSIOU AREOPAYITOU
PROPYLEON
EREKHTHIOU
See 'Pláka, Monastiráki & Sýndagma' map for detail
Acropolis Museum
Akropoli
Temple of Olympian Zeus
GARIVALDI
GALLI
MITSEON
MAKRIYIÁNNI
ATHANASIOU DHIAKOU
Dora Stratou Theatre
Filopáppou Hill
Monument of Filopappus
DHRAKOU
MOUSON
MARKOU BOTSARI
VEIKOU
LEOFOROS ANDHREA SYNGROU
ARISTONIKOU
ANAPAFSEOS
ROUMELIS
TZAMI KARATASI
DHIMITRAKOPOULOU
Syngrou-Fix
VOURVAHI
LEOFOROS VOULIAGMENIS
KAREA
KALLIRROIS
YENNEOU KOLOKOTRONI
PINOTSI
MATROZOU
NIKOLAOU
PLATIA KOUKAKIOU
ZAN MOREAS
OLYMBIOU
KOUKAKI
IRAKLEOUS
EVDHOXOU
ILIOUPOLEOS

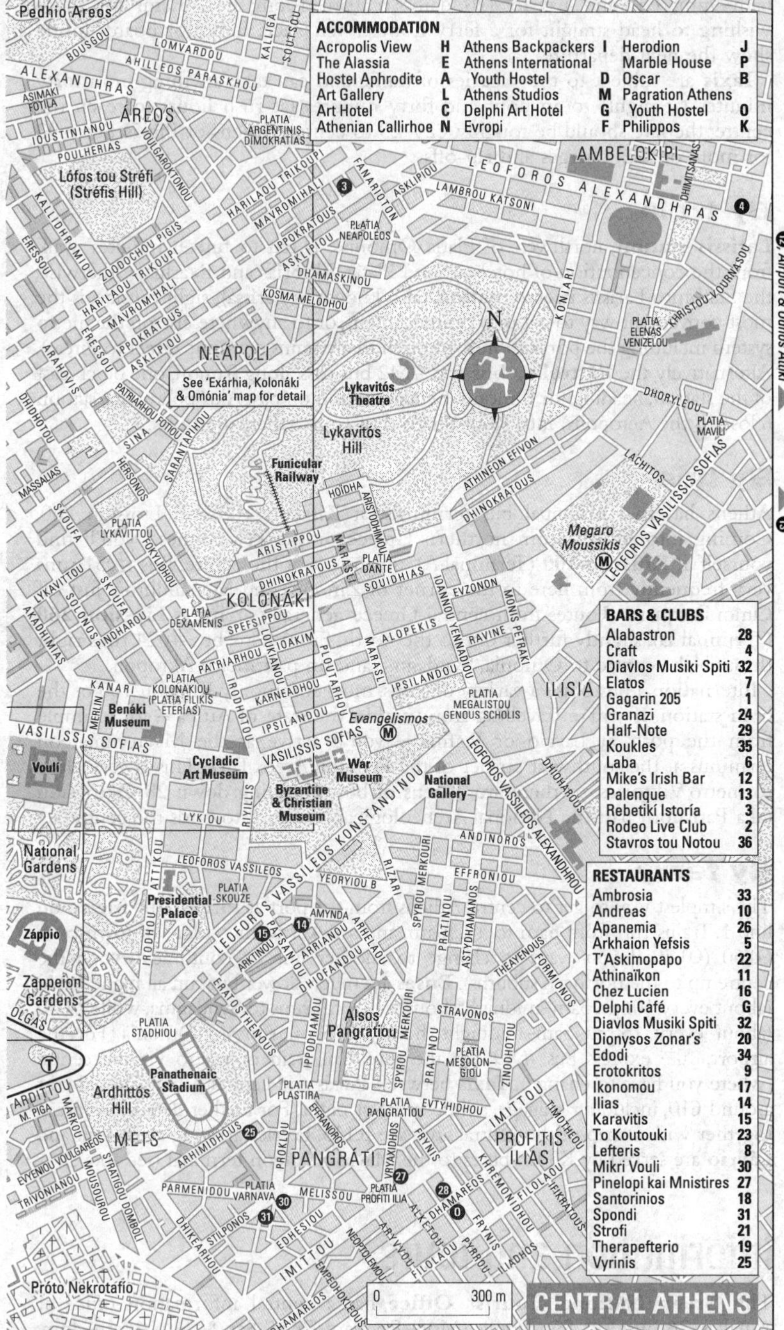
CENTRAL ATHENS
ACCOMMODATION
Acropolis View H
The Alassia E
Hostel Aphrodite A
Art Gallery L
Art Hotel C
Athenian Callirhoe N
Athens Backpackers I
Athens International Youth Hostel D
Athens Studios M
Delphi Art Hotel G
Evropi F
Herodion J
Marble House P
Oscar B
Pagration Athens Youth Hostel O
Philippos K
BARS & CLUBS
Alabastron 28
Craft 4
Diavlos Musiki Spiti 32
Elatos 7
Gagarin 205 1
Granazi 24
Half-Note 29
Koukles 35
Laba 6
Mike's Irish Bar 12
Palenque 13
Rebetikí Istoría 3
Rodeo Live Club 2
Stavros tou Notou 36
RESTAURANTS
Ambrosia 33
Andreas 10
Apanemia 26
Arkhaion Yefsis 5
T'Askimopapo 22
Athinaïkon 11
Chez Lucien 16
Delphi Café G
Diavlos Musiki Spiti 32
Dionysos Zonar's 20
Edodi 34
Erotokritos 9
Ikonomou 17
Ilias 14
Karavitis 15
To Koutouki 23
Lefteris 8
Mikri Vouli 30
Pinelopi kai Mnistires 27
Santorinios 18
Spondi 31
Strofi 21
Therapefterio 19
Vyrinis 25
Pedhio Areos
ÁREOS
Lófos tou Stréfi (Stréfis Hill)
NEÁPOLI
See 'Exárhia, Kolonáki & Omónia' map for detail
Lykavitós Theatre
Lykavitós Hill
Funicular Railway
AMBELOKIPI
LEOFOROS ALEXANDHRAS
12, Airport & Odhos Attiki
13
Megaro Moussikis
LEOFOROS VASILISSIS SOFIAS
KOLONÁKI
ILISIA
Benáki Museum
Vouli
Cycladic Art Museum
War Museum
Byzantine & Christian Museum
National Gallery
Evangelismos
National Gardens
Presidential Palace
Záppio
Zappeion Gardens
Alsos Pangratiou
Panathenaic Stadium
Ardhittós Hill
METS
PANGRÁTI
PROFITIS ILIAS
Próto Nekrotafio
0 300 m

6am–9pm; €3) and Lávrio (20 daily; 6.30am–10pm; €4), useful for those wishing to head straight for a ferry from either place. Indicator boards inside show the next departure.

Taxis are subject to the vagaries of traffic and can take anything from forty minutes (at night) to an hour and forty minutes (at rush hour) to reach the centre; the fare should be roughly €20–25 to central Athens or Pireás. See p.93 for more on taxi charges and rip-offs.

By train

Laríssis station, northwest of Platía Omonías, is ten to fifteen minutes' walk from the concentration of hotels around Platía Viktorías and Exárhia. Otherwise, the Stathmós Laríssis **metro station** (also known as Larissa), right outside, is the most convenient way to get into central Athens, or to anywhere else on the metro system including the port of Pireás (though many trains continue direct to Pireás). Alternatively, the **#1 trolley bus** and #M2 bus pass along Sámou, one block east of the station, heading for Omónia, Sýndagma and on past Akrópoli metro station (close to the Acropolis) into Koukáki. And of course there are **taxis**.

By bus

Athens has two principal bus terminals, at Kifissoú 100 and Liossíon 260. Coming into Athens from northern Greece or the Peloponnese, you'll find yourself at **Kifissoú 100** (Terminal A), northwest of the centre. Bus #051 runs very frequently from here to the corner of Zínonos and Menándhrou, just off Omónia square. Routes from central Greece generally arrive at **Liossíon 260** (Terminal B), slightly further out to the north. From here, bus #024 runs right through the centre to Omónia, Sýndagma and on past metro Akrópoli.

International buses use a variety of stops, most commonly Kifissoú 100 or the train station. If you're travelling from within the state of Attica – for example from the ports at Lávrio or Rafína – you'll arrive at the Mavrommatéon terminus at the southwest corner of the Pedhíon Áreos Park. This is very close to metro Viktorías, or there are dozens of buses heading down 28 Oktovríou (aka Patissíon) past the National Archeological Museum towards the centre.

By ferry

The simplest way to get to central Athens from the port at **Pireás** is by **metro** on line 1. Trains run from 5am to 12.30am, and a ticket to the centre of town costs €0.60 (€0.70 if you want to change to another line or continue beyond the centre up to the northern suburbs). **Buses** are much slower but run all night: #040 (about every 10min 5am–midnight; hourly 1–5am) runs to Sýndagma, while #049 (about every 15min 5am–midnight; hourly 1–5am) runs to Omónia. For the airport, take express bus #X96 or the suburban train or metro via the centre (where you have to change). **Taxis** between Pireás and central Athens should cost around €10, including luggage, a little more at night. For further details on Pireás, together with a map of the central area, see p.135. Ferries arriving at **Rafína** and **Lávrio** are served by KTEL buses to the Mavrommatéon terminal (see above).

Information and tours

The **Greek National Tourist Office** has a central information office at Amalías 26, just off Sýndagma (Mon–Fri 9am–7pm, Sat & Sun 10am–4pm;

> **The sites: opening hours and fees**
>
> Opening hours for the **sites** and **museums** in Athens are included with some trepidation; they are notorious for changing without notice, from one season to another, or even from one week to the next. To be sure of admission, it's best to visit in the morning, and to be wary of Mondays – when many museums and sites close for the whole day.
>
> Most government-run sites are free on Sundays during the off-season (Oct–March), and on some public holidays. Most sites and museums let EU students in free (others half price) and offer reduced senior (over 65), child and youth (under 18 or under 25) rates too.

Ⓣ210 33 10 392, Ⓦwww.gnto.gr). This is a useful first stop and they have a good free map as well as information sheets on current museum and site opening hours, bus schedules, and so on. If you are arriving by plane, you can save time by calling in at the similarly well-stocked airport branch.

City bus #400 offers a hop-on/hop-off tour passing all the major sites (€5; buy ticket on the bus; valid for 24 hours on this and all other city centre public transportation); handy stops include Omónia, Sýndagma and the National Archeological Museum. For kids especially, the Little Train, a thirty-minute trip around Pláka and the centre (€5 adults, €3 children), can be fun: it leaves from Eólou on the Platía Paliás Agorás, near the Roman Forum in Monastiráki. Most local travel agencies offer a variety of more formal tours ranging from a half-day bus drive around the highlights of the city, including guided tours of the Acropolis and Archeological Museum (for around €40), to walking tours of Pláka, day-trips to Soúnio or Delphi and cruises around the nearby islands of Égina, Póros and ýdhra. You'll find brochures in most hotels, or contact some of the travel agencies listed on p.156.

City transport

Athens is served by slow but ubiquitous **buses**, a fast, mostly modern **metro** system, and a **tram** service that runs from the centre to the beach suburbs. **Taxis** are also plentiful and, for short journeys in town, exceptionally cheap. Most public transportation operates from around 5am to midnight, with just a few buses – including those to the airport – continuing all night. **Driving** is a traffic-crazed nightmare, and parking far worse. If you do have a car, you're strongly advised to find somewhere to park it for the duration of your stay and not attempt to use it to get around the city centre.

The metro

The expanded **metro** system is much the easiest way to get around central Athens; it's fast, quiet and user-friendly. It consists of three lines: **Line 1** (green; Pireás to Kifissiá) is the original section, with useful stops in the centre at Thissío, Monastiráki, Omónia and Viktorías; **Line 2** (red; Áyios Antónios to Áyios Dhimítrios) has central stops at Omónia, Sýndagma and Akrópoli at the foot of the Acropolis; and **Line 3** (blue; Egaléo to the airport) passes through Monastiráki and Sýndagma. Some of the new stations are attractions in their own right, displaying artefacts discovered in their excavation (numerous important discoveries were made) and other items of local interest – Sýndagma and Akrópoli are particularly interesting central ones.

Trains run from roughly 5.30am to midnight. When travelling on the metro you need to know the final stop in the direction you're heading, as that is how the platforms are identified; there are plenty of maps in the stations.

Buses

The **bus network** is extensive and cheap, but also crowded and confusing. Routes, where relevant, are detailed in the text and at most of the major stops there are helpful information booths. Easiest to use are the **trolleybuses**: #1 connects the Baríssis train station with Omónia, Sýndagma and Koukáki; #2, #4, #5, #9, #11 and #15 all link Sýndagma with Omónia and the National Archeological Museum.

The tram

Athens' **tram** network was finished in a hurry for the 2004 Olympics – sometimes you can tell as it sways over lines that don't seem entirely straight. Nonetheless it's a great way to get to coastal suburbs and the beach. The tram runs from Leofóros Amalías just off Sýndagma to the coast, where it branches. To the right it heads northwest towards Pireás, terminating at SEF (the Stádhio Eirínis ké Filías or Peace and Friendship Stadium), an interchange with metro line 1 at Néo Fáliro and within walking distance of Pireás's leisure harbours. Left, the tram lines run southwest along the coast to Glyfádha. There are effectively three lines – #1, from Sýndagma to SEF; #2, from Sýndagma to Glyfádha; and #3, from SEF to Glyfádha. These numbers are displayed on

Bus, metro and tram tickets

The easiest and least stressful way to travel is with a **pass**. A **one-day imerísio** costs €3 and can be used on buses, trolleybuses, trams, metro and the suburban railway in central Athens (all lines except the airport route beyond Doukissis Plakentias and some long-distance bus lines). You validate it once, on starting your first journey, and it is good for 24 hours from then. A **weekly pass** costs €10 – again it must be validated on first use – while **monthly** passes are €38 (less for versions that don't include the metro). Passes can be bought from any metro ticket office and many places where bus tickets are sold (see below) – you can buy several daily passes at once and then validate them as necessary. A single ticket, valid for 90 minutes on all forms of transport (and transfers between them) is €1.

Otherwise, normal **metro tickets** cost €0.70 on Line 1 for journeys of no more than two of its three zones (this will get you from the centre to either end of the line), €0.80 for any other journey (valid for 90min from validation, for travel in one direction – for example you can change lines, but you can't go somewhere and come back). They're available from machines and ticket offices in any metro station, and must be validated before you start your journey, in the machines at the top of the stairs.

Bus tickets cost €0.50 and must be bought in advance from kiosks, certain shops and newsagents, or from booths near major stops – look for the brown, red and white logo proclaiming *Isitíria edhó* ("tickets here"). They're sold individually or in bundles of ten, and must be validated in the machine on board the bus. Validated tickets apply only to a particular journey and vehicle; there are no transfers.

Tram tickets are sold at machines on the stations. They cost €0.60, or €0.40 if your journey is less than five stops or you're transferring from another form of transport within 90 minutes. Tickets can be validated at machines on the platform or on board.

Fare-dodgers on any of the above risk an on-the-spot **fine** of sixty times the single fare.

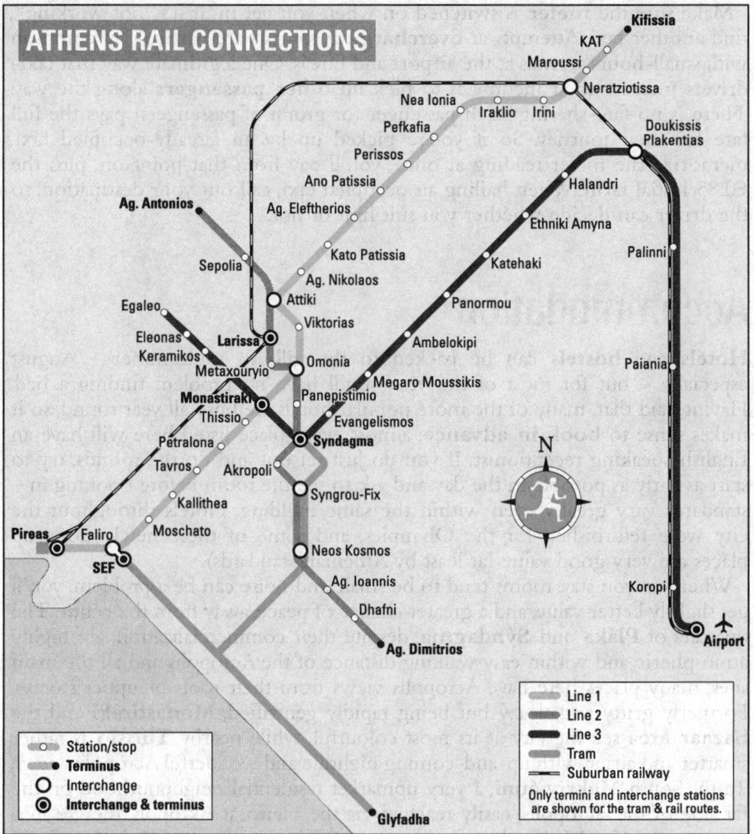

the front of the tram and are worth checking, as the electronic boards at the stations are erratic. The tram doesn't automatically stop at every station, so push the bell if you're on board, or wave it down if you're on the platform.

Taxis

Athenian **taxis** can seem astonishingly cheap – trips around the city centre will rarely run above €4, which means for a group of three or four they cost little more than the metro. Longer trips are also reasonable value: the airport only costing €20–25 and Pireás €8–12 from the centre – the exact amount determined by traffic and amount of luggage. All officially licensed cars are yellow and have a red-on-white numberplate. You can wave them down on the street, pick them up at ranks in most of the major travel termini and central squares, or phone one (or get your hotel to do it).

The meter starts at €0.85, with a minimum fare of €1.75: legitimate **surcharges** that will increase the cost include those for luggage; airport, sea-port or station trips; night-time journeys (midnight to 5am); ordering by phone and so on. Every taxi should display the rates and extra charges in English and Greek.

Make sure the **meter** is switched on when you get in. If it's "not working", find another taxi. Attempts at **overcharging** tourists are particularly common with small-hours arrivals at the airport and Pireás. One legitimate way that taxi-drivers increase their income is to pick up **other passengers** along the way. There is no fare-sharing: each passenger (or group of passengers) pays the full fare for their journey. So if you're picked up by an already-occupied taxi, memorize the meter reading at once; you'll pay from that point on, plus the €0.85 initial tariff. When hailing an occupied taxi, call out your destination, so the driver can decide whether you suit him or not.

Accommodation

Hotels and **hostels** can be packed to the gills in midsummer – August especially – but for most of the year you'll have no problem finding a bed. Having said that, many of the more popular hotels are busy all year round, so it makes sense to **book in advance**; almost every place listed here will have an English-speaking receptionist. If you do just set out and do the rounds, try to start as early as possible in the day and ask to see the room before booking in – standards vary greatly even within the same building. Hotels throughout the city were refurbished for the Olympics, and some of these newly done-up places are very good value (at least by Athenian standards).

Wherever you stay, rooms tend to be small, and noise can be a problem; you'll get slightly better value, and a greater chance of peace, away from the centre. The quarters of **Pláka** and **Sýndagma**, despite their commercialization, are highly atmospheric and within easy walking distance of the Acropolis and all the main sites; many places here have Acropolis views from their roofs or upper storeys. Formerly gritty and sleazy but being rapidly gentrified, **Monastiráki** and the **bazaar area** see the city at its most colourful, while nearby **Thissío** is rather smarter and airier, with up-and-coming nightlife and wonderful Acropolis views. To the south **Makriyiánni**, a very upmarket residential neighbourhood on the far side of the Acropolis, easily reached via the metro at Akrópoli, merges into more earthy **Koukáki** – close to the metro at Sýngrou-Fix, or on the #1 or #5 trolleybus routes from Sýndagma. East of the centre is the ritzy shopping district of **Kolonáki**, while to the north, **Platía Omonías** is still very much the city centre, with lots of large hotels on busy streets. In the marginally quieter neighbourhoods nearby – **Metaxouryío**, **Exárhia** and **Platía Viktorías** – you are again out of the tourist mainstream (though close to the archaeological museum), but benefit from good-value local restaurants and the proximity of cinemas, clubs and bars. These areas have clusters of good-value, mid-range hotels, just a short walk away from the train stations (and metros Omónia, Metaxouryío or Viktorías). Much further out, hotels in **Pireás** offer reasonably easy access to the centre of Athens, but you're only really likely to stay here if you're taking a ferry. Along the **coast**, many beach hotels are served by the new tram, and are also convenient for all-night bus routes to the airport.

Pláka, Monistiráki and Sýndagma

See map, p.109.

Acropolis House Kódhrou 6 ⓣ210 32 22 344, ehtlacrhs@otenet.gr. Metro Sýndagma. A rambling, slightly dilapidated 150-year-old mansion much loved by its regulars – mostly students and academics, many of whom leave behind books for other guests to read. Furnishings are individual and some rooms have baths across the hall; not all have a/c, though most are naturally cool. Rates include use of fridge. Discounts for longer stays. B&B ④

Adonis Kódhrou 3 ⓣ210 32 49 737, ⓦwww.hotel-adonis.gr. Metro Sýndagma. A 1960s low-rise *pension* across the street from *Acropolis House*, with some suites. Rather old-fashioned, but none the worse for it – rooms are comfortable with a/c and TV. The rooftop breakfast-bar has a stunning view of the Acropolis and central Athens. B&B ④

Athos Patröou 3 ⓣ210 32 21 977, ⓦwww.athoshotel.gr. Metro Sýndagma. Small hotel pleasantly refurbished in 2004, with comfortable, carpeted en-suite rooms (some a little cramped) with TV and a/c. Also a rooftop bar with Acropolis views. B&B ⑥

Ava Apartments & Suites Lysikrátous 9–11 ⓣ210 32 59 000, ⓦwww.avahotel.gr. Metro Akrópoli. Between the Temple of Zeus and the Acropolis, *Ava* offers luxurious two-room suites and apartments accommodating up to five people and ideal for families. All have balconies – some very large – with sideways Acropolis views, as well as small kitchens. ⑦

Central Apóllonos 21 ⓣ210 32 34 357, ⓦwww.centralhotel.gr. Metro Sýndagma. Completely refurbished in designer style, with seagrass or wooden floors, marble bathrooms and excellent soundproofing. Family and interconnecting rooms also available; all with a/c, TV and fridge. Large roof terrace with Acropolis views and hot tub. B&B ⑤–⑥

Electra Palace Nikodhímou 18 ⓣ210 33 70 000, ⓦwww.electrahotels.gr. Metro Sýndagma. Luxury hotel right in the heart of Pláka with every facility including both indoor and rooftop pools, small gym and sauna. Stunning if you have an upper-floor suite, whose large balconies have great Acropolis views, but standard rooms are rather dull. ⑧

Grande Bretagne Vassiléos Yioryíou 1, Platía Sýndagma ⓣ210 33 30 000, ⓦwww.grandebretagne.gr. Metro Sýndagma. If someone else is paying, try to get them to put you up at the *Grande Bretagne*, the grandest of all Athens' hotels with the finest location in town. Refurbished for the Olympics, it really is magnificent, with every conceivable facility. Treatments in the spa cost more than a night at many hotels; rooms are well over €300 even for an off-season special offer. ⑧

Hermes Apóllonos 19 ⓣ210 32 35 514, ⓦwww.hermeshotel.gr. Metro Sýndagma. Very classily renovated for the Olympics, with marble bathrooms, polished wood floors and designer touches in every room – some rooms are rather small; others have big balconies. There's also a roof terrace with Acropolis views. B&B ⑥

Kouros Kódhrou 11 ⓣ210 32 27 431. Metro Sýndagma. Faded but friendly and atmospheric *pension*, with fairly basic facilities: shared baths and sinks in rooms. Some rooms have balconies overlooking the pedestrianized street. ③

Metropolis Mitropóleos 46 ⓣ210 32 17 469, ⓦwww.hotelmetropolis.gr. Metro Sýndagma/Monastiráki. Right by the cathedral, the friendly Metropolis has simple, plainly furnished rooms with vinyl floors, each with a good-size balcony, a/c and TV, some with shared bathroom. Acropolis views from the upper floors. ④

Phaedra Herefóndos 16, cnr Adhrianoú ⓣ210 32 38 461, ⓦwww.hotelphaedra.com. Metro Akrópoli. Small, simple rooms with bare tiled floors, TV and a/c, not all en suite (but you get a private bathroom). Polite, welcoming management looks after the place well and it's quiet at night, thanks to a location at the junction of two pedestrian alleys. One of the best deals in Pláka. ③–④

The bazaar area, Psyrrí and Thissío

See map, p.125

Attalos Athinás 29 ⓣ210 32 12 801, ⓦwww.attalos.gr. Metro Monastiráki. Modern from the outside but traditional within, the Attalos has bright, comfortable rooms, well insulated from the noisy street, all with a/c and TV. Some balcony rooms on the upper floors have great views – there's also a roof-terrace bar in the evenings – but rooms facing the internal courtyard at the back are generally larger and quieter. Some triples. Buffet breakfast available at extra cost. ⑤

Cecil Athinás 39 ⓣ210 32 18 005, ⓦwww.cecil.gr. Metro Monastiráki. Loving restoration of a run-down 150-year-old *pension*; attractively decorated, good-sized rooms have polished wooden floors, a/c and TV. Helpful management; roof garden; B&B ⑤

Fresh Hotel Sofokléous 26, ⓣ210 52 48 511, ⓦwww.freshhotel.gr. Metro Omónia. Glossy, high-end "designer" hotel in the heart of the market area. Lavish use of colour, designer furnishings and great lighting and bathrooms, though you do wonder how long it will stay looking fresh. Wireless Internet access throughout, and an elegant rooftop pool, bar and restaurant. ⑦

Ochre and Brown Leokoríou 7 ⓣ210 33 12 950, ⓦwww.ochreandbrown.com. Metro Thissío. Understated designer hotel with just 11 rooms, one of which is a large suite with private terrace and views; all rooms have satellite TV, as well as DVD and CD players. Friendly and comfortable as well as elegant, plus a great location on the fringes of Psyrrí. ⑦

Phidias Apostólou Pávlou 39 ⓣ210 34 59 511, ⓦwww.phidias.gr. Metro Thissío. With an enviable position just down from the *Thission*, the *Phidias* shares similar views, though here only the front rooms have balconies. A little smarter than the *Thission*, with a/c and TV throughout, but still overdue for a makeover. ④

Tempi Eólou 29 ⓣ210 32 13 175, ⓦwww.travelling.gr/tempihotel. Metro Monastiráki. A long-time favourite with budget travellers: book exchange and shared kitchen, plus handy affiliated travel agency. Rooms are simple and tiny and most have shared facilities, but the view of the flower market at Ayía Iríni across the quiet pedestrian walkway is enchanting, and it's within walking distance of most central sights. ③

Thission Apostólou Pávlou 25 ⓣ210 34 67 634, ⓦwww.hotel-thission.gr. Metro Thissío. Virtually every room at the *Thission* has a balcony with a view of the Acropolis as good as any in Athens, and it lies at the heart of a newly fashionable area crammed with designer cafés. Which makes it even more amazing that nobody has got round to refurbishing the place; rooms are comfortable enough, with a/c and TV, but distinctly threadbare, and service can be slapdash. Pleasant roof-terrace café. ④

Omónia and around, Exárhia and Kolonáki

See maps, p.88 & p.131.

The Alassia Sokrátous 50 ⓣ210 52 74 000, ⓦwww.thealassia.com.gr. Metro Omónia. Refurbished for the Olympics in minimalist style with lots of dark wood veneer. Rooms are small but well soundproofed (you're just off Platía Omonías here) and with every comfort, including designer bathrooms. ⑥

Art Hotel Márni 27 ⓣ210 52 40 501, ⓦwww.arthotelathens.gr. Metro Omónia. Not the greatest location – on a rather noisy, scruffy street – but a very pleasant boutique hotel in a refurbished 1920s building with individually designed rooms. Thoughtful touches include Korres toiletries in the marble bathrooms, and there's a substantial buffet breakfast. ⑥

Delphi Art Hotel Ayíou Konstandínou 27 ⓣ210 52 44 004, ⓦwww.delphiarthotel.com. Metro Omónia. Right by the National Theatre and Áyios Konstantínos church, this 1930s mansion has been lavishly restored with Art Nouveau touches and eclectic, individual furnishings. Facilities include Internet access throughout, and Jacuzzi baths in some rooms. B&B ⑦

Evropi Satovriándhou 7 ⓣ210 52 23 081. Metro Omónia. Very basic but great value old-fashioned hotel with spacious rooms occupied only by bed, bedside table and ceiling fan, along with a concrete enclosure for en-suite shower. Reasonably quiet, despite being only a block from Platía Omonías; inexpensive singles available. ②

Exarchion Themistokléous 55, Platía Exarhíon ⓣ210 38 01 256, ⓦwww.exarchion.com. Metro Omónia. Big 1960s high-rise hotel that's a great deal less fancy inside than you might imagine. Vinyl-floored rooms, all with TV, a/c and fridge, are simply furnished and due for refurbishment. But that's reflected in the price, and it's good value if you want to be at the heart of Exarhía's nightlife. Upper-floor rooms are quieter, with better views. ③–④

Museum Bouboulínas 16 ⓣ210 38 05 611, ⓦwww.museum-hotel.gr. Metro Viktorías/Omónia. Very pleasant, international-style hotel (part of the Best Western chain), right behind the National Archeological Museum and the Polytekhnío. Rooms in the new wing, which has triples, quads and small suites, are more luxurious but slightly more expensive. ④–⑤

Orion and Dryades Emmanouíl Benáki 5 ⓣ210 36 27 362, ⓔorion-dryades@mail.com. Metro Viktorías/Omónia. Quiet, well-run twin hotels across from the Stréfis hill – a steep uphill walk from almost anywhere. Reception is in the cheaper Orion, which has shared bathrooms, a kitchen and communal area on the roof with an amazing view of central Athens. All rooms in the Dryades are en suite with a/c and TV. ②–④

Oscar Filadhelfías 25 ⓣ210 88 34 215, ⓦwww.oscar.gr. Metro Laríssis. Big, modern high-rise right in front of the station, so handy for late-night and early departures including suburban trains to the airport. This is its main recommendation, along with a rooftop pool and all the facilities of a large, comfortable hotel. ⑤

St George Lycabettus Kleoménous 75, Kolonáki ⓣ210 72 90 711, ⓦwww.sglycabettus.gr. A luxury boutique hotel and an Athenian classic, with a position high on Lykavitós hill overlooking the city. Abundant marble and leather in the public areas plus a welcome rooftop pool, and bars and restaurant popular with wealthy young Athenians. Some of the rooms are rather small, however, and there's no point staying here if you don't pay extra for the view. ⑦–⑧

Makriyiánni and Koukáki

See map, p.88

Acropolis View Webster 10 and Robérto Gálli ⓣ210 92 17 303, ⓦwww.acropolisview.gr. Metro Akrópoli. Small but well-furnished rooms with a/c, TV, fridge, balcony and tiny marble bathrooms in what looks like a 1970s apartment block. The roof garden has an amazing close-up view of the Acropolis. B&B ④

Art Gallery Erekhthíou 5 ⓣ210 92 38 376, ⓔecotec@otenet.gr. Metro Syngroú-Fix. A family-owned converted apartment block, this popular, slightly old-fashioned *pension* with many repeat customers is named for the original artworks that adorn every room. Knowledgeable and helpful staff, convenient location a short walk from the metro and a bountiful breakfast (extra) served on a terrace with Acropolis views. ⑤

Athenian Callirhoe Kalliróis 32, cnr Petmeza ⓣ210 92 15 353, ⓦwww.tac.gr. Metro Syngroú-Fix. Between Koukáki and the centre, the *Callirhoe* was one of Athens' first "designer" hotels. It's already starting to look slightly faded, but central location and good facilities – including Internet in the rooms and a small gym – make it popular with business and leisure travellers alike. It's worth checking for offers. ⑦

Athens Studios Veïkóu 3a ⓣ210 92 24 044, ⓦwww.athensstudios.gr. Metro Akrópoli. Newly furnished apartments for up to six with kitchen, sitting room, TV, a/c, phone, Internet access and linen provided. Run by the people from nearby *Athens Backpackers* (see p.98), and including use of their bar and facilities. Great value for groups; from €120 per apartment.

Herodion Robérto Gálli 4 ⓣ210 92 36 832, ⓦwww.herodion.gr. Metro Akrópoli. Lovely hotel, recently done up to very high standards, in an enviable position right behind the Acropolis. Comfortable rooms and a roof terrace looking almost straight down to the south slope of the Acropolis. ⑧

Marble House Cul-de-sac off A. Zínni 35A ⓣ210 92 34 058, ⓦwww.marblehouse.gr. Metro Syngroú-Fix. The best value in Koukáki, family run and friendly. Simple rooms with and without private bath, eight of which have a/c (for extra charge); also two self-catering studios for longer stays. Often full, so call ahead. ③

Philippos Mitséon 3 ⓣ210 92 23 611, ⓦwww.philipposhotel.gr. Metro Akrópoli. Sister hotel to the *Herodion*, the *Philippos* was also completely renovated for the Olympics though the interior is much less dramatic than the new facade. Very comfortable, well-appointed rooms with a/c. ⑦

Pireás and the coast

Acropole Goúnari 7, Pireás ⓣ210 41 73 313, ⓦwww.acropole-hotel.gr. See map, p.135. Metro Pireás. Very handy for ferries and metro, renovated for the Olympics with a variety of rooms including triples; some with Jacuzzi. Breakfast room (breakfast extra) and bar downstairs. ④

Astir Palace Appólonos 40, Vougliaméni ⓣ210 89 02 000, ⓦwww.astir-palace.com. This spectacular resort complex occupies some 75 acres of a private, pine-covered peninsula, 25km from downtown. There are three separate hotels (the *Arion*, the *Westin* and designer *W Athens*), plus private villas, pools, watersports, tennis courts, a spa and no fewer than six restaurants. A shuttle bus runs twice daily to central Athens, just in case the weather prevents you using the helipad. Can at times be dominated by groups attending conferences here. ⑧

Palmyra Beach Possídhonos 70, Glyfádha ⓣ210 89 81 183, ⓦwww.palmyra.gr. Tram Páleo Dimarhío. Well-run, mid-scale tourist hotel with a small pool. The beach of the name isn't up to much, but the hotel is within walking distance of the centre of Glyfádha, handy for the tram, and has plenty of other beaches nearby. There's a free shuttle from the airport during the day, plus the #X96 airport express bus stops nearby. B&B ⑥

Piraeus Dream Fílonos 79–81 & Notára 78–80, Pireás ⓣ210 41 10 555, ⓦ www.piraeusdream.gr. See map, p.135. Metro Pireás. Friendly hotel, handy for ferries, with quiet, recently refurbished rooms (with spectacular lighting); a/c and TV. Buffet breakfast included. ④

Airport

Holiday Inn Attica Avenue, Peánia, at exit 18 of the motorway ⓣ210 66 89 000, ⓦwww.hiathens.com/attica. It's only about 40min by train or metro to the centre of Athens, less by bus to hotels at Glyfádha (see coast above), but if you really need to stay at the airport then choose this brand-new hotel (a short ride on a free shuttle bus) rather than the outrageously expensive *Sofitel* right in the airport complex. ⑦

Hostels and campsites

There are quite a few hostels and backpackers in Athens – a good place to meet fellow travellers and find a ready-made social life. Note, though, that the central ones are pretty expensive; two people travelling together can often find a room for not much more than the price of two dorm beds. The city's **campsites** are out in the suburbs and also not especially cheap – they're only really worth using if you have a camper van; phone ahead to book space in season. There are more pleasant campsites further out on the coast – see p.159 and p.160.

Hostels

Hostel Aphrodite Inárdhou 12, between Alakmenous and Mikhaïl Vódha ⓣ210 88 39 249, ⓦwww.hostelaphrodite.com. See map, p.88. Metro Viktorías. Friendly, clean, IYHA-recognized hostel with some private en-suite doubles and triples, in a quiet residential neighbourhood. A/c available at extra charge; other facilities include breakfast room/bar, luggage storage and Internet access. Dorms €15–20, discounts for IYHA cardholders. ③

Athens Backpackers Mákri 12 ⓣ210 92 24 044, ⓦwww.backpackers.gr. See map, p.109. Metro Akrópoli. Very central Athenian-Australian run backpackers with few frills but clean rooms, communal kitchen, Internet access, rooftop bar with fabulous views, and great atmosphere. Probably the best spot in town to meet fellow travellers. Dorms €18–25.

Athens International Youth Hostel Víktoros Ougó 16 ⓣ&ⓕ210 52 32 540. See map, p.88. Metro Metaxouryío. A huge affair, with 140 beds over 7 floors in 2- and 4-bed rooms. Recently given a fresh coat of paint and still being done up, it is cheap and always busy. To be sure of a bed it's best to book in advance and this is essential if you want a private room – do it online at the hostel association website ⓦwww.hihostels.com. Dorms €12.25; non-members pay €2.50 extra per day. ①

Pagration Athens Youth Hostel Dhamáreos 75, Pangráti ⓣ210 75 19 530, ⓦwww.athens-yhostel.com. See map, p.88. Trolleys #2 and #11 from Omónia via Sýnttagma; bus #203 or #204 (or a 15–20min walk) from Metro Evangelismós. A bit out of the way but friendly, with no curfew and in a decent, quiet neighbourhood with plenty of local restaurants. Free use of kitchen and communal area with TV; charge for washing machine and hot water. There's no sign on the door, so look for the green gate. Basic 5/6-bed dorms €12.

Student & Traveller's Inn Kydhathinéon 16 ⓣ210 32 44 808, ⓦwww.studenttravellersinn.com. See map, p.109. Metro Akrópoli/Sýndagma. Very friendly, perennially popular travellers' meeting place; a mixture of hotel and hostel. Dorm beds from €25, depending on room size and facilities; private doubles, triples and quads, en suite or shared bath, are clean and comfortable, though not always the quietest. Small courtyard breakfast area/bar, Internet, luggage storage and travel agency. ④

Campsites

Athens Camping Leofóros Athinón 198–200 ⓣ210 58 14 114, ⓦwww.campingathens.com.gr. The closest campsite to the centre of Athens, just off the busy main road towards the Peloponnese; friendly and about as good as you could hope in this location. It has a minimarket, snack-bar and hot water. The Elefsína bus #A16 passes by.

Camping Nea Kifissia Potamoú and Dhimitsánis, Néa Kifissiá ⓣ210 80 75 579. More pleasant than *Athens Camping* but much further out, in the leafy suburb of Adames, with a swimming pool, bar and restaurant. Take the metro to Kifissiá and then bus #522/3.

The City

As a visitor, you're likely to spend most of your time in the central grid of Athens, a compact, walkable area well served by the metro. Only on arrival at, or departure from, the various far-flung stations and terminals do you have to confront the confused sprawl that surrounds the centre.

Finding your bearings is generally pretty easy: the **Acropolis** dominates most tourist itineraries and it's visible, around a corner, from almost any part of the city centre. Beneath the Acropolis to the east lies **Pláka**, the attractive old quarter where many tourists spend much of their time, with adjoining **Monastiráki** curling around to the north. **Sýndagma** (Platía Syndágmatos), the traditional centre of the city and home to the Greek Parliament, lies to the northeast of these two, midway between the Acropolis and the hill of **Lykavitós**. The ritzy **Kolonáki** quarter curls up the hill's slopes above Sýndagma, with a funicular to save you the final climb to the summit. Below Kolonáki many of the city's major museums can be found along the broad avenue of Leofóros Vassilísis Sofías, one of the main approaches to the city from the north and east. On the other side of the avenue, behind the Parliament, lie the jungly **National Gardens**.

To the north, more broad avenues lead from both Monastiráki and Sýndagma to **Omónia** (in full, Platía Omonías), the heart of commercial and business Athens. The **market and bazaar** area lies en route, while beyond to the north are the **National Archeological Museum** and the slightly alternative, studenty neighbourhoods of **Exárhia** and **Neápoli**, with a concentration of lively tavernas and bars. Close to the market you'll find the thriving nightlife of resurgent **Psyrrí**, whose modernizing influence spreads to the west in **Keramikós**, **Gázi** and **Metaxouryío**.

West and south of the Acropolis, newly pedestrianized streets open up the residential areas of **Thissío**, **Áno Petrálona**, **Makriyiánni** and **Koukáki** – all with excellent cafés and restaurants – as well as the wooded slopes of **Filopáppou Hill**. Adjoining these, and also accessible from Sýndagma via the National Gardens, the quiet, residential neighbourhoods of **Pangráti** and **Mets** are home to more local restaurants and bars. South beyond these districts, the traffic-laden axis of Leofóros Syngroú heads towards **Pireás and the coast**.

Metro and other **public transportation** information is given in the text where relevant, but it's worth knowing the main stops in the centre: **Sýndagma** for Sýndagma and Pláka; **Monastiráki** for Monastiráki, Psyrrí, the market area, the Ancient Agora and the northern approach to the Acropolis; **Akrópoli** for the southern approach to the Acropolis; and **Omónia** for Platía Omonías, the market area and the National Archeological Museum. A word of warning, too, on **pedestrian streets**: while these are generally free of cars, they are by no means traffic-free – mopeds and motorbikes see them as their property too.

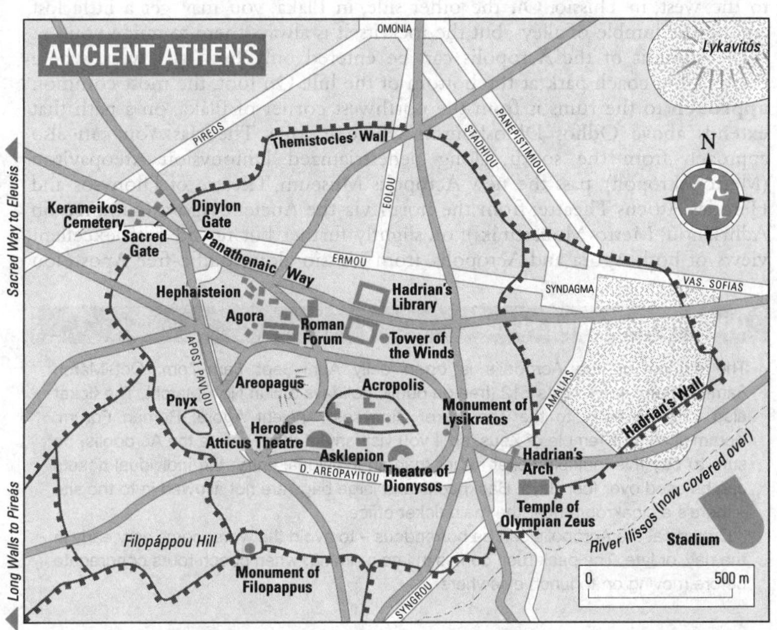

The Acropolis and ancient Agora

The **rock of the Acropolis**, crowned by the dramatic ruins of the Parthenon, is one of the archetypal images of Western culture. The first time you see it, rising above the traffic or from a distant hill, is extraordinary: foreign, and yet utterly familiar. The **Parthenon** temple was always intended to be a spectacular landmark and a symbol of the city's imperial confidence, and it was famous throughout the ancient world. But even in its creators' wildest dreams they could hardly have imagined that the ruins would come to symbolize the emergence of Western civilization – nor that, two-and-a-half millennia on, it would attract some two million tourists a year.

The Acropolis itself is simply the rock on which the monuments are built; almost every ancient Greek city had its acropolis (which means the summit or highest point of the city), but the acropolis of Athens is The Acropolis, the one that needs no further introduction. Its **natural setting**, a steep-sided, flat-topped crag of limestone rising abruptly 100m from its surroundings, has made it the focus of the city during every phase of its development. Easily defensible and with plentiful water, its initial attractions are obvious. Even now, with no function apart from tourism, it is the undeniable heart of the city, around which everything else clusters, glimpsed at almost every turn.

On top of the Acropolis stands the Parthenon, along with the Erechtheion, the Temple of Athena Nike and the Propylaia or gates to the Acropolis, as well as lesser remains of many other ancient structures. All of these are included in a single, fenced site. The South Slope of the Acropolis, with two great theatres and several smaller temples, has separate entrances and ticketing.

You can walk an entire circuit of the Acropolis and ancient Agora on **pedestrianized streets**, allowing them to be appreciated from almost every angle: in particular, the pedestrianization has provided spectacular new terraces for cafés to the west, in Thissío. On the other side, in Pláka, you may get a little lost among the jumble of alleys, but the rock itself is always there to guide you.

The summit of the Acropolis can be entered only from the west, where there's a big coach park at the bottom of the hill. On foot, the most common **approach** to the ruins is from the northwest corner of Pláka, on a path that extends above Odhós Dhioskoúron where it joins Theorías. You can also approach from the south, along pedestrianized Dhionysíou Areopayítou (Metro Akrópoli), past the new Acropolis Museum, Theatre of Dionysos and Herodes Atticus Theatre; from the north via the Ancient Agora (entrance on Adhrianoú; Metro Monastiráki); or, slightly further but repaid with excellent views of both Agora and Acropolis, from Thissío along traffic-free Apostólou

Opening hours and tickets

The summit of the Acropolis is **open** daily April–Sept 8am–7pm; Oct–March 8am–4.30pm; entry costs €12 (free on public holidays & Sun Nov–March). The ticket also includes entry to the Theatre of Dionysos, Ancient Agora, Roman Forum, Kerameikos and Temple of Zeus, so if you visit any of them before the Acropolis, be sure to buy this multiple ticket rather than an individual entry; the individual tickets can be used over four days. Backpacks and large bags are not allowed in to the site – there's a cloakroom near the main ticket office.

Crowds at the Acropolis can be horrendous – to avoid the worst come very early in the day, or late. The peak rush comes in late morning, when coach tours congregate before moving on to lunch elsewhere.

A brief history of the Acropolis

The rocky Acropolis was home to one of the earliest known settlements in Greece, its slopes inhabited by a **Neolithic** community around 5000 BC. In **Mycenaean** times – around 1500 BC – it was fortified with Cyclopean walls (parts of which can still be seen), enclosing a royal palace and temples to the cult of Athena. By the ninth century BC, the Acropolis had become the heart of Athens, the first Greek city-state, sheltering its principal public buildings. In 510 BC, the Oracle at Delphi ordered that the Acropolis should remain forever the **province of the gods**, unoccupied by humans. It was in this context that the monuments visible today were built. Most of the substantial remains date from the **fifth century BC** or later; earlier temples and sanctuaries were burned to the ground when the Persians sacked Athens in 480 BC. In 449 BC, with peace restored, the walls were rebuilt and architects drew up plans for a reconstruction worthy of the city's cultural and political ascendancy.

Pericles' rebuilding plan was both magnificent and enormously expensive but it won the backing of the democracy, for many of whose citizens it must have created both wealth and work. The project was under the general direction of the architect and sculptor **Fidias** and it was completed in an incredibly short time: the Parthenon itself took only ten years to finish.

The monuments survived unaltered – save for some modest Roman tinkering – for close to a thousand years, until in the reign of Emperor Justinian the temples were converted to **Christian** worship. Over the following centuries the uses became secular as well as religious, and embellishments increased, gradually obscuring the Classical designs. Fifteenth-century Italian princes held court in the Propylaia, the entrance hall to the complex, and the same quarters were later used by the **Turks** as their commander's headquarters and as a powder magazine. The Parthenon underwent similar changes from Greek to Roman temple, from Byzantine church to Frankish cathedral, before several centuries of use as a Turkish mosque. The Erechtheion, with its graceful female figures, saw service as a harem. A Venetian diplomat, Hugo Favoli, described the Acropolis in 1563 as "looming beneath a swarm of glittering golden crescents", with a minaret rising from the Parthenon. For all their changes in use, however, the buildings would still have resembled – very much more than today's bare ruins – the bustling and ornate ancient Acropolis, covered in sculpture and painted in bright colours.

Sadly, such images remain only in the prints and sketches of that period: the Acropolis buildings finally fell victim to the ravages of war, blown up during successive attempts by the Venetians to oust the Turks. In 1687, laying siege to the garrison, they ignited a Turkish gunpowder magazine in the Parthenon, and in the process blasted off its roof and set a **fire** that raged within its precincts for two days and nights. The process of stripping down to the bare ruins seen today was completed by souvenir hunters and the efforts of the first archeologists – see *The Elgin Marbles* on p.105.

Pávlou (Metro Thissío). **Bus** #230 from Sýndagma will also take you right to the entrance.

You can buy water and sandwiches, as well as guidebooks, postcards and so on, from a couple of stands near the main ticket office. There's also a handy branch of *Everest* right opposite Akrópoli metro station (at the corner of Makriyiánni and Dhiakoú) and plenty of similar places around Monastiráki metro. If you want to sit down to eat, there are cafés and tavernas nearby in almost every direction: Pláka (p.140), Monastiráki (p.140), Makriyiánni (p.145) and Thissío (p.142).

The Summit of the Acropolis

Today, as throughout its history, there's just one way up to the top of the Acropolis. In Classical times the Sacred Way extended along a steep ramp to a

▲ The Acropolis from Filopáppou Hill

massive monumental double gatehouse, the **Propylaia**; the modern path makes a more gradual, zigzagging ascent, passing first through an arched Roman entrance, the **Beule Gate**, added in the third century AD.

The Propylaia

The **Propylaia**, gateway to the Acropolis, were constructed by Mnesikles from 437–432 BC, and their axis and proportions aligned to balance the recently completed Parthenon. They – the name is the plural of propylon, gateway, referring to the fact that there are two wings – were built from the same Pentelic marble (from Mount Pendéli, northeast of the city) as the temple, and in grandeur and architectural achievement are almost as impressive. In order to offset the difficulties of a sloping site, Mnesikles combined, for the first time, standard Doric columns with the taller and more delicate Ionic order. The ancient Athenians, awed by the fact that such wealth and craftsmanship should be used for a purely secular building, ranked this as their most prestigious monument.

Walking through the gateway, which would originally have had great wooden doors, is your only chance to enter any of the ancient buildings atop the Acropolis; the rest are closed to protect them from the hordes of visitors. To the left of the central hall (which before Venetian bombardment supported a great coffered roof, painted blue and gilded with stars), the **Pinakotheke** was an early art gallery, exhibiting paintings of Homeric subjects by Polygnotus. The wing to the right is much smaller, as the original design trespassed on ground sacred to the Goddess of Victory and the premises had to be adapted as a waiting room for her shrine – the Temple of Athena Nike.

Beyond the gate can be seen one of the best-preserved sections of the Sacred or **Panathenaic Way**, the route of the great annual procession for ancient Athens' Panathenaic Festival. The procession – depicted on the Parthenon frieze – wound right through the Classical city from the gates now in the Kerameikos site (see p.126) via the Propylaia to the Parthenon and, finally, the Erectheion.

Here you can make out grooves cut into the rock and, to either side, niches for innumerable statues and offerings. In Classical times it ran past a ten-metre-high bronze statue of *Athena Promachos* (Athena the Champion), whose base can just about be made out. Created by Fidias as a symbol of the Athenians' defiance of Persia, the statue's spear and helmet were said to be visible to approaching sailors from as far away as Sounío. She was moved to Constantinople in Byzantine times and there destroyed by a mob who believed that the beckoning hand had directed the Crusaders to the city in 1204.

The Temple of Athena Nike

Simple and elegant, the **Temple of Athena Nike** stands on a precipitous platform overlooking the port of Pireás and the Saronic Gulf. It has only recently re-appeared, having been dismantled, cleaned, restored and reconstructed. Not for the first time either: demolished by the Turks in the seventeenth century, the temple was reconstructed from its original blocks two hundred years later.

In myth, it was from the platform beside the temple that King Aegeus maintained a vigil for the safe return of his son Theseus from his mission to slay the Minotaur on Crete. Theseus, flushed with success, forgot his promise to swap the boat's black sails for white on his return. Seeing the black sails, Aegeus assumed his son had perished and, racked with grief, threw himself to his death.

The Parthenon

The **Parthenon** was the first great building in Pericles' scheme, intended as a new sanctuary for Athena and a home for her cult image – a colossal wooden statue of Athena Polias (Athena of the City) overlaid with ivory and gold plating, with precious gems as eyes and sporting an ivory gorgon death's-head on her breast. Designed by Fidias, the statue was installed in the semi-darkness of the *cella* (cult chamber), where it remained an object of prestige and wealth,

Forty years of scaffolding

If you see a photo of a pristine Parthenon standing against a clear sky, it is almost certainly an old one. For most of the twenty-first century the Acropolis buildings have been swathed in **scaffolding** and surrounded by **cranes** – at times some structures have even been removed altogether, to be cleaned and later replaced. Though originally intended to be complete in time for the 2004 Olympics, the work is now set to continue for the foreseeable future – some claim that it will be forty years before the job is complete.

The monuments have suffered significant deterioration in modern times and as such there is little doubt that restoration was needed. Almost as soon as the War of Independence was over, Greek archeologists began clearing the Turkish village that had developed around the Parthenon-mosque. Much of this early work was destructive – iron clamps have rusted and warped, for example, causing the stones to crack – and in the meantime earthquakes have dislodged the foundations, generations of feet have slowly worn down surfaces and, more recently pollution has been turning the marble to dust.

In 1975 the imminent collapse of the Parthenon was predicted and visitors have been barred from its actual precinct – as well as the interiors of other structures on the Acropolis – ever since. The restoration process is aimed at ensuring that the Parthenon and its neighbours will continue to stand for another millennium or two, but, in the meantime, it's not improving the view.

if not veneration, until at least the fifth century AD. The sculpture has been lost since ancient times but its characteristics are known through numerous later copies (including a fine Roman one in the National Archeological Museum). However, the temple never rivalled the Erechtheion in sanctity, and its role tended to remain that of treasury and artistic showcase, devoted rather more to the new god of the polis than to Athena herself. The name "Parthenon" means "virgins' chamber", and initially referred only to a room at the west end of the temple occupied by the priestesses of Athena.

Originally the Parthenon's columns were brightly painted and it was decorated with the finest sculpture of the Classical age, also lavishly coloured. The Parthenon frieze and pediments are generally held to have depicted the Panathenaic procession, the birth of Athena and the struggles of Greeks to overcome giants, Amazons and centaurs, but there are alternative theories. Some say that the horsemen depicted represent the Athenians who died in the great victory at Marathon; or that the whole thing shows the sacrifice of the daughters of Erechtheus, ending the wars between Eleusis and Athens. The greater part of the pediments, along with the central columns and the *cella*, were destroyed by the Venetian bombardment in 1687. The best surviving examples are in the British Museum in London where they are known as the Elgin Marbles (see box opposite); the Acropolis Museum also has a few original pieces, as well as reconstructions of the whole thing, and there are good reproductions in Akrópoli metro station.

To achieve the Parthenon's extraordinary and unequalled harmony of design, its architect, Iktinos, used every trick known to the Doric order of architecture. The building's proportions maintain a universal 9:4 ratio, not only in the calculations of length to width, or width to height, but in such relationships as the distances between the columns and their diameter; many other proportions apparently follow the so-called "Golden Ratio" of 1:1.618. Additionally, any possible appearance of disproportion is corrected by meticulous mathematics and craftsmanship. All seemingly straight lines are in fact slightly curved, an optical illusion known as *entasis* (intensification). The columns (their profile bowed slightly to avoid seeming concave) are slanted inwards by 6cm, while each of the steps along the sides of the temple was made to incline just 12cm over a length of 70m.

The Erechtheion

To the north of the Parthenon, beyond the foundations of the Old Temple of Athena, stands the **Erechtheion**, the last of the great works of Pericles to be completed. Both Athena and the city's old patron of Poseidon-Erechtheus were worshipped here, in the most revered of the ancient temples, built over ancient sanctuaries, which in turn were predated by a Mycenaean palace. The site, according to myth, was that on which Athena and Poseidon held a contest, judged by their fellow Olympian gods, to determine who would possess Athens. At the touch of Athena's spear, the first ever olive tree sprang from the ground, while Poseidon summoned forth a fountain of sea water. Athena won, and became patron of the city.

Today, the many sacred objects within are long gone, but the series of elegant Ionic porticoes survives, the north one with a particularly fine, decorated doorway and blue marble frieze. By far the most striking feature, however, is the famous **Porch of the Caryatids**, whose columns form the tunics of six tall maidens. The statues were long supposed to have been modelled on the widows of Karyai, a small city in the Peloponnese that was punished for its alliance with the Persians by the slaughter of its menfolk and the enslavement of the women. There is, though, little suggestion of grieving or humbled

The "Elgin" Marbles

The controversy over the so-called Elgin Marbles has its origin in the activities of Western looters at the start of the nineteenth century: above all the French ambassador Fauvel, gathering antiquities for the Louvre, and **Lord Elgin** levering away sculptures from the Parthenon. As British Ambassador, Elgin obtained permission from the Turks to erect scaffolding, excavate and remove stones with inscriptions. He interpreted this concession as a licence to make off with almost all of the bas-reliefs from the Parthenon's frieze, most of its pedimental structures and a caryatid from the Erechtheion – all of which he later sold to the British Museum. While there were perhaps justifications for Elgin's action at the time – not least the Turks' tendency to use Parthenon stones in their lime kilns – his pilfering was controversial even then. Byron, for example, who visited in 1810–11 just in time to see the last of Elgin's ships loaded with the marbles, roundly disparaged all this activity.

The Greeks believe that the long-awaited completion of the new Acropolis Museum (p.106), would be a perfect opportunity for the British Museum to bow to pressure and return the Parthenon Marbles (as they are always known here). But despite a campaign begun by Greek actress and culture minister Melina Mercouri in the 1980s, there is so far little sign of that happening.

captives in the serene poses of the Caryatid women. Some authorities believe that they instead represent the Arrephoroi, young, high-born girls in the service of Athena. The ones *in situ* are replacements: five of the originals are in the Acropolis Museum, while a sixth was looted by Elgin, who also removed a column and other purely architectural features – they're replaced here by casts in a different-colour marble.

The South Slope of the Acropolis

Entrance to the **South Slope of the Acropolis** (daily: summer 8am–7.30pm; winter 8.30am–3pm; €2 or joint Acropolis ticket) is either by a path tracking around the side of the Acropolis from the area of the main ticket office, or from below, via pedestrianized Leofóros Dhionysíou Areopayítou close to Metro Akrópoli. The dominant structure here is the second-century Roman **Herodes Atticus Theatre** (Odeion of Herodes Atticus), which has been restored for performances of music and Classical drama during the summer festival (see p.60 & p.147). Unfortunately it's open only for shows; at other times you'll have to be content with spying over the wall.

The main reasons to visit, then, are the earlier Greek sites to the east. Pre-eminent among these is the **Theatre of Dionysos**, beside the lower site entrance, one of the most evocative locations in the city. It was here that the masterpieces of Aeschylus, Sophocles, Euripides and Aristophanes were first performed; it was also the venue for the annual festival of tragic drama, where each Greek citizen would take his turn as member of the chorus. Rebuilt in the fourth century BC, the theatre could hold some 17,000 spectators – considerably more than Herodes Atticus's 5000–6000 seats; twenty of the theatre's 64 tiers of seats survive. Most notable are the great marble thrones in the front row, each inscribed with the name of an official of the festival or of an important priest; in the middle sat the priest of Dionysos and on his right the representative of the Delphic Oracle. At the rear of the stage are reliefs of episodes in the life of Dionysos flanked by two squatting Sileni, devotees of the satyrs. Sadly, this area is roped off to protect the stage-floor **mosaic** – a magnificent diamond of multicoloured marble best seen from above.

All around the theatre a great deal of restoration and excavation work is ongoing, including the opening up of a new area on the eastern edge of the rock, above Pláka. It is all in something of a state of flux, but there are fine Byzantine cisterns to look out for, as well as numerous covered areas where groups of statues have been gathered together. Between the two theatres lie the foundations of the **Stoa of Eumenes**, originally a massive colonnade of stalls erected in the second century BC. Above the stoa, high up under the walls of the Acropolis, extend the ruins of the **Asklepion**, a sanctuary devoted to the healing god Asklepios and built around a sacred spring; restoration is ongoing, and there are extensive new signs in English. Nearby, above the Theatre of Dionysos, you can see the entry to a huge cave. This housed the **Choregic Monument of Thrasyllos**, and its entrance was closed off around 320 BC with a marble facade – this too is currently being restored. The cave was later converted to Christian use and became the chapel ofVirgin Mary of the Rocks, but an ancient statue of Dionysos remained inside until it was removed by Lord Elgin (it's now in the British Museum), while the Classical structure survived almost unchanged until 1827, when it was blown up in a Turkish siege.

The Acropolis Museum

After decades of delay, the **new Acropolis Museum** (Ⓦwww.newacropolismuseum.gr), by Metro Akrópoli below the South Slope site, should finally be open by the time you read this. It looks stunning. The architectural highlight is the top storey, an all-glass affair with a direct view up to the Parthenon. Here, it is hoped, the Parthenon Marbles (those already in the Acropolis Museum, plus the restored Elgin Marbles, see p.105) will finally be reunited in a fitting setting. To help bring this about, the Greeks have proposed that the Elgin Marbles come on loan, or that part of the museum be designated the "British Museum in Athens" so that ownership doesn't change. So far, all offers have been turned down by London, though some locals continue to believe that completion of the new museum – with gaps left for the missing items – will shame the British Museum into action.

Among the highlights from the old collection, far more of which will be on view in the new setting, are fragments of pedimental sculptures from the **old Temple of Athena** (seventh to sixth century BC), whose traces of paint give a good impression of the vivid colours that were used in temple decoration. Other sculpture includes the **Moschophoros**, a painted marble statue of a young man carrying a sacrificial calf, dated 570 BC and one of the earliest examples of Greek art in marble, and a unique collection of **Korai**, or maidens, dedicated as votive offerings to Athena at some point in the sixth century BC. Between them they represent a shift in art and fashion, from the simply contoured Doric clothing to the more elegant and voluminous Ionic designs; the figures' smiles also change subtly, becoming increasingly loose and natural. Look out too for a graceful and fluid sculpture, known as **Iy Sandalízoussa**, which depicts **Athena Nike** adjusting her sandal, and for four authentic and semi-eroded **caryatids** from the Erechtheion. On the lowest floor there's a raised, part-glass floor, added to the design to preserve and display remains of early Christian Athens, discovered during building work.

The Areopagus

Metal steps as well as ancient, slippery, rock-hewn stairs ascend the low, unfenced hill of the **Areopagus** immediately below the entrance to the

Acropolis. The "Hill of Ares" was the site of the Council of Nobles and the Judicial Court under the aristocratic rule of ancient Athens. During the Classical period the court lost its powers of government to the Assembly (held on the Pnyx) but it remained the court of criminal justice, dealing primarily with cases of homicide. In myth, it was also the site where Ares, God of War, was tried for the murder of one of Poseidon's sons; Aeschylus used the setting in *The Eumenides* for the trial of Orestes, who, pursued by the Furies' demand of "a life for a life", stood accused of murdering his mother Clytemnestra. The Persians camped here during their siege of the Acropolis in 480 BC, and in the Roman era Saint Paul preached the "Sermon on an Unknown God" on the hill, winning amongst his converts Dionysius "the Areopagite", who became the city's patron saint.

Today, there's little evidence of ancient grandeur, and the hill is littered with cigarette butts and empty beer cans left by the crowds who come to rest after their exertions on the Acropolis and to enjoy the views. These, at least, are good – down over the Agora and towards the ancient cemetery of Kerameikos.

The ancient Agora

The **Agora** or market (daily: summer 8am–7.15pm; winter 8.30am–3pm; €4 or joint Acropolis ticket) was the heart of ancient Athenian city life from as early as 3000 BC. Approached either from the Acropolis, down the path skirting the Areopagus, or through the northern entrance on Adhrianoú near Metro Monastiráki, it is an extensive and confusing jumble of ruins, dating from various stages of building between the sixth century BC and the fifth century AD. Originally, the Agora was a rectangle with an open space at its heart, divided diagonally by the Panathenaic Way and enclosed by temples, administrative buildings, and long, porticoed *stoas* (arcades of shops). As well as the marketplace, this was the chief meeting place of the city, where orators held forth, business was discussed and gossip exchanged – St Paul, for example, took the opportunity to meet and talk to Athenians here. It was also the first home of the democratic assembly before that shifted location to the Pnyx, and continued to be its meeting place when cases of ostracism were discussed for most of the Classical period.

The best overview of the site is from the exceptionally well-preserved **Hephaisteion**, or Temple of Hephaistos, which overlooks the rest of the site from the west. An observation point in front of it has a plan showing the buildings as they were in 150 AD, and the various remains laid out in front of you make a great deal more sense with this to help (there are similar plans at the entrances and upstairs in the Stoa of Attalos). The temple itself was originally thought to be dedicated to Theseus, because his exploits are depicted on the frieze (hence Thissíon, which has given its name to the area); more recently it has been accepted that it actually honoured Hephaistos, patron of blacksmiths and metalworkers. This was one of the first buildings of Pericles' programme, but also one of the least known – perhaps because it lacks the curvature and "lightness" of the Parthenon's design; the barrel-vaulted roof dates from a Byzantine conversion into the church of Saint George.

The other church on the site – that of **Áyii Apóstoli** (the Holy Apostles), by the south entrance – is worth a look as you wander among the extensive foundations of the other Agora buildings. Inside are fragments of fresco, exposed during restoration of the eleventh-century shrine.

The Stoa of Attalos

For some background to the Agora, head for the **Stoa of Attalos** (same hours as Agora but opens 11am Mon; upper floor Mon–Fri 9am–2.30pm). Originally constructed around 158 BC, the Stoa was completely rebuilt between 1953 and 1956 and is, in every respect except colour, an entirely faithful reconstruction; lacking its original bright red and blue paint or no, it is undeniably spectacular.

A small **museum** occupies ten of the 21 shops that formed the lower level of the building. It displays items found at the Agora site from the earliest Neolithic occupation to Roman and Byzantine times. Many of the early items come from burials, but as ever the highlights are from the Classical era, including some good red-figure pottery and a bronze Spartan shield. Look out for the *ostraka*, or pottery shards, with names written on them. At annual assemblies of the citizens, these *ostraka* would be handed in, and the individual with most votes banished, or "ostracized", from the city for ten years.

On the upper level, the **balcony** area has a sparse but fascinating little exhibition on the excavations of the Agora site and reconstruction of the Stoa, with various plans and it photos of buildings. The models especially help make sense of the rest of the Agora site.

Pláka and Monastiráki

The largely pedestrianized area of **Pláka**, with its narrow lanes and stepped alleys climbing towards the Acropolis, is, along with neighbouring **Monastiráki**, arguably the most attractive part of Athens, and certainly the most popular with visitors. Roughly delineated by Sýndagma and the National Gardens to the east, Odhós Ermoú in the north and the Acropolis to the west, this district was basically the extent of nineteenth-century, pre-independence Athens. In addition to a scattering of ancient sites and various offbeat and enjoyable museums, it offers glimpses of an older Athens, refreshingly at odds with the concrete blocks of the metropolis.

Although surrounded by huge, traffic-choked avenues, the area provides a welcome escape, its narrow streets offering no through-routes for traffic even where you are allowed to drive. Nineteenth-century houses, some grand, some humble, can be seen everywhere, their gateways opening onto verdant courtyards overlooked by wooden verandahs. Poor and working class for much of the twentieth century, the few private homes that remain are now thoroughly gentrified. With scores of **cafés and restaurants** to fill the time between museums and sites, and streets lined with touristy **shops**, it's an enjoyable place to wander, though things are noticeably more expensive in Pláka than in much of the rest of the city.

Kydhathinéon and Adhrianoú streets

An attractive approach to Pláka is to follow **Odhós Kydhathinéon**, a pedestrian walkway that starts near the **Anglican and Russian churches** on Odhós Filellínon, south of Sýndagma. It leads gently downhill, past the Museum of Greek Folk Art, through café-crowded Platía Filomoússou Eterías, to Hadrian's street, **Odhós Adhrianoú**, which runs nearly the whole length of Pláka from Hadrian's Arch past the ancient Agora. These two are the main commercial and tourist streets of the district, with Adhrianoú increasingly tacky and downmarket as it approaches Platía Monastirakíou and the Monastiráki Flea Market.

The Museum of Greek Folk Art

The **Folk Art Museum** (Tues–Sun 9am–2pm; €2), at Kydhathinéon 17, is one of the most enjoyable in the city, even though let down somewhat by poor

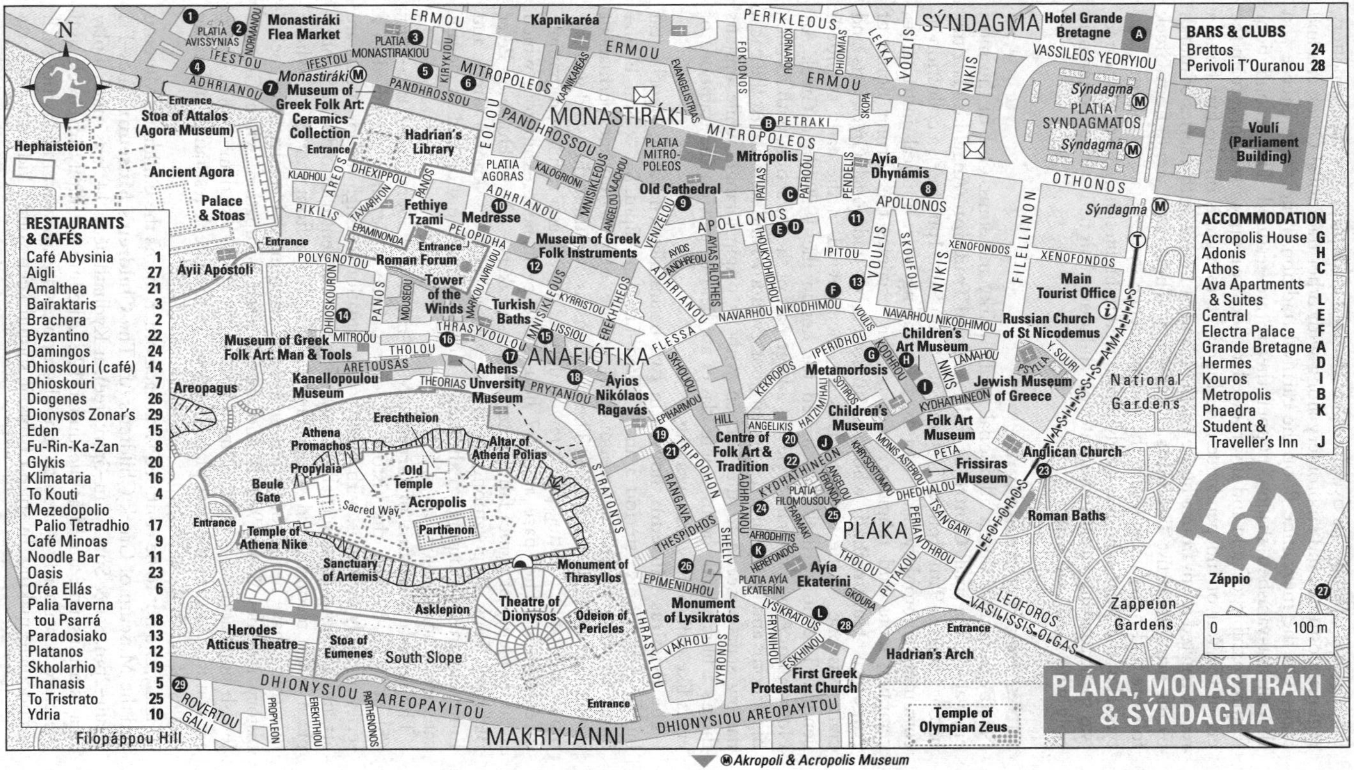

PLÁKA, MONASTIRÁKI & SÝNDAGMA

RESTAURANTS & CAFÉS

Café Abysinia	1
Aigli	27
Amalthea	21
Baïraktaris	3
Brachera	2
Byzantino	22
Damingos	24
Dhioskouri (café)	14
Dhioskouri	7
Diogenes	26
Dionysos Zonar's	29
Eden	15
Fu-Rin-Ka-Zan	8
Glykis	20
Klimataria	16
To Kouti	4
Mezedopolio Palio Tetradhio	17
Café Minoas	9
Noodle Bar	11
Oasis	23
Oréa Ellás	6
Palia Taverna tou Psarrá	18
Paradosiako	13
Platanos	12
Skholarhio	19
Thanasis	5
To Tristrato	25
Ydria	10

BARS & CLUBS

Brettos	24
Perivoli T'Ouranou	28

ACCOMMODATION

Acropolis House	G
Adonis	H
Athos	C
Ava Apartments & Suites	L
Central	E
Electra Palace	F
Grande Bretagne	A
Hermes	D
Kouros	I
Metropolis	B
Phaedra	K
Student & Traveller's Inn	J

lighting and labelling. Its five floors are devoted to displays of weaving, pottery, regional costumes and embroidery along with other traditional Greek arts and crafts. On the mezzanine floor, the carnival tradition of northern Greece and the all-but-vanished shadow-puppet theatre are featured. The second floor features exhibits of gold and silver jewellery and weaponry, much of it from the era of the War of Independence. The highlight, though, is on the first floor: a reconstructed room from a house on the island of Lesvós with a series of murals by the primitive artist **Theofilos** (1868–1934). These naive scenes from Greek folklore and history, especially the independence struggle, are wonderful, and typical of the artist, who was barely recognized in his lifetime. Most of his career was spent painting tavernas and cafés on and around his native island, often paid only with food and board.

More nearby museums

Nearby are half a dozen additional small, quirky museums. One of the most enjoyable is the small **Centre of Folk Art and Tradition** (Angelikís Hatzimiháli 6; Tues–Fri 9am–1pm & 5–9pm, Sat & Sun 9am–1pm; free), a collection of costumes, embroidery, lace and weaving, along with musical instruments, ceramics, icons and religious artefacts. This occupies the former home of **Angelikís Hatzimiháli**, whose championing of traditional Greek arts and crafts was one of the chief catalysts for their revival in the early twentieth century. The house itself – designed for her in the 1920s in a Greek Art Nouveau or Arts and Crafts style – is a large part of the attraction, with its cool, high rooms and finely carved wooden doors, windows and staircase. At the back, narrow stairs descend to the kitchen with its original range, while upstairs there's a library and rooms where classes are held to pass on the traditions of crafts like embroidery and weaving.

The **Frissiras Museum**, housed in two beautifully renovated, Neoclassical buildings at Monís Asteríou 3 and 7 (Wed–Fri 10am–5pm, Sat & Sun 11am–5pm; €6; Ⓦwww.frissirasmuseum.com), is the only significant permanent modern art collection in Athens. The museum has over three thousand works – mostly figurative painting plus a few sculptures, as well as a regular programme of exhibitions. The space at no. 7 houses the permanent exhibition, which includes plenty of names familiar to English-speakers – David Hockney, Peter Blake and Paula Rego among them – as well as many less known Greek and European artists. Temporary exhibitions, along with a fine shop and an elegant café, are at no. 3 a block away.

The **Jewish Museum of Greece** (Mon–Fri 9am–2.30pm, Sun 10am–2pm; €5), at Níkis 39, tells the history of Jews in Greece, elegantly presented in a series of dimly lit rooms, with plenty of explanation in English. Downstairs are art and religious paraphernalia, many of the pieces centuries old. The centrepiece is the reconstructed synagogue of Pátra, dating from the 1920s, whose furnishings have been moved here *en bloc* and remounted. Upstairs, more recent history includes World War II and the German occupation, when Greece's Jewish population was reduced from almost 80,000 to less than 10,000. There are features, too, on the part played by Jews in the Greek resistance, and many stories of survival.

Finally, and not to be confused with each other, there's the Children's Museum and the Museum of Greek Children's Art. The **Children's Museum** (Tues–Fri 10am–2pm, Sat & Sun 10am–3pm; free), at Kydhathinéon 14, is as much a play area as a museum, aimed at the under-12s. Labelling is entirely in Greek, and the place is primarily geared to school groups, who take part in activities such as chocolate making. In spite of this, it should keep young kids amused for a while. Permanent exhibits include features on the Athens metro, how computers work, and the human body. The **Museum of Greek Children's Art** (Tues–Sat 10am–2pm, Sun 11am–2pm, closed Aug; €2; ⓦ www.childrensartmuseum.gr) at Kódhrou 9, meanwhile, does exactly what it says on the label – displays art by Greek children. There are a few permanent exhibits, but mainly the works are the winning entries to an annual nationwide art contest open to children up to the age of 14. On the whole, it is wonderfully uplifting.

The Monument of Lysikratos and around

In the southeastern corner of Pláka, the **Monument of Lysikratos**, a graceful stone and marble structure from 335 BC, rises from a small, triangular open area overlooked by a quiet café/taverna. It's near the end of Odhós Tripódhon, a relic of the ancient Street of the Tripods, where winners of drama competitions erected monuments to dedicate their trophies (in the form of tripod cauldrons) to Dionysos; the Monument of Lysikratos is the only survivor of these triumphal memorials. A four-metre-high stone base supports six Corinthian columns rising up to a marble dome on which, in a flourish of acanthus-leaf carvings, the winning tripod was placed.

In the seventeenth century the monument became part of a Capuchin convent, which provided regular lodgings for European travellers – Byron is said to have written part of *Childe Harold* here, and the street beyond, Výronos, is named after him. The old Street of the Tripods would have continued in this direction, and many important ancient Athenian buildings are thought to lie undiscovered in the vicinity.

The church of **Ayía Ekateríni** – St Catherine's – (Mon–Fri 7.30am–12.30pm & 5–6.30pm, Sat & Sun 5–10pm; free) on Platía Ayía Ekateríni just round the corner from the monument, is one of the few in Pláka that's routinely open. At its heart is an eleventh-century Byzantine original, although this has been pretty well hidden by later additions. You can see it most clearly from the back of the church, while in the courtyard in front are foundations of a Roman building. Inside, the over-restored frescoes look brand new, and there are plenty of glittering icons.

Hadrian's Arch and the Temple of Olympian Zeus

Odhós Lysikrátous continues past Ayía Ekateríni to emerge at the edge of Pláka near one of the busiest road junctions in Athens, the meeting of Amalías and Syngroú. Across the way **Hadrian's Arch** stands in splendid isolation. With the traffic roaring by, this is not somewhere you are tempted to linger, but it's definitely worth a look on your way to the Temple of Olympian Zeus. The arch, 18m high, was erected by the emperor to mark the edge of the Classical city and the beginning of his own. On the west side its frieze is inscribed "This is Athens, the ancient city of Theseus", and on the other "This is the City of Hadrian and not of Theseus". With so little that's ancient remaining around it, this doesn't make immediate sense, but you can look up, westwards, to the Acropolis and in the other direction see the columns of the great temple completed by Hadrian.

Many more Roman remains are thought to lie under the Záppio area, and over towards the old Olympic Stadium. Concrete evidence of this lies in a large **Roman Baths** complex that was discovered alongside the Záppio Gardens during excavations for the Metro. Dating originally from the late third century

AD and substantially expanded over succeeding centuries, the baths are now visible under a metal and perspex cover alongside the busy avenue, 100m or so north of Hadrian's Arch. Complete rooms have been well preserved and are now exposed to the gaze.

Directly behind the arch, the colossal pillars of the **Temple of Olympian Zeus** (entrance on Vasilíssis Ólgas; summer daily 8am–7.30pm, winter daily 8am–3pm; €2 or joint Acropolis ticket) – also known as the Olympieion – stand in the middle of a huge, dusty clearing with excellent views of the Acropolis and constant traffic noise. One of the largest temples in the ancient world, and according to Livy, "the only temple on earth to do justice to the god", it was dedicated by Hadrian in 131 AD, almost 700 years after Peisistratos had begun work on it. Hadrian marked the occasion by contributing a statue of Zeus and a suitably monumental one of himself, although both have since been lost. Just fifteen of the temple's original 104 marble pillars remain erect, though the column drums of another, which fell in 1852, litter the ground, giving a startling idea of the project's size. To the north of the temple enclosure, by the site entrance, are various excavated remains including an impressive Roman bath complex and a gateway from the wall of the Classical city. The south side of the enclosure overlooks a further area of excavation (not open to the public) where both Roman and much earlier buildings have been revealed.

From the temple, a shady route up to Sýndagma or Kolonáki leads through the Záppio and the **National Gardens** (see p.117), while the Panathenaic Stadium is a short walk along Vasilíssis Ólgas.

Anafiótika

Heading northwest along **Adhrianoú** you enter the depressingly touristy home of the Manchester United beach towel and "Sex in Ancient Greece" playing cards. For a break, climb up into the jumble of streets and alleys that cling to the lower slopes of the Acropolis. Here, the whitewashed, island-style houses and ancient churches of the **Anafiótika** quarter proclaim a cheerfully architect-free zone. There's still the odd shop, and taverna tables are set out wherever a bit of flat ground can be found, but there are also plenty of hidden corners redolent of a quieter era. A particularly good view of this area can be had by following the paths that track around the base of the Acropolis, above the buildings.

Carry on round in this direction, keeping as high as you can under the looming Acropolis walls, and you'll eventally emerge by the eclectic **Kanellopoulou Museum** (currently closed for restoration) at Theorías 12. When open, it's well worth a look, both for the mansion itself and for a collection which has a bit of everything, all of the highest quality. Just below the Kanellopoulou, at Panós 22, the **Museum of Greek Folk Art: Man and Tools** (Tues–Sat 9am–2.30pm; free) is a new branch of the Greek Folk Art museum, set in another fine mansion and devoted to the world of work. Tiny but fascinating and with good English labelling, its exhibits of tools and antiquated machinery concentrate on the pre-industrial world: there's a wooden grape-press as well as tools used in traditional trades including agriculture, barrel-making, cobbling and metalwork. Also nearby, at Thólou 5, is the **Athens University Museum** (summer: Mon & Wed 5–9pm, Tues, Thurs & Fri 9.30am–2.30pm; winter: Mon & Wed 2.30–7pm, Tues, Thurs & Fri 9.30am–2.30pm; free). Occupying another old mansion, the site of Athens' first university, it has a great collection of old scientific and medical instruments, labelled in Greek only, and scintillating views, especially from its top-floor terrace.

The Roman Forum and Tower of the Winds

The **Roman Forum** (daily: April–Sept 8.30am–7.30pm; Oct–March 8.30am–3pm; €2 or joint Acropolis ticket; entrance on Pelopídhá, at the corner of Eólou) was built during the reign of Julius Caesar and his successor Augustus as an extension of the older ancient Greek Agora. Its main entrance was on the west side, through the **Gate of Athena Archegetis**, which is still among the most prominent remains on the site. This gate marked the end of a street leading up from the Greek Agora, and its four surviving columns give a vivid impression of the grandeur of the original portal. On the side facing the Acropolis you can still make out an engraved edict of Hadrian announcing the rules and taxes on the sale of oil. On the opposite side of the Forum, a second gateway is also easily made out, and between the two is the market-place itself, surrounded by colonnades and shops, some of which have been excavated. Inside the fenced site, but just outside the market area to the east, are the foundations of public latrines dating from the first century AD.

The best preserved and easily the most intriguing of the ruins inside the Forum site, however, is the graceful octagonal structure known as the **Tower of the Winds**. This predates the Forum, and stands just outside the main market area. Designed in the first century BC by Andronikos of Kyrrhos, a Syrian astronomer, it served as a compass, sundial, weather vane and water clock – the latter powered by a stream from one of the Acropolis springs. Each face of the tower is adorned with a relief of a figure floating through the air, personifying the eight winds. On the **north** side (facing Eólou) is Boreas blowing into a conch shell; **northwest**, Skiron holding a vessel of charcoal; **west**, Zephyros tossing flowers from his lap; **southwest**, Lips speeding the voyage of a ship; **south**, Notos upturning an urn to make a shower; **southeast**, Euros with his arm hidden in his mantle summoning a hurricane; **east**, Apiliotis carrying fruits and wheat; and **northeast**, Kaikias emptying a shield full of hailstones. Beneath each of these, it is still possible to make out the markings of eight sundials.

The semicircular tower attached to the south face was the reservoir from which water was channelled into a cylinder in the main tower; the time was read by the water level viewed through the open northwest door. On the top of the building was a bronze weather-vane in the form of the sea god Triton. In Ottoman times, dervishes used the tower as a *tekke* or ceremonial hall, terrifying their superstitious Orthodox neighbours with their chanting, music and whirling meditation.

Roman Athens

In 146 BC, the **Romans** ousted Athens' Macedonian rulers and incorporated the city into their vast new province of Achaia, whose capital was at Corinth. The city's status as a renowned seat of learning (Cicero and Horace were educated here) and great artistic centre ensured that it was treated with respect, and Athenian artists and architects were much in demand in Rome. Athens, though, was a backwater – there were few major construction projects, and what building there was tended to follow classical Greek patterns.

The one Roman emperor who did spend a significant amount of time in Athens, and left his mark here, was **Hadrian** (reigned 117–138 AD). Among his grandiose monuments are Hadrian's Arch, a magnificent and immense library and (though it had been begun centuries before) the Temple of Olympian Zeus. A generation later **Herodes Atticus**, a Roman senator who owned extensive lands in Marathon, became the city's last major benefactor of ancient times.

Turkish remains

It's not just Roman survivals that can be found in this corner of Monastiráki: around the Roman Forum are also some of the few visible reminders of the Ottoman city. The oldest mosque in Athens, the **Fethiye Tzami**, built in 1458, actually occupies a corner of the Forum site. It was dedicated by Sultan Mehmet II, who conquered Constantinople in 1453 (*fethiye* means "conquest" in Turkish). Sadly, you can't see inside the restored building, as it's used as an archeological warehouse. Across Eólou, more or less opposite the Forum entrance, the gateway and single dome of a **medresse**, an Islamic school, survive. During the last years of Ottoman rule and the early years of Greek independence, the building was used as a prison and was notorious for its harsh conditions; a plane tree in the courtyard was used for hangings. The prison was closed in the 1900s and the bulk of it torn down.

One local Ottoman survival you can visit is the site of the **Turkish Baths** (Mon & Wed–Sun 9am–2.30pm; free), nearby at Kirístou 8. Constructed in the 1450s, the baths were in use, with many later additions, right up to 1965. Newly restored, they now offer an insight into a part of Athens' past that is rarely glimpsed and well worth a look. Traditionally, the baths would have been used in shifts by men and women, although expansion in the nineteenth century provided the separate facilities you see today. The *tepidarium* and *caldarium*, fitted out in marble with domed roofs and rooflights, are particularly beautiful. The underfloor and wall heating systems have been exposed in places, while upstairs there are photos and pictures of old Athens. Labelling throughout is in Greek only, but an audio tour is available (€1, plus deposit).

For more on Ottoman Athens, check out also the nearby ceramic collection of the Museum of Greek Folk Art (see opposite) and the Benáki Museum of Islamic Art (p.126).

The Museum of Greek Folk Instruments

Also just around the corner from the Roman Forum, at Dhioyénous 1–3, the **Museum of Greek Folk Instruments** (Tues & Thurs–Sun 10am–2pm, Wed noon–6pm; free) traces the history and distribution of virtually every type of musical instrument that has ever been played in Greece. It's all attractively displayed in a fine mansion, with drums and wind instruments of all sorts (from crude bagpipes to clarinets) on the ground floor, lyras, fiddles, lutes and a profusion of stringed instruments upstairs. In the basement there are more percussion and toy instruments including some not-so-obvious festival and liturgical items such as triangles, strikers and livestock bells, along with carnival outfits. Reproductions of frescoes show the Byzantine antecedents of many instruments, and headphones are provided for sampling the music made by the various exhibits.

The museum shop has an excellent selection of CDs for sale, concentrating, not surprisingly, on traditional Greek music.

Hadrian's Library

Bordering the north end of the Forum site, and stretching right through from Eólou to Áreos, stand the surviving walls and columns of **Hadrian's Library** (daily: summer 8am–7.30pm, winter 8am–3pm; €2; entry on Áreos), an enormous building that once enclosed a cloistered courtyard of a hundred columns. Despite the name, this was much more than just a library – more a cultural centre including art galleries, lecture halls and a great public space at its centre. The site has only recently opened to the public and is still being excavated: for the moment remains are sparse and poorly labelled. Much of it has been built over many times, and a lot of what you can see today consists of the foundations and mosaic floors of later Byzantine churches. However, some of the original columns survive, and above all you get an excellent sense of the sheer scale of the original building, especially when you realize that the Tetraconch Church, whose remains lie at the centre of the site, was built entirely within the library's internal courtyard.

The Museum of Greek Folk Art: Ceramics Collection

Directly opposite Monastiráki metro station, squeezed between the walls of Hadrian's library and the shacks of Pandhróssou, the **Museum of Greek Folk Art: Ceramics Collection** (Mon & Wed–Sun 9am–2.30pm; €2) is housed in the former Mosque of Tzisdarákis at Áreos 1. Built in 1759, the building has had a chequered life, converted to a barracks and then a jail after Greek independence, before becoming the original home of the Greek Folk Art Museum in 1918. Today, as a branch of that museum, it houses the **Kyriazópoulos collection** of ceramics – the legacy of a Thessaloníki professor. Good as it is, the collection is, in all honesty, likely to excite you only if you have a particular interest in pottery; most will probably find the **mosque** itself, the only one in Athens open to the public, at least as big an attraction.

Though missing its minaret, and with a balcony added inside for the museum, plenty of original features remain. In the airy, domed space, look out for the striped *mihrab* (the niche indicating the direction of Mecca), a calligraphic inscription above the entrance recording the mosque's founder and date, and a series of niches used as extra *mihrabs* for occasions when worshippers could not fit into the main hall.

Platía Monastirakíou and around

Platía Monastirakíou marks a return to the traffic and bustle of commercial Athens. Full of fruit stalls, nut sellers, lottery vendors and kiosks, the square gets its name from the little monastery church (*monastiráki*) at its centre, possibly seventeenth-century in origin and badly restored in the early twentieth century. The area around has been a marketplace since Ottoman times, and it still preserves, in places, a bazaar atmosphere. The main market (see p.119) lies straight up Athinás from here, towards Omónia, but nearer at hand you'll see signs in either direction that proclaim you're entering the famous **Monastiráki Flea Market**. These days this is a bit of a misnomer – there's plenty of shopping, but mostly of a very conventional nature. **Odhós Pandhróssou**, to the east, is almost entirely geared to tourists, an extension (though not quite literally) of Adhrianoú. West of the square the flea market has more of its old character, and among the tourist tat you'll find shops full of hand-made musical instruments, or stalls selling nothing but chess and *tavlí* boards, as well as places geared to locals selling bikes, skateboards or camping gear. An alley off Iféstou is jammed with record and CD shops, with a huge basement second-hand bookshop. Around Normánou and **Platía Avyssinías** shops specialize in furniture and junky antiques: from here to Adhrianoú, the relics of a real flea market survive in hopeless jumble-sale rejects, touted by a cast of eccentrics (especially on Sundays). Odhós Adhrianoú is at its most appealing at this end, with a couple of interesting antique shops, and some shady cafés overlooking the metro lines, Agora and Acropolis.

The stretch of **Odhós Ermoú** fringing the flea market as it heads west from Platía Monastirakíou is the southern edge of fashionable Psyrrí, and among the workaday old-fashioned furniture stores here are some interesting new designer and retro shops; in the other direction, as it heads up towards Sýndagma, the street is much more staid. In the pedestrianized upper section are familiar high-street chains and department stores: if you're after Zara or Marks & Spencer, Mothercare or Benetton, this is the place to head.

Kapnikaréa and surrounding churches

The pretty Byzantine church of **Kapnikaréa** marks more or less the beginning of this upmarket shopping area and looks tiny, almost shrunken, in its high-rise, urban surroundings. Originally eleventh century, but with later additions, it has a lovely little dome and a gloomy interior in which you can just about make out the modern frescoes. The church is allegedly named after its founder, a tax collector: *kapnós* means smoke, and in the Byzantine era there was a tax on houses, known as the smoke tax.

Nearby **Platía Mitropóleos** – Cathedral Square – is home to not just one but two cathedrals. The modern **Mitrópolis** is a large, clumsy nineteenth-century edifice; the **old cathedral** alongside it is dwarfed by comparison, but infinitely more attractive. There is said to have been a church on this site since the very earliest days of Christianity in Athens. What you see now dates from the twelfth century: a beautiful little structure cobbled together with plain and carved blocks from earlier incarnations; some almost certainly from that original church. The Platía itself is a welcome spot of calm among the busy shopping streets that surround it. There are several other small churches nearby: look out especially for the dusty, tiny chapel of **Ayía Dhynámis** crouching surreally below the concrete piers of the Ministry of Education and Religion on Odhós Mitropóleos, a short way up towards Sýndagma.

Sýndagma and the National Gardens

All roads lead to **Sýndagma** – you'll almost inevitably find yourself here sooner or later for the metro and bus connections. Platía Syndágmatos, Constitution Square, to give it its full name, lies roughly midway between the Acropolis and Lykavitós hill. With the Greek Parliament building (the Vouli) on its uphill side, and banks, offices and embassies clustered around, it's the political and geographic heart of Athens. The square's name derives from the fact that King Otto was forced by popular pressure to declare a formal constitution for the new Greek state from a palace balcony here in 1844. It's still the principal venue for mass demonstrations and, in the run-up to elections, the major political parties stage their final campaign rallies here.

Vital hub as it is, the traffic and the crush ensure it's not an attractive place to hang around. Escape comes in the form of the National Gardens, a welcome area of greenery stretching out south from the parliament building and offering a traffic-free route down past the Záppio to Hadrian's Arch and the Temple of Olympian Zeus (see p.111) or across to the Panathenaic Stadium (see p.129). In other directions, Odhós Ermoú, prime shopping territory, heads west towards Monastiráki; Stadhíou and Panepistimíou stretch to the northwest towards Omónia; while to the north and east lies Kolonáki (see p.130) and the embassy quarter.

The square

With the exception of the Voulí, the Greek National Parliament, the vast **Hotel Grande Bretagne** – Athens' most impressive – is just about the only building on Sýndagma to have survived postwar development. Past the impressive facade and uniformed doormen, the interior is magnificently opulent, as befits a grand hotel established in the late nineteenth century. It's worth taking a look inside or having a drink at one of the bars: recent renovation included a new rooftop pool, bar and restaurant with great views across the city. The hotel has long been at the centre of Greek political intrigue: in one notorious episode, Winston Churchill narrowly avoided being blown up here on Christmas Day, 1944, when saboteurs from the Communist-led ELAS movement placed an enormous explosive charge in the drains. According to whom you believe, the bomb was either discovered in time by a kitchen employee, or removed by ELAS themselves when they realized that Churchill was one of their potential targets.

The **Voulí** presides over Platía Syndágmatos from its uphill (east) side. A vast, ochre-and-white Neoclassical structure, it was built as the royal palace for Greece's first monarch, the Bavarian King Otto, who moved in in 1842. In front of it, goose-stepping **evzónes** in tasselled caps, kilt and woolly leggings – a prettified version of traditional mountain costume – change their guard at regular intervals before the **Tomb of the Unknown Soldier**. On Sundays, just before 11am, a full band and the entire corps parade from the tomb to their barracks at the back of the National Gardens to the rhythm of innumerable camera shutters.

The National Gardens

The **National Gardens** (sunrise–sunset; free; entrances on Amalías, Vasilíssis Sofías and Iródhou Attikoú), spreading out to the south and east of the Voulí, are the most refreshing acres in the city – not so much a flower garden as a luxuriant tangle of trees, whose shade and duck ponds provide palpable relief from the heat of summer. They were originally the private palace gardens – a pet project of Queen Amalia in the 1840s; supposedly the main duty of the minuscule Greek navy in its early days was the fetching of rare plants, often the gifts of other royal houses, from remote corners of the globe. Despite a major pre-Olympic clear-out there's still something of an air of benign neglect here, with rampant undergrowth and signs that seem to take you round in circles. It's a great place for a picnic, though, or just a shady respite from the city streets. There are benches everywhere, ducks being fed in the ponds, and other attractions including a small zoo, a children's playground (on the Záppio side) and a botanical museum. The tiny **zoo** (signed Irattikou) has ostriches and some exotic fowl, but most of the cages these days are occupied by chickens, rabbits and domestic cats. The **Botanical Museum** occupies an elegant little pavilion nearby; closed for refurbishment at the time of writing.

To the south, the graceful crescent-shaped grounds of the Záppio are open 24 hours. Popular with evening and weekend strollers, they're more open and more formally laid out. The **Záppio** itself, an imposing Neoclassical edifice originally built as an exhibition hall, is not open to the public. Although it has no permanent function, the building has taken on prestigious roles such as headquarters of the Greek presidency of the European Union and of the 2004 Olympic bid. On the eastern side of the National Gardens, across Iródhou Attikoú, stands the **Presidential Palace**, the royal residence until King Constantine's exile in 1967, where more *evzónes* stand on duty.

Towards Omónia

Northwest from Sýndagma, the broad and busy avenues of **Stadhíou**, **Panepistimíou** (officially called Venizélou, though the name is rarely used) and **Akadhimías** head towards Platía Omonías. Initially lined with grandiose mansions, some converted to museums, squares with open vistas and opulent arcades with chi-chi shopping, they move steadily downmarket as you approach Omónia.

First of the museums, in the glorious former home of German archeologist Heinrich Schliemann (excavator of Mycenae and Troy) at Panepistimíou 12, just off Sýndagma, is the **Numismatic Museum** (Tues–Sun 8.30am–3pm; €3), with a collection of over 600,000 coins and related artefacts dating from Mycenaean times through Classical, Macedonian and Roman to Byzantine and the modern era. The nearby **National Historical Museum** (Tues–Sun 9am–2pm; €3), on Platía Kolokotróni, occupies a building that housed the parliament from 1874 until 1935. Its exhibits cover Greek history from the fall of Constantinople to the reign of King Otto, with particular emphasis on the Byzantine era. There's also a strong section on the War of Independence that includes Byron's sword and helmet. Unfortunately, minimal labelling leaves the visitor a little short on the historical context of the valuable pieces on display. Finally, the **City of Athens Museum** (Mon & Wed–Fri 9am–4pm, Sat & Sun 10am–3pm; €3) is at Paparigopoúlou 7, on Platía Klafthmónos. This was the residence of King Otto in the 1830s, and its exhibits cover Athens' history from Otto's time onwards. Some of the rooms have been restored to their state when the royals lived here, with exquisite period furnishings, and there are many artworks featuring the city as well as an interesting model of Athens in 1842, with just three hundred houses. A section of the ancient city walls can be seen in the basement.

Much cosmetic work was done in this area prior to the Olympics, and there's now a wonderful view up from **Platía Klafthmónos** towards three grand Neoclassical buildings on Panepistimíou. Here the planners' conceptualization of the capital of newly independent Greece can for once be seen more or less as they envisaged it, blending the nation's Classical heritage with modern, Western values. As you look up you see, from the left, the sober grey marble of the **National Library**, the rather racier **Akadhimía (University)**, enlivened by frescoes depicting King Otto surrounded by ancient Greek gods and heroes, and the frankly over-the-top **Academy of Science** with its pediment friezes and giant statues of Athena and Apollo. The garish decoration gives an alarming impression of what the Classical monuments might have looked like when their paintwork was intact. Behind these buildings, on Akadhimías, is a major terminus for **city buses**, from where you can get a connection to almost anywhere in the city or its suburbs.

The bazaar, Platía Omonías and north

While Pláka and Sýndagma are resolutely geared to tourists and the Athenian well-heeled, Platía Omonías (Omónia Square) and its surroundings represent a much more gritty city, revolving around everyday commerce and trade. Here the grand avenues imagined by the nineteenth-century planners have been subverted by time and the realities of Athens' status as a commercial capital. Heading up from Monastiráki, the **bazaar area** around Odhós Athinás is home to a bustling series of markets and small shops spilling into the streets and offering some of urban Athens' most compelling sights and sounds, as well as an ethnic mix that is a rare reminder of Greece's traditional role as a meeting place of East and West. From here to Omónia was once the city's red-light district and, though now much cleaned up, the square itself retains a distinct seediness. **Psyrrí**, southwest of the market area, is a former working-class district that is now home to Athens' busiest nightlife as well as some quirky shops; its gentrifying influence is rapidly spreading to surrounding neighbourhoods. North of Omónia, the **National Archeological Museum** is an essential visit: behind it, the perennially "alternative" quarter of **Exárhia** has plenty more nightlife and eating options.

The bazaar: from Ermoú to Omónia

The city's bazaar area is concentrated on **Athinás** and **Eólou streets**. Here the stores, though stocked mainly with imported goods, still reflect their origins in the Oriental souk system: their unaffected decor, unsophisticated packaging and, most strikingly, their specialization. Though it's a tradition that's gradually dying, each street still has a concentration of particular stores and wares. Hence the Monastiráki end of Athinás is dedicated to tools; food stores are gathered around the central market in the middle, especially along Evripídhou; there's glass to the west; paint and brasswork to the east; and clothes in Eólou and Ayíou Márkou. Always raucous and teeming with shoppers, *kouloúri* (bread-ring) sellers, gypsies and other vendors, the whole area is great free entertainment.

The lively heart of the neighbourhood is the central **meat and seafood market**, occupying almost an entire block bordered by Athinás, Evripídhou, Eólou and Sofokléous. The building itself is a grand nineteenth-century relic, with fretted iron awnings sheltering forests of carcasses and mounds of hearts, livers and ears – no place for the squeamish. In the middle section of the hall is the fish market, with all manner of bounty from the sea squirming and glistening on the marble slabs. Across Athinás is the colourful **fruit** and **vegetable** bazaar, surrounded by streets where grocers pile their stalls high with sacks of pulses, salt cod, barrels of olives and wheels of cheese. A clear sign of Athens' increasing **multi-ethnicity** is to be seen in the streets around Evripídhou just west of here, where a growing community from South Asia, predominantly Bengalis, gather in hordes around the spice-rich minimarkets and cheap and cheerful curry houses.

Odhós Eólou: The flower market and Platía Kótzia

Odhós Eólou seems far less frantic than parallel Athinás, partly because it is pedestrianized. Local businesses have taken advantage of this so that there are now café tables in the street, and benches to rest on. Its gentler nature must also reflect the goods sold here: where Athinás has power tools and raw meat, Eólou offers clothes and the **flower market**. The latter, gathered around the church of Ayía Iríni at the southern end of the street, has stalls through the week but really comes alive with the crowds on a Sunday morning.

At the northern end of the street, **Platía Kótzia** is a far more formal enclave, and one of the city's more impressive examples of Olympic refurbishment. Surrounded by the town hall and the weighty Neoclassical buildings of the National Bank, it's a rare glimpse of elegant old Athens, spoilt only by the crumbling modern blocks above the post office. In the middle of the square a large section of **ancient road** has been uncovered and can be seen in a fenced-off site – numerous tombs and small buildings lie alongside it. This road, just outside the walls, once led to one of the main **gates** of ancient Athens and this too has recently been excavated, during building work for a new Stock

Exchange. You can see this gate and some of the adjoining city wall underneath the new building, between Platía Kótzia and Sofokléous; nearby more sections of the ancient road and a drainage system are visible under glass pyramids in the middle of Eólou. The sight of the Acropolis from this street as you approached Athens in ancient times must have been awe-inspiring, and Eólou still has impressive views today, with the Erechtheion's slender columns and pediment peeking over the edge of the crag straight ahead.

Around Platía Omonías

Platía Omonías itself has little to offer in terms of aesthetics, but it is the heart of Athens for a good portion of the population. A continuous turmoil of people and cars, it is Athens at its earthiest and most urban. Cleaning-up and remodelling for the Olympics has removed much of the area's character – no bad thing, some would say, as that character derived from drug addicts, prostitutes and homeless Albanian refugees – and the new look is ugly, brutal and shadeless.

The streets surrounding the square are full of offices, high-rise hotels and functional shopping. To the west towards the rail stations, Metaxouryío is an area undergoing something of a revival as development spills over from fashionable neighbouring Psyrrí and Gázi; north and east lie Exárhia and the National Archeological Museum.

The Polytekhnío

Heading north, the **Polytekhnío**, a Neoclassical building housing the university's school of engineering and science, is on 28 Oktovríou (also known as Patissíon) just beside the National Archeological Museum. In November 1973, students here launched a protest against the repressive regime of the colonels' junta, occupying the building and courtyards, and broadcasting calls for mass resistance from a pirate radio transmitter. Large numbers came down to demonstrate support and hand in food and medicines. The colonels' regime was determined to smash the protest and, on the night of November 17, snipers were positioned in neighbouring houses and ordered to fire into the courtyards while a tank broke down the entrance gate and the buildings were stormed. Even today nobody knows how many of the unarmed students were killed – estimates range from twenty to three hundred.

Though a failure at the time, the protest arguably marked the beginning of the end for the colonels; its anniversary is still commemorated by marches and sombre remembrance ceremonies, and inside the main gates of the Polytekhnío you can still view the original entrance gates, mangled by the invading tank.

The National Archeological Museum

The **National Archeological Museum** (Mon 1–7.30pm, Tues–Sun 8.30am–7.30pm; closes 3pm Tues–Sun in winter; €7), at 28 Oktovríou 44, is an unrivalled treasure trove of ancient Greek art – and an essential Athens experience. However high your expectations, the museum seems effortlessly to surpass them, full of objects that seem familiar, so often have you seen them in pictures or reproductions. The interior is surprisingly plain – there's nothing flashy at all about the new displays, but the minimalist approach is clear and well labelled. You could easily spend an entire morning or afternoon here, but it's equally possible to scoot round the highlights in an hour or two; arriving early in the morning or late in the afternoon should mean you won't be competing with the tour groups for space. The nearest **metro** stations are at Viktorías or Omónia, but the museum is also very easy to get to by bus, with a local terminus outside on Vassiléos Iraklíou – look for *Mousseio*.

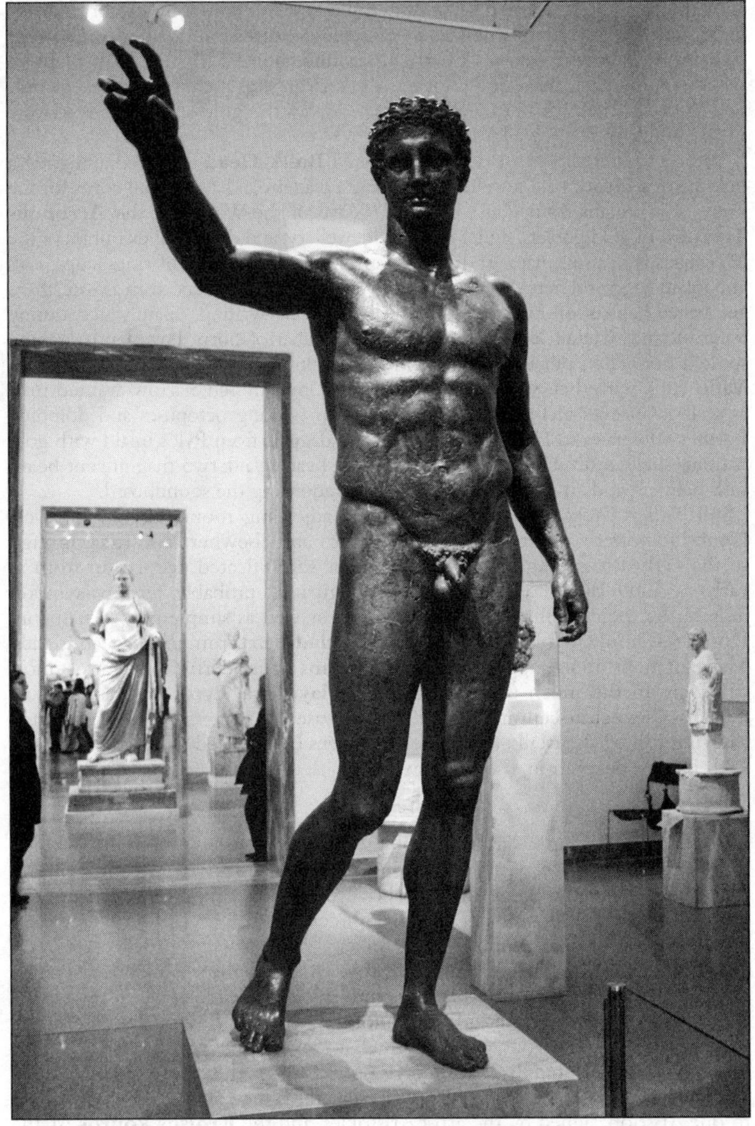

▲ Bronze figure, National Archeological Museum

Mycenaean and Cycladic art

Directly ahead of you as you enter, the **Mycenaean halls** have always been the biggest crowd pullers. Mycenaean culture flourished in the fifteenth and fourteenth centuries BC. The gold **Mask of Agamemnon**, arguably the museum's most famous piece, is almost the first thing you see. Modern dating techniques offer convincing proof that the funerary mask actually belonged to some more ancient Achaian king, but crowds are still drawn by its correspondence with the Homeric myth and compelling expression. Schliemann's other finds from Mycenae (see p.179) are all around, along with the fruits of more recent explorations there and at other Mycenaean sites including Tiryns (p.184) and Pylos (p.253). It's a truly exceptional display, the gold shining as if it were in the window of a jeweller's shop.

Among the highlights are a golden-horned **Bull's Head** displayed alongside a gold **Lion's Head**; gold jewellery including a diadem and a gold-foil cover for the body of an infant from Grave III (the "Grave of the Women"); the **Acropolis Treasure** of gold goblets, signet rings and jewellery; and dozens of examples of the Mycenaeans' consummate art, intricate, small-scale decoration of rings, cups, seals and inlaid daggers. There's work in silver, ivory, bronze and boars' tusks as well; there are baked tablets of Linear B, the earliest Greek writing (mainly accounting records) and Cretan-style frescoes depicting chariot-borne women watching spotted hounds in pursuit of boar and bull-vaulting. Other delights are the gold **Vafio** cups, with their scenes of wild bulls and long-tressed, narrow-waisted men as well as an eye-catching cup decorated with twining octopuses and dolphins. Further references to Homer abound: bronze daggers from Pylos inlaid with gold nautilus shells; a silver bowl with a gold bull's head inlaid; two magnificent boars' tusk helmets; and an ivory lyre with sphinxes adorning the soundboard.

Still earlier Greece is represented in the adjoining rooms. Room 5 covers Neolithic pottery and stone tools from Attica and elsewhere and runs through to the early Bronze Age. The pottery shows sophisticated decoration from as early as 5000 BC, and there are many figurines, probably fertility symbols judging by their phallic or pregnant nature, as well as simple gold ornaments. Room 6 is home to a large collection of **Cycladic art** from the Aegean islands. Many of these idols suggest the abstract forms of modern Cubist art – most strikingly in the much-reproduced **Man Playing a Lyre**. Another unusual piece is a sixteenth-century BC cylindrical vase depicting a ring of fishermen carrying fish by their tails, and there are dozens of so-called "frying pan" vessels with incised decoration, use unknown.

Sculpture

Sculpture makes up a large part of the museum's most important exhibits, following a broadly chronological arrangement in a clockwise direction around the main halls of the museum. This shows the gradual development from the stiff, stylized representations of the seventh century BC towards ever freer and looser naturalism in the following centuries.

Early highlights include a statue of a **kore** (maiden) from Merenda (Myrrhinous) in Attica, in room 11. Her elegantly pleated, belted *chiton* (dress) bears traces of the original paint and decoration of swastikas, flowers and geometric patterns. Nearby is a wonderful grave stele of a young *doryphoros* (spear-bearer) standing against a red background. Room 13 has the **Stele of a Young Warrior**, with delicately carved beard, hair and tunic-folds, a funerary tribute to one Aristion, signed by the artist Aristokles, and the **Kroisus kouros** (statue of an idealized youth), who looks as if he's been working out; both are from the late sixth century BC. Other delightful pieces here include a statueless plinth carved with reliefs showing, on one side, young men exercising in the gymnasium, on the other a group of amused friends setting a dog and cat to fight each other, and a statue of Aristodikos, whose sense of movement presages the development of early Classical art.

Just a few highlights of the massive **Classical art** collection can be mentioned. Room 15 boasts a mid-fifth-century BC bronze **Statue of Poseidon**, dredged from the sea off Évvia in the 1920s. The god stands poised to throw his trident – weight on the front foot, athlete's body perfectly balanced, the model of idealized male beauty. A less dramatic, though no less important, piece in the same room is the **Eleusinian Relief**. Highly deliberate in its composition, the relief shows the goddess of fertility, accompanied by her daughter Persephone, giving to mankind an ear of corn – symbol of the knowledge of agriculture and associated with the Mysteries of Eleusis (p.161). In Room 20 is a small marble statue of Athena, a copy of the great cult statue that once stood in the Parthenon. With shield and snake in her left hand, a winged, angel-like figure in her right and a triple crest of winged horses and sphinxes on her head it's a scary figure: the vast original, covered in gold and ivory, must have been extraordinary. The **Little Jockey of Artemission**, a delicate bronze figure seeming too small for his galloping horse, was found in the same shipwreck as the *Poseidon*; near it in room 21 is the **Atalante Hermes**, a wonderful funerary statue of a youth. Room 28 has some fine, fourth-century BC bronzes including the **Antikythira Youth**, thought to depict either Perseus or Paris, from yet another shipwreck, off Antikithira, and the bronze head of a *Boxer*, burly and battered. Still more naturalistic, in room 29, is the third-century BC bronze head of a **Philosopher**, with furrowed brow and unkempt hair. Too numerous to list, but offering fascinating glimpses of everyday life and also changing styles of craftsmanship and perception of the human form, are the many **stelae** and other grave monuments: rooms 16, 18, 23 and 24 are particularly rich in these.

The most reproduced of the **later sculptures** is a first-century AD statue of a naked and indulgent *Aphrodite* (room 30) about to rap Pan's knuckles for getting too fresh – a far cry (a long fall, some would say) from the reverent, idealizing portrayals of the gods in Classical times. There is also an extraordinary bronze equestrian portrait statue (without the horse) of the *Emperor Augustus*. Room 31A has a fascinating collection of portrait heads from the second and third centuries AD; probably officials of a Gymnasium, they offer a unique look at the ordinary citizens of Roman Athens.

Bronze, vases and frescoes

At the back of the museum, stairs lead up to the first floor, while below them is the entrance to the **bronze collection**. Despite being tucked away, this is by no means a poor relation – it is an exceptional display of thousands of items: weapons, figurines, axes, cauldrons, jewellery, mirrors, kitchen implements; even bronze sandals. Perhaps the highlight is the **Antikythera Mechanism**, at the far end. Dating from around 150–100 BC, this was discovered in a shipwreck off the island of Andikýthira in 1900, but modern scanning techniques have only recently revealed its full complexity. It is believed to be an astronomical computer capable of predicting the movements of stars and planets, and its sophisticated use of differential gears is unique – technologically, it is at least 1500 years ahead of its time.

Upstairs is a collection of hundreds of **vases**, if anything still more spectacular, with a full explanation of manufacturing techniques, changing styles of decoration and the uses of the different types of vessel. As ever, the highlights are from the Classical era. Among the exceptional black-figure and red-figure ceramics are, in case 105, a red-figure *pelike* depicting an adventure of Heracles and, in cases 130 and 131, amphorae awarded as prizes at the games of the Panathenaic Festival, when they would have been filled with oil. Also look out for cases 111 and 112, with entire graves from Kerameikos, complete with skeletons and offerings. Upstairs is a display on the excavations of Akrotíri on Thíra (p.582), including three wonderful Minoan frescoes.

Exárhia and Stréfis Hill

Exárhia, fifty-odd blocks squeezed between the National Archeological Museum and Stréfis Hill, is one of the city's liveliest neighbourhoods, especially at night. Traditionally the home of anarchists, revolutionaries, artists, students and anyone seeking an anti-establishment lifestyle in a conformist city, Exárhia is pretty tame these days, but it's still the closest thing in central Athens to an "alternative" neighbourhood. This means a concentration of ouzerís, nightclubs and genuine music tavernas by night, and during the day some interesting, off-beat clothing and music stores. The tiny, triangular, café-lined Platía Exarhíon is at the heart of it all; on Saturdays, locals flock to the colourful street market on Kallidhromíou from early morning till lunchtime.

Just above this, the little-visited Stréfis Hill (**Lófos toú Stréfi**) provides a welcome break from the densely packed streets and dull apartment blocks surrounding it. A labyrinth of paths leads up to the low summit, from where there are unexpectedly wonderful views – above all of the Acropolis with the Saronic Gulf and islands behind, but also across to nearby Lykavitós. Watch out for unguarded drops near the top and stick to the main paths as you walk up, in order to avoid one of the more obvious signs of the area's alternative lifestyle, discarded hypodermics.

Gázi and Thissío

Some of the most interesting up-and-coming areas of Athens – **Thissío**, **Gázi** and **Roúf** – lie to the west of the centre, where the new extension to Metro line 3 can only accelerate the pace of change. Nightlife and restaurants are the chief attractions here, but there's also a cluster of new museums and galleries, above all the Tekhnópolis centre and two annexes of the Benáki Museum, devoted to Islamic and modern art respectively. Here too is **Kerameikos**, site of a substantial section of the walls of ancient Athens and an important burial ground. South of Thissío, things are rather more traditional. Pedestrianized Apostólou Pávlou leads around the edge of the Agora and Acropolis sites, under the flanks of the hills of the Pnyx and Filopáppou, and offers a pleasant, green escape from the city as well as fine views. On the west side of the hills, the residential zone of **Áno Petrálona** is a real delight, entirely untouristy, with some excellent tavernas (see p.144) and a great open-air cinema, though absolutely nothing in the way of sights. On the east side of the hills, immediately south of the Acropolis, **Makriyiánni** is a far more upmarket residential neighbourhood, merging into rather earthier **Koukáki**. Again there are good, local restaurants here, but few sights.

Platía Thissíou to Gázi

From Monastiráki, Odhós Adhrianoú follows the edge of the ancient Agora site alongside the metro lines (here above ground) towards Platía Thissíou, in front of Thissío metro station. From here you can head south for Thissío proper and the traffic-free route round the Acropolis, west along a pedestrianized section of Ermoú past the Kerameikos site towards Gázi, or north towards a couple of interesting new museums.

The Islamic Art and Pottery museums

Two small new museums are just a short walk up Áyion Asomáton from Platía Thissíou. First, to the left on Melidhóni, is the **Museum of Traditional**

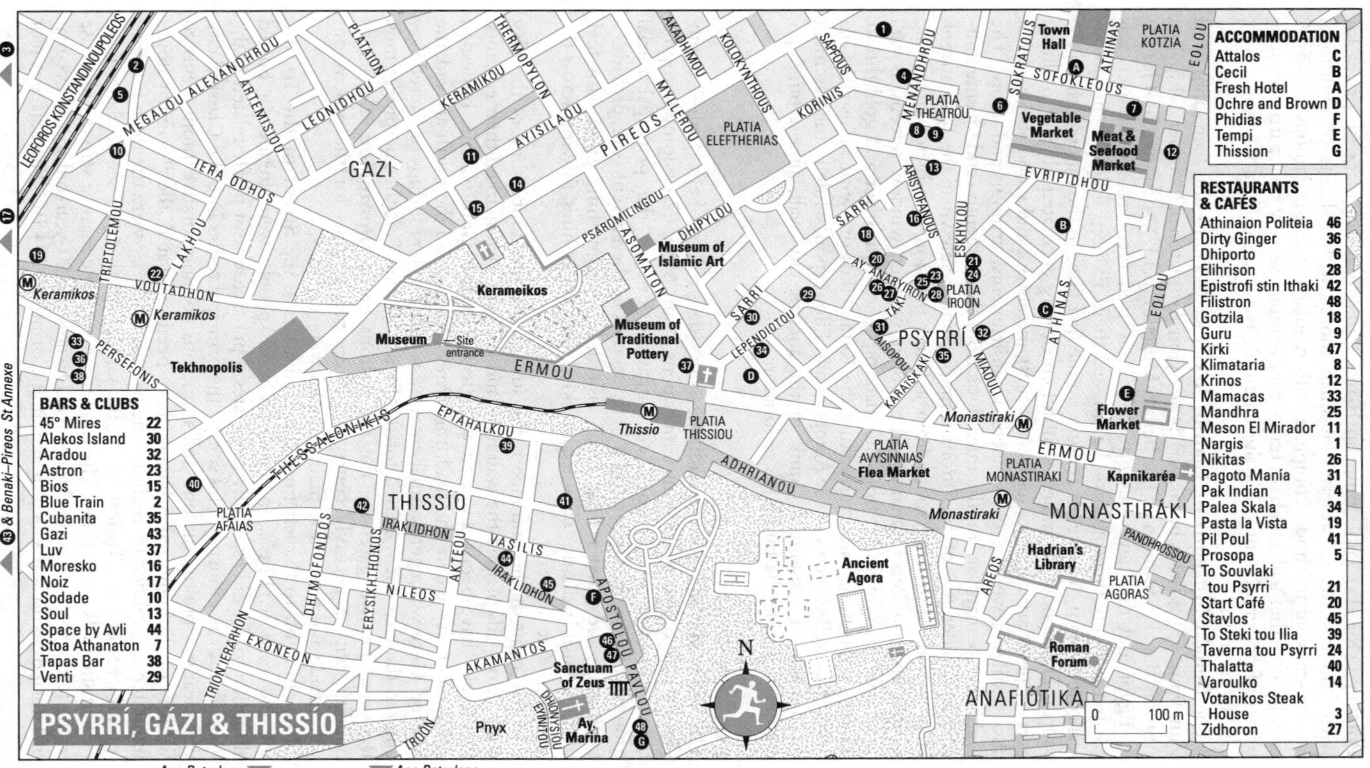
PSYRRÍ, GÁZI & THISSÍO
ACCOMMODATION
Attalos C
Cecil B
Fresh Hotel A
Ochre and Brown D
Phidias F
Tempi E
Thission G
RESTAURANTS & CAFÉS
Athinaion Politeia 46
Dirty Ginger 36
Dhiporto 6
Elihrison 28
Epistrofi stin Ithaki 42
Filistron 48
Gotzila 18
Guru 9
Kirki 47
Klimataria 8
Krinos 12
Mamacas 33
Mandhra 25
Meson El Mirador 11
Nargis 1
Nikitas 26
Pagoto Manía 31
Pak Indian 4
Palea Skala 34
Pasta la Vista 19
Pil Poul 41
Prosopa 5
To Souvlaki tou Psyrri 21
Start Café 20
Stavlos 45
To Steki tou Ilia 39
Taverna tou Psyrri 24
Thalatta 40
Varoulko 14
Votanikos Steak House 3
Zidhoron 27
BARS & CLUBS
45° Mires 22
Alekos Island 30
Aradou 32
Astron 23
Bios 15
Blue Train 2
Cubanita 35
Gazi 43
Luv 37
Moresko 16
Noiz 17
Sodade 10
Soul 13
Space by Avli 44
Stoa Athanaton 7
Tapas Bar 38
Venti 29
GAZI
PSYRRÍ
THISSÍO
MONASTIRÁKI
ANAFIÓTIKA
Town Hall
Vegetable Market
Meat & Seafood Market
Flower Market
Flea Market
Kapnikaréa
Museum of Islamic Art
Museum of Traditional Pottery
Kerameikos
Museum
Site entrance
Tekhnopolis
Ancient Agora
Hadrian's Library
Roman Forum
Sanctuam of Zeus
Ay. Marina
Pnyx
PLATIA KOTZIA
PLATIA THEATROU
PLATIA ELEFTHERIAS
PLATIA IROON
PLATIA THISSIOU
PLATIA AVYSINNIAS
PLATIA MONASTIRAKI
PLATIA AGORAS
PLATIA AFAIAS
Keramikos
Thissio
Monastiraki
LEOFOROS KONSTANDINOUPOLEOS
MEGALOU ALEXANDHROU
ARTEMISIOU
LEONIDHOU
PLATAION
KERAMIKOU
THERMOPYLON
AYISILAOU
PIREOS
MYLLEROU
AKADHIMOU
KOLOKYNTHOUS
KORINIS
SAPFOUS
MENANDHROU
SOKRATOUS
SOFOKLEOUS
ATHINAS
EOLOU
EVRIPIDHOU
ARISTOFANOUS
ESKHYLOU
SARRI
AY. ANARYIRON
TAKI
AISOPOU
KARAISKAKI
MIAOULI
LEPENDIOTOU
DHIPYLOU
PSAROMILINGOU
ASOMATON
IERA ODHOS
TRIPTOLEMOU
LAKHOU
VOUTADHON
PERSEFONIS
ERMOU
ADHRIANOU
EPTAHALKOU
THESSALONIKIS
IRAKLIDHON
VASILIS
AKTEOU
NILEOS
ERYSIKHTHONOS
DHIMOFONDOS
EXONEON
TRION IERARHON
AKAMANTOS
APOSTOLOU PAVLOU
DHIONYSIOU EYINITOU
TROON
AREOS
PANDHROSSOU
N
0 100 m
Ano Petralona
43 & Benaki–Pireos St Annexe

Pottery (Mon–Fri 9am–3pm, Sun 10am–2pm; €6). A tiny place (so pricey for what you get), it has a series of small rooms with exhibits of traditional pottery-making methods, complete with regular hands-on demonstrations. A couple of further galleries have temporary exhibits, usually on a particular style or era of pottery. Completing the ensemble is a small café and a shop selling quality ceramics.

The **Benáki Museum of Islamic Art** (Tues & Thurs–Sun 9am–3pm, Wed 9am–9pm; €5; Ⓦwww.benaki.gr) is at Áyion Asomáton 22, corner Dhípylou. Antonis Benakis, founder of the Benáki Museum (p.132), spent much of his life in Egypt and this new museum, in a converted Neoclassical mansion, was created to house the collection he amassed there. Exhibits follow a chronological course, from the seventh century on the first floor to the nineteenth on the fourth. Throughout there are beautiful, intricately decorated objects in almost every type of art: ceramics (especially tiles), metalwork and wood above all, but also textiles, jewellery, glass, scientific instruments, armour and more. The highlights, perhaps, are on the third floor, from the sixteenth- and seventeenth-century Golden Age of the Ottoman Empire under Suleiyman the Magnificent. Here is a reconstructed room from a Cairo mansion, complete with inlaid marble floor, sunken fountains and elaborate wooden window screens, as well as silk wall hangings (not from the mansion), shot with silver and gold thread. There's a top-floor café overlooking the Kerameikos site with industrial Gázi beyond, as well as views of the Acropolis and Filopáppou, while in the basement can be seen a substantial chunk of the ancient city wall, almost 6m high, preserved during the building's restoration.

Kerameikos

The **Kerameikos** (or Keramikós) site (daily: April–Sept 8am–7.30pm; Oct–March 8.30am–3pm; museum opens 11am Mon; €2 or joint Acropolis ticket; entrance on Ermoú), encompassing one of the principal burial grounds of ancient Athens and a hefty section of the ancient wall, provides a fascinating and quiet retreat. Little visited, it has something of an oasis feel, with the lush Iridhanós channel, speckled with water lilies, flowing across the site from east to west.

To the right of the entrance is the stream and the double line of the **city wall**. Two roads pierced the wall here, and the gates that marked their entrance to the city have been excavated: the great **Dipylon Gate** was the busiest in the ancient city, where the road from Pireás, Eleusis and the north arrived; the **Sacred Gate** was a ceremonial entrance where the Ierá Odhós or Sacred Way entered the city – it was used for the Eleusinian and Panathenaic processions. Between the two gates are the foundations of the **Pompeion**, a spacious building with a peristyle courtyard, where preparations for the processions were made and where the main vehicles were stored.

Branching off to the left from the Sacred Way is the **Street of the Tombs**, the old road to Pireás. In ancient Greece people were frequently buried alongside roads, and especially near gates, a practice at least partly related to the idea of death as a journey. This site, by the principal routes into the Classical city, was clearly a prestigious one and numerous commemorative monuments to wealthy or distinguished Athenians have been excavated, their original stones reinstated or replaced by replicas. The flat, vertical *stelae* were the main funerary monuments of the Classical world; the sarcophagi that you see are later, from Hellenistic or Roman times. The large tomb with the massive semicircular base to the left of the path is the *Memorial of Dexileos*, the 20-year-old son of Lysanias of Thorikos, who was killed in action at Corinth in 394 BC. The adjacent plot contains the *Monument of Dionysios of Kollytos*, in the shape of a pillar stele supporting a bull carved from Pentelic marble.

The **site museum** is a lovely, cool, marble-floored space displaying finds from the site and related material, above all stelae and grave markers. There are also many poignant funerary offerings – toys from child burials, gold jewellery and beautiful small objects of all sorts. The ceramics are particularly fine, including lovely dishes with horses on their lids (*pyxides*) from the early eighth century BC and some stunning fifth-century BC black-and-red figure pottery.

Gázi, Tekhnópolis and around

Gázi, to the west and north of Kerameikos, is a former industrial area where the reinvention of the old gasworks as the Tekhnópolis cultural centre has helped spark a rush of hip bars and restaurants, accelerated by the new Keramikós metro station. By day the streets tend to be deserted, and by night, with so many derelict buildings, they can feel threatening. In practice it's safe enough, but at night you may want to take a taxi down here; Gázi really comes into its own late on Friday night and over the weekend.

The former gasworks from which the Gázi district takes its name has been converted into a stunning series of spaces for concerts and exhibitions known as **Tekhnópolis** (daily 10am–10pm; ⓣ210 34 67 322). To get there continue along Ermoú past the Kerameikos site and you'll emerge on Odhós Pireós more or less opposite the entrance; there are also lots of buses on Pireós, or Keramikós metro is near the rear entrance. Two round gas-holders have become circular glass offices, while in the various pumping stations and boiler rooms surrounding them, galleries and exhibition halls of varying sizes have been created, many with parts of the original machinery preserved. There's also a café. The only permanent display here is a small **Maria Callas Museum** (Mon–Fri 10am–3pm; free), whose collection of personal letters and photos, plus a pair of gloves and a fur coat, is really for fans only. All sorts of temporary exhibitions and concerts take place, though, so it's well worth taking a look – or check local listings magazines for details.

Numerous other galleries and cultural spaces have sprung up in the surrounding area, with two of particular note. Some six long blocks southwest of Tekhnópolis, the **Benáki Museum Pireos St Annexe** (Wed, Thurs & Sun 10am–6pm, Fri & Sat 10am–10pm; €4; ⓣ210 34 53 111, ⓦwww.benaki.gr; Metro Petrálona, or many buses along Pireós including #049, #B18 and trolley #021), at Pireós 138, is symptomatic of the development that is transforming a formerly industrial part of the city centre. There's no permanent collection, but the prestige of the Benáki Museum can attract exceptional temporary shows so it's always worth checking out what's on. The vast industrial space, now clad in pink marble, has been converted to galleries on various levels around an internal courtyard: be sure to explore as it's not always obvious what's on where. An airy, upmarket indoor restaurant/café serves sandwiches and salads as well as more substantial dishes.

Further north, Ierá Odhós (following the line of the ancient Sacred Way) heads off from behind the Kerameikos site towards the **Athinaïs**, at Kastoriás 34–36 (ⓣ210 34 80 000; ⓦwww.athinais.com.gr). A magnificent restoration of an early twentieth-century silk factory, the Athinaïs complex contains a theatre, music space, movie screen, two restaurants, a bar and café, exhibition halls, a museum and, the real object of the place, a sizeable conference centre. The **Pierídhes Museum of Ancient Cypriot Art** (daily 9.30am–7pm; €3) is beautifully presented in four small galleries, with some top-class exhibits including ceramics and very early glassware. It does seem strange to be admiring these Cypriot objects in Athens, however. The museum shop is full of lavish (and lavishly priced) arty gifts, while upstairs are art galleries with temporary exhibitions. Details of what's on for both of the above can be found on the Athinaïs website or in the local press.

Thissío and views of the Acropolis

Head south from Metro Thissío and you can follow pedestrianized Apóstolou Pávlou right around the edge of the Ancient Agora and Acropolis sites to the new Acropolis Museum and Metro Akrópoli on the fringes of Pláka. It's an especially rewarding walk in the early evening, when the setting sun illuminates this side of the rock and the cafés of Thissío start to fill with an anticipatory buzz. As you follow the street round there are a number of small excavations at the base of the hills on your right. First, immediately below the church of Ayía Marína, is a rocky area identified as the earliest known **sanctuary of Zeus** in Attica; there's not a great deal to see through the fence, but it's clear that the rocks have been cut into terraces. A little further, the **Sanctuary of Pan** is on the lower slopes of the Pnyx just beyond the Thission open-air cinema. The cult of Pan was associated with caves, and in this fenced-off site you can see the opening to an underground chamber cut into the rock. Inside were found reliefs of Pan, a naked nymph and a dog. There's also a mosaic floor and, nearby, remains of an ancient road and two rock-cut, Classical-era houses. Just above the sanctuary is the so-called **Fountain of Pnyx**. Under Peisistratos a water system was engineered, with subterranean pipes bringing water from springs to rock-cut cisterns that supplied the city. This is believed to be one of those: behind a locked entrance is a chamber with a Roman mosaic floor where the water was collected. You can also see traces of the concrete used to seal the chamber during World War II, when valuable antiquities were stored inside.

Filopáppou Hill, the Hill of the Pnyx and the Hill of the Nymphs

From around the junction of Apóstolou Pávlou and Dhionysíou Areopayítou, a network of paths leads up **Filopáppou Hill**, known in antiquity as the "Hill of the Muses". Its pine- and cypress-clad slopes provide fabulous views of the Acropolis and the city beyond, especially at sunset (although night-time muggings have occurred here, so take care). This strategic height has played an important, if generally sorry, role in the city's history; in 1687 it was from here that the shell that destroyed the roof of the Parthenon was lobbed; more recently, the colonels placed tanks on the slopes during their coup of 1967. The hill's summit is capped by a grandiose monument to a Roman senator and consul, Filopappus, who is depicted driving his chariot on its frieze. To the west is the Dora Stratou Theatre (see p.151). On the way up the hill, the main path follows a line of truncated ancient walls, past the attractive sixteenth-century church of **Áyios Dhimítrios**, inside which are some original Byzantine frescoes. Further down, in the rock face near the base of the hill, you can make out a kind of cave dwelling, known (more from imagination than evidence) as the **prison of Socrates**.

North of Filopáppou, above the church, rises the **Hill of the Pnyx**, an area used in Classical Athens as the meeting place for the democratic assembly, which gathered more than forty times a year. All except the most serious political issues were aired here, where a convenient semicircular terrace makes a natural spot from which to address the crowd. All male citizens could vote and, at least in theory, all could voice their opinions, though the assembly was harsh on inarticulate or foolish speakers. There are some impressive remains of the original walls, which formed the theatre-like court, and of *stoas* where the assembly would have taken refreshment. This atmospheric setting provides commanding Acropolis views, while benches on the west side allow you to contemplate the vista across Pireás and out to sea. On the northern slope, above Thissío, stands the impressive Neoclassical bulk of the **National Observatory of Athens** (Ⓦwww.noa.gr; open first Fri of every month).

Over to the west a third hill rises – the **Hill of the Nymphs** (Lófos Nymfón). Nymphs were associated with the dusty whirlwinds to which this hill is particularly prone and it is said to be the location of the fairy sequences in Shakespeare's *A Midsummer Night's Dream*. Slightly lower and quieter than its better-known neighbours, this is a peaceful place with good views across to the western suburbs of Athens and beyond, as well as pleasant shaded walks.

Mets and Pangráti

For a taste of old Athens, head south and east of the National Gardens where **Mets** and **Pangráti** are just about the only central neighbourhoods outside Pláka to have retained something of their traditional flavour. In **Mets** especially, a steep hillside quarter on the southwest side of the Panathenaic Stadium, a few streets of pre-World War II houses survive almost intact; their tiled roofs, shuttered windows and courtyards with spiral metal staircases and potted plants offering an intimate glimpse at the more traditional side of the city. There are few sights here – just the stadium alongside the city's most prestigious cemetery. The residential district of **Pangráti**, beyond, has still less to see, but offers a wealth of small, homely tavernas and *mezedhopolía*. Platía Plastíra, Platía Pangratíou and, above all, Platía Varnáva are the focal points, while Odhós Arhimídhous, off Platía Plastíra, hosts an impressive street market every Friday.

The Panathenaic Stadium

The old Olympic Stadium or **Panathenaic Stadium** (aka Kalimármaro), is a nineteenth-century reconstruction on Roman foundations, slotted tightly between the pine-covered spurs of Ardhittós hill. You can't normally go inside, but you can go right up to the open end of its horseshoe shape, from where you get a very good view. An easy walk from the centre via the Záppio gardens, the stadium can also be reached by tram (Záppio stop).

This site was originally marked out in the fourth century BC for the Panathenaic athletic contests, but, in Roman times, as a grand gesture to mark the reign of Emperor Hadrian, it was adapted for an orgy of blood sports, with thousands of wild beasts baited and slaughtered in the arena. The Roman senator Herodes Atticus later undertook to refurbish the 60,000 seats of the entire stadium; the white marble from these was to provide the city with a convenient quarry through the ensuing seventeen centuries.

The stadium's reconstruction dates from the modern revival of the Olympic Games in 1896 and bears witness to the efforts of another wealthy benefactor, the Alexandrian Greek Yiorgos Averoff. Its appearance – pristine whiteness and meticulous symmetry – must be very much as it was when first restored and reopened under the Roman senator. Though the bends are too tight for major modern events, it's still used by local athletes, is the finishing point of the annual Athens Marathon and lays at the end of the 2004 Olympic marathon. Above the stadium to the south, on the secluded Hill of Ardhittós, are a few scant remnants of a Temple of Fortune, again constructed by Herodes Atticus, while beyond is the prestigious **Próto Nekrotafío** (First Cemetery), with the tombs of just about everybody who was anybody in nineteenth- and twentieth-century Greece, from Heinrich Schliemann to Melina Mercouri and former prime minister Andreas Papandreou.

Kolonáki, Lykavitós and the museum quarter

If you have money to spend, **Kolonáki** is the place to do it, catering as it does to every Western taste from fast food to high fashion. It's also from here that a funicular hauls you up **Lykavitós Hill**, where some of the best views of the city can be enjoyed. Close at hand, too, is a clutch of major museums. Near the National Gallery of Art lie what are believed to be the fourth-century BC foundations of **Aristotle's Lyceum** – where he taught for thirteen years and to which Socrates was a frequent visitor. Surrounded by museums, this seems an appropriate place for it, but important as the discovery is for scholars, there's nothing actually to see.

Kolonáki

Kolonáki is the city's most chic central address and shopping area. Walk up from Sýndagma, past the jewellery stores on Voukourestíou, and you can almost smell the money. The neighbourhood's lower limits are defined by the streets of Akadhimías and Vassilísis Sofías, where grand Neoclassical palaces house embassies and museums. The middle stretches of the quarter are taken up with shops, while the highest, wonderfully located on the southwest-facing slopes of Lykavitós, looking out over the Acropolis and National Gardens, are purely residential.

The heart of it all is a square officially called Platía Filikís Eterías, but known to all as **Platía Kolonakíou**, after the ancient "little column" that hides in the trees on the southwest side. Dotted around the square are kiosks with stocks of foreign papers and magazines, or in the library of the **British Council** you can check out the British press for free. The surrounding cafés are almost invariably packed with Gucci-clad shoppers – you'll find better value if you move away from the square a little. In the dozens of small, upmarket **shops** the accent is firmly on fashion and designer gear.

Lykavitós Hill

Lykavitós Hill offers tremendous views, particularly from late afternoon onwards – on a clear day you can see the mountains of the Peloponnese. After dark, the shimmering lights of Athens spread right across the Attica basin. To get to the summit you can take the **funicular** (daily 9am–3am; every 30min, more frequent at busy times; €4.50 return) or you can walk. The funicular begins its ascent from Odhós Aristípou, near the top of Ploutárhou. To get here is in itself something of a climb – though it doesn't look far from Kolonáki Square, it's a steep ascent through the stepped residential streets. To do the whole journey the lazy way take bus #060 to the base of the funicular – this starts its journey at the terminus beside the National Archeological Museum and has handy stops on Akadhimías. The principal path up the hill begins from the western end of

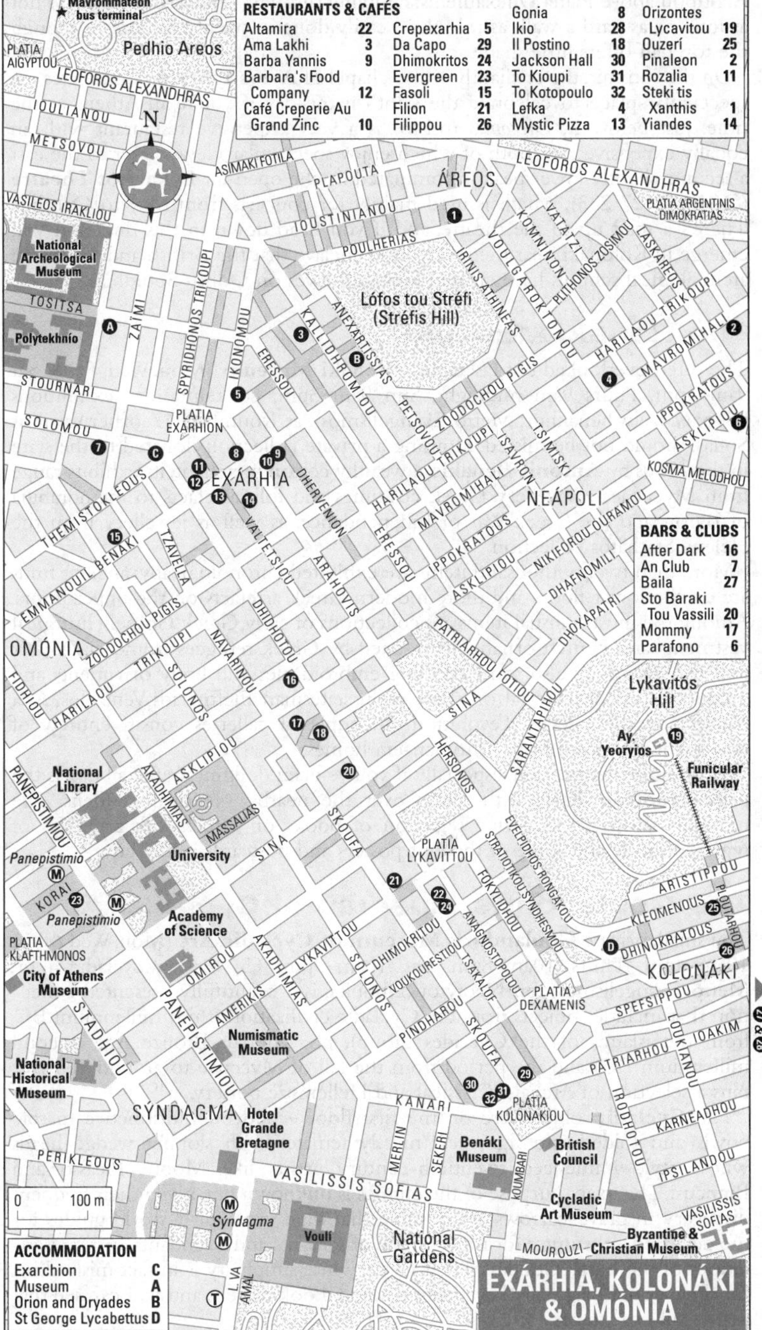
EXÁRHIA, KOLONÁKI & OMÓNIA
RESTAURANTS & CAFÉS
Altamira 22
Ama Lakhi 3
Barba Yannis 9
Barbara's Food Company 12
Café Creperie Au Grand Zinc 10
Crepexarhia 5
Da Capo 29
Dhimokritos 24
Evergreen 23
Fasoli 15
Filion 21
Filippou 26
Gonia 8
Ikio 28
Il Postino 18
Jackson Hall 30
To Kioupi 31
To Kotopoulo 32
Lefka 4
Mystic Pizza 13
Orizontes Lycavitou 19
Ouzerí 25
Pinaleon 2
Rozalia 11
Steki tis Xanthis 1
Yiandes 14
BARS & CLUBS
After Dark 16
An Club 7
Baila 27
Sto Baraki Tou Vassili 20
Mommy 17
Parafono 6
ACCOMMODATION
Exarchion C
Museum A
Orion and Dryades B
St George Lycabettus D
Mavrommateon bus terminal
Pedhio Areos
PLATIA AIGYPTOU
LEOFOROS ALEXANDHRAS
National Archeological Museum
Polytekhnío
ÁREOS
Lófos tou Stréfi (Stréfis Hill)
EXÁRHIA
PLATIA EXARHION
NEÁPOLI
OMÓNIA
Lykavitós Hill
Ay. Yeoryios
Funicular Railway
National Library
University
Panepistimio
Academy of Science
PLATIA KLAFTHMONOS
City of Athens Museum
Numismatic Museum
National Historical Museum
SÝNDAGMA
Hotel Grande Bretagne
PLATIA LYKAVITTOU
PLATIA DEXAMENIS
KOLONÁKI
PLATIA KOLONAKIOU
Benáki Museum
British Council
Cycladic Art Museum
Byzantine & Christian Museum
Vouli
National Gardens
Sýndagma
VASILISSIS SOFIAS
PLATIA ARGENTINIS DIMOKRATIAS
0 100 m
27 & 28

Aristípou above Platía Dhexamenís, rambling through woods to the top. It's not as long or as hard a walk as it looks – easily done in twenty minutes – though the top half offers little shade.

On the summit, the brilliantly white chapel of **Áyios Yeóryios** dominates – a spectacular place to celebrate the saint's name-day if you're in Athens at the time. Just below it, *Orizontes* (p.146) is a very expensive restaurant with an equally expensive café, both of which enjoy spectacular views. Over to the east a second, slightly lower peak is dominated by the open-air **Lykavitós Theatre** (Ⓣ210 72 27 233), which is used mainly for concerts from May to October. There's a road up to the theatre, and if you head down in this direction you emerge in Kolonáki near the lovely little enclave that the British and American archeological schools have created for themselves on Odhós Souidhías.

The Benáki Museum

The often overlooked but fascinating **Benáki Museum** (Mon, Wed, Fri & Sat 9am–5pm, Thurs 9am–midnight, Sun 9am–3pm; €6, temporary exhibitions €3–5; Ⓦwww.benaki.gr; Metro Evangelismós), at Koumbári 1/corner Vassilísis Sofías, should not be missed. Housing a private collection donated to the state in the 1950s by **Antonis Benakis**, a wealthy cotton merchant, its exhibits range from Mycenaean jewellery, Greek costumes and folk artefacts to memorabilia of Byron and the Greek War of Independence, as well as jewellery from the Hélène Stathatos collection.

More than twenty thousand items are exhibited chronologically; ancient finds are on the lower floors and more modern Greek artefacts on the upper floors. Among the most unusual items are collections of early Greek Gospels, liturgical vestments and church ornaments rescued by Greek refugees from Asia Minor in 1922. There are also some dazzling embroideries and body ornaments and unique historical material on the Cretan statesman Eleftherios Venizelos, Asia Minor and the Cretan Revolution. A couple of galleries consist entirely of reconstructed rooms from Ottoman-era homes.

An additional attraction, especially if you've been dodging traffic all day, is the pricey **rooftop café**, with views over the nearby National Gardens. The museum **shop** stocks a fine selection of books on Greek folk art, CDs of regional music and some of the best posters and postcards in the city.

The Goulandhrís Museum of Cycladic Art

The small, private **Goulandhrís Museum of Cycladic Art** (Mon, Wed & Fri 10am–4pm, Thurs 10am–8pm, Sat 10am–3pm; €5; Ⓦwww.cycladic-m.gr; Metro Evangelismós), on Neofýtou Dhouká, is a beautifully presented collection that includes objects from the Cycladic civilization (third millennium BC, from the islands of the Cyclades group), pre-Minoan Bronze Age (second millennium BC) and the period from the fall of Mycenae to around 700 BC, plus a selection of Archaic, Classical and Hellenistic pottery.

The **Cycladic** objects are on the first floor – above all, distinctive marble bowls and folded-arm figurines (mostly female) with sloping wedge heads whose style influenced twentieth-century artists like Moore, Picasso and Brancusi. The exact purpose of the effigies is unknown but, given their frequent discovery in grave-barrows, it's possible that they were spirit-world guides for the deceased, substitutes for the sacrifice of servants and attendants, or representations of the Earth Goddess. Their clean, white simplicity is in fact misleading, for they would originally have been painted. Look closely, and you can see that many still bear traces.

Of the ancient Greek art on the upper floors, the highlight is the superb black-figure pottery, especially a collection of painted **Classical-era** bowls, often showing two unrelated scenes on opposite sides – for example one of the star exhibits depicts revellers on one face and three men in cloaks conversing on the other. Others include, on the second floor, a depiction of Hephaistos' return to Olympus, with Hephaistos and Dionysos riding donkeys, and, on the top floor, a lovely *pyxis* with a lid of four horses.

On the ground floor and basement there's a tiny children's area and a good **shop**, as well as a pleasant **café** (with good vegetarian choices) in an internal courtyard. A covered walkway connects to the nineteenth-century **Stathatos House**, magnificently restored as an extension for temporary exhibitions.

The Byzantine and Christian Museum

The **Byzantine and Christian Museum** (Tues–Sun 7.30am–7.30pm; €4; Metro Evangelismós), at Vassilísis Sofías 22, was completely refurbished in 2004, and they did a wonderful job. Excellently displayed in a beautiful building, its collection is far more wide-ranging than you might expect from the name. The setting is a peaceful, courtyarded villa that once belonged to the Duchesse de Plaisance, an extravagantly eccentric French-American philhellene and widow of a Napoleonic general who helped fund the War of Independence.

The exhibits start with art from the very earliest days of Christianity, whose fish and dove motifs can't disguise their extremely close parallels with Classical Greek objects. There are displays on everyday Byzantine life; reconstructions of parts of early churches (mosaic floors and chunks of masonry, some even from the Christian Parthenon); a Coptic section with antique clothing such as leather shoes decorated with gold leaf; and tombs, in some of which offerings were left, again a reminder of a pagan heritage. But the highlights are the **icons**, with the earliest being from the thirteenth and fourteenth centuries. There are dozens of lovely examples, many of them double-sided, some mounted to be carried in procession, and you can follow the development of their style from the simplicity of the earliest icons to the Renaissance-influenced selections from the sixteenth century. Alongside the icons are some fine frescoes, including an entire dome reconstructed inside the museum.

The War Museum

The only "cultural" endowment of the 1967–74 junta, the **War Museum** (Tues–Sat 9am–2pm; free; Metro Evangelismós; limited English labelling), at Vassilísis Sofías 24, becomes predictably militaristic and right-wing as it approaches modern events: the Asia Minor campaign, Greek forces in Korea, and so on. One room devoted to Cyprus, in particular, has a virulently anti-Turkish message that seems extraordinary given current relations between the countries (it is also full of Cypriot antiquities, presumably to demonstrate the island's Greek heritage). However, the bulk of the collection consists of weaponry and uniforms, with a large collection of eighteenth- and nineteenth-century swords and handguns, and a particular concentration on the World War II era. Earlier times are also covered with displays on changing warfare from Mycenae through to the Byzantines and Turks, and an array of models of the acropolises and castles of Greece, both Classical and medieval. Outside are artillery pieces and planes, including a full-scale model of the *Daedalus*, one of the first-ever military aircraft, which dropped bombs on Turkish positions in December 1912 during the Balkan Wars.

The National Gallery

The **National Gallery and Alexándros Soútsos Museum** (Mon & Wed 9am–3pm & 6–9pm, Thurs–Sat 9am–3pm, Sun 10am–2pm; €6.50; Metro Evangelismós; Ⓦwww.nationalgallery.gr), at Vassiléos Konstandínou 50, is a bit of a disappointment. Its core collection is of Greek art from the sixteenth century to the present, and of the artists shown here only El Greco is well known outside Greece. One of the few modern painters to stand out is Nikos Hatzikyriakos-Ghikas (Ghika), well represented on the ground floor. On the mezzanine is a small group of canvases by the primitive painter Theophilos (more of whose work can be seen at the Museum of Greek Folk Art in Pláka – see p.115). Perhaps more interesting is the large temporary exhibition space, often hosting major travelling exhibitions; keep an eye out for posters or check the website or the *Athens News*.

The coast: Pireás to Glyfádha

Athens' coastline is often overlooked by visitors, who are here for their Classical fix and off to the islands for beaches. For Athenians, though, it's an essential summertime safety valve and they head down here in droves: not just for beaches, but for cafés, restaurants, nightlife and shops. Technically, **Pireás** and the "Apollo Coast" around **Glyfádha** are not part of Athens – indeed, Pireás is a proud municipality in its own right. In practice, though, they form part of a single, continuous conurbation, connected by excellent public transport and an unbroken ribbon of development. Thanks to the new tram it's easy to head down to the beach for a quick swim and be back in the centre just a couple of hours later; astonishingly, the water almost everywhere is clean and crystal clear. Pireás, meanwhile, has ferries to the islands, an excellent museum and some of the best seafood in town.

Pireás

PIREÁS (Piraeus) has been the port of Athens since Classical times, when the so-called Long Walls, scattered remnants of which can still be seen, were built to connect it to the city. Today it's a substantial metropolis in its own right. The port, whose **island ferries** (see p.137) are the reason most people come here, has a gritty fascination of its own, typified by the huge Sunday-morning **flea market**, concentrated around Odhós Skylítsi parallel to the rail tracks behind the metro station. It's not really a place to shop – the goods are mostly cheap clothing and pirated CDs, plus a few junky antiques – but it is quite an experience. The real attractions of the place, though, are around the small-boat harbours of Zéa Marina and Mikrolímano on the opposite side of the small peninsula. Here, the upscale residential areas are alive with attractive waterfront cafés, bars and restaurants and there's an excellent archeological museum.

Some history

The port at Pireás was founded at the beginning of the fifth century BC by **Themistocles**, who realized the potential of its three natural harbours. His work was consolidated by Pericles with the building of the **Long Walls** to protect the corridor to Athens, and the port remained active under Roman and Macedonian rulers. Subsequently, under Turkish control, the place

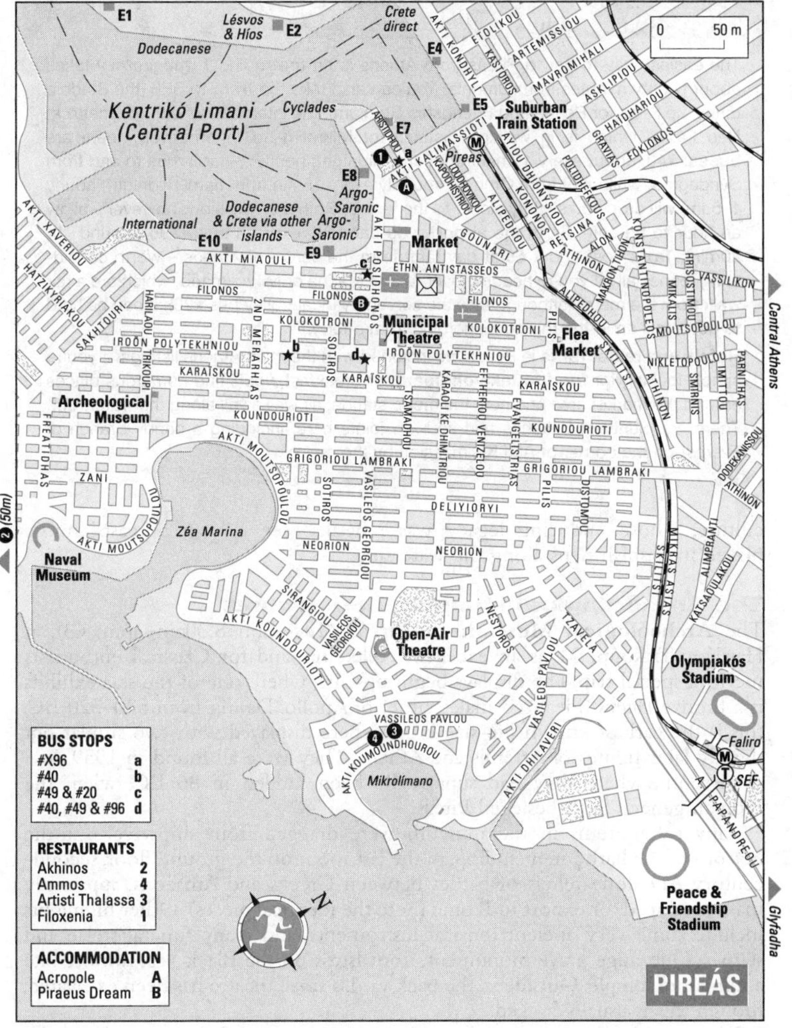

declined to the extent that there was just one building here, a monastery, by the end of the War of Independence. From the 1830s on, though, Pireás grew by leaps and bounds. The original influx into the port was a group of immigrants from Híos, whose island had been devastated by the Turks; later came populations from Ýdhra, Crete and the Peloponnese. By World War I, Pireás had outstripped the island of Sýros as the nation's predominant port, its strategic position enhanced by the opening of the Suez and Corinth canals in 1862 and 1893 respectively. Like Athens itself, the port's great period of expansion began in 1923, with the exchange of populations with Turkey. Over 100,000 Asia Minor Greeks decided to settle in Pireás, doubling the population almost overnight – and giving a boost to a pre-existing semi-underworld

Pireás transport and practicalities

The easiest way to get to Pireás from Athens is on **metro** line 1; the journey takes about twenty minutes from Omónia. You can also take the **tram** to SEF (the Stádhio Eirínis ké Fílias, or Peace and Friendship Stadium), the interchange with the metro at Néo Fáliro, which is in walking distance of Mikrolímano. Alternatively, there are **buses**: #40 (about every 10min from 5am–midnight; hourly 1–5am) runs to and from Sýndagma, while #49 from Omónia (roughly every 15min from 5am–midnight; hourly 1–5am) will drop you slightly closer to the ferries. Both are very slow, however – allow an hour to be safe. From the **airport**, you can take express bus #X96 (around 1hr 20min). **Taxis** cost about €8 at day tariff from the centre of Athens – worth considering, especially if you're heading over to Zéa Marina or Mikrolímano, which are a fair walk from the metro (although they are served by local trolley bus #20). It can be hard to get a taxi amid the throng disgorging from a ferry.

Hotels and restaurants in Pireás are included with the main Athens listings: if you're simply looking for **food to take on board**, or breakfast, you'll find numerous places around the market area and near the metro station, as well as all along the waterfront. There are plenty of bakeries and *souvláki* joints here, including a handy branch of *Everest* on the corner of Aktí Kalimassióti by the metro.

culture, whose enduring legacy was rebétika (see p.939), outcasts' music played in hashish dens along the waterside.

The Archeological Museum and around

The **Archeological Museum of Pireás** (Tues–Sun 8.30am–3pm; €3), at Haríláou Trikoúpi 31, is an excellent collection, and for Classical enthusiasts merits a special trip. The displays begin upstairs, where one of the star exhibits is a bronze *kouros* (idealized male statue) of Apollo. Dating from 530–520 BC, this is the earliest known life-size bronze, here displayed with two similar but slightly later figures of Artemis and Athena. They were all found in 1959, in a store-room, where they had supposedly been hidden in 86 BC, when the Roman general Sulla besieged Pireás.

Many other items in the museum were dragged from shipwrecks at the bottom of the harbour, including, in the last room on the ground floor, second-century AD stone reliefs of battles between Greeks and Amazons, apparently mass-produced for export to Rome (note the identical pieces). Other highlights include some very ancient musical instruments, and many funeral stelae and statues. One huge grave monument, from Istros on the Black Sea, is more like a miniature temple. Outside in the back yard, a small theatre has been excavated, though this is usually locked.

The route to the museum from the port takes you from one side of the peninsula to the other, over a hill. At the top are Pireás's main shopping and administrative streets, and at the bottom the very different atmosphere of the residential districts. Beyond the museum you can descend to **Zéa Marina** (aka Pasalimáni) to admire some of the monstrous gin palaces moored there. Nearby, on Aktí Themistokléous, the **Naval Museum** (Tues–Sat 9am–2pm, Sun 9.30am–2pm; €3) traces Greece's maritime heritage with models and actual sections of ancient triremes and modern warships. The museum is mainly of interest to specialists and small boys; anyone else might find their time better spent wandering around the harbours. The boats at **Mikrolímano** (known to many locals as Turkolímano) are more modest than those at Zéa, but the harbour itself is prettier, and there are more cafés to sit and enjoy it.

Glyfádha and Vouliagméni

Athens' southern suburbs form an almost unbroken line along the coast all the way from Pireás to Vouliagméni, some 20km away. This coast is Athens' summer playground and the centre of it – for shopping, clubbing, dining or posing on the beach – is **Glyfádha**, a bizarre mix of glitz and suburbia. At weekends, half of Athens seems to decamp down here. The epicentre is around the crescent of Leofóros Angélou Metáxa, lined with shops and malls, with the tram running down the centre and streets of cafés and restaurants heading off on either side. Glyfádha merges almost indistinguishably into its neighbour **Voúla**, and then into quieter, more upmarket **Kavoúri** and **Vouliagméni**. The latter is one of the city's posher suburbs, and its beautiful cove beaches are a traditional hang-out of Athens' rich and famous. Last stop for the local buses is **Várkiza**, more of a seaside resort pure and simple.

If you are prepared to walk a bit, or are driving and happy to battle the locals for parking space, then some of the best beaches can be found around the **Vouliagméni peninsula**, off the main road. Immediately after Voúla B pay beach, a road turns off to Kavoúri, past the *Divani Palace Hotel* and some packed free beaches with excellent tavernas. Further along on this Kavoúri side of the peninsula are some still better, less crowded, free beaches: the #114 bus runs a little way inland, not far from these. Carrying on round, you get to Vouliagméni itself, with beautiful little coves, a few of which remain free, and eventually rejoin the main road by Vouliagméni A Beach. Beyond Vouliagméni the road

Ferries from Pireás

Hundreds of ferries leave Pireás daily, so it's perhaps not surprising that a comprehensive list is hard to find: even the tourist office simply individual queries on the web (Ⓦwww.openseas.gr). The majority of the ships for the Argo-Saronic and the popular Cyclades leave between 7 and 9am. There is then another burst of activity between noon and 3pm towards the Cyclades and Dodecanese, and a final battery of departures in the evening, bound for a wide variety of ports, but especially night sailings to Crete, the northeast Aegean, the western Cyclades and Dodecanese.

There's no need to buy **tickets** for conventional ferries before you get here, unless you want a berth in a cabin or are taking a car on board; during Greek holidays (Aug and Easter especially) these can be hard to get and it's worth booking in advance – the big companies have Internet booking. Flying Dolphin hydrofoil reservations are also a good idea at busy times. In general, though, the best plan is simply to get to Pireás early and check with some of the dozens of **shipping agents** around the metro station and along the quayside Platía Karaïskáki (there are plenty of agents in central Athens too). Most of these act only for particular lines, so for a full picture you will need to ask at three or four outlets. Prices for domestic boat journeys vary little, but the quality of the craft and circuitousness of routes can be vastly different. If you are heading for Thíra (Santoríni) or Rhodes, for example, try to get a boat that stops at only three or four islands en route; for Crete settle for direct ferries only.

Boats for different destinations leave from a variety of points around the main harbour: it can be helpful to know the gate number, though these are primarily for drivers. Airport-style buses run from gate E5, near the metro, as far as E1, for the big ferries to Crete, the Dodecanese and the northwest. The main gates and **departure points** are marked on our map, but always check with the ticket agent as on any given day a ferry may dock in an unexpected spot. They all display signs showing their destination and departure time; you can't buy tickets on the boat, but there's usually a ticket hut on the quayside nearby.

Athens' beaches and coastal transport

People swim from the rocks or seawall almost anywhere on the coast southeast of Pireás – especially the older generation (the youth tend to head down towards the fleshpots and pay beaches of Glyfádha) – but the closest pleasant beach to the centre is **Edem**, reached by tram to the Edem or Váthis stops. A small patch of sand with cafés and tavernas, this is busy and urban but fine for a quick swim and sunbathe and, remarkably, has Blue Flag status. There are other small, free beaches near the Váthis and Flisvós tram stops. Almost all of the really good beaches within easy reach of Athens, however, demand **payment** for entry. For your money you'll get clean sand, lifeguards, somewhere to buy food and drink, a lounger (usually at extra cost) and a variety of other facilities including beach volleyball, massage, fun parks and all sorts of watersports. Some of the fanciest, in Glyfádha and Vouliagméni, charge upwards of €10 per person at weekends (the *Astir Palace* hotel charges an exorbitant €45); more basic places cost €3–5. There are plenty of places to **swim for free**, but this may mean from the rocks, or a long hike from the road. The best sandy beach with free access is at Skhiniás (p.160), but that's a long way out on the northeast Attic coast. On summer weekends, every beach – and the roads to them – will be packed.

Among the better **pay beaches** are Áyios Kósmas (summer daily 9am–8.30pm; €5, children €2), a relatively quiet choice at Ag. Kosmas 2 tram stop; Asteria (summer daily 8am–8pm; €5, €10 weekends, children half-price), a slightly glam and busy choice right in the heart of Glyfádha; Voúla A & B (summer daily 7am–9pm; €4), large twin beaches in Voúla between Glyfádha and Vouliagméni, cheap and cheerful with decent facilities; and Vouliagméni A (summer daily 8am–8pm; €5), on the main road in Vouliagméni, with few facilities but a lovely setting.

As far as Glyfádha, the easiest transport option is the **tram**, and at most stops you'll be able to find somewhere to swim. For the better beaches beyond Glyfádha, though, you'll have to transfer to the **bus**. The main routes from central Athens to Glyfádha are the #A2 or #2 express (which go as far as Voúla), #A3 or #B3 (to Vouliagméni) and the #22 (all the way down the coast to Saronídha), all of which leave from Akadhimías. The #A1 or #1 or #G1 run from Pireás all the way along the coast to Voúla. Local services #114 (Glyfádha–Kavoúri–Vouliagméni) or #115/6 (Glyfádha–Vouliagméni–Várkiza) are also useful. If you **drive**, be warned that parking is a nightmare, especially in Glyfádha and Vouliagméni; the pay beaches all have parking, though some charge extra.

runs high above the coast en route to Várkiza; the rocky shore a steep climb below, known as **Limanákia**, is largely nudist and has a large gay attendance.

Eating and drinking

As you'd expect in a city that houses almost half the Greek population, Athens has the best and the most varied **restaurants** and **tavernas** in the country – and many places are sources not just of good food but of a good night out too. Fast-food and takeaway places are also plentiful – the usual international chains keep a relatively low profile, and there are plenty of more authentic alternatives.

Most tourists never stray beyond the obvious central choices, but while Pláka's hills and narrow lanes can provide a pleasant, romantic evening setting, they also tend to be marred by high prices, aggressive touts and general tourist hype. Still in the centre, areas like Psyrrí and Thissío (or Gázi a little further afield) are where the locals go for a meal out; lively and fashionable. Omónia is business territory, a great place to grab a quick (or a long) lunch. For better value and traditional food, it's well worth striking out into the ring of **neighbourhoods** around, all of which have plenty of local tavernas: Exárhia, Neápoli, Áno Petrálona, Pangráti, Koukáki or the more upmarket Kolonáki are all good bets. None of these is more than a half-hour's walk, or a quick taxi or bus ride, from the centre – effort well repaid by more authentic menus and often a wonderful atmosphere. Further out along the coast the big attraction, not surprisingly, is fish. The pleasure harbours of **Pireás**, especially, are a favourite Sunday lunchtime destination. **Glyfádha** is

▲ Baïraktaris restaurant, Monastiráki

geared to crowds of shoppers and bar-hoppers, with busy, crowded "fun" restaurants, fast-food outlets and cafés. The northern suburb of **Kifissiá**, meanwhile, is a popular excursion with Athenians, for shopping and to meet up afterwards: there are plenty of cafés and restaurants, all of them relatively pricey, catering both to the more traditional, old-money locals and younger visitors.

Reservations are rarely necessary in ordinary Greek tavernas – indeed the simpler places probably won't have a reservation system (they can usually squeeze in an extra table if necessary) – but it is worth calling ahead at the fancier restaurants, or if you're planning a special trip across town.

Pláka, Monastiráki and Sýndagma

See map, p.109.

Restaurants, tavernas and ouzerís

Café Abysinia Kynétou 7, Platía Avysinnías, Monastiráki ⓣ210 32 17 047, ⓦwww.avissinia.gr. With two floors and a delicious, modern take on traditional Greek cooking (moussaka with spinach, for example, or mussel pilaf), *Café Abysinia* is always busy, popular with a local alternative crowd. Though more expensive than many, it's good value, and there's live music most weekday evenings and weekend lunchtimes. Tues–Sat 10.30am–1am, Sun 10.30am–7pm.

Aigli Záppio Gardens, Sýndagma ⓣ210 33 69 300, ⓦwww.aeglizappiou.gr. Pricey, smart restaurant with a fabulous setting, allegedly the haunt of the rich and famous and certainly popular with politicians and diplomats. "Modern Mediterranean" food, which here means Greek with French and Italian influences. A bar, open-air cinema and nightclub are part of the same complex.

Baïraktaris Mitropóleos 88, cnr Platía Monastirakíou, Monastiráki ⓣ210 32 13 036. Over a century old, this lively restaurant occupies two buildings whose walls are lined with wine barrels and photos of local celebrities. Some tables are set on the bustling pedestrian street, but for a cosier atmosphere, eat inside with the Greek regulars where there's often some impromptu live traditional music. The inexpensive menu includes *souvláki*, *yíros* and oven dishes such as soutzoukákia (meatballs in tomato sauce).

Brachera Platía Avysinnías 3, Monastiráki ⓣ210 32 17 202. Upmarket, modern Greek and Mediterranean café-bar-restaurant in a restored mansion overlooking the flea market. In summer, the roof garden offers views of the Acropolis. Dinner (from 9pm till the early hours) and Sunday lunch only. Closed Mon.

Byzantino Kydhathinéon 18 on Platía Filomoússou Eterías, Pláka ⓣ210 32 27 368. Reliable, traditional taverna that still attracts locals on this busy, touristy square. Take a look in the kitchen at the moderately priced daily specials, such as stuffed tomatoes or *youvétsi*.

Damingos (Ta Bakaliarakia) Kydhathinéon 41, Pláka ⓣ210 32 35 084. Open since 1865 and tucked away in the basement, this place has dour service, but the old-fashioned operation and the excellent *bakaliáro skordhaliá* (cod with garlic sauce) for which it is famed (and named) make up for it. Dinner only; closed mid-July to end Aug.

Dhioskouri Adhrianoú 37, Monastiráki ⓣ210 32 53 333. A very popular café-*mezedhopolío* with tables spreading across both sides of the pedestrianized street, some overlooking the metro lines. *Pikilía* – mixed *meze* plates – are good value at €10–15.

Diogenes Platía Lysikrátous, Pláka ⓣ210 32 24 845. Classy, upmarket taverna and café with a delightfully shady, tranquil location overlooking the Monument of Lysikratos.

Eden Lissíou 12, off Mnisikléous, Pláka ⓣ210 32 48 858. Closed for renovation in 2007, this is an established vegetarian restaurant – a rarity in Athens.

Evergreen Koräi 4, in Galleria Koräi off Platía Koräi, Sýndagma. See map, p.88. Healthy, fast-food style sandwiches, salads, juices and coffee served 24-hours. Some tables out on the square, and the Galleria is full of other fast-food options.

Fu-Rin-Ka-Zan Apóllonos 2, Sýndagma ⓣ210 32 29 170. Busy Japanese restaurant – popular at lunchtimes – with sushi, sashimi, yakisoba and the like at reasonable prices. Other Japanese and Asian restaurants nearby. Mon–Sat.

Klimataria Klepsýdhras 5, Pláka ⓣ210 32 11 215. Over a hundred years old, this unpretentious, pleasant taverna serves simple food – mainly grilled meat and fish. In winter, you're likely to be treated to live music, which inspires singalongs by the mostly Greek clientele. In summer, tables spill onto the vine-shaded alley outside. Dinner only.

To Kouti Adhrianoú 23, Monastiráki ⓣ210 32 13 229. Innovative Greek dishes as well as pasta and salads at this enjoyable, popular and slightly alternative restaurant. The menus are scrawled by hand in old children's books; the prices slightly higher than average.

Mezedopolio Palio Tetradhio Mnisikléous 26, cnr Thrassívoulou, Pláka ⓣ210 32 11 903. One of the touristy tavernas with tables set out on the stepped streets beneath the Acropolis. The food is a cut above that of most of its neighbours, though you pay for the romantic setting. Live music some evenings.

Noodle Bar Apóllonos 11, Pláka ⓣ210 33 18 585. Fairly basic and inexpensive place (takeaway too) serving decent Asian food – predominantly Thai but also with Indian, Chinese and Indonesian flavours.

Palia Taverna tou Psarrá Erekhthéos 16 at Erotókritou, Pláka ⓣ210 32 18 733. Large, classic Greek taverna around a restored old mansion with plenty of tables outside, on a tree-shaded and bougainvillea-draped pedestrian crossroads. You're best making a meal of the *mezédhes*, which include humble standards as well as seafood and fish concoctions.

Paradosiako Voulís 44a, Pláka ⓣ210 32 14 121. Tiny place on a busy street serving excellent, unpretentious, reasonably priced, fresh Greek food.

Platanos Dhioyénous 4, Pláka ⓣ210 32 20 666. A long-established taverna, with outdoor summer seating in a quiet square under the plane tree from which it takes its name. Reasonably priced traditional dishes such as chops and roast lamb with artichokes or with spinach and potatoes, and good house wine from vast barrels.

Skholarhio Tripódhon 14, Pláka ⓣ210 32 47 605, ⓦwww.sholarhio.gr. Attractive, split-level taverna with a perennially popular summer terrace, sheltered from the street. It has a great selection of *mezédhes* (all €2.50–5) brought out on trays so that you can point to the ones that you fancy. Especially good are the flaming sausages, *bouréki* (thin pastry filled with ham and cheese) and grilled aubergine. The house red wine is also palatable and cheap. All-inclusive deals for larger groups at €12 a head. Daily 11am–2am.

Thanasis Mitropóleos 69, Monastiráki. Rivals *Baïraktaris* for the title of best *souvláki* and *yíros* place in central Athens. Always packed with locals at lunchtimes. There's no booking so you may have to fight for a table, though there are plenty of them, especially in summer when they practically block the street.

Cafés

Amalthea Tripódhon 16, Pláka. Tasteful if pricey café-patisserie, serving yoghurt and crêpes as well as non-alcoholic drinks.

Dhioskouri Dhioskoúron, cnr Mitröon, Pláka. Popular café right on the edge of Pláka with great views over the ancient Agora. Simple food – salads and omelettes – as well as the inevitable frappés and cappuccinos.

Glykis Angélou Yéronda 2, Pláka. A secluded corner under shaded trees just off busy Kydhathinéon in Plaká, with a mouthwatering array of sweets.

Café Minoas Platía Mitropóleos cnr Venizélou, Monastiráki. A peaceful café on this pedestrianized square serving sandwiches, salads and ice cream.

Oasis West side of the National Gardens, opposite cnr of Amalías and Filellínon, Sýndagma. An unexpected shady haven just off the main avenue, offering light meals – sandwiches, pizza, pasta – ice cream and drinks.

Oréa Ellás Mitropóleos 59 or Pandhróssou 36, Monastiráki. Tucked away on the upper floor of the Kendro Ellinikis Paradosis store, this consciously old-fashioned *kafenío* offers a welcome escape from the crowded Flea Market. There's also a great view of the rooftops of Pláka on the slope towards the Acropolis. Open 9am–6pm.

To Tristrato Dedhálou 34, cnr Angélou Yéronda, Pláka. Lovely little traditional-style café just off the madness of Platía Filomoússou Eterías: coffee, juices, sandwiches, desserts and cakes.

Ydria Adhrianoú 68, cnr Eólou, Monastiráki. Platía Paliás Agorás, just round the corner from the Roman Forum, is packed with the tables of competing cafés: this is one of the best. A lovely place to sit outside for a quiet coffee or breakfast (they also serve meals), though, like its neighbours, very expensive.

Psyrrí and the bazaar

See map, p.125.

Restaurants, tavernas and ouzerís

Dhiporto Theátrou, cnr Sokrátous. Two brown-painted metal trapdoors in the pavement open to a steep stairway down into a basement that feels like it belongs in an Athens of fifty years ago. Simple, inexpensive Greek food – chick-pea soup, Greek salad, fried fish – washed down with retsina is enjoyed by market workers as well as tourists and office suits. Frequently as the afternoon wears on impromptu music breaks out. Mon–Sat 6am–6pm.

Elihrison Ayíon Anaryíron 6 ⓣ210 32 15 220. Huge new place at the heart of Psyrrí in a tastefully restored old building with tables on several levels, including a roof garden and an internal courtyard. Pricier than most, but classier too. Dinner only.
Gotzila Ríga Palamídhou 5 ⓣ210 32 21 086. Small sushi bar in this über-trendy little street off Platía Ayíon Anaryíron. Reasonably priced and mostly a late-night joint.
Guru Platía Theátrou 10 ⓣ210 32 46 350. High-fashion Thai restaurant plus late-night bar/club, whose artistically rusty iron facade is utterly out of keeping with the ugly concrete office blocks that surround it. Given the setting, the food is surprisingly authentic and not too pricey.
Klimataria Platía Theátrou 2 ⓣ210 32 16 629. Friendly, old-fashioned taverna serving ample portions of traditional fare at reasonable prices. Take a look at the daily specials in the kitchen; there are usually excellent vegetable dishes plus daily roast meats. Barrels of wine are just about the only decoration, but there's open courtyard seating in summer and live music at the end of the week. Open lunchtimes plus dinner Fri & Sat.
Mandhra Ayíon Anaryíron 8 cnr Táki ⓣ210 32 13 765. Popular place right at the heart of Psyrrí's restaurant quarter, with live music most evenings and standard taverna fare.
Nargis Sofokléous 60 ⓣ210 52 48 095. Tucked inside a tiny *stoa*, this basic Bengali canteen wins no prizes for decor, but has an authentic South Asian atmosphere and meat and vegetarian curries at very low prices.
Nikitas Ayíon Anaryíron 19 ⓣ210 32 13 765. A survivor from the days before Psyrrí was fashionable, and by far the least expensive option here, with excellent home-cooked taverna food and daily specials, plus great chips. Lunch (approx 11am–6pm) only.
Pak Indian Menándhrou 13, Platía Theátrou ⓣ210 321 9412. Handsomely decorated Indian restaurant, somewhat at odds with its grungey surroundings. The food is excellent – fresh and delicately spiced – and there's interesting taped music as well as the occasional live performance.
Palea Skala Lependiótou 25 near Leokoríou ⓣ210 32 12 677. Reasonably priced ouzerí with seating inside an old house and on a terrace in summer. Excellent *mezédhes* and wine to accompany the acoustic house band; generally packed and lots of fun. Tues–Sun dinner only till late.
To Souvlaki tou Psyrri Eskhýlou 14–16. Brightly-lit, busy spot serving inexpensive *souvláki*, grills and salads.
Taverna tou Psyrri Eskhýlou 12 ⓣ210 32 14 923. Some of the lowest prices and tastiest food in Psyrrí, so unsurprisingly popular. The menu is an unusual take on Greek classics, and is written in deliberately obscure Greek, so it may be easier to choose from the kitchen.
Zidhoron Táki 10, ⓣ210 32 15 368. A typical Psyrrí upscale *mezedhopolío*, painted bright yellow and in a great location offering a vantage point over the goings-on of the area. It serves tasty Middle Eastern-influenced foods like *pastourmás*, *haloúmi* and hummus, as well as Greek favourites such as baked feta, grilled peppers and baked aubergine.

Cafés

Krinos Eólou 87, behind the central market. Operating since 1922, though thanks to recent refurbishment the only signs of that are the old photos adorning the walls. Still popular for old-fashioned treats like *loukoumádhes* (doughnut-like puffs soaked in syrup) and *bougátsa* as well as sandwiches and ice creams.
Pagoto Mania Eisópou 21 cnr Táki, Psyrrí. Dozens of flavours of superb ice cream – an eight-year-old's heaven – as well as cakes, coffee and tea.
Start Café Platía Ayíon Anaryíron ⓣ210 32 18 285. It seems there's a café on every corner in Psyrrí, but this is one of the best. The building was once a *hamam*, and this provides the theme – *nargilehs* (hubble-bubble pipes) and floor cushions. Café by day and a chilled bar by night, with tables on the square and a summer roof terrace.

Thissío, Gázi and around

See map, p.125.

Restaurants, tavernas and ouzerís

Dirty Ginger Triptolémou 46, Gázi ⓣ210 34 23 809. Attracting a young crowd, *Dirty Ginger* is as much bar as restaurant, serving cocktails plus a tasty mixture of Greek and foreign food in a buzzy garden setting. Summer only, evenings and weekend lunchtimes.
Epistrofi stin Ithaki Iraklidhón 56, Thissío ⓣ210 34 72 964. Tiny, unpretentious place with just a couple of tables attached to an equally small organic food and craft shop, serving inexpensive organic *mezes*, including plenty of vegetarian choices. Mon–Sat 9am–9pm, Sun 1–9pm.
Filistron Apóstolou Pávlou 23, Thissío ⓣ210 34 22 897. Somewhat touristy, but worth it for the

roof terrace with great Acropolis view. Short menu of well-presented Greek food; good value given the location.

Mamacas Persefónis 41, Gázi ⓣ210 34 64 984. One of the restaurants that made Gázi fashionable, and still a favourite with the young, stylish and well-heeled. The white decor spreads through a house and across several terraces. Service can be slow, but the food – traditional Greek, *mezédhes*-style, with a modern twist – is reliably good. It's fairly pricey and doesn't get lively till late – some time after midnight, the DJs take over. Booking advised.

Meson el Mirador Ayisiláou 88, cnr Salamínos, Keramikós ⓣ210 34 20 007. Mexican restaurant in an elegant restored mansion. Makes a good effort at Mexican flavours and gets enjoyably rowdy later on. Closed Sun.

Pasta La Vista Voutádhon 58, Gázi ⓣ210 34 62 092. If you're after something simple to eat in Gázi, head here for inexpenzive pizza and pasta.

Pil Poul Apostólou Pávlou 51, cnr Poulopoúlou, Thissío ⓣ210 34 23 665. Fancy and expensive modern French/Mediterranean restaurant. The food is occasionally over-elaborate, but the roof terrace in this 1920s mansion offers immaculate Acropolis views in an incomparably romantic setting. There's a chilled-out bar/club (also Pil Poul) downstairs in the same building. Closed lunchtimes & Mon; booking essential.

Prosopa Konstantinoupóleos 84, Gázi ⓣ210 34 13 433. Very popular, somewhat upmarket restaurant serving excellent modern Mediterranean food – Greek with Italian and French influences. Tables are set out alongside the railway lines as well as indoors, in an area of Gázi with numerous gay clubs.

To Steki tou Ilia Eptahálkou 5, Thissío ⓣ210 34 58 052. Simple, inexpensive place on a pedestrianized street above the metro tracks that's so popular the owners have opened a second branch 200m further down (at Thessaloníkis 7). Renowned for some of the finest lamb chops in the city. Tables on the street in summer.

Stavlos Iraklidhón 10, Thissío ⓣ210 34 67 206, ⓦwww.stavlos.gr. Used as royal stables during the nineteenth century, Stavlos is now one of the area's more popular meeting points, with numerous seating areas including a large internal courtyard. Bar, gallery and club as well as an Italian-influenced restaurant. Mon–Thurs dinner only, Fri–Sun from midday.

Thalatta Vítonos 5, Gázi ⓣ210 34 64 204. A lovely, upmarket seafood restaurant (*Thalatta* means "sea" in Ancient Greek) with marine decor in a thoroughly unprepossessing location. Internal courtyard in summer. Closed lunchtimes & Sun.

Varoulko Pireós 80, Keramikós ⓣ210 52 28 400 ⓦwww.varoulko.gr. Chef Lefteris Lazarou earned a Michelin star for his restaurant in Pireás: the prices (€80 or more a head) reflect that and the new downtown location. When they come off, though, the elaborate and innovative seafood dishes are worth it, and the cool, modern setting includes a summer roof terrace with Acropolis views. Closed lunchtimes & Sun; booking essential.

Votanikos Steak House Kastoriás 34–36, Votanikós ⓣ210 34 80 000. Steaks, obviously, but also a broad menu of alternatives in this big, modern, brasserie-style place in the Athinaïs complex.

Cafés

Athinaion Politeia Akamántos 1 cnr Apóstolou Pávlou, Thissío. An enviable position in an old mansion, with great views from the terrace towards the Acropolis, make this a popular meeting place and a great spot to relax over a frappé. Light meals also served.

Kirki Apóstolou Pávlou 31, Thissío. Another café with a fabulous Acropolis view from its outdoor tables, serving good *mezédhes* as well as drinks and ice creams. Popular with the clientele of the late-night gay club (*Lizard*) upstairs.

Omónia and north: Platía Viktorías, Exárhia and Neápoli

See maps, p.88 & p.131.

Restaurants, tavernas and ouzerís

Ama Lakhi Kallidhromíou 69 or Methónis 66, Exárhia ⓣ210 38 45 978. A fine old mansion with a huge courtyard where tables are set out in summer: entry to the house from Kallidhromíou, to the courtyard from Methónis. The food is good-value, traditional taverna fare.

Andreas Themistokléous 18, Omónia ⓣ210 38 21 522. Like the *Athinaïkon* (below), a traditional ouzerí that's popular for long weekday lunches. Closed Sun.

Arkhaion Yefsis Kodhrátou 22, Metaxouryío ⓣ210 52 39 661, ⓦwww.arxaion.gr. The name means "ancient tastes" and this highly original restaurant claims to serve ancient Greek food, based on evidence from contemporary writings. It certainly makes for an enjoyable evening, in a lovely if slightly tacky setting with bare stone walls, statues, flaming torches and a courtyard. Dishes include wild boar cutlets and goat leg with mashed vegetables, cheese, garlic and honey (at €27 for two), as well as plenty of less meaty options.

Athinaïkon Themistokléous 2, cnr Panepistimíou, Omónia ☎210 38 38 485. Long-established, old-fashioned ouzerí with a huge variety of good-sized, mid-priced *mezédhes*: seafood – such as shrimp croquettes and mussels *saganáki* with cheese and peppers – is a speciality. Closed Sun & Aug.

Barba Yannis Emmanouíl Benáki 94, Exárhia ☎210 33 00 185. Popular neighbourhood treasure with a varied menu of home-style oven food (changes daily and displayed in large pots near entrance) in a relaxed atmosphere, aided and abetted by barrelled wine. Tables outside on pedestrianized street in summer. Open all day until the small hours.

Barbara's Food Company Emmanouíl Benáki 63-65, Exárhia ☎210 38 05 004. Colourful café-restaurant with wonderful salads and pasta dishes, plus daily specials from around the world, from meatballs to won-tons.

Erotokritos Kaníngos 3, Omónia. The streets around Omónia are full of small, fast-food lunch places serving sandwiches and kebabs. This is one such, with tables outside on a pedestrianized street.

Fasoli Emmanouíl Benáki 45, Exárhia ☎210 33 00 010. Fashionable, youthful *estiatório* with all-white decor, serving tasty modern Greek food.

Gonia Arahóvis 59, Exárhia. Mushroom *saganáki*, meatballs, spicy sausages and octopus are among the delights at this old-fashioned ouzerí near Platía Exarhíon.

Lefka Mavromiháli 121, Neápoli ☎210 36 14 038. Beloved old taverna with great *fáva* (hummus-like bean purée), black-eyed beans and baked and grilled meat with barrelled retsina. Summer seating in a huge garden enclosed by barrels. Closed Sun.

Lefteris Satovriándhou 20, Omónia ☎210 52 25 676. Very popular hole-in-the-wall *souvláki* place – eat standing up at high tables, or take away.

Mystic Pizza Emmanouíl Benáki 76, Exárhia ☎210 38 39 500. Tiny, unpretentious place serving pasta and salads as well as excellent, inexpensive pizzas. Takeaway and delivery service too.

Pinaleon Mavromiháli 152, Neápoli ☎210 64 40 945. A classic ouzerí-style establishment, serving rich *mezédhes* and meaty main courses, washed down with home-made wine, lovingly created by the chef/owner from Híos. Advance booking recommended. Open mid–Oct to early May only.

Rozalia Valtetsíou 58, Exárhia ☎210 33 02 933. Ever-popular, excellent-value *mezédhes*-plus-grill taverna, with renowned chicken and highly palatable barrelled wine. *Mezédhes* are ordered from the tray as the waiters thread their way through the throng; there's also a regular menu of grilled fish and meat. Garden seating in summer.

Steki tis Xanthis Irínis Athinéas 5, Neápoli ☎210 88 20 780. A delightful old mansion at the base of Stréfis Hill with a roof garden that offers fine views: approach from the hill, or up steep steps from Leofóros Alexandhrás. House specialities from a traditional menu include rabbit stew and schnitzel. Closed Sun.

Yiandes Valtetsíou 44, Exárhia ☎210 33 01 369. Modern and, for Exárhia, upmarket restaurant serving excellent food that's based on modern Greek cuisine with Asian influences. Pleasant courtyard next to the Riviera open-air cinema.

Cafés

Café Creperie Au Grand Zinc Emmanouíl Benáki 88, Exárhia. Cosy, quiet wood-lined interior makes a peaceful stop for coffee and crepes.

Crepexarhia Platía Exarhíon, Exárhia. Simple crêperie in a busy corner of the square, also serving coffee, sandwiches and ice cream.

Delphi Café Ayíou Konstandínou 27 below the *Delphi Art Hotel*, Omónia. A peaceful escape just a short way from Platía Omonías, with excellent coffee as well as hamburgers, omelettes, salads and sandwiches.

Áno Petrálona

See map, p.88.

Restaurants, tavernas and ouzerís

T'Askimopapo Iónon 61 ☎210 34 63 282. A wonderful taverna with *mezédhes* and unusual main dishes like meat in creamy sauces. Occasional live music. Closed Sun & mid-May to mid-Sept.

Chez Lucien Tróön 32 ☎210 34 64 236. Excellent French bistro with a short menu of authentic, well prepared dishes at reasonable prices; you may have to share a table. When busy (most of the time) there are two sittings, at 8 and 10.30pm. Tues–Sat dinner only.

Ikonomou Tróön 41, cnr Kydhantidhón ☎210 34 67 555. Wonderful, traditional taverna with home-cooked food served to packed pavement tables in summer. No menu, just a dozen or so inexpensive daily specials: check out what others are eating as the waiters may not know the names of some of the dishes in English. Closed Sun.

To Koutouki Lakíou 9 (reached from Filopáppou Bill, or by a tunnel under the main road) ☎210 34 53 655. Inexpensive traditional taverna with good *fáva* and grilled meat. Pleasantly rural atmosphere despite the proximity of the flyover, with no houses nearby and roof seating overlooking Filopáppou Hill. Closed Sun.

Santorinios Dhoriéon 8 ☎210 34 51 629. Unpretentious 'wine-taverna' whose main decoration is provided by vast barrels of Santorini wine. Wash it down with good *mezédhes* in the whitewashed courtyard.

Therapefterio Kydhantidhón 41 ☎210 34 12 538. The largest of a number of traditional tavernas near Ikonomou, also with pavement tables and excellent, inexpensive Greek dishes.

Koukáki and Makriyiánni

See map, p.88

Restaurants, tavernas and ouzerís

Ambrosia Dhrákou 3–5, Koukáki ☎210 92 20 281. A friendly *psistaría* (grill house) packed with locals, especially on summer nights when the tables spill out into the pedestrian walkway. Food is simple but delicious – succulent grilled chicken, pork chops, kebabs and Greek salads – and service friendly and attentive. Several other choices on this street.

Apanemia Erekthíou 2 and Veïkoú, Koukáki ☎210 92 28 766. Basic, inexpensive *mezedhopolío* with a wide selection of authentic *mezédhes* as well as good menu of Greek standards.

Edodi Veïkoú 80, Koukáki ☎210 92 13 013. Some say this is the finest restaurant in Athens, and if you want to splurge on exquisitely elaborate creations, this is the place. Starters such as lobster-tail with spinach or carpaccio of smoked goose go for €15–20, mains like sea bass with lavender or duck with cherries around €25; fancy desserts too. Before you choose, the waiter will display everything to you, raw. Booking essential. Closed Sun & all summer.

Strofi Robérto Gálli 25, Makriyiánni ☎210 92 14 130. A comfortable, old-fashioned taverna serving classic Greek dishes like *stifado*, lamb with aubergine, or chops. Higher-than-average prices, but worth it for the roof terrace with great Acropolis views.

Cafés

Diavlos Musiki Spiti Dhrákou 9, Koukáki. Music club by night, but by day a really welcoming café with Greek sweets and snacks.

Dionysos Zonar's Robérto Gálli 43, Makriyiánni ☎210 92 33 182. See map, p.125. Traditional upmarket patisserie relocated to a modern building. The unbeatable position opposite the Herodes Atticus Theatre is somewhat spoilt by being right above the main Acropolis coach park, and by the eye-watering prices. The complex also houses a pricey restaurant.

Pangráti

See map, p.88

Ilias Cnr Stasínou and Telesílis. A very good, popular taverna with a standard menu and wine from the barrel. Tables outside in summer. Dinner only.

Karavitis Arktínou 33, cnr Pafsaníou ☎210 75 15 155. Old-style taverna with barrelled wine, *mezédhes* and clay-cooked main courses. In summer there's outdoor seating in an enclosed garden. Dinner only.

Mikri Vouli Platía Varnáva 8 ☎210 75 65 523. Busy neighbourhood *mezedhopolío*, with tables out on the square in summer and excellent *meze*, including some unusual varieties. There are plenty of other places around the square.

Pinelopi kai Mnistires Ymittoú 130 on Platía Profíti Ilía ☎210 75 68 555. Lively and bustling, "Penelope and her Suitors" is a friendly, elegant place with no-nonsense Greek food and regular live music.

Spondi Pýrronos 5, just off Platía Varnáva ☎210 75 20 658, ⓦwww.spondi.gr. Long-time contender for the title of Athens' best restaurant, *Spondi* serves superb French-influenced cuisine, with fish a speciality. With starters – crab soup with ravioli scented with coriander, for example – from €25 and mains such as sea bass in fennel, olive oil and vanilla sauce or rabbit Provençal starting at €30 it's not cheap, but for a special occasion it's worth it. Dinner only; booking essential.

Vyrinis Arhimídhous 11 (off Platía Plastíra) ☎210 70 12 153. Classy, modern taverna, with prices slightly above average. Excellent house wine and a wide variety of interesting *mezédhes*. Tables in a garden courtyard in summer. Closed Sun.

Kolonáki

See map, p.131

Restaurants, tavernas and ouzerís

Altamira Tsákalof 36A ☎210 36 14 695. Multi-ethnic menu with Mexican, Indian, Asian and Arabic dishes – on the whole well done, and an interesting change from the usual Greek fare. The setting is lovely too, upstairs in an old mansion.

Dhimokritos Dhimokrítou 23 ☎210 36 13 588. Posh and perhaps a bit snooty – lots of suits at lunchtime – but a beautiful building and well-prepared, reasonably priced food from a vast menu, much of which is displayed in glass counters near the entrance. Closed Sun & late summer.

Filippou Xenokrátous 19 ☎210 72 16 390. This old-time taverna, a favourite of local office workers and residents, is liveliest at lunchtime – especially on Friday, when the street market is in full flow outside. Fresh food, moderately priced for the area, includes grills, stews and casseroles. Closed Sat lunch & Sun.

Ikio Ploútarhou 15 ☎210 72 59 216. The name means "homely", and that seems to be how the locals find it – a busy, reasonably priced neighbourhood restaurant with a slightly modern take on Greek classics and a short menu of daily specials, plus pasta and salads.

Il Postino Grivéon 3, in alleyway off Skoufá ☎210 36 41 414. Good-value modern Italian trattoria, serving freshly made pasta and simple Italian dishes in a friendly, bustling room.

Jackson Hall Milióni 4 ☎210 36 16 098. A very Kolonáki type of place; a big, busy, expensive American-themed diner – burgers, pasta, salads and the like – with a music bar upstairs.

To Kioupi Platía Kolonakíou 4 ☎210 36 14 033. Budget subterranean taverna with good, standard Greek fare such as moussaka and stuffed vine leaves. Closed Sun & Aug.

To Kotopoulo Platía Kolonakíou, north side. As the name indicates, this tiny hole-in-the-wall is the place for chicken – juicy, crispy, rotisserie-style. It's strictly no-frills, lit by fluorescent lights and packed with people at all hours. A few tables on the pavement too, or take away to eat in the nearby National Gardens or on the slopes of Lykavitós. Closed Sun.

Orizontes Lycavitou summit of Lykavitós Hill ☎210 72 10 701. Fabulous views from this glassed-in eyrie, or from its sheltered terrace. The prices are just as elevated, however, and the complex dishes (sea bass with green tagliatelle and moscato wine sauce with peanuts, for example, at around €30) don't always live up to their promise.

Ouzerí Kleoménous 22. Nameless, simply furnished and very inexpensive ouzerí with salads and sandwiches as well as good, plain *mezédhes*.

Cafés

Da Capo Tsákalof 1. One of the most popular of the many establishments on this pedestrianized street, just north of Kolonáki square. *Da Capo* is very chic and, unusually, self-service.

Filion Skoufá 34. A local institution for coffee, cakes, omelettes, salads and breakfast: busy at all times of day with a more sober crowd than the average Kolonáki café.

Pireás, Glyfádha and the coast

Restaurants, tavernas and ouzerís

Akhinos Aktí Themistokléous 51, Pireás ☎210 45 26 944. See map, p.135. Wonderful seafood and traditional Greek specialities served on a covered terrace overlooking a small beach just round the corner from the Naval Museum. Pricey if you go for the fish, but less so than harbourfront alternatives. Book at weekends.

Akti Possidhónos 6, Vouliagméni ☎210 89 60 448. On the main road just beyond the Vouliagméni peninsula, with waterfront tables and great views, this is a top-class fish taverna. Fish is expensive and so is Vouliagméni; by those standards €50–60 for a fish or lobster main course is reasonable value. Waterfront tables are very heavily in demand; booking essential.

Ammos Aktí Koumoundhoúrou 44, Mikrolímano, Pireás ☎210 42 24 633. See map, p.135. In contrast to the high-luxe places around it, *Ammos* goes for an island feel, with hand-painted tables and beach scenes. Still mainly fish, but a wide variety of *mezes* and slightly lower prices and a younger crowd than its neighbours.

Artisti Thalassa Aktí Koumoundhoúrou 38, Mikrolímano, Pireás ☎210 41 73 087. See map, p.135. Excellent, glamorous and inevitably expensive fish taverna; among the best of the harbourside places on Mikrolímano.

Buffalo Bill's Kýprou 13, Glyfádha ☎210 89 43 128. Get into the Glyfádha mood at this lively, atmospheric Tex-Mex joint. As you'd expect, tacos, steaks, chilli, and margaritas by the jugful. Dinner only; also lunch Sun.

George's Steak House Konstantinoupoléos 4, Glyfádha ☎210 89 46 020. Despite the name this is a fairly traditional Greek grill-house, large, reasonably priced and very popular. Located on a side street crowded with restaurants close to the main Platía Katráki tram stop. Excellent lamb chops and meatballs.

Island Limanakia Vouliagménis; km27 on Athens–Soúnio road between Vouliagméni and Várkiza ☎210 96 53 563. Beautiful bar /restaurant/club with a breathtaking clifftop setting; very chic and not as expensive as you might expect at €15–25 for a main course. Modern Mediterranean food and tapas lounge. Summer eves only 9.30pm–late (club from 11pm); booking is essential, especially at weekends.

Vincenzo Yiannitsopoúlou 1, Platía Espéridhon, Glyfádha ☎210 89 41 310. Good, reasonably priced Italian fare, including excellent pizzas from a wood oven.

Yevsis En Elladhi Marángou 4, Glyfádha ☎210 89 44 580. Simple, inexpensive but very good plain Greek food – *souvláki*, stuffed tomatoes and the like.

Cafés

Cosi Zissimopoúlo 12, Glyfádha. One of a host of packed, glam, upmarket café-bars on this street just off the main shopping drag in the heart of Glyfádha.

Filoxenia Aktí Tsélegi 4, Pireás. See map, p.135. Less manic than most around the port, with tables outside on a pedestrianized part of the waterfront just off Platía Karaïskáki, this café serves breakfast and light meals throughout the day.

Pagoto Mania Konstantinoupoléos 5, Glyfádha. As with the Psyrrí branch, wonderful ice cream in a huge variety of flavours, plus all the usual café fare.

Kifissiá

Restaurants, tavernas and ouzerís

Dos Hermanos, Kyriazí 24 ☎210 80 87 906. Decent Mexican food and tasty margaritas in a lively, late-opening bar-restaurant. Closed Mon.

Monippo Dhrosíni 12 ☎210 62 31 440. Wide range of *mezédhes* from all over Greece and smart, modern decor make this a typical Kifissiá hangout. Better value than most, though, and often has music on Fri and Sat nights.

Tesseres Epohes Platía Ayíou Dhimitríou 13 ☎210 80 18 233. The "Four Seasons" is an attractive bar-*mezedhopolío* where you can enjoy *mezédhes*, drinks, snacks and, on Thur to Sat evenings, excellent, unamplified live Greek music.

Cafés

Várson Kassavéti 5. This huge, old-fashioned café/patisserie is an Athens institution. Home-made yoghurts, jams and sticky cakes to take away or to enjoy with a coffee in the cavernous interior or in a quiet courtyard out back.

Entertainment, music and nightlife

When it comes to entertainment and nightlife, Athens is a very different place in winter than in summer. Perhaps surprisingly, to see the best live traditional **Greek music** you have to visit during the winter months, as in summer many musicians head off to tour the countryside and islands. This winter period – from around October to May – is also when the major **classical music**, **ballet** and **drama** performances are staged, and the **sporting** calendar is at its busiest. On the other hand, summer is the **festival** season. Most significant is the June-to-September **Hellenic Festival** of dance, music and ancient drama, but there

Listings information

Sources of information on **what's on** in English are somewhat limited. There are some listings in a number of free monthly or weekly publications distributed to hotels, but these are partial and not always accurate; better are the weekly *Athens News* (published Friday; www.athensnews.gr), with full movie lisitings and coverage of most major events, or the daily local edition of the *International Herald Tribune*. Much more exhaustive listings including music, clubs, restaurants and bars, but in Greek only, can be found in local weeklies *Athinorama* and *Exodos*. All of the above can be bought at kiosks anywhere in the city: look out too for the free weekly *Athens Voice* (again, Greek only), copies of which can be picked up in galleries, record shops and the like. Specialist record shops (see p.154) are also good sources of information in themselves, frequently displaying posters and selling tickets for rock, jazz or festival concerts.

are also annual rock, jazz and blues events, while you may see big international bands at one of the major outdoor venues.

More everyday nightlife in the form of **bars and clubs** shows a similar divide as, in summer, venues move out of the city centre to escape the heat and into temporary homes in the coastal suburbs.

Whatever time of year, most gigs start late – there's little point in arriving much before 10.30pm – and continue until 3 or 4am.

Traditional music

For an introduction to Greek **traditional** and **folk music** see Contexts, p.937.

Sto Baraki Tou Vassili Dhidhótou 3, Kolonáki ⓣ210 36 23 625, www.tobaraki.gr. Daily acoustic performances: a showcase for up-and-coming rebétika acts and popular singer-songwriters. Entry around €15, includes first drink.

Diavlos Musiki Spiti Dhrákou 9, Koukáki ⓣ210 92 39 588. Owned by popular singer Yiannis Glezos, who sometimes performs. Music ranges from rebétika to pop, with well-known singers often on the bill. Cover charge includes one drink. Thur night tango lessons are followed by open dancing. Wed–Sun; closed May–Sept.

Elatos Trítis Septemvríou 16, Omónia ⓣ210 52 34 262. An eclectic assortment of *dhimotiká* in this traditional, downtown basement club. Closed Wed.

Gazi Ierofándos 9 at Piréós, Roúf ⓣ210 34 74 477. Big *bouzoúki* club (glitzy modern Greek music) in an up-and-coming industrial area just down from Gázi – as a result attracts a younger crowd than some.

Laba Víktoros Ougó 22, cnr Akominátou, Metaxouryío ⓣ210 52 28 188. Big, central rebétika place that can attract big names. Drinks €10.

Perivoli T'Ouranou Lysikrátous 19, Pláka ⓣ210 32 25 558. Traditional rebétika club on the edge of Pláka (so used to tourists) with regular appearances by classy performer Babis Tsertsos. Closed Wed & summer.

Rebetikí Istoría Ippokrátous 181, Neápoli ⓣ210 64 24 937. A lovely old house with traditional rebétika sounds from a good company. Drinks from €6 and some tasty cold and hot dishes. Closed Wed & July–Aug.

Stoa Athanaton Sofokléous 19, in the meat market ⓣ210 32 14 362. Fronted by *bouzoúki* veterans Hondronakos and company. Good taverna food at reasonable prices but expensive drinks. Open 3–6pm & midnight–6am; closed Sun & May–Aug.

Rock, Jazz and Latin

The indigenous Greek **rock scene** is small but manages to support a number of local bands, while Athenian rock enthusiasts tend to be knowledgeable to the point of obsession. Major international bands generally appear in the summer to play open-air venues, either as part of the official Athens Festival or for other events that rarely seem to survive from year to year. For rock bars, clubs and record shops, Exárhia is the place to be. **Jazz** has only a small following in Greece, but there are still some good clubs that can attract touring bands of international repute. The major events take place as part of the **Jazz and Blues Festival** at the end of June; information and tickets are available from the Hellenic Festival box office (see p.151) and some record stores. **Latin** and other **world music** styles are also low-profile, but increasing in popularity.

After Dark Dhiodótou 31 & Ippokrátous, Exárhia ⓣ210 36 06 460. Rock, blues and soul, plus the occasional live performance by Greek indie bands to a young crowd. From 10pm. €5 entry.

Alabastron Dhamaréos 78, Pangráti, near Platía Profítis Ilías ⓣ210 75 60 102. Excellent atmosphere and live performances of a wide variety of music, from trad jazz to African and Latin. Closed summer.

An Club Solomoú 13–15, Exárhia ⓣ210 33 05 056. Basement club featuring live performances by local and lesser-known foreign rock bands.

Gagarin 205 Liossíon 205, near Metro Attikís ⓣ210 85 47 601, ⓦwww.gagarin205.gr. Probably the finest venue for live rock in Athens, where some 2000 fans can crowd in to see the best touring indie bands as well as local talent and club nights. In summer, the action moves down to Fáliro, on the coast, and *Gagarin on the Beach*.

Half-Note Trivonianoú 17, Mets ⓣ210 92 13 310. Athens' premier jazz club, with live jazz most nights and frequent big-name touring performers. Closed Tues & for much of the summer.

Palenque Farandáton 41, near Platía Ay. Thomá, Ambelókipi ⓣ210 64 87 748, ⓦwww.palenque.gr. Live Latin music by South American groups, salsa parties, flamenco music and dance lessons.

Parafono Asklipíou 130A, Neápoli ⓣ210 64 46 512, ⓦwww.parafono.gr. Excellent jazz and blues – mainly local groups – in a congenial, small cabaret-style club.

Rodeo Live Club Héyden 34, Platía Viktorías ⓣ210 88 14 702. Live rock bands and a friendly, alternative crowd.

Stavros tou Notou Tharípou 37, Néos Kósmos ⓣ210 92 26 975. One of the liveliest rock clubs in town, mostly featuring Greek artists, but plenty of touring foreigners too.

Bars and clubs

Athens has a huge array of **clubs**, few of which really start to warm up until after midnight, though some operate as quieter bars in the earlier evening; many close on Mondays, and all are busiest from Thursday to Saturday. There's every variety of music from trance to hip-hop (though little that's too far from the mainstream), but it pays to expect the unexpected: don't be surprised if the sound shifts to Greek or belly-dancing music towards the end of the night. In the city centre, the most vibrant nightlife is in and around Psyrrí, Gázi and Thissío, though there are clubs almost everywhere. As in any big city, venues come and go quickly, so it's worth asking around – especially at specialist record stores – or checking listings magazines and posters. Some central Athens air-conditioned clubs remain open year round, but in **summer** the scene really moves out to the long stretch of coast from Fáliro to Várkiza, where huge temporary clubs operate on and around the beaches. If you head out, bear in mind that the taxi fare will be just one of several hefty bills, although admission prices usually include a free drink. With drinks available at any café, and many cafés effectively becoming bars in the evenings, there aren't many simple **bars** as such in Athens. You can have a drink at almost any of the places in these music or club listings, but a few bars that are simply good places to meet, or to catch a football game on a big screen, are also included.

45° Mires Iákhou 18, cnr Voutádhon, Gázi ⓣ210 34 72 729. A big, lively, rock-music based bar/club with a rooftop terrace in summer.

Arodou Miaoúli 22, cnr Protoyénous, Psyrrí ⓣ210 32 16 774. Miaoúli, leading up from the metro into Psyrrí, is packed with bars and crowded with people every evening. *Arodou* is right at the heart – a big place with plenty of space both outside and in. Not fancy at all, but a good place to meet up before moving on, with decent food also available.

Astron Táki 3, Psyrrí ⓣ697 74 69 356. One of Psyrrí's busiest bars – partly because it's so small – which gets really packed when the guest DJs crank it up later on; electric techno and minimal sounds.

Baila Háritos 43, Kolonáki ⓣ210 72 33 019. "Freestyle" sounds in this busy Kolonáki club, where an adjoining café-bar (*City*) offers a quieter alternative and outdoor tables.

Bios Pireós 84, Gázi ⓣ210 34 25 335. Arty club (set among studios, with frequent exhibitions of its own) with late-night avant-garde sounds. Open as a café by day.

Brettos Kydhathinéon 41, Pláka ⓣ210 32 32 110. By day a store selling mainly the products of their own family distillery, at night *Brettos* is one of the few bars in Pláka. It's a simple, unpretentious place with barrels along one wall and a huge range of bottles, backlit at night, along another.

Craft Leofóros Alexándhras 205, Ambelókipi (by Metro Ambelókipi) ⓣ210 64 62 350. Vast, modern microbrewery bar with half a dozen styles of in-house draught beer available in jugs, and giant-screen TVs for entertainment.

Cubanita Karaïskáki 28, Psyrrí ⓣ210 33 14 605. Enjoyable Cuban-themed bar, with plenty of rum-based drinks, Cuban food and Latin music, occasionally live, till the early hours.

Envy Paralía Ayíou Kosmá, right by Áyios Kósmas beach ⓣ210 98 52 994. Huge complex right on the shore with café, restaurant and palm trees to complement the party-atmosphere club. Regular sunset parties and Greek nights make this typical of the slicker summer beach clubs.

Island km27 on Athens-Soúnio road between Vouliagméni and Várkiza ⓣ210 96 53 563. Stunning clifftop setting attracts a chic, stylish crowd. One way to be sure of making it past the queue and the bouncers is to book into the restaurant (see p.147).

Luv Asomáton 1, Platía Thissíou ⓣ210 32 24 553. Big mainstream dance club with DJ guest nights and a young crowd.

Mike's Irish Bar Sinópis 6, Ambelókipi ⓣ210 77 76 797. In the shadow of the Athens Tower, a huge American-style basement bar with a young crowd and big screens for sporting events. Karaoke on Mon and Tues, live music most weekends.

Mommy Dhelfón 4A, in an alley off Skoúfa, Kolonáki ⓣ210 36 19 682. Fashionable watering-hole for thirty-somethings, where soulful house is pumped out by resident DJs.

Moresko Aristophánous 17, Psyrrí ⓣ210 32 41 249. Moorish theme complete with belly dancers most nights in this ultra-cool, elegant club.

Soul Evripídhou 65, Psyrrí ⓣ210 33 10 907. Laid-back, popular upstairs cocktail bar (also serving Thai-influenced food), alternative sounds.

Space by Avli Iraklidhón 14, Thissío. In the heart of the Thissío bar area, this daytime café-bar on three floors evolves at night into a funky club with jazz and soul music.

Tapas Bar Triptolémou 44, Gázi ⓣ210 34 71 844. Despite the name you won't find many people eating the tapas here, but it's busy and buzzy till the early hours, handy for the Gázi clubs with good cocktails and a pleasant outdoor space. Closed Sun.

Venti Lepeniótou 20, Psyrrí ⓣ210 32 54 504. Elegant, upmarket bar/club/restaurant around a courtyard with opening glass roof. Dance music after midnight.

Gay and lesbian venues

Athens' **gay scene** is mostly very discreet, but the city has its share of established clubs. Gázi is the hot new area for bars and clubs, and some of the older places have moved down here: the area of Makriyiánni and Koukáki off Syngroú is home to some longer-established alternatives. For further information, check the gay sections in the listings magazines, buy the annual *Greek Gay Guide* (€16 from many kiosks), or check out the excellent website ⓦwww.gaygreece.gr.

Alekos Island Sarrí 41, Psyrrí. Alekos is one of Athens' more colourful bartenders, and his long-established, easy-going bar has moved down from Kolonáki to this more lively location near Metro Thissío. Low-key atmosphere and rock/pop music. Open nightly, year-round.

Blue Train Konstantinoupóleos 84, Gázi ⓣ210 34 60 677. Open from early evening, this is a popular gay meeting place before going on to the clubs, with a courtyard in summer. Upstairs, *Kazarma* (same phone) is one of the better clubs you could go on to, with dance music, laser shows and giant screens.

Granazi Lembési 20, Makriyiánni ⓣ210 92 13 054, ⓦwww.granazi.gr. Handy for Metro Akrópoli, a chilled bar with videos and quiet music early on, getting louder as the night progresses. Mostly Greek music, shows at weekends.

Koukles Zan Moreás 3, just off Syngroú, Koukáki ⓣ210 92 48 989. The name means "dolls" and the drag acts are said to be the best in Athens. Wed–Sun.

Noiz Konstantinoupóleos 70, Gázi ☎210 34 24 771. Lesbian bar-club with good international sounds and welcoming atmosphere. Open daily.

Sodade Triptolémou 10, Gázi ☎210 34 68 657 Ⓦwww.sodade.gr. Both lesbian- and gay-friendly, with a stylish crowd and great music – one room plays Greek and mainstream, the other quality dance music. Daily 11pm–3.30am.

Theatre, dance and classical music

Unless your Greek is fluent, the contemporary **Greek theatre** scene is likely to be inaccessible. As with Greek music, it is essentially a winter pursuit. **Dance** is easier to get to grips with and includes a fine show of traditional Greek dance by the **Dora Stratou Ethnic Dance Company** in their own open-air theatre at Arakínthou and Voutié on Filopáppou Hill (☎210 32 44 395 or 92 14 650; Ⓦwww.grdance.org). They combine traditional music, fine choreography and gorgeous costumes for an experience you'd be hard put to encounter in many years' travelling around Greece. Performances are held Tuesday to Saturday at 9.30pm, Sunday at 8.15pm from late May to late September. To reach the theatre, follow Dhionysíou Areopayítou along the south flank of the Acropolis, until you see the signs. Tickets (€15) can almost always be picked up at the door. Somewhat pricey snacks are on offer.

In the winter months, you may also be able to catch **opera** from the Greek National Opera Lyrikí Skiní, in the Olympia Theatre at Akadhimías 59 (Ⓦwww.nationalopera.gr) and also **classical events** either in the Mégaro Mousikís concert hall on Leofóros Vassilísis Sofías next to the US embassy (☎210 72 82 333, Metro Mégaro Mousikís), or at the Filippos Nakas Concert Hall, at Ippokrátous 41.

Film

Athens is a great place to catch a movie. In summer dozens of **outdoor** screens spring up in every neighbourhood of the city for a quintessentially

The Hellenic Festival

The annual **Hellenic Festival** encompasses a broad spectrum of cultural events: most famously **ancient Greek theatre** (performed, in modern Greek, at the Herodes Atticus Theatre on the South Slope of the Acropolis), but also modern theatre, traditional and contemporary dance, classical music, jazz, traditional Greek music and even a smattering of rock shows. The **Herodes Atticus Theatre** (see p.105) is a memorable place to watch a performance on a warm summer's evening – although you should avoid the cheapest seats, unless you bring along a pair of binoculars and a cushion. Other festival venues include the open-air **Lykavitós Theatre** on Lykavitós Hill, and the two ancient theatres at **Epidaurus** (see p.191). For the latter, you can buy inclusive trips from Athens from the festival box office, either by coach or boat – the two-hour boat trip includes dinner on board on the way home.

Performances are scheduled from late May right through to early October, although the exact dates vary each year. If you can, it's worth **booking** in advance (credit card bookings on ☎210 32 72 000 and at Ⓦwww.greekfestival.gr); tickets go on sale three weeks before the event at the box office. As well as online, **programmes** are available from tourist offices or from the **festival box office** in the arcade at Panepistimíou 39, downtown (Mon–Fri 8.30am–4pm, Sat 9am–2pm). There are also box offices at the Herodes Atticus Theatre (daily 9am–2pm and 5–8pm) and Epidaurus (Mon–Thurs 9am–2pm and 5–8pm, Fri & Sat 9.30am–9.30pm) for events at those venues only.

Greek film-going experience. There are also plenty of regular indoor cinemas, including a number in the centre, though a significant proportion of these, with no air-conditioning, close from mid-May to October. **Admission**, whether at indoor or outdoor venues, is reasonable: €6–7 for outdoor screenings, €7–8 for first-run fare at a midtown theatre. Films are almost always shown in the original language with Greek **subtitles** (a good way to increase your vocabulary, though remember that the original language may not be English). There are good listings in the *Athens News*, as well as all the Greek listings magazines.

The summer **outdoor screens** tend not to show brand-new films, or at least not mainstream ones, but they do have repeats of recent hits, new art-house and alternative offerings, classics and themed festival seasons. To attend simply for the film is to miss much of the point. You may in any case never hear the soundtrack above the din of Greeks cracking *passatémpo* (pumpkin seeds), drinking and chatting (sit near a speaker if you want to hear). Snack-bars serve sandwiches, popcorn, pizza, beer and wine. The first screening is usually at around 9pm early in the summer and 8.30pm later in the summer; at late screenings (usually 11pm), the sound is turned right down, so as not to disturb local residents. Among the most central and reliable **outdoor venues** are Cine Pari, Kydhathinéon 22, Pláka (☎210 32 22 071), a rooftop setting with a side view of the Acropolis; Thission, Apostólou Pávlou 7 in Thissío (☎210 34 20 864), another with an Acropolis view; Psyrrí, Sarrí 40-44, Psyrrí (☎210 32 47 234); Zefyros, Tróön 36 in Áno Petrálona (☎210 34 62 677), newly done up and a particular favourite; and Vox, Themistokléous 82 (☎210 33 01 020), and Riviera, Valtetsíou 46 (☎210 38 37 716), both in Exárhia.

Markets and shops

Shopping in Athens is decidedly schizophrenic. On the one hand the **bazaar area** is an extraordinary jumble of little specialist shops and stalls, while almost every neighbourhood still hosts a weekly **street market**. On the other, the upmarket shopping areas of the city centre, and the **malls** and fashion emporia of the ritzier suburbs, are as glossy and expensive as any in Europe. Somewhere between the extremes, in the city centre you'll find endless *stoas*, covered arcades off the main streets full of little shops. Some have been expensively refurbished and house cafés and designer-label stores; most, though, are a little dilapidated, and many still specialize in a single product – books here, computer equipment there, spectacles in another.

Even on a purely visual level, the **central bazaar** and nearby flower market (p.119) are well worth a visit, while the surrounding streets, especially Evripídhou, are full of wonderfully aromatic little shops selling herbs and nuts, and others concentrating on supplies for a peasant way of life that seems entirely at odds with modern Athens – rope, corks, bottles and preserving jars. The so-called **Monastiráki flea market** is, most of the time, no such thing – simply a continuation of the touristy shops you'll find lining Adhrianoú in Pláka. However, between Monastiráki and Thissío metro stations there are a few interesting, alternative stalls, while on Sunday mornings, from around 6am until 2pm, you will find authentic Greek junk (used phone cards and the like) spread out on the pavements, especially along the metro lines towards the Thissío end of Adhrianoú.

Among the best and most central **street markets** are: Mondays, Hánsen in Patissíon (Metro Áyios Eleftheríos); Tuesdays, Lésvou in Kypséli (Metro

Viktorías) and Láskou in Pangráti (trolley #2 or #11); Fridays Xenokrátous in Kolonáki, Dhragoúmi in Ilísia (Metro Evangelismós/Mégaro Mousikís), Tsámi Karatássou in Koukáki (Metro Akrópoli) and Arhimídhous in Mets, behind the Panathenaic Stadium; and on Saturdays Plakendías in Ambelókipi (Metro Ambelókipi) and Kallidhromíou in Exárhia. Usually running from 7am to 2pm, these are inexpensive and enjoyable, selling household items and dry goods, as well as fresh fruit and vegetables, dried herbs and nuts.

Handicrafts, antiques and gifts

Greek **handicrafts** are not particularly cheap but the standard of workmanship is usually very high. In addition to the stores listed below, several **museums** have excellent shops, including the National Archeological Museum, Benáki Museum and Cycladic Art Museum, which sell original designs as well as reproduction artworks.

Amorgos Kódhrou 3, Pláka (across from the *Acropolis House Hotel*). A small, old-fashioned shop filled with an eclectic collection of tasteful woodcarvings, needlework, lamps, lace, shadow puppets and other handicrafts.

Elliniko Spiti Kekropós 14, just off Adhrianoú, Pláka. Amazing artworks and pieces of furniture created from found materials, especially driftwood but also metal and marble. Probably too big to take home (for your wallet as well as your suitcase), but well worth a look.

Kendro Ellinikis Paradosis entrances at Mitropóleos 59 and Pandhróssou 36, Monastiráki. As the name, "Centre of Hellenic Tradition", suggests, this emporium has a wide selection of traditional arts and crafts, especially ceramics and woodcarving, with mercifully little of the hard sell often encountered in the nearby flea market.

Kori Mitropóleos 13 and Voúlis, Sýndagma. Very high-standard jewellery and crafts in silver, gold and ceramic with prices to match.

Studio Kostas Sokaras Adhrianoú 25, Monastiráki. Overlooking the Stoa of Attalos, this place is packed with a wonderful jumble of antiques and curiosities, including old shadow puppets, brass doorknobs, musical instruments, pistols and more.

Theotokis Normánou 7, Monastiráki. One of a number of quirky antique/junk shops in this narrow street in the Flea Market. Prints, posters, postcards, old radios, typewriters, military uniforms: if you are looking for something specific it's amazing what they can find among their stock.

Yiannis Samouelian Iféstou 36, Monastiráki. Long-established musical instrument shop in the heart of the Monastiráki flea market, selling hand-made guitars, *lyra* and the like.

Fashion and jewellery

Greeks love to shop, for **clothes** above all. On the whole it's familiar international labels you'll find here, in the main shopping area of **Ermoú** below Sýndagma, and in the dozens of malls in the suburbs. For high fashion, however, there's only one place to be, and that's **Kolonáki**, where wandering the narrow streets around the Platía will reward you with dozens of small boutiques. For something a little more alternative, wander over into adjoining **Exárhia**. If you do want to sample the suburban malls, probably the most authentic Athens shopping experience of all, then head for upmarket **Kifissiá**, where you'll find branches of Chanel and Gucci among the High Street labels, or the younger atmosphere of beachside **Glyfádha**.

Archipelagos Adhrianoú 142, Pláka. A small, inviting boutique with exquisite handmade jewellery and ceramics with a Greek theme.

Athena's Sandals Normánou 7 Ⓦwww.melissinos-sandals.gr. Stavros Melissinos, the "poet sandal-maker", was an Athens institution, numbering The Beatles, Anthony Quinn and Sophia Loren amongst his celebrity clients. Now retired, his daughter carries on his tradition, with interesting leather-work of all kinds alongside the sandals.

Attica Panepistimíou 9, Sýndagma. Athens' only fashion department store, with the finest window displays in the city. Convenient if you want to do everything under one roof, especially in the summer when it's hot, though the designer labels include nothing you wouldn't find at home.

Crop Circle Themistokléous 52 & 66, Exárhia. Reasonably priced vintage clothing and ethnic jewellery. The branch higher up the hill sells new stock, the lower one vintage.

Elena Votsi Xanthoú 7, Kolonáki. Home to Elena's innovative jewellery, which incorporates precious and semi-precious stones as well as shells and other materials.

Eleni Marneri Agathoupóleos 3, Kypséli (off 28 Oktovríou, north of Metro Viktorías). A beautiful contemporary jewellery shop whose decor reflects the innovative style of the various designers. Occasional exhibitions.

Free Shop Voukourestíou 50, Kolonáki. Upmarket contemporary boutique with own-label clothes, as well as up-and-coming Greek designers and international stalwarts like Balenciaga.

Ice Cube Tsakálof 28, Kolonáki. Beautiful designer boutique whose avant-garde designs are a breath of fresh air. Attracts a young but deep-pocketed crowd. Also in Glyfádha.

Lemisios Lykavitoú 6, Kolonáki. In business since 1912, Lemisios mainly make leather sandals and ballet flats of a much better quality than the tourist versions on sale in Pláka and Monastiráki. They even do custom-made if you can wait two weeks: take material along with you and they will make shoes up with it.

Mariana Petridi Háritos 34, Kolonáki. A showcase for Greek jewellery designers with varying styles, as well as work by Mariana Petridi herself.

Remember Adhrianoú 79, Pláka. Dimitris Tsouanato's shop has been around for 25 years but never seems to run out of inspiration: if there is one piece of clothing you should buy in Athens it's one of his hand-painted T-shirts. Also stocks rock memorabilia and has some amazing sculptures in the courtyard.

Shop Ermoú 112A, Psyrrí. Largest of a number of fashionable post-modern stores at the Psyrrí end of Ermoú, Shop deals in fashion labels including Custo, Energie and Miss Sixty as well as gifts, books, toys and music.

Le Streghe son Tornate Háritos 9, Kolonáki. One of the few vintage-clothes shops in Athens: mainly designer and top-end clothing, though, so few bargains.

Thallo Ploútarhou 25, Kolonáki. Small jewellery shop that's well worth a visit. Greek plants and flowers are coated in silver and gold to gorgeous effect and the prices are among the least intimidating in Kolonáki.

2morrow Kynéttou 3, Monastiráki, in the Flea Market. Yota Kayaba sells her designs on the first floor of the building where she also creates them. A small collection of interesting vintage and ethnic clothes too.

Food and drink

Aristokratikon Servías 9, Sýndagma. An old Athenian favourite for traditional Greek chocolates; try the chocolate-covered prunes. Also much-coveted pistachios, sugared almonds and sour cherry jam. A token from here is always welcome when visiting someone's home.

Bachar Evripídhou 31, central bazaar. A shop from another age: grains, seeds, candles, aromatic bags of teas, herbs and medicinal remedies doled out from vast sacks.

Biologicos Kyklos Skoufá 52, Kolonáki. Organic minimarket with fruit and veg, juice, yoghurt, cheese and wine as well as vitamins and essential oils.

Brettos Kydhathinéon 41, Pláka. A liquor store by day, bar by night. Sells mainly traditional products from the family distillery.

Elixirion Evripídhou 41, central bazaar. Soap, honey, pumice, herbs, cinnamon sticks and much more sold from a store with magnificent original fittings.

Eteria Hatzidhimia Evripídhou 32, central bazaar. Wonderfully old-fashioned liquor store with dozens of types of ouzo, brandies and wines.

Ikologi Elladas Panepistimíou 57, Omónia. Freshly-squeezed juices and vegetarian and organic foods to eat in or take away, plus a big health-food supermarket with alternative medicine practitioners in-store.

Lesvos Athinás 33, central bazaar. Very different from the traditional shops around the nearby market, this glossy and somewhat touristy deli sells high-quality wine, honey, preserves and olive oil as well as bread, cheese and deli meats.

Books, records and CDs

You'll find mainstream music stores in any of the main shopping areas; below are listings for places to explore Greek sounds, as well as classic vinyl (there are dozens of specialist stores, especially in Exárhia). Also listed are the main places to buy English-language books; again, studenty Exárhia is best for Greek texts.

7+7 Iféstou 7, Monastiráki. A choice selection of old and new rock and Greek music on vinyl and CD. This alley in the Flea Market has several other record and second-hand bookstores.

Art Nouveau Solomoú 23, Exárhia. Amazing collection of classic vinyl, new and secondhand. Mostly traditional rock, but also 1960s soul and all sorts of other gems.

Compendium Nikodhímou 5, cnr Iperídhou, Pláka. Long-established English-language bookshop: small secondhand section, noticeboards for travellers and residents, and regular poetry readings and other events.

Eleftheroudhakis Panepistimíou 17, Sýndagma. Five floors of books, with plenty in English; there's also an Internet café and an excellent café with a large selection of vegetarian dishes and sweets. Smaller branches at Níkis 20, Pláka, and in the basement beneath Starbucks, on Platía Mitropóleos.

Music Wave Iféstou 29, Monastiráki. Another excellent place for a rummage in the Flea Market.

Road Editions Sólonos 71, Exárhia. A good mix of English and Greek travel guides, plus maps.

Stoa tou Bibliou entered from Panepistimíou 49 or Pesmazogloú 5. A quiet arcade (or *stoa*) devoted entirely to books, with seating areas and frequent exhibitions. Almost all in Greek, but still worth a look – a couple of antiquarian dealers have old maps.

Xylouris Panepistimíou 39, Omónia, in Stoa Pesmazogloú. Run by the widow of the late, great Cretan singer Nikos Xylouris, this is currently one of the best places for finding Greek pop, folk and Cretan music.

Listings

Airlines Aegean ⓣ210 35 34 289, reservations ⓣ801 11 20 000; British Airways ⓣ210 35 30 453, reservations ⓣ801 11 56 000; Delta ⓣ800 44 12 9506; easyJet ⓣ210 35 30 300; Olympic, ticket office at Fillelínon 15 ⓣ210 92 67 555, main office at Syngroú 96 ⓣ210 92 69 111, reservations ⓣ801 11 44 444; Singapore Airlines ⓣ210 37 28 000; Swiss ⓣ210 61 75 320; Thai ⓣ210 96 92 012.

Airport enquiries For flight arrivals and departures, and all other airport information ⓣ210 35 30 000.

Banks and currency exchange Normal banking hours are Mon–Thurs 8am–2.30pm and Fri 8am–2pm and just about all banks can exchange money during those hours; several banks with longer hours can be found around Sýndagma, plus there are numerous currency exchange places (generally with worse rates) in Pláka and around Sýndagma, and hotels will change money at a worse rate still. Almost every bank in the centre has an ATM.

Buses For arrival points, see p.90. For information on buses out of Athens (and the respective terminals), see "Travel details" at the end of this chapter. There's excellent city bus information at ⓦwww.oasa.gr.

Car rental The vast majority of downtown car rental offices are on Leofóros Syngroú, mostly in the first section close to the Temple of Olympian Zeus. They include Antena at no. 36–38 ⓣ210 92 24 000, ⓦwww.antena.gr; Avance, no. 40–42 ⓣ210 92 00 100, ⓦwww.avance.gr; Europcar no. 43 ⓣ210 92 48 810; Hertz, no. 12 ⓣ210 92 20 102; Holiday Autos, no. 8 ⓣ210 92 23 088; and Thrifty, no. 25 ⓣ210 92 43 304. The local companies are generally cheaper; if you turn up in person and compare prices, you can often haggle a better rate.

Doctors and hospitals For emergencies, see p.156. You'll find a list of hospitals, and adverts for English-speaking doctors, in the weekly *Athens News*, or the US embassy website at ⓦwww.usembassy.gr has hospital addresses and a list of practitioners (look under US Citizen Services). Most doctors speak at least some English, and medical care is generally very good, though nursing and after-care tend to rely on the help of family. The largest central hospital is Evangelismós at Ipsilándhou 45, Kolonáki ⓣ210 72 01 000 (Metro Evangelismós).

Embassies and consulates Most major embassies are in Kolonáki or Ambelókipi, on or not far from Leofóros Vassilísis Sofías. They include: Australia, Level 6, Thon Building, cnr Kifissiás & Alexandhrás, Ambelókipi 7 ⓣ210 87 04 000, ⓦwww.ausemb.gr (Metro Ambelókipi); Canada, Ioánnou Yennadhíou 4 ⓣ210 72 73 400, ⓦwww.athens.gc.ca (Metro Evangelismós); Ireland, Vassiléos Konstandínou 7 ⓣ210 72 32 771, in Pangráti near the Panathenaic Stadium; New

Zealand (honorary consulate), Kifissiás 268, Halándri ⓣ210 68 74 700; South Africa, Kifissiás 60, Maroúsi ⓣ210 61 06 645, ⓦwww.southafrica.gr (Metro Panormóu); UK, Ploutárhou 1, Kolonáki ⓣ210 72 72 600, ⓦwww.british-embassy.gr (Metro Evangelismós); USA, Vassilísis Sofías 91 ⓣ210 72 12 951, ⓦwww.usembassy.gr (Metro Mégaro Mousikís).

Emergencies Ambulance ⓣ166; Fire ⓣ199; Police ⓣ100, or ⓣ112 from a mobile; Tourist Police ⓣ171. For details of emergency hospitals and duty doctors ⓣ1434, or English-speaking SOS doctors are on ⓣ1016 and will come to your hotel room – at a price.

Greek language courses Reliable schools include the long-established Athens Centre, Arhimídhous 48, Mets ⓣ210 70 12 268, ⓦwww.athenscentre.gr; and the Greek House, Dhragoúmi 7, Kifissiá ⓣ210 80 85 185, ⓦwww.greekhouse.gr.

Internet cafés Some of the more central and reliable Internet cafés are: Bits & Bytes, Kapnikaréas 19, off Adhrianoú, Pláka; Café 4U, Ippokrátous 44, Exárhia (24hr); Easy Internet Café, west side of Platía Syndágmatos above *Everest* (also in Kiffisiá, again above *Everest*, at Levídhou cnr Kassavéti); Futura, Víktoros Ougó 15, opposite the Youth Hostel (cheap; Mon–Sat 24hr); Internet World, 5th floor, Pandhróssou 29, Pláka; Museum Internet Café, 28 Oktovríou 46 by the Archeological Museum; and QuickNet, Gladhstónos 4, Omónia (cheap; 24hr). Charges vary from €1.50–4 per hour, with the cheapest rates at night.

Laundry Most hotels will do laundry but charge a fortune. Locations of laundromats that do service washes include: Angélou Yéronda 10, Pláka (Mon–Sat 8am–7pm, Sun 8am–1pm, €9 per load); National, Apóllonos 17, Pláka (Mon & Wed 7am–4pm, Tues, Thurs & Fri 7am–8pm; €5.50 per kilo, also offers dry cleaning); and Psárron 9, just off Platía Karaïskáki, Metaxouryío (Mon–Fri 8am–8pm, Sat 8am–5pm, Sun 8am–noon; €10).

Luggage storage Best arranged with your hotel; many places will keep the bulk of your luggage for free or for a nominal amount while you head off to the islands. Pacific Ltd, Níkis 26, Sýndagma ⓣ210 32 41 007, charges €2 per day for the first week, €1 thereafter for each item. Also at the airport.

Motorbike rental Avance Motorent, Robérto Gálli 1, cnr Kavalóti, Makriyiánni ⓣ210 92 34 939, ⓦwww.motorent.gr; and, Syngroú 40–42 ⓣ210 92 40 107.

Pharmacies There are a number of large general pharmacies (*farmakía*) around Omónia, especially on 28 Oktovríou (Patissíon) and Panepistimíou; many also sell homeopathic remedies. Bakakos, at Ayíou Konstandínou 3 just off Platía Omonías, is the largest general pharmacy in Athens and stocks just about everything. Standard hours are Mon & Wed 8am–2.30pm, Tues, Thurs & Fri 8am–2pm & 5.30–8.30pm. The weekly *Athens News* has listings of pharmacies open out-of-hours: a list of these is also on display at many pharmacies, or call ⓣ107.

Phones Phonecard booths are ubiquitous, and calling cards for cheap overseas calls are sold at many kiosks, especially around Omónia.

Police Dial ⓣ100 for emergency help (ⓣ112 from a mobile) or ⓣ171 for the Tourist Police; for thefts, problems with hotel overcharging, etc, it's the latter you should contact.

Post offices (*tahydhromía*) For ordinary letters and parcels up to 2kg, the branch on Sýndagma (cnr Mitropóleos) is open Mon–Fri 7.30am–8pm, Sat 7.30am–2pm, Sun 9am–1pm. There are machines selling stamps and phonecards. To send heavier parcels, use the post office at Mitropóleos 60, near the cathedral (Mon–Fri 7.30am–8pm) or at Koumoundhoúrou 29 by the National Theatre, Omónia. There are also major branches near Omónia at Eólou 100 (the central office for poste restante) and on Platía Kótzia. Queues can be enormous, so be sure you're at the right counter – there are often separate ones (with shorter lines) for stamps and parcels.

Rail tickets There are often huge queues for tickets at the station so book in advance at the ticket office at Sína 6 (off Panepistimíou), or call central reservations on ⓣ1110.

Travel agencies There are dozens of travel agencies, including many budget and youth or student-oriented ones, in the streets of Pláka just off Sýndagma, especially on and around Filellínon and Níkis. As well as ferry and plane tickets, many of these will offer island packages or tours of Greece. Among them are Magic Travel, Níkis 33 ⓣ210 32 37 471, ⓦwww.magic.gr; Pacific, Níkis 26 ⓣ210 32 41 007, ⓦwww.pacifictravel.gr; and Robissa/STA, Voúlis 43 ⓣ210 32 11 188, ⓦwww.robissa.gr. Closer to Omónia, try City of Athens, Efpólidhos 2, Platía Kótzia ⓣ210 32 47 557. Trekking Hellas, Filellínon 7, on the third floor of the arcade (ⓣ210 33 10 323, ⓦwww.trekking.gr), arrange particularly adventurous and well-run tours throughout Greece, including trekking, sea kayaking and sailing as well as more regular island hopping.

Around Athens: Attica

Attica (Attikí), the region encompassing the capital, is not much explored by tourists – only the great romantic ruin of the **Temple of Poseidon** at Soúnio is well known. The rest, if seen at all, tends to be en route to somewhere else – the airport or the Peloponnese (both unrelentingly ugly motorway drives) or the islands from the ports of **Rafína** or **Lávrio**, a fast and cheap route to many of the Cyclades.

At first sight the neglect is not surprising; the mountains of **Imittós**, **Pendéli** and **Párnitha**, which surround Athens on three sides, were devastated by forest fires in 2007, and in any event are progressively less successful in confining the urban sprawl, while the routes out of the city are unenticing to say the least. Yet a day-trip or two, or a brief circuit by car, can make a pleasant and rewarding break, with much of Greece to be seen in microcosm within an hour or two of the capital. There are rewarding archaeological sites at **Eleusis** and **Ramnous** as well as Soúnio, and **beaches** almost everywhere you turn, though none remote enough to avoid the Athenian hordes. Combine a couple of these with a meal at one of the scores of seaside *psarotavernas* (fish restaurants), always packed out on summer weekends, and you've got a more than worthwhile day out.

Cape Soúnio

Beyond the beaches at Várkiza the coast road south of Athens rapidly becomes much emptier, the countryside more barren. At Saronídha, the furthest outpost for city buses, roughly halfway from Várkiza to Soúnio, there's a large sandy beach with a gently shelving bottom, very popular with windsurfers. Neighbouring **Anávissos** has a row of *psarotavernas* along its more sheltered southern beach. Beyond here the coast starts to get rockier, the road more winding, looking out on small islands offshore, until finally you begin to catch glimpses of the Temple of Poseidon ahead.

Access to this part of southern Attica is straightforward. Orange KTEL Attikis **buses** leave from the terminal on Mavrommatéon at the southwest corner of the Pedhíon Áreos Park. For Soúnio via the coast (€4.60, roughly 2hr) they leave every hour on the half hour from 6.30am to 5.30pm; there's also a more central (but in summer, very busy) stop ten minutes later on Filellínon, south of Sýndagma (corner of Xenofóndos). Returns are hourly from 8am to 9pm. On the less attractive but marginally cheaper inland route to Lávrio and Soúnio there are half-hourly departures from 5.45am to 6.45pm, slightly less frequently to Lávrio from then until 10.30pm (one an hour continues to Soúnio). There are also direct buses to Lávrio from the airport. Drivers can take either route or complete a circuit, but there's little to see in the interior, where the road takes you via the airport and the toll motorway; and unless you're based in the northern suburbs it will probably be slower.

Cape Soúnio

Aktí Souníou – **Cape Soúnio** – on the southern tip of Attica some 70km from the city centre, is one of the most imposing spots in Greece, for centuries a landmark for boats sailing between Pireás and the islands, and an equally dramatic vantage point from which to look out over the Aegean. On its tip stands the fifth-century BC Temple of Poseidon, built in the time of Pericles as part of a major sanctuary to the sea god.

Below the promontory are several **coves** – the most sheltered a five-minute walk east from the car park and site entrance. The main Soúnio beach, a short distance to the north, is more crowded, but has a couple of tavernas at the far end.

The Temple of Poseidon

The **Temple of Poseidon** (daily 9.30am–sunset; €4) owes much of its fame to Lord Byron, who visited in 1810, carved his name on the nearest pillar (an unfortunate and much-copied precedent, which means the temple is now roped off) and immortalized the place in verse:

> Place me on Sunium's marbled steep,
> Where nothing, save the waves and I,
> May hear our mutual murmurs sweep;
> There, swan-like, let me sing and die:
> A land of slaves shall ne'er be mine –
> Dash down yon cup of Samian wine!
>
> from Don Juan

In summer, at least, there is little hope of silent solitude, unless you slip into the site before the tour groups arrive or after they've left. But the setting is still wonderful – on a clear day, the view takes in the islands of Kéa, Kýthnos and Sérifos to the southeast, Égina and the Peloponnese to the west – and the temple is as evocative a ruin as any in Greece. Doric in style, it was probably built by the architect of the Hephaisteion in the Athens Agora. That it is so admired and visited is in part due to its position, but also perhaps to its picturesque state of ruin – preserving, as if by design, sixteen of its original 34 columns.

The rest of the site is of more academic interest. There are remains of a fortification wall around the sanctuary; a **propylaion** (entrance hall) and **stoa**; and cuttings for two shipsheds. To the north are the foundations of a small **Temple of Athena**.

Practicalities

Places to stay are few, which means it's wise to book. The *Hotel Aegeon* (Ⓣ22920 39200, Ⓦwww.aegeon-hotel.com; B&B; ❻), on Soúnio beach itself, had a stunning Olympic makeover that has left it looking brand new, with warm, earthy tones, wood finishes and designer touches. Deals are often available. The *Hotel Saron* (Ⓣ22920 39144, Ⓦwww.saronhotel.com; ❹), about 4km round the coast road towards Lávrio, is substantially cheaper, with an attractive pool, but its rather basic rooms are not great value. Just beyond is *Camping Bacchus* (Ⓣ22920 39572), a pleasantly old-fashioned site among pine trees, where they have tents or permanent caravans that can be rented (❷).

The better of the **tavernas** on Soúnio beach is the simple *Akroyiali* (Ⓣ22920 39107), right down by the water, with seafood at reasonable prices (as ever, the fish is priced by weight). A good alternative is *Syrtaki* (Ⓣ22920 39125), on the road towards the *Hotel Saron*, with a more varied taverna menu and, again, seafood at fair prices.

The east coast

Central Attica has been blighted by the new airport and its associated motorways, and though there are still villages with Byzantine churches and countryside where wine is made, there's little incentive, when heading east, to stop anywhere before you reach the coast. This, as ever, is popular with weekending Athenians and the site of many of their second homes. Almost due east of Athens lies the port of **Rafína**, and to the north of here are **Marathon** and the isolated site of ancient **Ramnous**, as well as some relatively uncrowded beaches. South of Rafína the coast is largely unattractive, with continuous development all the way down through **Loútsa** (aka Artemis) towards **Pórto Ráfti**; it is also directly beneath the airport flight path.

KTEL **buses** to the east coast again leave from the Mavrommatéon terminal. Main services include those to Rafína every half hour from 6.45am to 5.15pm, and almost as frequently outside those hours from 5.30am to 10.30pm; to Pórto Ráfti and Avláki hourly from 5.45am to 7.45pm; and to Marathon half-hourly from 5.30am to 10.30pm – roughly half of these go via the local beaches. The main route for **drivers** is straight out on Messoyíon (following airport signs) onto the eastbound Leofóros Marathónos, which heads straight for Rafína and Marathon.

Rafína

The port of **RAFÍNA** has **ferries** and **catamarans** to the Cyclades, the Dodecanese and the northeast Aegean, as well as to nearby Évvia. Many Athenians have summer homes overlooking the attractive, rocky coast, but the beaches are tricky to reach even with a car, so for visitors the chief attraction, ferries aside, is gastronomic. Overlooking the harbour is a line of excellent **seafood restaurants**, many with roof terraces and a ringside view of the comings and goings at the harbour. They're interspersed with cafés and fishmongers, and the pick of them is *Ta Kavoúria tou Asimáki* (Ⓣ22940 24551), the first as you descend towards the harbour from the square. The pedestrianized square above the harbour is also a lively place, ringed with cafés and rather cheaper eating options: particularly good is the *Ouzeri Limeni*, at Platía Plastíra 17 (Ⓣ22940 24750). A lunchtime outing is an easy operation, given the frequency of the bus service. Evenings, when it's livelier, you need to arrange your own transport back, or stay. There are three very central **hotels**: cheapest and simplest, but still very comfortable, is the *Hotel Corali* (Ⓣ22940 22477; ❸), on the square at Platía Plastíra 11; the *Hotel Akti* (Ⓣ22940 29370, Ⓦwww.aktihotel.gr; ❹), towards the harbour at Arafinídhon Alon and Vithinías, has sea views from many of its rooms, along with satellite TV; while the designer-refurbished *Avra* (Ⓣ22940 22780, Ⓦwww.smartotel.gr; ❺) occupies a prime position on the opposite side of Arafinídhon Alon, perched high above the harbour, with luxury rooms and suites. There's also a beachside **campsite** at nearby Kókkino Limanáki (Ⓣ22940 31604; ❷), where permanent tents and huts are available.

Marathon and around

The site of the **battle of Marathon**, the most famous and arguably most important military victory in Athenian history, is not far from the village of **Marathónas**, 42km from Athens. Here, in 490 BC, a force of 9000 Athenians and 1000 of their Plataian allies defeated a 25,000-strong Persian army. After the victory a runner was sent to Athens to declare the news: having run the first marathon, he delivered his message and dropped dead. Just 192 Athenians died in the battle (compared to some 6,000 Persians), and the burial mound where they were laid, the **Týmfos Marathóna** (Tues–Sun 8.30am–3pm; €3), can still be seen, off the main road between Rafína and Marathónas. It is a quietly impressive monument, though surrounded now by one-way roads installed for the Olympic marathon race, which followed the route of the original marathon, over the hills from here to central Athens. The **Mound of the Plataians**, where the eleven Plataians (including a 10-year-old boy) who died were laid to rest, is about 5km away, near the edge of the mountain; there's also an **archeological museum** (Tues–Sun 8.30am–3pm; €3) here, with a sparse collection of artefacts mainly from the local Cave of Pan, a deity felt to have aided the victory.

MARATHÓNAS village itself is a dull place, though plentifully endowed with cafés and restaurants for the passing trade, and with now-neglected Olympic facilities (the rowing lake was also nearby).

Paralía Marathónas and Skhiniás

The coast around Marathon has some great stretches of sand. **ÁYIOS PANDELÍMONAS**, also known as Paralía Marathónas, is straight on past the burial mound. There's only a small beach here, but a string of waterfront fish tavernas and an open-air movie theatre ensure plenty of local visitors in summer. Of the places to eat, the pick is *Tria Adhelfia* (Ⓣ22940 56461), a simple seafood taverna with a stunning waterfront position 300m or so north of the village centre – follow the coast road round and you'll see signs. The *Marathon Hotel* (Ⓣ22940 55222; ❸), still with its original 1960s decor, is very basic, but great value if you get one of the rooms with sea views.

There's a far better **beach** to the north at **SKHINIÁS**, a long, pine-backed strand with shallow water, big enough to allow some chance of escaping the crowds. Marathon buses run along the road behind the beach, where there are a number of stops. At the southern end there's a **campsite**, *Camping Ramnous* (Ⓣ22940 55855), and several cordoned-off pay-beach sections offering cafés, showers, loungers and watersports; the central section of the beach, beyond the Olympic rowing and kayaking centre, is the least developed, with numerous tracks leading through the pines from the road to the sand. At the northern end there's some low-key development, mainly in the form of cafés and scattered **tavernas** on the sand – try *Glaros*. Towards Rafína, the coast around **Néa Mákri** is much more developed.

Ramnous

Further to the north, the little-visited ruins of **RAMNOUS** (summer daily 8am–5.30pm; winter Tues–Sun 8.30am–3pm; €2) occupy an isolated, atmospheric site above the sea, with magnificent views across the strait to Évvia. The site was an Athenian lookout point from the earliest times, and remains can be clearly seen continuing way below the fenced site, all the way down to the rocky shore. Within the site, the principal ruin is a Doric **Temple of Nemesis**, goddess of divine retribution. Pausanias records that the invading Persians incurred her wrath by their presumption in bringing with them a giant marble block upon which they intended to commemorate their victory. They met their nemesis, however, at the battle of Marathon, and the Athenians used the marble to create a statue instead. There are also the remains of a smaller temple dedicated to Themis, goddess of justice, and a section of ancient road.

Ramnous is not realistically accessible by public transport, though you might get a lift for the final few kilometres if you take a bus to **AYÍA MARÍNA** and hitch from the junction, some 5km from the site. There are frequent buses to

Ayía Marína, largely because from here eight ferries a day – more at weekends – make the short crossing to Néa Stýra on Évvia. There's a snack-bar on the quay, a rocky beach to swim from, and the attractive *Taverna Panorama* overlooking it all from the hillside.

Eleusis and west to the Peloponnese

The road from the centre of Athens **towards Kórinthos** (Corinth) follows the ancient Ierá Odhós – the Sacred Way – as far as Elefsína, ancient Eleusis. There's nothing sacred about it these days, though: this is as ugly a road as any in Greece, traversing a grotesque industrial wasteland. For the first 30km or so you have little sense of leaving Athens, whose western suburbs merge into Elefsína and then Mégara. Offshore, almost closing off the bay, is **Salamína** (ancient Salamis), these days just another suburb and not a dream island in anyone's book.

If the Peloponnese is your destination, there are only a couple of places you might break your journey on the way: at **ancient Eleusis** or the **monastery of Dhafní**. The latter, a beautiful example of Byzantine architecture at its best, is decorated with mosaics that are considered among the artistic masterpieces of the Middle Ages. Unfortunately, it was damaged by earthquake in 1999 and has missed numerous deadlines to reopen since, so check with the tourist office before visiting; it is easily accessible, right next to the main road or on the route of the #A16 bus (see Eleusis). **Drivers** should note that the Athens–Kórinthos non-toll road is notorious, switching from four-lane highway to a rutted two-laner without warning; the toll for the motorway is well worth paying. The Attikí Odhós motorway from the airport meets the road from Athens just outside Elefsína.

Eleusis

The **Sanctuary of Demeter** at **Eleusis** (Tues–Sun 8.30am–3pm; €3) was one of the most important in the ancient Greek world. For two millennia, the ritual ceremonies known as the Mysteries (see box) were performed here. Today, the extensive **ruins** of the sanctuary occupy a low hill on the coast right in the heart of modern Elefsína's industrial blight. The site offers something of an escape from its surroundings: from outside the museum, at one of the highest points, the gulf and its rusty shipping even manage to look attractive.

The best plan on arrival is to head straight for the **museum**, which features models of the sanctuary at various stages in its history: Eleusis is impressively large, with huge walls and gates, some of which date back to Mycenaean times, but the numerous eras of building can also be confusing, especially as signage is poor and mainly in Greek. As well as the models and maps, the museum has some excellent finds from the site, especially Roman statuary (though also some much older objects). Exploring outside, the most important structure of ancient Eleusis was the **Telesterion**. This windowless Hall of Initiation lay at the heart of the cult, and it was here that the priests of Demeter would exhibit the **Sacred Objects** and speak "the Unutterable Words".

Practicalities

The main road out of Athens towards Eleusis is the busy Leofóros Athinón, though it's also possible to follow the Ierá Odhós (Sacred Way) from the centre of town, which may have less traffic and certainly seems more appropriate. To

The Mysteries of Eleusis

The ancient **Mysteries** had an effect on their initiates that was easily the equal of any modern cult. According to Pindar, who experienced the rites in Classical times and, like all others, was bound on pain of death not to reveal their content, anyone who has "seen the holy things [at Eleusis] and goes in death beneath the earth is happy, for he knows life's end and he knows the new divine beginning."

Established in Mycenaean times, perhaps as early as 1500 BC, the cult centred around the figure of **Demeter**, the goddess of corn, and the myth of her daughter Persephone's annual descent into and resurrection from the underworld, which came to symbolize the rebirth of the crops and the miracle of fertility. By the fifth century BC the cult had developed into a sophisticated annual festival, attracting up to 30,000 people every autumn from all over the Greek world. The ceremonies lasted nine days: the **Sacred Objects** (identity unknown, but probably sheaves of fungus-infected grain, or vessels containing the magic potion) were taken to Athens, where they were stored in the Ancient Agora for four days. Various rituals took place in the city, many on the Acropolis but also mass bathing and purification in the sea at Fáliro. Finally a vast procession brought the objects back, following the Sacred Way to the sanctuary at Eleusis. Here initiates took part in the final rituals of *legomena* (things said), *dhromena* (things done) and *dheiknumena* (things shown). One theory suggests that these rituals involved drinking a potion containing grain-ergot fungus, producing similar effects to those of modern **psychedelic drugs**. The Mysteries survived well into the Christian era, but eventually fell victim to the new orthodoxy.

Demeter is said to have threatened to render the land permanently barren if her worship at Eleusis ever ceased. Looking at the ecological havoc wreaked by the area's industry, it would seem that the curse has been fulfilled.

get there by **bus**, take #A16, #B16 or express #16 from Platía Eleftherías (aka Platía Koumoundhoúrou), on Pireós. Between them they run several times an hour every day; the #16 doesn't stop at Dhafní. In Elefsína the buses head straight down the main street, Ierá Odhós: get off where you see the sign, and the sanctuary is a short walk down towards the sea. This is also the route to drive, ignoring confusing signs on the outskirts of Elefsína. There are plenty of small cafés and places to eat in Elefsína, including a good, nameless café almost directly opposite the site entrance.

On from Elefsína

Northwest from Elefsína, the **old road to Thebes and Delphi** heads into the hills. This route is described in Chapter Three (p.282), and is highly worthwhile, with its detours to **ancient Aegosthena** and the tiny resort of **Pórto Yermenó**. At Mégara another, more minor, road heads north to reach the sea at the village of Alepohóri, where it continues as a good road towards Pórto Yermenó.

Heading directly west, on towards the Peloponnese, there are shingle beaches – more or less clear of pollution – along the old coastal road at Kinéta and Áyii Theódhori. This highway, with the Yeránia mountains to the north and those of the Peloponnese across the water, has a small place in pre-Homeric myth, as the route where Theseus slew the bandit Skiron and threw him off the cliffs to be eaten by a giant sea turtle. Thus, Skiron met the same fate as the generations of travellers he had preyed upon.

You leave Attica at Isthmía, a village beside the **Corinth Canal** (see p.176), where buses tend to break the journey for a drink at the café by the bridge. To the north of the canal, Loutráki and Perahóra are technically part of Attica but, as they are more easily reached from Kórinthos, are covered in the Peloponnese chapter.

Travel details

Trains

Peloponnese Line to: Kórinthos (12 daily, plus 9 from airport; 1hr 30min), change there for: Kalamáta (3 daily; 7hr 30min from Athens); Pátra (8 daily; 4hr); Pýrgos (7 daily; 5hr 50min).
Northern Line to: Alexandhroúpoli (5 daily, 3 of which intercity; 14hr/10hr); Halkídha (19 daily; 1hr 30min); Thessaloníki (11 daily, 7 intercity; 7hr, intercity 5hr) via Livadhiá (1hr 30min/1hr 15min) and Lárissa (5hr/4hr); Vólos (1 direct daily; 5hr).

Buses

For details of termini see p.90. Journey times are approximate.
Mavrommatéon terminal Buses for most destinations in Attica including: Lávrio (half hourly 5.45am–6.45pm, less frequent until 10.30pm; 1hr 30min); Marathon (every 30min; 1hr 20min); Pórto Ráfti (hourly; 1hr 30min); Rafína (every 30min; 1hr); Soúnio via the coast (hourly on the half-hour; 2hr) or inland route (see Lávrio; 1hr 45min).
Kifissoú 100 Destinations in Peloponnese and western/northern Greece include: Árgos (hourly; 2hr); Árta (8 daily; 5hr 30min); Corfu (3 daily; 8hr 30min); Igoumenítsa (4 daily; 7hr 30min); Ioánnina (9 daily; 6hr 30min); Kalamáta (8 daily; 4hr 30min); Kefaloniá (3–4 daily; 8hr); Kórinthos (every 30min; 1hr 15min); Lefkádha (4 daily; 5hr 30min); Mycenae/Náfplio (hourly; 2hr 30min); Olympia (2 daily; 5hr 30min); Pátra (every 30min; 3hr); Pýlos (2 daily; 5hr 30min); Pýrgos (9 daily; 5hr); Spárti (11 daily; 3hr 30min); Thessaloníki (11 daily; 6hr 30min); Trípoli (16 daily; 2hr 30min); Zákynthos (4 daily; 6hr).
Liossíon 260 Buses for most other destinations in central Greece including: Áyios Konstandínos (hourly; 2hr); Delphi (6–8 daily; 3hr); Halkídha (every 30min; 1hr); Karpeníssi (3 daily; 4hr 30min); Kými, for Skýros ferries (2–4 daily; 3hr 30min); Ósios Loukás (8 daily; 2hr 30min); Thiva/Thebes (hourly; 1hr 30min); Tríkala (8 daily; 4hr 30min); Vólos (10–12 daily; 4hr 30min).

Island ferries, catamarans and hydrofoils

See the relevant island chapters.
Pireás Ferries and hydrofoils to the Argo-Saronic, Crete, the Cyclades, Dodecanese and northeast Aegean islands. Port authority ⓣ210 42 26 000; hydrofoils ⓣ210 41 99 200.
Lávrio Ferries daily to Kéa, Kýthnos and many of the Cycladic islands, twice or more a week to Tínos, Híos, Lésvos, Límnos, Áyios Efstrátios and Samothráki. Port authority ⓣ22940 25249.
Rafína Ferries and hydrofoils daily to Évvia as well as Ándhros, Tínos, Páros, Mýkonos, Ikaría and Sámos; most days also to Náxos and Amorgós. Port authority ⓣ22920 22481.

Domestic flights

Eleftherios Venizélos airport (see p.87) Olympic (ⓦwww.olympicairlines.com) and Aegean (ⓦwww.aegeanair.com) operate daily flights in summer to the following domestic destinations: Alexandhroúpoli, Astypálea, Haniá (Crete), Híos, Ikaría, Iráklion (Crete), Ioánnina, Kalamáta, Kárpathos, Kastoriá, Kavála, Kefaloniá, Kérkyra (Corfu), Kós, Kozáni, Kýthira, Léros, Límnos, Mílos, Mýkonos, Mytilíni (Lésvos), Náxos, Páros, Préveza, Ródhos (Rhodes), Sámos, Sitía (Crete), Skiáthos, Skýros, Sýros, Thessaloníki, Thíra (Santoríni) and Zákynthos. Na feuguer ostrud dolortie magnim velenis cidunt vulputpatis dignit, sumsandignit in

2

The Peloponnese

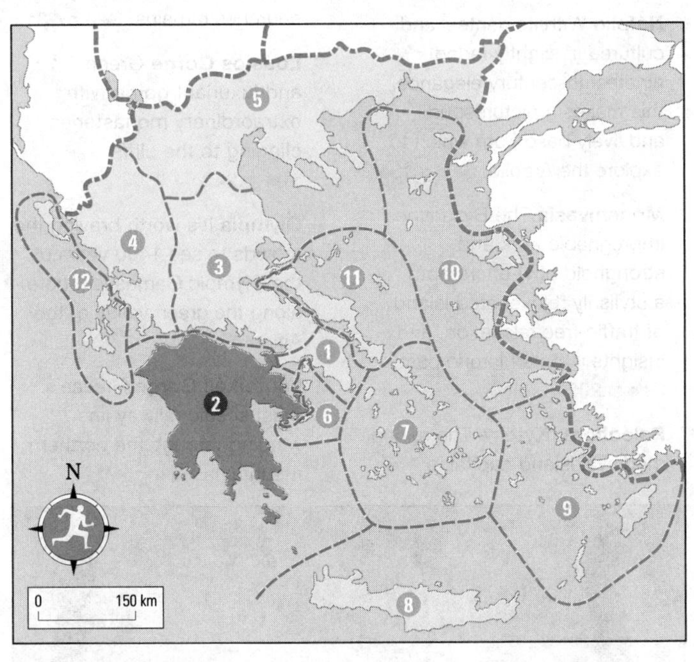

CHAPTER 2

Highlights

* **Acrocorinth** A huge, barren rock arising from and dominating the plains of Kórinthos, crowned by a great medieval fortress. See p.175

* **Mycenae** Agamemnon's legendary palace and possible site of his murder upon his return from the Trojan War. See p.179

* **Náfplio** With its genteel and cultured (if slightly faded) nineteenth-century elegance, this makes a picturesque and lively base from which to explore the Argolid. See p.185

* **Monemvasiá** The Byzantines' impregnable rock and stronghold now offers both a stylishly rejuvenated island of traffic-free relaxation, and insights into its historic past. See p.202

* **Paleohóra, Kýthira** The ruined medieval island capital; a fortified town, hidden between ravines. See p.210

* **Máni Towers** Anachronistic medieval architecture; high-rise internecine warfare in the deep south. See p.216 & p.222

* **Mystra** A visually stunning medieval city that once had a population of 20,000; a superb collection of frescoed Byzantine churches remains. See p.231

* **Loúsios Gorge** Green and luxuriant gorge with extraordinary monasteries clinging to the cliffs. See p.242

* **Olympia** It's worth braving the crowds to see 1400 years of the Olympic Games laid bare along the green valley of the Alfiós. See p.259

* **Vouraïkós Gorge** Greece's most scenic railway line, winding through the northern mountains. See p.271

▲ The Palaestra at Olympia

2

The Peloponnese

The appeal of the Peloponnese (Pelopónnisos) is hard to overstate. This southern peninsula, technically an island since the cutting of the Corinth Canal, seems to have the best of almost everything Greek. Its ancient sites include the Homeric palaces of Agamemnon at **Mycenae** and of Nestor at **Pýlos**, the best preserved of all Greek theatres at **Epidaurus**, and the lush sanctuary of **Olympia**, host to the Olympic Games for a millennium. The medieval remains are scarcely less rich, with the fabulous Venetian, Frankish and Turkish castles of **Náfplio**, **Methóni** and **Kórinthos**; the strange battle towers and frescoed churches of the **Máni**; and the extraordinarily well preserved Byzantine shells of **Mystra** and **Monemvasiá**.

Beyond this incredible profusion of cultural monuments, the Peloponnese is also a superb place to relax and wander. Its **beaches**, especially along the west coast, are among the finest and least developed in the country, and the **landscape** inland is superb – dominated by range after range of forested mountains, and cut by some of the lushest valleys and gorges to be imagined. Not for nothing did its heartland province of **Arcadia** give its name to the concept of a classical rural idyll.

The Peloponnese is at its most enjoyable and intriguing when you venture off the beaten track: to the old Arcadian hill towns like **Karítena**, **Stemnítsa** and **Dhimitsána**; the Maniot tower villages such as **Kítta** or **Váthia**; at **Voïdhokiliá** and **Elafónissos** beaches in the south; or the trip along the remarkable **rack-and-pinion railway** from the north coast at **Dhiakoftó** to **Kalávryta**.

Anciently known as the **Moreas**, from the resemblance of the outline to the leaf of a mulberry tree (*mouriá*), rounded at the top, with three long fingers below (from west to east, Messinía, the Máni, and Maléas), plus the thumb of the Argolid, it will amply repay any amount of time that you devote to it. The **Argolid**, the area richest in ancient history, is just a couple of hours from Athens, and if pushed you could complete a circuit of the main sights here – **Corinth**, **Mycenae** and **Epidaurus** – in a couple of days, making your base by the sea in Náfplio. Given a week, you could add in the two large sites of Mystra and Olympia at a more leisurely pace. To get to grips with all this, however, plus the wonderful southern peninsulas of the Máni and Messinía, and the hill towns of Arcadia, you'll need at least a couple of weeks.

If you were planning a combination of Peloponnese-plus-islands, then the **Argo-Saronic** or **Ionian islands** are most convenient, although you would be better off limiting yourself to the mainland on a short trip. The Argo-Saronic islands (see p.483) are linked by hydrofoil with the Argolid and Pireás. Of the Ionian islands, isolated **Kýthira** is covered in this chapter since closest access is from the southern Peloponnese ports, but **Zákynthos** (see p.881) or **Kefaloniá**

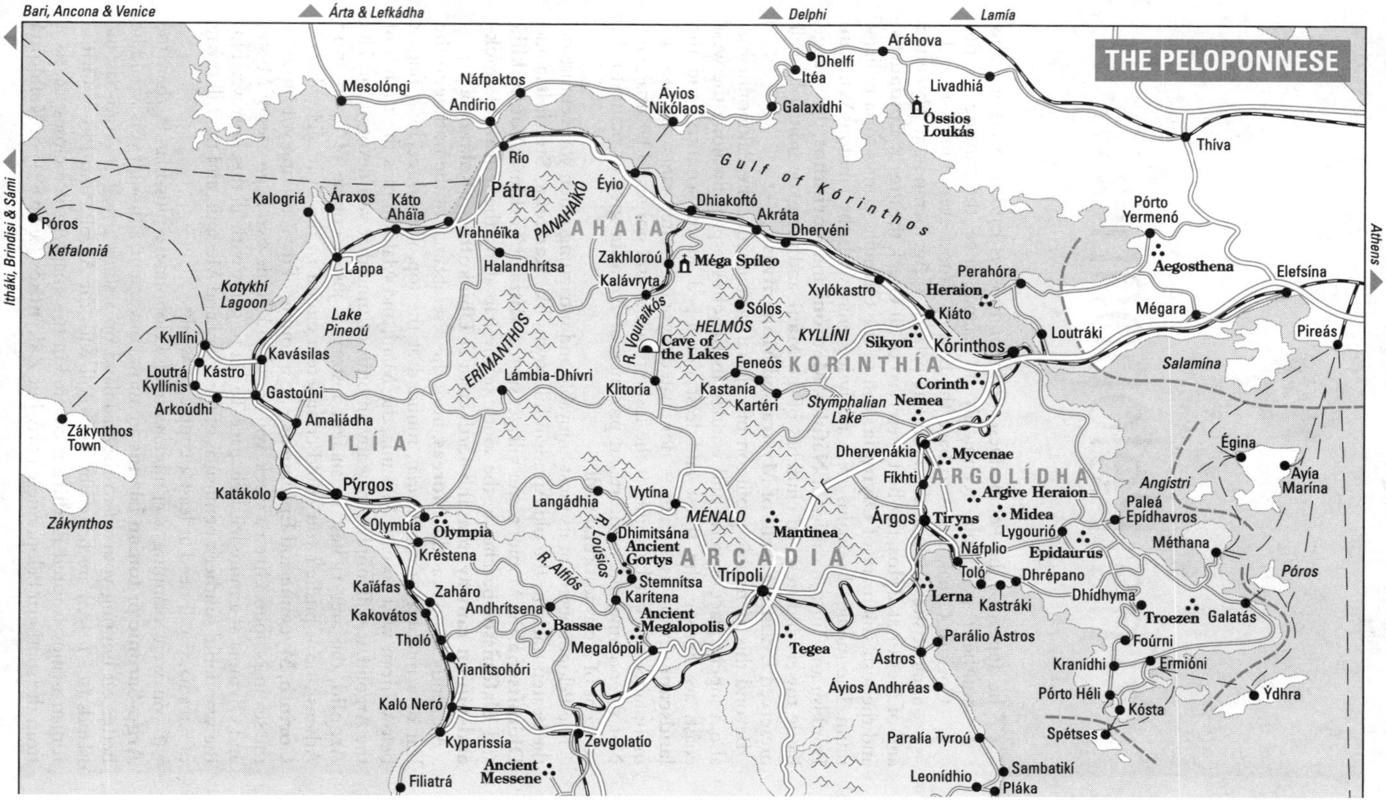

THE PELOPONNESE

Bari, Ancona & Venice
Árta & Lefkádha
Delphi
Lamía
Athens
Itháki, Brindisi & Sámi

Aráhova
Dhelfí
Itéa
Livadhiá
Óssios Loukás
Galaxídhi
Thíva
Mesolóngi
Náfpaktos
Andírio
Áyios Nikólaos
Río
Gulf of Kórinthos
Éyio
Pátra
PANAHAÏKÓ
Kalogriá
Áraxos
Káto Ahaïa
Vrahnéïka
A H A Ï A
Dhiakoftó
Akráta
Dhervéni
Pórto Yermenó
Aegosthena
Elefsína
Póros
Kefaloniá
Láppa
Halandhrítsa
Zakhloroú
Méga Spíleo
Kalávryta
Xylókastro
Perahóra
Heraion
Mégara
Kotykhí Lagoon
Lake Pineoú
ERÍMANTHOS
R. Vouraïkós
Sólos
HELMÓS
KYLLÍNI
Kiáto
Sikyon
Loutráki
Pireás
Kyllíni
Kavásilas
Cave of the Lakes
Kórinthos
Salamína
Loutrá Kyllínis
Kástro
Lámbia-Dhívri
Klitoría
Feneós
K O R I N T H Í A
Gastoúni
Kastanía
Kartéri
Corinth
Arkoúdhi
Amaliádha
Stymphalian Lake
Nemea
Zákynthos Town
I L Í A
Dhervenákia
Mycenae
Égina
Ayía Marína
Fíkhti
A R G O L Í D H A
Angístri
Pýrgos
Katákolo
Langádhia
Vytína
Argive Heraion
Paleá Epídhavros
MÉNALO
Midea
Zákynthos
Olymbía
Olympia
R. Loúsios
Mantinea
Árgos
Tiryns
Lygourió
Dhimitsána
Ancient Gortys
A R C A D I A
Náfplio
Epidaurus
Méthana
Kréstena
Stemnítsa
Tolό
Dhrépano
Póros
R. Alfiós
Trípoli
Kaïáfas
Zaháro
Karítena
Lerna
Kastráki
Dhídhyma
Kakovátos
Andhrítsena
Ancient Megalopolis
Troezen
Galatás
Bassae
Tegea
Parálio Ástros
Tholó
Megalópoli
Foúrni
Ástros
Kranídhi
Ermióni
Yianitsohóri
Áyios Andhréas
Pórto Héli
Ýdhra
Kaló Neró
Kósta
Kyparissía
Zevgolatío
Paralía Tyroú
Spétses
Ancient Messene
Sambatikí
Filiatrá
Leonídhio
Pláka

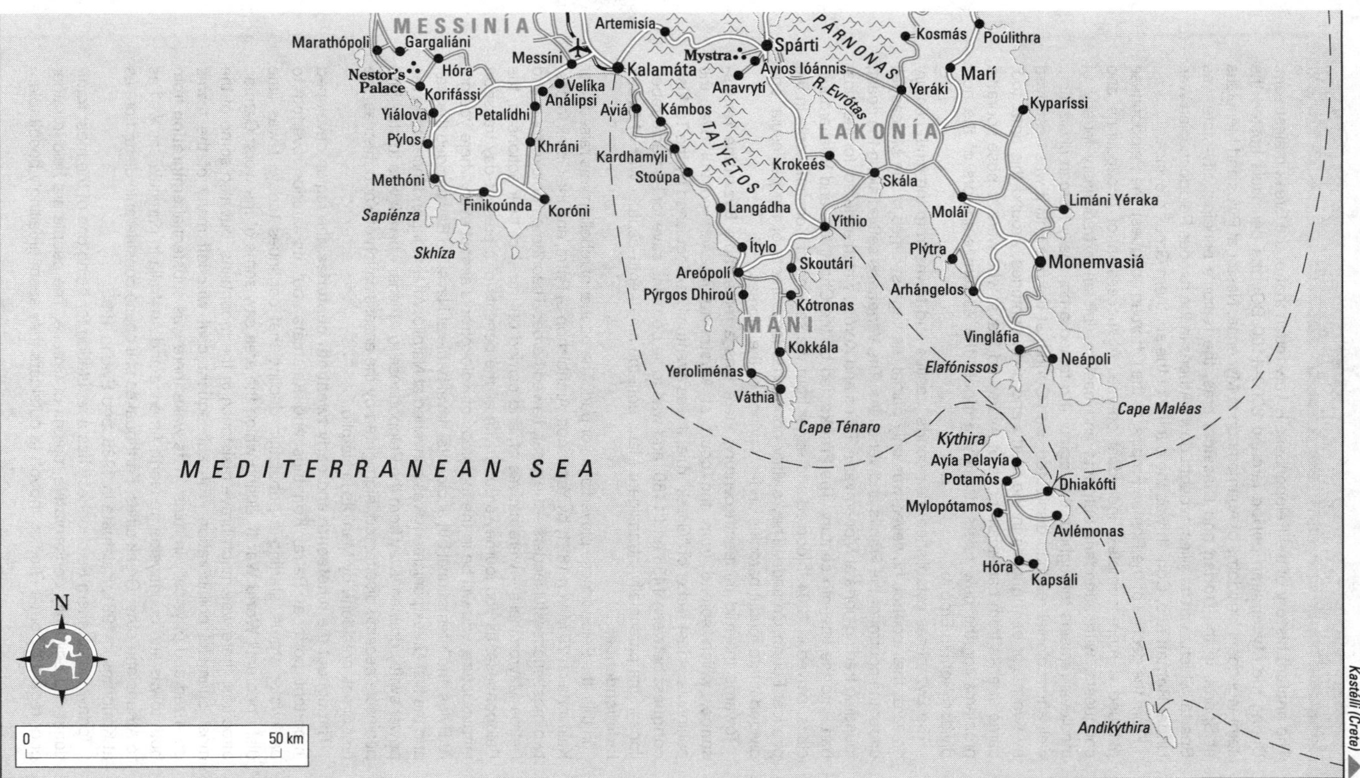
MESSINÍA
LAKONÍA
MÁNI
PÁRNONAS
TAÏYETOS
R. Evrótas
Marathópoli
Gargaliáni
Nestor's Palace
Hóra
Korifássi
Yiálova
Pýlos
Petalídhi
Messíni
Velíka
Análipsi
Khráni
Methóni
Finikoúnda
Koróni
Sapiénza
Skhíza
Artemisía
Kalamáta
Aviá
Kámbos
Kardhamýli
Stoúpa
Mystra
Spárti
Áyios Ioánnis
Anavrytí
Krokeés
Langádha
Ítylo
Areópoli
Pýrgos Dhiroú
Skoutári
Kótronas
Kokkála
Yeroliménas
Váthia
Cape Ténaro
Yíthio
Skála
Kosmás
Poúlithra
Marí
Yeráki
Kyparíssi
Moláï
Limáni Yéraka
Plýtra
Monemvasiá
Arhángelos
Vingláfia
Neápoli
Elafónissos
Cape Maléas
Kýthira
Ayía Pelayía
Potamós
Dhiakófti
Mylopótamos
Avlémonas
Hóra
Kapsáli
Andikýthira
Kastélli (Crete)
MEDITERRANEAN SEA
N
0
50 km

Pelopónnisos – Moreas: some history

The **ancient history** of the Peloponnese is very much that of the Greek mainstream. During the **Mycenaean period** (around 2000–1100 BC), the peninsula hosted the semi-legendary kingdoms of Agamemnon at Mycenae, Nestor at Pýlos and Menelaus at Sparta. In the **Dorian** and **Classical** eras, the region's principal city-state was Sparta, which, with its allies, brought down Athens in the ruinous Peloponnesian War. Under **Roman** rule, Corinth was the capital of the southern Greek province.

From the decline of the Roman Empire, to the Ottoman conquest, the Peloponnese pursued a more complex, individual course. A succession of occupations and conquests, with attendant outposts and castles, left an extraordinary legacy of medieval remains throughout the region. It retained a nominally Roman civilization, well after colonial rule had dissipated, with Corinth at the fore until it was destroyed by two major earthquakes in the fourth and sixth centuries. Around this time, too, came attacks from barbarian tribes of Avars and Slavs, who were to pose sporadic problems for the new rulers, the **Byzantines**, the eastern emperors of the now divided Roman Empire.

The Byzantines established their courts, castles and towns from the ninth century onward; their control, however, was only partial, as large swathes of the Moreas fell under the control of the Franks and Venetians. The **Venetians** settled along the coast, founding trading ports at Monemvasiá, Pýlos and Koróni, which endured, for the most part, into the fifteenth century. The **Franks**, led by the Champlitte and Villehardouin clans, arrived in 1204, bloodied and eager from the sacking of Constantinople in the piratical Fourth Crusade. They swiftly conquered large tracts of the peninsula, and divided it into feudal baronies under a prince of the Moreas.

Towards the mid thirteenth century, there was a remarkable **Byzantine renaissance**, which spread from the court at Mystra to reassert control over the peninsula. A last flicker of "Greek" rule, it was eventually extinguished by the **Turkish conquest** between 1458 and 1460, and was to lie dormant, save for sporadic rebellions in the perennially intransigent Máni, until the nineteenth-century **War of Greek Independence**.

In this, the Peloponnese played a major part. The banner of rebellion was raised near Kalávryta on 25 March 1821, by Yermanos, Archbishop of Pátra, and the Greek forces' two most successful leaders – the great, flawed heroes Theodhoros Kolokotronis and Petros Mavromihalis – were natives of, and carried out most of their actions in, the Peloponnese; as you journey around with all the benefits of a present-day transport infrastructure, you will be in the footsteps of Kolokotronis almost everywhere you go. At Pýlos, the international but accidental naval battle at Navarino Bay decided the war, and the first Greek parliament was convened at Náfplio. After independence, however, power swiftly drained away from the Peloponnese to Athens, where it was to stay. The peninsula became disaffected, highlighted by the assassination of Kapodhistrías, the first Greek president, by Maniots in Náfplio.

Throughout the **nineteenth** and **early twentieth centuries**, the region developed important ports at Pátra, Kórinthos and Kalamáta, but its interior reverted to backwater status, starting a population decline that continues today. It was little disturbed until **World War II**, during which the area saw some of the worst German atrocities; there was much brave resistance in the mountains, but also some of the most shameful collaboration. The subsequent **civil war** left many of the towns polarized and physically in ruins; in its wake there was substantial **emigration** from both towns and countryside, to North America and Australia in particular, as well as to Athens and other Greek cities. Earthquakes still cause considerable disruption, as at Kórinthos in 1981, Kalamáta in 1986, and Éyio in 1995.

Today, the southern Peloponnese has a reputation for being one of the most traditional and politically **conservative** regions of Greece. The people are held in rather poor regard by other Greeks, though to outsiders they seem unfailingly hospitable.

(see p.868) can be reached from the western port of Kyllíni, and Greece's second port city of **Pátra** is a gateway to Corfu and eastern Italy.

Travelling about the peninsula by **public transport**, you'll be dependent mostly on **buses**. These are fast and regular on the main routes between the seven provincial capitals, and from these towns go to most other places at least once a day; however, travelling between smaller towns in different provinces is considerably more complicated. The Peloponnese **train line** is gradually being upgraded, in particular with the Athens–Pátra section being converted to a high-speed track by 2008. The highly scenic southern loop still runs to a leisurely timetable but it does provide some direct connections and landscape views unavailable on buses.

Renting a **car** is worthwhile – even for just a few days – to explore the south from Kalamáta, Yíthio or Spárti, or coastal and heartland Arcadia from Náfplio.

Corinth and the Argolid

The usual approach from Athens to the Peloponnese is along the highway past Elefsína and over the Corinth Canal to modern-day **Kórinthos** (Corinth); buses and trains come this way almost every hour, the former halting at the canal (see p.176), while a fast train link (the Proastiakos) connects Athens with Kórinthos. A more attractive approach to the peninsula is by ferry or hydrofoil, from Pireás, via the **Argo-Saronic** islands (see p.483), with brief hops over to the Argolid ports of Ermióni and Pórto Héli.

The region that you enter to the south and southeast of Kórinthos, was known as the **Argolid** (Argolídha in modern Greek), after the city of Árgos, which held sway in Classical times. The greatest concentration of ancient sites in Greece is found in this compact peninsula, its western boundary delineated by the main road south from Kórinthos. Within less than an hour's drive of each other are Agamemnon's fortress at **Mycenae**, the great theatre of **Epidaurus**, and lesser sites at **Tiryns**, **Árgos**, **Lerna**, **Midea** and **Argive Heraion**. Inevitably, these, along with the great Roman site at **Ancient Corinth**, draw the crowds, and in peak season you may want to see the sites early or late in the day to realize their magic. When ruin-hopping palls, there are the small-town pleasures of elegant **Náfplio**, and a handful of pleasant **coastal resorts**.

Drivers heading from the north towards the Argolid (Mycenae, Tiryns, Náfplio and Epidaurus) should join the broad new road, south of Dhervenákia, which bypasses the chaotic streets of Árgos. Funding ran out before its completion, so at the southern end you follow farm roads to emerge near Tiryns.

Kórinthos

Like its ancient predecessor, the city of **KÓRINTHOS** (modern Corinth) has been levelled on several occasions by earthquakes – most recently in 1981, when a serious quake left thousands in tented homes for most of the following year. Repaired and reconstructed, with buildings of prudent but characterless

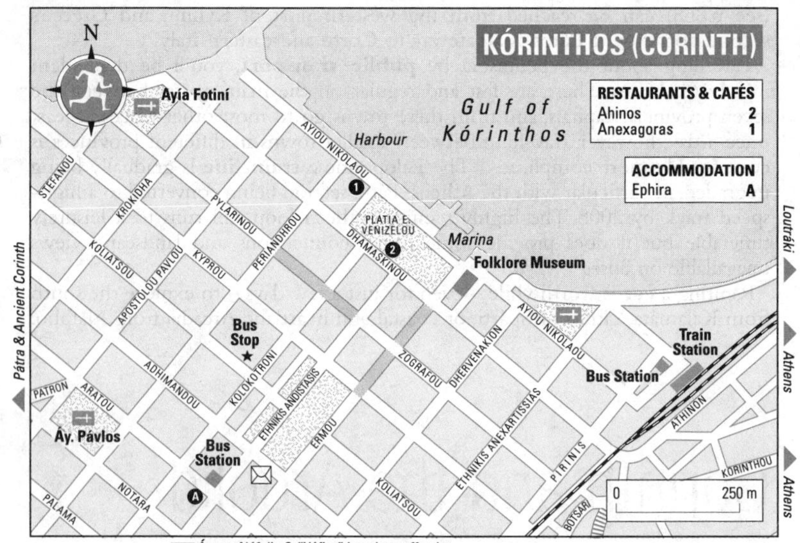

concrete, the modern city has little to offer the outsider; it is largely an industrial and agricultural centre, its economy bolstered by the drying and shipping of currants, for centuries one of Greece's few successful exports (the word "currant" itself derives from Corinth). As a first stop in the Peloponnese, it gives a poor impression: noisy, chaotic with traffic in the rush hour, and providing a fragmented and inconvenient transport system. In summer, it is the hottest, driest part of the peninsula. If you want to base yourself here for a night or two, you are unlikely to escape from the continuous traffic noise anywhere in the centre of town, so it is worth considering the small village of **Arhéa Kórinthos**; 7km to the southwest: it is a quieter, slightly cooler alternative, with magnificent views at night, and close to the remains of ancient and medieval Corinth. Kórinthos itself provides access to Perahóra and a couple of other minor sites.

The only specific sight in the modern city is the **folklore museum** (Tues–Sun 8.30am–1.30pm; €2), overlooking the marina and containing the usual array of peasant costumes, old engravings and dioramas of traditional crafts.

Practicalities

Orientation is straightforward. The centre of Kórinthos is its **park**, bordered on the longer side by Ermoú street and bisected by the parallel Ethnikís Andístasis. The **train station** is a few blocks to the east, opposite the KTEL **bus station** for Athens, Léheo, Kiáto and the campsites. Changing trains at Kórinthos is easy; changing buses can be a nightmare. Most buses between Athens and the Peloponnese avoid going in to town and either pass by on the New National Road (Néa Ethnikí Odhós) with a stop at Isthmós, or along the nearer Old National Road (Paleá Ethnikí Odhós). On the latter route, locals alight at "Yéfira" – a bridge under which you can access the town via a long walk along Ethnikís Andístasis. **Buses** to Ancient Corinth (Arhéa Kórinthos), Dhervéni, Kiáto, Léheo and Xylókastro go from outside the well-stocked *Erataino zaharoplastío* on Koliátsou, west of the park. Some **long-distance buses** to Argolídha

(Mycenae, Árgos and Náfplio), plus those to Ísthmia, Loutráki, Loutró Elénis (for Kekhriés) and Nemea, use a café near the *Ephira* hotel, at the corner of Ethnikís Andístasis and Arátou. Unlike others, this station – much used by tourists – has no signboard for destinations and times. Information and tickets are grudgingly provided by the café staff. You'll find various **banks** along northern Ethnikís Andístasis, and the main **post office** on Adhimandoú, on the south side of the park. There's a **tourist police** post at Ermoú 51 (Ⓣ27410 23282), and **taxis** wait along the Ethnikís Andístasis side of the park. If you want to rent your own **car**, try Vasilopoulos at Adhimandoú 30 (Ⓣ27410 28437), near the post office.

Accommodation

At most times of year, **hotel rooms** are reasonably easy to find, though almost all suffer from road noise: a good choice is the modern and comfortable *Ephira*, Ethnikís Andístasis 52 (Ⓣ27434 24021, Ⓕ27434 24514; B&B ④), one block south of the park and nearest to the long-distance bus station – the rear or interior rooms are quieter.

There are a couple of **campsites** along the gulf to the west: *Corinth Beach* (Ⓣ27410 27967; April–Oct) is 3km out at Dhiavakíta, opposite the Lechaion site – to reach the beach, such as it is, you must cross the coastal road and the train line. *Blue Dolphin* (Ⓣ27410 25766, Ⓦwww.camping-blue-dolphin.gr; April–Oct) is a bit further away at Léheo (part of Ancient Corinth), but is on the seaward side of the tracks, and offers free transfers from Kórinthos. For both sites, take the bus to Léheo from Koliátsou – or opposite the train station – in modern Kórinthos.

Eating and drinking

Kórinthos has many fast-food places along the waterfront, mostly reasonably priced, and only a few **tavernas**: *Anexagoras*, in a car park at Ayíou Nikoláou 31, west of the marina, has a good range of *mezédhes* and grilled meats, while *Ahinos*, by the marina, serves tasty, well-prepared seafood. Other than in the marina area, restaurants tend to be in uncomfortable proximity to relentless traffic. On the coast road near the *Corinth Beach* campsite, the *Arhontiko* (Ⓣ27410 27968) is very popular with the locals, so phone first.

Ancient Corinth

Buses to **ANCIENT CORINTH** (Arhéa Kórinthos) village leave modern Kórinthos ten minutes past every hour from 8am to 9pm and return on the half hour (20 min; €1). The ruins of the **ancient city**, occupy a rambling sequence of sites, the main enclosure of which is given a sense of scale by the majestic ruin of the Temple of Apollo. More compelling, though, are the ruins of the medieval city, which occupy the stunning acropolis site of **Acrocorinth**, towering 565m above the ancient city.

Ancient Corinth's ruins spread over a vast area, and include sections of ancient walls (the Roman city had a fifteen-kilometre circuit), outlying stadiums, gymnasiums and necropolises. Only the central area, around the Roman forum and the Classical Temple of Apollo, is preserved in an excavated state; odd patches of semi-enclosed and often overgrown ruin lurk unexpectedly about the village and up to Acrocorinth.

The overall effect is impressive, but it only begins to suggest the majesty of this once extremely wealthy city. Ancient Corinth was a key centre of the Greek and Roman worlds, whose possession meant the control of trade between northern Greece and the Peloponnese. In addition, the twin ports of **Lechaion**, on the Gulf of Kórinthos, and **Kenchreai**, on the Saronic Gulf, provided a trade link between the Ionian and Aegean seas – the western and eastern Mediterranean. Not surprisingly, therefore, the area's ancient and medieval history was one of invasions and power struggles that, in Classical times, was dominated by Corinth's rivalry with Athens, against whom it sided with Sparta in the Peloponnesian War.

Despite this, Corinth suffered only one major setback, in 146 BC, when the Romans, having defeated the Greek city-states of the Achaean League, razed the site. For a century the city lay in ruins before being rebuilt, on a majestic scale, by Julius Caesar in 44 BC; initially intended as a colony for veterans, it was later made the provincial capital. Once again Corinth grew rich on trade – with Rome to the west, and Syria and Egypt to the east.

Roman Corinth's reputation for wealth, fuelled by its trading access to luxury goods, was soon equalled by its appetite for earthly pleasures – including sex. Corinthian women were renowned for their beauty and much sought after as *hetairai* (courtesans); over a thousand sacred prostitutes served a temple to Aphrodite/Venus, on the acropolis of Acrocorinth. **St Paul** stayed in Corinth for eighteen months in 51–52 AD, though his attempts to reform the citizens' ways were met with rioting – tribulations recorded in his two letters to the Corinthians. The city endured until rocked by two major earthquakes, in 375 and 521, which brought down the Roman buildings and again depopulated the site until a brief Byzantine revival in the eleventh century.

The excavations

Inevitably, successive waves of earthquakes and destruction mean the **main excavated site** (daily: summer 8am–7.30pm; winter 8am–5pm; €6) is dominated by the remains of the Roman city. Entering from the north, you are in the Roman agora, an enormous marketplace flanked by the substantial foundations of a huge *stoa*, once a structure of several storeys, with 33 shops on the ground floor. Opposite the *stoa* is a *bema*, a marble platform used for public announcements. At the far end are remains of a **basilica**, while the area behind the *bema* is strewn with the remnants of numerous Roman administrative buildings. Back across the agora, hidden in a swirl of broken marble and shattered architecture, there's a fascinating trace of the Greek city – a grille-covered **sacred spring**, at the base of a narrow flight of steps.

More substantial is the elaborate Roman **Fountain of Peirene**, which stands below the level of the agora, to the side of a wide, excavated stretch of the marble-paved **Lechaion Way** – the main approach to the city. In the form of a colonnaded and frescoed recess, the fountain occupies the site of one of two natural springs in Corinth – the other is up on the acropolis – and its cool waters were channelled into a magnificent fountain and pool in the courtyard. The fountain house was, like many of Athens' Roman public buildings, the gift of the wealthy Athenian and friend of Emperor Hadrian, Herodes Atticus. Water still flows through the underground cisterns and supplies the modern village.

The real focus of the ancient site, though, is a rare survival from the Classical Greek era, the fifth-century BC **Temple of Apollo**, whose seven austere Doric columns stand slightly above the level of the forum, flanked by foundations of another marketplace and baths. Over to the west is the site **museum** (same hours as site; included in site admission), housing a large collection of domestic pieces, some good Greek and Roman mosaics from nearby and a frieze depicting some of the labours of Hercules. The city's other claim to mythic fame is as the home of the infant Oedipus and his step-parents, prior to his travels of discovery to Thebes.

A number of miscellaneous smaller excavations surround the main site. To the west, just across the road from the enclosing wire, there are outlines of two **theatres**: a Roman **odeion** (endowed by Herodes Atticus) and a larger Greek theatre, used by the Romans for gladiatorial sea battles. To the north are the inaccessible but visible remains of an **Asklepion** (dedicated to the god of healing).

Acrocorinth

Rising almost sheer above the lower town, **Acrocorinth** (summer daily 8am–7pm; winter Tues–Sun 8.30am–3pm; free) is sited on an amazing mass of rock, still largely encircled by 2km of wall. Once Corinth's ancient acropolis, it became one of Greece's most powerful medieval fortresses, besieged by successive waves of invaders, who considered it the key to the Moreas.

Despite the long, four-kilometre climb to the entrance gate (nearly an hour's walk) – or a taxi ride from Ancient Corinth – a visit to the summit is unreservedly recommended. Looking down over the Saronic Gulf and the Gulf of Kórinthos, you get a real sense of the strategic importance of the fortress's position. Amid the extensive remains is a jumble of chapels, mosques, houses and battlements, erected in turn by Greeks, Romans, Byzantines, Frankish crusaders, Venetians and Turks.

The Turkish remains are unusually substantial. Elsewhere in Greece evidence of the Ottoman occupation has been physically removed or defaced, but here, at the start of the climb to the entrance, you can see a midway point in the process – the still-used **fountain of Hatzi Mustafa**, Christianized by the addition of great carved crosses. The outer of the citadel's **triple gates** is also largely Turkish; the middle is a combination of Venetian and Frankish; the inner, Byzantine, incorporating fourth-century BC towers. Within the citadel, the first summit (to the right) is enclosed by a **Frankish keep** – as striking as they come – which last saw action in 1828 during the War of Independence. Keeping along the track to the left, you pass some interesting (if perilous) cisterns, the remains of a Turkish bathhouse, and crumbling Byzantine chapels.

In the southeast corner of the citadel, hidden away in the lower ground, is the **upper Peirene spring**. This is not easy to find: look out for a narrow, overgrown entrance, from which a flight of iron stairs leads down some 5m to a metal screen. Here, broad stone steps descend into the dark depths, where a fourth-century BC arch stands guard over a pool of (nonpotable) water that has never been known to dry up. To the north of the fountain, on the second and higher summit, is the site of the **Temple of Aphrodite**; after its days as a brothel, it saw use as a church, mosque and belvedere.

Practicalities: Arhéa Kórinthos

To explore both ancient and medieval Corinth you need a full day, or, better still, to stay here overnight. The modern **village** of **ARHÉA KÓRINTHOS** spreads around the edge of the main ancient site; the church has a memorial with, appropriately enough, a quotation from St Paul to the Corinthians. There is a scattering of **rooms** to rent – try *Tasos* (Ⓣ27410 31225; Ⓕ27410 31183; ❷) over the taverna of the same name. Another good option, just after the cemetery on the road in from Kórinthos, is the hospitable *Hotel Shadow* (Ⓣ27410 31481; B&B ❸); a restaurant downstairs includes an extensive collection of minerals, fossils, petrified wood and local relics. In the centre, the *Tasos* serves good, traditional Greek *psistariá* **food** at reasonable prices. The solitary modern building up on Acrocorinth is the *Acrocorinthos* café, which serves food until the early evening during the summer months.

Around Corinth

As well as the **Corinth Canal**, which you can't help but cross en route between Kórinthos and Athens, a number of minor sites are accessible by bus (at least most of the way) from Kórinthos, both on the Peloponnese and the western Attic peninsula of Yerània. Northwest of the canal are the spa of **Loutráki** and the classical **sanctuary of Hera** at **Perahóra** on Cape Melangávi.

Back in the Peloponnese proper, **Nemea** – home to the Lion of Hercules' labour – is a brief detour southwest of Kórinthos, off the road to Mycenae and Árgos. **Sikyon** is a bit more remote, 25km up the coast towards Pátra, but again accessible by bus.

The Corinth Canal

The idea for a **Corinth Canal**, providing a short cut and safe passage between the Aegean and Ionian seas, dates back at least to Roman times, when Emperor Nero performed initial excavations with a silver shovel and Jewish slave labour. It was only in the 1890s, however, that the technology became available to cut right across the six-kilometre isthmus. Opened in July 1893, the canal, along with its near-contemporary Suez, helped establish Pireás as a major Mediterranean port and shipping centre. Today supertankers have made it something of an anachronism and the canal has fallen into disrepair, but it remains a memorable sight nonetheless.

Approaching on the Athens road, you cross the canal near its southeastern end, often referred to as Isthmós. From Kórinthos you can use the Loutráki buses to get there and back. At both ends of the **bridge** there's a line of **cafés**, where buses from Athens usually stop – if they're going beyond Kórinthos – rather than into Kórinthos itself. At the Athens end of the bridge is a bus stop for buses to Athens and the Peloponnese, although getting onto buses here is a hit-or-miss affair, depending on seat availability and drivers who can be reluctant to pick up tourists with luggage. To get into Kórinthos, a taxi may be more practical. As you peer over from the bridge, the canal appears a narrow strip of water until a huge freighter, or cruise ship from Pireás to the Ionian islands, assumes toy-like dimensions as it passes nearly 80m below. Thrill-seekers can bungee jump with ZuluBungy (Ⓣ210 51 47 051, Ⓦwww.zulubungy.com; summer Wed–Sun, Apr Sun, May/Oct Sat–Sun) for around €60. At the northwestern end of the canal, by the old Kórinthos–Loutráki ferry dock, there are remains of the **diolkos** (summer Mon noon–7pm, Tues–Sun 8am–7pm; winter Tues–Sun 8.30am–3pm; free), a paved way along which a wheeled platform used to carry boats across the isthmus. In use from Roman times until the twelfth century, the boats were strapped onto the platform after being relieved temporarily of their cargo.

Loutráki and Perahóra

Some 6km north of the canal is the spa resort of **LOUTRÁKI**. The epicentre of the 1981 Corinth earthquake, today it has straight lines of unmemorable concrete buildings. The resort is, nonetheless, immensely popular, with a larger concentration of hotels than anywhere else in the Peloponnese. The visitors are mostly Greek or Italian, coming here since 1847 for the "cure" at the **hot springs**, and to sample Loutráki mineral water – the country's best-selling bottled brand. The thermal baths are at Lékka 24 (summer daily 6am–2pm; winter Mon–Fri 9am–noon & 4–6pm; ⓣ27440 61990). Others come for Greece's oldest **casino** at Posidhónos 48 (daily, open 24hr; ⓣ27440 65501) on the southwest seafront. Near the train station, there is a helpful **tourist kiosk** on E. Venizélou, the main road through town, four blocks south of the bus station, and a second near the baths. The local council has a choice range of well-produced brochures and a town map (ⓦwww.loutraki.gr) available at the kiosks. Loutráki is connected by bus and special summer trains with Athens, and by bus (every 30min) with Kórinthos.

En route to **Cape Melangávi** the road loops through the modern village of **Perahóra** (11km) before heading out to the cape along the shore of **Lake Vouliagméni**, a beautiful two-kilometre-wide lagoon with sheltered swimming. Perahóra is connected by hourly bus with Loutráki; in high season one daily bus makes the journey between Loutráki and Lake Vouliagméni.

Heraion Melangávi (summer daily 8am–7pm; winter Tues–Sun 8.30am–3pm; free) – also known as Ancient Perahóra or Peréa – stands just 1km from the western tip of the peninsula, commanding a marvellous, sweeping view of the coastline and mountains along both sides of the gulf. The site's position is its chief attraction, though there are the identifiable ruins of a sanctuary in two parts, the **Hera Akraia** (*akron* is the extremity of the peninsula) and **Hera Limenia** ("of the port"), as well as the *stoa* of the ancient harbour, which has great snorkelling opportunities. In mythology, it was here that Medea, having been spurned by her husband Jason at Corinth, killed their two children.

Nemea

Ancient **NEMEA**, the location for Hercules' (Herakles) slaying of its namesake lion (his first labour), lies 6km off the road from Kórinthos to Árgos. To get there by public transport, take the bus to modern Neméa and ask to be dropped at Arhéa Neméa, the small village just 300m west of the ruins.

Like Olympia, Nemea held athletic games for the Greek world from the sixth century BC, until these were transferred to Árgos in 270 BC. A sanctuary rather than a town, the principal remains at the **site** (summer daily 8am–7.30pm; winter Mon noon–7pm, Tues–Sun 8.30am–3pm; €3 for site and museum, €4 for site, stadium and museum) are of the **Temple of Nemean Zeus**, currently three slender Doric columns surrounded by other fallen and broken drums, but slowly being reassembled. Nearby are a **palaestra** with **baths** and a Christian **basilica**, built with blocks from the temple. There is also an excellent **museum** (same hours, except summer Mon noon–7pm; included in ticket price), with contextual models, displays relating to the biennial games and items from the area. Outside the site, 500m east, is the **stadium** (same hours as site; €2), which once seated 40,000 spectators. The vaulted entrance tunnel, now reconstructed, and complete with the graffiti of ancient athletes, is the oldest known. There is a guide available, written by archeologist Stephen Miller, who organized the (now quadrennial) **New Nemean Games** in 1996 as a non-commercial alternative to the Olympics; anyone can enter if they run barefoot and wear traditional tunics.

Signs locally indicate the Wine Road of Neméa, marking the notable **vineyards** of the area.

Xylókastro and the coast westward

A string of resorts, popular with Greeks despite the mountain backdrop being damaged by serious fires in 2000 and 2007, runs westwards along the Korinthian coast, accessible by bus or train from Kórinthos. There are hotels in Vraháti, Kokkóni, **Kiáto**, Melíssi and Sykiá, but **XYLÓKASTRO** is of more interest, with a marina, good beaches and accommodation, all in a pleasant setting backed by Mount Kyllíni. The main beach, Pefkiás, is lined by a strip of pine woodland. Cheapest of its dozen **hotels** is the basic but very hospitable *Hermes*, Ioánnou 95, near Pefkiás (ⓣ27430 22250, ⓔnikapos@panafonet.gr ;B&B ③). Others include the *Kyani Akti*, near the sea at Tsaldhári 68 (ⓣ27430 22225, ⓕ27430 28930; ③), and the *Apollon*, housed in a fine old building at Ioánnou 119 (ⓣ27430 22239, ⓔapollonx@otenet.gr; ④). The long seafront boasts a number of restaurants, of which *Zesti Gonia* is friendly and serves good fish, while *Palea Exedhra* has more variety. It is only possible to connect westwards with Pátra and Ahaïa by train, not by local bus, since the latter only run to and from Kórinthos.

The Stymphalian Lake

With your own transport, you can cut across the hills from Neméa towards Arcadia, via another Herculean locale, the **Stymphalian Lake** (around 35km from ancient Nemea). In myth, this was the nesting ground of man-eating birds that preyed upon travellers, suffocating them with their wings, and poisoned local crops with their excrement. Hercules roused them from the water with a rattle, then shot them down – one of the more straightforward of his labours. The lake is known in modern Greek as **Límni Stymfalías**, though it is really more of a swamp: an enormous depression with seasonal waters, ringed by reed beds, woods and the dark peaks of Mount Olíyirtos to the south. Between Stymfalía village and the lake are the extensive site of **ancient Stymfalos**, and the ruins of the thirteenth-century Frankish Cistercian **Abbey of Zaráka**, one of the few Gothic buildings in Greece. Signs around the lake mark suggested hiking routes, while a museum of traditional crafts and the local environment is due to open by 2008.

If you don't have your own transport, the most promising approach to the lake is from Kiáto on the Gulf of Kórinthos, where there are several hotels and rooms to rent; the road, much better than that from Neméa, has the occasional bus. The nearest place to stay is the pleasant – though very busy at weekends – *Hotel Karteri* (ⓣ27470 31203; B&B ③), behind the *Taverna Leonidas* in **Kartéri** village, 3km west of the lake. Some of the rustic-style rooms have their own working fireplaces.

Ancient Sikyon

Some 6km inland from Kiáto, ancient **SIKYON** (Sikyóna; summer daily 8.30am–3pm; winter Tues–Sun 8.30am–3pm; €2) is a fairly accessible if little-known site, which deserves more than the handful of visitors it attracts each year. Six buses a day run from Kiáto (on the bus and train routes from Kórinthos) to the village ofVasilikó, on the edge of a broad escarpment running parallel to the sea, from where it's a kilometre's walk to the site.

In ancient history, Sikyon's principal claim to fame came early in the sixth century BC, when the tyrant Kleisthenes purportedly kept a court of sufficient wealth and influence to entertain suitors for his daughter's hand for a full year. After his death the place was rarely heard of politically, except as a consistent ally of the Spartans, but a mild renaissance ensued at the end of the fourth century when Demetrios Polyorketes moved Sikyon to its present location from the plain below. The town became renowned for sculptors, painters and metallurgic artisans, and flourished well into Roman times; it was the birthplace of Alexander the Great's chief sculptor, Lysippos, and, allegedly, of the art of sculptural relief.

The road from Vasilikó cuts through the site, which is fenced off into a number of enclosures. To the right is the **Roman baths museum**, which shelters mosaics of griffins from the second to third centuries AD. To the left are the majority of the public buildings, with a theatre and stadium on the hillside above. As you enter the **main site** (unrestricted access), opposite the Roman baths, the foundations of the **Temple of Artemis** are to your left. Beyond it are traces of a **bouleuterion** (senate house) dating from the first half of the third century BC. In the far right-hand corner, at the base of the hill, are remains of the **Gymnasium of Kleinias**; this is on two levels, the lower dating from around 300 BC, the upper from Roman times.

Although only the first ten rows of seats have been excavated, the impressive outline of the **theatre** – larger than that of Epidaurus – is easy to distinguish. From the upper half there is a marvellous view encompassing the rest of the site, the village of Vasilikó, the lemon and olive groves around Kiáto, plus the Gulf of Kórinthos and distant mountains.

Mycenae (Mykínes) and around

Tucked into a fold of the hills just east of the road from Kórinthos to Árgos, Agamemnon's citadel at **MYCENAE** fits the legend better than any other place in Greece. It was uncovered in 1874 by the German archeologist Heinrich Schliemann (who also excavated the site of Troy), impelled by his single-minded belief that there was a factual basis to Homer's epics. Schliemann's finds of brilliantly crafted gold and sophisticated tomb architecture bore out the accuracy of Homer's epithets of "well-built Mycenae, rich in gold".

Mycenaean history and legend

The Mycenae-Árgos region is one of the longest occupied in Greece, with evidence of Neolithic settlements from around 3000 BC. But it is to the period from around 1550 to 1200 BC – that the citadel of Mycenae and its associated drama belong. This period is known as **Mycenaean**, a term that covers not just the Mycenae region but a whole Bronze Age civilization that flourished in southern Greece at the time.

According to the **legend** related in Homer's *Iliad* and *Odyssey*, and Aeschylus' *Oresteia*, the city of Mycenae was founded by Perseus, the slayer of Medusa the gorgon, before it fell into the bloodied hands of the **House of Atreus**. Atreus, in an act of vengeance for his wife's seduction by his brother Thyestes, murdered Thyestes' sons, and fed them to their father. Not surprisingly, this incurred the wrath of the gods: Thyestes' daughter, Pelopia, subsequently bore her father a son, Aegisthus, who later murdered Atreus and restored Thyestes to the throne. The next generation saw the gods' curse fall upon Atreus' son **Agamemnon**. On his return to Mycenae after commanding the Greek forces in the Trojan War – a role in which he had earlier consented to the sacrifice of his own daughter, Iphigeneia – he was killed in his bath by his wife Klytemnestra and her lover, the very same Aegisthus who had killed his father. The tragic cycle was completed by Agamemnon's son, Orestes, who, egged on by his sister

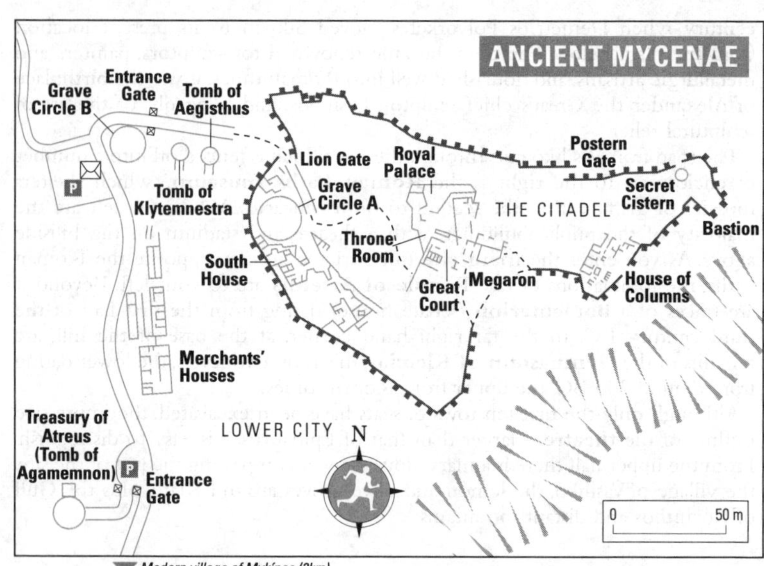

Elektra, took revenge by murdering his mother, Klytemnestra, and was pursued by the Furies until Athena finally lifted the curse on the dynasty.

The **archeological remains** of Mycenae fit remarkably easily with the tale, at least if it is taken as a poetic rendering of dynastic struggles, or, as most scholars now believe it to be, a merging of stories from various periods. The buildings unearthed by Schliemann show signs of occupation from around 1950 BC, as well as two periods of intense disruption, around 1200 BC and again in 1100 BC – at which stage the town, though still prosperous, was abandoned.

No coherent explanation has been put forward for these events, since the traditional "Dorian invasions" theory has fallen from favour; but it seems that war among the rival kingdoms was a major factor in the Mycenaean decline. These struggles appear to have escalated as the civilization developed in the thirteenth century BC: excavations at Troy revealed the sacking of that city, quite possibly by forces led by a king from Mycenae, in 1240 BC. The Mycenae citadel seems to have been replanned, and heavily fortified, during this period.

The Citadel

The **Citadel of Mycenae** (summer Mon 12.30–7.30pm Tues–Sun 8am–7.30pm; winter 8.30am–5pm; €8) is entered through the famous **Lion Gate**, whose huge sloping gateposts bolster walls which were termed "Cyclopean" by later Greeks in bewildered attribution to the only beings deemed capable of their construction. Above them a graceful carved relief stands out in confident assertion: Mycenae at its height led a confederation of Argolid towns (Tiryns, Árgos, Assine, Hermione – present-day Ermióni), dominated the Peloponnese and exerted influence throughout the Aegean. The motif of a pillar supported by two muscular lions was probably the symbol of the Mycenaean royal house, for a seal found on the site bears a similar device. Inside the walls to the right is **Grave Circle A**, the royal cemetery excavated by Schliemann who believed it contained the bodies of Agamemnon and his followers, murdered on their triumphant return from Troy. Opening one of the graves, he found a tightly fitting and magnificent gold mask that had somehow preserved the flesh of a Mycenaean noble; "I have gazed upon the face of Agamemnon," he exclaimed in an excited cable to the king of Greece. For a time it seemed that this provided irrefutable evidence of the truth of Homer's tale. In fact, the burials date from about three centuries before the Trojan War, though given Homer's possible combining of several earlier sagas, there's no reason why they should not have been connected with a Mycenaean king Agamemnon. They were certainly royal graves, for the finds (now in the National Archeological Museum in Athens) are among the richest that archeology has yet unearthed.

Schliemann took the extensive **South House**, beyond the grave circle, to be the Palace of Agamemnon. However, a building much grander and more likely to be the **Royal Palace** was later discovered near the summit of the acropolis. Rebuilt in the thirteenth century BC, this is an impressively elaborate and evocative building complex; although the ruins are only at ground level, the different rooms are easily discernible. Like all Mycenaean palaces, it is centred around a **great court**: on the south side, a staircase would have led via an anteroom to the big rectangular **throne room**; on the east, a double porch gave access to the **megaron**, the grand reception hall with its traditional circular hearth. The small rooms to the north are believed to have been **royal apartments**, and in one of them the remains of a red stuccoed bath have led to its fanciful identification as the scene of Agamemnon's murder.

With the accompaniment of the sound of bells drifting down from goats grazing on the hillsides, a stroll around the ramparts is evocative of earlier times. A more salutary reminder of the nature of life in Mycenaean times is the **secret cistern** at the eastern end of the ramparts, created around 1225 BC. Whether it was designed to enable the citadel's occupants to withstand siege from outsiders, rival Mycenaeans or even an increasingly alienated peasantry is not known. Steps lead down to a deep underground spring; it's still possible to descend the whole way, though you'll need to have a torch and be sure-footed, since there's a drop to the water at the final turn of the twisting passageways. Nearby is the **House of Columns**, a large and stately building with the base of a stairway that once led to an upper storey.

Only the ruling Mycenaean elite could live within the citadel itself. Hence the main part of town lay outside the walls and, in fact, extensive remains of **merchants' houses** have been uncovered near to the road. Their contents included Linear B tablets recording the spices used to scent oils, along with large amounts of pottery, the quantity suggesting that the early Mycenaeans may have dabbled in the perfume trade. The discovery of the tablets has also prompted a reassessment of the sophistication of Mycenaean civilization, for they show that, here at least, writing was not limited to government scribes working in the royal palaces as had previously been thought, and that around the citadel there may have been a commercial city of some size and wealth.

Alongside the merchants' houses are the remains of **Grave Circle B**, from around 1650 BC and possibly of an earlier, rival dynasty to those kings buried in Grave Circle A, and two **tholos** (circular chamber-type) tombs, identified by Schliemann as the **tombs of "Aegisthus" and "Klytemnestra"**. The former, closer to the Lion Gate, dates from around 1500 BC and has now collapsed, so is roped off; the latter dates from some two centuries later – thus corresponding with the Trojan timescale – and can still be entered.

The Treasury of Atreus

Four hundred metres down the road from the Citadel site is another, far more startling, tholos, known as the **Treasury of Atreus** or – the currently preferred official name – "Tomb of Agamemnon" (same hours as the Citadel; admission included in Citadel entrance fee). This was certainly a royal burial vault at a late stage in Mycenae's history, contemporary with the "Tomb of Klytemnestra", so the attribution to Agamemnon is as good as any – if the king were indeed the historic leader of the Trojan expedition. Whoever it belonged to, this beehive-like structure, built without the use of mortar, is an impressive monument to Mycenaean building skills. Entering the tomb through a majestic fifteen-metre corridor, you arrive at the chamber doorway, above which is a great lintel formed by two immense slabs of stone – one of which, a staggering 9m long, is estimated to weigh 118 tonnes.

Practicalities: Mykínes

The modern village of **MYKÍNES** is 2km from the main Kórinthos–Árgos road and the small train station at Fíkhti. Buses from Athens to Árgos or Náfplio usually drop passengers at Fíkhti (where the café sells bus tickets), rather than in Mykínes village; crowded local buses from Náfplio via Árgos serve the village and site. The site is a further two-kilometre walk uphill from Mykínes centre, and in season has a couple of canteens and a **post office** caravan.

Accommodation and eating

Unless you have your own transport, you might want to stay at Mykínes, which can be heavily touristy by day, but is quiet once the site has closed and the tour buses depart. Along the village's single street, there is quite an array of hotels – most of their names taken from characters in the House of Atreus saga – as well as a number of signs for rooms. Mycenae's two **campsites** are both centrally located, on the way into the village. Both open all year and there's not a great deal to choose between them, though *Camping Mykines* (Ⓣ27510 76121, Ⓕ27510 76247) is smaller and a little closer to the site than *Camping Atreus* (Ⓣ27510 76221, Ⓕ27510 76760).

All the **restaurants** cater mainly for lunchtime tour groups, so don't raise your expectations too high. Places worth trying are the *Electra*, the *King Menelaos* and the *Menelaos*, all along the main street.

Belle Helene Ⓣ27510 76225, Ⓔla_belle_helene@altecnet.gr. The second oldest (1885) hotel in Greece, converted from the 1862 house used by Schliemann during his excavations. Rooms with the original layout (so not en suite) are named after famous guests who have slept in them. Signatures in the visitors' books include Virginia Woolf, Henry Moore, Sartre and Debussy. Also has a good restaurant. B&B ❸

Rooms Dassis Ⓣ27510 76123, Ⓔdassisrooms@yahoo.com. A pleasant, well-organized setup, run – along with useful Internet facilities below – by Canadian Marion Dassis. Rooms have mosquito screening. Groups and students welcomed. Discounts for Rough Guide readers. B&B ❸

Klytemnestra Ⓣ27510 76451, Ⓕ27510 76731. Clean, pleasant, modern rooms run by friendly Greek-Australians. B&B ❸

Le Petite Planète Ⓣ27510 76240, Ⓦwww.petite-planet.gr. At the top end of the village, so the nearest hotel to the site, recently refurbished, with great views and a swimming pool. Open April–Oct, sometimes winter too. B&B ❹

The Argive Heraion and Ancient Midea

The little-visited **Argive Heraion** (daily 8.30am–3pm; free) is an important sanctuary from Mycenaean to Roman times and the site where Agamemnon is said to have been chosen as leader of the Greek expedition to Troy. It lies 7km south of Mycenae, off the new highway that continues to Tiryns, and with sweeping views out over the plain to Árgos. There are various Mycenaean tombs near the isolated site, but the principal remains of a temple complex, built over three interconnecting terraces, date from the seventh to fifth centuries BC. There are also Roman baths and a *palaestra* (wrestling and athletics gym). The central temple base is of a similar size to that of the Parthenon in Athens.

The Heraion makes a pleasant diversion for anyone driving between Mycenae and Náfplio, or an enjoyable afternoon's walk from Mykínes – it takes a little over an hour if you can find the old track southeast from the village, running parallel to the new road towards Ayía Triádha. Hónikas (Néo Iréo), 2.5km southwest from the site, has the occasional bus to Árgos; Ayía Triádha, 5km on, has more frequent connections to Náfplio.

Ancient Midea (daily; free), in gorgeous countryside between the villages of Midhéa and Dhendhrá, was the third fortified Mycenaean palace of the area, after Mycenae and Tiryns. Excavations have uncovered a fortified hilltop area of some six acres, the remains of a young girl – an earthquake victim in the thirteenth century BC – and numerous workshop items. However, the most famous find, from the ancient cemetery site at nearby Dhendhrá, is the remarkable Dendra cuirass, bronze body armour now in the archeological museum in Náfplio.

Árgos

ÁRGOS, 12km south of the Mykínes junction, is said to be the oldest continuously inhabited town in Greece (ca. 5000 years), although you wouldn't guess it from first impressions. However, this busy trading centre has some pleasant squares and Neoclassical buildings, and a brief stop is worthwhile for the excellent museum and mainly Roman ruins. Try to time your visit to coincide with the regular Wednesday and Saturday produce **market**, which draws locals from all the surrounding hill villages; the market square is between the Kapodhistría barracks' three-sided courtyard and the Neoclassical market building, and is unofficially referred to as the Laïkí Agorá.

The modern **archeological museum** (Tues–Sun 8.30am–3pm; €2, or €3 for the museum and theatre) is just off the pedestrianized Elgás street between the market square and the main church square, Platía Ayíou Pétrou. It makes an interesting detour after Mycenae, with a good collection of Mycenaean tomb objects and armour as well as extensive pottery finds. The region's Roman occupation is well represented here, in sculpture and mosaics, and there are also finds from Lerna on display.

Before leaving Árgos, visit the town's ancient remains which are ten minutes' walk down the Trípoli road – initially Fidhónos, then Theátrou – from the market square. The **site** (Tues–Sun 8.30am–3pm; €2) is surprisingly extensive and excavations continue. The Classical Greek **theatre**, adapted by the Romans, looks oddly narrow from the road, but climb up to the top and it feels immense. Estimated to have held 20,000 spectators – six thousand more than Epidaurus – it is matched on the Greek mainland only by the theatres at Megalopolis and Dodóna. Alongside are the remains of an **odeion** and **Roman baths**.

Above the site looms the ancient **acropolis**, on a conical hill capped by the largely Frankish **medieval castle** of Lárissa (Tues–Sun 8.30am–3pm; free), built on sixth-century BC foundations and later augmented by the Venetians and Turks. Massively walled, cisterned and guttered, the sprawling ruins offer wonderful views – the reward for a long, steep haul up, either on indistinct trails beyond the theatre, or a very roundabout road.

Practicalities

You may need to change **buses** in Árgos since some connections are better than those in Náfplio. There are local bus stops and a ticket kiosk on Kalléryi, at the southeast corner of the market square near the Dhikastikó Katástima building, for Mykínes and Nemea. Just around the corner, on Kapodhistría, is a KTEL office for buses back towards Athens, and for Trípoli, Spárti and south towards Leonídhio. **Taxis** go from Fidhónos, the market square's central street, as do buses to Kefalári and Kivéri (get off at Mýli for Lerna).

For a good meal between buses, try the *Retro* restaurant on the central square, although there are cheaper options in the backstreets. Staying overnight shouldn't prove necessary, unless you find Náfplio full – a possibility in high season. **Hotels** on the Ayíou Pétrou main square include the comfortable, air-conditioned *Morfeas* (Ⓣ27510 68317, Ⓦwww.hotel-morfeas.gr; B&B ❸) with balconies overlooking the square, and *Mycenae* (Ⓣ27510 68332, Ⓔmycenae@otenet.gr; B&B ❻), though the latter prefers longer-stay guests, groups, families or archeologists.

Tiryns (Tírynthos)

In Mycenaean times **TIRYNS** stood by the sea, commanding the coastal approaches to Árgos and Mycenae. The Aegean shore gradually receded, leaving the fortress stranded on a low hillock in today's plains, surrounded by citrus groves, and alongside the Argolid's principal modern prison. It's not the most enchanting of settings, which in part explains why this highly accessible, substantial site is undeservedly neglected and relatively empty of visitors. After the crowds at Mycenae, however, the opportunity to wander about Homer's "wall-girt Tiryns" in near-solitude is worth taking. The site lies just east of the main Árgos–Náfplio road, and half-hourly local buses stop for passengers outside.

The Citadel

As at Mycenae, Homer's epigrams correspond remarkably well to what you can see on the ground at Tiryns. The fortress, now over three thousand years old, is undeniably impressive, and the site itself had been occupied for four thousand years before that. The walls, 750m long and up to 7m thick, formed of huge Cyclopean stones, dominate the site; the Roman guidebook writer Pausanias, happening on the site in the second century AD, found them "more amazing than the Pyramids" – a claim that seems a little exaggerated, even considering that the walls then stood twice their present height.

The entrance to the site (daily 8.30am–3pm; €3) is on the far side of the fortress from the road, and visitors can only explore a restricted number of passages, staircases and the parts of the palace. Despite this, the sophistication and defensive function of the citadel's layout are evident as soon as you climb the **entrance ramp**. Wide enough to allow access to chariots, the ramp is angled to leave the right-hand, unshielded side of any invading force exposed for the entire ascent, before forcing a sharp turn at the top – surveyed by defenders from within. The **gateways**, too, constitute a formidable barrier; the outer one would have been similar in design to Mycenae's Lion Gate, though its lintel is missing, so there is no heraldic motif that could confirm a dynastic link between the sites.

Of the **palace** itself, only the limestone foundations survive, but the fact that they occupy a level site makes them generally more legible than the ruins of hilly and boulder-strewn Mycenae, and you can gain a clearer idea of its structure. The walls would have been of sun-dried brick, stucco-covered and decorated with frescoes. Fragments of the latter were found on the site, both now in the Náfplio museum: one depicting a boar hunt, the other a life-sized frieze of courtly women. From the forecourt one enters a spacious **colonnaded court** with a round sacrificial altar in the middle. A typically Mycenaean double porch leads directly ahead to the **megaron** (great hall), where the base of a throne was found – it's now in the Archeological Museum in Athens, with miscellaneous finds and frescoes from the site. The massive round clay hearth characteristic of these Mycenaean halls – there's a perfect example at Nestor's Palace (see p.256) – is no longer to be seen at Tiryns, because some time in the sixth century BC this part of the palace became the site of a temple to Hera, a structure whose column bases now pepper the ground. **Royal apartments** lead off on either side; the women's quarters are thought to have been to the right, while to the left is the bathroom, its floor – a huge, single flat stone – still intact. The **lower acropolis**, north of the megaron, is currently out of bounds due to the excavation of two underground cisterns discovered at its far end in the late 1980s.

A tower further off to the left of the megaron gives access to a **secret staircase**, as at Mycenae, which winds down to an inconspicuous **postern gate**, although currently both are closed off. The site beyond the megaron is separated by an enormous inner wall and can only be viewed from a distance.

Náfplio and around

NÁFPLIO (also sometimes known as Nauplia or Navplion) is a rarity amongst Greek towns. A lively, beautifully sited place, it exudes a grand, occasionally slightly faded elegance, inherited from the days when it was the fledgling capital of modern Greece. The seat of government was here from 1829 to 1834 and it was in Náfplio that the first president, Kapodhistrias, was assassinated by vengeful Maniot clansmen. It was here too that the young Bavarian Prince Otho, put forward by the European powers to be (briefly) the first king of Greece, had his initial royal residence from 1833 to 1834; he is commemorated by a new but locally unpopular statue. Since the 1980s the town has increasingly served as a popular year-round weekend retreat, with the result that hotel rooms and meals have crept up to Athens rates and above, but it remains by far the most attractive base for exploring the Argolid and resting for a while by the sea. The nearest good **beach** is at Karathónas, with others further afield at Toló, Kastráki, Dhrépano and Íria.

Arrival and information

Wedged between the sea and a doubly fortressed headland, the old part of Náfplio is an easy town to find your way around. Arriving by bus, you are set down at the **bus station** (Ⓣ27520 27323) on Syngroú, just south of the interlocking squares, **Platía Trión Navárhon** and **Platía Kapodhistría**. The **train** will deposit you near the junction of Polyzoïdhou and Irakléous, where a new station has been built, with two old carriages serving as ticket office and waiting room. The **tourist office** is at 25-Martíou 2 (daily 9am–1pm & 4–8pm; ⓣ27520 24444), but hours are unpredictable and the information provided is not always accurate.

Accommodation

Accommodation in Náfplio is generally overpriced for what you get, particularly in the old town, though out of season during the week most **hotels** drop their prices significantly. There are a number of private **rooms**, mostly clustered on the slope above the main squares. A few other hotels and rooms, generally the last to fill but often more reasonably priced, are located out in the modern town on the Árgos road (known locally as "stoús Argoús"). If you come by car, most old town hotels do not have easily driveable access, and finding a parking space near the old town is very difficult in summer – your best chance may be on the harbourfront. There is nowhere to **camp** in Náfplio itself, but southeast on the stretch of coast from Toló (11km from Náfplio) to Íria (26km away), there are a dozen or so campsites – see p.191.

Amymone Óthonos 39 ⓣ27520 99477, ⓦwww.amymone.gr. High-quality pension in a recently restored small mansion in the heart of the town. B&B ④–⑥

Byron Plátonos 2 ⓣ27520 22351, ⓦwww.byronhotel.gr. A beautifully restored old mansion just above Áyios Spyrídhon church. Some rooms have balconies and/or views. ③–④

Dioscouri Zygomála and Výronos 6 ⓣ27520 28550, ⓔdiosco1@otenet.gr. A friendly hotel, reached via a steep flight of steps. Rooms at the front overlook the old town and the port. ④

Economou Argonaftón 22 ⓣ27520 23955. To the northeast of town, near the Dia supermarket on the Árgos road. Recently refurbished, hospitable and excellent value – worth the 15min walk from the centre. Some dorm beds available (€15). ③

Kapodistrias Kokínou 20 ⓣ27520 29366, ⓦwww.hotelkapodistrias.gr. Beautifully decorated rooms, each one different, in a 200-year-old house just 50m from where Kapodhistrías was murdered. ③; weekends ④

King Othon 1 Farmakopoúlou 4 ⓣ27520 27585, ⓦwww.kingothon.gr. Popular, well-placed hotel, beautifully refurbished with an impressive staircase. There is a second, pricier, *King Othon 2* around the corner at Spiliádhou 5. April–Oct. ④–⑤

Leto Zygomála 28 ⓣ27520 28093, ⓦwww.leto-hotel.com. A friendly, recently refurbished hotel, with fridges in the rooms, located up against the Akronafplía fortress. March–Oct. Breakfast €6. ④

Marianna Potamiánou 9 ⓣ27520 24256, ⓦwww.pensionmarianna.gr. Very comfortable, restored house by the Akronafplía fortress walls, with some of the best views in town from the terrace where an organic breakfast is served. New maisonettes and apartments. Parking nearby. B&B ④

Park Dhervenakíon 1, off Platía Kapodhistría ⓣ27520 27428, ⓕ27520 27045. Large, well-run 1960s hotel – refurbished internally – which may have space when smaller old-town places are full. ⑤

The Town and around

There's ample pleasure in just wandering about Náfplio: looking around the harbourfront, walking the coastal circuit around to the rocky town beach and, when you're feeling energetic, exploring the great twin fortresses of **Palamídhi** and **Akronafplía** on the headland. Náfplio also offers some of the best **restaurants** and most varied and modern shops in the eastern Peloponnese, plus a range of facilities, including car rental.

Palamídhi

The **Palamídhi**, Náfplio's principal fort, was a key military flashpoint of the War of Independence. The Greek commander Kolokotronis – of whom there's

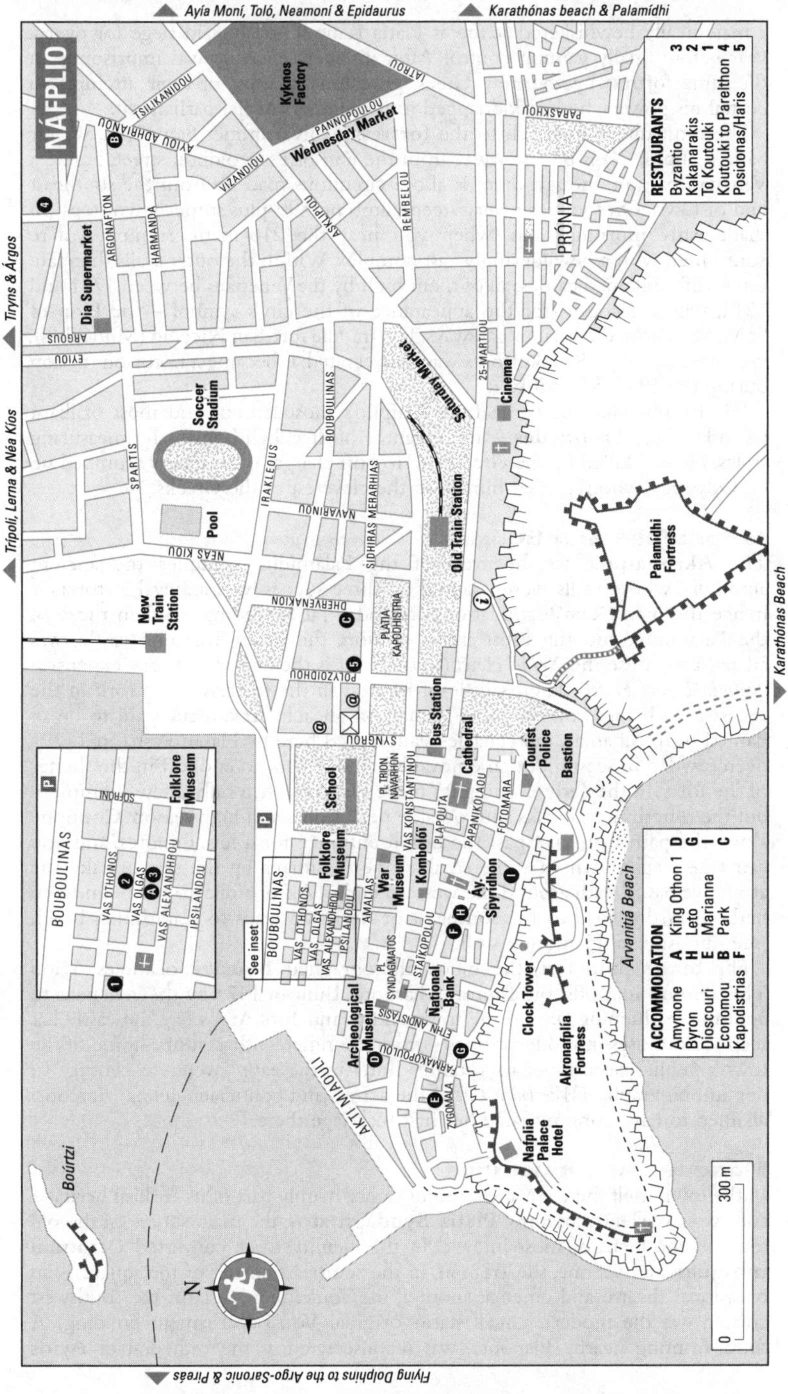

NÁFPLIO

▲ Trípoli, Lerna & Néa Kíos
▲ Tiryns & Árgos
▶ Ayía Moní, Toló, Neamoní & Epidaurus
▶ Karathónas beach & Palamídhi
▼ Karathónas Beach
◀ Flying Dolphins to the Argo-Saronic & Pireás

N

Boúrtzi

BOUBOULINAS
VAS OTHONOS
VAS OLGAS
VAS ALEXANDHROU
IPSILANDOU
SOFRONI
Folklore Museum

See inset

New Train Station
Pool
Soccer Stadium
Dia Supermarket
EYIOU
ARGOUS
ARGONAFTON
SPARTIS
HARMANDA
AYIOU ADHRIANOU
TSILIKANIDOU
VIZANDIOU
NEAS KIOU
IRAKLEOUS
Kyknos Factory
PANNOPOULOU
Wednesday Market
ASKLIPIOU
IATROU
REMBELOU
BOUBOULINAS
SIDHIRAS MERARHIAS
NAVARINOU
DHERVENAKION
POLYZOIDHOU
SYNGROU
School
AKTI MIAOULI
Archeological Museum
AMALIAS
War Museum
PL TRION NAVARHON
PLATIA KAPODHISTRIA
VAS KONSTANTINOU
PL SYNDAGMATOS
Kombolói
Bus Station
Saturday Market
Old Train Station
National Bank
STAÏKOPOLOU
ETHN ANDISTASIS
FARMAKOPOULOU
ZYGOMALA
PLAPOUTA
PAPANIKOLAOU
Cathedral
Áy. Spyridhon
FOTOMARA
25-MARTIOU
Cinema
Tourist Police
Bastion
Clock Tower
Nafplia Palace Hotel
Akronafplía Fortress
Arvanitiá Beach
Palamídhi Fortress
PRÓNIA
PARASKHOU

0 — 300 m

ACCOMMODATION

Amymone	A	King Othon 1	D
Byron	H	Leto	G
Dioscouri	E	Marianna	I
Economou	B	Park	C
Kapodistrias	F		

RESTAURANTS

Byzantio	3
Kakanarakis	2
To Koutouki	1
Koutouki to Parelthon	4
Posidonas/Haris	5

a majestically bewhiskered statue at Platía Kapodhistría – laid siege for over a year before finally gaining control. After independence, he was imprisoned in the same fortress by the new Greek government; wary of their attempts to curtail his powers, he had kidnapped four members of the parliament.

The most direct approach to the **fortress** (daily: summer 8am–7pm; winter 8am–6.30pm; €4) is by a stairway from the end of Polyzoïdhou street, beside a Venetian bastion, though there is also a circuitous road up from the southeast end of town. On foot, it's a very steep climb up 890-plus stone-hewn steps (in shade early morning) and, when you near the 216-metre summit, you're confronted with a bewilderingly vast complex. Within the outer walls there are three self-contained castles, all of them built by the Venetians between 1711 and 1714, which accounts for the appearance of the city's symbol – the Lion of St Mark – above the various gateways. The middle fort, San Niccolo (Miltiádhes), was the one where Kolokotronis was incarcerated; it became a notorious prison during the 1947–51 civil war.

The fortress takes its name from Náfplio's most famous and most brilliant legendary son, **Palamedes** – the inventor of dice, lighthouses and measuring scales. He was killed by the Greeks at Troy, on charges of treachery trumped up by Odysseus, who regarded himself as the cleverest of the Greeks.

Akronafplía and Boúrtzi

The **Akronafplía**, to the west of the Palamídhi, occupies the ancient acropolis, whose walls were adapted by three successive medieval restorers – hence the name. The fortifications are today far less complete than those of the Palamídhi, and the most intact section, the lower Torrione castle, was adapted to house the *Xenia Hotel* (to the west is the newer and very expensive *Nafplia Palace Hotel*). There's little of interest in the fortress, but a fork in the access road brings you down to a small pay-beach, **Arvanitiá** (said to be so named from Albanian mercenaries slaughtered here by Hasan Pasha in 1779), overcrowded in season but an enjoyable enough spot to cool off in the shelter of the forts. In the early evening it's more pleasant, with only a few swimmers, but the refreshment kiosks shut outside peak hours and high season. Continue along the path from just past the beach entrance for a few minutes, and you can take steps down to some small stone platforms by the sea, or take the attractive paved path around the western end of Akronafplía, to the main town harbour. A dirt road to the southeast of Arvanitiá leads to Karathónas beach (see opposite), a 45-minute walk.

The town's third fort, the much-photographed **Boúrtzi**, occupies Ayíou Theodhórou islet offshore from the harbour. Built in 1473 by the Venetians to control the shipping lane to the town and to much of Árgos bay, the castle has seen various uses in modern times – from the nineteenth-century home of the town's public executioner to a luxury hotel in the early twentieth century. In her autobiography *I Was Born Greek*, the actress and politician Melina Mercouri claimed to have consummated her first marriage there.

Mosques and museums

In the town itself there are a few minor sights, mainly part of its Turkish heritage, and two excellent museums. **Platía Syndágmatos**, the main square of the old town, is the focus of most interest. In the vicinity, three converted **Ottoman mosques** survive: one, the Trianón, in the southeast corner of the square, is an occasional theatre and cinema; another, the Vouleftikón, just off the southwest corner, was the modern Greek state's original **Voulí** (parliament building). A third, fronting nearby Plapoúta, was reconsecrated as the cathedral of **Áyios**

Yeóryios, having started life as a Venetian Catholic church. Nearby are a pair of handsome **Turkish fountains** – one abutting the south wall of the theatre-mosque, the other on Kapodhistría, opposite the church of Áyios Spyrídhon. On the steps of the latter, president Ioannis Kapodhistrías was assassinated by two of the Mavromihalis clan from the Máni in September 1831; there is a scar left in the stone by one of the bullets. The Catholic church, which has also been a mosque, on Potamiánou, has a monument to foreigners who died in the War of Independence, including Byron.

The **archeological museum** (Tues–Sun 8.30am–3pm, closed for refurbishment, due to reopen in 2008; €2) occupies a dignified Venetian mansion at the western end of Syndágmatos. It has some good collections, as you'd expect in a town near the Argolid sites, including a unique and more or less complete suit of Mycenaean armour, the Dendra cuirass from around 1400 BC, and reconstructed frescoes from Tiryns.

The fine **Peloponnesian Folklore Foundation Museum** (Mon, Wed–Sun 9am–3pm, closed Feb; €3), at Vassiléos Alexándhrou 1, features gorgeous embroideries, costumes and traditional household items from all over Greece. At Staïkopoúlou 25 is possibly the world's only **Komboloï (worry-beads) Museum** (daily 9.30am–8.30pm; €3), while a little further down at no. 40 you can see shadow puppets being made by Ilias Moros at the workshop To Enotion. The **War Museum** (Tues–Sun 9am–2pm; free) at Amalías 22 has weaponry, uniforms, illustrations and other military memorabilia from the War of Independence to the civil war, including a series of portraits of the heroes of the War of Independence, enabling you to put faces to all those familiar Greek street names.

Karathónas beach

The closest proper beach to Náfplio is at **Karathónas**, a fishing hamlet just over the headland beyond the Palamídhi fortress, which can be reached by a short spur off the drive going up to the ramparts. A more direct dirt road, theoretically closed to traffic, around the base of the intervening cliffs, can make a pleasant 45-minute walk; however, women alone are occasionally pestered by local scooter drivers. There are four morning bus services from Náfplio in season. The narrow **sandy beach** stretches for a couple of kilometres, with a summer taverna at its far end. Karathónas attracts plenty of Greek day-trippers in season, along with windsurfing foreigners in camper vans; in summer, cafés compete to provide the loudest music. There are some organized **rock climbing** routes between Náfplio and Karathónas (ask at the tourist office for information).

Eating, drinking and nightlife

Waterside **Bouboulínas**, where the locals take their early-evening *vólta*, is lined with luxurious cafés where the beautiful people meet; tourists not wearing designer clothes and gold jewellery may feel a little out of place here. A cosier place to start restaurant menu-gazing in Náfplio is **Staïkopoúlou**, with many enjoyable if touristy **tavernas**. For **breakfast** or coffee, there's the *Propylaion* right beside the bus station; assorted bakeries, ice-cream parlours and juice bars around Platía Syndágmatos are also worth investigating. Eating out is oriented towards dinner rather than lunch, and **nightlife** is mainly along Bouboulínas and Syngroú. A quieter drink can be had at the **cafés** on Platía Syndágmatos, which stay open late. The real night-out haunts are the numerous huge discos and expensive nightclubs on the coast road out towards Néo Kíos.

Byzantio Vassiléos Alexándhrou 15. Excellent and friendly taverna, on a quiet corner of a beautiful street, with a varied menu and large portions. Specialities include home-made sausages.

Kakanarakis Vassilísis Ólgas 18 ⓣ27520 25371. A lively place serving a variety of dependably good *mezédhes*, plus dishes such as braised cockerel (*kókoras*) with noodles, and *kokkinistó* (meat simmered in tomato sauce). Open evenings only; popular with locals so arrive early or book ahead.

To Koutouki Vassilísis Ólgas. Stylish taverna on square by Áyios Nikólaos church with good *mezédhes* and *mayireftá*.

Koutouki to Parelthon Profítis Ilías 12. The place to come for excellent *mezédhes* at very reasonable prices.

Posidonas/Haris Sidhirás Merarhías. Eating out in the park, with tasty, well-prepared *mezédhes*, at good prices.

Listings

Banks These are concentrated around Platía Syndágmatos and along Amalías; most have ATMs.

Bookshops Odyssey, on Platía Syndágmatos, has a good stock of English-language books, newspapers, cassettes, CDs and videos.

Car rental Avis, Bouboulínas 51 ⓣ27520 24160, ⓕ27520 24164; Safeway, Eyíou 2 ⓣ27520 22155; or Staïkos Travel, Bouboulínas 50 ⓣ27520 27950, ⓔstaikostravel@naf.forthnet.gr. They are agents for train tickets and can also book ferries and flights.

Cinema On Kyrinéas, near the junction of 25-Martíou and the Árgos road, showing English-language films with Greek subtitles.

Internet Posto, Sidhirás Merarhías.

Laundries 25-Martíou 28.

Post office The main branch (Mon–Fri 7.30am–2pm) is on the northwest corner of Platía Kapodhistría.

Scooter, motorbike and bicycle rental Bouboulínas 49; MotorTraffic, Sidhirás Merarhías 15 Nikopoulos.

Taxis There's a rank on Syngroú, opposite the bus station.

Tourist police Koundourióti ⓣ27520 28131. Helpful and open daily 7.30am–9pm.

Watersports Náfplio Diving Center ⓣ27520 27201, ⓦwww.nafpliodivingcenter.gr. Scuba instruction – also at Toló (Sékeri 67).

Beaches around Náfplio: Toló, Kastráki and beyond

Southeast from Náfplio are the ever-expanding resorts of **Toló** and **Kastráki** – popular and established enough to feature in some British package-holiday brochures. Inevitably, this means that they are busy at the height of the season, although they're still more tranquil than the big island resorts; you can always seek refuge at the low-key places further along the coast.

Toló (Tolon)

TOLÓ, 11km from Náfplio (hourly buses in season; last back at 10pm), is frankly overdeveloped, with a line of thirty or more hotels and campsites swamping its limited sands. Out of season it can still be quite a pleasant resort and the new bypass has, to some extent, improved traffic in the central area, but in summer it is about as un-Greek an experience as you'll find in the Peloponnese. Redeeming features include views of the nearby islets of Platía and Romví, and in summer a good range of watersports (windsurfing, waterskiing, paragliding) from operators such as *Poseidon* (ⓣ27520 59843), near the harbour, but the local mosquitoes can be a problem.

Hotels in Toló tend to be block-booked through the summer but you could try the *Artemis*, Bouboulínas 7A (ⓣ27520 59458, ⓦwww.hotelartemis.net; ❻), with a seafront taverna, or the nearby *Tolo*, Bouboulínas 15 (ⓣ27520 59686, ⓦwww.hoteltolo.gr; B&B ❺). For comfortable studios with pool, try the *Heliotopos* on Karaïskaki (ⓣ27520 58322, ⓕ27520 58324; ❹) or the *Panorama* (ⓣ27520 59788, ⓦwww.panoramatolo.gr; B&B ❺). It's usually possible to find

private rooms by asking around, but be prepared for inflated summer prices. The **campsites** charge similar rates to the rooms: try *Sunset* (ⓣ27520 59556; March–Oct) first; failing that, there's the quieter *Lido II* (ⓣ27520 59396). The taverna *Chez-Gilles*, at Bouboulínas 14, is highly rated, with well-prepared **food**, pricey but with large portions.

Kastráki and Dhrépano

A pleasant alternative to Toló, especially if you're looking for an inexpensive campsite, is the longer beach at **KASTRÁKI**, 2km to the east. Coming from Náfplio by bus, ask to be let off where the road reaches the sea – it forks right to Toló and left (500m) to Kastráki, marked on some maps as Paralía Asínis. Here, too, development is under way, but it's a fair bit behind that of Toló, with only a scattering of small-scale hotels and campsites. *Camping Kastraki* (ⓣ27520 59386, ⓕ27520 59572; April–Oct) is on the beach, and has windsurfing equipment, pedaloes and canoes for hire.

Further around the coast, 4km to the east of Kastráki, the road runs on to **DHRÉPANO**, a sizeable village with four **campsites** and a very expensive hotel. The best campsite is *Triton* (ⓣ27520 92128; March–Nov); it's 1.2km from the main square of Dhrépano – follow signs to the beach. The *Yefiraki* taverna overlooking the beach is popular with the locals both for its excellent fresh fish and seafood. Beyond Dhrépano, the **Vivári lagoon** has a couple of excellent **tavernas** on its shore, including the *Mermaid*, with good seafood and a wonderful view along the bay.

Epidaurus (Epídhavros) and around

EPIDAURUS is a major Greek site (daily: summer 8am–7.30pm; winter 8am–5pm; €6), visited for its stunning **ancient theatre**, built around 330–320 BC. With its extraordinary acoustics, this has become a very popular venue for the annual Athens Festival productions of **Classical drama**, which are staged on Friday and Saturday nights from June through until the last weekend in August (see also box, p.194). The works are principally those of Sophocles, Euripides and Aeschylus; given the spectacular setting, they are worth arranging your plans around, whether or not you understand the modern Greek in which they're performed. Note that for festival performances the theatre is open late, after the rest of the site is closed.

The theatre is just one component of what was one of the most important sanctuaries in the ancient world, dedicated to Asklepios (god of healing) and a site of pilgrimage for half a millennium, from the sixth century BC into Roman times, and now a World Heritage site. Restoration and reconstruction work is now underway, so varying areas of the site will be temporarily closed as this progresses.

The ancient theatre and Asklepian sanctuary

The dedication of the sanctuary at Epidaurus to **Asklepios**, the legendary son of Apollo, probably owes its origin to an early healer from northern Greece who settled in the area. There were Asklepian sanctuaries throughout Greece and they were sited, rationally enough, alongside natural springs. Epidaurus, along with the island of Kós, was the most famous and inspirational of them all,

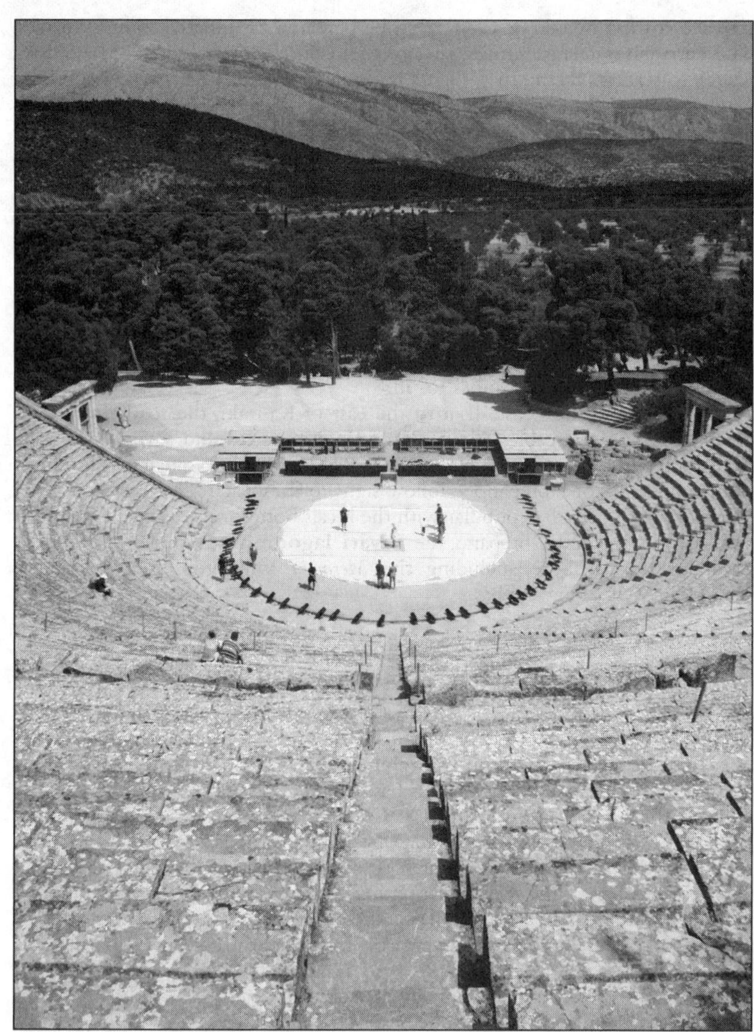

▲ The ancient theatre at Epidaurus

and probably the richest. The sanctuary was much endowed by wealthy visitors and hosted a quadrennial festival, including drama in the ancient theatre, which followed the Isthmian Games. Its heyday was in the fourth and third centuries BC, after which Rome, having been ravaged by an epidemic in 293 BC, sent for the serpent that was kept in the sanctuary.

This aspect of the site, however, along with much of the associated Asklepian ruins, is incidental for most visitors since Epidaurus's **ancient theatre** is the primary sight. With its backdrop of rolling hills, this 14,000-seat arena merges perfectly into the landscape, so well in fact that it was rediscovered and unearthed only in the nineteenth century. Constructed with mathematical precision, it has an extraordinary equilibrium and, as guides on the stage are forever demonstrating, near-perfect natural acoustics – such that you can hear coins, or even matches, dropped in the circular orchestra from the highest of the 54 tiers of seats. Constructed in white limestone (red for the dignitaries in the front rows), the tiered seats have been repaired, though the beaten earth stage has been retained, as in ancient times.

The museum

Close by the theatre is a small **museum** (summer Mon noon–7pm, Tues–Sun 8am–7pm; winter closes 5pm; entrance fee included in site ticket price), which is best visited before you explore the sanctuary. In 86 BC, with Epidaurus's reputation in decline, the Roman consul Sulla, leader of the forces invading the Peloponnese, looted the sanctuary and destroyed its buildings. Hence, most of the ruins visible today are just foundations, and a visit to the museum helps identify some of the former buildings. The finds displayed show the progression of medical skills and cures used at the Asklepian sanctuary; there are tablets recording miraculous and outrageous cures – like the man cured from paralysis after being ordered to heave the biggest boulder he could find into the sea – alongside quite advanced surgical instruments.

The sanctuary

The **Asklepian sanctuary**, as large a site as Olympia or Delphi, holds considerable fascination, for the ruins are all of buildings with identifiable functions: hospitals for the sick, dwellings for the priest-physicians, and hotels and amusements for the fashionable visitors to the spa. Their setting, a wooded valley thick with the scent of thyme and pine, is clearly that of a health farm.

The reasonably well-labelled **site** begins just past the museum, where there are remains of **Greek baths** and a huge **gymnasium** with scores of rooms leading off a great colonnaded court; in its centre the Romans built an **odeion**. To the southwest is the outline of the **stadium** used for the ancient games, while to the northeast, a small **sanctuary of Egyptian gods** suggests a strong influence on the medicine used at the site.

North of the stadium are the foundations of the **Temple of Asklepios** and beside it a rectangular building known as the **Abaton** or **Kimitirion**. Patients would sleep here to await a visitation from the healing god, commonly believed to assume the form of a serpent. He probably appeared in a more physical manifestation than expected; harmless snakes are believed to have been kept in the building and released at night to bestow a curative lick.

The deep significance of the serpent at Epidaurus is elaborated in the circular **Tholos**, one of the best-preserved buildings on the site. Its inner foundation walls form a labyrinth which is thought to have been used as a snakepit and, according to one theory, to administer a primitive form of shock therapy to the mentally ill. The afflicted would crawl in darkness through the outer circuit of the maze, guided by a crack of light towards the middle, where they would find themselves surrounded by writhing snakes. Another theory is that the labyrinth was used as an initiation chamber for the priests of Asklepios, who underwent a symbolic death and rebirth in it.

Practicalities

Most people take in Epidaurus as a day-trip; there are four buses daily from Náfplio to the site. They are marked "Theatre", "Asklipion" or "Epidavros" and shouldn't be confused with those to the modern villages of Néa or Arhéa (Paleá) Epídhavros. Alternatively, there are a couple of hotels in **LYGOURIÓ**

Tickets

Theatre tickets cost €15–50. In recent years there have been chaotic scenes with overselling and ticket-holders being turned away at the gates, so turn up early. Tickets for the plays are available in advance online, in Athens (at the festival box offices ⓣ210 32 72 000), or sometimes at the site (ⓣ27530 22009; Mon–Thurs 9am–2pm & 5–9pm, Fri & Sat 9.30am–9.30pm) during the festival, but, contrary to rumour, *not* at Náfplio bus station. Advance information is usually unavailable until just before the festival. In Athens, you can buy all-inclusive tickets for performances and return bus travel. There are also special evening buses from the site to Náfplio after the show; check at Náfplio bus station. English translations of the plays are available at the site and at the Odyssey bookshop in Náfplio (see p.190).

village, 25km from Náfplio and 5km northwest of the site. Possibilities include the basic *Alkion*, Asklipíou 195 (ⓣ27530 22002, ⓕ27530 22552; ❸), at the eastern end of the village, or the friendly nearby *Avaton* (ⓣ27530 22059, ⓔinfo@avaton.com.gr; ❸). Both hotels are open all year but fully booked long in advance for the festival period. Alternatively, it's possible to **camp** in the grass car park on performance days, though you must wait until an hour after the play's end before setting up a tent. Pleasant beachside accommodation is available at Paleá Epídhavros, 15km to the northeast (see below).

Lygourió itself has little of interest other than the Museum of Natural History (Tues–Sat 9am–5pm) at the western end of the village, the Byzantine church of Áyios Ioánnis Elémonos, and a Mycenaean pyramid on the northeast road.

For meals, the nearest **restaurant** is the *Oasis* on the Lygourió road, although there is a café at the site. Much better than either is *Taverna Leonidas* (ⓣ27520 22115), in the village proper, a friendly spot with a garden out the back; you'd be wise to book ahead if your visit coincides with a performance at the ancient theatre. Actors eat here after shows, and photos on the wall testify to the patronage of Melina Mercouri, the Papandreous, François Mitterrand and Sir Peter Hall.

Paleá Epídhavros

The closest beach resort to Epidaurus is **Paleá Epídhavros** (officially Arhéa Epídhavros; ⓦwww.epidavros.gr), which has expanded since the improvement of the direct coast road from Kórinthos, but remains pleasantly small scale. The recent discovery of ancient remains here means that some road signs for the beach now indicate "Ancient Epidavros", while the main inland site is referred to as "Ancient Theatre of Epidavros". As far as the remains are concerned, excavations are still in progress but they are worth a quick visit. A smaller classical theatre (Tues–Sun 8.30am–3pm; €6) on the headland, past the small town beach, is a festival venue for weekend musical shows in July and August, for which advance information is available at the *Hotel Christina* or from Athens (ⓣ210 92 82 900, ⓦwww.greekfestival.gr). You can find some small, open, Mycenaean tholos (tombs) behind the main street through town; turn inland up Ippokrátous by the BP petrol station, then left just above it.

Facing the harbour and town beach, there are a number of **hotels and rooms**, with more, plus campsites, on the 2km of road south to the narrow Yialási beach. All are full with festival patrons in season. Two friendly hotels to try are the *Christina* on the waterfront square (ⓣ27530 41451, ⓦwww.christinahotel.gr; ❸) and the *Marialena* apartments (ⓣ27530 41090; ❺), northwards on the Kórinthos road; both can provide excellent home-made breakfasts. Three **campsites** are on

Yialási beach, including *Nicholas II* (Ⓣ27530 41218, Ⓦwww.nikolasgikas.gr; April–Oct), whose owners also have rooms above the beachfront *Mouria* taverna (❸) and the *Gikas* studios next door (same contact details; Easter–Sept; ❹). **Buses** from Náfplio are scheduled to run late morning and return mid-afternoon, some via Epidaurus, though they can be unreliable; the central bus stop is at the *Platanos* café. **Taxis** can be called on Ⓣ27530 41723.

The Saronic ports: Méthana to Pórto Héli

The roads across and around the southern tip of the Argolid are sensational scenic rides, but the handful of resorts here lack character, have disappointing beaches and are generally overdeveloped. With a car, you can pick your route and take a leisurely drive back to Náfplio, perhaps exploring the site of **ancient Troezen** or volcanic **Méthana**. Otherwise, you'll probably travel this way only if heading for one of the **Argo-Saronic islands**: **Méthana** has local connections to Égina (Aegina) and Póros; **Galatás** to Póros; **Ermióni** to ýdhra (Hydra) and Spétses; and **Kósta** and **Pórto Héli** to Spétses. Geographically part of the Peloponnese, Galatás, Trizína and Méthana are, like the Argo-Saronic islands, administratively in the province of Pireás, and sometimes prices are inflated to match those on the islands.

Méthana and ancient Troezen

It's a sixty-kilometre drive from Epidaurus to the rugged **MÉTHANA** peninsula, the most volcanically active area in the Peloponnese. Méthana town is an unexciting spa, whose devotees are attracted by foul-smelling hot sulphur and saline springs. Of the half-dozen hotels, the most pleasant is the recently refurbished seafront *Avra* (Ⓣ22980 92382, Ⓦwww.ngb-hotelavra.gr; B&B ❹) with buffet restaurant. The **hydrofoil** agent is Palli at Aktí Saronikoú 34 (Ⓣ22980 92460).

The peninsula has 32 volcanoes but access to the most recent, **Ifestíou**, is via the town, or more directly by turning left at an unsigned fork just after the narrowest point of the neck of the peninsula. This new coastal road runs along to the pretty seaside resort of Paralía Paleókastro, with remnants of a Cyclopean-walled acropolis on a volcanic plug near the southeast end of the beach; there is a good, traditional fish taverna, the *Theoni*, on the shingle at the northwest end. Just beyond lies the sheltered little harbour of Vathý, with four tavernas, cafés, and some rooms. Continue northwest on the road above Vathý, to Kamméni Hóra ("Burnt Village"), huddled against the edge of a jagged lava flow from the semi-dormant **volcano Ifestíou**. The asphalt ends about 1km beyond, and a signed path through older lava leads, after about 15 minutes, to a distant viewpoint of the 25m-deep crater, but near to a cave-like exit vent. Strabo recorded an eruption here around 258 BC, but the most recent activity was in 1700 at the nearby undersea volcano Pausanias, 2km northwest of Méthana.

South and inland of the turning to the Méthana peninsula is the village of Trizína and the nearby ruins of ancient **TROEZEN**, legendary birthplace of Theseus and location of his complicated domestic dramas. Aphrodite, having been rejected by Theseus's virgin son Hippolytos, contrived to make Phaedra – Theseus's then wife – fall in love with the boy (her stepson). Phaedra, too, was rejected and responded by accusing Hippolytos of attempted rape. Hippolytos fled, but was killed when his horses took fright at a sea monster. Phaedra confessed her guilt and committed suicide. Originally told by Euripides (later reworked by Racine), a full account of the tragedy, together with a map of the ruins' remains, is on sale in the modern village.

The **remains** of the ancient town are widely spread. Most conspicuous are three ruined Byzantine chapels, constructed of ancient blocks, and a structure known as the Pýrgos Dhiatihísmatos or **Tower of Theseus**, whose lower half is third century BC and top half is medieval. This stands near the lower end of a gorge, the course of an ancient **aqueduct**, which you can follow in fifteen minutes' walk up a dirt road; a short, signed path leads to the **Dhiavoloyéfyro** ("Devil's Bridge"), natural rock formations spanning the chasm. On the far side, a short path to the right leads down to the lower bridge; a path to the left continues upstream past attractive rockpools.

Galatás

Workaday **GALATÁS** lies only 350m across the water from the touristy island of Póros, with which it is connected by a five-minute skiff ride; these cross almost continuously in the summer months. The town has a cluster of **hotels** on seafront 25-Martíou, including the friendly *Papasotiriou* (Ⓣ22980 22841, Ⓕ22980 25558; ❹), with large balconies and a taverna below; there are also **rooms** for rent around the waterfront, a **bike rental** place and **taxis**. The town is connected by daily buses with Epidaurus and Náfplio, and has local services to Trizína and Méthana.

Ermióni, Kósta and Pórto Héli

Continuing clockwise around the coast from Galatás, you follow a narrow road, cut to open up additional resorts close to Athens. **Plépi**, part of Aktí ýdhras ("Hydra Beach"), is a purpose-built strip of holiday villas behind sands, visited by boats from beachless ýdhra opposite. **ERMIÓNI** (ancient Hermione) is far better: a small town, on a rocky peninsula, overlooking Dhokós and ýdhra, and perhaps saved from development by lack of a sandy beach. It has separate access roads for the two sides of town – the northern entry is simpler for drivers and leads to the main waterfront, with tavernas, cafés, banks and ATMs. On Tuesdays there is a large market for local villages and islanders from ýdhra. The wooded tip of the peninsula – an archeological area – has pleasant walks. Ermióni's **accommodation** is mostly on the northern seafront, including the friendly *Pension Zoë* (Ⓣ27540 29565, Ⓔpensionzoe@altecnet.gr; B&B ❸) one row inland, and the *Ganossis Philoxenia* (Ⓣ27540 31218, Ⓦwww.philoxenia-ganossis.gr; ❸) with spacious apartments in the centre and at the eastern end of the northern seafront; they also have a seafront taverna-pizzeria, opened in 1918. On the southern side there are swimming places below the coastal road. The agent for the **hydrofoil** is Fun in the Sun Travel (Ⓣ27540 31514, Ⓦwww.ermionifuninthesun.gr).

Further southwest, **KÓSTA**, facing Spétses, and **PÓRTO HÉLI**, spread around two enclosed bays, are purpose-built resorts that have swallowed up their original hamlets. Kósta connects four times a day by **ferry** to Spétses (€2 one-way; buy tickets on board), as well as by fast water-taxi (€16 one-way). The **campsite** in Kósta, *Camping Costa*, is 1km to the west (Ⓣ27540 51113, Ⓦwww.costacamping.com; May–Oct). Much of the area east from Kósta through Áyios Emilianós has been covered with apartment complexes and holiday homes.

Much larger Pórto Héli has pretty waterfront views, numerous accommodation options, and facilities for yachters exploring the Argo-Saronic islands. Its fairly upmarket **hotels** include the comfortable, family-run, beachfront *Rozos* (Ⓣ27540 51416, Ⓦwww.hotelrozos.com; B&B ④), the well-equipped *Nautica Bay* (Ⓣ27540 51415, Ⓦwww.nauticabayhotel.gr; March–Oct; B&B; ⑤), and the luxury *AKS Porto Heli* (Ⓣ27540 53400, Ⓦwww.akshotels.com; B&B ④).

On the war memorial square is Hellenic Vision Travel (Ⓣ27540 51543, Ⓔevlassi@otenet.gr), which books **hydrofoils** and can find accommodation. There are numerous **restaurants** and cafés, one of the best of which is the sea-view *Kavouraki*, near the harbour, serving fresh fish since 1945. Much of the area east from Kósta through Áyios Emilianós has been covered with apartment complexes and holiday homes. With your own transport, you can go further to the very long, part-sand, part-pebble beach of Kranídhi bay, east across the peninsula from Pórto Héli.

The circuitous route back to Náfplio from Pórto Héli runs inland, via attractive Kranídhi (7km) village, then looping its way up through the mountains past the 1121-metre viewpoint peak of Mount Dhídhymo. It is covered three to four times daily by a bus, which usually dovetails in Pórto Héli and Kósta with ferries and hydrofoils to and from Spétses and elsewhere; in low season, however, you may have to change buses in Kranídhi.

Accessible by a 500m surfaced road from Dhídhyma village are two remarkable **doline craters**; the smaller Mikrí Spilia is accessed by a tunnel that takes you down and into the 80m-diameter crater, which has two small churches built in under the cliffs; the larger, 200m-diameter Megáli Spilia, visible from a considerable distance, is accessed by a stony track from the smaller. Nearby Dhídhymo summit has **rock climbing** routes, as does Mount Ortholíthi. Frágkhthi cave on the coast 4km west of Foúrni village, is a site of prehistoric human occupation as well as further routes. To the east, rock climbing is possible at several sites: between Fourní, Iliókastro and Thermisía, including Thermisía castle and the Katafiyi gorge. For these and other climbs in the area, see Ⓦwww.oreivatein.com or the book *Climb Argolis* by Titt & Zaczek.

The east coast: Náfplio to Leonídhio

The **coastline** between Náfplio and Leonídhio is mountainous terrain. Considering its proximity to Náfplio – and Athens – the whole stretch is enjoyably low key and comparatively unexploited, remaining more popular with Greek holiday-makers than with foreign tourists; the accommodation at resorts before Leonídhio may be fully booked well in advance for the mid-June to mid-August Greek school holidays.

Getting to the **beaches** – from Parálio Ástros to Pláka – is perhaps best done by car, though there are also **buses** two to three times daily, Monday to Friday, from Árgos to Leonídhio. Change money in advance, as there are few **banks** between Náfplio and Leonídhio. At the beginning of the route, around the coast from Náfplio, the minor site of **ancient Lerna** makes an interesting stop. If you are travelling by train from Árgos to Trípoli, you could stop off at the station of Mýli, only 500m from the site.

Ancient Lerna

The site of ancient **LERNA** (daily 8.30am–3pm; €2) lies 10km south of Árgos and 12km from Náfplio by the minor road around the coast via Néa Kíos. On the way in from Árgos there is an interesting detour possible to the picturesque, cave-lake **church of Panayía Kefalariótissa** at Kefalári, where even today some locals still wash their carpets in the nearby freshwater springs, although these springs are drying up as farmers extract increasing volumes of ground water upstream. The numerous tavernas here are very popular with locals. A further 4km inland is the remarkable fourth-century BC "**pyramid**" (Tues–Sun 8.30am–3pm; free) at Ellinikó village, actually a small fortress with inward-leaning walls, standing nearly at its original height on the ancient road from Árgos to Arcadia.

Ancient Lerna is at Mýli, on the bus and train routes from Árgos to Trípoli; there is a small **taverna** on the southeast side of the T-junction that is considered by Náfplians to make the best *souvláki* in the area. Just south of the straggle of the village a narrow lane leads to the small prehistoric site, which lies between the main road and the railway. This is one of Greece's most important Bronze Age sites, but most of it is now under a hideous concrete roof. American excavations carried out in the 1950s unearthed ruins of an early **Neolithic house** and a well-preserved **fortification wall**, revealing it as one of the most ancient of Greek settlements, inhabited from as early as 5500 BC.

Another large house at the north end of the site is thought to have been an early palace, but was superseded by a larger and more important structure known as the **House of Tiles**. Measuring approximately 24m by 9m, this dwelling, labelled as another palace, takes its name from the numerous terracotta roof tiles found inside, where they are thought to have fallen in approximately 2200 BC when either lightning or enemy raiders set the building ablaze. The house is the earliest known instance of the use of terracotta as a building material, and is the most impressive pre-Helladic structure so far unearthed on the Greek mainland. A symmetrical ground plan of small rooms surrounding larger interior ones has stairs mounting to a now-vanished second storey. The substantial walls, made of sun-dried brick on stone foundations, were originally covered with plaster. Even after its destruction, this palace may have retained some ritual significance, since two Mycenaean **shaft graves** were sunk into the ruins in around 1600 BC, and the site was not completely abandoned until around 1250 BC at the end of the Mycenaean period. Further excavations are taking place in Mýli itself, and an archeological park has been proposed, to connect the two sites.

As implied by the chronology, the founders and early inhabitants of Lerna were not Greeks. Certain similarities in sculpture and architecture with contemporary Anatolia suggest Asiatic origins, but this has yet to be proved conclusively. Excavated finds, however, demonstrate that the Lerneans traded across the Aegean and well up into the Balkan peninsula, cultivated all the staple crops still found in the Argolid, and raised livestock, as much for wool and hides as for food. Elegant terracotta sauce tureens and "teaspoons" (now in the Árgos archeological museum) hint at a sophisticated cuisine.

Coastal Arcadia: Parálio Ástros, Ástros and Sambatikí

The initial section of coast from Lerna to Ástros is low-lying and less spectacular than the sections further south. The first resort of any size is **PARÁLIO ÁSTROS**, whose older houses are tiered against a headland shared by a medieval **fort** (Tues–Sun 8.30am–3pm; free) and the ruins of a thirteenth-century BC acropolis. Back from the northern end of the sand-and-gravel beach, which extends 6km south of the fishing harbour, there are a few tavernas, more cafés, numerous rooms to let and some **hotels**: just south and inland of the main seafront square is the *Crystal* (Ⓣ27550 51313, Ⓔhotelcrystal@hotmail.com; ❹), with fridges in the rooms – family apartments are also available. The *Alexandros* (☎27550 21743, ✉info@alexandrosastros.gr; ⑤) is nearer the castle, and has well-appointed studio rooms; both have parking. The beautiful *Il Gusto* (also called *Maglis*) apartments (☎27550 52733; ⑤–⑥) have large balconies directly overlooking the beach near the square. The nearest **campsite** is *Thirea*, 3km south at Meligoú Beach (☎27550 51002, Ⓕ27550 29206; May–Sept).

To the west and south, a trio of surprisingly neat and compact villages – **ÁSTROS** (site of the second National Assembly in 1823), Korakavoúni and Áyios Andhréas – perch at the foothills of **Mount Párnonas** where it meets the lush, olive-green plain. The **Kynouria archeological museum** (Tues–Sun 8.30am–3pm; €2) in a traditional building (the Karytsióti School) in Ástros contains local finds – including a collection from the Roman villa of Herodes Atticus at Éva Dholianón, 5km inland on the road to Trípoli.

Some 40km south, en route to Leonídhio, a good fish taverna, *Klimataria*, sits above the very pretty **SAMBATIKÍ** fishing beach. A circuitous road leads down to the beach itself and **accommodation**: the *Porto Sambatiki* (☎27570 61316, ✉tasoslys@forthnet.gr; ②), with a taverna underneath, and the *Armenaki* (☎27570 61274, Ⓕ27570 61040; ③), with comfortable studios.

Leonídhio, Pláka and Poúlithra

Gigantic ochre cliffs that wouldn't look out of place in deserts of the American Southwest or the Canary Islands confine red-roofed **LEONÍDHIO** (Leonídhion in formal Greek). Set inland, with rich agricultural land spreading down to the sea, this prosperous and traditional market town sees little need to pander to tourists, most of whom head for the coast at Leonídhio's diminutive port, Pláka. The **Tsakonic dialect** – a form of ancient Doric – is still used locally, notably for the Easter Sunday Mass. Also unique is the streaky, pale purple, sweet-tasting Tsakonikí aubergine, celebrated in a Pláka festival each August. There are some enjoyable, small-town **tavernas**, such as the *Mouria* near the small square.

PLÁKA, 4km away, is a delightful place consisting of a harbour and some **eateries**. It also has a fine pebble beach, which in recent years has become popular with Greek and European tourists, plus a sporadic influx of yachters. The Bekarou family have run the central *Michael & Margaret* taverna here since 1830.

Accommodation is much easier to find 3km south of Pláka in the attractive small resort of **POÚLITHRA**, from where the coast road heads inland to small, isolated, mountain villages. With little development to distract you, this makes a relaxing staging post. There are tavernas near the narrow strip of beach, although prices can be high. The friendly, family-run **hotel** ✱ *Akroyiali* (☎27570 29106, Ⓕ27570 51262; ④), has spacious studios by the sea, while rooms are available at the *Kyma* (☎27570 51250; ③).

Inland from Leonídhio

The route inland from **Leonídhio** is worth taking for its own sake, climbing through the huge **Dhafnón gorge**, past the **monastery of Élonas** – although the views are even better if this route is covered in the reverse direction, descending through the gorge to Leonídhio. The road peaks at the high mountain village of **Kosmás**, providing a temperature shock in the height of summer, but a great place to stop and enjoy the fresh mountain air over a drink in the shady square. The route brings you out near the Byzantine site of **Yeráki** (see p.201); from there, you have a choice of roads – to Spárti or Yíthio (Gythion) via Skála, or to Monemvasiá and Neápoli via Moláï. An alternative route south, to Monemvasiá or Neápoli, is the now surfaced road from Leonídhio via Poúlithra, Marí and Apidhiá. Without a car, you'll have to plan very carefully: a weekly bus runs from Leonídhio to Yeráki, with a few onward connections to Spárti – but check with the Náfplio bus station (Ⓣ27520 27323) first.

Moní Panayía tís Elónis

The **Panayía tís Elónis** (Élonas) monastery stands out as a white slash in the mountainside – though as you twist around and up the ravine, it drops away from view. The turn-off to the monastery (visitors permitted from sunrise to sunset) comes 16km from Leonídhio, via a short approach road which ends at a gateway and parking area. A cliff path leads you on to the main building, where you can wander down to a small church (closed during siesta) crammed with icons and lanterns, and to an *ayíazma* (spring), where water dribbling from the cliff has supposedly curative powers. Most of the monastery, originally founded in medieval times following the miraculous appearance of an icon in a seemingly inaccessible position, was rebuilt following the War of Independence, becoming a nunnery in 1972. The icon, said to be by St Luke, was stolen and recovered in 2006.

Kosmás

Continuing south, 15km past the Elónis turning, you reach **KOSMÁS**, a handsome alpine village set about a grand platía and giant plane tree, with several **tavernas**. Straddling the most important pass of Párnonas, at 1150m, it can be a chilly place during the spring or winter, but very beautiful, too, with its streams, cherries and walnut trees, and can make a pleasant base for mountain walking. The central *Xenonas Maleatis Apollo* (Ⓣ27570 31494; ③) has studios in a refurbished eighteenth-century building. Just at the edge of the village, on the Leonídhio side, and with countryside views, are the *Kosmas* studios (Ⓣ27570 31483; ③). The taverna *O Navarhos* on the platía has good food and prices. Beyond Kosmás the road runs through a pass, then sweeps down the valley through fir forests to the village and Byzantine ruins of Yeráki.

The southeast: Lakonía

Lakonía, the ancient territory of the Spartans, covers the area between the high ridges of Mount Taïyetos and Mount Párnonas and everywhere to the south. Apart from the lush Evrótas valley, with Spárti itself and Mystra, it is a dramatic and underpopulated landscape of harsh mountains and poor, dry, rocky soil. Landforms apart, the highlights here are the extraordinarily preserved Byzantine town of **Monemvasiá** – an essential visit for any tour of the southern Peloponnese – and the aridly remote **Máni** peninsula, with its bizarre history of violence, piety and feuds, and its unique tower-houses and frescoed churches with barrel roofs. **Kýthira** and **Elafónissos**, historically Ionian islands but now under the administration of Pireás and Lakonía respectively, are reached from the Peloponnese, so are covered in this chapter.

Yeráki

If you choose the southeastern route over Mount Párnonas from Leonídhio then it is worth making the effort to visit the **Byzantine antiquities** at **YERÁKI**. With its **Frankish castle** and fifteen **chapels** spread over a spur of the mountain, Yeráki stands a creditable third to the sites of Mystra and Monemvasiá. The "modern" village of Yeráki has no regular **accommodation**, though rooms may be negotiable through **cafés** in the square. If you're dependent on public transport, you'll need to take in Yeráki as a day-trip from Spárti: **buses** run several times daily, but only once a week along the splendid route from Leonídhio.

Medieval Yeráki

Yeráki (Tues–Sun 8.30am–3pm; free) was one of the original twelve **Frankish baronies** set up in the wake of the Fourth Crusade, and remained an important Byzantine town through the fourteenth century, straddling the road between Mystra and its port at Monemvasiá. The site is spectacular, with sweeping vistas over the olive-covered Evrótas plain and across to Taïyetos. It stands 4km outside and overlooking the current village of Yeráki, where the bus stops.

All the main churches – many incorporating material from Yeráki's ancient predecessor, Geronthrai – are kept locked, and to visit them you should, theoretically, enquire at the caretaker's office (red door) near the rural doctor by the town square. You may be given a tour (tip expected), clambering around the rocks to the best-preserved **chapels**, including **Zoödhóhos Piyí** and **Ayía Paraskeví**, both of which have restored fifteenth-century frescoes. However, they may only open for organized excursions from the larger resorts or Athens.

The most substantial remains of the medieval town are of its fortress, the **Kástro**, built in 1256 by the local Frankish baron, Jean de Nivelet; its heavily fortified design is based on that of the Villehardouin fortress at Mystra, for this was one of the most vulnerable Frankish castles of the Moreas, intended to control the wild and only partially conquered territories of Taïyetos and the Máni. In the event, the castle was surrendered to the Byzantines just six years later. In the late seventeenth century it became Venetian, then Turkish in 1715 until being abandoned in the late eighteenth century. Within the fortress are huge **cisterns** for withstanding sieges, and the largest of Yeráki's churches: the thirteenth-century **Mitrópolis**, also known as **Áyios Yeóryios**, which features Byzantine frescoes, a Frankish iconostasis and the Villehardouin arms.

Kyparíssi

The Lakonía coastline between Poulíthra and Monemvasiá is wild and sparsely inhabited, with just a couple of isolated coastal settlements – Kyparíssi and Limáni Yéraka – cut into the cliffs. By road, it's a roundabout route to Kyparíssi: 45km from Moláï on the Spárti–Monemvasiá road, via a 900-metre col; 51km from Yeráki via Ágios Dimítrios; or 53km from Monemvasiá via Rikhiá. All routes take in a final, spectacular, precipitous corniche beyond Hárakas.

KYPARÍSSI is a verdant Shangri-La, sandwiched between huge cliffs and the sea, and divided into three settlements: inland Kyparíssi, Mitrópoli and Paralía. **Mitrópoli** at the northern end of the bay has the *Tiris* and *Poulaki* tavernas, both with good seafood at reasonable prices. Behind them is a small supermarket; at the far end is a petrol station. The jetty is at **Paralía** at the southern end, where there is studio **accommodation**, including the sea-view *Helioti* (☎27320 55238; ⑤) with its own taverna next door, and the *Myrtoo* (☎27320

55327, Ⓦwww.myrtoo.com; ④); both are well-placed for the sea, between the harbour and Megáli Ámmos beach on the coast road to Mitrópoli. On the inland road to Mitrópoli are the attractively refurbished *Kyfanta* studios (Ⓣ27320 55356 Ⓦwww.kyparissi.info; ④), set in their own large olive garden. Accommodation prices drop considerably outside July and August.

Monemvasiá

MONEMVASIÁ, standing impregnable on a great island-like irruption of rock, was the medieval seaport and commercial centre of the Byzantine Peloponnese, the secular counterpart of Mystra. Nowadays the lower town is a fascinating mixture of atmospheric heritage, careful restoration and sympathetic redevelopment in matching stone and style – and an experience that should not be missed.

The town's name, an elision of Moni Emvasis, "single entrance", is a reference to its approach from the mainland, across a kilometre of causeway and a small twentieth-century bridge built to replace earlier wooden bridges. Such a defensible and strategic position gave it control of the sea lanes from Italy and the West, to Constantinople and the Levant. Fortified on all approaches, it was invariably the last outpost of the Peloponnese to fall to invaders, and was only ever taken through siege. Even today, it differs deeply in character from the nearby mainland.

Some history

Founded by the **Byzantines** in the sixth century, Monemvasiá soon became an important port. It later served as the chief commercial port of the Despotate of Mystra and was for all practical purposes the Greek Byzantine capital. Mystra, despite the presence of the court, was never much more than a large village; Monemvasiá at its peak had a population of almost 60,000. Like Mystra, Monemvasiá had something of a golden age in the thirteenth century, when it was populated by a number of noble Byzantine families, and reaped considerable wealth from estates inland, from the export of wine (the famed Malmsey – *Malvasia* – mentioned in Shakespeare's *Richard III* and now being replanted locally) and from roving corsairs who preyed on Latin shipping heading for the East. When the rest of the Moreas fell to the Turks in 1460, Monemvasiá was able to seal itself off, placing itself first under the control of the papacy, later under the **Venetians**. Only in 1540 did the **Turks** gain control, the Venetians having abandoned their garrison after the defeat of their navy at Préveza.

Turkish occupation precipitated a steady decline, both in prestige and population, though the town experienced something of a revival during the period of Venetian control of the Peloponnese (1690–1715). Monemvasiá was again thrust to the fore in the **War of Independence**, when, in July 1821, after a terrible siege and wholesale massacre of the Turkish inhabitants, it became the first of the major Turkish fortresses to fall.

After the war, there was no longer the need for such strongholds, and, at the end of the nineteenth century, shipping routes changed too, with the opening of the Corinth Canal. The population plummeted and the town drifted into a village existence, its buildings for the most part allowed to fall into ruin. By the time of World War II – during which four thousand New Zealand troops were dramatically evacuated from the rock – only eighty families remained. Today just a handful are in permanent residence, but much restoration work has been done to the houses, walls and many of the churches.

The rock: medieval Monemvasiá

From the mainland village of **Yéfira** – where the causeway to **Monemvasiá** (or **Kástro**, as locals call it) begins – nothing can be seen of the medieval town, which is built purely on the seaward face of the rock. Little more is revealed as you cross the causeway, but the long entrance road, used for **parking**, brings you to castellated walls. In peaceful times, the town was supplied from the tiny external harbour, **Kourkoúla**, below the road as you approach the entrance gateway. Once through the fortified entrance gate, narrow and tactically z-shaped, everything looms into view: clustered houses with tiled roofs and walled gardens, narrow stone streets, and distinctively Byzantine churches. High above, the extensive castle walls protect the upper town on the summit.

The Lower Town

The **Lower Town** once numbered forty churches and over eight hundred homes, an incredible mass of building, which explains the intricate network of alleys. A single main street – up and slightly to the left from the gateway – is lined with cafés, tavernas and souvenir shops. One of the tavernas is owned by relatives of Yannis Ritsos, one of Greece's leading poets and a lifelong communist, who was born on the rock; a plaque and bust statue at a house above the main gate commemorate his birthplace, and he is buried in the cemetery outside the walls, his gravestone inscribed with a poem.

At the end of this street is the lower town's main square, a beautiful public space, with a cannon and a well in its centre, and the setting for the great, vaulted **cathedral**, built by the Byzantine emperor Andronikos II Komnenos when he made Monemvasiá a see in 1293. The largest medieval church in southern Greece, it is dedicated to Christ in Chains, Elkómenos Khristós. Across the square is the domed church of **Áyios Pétros**, originally a sixteenth-century mosque, which was reconverted by the Turks back into a mosque in the eighteenth century and now houses a small museum of local finds (officially Tues–Sun 8.30am–3pm, but unpredictable; free). Unusually for Ottoman Greece, the Christian cathedral was allowed to function during the occupation, and did so beside this mosque, hence the name of this square, Platía Tzamíou – "the square of the mosque".

Down towards the sea is a third notable church, the seventeenth-century **Khrysafítissa**, whose bell hangs from a bent-over old acacia tree in the courtyard. It was restored and adapted by the Venetians in their second, eighteenth-century, occupation. The **Portello** is a small gate in the sea wall, due south of Platía Tzamíou; you can **swim** off the rocks here. There are two minor churches just off the main street. **Panayía Myrtidhiótissa**, to the north of the cathedral, is a small, single-aisled basilica with a single dome; inside there is a beautifully carved iconostasis.

The Upper Town

The climb to the **Upper Town** is highly worthwhile – not least for the solitude, since most day-trippers stay down below – and it is less strenuous than it initially looks. To get the most from the vast site, it's a good idea to bring some food and drink (from Yéfira, since Monemvasiá has no proper supermarket), so you can explore at leisure. There are sheer drops from the rockface, and unguarded cisterns, so descend before dusk.

The fortifications, like those of the lower town, are substantially intact, with even the **entrance gate** retaining its iron slats. Within, the site is a ruin, unrestored and deserted – the last resident moved out in 1911 – though many structures are still recognizable, and there are information boards. The only building that is relatively complete, even though its outbuildings have long since crumbled to foundations, is the beautiful thirteenth-century **Ayía Sofía** (usually locked), a short distance up from the gateway. It was founded on the northern rim of the rock as a monastery by Andronikos II, along a plan similar to that of Dhafní.

Beyond the church extend acres of ruins; in medieval times the population here was much greater than that of the lower town. Among the remains are the stumpy bases of Byzantine houses and public buildings, and, perhaps most striking, vast **cisterns** to ensure a water supply in time of siege. Monemvasiá must have been more or less self-sufficient in this respect, but its weak point was its food supply, which had to be entirely imported from the mainland. In the last siege, by Mavromihalis's Maniot army in the War of Independence, the Turks were reduced to eating rats and, so the propagandists claimed, Greek children.

Practicalities

Direct **buses** connect with Spárti three times daily – although they are not timed to allow a day visit from there – and occasionally with Yíthio; the change of bus at Molái can involve a lengthy wait. Buses arrive in the modern mainland village of Yéfira (see below), from where a minibus shuttles across to the rock every 20 minutes from 8am–11pm (€0.50). Yéfira is little more than a straggle of hotels, rooms and restaurants for the rock's tourist trade, with a pebble beach; though for a **beach** day-trip, it's best to head 3–4km north along the coast to Porí beach, or via a separate road to the very clean, northern, Kastráki end of the beach, by the Cyclopean walls of ancient **Epidavros Limira**. Snorkellers can see further marble remains from the site, now underwater, as well as the wreckage of a sunken German warship.

Accommodation on the rock is expensive – in season and out – and from June to September you should book ahead. Within the walls, the choice includes some very upmarket **hotels**, with attractively restored and traditionally furnished rooms. The *Malvasia* (Ⓣ27320 61323, Ⓔmalvasia@otenet.gr; ❹–❼), occupies three separate locations between the main street and the sea; call first at the hotel reception, well signposted from just inside the main gateway. The similarly characterful *Byzantino* (Ⓣ27320 61254, Ⓕ27320 61436; ❹–❻), further along the main street, is usually more expensive; they also own the separate *Enetiko* café and the *Xenonas Hamam* (❻–❼) with beautiful, eclectic suites in the restored baths: ask at the café at the *Byzantino* or their office. The *Xenonas Goulas* has rooms and studios (Ⓣ27320 61223, Ⓔgialos@gialos.gr; ❺–❼). There are other **furnished apartments** and **traditional hotels** on the rock: ask around at the shops and tavernas on the main street, or seek the help of Malvasia Travel in Yéfira (see below). **Eating out** in the old village is enjoyable, as much for the location as for its food. Of the several restaurants, the best all-round place is *Matoula*, going since the 1960s, and with a leafy garden overlooking the sea.

Yéfira

There's more accommodation in **YÉFIRA**, along with various other useful tourist services including a **bank**, three **ATMs**, a **post office** and a **travel agent**, Malvasia Travel (Ⓣ27320 61752, Ⓔmalvtrvl@otenet.gr), which can help with rooms and **scooter** rental. There are several **hotels** near or just north of the causeway. North of the road are the comfortable *Filoxenia* (Ⓣ27320 61716, Ⓦwww.filoxenia-monemvasia.gr; ❹) and the friendly, good-value *Pramataris* (Ⓣ27320 61833, Ⓦwww.pramatarishotel.gr; ❸), with some balconies overlooking the sea and an excellent buffet breakfast; just inland of the road is the *Flower of Monemvasia* (ⓣ27320 61395, ⓦwww.flower-hotel.gr; B&B ⑤); rooms have a kitchenette. There are good **rooms** for rent such as the hospitable, stone-clad *Petrino* (ⓣ & ⓕ27320 61136; B&B ④) on the southern seafront. A little further north (4.5km), there is some accommodation at Porí beach and (7km) at the little village of Paliá Monemvasiá, beyond Epidavros Limira, on the northern side of the bay where the *Hotel Annema* (ⓣ27320 68381, ⓦwww.annema.co.uk; B&B; ④) has a pool and wonderful sea views across the bay to Monemvasiá, sometimes with sightings of seals and dolphins. The nearest **campsite** is 3km to the south, along the coast road; *Kapsis Paradise* (ⓣ27320 61123, ⓦwww.camping-monemvasia.com) is open year-round, and has water-skis and scooters for rent.

Back in Yéfira, on the south side, good **food** with a sea view is available at *Skorpios,* near the *Petrino*; if you have transport, you could also try the *Pipinelis* (ⓣ27320 61044; May–Oct), about 2km out on the road south to the campsite, but indoor seating is limited so call first to make a reservation if the weather's cool. Even closer to the campsite is the pleasant *Kamares* taverna with good food. Yefira's numerous *zaharoplastía* all have the local speciality, *amygdhalóta* (almond biscuits). For nightlife in Yéfira, try the popular *Rock Café* bar on the southern seafront.

South to Neápoli and Elafónissos

The isolated southeasternmost "finger" of the Peloponnese below Monemvasiá, locally known as Vátika, is little visited by tourists, except for the area around **Neápoli**, the most southerly town in mainland Greece, which offers access to the islet of **Elafónissos**, just offshore, and to the larger islands of Kýthira and Andikýthira, midway to Crete. Beyond Neápoli, the Peloponnese ends at Akrotíri (Cape) Maléas, a cluster of tiny monasteries known as "Mikró Áyion Óros", and a petrified forest. From Monemvasiá the southerly route high over the central ridge via Ellinikó village is the slower but more attractive of the two roads to Neápoli; the other, longer route has been extensively widened and straightened.

Neápoli

NEÁPOLI (full name Neápoli Vión) is a mix of old buildings and modern Greek concrete behind a grey-sand beach with views of Kýthira and Elafónissos islands – and mainly of interest for its ferry connections. For such an out-of-the-way place, it is surprisingly developed, catering mostly to Greek holiday-makers. Besides rooms, there are some modest **hotels** including the older-style *Aïvali* (ⓣ27340 22287, ⓕ27340 22777; ③) on the seafront and, more quietly situated, the newer, friendly *Vergina* (ⓣ27340 23443, ⓦwww.verginahotel.com; ④); both may need to be booked ahead in summer. The agency for the Kýthira **ferry** is Vatika Bay at Ayías Triádhas 3, a side street near the jetty (ⓣ27340 24004, ⓕ27340 22660). Neápoli has several **banks**; **taxis** can be ordered on ⓣ27340 22590; and the KTEL **bus** office is on Dhimokratías, opposite the bus park. A signboard here has a map detailing hiking routes in Vátika.

Neápoli **beach** extends northwest to Vingláfia village and the little harbour of **Poúnda**, which has between five and 26 daily vehicle ferry crossings over the short strait to Elafónissos (10min; ⓣ27340 61117, ⓦwww.elafonisos.net/dromolo.htm; pay on the boat; €2). The short hop makes a day-trip to the island practical, even with a car. Nearby Lake Strongylí, south of Áyios Yeóryios, is a nature reserve.

Elafónissos island

Part of the mainland until 375 AD, when an earthquake separated it, **Elafónissos** is very busy in the short summer season, when its 700-odd resident population is vastly outnumbered by visitors, mainly Greek. The island's eponymous town is largely modern, but has plenty of rooms, mostly in the narrow backstreets, plus some good fish tavernas. **Hotels** include the *Asteri*, one row back from the western seafront (Ⓣ27340 61271, Ⓕ27340 61077; ④) and the *Exantas* (Ⓣ27340 61024; ③), which has sea views and is conveniently positioned for the tavernas on the northern seafront near the ferry dock. Details of other accommodation are available at Ⓦwww.elafonisos.net; those on the western shoreline can have wonderful sunset views. Near the main church on its tiny peninsula, the *Spyros & Spyroula* taverna has well-prepared traditional food.

One of the island's two surfaced roads leads 5km southeast to **Símos**, one of the best **beaches** in this part of Greece, a large double bay with fine pale sand heaped into dunes and views to Kýthira; a *kaïki* (boat) leaves from the town to Símos every morning in summer. There's a seasonal café at the eastern end of the beach, and the well-equipped *Simos Camping* and bungalows (Ⓣ27340 22672, Ⓦwww.simoscamping.htm; June–Sept; ④) at the western end. To the southwest of town is the small, scattered settlement of Káto Nisí, and **Panayítsa** beach, quieter than Símos but almost as beautiful, with views to the Máni peninsula. There is a petrol station on the Panayítsa road.

Arhángelos

Further up the coast from Neápoli, just off the more northerly route from Monemvasiá, **ARHÁNGELOS** is a pleasant little resort at the southern end of a quiet, sandy and deserted bay. The smart, apricot-coloured *Hotel Palazzo* (Ⓣ27320 54111, Ⓦwww.palazzo.gr; ⑤) has luxurious rooms, and a seafront café and restaurant; it's open all year and the owners are hospitable and knowledgeable. The nearby *Anokato* is a popular hangout for the whole peninsula, especially in winter. By a quaint twist the village, whose name means "archangel", is the harbour for Dhemonía ("devilry") several kilometres up the coast, which has tavernas, cafés and a big, empty beach.

Kýthira and Andikýthira islands

Isolated at the foot of the Peloponnese, the island of **Kýthira** traditionally belongs to the Ionian islands, and shares their history of Venetian and, later, British rule; under the former it was known as Cerigo. Administratively it is part of Piréas in mainland Attica – like the Argo-Saronic islands. For the most part, similarities end there. The island architecture of whitewashed houses and flat roofs looks more like that of the Cyclades, albeit with an ever-stronger **Venetian** influence. The landscape is different, too: wild scrub- and gorse-covered hills, or moorland sliced by deep valleys and ravines.

Depopulation has left the land underfarmed and the abandoned fields overgrown – since World War II, most of the islanders have left for Athens or Australia, giving Kýthira a reputation for being the classic emigrant island; it is known locally as "Australian Colony" or "Kangaroo Island", and Australia is referred to as "Big Kýthira". Many of the villages are deserted, their platíes empty and the schools and *kafenía* closed. Kýthira was never a rich island, but,

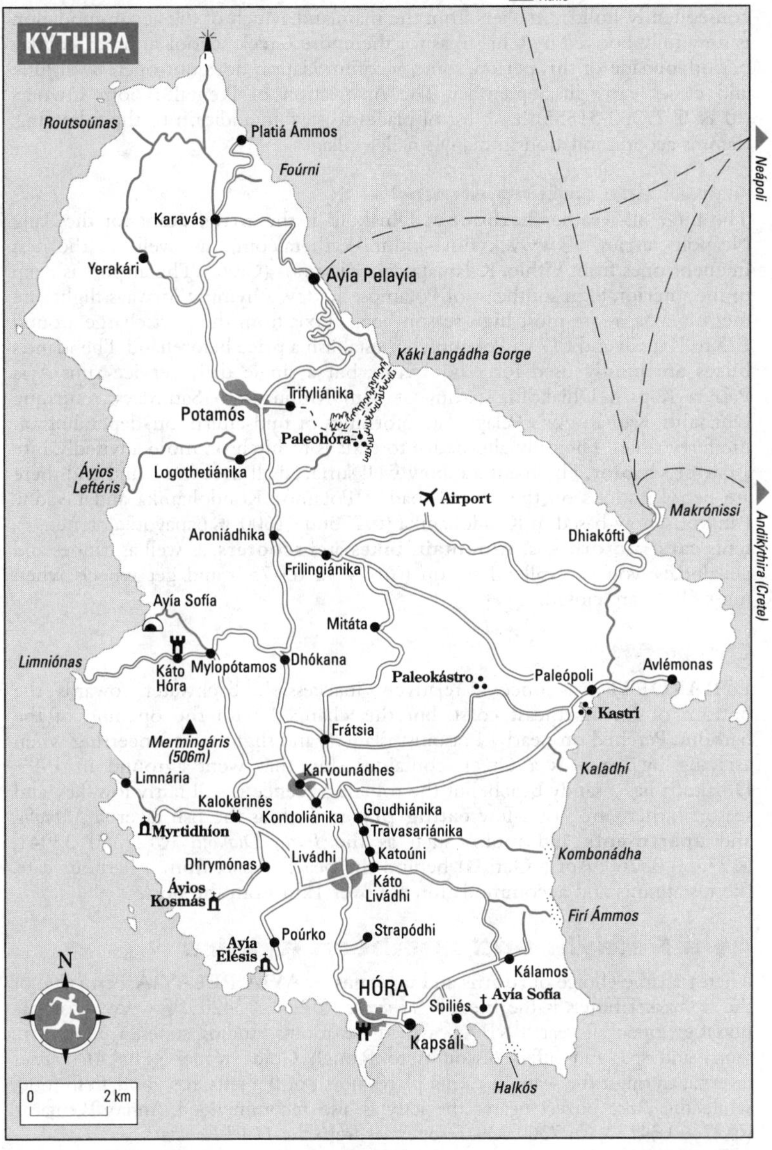

along with Monemvasiá, it did once have a military and economic significance – which it likewise lost with Greek independence and the opening of the Corinth Canal. These days, tourism has brought prosperity (and a few luxury hotels), but most summer visitors are Greeks and especially Greek Australians. For the few foreigners who reach Kýthira, it remains something of a refuge, with its undeveloped **beaches** a principal attraction. However, Greek film and television exposure has attracted a huge amount of domestic attention and, consequently, holiday-makers from the mainland. Much of the accommodation is now fully booked by Christmas for the entire Greek school summer holiday period; outside of this period, some accommodation does not open until June and closes early in September. The Association of Rental Room Owners (Ⓣ & Ⓕ27360 31855) has a list of places to stay: in addition to the following, there is accommodation in many smaller villages.

Arrival and getting around

The huge all-weather **harbour** at Dhiakófti is the arrival point for the daily Neápoli ferries (Ⓦwww.kythira-kithira-kythera.com), as well as the less frequent ones from Yíthio, Kalamáta and Kissamos (Crete). The airport is deep in the interior, 8km southeast of Potamós; the few Olympic Airways flights are met by taxis, as are most high-season boats. Taxis from the port charge around €25 to Kapsáli and €17 to Potamós, but establish a price beforehand. The island's **buses** are mostly used for school runs, but a single daily service runs Ayía Pelayía–Kapsáli–Dhiakófti, starting at 9am Mondays to Saturdays, returning Dhiakófti–Kapsáli–Ayía Pelayía late mornings or mid-afternoon, depending on the ferry times. The only alternative to taxis is to hitch or, more advisedly, hire a **car** or **scooter**. The roads are now well surfaced all over the island and there are petrol stations on the central road at Potamós, Kondoliánika and Livádhi. Panayotis, now based in Kondoliánika (Ⓣ27360 31600, Ⓔpanayoti@otenet.gr), rents **cars**, **motorbikes**, **mountain bikes** and **scooters**, as well as canoes and pedalboats; you can call off-season (Ⓣ694 42 63 757) and get wheels when most places are closed.

Dhiakófti

DHIAKÓFTI was once a relatively inaccessible backwater towards the bottom of the northeast coast, but this changed with the opening of the harbour. Perched on nearby Prasónisi island – and slightly disconcerting when arriving by sea – is a Greek container ship that went aground in 1999. Dhiakófti has a sandy beach, but the tourist presence is still fairly low-key and seasonal; there are just a few **eating places**, such as the fish taverna *Manolis*, and **apartments** and rooms such as the *Porto Diakofti* (Ⓣ27360 33041, Ⓕ27360 33760; April–Oct; ⑥) behind the beach. Apart from a harbour café, the restaurants and accommodation are over 1km from the port.

Ayía Pelayía and northern Kýthira

There's a large choice of **rooms** and **tavernas** in **AYÍA PELAYÍA**; best value of the upmarket hotels is the friendly *Venardos* (Ⓣ27360 34205, Ⓦwww.venardos-hotels.gr; open all year; B&B ⑤), which has rooms, studios, suites, a pool, gym, sauna and spa, and offers discounts to Rough Guide readers. The *Moustakias* taverna, amongst the seafront eating places north of the jetty, has good, fresh food, while the *Paleo* ouzerí nearer the jetty is also recommended. Anna's Rentacar (Ⓣ27360 34153, Ⓕ27360 33915) operates from the *Hotel Romantica*.

The main beaches are cleaner since the ferries stopped coming here, but the beach at Kalamítsa, a two-kilometre dirt track away to the south, is better – the track continues on to the mouth of the Káki Langádha gorge (see p.210). In summer, boat trips are available to Elafónissos island to the north (see p.206).

Potamós and around

From Ayía Pelayía, the main road winds up the hillside towards **POTAMÓS**, Kýthira's largest town – a pleasant and unspoilt place which, if you have your own transport, makes a good base for exploring the island. It has a few **studios**, such as those at the *Xenonas Porfyra* (Ⓣ27360 33329, Ⓕ27360 33924; ③), just north of the centre, which has a pretty terrace and courtyard. In addition to **tavernas**, a **bank**, a **post office** and **petrol stations**, facilities include an Olympic Airways office (Ⓣ27360 33362). Most of the shops on the island are here, too, as is the **Sunday market**, Kýthira's liveliest regular event – the *Lilis* or *Astikon* cafés have live music to coincide with this. The *Selana* café-pizzeria has **Internet** facilities, while more serious nightlife is at the *Vergadi* club (open all year), just south of town. The *Mare Nostrum* camping and outdoor shop

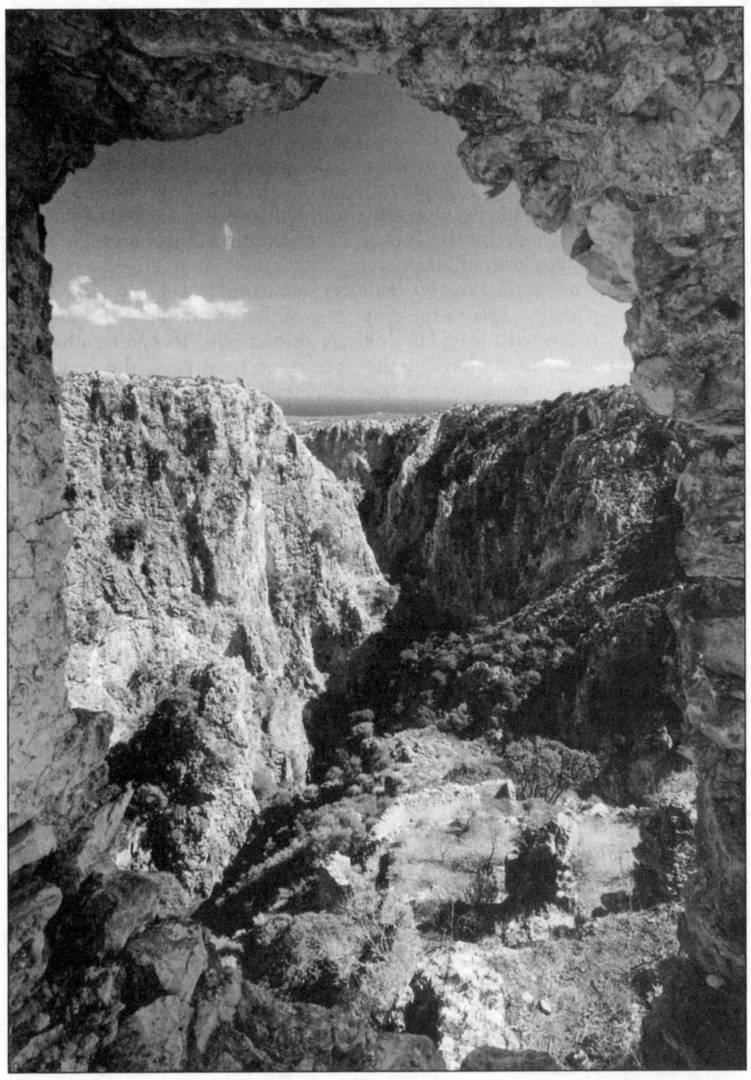

▲ Káki Langádha Gorge, Kýthira

southwest of the platía (☎27360 33573, ⓔchronisdiver@hotmail.com) can organize guided walks down through the Káki Langádha Gorge (see p.208 under Paleohóra) to the coast a couple of kilometres south of Ayía Pelayía.

Paleohóra

The main reason for visiting Potamós is to get to **PALEOHÓRA**, the ruined **medieval capital** (then called Áyios Dhimítrios) of Kýthira, 3km to the east of the town. Few people seem to know about or visit these remains, though they constitute one of the best Byzantine sites around. The most obvious comparison is with Mystra, and although Paleohóra is much smaller – a fortified village rather than a town – its natural setting is perhaps even more spectacular. Set on a hilltop at the forked head of the **Káki Langádha Gorge**, it is surrounded by a sheer hundred-metre drop on three sides.

The site is lower than the surrounding hills and invisible from the sea and most of the island, which served to protect it from the pirates that plagued Paleohóra through much of its history. The town was built in the thirteenth century by Byzantine nobles from Monemvasiá, and when Mystra fell to the Turks, many of Mystra's noble families sought refuge here. Despite its seemingly concealed and impregnable position, the site was discovered and sacked in 1537 by Barbarossa, commander of the Turkish fleet, and the island's seven thousand inhabitants were killed or sold into slavery.

The town was never rebuilt, and tradition maintains that it is a place of ill fortune, which perhaps explains the emptiness of the surrounding countryside, little of which is farmed today. The hills are dotted with Byzantine **chapels**, which suggests that, in its heyday, the area must have been the centre of medieval Kýthira; it is rumoured to have once had eight hundred inhabitants and 72 churches. Now the principal remains are of the surviving churches, some still with traces of frescoes (but kept firmly locked), and the castle. The site is unenclosed and has never been seriously investigated. The 4.5km road to Paleohóra is signposted off the main road from Potamós just north of Aroniádhika: the first 2.4km is asphalt, the remainder driveable gravel.

Karavás

The architecture and setting of **KARAVÁS**, 6km north of Potamós, above a deep, partly wooded valley with a stream, are reminiscent of the Ionian islands. There is nowhere to stay, but there is a popular **café-bar**, *Amir Ali*, providing a large range of *mezédhes* (and sometimes live music) in a shady, streamside setting at the northern end of the village, down a narrow lane off the road to Platiá Ámmos. At the northeast end of the village, the new *Artopiío tou Karava* bakery is in a former agricultural building, with beautifully restored olive press machinery on display; a café is planned.

Platiá Ámmos, at the end of the valley, en route to the lighthouse at the island's northern tip, is a small, scattered village behind an attractive sandy beach. On the headland just beyond, the popular *Varkoula* taverna has live rebétika music (Saturdays in winter; daily in summer). There is also an ouzerí, a café, the *Modeas* restaurant, and several establishments with **rooms**, of which the best is the *Akrotiri* (☎27360 33216; ❸). There's an even more attractive little pebble beach at **Foúrni**, 2km south by dirt road.

Kapsáli

KAPSÁLI, on the south coast, is largely devoted to tourism – much of it closes down from September to June. Most foreign visitors to Kýthira in summer stay here, and it's a popular port of call for yachts, particularly since it is sheltered from the strong north winds of summer. Set behind double pebble-and-sand bays, overlooked by Hóra castle, and backed by high grey cliffs on which the tiny white monastery of Áyios Ioánnis Éngremmos perches, it is certainly picturesque. The larger bay has a line of **tavernas**: *Vlastos* is one of the earliest to open in the season, with fish, local dishes and its speciality, cockerel (*kókoras*) in wine; *Zeidoros* (Ⓣ27360 38212, Ⓦwww.zeidoros.gr), halfway along the seafront, has an exhibition hall in a restored Venetian building, organizes summer concerts, and serves food in the atmospheric olive garden behind; *Idragogio* at the Hóra end of the beach serves up good veggie options.

The best **accommodation** is in high demand and expensive. Top of the tree is the *Porto Delfino* (Ⓣ27360 31940; April–Oct; ❼). Nearer the beach, the attractive *Afroditi Apartments* (Ⓣ27360 31328; Ⓔafrodite@aias.gr; open all year; ❺), has more reasonable rates, a pleasant rear garden, and Internet facilities for guests. The *Vasili Spitia* (Ⓣ27360 31125, Ⓦwww.kythirabungalowsvasili.gr; April–Oct; B&B ❺) a short way up the hill, has comfortable rooms and studios, most with sea views. A basic **campsite** (Ⓣ27360 31580; June–Sept) nestles in the pine trees below the *Porto Delfino* entrance road.

Hóra

HÓRA (or Kýthira Town), a steep two-kilometre haul above Kapsáli, has an equally dramatic position, its Cycladic-style houses tiered on the ridge leading to the Venetian **castle**. Access to the fortress is up a modern pathway, but, to the right of this, the original narrow tunnel entrance is still usable. Within the walls, most of the buildings are in ruins, except the paired churches of Panayía Myrtidhiótissa and the smaller Panayía Orfáni (Catholic and Orthodox respectively, under the Venetian occupation), and the office of the archives of Kýthira opposite. There are spectacular views down to Kapsáli and out to sea to the chunk of inaccessible islet known as Avgó (Egg), legendary birthplace of Aphrodite. On the cliffs grow the yellow-flowered everlasting (*sempreviva*), used locally for making small dried flower arrangements. Below the castle are both the remains of older Byzantine walls and, in Mésa Vouryó, numerous well-signed but securely locked Byzantine churches. A small **museum**, at the junction of the Hóra–Kapsáli road – currently closed following 2006 earthquake damage – houses modest remnants (labelled in Greek only) of the island's numerous occupiers, in particular Minoan finds from excavations at Paleópoli and an Archaic stone lion, as well as a telling selection of unexpectedly youthful soldiers' gravestones from the English cemetery. The Stavros bookshop, almost opposite, sells a book of walks (mainly around the southern half of the island).

Compared with Kapsáli, Hóra stays quieter in summer and many places have an even shorter season. Facilities include a couple of **banks** with **atms** and a **post office** on the main square, a branch of Panayotis vehicle rental (Ⓣ27360 31004) and the office of Kýthira Travel (Ⓣ27360 31390, Ⓔkkmk@otenet.gr), the island's agent for the Neápoli ferry. A few **tavernas** open in summer, of which *Zorba* is by far the best, but the climb from Kapsáli discourages the crowds. A popular café-bar is *Mercato*, which stays open in the winter and also has exhibitions of local art. The nearest bakery is at Livádhia, 4km north. **Internet** facilities are available at the *Photo Cerigo* shop just above the square. **Accommodation** is slightly easier to find than in Kapsáli. Options include the *Castello* (Ⓣ27360 31069, Ⓦwww.castelloapts-kythera.gr; ❸) on the Kapsáli side, the *Hotel Margarita* (Ⓣ27360 31711, Ⓦwww.hotel-margarita.com; B&B ❺) in a beautiful 1840s house below the main street, or the gorgeous *Xenon Nostos* (Ⓣ27360 31056, Ⓦwww.nostos-kythera.gr.com; B&B ⑤) in a nineteenth-century house at a fork of the main street.

North and west of Hóra

LIVÁDHI, 4km north of Hóra, has rooms and, on the main road, a hotel, the *Aposperides* (Ⓣ27360 31656, Ⓔaposperides@freemail.gr; B&B ④), as well as two tavernas, a supermarket, a bakery and *zaharoplastía*. Livádhi is also home to one of the most efficient travel agencies on the island, Porfyra Travel, which is the main ANEK/ANEN and Olympic Airways agent (Ⓣ27360 31888, Ⓦwww.kythira.info), with exchange and car rental; they can also arrange accommodation and transfers. There are Internet facilities at the Polyedro shop; for nightlife, head 5km north to the *Camelot* dance club (open Fri–Sat in low season, daily in high season), near Frátsia.

At **Káto Livádhi**, 1km east of Livádhi, there is a small **museum** of Byzantine and post-Byzantine art (July–Oct Tues–Sun 8am–3pm; Nov–June Mon–Fri 8.30am–2pm; free) next to the large central church. It contains frescoes, painstakingly removed from island churches, dating from the twelfth to the eighteenth centuries, a seventh-century mosaic floor and some portable icons (labelling in Greek only). A few minutes' walk away there is also a cooperative pottery workshop (open mornings and evenings, with a 2–4pm break) and, on the road to Katoúni, a multiple-arched bridge, said to be the longest stone bridge in Greece and a legacy of the nineteenth century when all the Ionian islands were a British protectorate; like others on the island it was built by a Scottish engineer called McPhail. The best view of it is from beside *Rena's zaharoplastío* in Livádhi. A popular **taverna** nearby is the *Theofilos*.

From Livádhi, a side road heads west to Kalokerinés, and continues 3.6km further to the island's principal monastery, **Myrtidhíon**, set above the wild and windswept west coast, among a dead forest of pines burned in June 2000. The monastery's main icon is said to date from 1160. An early left fork off the Myrtidhíon road out of Livádhi brings you through the hamlet of Poúrko: from here, an increasingly steep road leads up to the **Ayía Elésis**, a nineteenth-century monastery marking the martyrdom of the saint on the hilltop in 375 AD, an event depicted in modern wall-paintings inside the church. For many visitors, however, the breathtaking view from the western side of the courtyard is the main reason to visit.

Mylopótamos, Káto Hóra and the Ayía Sofía cave

North of Livádhi, just beyond Dhókana, it is worth making a detour off the main road for **MYLOPÓTAMOS**, a lovely traditional village and an oasis in summer, set in a wooded valley with a small stream. The shady *Platanos* café-taverna makes a pleasant stop for a drink above the village's springs, and the music bar *Kamari* serves snacks and drinks on a lower waterside terrace. Follow the signs for "Katarráktis Neráïdha" to find a waterfall, hidden from view by lush vegetation, next to a long-closed café.

Káto Hóra (also called Kástro Mylopotamoú), 500m down the road, was Mylopótamos's predecessor, and remains half-enclosed within the walls of a Venetian fortress – it is signposted only as Áyios Ioánnis Pródromos, the main church. The fortress is small, full of locked, well-labelled churches, and has a rather domestic appearance: unlike the castle at Hóra, it was built as a place of refuge for the villagers in case of attack, rather than as a base for a Venetian garrison. All the houses within the walls are abandoned – as are many outside

– but are open and accessible. The traditional style of two-floored Cycladic *kástro* houses, with separate dwellings on each floor, can be seen in the village's main street.

Most visitors come to Mylopótamos to see the **cave of Ayía Sofía**, the largest and most impressive of a number of caverns on the island. A half-hour signposted walk from the village, or a short drive along a dirt road off the Limniónas road, the cave is open from mid-June to mid-September (Mon–Fri 3–8pm, Sat & Sun 11am–5pm; €3). When the cave is closed, you can probably find a guide in Mylopótamos; ask at the village, giving a day's notice if possible. The cave's entrance has been used as a church and has an iconostasis carved from the rock, with important Byzantine frescoes on it. Beyond, the cave system comprises a series of chambers, which reach 250m into the mountain, although the thirty-minute guided tour (in Greek and English) only takes in the more interesting outer chambers.

The southeast coast

The beach at Kapsáli is decent but not large and gets very crowded in July and August. For quieter, undeveloped beaches, it's better to head out to the southeast coast, towards Avlémonas.

Firí Ámmos, Kombonádha and Halkós beaches

Firí Ámmos, the nearest good sand beach to Kapsáli, is popular but not overcrowded, even in summer. To get there, follow paved roads from Kapsáli or Livádhi as far as the *Filio* taverna (June–Sept), which serves good traditional food and local specialities, in the scattered settlement of Kálamos; the onward road becomes a four-kilometre dirt track to the beach. Firí Ámmos can also be reached by a second dirt track off the Livádhi–Kálamos road, while another, longer, surfaced road, off the Káto Livádhi–Frátsia road, leads to **Kombonádha**, the next beach north. There are summer canteens at both beaches. Much smaller, but prettier, pebbly **Halkós** beach near the southeast corner of the island is signposted from the crossroads at the entrance to Kálamos.

Paleópoli and Avlémonas

PALEÓPOLI, a hamlet of a few scattered houses, is accessible by asphalt roads from Aroniádhika, Frátsia and Kondoliánika. The area is the site of the ancient city of **Skandia**, and excavations on the headland of **Kastrí** have revealed remains of an important Minoan colony. There's little visible evidence, apart from shards of pottery in the low crumbling cliffs, but tourist development in the area has been barred because of its archeological significance. Consequently, there's just one solitary **taverna**, the *Skandia* (June–Oct), behind the two-kilometre sand-and-pebble **beach** that stretches to either side of the headland – they have some rooms on the hillside above.

Paleokástro, the mountain to the west, is the site of ancient Kýthira where there was a sanctuary of Aphrodite, but again, there's little to be seen today. Heading west from Paleópoli, and crossing the river bridge onto the Kondoliánika road, an unpaved road off to the left leads up to a tiny, white-washed church. From there, a rougher track leads down to **Kaladhí**, a beautiful cliff-backed pebble beach with caves, and rocks jutting out to sea.

AVLÉMONAS, on a rocky shoreline 2km east of Paleópoli beach, is a small fishing port with an end-of-the-world feel as you approach from a distance. It becomes much more attractive once reached, and has a remarkable coordination of colour schemes throughout the village. There is a small, unimpressive Venetian fortress, and two **tavernas**, *Korali* and *Sotiris*, both offering a wide selection of fresh, well-prepared and reasonably priced fish dishes. There are a number of **rooms**, including the apartments of *Popi Kastrisiou* (Ⓣ27360 33735; ❹), and the rooms at *Manti* (Ⓣ27360 33039, Ⓦwww.manti.gr; ❹–❻).

Andikýthira island

Thirteen kilometres to the south of Kýthira, the tiny, wind-blown 22-square-kilometre island of **ANDIKÝTHIRA** (Ⓦwww.antikythira.gr) has, theoretically, a twice-weekly connection with Crete on the Kýthira–Kastélli–Kýthira run (Ⓦwww.anen.gr), but landings are often impossible due to adverse weather. There are attempts to organize a ferry from Kýthira for the festival of Áyios Mýron on August 17 at Galanianá – an annual reunion jamboree for the Andikytheran diaspora – returning the following day, but these are often thwarted by the wind. Rocky and poor, and a site of political exile until 1964, the island only received electricity in 1984, but the island has one remarkable claim to fame: the **Andikythera Mechanism** (see p.123). Local attractions include good birdlife (a bird observatory has been built in the old school at Lazianá) and flora, but it's not the place if you want company: with only 45 residents divided among a scattering of settlements – mainly in **Potamós**, the harbour, and **Sohória**, the village – people are rather thin on the ground. The only official accommodation is the set of **rooms** run by the local community (Ⓣ27360 33004, Ⓔinfo@antikythera.gr; ❷) at Potamós, which also has a couple of **tavernas**, but you'd be wise to bring plenty of supplies with you. In Sohória the only provisions available are basic foodstuffs at the village shop.

Recent excavation work above Xeropótamos has revealed the site of ancient **Aigila**, a 75-acre fortress city of the Hellenistic period. At the harbour below are the remains of one of ancient Greece's best-preserved warship slipways, a *neosoikos*, carved out of the rock. Archeologist Aris Tsaravopoulos (Ⓣ697 30 50 204) can sometimes arrange volunteer excavation work at the sites.

The Máni

The southernmost peninsula of Greece, **the Máni**, stretches from Yíthio in the east to Kardhamýli in the west and terminates at Cape Ténaro, the mythical entrance to the underworld. Its spine, negotiated by road at just a few points, is the vast grey mass of Mount Taïyetos and its southern extension, Sangiás. It is a wild landscape, an arid Mediterranean counterpart to Cornwall or the Scottish highlands, with an idiosyncratic culture and history to match. Nowhere in Greece does a region seem so close to its violent medieval past – which continued largely unaltered until the end of the nineteenth century. Despite, or perhaps because of this, the sense of hospitality is, like nearby Crete, as strong as anywhere in Greece.

The peninsula has two distinct regions: the Éxo (Outer) Máni and the Mésa (Inner or Deep) Máni. The **Mésa Máni** – the part of the peninsula south of a line drawn between Ítylo and Vathý bay – is classic Máni territory, its jagged coast relieved only by the occasional cove, and its land a mass of rocks. It has one major nonhistorical sight, the remarkable caves at **Pýrgos Dhiroú**, which are now very much on the tourist circuit, but beyond this point visitor numbers thin out fast. Attractions include the coastal villages, like **Yeroliménas** on the west coast, or **Kótronas** on the east, but the pleasure is mainly in exploring the **tower-houses** and **churches**, and the solitude. A fair number of the towers survive, their groupings most dramatic at **Kítta**, **Váthia** and **Flomohóri**. The churches are subtler and harder to find, often hidden away from actual villages, but worth the effort to locate them. Many were built during the tenth and twelfth centuries, when the Maniots enthusiastically embraced Christianity; almost all retain at least traces of frescoes, though most are kept locked, with elusive wardens. The well-illustrated website of John Chapman (Ⓦwww.zorbas.de/maniguide) is a comprehensive information source on the Máni, in particular its history, churches and frescoes.

The **Éxo Máni** – the coast up from Areópoli to Kalamáta, mostly in Messinía province – sees the emphasis shift to walking and beaches. **Stoúpa** and **Kardhamýli** are both attractive resorts, developing but far from spoilt. The road itself is an experience, threading up into the foothills of Taïyetos before looping back down to the sea. Some of the finest views of the whole western coast and the southernmost point of the Máni are from the Kalamáta–Kýthira ferry.

Some Maniot history

The **mountains** offer the key to Maniot history. Formidable natural barriers, they provided a refuge from, and bastion of resistance to, every occupying force of the last two millennia. The Dorians never reached this far south in the wake of the Mycenaeans. Roman occupation was perfunctory and Christianity did not take root in the interior until the ninth century (some five hundred years after the establishment of Byzantium). Throughout the years of Venetian and Turkish control of the Peloponnese there were constant rebellions, climaxing in the Maniot uprising on March 17, 1821, a week before Archbishop Yermanos raised the Greek flag at Kalávryta to officially launch the War of Independence.

Alongside this national assertiveness was an equally intense and violent internal tribalism, seen at its most extreme in the elaborate tradition of **blood feuds** (see box, p.216), probably prolonged, and certainly exploited, by the **Turks**. The first Maniot uprising against them took place in 1571, a year after the Ottoman

Practicalities in the Máni

Getting around can be time-consuming unless you have your own transport, and you may want to consider renting a car from Stoúpa or Kalamáta or a motorbike from Yíthio or Kalamáta. Without a vehicle, you will need to walk or hitch to supplement the buses. In Mésa Máni, there are just two services: Areópoli–Yeroliménas–Álika–Váthia, although the Váthia section is unreliable (daily in summer; three weekly out of season), and Areópoli–Kótronas–Láyia (daily). An alternative is to make use of the handful of taxis, generally negotiable, at Areópoli, Yeroliménas, Kótronas and Yíthio; currently, a taxi from Areópoli to Váthia would cost €30.

There is a **bank** at Areópoli. You can sometimes change cash at the **post offices** (Mon–Fri 7.30am–2pm) in Yeroliménas or Areópoli, but it's wiser to bring as much as you think you'll need. **Opening hours** of shops, tavernas, petrol stations and almost anything else can be idiosyncratic in the Mésa Máni, so it may also prove wise to bring some general supplies with you – there are well-stocked **supermarkets** in Areópoli, Kalamáta, Kardhamýli, Stoúpa and Yíthio, and smaller ones in Pýrgos Dhiroú and Yeroliménas. Always try and book in advance for any **accommodation** that is not a hotel – owners can be very hard to locate.

A good, large-scale **map** is invaluable for navigating among the innumerable tiny settlements of the Mésa Máni: both Road Editions and Anavasi have a 1:50 000 scale map of the area, while Anavasi also produce a 1:25 000 map of the southernmost half. Recently, a number of walk routes have been signed in the area, with useful map boards at the start points.

occupation. There were to be renewed attempts through the succeeding centuries, with plots involving the Venetians, French and Russians. But the Turks, wisely, opted to control the Máni by granting a level of local autonomy, investing power in one or other clan whose leader they designated "bey" of the region. The position provided a focus for the obsession with arms and war and worked well until the nineteenth-century appointment of **Petrobey Mavromihalis**. With a power base at Liméni he united the clans in revolution, and his Maniot army was to prove vital to the success of the War of Independence.

Unsurprisingly, the end of the war and the formation of an **independent Greece** did not mark the end of Maniot rebellion. Mavromihalis swiftly fell out with the first president of the nation, Kapodhistrías and, with other members of the clan, was imprisoned by him at Náfplio – an act which led to the president's assassination at the hands of Petrobey's brothers. The monarchy fared little better until one of the king's German officers was sent to the Máni to enlist soldiers in a special Maniot militia. The idea was adopted with enthusiasm, and was the start of an enduring tradition of Maniot service in the modern Greek military.

In the twentieth century, the area slipped into decline, with persistent **depopulation** of the villages. In places like Váthia and Kítta, which once held populations in the hundreds, the numbers are now down to single figures, predominantly the old. Socially and politically the region is notorious as the most conservative in Greece. The Maniots reputedly enjoyed an influence during the colonels' junta, when the region first acquired roads, mains electricity and running water. They voted almost unanimously for the monarchy in the 1974 plebiscite, and this is one of the very few parts of Greece where you may still see visible support for the ex-king or the far-right National Party. Recently, there has been an influx of

Maniot blood feuds

Blood feuds were the result of an intricate feudal society that seems to have developed across the peninsula in the fourteenth century. After the arrival of refugee Byzantine families, an aristocracy known as Nyklians arose, and the various clans gradually developed strongholds in the tightly clustered villages. The poor, rocky soil was totally inadequate for the population and over the next five centuries the clans clashed frequently and bloodily for land, power and prestige.

The feuds became ever more complex and gave rise to the building of **strongholds**: marble-roofed battle towers that, in the elaborate mores of the peninsula, could be raised only by those of Nyklian descent. From these local forts the clans – often based in the same village – conducted vendettas according to strict rules and aims. The object was to annihilate both the tower and the male members of the opposing clan. The favoured method of attack was to smash the prestigious tower roofs; the forts consequently rose to four and five storeys.

Feuds would customarily be signalled by the ringing of **church bells** and from this moment the adversaries would confine themselves to their towers, firing at each other with all available weaponry. The battles could last for years, even decades, with women (who were safe from attack) shuttling in food, ammunition and supplies. During the really prolonged feuds, temporary truces were declared at harvest times; then, with business completed, the battle would recommence. Ordinary villagers – the non-Nyklian peasantry – would, meanwhile, evacuate for the duration of the worst conflict. The feuds would end in one of two ways: destruction of a family in battle, or total surrender of a whole clan in a gesture of *psyhikó* ("a thing of the soul"), when they would file out to kiss the hands of enemy parents who had lost "guns" (the Maniot term for male children) in the feud; the victors would then dictate strict terms by which the vanquished could remain in the village.

money, and considerable refurbishment: many postwar concrete houses have now acquired "traditional" stone facings, as indeed have the shed-like, concrete box-tombs in cemeteries.

Yíthio (Gythion)

YÍTHIO, Sparta's ancient port, is the eastern gateway to the dramatic Máni peninsula, and one of the south's most attractive seaside towns in its own right. Its somewhat low-key harbour, with occasional ferries to Pireás and Kýthira, gives onto a graceful nineteenth-century waterside of tiled-roof houses – some of them now showing their age. There are beaches within walking distance, and rooms are relatively easy to find. In the bay, tethered by a long, narrow jetty, is the islet of **Marathoníssi**, ancient Kranae, where Paris of Troy, having abducted Helen from Menelaus's palace at Sparta, dropped anchor, and where the lovers spent their first night.

Arrival and information

The **bus station** is close to the centre of town, with the main waterfront street, **Vassiléos Pávlou**, ahead of you, and several **banks** nearby. The helpful Rozaki Shipping and Travel Agency on the waterfront (Ⓣ27330 22650, Ⓔrosakigy@otnet.gr) can provide **ferry** sailing times and **car rental** and will also change money. There is a small EOT **tourist office** at Vassiléos Yeoryíou 20.

A trip of at least three days is worth considering for the Máni; the extensive Hasanakos **bookstore** at Vassiléos Pávlou 39 is worth scouring for books on that area, and food supplies can be bought from the large supermarket behind the bus station. **Internet** facilities are available at the *Mystery* café just beyond the supermarket.

Accommodation

Finding **accommodation** shouldn't be hard, with a fair range in town – most hotels are along the waterfront. Despite double glazing in a number of the waterfront rooms on Vassiléos Pávlou, there is late-night noise from the many bars. Numerous cheaper rooms are signposted up the steps behind the waterfront, or facing Marathoníssi islet. Out along **Mavrovoúni** beach, which begins 3km south of the town off the Areópoli road, there are numerous rooms and three **campsites**, the nearest and best of which is the *Meltemi* (Ⓣ27330 23260, Ⓦwww.campingmeltemi.gr; April–Oct).

Demestihas Mavrovoúni Beach Ⓣ27330 22775, Ⓦwww.demestihas.gr. Immediately behind the beach, in a large garden, with a variety of rooms, studios and apartments, many refurbished in 2007. ❸

Gythion Vassiléos Pávlou 33 Ⓣ27330 23452, Ⓦwww.gythionhotel.gr. A fine old (1864) hotel with period decorated rooms on the waterfront, and above a *Dodoni* ice cream parlour. Guests can use the Gythion Bay campsite's facilities. March–Oct. B&B ❺

Grigoris-Matina Vassiléos Pávlou 19 Ⓣ27330 22518. A small, friendly pension (formerly *Kondogiannis*), up steep steps alongside the management's jewellery shop. Some internal rooms, some with sea view. Shared coffee-making facilities. ❸

Kalypso Just off the main road in Mavrovoúni village, opposite the *Milton Hotel* Ⓣ27330 24449, Ⓦwww.kalypso-studios.com. Very good-value, spacious studios and magnificent sea views north over Yíthio Bay. ❹

Saga Tzanetáki Ⓣ27330 23220, Ⓕ27330 24370. Comfortable seafront pension run by a friendly, knowledgeable French-Greek family, with a good restaurant on the ground floor, overlooking the Marathoníssi islet. ❸

The Town and around

Marathoníssi islet is the town's main attraction, with swimming possible off the rocks towards the lighthouse. Amid the island's trees and scrub stands the restored Tzanetákis tower-fortress, built around 1810 by the Turkish-appointed Bey of the Máni, to guard the harbour against his lawless countrymen. It now houses a **Museum of the Máni** (officially Tues–Sun 9.30am–3pm, though often closed; €2), which deals with the exploration of the Máni from Ciriaco de Pizzicoli (1447) to Henri Belle (1861), with labels in Greek and English.

Much of the lower ancient site now lies submerged, but there are some impressive remains of a **Roman theatre** at the northeast end of the town. Follow the road past the post office for about 300m until you reach the army barracks – the site stands just to the left, inside the outer gate. With most of its stone seats intact, and 50m in diameter, the theatre illustrates perfectly how buildings in Greece take on different guises through the ages: to one side is a Byzantine church (now ruined) which, in turn, functions as an outer wall of the barracks. The archeological museum is currently under restoration, but possesses items from Yíthio and the Lakonian Máni. For some more recent history, visit poet Kostas Vrettos' antiques shop, Paliatzoures, at Vassiléos Pávlou 25.

Eating and drinking

For **meals**, the waterside is the obvious location – though many have inflated prices for fish and seafood. At the inner end of the harbour, near the jetty, the unpretentious but popular *Iy Nautilia* ouzerí has water's-edge tables, excellent seafood and tasty *mezédhes*, and fine views of the waterfront, sunsets and Mount Profitis Ilías. *Poulikakos* on the nearby square is recommended for its simple but good food.

Into the Máni: Yíthio to Areópoli

The road from Yíthio into the Máni begins amid a fertile and gentle wooded landscape, running slightly inland of the coast and Mavrovoúni beach, through tracts of citrus and olive groves and between hilltop towers. About 12km beyond Yíthio, the Máni suddenly asserts itself as the road enters a valley below the **castle of Passavá**. Shortly after, a turning to the left leads down to an attractive long sandy beach at **Vathý Bay** (Vathý Ayéranou), which is mostly used by German tourists. At the southern end of the beach is the *Hotel Belle Helene* (Ⓣ27330 93001, Ⓕ27330 93006; April–Oct; ⑤), often block-booked by German groups; towards the north end, behind the reasonable *Gorgona* restaurant, the *Kronos* campsite (Ⓣ27330 93320; April–Oct) is well suited to families.

Continuing towards Areópoli from Passavá, the landscape remains fertile until the wild, scrubby mass of Mount Kouskoúni signals the final approach to the Mésa Máni. You enter another pass, with **Kelefá castle** (see p.225) above to the north, and beyond it several southerly peaks of the Taïyetos ridge. Areópoli, as you wind down from the hills, inspires a real sense of arrival.

Areópoli and around

An initially austere-looking town, **AREÓPOLI** (Aerópoli) sets an immediate mood for the region. Until the nineteenth century it was secondary to Ítylo, 11km north and the gateway to the Mésa Máni, but the modern road has made it, to all intents, the region's centre, and many of the stone buildings are now undergoing (mostly) tasteful renovation. Formerly Tsímova, its present name "Town of Ares" (the god of war) was bestowed for its efforts during the War of Independence. It was here that Mavromihalis (commemorated by a statue in the main platía) declared the uprising.

The town's sights are archetypally Maniot in their anachronisms. The **Áyii Taxiárhes** Cathedral, for example, has primitive reliefs above its doors which

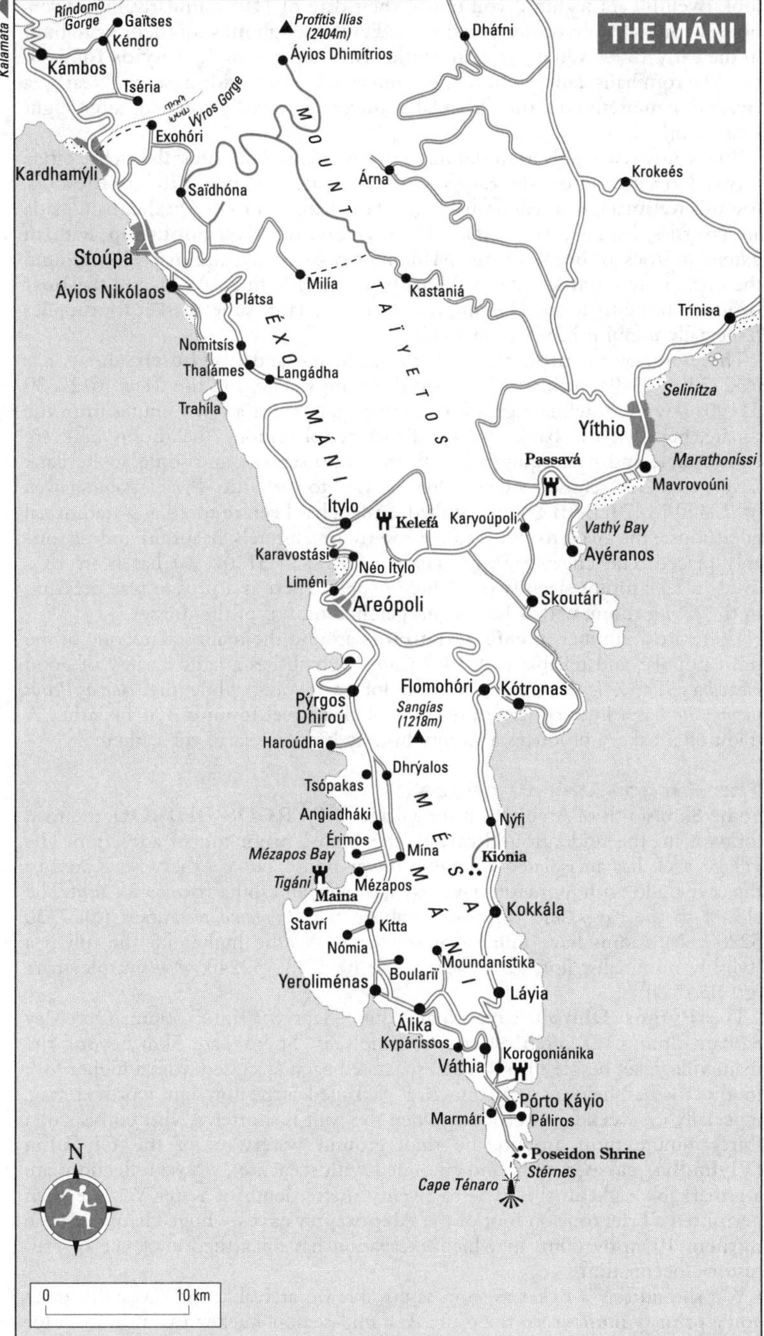
THE MÁNI
Spárti
Kalamáta
Yeráki, Molái & Monemvasiá
Ríndomo Gorge
Gaïtses
Kéndro
Kámbos
Tséria
Výros Gorge
Exohóri
Kardhamýli
Saïdhóna
Stoúpa
Áyios Nikólaos
Plátsa
Nomitsís
Thalámes
Langádha
Trahíla
Profítis Ilías (2404m)
Áyios Dhimítrios
Dháfni
Árna
Krokeés
MOUNT TAÏYETOS
Milía
Kastaniá
ÉXO MÁNI
Trínisa
Selinítza
Yíthio
Marathoníssi
Passavá
Mavrovoúni
Ítylo
Kelefá
Karyoúpoli
Vathý Bay
Ayéranos
Karavostási
Néo Ítylo
Liméni
Areópoli
Skoutári
Flomohóri
Kótronas
Pýrgos Dhiroú
Sangías (1218m)
Haroúdha
Dhrýalos
Tsópakas
Angiadháki
Érimos
Mézapos Bay
Mína
Nýfi
Kiónia
MÉSA MÁNI
Tigáni
Maina
Mézapos
Kokkála
Stavrí
Kítta
Nómia
Moundanístika
Boularií
Yeroliménas
Láyia
Álika
Kypárissos
Korogoniánika
Váthia
Pórto Káyio
Marmári
Páliros
Poseidon Shrine
Stérnes
Cape Ténaro
N
0
10 km

look twelfth century until you notice their date of 1798. Similarly, the tower-houses could readily be described as medieval, though most of them were built in the early 1800s. On its own, in a little platía, is the church of **Áyios Ioánnis**, the Mavromihalis' family church; the interior is lined with frescoes. Nearby, a Byzantine museum in the Pikoulakis tower, has finally opened, after eight years' work.

Buses leave Areópoli from the main square, Platía Athánatos; the ticket office is two doors down from the *Europa Grill*. If you are heading north into Messinía, towards Kalamáta, you will probably need to change in Ítylo. On the main platía are tavernas, several *zaharoplastía*, and the Adhou oti Mani **bookshop**, with an extensive stock of books on the Máni, mostly in Greek, and maps; just around the corner are a **bank** (Tues & Thurs 9am–1pm) with an ATM, and the **post office**. On the main road behind the square is a large supermarket for supplies (especially useful if heading on south).

There are several **rooms** around the cathedral and two **hotels**: the *Kouris* (Ⓣ27330 51340; breakfast €7; ❸) on the main square, and the *Mani* (Ⓣ27330 51190, Ⓦwww.hotelmani.gr; B&B ❹) in a quiet street a few minutes from the square, between the bank and the EKO petrol station. The rooms here are comfortable and well equipped, with mosquito screens, and some at the back have wonderful sunset views. One of the towers, the *Pyrgos Kapetanakou* (Ⓣ27330 51479; B&B ❹), in a walled garden, has been restored as a traditional guesthouse; the two- to five-bedded rooms are austerely beautiful and reasonably priced. The cheaper *Pyrgos Tsimova* (Ⓣ27330 51301; ❹) has more of a lived-in feel; rooms sleep two or three people. There is a private war museum in the living room, with a Lewis gun perched on top of the dresser.

There are a number of **café-restaurants** around the main square; one of the most popular and reliable is *Nicola's Corner*, which has a large variety of good *mezédhes*. The *Alepis psistariá* is good for carnivores, while the *Barba Petros inomayirio* has a little courtyard off the cobbled street towards Áyii Taxiárhes. A traditional bakery produces a variety of tasty breads next to the cathedral.

The Pýrgos Dhiroú caves

Some 8km south of Areópoli, at the village of **PÝRGOS DHIROÚ**, the road forks off to the underground caves – the Máni's major tourist attraction. The village itself has an isolated 21-metre tower-house, but is otherwise geared to the cave trade, with numerous tavernas and cafés, and some **rooms** for rent. The closest to the caves, and the sea, are above the *Panorama* restaurant (Ⓣ27330 52280; ❸); rooms have impressive sea views. A little higher up the hill is a stylishly minimalist hotel, the *Sole e Mare* (Ⓣ27330 52240, Ⓦwww.soleemare.gr; B&B ❻).

The **Pýrgos Dhiroú caves** (daily: June–Sept 8.30am–5.30pm; Oct–May 8.30am–3pm; €12), often referred to simply as "Spílea", are 5km beyond the main village, set beside the sea and a separate beach (accessed from a higher fork in the road). They are very much a packaged attraction but worth a visit, especially on weekday afternoons when the wait is shorter. A visit consists of a thirty-minute punt around the underground waterways of the **Glyfádha (Vlyhádha) caves**, well lit and crammed with stalactites, whose reflections are a remarkable sight in the two- to twenty-metre depth of water. You are then permitted a brief tour on foot of the **Alepótrypa caves** – huge chambers (one of them 100m by 60m) in which excavation has unearthed evidence of prehistoric occupation.

You should buy a ticket as soon as possible on arrival at the caves: this gives you a priority number for the tours. At a mid-season weekend you can wait for an hour or more, so it's best to arrive as early as possible in the day with gear to make the most of the adjacent beach. If time is short, taxis from Areópoli will take you to the caves, then wait and take you back; prices, especially if split four ways, are reasonable. The nearby **museum** (Tues–Sun 8.30am–3pm but unreliable; €3), on a bend of the road, contains interesting Neolithic finds from the caves; the few labels are in Greek.

South towards Yeroliménas

The narrow, raised coastal plain between Pýrgos Dhiroú and Yeroliménas is one of the more fertile parts of the Mésa Máni with a uniform sprinkling of dwarf olive trees. This seventeen-kilometre stretch of the so-called "shadow coast" supported, until the twentieth century, an extraordinary number of small villages. The main road carefully avoids most of them, but many are sited just a kilometre or so to the east or west of it. Few villages have shops, or facilities such as public phones, so you should carry sufficient water if walking. Drivers will find the road surfaces patchy: new in places, potholed elsewhere. There are numerous road signs, although a number are used for firearms target practice.

The area retains a major concentration of **churches**, many of them Byzantine, dating from the ninth to the fourteenth centuries. Though many are now signposted, they can still be hard to find, but are well detailed in Peter Greenhalgh and Eliopoulos *Deep Into Mani* (see p.963). The main feature to look for is a barrel roof. Almost all are kept locked, though a key can sometimes be found by asking around. Among Greenhalgh's favourites on the seaward side are the eleventh-century **church of the Taxiárhes** at Haroúdha (3km south of Pýrgos Dhiroú), the semi-ruined **Trissákia church** west of Tsópakas (5km south of Pýrgos Dhiroú) and the twelfth-century **Ayía Varvára** at Érimos (8km south of Pýrgos Dhiroú).

At **Angiadháki**, the hospitable, stone-built *Villa Koulis* (aka *Xenonas Strilakou*; ⓣ27330 52350; ❸–❹) has rooms and apartments set in a pleasant garden and orchard, and a shared kitchen.

Mézapos, the Castle of the Maina, and Kítta

An easy excursion from the main road is 2km down to the small hamlet of **MÉZAPOS**, whose deep-water harbour made it one of the chief settlements of Máni, until the road was built in the twentieth century. From the main road, take the side lane to Áyios Yeóryios and then to Mézapos, where there are a few rooms, a fish taverna, a small pebble beach, and some spectacular sculpted cliffs. The best of some fine coastal walks leads to the twelfth-century **church of Vlahérna**, which has a few fresco fragments, including a memorable John the Baptist. If you ask at one of the cafés in Mézapos, it's sometimes possible to negotiate a boat trip out to Tigáni, or even around the cape to Yeroliménas.

The nearby village of **STAVRÍ** (3km from the main road) offers traditional **tower-house accommodation** in the converted *Tsitsiris Castle* complex (ⓣ27330 56297, ⓕ27330 56296; B&B ❹), similarly priced to the tower hotels in Areópoli, though much bigger and in a more remote, exciting setting – and well placed for local hiking. The broad plateau here has a confusing network of small, unsigned roads, and many maps are hopelessly inadequate. To the northeast of Stavrí, but within walking distance, is the twelfth-century **Episkopí church**, in Katayióryis hamlet; the roof has been restored, while inside there are fine but faded frescoes, and columns crowned by Ionic capitals, with a surprising marble arch at the entry to the iconostasis. Head from Stavrí to the deserted hamlet of **Ayía Kyriakí** for good views, and access to the castle

(2.5km) on the bare **Tigáni** ("Frying Pan") **peninsula**. The fortress, by general consensus, seems to have been the **Castle of the Maina**, constructed like those of Mystra and Monemvasiá by the Frankish baron, Guillaume de Villehardouin, and ceded with them to the Byzantines in 1261. Tigáni is as arid a site as any in Greece, and the fortress scarcely seems man-made, blending as it does into the terrain. It's a jagged walk out to the castle across rocks fashioned into pans for salt-gathering; within the walls are ruins of a huge Byzantine church and numerous cisterns.

Further along the main road, **KÍTTA**, once the largest and most powerful village in the region, boasts the crumbling remains of more than twenty tower-houses. It was here in 1870 that the last feudal war took place, only being suppressed by a full battalion of four hundred regular soldiers. Over to the west, visible from the village, is another eruption of tower-houses at Kítta's traditional rival, Nómia.

Yeroliménas and Cape Ténaro

After the journey from Areópoli, **YEROLIMÉNAS** (Yerolimín) feels like a village in limbo, of uncertain purpose, but it does make a good base for exploring the southern extremities of the Máni. The village was only developed as a trading centre in the 1870s, around the jetty and warehouses of a trading post built by a local who had made good on the island of Sýros – quails were one of the main exports. There are a few shops, a **post office**, a couple of **cafés** and several **hotels**, including the long-established *Akroyiali* (Ⓣ27330 54204, Ⓦwww.gerolimenas-hotels.com), with air-conditioned rooms (❸), apartments (❹), and a traditional stone-built hotel (❹–❻). The *Kyrimai* (Ⓣ27330 54288, Ⓦwww.kyrimai.gr; ❺), at the southeastern end of the bay, is in a restored 1870 building, with an old library, a pool and stylish rooms. There are several **eating options** nearby, but the baked fish in lemon juice and olive oil served at the *Akroyiali* takes some beating.

At the dock, occasional boat trips are offered around Akrotíri Ténaro, formerly known as Cape Mátapan (see opposite). The petrol station just beyond Yeroliménas is currently the southernmost of the peninsula.

Álika to Pórto Káyio and Marmári

South from Yeroliménas, the scenery becomes browner, treeless, and more arid; a good road (and the bus) continues to **Álika**, where it divides. One fork leads east through the mountains to Láyia (see p.224), and the other continues southwards to Váthia and across the Marmári isthmus towards Ténaro. Between Álika and Váthia there are good coves for swimming. One of the best is **Kypárissos**, reached by following a dry riverbed about midway to Váthia. On the headland above are scattered Roman remains of ancient Kaenipolis, including (amid the walled fields) the excavated ruins of a sixth-century basilica.

VÁTHIA, a photogenic group of tower-houses set uncompromisingly on a high hillside outcrop, is one of the most dramatic villages in the Mésa Máni. It features in Colonel Leake's account of his travels, one of the best sources on Greece in the early nineteenth century. He was warned to avoid going through the village in 1805 as a feud had been running between two families for the previous forty years. Today it has the feel of a ghost town. The EOT-restored inn, occupying a dozen tower-houses, has been bankrupt and inactive for some years now, though there is a seasonal café.

From Váthia the road south to the cape edges around the mountain, before slowly descending to a couple of junctions. Left at the second brings you steeply

▲ Váthia village, the Máni

down to the beach and laid-back hamlet of **PÓRTO KÁYIO** ("Bay of Quails", 6km from Váthia). There are comfortable **rooms** at the *Akrotiri* (ⓣ27330 52013, ⓦwww.porto-kagio.com; ④) and the *Hotel Psamathous* (ⓣ27330 52033, ⓦwww.portokayio.com; B&B ④), both of which have popular **fish tavernas**; the latter also has an art gallery. A pleasant short walk goes out to the Ágios Nikólaos chapel on the southeastern headland of the bay, while across the bay on the north side are the spectacular ruins of a Turkish fortress contemporary with Kelefá and the monastery of Korogoniánika.

Above Pórto Káyio, the right branch of the road goes south along the headland, capped by the Grigorákis tower, to pleasant sandy **beaches** at the double bay of **Marmári**. A variety of rooms is available above the beach at *Marmari* (ⓣ27330 52101; Easter–Oct; ④–⑤), which has sea views and serves good food.

On to Cape Ténaro

Starting from the left fork before Marmári, follow the surfaced road and signs for the fish taverna, passing a turning for Páliros and making your way along the final barren peninsula, to Stérnes (Kokkinóyia). The road ends at a knoll crowned with the squat **chapel of Asómati**, constructed largely of materials from an ancient temple of Poseidon. The nearby taverna *Akron Tainaro* (ⓣ27330 53064; ③) has good, locally caught fish, and rooms.

To the left (east) as you face the chapel is the little pebbly **bay of Asómati**; on the shore is a small **cave**, another addition to the list of mythical entrances to the underworld. To the right (west) of Asómati, the marked main path continues along the edge of another cove and through the metre-high foundations of a **Roman town** that grew up around the Poseidon shrine; there is even a mosaic in one structure. From here the old trail, which existed before the road was bulldozed, reappears as a walled path, allowing 180-degree views of the sea on its twenty-five-minute course to the lighthouse on **Cape Ténaro**.

The east coast

The east coast of the Mésa Máni is most easily approached from **Areópoli**, where there's a daily **bus** through Kótronas to Láyia. However, if you have transport, or you're prepared to walk and hitch, there's satisfaction in doing a full loop of the peninsula, crossing over to Láyia from Yeroliménas (Álika) or Pórto Káyio. The landscape of the eastern side, the "sunward coast", is different from the western "shadow coast". There are few beaches, and less coastal plain, with larger, more scattered villages hanging on the hillsides. Road signs are fewer than in the west.

Láyia to Kokkála

From the fork at Álika (see p.222), it's 10km by road to **LÁYIA**, one of the highest villages (400m) in the Mésa Máni. A turning off the road, not far above Álika, takes you to Moundanístika, the Máni's highest village – recommended for spectacular views. Láyia itself is a multi-towered village that perfectly exemplifies the feudal setup of the old Máni. Four Nyklian families lived here, and their four independently sited settlements, each with its own church, survive. One of the taller towers, so the locals claim, was built overnight by four hundred men of one clan, hoping to gain an advantage at sunrise. During the eighteenth century the village was home to a Maniot doctor – a strategic base from which to attend profitably to the war-wounded all across the peninsula. Today, a council-owned café faces the main church and the village shows healthy signs of revival, with the ongoing refurbishment of a number of houses.

Leaving Láyia northwards, the spectacularly descending road has possibly the best views in the Máni – of most of the northeast coast. Some 7km on is **KOKKÁLA**, a larger, though visually unexciting, village, with a small harbour and scruffy beach, a longer beach to the north and walking possibilities. The village boasts several café-restaurants, and rooms for rent above the *Taverna Marathos* (Ⓣ27330 21118; summer only; ❸) on the beach. More central is the friendly *Hotel Soloteri* (Ⓣ27330 21126; ❸), which may be the only place open out of high season. On the mountainside above Nýfi, 3km northwest, is one of the area's few ancient sites, a spot known as Kiónia (columns), with the foundations of two Doric temples.

Flomohóri and Kótronas

After 22km northwards from Kokkála, you reach **FLOMOHÓRI**; the land below is relatively fertile, and the village has maintained a reasonable population as well as a last imposing group of tower-houses. **KÓTRONAS**, a few kilometres downhill, feels less harsh than the rest of the Máni. It is still a fishing village, and its pebble beach (there are sandy strips further around the bay) and causeway-islet make it a good last stop in the region. The village is frequented by a fair number of tourists each summer, and has a trio of pensions. The most pleasant is the well-priced *Kali Kardia* (also known as *4-Asteria*; Ⓣ27330 21246; ❷) above a seafront café. The attractive *Kotronas Bay* studios (Ⓣ27330 21340, Ⓦwww.kotronasbay.gr; April–Nov; ❻) are set in a large garden overlooking the sea, northeast along the coastal road. The coastal road from here to Skoutári, and thence Yíthio, has been widened and paved in 2007, offering an alternative to the picturesque inland route from Flomohóri to Areópoli.

The Éxo Máni: Areópoli to Kalamáta

The forty kilometres of road into Messinía, between Areópoli and Kalamáta, are as dramatic and beautiful as any in Greece, almost a corniche route between the **Taïyetos** ridge and the **Gulf of Messinía**. The first few settlements en route are classic Maniot villages, their towers packed against the hillside. As you move north, with the road dropping to near sea level, there are several small resorts, which are becoming increasingly popular. For walkers, there is a reasonably well-preserved *kalderími* (footpath) running parallel to (or short-cutting) much of the paved route, with superb **gorge hikes** just east of Kardhamýli, a good base for local exploration and touring.

North to Liméni

Areópoli stands back a kilometre or so from the sea. **LIMÉNI**, the town's tiny traditional port, lies 3km to the north: a handful of houses dominated by the restored tower-house of Petrobey Mavromihalis, which resembles nothing so much as an English country parish church. On one of the bends on the road down to Liméni is the *Limeni Village* (ⓣ27330 51111, ⓕ27330 51182; ⑥), an externally austere re-creation of Maniot houses, high above the rocky shore and with its own swimming pool. Further round the bay, on the waterside, there are a few tavernas, including *Limeni*, and some basic rooms.

Ítylo and around

ÍTYLO (Oítylo), 11km from Areópoli, is a transport hub. If you are heading by bus into Messinía province towards Kalamáta, either from Yíthio or Areópoli, you will probably need to change here, at the *Petrini Gonia* café. The village is currently experiencing a resurgence in fortunes, with many crumbling old houses being restored. In earlier times, Ítylo was the capital of the Máni, and from the sixteenth to the eighteenth century it was the region's most notorious base for piracy and slave trading. The Maniots traded efficiently in slaves, selling Turks to Venetians, Venetians to Turks, and, at times of feud, the women of each other's clans to both. Irritated by the piracy and hoping to control the important pass to the north, the Turks built the sprawling **castle of Kelefá** in 1670. This is just a kilometre's walk from Ítylo across a gorge, and its walls and bastions, built for a garrison of five hundred, are substantially intact. Also worth exploring is the **monastery of Dhekoúlou**, down towards the coast; its setting is beautiful and there are some fine eighteenth-century frescoes in the chapel.

There are a few **rooms** to rent in Ítylo, and a smart guesthouse with a pool just south of town: the *Pyrgos Alevras* (ⓣ27330 59388, ⓦwww.alevrastower.gr; ④), with studios and views – well positioned if you have your own transport. Accommodation by the beach is also to be found in **NÉO ÍTYLO**, just round the bay from Ítylo's ancient and modern seaport, Karavostási. Néo Ítylo is a tiny hamlet, but as well as rooms for rent it boasts the comfortable *Hotel Ítylo* (ⓣ27330 59222, ⓦwww.hotelitilo.gr; ④), which also runs the slightly cheaper *Alevras* (④) guesthouse. The *Faros* taverna in Karavostási makes good fish dishes, and also has en-suite rooms (ⓣ27330 59204; ③).

Langádha, Nomitsís and Thalámes

If you want to walk for a stretch of the onward route, you can pick up the *kalderími* just below the main road out of Ítylo. As it continues north, the track occasionally crosses the modern road, but it is distinct at least as far as Kotróni or Rínglia. The most interesting of the villages along the way are **LANGÁDHA**, for its setting that bristles with towers, and **NOMITSÍS**, with its trio of frescoed Byzantine churches strung out along the main street. Just before Nomitsís, you pass the hamlet of **THALÁMES**, where a local enthusiast has set up a widely advertised **Museum of Maniot Folklore and History** (April–Sept daily 9am–4pm; €2.50). The tag "museum" is perhaps a bit inflated for what is really an unlabelled collection of junkshop items, but it's a nice stop nonetheless and it also sells local honey and olive oil.

Áyios Nikólaos and Stoúpa

The beaches of the Éxo Máni begin south of **ÁYIOS NIKÓLAOS** (Selenítsa), at the pleasant, tree-shaded Pantazí beach. The village's delightful little harbour is flanked by old stone houses, cafés and tavernas overlooking the fishing boats. The *Limani* taverna at the southern end of the harbour, with a small shaded extension over the water, does excellent fresh fish, while *Kamares* next to the bus stop and post office is open most of the year and its varied menu is popular with the locals. There are a few **rooms** and apartments; one of the best is the *Skafidakia* (Ⓣ27210 77698, Ⓕ27210 77947; ④) in a stone building near the OTE mast, and near a hidden swimming jetty known as Gnospí; the owner can suggest local walks.

Just to the north of Áyios Nikólaos, **STOÚPA** is much more developed, particularly with British package holidaymakers and holiday home owners. It has possibly the best sands along this coast, with two glorious **beaches** (Stoúpa and the smaller, deeper Kalogriá) separated by a headland, each sloping into the sea and superb for children. Submarine freshwater springs gush into the bay, keeping it unusually clean, if a bit cold. A ten-minute walk to the north of Kalogriá beach is the delightful and often deserted cove of Dhelfíni. A further 600m brings you to the pebble beach of Fonéa, wrapped around a rock outcrop and tucked into a corner of the hillside. Stoúpa was home in 1917–18 to the wandering Cretan writer, Nikos Kazantzakis, who is said to have based the title character in *Zorba the Greek* on a worker at the lignite mine in nearby Pástrova, though the book itself was written later on Égina island in the Saronic Gulf.

Out of peak season, Stoúpa is certainly recommended, though in July and August, and any summer weekend, you may find the crowds a bit overwhelming and space at a premium. A popular walking-guide booklet and large-scale map are available: ask at the efficient Doufexis Travel (Ⓣ27210 77677, Ⓔdouftvl@hellasnet.gr), who can also find accommodation and organize car hire (including for the southern Peloponnese during the winter), as well as exchange money. In the resort there are numerous **rooms** and apartments, and several **hotels**. The *Lefktron* (Ⓣ27210 77322, Ⓦwww.lefktron-hotel.gr; ④), with Internet access, and the *Stoupa* (Ⓣ27210 77308, Ⓕ27210 77568; ④) are upmarket but very friendly and reasonably priced. Over the road from Kalogriá beach is *Kalogria Camping* (Ⓣ27210 77319; May–Oct). Towards Kardhamýli, above Dhelfíni beach, there is another, livelier, **campsite**, *Ta Delfinia* (Ⓣ27210 77318; April–Sept). There are plenty of **tavernas**, but *Akroyiali* at the southern end of the main beach not only has well-prepared food, but also has views after dark of the lights of the mountain village Saïdhóna which look remarkably like an extra constellation of stars. The *Gelateria,* a home-made ice cream place at the other end of the beach, is justifiably famous. Bus services can be unreliable on the Kalamáta–Ítylo route, and **taxis** are in short supply locally; the Stoúpa taxi is on Ⓣ27210 77477 and the nearest to Áyios Nikólaos is at Plátsa on Ⓣ27210 74226.

Kardhamýli

KARDHAMÝLI, 8km north of Stoúpa, is also a major resort, by Peloponnese standards at least, and suffering from the busy main road that splits it. But once again the **beach** is good, though not sandy – a long pebble strip north of the village and backed by acres of olive trees.

The area is an excellent base for walkers, with interesting villages and a network of paths that includes some magnificently engineered *kalderímia*. Inland from the platía, it's a nice walk up to "Old Kardhamýli": a partly restored citadel of nineteenth-century houses, gathered about the eighteenth-century church of **Áyios Spyrídhon** with its unusual multi-storey bell tower, and the courtyard where the Maniot chieftains Kolokotronis and Mourtzinos played human chess with their troops during the War of Independence. Part of the area is an interesting museum (Tues–Sun, 9am–2pm). Further back, on the *kalderími* up to Ayía Sofía, is a pair of ancient tombs, said to be of the **Dioskoúri** (the Gemini twins).

On the main road south of the platía, you'll find a bookshop, a **post office** (Mon–Fri) and a good bakery. **Accommodation** includes the upmarket and spacious *Melitsina Village Hotel* (Ⓣ27210 73334, Ⓦwww.melitsina.com; ❺) at the northern end of Ritsa beach, while just off the square are the well equipped *Kipos tis Skardamoulas* studios (Ⓣ27210 73516, Ⓔgeo55@mail.gr; ❹), above the taverna of the same name. Also recommended are the *Notos* (Ⓣ27210 73730, Ⓦwww.notoshotel.gr ❺), on the hill behind town, and the shoreline *Anniska* (Ⓣ27210 73600, Ⓦwww.anniska.gr ❹), southwest of the square. The **campsite**, *Melitsina* (Ⓣ27210 73461; May–Sept), is 2km north of the village. Among Kardhamýli's **tavernas**, try *Kiki's* below *Kipos tis Skardamoulas*, as well as the excellent, traditional *Kyria Lela's*, near the harbour. There is an **ATM** at the bank, next to the bridge and two well-stocked supermarkets.

Inland to the Výros Gorge

North of Kardhamýli the road leaves the coast, which rises to cliffs around a cape, before finally dropping back to the sea in the bay near Kalamáta. But before moving on, a day or two spent exploring Kardhamýli's immediate environs on foot is time well spent.

The giant **Výros Gorge** plunges down from the summit ridge of Taïyetos to meet the sea just north of the village, and tracks penetrate the gorge from various directions. From Kardhamýli, the *kalderími* from the citadel continues to the church and village of Ayía Sofía, and then proceeds on a mixture of tracks and lanes either across the plateau up to the hamlet of Exohóri, or down into the gorge, where two **monasteries** nestle deep at the base of dramatic cliffs. An hour or so inland along the canyon, more cobbled ways lead up to either Tséria on the north bank (there's a taverna, but no accommodation) or back towards Exohóri on the south flank. Linking any or all of these points is a reasonable day's hiking at most; forays further upstream require full hiking gear and detailed topographical maps. Exohóri itself has a **hotel** and café, *Farangi* (Ⓣ27210 73372, Ⓕ27210 73392; ❹), well placed for starting walks, or simply for magnificent views.

Spárti, Mystra and Taïyetos

The central core of the Peloponnese is the luxuriantly spreading Mount Ménalo; but due south, in the Lakonian Evrótas valley, are **Spárti** and its Byzantine companion, **Mystra**, both overlooked and sheltered from the west by the massive and astonishing wall of the **Taïyetos** mountain ridge. Spárti was inextricably entwined with the development of ancient Greece, while Mystra, arrayed in splendour on its own hillside, is one of the country's most compelling historical sites of the last two millennia.

Spárti (Sparta)

Thucydides predicted that if the ancient city of **Sparta** were deserted, "distant ages would be very unwilling to believe its power at all equal to its fame". The city had no great temples or public buildings and throughout its period of greatness it remained unfortified: Lykurgos, architect of the Spartan constitution, declared that "it is men not walls that make a city". Consequently, modern **SPÁRTI**, laid out on a generous grid in 1834, has few ancient ruins, and is today the pleasant organizational centre of a huge agricultural plain. Spárti's appeal is its ordinariness – its pedestrianized side streets, café-lined squares, orange trees and evening *vólta*. The reason for coming here is basically to see **Mystra**, the Byzantine town, 5km to the west, which once controlled great swaths of the medieval world.

Arrival and information

If it is Mystra that brings you here, and you arrive early in the day, you may well decide to move straight on. Getting out of Spárti is straightforward. The **main bus terminal** (for Trípoli, Athens, Monemvasiá, Kalamáta and the Máni) is on the eastern edge of town at the far end of Lykoúrgou, but for the centre the locals alight earlier on Lykoúrgou, near the archeological museum. Buses for **Mystra** leave (hourly; less frequently at lunchtime and on Sun) from the main terminal. Parking tickets need to be bought for certain times in the central area. Most of the **banks** are on Paleológou. There is a good **bookshop** and map stockist near the corner of Paleológou and Lykoúrgou, and **Internet** facilities at the Cosmos video shop at Paleológou 34.

Accommodation

There are usually enough **hotels** to go around, many of them on the main avenue, Paleológou (street noise can be a problem): at no. 25, the *Cecil* (Ⓣ27310 24980, Ⓕ27310 81318; ③) is small and recently renovated, with very friendly and knowledgeable owners; at no. 61, *Lakonia* (Ⓣ27310 28951, Ⓕ27310 82257; ③) is well priced; opposite at no. 72–76, the modern *Maniatis* (Ⓣ27310 22665, Ⓦwww.maniatishotel.gr; ⑤) has good facilities, including its in-house *Zeus* restaurant, recommended for its excellent Greek cuisine. The *Sparta Inn* (Ⓣ27310 21021, Ⓕ27310 24855; ④), at Thermopýlon 105, is huge and modern, with a roof garden and two swimming pools.

Camping is available at two sites out along the Mystra road; both can be reached via the Mystra bus, which will stop by the sites on request. The nearest, 2.5km from Spárti, is *Paleologio Mystra* (Ⓣ27310 22724), open year-round. The *Castle View* (Ⓣ27310 83303, Ⓦwww.castleview.gr; April–Oct), 2km closer to Mystra, is a very clean, well-managed site, with a pool, and a bus stop outside.

Ancient Sparta

Descending from the mountains that ring Spárti on three sides, you get a sense of how strategic the location of the ancient city-state of **SPARTA** was. The ancient "capital" occupied more or less the site of today's town, though it was in fact less a city than a grouping of villages, commanding the Lakonian plain and fertile Evrótas valley from a series of low hills just west of the river.

The Greek city was at the height of its power from the eighth to the fourth century BC, a period when Sparta structured its society according to the laws of **Lykurgos**, defeated Athens in the Peloponnesian War, established colonies around the Greek world, and eventually lost hegemony through defeat to

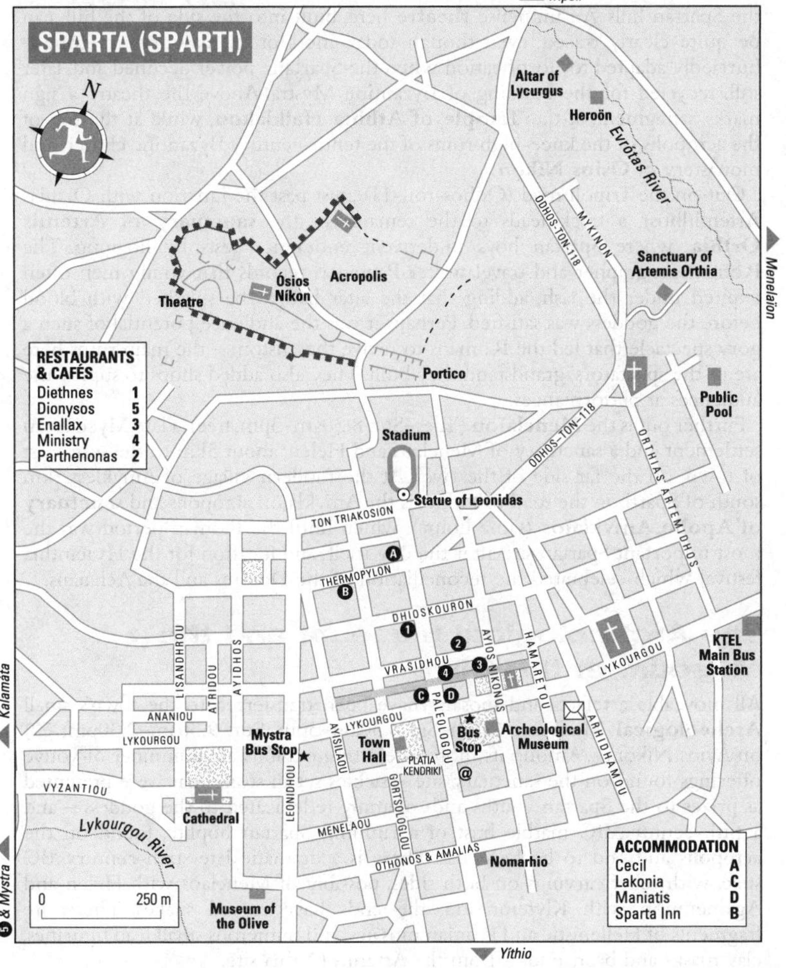

Thebes. A second period of prosperity came under the Romans – for whom this was an outpost in the south of Greece, with the Máni never properly subdued. However, from the third century AD, Sparta declined as nearby Mystra became the focus of Byzantine interest.

The annual September **Spartathlon**, a 246-kilometre run from Athens to Spárti, commemmorates the Athenian messenger Pheidippides who ran the same route in 490 BC between dawn and dusk of the following day: the current course record is 20 hours and 25 minutes.

The sites

Traces of ancient Spartan glory are in short supply, but there are some ruins to be seen to the north of the city (daily 8.30am–3pm; free). From the bold **Statue of Leonidas**, hero of Thermopylae, at the top of Paleológou, follow the track around and behind the modern stadium towards the old **Acropolis**, tallest of the Spartan hills. An immense **theatre** here, built into the side of the hill, can be quite clearly traced, even though today most of its masonry has gone – hurriedly adapted for fortification when the Spartans' power declined and, later still, recycled for the building of Byzantine Mystra. Above the theatre a sign marks a fragment of the **Temple of Athina Halkiakou**, while at the top of the acropolis sit the knee-high ruins of the tenth-century Byzantine church and monastery of **Ósios Níkon**.

Out on the Trípoli road (Odhós-ton-118, just past the junction with Orthias Artémidhos), a track leads to the remains of the **sanctuary of Artemis Orthia**, where Spartan boys underwent endurance tests by flogging. The Roman geographer and travel writer Pausanias records that young men often expired under the lash, adding that the altar had to be splashed with blood before the goddess was satisfied. Perhaps it was the audience potential of such a gory spectacle that led the Romans to revive the custom – the main ruins here are of the spectators' grandstand they built. They also added shops to supply the audiences at performances.

Further out is the **Menelaïon** (Tues–Sun 8.30am–3pm; free), a late Mycenaean settlement and a sanctuary of Menelaus and Helen, about 5km to the southeast of town, on the far side of the river. At the modern village of Amýkles, 7km south of Spárti on the road to Yíthio, is the Amyklaïon acropolis and **sanctuary of Apollo Amyklaïos** (same hours), which until the Roman period was the most important Spartan site after the city itself, and location for the Hyacinthia festival which celebrated the reconciliation of the Dorians and the Achaians.

The Archeological Museum and the Museum of the Olive

All moveable artefacts and mosaics have been transferred to the town's small **Archeological Museum** (Mon–Sat 8.30am–3pm, Sun 9.30am–2.30pm; €2) on Áyios Níkonos. Among its more interesting exhibits are a number of votive offerings found on the sanctuary site – sickles set in stone that were presented as prizes to the Spartan youths and solemnly rededicated to the goddess – and a fifth-century BC marble bust of a running Spartan hoplite, found on the acropolis and said to be Leonidas. There is a dramatic late sixth-century BC stele, with relief carvings on both sides, possibly of Menelaos with Helen and Agamemnon with Klytemnestra; the ends have carved snakes. There are fragments of Hellenistic and Roman mosaics, and numerous small lead figurines, clay masks and bronze idols from the Artemis Orthia site.

At the southwest corner of town is the **Museum of the Olive and Greek Olive Oil** (Wed–Mon: summer 10am–6pm; winter 10am–5pm; €2; Ⓦwww.piop.gr), at Óthonos & Amalías 129, worth a visit for its informative displays covering the history, uses and production technology of the olive.

Eating and drinking

Most **restaurants** and **tavernas** are concentrated on the main street, Paleológou. *Diethnes*, at Paleológou 105, is a local favourite with an extensive menu of traditional dishes; the interior lacks atmosphere, but a delightful garden behind with orange and lemon trees compensates. Nearby *Parthenonas*, next to the cinema on Vrasídhou, is a *psistariá* serving well-priced, traditional Greek food (also to take away). *Dionysos*, 1500m out on the road towards Mystra, serves up expensive dishes with style, with tables outdoors in summer. The most consistently popular music **bars** are *Ministry* opposite the *Maniatis* hotel, or *Enellax* along the side-street behind *Ministry*.

Mystra (Mystrás)

A glorious, airy place, hugging a steep, 280-metre-high foothill of Taïyetos, **MYSTRA** is one of the most exciting and dramatic sites that the Peloponnese can offer. Winding up the lushly vegetated hillside is a remarkably intact Byzantine town that once sheltered a population of some 20,000, and through which you can now wander. Winding alleys lead through monumental gates, past medieval houses and palaces and above all into the churches, several of which yield superb and radiant frescoes. The overall effect is of straying into a massive museum of architecture, painting and sculpture – and into a different age.

There are no facilities at the site itself, so you'll need to base yourself either at the nearby modern settlement of Néos Mystrás (see p.236) or at Spárti (see p.228). If not taking the local bus from Spárti, you can walk a reconstructed stone path to the site. Head westwards on Lykoúrgou, turn left at the end and follow the road (no pavement), then join the start of the path opposite the *Dionysos* taverna. The path and some dirt tracks bring you up to the entrance of the site in about one hour.

Some history

Mystra was basically a Frankish creation. In 1249, Guillaume II de Villehardouin, fourth Frankish prince of the Moreas, built a castle here – one of a trio of fortresses (the others at Monemvasiá and the Máni) designed to garrison his domain. The Franks, however, were driven out of Mystra by the Byzantines in 1262, and by the mid-fourteenth century this isolated triangle of land in the southeastern Peloponnese, encompassing the old Spartan territories, became the **Despotate of Mystra**. This was the last province of the Greek Byzantine empire and, with Constantinople in terminal decay, its virtual capital.

During the next two centuries, Mystra was the focus of a defiant rebirth of Byzantine power. The despotate's rulers – usually the son or brother of the eastern emperor, often the heir apparent – recaptured and controlled much of the Peloponnese, which became the largest of the ever-shrinking Byzantine provinces. They and their province were to endure for two centuries before eventual subjugation by the Turks. The end came in 1460, seven years after the fall of Constantinople, when the last despot Demetrios Paleologos, feuding with his brothers, handed the city over to the sultan Mehmet II.

Mystra's political significance, though, was in any case overshadowed by its **artistic achievements**. Throughout the fourteenth century and the first decades of the fifteenth, it was the principal cultural and intellectual centre of the Byzantine world, sponsoring, in highly uncertain times, a renaissance in the arts and attracting the finest Byzantine scholars and theologians – among them a number of members of the imperial families, the Cantacuzenes and Paleologues. Most notable of the court scholars was the humanist philosopher **Gemisthus Plethon**, who revived and reinterpreted Plato's ideas, using them to support his own brand of revolutionary teachings, which included the assertions that land should be redistributed among labourers and that reason should be placed on a par with religion. Although his beliefs had limited impact in Mystra itself – whose monks excommunicated him – his followers, who taught in Italy after the fall of Mystra, exercised wide influence in Renaissance Florence and Rome.

More tangibly, Mystra also saw a last flourish of **Byzantine architecture**, with the building of a magnificent palace for the despots and a perfect sequence of churches, multi-domed and brilliantly frescoed. These, remarkably

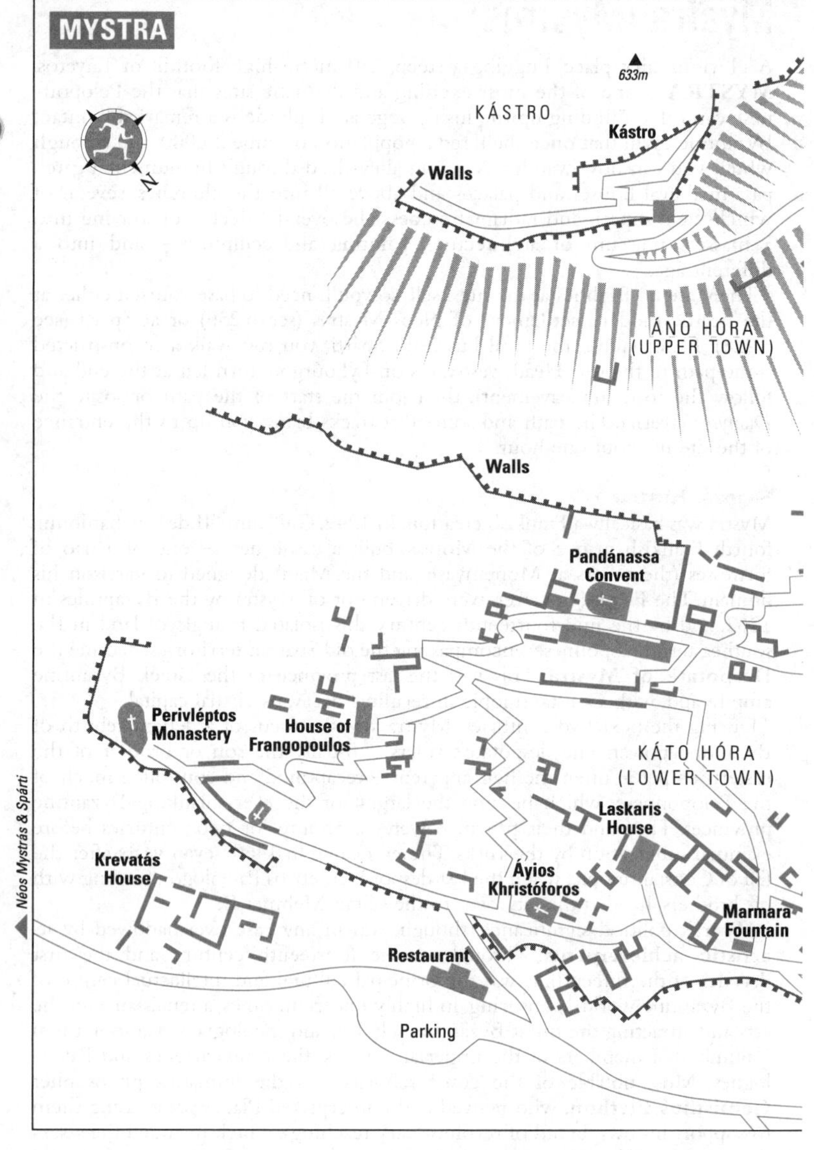

preserved and sensitively restored, provide the focus of this extraordinary site. In the frescoes, it is not hard to see something of the creativity and spirit of Plethon's court circle, as the stock Byzantine figures turn to more naturalistic forms and settings.

The town's **post-Byzantine history** follows a familiar Peloponnesian pattern. It remained in Turkish hands until 1687 when it was captured, briefly,

by the Venetians under Francesco Morosini, under whom the town prospered once more, attaining a population of 40,000. Decline set in with a second stage of Turkish control, from 1715 onwards, culminating in the destruction that accompanied the War of Independence, the site being evacuated after fires in 1770 and 1825. Restoration begun in the first decades of the twentieth century was interrupted by the civil war – during which it was, for a while, a battle site, with the ruins of the Pandánassa convent sheltering children from the lower town – and renewed in earnest in the 1950s when the last inhabitants were relocated.

The Byzantine city

The site of the Byzantine city (daily: summer 8am–8pm; winter 8am–2pm; €5) comprises three main parts: the **Káto Hóra** (lower town), with the city's most important churches; the **Áno Hóra** (upper town), grouped around the vast shell of a royal palace; and the **Kástro** (castle). There are two entrances to the site, at the base of the lower town and up near the Kástro; once inside, the site is well signposted. A road loops up from the modern village of Néos Mystrás to Trýpi, passing near both upper and lower entrances. Buses from Spárti stop at the lower entrance, and usually go up to the top as well (which saves a considerable climb). It's a good idea to stock up on refreshments before setting out: there's a mobile snack-bar at the lower gate, serving freshly pressed orange or lemon juices, but nothing in the site itself. This lack of commercialism within the site contrasts distinctly with Monemvasiá and contributes to the powerfully historic atmosphere at Mystra.

The Upper Town and Kástro

The **Kástro**, reached by a path direct from the upper gate, maintains the Frankish design of its original thirteenth-century construction, though it was repaired and modified by all successive occupants. There is a walkway around most of the keep, with views of an intricate panorama of the town below. The castle itself was the court of Guillaume II de Villehardouin but in later years was used primarily as a citadel.

Following a course downhill from the upper entrance, the first identifiable building you come to is the church of **Ayía Sofía** (1350), which served as the chapel for the Despots' Palace – the enormous structure below. The chapel's finest feature is its floor, made from polychrome marble. Its frescoes, notably a *Pandokrátor* (Christ in Majesty) and *Nativity of the Virgin*, have survived reasonably well, protected until recent years by coatings of whitewash applied by the Turks, who adapted the building as a mosque. Recognizable parts of the refectory and cells of its attached monastery also remain.

Heading down from Ayía Sofía, you have a choice of routes. The right fork winds past ruins of a Byzantine mansion, one of the oldest houses on the site, the **Palatáki** ("Small Palace"; 1250–1300), and **Áyios Nikólaos**, a large seventeenth-century building decorated with unsophisticated paintings. The left fork is more interesting, passing the fortified **Náfplio Gate**, which was the principal entrance to the upper town, and the vast, multistoreyed, Gothic-looking complex of the **Despots' Palace** (1249–1400; currently undergoing extensive rebuilding and restoration). Parts of the palace probably date back to the Franks. Most prominent among its numerous rooms is a great vaulted audience hall, built at right angles to the line of the building, with ostentatious windows regally dominating the skyline; this was heated by eight great chimneys and sported a painted facade. Behind it were various official public buildings, while to the right of the lower wing, flanking one side of a square used by the Turks as a marketplace, are the remains of a **mosque**.

The Lower Town

At the **Monemvasiá Gate**, which links the upper and lower towns, there is a further choice of routes: right to the Pandánassa and Perivléptos monasteries or left to the Vrondohión monastery and cathedral. If time is running out, it is easier to head right first, then double back down to the Vrondohión.

When excavations were resumed in 1952, the last thirty or so families who still lived in the lower town were moved out to Néos Mystrás. Only the nuns of the **Pandánassa** ("Queen of the World") **convent** have remained; they have a reception room where they sell their own handicrafts and sometimes offer a cooling *vyssinádha* (cherryade) to visitors. The convent's church, built in 1428, is perhaps the finest surviving in Mystra, perfectly proportioned in its blend of Byzantine and Gothic. The **frescoes** date from various centuries, with some superb fifteenth-century work, including one in the gallery that depicts scenes from the life of Christ. David Talbot Rice, in his classic study, *Byzantine Art*, wrote of these frescoes that "Only El Greco in the west, and later Gauguin, would have used their colours in just this way." Other frescoes were painted between 1687 and 1715, when Mystra was held by the Venetians.

Further down on this side of the lower town is a balconied Byzantine mansion, the **House of Frangopoulos**, once the home of the Despotate's chief minister – who was also the founder of the Pandánassa. Beyond it is the diminutive **Perivléptos monastery** (1310), whose single-domed church, partially carved out of the rock, contains Mystra's most complete cycle of frescoes, almost all of which date from the fourteenth century. They are in some ways finer than those of the Pandánassa, blending an easy humanism with the spirituality of the Byzantine icon traditions, and demonstrating the structured iconography of a Byzantine church. The position of each figure depended upon its sanctity, and so upon the dome the image of heaven is the *Pandokrátor* (the all-powerful Christ in glory after the Ascension); on the apse is the Virgin; and the higher expanses of wall portray scenes from the life of Christ. Prophets and saints could only appear on the lower walls, decreasing in importance according to their distance from the sanctuary.

Along the path leading from Perivléptos to the lower gate are a couple of minor, much-restored churches, and, just above them, the **Laskaris House**, a mansion thought to have belonged to relatives of the emperors. Like the House of Frangopoulos, it is balconied; its ground floor probably served as stables. Close by, beside the path, is the old Marmara Turkish Fountain.

The **Mitrópolis** or cathedral, immediately beyond the gateway, is the oldest of Mystra's churches, built between 1270 and 1292 under the first Paleologue ruler. A marble slab set in its floor is carved with the double-headed eagle of Byzantium, commemorating the 1448 coronation of Constantine XI Paleologos, the last Eastern emperor (also celebrated in a statue in Néos Mystrás); he was soon to perish, with his empire, in the Turkish sacking of Constantinople in 1453. A stone with red stains is said to mark where Bishop Ananias Lambadheris was murdered in 1760. Of the church's frescoes, the earliest, in the northeast aisle, depict the torture and burial of Áyios Dhimítrios, the saint to whom the church is dedicated. The comparative stiffness of their figures contrasts with the later works opposite. These, illustrating the miracles of Christ and the life of the Virgin, are more intimate and lighter of touch; they date from the last great years before Mystra's fall. Adjacent to the cathedral, a small **museum** (included in main admission charge) contains various fragments of sculpture and pottery.

Finally, a short way uphill, is the **Vrondohión monastery**. This was the centre of cultural and intellectual life in the fifteenth-century town – the cells of the monastery can still be discerned – and was also the burial place of the despots. Of the two attached churches, the further one, **Odhiyítria** (Afendikó; 1310), has been beautifully restored, revealing early fourteenth-century frescoes similar to those of Perivléptos, with startlingly bold juxtapositions of colour.

Practicalities: Néos Mystrás

Buses run all day from Spárti to the lower Mystra site entrance, stopping en route at the modern village of **NÉOS MYSTRÁS**. This small roadside community has a small square with several often pricey tavernas, crowded with tour buses by day but low-key at night, except at the end of August when the place buzzes with live music during the week-long annual *paniyíri* (fête).

In general, it's worth paying a bit extra to stay in Néos Mystrás rather than Spárti, for the setting, relative quiet, and easy access to the site – though you will need to book ahead, or arrive early in the day, to find a place. **Accommodation** is limited to two hotels, the refurbished and very pleasant *Byzantion* (ⓣ27310 83309, ⓔbyzanhtl@otenet.gr; April–Oct; B&B ❸), which has a garden and pool and can be oversubscribed for much of the year, and the *Pyrgos Mystra* (ⓣ27310 83309; ⓦwww.pyrgosmystra.com; B&B ❽), in a beautifully restored and luxurious mansion near the start of the side road to Taïyéti, plus the *Vahaviolou* rooms (ⓣ27310 20047; ❸). There are also a small number of other rooms along the main street. The friendly *Ellinas* **taverna** on the main square is recommended for good food and service.

Walks from Mystra

There are a number of marked paths heading into the Taïyetos foothills behind Mystra, with signs at the start of each detailing the options; a good circular route of about 12km goes up through the narrow valley immediately south of the site, via the hamlets of Taïyéti and semi-deserted Pergandéïka, then down, past the monastery of Faneroméni and the cliff-hung monastery of Panayía Zayoúna (Zoyéni), to Paróri village. From there it's just a couple of kilometres back to Néos Mystrás, with a short detour into a gorge to visit the cave-church of Panayía Langadhiótissa.

A second option is to set off from Paróri, on the spectacular cliff path up through the Langadhiótissa Gorge, then join the E4 footpath to Faneroméni (4km). Take the surfaced road towards Anavrytí, but about 700m along join an old path to enter **ANAVRYTÍ**, which boasts superb vistas, and a **hotel** – the *Antamoma* (ⓣ27310 81595, ⓦwww.antamoma.com; B&B ❸). **Buses** run from Spárti to Anavrytí three times a week, early morning and early afternoon (Mon, Wed & Sat). From Anavrytí, take the road to Spárti, but follow signs off left at the edge of the village to join a remarkable *kalderími* through the Marousó valley (3km). Rejoin the road at the Ágios Geórgios church, from where it is 3.5km downhill to Áyios Ioánnis village (6 weekday buses to Spárti, 5km away). This is a straightforward hike, but most expeditions beyond Anavrytí need experience and proper equipment, including the relevant Anavasi Editions maps, and should definitely not be undertaken alone – a sprained ankle could be fatal up here. The area is prone to flash floods, so check locally. If you are confident, however, there are various routes to the Profítis Ilías summit and beyond. The EOS at Gortosológlou 97 in Spárti (ⓣ27310 22574) can give advice.

Mount Taïyetos and the Langádha pass

From Spárti, there is a tough choice of routes: west over the Taïyetos ridge, either on foot or by road through the dramatic **Langádha pass** to Kalamáta; east to the Byzantine towns of Yeráki and Monemvasiá; or south, skirting the mountain's foothills, to Yíthio and the Máni. For anyone wanting to get to grips with the Greek mountains, there is **Mount Taïyetos** itself. Although the range is one of the most beautiful, dramatic and hazardous in Greece, with vast grey boulders and scree along much of its length, it has one reasonably straightforward path to the highest peak, Profítis Ilías. Three areas, covering different and specialized ecological habitats, in the higher mountains and the gorges of Langádha and Nédhondas, were included for conservation under the EU's NATURA 2000 programme.

Spárti to Kalamáta: the Langádha pass

The **Langádha pass**, the sixty-kilometre route over the Taïyetos from Spárti to Kalamáta, was the second ancient crossing after the Kakí Skála and is still the only fully paved road across the mountain. Remote and wild, with long uninhabited sections, it unveils a constant drama of peaks, magnificent at all times but startling at sunrise; sadly the pine forests suffered extensive damage in recent fires. This route was taken by Telemachus in the *Odyssey* on his way from Nestor's palace near Pýlos to that of Menelaus at Sparta. It took him a day by chariot – good going by any standards, since today's buses take four hours.

From Spárti, the last settlement is **TRÝPI**, 9km out, where there is one of the best **tavernas** in the Spárti area, *Barba Vozola*. Just beyond the village, the road climbs steeply into the mountains and enters the **Gorge of Langádha**, a wild sequence of hairpins. At the rock of Keádhas, high above the southern side of the road a short distance from the village, the Spartans used to leave their sick or puny babies to die from exposure. Above Keádhas is a **climbing park** (grades 5–8b+; guidebook *Rock Climbing in Langada* is available locally) with marked routes for rock-climbers. Beyond the gorge, just before the summit of the pass, 22km from Spárti and 37km from Kalamáta, the *Canadas* **guesthouse** (Ⓣ27210 99281; ❶), built in the style of an alpine chalet, is excellent value, with a restaurant that serves good *bakaliáros* (cod or hake), *loukániko* (sausage), smoked pork, and (in winter) bean soup. It's also a good place to sample mountain tea, made from the local herb *sidherítis*, and a fine local *rakí*. At the **pass**, Selibovés, 3km further on and 125m higher at 1375m, is the *Touristiko Taïyetou* (Ⓣ27210 99236, Ⓕ27210 98198; ❷) hotel, also open all year. This has a very good **restaurant**, with tasty home cooking and panoramic alpine views. From here tracks and paths head north and south along the mountain ridge – peaks up to 1900m are accessible in a day's outing.

The first actual village on the Kalamáta side is **Artemisía**, where the buses from one side meet those from the other, and from where you enter the **Nédhondas** Gorge for the final zigzagging descent to Kalamáta. There is basic accommodation here, in rooms above one of the cafés, but the *Canadas* and *Touristiko Taïyetou* are far better value for little more cost.

Arcadia

Arcadia (Arkadhía in modern Greek), the heartland province of the Peloponnese, lives up to its name. It contains some of the most beautiful landscapes in Greece, though fire damage in summer 2000 took its toll on the fir forests (ironically, the first woodlands in Greece to receive international certification for sustainable management) and the huge wildfires in August 2007 destroyed much of the oak woodland of the plains.

Dramatic hills are crowned by a string of medieval towns, and the occasional Classical antiquity. The best area of all is around **Andhrítsena**, **Stemnítsa** and **Karítena**, where walkers are rewarded with the luxuriant **Loúsios Gorge**, and archeology buffs with the remote, though permanently covered, **Temple of Bassae** (Apollo Epikourios). En route, if approaching from **Trípoli**, you may also be tempted by the ancient theatre at **Megalópoli**. Drivers should be aware that Arcadia's highways, some of the broadest and emptiest in the Peloponnese, are shared with sheep- and goat-herds moving their flocks.

Trípoli

Trípoli is a major crossroads of the Peloponnese, from where most travellers either head **northwest** through Arcadia towards Olympia or Pátra, or **south** to Spárti and Mystra or Kalamáta. To the **east**, a decent road, looping around Mount Ktenías, connects Trípoli with Árgos and Náfplio, via Lerna. A second road runs southeast across the Tegean plain, then east down to Ástros. To the **southwest**, a winding road (a more direct road is under construction) over the intervening ridge leads to Megalópoli from where a faster road reaches the coast near Kyparissía. To the **northeast**, a fast (toll) highway starting near Megalópoli links Trípoli, via the Artemisíon Tunnel, with Kórinthos and Athens.

The Peloponnese **railway** also passes through Trípoli, continuing its meandering course from Kórinthos and Árgos to Kyparissía or Kalamáta. Those with passes might be tempted to use the train to Trípoli and then take a bus to Spárti, but it's not a good idea, as Árgos–Spárti buses are not scheduled to meet trains in Trípoli and furthermore they often pass through full; it's better to take a direct bus (7–9 daily from Athens to Spárti, via Árgos and/or Trípoli).

The Town

Set in a huge upland plain, and surrounded by spectacular mountains, the Arcadian capital doesn't live up to expectations: **TRÍPOLI** is a large, modern town, and home to one of the country's biggest army barracks. It doesn't pander to tourism and has few obvious attractions, although the **Panarcadic Archeological Museum**, Evangelistriás 6 (Tues–Sun 8.30am–3pm; €2), signposted off Vassiléos Yeoryíou (which leads off the central square, Platía Kolokotróni) and housed in a Neoclassical building with a beautiful rose garden, makes a pleasant diversion; the collection includes finds from much of Arcadia, from Neolithic to Roman.

The town's altitude of 665m means an often markedly cooler summer climate and harsh winters. Traffic can be chaotic and you may wish to escape to the quiet greenery of Platía Áreos. Medieval Tripolitsa was destroyed by retreating Turkish forces during the War of Independence, when the Greek forces, led by Kolokotronis in one of their worst atrocities, had earlier massacred the town's Turkish population.

Practicalities

Getting in and out of the town can be fairly complicated. The new, main **bus terminal**, serving all destinations in Arcadia and the northern Peloponnese, is 1.25km from the centre on the Akhladókambos road, to the southeast of town.

Services to Messinía, Kalamáta, Pýlos, the Máni and Spárti leave from the corner café on Lagopáti, directly opposite the train station, 1.5km away at the south-eastern edge of town. There are several comfortable **hotels**, including the central *Alex*, Vassiléos Yeoryíou 26 (Ⓣ27102 23465; B&B ④); and the very friendly *Anactoricon*, Ethnikís Andístasis 48 (Ⓣ27102 22545, Ⓔroinioti@compulink.gr; ④). Eating establishments are mostly functional, but for decent food in more pleasant surroundings there are a couple of **tavernas**, *Neos Dionysos* and *Klimataria*, almost adjacent to one another on Kalavrýton, beyond the Aello cinema and about 100m past the far end of Platía Áreos.

Ancient Mantinea

ANCIENT MANTINEA (Tues–Sun 8.30am–3pm; free), known to Homer as "pleasant Mantinea", was throughout its history a bitter rival of nearby Tegea, invariably forming an alliance with Athens when Tegea stood with Sparta, then switching allegiance to Sparta when Tegea allied with Thebes. It stands 15km north of Trípoli, between the road to Pátra and the Trípoli–Kórinthos highway, and is served by hourly buses from Platía Kolokotróni in Trípoli. The principal remains are a circuit of the 4km of fourth-century BC **walls**, still more or less intact, though much reduced in height – originally they had around ten gates and 120 towers – and a few tiers of its ancient theatre.

Alongside the site is one of the most bizarre sights in Greece: the modern **church of Ayía Fotiní** constructed in the 1970s, from ancient building stones, in an eclectic pastiche of Byzantine and Egyptian styles. It is dedicated to "The Virgin, the Muses and Beethoven".

Megalópoli

Modern **MEGALÓPOLI** is an important road junction and hub for buses, and your first thoughts on arrival may be directed towards getting out. It's a rather characterless place, with a military presence and two monstrous power stations nearby that consume lignite from vast open-cast mines. The adoption of its ancient name, "Great City", was an altogether empty joke. However, the impulse to move on should be resisted, because just outside the city to the northwest is one of the most extensive sites in the Peloponnese: **ancient Megalopolis**.

Practicalities

Megalópoli has regular **bus connections** with Trípoli (and on to Árgos and Athens) and Kalamáta. Moving north or west into Arcadia is slightly more problematic, with just two buses daily to Karítena and Andhrítsena. However, hitching is a viable proposition along this route, as local drivers are aware of the paucity of transport, and it's also possible to negotiate a **taxi** to Karítena. Facilities such as **banks** and a **post office** are around the central Platía Gortynías. There are several **hotels** in Megalópoli, catering mostly to local business travellers rather than tourists. Most are in the vicinity of the central platía, of which the best is *Paris*, Ayíou Nikoláou 5 (Ⓣ27910 22410; ④). The *Leontara* **restaurant** on the main square is good for baked dishes.

Ancient Megalopolis

Ancient Megalopolis (theoretically Tues–Sun 8.30am–3pm, but often closed; free) was one of the most ambitious building projects of the Classical age. The

Theban leader Epaminondas, who oversaw construction from 371 to 368 BC, intended the city to be the finest of a chain of Arcadian settlements designed to hold back the Spartans. However, although no expense was spared on its construction, nor on its extent – 9km of walls alone – the city never took root. It suffered from sporadic Spartan aggression, and the citizens, transplanted from forty local villages, returned to their old homes. Within two centuries it had been broken up, abandoned and ruined.

As you approach the site, along a 250-metre tree-lined track off the Andhrítsena road (signposted "Ancient Theatre"), the ruins are hidden from sight. Suddenly, you reach a hill with the largest **theatre** built in ancient Greece. Only the first few rows are excavated, but the earthen mounds and ridges of the rest are clearly visible as stepped tiers to the summit where, from the back rows, trees look on like immense spectators. Restoration work is planned. The theatre was built to a scale similar to those at Árgos and Dodona, and could seat 20,000; the **Thersileion** (Assembly Hall) at its base could hold 16,000. Today you're likely to be alone at the site, save perhaps for the custodian. Out beyond the enclosed part of the site you can wander over a vast area, and with a little imagination make out the foundations of walls and towers, temples, gymnasiums and markets. "The Great City", wrote Kazantzakis in *Journey to the Morea*, "has become a great wasteland".

Megalópoli to Vytína

North of Megalópoli, the best of Arcadia lies before you: minor roads that curl through a series of lush valleys and below the province's most exquisite medieval hill towns. The obvious first stop is **Karítena**. From here, there is a choice of roads. The "main" route loops west through Andhrítsena to Kréstena, from where irregular buses run to Olympia. An alternative route to the northwest winds up around the edge of the Ménalo mountains to the delightful towns of **Stemnítsa** and **Dhimitsána**, meeting the main Trípoli–Langádhia–Olympia–Pýrgos road at Karkaloú. From either of these you can visit the dramatic and remote site of **ancient Gortys** and explore the **Loúsios Gorge**, above which, outrageously sited on 300-metre-high cliffs, is the eleventh-century **Ayíou Ioánnou Prodhrómou Monastery** (commonly abbreviated to Prodhrómou). North of Dhimitsána is modern **Vytína**, a ski centre with more extensive tourist facilities – snow chains may be necessary if driving around the Ménalo villages in the winter.

Karítena

Picturesquely set, high above and guarding the strategic Megalópoli–Andhrítsena road, **KARÍTENA** may look familiar to Greece aficionados; with its medieval bridge over the River Alfiós (Alpheus), it used to grace the 5000-drachma note. Like many of the Arcadian hill towns hereabouts, its history has Frankish, Byzantine and Turkish contributions, the Venetians having passed over much of the northern interior. It was founded by the Byzantines in the seventh century and had attained a population of some 20,000 when the Franks took it in 1209. Under their century-long rule, Karítena was the capital of a large barony under Geoffroy de Bruyères, the paragon of chivalry in the medieval ballad *The Chronicle of the Morea*, and probably the only well-liked Frankish overlord.

These days the village has a population of just a couple of hundred, but as recently as the beginning of the nineteenth century there were at least ten times that figure. Stop on the south side of the modern bridge over the Alfiós and follow a short track down to the **medieval bridge**, almost underneath the new. It is missing the central section, but is an intriguing structure nonetheless, with a small Byzantine chapel built into one of the central pillars.

From the main road, there's a winding three-kilometre road up to the village, in the upper part of which is a small central platía with a *kafenío*. Off the platía are signposted two Byzantine churches: the fourteenth-century **Zoödhóhos Piyí** (with a Romanesque bell tower) and the late seventeenth-century **Áyios Nikólaos** (with crumbling frescoes) to the west, down towards the river; ask at the *kafenío* for the keys. Also off the platía is the **Froúrio**, the castle built in 1245 by the Franks, with added Turkish towers. It was repaired by Theodhoros Kolokotronis and it was here that he held out against Ibrahim Pasha in 1826 and turned the tide of the War of Independence – hence the view of Karítena on the old 5000-drachma note and a portrait of Kolokotronis on the reverse.

The best choice for **rooms** is the *Vrenthi* (Ⓣ27910 31650; ❷, weekends ❸) on the right just before the main square: ask at the *Vrenthi* café on the left just beyond. **River rafting** is organized by the Alpin Club (Ⓦwww.alpinclub.gr), near the bridge.

Stemnítsa

STEMNÍTSA (Ypsoúnda in its official Hellenicized form – Ypsoús on many maps), 15km north of Karítena and at an altitude of 1050m, was for centuries one of the premier metal-smithing and goldworking centres of the Balkans. Although much depopulated, it remains a fascinating town, with a small folklore museum, an artisan school and several quietly magnificent medieval churches.

The town is divided by ravines into three distinct quarters: the Kástro (the ancient acropolis hill), Ayía Paraskeví (east of the stream) and Áyios Ioánnis (west of the stream). The **folklore museum** (summer Mon & Wed–Fri 6–8pm, Sat 11am–1pm & 6–8pm, Sun 11am–1pm; winter Mon 4–6pm, Wed, Thurs & Sat 11am–1pm & 6–8pm, Sun 11am–1pm; closed Feb; free) is just off the main road in the Ayía Paraskeví quarter, and repays the trip out in itself. The ground floor is devoted to mock-ups of the workshops of indigenous crafts such as candle-making, bell-casting, shoe-making and jewellery. The next floor up features re-creations of the salon of a well-to-do family and a humbler cottage. The top storey is taken up by the rather random collections of the Savopoulos family: plates by Avramides (a refugee from Asia Minor and ceramics master), textiles and costumes from all over Greece, weapons, copperware and eighteenth- and nineteenth-century icons. Across the way is the seventeenth-century **basilica of Tríon Ierarhón**, the most accessible of the town's Byzantine churches; its caretaker lives in the low white house west of the main door.

Accommodation options include the hospitable and homely *Xenonas Stemnitsa* (Ⓣ27950 29504; ❸, winter ❹) off the northern end of the main square, and to the east is the very comfortable but expensive *Trikolonion Country Club* (Ⓣ27950 29500; www.countryclub.gr; B&B ❺–❻, winter ❻–❽. You can eat in town at the simple *Klinitsa* on the square or pleasant *Kastro* near the hill; vegetarians, however, may find suitable dishes limited both here and at Dhimitsána. There is one bus a day linking Stemnítsa with Trípoli via Dhimitsána.

Ancient Gortys and the Loúsios River valley

The site of **ancient Gortys** can be approached either from Karítena or from Stemnítsa (8km northwest of the site). **From Karítena** the most direct route to the valley runs up and through the town to Astíholos (11km), a village 3km southwest of the site. The last section is no more than a jeep track, but is well used. If you don't have your own transport, bus or hitch to Ellinikó, 6km up the Stemnítsa road. From the edge of Ellinikó, a six-kilometre side road descends northwest to the bank of the Loúsios River. Here, across an old bridge, is the site of ancient Gortys. It is possible to stay at the nearby monastery of Prodhrómou. The towns of Stemnítsa or Dhimitsána, the latter with more choice of accommodation, make the best bases for exploring the area, and walkers may want to follow the Stemnítsa–Gortys–Prodhrómou–Filosófou–Dhimitsána route.

If walking **from Stemnítsa**, head out of town on the paved road to Dhimitsána and, 500m after the town-limits sign, bear down and left onto the obvious beginning of an old *kalderími*. The shrub-lined path with fine views takes you down, in around 75 minutes, to near a surfaced road T-junction at the Prodhrómou parking area. Turn left and down towards Gortys (3.5km), but before doing so it is worth going to the parking area and the church viewpoint beyond, perched over the rim of the gorge.

Ancient Gortys

Ancient Gortys is one of the most stirring of all Greek sites, set beside the rushing river known in ancient times as the Gortynios. The remains are widely strewn over the hillside on the west bank of the stream, but the main attraction, below contemporary ground level and not at all obvious until well to the west of the little chapel of Áyios Andhréas (by the old bridge), is the huge excavation containing the remains of a **temple to Asklepios** and an adjoining **bath**, both dating from the fourth century BC.

The most curious feature of the site is a circular **portico** enclosing round-backed seats, which most certainly would have been part of the therapeutic centre.

The Loúsios Gorge and Monastery of Prodhrómou

The farmland surrounding ancient Gortys belongs to the monks of the nearby **Prodhrómou Monastery**, who have carved a path along the **Gorge of the Loúsios** between Áyios Andhréas and the monastery. It's about forty minutes' walk upstream, with an initially gradual and later steady ascent up a well-graded trail. If you look up through the trees above the path, the monastery, stuck on to the cliff like a swallow's nest, is plainly visible a couple of hundred metres above. A set of park benches by a formal gate indicates the entrance.

The interior of the monastery does not disappoint; the local villagers accurately describe it as *politisméno* (cultured) as opposed to *ágrio* (wild). Once inside, it is surprisingly small; there were never more than about fifteen tenants, and currently there are twelve monks, many of them very young and committed. Visitors are received in the *arhondaríki* (guest lounge and adjoining quarters), and then shown the tiny frescoed *katholikón*. Strict dress rules apply. The monastery is also accessible along an asphalt lane that makes a circuitous seven-kilometre descent from the Stemnítsa road.

Prodhrómou to Dhimitsána

Beyond Prodhrómou the path continues clearly to the outlying monasteries of **Paleá** and **Néa Filosófou** on the opposite side of the valley. The older, dating from the tenth century, is virtually ruined and easy to miss, since it blends into the cliff against which it is flattened. The newer (seventeenth-century) monastery has been restored and recently expanded considerably, but retains frescoes from 1663 inside; there is a permanent caretaker monk. Accommodation is sometimes possible, but mosquitoes can be a problem. From here, paths follow the west, then east banks of the river, to reach Dhimitsána via Paleohóri in under two hours.

Dhimitsána

Like Stemnítsa, **DHIMITSÁNA** has an immediately seductive appearance, its cobbled streets and tottering houses straddling a twin hillside overlooking the Loúsios River. Views from the village are stunning: it stands at the head of the gorge, and looking downriver you can just see the cooling towers of the Megalópoli power plant and the bluff that supports Karítena. To the east are the folds of the Ménalo mountains, most visible if you climb up to the local **kástro**, whose stretch of polygonal walls attests to its ancient use.

In the town, a half-dozen churches with tall, squarish belfries recall the extended Frankish, and especially Norman, tenure in this part of the Moreas during the thirteenth century. Yet no one should dispute the deep-dyed Greekness of Dhimitsána. It was the birthplace of Archbishop Yermanos, who first raised the flag of rebellion at Kalávryta in 1821, and of the hapless patriarch, Grigoris V, hanged in Constantinople upon the sultan's receiving news of the insurrection mounted by the patriarch's coreligionist, and of the massacre at Tripolitsa. Grigoris' house is now an **Ecclesiastical Art Museum** (daily except Wed & Fri 10am–1pm & 4–6pm; free). During the hostilities the ubiquitous Kolokotronis maintained a lair and a powder mill in the then almost inaccessible town. Before the War of Independence, the nunnery of **Emyalón** (daylight hours except 2–5pm), 3km south towards Stemnítsa, was used by the Kolokotronis clan as a hideout. About 2km south of Dhimitsána, the excellent **Open-Air Water-Power Museum** (summer daily 10am–6pm; winter Wed–Mon 8.30am–3pm; €3; Ⓦwww.piop.gr) has a reconstructed watermill, tannery and powder mill, with exhibitions on the processes involved.

Accommodation

Though quite a small resort, there is now a selection of very good accommodation, making Dhimitsána a prime base for exploring the centre of the Peloponnese. The refurbished *Dimitsana* (Ⓣ27950 31518, Ⓦwww.dimitsanahotel.gr; ❹, winter ❺), a popular hotel 1km out on the road to Stemnítsa, is easiest for parking. In the northwest corner of town, *Pyrgos Xeniou* (Ⓣ27950 31750, Ⓦwww.pyrgos-xenioy.gr; ❻–❼, winter ❻–❽) is a luxurious, restored five-storey tower, said to be the tallest building constructed in Greece in the mid-nineteenth century; the *Velissaropoulos* (Ⓣ27950 31617; ❷–❸, winter ❸–❹) next door has good-value studios and apartments. Below the village, the *Tefthys* (Ⓣ27950 32604; B&B ❹, winter ❺) is a hospitable, beautifully constructed hotel; most rooms have gorgeous views down to the Lousios valley.

Eating

The **taverna** *Kali Thea*, just across the road from the *Dimitsana*, is good and reasonably priced. At the southern entrance to town, the cosy *Drymonas* has a large variety of *mezédhes* and local dishes. In nearby **Zátouna** village, 4km southwest, the *Kaffenio tou Kentron* of Barba Nikita is a picture-crammed café, preserved as it was in the 1930s.

Vytína

A further 19km clockwise around the Ménalo mountains brings you to the small town of **VYTÍNA**. Local accommodation is intended mainly for winter use during the skiing season, and the town has up to six buses a day to and from

Trípoli. Hidden in the fir forest, above the nearby village of **Eláti**, at 1220m, is the luxurious *Salé (Chalet) Elati* (Ⓣ27950 22906, Ⓦwww.sale-elati.gr; B&B ❻, winter ❼). In Vytína, the **taverna** *Ta Kokkina Pytharia* offers a wide choice of well-prepared local dishes, including a reasonable choice for vegetarians and local wild boar or venison for the carnivores.

Moving on to Olympia

Through buses from Stemnítsa and Dhimitsána are scarce, and you may well need to hitch or take a taxi to Karkaloú junction (or to Vytína), on the main Trípoli–Pýrgos road, where you can pick up buses more easily. You may find that you have fewer changes and stops if you backtrack south to join the Karítena–Andhrítsena route and travel on to Olympia from there.

Andhrítsena and the Temple of Bassae

Moving west from Karítena towards Andhrítsena, the Alfiós River falls away to the north and the hills become mountains – sacred Lýkeo to the south and Mínthi to the west. The route, only slightly less remote than the twists of road around Dhimitsána, is a superb one for its own sake, with the added attractions of **Andhrítsena**, a traditional mountain town, and the **Temple of Apollo Epikourios** at **Bassae** up on the flanks of Mount Lýkeo.

Andhrítsena

ANDHRÍTSENA, 28km west of Karítena, is a beautiful stop, and the traditional base from which to visit the Temple of Apollo at Bassae up in the mountains to the south. Though very much a roadside settlement today, it was a major hill town through the years of Turkish occupation and the first century of independent Greece. It remains remarkably untouched, with wooden houses spilling down to a stream, whose clear ice-cold headwaters are channelled into a fountain set within a plane tree in the central platía.

Hotel accommodation is available at the renovated, friendly *Epikourios Apollon* (Ⓣ26260 22640; Ⓕ26260 22992; ❹) on the central platía. For **meals**, try the small, central *Tsigouri* taverna, which serves local specialities.

The Temple of Apollo Epikourios at Bassae

Some 14km into the mountains south of Andhrítsena, and a World Heritage Site, the **Temple of Apollo** at **BASSAE** (Vásses; summer daily 8am–7.30pm; €3) is one of the most remote, highest (1131m), and arguably most spectacular site in Greece. In addition, it is, after the Hephaisteoin in Athens, the best-preserved Classical monument in the country, and for many years was considered to have been designed by Iktinos, architect of the Parthenon – though this theory has fallen from favour.

There the superlatives must cease. Romantic though the temple was in the past, it is now swathed in a gigantic grey marquee supported on metal girders; its entablature and frieze lie dissected in neat rows on the ground to one side. No doubt the **restoration** is badly needed for its preservation – and the marquee is quite a sight in itself – but visitors are likely to be a bit disappointed. If you are not put off, take the Kréstena road out of town and then, almost immediately, turn off to the left and you begin the climb to the temple. Without transport, the simplest approach is to share a taxi, which should charge around €35 for the round trip, waiting an hour at the site. On foot it's a tiring ascent, with little likelihood of a lift. The site has a full-time guardian who lives alongside, but it's a lonely place, and must have felt even more isolated in ancient times.

The temple was erected in dedication to **Apollo Epikourios** ("the Succourer") by the Phigalians. It's known that they built it in gratitude for being spared from plague, but beyond this it is something of a puzzle. It is oddly aligned on a north-south axis and, being high up in the mountains, is only visible when you are comparatively near. There are also oddities in the architecture: the columns on its north side are strangely thicker than in the rest of the building, and incorporated into its *cella* was a single Corinthian column, the first known in Greece (though now vanished save for its base). Unusually again, the cult statue, probably a four-metre-high bronze, would have stood in front of this pillar. Many of the frieze marbles are now in London's British Museum.

Moving on from Bassae or Andhrítsena

Leaving the Bassae-Andhrítsena area, there are a number of choices: from Andhrítsena two daily **buses** head back up towards Karítena and Megalópoli and two go down to Pýrgos (for **Olympia**).

A well-surfaced road winds through the mountains from Bassae down to the coast at **Tholó**. It takes quite a while to cover the 46km, but for the unhurried there's an opportunity to stop at **Perivólia** (10km on), which is a surprisingly lively little place with a couple of restaurants, cafés and a bar. This mountain hamlet has a short road connecting it with the similarly diminutive Figália, close by the ruins of the enormous Classical walls of **ancient Phigalia** and remarkable views over the Nédha Gorge.

Messinía: Kalamáta to Kyparissía

The province of **Messinía** stretches from the western flank of the Taïyetos ridge across the plain of **Kalamáta** to the hilly southwesternmost finger of the Peloponnese. Green, fertile and luxuriant for the most part, it is ringed with a series of well-preserved castles overlooking some of the area's most expansive beaches. The pale curve of fine sand at the bay of **Voïdhokiliá**, near Yiálova, sandwiched between sea, rock and lagoon, is one of the most beautiful in Greece. Smaller beaches at **Koróni**, **Methóni** and **Finikoúnda** draw the crowds, but Messinía's important archeological sites, such as **Nestor's Palace** near Hóra, rarely see visitors in the quantity of the Argolid sites.

Kalamáta and around

KALAMÁTA is by far the largest city in the southern Peloponnese, spreading for some 4km back from the sea, and into the hills. It's quite a metropolitan shock after the small-town life of the rest of the region. The city has a long-established export trade in olives and figs from the Messinian plain, flourishing as a commercial centre during the Turkish period and as one of the first independent Greek towns in 1821, with the first newspaper to be printed on Greek soil five months later. In 1986, however, Kalamáta was near the epicentre of a severe **earthquake** that killed twenty people and left 12,000 families homeless. But for the fact that the quake struck in the early evening, when many people were outside, the death toll would have been much higher. As it was, large numbers of buildings were levelled throughout the town.

Arrival

If you're looking to get transport straight through, arrive early to make connections. The **bus station** (Ⓣ27320 23145) is nearly 1km north of the centre; follow the river, partly covered with car parks, along Nédhondos. The most regular buses run north to Megalópoli, Trípoli and Athens, and west to Messíni, Koróni or Pýlos; the magnificent route over the Taïyetos ridge to Spárti is covered twice daily, and the one to Kardhamýli, Stoúpa and Ítylo (connection to Areópoli) four times daily. Trípoli/Náfplio/Árgos buses leave from outside the Arkadia bus office 200m down the road. The local #1 bus (buy tickets on the bus) starts from Platía 23-Martiou, about a 600m walk from the bus station, and heads south through the centre to run the length of the Navarínou seafront and beach as far as the *Filoxenia Beach Hotel*.

The **train station** is on Frantzí, 200m to the west of the central Platía Konstandínou Dhiadhókhnou. Kalamáta is the railhead for trains chugging along the pretty, but slow and at times uncomfortable, route to Kyparissía (and ultimately to Pátra, with a possible detour to Olympia), or even more scenically, inland to Trípoli and Árgos.

The **airport** (Ⓣ27210 69442) is 10km west of Kalamáta on the highway to Messíni, Pýlos and Koróni, and buses to these destinations pass the entrance. In season there are four charters a week from the UK, all on Sundays. The small terminal has an automatic **exchange** machine, and a helpful tourist office, open when flights are due, that will book accommodation. There is an **EOT tourist office** upstairs at Polyvríou 6 (Ⓣ27210 86868), near the top of Aristoménous.

Drivers going through Kalamáta between the Máni and Arcadia or the west, should follow the signed southern route through the city, along Kritís, Lykourgoú and Artémidhos, and then on the western bypass (which partly follows the train line); drivers to or from Spárti must brave the narrower crowded streets of the northern part of town.

Accommodation

In the city centre, there are very few mid-range **hotels**, so you'll do better down by the waterfront, where there are many more hotels, some of them expensive, though they seem to spend more on the reception areas than the bedrooms, and can be noisy. However, they are often full by mid-afternoon and if you have not booked ahead, particularly at weekends, you may have to look around.

Akti Taygetos Mikrá Mandínea Ⓣ27210 42000, Ⓦwww.aktitaygetos.gr. Luxurious rooms and studios, in large and attractive gardens near the sea, with pool and disabled access. About 5km outside town to the southeast. B&B ❺

Flisvos Navarínou 135 Ⓣ27210 82177, Ⓕ27210 226 179. Quiet, comfortable rooms, on the waterfront next to the church of Ayía Anástasi. ❹

Fotini Vérga Ⓣ27210 93494, Ⓦwww.hotel-fotini.gr. Spacious apartments, with kitchens. mosquito

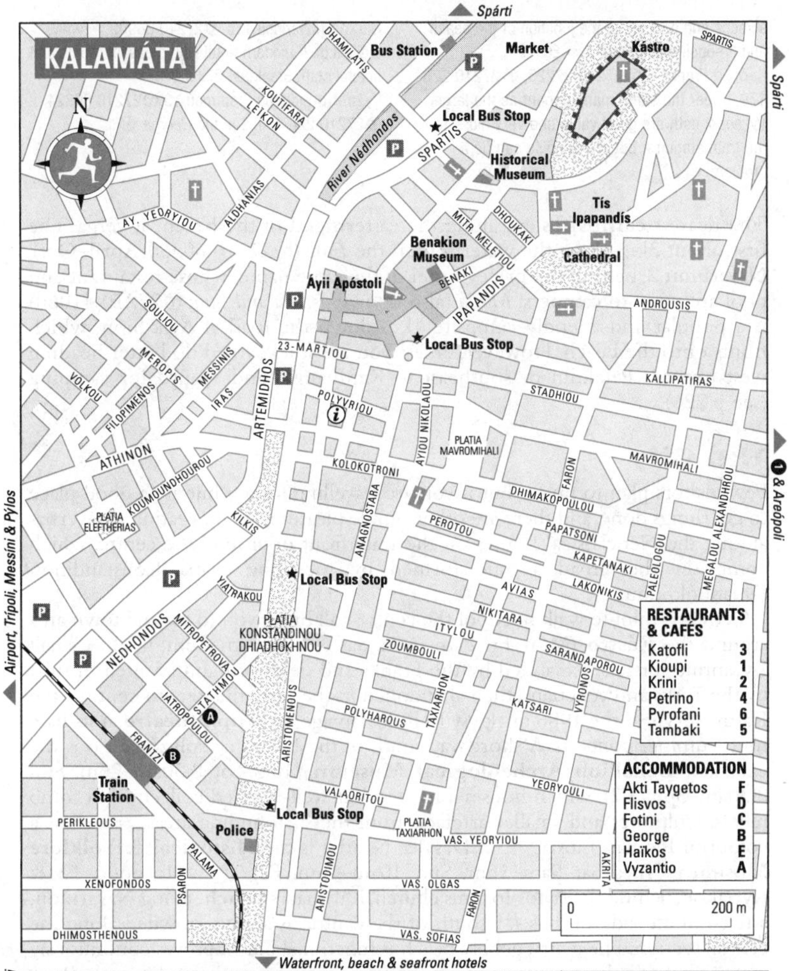

KALAMÁTA

Spárti
Spárti
❶ & Areópoli
Airport, Trípoli, Messíni & Pýlos
Waterfront, beach & seafront hotels

Bus Station
Market
Kástro
Local Bus Stop
Historical Museum
Tís Ipapandís
Benakion Museum
Cathedral
Áyii Apóstoli
Local Bus Stop
Local Bus Stop
Local Bus Stop
Train Station
Police
PLATIA MAVROMIHALI
PLATIA ELEFTHERIAS
PLATIA KONSTANDINOU DHIADHOKHNOU
PLATIA TAXIARHON
DHAMILATIS
SPARTIS
KOUTIFARA
LEÏKON
River Nédhondos
ALDHANIAS
AY. YEORYIOU
MITR. MELETIOU
DHOUKAKI
BENAKI
IPAPANDIS
ANDROUSIS
KALLIPATIRAS
SOULIOU
MEROPIS
MESSINIS
VOLKOU
FILOPIMENOS
IRAS
23-MARTIOU
ARTEMIDHOS
POLYVRIOU
AYIOU NIKOLAOU
STADHIOU
ATHINON
KOUMOUNDHOUROU
KILKIS
KOLOKOTRONI
ANAGNOSTARA
FARON
MAVROMIHALI
DHIMAKOPOULOU
PEROTOU
PAPATSONI
KAPETANAKI
LAKONIKIS
PALEOLOGOU
MEGALOU ALEXANDHROU
AVIAS
NIKITARA
ITYLOU
ZOUMBOULI
SARANDAPOROU
YIATRAKOU
NEDHONDOS
MITROPETROVA
STATHMOU
IATROPOULOU
FRANTZI
ARISTOMENOUS
POLYHAROUS
TAXIARHON
KATSARI
VYRONOS
VALAORITOU
YEORYOULI
VAS. YEORYIOU
PERIKLEOUS
PALAMA
PSARON
XENOFONDOS
ARISTODIMOU
VAS. OLGAS
FARON
AKRITA
DHIMOSTHENOUS
VAS. SOFIAS
0 200 m

RESTAURANTS & CAFÉS

Katofli	3
Kioupi	1
Krini	2
Petrino	4
Pyrofani	6
Tambaki	5

ACCOMMODATION

Akti Taygetos	F
Flisvos	D
Fotini	C
George	B
Haïkos	E
Vyzantio	A

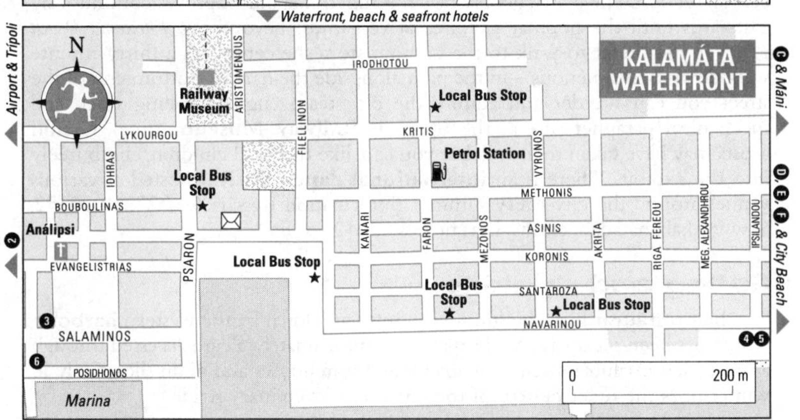

screens and parking, at the junction of the beach and Areópoli roads. Breakfast €6. ❹

George Frantzí 5 ⓣ27210 27225, ⓕ27210 226 179. Under the same management as the larger *Vyzantio*, both are good value and very close to the train station – but street noise can be a problem. ❸

Haïkos Navarínou 115 ⓣ27210 88902, ⓦwww.haikos.gr. A modern hotel with pleasant rooms and helpful staff. Breakfast €7. ❹

Vyzantio Sidhiroú Stathmoú 13 ⓣ27210 86824, ⓕ27210 226 179. See the *George*. ❸

The nearest **campsites** are along the eastern end of the beach, at Vérga. The first, about 3km along the waterfront, is the *Elite* (ⓣ27210 80365; April–Oct), Navarínou 2, behind the pricey hotel of the same name, whose restaurant and pool are open to campers; *Maria* (also known as *Sea and Sun*; ⓣ27210 41060) is a popular and friendly campsite 1km down the road at Ayía Sión, which fronts onto the beach. However, unless you are stuck, you'd do better heading west towards Petalídhi or southeast to Kardhamýli and Stoúpa for camping (see p.226)

The City

Few visitors plan to linger, but if you are travelling for a while it's a good place to get things done, and there are other simple pleasures such as eating at tavernas among the Neoclassical houses on the waterfront or around the centre, which comprises the broad avenue formed by the long Platía Konstandínou Dhiadhókhnou.

A twenty-minute walk north of the centre will bring you to the old town area around the **Kástro** (Mon–Fri 8am–2pm, Sat & Sun 9am–3pm; free). A small Byzantine fortress, expanded by the Franks and destroyed and adapted in turn by the Turks and Venetians, then abandoned in the early nineteenth century, the Kástro survived the 1986 quake with little damage; an **amphitheatre** at its base hosts summer concerts. A short way south of the Kástro at Polyzóglou 6 is the excellent **Benakion Archeological Museum** (Tues–Sat 8.30am–2pm, Sun 8.30am–3pm; €2), which houses a modest but well-labelled collection of tomb reliefs, sculptures and smaller artefacts from the surrounding areas, as well as a colourful Roman mosaic from Desylla. Nearby is the **Historical & Folklore Museum** (Tues–Sat 9am–1pm, Sun 10am–1pm; €2) at Ay. Ioannou 12 & Kyriakou, behind the Áyios Ioánnis church. Kalamáta's **beach**, along Navarínou, a ten-minute ride on bus #1 south of the centre, is always crowded along the central section. The gritty, pebbly beach is functional but improves continuously eastwards until the popular gay area at Vérga, just beyond the *Filoxenia Beach Hotel*. If you prefer to walk to the harbour from the centre, it's a thirty-minute walk down Aristoménous – in the park alongside the narrow bottom end of the street you can wander and admire the old steam engines, rolling stock and mechanical paraphernalia at the open-air **Railway Museum** (free). Graffiti artists may have taken their toll, but you can, like the local children, climb freely into the exhibits. There is an **international dance festival** hosted at various venues around the city every summer (information Kessári 6, ⓣ27210 20352, ⓦwww.kalamatadancefestival.gr; tickets €20–23).

Eating and drinking

The best **restaurants** in the summer months are down by the western **harbour**, which has been set up as a yacht marina – unfortunately all are accessed through a somewhat insalubrious area of abandoned warehouses and grain silos. Only in winter does the older **centre** of town get into its culinary stride.

There are a couple of well-priced **cafés** directly opposite the bus station, and a plethora of cafés, bars, ice-cream parlours and eating places along waterfront Navarínou. For afternoon or evening drinks, the cafés along the central broad Platía Konstandínou Dhiadhókhnou are very pleasant, and less noisy with traffic. Round the corner, the pace heats up in the **bars** along Frantzí and by the train station, of which *Stathmos*, opposite, is one of the most popular.

Katofli Salamínos 20. Near the marina; outdoor summer seating and a huge menu.
Kioupi Alexíki 52 (off the Areópoli road). Idiosyncratically decorated and with clay-pot cooking: fish, *mezédhes* and *mayireftá*.
Krini Evangelistrías 40. Near the marina; a neighbourhood fish-and-wine taverna open most of the year.
Petrino Navarínou 93. A good selection of *mezédhes*; also open for seafront breakfasts.
Pyrofani Spetson/Posidhonos. At a corner on the waterfront with views of the marina and the lights of the eastern villages. A large selection of meat and vegetarian dishes and good local wine.
Tambaki Navarínou 91. A wide menu, tasty food and cheerful service by the sea.

Listings

Banks and ATMs Most are on Aristoménous or adjacent Platía Konstandínou Dhiadhókhnou and Sidhiroú Stathmoú.
Bike & scooter rental Bastakos, Fáron 190 ⓣ27210 26638.
Car rental Agni Travel, Kessári 2 ⓣ27210 20352, ⓕ27210 22428; Maniatis, Iatropoúlou 1 ⓣ27210 27694, ⓔmaniatis@kal.forthnet.gr; Stavrianos, Nédhondos 89 ⓣ27210 23041, ⓕ27210 25370.
Cinemas There are several cinemas near Platía Konstandínou Dhiadhókhnou; English-language films are shown with Greek subtitles.
Ferry agent Maniatis, Psaron 148 ⓣ27210 20704, ⓔmantrv@acn.gr. Agent for ANEN.
Market The Wed and Sat produce market, one of the region's most colourful, is across the bridge from the bus station, below the castle.
Post office Near the customs house beyond the park at the seaward end of Aristoménous.
Taxis Ranks on Aristoménous, Nédhondos and Navarínou.
Tourist police Miaouli, near the harbour ⓣ27210 95555.

Ancient Messene

The ruins of **ancient Messene** (Ithómi) lie 30km northwest of Kalamáta and 22km north of modern Messíni. The ancient city was the fortified capital of the Messenians, and achieved some fame in the ancient world as a showcase of military architecture. The highlights of the widely dispersed site are the outcrops of its giant walls, towers and gates. The ruins share the lower slopes of Mount Ithómi (800m) with the pretty village of **Mavromáti**. An hour's climb to the summit is rewarded with spectacular views of the region of Messinía and the southern Peloponnese. If you wish to stay and see the sunset from the site of the temple of Zeus which crowns this peak, there are some **rooms** in the village. The site is a tricky place to get to, unless you're driving. Buses run only twice a day from Kalamáta (very early morning and early afternoon). With a car it's a slow detour en route to either the west coast or Arcadia.

The site

Messene's fortifications were designed as the southernmost link in a defensive chain of **walled cities** (which included Megalopolis and Árgos) masterminded by the Theban leader Epaminondas to keep the Spartans at bay. Having managed to halt them at the battle of Leuctra in 371 BC, he set about building an astonishing nine-kilometre circuit of ten-metre-high walls (which lasted almost undamaged for 750 years) and restoring the Messenians to their native acropolis. The Messenians, who had resisted Spartan oppression from the eighth century

BC onwards, wasted no time in re-establishing their capital; the city, so chronicles say, was built in 85 days.

The remains include the **Arcadia gate** at the north end of the site, through which the nine-kilometre side road to the village of Meligalás still runs. It consisted of an outer and inner portal separated by a circular courtyard made up of massive chunks of stone precisely cut to fit together without mortar. The outer gate, the foundations of which are fairly evident, was flanked by two square towers from where volleys of javelins and arrows would rain down on attackers. The inner gate, a similarly impregnable barrier, comprised a huge monolithic doorpost, half of which remains. In paved stretches within the gateway you can still trace the ruts of chariot wheels.

Further south, just northwest of Mavromáti and signposted "Ithomi", is the main site (summer Tues–Fri 8am–7pm, Sat & Sun 8.30am–5pm; winter Tues–Sun 8.30am–3pm; free). The **sanctuary of Asklepios** consisted of a temple surrounded by a porticoed courtyard; the bases of some of the colonnades and traces of benches have been unearthed. To the north is the fine Roman theatre, while to the south the spectacular stadium has restored seating.

Koróni, Finikoúnda and Methóni

The twin **fortresses** at Koróni and Methóni were the Venetians' oldest and longest-held possessions in the Peloponnese: strategic outposts on the route to Crete and known through the Middle Ages as "The Eyes of the Serene Republic", when Koróni was also noted for the manufacture of siege-engines. Today they guard three of the more attractive small resorts in the south: Koróni, Finikoúnda and Methóni.

Public **transport** around the Messinian peninsula has improved of late and there are good bus connections between Kalamáta and Koróni, or Pýlos, plus several buses a day from Pýlos to Methóni and Finikoúnda. Direct bus connections between Methóni and Koróni are still elusive, although a new fast road has been built connecting the two. In season, one or two buses a day (usually early morning and mid-afternoon) on the Kalamáta–Koróni route continue to Finikoúnda. If moving on from Koróni to Pýlos, you can change from the Koróni–Kalamáta bus to the Kalamáta–Pýlos bus at the café at Rizómylos junction.

Koróni

KORÓNI has one of the more picturesque locations in Greece, stacked against a fortified bluff and commanding grand views across the Messenian gulf to the Taïyetos peaks. The town is rustically beautiful in itself, with tiled and pastel-washed houses arrayed in a maze of stair-and-ramp streets that can have changed little since the medieval Venetian occupation (1206–1500) when it was a fleet supply base. Buses terminate in the square below the main church, outside a café and excellent *zaharoplastío* and one row back from the waterfront. Koróni's **citadel** is one of the least militaristic-looking in Greece, crowning rather than dwarfing the town. Part of the interior is given over to private houses and garden plots, but the greater part is occupied by the nunnery of **Timíou Prodhrómou**, whose chapels, outbuildings and flower-strewn gardens occupy nearly every bastion.

Continuing downhill, you reach **Zánga beach** which runs into **Mémi beach**, making a two-kilometre stretch of sand and preternaturally clear water that sets the seal on Koróni as a place to relax, drink wine and amble about a countryside lush with vineyards and olive groves. The beach is about the only place to go during the afternoon, when Koróni strictly observes siesta.

Practicalities

To be sure of a room in summer, it's worth trying to phone ahead. The only large hotel, the *Auberge de la Plage* (Ⓣ27250 22401, Ⓦwww.delaplage.gr; ④), is in a fine position, with a large restaurant verandah overlooking the sea, out on the road towards Mémi beach. If you're looking for private **rooms** on arrival, try the places to the right of the fishing port as you face the water, and don't leave it too late in the day; there are also cheaper, quieter rooms in the Panórama district, up behind Zánga beach. Several of the town tavernas rent rooms, including the *Parthenon* (Ⓣ27250 22146; ③) on the seafront corner below the square and being renovated in 2007. An attractive and only slightly more expensive option, with a leafy setting and views of the bay and castle, is *Marinos Bungalows* (Ⓣ & Ⓕ27250 22522; April–Oct; ③) on the road north just out of town. There are two **campsites**: *Memi Beach* (Ⓣ27250 22130, Ⓦwww.memibeachcamping.gr; June–Sept), 2km south of Koróni on the Vasilítsi road, and *Koroni* (Ⓣ27250 22884, Ⓕ27250 22119; April–Oct), 100m from the *Marinos*; both have sandy beaches, though from *Memi Beach* you have to cross the road.

There is a reasonable selection of **restaurants** on the waterfront, and some authentic **tavernas** (barrel-wine and oven-food places) along the main shopping street. The *Flisvos* has good seafood at reasonable prices, and the *Symposion* serves moussaka, grills and seafood. The recommended *Boyris psistaria* is in a pleasant garden at the back of the school car park.

Many people make wine or *raki* in their basement, and the heady local tipple figures prominently in the **nightlife**. The main venues are the sprawling *Astra Club* out towards Mémi beach and the *Zanza Club*. Koróni has two **banks** and **ATMs**, and a **post office**. Mountain bikes are available from the Makrisa shop on the main street.

Finikoúnda

FINIKOÚNDA, 18km west of Koróni, is a small fishing village with a superb cove-beach, with another to the east, and a gigantic strand to the west. Over recent years it has gained a reputation as a backpackers' – and especially windsurfers' – resort, with half the summer intake staying at a trio of campsites on either side of the village, the others housed in a variety of rooms including some block-booked by British package companies.

To book **rooms** in advance, try the central, laid-back hotel *Finikounda* (Ⓣ27230 71208, Ⓔkarhotel@otenet.gr; B&B ④), the beachfront *Porto Finissia* (Ⓣ27230 71358, Ⓕ27230 71458; May–Oct; B&B ④), or the nearby *Korakakis Beach* (Ⓣ27230 71221, Ⓔkorakaki@otenet.gr; B&B ④), which also has apartments at similar prices. The local **campsites** are the well-equipped *Anemomylos* (Ⓣ27230 71120, Ⓕ27230 71121), 500m west of town; *Ammos* (Ⓣ27230 71262, Ⓕ27230 71124; May–Oct), 3km west of the village; and the *Loutsa* (Ⓣ27230 71169, Ⓕ27230 71445; June–Sept), 2km to the east. Among the **tavernas**, *Elena* is recommended for its good, traditional fare and harbour view, while *Psychos* has tasty food, including pasta and pizza, at good prices. *Theasis* **bar** features a mixture of old and new rock **music**.

Methóni

In contrast to the almost domestic citadel at Koróni, the huge fortress at **METHÓNI** is as imposing as they come – massively bastioned, washed on three sides by the sea, and cut off from the land by a great moat. It was maintained by the Venetians in part for its military function, in part as a staging post for pilgrims en route, via Crete and Cyprus, to the Holy Land, and from the thirteenth to the nineteenth centuries it sheltered a substantial town. It was from here, in 1825, that Ibrahim Pasha launched his destructive reinvasion of the Peloponnese that was only finally stopped by the events at Navaríno in 1827 (see box, p.254).

Within the **fortress** (Mon 8.30am–3pm, Tues–Sun 8am–7pm; until 3pm in winter; free), entered across the moat along a stone bridge, are the remains of a Venetian cathedral (the Venetians' Lion of St Mark emblem is ubiquitous), along with a Turkish bath, the foundations of dozens of houses and some awesome, but mostly cordoned-off, underground passages. Walk around the walls and a sea gate at the southern end leads out across a causeway to the **Boúrtzi**, a small fortified island that served as a prison and place of execution. The octagonal tower was built by the Turks in the sixteenth century to replace an earlier Venetian fortification.

Practicalities

The **bus** from Pýlos stops at the first forked junction in town, near the **bank** and **atm**, but if planning a day-trip check return times with the driver. The rather scruffy beach runs eastwards from the castle, although the small Paralías square has been recently paved and revamped. In high season, there are occasional boat trips out to the southern islands of Skhíza and Sapiénza.

Methóni is geared more conspicuously to tourism than Koróni and gets very crowded in season, when **accommodation** can be expensive and often oversubscribed; out of season, the hotels are cheaper. The upmarket *Methoni Beach* (Ⓣ27230 28720, Ⓦwww.methonibeachhotel.gr; B&B ❸) has very comfortable rooms and its own restaurant for buffet breakfast overlooking the sea. The well-priced *Castello* (Ⓣ27230 31300, Ⓦwww.castello.gr; May–Oct ❸) is near the entrance to the fortress, with beautiful gardens, balconies and a stunning view; the friendly *Aris* (Ⓣ27230 31125, Ⓕ27230 31336; ❸) is on the

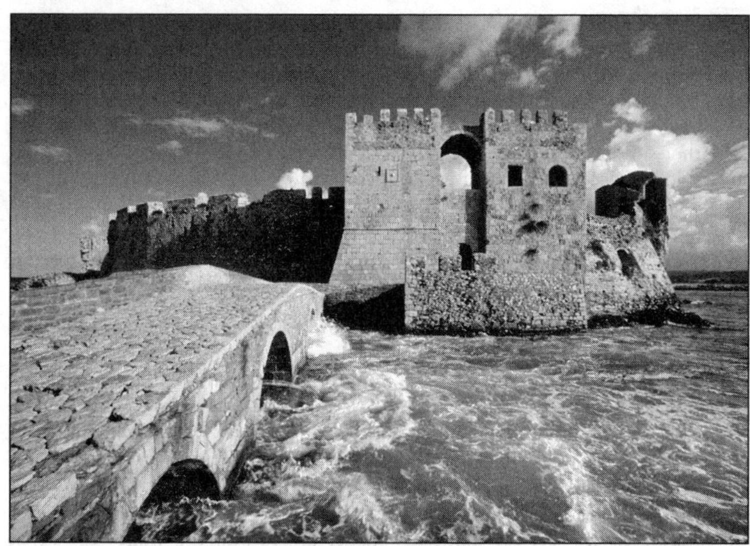

▲ The Boúrtzi, Methóni

small Platía Syngroú behind *Castello*. Cheaper **rooms** are to be found at the fortress end of town. At the east end of the beach is a popular municipal **campsite**, the *Methoni* (☎27230 31228; May–Oct); the facilities are good and the beach here reasonable, so it can get crowded.

Methóni has several **restaurants**, including the pricey *Klimataria* (May–Oct, evenings only), which serves well-prepared dishes (including good veggie choices) in a courtyard garden opposite the *Castello*. A more traditional favourite is the *Nikos*, almost next door. Among the dozen or so other eateries, *Sapienza*, set back from the seafront on the Finikounda road, is recommended for fresh fish. **Internet** facilities are available at the *Doureos Ippos* café, opposite the *Nikos*.

Pýlos and around

PÝLOS is a compact but surprisingly stylish town for rural Messinía; guarded by a pair of medieval castles, it occupies a superb position on one of the finest natural harbours in Greece, the almost landlocked **Navarino Bay**. Given the town's associations with the Battle of Navarino, and, more anciently, with Homer's "sandy Pýlos", the domain of "wise King Nestor" whose palace (see p.256) has been identified 16km to the north, it makes a good base for exploring this part of the Peloponnese, particularly if equipped with a car. Relying on public transport, you'll find that long afternoon gaps in services make complex day-trips impractical.

The Town

The main pleasures of Pýlos are exploring the hillside alleys, waterside streets and fortress. Getting your bearings is easy as it's not a large town, and the main square facing the port is very much the heart of the town.

Shaded by a large plane tree and several of its offspring, **Platía Trión Navárhon** is a beautiful public space, encircled by cafés and colonnaded shops. At its head is a **war memorial** commemorating the admirals Codrington, de Rigny and von Heyden, who commanded the British, French and Russian forces in the Battle of Navarino (see box, p.254). Nearby, just uphill on the Methóni road, the little **Antonopouleion Museum** (Tues–Sun 8.30am–3pm; €2) boasts remains from the battle, along with archeological finds from the region.

Further memories of the Navarino battles can be evoked by a visit to the **island of Sfaktiría**, across the bay, where there are various tombs of Philhellenes, a chapel and a memorial to Russian sailors. You can also hire a **boat** from the port and snorkel to see the remains of the Turkish fleet lying on the sea bed; ask at the harbour office or cafés by the port.

The principal sight in town, however, is the **Néo Kástro** (Tues–Sun 8.30am–3pm; €3), further up the Methóni road from the museum. The huge "new castle" was built by the Turks in 1572, and you can walk around much of the 1500m of arcaded battlements. For most of the eighteenth and nineteenth centuries, it served as a prison and its inner courtyard was divided into a warren of narrow yards separated by high walls, a design completely at odds with most Greek prisons, which were fairly open on the inside. This peculiar feature was necessitated by the garrison's proximity to the Máni. So frequently was it filled with Maniots imprisoned for vendettas, and so great was the crop of internal murders, that these pens had to be built to keep the imprisoned clansmen apart.

The battles of Navarino Bay

As you arrive at Pýlos, your gaze is inevitably drawn to the bay, almost landlocked by the long offshore island of Sfaktiría (Sphacteria). Its name, Órmos Navarínou – Navarino Bay – marks the **battle** that effectively sealed implementation of Greek independence from the Turks on the night of October 20, 1827, though the battle itself seems to have been accidental. The Great Powers of Britain, France and Russia, having established diplomatic relations with the Greek insurgent leaders, were attempting to force an armistice on the Turks. To this end they sent a fleet of 27 warships to Navarino, where Ibrahim Pasha had gathered his forces – 16,000 men in 89 ships. The declared intention was to coerce Ibrahim into leaving Messinía, which he had been raiding ruthlessly.

In the confusion of the night an Egyptian frigate, part of the Turks' supporting force, fired its cannons, and full-scale battle broke out. Without intending to take up arms for the Greeks, the "allies" responded to the attack and, extraordinarily, sank and destroyed 53 of the Turkish fleet without a single loss. There was considerable international embarrassment when news filtered through to the "victors", but the action had nevertheless effectively ended Turkish control of Greek waters and within a year Greek independence was secured and recognized.

Navarino Bay also features in one of the most famous battles of **Classical times**, described in great detail by Thucydides. In 425 BC, during the Peloponnesian War, an Athenian force encamped in Kástro Navarínou (the old castle of Pýlos) laid siege to a group of Spartans on the island of **Sfaktiría**, just across the straits. In a complete break with tradition, which decreed fighting to the death, the Spartans surrendered. "Nothing that happened in the war surprised the Hellenes as much as this," commented Thucydides.

The pens and walls have been pulled down as part of an ongoing programme to restore and convert the castle into a **museum** for underwater archaeology. So far, the only attraction is René Puaux's extensive collection of historical pictures and cartoons.

Practicalities

The National Bank is on the central platía, and the **post office** on Niléos, just west of the **bus station** (ⓣ27230 22230). **Car rental** (also at Kalamáta airport) is available through AutoUnion (ⓣ27230 22393, ⓔautounionkalamata @mailbox.gr) on the Kalamáta road, and from the *Miramare* hotel.

Pýlos has somewhat limited accommodation; in the summer months you should definitely try to phone ahead. Among the **hotels** are the *Galaxy*, on the platía (ⓣ27230 22780, ⓕ27230 22208; B&B ④) and the posher *Karalis*, Kalamátas 26 (ⓣ27230 22960, ⓔhotel_karalis@yahoo.gr; B&B ⑤), an attractive sea-view hotel. The *Miramare*, Myrtidhiotíssis 35 (ⓣ27230 22751, ⓔmmpylos @otenet.gr; April–Sept; B&B ③), near the port, has fine views, while the smaller *Nilefs*, René Pyot 4 (ⓣ27230 22518, ⓕ27230 22575; April–Sept; ③), just behind, is recommended. There are many **rooms** around the winding main road on the hill out towards Kalamáta and Kyparissía, and a few near the castle and the *Miramare*. A more relaxed alternative to staying in Pýlos is the beachfront part of Yiálova (see opposite).

For **drinks**, the Platía Trión Navárhon cafés are the obvious choice, although they can be pricey. Among the **tavernas**, try *Lykourgos* for *mayireftá* on the small street northeast from the platía, or *Gregory's*, at the T-junction at the top of the same street. Nightlife revolves around bars on the square, and the larger, summer-only **clubs** *Gigi's* and *Zoglo Summer Matter*, both a little out of town. There is also an outdoor summer **cinema**, south of the square.

The northern rim of Navarino Bay

YIÁLOVA, 6km north out of Pýlos, has tamarisk trees shading its sandy beach, and makes a delightful base for walkers, naturalists or beach-lovers. The *Navarino* **campsite** (ⓣ27230 22761, ⓦwww.navarino-beach.gr; April–Oct) has good facilities including a recommended restaurant, and is popular with windsurfers. A second campsite, *Erodios* (ⓣ27230 28240, ⓦwww.erodios.gr; March–Oct), is on the Golden Beach road and has studios (❸) and watersports facilities. Nearer the central jetty there is a **hotel**, the *Zoe* (ⓣ27230 22025, ⓦwww.hotelzoe.com; ❹), whose owner has an interest in the wildlife that inhabits the local lagoons and can suggest walks; the cheaper *Helonaki* (ⓣ27230 23080, ⓔhelonaki@panafonet.gr; ❷) has a variety of rooms and apartments. Both have good **tavernas** underneath, and great views, though for meals, you can't beat the excellent home cooking at *To Spitiko* or at *Farmakio*, just south of the corner of the pier. There is a small **shop** for picnic supplies between the pier and the main road; northwards along the main road is more, though less well-positioned, accommodation.

Pýlos's northern castle and ancient acropolis, **Kástro Navarínou** (Paleó Kástro), stands on a hill ridge almost touching the island of Sfaktiría, at the end of the bay 5km west of Yiálova. It has substantial walls and identifiable courtyards and cisterns within fortifications, which are a mix of Frankish and Venetian, set upon ancient foundations. The panoramic outlook over one of the best beaches in the Peloponnese – a gorgeous crescent of fine sand curling around the spectacular **Bay of Voïdhokiliá** – is tremendous, but the interior is a jungle of shrubs and other vegetation that makes progress through it difficult. It's a ten- to twelve-kilometre trip from Pýlos, for which you'll need some transport. Go north through Yiálova, turn left at the sign to Voïdhokiliá and Golden Beach (the Pýlos–Hóra bus will bring you this far); at the end of the surfaced road, go left until the dirt road ends below the castle hill. From here, proceed left up to the castle, or head right along the footpath between the lagoon and the hill until you reach the Voïdhokiliá dunes and beach. With your own transport, follow the main road north towards Hóra, and when the road swings right to Korifássi, go left on a side road signed to Romanós and Navarino castle. Continue on the increasingly badly surfaced roads and you will end up at Voïdhokiliá.

The **lagoon** behind the beach is an important bird conservation area, and vehicles are not allowed on the earth road around its eastern rim. Near the end of the Golden Beach asphalt, a signed **nature trail** has been laid out. Turtles still breed at Voïdhokiliá (and at the beaches of Romanoú and Máti, further north), but a tiny population – the only one in mainland Europe – of slow-moving chameleons amongst the dune shrubs is endangered by illegal drivers, camper vans and reptile collectors. A large golf resort, one of three for the Navarino area, is planned for the area immediately behind Romanós beach.

A path from the southern Voïdhokiliá dunes ascends to the **Spílio toú Nestóros** (Nestor's Cave), and then (head right, up steep rocky steps) to the castle. This impressive bat cave with a hole in the roof is fancifully identified as the grotto in which, according to the *Odyssey*, Nestor and Neleus kept their cows, and in which Hermes hid Apollo's cattle. It is not impossible that the cave sparked Homer's imagination, for this area is reckoned by archeologists to have been the Mycenaean-era harbour of King Nestor, and later of the Classical town of Korifasio.

North to Nestor's Palace

Nestor's Palace (also known as the Palace of Áno Englianós, after the hill on which it stands) was discovered in 1939, but left virtually undisturbed until after World War II; thus its excavation – unlike Mycenae, or most of the other major Greek sites – was conducted in accordance with modern archeological techniques. In consequence, its remains are the best preserved of all the Mycenaean royal palaces, though they shelter rather prosaically beneath a giant metal roof. The site guide by excavators Carl Blegen and Marion Rawson is an excellent buy.

The palace is located some 17km – a half-hour drive – from modern Pýlos. Using public transport, take any of the **buses** from Pýlos towards Hóra (3–6 daily); these follow the main road inland past Korifássi to the site and its museum at Hóra (4km to the east).

The palace site

Flanked by deep, fertile valleys, the **palace site** (summer Tues–Fri 8am–7.30pm, Sat & Sun 8.30am–3pm; winter daily 8.30am–3pm; €3) looks out towards Navarino Bay – a location perfectly suiting the wise, measured and peaceful king described in Homer's *Odyssey*. The scene from the epic that is set here is the visit of Telemachus, son of Odysseus, who had journeyed from Ithaca to seek news of his father from King Nestor. As Telemachus arrives at the beach, accompanied by the disguised goddess Pallas Athena, he comes upon Nestor with his sons and court sacrificing to Poseidon. The visitors are welcomed and feasted, "sitting on downy fleeces on the sand", and although the king has no news of Odysseus he promises Telemachus a chariot so he can enquire from Menelaus at Sparta. First, however, the guests are taken back to the palace, where Telemachus is given a bath by Nestor's "youngest grown daughter, beautiful Polycaste", and emerges, anointed with oil, "with the body of an immortal".

By some harmonious twist of fate, a bathtub was unearthed on the site, and the palace ruins as a whole are potent ground for Homeric imaginings. The walls stand a metre high, enabling you to make out a very full plan. Originally, they were half-timbered (like Tudor houses), with upper sections of sun-baked brick held together by vertical and horizontal beams, and brilliant frescoes within. Even in their diminished state they suggest a building of considerable prestige. No less should be expected, for Nestor sent the second largest contingent to Troy – a fleet of "ninety black ships". The remains of the massive complex are in three principal groups: the **main palace** in the middle, on the left an earlier and **smaller palace**, and on the right either **guardhouses** or **workshops**.

The basic design will be familiar if you've been to Mycenae or Tiryns: an internal court, guarded by a sentry box, gives access to the main sections of the principal palace. This contained some 45 rooms and halls. The **megaron** (throne room), with its characteristic open hearth, lies directly ahead of the entrance, through a double porch. The finest of the frescoes was discovered here, depicting a griffin (perhaps the royal emblem) standing guard over the throne; this is now in the museum at Hóra. Arranged around are domestic quarters and **storerooms**, which yielded thousands of pots and cups during excavations; the rooms may have served as a distribution centre for the produce of the palace workshops. Further back, the famous **bathroom**, with its terracotta tub in situ, adjoins a smaller complex of rooms, centred on another, smaller, megaron, identified as the **queen's quarters**. Finally, on the other side of the car park there is a tholos tomb, a smaller version of the famous ones at Mycenae.

Archeologically, the most important find at the site was a group of several hundred tablets inscribed in **Linear B**. These were discovered on the first day of digging, in the two small rooms to the left of the entrance courtyard. They were the first such inscriptions to be discovered on the Greek mainland and proved conclusively a link between the Mycenaean and Minoan civilizations; like those found by Sir Arthur Evans at Knossos on Crete, the language was unmistakeably Greek. The tablets were baked hard in the fire which destroyed the palace at the time of the Dorian invasion around 1200 BC, perhaps as little as one generation after the fall of Troy.

The museum at Hóra

At **Hóra** (Hóra Trifylías), a small town despite the name "village", the **museum** (officially Tues–Sun 8.30am–3pm, but can be erratic; €2) on Marinátou, signed above the main square (with Friday-morning produce market), adds significantly to a visit to the site. If you've no transport, it might be better to take a bus here first, to the central bus station stop, and then walk the 45 minutes to the site after viewing the exhibits. In hot weather, or if pressed for time, you might be able to hitch, or get a taxi.

Pride of place in the display goes to the **palace frescoes**, one of which, bearing out Homer's descriptions, shows a warrior in a boar-tusk helmet. Lesser finds include much pottery, some beautiful gold cups and other objects gathered both from the site and from various Mycenaean tombs in the region.

The coast north of Pýlos

The stretch of **coast** between Pýlos and Pýrgos is defined by its **beaches**, which are on a different scale to those elsewhere in the Peloponnese, or indeed anywhere else in Greece – fine sands, long enough (and undeveloped enough) to satisfy the most jaded Australian or Californian. Their relative anonymity is something of a mystery, though one accounted for in part by poor communications. For those without transport this entails slow and patient progress along the main "coast" road, which for much of the way runs 2 to 5km inland, and a walk from road junction to beach.

Heading north from the Bay of Voïdhokiliá, near the turning inland to Korifássi and Nestor's Palace, you can take a paved road, flanked by orange and olive orchards. This keeps close to the sea for most of the way to Kyparissía, allowing access to isolated beaches and villages.

If you're travelling to Olympia by **train** from this coast, you can save the detour to Pýrgos (not an exhilarating town – see p.265) by getting a connection at Alfiós, a tiny station at the junction of the Olympia line and as bucolic a halt as any on the network (but not to be confused with next stop Alfioúsa station). Alfiós is seven minutes down the line from Pýrgos, and thirteen from Olympia.

Marathópoli and Kyparissía

If you are looking for little more than accommodation and a village café, then **MARATHÓPOLI**, the harbour of Gargaliáni, holds most promise. It has a long beach, rockier than most along this coast, and faces the islet of Próti, shaped like a long-tailed turtle and once a pirate refuge. The better hotel is the popular beachfront *Artina* (T 27230 61400, W www.artina.gr; 4) with pool; book ahead. There are some **rooms** for rent; a **campsite**,

Proti (Ⓣ27230 61211, Ⓕ27230 29806; May–Oct), with a swimming pool; and two or three summer **tavernas** by the sea. A small taxi boat makes the short crossing to the islet of **Próti**, with its sandy beach and monastery, but can be expensive – ask at the supermarket.

KYPARISSÍA is a small, congenial agricultural and market town, positioned in the shadow of the eponymous peak, part of the spectacular Egáleo mountain ridge. On a lower outcrop of the range is a Byzantine-Frankish **castle** (free), around which spreads the **old town**. Its ochre-hued mansions suffered heavy damage during the civil war, but there are some **tavernas** here.

Below the hill, the modern town is a functional but pleasant place. A few tourist boutiques and a nightclub or two have sprung up recently, and it is possibly preferable to a night in Kalamáta if you're on your way to Olympia by bus or train (Kyparissía is the junction of the Kalamáta and Pýrgos lines). Within walking distance of town are long, near-deserted sands – turtle breeding-grounds – and rocky cliff paths.

Practicalities

The centre of the modern town, just south of the adjacent **bus** (Ⓣ27610 22260) and **train stations** (Ⓣ27610 22283), is Platía Kalantzákou, where you'll find several **banks**, the **post office** and a remarkable number of cafés. Accommodation consists of a half-dozen **hotels**, divided between the town and the beach. The cheapest place to stay in town is the *Trifolia*, 25-Martíou 40 (Ⓣ27610 22066; ❷), a down-to-earth and welcoming pension, just east of the square and round the corner from the bus station; the comfortable and friendly *Ionion* (Ⓣ27610 22511, Ⓕ27610 22512; ❸), faces the train station; by the beach is the well-equipped **campsite**, *Kyparissia* (Ⓣ27610 23491, Ⓕ27610 24519; April–Oct). Beyond this beach, over a small rocky headland there's a better beach used by naturists, though it has strong currents at times. At Kaló Neró beach, 7km north, are the studios of the *Irida Resort* (Ⓣ27610 71386, Ⓦwww.iridaresort.gr; ❺). There are a handful of no-nonsense **restaurants** and pizzerias in the streets around Platía Kalantzákou; one of the best is *Stars*, at the southwest corner of the main square. For atmosphere it's better to eat down at the beach, where the taverna *Ta Porakia*, towards the campsite, is a fine choice, or up at the old town, where the liveliest place to dine is the *psistariá Arcadia*.

Ilía and Ahaïa: the northwest

Dominated economically by the sprawling city of **Pátra**, the large province of **Ahaïa** combines high mountains and a narrow, densely populated coastal strip. From **Dhiakoftó** in the north, one of Greece's most remarkable railway lines follows the dramatic **Vouraikós Gorge**, up to Kalávryta. To the southwest of Ahaïa, the flat coastal plains of **Ilía** support a series of undistinguished market towns and are bordered on the west by long, narrow, often underused beaches. The **Olympia** archeological site is the jewel of the fertile Alfíos valley and this area's main tourist attraction.

Olympia (Olymbía)

The historic associations and resonance of **OLYMPIA**, which for over a millennium hosted the most important **Panhellenic games**, are rivalled only by Delphi or Mycenae. It is one of the largest ancient sites in Greece, spread beside the twin rivers of Alfiós (Alpheus) – the largest in the Peloponnese – and Kládhios, and overlooked by the Hill of Krónos. The site itself is picturesque, but the sheer quantity of ruined structures can give a confusing impression of their ancient grandeur and function; despite the crowds, tour buses, souvenir shops and other trappings of mass tourism, it deserves a lengthy visit.

The modern village of Olymbía acts as a service centre for the site, and has little in the way of other distractions, save for three somewhat dutiful minor museums. The **Museum of the Modern Olympic Games** (Mon–Sat 8am–3.30pm, Sun 9am–4.30pm; €2), on the street above the *Hotel Phedias*, has commemorative postage stamps and the odd memento from the modern games, including the box that conveyed the heart of Pierre de Coubertin (reviver of the modern games) from Paris to its burial at Olympia. The **Museum of the History of the Olympic Games in Antiquity** and the **Museum of the History of Excavations in Olympia** (both: summer daily 8am–7.30pm, winter Tues–Sat 8.30am–3pm; free) lie above the coach park at the eastern end of the village, en route to the main site.

The site

From its beginnings the **site** (May–Oct daily 8am–7pm; Nov–April Mon–Fri 8am–5pm, Sat & Sun 8.30am–3pm; €6, or €9 for combined site and archeological museum) was a sanctuary, with a permanent population limited to the temple priests. At first the games took place within the sacred precinct, the walled, rectangular **Altis**, but as events became more sophisticated a new **stadium** was built to adjoin it. The whole sanctuary was, throughout its history, a treasure trove of public and religious statuary. Victors were allowed to erect a statue in the Altis (in their likeness if they won three events) and numerous city-states installed treasuries. Pausanias, writing in the second century AD, after the Romans had already looted the sanctuary several times, fills almost a whole volume of his *Guide to Greece* with descriptions.

The entrance to the site leads along the west side of the Altis wall, past a group of public and official buildings. On the left, beyond some Roman baths, is the **Prytaneion**, the administrators' residence, where athletes stayed and feasted at official expense. On the right are the ruins of a **gymnasium** and a **palaestra** (wrestling school), used by the competitors during their obligatory month of pre-games training.

Beyond these stood the Priests' House, the **Theokoleion**, a substantial colonnaded building in whose southeast corner is a structure adapted as a Byzantine church. This was originally the **studio of Fidias**, the fifth-century BC sculptor responsible for the great chryselephantine (gold and ivory) cult statue in Olympia's Temple of Zeus. It was identified by following a description by Pausanias, and through the discovery of tools, moulds for the statue and a cup engraved with the sculptor's name. The studio's dimensions and orientation are exactly those of the *cella* in which the statue was to be placed, in order that the final effect and lighting matched the sculptor's intentions.

To the south of the studio lie further administrative buildings, including the **Leonidaion**, a large and doubtless luxurious hostel endowed for the most

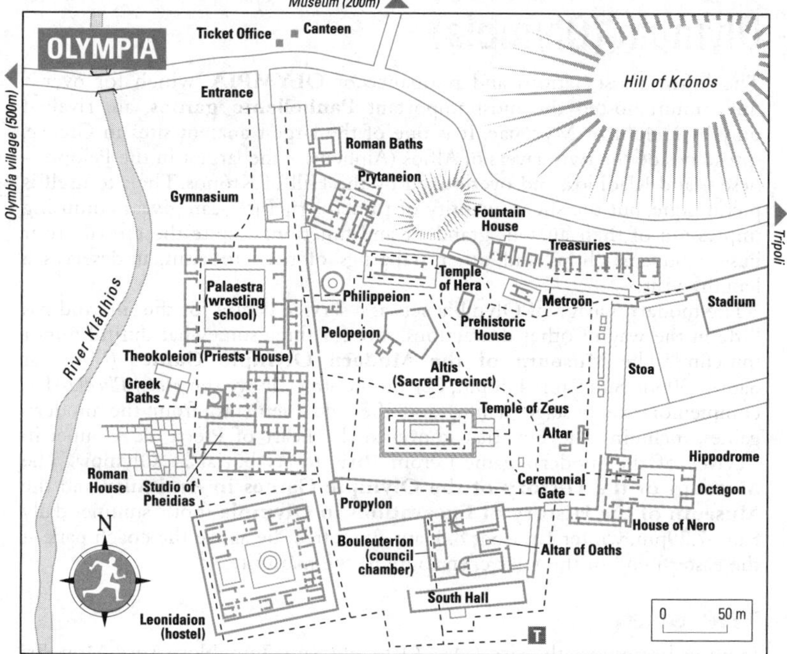

important of the festival guests. It was the first building visitors would reach along the original approach road to the site.

The Altis

In the earlier centuries of the games, admission to the **Altis** was limited to freeborn Greeks – whether spectators or competitors. Throughout its history it was a male-only preserve, save for the sanctuary's priestess. A woman from Rhodes disguised herself as her son's trainer to gain admission, but revealed her identity in joy at his victory. Though she was spared the legislated death penalty, all subsequent trainers had to appear naked.

The main focus of the precinct is provided by the great Doric **Temple of Zeus**. Built between 470 and 456 BC, it was as large as the almost contemporary Parthenon, a fact quietly substantiated by the vast column drums littering the ground. The temple's decoration, too, rivalled the finest in Athens; partially recovered, its sculptures of Pelops in a chariot race, of Lapiths and Centaurs, and the Labours of Hercules, are now in the museum. In the *cella* was exhibited the (lost) cult statue of Zeus by Fidias, one of the seven wonders of the ancient world. Here, too, the Olympian flame was kept alight, from the time of the games until the following spring – a tradition continued at an altar for the modern games.

The smaller **Temple of Hera**, behind, was the first built in the Altis; prior to its completion in the seventh century BC, the sanctuary had only open-air altars, dedicated to Zeus and a variety of other cult gods. The temple, rebuilt in the Doric style in the sixth century BC, is the most complete building on the site, with some thirty of its columns surviving in part, along with a section of the inner wall. The levels above this wall were composed only of sun-baked brick, and the lightness of this building material must have helped to preserve the sculptures – most notably the *Hermes of Praxiteles* – found amid the earthquake ruins.

Between the temples of Hera and Zeus is a grove described by Pausanias, and identified as the **Pelopeion**. In addition to a cult altar to the Olympian hero, this enclosed a small mound formed by sacrificial ashes, among which excavations unearthed many of the terracotta finds in the museum. The sanctuary's principal altar, dedicated to Zeus, probably stood just to the east.

West of the Temple of Hera, and bordering the wall of the Altis, are remains of the circular **Philippeion**, the first monument in the sanctuary to be built to secular glory. It was begun by Philip II after the Battle of Chaironea gave him control over the Greek mainland, and may have been completed by his son, Alexander the Great. To the east of the Hera temple is a small, second-century-AD **fountain house**, the gift of the ubiquitous Herodes Atticus. Beyond, lining a terrace at the base of the Hill of Krónos, are the **state treasuries**. All except two of these were constructed by cities outside of Greece proper, as they functioned principally as storage chambers for sacrificial items and sporting equipment used in the games. They are built in the form of temples, as at Delphi; the oldest and grandest, at the east end, belonged to Gela in Sicily. In front of the treasuries are the foundations of the **Metroön**, a fourth-century BC Doric temple dedicated to the mother of the gods.

The ancient ceremonial entrance to the Altis was on the south side, below a long **stoa** taking up almost the entire east side of the precinct. At the corner was a house built by the Roman emperor Nero for his stay during the games. He also had the entrance remodelled as a triumphal arch, fit for his anticipated victories. Through the arch, just outside the precinct, stood the **Bouleuterion** or council chamber, where before a great statue of Zeus the competitors took their oaths to observe the Olympian rules. As they approached the stadium, the gravity of this would be impressed upon them: lining the way were bronze statues paid for with the fines exacted for foul play, bearing the name of the disgraced athlete, his father and city.

The stadium

In the final analysis, it is neither foundations nor columns that make sense of Olympia, but the two-hundred-metre track of the **stadium** itself, entered by way of a long arched tunnel. The starting and finishing lines are still there, with the judges' thrones in the middle and seating ridges banked to either side. Originally unstructured, the stadium developed with the games' popularity, forming a model for others throughout the Greek and Roman world. The tiers here eventually accommodated up to 20,000 spectators, with a smaller number on the southern slope overlooking the **hippodrome** where the chariot races were held. Even so, the seats were reserved for the wealthier strata of society. The ordinary populace – along with slaves and all women spectators – watched the events from the Hill of Krónos to the north, then a natural, treeless grandstand. The stadium was unearthed only in World War II, during a second phase of German excavations between 1941 and 1944, allegedly on the direct orders of Hitler.

The Archaeological Museum

Olympia's site **museum** (May–Oct Mon noon–7.30pm, Tues–Sun 8am–7.30pm; Nov–April Mon 10.30am–5pm, Tues–Sun 8.30am–5pm; €6) lies a couple of hundred metres north of the sanctuary. It contains some of

The Olympic games: some history

The origins of the games at Olympia are rooted in **legends** – often relating to the god Pelops, revered in the region before his eclipse by Zeus, or to Hercules (Herakles), one of the earliest victors. Historically, the contests probably began around the eleventh century BC, growing over the next two centuries from a local festival to the quadrennial celebration attended by states from throughout the Greek world.

The impetus for this change seems to have come from the Oracle of Delphi, which, with Iphitos, the local ruler of Elis, and the Spartan ruler Lykurgos, helped codify the Olympic rules in the ninth century BC. Among their most significant introductions was a sacred truce, the **Ekeheiria**, announced by heralds prior to the celebrations and enforced for their duration. It was virtually unbroken throughout the games' history (Sparta, ironically, was fined at one point) and as host of the games, Elis, a comparatively weak state, was able to keep itself away from political disputes, meanwhile growing rich on the associated trade and kudos.

From the beginning, the main Olympic **events** were athletic. The earliest was a race over the course of the stadium – roughly 200m. Later came the introduction of two-lap (400m) and 24-lap (5000m) races, along with the most revered of the Olympiad events, the pentathlon. This encompassed running, jumping, discus and javelin events, the competitors gradually reduced to a final pair for a wrestling-and-boxing combat. It was, like much of these early Olympiads, a fairly brutal contest. More brutal still was the *pancratium*, introduced in 680 BC and one of the most prestigious events. *Pancratium* contestants fought each other, naked and unarmed, using any means except biting or gouging each other's eyes; the olive wreath had on one occasion to be awarded posthumously, the victor having expired at the moment of his opponent's submission. Similarly, the chariot races, introduced in the same year, were extreme tests of strength and control, only one team in twenty completing the seven-kilometre course without mishap.

The great gathering of people and nations at the festival extended the games' importance and purpose well beyond the winning of olive wreaths; assembled under the temporary truce, nobles and ambassadors negotiated treaties, while merchants

the finest Classical and Roman sculptures in the country, all superbly displayed.

The most famous of the individual sculptures are the **head of Hera** and the **Hermes of Praxiteles**, both dating from the fourth century BC and discovered in the Temple of Hera. The Hermes is one of the best preserved of all Classical sculptures, and remarkable in the easy informality of its pose; it retains traces of its original paint. On a grander scale is the **Nike of Paionios**, which was originally 10m high. Though no longer complete (it's well displayed in a special area), it hints at how the sanctuary must once have appeared, crowded with statuary.

The best of the smaller objects include several fine bronze items, among them a **Persian helmet**, captured by the Athenians at the Battle of Marathon, and displayed alongside the **helmet of Miltiades**, the victorious Athenian general; both were found with votive objects dedicated in the stadium. There is also a superb terracotta group of **Zeus abducting Ganymede** and a group of finds from the workshop of **Fidias**, including the cup with his name inscribed.

In the main hall of the museum is the centrepiece of the Olympia finds: statuary and sculpture reassembled from the **Temple of Zeus**. This includes three groups, all of which were once painted. From the *cella* is a frieze of the **Twelve Labours of Hercules**, delicately moulded and for the most part chased contacts and foreign markets. Sculptors and poets, too, would seek commissions for their work. Herodotus read aloud the first books of his history at an Olympian festival to an audience that included Thucydides – who was to date events in his own work by reference to the winners of the *pancratium*.

In the early Olympiads, the **rules** of competition were strict. Only free-born male Greeks could take part, and the rewards of victory were entirely honorary: a palm, given to the victor immediately after the contest, and an olive branch, presented in a ceremony closing the games. As the games developed, however, the rules were loosened to allow participation by athletes from all parts of the Greek and Roman world, and nationalism and professionalism gradually crept in. By the fourth century BC, when the games were at their peak, the athletes were virtually all professionals, heavily sponsored by their home states and, if they won at Olympia, commanding huge appearance money at games elsewhere. Bribery became an all too common feature, despite solemn religious oaths sworn in front of the sanctuary priests prior to the contests.

Under the Romans, predictably, commercialization accelerated. Palms and olive branches were replaced by rich monetary prizes, and a sequence of new events was introduced. The nadir was reached in 67 AD when Emperor Nero advanced the games by two years so that he could compete in (and win) special singing and lyre-playing events – in addition to the chariot race in which he was tactfully declared victor despite falling twice and failing to finish.

Notwithstanding all this abuse, the Olympian tradition was popular enough to be maintained for another three centuries, and the games' eventual **closure** happened as a result of religious dogma rather than lack of support. In 393 AD Emperor Theodosius, recently converted to Christianity, suspended the games as part of a general crackdown on public pagan festivities. This suspension proved final, for Theodosius's successor ordered the destruction of the temples, a process completed by barbarian invasion, earthquakes and, lastly, by the Alfiós River changing its course to cover the sanctuary site. There it remained, covered by 7m of silt and sand, until the first excavation by German archeologists in the 1870s.

identifiably preserved. The other groups are from the east and west pediments. The east, reflecting Olympian pursuits, depicts Zeus presiding over a **chariot race** between Pelops and Oinamaos. The story has several versions. King Oinamaos, warned that he would be killed by his son-in-law, challenged each of his daughter Hippomadeia's suitors to a chariot race. After allowing them a start he would catch up and kill them from behind. The king (depicted on the left of the frieze) was eventually defeated by Pelops (on the right with Hippomadeia), after – depending on the version – assistance from Zeus (depicted at the centre), magic steeds from Poseidon or, most un-Olympian, bribing Oinamaos's charioteer to tamper with the wheels.

The west pediment, less controversially mythological, illustrates the **Battle of the Lapiths and Centaurs** at the wedding of the Lapith king, Peirithous. This time, Apollo presides over the scene while Theseus helps the Lapiths defeat the drunken centaurs, depicted attacking the women and boy guests. Many of the metope fragments are today in the Louvre in Paris, and some of what you see here are plaster-cast copies.

The last rooms of the museum contain a collection of objects relating to the games – including *halteres* (jumping weights), discuses, weightlifters' stones and other sporting bits and pieces. Also displayed are a number of **funerary inscriptions**, including that of a boxer, Camelos of Alexandria, who died in the stadium after praying to Zeus for victory or death.

Practicalities: Olymbía

Modern **OLYMBÍA** is a village that has grown up simply to serve the excavations and tourist trade. It's essentially one long main avenue, **Praxitéles Kondhýli**, lined with gold shops, and with a few short side streets. Nevertheless, Olymbía is quite a pleasant place to stay, and is probably preferable to Pýrgos, with the prospect of good countryside walks along the Alfiós River and around the Hill of Krónos.

Most people arrive at Olymbía **via Pýrgos**, which is on the main Peloponnese rail line and has frequent bus connections with Pátra and four daily with Kyparissía. The refurbished **train** link from Pýrgos to Olymbía has five daily services. **Buses** leave hourly between Pýrgos and Olymbía, from 5.15am to 9.45pm, some signed to "Vasiláki" beyond Olymbía. The only other direct buses to Olymbía are **from Trípoli**, via Langádhia. These run twice daily in either direction.

There is a **tourist office** (Mon–Sat: May–Oct 9am–3pm; Nov–April 11am–5pm; ⓣ26240 23100), on the right of Praxitéles Kondhýli, as you come into town from Pýrgos. Olymbía has three **banks** on the main avenue, and a **post office** just uphill. **English-language books** are to be found in a couple of shops near the site end of town.

Accommodation

Accommodation is fairly easy to come by, with a swift turnaround of clientele and a range of hotels and private rooms whose prices are kept modest by competition. As elsewhere, rates can drop substantially out of season (never precisely defined, but essentially June–Sept), though many of the smaller and cheaper places close; it's best to check in advance. The centre of town can be very noisy at night.

There are three **campsites**, closest of which is *Diana* (ⓣ26240 22314, ⓕ26240 22425; March–Nov), 1km from the site, with a pool and good facilities.

Europa Dhroúva 1 ⓣ26240 22650, ⓦwww.hoteleuropa.gr. A popular, well-run and comfortable hotel, part of the *Best Western* chain, situated near the top of the hill to the southwest. B&B ❻

Hercules Tsoúreka 2 ⓣ26240 22696 ⓦwww.hotelhercules.gr. A congenial small hotel by the church and school on a side street off Praxitéles Kondhýli. Wi-Fi available. B&B ❸

Kronio Tsoúreka 1 ⓣ26240 22188, ⓦwww.hotelkronio.gr. A friendly, comfortable hotel, with Wi-Fi access in rooms. ❸

Pelops Varélas 2 ⓣ26240 22543, ⓦwww.hotelpelops.gr. On a square by the church and school; a hotel run by a Greek-Australian couple and recently extensively refurbished. March–Oct. B&B ❸

Youth Hostel Kondhýli 18 ⓣ26240 22580, ⓕ26240 23125. Average facilities, but warm water in the showers; good value. Dorms €9

Eating and drinking

The main avenue is lined with **tavernas**, which offer standard tourist meals at notably inflated high-season prices – some cafés charging at Athenian levels – but there is a growing number of fast-food kerbside cafés which are often far better value. The *Aegean*, just off the main street, has good food at average prices. The *Klimataria Taverna* in **Kokkinés** village, a few kilometres northeast, is also recommended.

The northwest coast to Pátra

Despite the proximity of Olympia and Pátra, the northwest corner of the Peloponnese is not much explored by foreign visitors. Admittedly, it's not the most glamorous of coasts, although there are some very attractive beaches including the glorious one at **Kalogriá**, but a visit around **Loutrá Kyllínis** or **Arkoúdhi** can provide a pleasant enough diversion. From Kyllíni there are regular crossings to Zákynthos, and in summer to Kefaloniá.

Pýrgos

PÝRGOS has a grim recent history. When the Germans withdrew at the end of World War II, it remained under the control of Greek Nazi collaborators. These negotiated surrender with the Resistance, who were met by gunfire as they entered the town. Full-scale battle erupted and for five days the town burned. Today, it's a large, friendly and modern town with a pleasantly pedestrianized centre. Serious diversions are nonexistent for the tourist, except for the avid clothes shopper (clothes shops here are abundant, well stocked and well priced), although there are plans to convert the Neoclassical Central Market building into an archeological museum. For an overnight **stay**, a convenient hotel is the *Pantheon*, Themistokléous 7 (ⓣ26210 29748, ⓔpantheon@mailbox.gr; ④).

The main escape routes are by **train** or **bus** to Pátra, Olympia or Kyparissía – though services to the last are not well timed for onward connections; the new bus station is to the west of town, and the train station fifteen minutes away at the bottom on Ypsilándou, so allow time for interchange. Drivers should be aware that the main road from Pýrgos to Pátra, though level and comparatively straight, is a scary mix of very fast and very slow traffic, bad driving and numerous stray dogs.

The cape north of Pýrgos

North from Pýrgos, road and rail meander through a series of uneventful market towns, but there are two forks west to a sandy cape and the coast. The first is at Gastoúni and heads for the spa of **Loutrá Kyllínis** (1–3 daily buses from Pýrgos and Pátra) and beaches to the south; the second is at Kavásilas, where a side road heads down to **Kyllíni** port proper (3–4 daily buses from Pýrgos and Pátra). Take care not to confuse the two.

LOUTRÁ KYLLÍNIS has a long beach, and a crop of upmarket **hotels** catering for the resort's spa trade. It's better to continue south for places to stay. Only a few kilometres south, near the point where this most westerly coast of the Peloponnese bends back east into the long bay that curves towards Katákolo, is **ARKOÚDHI**, a compact village resort that has something of an island feel to it, and a fine sandy bay enclosed by a rocky promontory. As well as a **campsite**, there is a surprising number of **hotels** and **rooms**. On the edge of the village is the posh but good-value hotel *Arkoudi* (ⓣ26230 96480; April–Oct; B&B ⑤), which has a pool. In the village centre, apartments with kitchen and fridge are available at *Soulis* (ⓣ26230 96379; ④). For meals try the central *Spyros psistariá*, or the *Akrogiali*, which offers a sea view and a wide selection of dishes.

At **PARALÍA GLÝFA**, 3.5km from Arkoúdhi, there are two **campsites** – the *Anginara Beach* (ⓣ26230 96211, ⓕ26230 96157) and the *Ionian Beach* (ⓣ26230 51300, ⓦwww.ionianbeach.gr), both bordered by trees and beaches of fine shingle and sand and best approached via Lygiá on the road from Gastoúni.

Cheerless little **KYLLÍNI** (accessible by taxi from Loutrá Kyllínis) has little more to offer than its **ferry connections** (ⓦwww.ionianferries.gr). It is the principal port for **Zákynthos** (4–7 daily; cars €31.50, passengers €6.90; Maniatis ⓣ26230 92100) and **Kefaloniá** (to Argostóli: summer 1 daily; to

Póros: summer 5–6 daily, winter 1–2 daily; cars €39.60, passengers €8.40; ⓣ26230 92013). Buses coming off the ferry, to Pátra and Athens, are often full and will not take extra passengers. If you're stuck overnight in Kyllíni, **places to stay** are limited: the choice is between the *Hotel Ionian* (ⓣ26230 92318; ❹) on the main street where some rooms have private facilities, private rooms (also on the main street) – or sleeping on the beach. The *Taverna Anna*, beyond the harbour, serves a wide range of traditional dishes and is particularly popular with locals at Sunday lunchtimes.

Using Loutrá Kyllínis, Arkoúdhi or Kyllíni as a base, it's worth taking time to hitch or walk to the village of **KÁSTRO**, at the centre of the cape. Looming above the village and visible from miles around is the Frankish **castle of Khlemoútsi** (Castel Tornese; summer daily 8am–7pm; winter Tues–Sun 8.30am–3pm; €3), a vast hexagonal structure built in 1220 by Geoffrey de Villehardouin. Its function was principally to control the province of Ahaïa, though it served also as a strategic fortress on the Adriatic. Haze permitting, there are sweeping views across the straits to Zákynthos, and even to Kefaloniá and Itháki, from the well-preserved and restored ramparts. Kástro has the welcoming *Katerina Lepidas* (aka *Chryssi Avgi*) rooms with kitchen facilities, at Loutrópoleos 9 (ⓣ26230 95224; May–Oct; ❹). You can **dine** well at the nearby *Apollon* taverna.

Kalogriá

Midway between Kyllíni and Pátra, **KALOGRIÁ** (locally Kalógria) is a seven-kilometre strand of beach, partly naturist, bordered by a swathe of **umbrella pine forests**. A fair proportion of Pátra, including the gay community, descends here at the weekend as it's the nearest good **beach** to the city. The whole area is protected as part of the Strofyliá Forest-Kotýkhi Wetland National Park, which covers beach dunes, the forest, and lagoons with their rare birdlife, and permanent development remains low-key. There is an enthusiastic information and environmental monitoring centre (Mon–Fri, 8am–2pm; ⓣ26930 31651, ⓔciks@otenet.gr) for the park at nearby Láppa, in a building opposite the train station. Kalogriá is not actually a village – the nearest bona fide town is Metóhi – but rather a small cluster of tavernas and stores. At the far north end of the beach there's the *Kalogria Beach* (ⓣ26930 31276, ⓔkalogria@otenet.gr; ❺), a large, French-oriented **hotel complex** with many sports facilities. For a quieter stay there's the *Amalia Hotel* studios (ⓣ26930 31100, ⓦwww.amaliahotel.gr; breakfast €5; ❸), hidden in a large garden behind their own good taverna. Behind the hotels, the 200-metre outcrop Mávra Voúna has a number of organized climbing routes (ⓦwww.geocities.com/patrasclimbing).

Pátra

PÁTRA (Patras) is the largest city in the Peloponnese and, after Pireás, the major port of Greece; from here you can go to Italy as well as to certain Ionian islands. The city is also a hub of the Greek-mainland transport network, with connections throughout the Peloponnese and, via the ferry at Río, across the straits to Delphi or western Greece.

Unless you arrive late in the day from Italy, you shouldn't need to spend more than a few hours in the city. A conurbation of close to a quarter of a million souls, it's not the ideal holiday retreat: there are no beaches and no major sights. Traffic noise goes on well into the night and starts earlier than you'd want to get up. However, it is an opportunity to experience a vibrant and reasonably civilized city life, unrelated to tourism. There is a **summer festival** which sponsors events from late June to mid-September, including Classical plays, the occasional rock concert in the Roman **odeion**, and art and photographic exhibitions that bring a bit of life to the warehouses by the harbour (details from the tourist office or the Apóllon Theatre on Platía Yeoryíou). The three-week **carnival** (Ⓦwww.carnivalpatras.gr), one of Greece's largest, ends on the Sunday before Lent Monday (Katharí Dheftéra) with a grand parade through the city centre.

Arrival and information

If you are driving in or through Pátra, you will find the traffic and one-way system no less frustrating than in Athens; a map showing the direction of traffic, if not vital, will at least save time and probably maintain sanity. If going beyond Pátra, then there is a fast bypass to the east. The **train station** is on Óthonos & Amalías. Trains travel south (changes at Alfiós or Pýrgos for Olympia) to Kaló Neró (for Kyparissía) then on to Kalamáta; north and east to Dhiakoftó, Kórinthos (change for Árgos, Náfplio or Trípoli), Athens and Pireás.

Buses for the Peloponnese, Athens, Ioánnina, Thessaloníki and Vólos depart from the main bus station (Ⓣ26106 23 886), a short distance northeast of the train station. Buses for Zákynthos go from Óthonos & Amalías 47 (Ⓣ2610 220 993), for Lamía, Tríkala, Kefaloniá and Crete from Óthonos & Amalías 58 (Ⓣ2610 274 938), and for Mesolóngi, Agrínio, Náfpaktos and Delphi from Nórman 5 (Ⓣ2610 421 205). Local buses go from Óthonos & Amalías north of the main bus station; tickets are available from kiosks, and are cheaper than when bought from the driver. For **tourist information**, the city has opened the helpful Info Center Patras in an old raisin-processing factory at Óthonos & Amalías 6 (daily 8am–10pm; Ⓣ2610 461 740, Ⓦwww.infocenterpatras.gr), with a good photographic gallery of the province's attractions; they offer free Internet (30min) and free bike loan (3hr; passport/ID necessary). They also have a kiosk on Platía Trión Symáhon (daily 9am–1pm & 5–8pm), with Wi-Fi access. The **tourist police** (daily 7am–11pm; Ⓣ2610 452 512) are at the western end of Nórman near the new Italy ferry terminal, where the **EOT** office is also located (Mon–Fri 7am–9pm; Ⓣ2610 430 915).

Accommodation

Most of Pátra's **hotels** are on Ayíou Andhréou, one block back from Óthonos & Amalías, or on Ayíou Nikoláou, which runs back from the sea, near the train station and Platía Trión Symáhon. Don't expect too much in the way of standards, value for money or quiet nights; most of the places cater for a very passing trade and don't make great efforts. Many of the older hotels nearer the waterfront have closed, or indeed collapsed. Of those still standing, choices include the following:

Adonis Kapsáli 9, cnr Záïmi Ⓣ2610 224 213, Ⓔhoteladonis@pat.forthnet.gr. Well furnished and maintained; good value. ❹

Atlanta Záïmi 10 Ⓣ2610 220 098, Ⓔatlanta@pat.forthnet.gr. Central hotel, but still good value; out of season you should get a competitive price. ❻

El Greco Ayíou Andhréou 145 Ⓣ2610 272 931, Ⓕ2610 272 932. A good-value hotel and top of its class with refurbished rooms. ❻

Galaxy Ayíou Nikoláou 9 Ⓣ2610 275 981, Ⓕ2610 278 815. A well-placed hotel, if a touch pretentious in decor; serves a good breakfast. B&B ❹

Méditerranée Ayíou Nikoláou 18 Ⓣ2610 279 602, Ⓦwww.mediterranne.com. Modern, adequate hotel, with helpful staff. Both the *Galaxy* and the *Méditerranée* are on a pedestrian street packed with popular bars and cafés. B&B ❼

Youth Hostel Iróön Polytekhníou 62 Ⓣ2610 427 278. Set in a pleasant tree-filled garden opposite the marina, but a 1.5km walk from the centre. Dorms €9.

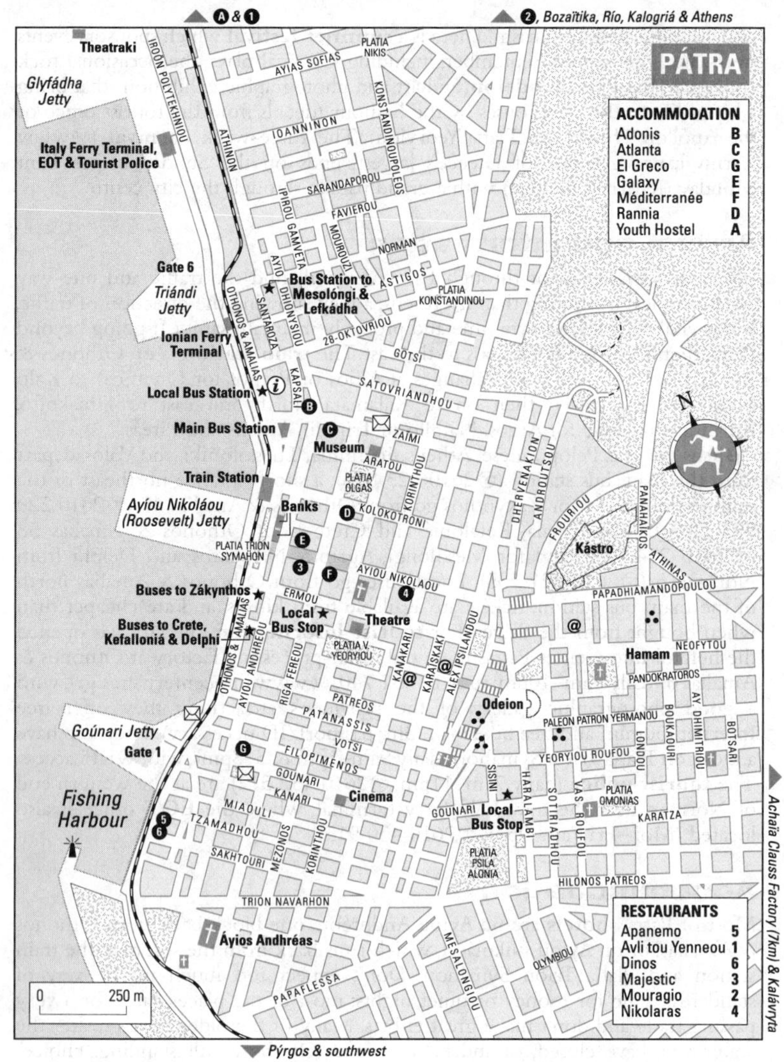

The City

For relaxation, the best places to make for are the café-filled squares **Vassilísis Ólgas** and **Psilá Alónia**, or Vassiléos Yeoryíou with the Neoclassical, Schiller-designed **Apollon Theatre** (Mon–Fri 8am–1.30pm). Alternatively, head up to the **Kástro** (Mon–Fri 8am–7pm, Sat & Sun 8am–5pm; free), a mainly Frankish-Byzantine citadel fifteen minutes' walk up from the water; this partly restored fortress is not particularly exciting, but it is away from the city bustle, surrounded by a small park and with woodland beyond. Nearby, at Boukaoúri 29, is the **hamam** (Ⓣ2610 274 267), still functioning after six hundred years, and the Roman **odeion** (Tues–Sun 8.30am–3pm; free) on Sotiriádhou. Like many a Greek metropolis in summer, Pátra is perhaps at its best after dark, when the heat is less oppressive, the concrete structures less overpowering, and the city life and lights rather brighter; a stroll down to the huge jetty at the foot of Ayíou Nikoláou can bring you to cool sea breezes – and takeaway refreshments at the port kiosk just over the railway lines. Join the evening *vólta* here, or watch the sunset and departing ferries. The pedestrianized bottom end of Ayíou Nikoláou is a very lively area at night, with busy cafés spread across the street. To the north, just beyond the Glyfádha jetty, is the Theatráki ("little theatre"; contact the Info Center for details) and marina cafés.

In the centre, on the corner of Mézonos and Arátou, a small **archeological museum** (Tues–Sun 8.30am–3pm; free) contains a number of exquisite objects from the province of Ahaïa dating from the Mycenaean to the Roman eras. Opened in 1979, the huge neo-Byzantine **church of Áyios Andhréas** (daily 8–11am, 4.30–7pm) lies at the southwest end of the waterfront on a spot where St Andrew, whose relics the church houses, is said to have been martyred in 69 AD. It is a massive confection of yellow-and-cream walls, blue-tiled domes and an excess of marble pillars and arches. The nearby seafront space has been converted into a pleasant grassed area.

Swimming near Pátra isn't advisable – the sea is polluted for some kilometres to the southwest. Locals go to the **beaches** around Río (7km northeast; bus #6) or to Kalogriá (46km southwest).

The Achaïa Clauss winery

The **Achaïa Clauss** winery (☎2610 368 100; daily tours 11am–7pm), founded in 1854, is at Petrotó, 8km southeast of Pátra; those with an interest in modern wine-making should take the #7 bus (half-hourly; stops are on Ermoú and Gounári; €0.70). Tours show you the wine-making process, and feature some treasured, century-old barrels of Mavrodhafni – a dark dessert wine named after the woman Clauss wanted to marry. You're given a glass of white wine to sample on reaching the winery's rather Teutonic bar, an echo of its founder's nationality. Along the walls are signed letters from celebrity recipients of Mavrodhafni. A shop sells all the winery's products.

Eating and drinking

Pátra's **restaurants** are sometimes uninspiring, with countless fast-food places – many of which offer discounts to ISIC card-holders – around Platía Trión Symáhon, and along Ayíou Andhréou and Ayíou Nikoláou. But even here there are some reliable restaurants with character, and some mouth-watering patisserie-bakeries. For fish, the best places are a couple of tavernas down by the fishing harbour.

If you're stuck for the night and feel the urge to escape to a quieter stretch of sea, hop on any #5 blue bus labelled "Tsoukaleíka" or "Vrahnéïka" and alight at either **Monodhéndhri** or **Vrahnéïka** (€0.90) 10km southwest of the city. There is now a practically unbroken chain of tavernas stretching 2km between these resorts. They vary in price, range and quality, but all share the seaside and sunset view. Choices in Pátra include the following:

Apanemo Óthonos & Amalías 107. Seafood taverna opposite the fishing harbour, with good fresh fish and noted for its *galaktoboúreko* (custard pudding).

Avli tou Yenneou (aka *Nirika*) Paraskhoú ☎2610 429 521. Hidden behind waterfront apartments in Terpsithéa, not far north of the youth hostel. Recommended for seafood.

Dinos Óthonos & Amalías 102. Long-established taverna, providing tasty seafood and salads.

Majestic Ayíou Nikoláou 2–4. Old-style restaurant where you can choose from the day's tasty hot dishes; can be expensive.

Mouragio Kastellókambos, Boznitika; 6km north of Pátra, towards the university; bus #6. Specialities include artichoke soufflé and seafood pasta served in a conch shell; prices are mid-range.

Nikolaras Ayíou Nikoláou 50. Another old-style restaurant serving good, traditional food on a self-serve basis.

Listings

Airlines Olympic, Arátou 8 ⓣ2610 222 901.
Banks and money exchange National Bank of Greece, Platía Trión Symáhon (normal banking hours plus 6–8pm); several banks in the area have ATMs. Kapa foreign exchange bureau, Ayíou Andhréou 97.
Books and newspapers Book's Corner, Ayíou Nikoláou 32, stocks useful maps and English-language newspapers; the latter are also available from kiosks on the waterfront; Lexis, Mézonos 38 and Patréos 90, stocks maps and a selection of books in English; the Ermis bookshop at Zäími stocks Road's map of Ahaïa.
Car rental Alamo/National, Ayíou Andhréou 1 ⓣ2610 273 667, ⓕ2610 277 864; AutoUnion/Thrifty, Ayíou Dhionysíou 2 ⓣ2610 623 200, ⓕ2610 622 201; Avis, 28-Oktovríou 16 ⓣ2610 275 547; Delta, Óthonos & Amalías 44 ⓣ2610 272 764; Eurodollar, Albatros Travel, Óthonos & Amalías 48 ⓣ2610 220 993; Hertz, 28-Oktovríou 2 ⓣ2610 220 990; InterRent-EuropCar, Ayíou Andhréou 6 ⓣ2610 621 360; Sixt, Ayíou Andhréou 10 ⓣ2610 275 677.
Consulate Britain, Vótsi 2 ⓣ2610 277 079, ⓕ2610 225 334.
Internet Netrino, Karaïskaki 133; others in nearby Yerokostopoúlou. Most are very well priced.
Post office Cnr Mézonos and Zäími (Mon–Fri 7.30am–8pm); also near cnr Gounári and Ayíou Andhréou (Mon–Fri 7.30am–2pm).

The north coast and the Kalávryta railway

From Pátra you can reach Kórinthos in two hours by **train** or **bus** along the national highway; the onward journey to Athens takes another ninety minutes. The resorts and villages lining the Gulf of Kórinthos are undistinguished, though none of them is overdeveloped. At most of them you find little more than a narrow strip of beach, a campsite, a few rooms for rent and a couple of seasonal tavernas. At **Río** you can cross the gulf to the mainland by the **new bridge** across the Gulf of Kórinthos to Andírio, or by ferry, and at **Éyio** by ferry. Beyond **Dhiakoftó**, if you're unhurried, it's worth taking the old **coast road** along the Gulf of Kórinthos; this runs below the national highway, often right by the sea. However, to travel from Pátra to Kórinthos without taking the time to detour along the **Kalávryta railway** from Dhiakoftó would be to miss one of the finest train journeys in Greece. Even if you have a car, this trip should still be part of your plans.

Río and Éyio

RÍO (Ríon), connected by local bus #6 to Pátra in thirty minutes (or by train in ten, though with a long walk from the station to the harbour), signals the beginning of swimmable water, though most travellers pass through for the suspension bridge across the gulf to Andírio (5 min; €10 car toll). Surprisingly, the ferry (every 30 min; ⓣ29320 74717; €6 including driver, passengers €0.50) that functioned before the opening of the bridge in autumn 2004 continues to flourish, with many drivers preferring the cheaper fares and short break from driving.

Further east, a **ferry** from Éyio crosses the gulf four times daily (7.30am–5pm; €10 cars including driver, €1.60 passengers; ⓣ26910 22792) to Áyios Nikólaos, well placed for Delphi. Buses from Pátra stop at the bus station on the inland side of town, a considerable and inconvenient distance from the harbour or the train station.

Dhiakoftó and around

It is from **DHIAKOFTÓ** (officially Dhiakoptó) that the rack-and-pinion railway heads south up into the Vouraïkós gorge for Kalávryta (see p.272). If you arrive late in the day, it's worth spending the night here and making the train journey in daylight; the town can, in any case, be an attractive alternative to staying overnight in Pátra. The climate is very pleasant: less humid than Pátra and less furnace-like than Korinthía province to the east. There are several **hotels**, including the central, upmarket *Chris-Paul* (ⓣ26910 41715, ⓦwww.chrispaul-hotel.gr; ❹), which has a pool, and the small, friendly *Lemonies* (ⓣ26910 41229, ⓕ26910 43710; ❸), with comfortably refurbished rooms, opposite the school on the road to the beach, so well positioned for both sea and train. The seafront *Kohyli* **taverna** on the corner of the beach road has excellent seafood. A few minutes inland of the station, on the road out to the main highways, there is a map stockist and bookshop, Epi Hartou, carrying a comprehensive range of Anavasi and Road maps. Some 5km east of Dhiakoftó there is a better beach at **Paralía Trápezas**.

Dhiakoftó to Kalávryta: the rack-and-pinion railway

Even if you have no interest in trains, the **rack-and-pinion railway** from Dhiakoftó to Kalávryta is a must. The journey can be hot, crowded and uncomfortable, but the track is a crazy feat of Italian engineering, rising at gradients of up to one in seven as it cuts inland through the **Vouraïkós gorge**. The route is a toy-train fantasy of tunnels, bridges and precipitous overhangs.

The railway was built between 1889 and 1896 to bring minerals from the mountains to the sea. Its 1896 steam locomotives were replaced some years ago – one (*O Moutzouris*) remains by the line at Dhiakoftó station (ⓣ26910 43206) with other relics, and another at Kalávryta – but the track itself retains all the charm of its period. The tunnels, for example, have delicately carved window openings, and the narrow bridges zigzagging across the Vouraïkós seem engineered for sheer virtuosity.

It takes around 45 minutes to get from Dhiakoftó to Zakhloroú (confusingly listed on timetables as Méga Spiléo), and about another twenty minutes from there to Kalávryta. The best part of the trip is the stretch to **Zakhloroú** (see below), along which the gorge narrows to a few feet at points, only to open out into brilliant shafts of light beside the Vouraïkós, clear and fast-running even in midsummer. In peak season the ride is very popular (there are just four to six trains a day), so you'll probably need to buy tickets in advance of your preferred departure (including the return journey); inflated ticket prices reflect the popularity. Despite only covering some 22km, trains on this line can be subject to the same lengthy delays (or cancellations) as their grown-up counterparts on the main line below.

Zakhloroú and Méga Spiléou

ZAKHLOROÚ is as perfect a train stop as could be imagined: a tiny hamlet echoing with the sound of the Vouraïkós River, which splits it into two neighbourhoods. It's a lovely, peaceful place with an old hotel, the *Romantzo* (ⓣ26920 22758; ❸), with en-suite rooms and a taverna opposite. The adjacent *Messina* restaurant has basic rooms: coming down to the station it could be mistaken for the *Romantzo*.

The eight-storey **Monastery of Méga Spiléou** ("Great Cave"; ⓣ26920 23130; open roughly 8am–1pm, 5–7pm), built at a sixty-metre cave entrance under a 120-metre cliff, is a 45-minute walk from the village, up a rough donkey track along the hillside; this joins a road, then an access drive along the final stretch, often chock-a-block with tour buses. Reputedly the oldest monastery in Greece, it has been burned down and rebuilt so many times that you'd hardly guess at its antiquity – from a distance it looks like a misplaced hotel. The last major fire took place in 1934, after a keg of gunpowder left behind from the War of Independence exploded. In 1943, the Nazis killed many of the residents and looted seventy lorryloads of furniture and relics, much of it later recovered. Dress conduct for visitors is strict: skirts for women, and long sleeves and trousers for men. Only men are allowed to stay overnight, at the precipitous *xenónas*, and the monks like visitors to arrive before 8pm, serving up a rough repast before closing the gates.

The view of the gorge valley from the monastery is for many the principal attraction. However, the cloister once housed 450 monks and was among the richest in the Greek world, owning properties throughout the Peloponnese, in Macedonia, Constantinople and Asia Minor; in consequence, its treasury, arranged as a small **museum** (€1), is outstanding. In the main church, among its icons is a charred black wax and mastic image of the Virgin, one of three in Greece said to be by the hand of St Luke (but probably from the tenth century); a smaller chapel houses a remarkable collection of body parts from various saints. The monastery was founded by Saints Theodhoros and Simeon, after a vision by the shepherdess Euphrosyne in 362 AD led to the discovery of the icon in the cave (Ayíazma) behind the site of the later church; cardboard cutouts now model the story, including flames leaping from the icon to destroy a serpent.

If returning to Dhiakoftó from Zakhloroú, it is possible to walk alongside the 12km of railway line down through the gorge (part of the **E4 walk route**) in 2–3 hours, although in places you need to walk on the rail sleepers. You should of course be aware of the times that trains are due on that section of line – the most photogenic points are around the 5.8-kilometre mark above Dhiakoftó. The walk may not be easy for vertigo sufferers, since it involves crossing some rather precipitous bridges. The southward E4 continues through Kalávryta, Vytína, Trípoli, Spárti, Mystra and Taïyétos to Yíthio.

Kalávryta and around

From Méga Spiléou a scenic road has been constructed 28km down to coastal Trápeza, and another has been hacked 10km through to **KALÁVRYTA**. The train line is more in harmony with the surroundings, but coming from Zakhloroú the drama of the route diminishes as the gorge opens out. Kalávryta itself is beautifully positioned, with Mount Helmós as a backdrop, but has a melancholy atmosphere. During World War II, on December 13, 1943, the German occupiers carried out one of their most brutal reprisal massacres because of partisan activity in the area, killing the entire male population – 1436 men and boys – and leaving the town in flames. Rebuilt, it is both depressing and poignant. The first and last sight is a mural, opposite the station, that reads: "Kalávryta, founder member of the Union of Martyred Towns, appeals to all to fight for world peace." The left clocktower on the central church stands fixed at 2.34pm – the hour of the massacre. In the old primary school is the **Museum**

of the Sacrifice of the People of Kalávryta (daily 9am–4pm; free), while out in the countryside behind the town is a shrine to those massacred, with the single word "Peace" (*Iríni*).

The Nazis also burned the tenth-century **monastery of Ayías Lávras** (open roughly 8am–1pm, 4–6pm), 6km out of Kalávryta. As the site where Yermanos, Archbishop of Pátra, raised the flag to signal the War of Independence, the monastery is one of the great Greek national shrines. It, too, has been rebuilt, along with a small historical museum.

Staying at Kalávryta has a sense of pilgrimage about it for Greeks; it's crowded with school parties during the week and with families at weekends. The general attitude to foreigners is business-like rather than overtly friendly, and the town will probably not have the same appeal for the casual visitor. If you miss the last train back to Zakhloroú (currently at 3.50pm, but check upon arrival), there are several pleasant **hotels** whose rates drop outside of winter weekends. Among them are the hospitable *Polyxeni*, Lohagón Vassiléos Kapóta 13 (Ⓣ26920 22141; ❷) and the friendly, good-value and luxurious *Filoxenia*, Ethnikís Andístasis 20 (Ⓣ26920 22422, Ⓦwww.hotelfiloxenia.gr; B&B ❹, winter ❺). The Info Center in Pátra has an extensive list of **rooms** in Kalávryta. There are several adequate **restaurants** around the square – *To Tzaki* has a nice atmosphere and good, mostly grilled, food. Kalávryta is also the main base for the **Helmós Ski Centre** (Dec–April daily 9am–4pm; Ⓣ26920 24451, Ⓦwww.kalavrita-ski.gr), which is rapidly growing in popularity; the website also carries contact details for accommodation in nearby villages. There are a number of shops that rent out equipment, give information about the state of the slopes and can sometimes help with transport up to the centre.

A thirty-minute drive south of Kalávryta, and 1.5km north of Kastriá, is the Spílio tón Limnón or **Cave of the Lakes** (summer daily 9am–6pm; winter Mon–Fri 9.30am–4.30pm, Sat & Sun 9.30am–6.30pm; Ⓣ26920 31633, Ⓦwww.kastriacave.gr; €8). Mineral-saturated water trickling through a two-kilometre cavern system from the Apanókambos plateau has precipitated natural dams, trapping a series of small underground lakes. As yet, only the first 500m or so are open to the public, and the guided tour can be short and hurried. The cave is on the same **bus** line from Kalávryta as the villages of Káto Loussí, Kastriá and Planitéro, and is 2km north of Kastriá. Buses also run from Kalávryta to Pátra four times daily.

Travel details

Trains

There are two main Peloponnesian lines:
Athens–Kórinthos–Dhiakoftó–Éyio-Pátra–Pýrgos–Kyparissía; two trains daily cover the full route, with onward connections to Kalamáta.
Kórinthos to: Dhiakoftó (3 daily; 1hr–1hr 30min); Kyparissía (2 daily; 1hr–1hr 35min). Pátra (3 daily; 45min–1hr 25min); Pýrgos (3 daily; 1hr 30min–2hr 15min);
Pátra to: Kalamáta (1 daily; 4hr 45min); Kyparissía (4 daily; 3hr); Pýrgos (4 daily; 1hr 30min–2hr).
Pýrgos to: Kalamáta (2 daily; 3hr); Kyparissía (6 daily; 1hr 20min).
Kyparissía to: Kalamáta (4 daily; 1hr 30min).
Athens (starts in Pireás)–Kórinthos–Mykínes (Mycenae)–Árgos–Trípoli–Diavolítsi–Kalamáta; three trains daily cover the full route.
Kórinthos to: Árgos (10min); Kalamáta (2hr–2hr 20min); Mykínes (50min); Trípoli (1hr 20min–1hr 35min).
In addition, there are the following branch lines and extra seasonal services on the main lines:
Árgos–Náfplio currently closed for reconstruction.
Dhiakoftó–Zakhloroú–Kalávryta 4–6 daily (Dhiakoftó–Zakhloroú 46min; Zakhloroú–Kalávryta 21min).
Isthmós–Loutráki 3 daily in summer (13min).

Pátra–Éyio–Dhiakoftó (3 daily in summer Mon–Sat; 45min–1hr).
Pýrgos–Olymbía 5 daily (27min).

Buses

Buses detailed usually have similar frequency in each direction, so entries are given just once; check under both starting point and destination. Bus station timetables rarely indicate when there is a change of bus en route – this can involve a long wait. Long-distance buses from Athens sometimes have a break at Isthmós, by the Corinth Canal.

Connections with Athens: Árgos (hourly; 2hr 15min); Hóra (4 daily; 5hr 30min); Kalamáta (12–13 daily; 4hr 30min); Kalávryta (1–2 daily; 3hr 30min); Kórinthos (hourly; 1hr–1hr 30min); Koróni (1 daily; 7hr); Kyparissía (4 daily; 5hr 30min); Loutráki (9 daily; 1hr 30min); Monemvasiá (2 daily; 6hr); Mykínes–Fíkhti (for Mycenae; hourly; 2hr); Náfplio (hourly; 3hr); Olymbía (4 daily; 5hr 30min); Pátra (33 daily, 2.30am–9.45pm; 3hr); Poulíthra (1 daily via Leonídhio; 4hr 30min); Pýlos (2 daily; 5hr 30min–7hr); Pýrgos (8 daily; 5hr); Spárti (9 daily; 4hr); Tiryns (hourly; 2hr 45min); Trípoli (14 daily; 2hr 30min–3hr); Yeroliménas (2 daily in season only; 7hr); Yíthio (4–6 daily; 5hr).

Areópoli to: Ítylo (4 daily, 20min); Kalamáta (4 daily changing at Ítylo; 1hr 30min–2hr 30min); Láyia (daily; 1hr); Spárti (2 daily; 2hr); Váthia (daily in season; 1hr 30min); Yeroliménas (2 daily in season; 1hr); Yíthio (4 daily; 35–50min).

Árgos to: Andhrítsena (1 daily; 3hr); Ástros (3 daily Mon–Fri; 1hr); Ayía Triádha (8 daily; 20min); Kórinthos (15 daily; 1hr); Leonídhio (3 daily Mon–Fri; 3hr); Midhéa (3 daily; 40min); Mykínes (Mycenae, 5 daily; 30min); Mýli (for Lerna, 5–10 daily; 25min); Náfplio (15–32 daily, every 30min; 30min); Nemea (2 daily; 1hr); Néo Kíos (11 daily; 20min); Olymbía (3 daily on weekdays; 4hr 30min); Pátra (1 Sundays; 4hr), Spárti (8 daily; 3hr); Tiryns (every 30min; 15min); Trípoli (4 daily Mon–Fri, 3 daily Sat & Sun; 1hr 20min).

Galatás to: Méthana (2–4 daily; 45min); Náfplio (1–3 daily; 2hr); Trizína (4 daily; 15min).

Kalamáta to: Exohóri (2 daily; 1hr 30min); Finikoúnda (4 daily, changing at Pýlos, 2 daily via Koróni; 2hr 15min); Hóra (4 daily, changing at Pýlos, plus 4 direct; 2hr); Kardhamýli (4 daily; 50–75min); Kórinthos (7 daily; 3hr 15min–4hr); Koróni (8 daily; 1hr 20min–2hr); Kyparissía (5 daily; 2hr); Megalópoli (8 daily; 1hr 15min); Messíni (frequent except Sun; 25min); Methóni (4 daily, via Pýlos; 2hr); Pátra (2 daily, via Pýrgos; 4hr–4hr 30min); Petrálona (for Ancient Messini, 2 daily); Pýlos (5–9 daily; 1hr 20min); Pýrgos (2 daily; 2hr); Saïdhóna (2 daily; 1hr 30min-2hr); Spárti (2 daily, changing at Artemisia; 2hr–2hr 30min); Stoúpa (4 daily; 1hr-1hr 30min); Trípoli (8 daily; 1hr 45min–2hr).

Kórinthos to: Loutráki (every 30min; 20min); Mykínes (Mycenae, hourly; 30min); Náfplio (7 daily; 1hr 20min); Nemea (5 daily; 45min); Spárti (8 daily; 4hr); Tiryns (hourly; 1hr 15min); Trípoli (9 daily; 1hr 30min); Xylókastro (every 30min 1hr; 45min).

Kyparissía to: Filiatrá (7 daily; 20min); Pýlos (5 daily changing at Hóra; 2hr); Pýrgos (2–4 daily; 1hr); Trípoli (2 daily; 1hr 30min–2hr); Zaháro (4 daily; 25min).

Megalópoli to: Andhrítsena (2 daily; 1hr 15min); Pýrgos (2 daily; 4hr).

Náfplio to: Dhrépano (6–8 daily, except Sun; 20min); Epidaurus ("Asklipio", 4–5 daily; 45min); Ermióni (3–4 daily; 2hr 15min); Galatás for Póros (1–3 daily; 2hr); Íria (2 daily; 1hr); Isthmós (14 daily; 1hr 20min); Karathónas beach (4 daily; 20min); Kósta (3–4 daily; 2hr 15min); Kranídhi (3–4 daily; 1hr 50min); Lygourió (7 daily; 40min); Méthana (2 daily; 2hr); Midhéa (5 daily; 40min); Mykínes (Mycenae, 3–4 daily; 1hr); Néo Kíos (11 daily; 20min); Paleá Epídhavros (3 daily; 1hr); Pórto Héli (3–4 daily; 2hr); Tiryns (every 30min; 15min); Toló (14 daily; 25min); Trípoli (2–4 daily; 2hr).

Pátra to: Agrinio (8–9 daily; 1hr 45min); Ahaïa (every 30–45min; 40min); Árgos (1 Fridays; 4hr), Crete (5 weekly, via Pireás; 16hr); Éyio (12–16 daily; 1hr); Itéa (for Delphi, 2 daily, Mon–Sat; 3–4hr); Ioánnina (2–4 daily; 5hr); Itháki (1 daily, via Kefaloniá; 6hr), Kalamáta (2 daily; 4hr); Kalávryta (2–4 daily; 2hr 15min); Kalogriá (3–5 daily in season; 1hr 15min); Kefaloniá (3 daily; 4hr); Lápas/Metóhi (for Kalogriá; 6–10 daily; 50–1hr): Lefkádha (2 weekly; 3hr 30min); Mesolóngi (8–10 daily; 1hr); Náfpaktos (1–7 daily; 1hr); Pýrgos (6–10 daily; 2hr); Thessaloníki (4 daily; 9–10hr); Trípoli (1–2 daily, via Lámbia; 3–4hr); Vólos (1 daily, except Sat; 6hr); Zákynthos (4 daily; 2hr 30min including ferry from Kyllíni).

Pýlos to: Finikoúnda (3–5 daily; 45min); Filiátra (2–6 daily, usually changing at Hóra; 1hr 30min) Hóra (2–6 daily; 40min); Kyparissía (1–5 daily, usually changing at Hóra; 2hr); Methóni (3–6 daily; 20min); Yiálova (2–8 daily; 20min).

Pýrgos to: Andhrítsena (2 daily; 2hr); Katákolo (9 daily; 30min); Kyllíni (3 daily; 1hr); Olymbía (hourly, but none 12.30–3.30pm; 45–1hr); Trípoli (3 daily; 3hr).

Spárti to: Moláï (6 daily; 1hr 40min–2hr); Monemvasiá (3 daily, 2 on Sun, changing at Moláï; 2hr 30min–3hr); Mystra (11 daily, 4 on Sun; 15–30min); Neápoli (3–4 daily; 4hr); Pýrgos Dhiroú (1 daily; 2hr 30min); Trípoli (9–10 daily; 1hr–1hr 20min); Yeroliménas (2 daily; 3hr); Yíthio (5–6 daily; 1hr).

Trípoli to: Andhrítsena (2 daily; 1hr 30min); Ástros (2 daily Mon–Sat; 1hr 30min); Dhimitsána (1 daily; 1hr 30min); Kalávryta (1 daily; 2hr 30min); Karítena (2 daily; 1hr); Klitoría (1–2 daily; 2hr); Leonídhio (1–2 daily; 3hr 30min); Megalópoli (9 daily Mon–Fri, 6 daily Sat & Sun; 40min); Neápoli (2 daily; 5hr 30min); Olymbía (2 daily Mon–Fri, 1–3 Sat & Sun; 5hr); Pýlos (3 daily; 3hr); Stemnítsa (1 daily; 1hr 15min); Tegéa (hourly; 20min); Vytína (6 daily; Mon–Fri, 4 Sat & Sun; 1hr 15min); Yíthio (3 daily; 2hr 30min).
Yíthio to: Láyia (daily; 1hr); Mavrouvoúni ("Kamping" 4 daily; 15–20min); Monemvasiá (2 daily in high season; 2hr 30min); Pýrgos Dhiroú ("Spílea" 1 daily; 1hr 10min); Váthia (1 daily, Mon, Wed, Fri; 2hr); Yeroliménas (2–3 daily; 2hr).

Ferries

Across the Gulf of Kórinthos: Andírio–Río (every 15min, every 30min between 11pm and 7am; 10–20min); Éyio–Áyios Nikólaos (4 daily; 7.30am–5pm; 35–50min).
Galatás to: Póros (every 15min from dawn till past midnight; 5min).
Kalamáta to: Kastélli, Crete (1 weekly in season; 8hr 30min); Kýthira (1 weekly in season; 5hr 30min).
Kósta to: Spétses (4 daily; 7.20am–4.30pm; 20min).
Kyllíni to: Zákynthos (4–7 daily; 1hr); Kefaloniá Póros (5 daily summer, 2–3 daily winter; 1hr 15min–2hr 15min), Kefaloniá Lixoúri–Argostóli (1 daily summer; 2hr 30min).
Kýthira to: Andikýthira (2 weekly in season); Kastélli, Crete (4–6 weekly in season; 2hr 15min; 5hr via Andikýthira); Pireás (2 weekly in season; 5hr).
Neápoli to: Kýthira (2–3 daily mid-season, 3–4 daily late July–Aug; 1hr).
Neápoli (Poúnda) to: Elafónissos (5–15 daily; 10min).
Pátra to: Igoumenítsa and Corfu (2–3 daily; 6–11hr/8–11hr); Kefaloniá and Itháki (1–2 daily; 2hr 30min/3hr 45min); also to Brindisi, Ancona, Bari, Trieste and Venice (Italy).
Yíthio to: Kýthira (1–5 weekly in season; 2hr 30min); contact Rozaki (☎27330 22650) for current information.

Hydrofoils

For details and frequencies of services, which vary drastically with the seasons, contact local agents or the Minoan Flying Dolphins' main office in Pireás (Aktí Themistokléous 8 ☎210 41 28 001).
Flying Dolphin hydrofoils run between the following ports: **Ermióni** to: Spétses, Pórto Héli, ýdhra, Póros, Méthana and Pireás.
Méthana to: Póros, ýdhra, Ermióni, Égina and Pireás. Summer-only excursion boats
Kósta and Pórto Héli: Water-taxis to Spétses according to demand (10–20min).

3

Thessaly and central Greece

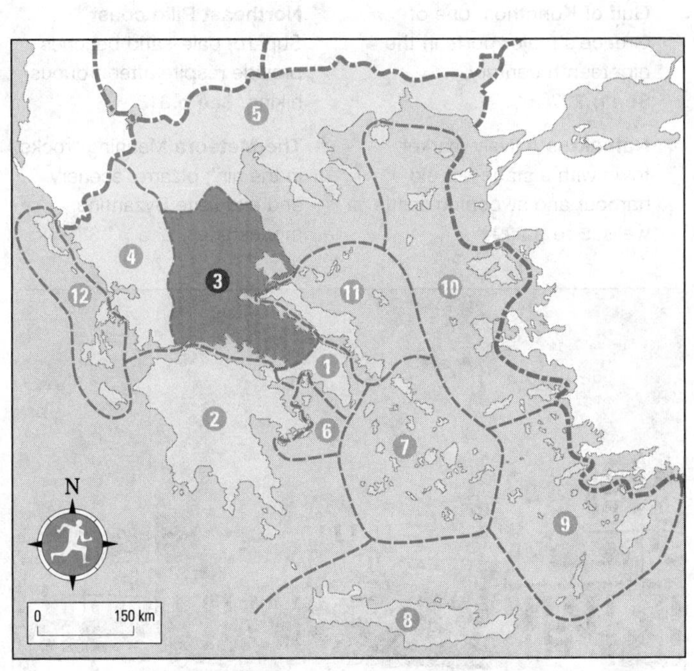

CHAPTER 3

Highlights

* **Ósios Loukás** A remote Byzantine monastery with vivid eleventh-century mosaics. See p.285
* **Delphi** Spectacularly set ruins of an oracle believed in ancient times to be the centre of the earth. See p.288
* **Galaxídhi** The best preserved settlement on the Gulf of Kórinthos, one of Greece's major ports in the nineteenth century. See p.297
* **Náfpaktos** A lively market town with a stage-set old harbour and swooping castle walls. See p.299
* **Karpenisiótis valley** This alpine valley, nicknamed the "Greek Switzerland", is a major springtime river-sport venue. See p.305
* **Mount Pílio** Hiking trails link mansion-filled villages clinging to wooded hillsides, the mythical home of the centaurs. See p.314
* **Northeast Pílio coast** Superb, pale-sand beaches provide respite after arduous hiking. See p.318
* **The Metéora** Meaning "rocks in the air"; bizarre, scenery and exquisite Byzantine monasteries. See p.338

▲ Marina, Náfpaktos Town

3

Thessaly and central Greece

Central Greece offers scattered highlights –especially the site of the ancient oracle at **Delphi** (modern Dhelfí), and, further north, the other-worldly rock-top monasteries of **Metéora**. Overall the region, dominated by the vast agricultural plain of Thessaly, is less memorable, with mostly drab market and industrial towns. The area south of Thessaly is known as **Stereá Elládha** – literally "Greek Continent", reflecting its mid-nineteenth-century past as the only independent Greek mainland territory, along with Attica and the quasi-island of the Peloponnese. It encompasses the ancient districts of Boeotia and Phokis, the domains respectively of Thebes (modern Thíva) and Delphi. Most visitors head straight to Delphi, but those with extra time make a rewarding detour to **Ósios Loukás** monastery – containing the finest Byzantine mosaics in the country.

The basin of **Thessaly** (*Thessalía* in Greek) formed the bed of an ancient inland sea – rich agricultural land ceded reluctantly to the modern nation by the Ottomans in 1881. Thessaly's attractions lie at its periphery, defined by the mountain ranges of Ólymbos (Olympus), Píndhos (Pindus), Óssa and Pílio (Pelion). East from the major port city of Vólos extends the hilly peninsula of **Mount Pílio**, whose luxuriant woods and idyllic beaches are easily combined with island-hopping to the Sporades. Less frequented **Mount Óssa** is usually visited en route to northern Greece, lying between the sea and the motorway to Thessaloníki. To the west, **Kalambáka** gives access to the unmissable Metéora, and to Epirus via the dramatic **Katára Pass** over the Píndhos.

Stereá Elládha

The inevitable mecca of Stereá Elládha is **Delphi**, 175km northwest of Athens. Buses regularly cover the route from the capital, or they can be picked up at

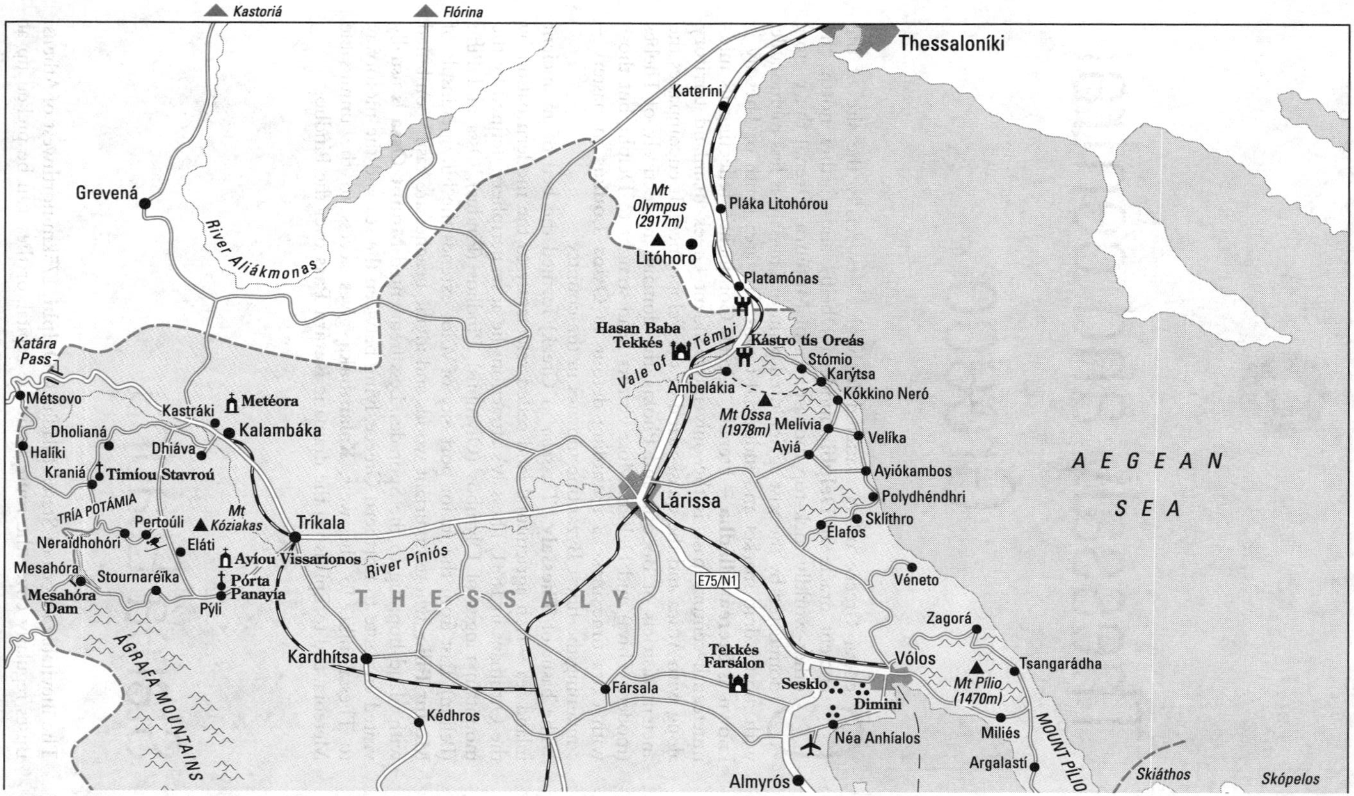

Kastoriá
Flórina
Thessaloníki
Kateríni
Mt Olympus (2917m)
Pláka Litohórou
Litóhoro
Grevená
River Aliákmonas
Platamónas
Ioánnina
Katára Pass
Hasan Baba Tekkés
Vale of Témbi
Kástro tís Oreás
Stómio
Karýtsa
Ambelákia
Kókkino Neró
Mt Óssa (1978m)
Melívia
Velíka
Ayiá
Ayiókambos
AEGEAN SEA
Métsovo
Meteora
Kastráki
Kalambáka
Dholianá
Dhiáva
Halíki
Kraniá
Timíou Stavroú
Lárissa
Polydhéndhri
Sklíthro
Élafos
TRÍA POTÁMIA
Mt Kóziakas
Pertoúli
Tríkala
Neraïdhohóri
Eláti
Ayíou Vissaríonos
River Piniós
Mesahóra
Stournaréïka
Pórta Panayía
Mesahóra Dam
Pýli
THESSALY
E75/N1
Véneto
Árta
Zagorá
ÁGRAFA MOUNTAINS
Kardhítsa
Tekkés Farsálon
Vólos
Mt Pílio (1470m)
Tsangarádha
Sesklo
Dimini
Fársala
Kédhros
Miliés
Néa Anhíalos
MOUNT PÍLIO
Argalastí
Almyrós
Skiáthos
Skópelos

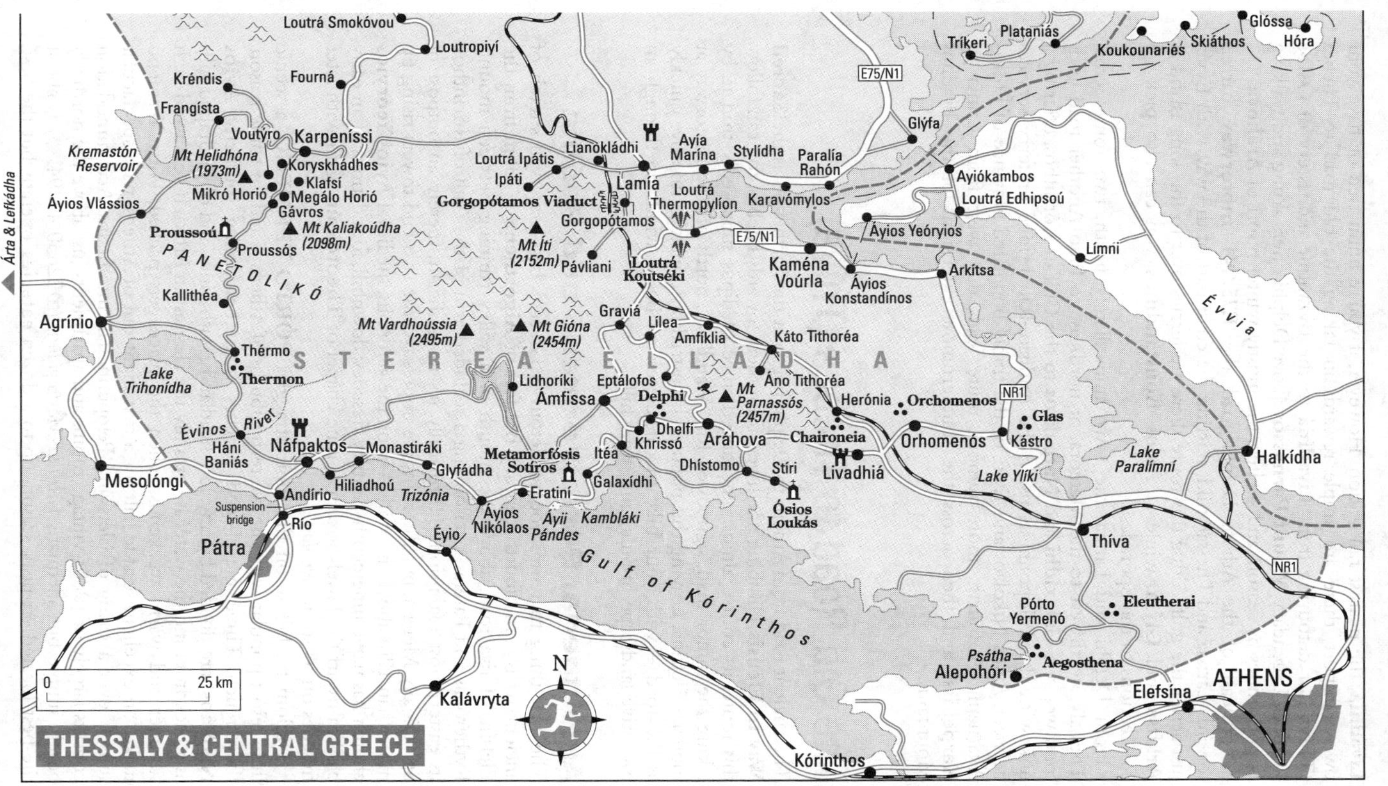
THESSALY & CENTRAL GREECE
Árta & Lefkádha
Loutrá Smokóvou
Loutropiyí
Kréndis
Fourná
Frangísta
Voutýro
Karpeníssi
Kremastón Reservoir
Mt Helidhóna (1973m)
Koryskhádhes
Klafsí
Mikró Horió
Megálo Horió
Gávros
Áyios Vlássios
Proussoú
Mt Kaliakoúdha (2098m)
Proussós
PANETOLIKÓ
Kallithéa
Agrínio
Thérmo
Thermon
Lake Trihonídha
Évinos River
Háni Baniás
Náfpaktos
Mesolóngi
Andírio
Suspension bridge
Río
Pátra
Monastiráki
Hiliadhoú
Glyfádha
Trizónia
Metamorfósis Sotíros
Eratiní
Galaxídhi
Áyios Nikólaos
Áyii Pándes
Kambláki
Éyio
Kalávryta
Gulf of Kórinthos
Kórinthos
Loutrá Ipátis
Ipáti
Gorgopótamos Viaduct
Gorgopótamos
Mt Íti (2152m)
Pávliani
Lianokládhi
Lamía
Ayía Marína
Stylídha
Paralía Rahón
Loutrá Thermopylíon
Karavómylos
Loutrá Koutséki
Kaména Voúrla
Áyios Konstandínos
Mt Vardhoússia (2495m)
Mt Gióna (2454m)
Graviá
Lílea
Amfíklia
Káto Tithoréa
STEREÁ ELLÁDHA
Lidhoríki
Eptálofos
Ámfissa
Delphi
Dhelfí
Khrissó
Itéa
Mt Parnassós (2457m)
Áno Tithoréa
Aráhova
Dhístomo
Stíri
Ósios Loukás
Herónia
Chaironeia
Livadhiá
Orchomenos
Orhomenós
Glas
Kástro
NR1
Lake Ylíki
Lake Paralímní
Halkídha
Thíva
Eleutherai
Pórto Yermenó
Psátha
Aegosthena
Alepohóri
Elefsína
ATHENS
Glýfa
E75/N1
Ayiókambos
Loutrá Edhipsoú
Áyios Yeóryios
Límni
Arkítsa
Évvia
Tríkeri
Plataniás
Koukounariés
Skiáthos
Glóssa
Hóra
0
25 km
N

Livadhiá, the nearest rail station. However, if you're unhurried or have your own transport, there are ample rewards in taking the old road to Thebes (**Thíva**), or detouring from **Livadhiá** to the Byzantine monastery of **Ósios Loukás**. Legendary **Mount Parnassós** above Delphi offers skiing and walking opportunities by season, and shelters the mostly winter resort of **Aráhova**.

Northeast of the Athens–Delphi road, the **E75/N1 motorway** barrels towards Lárissa and Thessaloníki, skirting the coast part of the way, with Évvia just across the gulf. Along this route there are ferries over to this long island at **Arkítsa** and **Glýfa**, while at **Áyios Konstandínos** you can also pick up connections to the Sporades.

From Delphi and Lamía, the town immediately north, two routes cross Thessaly: northwest to the Metéora, or northeast to Pílio. Another road leads southwest via **Galaxídhi** and **Náfpaktos** to the Gulf of Kórinthos, offering a link with the Peloponnese, using the Andírio–Río bridge or ferry services between Áyios Nikólaos and Éyio, or the thinly populated province of Étolo-Akarnanía. A fourth, more remote, route leads due west from Lamía to **Karpeníssi** and then across the southernmost extensions of the Píndhos Mountains.

The Old Road to Thebes (Thíva)

The ancient road from Athens to Delphi began at the Parthenon as the **Sacred Way to Eleusis**, climbing northwest from there towards Thebes. You can follow this route, its course almost unchanged since Oedipus supposedly trod it, by taking the minor road, signposted for "Mándhra", north off the motorway at modern Elefsína. Leaving this polluted industrial port, matters improve quickly, as the road – with your bike or car, there's no bus – winds up through an evocative landscape of pines and stony hills.

Aigosthena, Pórto Yermenó and Psátha

The first thing to tempt you to detour is Greece's best-preserved stretch of ancient walls – the fourth-century BC fort of **Aigosthena** – 23km from the Elefsína–Thíva road, above the mouth of a valley running between mounts Kytherónas and Patéras, overlooking a secluded arm of the Gulf of Kórinthos, its easternmost extension. Historically it's insignificant, merely an outpost of Sparta's ally Megara, but the ruins are impressive, the two end towers rising up more than 12m above the walls. Up on the acropolis, medieval **Áyios Yeóryios** church has naive nineteenth-century frescoes; downhill, foundations of an early basilica dwarf the jewel-box Byzantine chapel of **Theotókou**, again with later frescoes on its stone *témblon*.

A kilometre below on the shore straggles **PÓRTO YERMENÓ**, a scenic little resort popular with the western suburbs of Athens – and for some reason, the French. Three gravel-sand beaches here (best being southerly **Áyios Nikólaos**) are divided by tiny, low headlands, with pine- and olive-draped hills as a backdrop, and the water is certainly the cleanest in Attikí. If you avoid high summer and warm weekends, when the place gets packed, Pórto Yermenó makes an excellent seaside halt for a first night out of Athens, with spectacular sunsets over a string of islets and Peloponnesian mountains. Accommodation consists largely of 1980s-vintage rooms and apartments just above the northerly beach: simple but adequate *Vassiliki Mastroyianni* (☎22630 41394; ❷) is about the best located. At peak season, up to a dozen **eateries** operate, but the best, most reliable year-round taverna, at the north end of the esplanade, is *Akrotiri* (*Tis Marias*), with enormous portions, its own wine from the nearby uplands and fresh *bakaliáros*, *koutsoumoúres* and *karavídhes*, local seafood especially abundant in spring. *Avra* next door also works all year and serves similar fare.

From a junction just uphill from Pórto Yermenó, a steep, winding road through the pines leads 8km to **Psátha**, a longer (2km) and trendier beach than its neighbour – there are two all-day bars/nightclubs at mid-strand. Otherwise, it's surprisingly undeveloped – there's no accommodation – but plenty of fish **tavernas** at the north end of the sand, where *Limanaki* and *Angelos* operate most of the year, the latter fair value, featuring local fish such as sardines and *melanoúri*.

Eleutherai and Thíva (Thebes)

Back on the Thebes road, 1km north of the Pórto Yermenó turning, you pass within 400m of another fortress defending a critical pass: fourth-century BC **Eleutherai** (unfenced, signposted from the road). The northeast side of the fort stands almost intact, with six towers surviving to varying degrees.

The modern town of **THÍVA** lies 20km north of Eleutherai, built atop its mighty predecessor, birthplace of Pindar and Epaminondas. Thus there are few visible traces of its past: archeologists have been unable to excavate the crucial central areas. The excellent **archeological museum** at the downhill end of Pindhárou, with an enormous Frankish tower in its forecourt, is closed indefinitely for a ground-up reconstruction. Whenever it re-opens, star exhibits from ancient Boeotia are still likely to include an Archaic funerary stele depicting a youth holding a cockerel and sniffing a lotus; two *kouroi* (idealized Archaic male figures) from the Apollo shrine at Ptóön; and painted *larnakes* (sarcophagi) from Mycenaean Tanagra, featuring well-observed hunting scenes and women lamenting their dead.

There are no direct **buses** from Thíva to Delphi, but services run frequently to Livadhiá (where there are better connections), and the town straddles the main Athens–Thessaloníki **rail line**. Until the museum re-opens you're unlikely to stay the night, though best-value of three central hotels is the welcoming, well-kept *Niovi* at Epaminónda 63 (Ⓣ22620 29888, Ⓦwww.hotelniovi.gr; ③), breakfast extra. The main **taverna** district occupies the pedestrianized section of Epaminónda north of the square; here *Ladhokolla* at no. 105 is a popular choice for traditional *mayireftá*.

Livadhiá and around

Livadhiá lies at the edge of a great agricultural plain, much of it reclaimed lake bed scattered with minor archeological sites, including ancient **Orchomenos** and **Chaironeia**. It's a little-touristed region; most visitors are intent on reaching the Parnassós country just to the west, and will mainly interest veteran travellers to Greece with their own transport.

Livadhiá

LIVADHIÁ is a pleasant cotton-milling town on the banks of the Érkyna, a river emerging from a narrow gorge at the base of a fortress. Ancient and medieval monuments, along with landscaping and gentrification by the river springs, make it an enjoyable midday pause before, or after, Delphi. But if you're without transport, and on a budget, check the last bus or train connection out, since there are no cheap places to stay.

The older curiosity is the **Oracle of Trophonios**, a ten-minute walk from the main square, beside an Ottoman-era bridge, near where the Érkyna rises. Above its springs, cut into the rock, are niches for votive offerings – in one large chamber with a bench, the local Ottoman governor would sit for a quiet smoke. In antiquity, petitioners of the Oracle of Trophonios first had to bathe in the Springs of Memory and Forgetfulness. The oracle, a circular structure which led to caves deep in the gorge, has been tentatively identified at the top of the hill.

The fourteenth-century **kástro** overlooking the springs provides the medieval interest; its entrance lies just around the corner, uphill and west. An impressive, well-bastioned square structure, it was a key early insurgent conquest in the War of Independence. Originally the castle was the stronghold of the Catalan Grand Company, who wrested control of central Greece from the Franks in 1311 and held it for sixty years. The outnumbered Catalans dispensed with the Frankish nobility based at Thebes by diverting the river to flood the plain as their adversaries approached Livadhiá; the Frankish cavalry foundered in the unexpected marsh and were cut down to a man.

Practicalities

Buses arrive near the central square, **Platía Lámbrou Katsóni**; in season services towards Delphi often arrive and leave full. The **train station** is 6km out; arrivals should be met by an OSE shuttle bus into town – otherwise use a taxi.

The more central of two overpriced hotels is the *Levadia* on Platía Lámbrou Katsóni at the main junction (℡22610 23611; ④). **Eating and drinking** here is a better proposition; in the pedestrianized zones surrounding the riverside park are a number of establishments. *Neromylos*, housed in a converted water mill, is a conventional dinner-only taverna, moderately priced, with the old sluice running through its premises; for lunch, *Iy Krya* at Trofoníou 13 (first on the right, facing upriver) is a simple grill. Between these two, sample good coffees and desserts at *Kafe Erkyna*.

Orchomenos and Chaironeia

Just 10km northeast of Livadhiá (on bus routes) is the site of **ancient ORCHOMENOS**, one of the wealthiest Mycenaean cities. Near the edge of modern Orhomenós, along the road towards Dhiónysos village, stands the "**Treasury**" **of Minyas** (Tues–Sun 8.30am–3pm; €2), a tholos-type tomb similar to those at Mycenae, and also excavated by Heinrich Schliemann. The roof has collapsed but it's otherwise complete, with an intricately carved marble ceiling inside. Nearby are the remains of a fourth-century BC **theatre** (locked), and the ninth-century Byzantine **church of Panayía tís Skripoús**, built entirely of masonry from the theatre and a Classical temple. The triple-apsed church has some fine reliefs, including a sundial on the south transept.

Directly north of Livadhiá, on the Lamía road, lies **Chaironeia**, site of one of the most decisive **ancient Greek battles**. Here, in 338 BC, Philip of Macedon won a resounding victory over an alliance of Athenians, Thebans and Peloponnesians. This ended the era of city-states, from whom control passed forever into foreign hands: first Macedonian, later Roman. Beside the road, at modern **Herónia**, stands a six-metre-high **stone lion**, part of the funerary monument to the Thebans killed in the battle; adjacent is a small **museum** of local finds.

The Oedipus junction, Ósios Loukás and Aráhova

West from Livadhiá, the landscape becomes ever more striking as Mount Parnassós and its outriders loom overhead. After 22km, about halfway to Delphi, you reach the vicinity of the so-called **Schist** (Split) or **Triodos** (Triple Way) **junction**, intersection of the ancient roads from Delphi, Daulis (today Dhávlia), Thebes (Thíva) and Ambrossos (modern Dhístomo). The Thebes-Delphi road actually lay 1km or so north, in the Stení Rematiá Gorge, still with a minor track through it.

Pausanias identified this crossroads as the site of Oedipus's murder of his father, King Laius of Thebes, and most of his retainers. According to myth, Oedipus was returning on foot from Delphi while Laius and his entourage were speeding towards him from the opposite direction on a chariot. Neither would give way, and in the ensuing altercation Oedipus killed them, ignorant of who they were. It was, in Pausanias's supreme understatement, "the beginning of his troubles". Continuing to Thebes, Oedipus solved the riddle of the Sphinx – which had been ravaging the area – and took widowed Queen Iokaste as his wife – unaware that he was marrying his own mother.

Ósios Loukás monastery

Some 8km east of Dhístomo is the **monastery of Ósios Loukás**. There are numerous daily **buses** from Livadhiá to Dhístomo, but nothing towards Stíri, the village 3.5km west of the monastery (the last 2.5km on a spur road). There's a scenic, more direct route of 35km from Livadhiá, practicable **by taxi or your own transport**; this goes over a fir-covered pass on Mount Elikónas, then descends via Kyriáki (tavernas), a village 14.5km east of Ósios Loukás.

Ósios Loukás monastery (daily: May 3–Sept 15 8am–2pm & 4–7pm; rest of year 8am–5pm; €3) was a precursor of the final flourish of **Byzantine art** found in the great churches at Mystra in the Peloponnese. From an architectural or decorative standpoint it ranks as one of the great buildings of medieval Greece; the remote setting is exquisite as well, especially in February when the many local almond trees bloom. Approaching along the last stretch of road, Ósios Loukás suddenly appears on its shady terrace, overlooking the highest summits of the Elikónas range and a deserted valley. The complex comprises two domed churches, the larger **katholikón** of Ósios Loukás (a local beatified hermit, Luke of Stiri, not the Evangelist) and the adjacent chapel of **Theotókos**. A few monks still live in the cells around the courtyard, but the monastery is essentially a museum, with a café and souvenir stalls in the grounds.

The Dhístomo massacre

Drab Dhístomo is distinguished by one of the worst World War II atrocities in Greece: German occupying forces shot 232 inhabitants on June 10, 1944, looting and burning part of the village for good measure. The event is immortalized in a bleak grey-and-white marble **memorial**, erected in 1996 on a nearby hilltop – follow the signs to the "mausoleum". On one plaque are the names of the victims; on two others apologetic sentiments from a German citizens' group and then-president Roman Herzog. This has not mollified the survivors a bit, who continue to pursue the unified German State through successive court cases in Greece, Italy and Strasbourg for more monetary compensation than was paid by West Germany in 1960.

The katholikón

The design of the **katholikón**, built around 1040 to a cross-in-square plan, strongly influenced later churches at Dhafní and at Mystra. Externally it is unassuming, with rough brick-and-stone walls topped by a well-proportioned octagonal dome. The interior, however, is startling, with multicoloured-marble walls contrasting with gold-background mosaics on the high ceiling. Light filtering through marble-encrusted windows reflects from the curved mosaic surfaces onto the marble walls and back, bringing out subtle shading.

The **mosaics** were damaged by an earthquake in 1659, replaced at many points by unremarkable frescoes, but surviving examples testify to their glory. On the right as you enter the narthex are a majestic *Resurrection*, rivalled only by the version at Néa Moní on Híos (see p.768), and *Thomas Probing Christ's Wound*. The mosaic of the *Niptir* (*Washing of the Apostles' Feet*) on the far left (north side) of the narthex is one of the finest here, the expressions of the Apostles ranging between diffidence and surprise. This humanized approach is again illustrated by the *Baptism*, up in the northwest squinch (curved surface supporting the dome). Here Jesus reaches for the cross amidst a swirling mass of water, an illusion of depth created by the curvature of the wall. On other squinches, the Christ Child reaches out to the High Priest Simeon in *The Presentation*, while in *The Nativity*, angels predominate rather than the usual shepherds. The church's original **frescoes** are confined to vaulted chambers at the corners of the cross plan and, though less imposing than the mosaics, employ subtle colours, notably in *Christ Walking towards the Baptism*.

The Theotókos chapel and crypt

The chapel of **Theotókos** ("God-Bearing", ie the Virgin Mary), built shortly after Luke's death, is nearly a century older than the *katholikón*. From outside it overshadows the main church with elaborate brick decoration culminating in a marble-panelled drum, but the interior seems mean by comparison, enlivened only by a couple of fine Corinthian capitals and the original floor mosaic, its colours now faint.

Finally, do not miss the vivid frescoes in the **crypt** of the *katholikón*, entered on the lower south side of the building. Bring a torch, since illumination is limited to three spotlights to preserve the colours of the post-Byzantine frescoes.

Aráhova

Arriving at **ARÁHOVA**, the last town east of Delphi (just 11km further), you are well into Parnassós country. The peaks rise tiered above, sullied somewhat by the wide asphalt road cut to a ski-resort – the winter-weekend haunt of well-heeled Athenians. Also notable is the local **festival of Áyios Yeóryios** (April 22–25, or around Easter Monday if the date range falls within Lent), centred on the hilltop church.

Arrival and information

Buses use a stop on the platía at the west end of town (still dubbed "Xenías" after the eponymous, now-renamed, hotel) heading in both directions. A few paces away is the post office, and a municipal **tourist office** (Greek-signed as ΔΕΤΠΑ; variable hours; ⓣ22670 29170, ⓦarachova.tripod.com), which can help on a number of matters, including bus schedules. There are also several **bank ATMs**.

Accommodation

In the summer, most people just stop for a meal and to souvenir shop, so finding **accommodation** is easy, even though several establishments close down. In winter, particularly at weekends, rooms are at a premium in all senses, with prices bumped up at least two categories.

Apollon Inn Delphi end of town ⓣ22670 31057, ⓔapolloninn-arahova@united-hellas.com. Budget option whose pine-and-white tile en-suite rooms are plain but spacious. ❷

Lykoreia West edge of town ⓣ22670 32132, ⓦwww.lykoria.com.gr. Huge standard balconied doubles, plus a few suites, were renovated up to 2007, emerging with designer baths and Wi-Fi. Amenities include a terrace garden, pool, gym/sauna and buffet breakfast served in a somewhat dark salon; easy parking. Summer ❹, winter ❻

Paradhosiakos Xenonas Maria Village centre, just up a pedestrian lane from through road ⓣ22670 31803, ⓦwww.mariarooms.com. One of Aráhova's better restoration inns, occupying a pair of lovely old buildings with an array of rustic-decor doubles, triples and quads. B&B summer ❸, winter ❹; family quads €80–150 by season.

Xenonas Generali Down stair-path at eastern outskirts, below the primary school, clocktower and church ⓣ22670 31529, ⓦwww.generalis-xenon.com. Aráhova's "other" restoration inn, offering the best standard in town: nine very different rooms, most with fireplace; the decor of some can be too cute, but the welcome's warm and the breakfasts are more elaborate in winter. An indoor pool (winter only), spa, *hamam* and sauna are all popular with the après-ski set. B&B summer ❹, winter weekdays ❺, weekends ❻

Xenonas Petrino Village centre, south of the through road ⓣ22670 31384, ⓕ22670 32663. Small stone-clad inn with a basement breakfast salon; upstairs galleried rooms (sleeping four) are more exciting than the conventional ground-floor doubles. B&B summer ❸, winter ❹

Xenonas Ro Platía Xenías ⓣ22670 29180 or 697 76 18 994, ⓦwww.arahova-ro.gr. Wood-floored rooms are on the small side (except for the family suites), but tastefully appointed, and some have balconies and mountain views; pleasant breakfast salon. Summer ❸, winter weekdays ❸, weekends ❹

The Town

The town centre is appealing, despite being sundered by the Livadhiá–Delphi road, ever-mushrooming chalet construction on the outskirts, and fairly comprehensive après-ski commercialization. If you're not making for any other mountain areas, Aráhova is worth an afternoon's pause before continuing to Delphi; those with their own transport may prefer staying here, as opposed to modern Dhelfi. A small number of houses in Aráhova retain their vernacular architecture or have been restored in varying taste, flanking narrow, often stepped lanes twisting north up the slope or poised to the south on the edge of the olive-tree-choked Plistós Gorge. The area is renowned for its strong purplish

Skiing on Parnassós

There are two main **skiing** areas developed on the northwest flank of Mount Paranassós: Kelária (23km from Aráhova) and Fterólakka (29km). The top point for each is about 2200m, descending to 1600–1700m when conditions permit; the twenty or so runs are predominantly red-rated, making this a good intermediate resort, and served by fourteen lifts, of which about half are bubble-chair type. Most **facilities** (and the biggest car park) are at Kelária, but Fterólakka has longer, more challenging runs.

Equipment is rented on a daily basis at the resort, or for longer term in Aráhova (which teems with seasonal sports equipment shops). The main problem is high winds, which often close the lifts, so check the forecast before setting off. The skiing season is generally from mid-December to April, sometimes into May in increasingly rare long winters.

wines, *tsípouro*, honey, candied fruits and nuts, cheese (especially cylindrical *formaélla*), the egg-rich noodles called *hilopíttes*, and woollen weavings; all are prominent in the roadside shops, though most woven goods are imported from elsewhere and/or machine-loomed.

Eating and drinking

During summer, about half of Aráhova's eateries shut, as do most of the bars, music clubs and sweet shops pitched at trendy local youth as well as visiting Athenians. More traditional *kafenío* and ouzerí tables on the main fountain-square attract an older crowd all year until late. Reliably good and usually open central **tavernas** include meat-strong *Dhasaryiris* (closed Aug and lunchtime) and *Karmalis*, both on the through road; or *To Kalderimi*, downhill from *Dhasaryiris*, with high-quality traditional cuisine. Way up the steps behind Áyios Yeóryios next to a fountain, also accessible via a roundabout drive, *Panayiota* (weekends only outside ski season) sets tables out under poplar and plane to take advantage of an unbeatable setting; the food is decent if not exceptional value, though service is good and there's usually a sweet offered on the house.

Delphi (Dhelfí)

Occupying a high mountain terrace dwarfed either side by the ominous crags of Parnassós, it's easy to see why the ancients considered **DELPHI** the centre of the earth. But more than the setting or the occasional earthquake and avalanche were needed to confirm a divine presence. This, according to Plutarch, was achieved through the discovery of a rock chasm that exuded strange vapours and reduced supplicants to frenzied, incoherent and undoubtedly **prophetic** mutterings.

The oracle: some history

The **first oracle** established here was dedicated to Gaia ("Mother Earth") and Poseidon ("Earth Shaker"). The serpent Python, son of Gaia, dwelt in a nearby chasm, and communication was made through the Pythian priestess. Python was later slain by young Apollo, who supposedly arrived in the form of a dolphin – hence the name Delphi. The **Pythian Games** were held periodically in commemoration, and perhaps also to placate the deposed deities.

Following the supplanting of Python by Apollo in the ninth century BC, the sanctuary became the centre of an association of city-states known as the **Amphyctionic League**. The precinct still belonged, however, to the nearby town of Krissa, which – as the oracle gained popularity – began to extort heavy tolls from the pilgrims arriving at the port of Kirrha (modern Itéa). Around 600 BC the **First Sacred War** broke out, with the League destroying Krissa and Kirrha, making Delphi autonomous. Delphi subsequently became one of the major sanctuaries of Greece, its increasingly respected oracle widely regarded as the most truthful in the known world.

For over a millennium thereafter, a steady stream of **pilgrims** converged on Delphi to seek divine direction in matters of war, worship, love or business. On arrival they would pay a set fee (the *pelanos*), sacrifice a goat, boar or even a bull, and – depending on the omens – wait to submit questions inscribed on lead tablets. The Pythian priestess, a village woman over fifty years of age, would chant her prophecies from a tripod positioned over the oracular chasm. Crucially, an attendant priest would then "interpret" her utterings in hexameter verse.

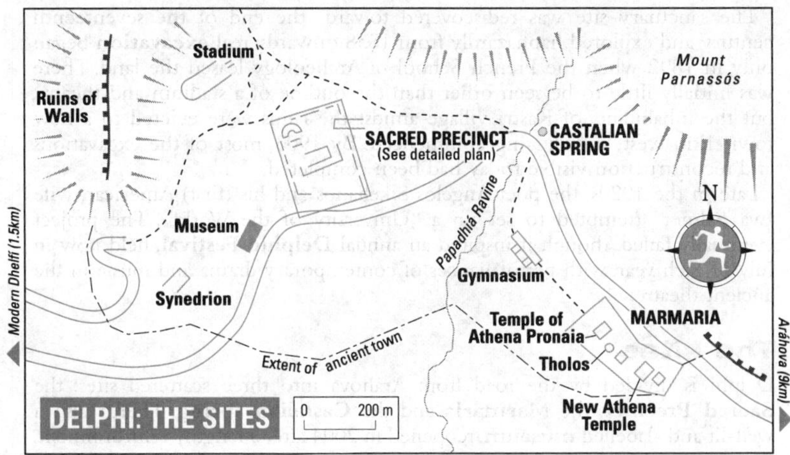

Many **oracular answers** were pointedly ambiguous: Croesus, for example, was told that if he commenced war against Persia he would destroy a mighty empire; he did – his own. But the oracle would hardly have retained its popularity for so long without offering predominantly sound advice, largely because the Delphic priests were better informed than any other corporate body of the time. With the Amphyctionic League functioning as a "United Nations" of the Greek city-states, they were able to amass a wealth of political, economic and social information and, from the seventh century BC onwards, had their own network of agents throughout the Greek world.

The **influence** of the oracle spread during the Classical age of colonization and its patronage grew, peaking during the sixth century BC, with benefactors such as King Amasis of Egypt and the hapless King Croesus of Lydia; Greek city-states also dedicated treasuries. Its position and wealth, however, made Delphi vulnerable to Greek rivalries; by the mid-fifth century BC, the oracle became the object of a struggle between Athens, Phokia and Sparta, prompting the **Second Sacred War**. Worse, it had maintained an almost treasonous attitude towards the Persian invasions – only partially mitigated when a Persian force, sent by Xerxes to raid Delphi, was crushed at the entrance to the sanctuary by a well-timed landslide.

The oracle never quite regained the same level of trust after these episodes of bias and defeatism. However, real **decline** did not set in until 356 BC, when the Phokians seized the sanctuary, leading to Philip of Macedon's intervention (the **Third Sacred War**) to restore the Amphyctionic League's authority. In 339 BC, the League invited Philip to settle a dispute provoked by the Amphissans; he responded by invading southern Greece, crushing the city-states in 338 at the Battle of Chaironeia. Delphi's political intriguing was effectively over.

Under **Macedonian** and later **Roman** control, the oracle's role became increasingly domestic, dispensing advice on marriages, loans, voyages and the like. The Romans thought little of its utterances, rather more of its treasure: Sulla plundered the sanctuary in 86 BC and Nero, outraged when the oracle denounced him for murdering his mother, carted away five hundred bronze statues. Upon the proscription of paganism by Theodosius in 391 AD, the oracle ceased.

The sanctuary site was rediscovered towards the end of the seventeenth century and explored haphazardly from 1838 onwards; real **excavation** began only in 1892 when the French School of Archeology leased the land. There was initially little to be seen other than the outline of a stadium and theatre, but the inhabitants of Kastrí village amidst the ruins were evicted to a new town 1km west, and digging commenced. By 1903, most of the excavations and reconstruction visible today had been completed.

Late in the 1920s, the poet Angelos Sikelianos and his (first) American wife Eva Palmer attempted to set up a "University of the World". The project eventually failed, though it inspired an annual **Delphic Festival**, held now in July of each year, with performances of contemporary drama and music in the ancient theatre.

The sites

Delphi is divided by the road from Aráhova into three scattered sites: the **Sacred Precinct**, the **Marmaria** and the **Castalian spring**. There's also a well-lit and -labelled **museum**, reopened in 2004 after a lengthy refurbishment. The attractions are best taken in two stages, with the sanctuary ideally at the beginning or end of the day, or (in winter) at lunchtime, to escape the coached-in crowds. Lots of clambering up rough stone steps and paths means taking sturdy footwear and a water bottle; the little café opposite the Castalian spring is more appealing than the one in the museum.

The Sacred Precinct

The **Sacred Precinct** (daily: summer 7.30am–7.30pm, but all are urged out at 7pm; winter 8am–5pm, evacuation starts 4.30pm; €9 joint ticket with museum), or Temenos (Sanctuary) of Apollo, is entered – as in ancient times – by way of a small **agora** enclosed by ruins of Roman porticoes and shops for selling votive offerings. The paved **Sacred Way** begins after a few stairs, zigzagging uphill between the foundations of memorials and treasuries to the Temple of Apollo. Along each edge is a jumble of statue bases where gold, bronze and painted-marble figures once stood; Pliny counted more than three thousand on his visit, and that was after Nero's infamous raid.

The style and positioning of these **memorials** were dictated by more than religious zeal; many were used as a deliberate show of strength or as a direct insult against a rival Greek state. For instance, the **Offering of the Arcadians** right of the entrance (a row of nine bronzes) was erected to commemorate their invasion of Laconia in 369 BC, and pointedly placed in front of the Lacedaemonians' own monument. Besides this, following the same logic, the Spartans celebrated their victory over Athens by erecting their **Monument of the Admirals** – a large recessed structure, which once held 37 bronze statues of gods and generals – directly opposite the Athenians' **Offering of Marathon**.

Further up the path, past the Doric remains of the **Sikyonian Treasury** on the left, lie the foundations of the **Siphnian Treasury**, a grandiose Ionic temple erected in 525 BC. Ancient Siphnos (Sífnos) had rich gold mines and intended the building to be an unrivalled show of opulence. Above this is the **Treasury of the Athenians**, built, like the city's "offering", after Marathon (490 BC). It was reconstructed in 1904–1906 by matching the inscriptions – including a hymn to Apollo with musical notation – that completely cover its blocks.

Next to the Treasury are the foundations of the **Bouleuterion**, or council house, a reminder that Delphi needed administrators, and above stretches the remarkable **Polygonal Wall** whose irregular interlocking blocks have withstood,

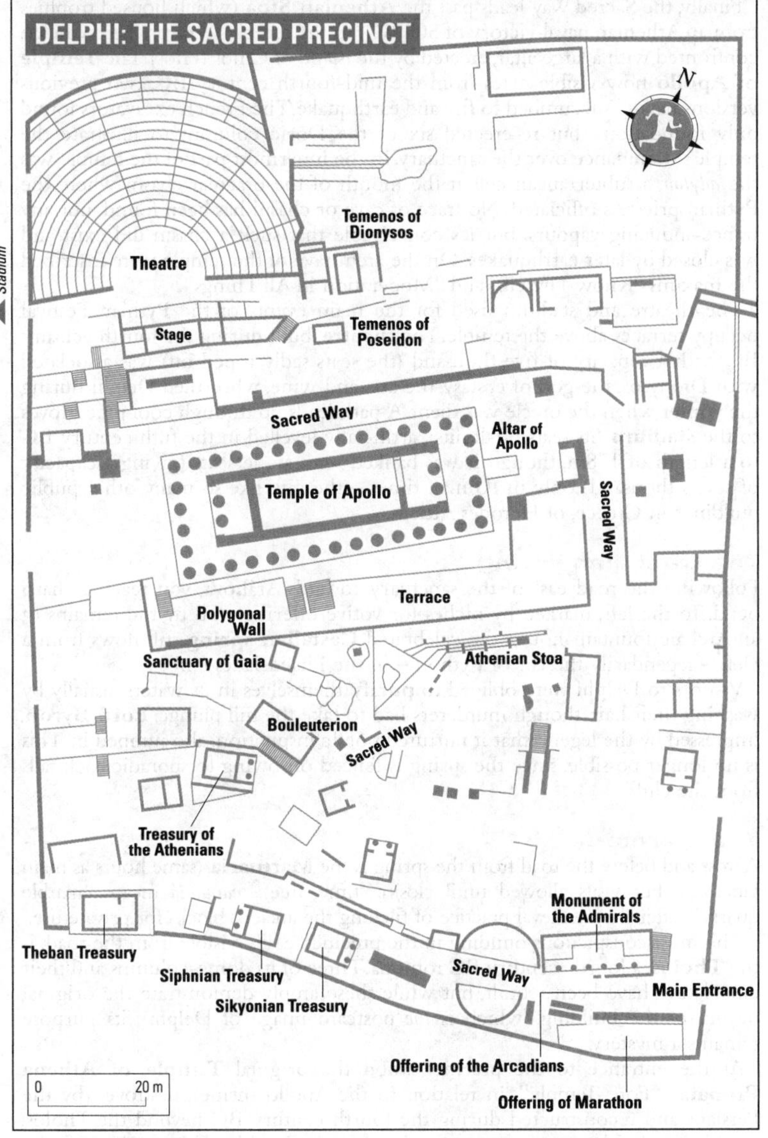

intact, all earthquakes. It, too, is covered with inscriptions, mostly referring to the emancipation of slaves; Delphi was one of the few places where such freedom could be made official by an inscribed register. An incongruous outcrop of rock between the wall and the treasuries marks the original **Sanctuary of Gaia**. It was here, or more precisely on an artificially built-up rock, that the Sibyl, an early itinerant priestess, was reputed to have uttered her prophecies.

Finally, the Sacred Way leads past the **Athenian Stoa** (which housed trophies from an Athenian naval victory of 506 BC) to the temple terrace where you are confronted with a large altar, erected by the island of Chios (Híos). The **Temple of Apollo** now visible dates from the mid-fourth century BC, two previous versions having succumbed to fire and earthquake. The French excavators found only foundations, but re-erected six of the Doric columns to illustrate the temple's dominance over the sanctuary. In the innermost part of the temple was the *adyton*, a subterranean cell at the mouth of the oracular chasm where the Pythian priestess officiated. No trace of cave or chasm has been found, nor any trance-inducing vapours, but it's conceivable that such a chasm did exist and was closed by later earthquakes. On the architrave of the temple were inscribed the maxims "Know Thyself" and "Moderation in All Things".

The theatre and stadium used for the main events of the Pythian Festival occupy terraces above the temple. The **theatre**, built during the fourth century BC with a capacity of five thousand (the seats sadly roped off) was associated with Dionysos, the god of ecstasy, the arts and wine, who ruled Delphi during the winter when the oracle was silent. A path leads up through cool pine groves to the **stadium** (its seats off-limits), artificially levelled in the fifth century BC to a length of 178m, though it was banked with stone seats (giving a capacity of seven thousand) only in Roman times – the gift, like so many other public buildings in Greece, of Herodes Atticus.

The Castalian spring

Following the road east of the sanctuary, towards Aráhova, you reach a sharp bend. To the left, marked by niches for votive offerings and by the remains of an Archaic fountain-house, the celebrated **Castalian spring** still flows from a cleft – legendarily the lair of Python – in the Phaedriades cliffs.

Visitors to Delphi were obliged to **purify** themselves in its waters, usually by washing their hair, though murderers had to take the full plunge. **Lord Byron**, impressed by the legend that it nurtured poetic inspiration, also jumped in. This is no longer possible, since the spring is fenced off owing to sporadic rock falls from the cliffs.

The Marmaria

Across and below the road from the spring is the **Marmaria** (same hours as main sanctuary, but visits allowed until closing time; free); *marmariá* means "marble quarry", after the medieval practice of filching the ancient blocks for private use.

The most conspicuous building in the precinct, easily visible from the road, is the **Tholos**, a fourth-century BC rotunda. Three of its dome-columns and their entablature have been rebuilt, but while these amply demonstrate the original beauty of the building (which is *the* postcard image of Delphi), its purpose remains a mystery.

At the entrance to the precinct stood the original **Temple of Athena Pronaia** ("Fore-Temple", in relation to the Apollo shrine), destroyed by the Persians and reconstructed during the fourth century BC beyond the Tholos; foundations of both structures can be traced. Outside the precinct on the northwest side (above the Marmaria) is a **gymnasium**, again built in the fourth century BC, but later enlarged by the Romans; prominent among the ruins is a circular plunge-bath for athletes' refreshment after their exertions.

The museum

Delphi's **museum** (summer Mon 12.30–6.30pm, Tues–Sun 7.30am–7.30pm; winter daily 8.30am–2.45pm; included in site ticket) contains a rare and exquisite collection of sculpture spanning the Archaic to the Roman eras, matched only by finds on Athens' Acropolis. It also features pottery, bronze articles and friezes from the various treasuries and temple pediments, which give a good picture of the sanctuary's riches.

The most famous exhibit, with a room to itself at the south end of the galleries, is the **Charioteer**, one of the few surviving bronzes of the fifth century BC, unearthed in 1896 as part of the "Offering of Polyzalos", toppled during the earthquake of 373 BC. The charioteer's eyes, made of onyx and set slightly askew, lend it a startling realism, while the serene expression suggests a victory lap. The odd proportions of the body – the torso seems far too abbreviated viewed straight on – were probably designed by the sculptor with perspective in mind; they would be "corrected" when the figure was seen, as intended, from below.

Other major pieces include two huge **kouroi** from the sixth century BC, betraying clear Asiatic/Egyptian stylistic traits; a life-size, sixth-century BC votive **bull** fashioned from hammered silver and copper sheeting; and the elegant Ionic winged **Sphinx of the Naxians**, dating from 565 BC. Other notable works of the same period include two lion-spouted marble rain gutters from the Temple of Apollo, as well as bronze *protomes* or **griffin heads**, used extensively during Archaic times on the edge of cauldrons. Large chunks of the beautiful and meticulously carved **Siphnian frieze**, in the same northernmost gallery as the Naxian sphinx, depict Zeus and other gods looking on as the Homeric heroes fight over the body of Patroclus, as well as Hercules (Herakles) and Apollo engaged in a tug-of-war over an oracular tripod. Another portion of this frieze shows a battle between gods and giants, including a lion graphically mauling a warrior.

The **Athenian Treasury** is represented by fragments of the metopes (friezes) which depict the labours of Hercules, the adventures of Theseus and a battle with Amazons. A group of three colossal if badly damaged **dancing women**, carved from Pentelic marble around an acanthus-topped column – probably a tripod-stand – dates from the fourth century BC and probably represents the daughters of Kekrops. Among later works is an exquisite second-century AD figure of **Antinoös**, favourite of Roman emperor Hadrian.

Modern Dhelfí

Modern Dhelfí is as inconsequential as its ancient namesake, 1500m to the east, is impressive. The village is notorious as one of the most right-wing towns in Greece, with perhaps the last street in the country honouring post-war King Paul and his quasi-fascist consort Frederika. Entirely geared to tourism (including Greek skiers), Dhelfí's attraction lies in its cliffside setting, proximity to the ruins and access to Mount Parnassós (see p.294).

There's a single **bus terminal** at the Itéa (west) end of town, where the upper and lower commercial streets link up. Westbound buses go to Ámfissa (for onward connections north), Itéa and (usually with a change) Náfpaktos, while eastbound services go to Aráhova, Livadhiá or Athens. The main problem, since all coaches originate elsewhere, is that seats allocated for the Dhelfí ticket booth are limited and sell out quickly. Bus timetables are available from the helpful **tourist office** (Mon–Fri 8am–2.30pm; ⓣ22650 82900) in the town hall on lower main thoroughfare Vassiléos Pavloú kéh Fridheríkis. Other amenities, along the same street, include several **bank ATMs**, a **post office** and a number of bar-cafés, at least one of which will be offering **Internet access**.

Accommodation

Accommodation is plentiful if not always good value, with the fancier hotels often booked by coach tours; like most archeological-site villages, Dhelfí has quick visitor turnover so, with over twenty hotels and pensions, finding a vacancy should present few problems. However, there is no set peak season – indeed winter weekends can see top rates charged, courtesy of the ski trade – so scope for bargaining depends on current traffic. As an alternative to Dhelfí or Aráhova, you might consider **KHRISSÓ** village, 13km downhill towards the gulf; it's far less touristy, with considerable character in its centre where there's one central **inn** (T 22650 83220, W www.guestinn.com; 3) and a few **tavernas** under the plane trees, the more popular being *Fourlas* (dinner only except summer) and *O Platanos*, in the upper quarter.

There are three **campsites** in the immediate area. The closest two are *Camping Apollon* (T 22650 82762; May–Sept), alongside the road to Ámfissa/Itéa and 1km west of Dhelfí, with a pool, restaurant and more caravan space than tenting turf; and *Camping Delphi* (T 22650 82209; April–Oct), 3km further along the same road, just above Khrissó.

Acropole Filellínon 13 T 22650 82675, W www.delphi.com.gr. On the quietest, lowest street of the village, with unbeatable views out back over the Plistós Gorge, this hotel's rooms were refurbished in 2006, with marble dresser tops, some double beds, and three attic rooms with fireplace. Unchanged, small bathrooms remain a weak spot; it's also a good idea also to book a triple as a double. Good buffet breakfast. 4

Athina Pávlou ké Fredherícis 55 T 22650 82239 or 697 38 81 509, F 22650 82239. Near the bus station at the Itéa (west) end of town, this hotel has wood decor, well-kept if smallish rooms, mostly en suite, and views of the gulf from rear rooms. Closed Nov–Christmas and weekdays Christmas–end March. B&B 2

Odysseus Pension Iséa 1, cnr Filellínon, the street below and parallel to Pávlou ké Fredherícis T 22650 82235. Spartan 1970s-vintage rooms with shared bathrooms, but this is the quietest spot in town. A flowered terrace offers unobstructed views and - keen walkers take note - overlooks the start of marked paths to Khrissó and Dhésfina villages. 1

Orfeas Ifiyenías Syngroú 35 T 22650 82077, E zdroserou@hol.gr. Rooms are spacious and well maintained, the top floor completely redone (versus light touch-up elsewhere), with superb views and air conditioning. Better-than-average parking; substantial discount to Rough Guide readers. B&B 3

Pan Pávlou ké Fredherikis 53 T 22650 82294 or 22650 82494, W www.panartemis.gr. All rooms, including attic quads, emerged from a 2006 refit with new tiles, paint job, a/c and bathrooms with tubs, exploiting existing balconies with fine views to the gulf. Immediately opposite is the annexe, the *Artemis*, with rooms of equal standard, but you sacrifice views. Summer 2, Aug/ski season 4

Sibylla Pávlou ké Fredherikis 9 T 22650 82335, W www.sibylla-hotel.gr. 2005-overhauled furnishings in small-to-medium-sized en-suite rooms; there are fans rather than a/c, and balconies overlooking the gorge. 1

Sun View Pension Apóllonos 84, far west end of upper commercial street, near *Amalia Hotel* T 22650 82349, E dkalentzis@internet.gr. Fair-sized rooms in pastel colours with art on the walls; rear-facing ones are a bit dark. Pleasant breakfast area; parking adjacent. B&B 2

Eating and drinking

Restaurants are not a Dhelfí strong point, despite wintertime skier custom. The best choices include *Iy Skala*, up steps from nearby hotel *Sibylla*, for cheap and honest fare, or *Garganduas* at the west end of town by the BP petrol station, with a broad menu encompassing *kondosoúvli* and *kokorétsi*. Another good-value carnivorous option is *Hasapotaverna Panagakos* (Sept–June), opposite the *Athina* hotel.

Mount Parnassós

For a taste of the Greek mountains, **Parnassós** is probably the most convenient peak, though its heights no longer rank as unspoilt wilderness, having been disfigured by the ski-station above Aráhova and its accompanying paraphernalia. The best routes for walkers are those up from Dhelfí to the **Corycian cave** (practicable April–Nov, but not in midsummer without a dawn start), or the more strenuous **Liákoura summit ascent** (May–Oct only). For any explorations, Road Editions' 1:50,000 **map** no. 42, or Anavasi Editions' 1:55,000 map no. 1, both entitled *Parnassos*, are wise investments, though neither is infallible.

Dhelfí to the Corycian cave

Allow a full day for this outing (4hr for ascent to cave, 3hr 30min back to Dhelfí) and take ample food. To reach the **trailhead** for this walk – and the initial path up the mountain – follow signposting up through Dhelfí village to the Dhelphi Festivals Museum (daily except Tues & Wed 8.30am–3pm; €2), where the poet **Angelos Sikelianos** once lived; exhibits mostly concern the events which he and Eva Palmer organized in 1927–30.

Continue climbing from here to the highest point of the fence enclosing the sanctuary ruins. Where the track ends at a gate, take a trail on your left, initially marked by a black-and-yellow rectangle on a white background; these, repeated regularly, indicate the trail is part of the **E4 European long-distance route**. Initially steep, the way soon flattens out on a grassy knoll overlooking the stadium, and continues along a ridge. Soon after, you join an ancient cobbled trail coming from inside the fenced precinct – the **Kakí Skála**, which zigzags up the slope above you in broad arcs. The cobbles end near two concrete inspection covers for Dhelfí's water supply, an hour-plus above the village, at the top of the **Phaedriades** cliffs. From one of several nearby rock pinnacles those guilty of sacrilege in ancient times were thrown to their deaths – a custom perhaps giving rise to the name Kakí Skála or "Evil Stairway".

E4 markers remain visible in the valley ahead of you as the principal route becomes a gravel track bearing northeast; ignore this and follow instead a metal sign pointing toward the cave, taking the right fork near the **Krokí spring** and watering troughs, with a complex of summer cottages on your right. This track, now intermittently paved, passes a picnic ground and a chapel of Ayía Paraskeví within fifteen minutes. Continue for some forty minutes beyond the chapel, heading gently downhill and passing another sign for the cave, until you emerge from the fir woods (2hr 40min from Dhelfí) with a view east and ahead to the rounded mass of the Yerondóvrahos peak (2367m) of the Parnassós massif.

The Corycian cave (Korýkio Ándro)

Another fifteen minutes bring you to a second chapel (of **Ayía Triádha**) on the left, with a spring and picnic ground. To the left rises a steep ridge, on whose flank lies the ancient **Corycian cave**. Ignore the Greek-only sign behind the chapel indicating a dangerous, disused old trail, and persevere along the road for five more minutes to where a white bilingual sign indicates a newer path, marked by orange paint splodges and red-triangle signs. After forty minutes' climb on this, you meet another dirt road; turn left and follow it five minutes more to the end, just below the conspicuous cave mouth at an altitude of 1370m.

In ancient times the cave was sacred to Pan and the nymphs, the presiding deities of Delphi during winter when Apollo forsake the oracle. Orgiastic rites were celebrated in November at the cave by women acting as nymphs, who made the long hike up from Delphi on the Kakí Skála by torchlight. If you look carefully with a torch you can find ancient inscriptions near the entrance; without artificial light you can't see more than 100m into the chilly, forbidding cavern. By the entrance you'll also notice a rock with a man-made circular indentation – possibly an ancient altar for libations.

Liákoura summit

Liákoura is Parnassós's highest peak (2457m), approachable either from the Delphi/Aráhova side or from the northeastern foothills of the mountain. The latter hike, starting from **Tithoréa**, is best, but involves taking a bus or train and then taxi to the trailhead – plus probably camping out on the mountain. For a more casual look at Parnassós, it's probably better to walk up from the **Dhelfí side** as a continuation of the Corycian cave outing, staying overnight at the hamlet of **Kalývia** on the Livádhi plateau, some 45 minutes' walk east of the cave. Here there are numerous tavernas, many shut during summer, and chalet-hotels for skiers.

Energetic trekkers can traverse the whole massif in a single long day's walk, starting **from Zemenó** (2 roadside hotel-restaurants), between Aráhova and the Triodos of Oedipus, and descending to Áno Tithoréa, or vice versa. A trail marked initially as part of local path 22 ascends 1200m to Baïtanórahi and then the pass known as Sidherópорta before joining the route up from Tithoréa (see below). You should, however, take a day's food, three litres of water per person and basic bivouacking supplies, as bad weather can descend without warning, springs are poorly spaced, and alpine shelters near the summit are apt to be locked or very primitive.

Tithoréa to Liákoura via the Velítsa ravine

The principal surviving wilderness route up Parnassós to Liákoura begins from **TITHORÉA**, 6km above Káto Tithoréa on the Livadhiá–Amfíklia road and the Athens–Thessaloníki railway. The village is a beauty, its stone houses interspersed with patches of **ancient wall** (including an elaborate tower) and the little chapel of Áyios Ioánnnis Theológos, containing an exquisite **Paleochristian mosaic** under glass (illuminated on entry). There are plenty of **tavernas** off the scenic platía, though only one official **rooms** establishment, the *Tithorea* at the outskirts approaching from downhill (☎22340 71021; ❸).

Allow at least six hours for the ascent from Tithoréa with a day-pack, and around four and a half hours for the descent, so set out early in June or July. From the platía, head southwest past a church with a few graves adjacent, and the secondary Platía Andhroútsou (with a bust of that Greek Revolutionary). Continue up a flagstoned lane, past the last houses, towards the first red-on-white painted-diamond waymark, beyond which lies another flagstoned, half-circular platía overlooking the giant **Velítsa ravine**. Guided onward by the diamond waymarks – and the appropriate section of *The Mountains of Greece* (see "Books" p.962) – you follow the proper trail, momentarily descending into the ravine. The path stays in fir forest much of the time, though there's reliable water only about half way along at the Tsáres spring. Just past this there's the junction with the route over Baïtanórahi from Zemenó, and shortly after the base of Liakoúra peak. The **final ascent** is an easy scramble more or less up to the ridge line. On a clear day you can see Mount Olympus in the north, the Aegean to the east, the Ionian to the west and way down into the Peloponnese to the south.

Along the gulf: Itéa to Náfpaktos

The train-less, almost beach-less north shore of the **Gulf of Kórinthos** is far less frequented than the south coast. Its arid landscape, with harsh mountains inland, can be initially off-putting, but there are patches of cultivated valley and coastal plain, and attractive, low-key resorts in **Galaxídhi** and **Náfpaktos**, both well connected by bus. This coast also offers convenient access south to the Peloponnese, via car-ferries at Áyios Nikólaos–Éyio and Andírio–Río, the latter straits also spanned by a futuristic bridge completed in 2004. At both Éyio and Río, you are on the main rail and road routes between Kórinthos and Pátra.

All buses heading southwest of Delphi towards the Gulf of Kórinthos stop first at Itéa, with a possible change of buses for the onward journey. **ITÉA** is more pleasant than the purplish-red bauxite tailings of the huge aluminium works on the western outskirts would suggest, with two **hotels** and a half-dozen **tavernas** on the seafront; the adjacent *Park* or *Skala* halfway along are both fine for an inexpensive seafood meal.

Galaxídhi

GALAXÍDHI, a quiet port rearing mirage-like out of an otherwise lifeless shore 17km southwest of Itéa, is the first place you'd probably choose to break a journey. Amazingly, Galaxídhi was once one of Greece's major harbours, with a fleet of over four hundred two- and three-masted *kaïkia* and schooners, which traded as far afield as the UK. But shipowners failed to convert to steam power after 1890, and the town's prosperity vanished. Clusters of nineteenth-century shipowners' mansions, reminders of those heady days, don't match the rest of Fokídha province architecturally, but reflect borrowings from Venice, testament to the sea captains' far-flung travels. Lately they've become the haunt of Athenian second-homers, but despite their restorations and a bit of a marina ethos down at the main southeasterly harbour, the town still remains just the right side of twee, with an animated commercial high street (Nikólaou Máma) and a good range of places to eat and drink.

Arrival, information and accommodation

Buses call at the landscaped, central Platía Iróön; Galaxídhi is large enough to support a **post office** and a **bank ATM**.

Accommodation is on the pricey side and can be scarce in summer, or at weekends year-round, though all of it is en suite and usually air conditioned. Most of the best outfits are housed in converted seafarers' mansions.

Arhondiko ⓣ22650 42292 or 697 25 55 488. Recently built, mock-trad complex in a secluded spot beyond Hirólakkas with easy parking, partial sea views, themed rooms (including one with a mirrored ceiling) and self-catering breakfast facilities, though breakfast served on request in the basement salon or out in the rock-garden courtyard. ④

Galaxa ⓣ22650 41620, ⓕ22650 42053. Somewhat casually run hillside hotel above the northwest shore of Hirólakkas with private parking; most of the rooms have some sort of water view (the best in town), all have blue-and-white decor, fridges, phones and small bathrooms. Manolis, your genial host, presides over the popular garden-bar where breakfast is served. B&B ④

Ganimede/Ganymidis Nikólaou Gourgoúri 20 (southwest market street) ⓣ22650 41328 or 693 71 54 567, ⓦwww.ganimede.gr. Under the energetic management of the Papalexis family since 2004, who have thoroughly overhauled the rooms. There are four doubles in the old house (best is no. 1), with fridges and satellite TV, and a family suite (€150 for 4) with loft and fireplace across the courtyard-garden where a copious breakfast is served, still featuring founder Bruno's exquisite recipes for pâtés and jams, plus novelty breads from the Papalexis bakery. Free Wi-Fi access, and longer-term apartments out back. B&B ④

Hirolakas ⓣ22650 41170 or 693 69 99 327. A mix of standard doubles, studios and family suites, with fridge, a/c and TV, at this pension set just back from the water. ③

Votsalo Pension ⓣ22650 41788 or 697 79 94 227. Just three en-suite rooms with a/c on the east shore of Hirólakkas, in a refurbished 1861 house; simple breakfast. ③

The Town

The old town stands on a raised headland, crowned by the eighteenth-century church of Ayía Paraskeví (the old basilica, not the more obvious belfried Áyios Nikólaos, patron saint of sailors). With its protected double harbour, the place proved irresistible to early settlers, which explains stretches of walls – all that's left of **ancient Chaleion** and its successor **Oianthe** – between the two churches and the water on the headland dividing the two anchorages. What you see dates from 1830–70, as the town was largely destroyed during the War of Independence.

Just uphill from the main harbour is the **Nautical and Historical Museum** (daily: June–Sept 10.10am–1.30pm & 5.30–8.30pm; Oct–May 10.10am–4.15pm; €5), whose galleries do a well-labelled, clockwise gallop of this citadel-settlement in all eras. Ancient Chaleion is represented by painted pottery and a bronze folding mirror, then it's on to the chronicles of Galaxídhi –the place's name from Byzantine times onwards – and its half-dozen shipyards, mostly alongside the northwesterly Hirólakkas anchorage. The local two- and three-masters are followed from their birth – primitive, fascinating ship-building and sail-making tools – to their all-too-frequent sudden violent death. Along the way are propeller-operated logs, wooden rattles to signal the change of watches, a *bouroú* or large shell used as a foghorn and – best of all – superb polychrome figureheads.

Strolling or driving around the pine-covered headland flanking the south-eastern harbour leads to tiny pebbly **coves** where most people swim (accessed by steps from the narrow road), with chapel-crowned islets offshore. The closest "real" beaches are at the end of this road, or at **Kalafátis** just north of town, though neither is brilliant – harsh shingle underfoot and occasionally turbid water. With transport, head for better beaches at Kambláki (4km west) or Áyii Pándes (11km west).

Eating and drinking

Tavernas, mostly on the southeasterly quay (Iánthi), are generally adequate, though an obvious cluster at the head of the port is worth avoiding. An exception to that rule, one block inland, is the good, inexpensive seafood ouzerí *To Maistrali*, with all the usual (fried) standards. The only other budget choice is friendly ✱ *Albatross*, inland on the street between the two churches, purveying well-executed *mayireftá* from a short daily menu which might stretch to octopus, spinach/cheese pie, rabbit stew, pale *taramosaláta* and the house speciality *samári* (pancetta in savoury sauce). On the water, *Anamniseis ap' ta Limania* (which has its own fishing boat) is a good choice for seafood and starters at fair prices, while pricier *Barko Maritsa* (weekends only in winter, daily otherwise) near the far northeastern end of the esplanade features savoury, non-greasy *píttes* and an approximation of seafood risotto. For those with a sweet tooth, there are an improbable number of oriental pastry shops on Nikoláou Máma, between Platía Iróön and Iánthi.

Nightlife comprises a dozen quayside cafés and bars catering to sophisticated Athenian forty- and fifty-somethings. Beyond traces of the ancient walls at the lighthouse, a late-night music club incorporates a sand-strewn lido, while *Oianthe* nestles below the pines across the harbour. The only establishment at Hirólakkas is *Paleo Liovtrivi*, ideal for a snack, a home-made dessert or a nightcap at the water's edge.

West of Galaxídhi

West of Galaxídhi lies some of the sparsest Greek coastal scenery; there are just a handful of villages with scrappy beaches, few warranting a stop. At **Áyios**

Nikólaos, however, there's a year-round, roll-on-roll-off **ferry** (€2.20 passengers, €11 small car) across the gulf to the Peloponnese – an alternative to the straits at Andírio–Río, 60km further west (see p.300). Westbound bus timings just miss coinciding with ferry departures; if you don't catch the last sailing, there are at least three **accommodation** establishments and a like number of tavernas at various points along the pebble beach.

Trizónia and Monastiráki

The Gulf of Kórinthos has a dozen islets, but **TRIZÓNIA** – halfway between Áyios Nikólaos and Náfpaktos, just across a narrow strait – is the largest and only inhabited one (permanent population around 55). Well-vegetated and blissfully vehicle-free (except for a few service trucks), it has long been a favourite amongst yachties, and makes an idyllic retreat for conventional travellers despite having few beaches. To reach Trizónia, follow signs from the main highway down to the settlement of Hánia, where a little boat shuttles across eleven times daily until about 9pm (5min; more frequent in midsummer) to the appealing fishing harbour with its three fish **tavernas**. **Accommodation** includes the modern, well-designed *Hotel Drymna* (Ⓣ22660 71204, Ⓦwww.drymna.gr; B&B ④), most of whose wood-trimmed rooms overlook the yacht anchorage – and *Lizzie's Yacht Club* on the hillside opposite, a revered institution constituting the island's main **nightlife**. The access track to it continues towards Trizónia's southeast tip, where the small, red-sand beach at **Poúnda**, a half-hour in total from the village, is the best of several swimming coves on the far side of the island.

Beyond Trizónia, the most pleasant spot is **MONASTIRÁKI**, some 11km shy of Náfpaktos. Monastiráki retains plenty of old stone houses, along a serpentine, tree-studded quay; there are no short-term places to stay but there is a handful of **seafood tavernas**, the most popular *Iliopoulos* around the easterly headland. This has a good selection of wild-caught fish, cheaper seafood appetizers, good bulk wine and home-made *píttes* – but brusque service at busy times. For a pre- or post-prandial swim, there's a pebble **beach** adjacent, or much larger, less windy but shadeless **Parathálasso** west of the main port, backed by a lagoon and a few seasonal beach-bars. There's a sandier, 1300-metre beach – exposed and not always clean – 3km further west at **Hiliadhoú**, with showers, beach-bars, accommodation and tavernas.

Náfpaktos

The other distinctive place west of Galaxídhi – indeed the largest settlement on the gulf's north shore – is **NÁFPAKTOS**, a lively market town and resort which straggles along a plane-tree-shaded seafront, below its rambling Venetian castle. The planes are nurtured by numerous running springs, which attest to water-rich, deceptively gaunt mountains just inland. Some two hours' drive from Dhelfí, or an hour by road and ferry from Pátra, it makes a convenient, attractive stopover, and a new bypass road should siphon off some of the heavy through traffic which dents the town's charm.

Arrival, information and accommodation

Náfpaktos has two **bus** stations: the KTEL Etoloakarnanías at the corner of Manássi and Bótsari, handling services to Pátra, and the KTEL Fokídhas on Asklipíou, corner Kefalóvrysou, for eastward departures. Local blue-and-white city bus #5 goes west frequently (6am–9pm) to Andírio, where you can intercept buses north from Pátra to Ípiros, or catch a ferry across to the Peloponnese. The post office is on Tzavéla just east of the harbour; bank **ATMs** cluster further east on the same boulevard.

Despite ten hotels and nearly as many rooms/apartments, **accommodation** can be scarce in summer, and noisy at mid-town. The cleaner, more popular west beach of **Psáni**, with its frontage road Navmahías, is central and relatively quiet; top choices here are the *Plaza*, Navmahías 37 (Ⓣ26340 22226, Ⓦwww.plaza-hotel.gr; ④), renovated, (especially the bathrooms) in 2007, with Wi-Fi, or the slightly noisier apartments *Regina* at the east end of the esplanade near the old port (Ⓣ26340 21555, Ⓕ26340 21556; ③). About 250m inland, at Daliáni 7 in Botsaréïka at the base of the kástro, the *Ilion* (Ⓣ26340 21222; ③) has the best views in town from both rooms – redone in 2006 with mock-antique furniture and wood floors – and terrace bar, where a bacon-and-egg breakfast can be had, though it's a fair climb up with no easy parking nearby.

For even more tranquillity and comfort (and easier parking), head for the easterly beach of **Grímbovo** (Paralía Grimbóvou), 1km east of the old port – though swimming here is unwise, as foul-smelling culverts drain straight into the sea. Here the best-value choice, right beside the untainted creek-fountain flowing to the sea, is *Akti* (Ⓣ26340 28464, Ⓔakti@otenet.gr), with gulf views from about half the rooms, an antique-crammed lobby and an airy, cheerful breakfast salon. Standard doubles (B&B ④) were refurbished with butler sinks, marble dresser tables and the like in 2005–06, while three palatial rooftop suites are worth the splurge (⑥).

The Town

The vast, pine-tufted **kástro** provides a picturesque backdrop; most of it dates from the Venetians' fifteenth-century tenure. A complete tour is only possible by driving the well-marked 2.5km to the car park at the highest citadel, passing en route a clutch of cafés taking advantage of the view. At the summit are the remains of Byzantine baths and an Ottoman mosque, both converted into chapels. The curtain walls plunge down to the sea, enclosing the higher neighbourhoods and oval-shaped old harbour in crab-claw fashion (you can climb each rampart for free), with the original westerly gate giving access to Psáni beach.

The castle formed an essential part of the Venetian defences, and the **Battle of Lepanto** (Náfpaktos's medieval name) was fought just offshore on October 7, 1571. An allied Christian armada commanded by John of Austria devastated an Ottoman fleet – the first European naval victory over the Turks since the death of the dreaded pirate-admiral Barbarossa. Cervantes, author of *Don Quixote*, lost his left arm to a cannonball during the conflict; a Spanish-erected statue honours him at the old harbour. But Western naval supremacy

Andírio and the Andírio–Río suspension bridge

The roll-on-roll-off ferries that for decades crossed the straits between Andírio and Río, on the opposite side of the Gulf of Kórinthos, were in August 2004 joined by a futuristic antiseismic suspension bridge completed by a French consortium. Spanning a three-kilometre channel, it's the world's longest, plainly visible to approaching airline passengers from 30,000 feet (as pilots never tire of pointing out). The ferries have survived largely because their fares for a car and driver cost about half the stiff bridge toll – €10.50 for ordinary passenger cars and rising. The #5 bus from Náfpaktos deposits you at whichever quay is being used (according to weather and currents), where you can cross to Río and its train station, or retire to the handy KTEL booth at the west quay for all passing services between northwestern Greece, Pátra and Athens.

proved fleeting, since the Ottomans quickly replaced their ships and had already wrested Cyprus from the Venetians that same year.

Eating and drinking

Most of Náfpaktos's full-service **tavernas** line the plane-tree esplanade at Grímbovo, some half-dozen strong and all fairly comparable in quality. The only eateries near the old port are *Tsaras* (Wed–Sun only), dedicated to a limited range of daily-changing *mayireftá*, and popular *Papoulis* on the pedestrian zone near the Fetiye mosque missing its minaret. The latter comprises two adjacent premises – an ouzerí and a taverna, with large-portioned, well-executed fare and good service at both, local wine and seating both indoors and out. Otherwise, the medieval harbour and the Stenopázaro lane just inland arelined by *frappádhika* and bars which provide most of the town's **nightlife**.

North to Lamía

Lamía is a half-day's journey north from Dhelfí by bus, with a connection at Ámfissa (but under three hours with your own car): a pleasant route skirting mounts Parnassós, Gióna and (to the northwest) Íti. Just west of the historic pass of **Thermopylae**, at the open-air hot springs of **Loutrá Koutséki**, 12km shy of Lamía, the road joins the **coastal highway** from Athens.

Inland: Ámfissa to Gorgopótamos

The inland road west from Dhelfí climbs slowly through a sea of groves, source of the acclaimed local green olives, to **ÁMFISSA**, a small town below Mount Gióna. Its medieval name of Sálona is still used; like Livadhiá, this strategic location was a base for the Catalan Grand Company, who left their mark on the originally thirteenth-century **castle**. If you have time to kill between buses (the **KTEL** is on the main square), its ruins, including Classical polygonal masonry of the ancient acropolis, make for a pleasant walk.

Most travellers continue north along the scenic **Lamía road**, dividing mounts Parnassós and Gióna; the area is thinly populated, with few amenities. The only reliable ones between Itéa and Lamía are at **GRAVIÁ**, 30km beyond Ámfissa, where either of two grills – *Ble Gonia*, on the through road, or *O Lefteris*, a few paces away – are both popular, salubrious and inexpensive.

Just beyond Graviá, you cross the **rail line** between Livadhiá and Lamía: one of the most dramatic stretches of railway in Greece, with a history to match. It traveses the foothills of Parnassós, Kallídhromo and Íti, and over the precipitous defile of the **Gorgopótamos River**, where on November 25, 1942 the Greek Resistance – all factions united for the first and last time under British intelligence officer Eddie Meyers – blew up a critical **railway viaduct**, cutting one of the Germans' supply lines to North Africa for three months. At the replacement viaduct, just upstream from **GORGOPÓTAMOS** village, there's a commemorative plaque – not to the intrepid guerrillas, but to sixteen local hostages executed in reprisal by the Germans on December 1, 1942. The village proper is a minor resort, with a hotel and several tavernas; for a less commercialised alternative, head 500m north to Zakéïka district, where *O Pardhalis* is a welcoming **psistariá** featuring pork *exhohikó*, mutton *kondosoúvli*, and offal, from 9pm till late (call ⓣ22310 96192 to verify opening days).

The coastal highway

The **Athens–Lamía** four-to-six-lane **motorway** is fast and dull, completed up to just east of Áyios Kondstandínos, beyond which the "Maliakó Petalídhi" ("horseshoe" around the Maliakós Gulf) is under construction, extremely hazardous, and to be avoided by night. En route there are various links with the island of **Évvia** (see p.828): first at Halkídha (where there's a causeway), then by ferry at **Arkítsa** to Loutrá Edhipsoú.

Áyios Konstandínos and Kaména Voúrla

ÁYIOS KONSTANDÍNOS is the closest port to Athens for the Sporades islands, with daily catamaran or car-ferry departures to Skiáthos, Skópelos and Alónissos. For current information consult central agencies Bilalis (Ⓣ22350 31614, Ⓦwww.bta.gr), for Saos Ferries and some Hellenic Seaways departures, or Alkyon (Ⓣ22350 32444, Ⓦwww.alkyontravel.com), handling other Hellenic Seaways sailings, GA boats plus a link to Áyios Yeóryios (Évvia). There's no reason to **stay**; if necessary, **KAMÉNA VOÚRLA** spa 9km west, proves slightly more attractive. Thermal properties aside, its resort status is somewhat mysterious, given a truly awful mud-and-shingle beach dominated by neon-garish, traffic-buzzed mega-hotels and lapped by murky water. For most the utility of the place is confined to several harbourside fish tavernas at the end of Ayíou Pandelímona, best being *Ta Falareïka*, with good seafood and local wine but poor *mezédhes*. The local KTEL is at the base of the same shoreline street, while for an emergency overnight, *Hotel Parnassos* (Ⓣ22350 22391; ③), a block inland behind the *dhimarhío*, offers decent value, easy parking and calm.

Thermopylae and Loutrá Koutséki

Just before joining the road coming north from Graviá, the highway enters the **Pass of Thermopylae** (Thermopýles), where Spartan King **Leonidas** and his entourage made their stand against Xerxes' thirty-thousand-strong Persian army in August 480 BC. The pass was far more defined in ancient times: a narrow defile with Mount Kallídhromo on the south and the sea, now 4km distant, just north. The Spartans' bravery is described by Herodotus (and more recently, comic-book style, by Zack Snyder's hokey film *300*). Leonidas held the pass, the only approach an army could take to enter Attica from Thessaly, for two days with a mixed force of 7000 Spartans, Phokians, Thebans and helots. By night, however, Xerxes – tipped off by the traitor Ephialtes – sent an advance party along a little-used mountain trail and skirted the pass to attack the Greeks from behind. Leonidas ordered a retreat of the main army, but remained in place with a rearguard of about 2300, including 300 Spartans (thus the film's title), to delay the Persians' progress. All but two of them fought to their deaths on the third day.

Loutrá Thermopylíon, midway through the pass, are thermal springs exploited here since antiquity. The grave mound of the fallen rearguard lies 500m away, opposite a gloriously heroic statue of Leonidas. The **spa** and restaurant facilities are tatty, but off to one side you can bathe undisturbed in open-air hot cascades. For an even better outdoor **hot springs** experience, leave the main road heading southwest on the minor road to Dhamásta, and after 750m bear left onto an unmarked road; you'll see some streetlights ahead, seemingly in the middle of nowhere. Road's end is a car park beside a long, narrow pond, over a metre deep; this is **Loutrá Koutséki** (free, unenclosed). The clean water ranges from 30–33°C, so proves tolerable for long dips even in summer. The place is popular with Lamians, who bob about in the shadow of hillside greenery or apply facial mudpacks. It's an idyllic spot, more so at night when the high-voltage lines overhead are less obvious (though road noise always intrudes).

Lamía and around

LAMÍA (population approx. 50,000) is the busy capital of Fthiotídha province, and an important transport hub. There's a choice of three **onward routes**: north to Lárissa or Tríkala, west to Ypáti and Karpeníssi, or northeast to Vólos. The northerly option is the dullest; the routes west and east have more to delay your progress. Lamía itself sees few overnight visitors, but has a worthwhile sight in its combined castle-museum, and abounds in excellent restaurants.

The town centre is defined by four main squares: Platía Párkou, Platía Eleftherías, Platía Laoú and Platía Dhiákou. **Platía Eleftherías** is the traditional social hub and venue for the evening *vólta*, with a few outdoor café tables and a little bandstand-gazebo. The cathedral and Neoclassical provincial government building flank the square on the north, with the Galaxias three-screen **cinema** tucked into the southwest corner. Just east and downhill from Eleftherías is atmospheric, plane-tree shaded **Platía Laoú**, site of an equestrian statue of controversial wartime Resistance leader Aris Velouhiotis, a native of the town. Overlooking Lamía from the north is the fourteenth-century Catalan **castle**, which besides superb views houses an **archaeological museum** (both Tues–Sun 8.30am–3pm; €2 for museum) exhibiting a variety of finds from the Neolithic through to the Roman eras in a former 1850s-vintage barracks; the displays, mostly from nearby ancient tombs, are well arranged but often labelled in Greek only.

Practicalities

Buses, including a local service from Lianokládhi main-line **train station** (6km out, but in-town OSE office at Avérof 28, southwest of Platía Párkou), arrive at several scattered terminals, though none is much further than ten minutes' walk away from Platía Párkou. Services for Karpeníssi and western Fthiotídha in general call at a terminal at Márkou Bótsari 3, near the little-used, in-town train station on the Stylídha–Lianokládhi spur line; buses for Dhelfí and Tríkala stop out on Thermopýlon near the corner of Nikopóleos, past the train tracks; those for Vólos use a central stop at the corner of Kapodhistríou and Rozáki-Ángeli; while buses for Athens and Thessaloníki go from the corner of Papakyriazí and Satovriándou, near the Karpeníssi station. The most convenient **taxi** rank (red vehicles) is at the top end of Andhroútsou, behind the cathedral. **Drivers** will find **parking** nearly impossible in the centre, though the pay-and-display scheme appears to have been abandoned. Heart of the shopping district is **Platía Párkou**, with several **bank** ATMs around it, and the blue city-bus terminus, while west and uphill from here is diminutive **Platía Dhiákou**, with a few more cafés, the **post office** and an adjacent **Internet** café, Terminal.

Accommodation

Accommodation prospects in Lamía are noisily sited, but well priced and well maintained. On Rozáki-Angelí are two budget choices opposite each other, both renovated since 2003: the *Thermopyles* at no. 36 (Ⓣ22310 21366, Ⓕ22310 26645; ❸), in a mosaic-floored, 1960s building with en-suite a/c rooms, or the helpful *Athina* at no. 41 (Ⓣ22310 20700; ❸), which has the additional bonus of a car park. Moving up a notch, the *Apollonio* at one corner of Párkou (entrance at Hatzopoúlou 25; Ⓣ22310 22668, Ⓕ22310 23032; ❹) has medium-sized, double-glazed rooms.

Eating, drinking and nightlife

Lamía abounds in **eating and drinking** options, making it a good lunch-hour halt. Lunch options on or just off Platía Laoú include *Fytilis* at no. 6, a good all-rounder specializing in bacon-and-cheese-stuffed *biftéki*; the *Ilysia* at Kalyvá Bakoyiánni 10, offering a variety of reasonably priced *mayireftá*; and (best of all) *Ouzou Melathron*, in an old house up some steps at Aristotélous 3, with reasonably priced portions of rich Middle Eastern and Macedonian recipes washed down by Límnos wine, served in a pleasant courtyard in summer or a stunning interior. Nearby, Odhysséa Andhroútsou, a pedestrianized lane threading south-to-north between Laoú and Eleftherías, opens onto tiny Platía Kaïla with its fountain-spring, crammed full of attractive ouzerís; *Aman Aman*, *Odhos Onirou* (both dinner only) and *Alaloum* (lunch too, next to *Aman Aman*) are the best. The trendiest **nightlife** venues and **frappádhika**, their identities shifting yearly, cluster on Athanasíou Dhiákou between Platía Eleftherías and Platía Dhiákou.

East of Lamía: Paralía Rahón and Glýfa

The **Vólos-bound road** initially leads east along the coast of the shallow Maliakós Gulf. Once past the gritty industrial town of Stylídha, the first spot to tempt a stop – and the best place to break a journey between Athens or Lamía and Vólos – would be **PARALÍA RAHÓN**, 35km from Lamía, with scrappy beaches but stunning views south to mountainous horizons, and a lively boating culture. Among many **tavernas**, *To Yiousouri* (no sign, under two plane trees) is the place for seafood and good vegetarian *pikilíes*; *Kostas* at the far east end of the shoreline strip is the most popular meat specialist.

GLÝFA 26km further east (actually 11km off the resumed motorway) has better beaches but more importantly the mainland's northernmost ferry **crossing to Évvia**; if you miss the last departure (check times on ⓣ22380 61288), there's ample accommodation.

West of Lamía: Ypáti and Mount Íti

The road west from Lamía **towards Evrytanía** province traces the preternaturally lush Sperhiós Valley, with more pistachio orchards than Égina island, and glimpses south to mounts Íti, Gióna and Vardhoússia. Satisfying **hiking** is available on Mount Íti (the Classical Oeta), easiest approached from the village of Ypáti.

Mount Íti is one of the most beautiful of Greek mountains – its green northeast slopes constituting a national park – and also unusually accessible by Greek standards. Almost hourly buses cover the 22km from Lamía to Ypáti, the usual trailhead; if you arrive by train, these can be picked up en route at the main Lianokládhi station. Be sure not to get off the bus at Loutrá Ypátis spa, 5km before Ypáti proper.

Medium-sized **Ypáti** village clusters below a much-ruined Byzantine/Catalan castle. Though Loutrá Ypátis has most local **hotels**, Ypáti can offer the courteous, slightly dated *Panorama* (ⓣ22310 98222; April–Oct; ❷), just above the square, or the more comfortable *Arhondiko Ziaka* (ⓣ22310 98080, ⓦwww.xani.gr; open all year; ❹). There are a few reasonable **tavernas** and **ouzerís**, both on the platía and on the road into town.

Two topographic **maps** of Mount Íti are available, published by Road Editions (no. 43, 1:50,000, with route summaries in English) and Anavasi (no. 10, 1:50,000), also with a useful booklet in bilingual text. The classic **full traverse** of the range from Ypáti to Pávliani, taking in 2150-metre Pýrgos summit, takes about eleven hours, best spread over two days (described in reverse in *The Mountains of Greece*; see "Books" p.962). The flat-topped peak of Pyrá ("the pyre") is where in legend Hercules immolated himself to escape the agony of the poisoned tunic which his wife Deinaneira had given him. **PÁVLIANI**, with upper and lower quarters, has abundant **accommodation**, including the wood-and-stone-trimmed *Hotel Katerina* (Ⓣ22310 83009, Ⓦwww.hotelkaterina.gr; ❸), with a **taverna**, but patchy (if any) bus connections back to Lamía.

Alternatively, a rewarding **one-day outing** through Íti's sheer rock ramparts and lush meadows involves two overnights in Ypáti. The way uphill, starting from the square, is marked with red paint splodges or square placards; the actual path from the top of the village leads in around four hours to an EOS refuge at **Trápeza** (usually locked, but with a spring nearby). From there you could return on a different path via Zapandólakka to Ypáti for a circular hike.

Karpeníssi and around

West of Mount Íti, the **Karpenisiótis Valley** – heart of Evrytanía – is surrounded by dark fir forest and snow-fringed (Dec–May) mountains, a region promoted (with some justice) as "the Greek Switzerland". Skiing on **Mount Tymfristós (Veloúhi)** and springtime rafting or summer canyoning along local rivers are the main outdoor activities. Seasonal tourism, mostly domestic, is well established, such that accommodation prices in the region area are also authentically Swiss, boosted by a clientele of wealthy Athenians and Thessalonians, although reality has finally bitten, with arrival numbers stagnant and rates frozen. Budget travellers don't really get a look-in unless they're part of an organized adventure group. Many local businesses close weekdays in low season; we've listed more reliably open ones.

The main road in from Lamía, after scaling a spur of Mount Tymfristós, drops down to **KARPENÍSSI**; a 1400-metre tunnel below the snow line guarantees year-round access and spares drivers at least twice that distance of curvy road over the pass. Karpeníssi's site is spectacular – huddled at the base of the peak and head of the valley, which extends south all the way to wall-like Mount Panetolikó – but the town itself is entirely nondescript, having been destroyed in World War II by the Germans and again in the civil war.

Practicalities

Arriving **by bus** is inconvenient, since the KTEL has been exiled 1.5km out on the bypass road, though shuttles occasionally do a run into town, along main drag Zinopoúlou, to the leafy, café-table-crowded platía, its **taxi** rank and adjacent, basement tourist office (Mon–Sat 9am–2pm & 5–8pm, Sun 10am–2pm; Ⓣ22370 21016, Ⓦwww.karpenissi.gr). **Parking** in the centre is difficult and heavily controlled, so we've indicated lodging where this is easier.

Except on summer weekends or during skiing season, **accommodation** is easily found, if not inspiring; many of the eight hotels are noisy or overpriced, though bargaining at midweek is productive. Quiet budget **rooms** are to be found at *Kostas Koutsikos*, up some steps opposite the town hall (Ⓣ22370 80183; ❷), or the *Hotel Galini* (Ⓣ22370 22914; ❸) on Ríga Feréou 3, a backstreet (parking feasible) downhill from the main thoroughfare, 250m southeast of the *Panorama* restaurant (see p.306). For more comfort, try the externally unprepossessing *Hotel Elvetia*, Zinopoúlou 17 (Ⓣ22370 22465, Ⓦwww.elvetiahotel.gr; doubles ❺, suites ❻), where attractive communal areas (including an arcaded stone-and-wood bar) and helpful management make up for somewhat small rooms, or the chalet-style *Anesis*, Zinopoúlou 50 (Ⓣ22370 80700, Ⓦwww.anesis.gr; summer ❸, winter ❺), mainly worth it if you get one of the rooms with stunning valley views.

Eating options are surprisingly limited amidst a plethora of fast-food outlets, cafés and après-ski bars. The only real full-service tavernas downtown are the *Panorama* (lunch and dinner) at Ríga Feréou 18, well signed two blocks below an unfinished hotel, which offers well-executed *mayireftá* and grills in a tranquil garden, and newcomer *En Elladhi* just off the main square on Koutsímbou, with more hearty casserole fare.

The more reliable of two locally based **activity operators** is Ev Zein, beyond the *Anesis* at Zinopoúlou 61 (Ⓣ22370 80150, Ⓦwww.fzein-evryt.gr); their main rafting season is April to early May, at the Dhipótama site and on the Távropos River. Snow conditions at the downhill ski centre, 11km above town, can disappoint as the twelve runs and four chair lifts have a top point of only 2040m.

South of Karpeníssi

Your first conceivable stop in the Karpenisiótis Valley, 5km south of town, is the rather embalmed village of **KORYSKHÁDES**, its stone houses famous for their wooden balconies facing Mount Kaliakoúdha. All but ten of the permanent population have decamped, selling up to an enterprise which has meticulously restored or built six mansions as premier **accommodation** – rooms, suites and family apartments (Ⓣ22370 25102, Ⓦwww.korys.gr; summer ❹, winter weekends ❻). The only place to **eat** or **drink** is the scheme's *kafenío*-restaurant-breakfast salon, on the platía.

For villages with a more lived-in feel to them, return to the valley floor and head a kilometre or two downriver to the respective signposted turnings to Klafsí (east) and Voutýro (west). At the church-platía in **KLAFSÍ**, there are superb views, **rooms** offered by the Mathes brothers (Ⓣ22370 22397; ❸) and three tavernas; best of these is cosy *To Steki* (supper only), with smallish portions but also smallish prices, featuring *lahanodolmádhes*, *gardoúmba* (baked offal) and good bulk wine.

Up its own side-valley, **VOUTÝRO** has two **tavernas**, *O Avstralos* and *O Spithas*, on its square, plus a superior **inn**, ✱ *Amadryades* (Ⓣ22370 80909, Ⓦwww.amadryades.gr; rooms ❹, quad suites ❻), arrayed over two restored buildings dwarfed by a lawn-terrace (with parking underneath), where large rooms have fireplaces or balconies (or both), and a normal-priced café operates on-site (8am–midnight in season).

Megálo Horió and Gávros

From Karpeníssi it's 16km down the valley to Megálo Horió and Mikró Horió ("Big Village" and "Little Village"); buses make the trip from Karpeníssi twice daily. **MEGÁLO HORIÓ**, on the east side of the valley, is a pleasant if architecturally heterogeneous place set right under Mount Kaliakoúdha. There are several places to stay, but no bargains. The friendliest, best sited and least expensive is *Agnandi* (Ⓣ22370 41303 or 697 27 76 522; summer ❸, winter ❺), to your left on the approach road, which has modern but tasteful rooms with knockout views across the village to the mountains, and a communal ground-floor kitchen providing self-service breakfast (extra). There are no serious restaurants in the village centre; for meals head down to nearby **GÁVROS** on the valley floor. Among several **tavernas** lining the through road, *To Spiti tou*

Psara gets top marks for grilled trout, *píttes*, dips and local wine, with seating on the rear terrace overlooking the riverside trees. There's also **accommodation** here well worth considering, by the bridge and church: *Pension Agrambeli* (☎22370 41148; Ⓦwww.agrampeli.gr; all year; B&B summer ❸, winter ❹), with seven 2006-redone rooms, many with fireplace, self-catering area and stone floor; full buffet breakfast served in the bar-salon and a medium-size swimming pool sharing space on a riverside lawn.

Mikró Horió

MIKRÓ HORIÓ, visible opposite Megálo at the foot of Mount Helidhóna, was a major centre for the leftist ELAS resistance during World War II. Then on Sunday, January 13, 1963, after two weeks of uninterrupted rain, an avalanche wiped out most of the original village, killing thirteen (the death toll would have been far higher except that many locals were in church). The place was already under suspicion because of its wartime stance, and every government since the disaster has exerted pressure to move the survivors 4km downhill to the replacement community of **Néo** (New) **Mikró Horió**. Here "Swiss" pricing policies apply at the *Hellas Country Club* (☎22370 41570, Ⓦwww.countryclub.gr; summer ❺, winter ❼), where you can spend €350 on a luxury suite if you're so inclined; the best rooms face the garden and Mount Kaliakoúdha, while common facilities include a gym and café. There are a half-dozen other more reasonable **rooms** outfits lining the grid of streets in the purpose-built village, its stone-built houses not so wretched as many such disaster responses are. Two of the best, both well-signposted, are *Iy Gonia* near the top of the hill (☎22370 41393, Ⓦwww.giannakopoulos-g.gr; summer ❸, winter ❹), five stone-clad, fireplace rooms upstairs with mountain views and two apartments downstairs, or (200m downhill on the same street) the friendly *Fotini Zara*'s units (☎22370 41236; summer ❸, winter ❹), standard doubles or wood-panelled suites with fireplaces. The favourite local **taverna** is *To Horiatiko* down on what passes for the platía, with well-priced grills and *mayireftá*; book on ☎22370 41257 at peak times.

You might prefer to continue to road's end at **Paleó** (Old) **Mikró Horió**, where the five-room, en-suite *Xenonas Iy Helidhona* (☎22370 41221, Ⓦwww.ihelidona.gr; summer ❸, winter ❹) by the fountain complex and plane tree is the most reasonable lodging in the valley, with knockout views from Rooms 1 to 3 towards Mount Tymfristós. The serviceable ground-floor restaurant, *Iy Kyra Maria*, puts tables out under the tree by the spring in fair weather. Your alternative, by the church, is the lawn-fronted *Studio Merses* complex (☎22370 41444, Ⓦwww.merses.gr), with rustic-style doubles (summer ❹, winter ❺) and quad suites (€90–145) with fireplaces, enjoying the same views as the on-site bar-café where breakfast (extra) is served. The three-hour hike west **up Mount Helidhóna** (1973m) is indicated by blue or yellow waymarks, though the first half is along forestry track, rather than path. The other local sight is a small **natural lake** near the village entrance, the path there beginning by a memorial to the 1963 landslide victims, and signed in Greek ("Límni, 200m"). The lake proves pleasant and clean if shallow, swimmable in July or August.

Mount Kaliakoúdha

The eight-hour **hike** up and down **Mount Kaliakoúdha** (2098m), which dominates Megálo Hório, is one of the most popular outings in the Karpenisiótis Valley. There's a good, waymarked path much of the way, but some track-tramping near the top, and the final ascent conquers a pretty sharp grade – peak-bagging skills are essential. The route and its features are shown reasonably accurately on Anavasi Editions 1:50,000 map no. 13, *Karpenisi*

Prousos. With an early start, you'll polish off most of the 1250-metre altitude difference before the sun catches you.

From Megálo's square with its bars and cafés, head southeast, following painted red or yellow waymarks on walls until a proper path leaves the village. This passes one water source and climbs steadily through fir forest where many trees are dead or dying due to climate change, but the survivors provide welcome shade. About two hours above the village, and frequent crossing of the dirt track, the path ends temporarily just below the tree line at **Malakássa**, near the only other reliable **spring** this side of the mountain. You're forced onto the track for about another hour (unless you use some trail shortcuts) to a saddle at the northeast flank of the peak. The track continues down and south towards Stournára and Pandavréhi (see below); for Kaliakoúdha, head west and relentlessly up, following red-paint waymarks. The trail is poor to nonexistent, often strewn with scree, but there's little danger of getting lost and on a fine day you'll have company. Just under an hour (roughly 4hr from the village) should see you on the **summit** with its trig point; staggering **views** over central Greece are your reward. Vardhoússia and Íti loom to the east; the Ágrafa region unfolds beyond Mount Tymfristós to the north-northeast; while Mount Panetolikó approximates the provincial border south-southwest.

Due south lies Stournára village in the Krikellopótamos Valley, poised just above **Pandavréhi**, the other big local attraction, where waterfalls pour year-round from the walls of a narrow gorge of the Krikellopótamos. As there are no reliable facilities in Stournára, most people visit Pandavréhi by car; from the signposted junction just below Megálo Horió, it's 23km there along the track system.

Proussós village and Proussoú monastery

Beyond Gávros, the valley becomes a spectacular **gorge** with two narrows at Klidhí and Patímata tís Panayías ("Footsteps of the Virgin") before emerging at Dhipótama, the mingling of the Karpenisiótis and Krikellopótamos rivers to form the Trikeriótis, a site (with photogenic old bridge) much used by rafting outfitters. A paved if narrow and steep road through the canyon makes access to the monastery and village of **PROUSSÓS** (33km from Karpeníssi) straightforward, though only a few weekly buses call. The **monastery**, wedged into a cliff in a bend of a tributary to the Krikellopótamos, opposite two rock pinnacles, is flanked by two eighteenth-century defensive towers associated with revolutionary fighter Yiorgos Karaïskakis. Massive and repeatedly rebuilt after fires, **Proussoú** (its official name) is presently inhabited by just three monks, plus some layworkers. Coachloads of pilgrims collect holy water from the *ayíasma* and revere the resident icon in the tiny, frescoed ninth-century *katholikón* tucked under a rock overhang.

The village's houses, 1km further on, are dispersed across incredibly steep slopes, plagued by the sort of earth movements that did for Mikró Horió. The central neighbourhood has a drab, sporadically open community **hotel**, *Agathidis* (☎22370 80813; ❸), and two carnivorous tavernas by the central square; most reliable for a lamb-chop lunch is *O Platanos*, with tables under a plane tree.

Proussós to Náfpaktos

The road south of Proussós creeps over **Panetolikó**, dividing Evrytanía province from Étolo-Akarnanía, en route **to Náfpaktos**, a three-hour drive. This scenic route is entirely paved but there's no public transport, and the first 35km is extremely narrow and slow-going. Landslides are nibbling away at the pavement up to the Arapokefála pass in Panetolikó and a last panorama of Evrytanía, before the drop to Lambíri. This and subsequent villages up to Kallithéa have a wild, God-forsaken aspect; there's little evidence hereabouts of the tourism-based prosperity in the Karpenisiótis Valley. At livelier Kallithéa there are sweeping views of **Lake Trihonídha**, Greece's largest natural body of fresh water. It's largely for irrigational rather than recreational use, the shore by turns sheer or reedy except for beaches near Myrtiá, but in good ecological shape.

About ninety minutes out of Proussós you reach **THÉRMO**, a small town dominating a fertile upland invisible from the lake; it has a pleasant, plane-shaded square, a filling station, **bank** ATMs, shops, **tavernas** and regular **buses** to Agrínio if needed. Of potentially more interest is **ancient Thermon** (Tues–Sun 8.30am–3pm; free, photography forbidden), well signposted 1.5km southeast of the centre. This, still under excavation, was the walled political capital and main religious sanctuary of the Aetolians. The main temple, orientated north-to-south rather than the usual west-to-east, was dedicated to Apollo Thermios; just east lies an older, smaller shrine to Apollo Lyseios, while to the northwest are foundations of an Artemis temple. South of the main temple – off limits like much of the site – the sacred spring still flows, full of frogs. Beyond the spring extend two long *stoas* (with the occasional *exedra*), terminating at a *bouleuterion*. The keeper will unlock the small, one-room museum, crammed with unlabelled finds.

Beyond Thérmo the route drops to the intensely cultivated southeast lakeshore, climbing again over surprisingly green hills into the valley of the **Évinos River**, its lower reaches undammed. Accordingly, there are a handful of **rafting operators** near **Háni Baniás** at the river bridge, as well as restaurants and a *xenónas*; these work primarily March to May after increasingly rare rainy winters, with most clients day-tripping in from Náfpaktos, 15km further. Reversing these directions from Náfpaktos, take the road west of town signed as "Thérmo 46".

Routes west and north from Karpeníssi

Roads west or north from Karpeníssi thread through the **Ágrafa mountains**, the southernmost extension of the Píndhos. As with the Arapokefála saddle above Proussós, critical passes are generally closed in winter, but all summer they're open. Any of these routes is intrinsically enjoyable, and much the quickest way out in the directions indicated.

West to Agrínio or Amfilohía

The road west from Karpeníssi, then southwest to Agrínio, is well paved and broad, but extremely sinuous, so it still takes the daily bus from Karpeníssi three-and-a-half hours to cover the 114km (cars will make it in 3hr). The beauty of the first three-quarters of the journey until Áyios Vlássios cannot be overemphasized; it's empty country, with the only significant place being the double village of **FRANGÍSTA**, which straddles a compact valley – Anatolikí Frangísta, 39km from Karpeníssi, with six simple inns, and Dhytikí Frangísta, 3km further, offering more accommodation, a filling station and two **psistariés**. Beyond Frangísta, a causeway crosses the giant, surprisingly scenic **Kremastón reservoir** on the Tavropós, Trikeriótis and Ahelóös rivers, with two fish tavernas (exactly halfway to Agrínio) on the far side. Next, the route climbs again until the fir trees stop at Áyios Vlássios and a narrower road winds down through tobacco-planted hills to Agrínio.

With a sturdy car or motorbike, you can detour west over the Kremastón dam itself to emerge at Amfilohía in the same time as the journey to Agrínio. There are, however, 12km of bad dirt road before rejoining paved surface at Alevrádha and Petróna, and no facilities until Podhogorá.

North to Kardhítsa

Again with your own transport, one of the best options – giving direct access to the Metéora (see p.338) – is the **route north to Kardhítsa**, which begins from the top of the pass east of Karpeníssi, directly above the tunnel. Except for landslip-damaged stretches, the way is paved and wide, a beautiful drive where sweeping vistas of central Greece alternate with fir forest. It's 28km around Mount Tymfristós to **FOURNÁ** with its hotel, *Wild Beauty* (☎22370 51223; ③), if needed. Kardhítsa is 64km further, with little in-between other than **Loutropiyí** (*souvláki* stalls); **Loutrá Smokóvou** and its little spa; and Kédhros, with the first fuel since Karpeníssi, and where the road straightens out for the final flat approach to Kardhítsa. Allow just over two hours of driving from Karpeníssi.

Thessaly

The highlights of **Thessaly** are easily summarized. On the east, the mountainous **Pílio** (Pelion) peninsula curls down from the port-city of **Vólos**. Villages on its lush, orchard-covered slopes are among the most beautiful in the country – a long-established target for Greeks and foreigners, though still with unspoilt corners. To the west tower the unmissable, extraordinary "monasteries in the air" of the **Metéora**.

The **central plains** are for passing through, rather than visiting. That said, **Tríkala**, capital of the eponymous province, proves a relatively pleasant city, besides providing efficient connections by bus to nearby **Kalambáka**, gateway to the Metéora, and to Vólos (via dreary **Lárissa**).

Mountain ranges straddle or flank roads north or west from Lárissa. One dramatic route over the Píndhos, from Kalambáka to Ioánnina, is covered in Chapter 4, though the less-travelled but equally scenic passage from **Pýli towards Árta** is detailed on p.337. North from Kalambáka there are reasonable roads, if few buses, into western Macedonia, specifically the lakeside town of Kastoriá. Most travellers, however, head north from Lárissa towards Thessaloníki, an attractive route in the shadow of Mount Olympus; with your own transport it's worth detouring via the hill villages or underrated coast of **Mount Óssa**.

Vólos and around

The resolutely industrial outskirts of **VÓLOS** give little hint of Pílio's promise. Neither is it easy to imagine this busy modern port's mythological past, but 4km west lies the site of ancient Iolkos, from where Jason and the Argonauts legendarily embarked on their quest for the Golden Fleece. With a population approaching 150,000, Vólos ranks as the fifth-largest Greek town, rebuilt in utilitarian style after a series of devastating earthquakes between 1947 and 1957, and now edging to its natural limits against the Pílio foothills. University of

Thessaly students make it a lively place, and you could do worse than spend a few hours or even a night here while waiting for a bus into Pílio or a boat to the Sporades islands, for which Vólos is the **main port**.

Vólos was historically home to one of the larger **Jewish communities** of central Greece. Local Jews were well integrated into local social and political life, such that during World War II only 155 out of the thousand-strong community were detained and murdered by the Nazis; the rest joined the resistance (there's a monument to a Jewish ELAS-ite in Tsangarádha, caught and executed with six comrades in 1944) or were otherwise hidden on Mount Pílio. The unlucky victims have a prominent, sculpted memorial at one corner of Platía Ríga Feréou, just two blocks from the modern, post-earthquake synagogue.

Arrival and information

The nearest **airport**, receiving overseas charters (but not domestic flights), is 26km southwest, beyond Néa Anhíalos. Ferries and hydrofoils call at the **main quay**; most other services are found within a few blocks. An exception is the **KTEL** with its adjacent **taxi rank** and **city bus terminal** on Sekéri, just off Grigoríou Lambráki, ten minutes' walk southwest of the main square, **Platía Ríga Feréou**, with the **train station** just off the latter. **Drivers** should beware the comprehensive central pay-and-display schemes – either **park** in outlying residential areas, or use the covered car-park on Ógl. The following agencies rent cars for exploring Mount Pílio: Avis, Argonaftón 41 (Ⓣ24210 28880); Budget, Polyméri 27 (Ⓣ693 61 13 027); or helpful and efficient Hertz, Iássonos 90 (Ⓣ24210 22544).

Vólos has daily **car ferries** and – in summer – frequent hydrofoils or catamarans to the Sporades. Sporades Travel at Argonaftón 33 (Ⓣ24210 23400) is the central **agent** for Hellenic Seaways, open Sundays too; Vis Travel around the corner at Andonopoúlou 3 (Ⓣ24210 25666 or 24210 31059) represents Saos Ferries and the tiny "jet boats" to Tríkeri and northern Évvia. For information after-hours try the dockside port police (Ⓣ24210 38888).

Vólos has a helpful, cutting-edge "Information Centre" opposite the KTEL (April–Oct daily 8am–9pm, Nov–March Mon–Sat 8am–8pm, Sun 8am–3.30pm; Ⓦwww.volos.gr), with copious leaflets on every conceivable local topic. Commercial maps plus a selection of foreign-language books and magazines, can be found at Papasotiriou, on Dhimitriádhos, corner of Koumoundoúrou, or Newsstand, Iássonos 80. A CD books and electronics megastore (good for Greek and international CDs), at Ioánnou Kondarátou 9, has two free Internet terminals.

Accommodation

Hotels are fairly plentiful if not often great value, with a concentration of acceptable ones behind the port. Budget options (relatively speaking) include the double-glazed, air-conditioned *Iasson* (Ⓣ24210 26075; ❸), partly facing the port at Pávlou Melá 1 or, further out at Iatroú Tzánou 1, corner of Plastíra 16, the en-suite *Roussas* (Ⓣ24210 21732, Ⓕ24210 22987; ❸), easily the best deal so in demand, with relatively easy parking, convenience to tavernas, and helpful staff, though no breakfast facilities. Luxurious places include the well-sited *Park*, just inland from Platía Yeoryíou at Dheliyióryi 2 (Ⓣ24210 36511, Ⓦwww.amhotels.gr; ❻), a classic business hotel whose rooms, with dark walls, are on the small side, but well-equipped, with marble trim and state-of-the-art baths, and the 2006-refurbished *Xenia Domotel* in seafront grounds off Plastíra 1

(Ⓣ24210 92700, Ⓦwww.xeniavolou.gr; ❼), with a pool, spa, fitness centre and copious buffet breakfast.

The Town

The most attractive place to linger is along the eastern **waterfront esplanade**, between landscaped **Platía Yeoryíou** and the **archeological museum** (Tues–Sun 8.30am–3pm; €2). A lengthy overhaul has resulted in exemplary labelling and well-lit galleries, one reserved for changing exhibits. Highlights of the permanent collection include one of the best European assemblages of Neolithic (6500–3500 BC) figurines from various surrounding sites; faint but expressive painted grave stelae from Hellenistic Dimitrias depicting everyday scenarios of fifth-century BC life, with some inscriptions helpfully translated; and a massive quantity of items, including superb stone and gold jewellery, from tombs of all eras across Thessaly. Folk-art buffs might want to drop in at the nearby **Kitsos Makris Folk Art Centre** on Kítsou Makrí 38 (Mon–Fri 8.30am–12.30pm, Sun 10.30am–2pm), containing 25 paintings by naïve artist Theophilos (see p. 000).

Eating and drinking

Vólos specializes in one of Greece's most endearing and enduring institutions – the authentic **ouzerí** or **tsipourádhiko**, serving various *mezédhes* washed down not necessarily with ouzo but with *tsípouro*, the favoured spirit of the northern mainland. The western third of Argonaftón supports half-a-dozen (out of the city's reputed four hundred), adequate but pricey; most Voliots themselves go elsewhere, for example to *Iy Marina* out in Néa Ionía at Magnisías 13. To reach it, head out on Dheftéris Noemvríou, passing the drainage ditch, bear right at the stoplights onto Dhimokratías, then take the third left. Service can suffer, as it's just Marina at the grill and her son serving at tables outside, but each *tsípouro* comes with random titbits which might be *kténia* (scallops), grilled octopus or fish of the day. There are a few more such establishments on Nikifórou Plastíra, near the enormous Áyios Konstandínos church, poshest and most durable being *Monosandalos*, most reliably open evenings and all day weekends, with waterside seating and the house special, *garidhokrokétes* (shrimp patties). Continuing a few steps east to *Ta Palia Kalamakia* at Plastíra 10 will save you a few euros, sacrificing the direct sea view (but not quality) for grilled fresh squid or scaly fish in the cooler drawer. If seafood and ouzerís are not your thing, look no further than air-conditioned, pleasantly appointed *Haliambalias* (aka *Zafiris*; closed Sun), inland at pedestrianized Kondarátou 8, corner Skýrou; founded in 1947 and a lodestar of affordable *mayireftá*; the menu never varies much from vegetarian *tourloú*, baked *pérka* fish and a few stews. The daytime **frappádhiko** nucleus, with eight contenders, lies towards the pedestrianized east end of Argonaftón, by the main university building, the unmissable Art Deco Papastratos ex-tobacco factory.

Entertainment and nightlife

Concerts and plays are performed at either the open-air or covered **theatres** on Platía Ríga Feréou. There's a **summer cinema** off Platía Yeoryíou, the Exoraïstiki, unusually specialising in art-house fare; in winter film action moves to the Art Deco Ahilleion multi-plex on Koumoundoúrou. The most central nightlife zone, comprising intimate **live-music venues** and café-bars where

An Orthodox nation

The rituals of the Greek Orthodox church permeate every aspect of Greek society and, with over ninety-five percent of the population describing themselves as Orthodox, Greece is, in this sense, an extraordinarily homogeneous nation. For most, religion is a constant but almost unnoticed part of everyday life – taxi drivers cross themselves as they pass a church, not pausing for a moment in their animated discussion of last night's match; shoppers pop into the church to rest their feet and light a candle before continuing with the errands; and lamps are lit daily in front of icons in most homes.

Icon procession, Kárpathos, the Dodecanese ▲

The black-clad Papas or priest is an everyday sight, not just in the island villages – where as often as not he'll be a fixture in the kafenío – but also in the cities, astride a moped or out shopping.

Orthodox priest, Athens ▼

Easter

Easter is by far the biggest and holiest of the Orthodox festivals. On **Good Friday** images of Christ are taken from churches and paraded through the local town or village in a flower-strewn casket, symbolizing Christ's tomb. The highlight is on the evening of **Easter Saturday**, when everyone attends church carrying an unlit candle. At the stroke of midnight all the lights in every crowded church are extinguished, and the congregation plunged into the darkness which enveloped Christ as He passed through the underworld. Then there's a faint glimmer of light behind the altar screen before the priest appears, holding aloft a lighted taper and chanting *Avtó to Fós* ("This is the Light of the World"). Intoning *Dévte, Lévete Fós* ("Come, take the Light"), he touches the flame to the candles of the nearest worshippers. From here light spreads again throughout the church and out into the street as candles are lit from candles and the cry of "*Christos Anesti*" ("Christ is Risen") rings out everywhere, along with a wilder celebration of fireworks and food to break the fast.

If you have the inclination to listen, the chanting from midnight to 2am in the half-empty churches is actually the most beautiful part of the Resurrection liturgy. Most worshippers, however, have long since taken their candles home through the streets; they are said to bring good fortune to the house if they arrive still burning. On reaching the front door it is common practice to make the sign of the cross on the lintel with the flame, leaving a black smudge visible for the rest of the year.

Although Easter celebrations follow the same broad pattern throughout Greece, there are plenty of local twists. Easter Saturday on **Corfu**, for example, sees locals throwing great ceramic pots (often filled with water to increase the dramatic impact) out of their windows to smash on the ground. And on **Híos**, a very un-Christian war breaks out every Easter, when two rival churches in the town of Vrondádhos fire thousands of home-made fireworks at each other, in an attempt to hit the other's bell during the service.

Breaking the fast

Many Greeks still **fast** in the week leading up to Easter weekend (or even for the whole of Lent), when restaurants serve special fasting dishes known collectively as **nistísima** which avoid meat, dairy, fish and even olive oil and wine at the most extreme. The fast is traditionally broken in the early hours of Easter Sunday with a meal of **mayerítsa**, a soup made from lamb's tripe, rice, dill and lemon. The rest of the lamb will be roasted on a spit to be eaten for lunch, a festive meal that is likely to continue for the rest of the day. The Greek equivalent of **Easter eggs** are red-painted hard-boiled eggs, which are baked into twisted, sweet bread-loaves (*tsourékia*) or distributed on Easter Sunday. People rap their eggs against their friends' eggs, and the owner of the last uncracked egg is considered lucky.

The holy flame

The flame from which all the Easter candles are lit has its source at Christ's Tomb in the Church of the Holy Sepulchre in Jerusalem; here the Patriarch of the Greek Orthodox church celebrates the ceremony of the Holy Fire each Holy Saturday. From here it is transported every year on a special flight to Athens, and distributed within hours by land, sea and air to churches throughout the country.

▲ Girls in traditional costume, Kárpathos, the Dodecanese

▼ Traditional Easter loaves and red-painted eggs

▼ Lighting Easter candles

Byzantine fresco of Áyios Yitóryios (St George) ▲

Orthodox priest, western Macedonia ▼

Name days

In Greece, everyone gets to celebrate their birthday twice a year. More important, in fact, than your actual birthday, is the feast day of the saint whose moniker you share – their **name day**. Greek ingenuity has stretched the saints' names (or invented new saints) to cover almost every single forename, so even pagan Dionysos or Socrates get to celebrate. If yours isn't covered, no problem – your party is on All Saints' Day, eight weeks after Easter.

The big name day **celebrations** (such as for Iannis and Ianna on January 7, and Yioryios on April 23) can involve thousands of people, and tradition guarantees that families get to celebrate together. In most families, for example, the eldest boy is still named after his paternal grandfather, and the eldest girl after her grandmother, so that all the eldest cousins will share the same name, and the same name day. Any church or chapel bearing the saint's name will mark the event – some smaller chapels will open just for this one day of the year – while if an entire village is dubbed after the saint, you can almost guarantee a festival.

Ancient echoes

Many Greek Easter traditions can trace their lineage to ancient Greek customs and practices. The ceremonies around the **rebirth of light**, above all, closely mirror the ancient worship of Persephone, daughter of Demeter, goddess of the earth. In legend, Persephone was banished to the darkness of Hades for the winter, returning joyously to the light of day every spring. Greek children often wear a red-and-white band – a Marti or March thread – around their wrists throughout Lent. Initiates of the Mysteries of Eleusis, heart of the cult of Demeter and Persephone, wore exactly such bands of red and white wool around their wrists.

conversation is possible, fills the grid of pedestrianized lanes east of Koumoundoúrou and north of Dhimitriádhos; a few indoor **clubs** survive at the west edge of town near the KTEL, particularly on Lahaná.

Around Vólos: Dimini, ancient Sesklo, Néa Anhíalos and Tekkés Farsálon

Ancient Dimini (Tues–Sun 8.30am–3pm; €2), west of Vólos, preserves its circuit of low Neolithic walls and exposed foundations, plus two Mycenaean tholos-type tombs; only the one with a collapsed dome, inside the Neolithic town, is visitable. Adjacent sprawls a vast Mycenaean palace complex (closed for excavations) which is thought to be ancient Iolkos. Vólos city bus #8 covers the 3km to modern Dhimíni village, 400m away.

You'll need your own transport to reach **ancient Sesklo** (Tues–Sun 8.30am–3pm; €2), 15km from Vólos. The acropolis, inhabited from about 7000 to 3000 BC, occupies the hill of Kastráki overlooking a secluded valley near modern Sésklo. Vividly coloured pottery, displayed at the Vólos museum, was the distinguishing feature of the local culture.

NÉA ANHÍALOS, 17km southwest of Vólos, was settled post-1923 by wine-making refugees from the Bulgarian Black Sea coast, atop two ancient predecessors: Pyrassos and Phthiotic Thebes. Ruins of the latter (daily 8.30am–3pm; free), specifically several **early Christian basilicas,** may prove frustrating as none of their intricate mosaic floors are viewable. Of more interest is the long beach of coarse red-brown sand – best on the Pagasitic, with showers and shade from tamarisks. *To Yiousouri* is the best of an average lot of *tsipourádhika* on the front; there are also two hotels.

Tekkés Farsálon (Turbali Tekke)

About 25km west of Néa Anhíalos stands the largest rural Muslim monument in Greece, the **Tekkés Farsálon (Turbali Tekke)**, a lodge of Bektashi dervishes, the dominant Islamic mystical order in the Balkans during Ottoman times. To reach it, leave the E75 at the Aerinó exit and follow signs through Perívleptos, forking right (northwest) at the village outskirts towards the border with Lárissa province; just beyond the pass marking it, some 12km from the motorway, a fading signpost points south to "Moní (Monastery) Tekké Farsálon". Ascend the steep, 400-metre track indicated to the spring-fed oasis here; the *tekkés*, studded by prominent cypresses, is a short walk uphill.

To one side, the large stone-and-plaster complex – the actual Bektashi "monastery" – is derelict, though it was inhabited by Albanian-speaking Tsamídhes until 1964. Of primary interest are the two sixteenth-to-seventeenth-century, domed *türbes* (**marabouts**) with schist-slab roofs on your left, arcaded on their east side. The northerly building, built of brick and rubble, has gaily painted stalactite vaulting and floral decoration on its portal. Below the portico, a small graveyard musters calligraphic headstones of perhaps twenty dervishes, with the ornate grave of the last *şeyh* or spiritual leader to one side. Up in the *türbes*, and in a newer linking structure, are tombs of five more *şeyhs* and a trio of Ottoman-era warriors. All are still venerated with floral offerings, candles, libation water and bath-towels draped over the sarcophagi – most likely by the villagers of nearby Lefkóyia, Christianized descendants of the dervishes. Throughout former Ottoman territory, it is still common for the closest such shrine to be tended by locals of whatever creed, to obtain favours from the saintly deceased.

The Mount Pílio (Pelion) peninsula

The **Mount Pílio peninsula**, with its lush orchards of apple, pear and nut trees and dense forests of beech and oak, seems designed to confound stereotypical images of Greece. Scarcely a rock is visible along the slopes, and water gurgles up from fountains or aqueducts beside every track; summer temperatures here can be a good 5°C cooler than on the baking Thessalian plains. Pílio was reputedly the haunt of the mythical centaurs – thus the name *Kentavros* (Centaur) for various hotels and bars – and the site of revelries by ancient gods.

Pílio **villages** are often spread out widely due to the easy availability of water, their various quarters linked by winding cobbled paths. The mountain formed a semi-autonomous district throughout the Ottoman era, and during the eighteenth century became a nursery for Greek nationalism and culture, fostered by church-sponsored education and a revival of **folk art** and **traditional architecture**. There is also a distinct regional **cuisine**, with specialities such as *spedzofáï* (sausage and pepper casserole) and *gídha lemonáti* (goat stew with lemon sauce); seafood is often garnished with *krítamo* (pickled rock samphire) or *tsitsíravla* (pickled April-shrubbery shoots). To wash it down, palatable wine from the Dhimitra Co-op at Néa Anhíalos is widely available. Herbs, fruit, home-made preserves and honey are important local products and souvenirs; the only significant non-touristic enterprises are timber-cutting, quarrying of the famous local schist stone, and nurseries propagating every sort of shade-loving plant.

Many communities have changed little in appearance over the centuries, and their ornate mansions, churches and sprawling platíes – invariably shaded by vast plane trees, and flanked by *kafenía* or *tsipourádhika* – make rewarding targets. Distinctive, stone-roofed **churches** are built low and wide, often with a detached bell tower, marble reliefs on the apse and interior ornamentation with carved wood. Two villages, **Makrynítsa** and **Vyzítsa**, have been designated as protected showpieces, but almost every place offers attractions.

Add the delights of numerous excellent **beaches**, plus various recognized **hiking** routes (see box, p.316), and you have a recipe for an instant holiday idyll – or disaster, if you time it wrong. Lying conveniently between Athens and Thessaloníki, Pílio is a long-established favourite with Greek holiday-makers, who inundate the place at Eastertime or Christmas week, mid-summer and during any three-day weekend year-round. At such times you're pushing your luck to show up without a reservation, when – in any case – prices are among the highest on the mainland. Additionally, many mansions restored as accommodation are typically unattended, their owners absent in Vólos unless they know they'll have customers; it's essential to reserve such lodging in advance year-round.

Arriving fairly directly in Pílio **from overseas** is now possible, thanks to May–October charter flights to either Skiáthos (frequent) or Néa Anhíalos (Almyrós) airport, near Vólos (Fridays), followed by a short transfer. Package companies monopolize most such flights, so tickets on a flight-only or fly-drive basis are scarce.

Getting around the peninsula

The peninsula divides into three regions, the best concentration of traditional communities lying just **north and east** of Vólos and along the **northeast coast**. The **southwest coast** up to Áfyssos is less memorable, with concentrated development along the Pagasitic Gulf despite no decent beaches. The **far south**,

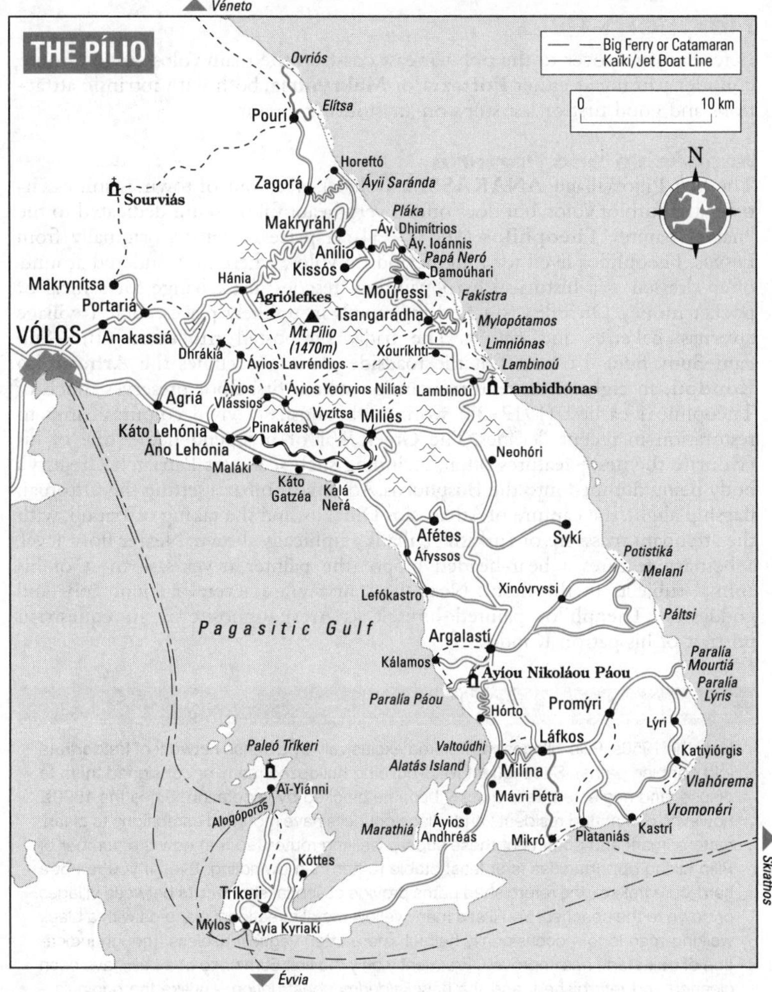

relatively low-lying and sparsely populated, has just two major resorts – Plataniás and Milína – plus a few inland villages.

Travelling around can be tricky without your own transport. **Buses** to the east cover two main routes: Vólos–Hánia–Zagorá and Vólos–Tsangarádha–Áyios Ioánnis, with scarce services linking Zagorá and Tsangarádha to complete a loop. The far south is equally infrequently served with departures to Milína, Tríkeri, Plataniá and Katiyiórgis, though the respective northern and western highlights Makrynítsa and Vyzítsa both have more frequent connections, as does Áfyssos.

Alternatives include **renting a car** in Vólos or walking. Any transport mode means slow progress, since perilously narrow roads snake around ravine contours, seemingly never getting closer to villages just across the way.

Northern Pílio

Before crossing over to the popular east coast on the main Vólos–Zagorá route, consider pausing at either **Portariá** or **Makrynítsa**, both with intrinsic attractions and good first or last stops on any touring circuit.

Anakassiá and Portariá

The first Pílio village, **ANAKASSIÁ** (Iolkós), 4km out of town, is still essentially a suburb of Vólos, but does offer a very beautiful museum dedicated to the "naive" painter **Theophilos** (1873–1934). A prize eccentric, originally from Lésvos, Theophilos lived for long periods in Vólos, where he wandered around, often dressed as a historical hero, painting frescoes in exchange for a meal or pocket money. On Pílio you find his murals in unlikely places, such as village tavernas, bakeries and *kafenía*. The badly signposted **museum** (Tues–Sun 8am–3pm; free) – turn off at the roadside platía – occupies the **Arhondikó Kondoú**, an eighteenth-century mansion whose first floor preserves much of Theophilos's earliest (1912–27) work, with unusually vivid colours thanks to restoration in recent decades. The Greek War of Independence – one of his favourite themes – features often, including such scenes as Patriarch Gregory's body being dumped into the Bosphorus, Admiral Tombazis setting the Ottoman flagship alight, the capture of Athanasios Dhiakos, and the taking of Tripoli, with the attendant massacre of Turkish civilians graphically shown. Nearer floor level, a bestiary features a bear-headed hippo (the painter never saw most of his animal subjects in the flesh). Near the stairway are several ancient gods and goddesses (Theophilos painted himself as Ares); opposite is an equestrian portrait of his patron Kondos.

Walking on Mount Pílio

Until the 1950s, Pílio villages were linked exclusively by a dense network of **kalderímia** (old cobbled paths). Subsequent road-building bulldozed many or consigned them to disuse, and neglected trails quickly became blocked by vegetation. Since the 1990s, however, committed residents and village councils have mounted campaigns to clean, restore, mark and document these superb walking routes, so that now the number of Pílio hiking opportunities is at least stable rather than dwindling. Even if you're not a hard-core trekker, the refurbished paths provide essential **short-cuts** between villages or down to the beaches. You'll see many yellow metal directional placards with a black walking-man logo – occasionally helpful, more often vaguely useless, though indication of trail-starts has improved. Frequently only the first 50m or so of a trail have been cleaned and refurbished, and the new *kalderími* construction – unlike the originals – has been done too superficially to last.

The best **walking seasons** are late April through early June, and early September through October; summer is hot and humid, and the winter mist- and snow-line in the north can dip well below the villages. If you're serious about hiking here, obtain Anavasi's 1:25,000 **map** *Pílio* (covering the centre of the peninsula) plus their 1:50,000 *North Pílio-Mavrouvoúni* and *South Pílio* sheets. Road Editions' 1:50,000 map no. 33 *Pílio* is a good touring map, but does not trace all paths or minor roads accurately. Nikos Haratsis' *A Hiker's Guide to Mount Pelion* (Epikinonia Editions, Vólos) has non-scale, hand-drawn maps, and some imprecise or obsolete text directions; the Vólos Information Centre hands out extracts. Lance Chilton's *Walks in The Pilion* (with detailed map; see "Books", p.962) is excellent, but does not estimate hiking times, and covers only the east-coast villages from Anílio to Tsangarádha. In this chapter, we have indicated the most useful routes, with estimated times, start points and brief summaries.

PORTARIÁ, 14km east of central Vólos, grew up around the tiny, frescoed Byzantine chapel (1273) of Panayía tis Portariás. Regrettably, areas closest to the busy road have become tacky and commercialized (including a convenient **ATM**), but the backstreets are still rewarding. The chief glory, as so often in Pílio, is the main square, shaded by tremendous plane trees, one planted in 1220; nearby, the *Belle Époque Hotel Theoxenia*, once the grandest in the Balkans – where Venizelos stayed during its prime – is being restored. **Accommodation** comprises a dozen-plus traditional mansions and conventional hotels; much the best of the former is *Despotiko* (Ⓣ24280 99046, Ⓦwww.despotiko-portaria.com; B&B summer ④, winter ⑤), down a *kalderími* from the big church and playground. Guest rooms with contemporary furnishings occupy the most sumptuous *arhondikó* in the village; breakfast and café staples are served inside the former stables opposite, or on a sunny terrace in the lovely grounds. Among hotels, the clear winner is *Kritsa* on the platía (Ⓣ24280 99121, Ⓦwww.hotel-kritsa.gr; summer ③, winter ④), an interwar building tastefully refurbished into an eight-room hotel (including two suites at ④) of top standard; the hearty €8 breakfasts, with their array of breads, cheese, eggs, turnovers and savoury titbits, are a model of what hotel breakfasts should be. **Eating** out, the congenial dining room of the *Kritsa* stands head and shoulders above the rest, with large portions, professional service, proper table linen and specialities such as parsley-purée dip, *hórta mé avga (*eggs with greens*),* Skópelos olive biscuits and a hearty rendition of *spetzofái*, accompanied by excellent local wine.

Makrynítsa

From Portariá you can detour 2km northwest to **MAKRYNÍTSA**, 17km from Vólos, where stone houses straggle picturesquely 200m down the mountainside. Founded in 1204 by refugees from the Fourth Crusade's sacking of Constantinople, it offers six churches plus a monastery, and various **traditional mansions** – many restored as accommodation. Inevitably, the main lane into the centre is blighted by tatty souvenir shops, and plenty of (Greek) day-trippers, but both are easy to escape, and the views are splendid.

Most impressive of the churches are **Áyios Ioánnis**, next to the fountain on the shady main platía, and the beautiful eighteenth-century **monastery of Panayía Makrynítissa**, beneath the clocktower. The marble relief work on Áyios Ioánnis' apse, plus that on the fountain opposite, are among the best of its type in Greece. A few paces above the Áyios Ioánnis square there's a **Theophilos fresco** in the right-hand café, showing revolutionary chieftain Katsandonis and his men merry-making.

If you are looking for a **challenging walk**, Makrynítsa is the starting point for the three-and-a-half-hour trek to the deserted, frescoed **monastery of Sourviás**, mostly on *kalderími* and path surface. The route starts from a steep cement track west of the monastery of Ayíou Yerasímou, though trail resumes for most of the way once Makrynítsa is out of sight.

Accommodation in Makrynítsa abounds. Among the more affordable options, all just above the lane in from the Platía Bráni car park, are *Theophilos* (Ⓣ24280 99435; summer ②, winter ④), with bright, salubrious if rather kitsch rooms; cosy, en-suite *Arhondiko Routsou* (Ⓣ24280 99090; summer ②, winter ④); and the *Arhondiko Repana* (Ⓣ24280 99067, Ⓕ24280 99548; ③), its rooms a bit over-restored but the best value here. Drivers are better off at more upmarket lodgings along the road descending just before Platía Bráni. Best of these, about 300m along on the right (inconspicuous sign) is *Arhondiko Pandora* (Ⓣ24280 99404, Ⓦwww.pandoramansion.gr; ⑥–⑦), with deceptively large grounds behind the gate, including a café-restaurant serving meals in the lovely courtyard.

Seven rooms and suites are unique and tastefully appointed, as you'd expect from an architect-owner. There are a few rather commercialized **tavernas** right on the platía; it's best to continue 100m beyond, along a gravel path, to *Alfa ke Vita*.

Hánia and Agriólefkes

Beyond Portariá, the road hairpins up to the **Hánia Pass** and the cheerless eponymous "village", a string of modern houses and hotels which see little use except in winter. A minor road leads 4km southeast to the **Agriólefkes ski resort** (two lifts and three runs plus a long nordic piste; top point 1473m); it's open January to March (daily 9am–4pm) as a rule, into April if snow permits. Once past Hánia, the view opens to encompass the whole northeast coast of the peninsula as you spiral down to a fork: the left turning leads to Zagorá, the right towards Tsangarádha.

The northeast Pílio coast

Pílio's best (and most popular) beaches, and its lushest scenery, are found on the Aegean-facing **northeast coast**, which bears the brunt of winter storms. A relatively humid climate and shady dells nurture exotic flowers such as hydrangeas, gardenias and camellias, locally bred and sold at the roadside. The "county town" of the region is **Zagorá**, self-proclaimed apple capital of Greece.

Zagorá and Pourí

The largest Pílio village, **ZAGORÁ** has a life more independent of tourism than others, though studies give the fruit orchards only until the year 2020 to survive, owing to depleted soil and overuse of pesticides. Other crops (kiwis, raspberries) are being considered as a potential breakaway from apple monoculture.

Visitors often jump to unfavourable conclusions from the workaday main street where the bus calls; in fact, there are four well-preserved and architecturally varied parishes with handsome Neoclassical mansions, arrayed around the squares of **Ayía Paraskeví**, **Ayía Kyriakí**, **Áyios Yeóryios** and **Metamórfosis (Sotíra)**, strung out over 5km. Coming from Vólos, turn left at the first filling station to find Ayía Paraskeví (Perahóra), with its pleasant, unvisited platía. Ayía Kyriakí is effectively the centre of Zagorá. Bearing left away from the turning for Horeftó will bring you to the broad platía of Áyios Yeóryios, in the shadow of its plane tree and beautiful eighteenth-century church, while Sotíra lies beyond this, above the road to Pourí.

The prime **accommodation** choice in Zagorá is impeccably restored ✱ *Arhondiko Gayanni* (Ⓣ24260 23391, Ⓦwww.villagayannis.gr; B&B summer ④, winter ⑤), a gorgeous three-storey mansion dating from 1770, with a beautiful garden, ample parking, genial hosts and copious breakfasts. Families should head for the *Xenonas Stefania* on the road to Horeftó (Ⓣ24260 23666, Ⓦwww.pelion.com.gr/stefania.htm; summer ③, winter ④), whose air-conditioned studios with fireplaces and terraces sleep up to four. Zagorá has more budget lodging than elsewhere nearby, for example friendly *Yiannis Halkias* (Ⓣ24260 22159; ②), in Áyios Yeóryios by the turning for Horeftó. All four parishes host **grill-tavernas**, though best-in-show are *Tsipouradhiko To Meïdani* by the roadside in Sotíra, where you fight for one of the few seats on the flower-lined balcony, and *O Petros* (alias *Fani's*; open all day every day), off the *kalderími* above Áyios Yeóryios square, where the quality of the cooking and views over the church to the Sporades offset somewhat small portions. There's also a **post office** in Áyios Yeóryios and a bank **ATM** in Ayía Kyriakí.

The road beyond Zagorá continues to **POURÍ**, one of the remotest – and most spectacularly sited – communities on Pílio. Theoharis Hiotis rents **rooms** (☎24260 23168; ❷) in his modern pension 250m beyond the square; the only **taverna** is *To Balkoni*, below the square. The nearest beach is **Elítsa**, 4km below by paved, then dirt, road; it's tiny and functional, but a welcoming **taverna**, *Plymari*, straddles the final approach. Superior **Ovriós** beach is reached by a different track off from the Elítsa road just below the village. Pourí is also a major trailhead for ambitious **treks** such as the seven-hour hike to Makrynítsa, or the eight-hour expedition to Véneto, the northernmost village in Pílio, via abandoned Paleá Mintzéla. Both require more stamina, planning and orientation skills than the usual Pílio outing.

Horeftó

Eight twisting kilometres down the mountain, **HOREFTÓ** (infrequent bus from Zagorá) makes an excellent coastal base. There is ample choice of **beaches**: a long, decent one in front of this former fishing village; secluded Áyii Saránda 2km south (see below); and two coves at Análipsi, just north – a brief hike brings you to the first cove, a little paradise popular with nudists and rough campers taking advantage of a spring behind the sand. Determined explorers can follow the coastal path for twenty minutes more to the northerly cove, road-accessible and rockier. There are also two hour-long *kalderímia* up to Zagorá, which can be combined to make an enjoyable loop.

Horeftó supports half-a-dozen hotels and an equal number of studio apartments for rent. The best-value and best-located **hotels** – near the quieter, south end of the shoreline road – are the high-standard *Hagiati* (☎24260 22405, Ⓦwww.pelion.com.gr/hagiati.htm; all year; ❹), with off-street parking, spacious garden bar, wheelchair access and fridges in the mostly sea-view rooms, or the simpler *Erato* (☎24260 22445; ❸), a 1970s block with partial sea views and fridges. There's a basic municipal summer **campsite** (no phone) beyond these two hotels; continue past this to the signposted and very useful shortcut up to Makryráhi, saving the long way around back through Zagóra. This passes the steep, one-kilometre driveway down to **Áyii Saránda** beach, 700m of sand punctuated by rock outcrops (one with a whimsical statue on top), halting just below one of the liveliest day-and-night **clubs** in the region, with paddle-ballers out in force and nocturnal noise making the non-en-suite rooms (❶) above the lone, basic **taverna**, *In Front of the Sea*, a bit of a non-starter.

Eating options in Horeftó are decent, with our recommendations open much of the year. *O Petros* is a meat specialist, while its affiliate *Petros O Sogrambos* does only seafood. *Ta Dhelfinia* by contrast is a popular and very reasonable *mayireftá* taverna, with grills at weekends.

Kissós

The easterly option at the junction below Hánia leads through resolutely untouristy Makryráhi, a perennial traffic bottleneck; north-facing Anílio ("Sunless"); and the upper edge of Áyios Dhimítrios before reaching the turning for **KISSÓS**. Virtually buried in foliage 1km off the main road, its residential quarters ascend in terraces either side of eighteenth-century **Ayía Marína**, one of the finest churches on the peninsula. It's frequently open, especially Sunday, but you can always admire fine frescoes around the south door. The interior of this three-aisled basilica contains an extravagant *témblon* and hard-to-see ceiling frescoes.

Accommodation here tends to be simple but good value, for example the modern, bland *Rooms Sofia Gloumi-Hanou* (☎24260 31267 or 697 28 21 841; ❸), uphill from the multilevel platía – the largest on the mountain – with limited parking and an evening-only *psistariá* downstairs. The smallish rooms at *Xenonas Kissos* (☎24260 31214; ④, also triples and quads), opposite the church, have wood trim, bright curtains and fridges. Its ground-floor **taverna**, *Iy Klimataria*, has a fine terrace, but the more prosaically set *Ta Pende Fi* (aka *Makis*) across the street pips it for value with *mayireftá* (such as rabbit stew, broccoli, potato croquettes, beans) all year, plus grills in high season.

Áyios Dhimítrios and Áyios Ioánnis

Heading for the coast instead, you tackle 6km of twisting paved road via **ÁYIOS DHIMÍTRIOS**, whose main bright spot is a **taverna** on the lowermost Platía Xyróvrysi, *Ta Pende Platania* (dinner daily May–Sept, also lunch Aug), named for the five plane trees which grace the square and a reliable source of eminently reasonable, simple and salubrious grills with vegetable *mezédhes*.

ÁYIOS IOÁNNIS, 2km below, was once the port and boatyards for Áyios Dhimítrios but is now eastern Pílio's main resort. Numerous hotels and *dhomátia* were erected during the 1980s to a density no longer allowed, but despite this, finding a bed here in peak season is as problematic as anywhere on the peninsula. Budget **accommodation** options include the *Hotel Marina* (☎24260 31239 or 24260 31097; ②), in a peaceful cul-de-sac at the south end of the strip. With a bit more to spend, try the tasteful *Anesis* (☎24260 31123, Ⓦwww.hotelanesis.gr; ③), with a slightly alternative ambience and pastel-coloured rooms; the *Sofokles* (☎24260 31230, Ⓦwww.sofokleshotel.com; ⑤), towards the northern end of the front, with a stone-walled lounge, sea views from most of the rooms, and an attractive terrace-pool; or the somewhat impersonal but comfortable *Aloe* (☎24260 31240; ⑤), sprawling just inland behind its garden.

Restaurants along the front are mostly similar and touristy, but *Poseidhonas* proves an excellent, all-year seafood taverna kept by a fishing family who only purvey their own fresh catch – and who therefore can run out of food early. For something unusual, well-signed *Ostria* uphill features Mediterranean recipes making use of herbs and strong flavourings – proprietress Hariklia spent years in Florence, so pasta dishes are prominent; reserve tables in season (☎24260 32132).

The **beach** at Áyios Ioánnis, though of average quality, is equipped with windsurf boards for rent. For more ambitious activities, such as sea-kayaking or mountain-biking, contact local travel agency Les Hirondelles (☎24260 31181, Ⓦwww.les-hirondelles.gr), which also represents most of the ocean-view studios in the area. For a quieter time and finer sand, walk either ten minutes north to **Pláka** beach, with a young, Greek clientele and popular beach bar-taverna, or fifteen minutes south (past the summer **campsite**) to **Papá Neró** beach, the best tanning spot in the vicinity, and accordingly cluttered with sunbeds. At sea level, cars are banned all day in summer, and there are just a few **rooms** for rent – such as *Iy Orea Ammoudhia* (☎24260 31219, Ⓔpapanero@internet.gr; Easter–Oct; ③), pine-and-tile-bedecked rooms with sea view. Downstairs is the better of two **tavernas** here, known also as *Papoutsis* after the founder; the fare's a mix of humbler fish species and *mayireftá*, with nice touches like *toursí* (pickled vegetables) mix and samphire on the salads, plus real table linen.

Damoúhari

South of Áyios Ioánnis's campsite, a narrow paved road leads up over a low ridge and down through olive groves to **DAMOÚHARI** hamlet, bordering a stageset-perfect port indeed used for film shoots. The construction of a broader road down from Moúressi ended its seclusion, and villas have sprung up mushroom-like amongst the olive trees. However, cars are excluded from the shoreline, which offers a large pebble beach, the overgrown ruins of a Venetian castle, and several **tavernas**, most atmospheric being fish specialist *Barba Stergios*, though *Karagatsi* opposite is more reliably open at lunch. Top **accommodation** choice here is the attractive, unobtrusive *Hotel Damouhari* (Ⓣ24260 49840, Ⓕ24260 49841; ④), a "village" of stone-built studio cottages and rooms below a small infinity pool, with antiques and wood trim in the rooms and *objet-trouvé* decor in its *Kleopatra Miramare* bar. There's an excellent waterside annexe of five state-of-the-art rooms (③), above the *Karagatsi*.

From Damoúhari, you can **walk to Tsangarádha** in 75 minutes, a popular and rewarding trip (though most folk do it downhill in under an hour). At the mouth of the ravine descending to the larger bay, a spectacular *kalderími* begins its steep ascent, allowing glimpses of up to six villages simultaneously, plus the Sporades on a clear day, from points en route. Then there is deep shade, and a potable spring approaching Ayía Kyriakí; the path emerges in the Ayía Paraskeví quarter of Tsangarádha, just downhill from the post office.

Tsangarádha

TSANGARÁDHA is the largest northeastern village after Zagorá, though it may not seem so at first, since it's also divided into four distinct quarters – south to north, **Taxiárhes, Ayía Paraskeví** (**post office** and bank **ATM**), **Ayía Kyriakí** and **Áyios Stéfanos** – strung along several kilometres of road. Each of these focuses on a namesake church and platía, the finest being **Ayía Paraskeví**, shaded by reputedly the heftiest plane tree in Greece – about a thousand years old, and requiring eighteen men to encircle – and Taxiárhes, with a tree nearly as large and a four-spouted fountain from 1909. More Taxiárhes botanical prodigies are found at the **Serpentin Garden** (visits by appointment only, Ⓣ24260 49060, Ⓦwww.serpentin-garden.com), a hillside Eden featuring many heirloom roses and other rare plants.

Most local **accommodation** is overpriced and/or along the noisy main road. Exceptions include *Arhondiko Hatzakou* (Ⓣ24260 49911; ④), a somewhat over-modernized mansion well below the highway in Taxiárhes; or the good-value *Konaki Hotel* (Ⓣ24260 49481; ③), just south of the Ayía Paraskeví square but set back from the road. All rooms have fridges and views, some have balconies, and there's a pleasant basement breakfast area. Just off Ayía Paraskeví's platía, *The Lost Unicorn* (Ⓣ24260 49930, Ⓦwww.lostunicorn.com; shut one month winter; B&B ⑤), under the sympathetic management of Claire and Christos Martzos, scores as much for its common areas – kitted out like a British gentlemen's club – and champagne breakfasts as for the eight antique-furnished, terrazzo-floored rooms in the 1890s building; a roof terrace is planned, and a pricey on-site "continental cuisine" restaurant operates five nights weekly. Independent **eating** options are best in Taxiárhes, where two upscale tavernas – *Agnandi* and *To Kalyvi* – put out tables on the platía; the latter has a limited menu of grills and *mayireftá* like Pílio-style eggplant and *yiortlú kebáb*.

Moúressi

More meals are found at **tavernas** in **MOÚRESSI**, 3km northwest of Áyios Stéfanos. Both *To Tavernaki* and *Iy Dhrosia* up on the main highway are famously dour, but serve *fasólies hándres* (delicately flavoured pinto beans) and assorted offal on a spit. Good food at *To Kentriko* on Moúressi's linden-shaded platía offsets a clinical atmosphere and *Fawlty Towers*-style service. Approaching the village centre on the access road, there's also a prime en-suite **accommodation**

▲ Taverna tables, Tsangarádha, Pílio

choice: *The Old Silk Store* (Ⓣ24260 49086 or 693 71 56 780, Ⓦwww.pelionet.gr; closed Feb; B&B ④), a lightly restored nineteenth-century mansion with a lush garden, barbecue area and high-ceilinged, wood-floored rooms (plus a self-catering studio cottage ④). Breakfasts change daily but always include excellent bread and home-made preserves. Proprietress Jill also runs Mulberry (same phone), which helps with incoming travel arrangements, acts as the local Hertz **car rental** rep and leads regular walking tours. An excellent short stroll, very useful for reaching the beach or completing a loop via Áyios Ioánnis, is the 45-minute descent to Damoúhari; look for the signposted start of the trail on the bend in the road just past the minimarket/newsagent.

Fakístra and Mylopótamos to Lambinoú

From Taxiárhes Tsangarádha, a soon-to-be-cleaned, ninety-minute path, or a seven-kilometre hairpin road, snake down to **Mylopótamos** and its two attractive if hugely popular pebble coves, with afternoon shade from caves and overhangs. The pair are separated by a naturally tunnelled rock, with a music bar just above. Beachgoers pack into **accommodation** lining the approach road; the nearest is *Diakoumis* (Ⓣ24260 49203, Ⓦwww.diakoumis.gr; ❸), with wood-trimmed rooms and studios spread over two rambling buildings, and spectacular views from wooden terraces. At road's end, above the first cove, stands welcoming, efficient *Angelika* **taverna** (daily Easter–Oct, weekends otherwise); the fish is fresh if expensive but other seafood, *mezédhes* and *mayireftá* are tasty and reasonably priced.

For more solitude, try **Fakístra beach**, the next cove north of Mylopótamos. This is most satisfyingly reached on foot from Damoúhari, via a coastal corniche trail which starts between two prominent stakes, fifteen minutes uphill from the latter beach. Just beyond, there's disruption from an illegal road threatening the *kalderími*, but persevere – the way goes through; green-dot waymarks lead you down towards sea level through olive groves. After about half an hour, you cross Makrolítharo bay with its rocky shore and striking promontory; the path continues from the far side, climbing gradually through more olives to a spectacular viewpoint towards a cliff-cave, signposted spuriously as a "secret school". Some thirty minutes past Makrolítharo, you pass the marked side-trail accessing the cave, and then almost immediately the end of the road down from Ayía Kyriakí, with a tiny parking area. It's a few minutes more (total 80min from Damoúhari) to the cliff-girt, pea-gravel-and-sand bay with a shattered castle overhead, nudists, rough campers – and no amenities.

Southeast of Mylopótamos lie two more attractive **beaches**: Limniónas and Lambinoú. You can arrive on foot from Mylopótamos, but most people get there via Lambinoú village (no reliable facilities), from where a paved road leads 3km down past the restored eighteenth-century **Lambidhónas monastery**, its *katholikón* locked but sporting fine frescoes over the doors. **Lambinoú** cove, with a seasonal snack-bar, is a narrow, deep square of sand where four parties constitute a crowd; continue to much larger, more scenic Limniónas, mostly on path, along the coast, or by a separate track system from Lambinoú village. **Limniónas** has a fresh-water shower but no other reliable amenities, though further north stands the *Faros Hotel* (Ⓣ24260 49994, http://pelion.org/faros/index.asp; ❹), a secluded spot popular with hikers and horse-riders.

Hikes from Xouríkhti

Just above the main road between Tsangarádha and Lambinoú, workaday Xouríkhti, served by path from Tsangarádha, is the start-point for more **walks**. Near the lower end of the village, a yellow walking-man sign points down a weedy **path towards Lambinoú**; within twenty minutes you're out onto the asphalt, along which you must walk south 2km until the resumption of the path (signed), near a circular wooden gazebo below the highway. The route, now maintained, reaches Lambinoú village and then descends sharply to the eponymous monastery, nicely short-cutting the road; then it's briefly road to Lambinoú cove, mostly path to Limniónas, and then coastal track to Mylopótamos past *Faros Hotel*, the final ten minutes on path and steps emerging at the *Angelika* taverna. Total walking time from Xouríkhti is just over two hours; arrange a taxi out of Mylopótamos, instead of attempting a loop back to Xouríkhti (something encouraged by both Road and Anavasi maps) – the path up from Mylopótamos has been mostly destroyed by bulldozing and quarrying.

Xouríkthi is also the eastern trailhead for an enjoyable three-hour **hike to Miliés**, one of the classic Pílio treks. The path proper, wending its way through a mix of open hillside and shady dell, starts about fifteen minutes southwest of the platía (follow signage to Áyios Dhimítrios), branching left off the track system; beyond here the route is well-marked, with stretches of restored *kalderími*. Before the road via Lambinoú and Kalamáki was opened in 1938, this was the main thoroughfare between Miliés and Tsangarádha. With planning, you can do this walk one-way and then take an afternoon KTEL back to your starting point.

Western Pílio

Lying in the "rain shadow" of the mountain, the western Pílio has a drier, more Mediterranean climate, with olives and arbutus predominating except in shady, damp ravines. The beaches, at least until Kalá Nerá, are far more developed than their natural endowments merit and lack the character of those on the east shore. Inland it is a different story, with pleasant foothill villages and decent bus services. **Vyzítsa** and **Pinakátes** in particular both make good bases for car-touring or hiking.

Miliés

Like Tsangarádha, the sizeable village of **MILIÉS** (sometimes Miléës or Mileai) was an important cultural refuge during the eighteenth century. It retains some imposing mansions and Pílio's most interesting church, **Taxiárhis** (usually open around 6pm). Its narthex frescoes are the oldest (eighteenth century) and most unusual, including scenes from Noah's Flood (with two elephants boarding the Ark) and, in one corner, a three-ringed mandala showing the seasons, the zodiac and the cycle of human existence. With five wells under the floor and 48 clay urns secreted in the walls, the church's acoustics are superb, so it's occasionally used for concerts of sacred music.

The Pílio trenáki

A prime west-Pílio attraction is the *trenáki*, or **narrow-gauge railway**, which originally ran between Vólos and Miliés. The sixty-kilometre line, in normal service until 1971, was laid out between 1894 and 1903 by an Italian consortium under the supervision of engineer Evaristo de Chirico, father of famous artist Giorgio de Chirico. The boy, born in Vólos in 1888, spent his formative years with his father on the job-site, which accounts for the little trains which chug across several of his paintings (such as *The Hour of Silence* and *The Seer's Reward*, both from 1913). To conquer the 2.8-percent gradient and numerous ravines between Áno Lehónia and Miliés, the elder de Chirico designed six multiple-span stone viaducts, blind-arch buttressing, tunnels and a riveted **iron trestle bridge**, all justly considered masterpieces of form and function. The bridge, some 700m west of the terminus below Miliés, spans a particularly deep gorge and can be crossed on a **pedestrian catwalk**; indeed, following the entire route down to Áno Lehónia is a popular 5hr 30min walk, with occasional springs en route.

An **excursion service**, using one of the original Belgian steam locomotives (since converted to diesel), is now a tourist attraction during weekends and holidays Easter–October (daily July–Aug), and several of the *Belle Époque* stations have been restored. The train leaves Áno Lehónia (city bus #5 from Vólos) on the coast at 11am, taking 95min to reach Miliés, from where it returns at 4pm. Tickets are currently €13 adults, €8.50 kids, one-way or round trip, and go on sale at 10.30am (start queuing at 10am), at either Vólos or Áno Lehónia. However, groups often book out the three carriages, so best make enquiries at Vólos station a few days in advance.

Accommodation is limited compared to nearby Vyzítsa; the choice boils down to either *Eskitzi Rooms* just east of town (Ⓣ24230 86789, Ⓦwww.eskitzirooomspelion.com; ④) or *O Palios Stathmos* (Ⓣ24230 86425, Ⓦwww.paliosstathmos.com; ④), down by the train line, whose very plain rooms are only worth it if you get a balconied front unit; both operate all year. Quality **restaurant** options are also limited; the simple grill *Panorama*, occupying a wedge-shaped building just above the platía, is the most consistent. The most distinctive food emerges from the *Othon Korbas* bakery down by the bus stop, selling every kind of bread, pie and turnover imaginable, including *eleópsomo* and *tyrópsomo* suitable for hikers.

Vyzítsa

VYZÍTSA, 3km west of Miliés and alive with water in streams and aqueducts, has a more open and less lived-in feel than either Makrynítsa or Miliés, though it draws crowds of day-trippers in summer. Nonetheless it's an excellent base, with several **accommodation** options in converted mansions. The pick of these in terms of decor and quiet is *Arhondiko Karagianopoulou* (Ⓣ24230 86717, ④), 200m uphill from the village through-road, with well-restored rooms and breakfast served in the courtyard; it's also worth trying the slightly plainer but airy *Arhondiko Kondou* (Ⓣ24230 86793, Ⓦhttp://kontos.hid.gr/; ④), also a five-minute walk uphill from the car-park platía. About the best value, if not the most inspired restoration job, is *Thetis* (Ⓣ24230 86111; B&B summer ②, winter ③), just west of the central car park but calm enough, with good breakfasts at the adjacent stone-built café. The approach road from Miliés to the village is lined with more prosaically located inns, including modern *Hotel Stoïkos* (Ⓣ24230 86406, Ⓕ24230 86061; ④), most of whose well-executed, mock-traditional rooms have views. The tiered upper platía with its fountains and trio of plane trees, each larger than the last, offers three unremarkable **tavernas**; the best eating is at *O Yiorgaras*, next to *Hotel Stoïkos*.

Hikes around Vyzítsa

Vyzítsa sits at the nexus of several trails down to the coast, which can be combined into half-day **loop-hikes**. From the chapel of Zoödhóhou Piyís, just below Vyzítsa's platía, a sporadically marked route takes you around a vast landslip zone, and then across two ravines (bridges provided) and a brief stretch of farm track until dropping to Kalá Nerá, via Aryiréïka hamlet, just under two hours later. Once on the main highway in Kalá Nerá, you can bear left (east) and adopt the oblique cemetery track, start of the ninety-minute hike up to Miliés. There is a signposted *kalderími* from Miliés to Vyzítsa, which takes less than an hour.

Alternatively, turn right (west) at Kalá Nerá and complete a circuit by turning onto the well-indicated *kalderími* beginning just before the petrol station, opposite the telecoms building. This climbs, in slightly over two hours, to Pinakátes, almost entirely along a cleaned and meticulously restored *kalderími* (shortcutting a paved road), with superb views over the ravine separating Oglá hamlet from Aryiréïka, and de Chirico's five-arched rail bridge there. Once in Pinakátes, however, you'll have to take a taxi or walk along the road back to Vyzítsa, since the path between there and Pinakátes, described in some sources, is no longer passable.

Pinakátes

PINAKÁTES, at the top of a densely forested ravine, was once among the least visited and most desolate of the west Pílio villages, following a 1955 phylloxera outbreak which ended its status as vineyard capital of Pílio. No longer: the surfacing of roads in from three directions, and trendy Greeks buying up crumbling mansions for restoration, have seen to that. For now it remains a superbly atmospheric spot, with just enough food and accommodation to make it a practical base. The two mansion-**inns** are *Alatinou*, a few steps below the square (ⓣ24230 86995 or 697 28 38 282; ④), offering simple en-suite rooms with dark-wood decor and a basement breakfast salon; and much grander *Xiradhakis* (ⓣ & ⓕ24230 86375; summer ④, winter ⑤), a bit further down the same lane. The shaded platía has a single **taverna**, but the best eating for some distance around – and where the villagers themselves hang out – is at *Iy Dhrosia* (alias *Taverna tou Papa*), at the far western edge of Pinakátes. The food – including *dolmádhes* and *gídha lemonáti* (goat stew with lemon sauce) – uses free-range meat and poultry, washed down by a jug of deceptively potent red wine from some of the few surviving local vineyards. Alternatively, excellent off-menu *mezédhes* accompany a *karafáki* of *tsípouro*.

Áyios Yeóryios Nilías to Áyios Lavréndios – and more walks

The next village on the road (and bus route) west to Vólos, **ÁYIOS YEÓRYIOS NILÍAS**, could be a mecca for walkers – except that **accommodation** is very pricey, none more so than at the stone-built luxury *Anovolios Resort* at the village's west entrance (ⓣ24280 86893, ⓦwww.anovolios.gr; ⑦–⑧). Less expensive nineteenth-century mansion-inns include *Vogiatzopoulou* (ⓣ24280 93135, ⓦwww.vogiatzopoulou.gr; summer ⑤, winter ⑥), with warm decor, and the nineteenth-century *Arhondiko Tzortzis* (ⓣ24280 94923, ⓕ24280 94252; summer ⑤, winter ⑥), at the start of the path up the mountain. Among platía **tavernas**, *O Tsakitzis* is the most consistently open, with reliable meat from its own butcher's downstairs.

Two long **hikes** from here are worthwhile; both initially use the same path, but 25 minutes above the village, at a cement aqueduct, there's a division, with a left turn taking you up to Agriólefkes ski centre within three-and-a-half hours, through beech woods with long stretches of path.

Continue straight rather than left, following profuse red or blue paint dots or arrows (as well as the occasional sign), and you will arrive at **Taxiárhes of Tsangarádha** within five hours from Áyios Yeóryios Nilías. This scenic, trans-Pelion traverse adopts a higher contour than the Xouríkhti–Miliés one (see p.324), topping out just two hours along Kourvéndelis (1057m). The changes in landscape – from apple orchards to dense beech forest – are marvellous, drinking water abundant, and the views southeast magnificent; the main drawback is that nearly half the distance is along track rather than trail.

Other, briefer *kalderímia* link Áyios Yeóryios with Áno Lehónia via Áyios Vlássios (1hr), down to Áno/Káto Gatzéa (90min) or northwest to **ÁYIOS LAVRÉNDIOS**, an architecturally hotch-potch village with another lovely platía. **Accommodation** includes the luxuriously restored *Paleo Eleotrivio* (ⓣ24280 96481; ⑥), or the more affordable, wood-floored *Rooms Thalpori* (ⓣ24280 96310; ③). This village is in turn connected with Káto Lehónia by a well-marked *kalderími* (90min).

Southern Pílio

South of the road linking Kalá Nerá, Miliés and Tsangarádha, Pílio becomes drier, lower and more stereotypically Mediterranean; the terrain overall is less dramatic, the villages more scattered. The region has been hit hard by forest fires – in particular a June 2007 blaze which burnt the entire coast from

Argalastí to Áfyssos, and across the peninsula to Potistiká – such that the only undamaged pines grow around Neohóri, southeast of Miliés, and above Katiyiórgis. There are, however, interesting corners, and considerably less tourism inland, while a number of busy coastal resorts attract a mixed clientele of foreigners and Greeks.

The area can be reached a little tortuously by bus or car from Vólos, or more directly by sea, via speedboats to Ayía Kyriakí (Tríkeri) and Tríkeri island from Vólos or northern Évvia.

Argalastí and around

AFÉTES is the first village southeast of Miliés, worth the brief detour for its vast platía with five plane trees, ornate church, well-preserved houses with slate roofs and two dinner-only **tavernas**; at lunch-time the rough-and-ready *Rematia* taverna by the car park doles out better, cheaper fare than appearances suggest. A few kilometres downhill lies **ÁFYSSOS**, a busy but pleasant resort with a shady waterfront square and and a half-dozen tavernas (*O Varkalas* the most Greek-attended) along the front, its development courtesy of Ambovós town beach, more scenic Kalliftéri to the north, and other secluded ones along 3km of road south to Lefókastro, whose average beach is lined with studios and sleepier tavernas.

ARGALASTÍ, 12km southeast of Afétes, is the biggest place in the south, with a **post office**, **bank** ATM by the church, petrol stations and shops, as well as car rental from Pelion Rent (Ⓣ24230 54365, Ⓦwww.pelionrent.com), also present in Áfyssos and Milína. You can **stay** a bit west of the main through road at the high-standard *Agamemnon* (Ⓣ24230 54557, Ⓦwww.agamemnon.gr; ❹), a well-restored, eighteenth-century mansion-hotel with a swimming pool, common areas stuffed with antiques, and Wi-Fi access; rooms, some with fireplaces, have stone or wood floors. On the platía, *Sfindio Ouzeri* is the most reliable **and** efficient spot to eat, while *O Kaloyeros (Tis Nikolettas)* across the way does fuller meals. Around the corner just west, *Iy Artemis* is good for meat grills and a few dishes of the day; nearby is the former basement wineshop where poet Kostas Varnalis, a teacher here in the 1930s, wrote the lyrics of the much-loved Theodhorakis song *Mes'tin Ipoyia tin Taverna*.

Argalastí is close to the Pagasitic Gulf, with two beaches just a brief drive (or short walk) west. **Kálamos** is about the longest and sandiest on the Pagasitic side, but the road runs just behind it; there are dozens of apartments and two tavernas. Secluded **Paralía Páou**, reached by a different, dead-end road, is by contrast fine gravel, one of the best on the Pagasitic, but without amenities. En route there, stop at **Ayíou Nikoláou Páou monastery**, restored as a conference and New-Age seminar centre but usually open to permit viewing its **frescoes** dated to 1794; particularly fine are an Ancient of Days in the narthex dome, townscapes with ships and a Pandokrátor in the sanctuary dome.

Potistiká to Páltsi: the east coast

Better, less developed beaches line the east coast, with fine views across to Skiáthos, Skópelos and Alónissos, though fire damage has sullied their hinterlands. Closest (10km) to Argalastí is stunning, if often windy, **Potistiká**; huge rock formations and sunbeds at the south end separate it from more secluded Melaní (walkable; see p.328 for road access). Potistiká is a potential base, courtesy of a welcoming **hotel**, *Elytis* (Ⓣ & Ⓕ24230 54482 or 697 75 90 657; Easter-Nov; ❷), whose bland, white-tiled rooms all face the sea, with heating for cooler months and the only local full-service **taverna** (though there are snack bars by the beach). For other meals, the platía of **Xinóvryssi** offers two nocturnal eateries.

The beach at **Páltsi** lies 13km from Argalastí via a paved turning from the Xinóvryssi road (officially, confusingly, signposted as "Áyios Konstandínos"). The sandy beach is marred somewhat by a reef in the middle, but the edges are fine, with islets and outcrops to dive off or swim towards. **Melaní** Beach (no facilities) is accessed by a paved road (2.5km) from the inland side of Páltsi hamlet. Páltsi facilities comprise three **tavernas** and a number of **rooms**, for example *Olga* (ⓣ24230 55300 or 697 47 23 598; ❷), right behind the beach.

Hórto to Marathiá via Láfkos: the west coast

Continuing south from Argalastí, you reach the sea again after 7km at **HÓRTO**, a quiet little resort largely ensured against exploitation by its mediocre beaches. **Accommodation** is self-catering, and handled by tour companies; the best standard is offered by mock-trad complex *Diplomats' Holidays* (ⓣ24230 65497, ⓦwww.diplomatsholidays.com; ❺), with pool, tennis court and private beach. Three **tavernas** grace a like number of coves here; *Flisvos*, left of the creek mouth as you face the sea, is the cheap-and-cheerful option favoured by locals.

Just 3km further, **MILÍNA** seems far more commercialized; the beach is the scanty Pagasitic norm, making it mostly a place to watch magnificent sunsets over the offshore islets and distant mainland ridges from one of the waterside **bar-cafés**. A score of **accommodation** establishments also overlook the water or line the inland street grid. Plain but serviceable *Xenon Athina* (ⓣ24230 65473, ⓦwww.athina-pelion.com; ❸) on the front is worth it only if you get a sea view; a block inland from the south end of the quay, vine-covered *Xenon Xenios* studios (ⓣ24230 65227; ❹) have air conditioning and easier parking. For more choice, refer to the local office of recommended Houses of Pelion agency (ⓣ24230 65471, ⓕ24230 65910; see p.33), which can fix you up with one of their premises in the area, though they're mostly geared to packages based on Friday charter arrivals and departures. Among half-a-dozen **tavernas**, ★ *O Sakis* is much the best and has the most genuinely Greek feel, where you can assemble a tasty meal of seafood, two *mezédhes* and local wine for €14 – or scaly fish for a bit more.

Milína is one terminus of a pair of hour-long *kalderímia* linking the coast with the inland village of Láfkos, which can be combined for an enjoyable walking circuit. Starting from the shoreline church in Milína, head ten minutes inland walking along the side road until you see the *kalderími* erupting in an olive grove; from Láfkos, the return route starts at the far end of its platía, exiting the village from its lowest houses.

LÁFKOS itself is a handsome, ridgetop village in the throes of restoration, graced by another sumptuous, car-free platía with a record number of plane trees, a **ATM** and three **tavernas**, of which eccentrically managed *Pigasos* is the best all-rounder, especially for grills; *Sipiada* opposite is more stylish, with good *mayireftá*, but poor grills. Near the south edge of the village is one of the last wood-fired bakeries in the region, ace for pies and turnovers. Just off the start of the path down to Milína are two high-standard restoration **inns**, the better of which is sumptuous *Arhondiko Parissi* (ⓣ24230 65856 or 697 81 91 851; ❹), with iron beds, a swimming pool and a full breakfast on offer.

Beyond Milína, there are no more shoreline villages and the landscape becomes increasingly bleak, with only the occasional weekend villa or moored boat to vary the horizon. Some 2km along, at nearly landlocked **Valtoúdhi bay**, yachts anchored in the lee of Alatás islet outnumber fishing boats; here Pelion Sail and Cycle (ⓣ24230 65365, ⓦwww.pelionsailandcycle.com) rents sailboats, windsurf-boards, kayaks and bikes. About 4km past Milína, a side road leads to diminutive **Áyios Andhréas** anchorage, where fishermen sit about talking shop and *O Pingoúinos* is another good bet for somewhat pricey fish. People play on the water rather than in it hereabouts, as the gulf tends to be unpalatably warm, with flotsam and jetsam. About the best swimming beach locally is at **Marathiá(s)**, 7km further on, offering two tavernas and sun loungers.

The lower southeast coast: Paralía Mourtiá to Kastrí

Heading east from Láfkos, you'll again find better beaches on the east-facing coast. About halfway to the Aegean, **PROMÝRI** spills down the slope where it's hidden, out of sight from the sea and prying pirate eyes; this marks the start of an excellent three-hour **walk** to Plataniás, shown correctly on both recommended hiking maps. If necessary, get up the hill from Plataniás with a taxi or morning bus; just south of Promýri, damage to the *kalderími* from rubble-dumping has been cleaned and marked somewhat, after which it's plain sailing to the ridge and asphalt road down to Plataniá. Cross this for a brief stretch on track, then descend a shady canyon (old working fountain en route), sticking to path and *kalderími* until the last moments where you're in the stream bed, emerging on the asphalt about 700m before Plataniás.

After climbing northeast out of the ravine beyond the village, the onward road from Promýri passes the turning for **Paralía Mourtiá**, a tiny but fairly attractive beach, and then the side-road to subsequent **Paralía Lýris**, bigger and sandier, with a **taverna** and **rooms**. The main road threads through Lýri (no facilities) before arriving at the little port of **KATIYIÓRGIS**, the only sizeable coastal settlement in these parts, and terminus of a bus line from Vólos, 66km away. The minuscule sandy bay here isn't great for swimming, owing to fishing boats and yachts at anchor, but Katiyiórgis makes a good lunch stop, with terrace seating opposite Skiáthos, just three nautical miles distant. The more venerable of two **tavernas** is *Flisvos* (April–Oct), with *mayireftá* and famously fresh fish served at tables on the sand, at only slightly bumped up prices; dishes may be garnished with *ftéri* (fried fern) and *tsitsíravla*. They also have self-catering **rooms** upstairs (ⓣ24230 71071, ⓦwww.flisvospelion.com; ❷) – basic but perfectly adequate, even better if you get one with a sea-view balcony. There's more accommodation on the hillside just south (❷–❸), with a significant UK package-holiday presence; clients support a little waterside breakfast café/sweetshop, *Iy Avra*. For better, more secluded, beaches, take the well-defined path beginning below the last private villa, which leads within fifteen minutes to the secluded sandy covelet of **Vlahórema**, continuing another fifteen minutes over a ridge to larger **Vromonéri**, which also has track access from the west and a *kantína*.

From 500m north of Katiyiórgis quay, a paved road heads southwest through as-yet-unburnt olives and pines, with eyefuls of Skiáthos and Évvia across the straits. After 7km it emerges on the paved road linking Plataniás with **KASTRÍ**. Bearing left leads to the latter, a large, slightly exposed, sandy bay with a small **campsite** (ⓣ24230 71209; June–Sept), a beachfront **taverna**, plus two **studio** outfits: *Kastri* (ⓣ24230 71201; ❸) and *Ktena* (ⓣ24230 71345; ❸).

Plataniás and Mikró

Turning down and right from the above-cited junction brings you shortly to **PLATANIÁS** (or "Plataniá"), on Pílio's south coast, 10km from Láfkos. Named for the robust plane trees in the stream valley meeting the sea here, this is the biggest southern resort after Milína, with bus service from Vólos, and excursion *kaïkia* – on which you can arrange passage – calling most days from Skiáthos. The small beach is fine, but always busy; from the olive grove just inland an obvious path, threading spectacularly above the coast, leads twelve minutes west to the much bigger and better strand of **Mikró**, with naturist covelets in-between. Plataniás is also the destination of the excellent **walk** in from Promýri (see p.328), but the hike to Láfkos, shown on the Road Editions map, is no longer followable and should not be attempted.

One of the earliest Pílio beach resorts, Plataniás is essentially a collection of low-rises interspersed with restored vernacular houses. Among six licensed **hotels**, best and quietest is the *Platania*, east of the river mouth, on the waterfront (Ⓣ24230 71240; all year; ❸). At this rambling complex, all rooms have a fridge and balcony, and mostly mountain rather than sea views; there are also family units suitable for four, and a respectable **taverna** (*To Steki*) – one of several in a row – on the ground floor. Accommodation alternatives include *dhomátia* establishments to the west (right) of the seaside bridge, calmest of these at the end of the quay and then 50m inland (Ⓣ24230 71263; ❸). On the access road 600m inland there's also a large **campsite**, the *Louisa* (Ⓣ24230 71260).

MIKRÓ is arguably more attractive as a base, served by an 8.5-kilometre dirt road from the Láfkos–Promýri asphalt. There are **tavernas** at each end of the sand, and a handful of **rooms** outfits, the *Mikro* (Ⓣ24230 71212, Ⓦwww.mikrobeachhotel.com; ❸), halfway along, being the most established.

Tríkeri, Ayía Kyriakí and Kóttes

Until 1974 no road linked southwesterly **Tríkeri** with the rest of Pílio; though a broad highway now connects it with Milína in less than 45 minutes, this crab-claw-shaped peninsula still feels remote and insular. During the War of Independence, the Trikeriots donated numerous ships to the insurrection, and later the local sponge fleet rivalled the more renowned ones of the Argo-Saronics and Dodecanese. More recently, the area was used during and after the 1946–49 civil war for exiling political prisoners, and Paleó Tríkeri islet housed a detention camp for women leftists.

The hilltop village of **TRÍKERI** ("Horió" in local parlance) has few amenities for outsiders other than some simple *kafenía* and grills on the little square, shaded in this arid climate by pea-family trees rather than the usual planes. The road in has prompted a spate of cement construction and re-roofing, though a few *arhondiká* with views over the straits to Évvia survive in the maze of back lanes, densely packed in the manner of a typical island village. Transport by donkeys and mules is on the wane, but the 1500-metre *kalderími* down to **AYÍA KYRIAKÍ** is still well used (drivers tackle a winding, six-kilometre road). This is a working port with multicoloured fishing smacks at anchor, and much the most attractive spot on this coast. In the boatyard, a variety of craft are still built as they always have been, continuing the local seafaring tradition. There are a few **rooms** to rent here and at Mýlos cove, 1km west, but otherwise minimal tourist facilities, perhaps because there's no good beach nearby. East of the car park and bus turnaround area are two seafood **tavernas**, *Manolas* and *Mouragio*, the former more accomplished and popular but both surprisingly expensive considering their situation. Greeks in the know repair instead to Tríkeri's winter port, **KÓTTES**, on the other side of the isthmus, where *O Khristos* is the most reliable of three less expensive **tavernas** serving up unfarmed fish.

Paleó Tríkeri islet

Balanced just north of the tip of the "crab claw" is **Paleó Tríkeri** (aka Nisí Tríkeri). The only inhabited islet in the Pagasitic Gulf was settled from prehistoric times until sixteenth-century piracy compelled its abandonment and the move to "Horió"; today there's a population of under fifty, but burgeoning second-home sales (as everywhere on Pílio). Little more than 1700m from end to end, tranquil Paleó Tríkeri consists of olive-covered hills, some dirt tracks for service vehicles (but no saloon cars or asphalt) and two miniscule, rocky beaches on the north shore.

The lone port-village of **AÏ-YIÁNNI** has a single shop and one **bar/café** patronized by the many yachts calling here, and two friendly, almost normal-priced waterside tavernas: *Isalos* and *Dhiavlos* (☎24230 55210), the latter with a few **rooms** (❶) upstairs. There's also a small **hotel** with a pool in the village "centre", *Galatia* (☎24230 55505; ❸). If you don't catch one of the several daily "jet-boats" calling at Paleó Tríkeri, the only means of **arrival** besides a yacht is by following the paved road 6km from just north of "Horió" to **Alogóporos** ("Ford of the Horse"), the traditional crossing point, with a large fee car park. Water-taxis can be called on ☎697 34 10 908 or 697 74 12 169 (fare €5 each way per boatload; 10 people max).

From Aï-Yiánni, a fifteen-minute path/track leads up to the nineteenth-century **monastery** (daily 8am–1.30pm & 5–8pm) of Evangelistrías near the middle of the islet. Left of the door, a sombre plaque commemorates the five thousand female exiles interned here between 1948 and 1953. Inside beckons a lovely courtyard, with marble mosaics under the portico; the cells are being restored for future re-inhabitation by nuns.

Lárissa

LÁRISSA, approached across a prosperous but dull landscape of wheat and corn fields, is both marketplace and major garrison: army camps ring it, the airport remains monopolized by the Greek Air Force, and the southwestern part of the city – with nearly 140,000 inhabitants – is dominated by ranks of military housing.

Despite such an unpromising introduction, modern and unremarkable Lárissa retains a few streets reflecting its distant past as ancient and Byzantine Larissa, and later the Ottoman provincial capital ofYeniehir. The ancient Áyios Ahíllios **acropolis** sports the remains of a medieval **froúrio**, home to an Ottoman **bezesténi** (lockable bazaar), a popular café and the foundations of an ancient **Athena temple**. Just south and below you can spy the excavated, remains of the **ancient theatre** (closed). Further south in the flatlands, two landscaped squares (Sapká and Makaríou), connected by pedestrianized streets lined with upmarket boutiques, define the city centre. Spare a few minutes for the **archeological museum** in the old mosque at 31-Avgoústou 2 (Tues–Sun 8.30am–3pm; €2), with its collection of Neolithic finds and grave stelae. Otherwise, the **Alkazar Park** beside the Piniós, Thessaly's major river, keeps relatively cool through the summer, when Lárissa otherwise bakes.

Practicalities

As a major **road and rail junction**, Lárissa has efficient connections with more alluring places. The main **KTEL** is on Yeoryiádhou at the far north end of Olýmbou, 200m east of the acropolis, but all buses towards Tríkala leave from a station on Iróön Polytekhníou southwest of the centre, and a few other random services use a third stop on Ptoleméou, opposite the **train station**, 1km southeast of downtown. **Drivers** will find **parking** easiest and relatively unrestricted in the streets east of the acropolis.

You probably won't need or choose to **stay**, though there are numerous, usually pricey, **hotels**. Among a trio by the train station, the *Dhiethnes* (☎24102 34210; ❸) is the most appealing. Best central option is popular, cheerfully decorated *Metropol* at Roosevelt 14 one block southeast of Sápka (☎24105 37161, Ⓦwww.hotelmetropol.gr; B&B ④), its garage a blessing in a town with difficult parking.

More probably you'll just stop for a **meal**. There's a reliable ouzerí (*To Ayioklima*) near the museum-mosque at Olýmbou 9 by Platía Laoú, while *To Syndrivani* at Protopapadháki 8, on the south side of Platía Makaríou, purveys a variety of *mayireftá*, with tables outside in summer. Makaríou itself, with flower-beds and fountains, is the hub of daytime *frappádhika* life, but **after dark** the action shifts to pedestrianized, old-bazaar lanes around the *froúrio* like Fillelínon and Papaflέssa, currently threatened by a "redevelopment" scam. Café/bar prices here are eye-popping, at Athens levels without Athenian style or substance. Touring rock groups appear at the ex-industrial *Mylos* complex on Yeoryiádhou by the KTEL, a frank imitation of Thessaloníki's namesake facility, also with a cinema, theatre, bar and exhibition space.

North of Lárissa: Témbi and the Óssa coast

Travelling north from Lárissa, the motorway heads towards Thessaloníki via the scenic **Vale of Témbi**, between mounts Olympus and Óssa, before emerging on the coast. Accounts of the valley and the best of the **beaches** east of **Mount Óssa** follow; for details of Mount Olympus, see p.430.

Ambelákia

If you have time, or your own transport, a worthwhile stop in the Témbi region is **AMBELÁKIA**, a large village on Mount Óssa's west flank. You can walk up from the Témbi train station in about an hour along a cobbled way, part of the **O2 long-distance trail**, which continues over Mount Óssa to the coast at Stómio or **Karýtsa**.

During the 1700s, Ambelákia supported the world's first **industrial cooperative**, based on weaving and dying of textiles. At a time when much of Greece lay stagnant under Ottoman rule, Ambelákia was prosperous and largely autonomous, subsidizing a variety of social services including performances of ancient drama. This brave experiment lasted over a century, eventually succumbing to the triple ravages of war, economics and the industrial revolution's aniline dyes. In 1811 Ali Pasha raided Ambelákia, and a decade later the Viennese bank in which the town's wealth was deposited collapsed.

Until World War II, however, over 600 mansions survived here. Today there are just 36, many dilapidated but some finally benefiting from renovation. You can get an idea of the former prosperity by visiting the **Mansion of George Schwarz** (Tues–Sat 9am–3pm, Sun 9am–2.30pm; €3), the cooperative's last president, built in grand, old-Constantinople style. The outside has been admirably restored, as has the elaborately frescoed interior. Schwarz, incidentally, was Greek, despite the German-sounding name, merely the Austrian bank's translation of his real surname, Mavros (Black).

Without being twee, Ambelákia is an attractive, unpretentious place, with a cobbled high street, two old-fashioned bakeries and three *psistariés* on the plane-and-mulberry-shaded square. Simple **rooms** are available through the Women's Agrotourism Cooperative (☎24950 93487; ②), contactable in person at their café, *To Rodi*. There's also a **hotel**, the *Ennea Mousses* (☎24950 93405; ③), on the left just before the square, with somewhat dated wood-trimmed rooms but its own parking (problematic here).

The Vale of Témbi

At the edge of **TÉMBI** village, visible from the north-bound toll post and turning to Ambelákia, is Thessaly's other surviving (if scaffolded) Bektashi **tekkés** (see p.313), that of **Hasan Baba**. It's accessible by crossing an almond grove, and worth the effort for the sake of a fine dome with stalactite vaulting and three bands of Arabic calligraphy.

Some 2km beyond the Ambelákia turning, you enter the actual **Vale of Témbi**, a valley cut over the eons by the Piniós, which runs for nearly 10km between steep cliffs of the Olympus (Ólymbos) and Óssa ranges. In antiquity it was sacred to Apollo and constituted one of the few practicable approaches into central Greece – being the route taken by both Xerxes and Alexander the Great – and it remained an important passage from the Middle Ages to World War II. Despite traffic noise, the river here is popular with rafters – the main outing organizer is Olympos Trek, based in Lárissa (ⓣ24109 21244, ⓦwww.olympostrek.gr) – with Grade IV rapids at Vernézi (€60 for an outing). Halfway through the vale (on the southeast flank) are the ruins of **Kástro tís Oreás** ("Castle of the Beautiful Maiden"), one of four local Frankish guard-posts, while marking the northern end – and the border with Macedonia – is the Platamónas **fortress** (summer Tues–Fri 8am–7pm; winter Tues–Fri 8.30am–5pm; all year Sat & Sun 8.30am–3pm), also Crusader-built. An impressive citadel, it's a prime venue for the summer Olympos Festival; a 2004-bored rail tunnel goes right under it, so that the train no longer stops here, but 4km before at Néi Póri. A steep dirt track leads to the fort from the busy main highway, for the expected views.

The Óssa coast: Stómio to Polydhéndhri

A side road near the Kástro tís Oreás takes you 12km to **STÓMIO**, a cheerfully downmarket and resolutely Greek working-class seaside village near the mouth of the River Piniós. The beach here is relatively new – a 1950s flood changed the river's course, creating a vast sandspit behind the abandoned riverbed. The dense beech and linden forest of Óssa marches down almost to the shore, masking some of Stómio's more uninspired recent construction, mixed in with old stone houses and EU-funded cosmetic improvements. The marshes flanking the old river-branch provide excellent bird-watching, while the five-star-quality sand at Stómio merges seamlessly with **Stríntzo** beach, extending northeast to the current river-delta near Kouloúra.

Outside July and August you shouldn't have any trouble finding **accommodation**, though rooms close to the waterfront may be noisy. A prime choice is *Hotel Alexiou* (ⓣ24950 91210, ⓦwww.hotel-alexiou.gr; ❸), in a calm uphill setting, with somewhat small rooms but ample parking and a roof-restaurant. A municipal beachside **campsite** is well equipped with hot showers and power hook-ups for caravans. Of the four **tavernas** on the shore road leading to the fishing port, the two best are *To Tsayezi* ("river-mouth" in Turkish) and *Iy Gorgona*, though seafood is pricey.

Much the highest-standard **accommodation** in the region is 6km south and uphill at **KARÝTSA**, where Yiorgos and Stella's ★ *Dohos Katalymata* (ⓣ24950 92001; ❹) takes in a view extending from Káto Ólymbos to the Sithonía peninsula, from a perch amidst Greece's only true cloud-forest environment. Choose between huge wood-floored rooms or suites, all with sea-facing balconies and music systems, as well as a free-standing circular wigwam; in winter you'll appreciate the fireplaces. The common areas, crammed with a museum's worth of antiques, include a concert hall – hosting special events all summer – two pools, a sauna/*hamam* and a bar and breakfast salon. If it's full, continue another 6km to the Platánia district of **KÓKKINO NERÓ**, where *Hotel Hlidhi* (Ⓣ24950 92111; ③) has plush rooms with fridges, large baths and sea or mountain views; you'll be encouraged to patronize affiliated *Akrotiri*, one of several serviceable waterside fish **tavernas**.

Between Stómio and Cape Dhermáti, the steep shoreline is punctuated by secluded light-sand coves like Platýs Ámmos, often with rough access tracks; the direct Kókkino Neró–Stómio bypass makes them easier to reach. Between Kókkino Neró and the cape are larger, congenial beaches at **Koutsoupiá** and **Paliouriá**, but further south the coast subsides into uninterrupted but featureless, exposed beaches at Velíka, Sotirítsa and Ayiókambos. Except for some Czech and Polish tourists, the area is effectively the summer-weekend villa-annexe of Lárissa. You're best off continuing straight through to **POLYDHÉNDHRI** 3km south, with **rooms**, three **tavernas**, and a charming small beach popular with campers; from here the paved road veers scenically inland via the mountain villages of Sklíthro and Élafos on its way back towards Lárissa.

West from Lárissa: Tríkala, the Pýli region and routes to Epirus

West from Lárissa, the road follows the River Piniós to **Tríkala**, an enjoyable provincial capital with important Byzantine monuments nearby. For most travellers, it's merely a staging post en route to the Metéora, with the rail line connecting Lárissa and Tríkala continuing to Kalambáka. Frequent buses also call from Lárissa, with additional services west into Epirus.

Tríkala

TRÍKALA (population 50,000) is quite attractive and manageable compared to most Thessalian towns; it's evenly divided by the Lethéos, a tributary of the Piniós – clean enough to harbour trout – and backed by the Kóziakas range rising abruptly to the west. Almost uniquely in Greece, it's **bicycle-friendly**, if not actually bicycle-besotted; people of all ages pedal about and there are even municipally provided racks for locking up.

Tríkala was the capital of a nineteenth-century Ottoman province and retains lanes full of variably restored houses from that era, in the **Varoúsi** district below the fortress clocktower at the north end of town. Downriver from the bus station on the same bank, the **Koursoúm Tzamí** (signed by its alias "**Osman Shah**"), a very elegant restored mosque built 1567–70 by the legendary architect Sinan, also survives; it's locked except for art exhibits but you may peer in the windows, as you can with the octagonal dervish ceremonial hall – or possibly mausoleum – just southeast.

The town's inner **fortress**, a Turkish and Byzantine adaptation of a fourth-century BC citadel, is also closed to the public except for special events (including summer film showings), but the outer walls host attractive gardens and a terrace café. Down in the flatlands, on busy Saráfi, lie the meagre, half-excavated remains of a **sanctuary of Asklepios**; the cult of the healing god probably originated here in ancient Trikke. The liveliest part of town, encompassing what remains of the **old bazaar**, are the streets around the central, riverside **Platía Iróön Polytekhníou** with its statue of local hero Stefanos Sarafis, commander of ELAS from 1943 to 1945. Rebétika great Vassilis Tsitsanis (see Contexts p.942) also hailed from here, and he too is honoured by the street bearing his name, heading east from the platía.

Practicalities

The long-hours **post office** is at Stefánou Saráfi 15 off Platía Iróön Polytekhníou, as are several bank **ATMs**. The **KTEL** is on Óthonos on the southwest bank of the river, 300m southeast of the square; the main **taxi** ranks are on Iróön Polytekhníou and its continuation across the river (via an 1886-built iron bridge), Platía Ríga Feréou. **Drivers** should be mindful of the prevailing pay-and-display **parking** scheme, easily enough avoided by parking slightly out of the centre – or following signs to attended fee car parks.

Three mid-range **hotels** are pretty comparable in price, so you may as well plump for the most distinctive and historic: the Neoclassical *Panellinion* on Platía Ríga Feréou (Ⓣ24310 73545, Ⓦwww.panellinion.com; ❹), away from traffic noise. Dating from 1914, it hosted leading Greek politicians and artists of the era, and served as the Italian and German HQ during World War II. En-suite rooms are parquet-floored and air conditioned, some with balconies and small tubs; there's a mezzanine bar and a decent ground-floor restaurant, the *Aigli*, where breakfast is offered.

Other **tavernas** are scattered on either bank of the river; *psistariés* abound, as Tríkala province is renowned for its fine meat. A salubrious *mayireftá* lunch amidst updated decor can be had at *Selemekos*, Óthonos 10, near the KTEL. Pedestrianized Asklipíou, forging southwest from Ríga Feréou towards the train station, is the hub of **daytime café** society, but **after dark** the action moves to the partly pedestrianized **Manávika** quarter of the east-bank bazaar, especially on and just off Ypsilándou. Gentrification here isn't quite complete, as ouzerís and **clubs** still coexist with cobblers and tinsmiths; most clubs change constantly, but from October to May Tríkala honours its heritage at long-running *Orfeas*, Amalías 8 (opposite the iron river-bridge; reserve on Ⓣ24310 38486), where contemporary rebétika stars perform. There's also a **summer cinema** in the Mylos Matsopoulou complex, an ex-industrial premises at the northeast edge of town.

Consistent **eateries** in Manávika – open lunchtime as well – include cavernous, brick-interior *Ta Mezedhokomomata* at Ypsilándou 16–18, offering good value for somewhat heavy food; or superior ★ *Palia Istoria* at no. 3 with a lighter touch and fair prices for sardines, grilled mushrooms, ostrich steak, *imám baildí* and hot peppers.

Pýli and around

It takes some exercise of will to delay immediate progress from Tríkala to the Metéora. Byzantine aficionados, however, should make a detour to **PÝLI**, 19km southwest, for the thirteenth-century church of **Pórta Panayía**, one of the unsung beauties of Thessaly, in a superb setting at the mouth of a gorge. Nearby, there are outstanding frescoes at the monastery of **Ayíou Vissaríonos Dousíkou**, which might be a major tourist attraction were it not overshadowed by the neighbouring Metéora.

Buses run to Pýli from Tríkala almost hourly during the day. Near Pórta Panayía and beside a fountain-fed oasis on the north bank there is a simple **psistariá** with **rooms**, the *Porta Panayia* (Ⓣ24310 22691; ❷), though the

Hotel Pyli a bit further upstream on the same bank (Ⓣ24310 23510, Ⓦwww.hotelpyli.gr; all year; ④) is more comfortable, with a mix of wood- and tile-floored balconied rooms.

Pórta Panayía

Pórta Panayía church (daily: summer 8am–noon & 4–8pm; winter 9am–noon & 3–5pm; €2) is a ten-minute walk uphill from the bus stop in Pýli village. Cross the Portaïkós River on the footbridge, then bear left on the far bank until you see its dome above a clump of trees below the north-bank frontage road; cars must use a slightly longer route via a one-lane vehicle bridge. The caretaker is often found in the excellent, reasonable **café/bar** a few paces upstream from the church, and may admit you outside of the stated hours.

Much of the current church was completed in 1283 by Prince Ioannis Doukas of the Despotate of Epirus, atop an ancient Athena temple (its masonry liberally recycled into the walls); the domed narthex, Serbian built, was added a century later. In the three-aisled Doukas section, perpendicular barrel vaults over a narrow transept and more generous nave lend antiseismic properties, with further support from six columns.

The highlights of the interior are two **mosaic icons** depicting the adult Christ plus the Virgin holding the Child right-handedly, contrary to the usual iconography. Slightly later **frescoes**, many pigmented with Kozáni crocus, have fared less well, either blackened by fires or long covered by plaster. The most interesting are the *Metastási* (Assumption) of the Virgin on the west wall, reflecting the church's August 23 festival; a lunette over Ioannis Doukas's (empty) west-wall tomb, where the Archangel Michael leads Doukas by the hand to the enthroned Virgin with Child; and a late-medieval Holy Trinity over the apse, showing Renaissance influence.

A kilometre upstream, easiest reached along the Pýli bank of the river, a graceful **medieval bridge**, built in 1514 by St Vissarionos (see below), spans the Portaïkós at the point where it exits a narrow gorge. A couple of cafés take advantage of the setting; the whole area being a very popular weekend venue for the locals, it's best appreciated on a weekday.

Ayíou Vissaríonos Dhousíkou

Ayíou Vissaríonos Dhousíkou monastery (daily: summer 8am–noon & 4–8pm, winter 9am–noon & 3–5pm) – known locally as Aï-Vissáris – has a stunning setting, 500m up Mount Kóziakas, looking east over much of Thessaly. Its small community of monks seems keen to maintain its isolation, denying women admission and admitting foreign men with occasional reluctance, preference being given to the Orthodox and/or Greek-speakers. To reach the monastery, cross the single-lane road bridge over the Portaïkós as if heading for Pórta Panayía, but turn right instead, then left almost instantly onto a signed paved road climbing 4.5km.

The monastery was founded in 1530 by Vissarionos (Bessarion) of Pýli, and contains a perfect cycle of **frescoes** by Tzortzis – one of the major painters of Mount Athos – executed between 1550 and 1558 and restored to brilliance in 1992–93. These, and the institution overall, miraculously escaped damage in 1940, when two Italian bombs fell in the courtyard but failed to explode.

Originally, the monastery perched on a precipitous cliff, but in 1962 the abyss was filled in with kitchen gardens, and the road to the current entrance graded. This rendered ornamental the pulleys and ladder on the east wall, which, like much of the place, had survived intact since its foundation. Once nearly three hundred monks lived here; now there are around ten.

Routes to Epirus and alpine resorts

West of Tríkala and Pýli lies a wild, impressively scenic alpine region long frequented by Greek vacationers, which is now pitching itself to foreigners. Villages and attractions line a reasonable road network, which (with a few remaining unmade patches) can also be followed southwest all the way to Árta (see p.398). During summer, with a sturdy, high-clearance vehicle, you can also cross northwest over a Píndhos ridge in considerably less time, emerging at Métsovo (see p.356).

The Mesahóra dam

Just 4km west of Pýli, signs point left for the most direct way to Árta, via Stournaréïka. It's 142km to Árta from Pýli, paved except for 10km, with some massive tunnels (including a five-kilometre one near Lafina) to be finished by 2008. Unless bicycles are banned in the tunnels, this road is much the best (and most scenic) choice for cyclists as the gradients are easier and traffic lighter than on the usual Kalambáka–Métsovo route. There is, however, no food or petrol between Stournaréïka and Athamánio – pretty much half the distance – and curves plus lingering rough patches mean that drivers should allow well over three hours for the traverse.

En route, about 40km from Pýli, stands the completed, but thus-far empty, **Mesahóra dam**, Greece's most controversial **hydroelectric project**, approved by ex-PM Constantine Mitsotakis in 1993 despite strenuous opposition. Although the EU pulled the financial plug on the project, construction proceeded. The scaled-down compromise is supposedly only for power generation, omitting a water-diversion scheme for agricultural use, though this could be revived as litigation proceeds. The dam remains empty while the inhabitants of three upstream villages to be flooded resist eviction through court action.

Eláti, Pertoúli and Neraïdhohóri

Most people continue from the cited junction another 10km on the wider road to **ELÁTI**, a "hill station" for Trikalans nestled in fir trees. There are numerous amenities, though **accommodation** (except during the dozy off season) could be noisy – on the upper, through highway from traffic, on the lower street from late-night revelling. *Lingeri* on the upper road (Ⓣ24340 71454, Ⓦwww.ligerihotel.gr; B&B summer ❹–❺, winter ❺–❻) is a modern but stone-clad structure with three grades of wood-floored rooms and suites, the plushest with fireplaces. More affordable is *Koziakas* down on the commercial street (Ⓣ24340 71270; ❹), whose ground-floor **restaurant** *Kalamaras* runs to such exotica as ostrich steak in plum sauce, venison, wild-boar chop and an eighty-label-strong wine cellar.

Another 10km takes you to a junction with the side road north marked "Kalambáka 37km". It's actually more like 51km, but still a quicker way to the Metéora region than retracing your tyre treads, and allows a satisfying circuit of mounts Kóziakas and Kerkétio via Khryssomiliá. The uplands here – the Pertouliótika Livádhia – form part of the Píndhos watershed; behind you all rivers drain into the Aegean, while from all points west streams find their way into the Ahelóös and eventually the Ionian Sea.

PERTOÚLI village itself lies 4km west of this intersection in dense stands of local fir. It's more attractive and upmarket than Eláti, with **accommodation** priced accordingly. The stone-built *Arhondiko Dhivani* (Ⓣ24340 91252, Ⓕ24340 91111; summer ❺, winter ❻), with carved-wood furniture, fireplaces in some rooms and a lounge with wood stove, is typical of offerings here, though true luxury is available at the ★ *Arhondiko Hatzigaki* (☎24340 91146, ⓦwww.chatzigaki.gr; open all year; obligatory HB ❼), a restored 1890-vintage villa set in lovely grounds with an outdoor pool and other resort trappings (sauna, gym, conference rooms). The cost-conscious might continue another 3km to **NERAÏDHOHÓRI**, the last place of any size and the end of the bus line. A collection of scattered buildings looking southwest to 2148-metre Avgó includes roadside **lodgings** like the *Hotel Niavis* (☎24340 91201; ❹) and a **taverna**, *Margaritis*, specializing in own-raised meat. In summer both Pertoúli and Neraïdhohóri are start-points for day-walks up the peaks immediately north.

Tría Potámia to Métsovo

Just 2km west of Neraïdhohóri, medieval roadside **Ayía Paraskeví church** – with its high hexagonal cupola, carved portal and slate roof – is the last trace of civilization for some time. Beyond, the valley opens up dramatically, with bony ridges rising everywhere above the fir forest. Villages are tucked away up side canyons, though not remotely enough to have saved them from the German army's pyromaniac vengeance in late 1943; it's lonely country, with only the occasional goatherd and his flock for human scale.

At **Tría Potámia**, the Aspropótamos and the Komnaïtikos unite to form the Ahelóös – thus the "Three Rivers" of the name. It's a popular **kayaking and rafting venue**, but for how much longer is a moot point, as the Mesahóra dam waters will conceivably rise as far as the nearby Alexíou bridge.

If you bear right (north), away from the turnings for Gardhíki and Mesohóra, and follow the Aspropótamos upstream to another fork (67km from Pýli) and then veer right again, you reach *Pyrgos Mantania* (☎24320 87351, ⓦwww.mantania-ae.gr), the region's most interesting and best-value **accommodation**. Rooms in the original stone-built hotel vary from large, tasteful doubles (summer ❹, winter ❺) to even bigger top-floor family suites with fireplaces (summer ❻, winter ❼). Five new units by an outdoor pool were added in 2007, and the **bar-restaurant** feeds large numbers of weekend trippers on cuts of roast beast, game, sausages, vegetables and baked-apple dessert.

Veering left instead at this last fork takes you up another stream valley for 16km to **HALÍKI** village, end of the asphalt and last settlement in the province, with an eight-room **inn-taverna** (☎24320 87239; all year; ❸). Beyond Halíki, a dirt road – open from mid-May to October – continues some 25km to Anílio, by Métsovo in Epirus. There may be rutted, muddy patches along the first 7km to a saddle (the provincial border) in the Lákmos range, but thereafter it's a pretty easy descent through forest. Allow an hour from Halíki to Métsovo, and don't try this in a small rental car.

The Metéora and around

The **monasteries of the Metéora** are indisputably one of the great sights of mainland Greece. These extraordinary buildings, perched on seemingly inaccessible rock pinnacles, occupy a valley just north of **Kalambáka**; *metéora* means "suspended in mid-air", while *kalabak* is an Ottoman Turkish word meaning cliff or pinnacle. Arriving at the town, you glimpse the closest of the monasteries, Ayíou Stefánou, firmly ensconced on a massive pedestal; beyond stretches a chaos of greyish pinnacles, cones and stubbier, rounded cliffs. These are remnants of river sediment which flowed into a prehistoric sea that covered the plain of Thessaly around 25 million years ago, subsequently moulded into bizarre shapes by the combined action of fissuring from tectonic-plate pressures and erosion by the infant River Piniós.

Some history

Legend credits **St Athanasios**, who founded Megálou Meteórou – the earliest community – with flying up the rocks on the back of an eagle. More prosaically, the villagers of Stági, the Byzantine precursor of Kalambáka, may have become adept at climbing, and helped the original monks up. The difficulties of access and building are hard to overstate; almost all Metéora rock-climbing routes are rated "advanced", even with high-tech climbing gear.

The earliest religious communities appeared here late in the tenth century, when **hermits** occupied the caves scoring many of the rocks. In 1336 they were joined by two Athonite monks: **Gregorios** and his disciple **Athanasios**. Gregorios soon returned to Áthos, having ordered Athanasios to establish a monastery. This Athanasios did around 1344, whether supernaturally assisted or not, imposing a particularly austere rule. He was quickly joined by other monks, including (in 1381) **John Uroş**, who renounced the throne of Serbia to become the monk Ioasaph.

Royal presence was instrumental in **endowing** monasteries and hermitages, which multiplied on all the (relatively) accessible rocks to 24 institutions during the reign of Ottoman sultan Süleyman the Magnificent (1520–66). The major establishments flourished on revenues of estates granted them in distant Wallachia and Moldavia, as well as in Thessaly; they retained most of these estates until the eighteenth century, when monasticism throughout Greece began to wane.

Over the centuries, numerous disputes arose over power and precedence among the monasteries. However, the principal causes of Metéora's **decline** were physical and economic. Many buildings were simply not designed to withstand centuries of the harsh climate; neglected or unoccupied, they gradually disintegrated. The grander monasteries suffered depopulation, especially during the nineteenth century as a modern Greek state was established to the south – with Thessaly excluded until 1881 – and monasticism lost its exclusive identification with Greek nationalism and resistance to Turkish rule.

The crisis accelerated after monastic lands and revenues, already much reduced from their heyday, were expropriated by the state for use by Greek Asia Minor refugees after the Greco-Turkish war of 1919–22. By the late 1950s, there were just four active monasteries, struggling along with barely a dozen monks between them – an era chronicled in Patrick Leigh Fermor's *Roumeli*. Ironically, before being overtaken by **tourism** in the 1970s, the monasteries had begun to revive, attracting younger and more educated brothers; today about sixty monks and fifteen nuns dwell in the six extant foundations. Put firmly on the map by appearances in such films as James Bond's *For Your Eyes Only*, the four most visited monasteries and convents are essentially museum-monuments. Only **Ayías Triádhos** and **Ayíou Stefánou** still function with a primarily religious purpose, though everywhere there has been a notable recent increase in **pilgrimage** by devout Romanian and Russian Orthodox.

Practicalities: Kalambáka and Kastráki

Seeing the Metéora requires a full day, which means staying at least one night in **Kalambáka** or, preferably, **Kastráki** village, 2km northwest, which wins hands down on atmosphere and a situation enveloped by the rocks, and usually offers better value for money.

Kalambáka

KALAMBÁKA has no particular appeal, save for its position below the rocks. The town has tried valiantly to gentrify itself, with fountains in every square, but the effort founders on the fact that Kalambáka was burned by the Germans during World War II and very few prewar buildings remain. Among these are the ninth-to-eleventh-century **Mitrópolis** or old cathedral, dedicated to the Kímisis tís Theotókou ("Dormition of the Virgin"; daily 8am–1pm & 4–6pm; €2), at the top of town. It was first erected in the sixth century on the site of an Apollo temple and incorporates Classical masonry in its erratically designed walls. The interior is overarched by a coffered-wood ceiling and dominated, unusually for a Greek church, by a great double marble pulpit – like an Islamic *mimber* or oratory – in the central aisle, itself staked out by marble columns. Thirteenth- and fourteenth-century Byzantine frescoes are best preserved in the narthex, emphasizing miracles of Christ (*Healing the Paralytic, The Storm on Galilee, Raising Lazarus, The Wedding at Cana*), though there's also a vivid portrayal of Hell on the south wall.

Practicalities

The **train station** is on the ring road at the south edge of town; incoming **buses** stop at central Platía Dhimarhíou, but the KTEL is just downhill on Ródhon. Diagonally opposite a useless, limited-hours **tourist information** post, better documentation – maps, foreign-language guides, papers and magazines – is found at the **bookshop-newsagent** on the west side of the same plaza, corner Ioannínon and Patriárhou Dhimitríou. Arrivals may be met by **accommodation touts**; you are advised to ignore them, following numerous complaints about substandard rooms and price-fiddling. You also won't get much joy from the main street's undistinguished hotels, filled with coach tours and plagued by traffic noise despite double glazing.

One good **budget** choice is *Hotel Meteora* (Ⓣ24320 22367, Ⓦwww.meteorahotels.com; B&B ❷) at Ploutárhou 13, a quiet side-street towards the foot of the rocks as you leave Kalambáka for Kastráki. This has variable en-suite rooms, as well as adequate parking; breakfasts are enhanced with cheese and home-made cakes. In the upper, most village-like, quarter, some 700m uphill from either of the two main squares, near the Mitrópolis, are two more options. More comfortable is *Alsos House* at Kanári 5 (Ⓣ24320 24097, Ⓦwww.alsoshouse.gr; ❸), where rooms comprise doubles, triples and a quad suite, plus a well-appointed communal kitchen; helpful owner Yiannis Karakantas speaks good English. Classic backpackers' hangout *Koka Roka Rooms* (en suite and not) is nearby at no. 21 (Ⓣ24320 24554, Ⓔkokaroka@yahoo.com; ❶). Service at its cheap-and-cheerful ground-floor grill can be leisurely; there's also **Internet** access for all comers.

Mid-range choices include the well-run ✱ *Odysseon* (Ⓣ24320 22320, Ⓦwww.hotelodysseon.gr; ❹) on the main through road at the Kastráki end of things, but fairly quiet since set back; rooms were redone 2004–2006, with a mix of tile or parquet floors, and showers or tubs. There's a bright breakfast salon here and a **luxury** six-suite annexe in Kastráki (see opposite), *Archontiko Mesohori* (Ⓣ24320 77125, Ⓦwww.archontikomesohori.com; ❺). With transport, head east out of town to family-run *Pension Arsenis* (Ⓣ24320 24150, Ⓦwww.arsenis-meteora.gr; ❸), worth the effort for its bucolic setting, high-standard rooms and competent on-site restaurant.

A sterling exception to Kalambáka's mainly mediocre **tavernas**, 150m past the *Divani* Hotel on the west edge of town, is *O Skaros* (open all year; book large parties on Ⓣ24320 24152). Not many tourists find it, but locals certainly know about its excellent *kebáb* (called *kondosoúvli* elsewhere), chops and own-grown vegetables. Popular *Panellinion* on central Platía Dhimarhíou has rustic-kitsch decor and bumped-up prices, justified by high-quality ingredients, good brown bread and fresh-cut chips.

Kastráki

KASTRÁKI is twenty minutes' walk out of Kalambáka along the busy and somewhat dangerous road; in season (May 15–Sept 15) there are regular bus services throughout the day. Kastráki was also burnt by the Nazis, but a few older houses survive in the upper quarter.

Entering the downhill end of the village, you pass the better-equipped and -managed of two **campsites**, *Camping Vrachos* (Ⓣ24320 22293), where a resident outfitter (No Limits, Ⓣ24320 79165) offers adventure sports across the region. *Camping Boufidhis–The Cave* (Ⓣ 24320 24802; May–Oct), at the top end of the through road, is cramped and neglected, if incomparably set with Ayíou Nikoláou Anapavsá and Roussánou visible overhead; both sites have pools.

Kastráki has scores of **mid-range dhomátia**, mostly high standard, as well as several hotels. It's vital, however, to shun the main road, where coaches rumble through much of the day (and scooters buzz along by night). Meeting this criterion admirably is *Doupiani House* (Ⓣ24320 77555, Ⓔdoupiani-house@kmp.forthnet.gr; closed Dec–Feb except hols; ③), well signposted left of the road near *The Cave*, with superb views from the front-facing, 2007-redone rooms; proprietors Thanassis and Toula serve breakfast in the finest hotel garden of Kastráki, and can point walkers to the start of various hikes. Reservations are essential, even though a luxurious 2007-built annexe (④) adjacent brings their air-conditioned room total to 20. *Vassiliki Zioga Rooms* (Ⓣ24320 24037; ②), further downhill and again well back from the road, offers simple balconied, heated, marble-floored rooms, most with superb views, above a huge breakfast salon. Closer to the road, but still peaceful if you get one of the rear-facing pine-and-white-tile rooms, friendly, spotless *Hotel Tsikelli* (Ⓣ24320 22438; ③), has parking and a pleasant garden café. Apart from the annexes of *Doupiani House* and *Odysseon* (see opposite), **luxury** in Kastráki means either the 2007-built, wood-floored *Pyrgos Adrachti* (Ⓣ24320 22275, Ⓦwww.hotel-adrachti.gr; ⑤) at the top of the old quarter – a steep drive up but ample parking on arrival – or nearby five-room *Guesthouse Sotiriou* (Ⓣ24320 78105, Ⓦwww.guesthouse-sotiriou.gr; ⑤), three with fireplaces, in an impeccably restored, 1845-vintage mansion.

Among a dozen **places to eat** (mostly *psistariés*), the best all-rounder is *Paradhisos* on the through road, which besides excellent *kokorétsi* and *biftéki* features *moussakás*, starters and *ravaní* by owner-chef Koula, long experienced cooking abroad and in Thessaloníki. On summer nights, an atmospheric, inexpensive choice is *Bakalarakia*, behind the church and below the central platía, a little *koutoúki* (joint) limited to grills, salads, *bakaliáros* (of course) and local wine. With transport, don't miss well-signed *Neromylos* at the far end of **DHIÁVA** village, 4km southwest. The high-ceilinged interior was the owner's grandfather's watermill; outdoor seating near the trout-tanks is equally attractive. Besides trout, high-calibre ingredients include their own meat and *galotýri* as well as vegetarian *mezédhes*, the large portions washed down by a light *hýma* wine.

Ayíou Nikoláou Anapavsá and around

Beyond Kastráki the road threads between the huge monoliths of Áyion Pnévma and Doúpiani, the latter adorned with ruined **Pandokrátor**, among the earliest monastic settlements. To avoid road walking, follow instead the street

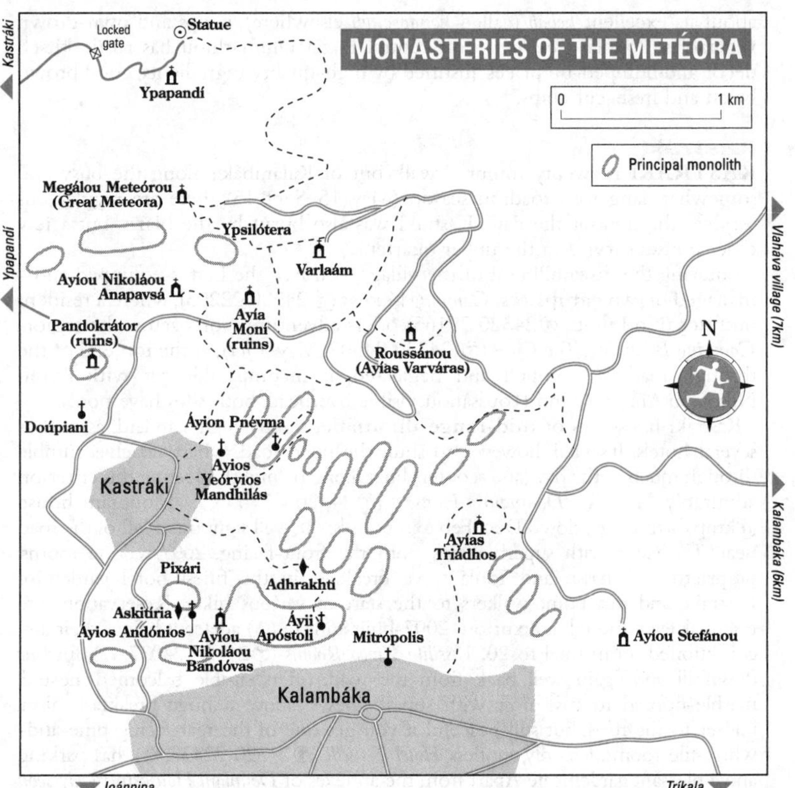

– later a track – that starts from the northwest corner of Kastráki's village square. This passes right under the cave-shrine of **Áyios Yeóryios Mandhilás**, low on the flank of Áyion Pnévma, its cavity marked by what looks like a lot of colourful washing hung up to dry. These are votive kerchiefs or *mandhília* (hence the saint's epithet), changed annually on April 23 by a couple of hundred daredevil youths, both local and from wider Greece, who climb or abseil up and retrieve last year's kerchiefs for luck. The rite is televised nationally, sometimes with a grisly conclusion; the final overhang is exceptionally challenging, and many have quite literally fallen from the saint's favour.

The track deposits you, after twenty minutes, at the base of the stair-path up to diminutive **Ayíou Nikoláou Anapavsá** (Mon–Thurs, Sat & Sun 9am–3.30pm; closes 3pm Nov–March). This has superb frescoes from 1527 by the Cretan painter Theophanes in its tiny *katholikón* (main chapel), which unusually faces almost due north rather than east because of the rock's shape. On the east wall of the naos over the window, a shocked disciple somersaults backwards at the *Transfiguration*, an ingenious use of the cramped space; in the *Denial of Peter* on the left door-arch as you enter the naos, the protagonists warm their hands over a fire in the pre-dawn, while above the *ierón* window is the *Sacrifice of Abraham*. On the west wall of the narthex, a stylite (column-dwelling hermit) perches in a wilderness populated by wild beasts, while an acolyte prepares to hoist up a supply basket – as would have been done just outside when the fresco was new. Other Desert Fathers rush to attend the funeral of St Ephraim the Syrian: some riding beasts, others – crippled or infirm – on litters or piggyback on the strong. There are also post-Theophanes, naïve images, such as Adam naming the animals (including a mythical basilisk), low on the west wall below Ephraim's funeral.

Megálou Meteórou (Great Meteoron)

Next to Ayíou Nikoláou, on a slender shaft, perch the shattered fragments of **Ayía Moní**, abandoned after an earthquake in 1858. Beyond this, some 250m past the Ayíou Nikoláou stairs, a cobbled, partly shaded path (signposted for Varlaám) leads northwest from the road; fifteen minutes up this trail, bear right at a T-junction to reach Varlaám monastery in ten minutes, or left for Megálou Meteórou within ten slightly steeper minutes. There is no other direct route between the two (besides the unpleasantly cluttered access roads serving both).

The **Megálou Meteórou** (aka **Metamorfóseos**; summer Mon & Wed–Sun 9am–5pm; winter Mon & Thurs–Sun 9am–4pm) is the highest monastery, built on the Platýs Líthos ("Broad Rock") 615m above sea level. It enjoyed extensive privileges and dominated the area for centuries: in an eighteenth-century engraving (sold as a reproduction) it dwarfs its neighbours.

Visiting Metéora's monasteries

There are six major monasteries, keeping slightly different visiting hours/days. To see them all in one day, start early to take in Ayíou Nikoláou Anapavsá, Varlaám and Megálou Meteórou before 1pm, leaving the afternoon for Roussánou, Ayías Triádhos and Ayíou Stefánou.

The road from **Kastráki to Ayíou Stefánou** is nearly 10km, often narrow and dangerous with speeding cars; if you're on foot, follow the hiking directions – by using available trails and dirt tracks you avoid most of the asphalt. Ayíou Stefánou is in a cul-de-sac for both drivers and hikers; the through road signposted to Kalambáka just before Ayías Triádhos is a fairly indirect 6km. In season there are daily **buses** (usually at 9am and 1pm) from Kalambáka up the road as far as Megálou Meteórou/Varlaám; even taken just part-way, they will provide the necessary head start to make a hiking day manageable.

You may want a local **map** in addition to that provided opposite, especially if you intend to leave the beaten track; the only two products worth having are stocked at the recommended Kalambáka newsagent. The *Panoramic Map with Geology* (co-produced by Karto Atelier, Switzerland and Trekking Hellas) is fairly accurate despite its aerial-view format and sufficient to follow the main routes. Andonis Kaloyirou's *The Footpaths of Meteora* (Kritiki Editions), with topographic map included, is superior, the map alone worth the investment.

Before setting out, buy **food and drink** to last the day; there are only a few *kantínas* by Varlaám and Megálou Meteórou. Each monastery levies an **admission charge** – currently €2, with student discounts generally not given. All monasteries enforce a strict **dress code**: both sexes must cover their shoulders; women wear a long skirt not trousers; men, long trousers, not shorts. Skirts or wraps are often lent to female visitors, but don't rely on this. Finally, it's worth noting that **photography** and **videoing** are **forbidden** inside all monasteries.

Metéora is really best visited out of season, when the leaves turn or snow blankets the pinnacles. During **midsummer**, the commercialization, traffic and crowds (plus the shocking amount of roadside litter) detract from the wild, spiritual romance of the valley. In this period you're better off at less visited monasteries such as Ayíou Nikoláou or Ayías Triádhos.

The monastery's cross-in-square **katholikón**, dedicated to the Transfiguration, is Metéora's most imposing; columns and beams support a lofty dome with a *Pandokrátor*. It was enlarged in the 1500s and 1600s, with the original chapel, constructed by the Serbian Ioasaph in 1383, now the *ierón* behind the intricately carved *témblon*. Frescoes, however, are much later (mid-sixteenth century) than at most other monasteries and artistically undistinguished; those in the narthex concentrate almost exclusively on grisly martyrdoms.

Elsewhere in this vast, arcaded cluster of buildings, the *kellári* (cellar) hosts an exhibit of rural impedimenta; in the domed, vaulted refectory, still set with the traditional silver/pewter table service for monastic meals, a **museum** features exquisite carved-wood crosses and rare icons. The ancient smoke-blackened kitchen adjacent preserves its bread oven and soup-hearth.

Ypapandí

For a real escape, walk briefly north from Megálou Meteórou to its dependency, **Ypapandí**. From Megálou Meteórou's car park, head northeast along multiple trail tracings visible beside a downed metal fence; after five minutes, you'll reach a prominent pass in the ridge where several trails cross and the main, wide path begins descending, still northeast, through oak woods. The path arcs twice around the tops of ravines, until some thirty minutes along you meet the rough service track leading ten more minutes west towards Ypapandí hermitage, now visible wedged into its cliff face. Although restored in the 1990s, there are not yet any resident monks to receive visitors who might come to admire the chapel's fine fourteenth-century frescoes. Until and unless this happens, the best view is from the next round-topped monolith along, with its statue of a heroic monk, and circular area with flagpole. You can follow the service track about 3km southwest, then southeast as it loops around rock formations to emerge on the paved road between Áyiou Nikoláou and Doúpiani; ordinary cars can approach in the opposite direction, up to a locked gate about 500m before Ypapandí.

Varlaám (Barlaam)

Varlaám (summer daily 9am–4pm; winter Mon–Wed, Sat & Sun 9am–3pm) is among the oldest monasteries, replacing a hermitage established by St Varlaam shortly after Athanasios' arrival. The present building, now home to seven monks and one of the most beautiful in the valley, was constructed by the Apsaras brothers from Ioánnina in 1540–44.

The monastery's *katholikón*, dedicated to Ayíon Pándon (All Saints), is small but glorious, supported by painted beams, its walls and pillars totally covered by frescoes (painted 1544–66), dominated by the great *Pandokrátor* of the inner dome. Among the more unusual are a beardless Christ Emmanuel in the right transept conch, and the Parliament of Angels on the left; on one pier, the Souls of the Righteous nestle in the Bosom of Abraham, while the Good Thief is admitted to Paradise. On the inner sanctuary wall, there's a vivid Crucifixion and a Dormition of the Virgin with, lower down, an angel severing the hands of the Impious Jew attempting to overturn her funeral bier. The treasury-museum features crucifixes and silver items; elsewhere the monks' original water barrel is on show.

Varlaám prominently displays its old **ascent tower**, comprising a reception platform, well-worn windlass and original rope-basket. Until the 1930s the only way of reaching most Meteoran monasteries was by being hauled up in said rope-basket, or by equally perilous retractable ladders. A nineteenth-century abbot, asked how often the rope was changed, replied, "Only when it breaks."

Steel cables eventually replaced ropes, and then steps were cut to all monasteries by order of the Bishop of Tríkala, unnerved by the vulnerability of his authority on visits. Today rope-baskets figure only as museum exhibits, supplanted by square metal cage-buckets along aerial cables bridging chasms from the nearest car park.

Roussánou

The following hiking route from Varlaám to Roussánou involves the least unnecessary altitude change and road-tramping. Proceed down the access road for Varlaám to a point about 150m past where the access drive for Megálou Meteórou joins up. Leave the road by the guard rail, keeping an eye out for blue-paint waymarks, and take paths with (except initially) decent surface underfoot; thread around (and briefly over) some minor, rounded monoliths, the Plákes Kelaraká, until you reach the bed of a ravine, just above the road. Cross the streambed and head briefly up the canyon on the far bank, then bear right into the trees on another path after about 50m. You'll emerge on the road, right below Roussánou, some 35 minutes after leaving Varlaám, with only a final twenty-metre scramble where the path has been ruined by rubble-dumping.

More or less opposite, a signed, cobbled path ascends to the compact convent of **Roussánou** (summer daily 9am–6pm; winter Mon, Tues & Thurs–Sun 9am–2pm), aka **Ayías Varváras**; there's another descending stair-path off a still higher loop of road, but in either case the final approach is across a vertiginous bridge from an adjacent rock. Roussánou, founded in 1545, has an extraordinary, much-photographed situation, its walls edging to sheer drops all around. Inside, the narthex of its main chapel has particularly gruesome frescoes (1560) of martyrdom and judgement, the only respite from sundry beheadings, spearings, crushings, roastings and mutilations being the lions licking Daniel's feet in his imprisonment (left of the window); diagonally across the room, two not-so-friendly lions proceed to devour Saint Ignatios Theoforos. On the right of the transept there's a vivid *Transfiguration* and *Entry to Jerusalem*, while to the left are events after Christ's Resurrection. On the east of the wall dividing naos from narthex is an exceptionally vivid Apocalypse.

To return to Kastráki directly from Roussánou, there's a trail shortcut. From the lower access path, walk downhill some thirteen minutes, through the first hairpin bend, to another roadside "sharp-bend" warning sign and a transformer pole. Take the path which drops from here to the course of the Paleokraniés stream, and then follow this until you emerge at a small pumping station on the Kastráki–Ayíou Nikoláou farm track. This takes about twenty minutes, saving nearly as much compared to using the road.

Ayías Triádhos

Alternatively, from the base of Roussánou's lower access path, descend the main road for just seven minutes until the first curve and then take the path signposted for Ayías Triádhos. Ten minutes' climb brings you to a ridge, beyond which lies the rugged canyon called Houní Ayías Triádhos. There's no way directly across this; instead bear left, following red paint-dots on the rocks, to climb more gently to a point on the circuit road about 600m shy of your goal – this won't save much time compared to the half-hour road-walk from Roussánou, but is far more pleasant. The final approach from the end of the lane down from the parking area of **Ayías Triádhos** (daily except Thurs: summer 9am–5pm; winter 9am–12.30pm & 3–5pm) consists of 130 steps carved into a rock-tunnel. You emerge into a cheerful compound with small displays of kitchen/farm implements, plus an old ascent windlass, but in lieu of labelling, maxims from Corinthians 1:13 appear everywhere: "Love is Patient", "Love Does not Criticize", etc. Few tour buses stop here, and life remains essentially monastic, even if there are only three brothers to maintain it.

The seventeenth-century frescoes in the *katholikón* have been completely cleaned and restored, fully justifying a visit. On the west wall, the *Dormition* is flanked by the *Judgement of Pilate* and the *Transaction of Judas*, complete with the thirty pieces of silver and subsequent self-hanging. Like others at the Metéora, this church was built in two phases, as evidenced by two domes, each with a *Pandokrátor* (the one above the *témblon* very fine), and two complete sets of Evangelists on the squinches. In the arch right of the *témblon* is a rare portrait of a beardless Christ Emmanuel, borne aloft by four seraphs; on the arch supports to the left appear the *Hospitality of Abraham* and *Christ the Righteous Judge.*

Although Ayías Triádhos teeters above a deep ravine and the little garden ends in a precipitous drop, an obvious, well-signposted **path** from the bottom of the monastery's access steps leads back to the upper quarter of **Kalambáka**. This 45-minute descent saves a tedious retracing of one's steps; it's a partly cobbled, all-weather surface in decent shape.

Ayíou Stefánou

Ayíou Stefánou (Tues–Sun: summer 9am–2pm & 3.30–6pm; winter 9am–1pm & 3–5pm), the last, easternmost monastery, is fifteen minutes' walk beyond Ayías Triádhos (no path short-cuts), appearing suddenly at a bend in the road. It's occupied by nuns keen to peddle trinkets, but the buildings – bombed during World War II and then raided during the civil war – are disappointing: the obvious one to miss if you're short of time. That said, the fifteenth-century refectory contains an apsidal fresco of the Virgin, beyond the museum graced by a fine *Epitáfios* (Good Friday bier) covering embroidered in gold thread. The trail towards Kalambáka from Ayíou Stefánou is disused and dangerous – return to Ayías Triádhos to use the descending path described above.

Other local walks

Once they've toured the monasteries, many visitors – especially during low season – are seduced into staying an extra day by the otherworldly scenery. There are several other hikes to hidden attractions on and around certain lesser monoliths, where you're virtually assured solitude.

One of the easier walks is to **Áyion Pnévma**. From Kastráki's platía, take the fieldstoned lane just above and north, heading northeast on this side of the ravine dividing the village. Behind the last house a clear if unmarked path heads off through some abandoned fruit and nut groves, before entering scrub and boulder-falls, with the wall-like Áyion Pnévma monolith to your left. Roussánou pops into sight as the trail executes a hairpin and begins scaling a a fissure in the side of the rock. Some 35 minutes out of town you'll reach a level spot cradled by the monolith; to the right the **cave-chapel** of Áyion Pnévma has been hollowed out of the rock as a hermit's quarters. Inside – otherwise all whitewash and modern icons – you'll see a sarcophagus for his (vanished) bones, again carved from the rock. Left of the chapel door is the rain cistern which supplied the hermit; the adept can scramble a few minutes further, onto the surface with the metal belfry, for superb views. On Pentecost Monday, half the village ascends for a liturgy (8–10am) in the cave, and the bolder lads abseil down the cliff to a remote cross and change its *mandhília* (see p.342).

A more advanced stroll – though not quite up to abseiling standard – is the steep scramble from upper Kastráki to the partly frescoed **cave-church of Áyii Apóstoli**, atop its 630-metre namesake monolith, highest at the Metéora. From beside the village cemetery, a good path climbs steeply for fifteen minutes to the obvious Adhrakhtí "finger"; the easy going is over now, and you must find the hard-to-spot continuation of the route up the steep gully to the right, keeping to the left side. After five minutes on all fours, you reach the proper onward path; there's a ladder near the top, but this isn't an outing for acrophobics.

On the southeastern outskirts of Kastráki, opposite *Taverna To Harama*, turn onto the narrow road signposted "Old Habitation of Kastráki" in English. After a short distance along this, bear right onto a one-lane cement drive which soon becomes dirt, then stops at a modern but attractive chapel built in traditional style (you can also arrive here from upper Kastráki). Overhead to the east, wedged into the cliff face, is the restored monastery of **Ayíou Nikoláou Bandóvas** (visits strictly forbidden), a dependency of Ayías Triádhos. But the real reason you've come here, ideally at sunset, is bang in front of you, on the side of the Pixári monolith: the **cave-chapel of Áyios Andónios** (restored 2005–2006; locked) and a series of rickety wooden platforms jammed into natural cavities in the cliff face, with dangling, half-rotten ladders. These **askitíria** or extreme hermitages are now home only to rock doves, but they were inhabited into the 1920s, and on their patron saint's day a monk used to be levered up to conduct a liturgy until the 1960s. Here in the raw, without souvenirs, multilingual guides and tour buses, are the origins and impulse of Metéora contemplative life.

Timíou Stavroú church

With your own transport, the flamboyant monastic **church of Timíou Stavroú**, 42km west of Kalambáka at 1150m altitude, between the villages of Kraniá and Dholianá, well rewards a visit (April–Oct daily except Wed

▲ Timíou Stavroú church

10am–6pm; free). The church itself, dating from 1770 but seeming far older, is a masterpiece of whimsy, matched in concept only by specimens in Romania and Russia. It musters thirteen turret-like cupolas, higher than they are wide, and is in excellent external repair, thanks to postwar restoration (it was burnt by the Germans in 1943); there are wonderful relief carvings outside on the south transept, showing Saint George (left), Saint Demetrios (right) plus Constantine and Helen with their Jerusalem-found cross in the middle. Inside, supposedly never frescoed, round piers uphold the vaults; a stone *sýnthronon* or bishop's bench occupies the apse.

Practicalities

To reach the church from Kalambáka, first head towards Dhiáva, then bear right following an "Aspropótamos 52" road sign. Climb steadily over a pass on the shoulder of Mount Tringía, via Kastaniá village, and then drop sharply into the densely forested **valley of the Aspropótamos River**, one of the loveliest in the Píndhos (see Ⓦwww.aspropotamos.org for the full story). From the unsigned taverna by the Dholianá turning, continue 1.5km further south to a tiny bridge and a wide track on the left, signposted "Ierá Moní Timíou Stavroú", which leads 750m to the church.

There's a **bus** from Tríkala to nearby **KRANIÁ** most days in the summer; on the village platía there's a stone-built **hotel-taverna**, the *Aspropotamos* (Ⓣ24320 87235; June–Sept; ③). From either church or Kraniá it's an easy matter to continue 7km down-valley to *Pyrgos Mantania* (see p.338), or 17km further to Tría Potámia, where you can loop east to Tríkala via Pertoúli and Pýli.

Travel details

Trains

Athens–Lárissa: 13 daily each direction; 3hr 15min–4hr 30min.
Athens–Lianokládhi (Lamía) 16 daily each direction; 2hr 15min–3hr; 2 services serve Lamía itself (20min extra).
Athens–Livadhiá 13 daily each direction; 1hr 25min.
Lárissa–Thessaloníki 11 daily each direction; 1hr 10min–1hr 45min.
Kalambáka–Athens 2 daily through services each direction; 4hr 30min–4hr 45min.
Vólos–Athens 1 daily through express service in each direction via Lárissa, otherwise change trains there; 4hr 30min.
Vólos–Lárissa 15 daily each direction; 52min.

Buses

Departures have similar frequency in each direction, so are given just once; check under both starting point and destination.
Ámfissa to: Lamía (3 daily; 1hr 30min).
Athens to: Dhelfí (6 daily; 3hr); Karpeníssi (3 daily; 4hr 30min); Lamía (hourly; 3hr); Lárissa (6 daily; 4hr 15min); Livadhiá (hourly; 2hr); Thíva (hourly; 1hr 30min); Tríkala (7 daily; 4hr 30min); Vólos (11–12 daily; 4hr 30min–5hr).
Dhelfí to: Ámfissa (6 daily; 30min); Itéa (5 daily; 30min); Pátra (1 daily; 3hr).
Galaxídhi to: Itéa (5 daily Mon–Fri, 4 Sat–Sun; 30min); Náfpaktos (6 daily Mon–Sat, 3 Sun; 1hr 15min).
Kalambáka to: Grevená (1 daily; 1hr 30min); Ioánnina (2 daily; 3hr 20min); Métsovo (2 daily; 1hr 30min); Vólos (4 daily; 3hr).
Karpeníssi to: Agrínio (1 at 9am Mon–Sat, 1pm Sun; 3hr 30min); Megálo/Mikró Horió (2 daily; 15min); Proussós (Mon & Fri at 5.30am & 1pm; 1hr).
Lamía to: Karpeníssi (4–5 daily; 1hr 45min); Thessaloníki (2 daily; 4hr); Tríkala (4 daily; 2hr 30min); Vólos (2 daily; 2hr).
Lárissa to: Ambelákia (Mon–Sat 2 daily, Sun 1; 30min); Kalambáka (hourly; 1hr 15min); Stómio (2 daily; 40min); Tríkala (hourly; 1hr); Vólos (almost hourly; 1hr).
Livadhiá to: Aráhova (6 daily; 40min); Dhelfí (6 daily; 50min); Thíva (hourly; 40min).
Tríkala to: Ioánnina (2 daily; 4hr); Kalambáka (at least hourly 6am–10pm; 15min); Métsovo (2 daily;

2hr); Pertoúli, via Eláti (3 daily Mon–Fri, 1 Sat & Sun; 1hr 15min); Pýli (14 daily Mon–Fri, 12 Sat & Sun; 20min).
Vólos to: Áfyssos (6 daily Mon–Fri, 5 Sat & Sun; 1hr); Áyios Ioánnis (2 daily Mon–Fri, 1 Sun; 2hr 15min); Katiyiórgis (2 daily Mon–Fri, 1 Sat & Sun; 2hr); Makrynítsa (9 daily Mon–Fri, 7 Sat & Sun; 50min); Miliés (6 daily Mon–Fri, 4 Sat & Sun; 1hr); Milína via Hórto (4 daily; 1hr 30min); Plataniás (3 daily Mon–Fri, 2 Sat & Sun; 2hr); Portariá (9 daily Mon–Fri, 7 Sat & Sun; 40min); Thessaloníki (8–9 daily; 3hr); Tríkala (4 daily; 2hr 30min); Tríkeri (2 daily Mon–Fri, 1 Sat & Sun; 2hr 30min); Tsangarádha (2 daily; 1hr 45min); Vyzítsa (6 daily Mon–Fri, 4 Sat & Sun; 1hr 10min); Zagorá (3 daily Mon–Fri, 2 Sat & Sun; 2hr–2hr 30min).
Zagorá to: Horeftó (1–2 daily; 15min); Pourí (4 daily Mon–Fri, 2 Sat & Sun; 15min).

Ferries and catamarans

"In season" means late June to early September; "otherwise" means mid-April to late June and early September to end October.
Áyios Konstandínos to: Alónissos (2 daily in season; 3hr); Skiáthos (2 daily in season; 1hr 45min); Skópelos, both ports (2 daily in season; 2hr–2hr 45min), on Hellenic Seaways.
Áyios Konstandínos to: Alónissos (4 weekly in season); Skiáthos (daily in season); Skópelos, both ports (daily in season), on GA Ferries; journey times as above.
Vólos to: Alónissos (1 daily car ferry July & Aug, 3 weekly otherwise; 4hr 45min–5hr; daily catamaran, 3hr); Skiáthos (2 daily car ferries in season, 1 daily otherwise; 2hr 15min; daily catamaran, 1hr 20min); Skópelos, both ports (2 daily car ferries in season, 1 daily otherwise; 3hr 30min; daily catamaran, 2hr–2hr 30min).
For current details, ring ⓣ24210 23400 for Hellenic Seaways services, ⓣ24210 31059 for other companies (eg Saos Ferries).
To Évvia Arkítsa–Loutrá Edhípsou (at least hourly July–Sept 15, every 2hr otherwise, last sailing at 11pm/10pm; 45min); Áyios Konstandínos–Áyios Yeóryios (June–Sept 5–6 daily, except Wed; April, May, Sept & Oct 4–5 daily, except Tues; 35min); Glýfa–Ayiókambos (10 daily summer, 8 winter; last sailing at 8.30pm/6.30pm; 30min).
Across the Gulf of Kórinthos Andírio–Río (every 15min, much less often after midnight; 15min); Áyios Nikólaos–Éyio (4 daily year-round except major hols, well-spaced 8.30am–6pm; 45min; ⓣ22660 31854 or 26910 22792 for current info).

Hydrofoils and "jet boats"

Vólos 1 daily Hellenic Seaways hydrofoil in season to: Skiáthos (1hr 30min), Skópelos (2hr–2hr 30min) and Alónissos (3hr).
Tiny "jet boats" run by Thalássies Synkinoníes Evoïkoú (ⓣ22260 72900, ⓦwww.evoikos-seatransports.gr) as follows:
Vólos 3–4 daily May–Sept to Nisí Tríkeri (1hr), Ayía Kyriakí (1hr 10min) and Oreí, Évvia (1hr 45min).

Epirus and the west

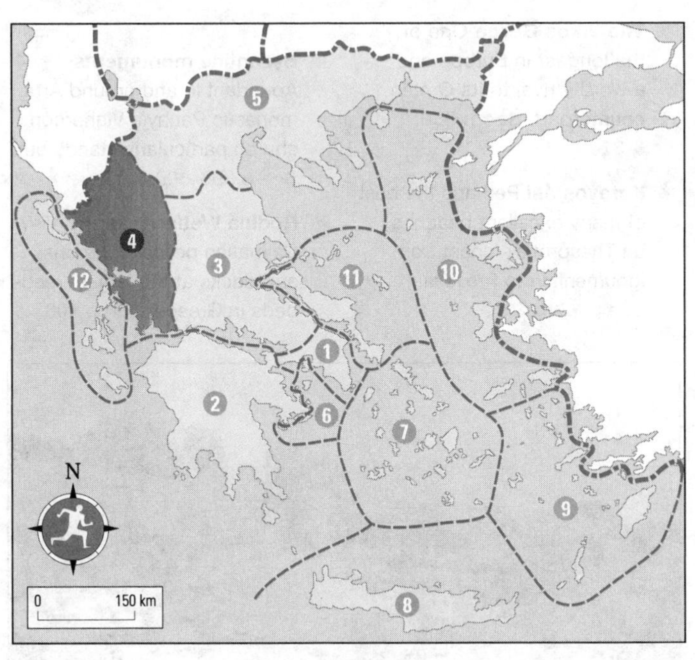

CHAPTER 4

Highlights

* **Ioánnina** The Ottoman citadel, lakefront and island associated with locally infamous hero/villain Ali Pasha. See p.359

* **Zagóri** Stone-built mansions and villages set in rugged mountain scenery. See p.368

* **The Víkos Gorge** One of the longest in Europe and a worthy rival to its Cretan counterpart. See p.369 & 373

* **Karavostási** Perhaps the best of many excellent beaches on Thesprotía's coast from Igoumenítsa to Préveza. See p.388

* **The Ahérondas River** A delight, from the gorge at its wild upper reaches to the sea at Ammoudhiá. See pp.393–394

* **Ancient Kassope** Underrated, atmospheric remains of a fortified town, abandoned in 31 BC. See p.396

* **Byzantine monuments** Abundant in and around Árta; monastic Panayía Vlahernón church particularly stands out. See p.398–399

* **Rodhiá Wetland Centre** View Dalmatian pelicans, herons and ducks at the largest reed-beds in Greece. See p.400

▲ Ancient Kassope

Epirus and the west

Epirus (*Ípiros* in modern Greek) has one of the strongest regional identities in mainland Greece, thanks to the unrelentingly rugged peaks, forested ravines and turbulent rivers of the **Píndhos** (Pindus) **range**. The **climate** is **wet** almost everywhere, much of the year, with thundery squalls bouncing off lower coastal ranges to dissipate a short distance offshore. These mountains have always protected Epirus from outside interference, securing it a large measure of autonomy even under Ottoman rule.

Because of this remoteness, the region was peripheral to ancient Greek culture; there are just four significant archeological sites, two of them isolated oracles. At **Dodona**, the sanctuary includes a spectacular Classical theatre; at **Ephyra**, the eerie remains of a Nekromanteion (Oracle of the Dead) was legendarily the gateway to Hades. **Kassope** and **Nikopolis**, near Préveza, are more conventional ancient cities. More recently, **Lord Byron** was the region's greatest publicist. He passed through in 1809 when tyrannical local ruler Ali Pasha was at the height of his power, and the poet's tales of intrigue and brigandage sent a shiver down romantic Western spines. Byron went on to distinguish himself in southerly **Étolo-Akarnanía** by supplying and training troops for the Greek War of Independence, and by dying during it at **Mesolóngi**.

The Ottomans were not finally ousted from Epirus – disputed frontier territory from the 1870s onwards – until March 1913, and the region never recovered its late-medieval prosperity. After 1923, **refugees** from Asia Minor were resettled on ex-Muslim holdings around Ioánnina, Préveza and across Thesprotía, the westernmost county of Epirus. After the Italians invaded in 1940, followed by the Germans in 1941, the Píndhos became first a stronghold of the **Resistance**, then the chief bastion of the Communist "Democratic Army" during the **civil war**. These events (see box, p.354) still reverberate today, not least in Epirus's consistent EU ranking as one of the poorest parts of Europe.

However, the **mountains** provide much of the attraction of Epirus. Their physical beauty is stunning, with limestone peaks and dense forest contrasting with stone-built villages and arched packhorse bridges. The most accessible and rewarding walker's target is **Zagóri**, particularly the magnificent **Víkos** and **Aóös gorges**, while **mounts Gamíla** and **Smólikas** provide several days of serious trekking. Above the villages, a few Latinate-speaking Vlach and Grecophone Sarakatsan transhumant shepherds still bring their sheep to the alpine pastures in summer, though owing to changed EU subsidy policies, unattended cattle are now more common. The wild fauna is impressive: there's good birdwatching, increasing numbers of wolves, plus legally protected brown bears who leave footprints in riverside mud.

Certain road itineraries offer less strenuous travelling, though many two-lane highways will soon be superseded by motorways. The route from Mesolóngi to Ioánnina via Árta should become the **Ionian Highway** as of 2011 – Árta to Filipiádha is already open. The old Kalambáka–Ioánnina highway is being eclipsed by the showcase **Vía Egnatía**, which will, by 2009, seamlessly link Igoumenítsa and Ioánnina with Métsovo, Grevená and Macedonia (the Igoumenítsa–Ioánnina section is complete).

Roughly halfway between Ioánnina and the Metéora stands **Métsovo**, the easiest venue for a taste of mountain life, albeit with a fair dose of commercialization. The two urban attractions are characterful **Ioánnina**, Ali Pasha's capital with its fortress, island and lake, and **Árta**, prettily set and blessed with a fine group of Byzantine churches and monasteries.

The coast, in both Epirus and Étolo-Akarnanía just south, is generally low-key, with sandy, not overly spoilt **beaches** between **Igoumenítsa** – the main ferry terminal for Corfu and Italy – and sleepy **Préveza**, boosted by proximity to those beaches and its airport. In between lies photogenic **Párga**, the main – often oversubscribed – Epirot resort. Inland the eminently scenic **gorge of the**

World War II and the civil war in Epirus

In **November 1940**, the **Italians** invaded Epirus from Albania; the Greeks repulsed the attack at Kalpáki, south of Kónitsa, and captured southern Albania in turn, humiliating Mussolini. However, euphoria was short-lived, since in April 1941 German armoured divisions rapidly overran Greece. When handing over various portions of the country to their allies for administration, the Germans assigned Epirus to the Italians, who trod lightly in the province where they had been so soundly beaten. After the Italian capitulation in September 1943, the Germans assumed direct control of Epirus, and conditions worsened. Together with the mountains of central Greece, the Epirot Píndhos was the main redoubt of various **partisan bands**, especially Communist-dominated **ELAS**. Harassment and ambush of the occupying forces incurred harsh reprisals, including the burning in early 1944 of almost every village along the Aóös River.

Emigration to the cities was greatly accelerated by these atrocities, and the subsequent **civil war** (1946–49) dashed any lingering hope of a reasonable existence in the mountains. Victims of reprisals by either the Communists or the Royalist/Nationalist central government, villagers continued fleeing to urban safety, or abroad, and many never returned.

After 1975, many men (and a few women) who fought in ELAS or the Communist Democratic Army, either as volunteers or conscripts, returned to Greece – often after more than three decades of exile in the USSR or its satellites. Others had been carried off as children to Albania, before being sent to various East European states for institutional upbringing. The political Right claims that this *pedhomázema* (roundup of children) was a cynical ploy to indoctrinate an army of dedicated future revolutionaries; the Left retorts that it was a humane evacuation of noncombatants from a war zone.

Whatever the truth, the Right won, with British and – after 1947 – American backing, and they used that victory to maintain an undemocratic, vengeful regime for the next 32 years. Many Epirot villagers, regardless of political conviction, believe that the poverty in which their communities long remained was deliberate punishment for falling within Communist-held territory during the civil war. Until 1981 they were routinely denied various licences and certificates needed to obtain public-sector work, to travel, to put children in better schools, or to run their own businesses. Only after the election of Greece's first PASOK government that year did things really change, and the past was finally treated as a separate age.

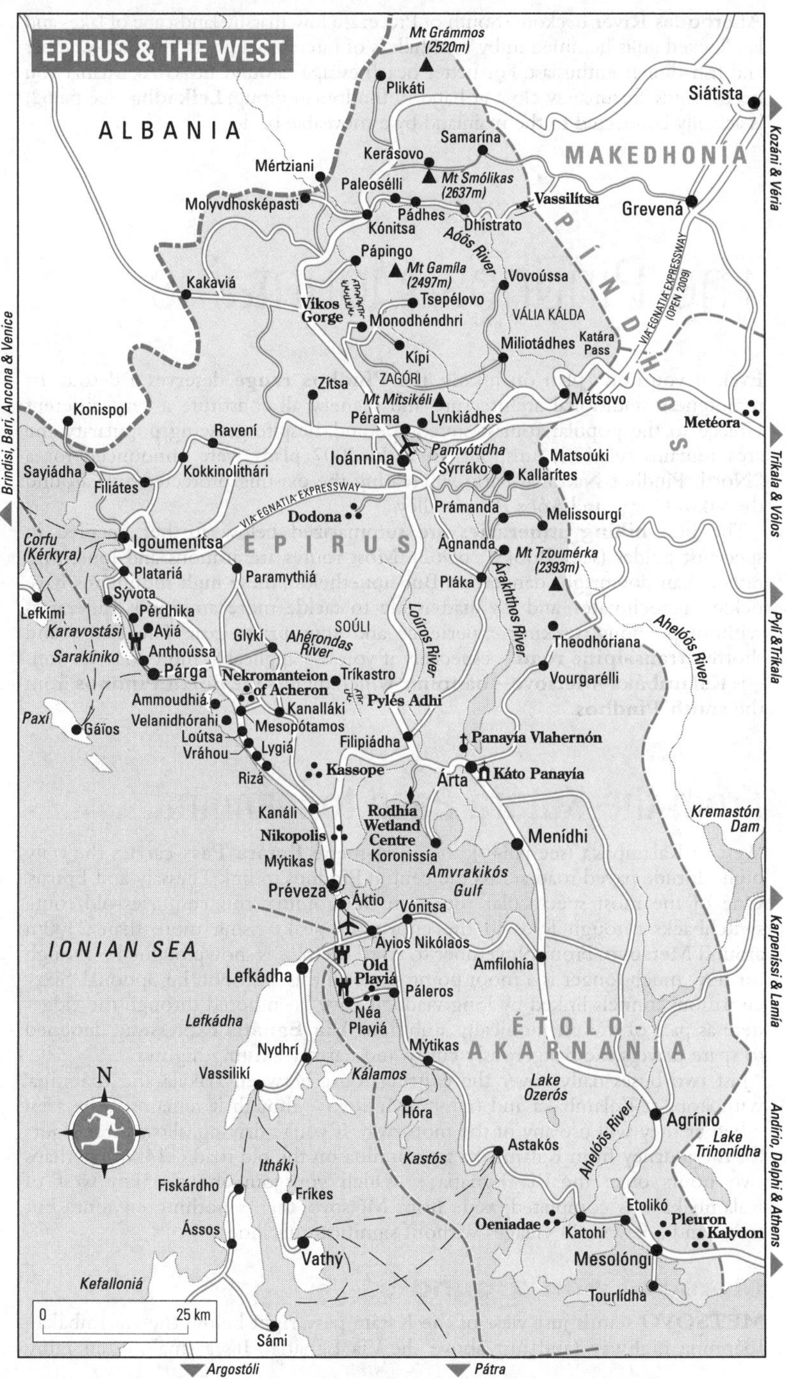

EPIRUS & THE WEST
ALBANIA
MAKEDHONÍA
PÍNDHOS
EPIRUS
ÉTOLO-AKARNANÍA
IONIAN SEA
Mt Grámmos (2520m)
Plikáti
Siátista
Samarína
Kerásovo
Mt Smólikas (2637m)
Mértziani
Paleosélli
Molyvdhosképasti
Pádhes
Vassilítsa
Grevená
Kónitsa
Dhístrato
Aóös River
Pápingo
Mt Gamíla (2497m)
Vovoússa
Kakaviá
Víkos Gorge
Tsepélovo
VÁLIA KÁLDA
Monodhéndhri
Miliotádhes
Katára Pass
VIA EGNATIA EXPRESSWAY (OPEN 2009)
Kípi
ZAGÓRI
Zítsa
Mt Mitsikéli
Métsovo
Konispol
Pérama
Lynkiádhes
Metéora
Raveni
Pamvótidha
Ioánnina
Matsoúki
Sayiádha
Kokkinolithári
Syrráko
Kallarítes
Filiátes
VIA EGNATIA EXPRESSWAY
Dodona
Prámanda
Melissourgí
Igoumenítsa
Corfu (Kérkyra)
Ágnanda
Mt Tzoumérka (2393m)
Plataria
Paramythiá
Pláka
Sývota
Lefkími
Pérdhika
Árakhthos River
Karavostási
Ayiá
Loúros River
Ahelóös River
SOÚLI
Glykí
Ahérondas River
Theodhóriana
Sarakíniko
Anthoússa
Vourgarélli
Párga
Nekromanteion of Acheron
Tríkastro
Ammoudhiá
Pylés Adhi
Velanidhórahi
Kanalláki
Paxí
Gáïos
Mesopótamos
Loútsa
Filipiádha
Panayía Vlahernón
Vráhou
Lygiá
Kassope
Árta
Káto Panayía
Rizá
Kanáli
Rodhía Wetland Centre
Kremastón Dam
Nikopolis
Menídhi
Koronissía
Mýtikas
Amvrakikós Gulf
Préveza
Áktio
Vónitsa
Áyios Nikólaos
Amfilohía
Lefkádha
Old Playiá
Páleros
Néa Playiá
Lefkádha
Nydhrí
Mýtikas
Vassilikí
Kálamos
Lake Ozerós
Hóra
Agrínio
Astakós
Ahelóös River
Lake Trihonídha
Ithákí
Kastós
Fiskárdho
Fríkes
Etolikó
Oeniadae
Katohí
Pleuron
Kalydon
Ássos
Vathý
Mesolóngi
Kefalloniá
Tourlídha
0
25 km
Sámi
Argostóli
Pátra
Brindisi, Bari, Ancona & Venice
Kozáni & Véria
Tríkala & Vólos
Pylí & Tríkala
Karpeníssi & Lamía
Andírio, Delphi & Athens
N

Ahérondas River beckons. South of Préveza, a low, marshy landscape of lakes and landlocked gulfs hemmed in by bare hills is of interest mainly to the bird-watcher and fish-dinner enthusiast. For better beach escapes around Étolo-Akarnanía you need islands, fortunately close at hand in the Ionian group; **Lefkádha** (see p.862) is actually connected to the mainland by a moveable bridge.

The Píndhos Mountains

Even if you don't plan on hiking, the **Píndhos range** deserves a detour. Its remoteness, traditional architecture and scenery all constitute a very different Greece to the popular tourist stereotype and, despite growing popularity, the area remains relatively unspoilt. In early 2007 plans were announced for a "North Píndhos National Park", increasing the existing protected area around the Víkos Gorge and Aóös River valley.

The best **hiking itineraries** are summarized below, further detailed in specialist guides (see "Books", p.962). Most routes are arduous and lonesome, rather than downright dangerous. But nonetheless, these high mountains have fickle microclimates, and it's inadvisable to tackle more ambitious itineraries without previous trekking experience and appropriate gear. The easiest and shortest **transalpine road** – especially if you use applicable motorway sections – is **Kalambáka–Métsovo–Ioánnina**, which divides the **north Píndhos** from the **south Píndhos**.

From the Katára Pass to Ioánnina

West of Kalambáka (see p.340), the 1694-metre **Katára Pass** carries the only high-altitude paved road across the central Píndhos to link Thessaly and Epirus. One of the most spectacular routes in the country, this centuries-old route switchbacks through folds in the enormous peaks rising more than 2300m around **Métsovo**. From November to April the pass is snowploughed – though for how much longer is a moot point, since all this will soon be optional. Sixty enormous tunnels linked by long viaducts have been bored through the ridges here as part of the pharaonically ambitious **Vía Egnatía** expressway, designed to spare drivers the dangerously curvy and narrow existing highway.

Just two buses daily cover the existing route between Tríkala and Ioánnina, with stops at Kalambáka and (rarely) Métsovo – though it remains to be seen whether they will use any of the motorway. If you're driving, allow three hours for the journey from Kalambáka to Ioánnina on the old road (114km), perhaps two hours once the Vía Egnatía – which you join about 35km west of Kalambáka – is completed; aside from Métsovo, there's nothing en route but forest and a few small villages without significant facilities.

Métsovo and around

MÉTSOVO stands just west of the Katára pass, right below the Kalambáka–Ioánnina highway (and just above the Vía Egnatía). It's a small, often rainy, alpine town, occupying two sides of a ravine and guarded by forbidding peaks to the south and east. Its tiers of eighteenth- and nineteenth-century stone houses spill downhill to and past the main platía, where a few old men still loiter after Sunday Mass in traditional dress, from black caps to pompom-ed shoes, chatting in Vlach (or, more properly named, Aroman). Women's garb, incorporating rich blue fabric and a headscarf, is less flamboyant but more regularly seen.

If you avoid the high seasons (midsummer and Christmas/Easter weeks), stay overnight and take in the surroundings, the place can seem magical. In season, Métsovo makes a favourite target for tour-buses full of Greeks, its ethos a numbing combination of the studiously twee and the relentlessly commercial, with shops selling kitsch wooden souvenirs and "traditional" weavings (mostly mass-produced these days). Even the garish roof pantiles are replacements for the stone originals, which apparently required too much maintenance.

Nonetheless, it would be a shame to omit Métsovo altogether, for its history and status as the Vlach "capital" are unique. Positioned astride the most viable route over the Píndhos, it secured a measure of independence, both political and economic, in the earliest days of Ottoman rule. Such privileges were elaborated in 1659 by a grateful Turkish vizier who, returned to the sultan's favour, wanted to reward the Metsovot family who had protected him during his disgrace and exile. Métsovo's continued prosperity and preservation of some traditions is largely due to Baron Mihaïl Tositsas (1888–1950), banker offspring of a Metsovot family living in Switzerland, who left his colossal fortune to an endowment that supports industries and crafts in and around the town. The eighteenth-century **Arhondikó Tosítsa** (daily except Thurs: summer 9.30am–1.30pm & 4–6pm; winter 3–5pm; only group entry every 30min; €3) just off the main thoroughfare has been restored to full glory as a **museum**; panelled rooms, rugs and a fine collection of Epirot crafts and costumes give a sense of the town's opulence in that era.

Practicalities

The **bus stop** is on the main platía, the **post office** is on the main street 200m uphill, while five **bank** ATMs are scattered between the two.

Meals are overwhelmingly meat-oriented, as befits a pastoral centre. Best – and most secluded – of several grills is friendly, big-portioned *Kamares* next to the police station, functioning principally in the evening. The main vegetarian or lunchtime options are the central *Hotel Galaxias*, where a limited but tasty menu is served on the lawn under giant trees, or *Metsovon Yevseis* just below the main square, reincarnation of the venerable *Athinae*. **Wine** buffs may want to try the fabled Katóyi, available at restaurants, local shops and indeed across Greece. It's a moderately expensive limited bottling from vineyards along the Árakhthos River, though quality of the main Averoff label varies (the Ktima line is best). This, and other **local specialities** such as *trahanádhes* (a porridge of milled wheat and soured sheep's milk, either sweet or savoury), the smoked *metsovóne* cheese and *hilópites* (like tagliatelle, long or diced, with added egg), can be obtained at local shops such as Iy Piyi or O Vlahos, just downhill from *Hotel Bitouni*.

Accommodation

Métsovo has a wide range of **accommodation**, with thirteen hotels plus quite a few inns or *dhomátia*, nearly all en suite. Outside Christmas/Easter weeks, the local festival (July 26) or August, you should have little trouble in getting a bed or bargaining indicated rates down a category.

Adonis Just above the main square ⓣ26560 42300, ⓦwww.metsovohotels.com. Quietly sited and with the largest, plushest rooms (all with fireplace) in town; if they're full or not affordable, try one of their affiliates, the *Hotel Apollon* (❹) or the adjacent *Anostro Guesthouse* (❸), below the main square. B&B peak season ❺, rest of year (room only) ❹

Bitouni Top of the main street ⓣ26560 41217, ⓦwww.hotelbitouni.com. *Bitouni*'s affable proprietor speaks fluent English, the result of eight years' residence in London. Most rooms have balconies with valley views; there are attic suites suitable for four, plus a sauna. ❹

Filoxenia Just behind the grassy central-park hillock ⓣ26560 41021, ⓕ26560 42009. Officially *dhomátia* (rooms), these en-suite units are excellent value, with valley views out of the rear rooms and some pricier, plusher units. ❷–❸

Kassaros On street leading south from the square ⓣ26560 41800, ⓦwww.kassaros.gr. Most rooms and suites at this large hotel have views over to Anílio, there's a sauna/*hamam*, and the management organizes summer or winter activities in the nearby mountains. ❺

Around Métsovo

Outside Métsovo, the main attraction is the monastery of **Áyios Nikólaos**, signposted from the main platía but in fact fifteen minutes' walk below town; it is reached just off the half-cemented *kalderími* bound for **Anílio**, the village across the ravine. The monastery's *katholikón*, topped by a simple barrel vault, was built in the fourteenth century to an unconventional plan; what might once have been the narthex eventually became a *yinaikonítis* or women's gallery. Brilliantly coloured, unconventional **frescoes** date from 1702, cleaned and illuminated courtesy of the Tosítsa Foundation. Since there's no dome, the Four Evangelists are painted on four partly recessed columns; between them are scenes from the life of Christ, and assorted martyrdoms. The barrel vault features the Virgin and Child, the Holy Trinity, an Archangel and a *Pandokrátor* in medallions, forming an unusual sequence. Otherwise the iconography is the norm for post-Byzantine churches: a *Crucifixion* on the west wall, and a *Virgin Enthroned* in the conch of the apse, flanked by the *Communion of the Apostles* (six to each side). A guardian family lives on the premises and receives visitors until 7.30pm (purchase of postcards or souvenirs expected). You'll also be shown the monks' former cells, with insulating walls of mud and straw, and the abbot's more sumptuous quarters.

Eastern Zagóri: Vovoússa and the Vália Kálda

For lonelier scenery, and a truer picture of contemporary mountain life, follow the paved road into **eastern Zagóri** from the Baldhoúma bridge on the old Métsovo–Ioánnina highway. This precipitous route snakes north along the Várdhas River valley through a landscape of broad-leafed trees and scrub. At Grevenítí, 21km along and the first of several Vlach villages, a mixed black-pine-and-beech forest emerges, cloaking the Píndhos almost to Albania. Beyond Flambourári – like its neighbours badly depopulated, and burnt by the Germans in reprisal for Resistance activities, with only fine stone churches spared – the road becomes ever more twisty. Hazardous driving conditions are aggravated by lumber trucks hauling logs out from the sawmill at **VOVOÚSSA**, which, 51km from the main highway, straddles the Aóös River. Its milky-green waters are spanned by a high-arched, eighteenth-century **bridge**. On either side, wooded ridges rise steeply to the skyline, culminating in 2177-metre Avgó peak presiding over the **Vália Kálda**, heart of a small national park, traversed by the E6 long-distance trail and home to bears, thus the Arkoudhórema (Bear Stream) threading through the valley.

Like its southerly neighbours, Vovoússa (except for bridge and church) was torched by the Germans; the village, the last before the border with Grevená province in Macedonia, serves as the gateway to the national park. **Accommodation** includes the very basic *Xenon Perdhiki* (Ⓣ26560 22850; ❶) at the riverside, or, 500m upstream in the small west-bank quarter, *Xenonas Dhrouyia* (Ⓣ26560 22555 or 697 70 27 207; all year; ❸), with sparsely furnished but good-standard doubles, triples and quads, plus an on-site taverna. The main independent **taverna** is *Psistaria Angelos* back on the main street, with terrace seating overlooking the river.

For visiting the Válìa Kálda, the *Katafíyio Valia Kalda* (Ⓣ26510 29445, Ⓦwww.katafigiovaliacalda.com; dorms €10), 3.5km south of Vovoússa near the edge of the park, is possibly a better base. There are multi-bed dorms as well as five-person family rooms, a lounge, and cheapish meals on offer. Kostas Yiannoulis, the full-time warden, is a mine of information on the area and can advise on excursions into the Válìa Kálda ("Warm Valley" in Vlach, named ironically, as it has one of the coldest climates in Greece). The postcard-starring twin **tarns of Flénga**, just below the eponymous 2159-metre peak of the lightning-blasted Mavrovoúni ridge bounding the park on the south, are a favourite destination, just feasible as a day-trip with an early start.

The bus service to or from Vovoússa has been abolished, so you've either driven your own car or walked here. Leaving on foot, you can follow a marked long-distance route down the Aóös River valley to the village of Dhístrato (see p.381); the trek, partly along trail and partly on forestry track, keeps to the east bank of the Aóös, and takes a full day.

Ioánnina and around

Moving west from Métsovo, the old road drops first into the Árakhthos River valley, then climbs again over a shoulder of Mount Mitsikéli before the final descent to the great, reed-fringed **lake of Pamvótidha** (or Pamvótis). On its south shore, the old town of **IOÁNNINA** (aka Yiánnena) covers a rocky promontory jutting out into the water, its fortifications punctuated by minarets. From this stronghold, Ali Pasha carved out a semi-autonomous fiefdom that encompassed much of western Greece and present-day Albania: a localized rebellion that prefigured wider defiance in the Greeks' own War of Independence.

Although much of the city is modern and undistinguished – thanks not to Ali (though he did raze numerous buildings while under siege in 1821) but to 1960s developers – the old town remains one of the more characterful in Greece. There are stone-built **mosques** (and a **synagogue**) to evoke the Ottoman era, and Ali Pasha's citadel, the **Kástro**, survives more or less intact; **Nissí island** has a car-free if overly prettified village, and frescoed **monasteries**. Ioánnina is also a springboard for visits to the **caves of Pérama**, among the country's largest, on the western shore of the lake, and the longer excursion to the mysterious and remote Oracle of Zeus at **Dodona**, as well as to Epirus's most rewarding corner, **Zagóri**.

Modern Ioánnina is one of Greece's fastest-growing provincial capitals, with the city and suburbs' **population** doubling since the 1970s to 130,000. Much of this has been decanted from moribund villages in the corners of the province, but it also includes some 25,000 students at the major university here, plus military personnel; Ioánnina has been a strategic garrison town since its incorporation into Greece.

Arrival, information and town transport

Ioánnina **airport** is on the road to Pérama, 5km from the centre (city bus #7 links it with town). Drivers will find **parking** nightmarish and the city's pay-and-display scheme comprehensive, permitting only two hours at a time – it's easiest to use the car park shown on the map, or try for unregulated spaces in the Kástro.

KTEL buses currently arrive at one of three terminals, though these will soon be moved to one station on Yeoryíou Papandhréou. A current terminal at Zozimádhon 4, north of Platía Pýrrou, serves most points north and west, including Métsovo, Kalambáka, Igoumenítsa, Kónitsa and the Zagóri villages. Another station at Bizaníou 19 connects Árta, Préveza, Dodona and all villages in the south or east parts of Epirus, though this shuts at weekends when all services use the Zozimádhon terminal. Kastoriá services use a third terminal at Yeoryíou Papandhréou 58. It's advisable on summer weekends to buy tickets for both coast and mountains the day before. Local blue-and-white **city buses** leave from a cluster of stops below the central Platía Pýrrou; buy tickets from adjacent booths beforehand, and cancel them when boarding. Information on current KTEL timetables is most easily obtained from the **EOT** at Dhodhónis 39 (Sept–June Mon–Fri 7.30am–2.30pm), though they keep little other literature in English. The local **taxis** are dark green; central ranks are marked on the map.

Accommodation

Many Ioánnina **hotels** are noisy, badly placed and expensive for what's on offer, though off-season prices drop a category. High season tends to be Christmas and Easter more than summer, and weekends year-round see the better places packed out. Given the town's traffic congestion, hotels with unrestricted street parking or their own garages are indicated.

If you're willing to sacrifice midtown convenience for better value, there are about twenty licensed **dhomátia** in Pérama village (see p.366). If you can afford the better Ioánnina hotels, pay about the same (or less) for quality lodgings 12km away in stunningly set Lynkiádhes, halfway up Mount Mitsikéli, overlooking the lake.

Camping, unusually for a town, is an attractive option. Lakeside *Camping Limnopoula* (☎26510 25265), 1500m west of Platía Mavíli (city bus #2 or 20min walk), is well-equipped and mosquito-free, though a bit cramped and more geared towards camper-vans than tents.

Central Ioánnina

Filyra Alley off Andhroníkou Paleológou 18 ☎26510 83560 or 693 26 01 240. Four appealing studios (some triple) in a restored old building, with full kitchens (though breakfast is offered) and a young, trendy clientele. B&B ❹

Galaxy Platía Pýrrou, south cnr ☎26510 25056, ⓕ26510 30724. Comfortable and quiet rooms with spectacular mountain/lake views from the balconies, a/c and small tubs in the bathrooms. You don't get much more central; limited street parking. ❹

Kastro Andhroníkou Paleológou 57 ☎26510 22866, ⓦwww.epirus.com/hotel-kastro. A tastefully restored inn at the base of the ramp up to "Its Kale", whose seven unique rooms are mostly equipped with double beds. Downstairs rooms are cooler (fans but no a/c) and cheaper. Adequate street parking. B&B ❺

Kentrikon Kolléti 5a ☎26510 71771, ⓦwww.hotel-kentrikon.gr. As the name says ("central"); a boutique hotel in a restored building, with exposed stonework, flat-screen TVs and quality furnishings in variably sized rooms (doubles and two galleried family suites). Small breakfast salon, pleasant rear courtyard with rain roof. ❹

Olympic Melanídhis 2 ☎26510 25888, ⓦwww.hotelolymp.gr. The highest-standard hotel in the city centre, in a fairly quiet spot. Well-appointed rooms (plus a few suites) have music systems, safes, small but well-executed designer bathrooms with tubs, and balconies or large terraces. Full-service restaurant on-site; private parking. ❻

Politeia Anexartissías 109 ⓣ 26510 22235, ⓦ www.etip.gr. Built on the site of an old tradesmen's hall, this hotel retains some period details and its arrangement around a courtyard. Handy for the bus station, but an oasis of calm in the bazaar; choose between standard rooms at the back or palatial upstairs suites which sleep four. Some free off-street parking; breakfast available in the bar-café flanking the courtyard. Rooms B&B ⑤, suites ⑦

Tourist Kolétti 18, cnr Krystálli ⓣ 26510 25070, ⓦ www.hoteltourist.gr. The only recommendable quasi-budget digs in town. Overhauled rooms are all en suite with a/c, but bathrooms remain basic, there are few balconies, and most renovation funds seem to have been spent on the lobby. ③

Lynkiádhes and Nissí

Mitsikeli Lynkiádhes village ⓣ 26510 81964 or 697 88 95 106. Simple but serviceable en-suite rooms, heated but with no balconies, above an eponymous, limited-menu grill-taverna. Easy access and parking. ③

Orizon/Horizon Lynkiádhes village ⓣ 26510 86180 or 697 60 06 756, ⓦ www.hotel-horizon.gr. The name says it all – views over the entire lake basin from this modern hotel, which got new beds, furniture and plasma TVs in 2007. Seven en-suite, double-glazed, wood-floored rooms are huge, all with balconies, four with fireplaces and some with tubs in the bathrooms. Breakfast is served out on the terrace or in the lounge, and own-label wine is on offer. Adequate parking, but a steep, hairpin drive to reach it. ⑤

Sotiris & Evangelos Dellas Nissí island ⓣ 26510 81494. Simple *pension* with several rooms sharing bathrooms; you'll find the proprietors at the house right next to the school, or in the ground-floor café-bar of the inn-building (can be noisy at night). ①

The Town

Once through its extensive modern suburbs, **orientation** in central Ioánnina is straightforward. Main drag Avéroff leads from the gate of the lakeside Kástro, past the dense grid of lanes in the old bazaar area, to central Platía Pýrrou, before continuing south as Dhodhónis.

The Kástro

In its heyday the **Kástro**'s walls dropped abruptly to the lake, and were moated on their landward (southwest) side. The moat has been filled in, and a quay-esplanade now extends below the lakeside ramparts, but there is still the sense of a citadel, with narrow alleys and shops.

Signs inside point to the **Municipal Ethnographic Museum** (daily: May–Sept 8am–8pm; Oct–April 9am–4pm; €4.40), an elegantly arranged collection of Epirot costumes, guns, silver-work and Islamic art, housed in the well-preserved, floodlit **Aslan Pasha Tzamí**, allowing a rare glimpse inside an intact Greek mosque. It dates from 1618, built on the site of an Orthodox cathedral pulled down in reprisal for a failed local revolt of 1611. The interior retains painted decoration in its dome and *mihrab* (niche indicating direction of Mecca), as well as a vividly coloured *mimber* or pulpit, nicely complementing a walnut and mother-of-pearl suite on display in the "Muslim section".

Ali Pasha

Ali Pasha, a decidely ambivalent "heroic rebel", is the major figure in late medieval Epirot history. The so-called "Lion of Yiannena", on balance a highly talented sociopath, pursued policies consistent only with his self-interest. Ali's attacks on the Ottoman imperial government alternated with acts of vindictive **savagery** against his largely Orthodox Christian subjects. Despite this, he is still held in some regard by locals for his perceived role as a defier of Istanbul, the common enemy – folk postcards of the man abound, and a platía in the citadel is even named after him.

Ali was born in 1741 in Tepelene, now in modern Albania, and by 1787 had been made pasha of Tríkala as a reward for his efforts in the war against Austria. His ambitions, however, were larger, and the following year he **seized Ioánnina**, an important town since the thirteenth century, with a population of 30,000 – probably the largest in Greece at the time. Paying sporadic tribute to the sultan, he operated from here for the next 33 years, allying himself in turn, as strategy required, with the Ottomans, the French or the British.

In 1809, when his dependence upon the sultan was nominal, Ali was visited by young **Lord Byron**, whom he overwhelmed with hospitality. (The tyrant's sexual tastes were famously omnivorous, and he was particularly taken with the poet's "small ears", a purported mark of good breeding.) Byron, impressed for his part with Ali's stature, and the **revival of Greek culture** in Ioánnina, commemorated the meeting in *Childe Harold*. This literary portrait was ambiguous, however, since Byron well knew that behind Ali's splendid court and deceptively mild countenance were "deeds that lurk" and "stain him with disgrace".

Ali met a suitably grisly end. In 1821, resolved to eliminate the Epirot threat to his authority before tackling the Greek insurgency, the Ottoman sultan sent an army of 50,000 to capture Ali. Lured from the security of Ioánnina citadel with false promises of lenient surrender terms, he was ambushed, shot and decapitated instead. His severed head was displayed in all the provinces he had terrorized, to assure folk that the monster was dead – and that the sultan's writ ran once more – before being sent to Istanbul. The rest of Ali supposedly lies in the northeast corner of the citadel.

More poignant is a section devoted to synagogue rugs and tapestries donated by the dwindling Jewish community of about fifty; their **synagogue** at Ioustinianoú 16 can be visited on application (8am–2pm) to the community office at Iosef Eliyiá 18B (an unmarked, ground-floor storefront – only Greek or Hebrew spoken – where there's a good, brief display on the community's history). Some 150m west of the clocktower over the *kástro* gate, a municipally erected, trilingual **memorial** honours the 1850 local Jews deported on March 25, 1944 to Auschwitz.

In the arcaded *medresse* or Muslim seminary next to Aslan Pasha, tradition places Ali's attempted 1801 rape of Kyra Frosyni, mistress of his eldest son. Having refused the 60-year-old tyrant's advances, she was bound, weighted and thrown alive into Lake Pamvótidha, together with seventeen companions. The incident gave rise to several folk songs (and various kitsch postcards); her ghost is still said to hover over the water on moonlit nights. The *medresse* houses the **Fotis Rapakousis Museum** (same hours as Ethnographic Museum; free, Greek-only labelling), a huge collection of medieval weaponry and jewellery.

The inner citadel (Its Kale)

Southeast of the Aslan Pasha Tzamí lies the "**Its Kale**" or **inner citadel** of the fortress (daily 8am–10pm; free); the grounds are occasionally used for concerts after-hours, and there's a pleasant café near the entrance, occupying the garrison's former mess. The citadel was used for decades by the Ottoman, then Greek, military, and most buildings have unfortunately been razed, or overhauled in such a way that few can be recognized as eighteenth-century structures. One of two Ottoman graves beside the old **Fethiye Tzamí** ("Victory Mosque"), surmounted by an elegant wrought-iron cage, is probably that of Ali Pasha, while the other contains his first wife Emine and one son; the mosque, remodelled by Ali, was built atop the remains of a thirteenth-century cathedral. On the site of Ali's vanished palace, where Byron was entertained, stands the **Byzantine Museum** (summer Mon 12.30–7pm, Tues–Sun 8am–7pm; winter Tues–Sun 8am–5pm; €3), a thin, largely post-Byzantine collection that can be skipped if time is short or if you'll be in Kastoriá. The displays mostly comprise masonry, coins, pottery, icons and colour prints of frescoes from various ages; the only Byzantine painting is a fresco fragment of *The Betrayal*, from a church near Vourgarélli (see p.384). A few paces away, in the purported treasury of Ali Pasha's seraglio, is a more interesting auxiliary exhibit, labelled as the **Silver-work Hall**, devoted to Ioánnina's long-running silver industry.

The rest of the town

Apart from the Kástro, the town's most enjoyable district is the **old bazaar and Jewish quarter**, a warren of narrow lanes between the citadel's main gate and Anexartissías avenue bounding it on the south. It retains a cluster of Ottoman-era buildings (including imposing mansions with ornate window grilles and founding inscriptions), as well as a scattering of copper- and tinsmiths, plus the silversmiths who were long a mainstay of the town's economy. Retail **silver** outlets cluster either side of Kástro's gate; you'll find the last traditional **tinsmiths** at Anexartissías 84, and the last **copper-mongers** at no. 118–122. *Stoas* off Anexartissías serving old warehouses, now being gentrified, can also be rewardingly explored.

Just off central Platía Dhimokratías (officially renamed Andhréa Papandhréou), beside a small park behind the National Bank, is the **archeological museum** (closed indefinitely). When and if it reopens, a fascinating collection of lead tablets inscribed with questions to the oracle at Dodona should return to view, along with a variety of bronze and ceramic artefacts from Neolithic to Roman times, from across Epirus.

Nissí island

The island of **Nissí** in Lake Pamvótidha is connected by water-buses (half-hourly in summer, hourly otherwise; 8am–11pm, return journey 6.30am–11pm; €1.50 each way) from the Mólos quay on Platía Mavíli. Only islanders' cars are allowed, hauled across on a chain-barge to the mainland opposite. The beautiful island village, founded during the sixteenth century by refugees from the Máni, is flanked by several **monasteries**, worthy targets for an afternoon's visit. By day the main lane leading up from the boat dock is crammed with stalls selling jewellery and kitsch souvenirs. Except at three overpriced waterfront restaurants and another cluster by Pandelímonos, quiet descends with the sun setting vividly over the reed beds that fringe the island.

The **monastery of Pandelímonos**, just east of the village, is the most evocative of Ioánnina's Ali Pasha sites, though it is in fact a complete reconstruction, as the original building was smashed years ago by a falling tree. In January 1822 Ali, trapped on the upper storey by the sultan's men, was shot from the floor below, then decapitated (supposedly on the second step from the top). The fateful bullet holes form the centrepiece of a small **museum** (daily: summer reasonable daylight hours; winter hours vary; €2) devoted to Ali, along with numerous wonderful period prints and a splendid hubble-bubble.

Three other clearly signposted **monasteries** – **Filanthropinón**, **Ayíou Nikólaou Stratigopoúlou** or **Dilíou**, and **Eleoússas** (closed) – lie south of the village in the order cited. They stand within a few hundred yards of one another along a tree-lined lane; the first two have resident families, who allow brief visits except during siesta hours (knock for admission if doors shut) to the main chapel, or *katholikón*, which feature late- and post-Byzantine **frescoes** in various states of preservation.

The finest are at Filanthropinón, a simple barrel-vaulted structure with a blind narthex and two side chapels. A complete cycle of Christ's life in the

Lake Pamvótidha and its ecology

Murkily green and visibly polluted, **Lake Pamvótidha** is in desperate straits. The springs that historically fed it along its north shore now flow fitfully, leaving **runoff** as its main replenishment. This – from Ioánnina and surrounding farmland – is heavily **contaminated** with tyre and brake-lining particles, pesticides and fertilizers. The lake only drains in winter, via ditches near Pérama linking it to the Kalamás River; in dry years Pamvótidha may not drain at all, with water levels falling 2m in a lake that's barely 15m deep. Swimming is forbidden, though few would care to in such conditions; after a nadir at the millennium when eighty percent of its fish died, Pamvótidha – and a variable zone along the shoreline – has been officially protected since 2003, with Greek President Karolos Papoulias – his mother a Nissí native – helping to push for cleanup funding.

Despite all this, Nissí's inhabitants struggle to continue **fishing**, to pass the time and supplement island diets. The lake was stocked with several Hungarian species from 1986 onward, though only the hardy *kyprínos* (carp), and a bass-like leviathan that attains fifteen kilos in weight, managed to thrive. Ioánnina inhabitants understandably refuse to eat anything caught in Pamvótidha, so the islanders must sell their catch at a pittance to Thessaloníki. The only lake items on Nissí restaurant menus are the legs of frogs from the surrounding reed beds, some of the eels, and *kyprínos*.

inner nave dates from just after the monastery's foundation in 1292; there are plenty of episodes on boats in the Sea of Galilee, as befits a lake-island church. Lower down, throughout the building, are saints; higher up, in the outer nave and north chapel, graphic martyrdoms predominate – sundry beheadings, draggings, impalings and boilings. At the east end of the north chapel, Adam names the beasts in the Garden of Eden, while the narthex ceiling bears a fine *Transfiguration*. In the south chapel, just west of the door, ancient Greek sages (Solon, Aristotle, Plutarch) make a rare appearance.

The frescoes in Ayíou Nikólaou Stratigopoúlou are being slowly cleaned, and should eventually equal Filanthropinón's in interest. Currently the narthex offers, from the Life of the Virgin, a fine *Adoration of the Magi* and a *Flight into Egypt* on the west wall, plus a typically surreal *Apocalypse* over the door. There's a fine touch to the *Nativity*, where an angel sternly awakens Joseph with a wagging finger.

Beyond these three monasteries the track loops anticlockwise around the island up to a fourth monastery, **Ioánnou Prodhrómou**, right behind Pandelímonos, which holds the keys. However, the interior is far less interesting than the exterior's three-windowed gables and brickwork.

Eating and drinking

Ioánnina offers numerous **restaurants** both in town and across the lake. The most obvious concentration of eateries, offering meat and seafood, lines part-pedestrianized Pamvótidhas northwest of Mólos quay (though addresses are cited as Stratigoú Papágou, the parallel back alley). Just outside the *kástro* gate are a few traditional Greek tavernas and *psistariés*. On Nissí Island, the obvious dockside tavernas are atmospheric but overpriced, mediocre venues for fresh-water specialities like eel (*héli*), crayfish (*karavídhes*), carp (*kyprínos*) and frogs crammed rather off-puttingly into glass tanks outside. Most Ioanninots, if they want a meal out of town, head for Amfithéa or Lynkiádhes on Mount Mitsikéli, the latter always several degrees cooler year-round.

Restaurants

Exostis Lynkiádhes village. The most reliably open, of three tavernas here, providing good-value, locally sourced grills and *mezédhes* on an airy terrace. Dinner only except summer.

Fysa Roufa Avéroff 55. Traditional *mayireftá* such as *patsás*, *mayirítsa*, baked fish, suckling pig and *spetzofáï*, whose slightly bumped-up prices are amply justified by the calibre of the cooking, the service, a pleasantly upmarket environment and large portions; unusually, there's a full line of desserts too. Cosy loft seating for winter, and a decor of archival photos from Párga, the proprietor's birthplace, and Greek theatre actors. Open 24hr.

Limni Stratigoú Papágou 26. More likely than its neighbours to have seafood, and slightly elevated prices are compensated for with large, salubrious portions.

To Metsovo Ethnikís Andístasis 6. Very popular with the locals at night, serving all manner of roast beast washed down with bulk wine. Dinner only.

Stin Ithaki Stratigoú Papágou 20A. The most ambitious menu on the lakefront, encompassing Turkish-style kebabs, Cypriot specialities and Smyrna recipes as well as Epirot standards such as trout, *píttes*, cheeses and mushrooms in various guises. With such a range, some duff platters are inevitable, but the kitchen succeeds more often than not. Don't over-order starters; they're big, and often better value than main courses.

Iy Veranda Amfithéa, 7km out of Ioánnina, on the highway. Well-executed *mezédhes* and grills, with views over the island and lake. Closed Mon, and lunch except summer.

Snacks and cafés

Ioánnina is the original home of **bougátsa** (custard tart; served with a salty *kouloúra* or round biscuit), fresh at breakfast time with sweet or savoury fillings from *Select* at Platía Dhimokratías 2, its decor of terrazzo floor and marble tables unchanged for forty years. Its rival, with a more updated design sense, is *Paleopanos* at Avéroff 3. The patisserie *Vrettania*, under the eponymous hotel at Platía Dhimokratías 11A, has excellent own-brand ice cream as well as all imaginable sticky cakes.

Nightlife and entertainment

The large local student population keeps Ioánnina lively after dark. **Nightlife** and **frappádhiko society** oscillates between the calmer **cafés** around Platía Pýrrou and along nearby Dhodhónis, and the more nocturnal café-bars, patisseries and ice-cream parlours on Platía Mavíli, heart of the **Mólos** or lakefront, where a gas-lantern-lit carnival atmosphere prevails thanks to sellers of Fársala *halvás* (sweetmeat) and roast corn. There are more wine bars, crêperies and the odd "pub" scattered across the approaches to the castle, especially along Karamanlí.

After-hours **bars** concentrate at the southern corner of the citadel, in the little platía of a former craftsmen's bazaar off Ethnikís Andístasis; premises all merge anonymously together into one giant seating area. Posters announce hangar-like summer **music clubs** out on the lakeshore.

Back up around Platía Pýrrou, there are three **cinemas**, which usually host decent first-run films, as does the Odeon five-screen at the Paralimnio Centre, out in Votanikós district. Various formal music/theatre events occur in midsummer; get information and tickets from the EOT office.

Listings

Adventure specialist For rafting, canyoning, caving and other activities in the Píndhos, contact Alpine Zone, Ioséf Eliyía 16 ⓣ26510 23222, ⓦwww.alpinezone.gr.

Books, maps and newspapers For quality maps and a respectable stock of books in English, head for Papasotiriou bookstore at Mihaïl Angélou 6, just off Platía Pýrrou; Newsstand at Pyrsinélla 14 has foreign newspapers.

Car rental Most rental offices are on Dhodhónis: Avis, no. 71 ⓣ26510 46333; Budget, no. 109 ⓣ26510 43901; Tomaso, no. 42 ⓣ26510 66900; National/Alamo, no. 10 cnr Kaliáfa 3G ⓣ26510 47444; and Hertz, no. 105 ⓣ693 70 96 377. Hertz and Avis also have booths at the airport.

Internet *On-Line*, on Pyrsinélla, behind the provincial government HQ; open 24hr with cheap rates.

Post office Both the central post office (Mon–Fri 7.30am–8pm) and the secondary one (normal hours), have long queues; take a number and wait.

The Pérama caves and lake circuit

Some 5km north of Ioánnina, the village of **PÉRAMA** claims to have Greece's largest system of **caves** (daily 8am–8pm; €6), extending for kilometres beneath a low hill. They were discovered during late 1940 by locals attempting to find shelter from Italian bombing raids. The one-hour mandatory tours of the complex are primarily in Greek (commentary repeated in passable English) and make some effort to educate, though inevitably there's recitation of various suggestively shaped formations.

To reach the caves on public transport, take a #8 blue city bus from the terminal below Platía Pýrrou to Pérama village; the caves are a ten-minute walk inland from the bus stop. Once beyond the cave, drivers can **make a circuit** of the lake. The road splits shortly after Pérama, at Amfithéa: the lower option hugs the lakeshore, passing – about halfway around – the **monastery of Dhouraháni**, now a vocational school. The name stems from Durahan Pasha, an

Ottoman general who founded it in 1434 as thanks for being miraculously saved by the Virgin while unwittingly crossing the frozen lake.

Dodona: the Oracle of Zeus

DODONA, 22km southwest of Ioánnina in a once-isolated valley, comprises the ruins of the ancient **Oracle of Zeus** (daily 8.30am–3pm, may close 6pm mid-summer; €3) and a vast **theatre**. "Wintry Dodona" was mentioned by Homer, and religious life here seems to have begun with the first Hellenic tribes who arrived in Epirus around 1900 BC.

The origins of the oracle – oldest in Greece – are shadowy. Herodotus records the arrival of a *peleiae* from Egypt which alighted on an oak tree and ordered the founding of a divination shrine. In ancient Greek, *peleiae* meant either "dove" or "old woman", so the tale conceivably refers to a priestess – perhaps captured from the Middle East and versed in Asiatic cults and divination. The oak tree, embossed on local ancient coins, was central to the cult. Herodotus also related that the oracle spoke through the rustling of the oak's leaves, amplified by copper vessels suspended from its branches. These sounds would then be interpreted by frenzied priestesses and strange priests who slept on the ground and never washed their feet. The Argonauts legendarily used timber from this oak for their ship, with the charmed properties of the wood enabling them to get out of numerous predicaments.

Dodona occasionally hosts **musical and ancient drama performances** on summer weekends, though sadly since 2000 these are staged on modern wooden bleachers rather than in the ancient theatre.

The site

Entering the site past a few tiers of a third-century BC **stadium**, you are immediately confronted by the massive western wall of the **theatre**. Built during the reign of King Pyrrhus (297–272 BC), this was one of the largest in Greece, rivalled only by those at Argos and Megalopolis. The Romans added a protective wall and a drainage channel around the orchestra as adaptations for their blood sports. What's now visible is a meticulous late nineteenth-century reconstruction of what until then had been a chaotic jumble of stones. Alas, almost all of it is now off-limits, though it's worth following a path around to the top of the *cavea* (seating curve) to fully savour the glorious setting, looking across a green, silent valley to Mount Tómaros. A grand entrance gate leads into the overgrown **acropolis**, with Hellenistic foundations up to 5m wide.

Beside the theatre, tiered against the same slope, are the foundations of a **bouleuterion**, beyond which lie the complex ruins of the **Sanctuary of Zeus**, site of the oracle itself. There was no temple per se until late in the fifth century BC; until then, worship had centred upon the sacred oak, inside a circle of votive tripods and cauldrons. Building began with a small *iera oikia* (sacred house), later flanked by Ionic colonnades and **temples** to the minor goddesses **Dione and Themis** in the time of Pyrrhus. After a 219 BC sacking by the Aetolians, a larger temple was constructed, surviving until the fourth century AD, when the oak tree was chopped down by Christian zealots. The remains of the Pyrrhian and later sacred precinct can be seen today, with a modern **oak tree** planted at the centre of the *iera oikia* by a helpfully reverent archeologist. Ruins of an early Christian **basilica**, constructed partly atop a **sanctuary of Hercules** (**Herakles**), are also prominent nearby – distinguished by round column stumps, and a useful placard detailing the entire site.

Excavations by the University of Ioánnina have resumed, which should eventually result in greater comprehensibility. Many **oracular inscriptions** were found when the site was first systematically dug in 1952, demonstrating the oracle's lingering influence even after its eclipse by Delphi – and the fears and inadequacies motivating pilgrims of the era in such questions as: "Am I her children's father?" and (bathetically) "Has Peistos stolen the wool from the mattress?"

Practicalities

Public transport to Dodona (and its modern village) is hopelessly sparse and mostly doesn't really show up until almost closing time. A round trip by **taxi** from Ioánnina with an hour at the site can be negotiated for a reasonable amount – about €24 per carload. **Drivers** will find the Vía Egnatía (exit "Dhodhóni") only slightly quicker than the old secondary roads for arrival from Ioánnina.

Local **accommodation** and **taverna** options have multiplied, as much with an eye to passing trade from the nearby motorway as to site visitors. The closest hotel is *Andromachi* (Ⓣ26510 82296; ③), offering simple but adequate, cheerful 1970s-vintage rooms and a decent, popular taverna. The same management owns the more comfortable, good-value *Thea Dodoni* in **MANDÍO** village 600m distant (same phone; Ⓦwww.theadodoni.gr; ④), with pastel-coloured rooms and another restaurant. Also in Mandío, the Michelis family's *Mirtali Art Motel* (Ⓣ26510 82288, Ⓦwww.mirtali.gr; doubles ⑤–⑥, suites ⑦–⑧) is an ultra-contemporary designer hotel with ten ancient-deity-themed units, some glimpsing the theatre; the higher in the building, which includes an upmarket restaurant, the pricier. Diametrically opposite to this, in **DHODHÓNI** village, is the all-in-one taverna-grocer's-post office-*dhomátia* of Stefanos Nastos (Ⓣ26510 82289; ②) – basic in all respects, but with unbeatable views from the lawn tables.

Zagóri

Few parts of Greece are more surprising or more beguiling than **Zagóri**. A wild, thinly populated region, it lies north of Ioánnina, bounded by the roads to Kónitsa and Métsovo on the west and south, and the Aóös River valley to the northeast. The beauty of its landscape is unquestionable: dense forest, bare limestone and flysch badlands, rugged mountains furrowed by foaming rivers and partly subterranean streams. But there is hardly an arable inch anywhere, and no non-touristic livelihood for its few remaining inhabitants besides herding livestock or cutting timber. The last place, in fact, that one would expect to find some of the most imposing architecture in Greece.

Yet the **Zagorohória**, as the 46 local villages are called, are full of grand stone *arhondiká* (mansions), often with enclosed courtyards whose deep-eaved gateways open onto immaculately cobbled streets. Though they look older, the *arhondiká* date mostly from the late eighteenth or early nineteenth century. By the 1960s, many had become derelict or been insensitively restored, but the authorities now ensure (in several listed villages, anyway) that repairs are carried out using proper materials, rather than cheap brick and sheet metal; new structures are required to have local stone cladding.

Inside, the living quarters are upstairs, arranged on an **Ottoman** model. Instead of moveable furniture, low platforms line the rooms on either side of a hooded

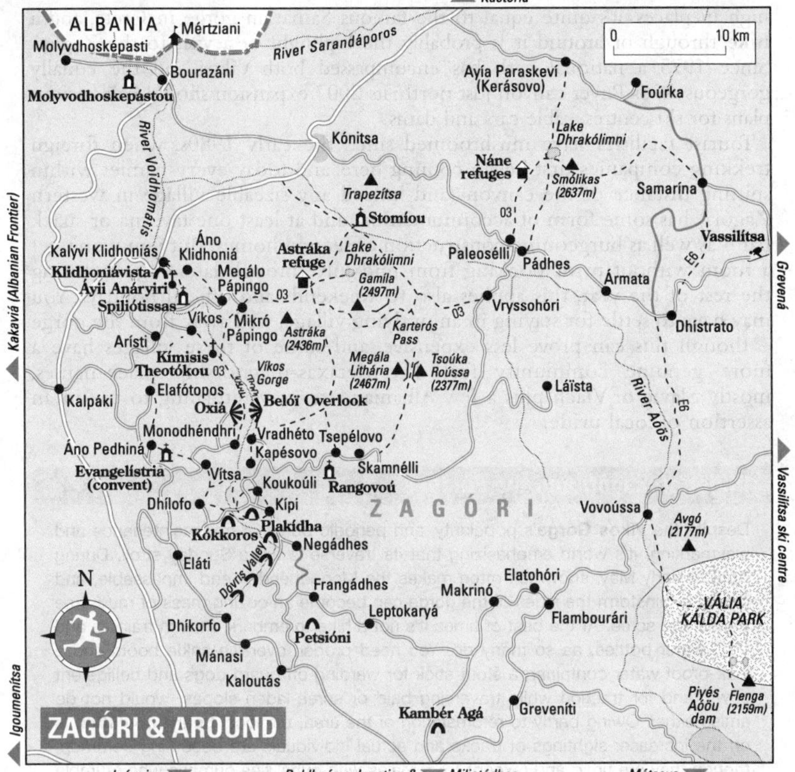

fireplace; strewn with rugs and cushions, they serve as couches for sitting during the day and sleeping at night. The wall facing the fire is usually lined with panelled and sometimes painted storage cupboards called *misándres*; in the grander houses intricately fretted wooden ceilings are often also coloured. Additionally, most houses have a *bímtsa* (fireproof bunker) for hiding the family gold and perhaps a wife and child or two whenever marauders threatened; even if the house was torched, survivors could dig out their wealth and start over again.

As for the countryside, the best way to savour it is by **hiking** numerous paths which, gliding through forest and pasture or slipping over passes and hogbacks, connect the villages. The most popular outing is along the awesome **Víkos Gorge** and then up over the Astráka pass to an alpine lake. It's not to be missed, though for more of a backcountry feel, you may want to continue northeast over **Mount Gamíla**, towards the remoter villages at the base of **Mount Smólikas** (see p.381). Lately other more organized activities in the area – canyoning, paragliding, kayaking and rafting on the lower Voïdhomátis – are beginning to take precedence, courtesy of various local expedition outfitters (cited in the text).

The Víkos Gorge and western Zagóri

The **Víkos Gorge** cuts right through the limestone uplands of Mount Gamíla, separating the villages of western and central Zagóri. With walls almost 1000m high in places, it's quite equal to the famous Samarian gorge in Crete, and a **hike** through or around it is probably the highlight of a visit to the Zagóri. Since 1975 a national park has encompassed both Víkos and the equally gorgeous Aóös River canyon just north; its 2007 expansion should halt various plans for ski centres, cable cars and dams.

Tourist facilities have mushroomed since the early 1980s, when foreign trekking companies first began coming here, and today every hamlet within spitting distance of the canyon (and indeed any sizeable village in western Zagóri) has some form of accommodation, and at least one taverna or snack bar – as well as burgeoning construction of second homes. But you won't get a room without prior booking from mid-July through late August; during the rest of the year, this applies also to weekends and official holidays. You may have to settle for staying in an outlying village, well away from the gorge – though this can prove less expensive, and some of these villages have a more genuine community feel. Pre-Metaxas-dictatorship place-names, mostly Slavic or Vlach plus a few Albanian, are now returning to use in an assertion of local pride.

Hiking in Zagóri and the Píndhos

Despite the **Víkos Gorge**'s popularity, and periodic bouts of trail maintenance and waymarking, it's worth emphasizing that its traverse is not a Sunday stroll. During April or early May, snowmelt often makes the Monodhéndhri end impassable, and during a rainstorm the sides of the gorge can become an oozing mass of mud, tree trunks and scree. At the best of times it's not a hike to embark on with trainers and PVC water bottles, as so many do. You need proper, over-the-ankle boots and a leak-proof water container; a stout stick for warding off guard dogs and belligerent cows, and for traction while traversing bald or scree-laden slopes, would not go amiss either. Owing partly to reforestation of the area, the local **bear population** is on the increase; sightings of tracks and actual individuals are becoming common, though they are timid and (except for females with cubs) flee humans who stumble upon them.

In 1995, an EU-funded programme indicated some thirty **"Z"-prefixed** trails and tracks in western and central Zagóri, but walking times given on various signposts are often unreliable, waymarking en route – often vandalized by hunters and other interested parties – can be haphazard, and trail maintenance has been almost nonexistent. Treks over the **high ridges of Gamíla or Smólikas** fall into a different category – you must be a fit, experienced hill-walker used to carrying fifteen-to-twenty-kilo loads. Optimal seasons are late May to late June and mid-September to mid-October; hike in July (let alone Aug) and you'll be cooked by the sun at all altitudes, and eaten alive by the fierce *davánia* (deer-flies). You should have at least two days' supply of food in your pack; few villages have any sort of shop at all, and where they exist, stocks are limited to the odd carton of juice, eggs and tin of sardines. Given the region's severe depopulation, buses do not run daily (or at all) to/from critical trailhead villages, so you will probably have to use taxis or do a lot of road-trudging before or after your trek. If you get into difficulties, the best strategy is to ring the warden of the Astráka hut (see p.375) who will summon rescue services from Ioánnina if needed. The approaching end of traditional pastoral life means that shepherds – traditionally an excellent source of guidance, emergency shelter and food – do not reliably occupy the high meadows.

The best **topographical maps** for the region, sturdy and waterproof, are Anavasi Editions' 1:50,000 *Pindus Zagori* (for Mt Gamíla, Víkos and the Aóös) and their 1:25,000 *Smólikas Trapezítsa* (for Mt Smólikas), available in Athens, Ioánnina or map specialists abroad.

Monodhéndhri is the most popular starting point for a gorge traverse, but far from the only one; local explorations lend themselves to linear or loop trips of some days, rather than basing yourself somewhere for a week.

Monodhéndhri

Near the south end of the gorge, at 1150-metre elevation, stands handsome **MONODHÉNDHRI**, which like all western Zagóri villages escaped the wartime devastation suffered by their eastern cousins – though it's now somewhat disfigured by tourist shops and parked coaches. Just before the flagstoned platía with its giant tree, the seventeenth-century church of **Áyios Minás** is locked, but the narthex, with fine eighteenth-century frescoes, is open. The wide, artless modern *kalderími* leading from the far end of the platía reaches, after 900m (not "600m" as signed) the eagle's-nest monastery of **Ayía Paraskeví** (built 1412), teetering on the brink of the gorge (there's a viewing platform just behind) and now empty, though left open. If you've a head for heights, continue around the adjacent cliff face on a path to a stair-trail climbing to **Megáli Spiliá**, a secluded cave where villagers once barricaded themselves in times of danger. The views over the gorge en route are spectacular, as they also are from **Oxiá** (7km by car, less by the Z8 path), where a short *kalderími* leads from the road's end onto a natural balcony with all of Víkos spread vertiginously at your feet.

Buses from Ioánnina call only two days weekly; drivers should leave vehicles at the car park by the lower platía (the spur road's marked for Víkos Gorge and Ayía Paraskeví). The handful of **inns** along the upper, asphalted road-curve are mostly expensive; one better-value establishment is quiet and well-placed *Arhondiko Kalderimi* (Ⓣ26530 71510 or 694 52 11 241; summer ❸, winter ❹) with wood-floored rooms, some balconied, and snug breakfast bar. The only real budget option is *Monodendri Pension* (aka *Katerina's*; Ⓣ26530 71300; ❸), with plain but adequate rooms either en suite or not. The best, most reliably open **tavernas** are *Iy Pyli tou Viko*, offering salads, dips and grills opposite Áyios Minás church, or pricier *Pitta tis Kikitsas* on the platía, specializing in *alevrópitta* (a heavy dish made from dough, egg and cheese). There is no shop, so come equipped with trekking supplies.

Vítsa and the Skála Vítsas

During busy seasons, you may choose – or be forced – to stay in other nearby villages. **VÍTSA** (alias **Vezítsa**), 2km below Monodhéndhri, is to many tastes less claustrophobic and more attractive than Monodhéndhri. **Accommodation** includes the slightly kitsch but homey en-suite rooms, approached through a long vegetable patch, of Eleni Kondou (Ⓣ26530 71464; ❸), in the lower of two neighbourhoods, and a restored-mansion inn just below the fine platía, *O Troas* (Ⓣ26530 71123; summer ❸, winter ❹), featuring five large rooms with modern baths, an old mural of Sebastopol in the upstairs lounge, and a pleasant breakfast café/courtyard. Among several **tavernas**, mostly on the through road, most interesting (if pricey) is *Kanella ke Garyfallo* at the curve, run by a returned Canadian-Greek mycologist who unsurprisingly features mushrooms on his menu. There's also access to the gorge via the signposted **Skála Vítsas**, a half-hour's gentle descent from the platía along the **Z9** – mostly on engineered stair-path – to the handsome single-arched **Misíou bridge**; from there one can continue upstream to Kípi village via the O3 path, or downstream along the heart of the gorge.

Dhílofo, Eláti, Dhíkorfo and the Kaloutás bridge

From either Vítsa or the Misíou bridge, the **Z15** leads south to Dhílofo; the path-start in Vítsa is trickier to find than the branch leading from the bridge, but once done it's a twenty-minute descent to a stream bed, where the Misíou branch links up, then a climb along a crumbled *kalderími* which peters out in flysch badlands. After another stream crossing, the path resumes before becoming a track to the outskirts of **DHÍLOFO**, just over an hour along. One of the most handsome Zagorian villages, formerly **Sopotséli**, it also has road access (cars must be left at the outskirts). You can **stay** at the sumptuous *Arhondiko Dhilofo* (☎26530 22455, ④), while the most reliable if simple **taverna** – on the lovely central platía – is *To Sopotseli*, featuring grills and *mezédhes*.

From Dhílofo, walkers can continue down to Áyios Minás chapel on the main road and thence to Eláti on the **Z24**, but nearly half the way (90min) is along asphalt or bulldozer track, so you may as well visit **ELÁTI** (ex-Boúltzi) by car. You're rather distant here from the gorge, but there are fine views north to the peaks of Gamíla, plus a good **hotel**, *Elati* (☎26530 71181, Ⓦwww.hotelelati.gr; B&B ④), run by Canadian-Greek Alex Yiannakopoulos. There's an excellent independent **restaurant** down the street, *Sta Riza* (closed Tues, also Thurs low season; ☎693 70 37 544), doing local *píttes*, vegetarian starters and cooked dishes at fair prices, with good bulk wine.

The next village, **DHÍKORFO (Tzódhila)**, proves a beauty with its grand houses and unusual, minaret-like belfry of Áyios Minás church; on the platía is *To Milo* **taverna**, which also rents a villa to groups (☎26530 71174). Beyond Dhíkorfo the chief attraction is the enormous **triple-arched bridge** below **Kaloutás**, about 250m off the paved road by dirt track – initially follow signage for Visóka monastery. All villages past Kaloutás were burnt by the Germans, but the road continues paved to Miliotádhes and thence the old Ioánnina–Métsovo highway – a very useful short-cut. Alternatively, a paved side-road just past Kaloutás leads to Frangádhes (see p.378).

Áno Pedhiná and Elafótopos

ÁNO PEDHINÁ (formerly **Soudhená**), 4km west of Vítsa and Monodhéndhri and sharing the same bus service, offers a few rooms establishments and some superior **hotels**. Best of these is Dutch co-managed *Porfyron* (☎26530 71579, Ⓦwww.porfyron.com; all year; ⑤) beside Áyios Dhimítrios church, a lovingly restored mansion whose rooms have painted or carved ceilings and antique furnishings; there's a large garden and indoor taverna open to all. Otherwise try the *Ameliko* (☎26530 71501 or 694 47 72 638, Ⓦwww.ameliko.gr; B&B ⑤), whose simply appointed rooms with working fireplaces occupy three buildings, with an on-site restaurant. At the lower entrance to the village is your best **taverna** option, *Ta Soudhena*, with hearty food served in a rustic atmosphere. Also at the base of the village stands the restored **convent of Evangelístria**, currently untenanted. Should you gain admission, you'll see the *katholikón's* magnificent carved *témblon* and vivid, cleaned frescoes from 1793, though the structure is much older. Nearby Káto Pedhiná is headquarters for worthwhile **activity organizer** Compass Adventures (☎26530 71770, Ⓦwww.compassadventures.gr), offering local skiing, hiking and rafting.

From Áno Pedhiná, the **Z5** (very overgrown in places) and **Z4** (much clearer) routes, via Elafótopos, take you around the Víkos Gorge when that is impassable, ending up at Víkos village (see opposite) after three-and-a-half hours. **ELAFÓTOPOS** itself (**Tservári**), on a bare hillside, has an attractive stone-built **hotel/restaurant**, the *Paradhosiako Katalyma Elafotopos* (☎26530 71001; July–Sept, weekends only otherwise; ③) at the village entrance; supper is also available at nearby grill *T'Alonia*.

Through the gorge: Monodhéndhri to Pápingo

The most-used **path down to the gorge** begins beside handsome arcaded Áyios Athanásios church in Monodhéndhri; a sign promises fairly accurate walking times of four-and-a-half hours to Víkos village, six hours to either of the Pápingo villages. Once past Monodhéndhri's municipal amphitheatre, the path is cobbled for most of the forty minutes down to the riverbed, whose stony course you follow for another few minutes before shifting up the west (true left) bank, reaching the best viewpoint at a saddle ninety minutes from the village.

The entire route is waymarked, sometimes faintly, by red-paint dots and white-on-red stencilled metal diamonds with the legend "**O3**". This refers to a long-distance path, which begins south of Kípi at Lynkiádhes on Mount Mitsikéli, traverses Mount Gamíla and ends beyond Mount Smólikas. However, the surface underfoot is arduous, with some boulder-hopping in the gorge bed, metal or felled-branch ladders getting you over tricky bits on the bank, plus slippery, land-slid patches.

About two hours out of Monodhéndhri you draw even with the **Mégas Lákkos ravine**, the only major breach in the east wall of the gorge; a spring here has been piped to make it more usable in summer. Another thirty minutes' level tramping takes you past the small, white shrine of **Ayía Triádha**; a further half-hour (around 3hr from Monodhéndhri) sees the gorge begin to open out and the sheer walls recede.

Víkos village and the Voïdhomátis springs

As the gorge widens you must make a choice. Continuing straight, the best-defined path takes you past the side trail to beautifully set eighteenth-century **Kímisis Theotókou** chapel (unlocked; excellent frescoes well worth the fifteen-minute round-trip detour). Beyond here, the route becomes a well-paved *kalderími*, climbing up and left to **VÍKOS** (**Vitsikó**; 870m elevation), four-plus hours from Monodhéndhri and also accessible by a five-kilometre paved road from Arísti. This underrated village has two **inns**, the better being the one kept by Ioannis Dinoulis (☎26530 42112; ④), right where the gorge trail arrives, with modern, comfortable rooms and a small restaurant-bar. Up on the square, with its exceptionally handsome church of **Áyios Trýfon**, there's Khristoforos Tsoumanis' independent **restaurant**, reliably open with good Zagorian *píttes*, grills, local wine and *mayireftá*.

Most walkers, however, prefer to follow the marked O3 route to the two **Pápingo villages**, crossing the gorge bed at the **Voïdhomátis springs**, some three-and-a-half hours from Monodhéndhri. It's about two hours' walk from the springs up to Mikró Pápingo, slightly less to Megálo, with the divide in the trail nearly ninety minutes above the riverbed crossing. After an initial steep climb, there's a fine view down into the gorge near some weathered, tooth-like pinnacles, before the trail traverses a stable rock slide to the fork. Should you be reversing this route, the path-start in Mikró Pápingo village is signposted bilingually, and marked by a fancy stone archway in Megálo Pápingo.

The Pápingo villages and Áno Klidhoniá

MEGÁLO PÁPINGO is the larger of these paired villages, comprising two distinct quarters of 25 or so houses each along a tributary of the Voïdhomátis. It has served as the location for Jonathan Nossiter's 2000 film *Signs and Wonders*, starring Charlotte Rampling, plus countless Greek advertising shoots. Even before this, Megálo was a haunt of wealthy, trendy Greeks, making it a dubious target in peak season, though it is still delightful at other times. The fact that large coaches can't scale the steep hairpin road from the Voïdhomátis valley has made all the difference between here and Monodhéndhri; in peak season you must leave cars at the outskirts.

Accommodation is abundant if not generally budget-priced. Dead-central *Xenonas tou Kouli* (Ⓣ26530 41115 or 693 28 47 752; ❸) is the historic original inn, its now en-suite rooms fitted with TVs and fridges; Koulis has retired, and English-speaking sons Nikos and Vangelis Khristodhoulou (Ⓣ693 28 47 752) manage it, as well as the lively **café-bar** out front. Above the main shop across the way, the rooms kept by Lakis Kotsoridhis (Ⓣ26530 41087; ❸) are more modern but excellent value. Just across the street, between the two churches and arranged around a narrow courtyard, are the variable-sized, traditional rooms (Ⓣ26530 41893 or 697 36 82 252; ❹) of Nikos and Ioulia Tsoumani attached to their **restaurant**, best in the village, with tasty soufflés, lamb and regional dishes, an understatedly classy dining room (the old barn) for winter, plus an unbeatable view of Mount Astráka from the summer terrace. The rooms – best being the family suite – have quality furniture and down quilts. Equally comfortable, with a homey, non-institutional ethos, off at the far north end of the village, is the *Xenonas Papaevangelou* (Ⓣ26530 41135, Ⓦwww.papevangelou.gr; rooms ❹, studios ❻), with large, variable rooms – many with fireplace – and four self-catering studios amidst well-tended gardens, family-friendly common areas and a genial, multilingual proprietor, Yiorgos. On the south side of the village, *Xenonas Kalliopi* (Ⓣ26530 41081, Ⓦwww.epirus.com/kalliopi; ❸), offers dated but cheerful en-suite rooms, and home-style meals at their year-round taverna.

Megálo Pápingo is linked to its smaller namesake by a three-kilometre surfaced road; walkers should take the marked, restored *kalderími* off the road, via a historic bridge, which shortcuts the journey to half an hour. If you do take the road, just before the bend – at an obvious spot adorned by low masoned walls – you can detour to the **kolymvitíria** or natural swimming pools, a few paces up the stream bed of the Rongovós canyon.

MIKRÓ PÁPINGO, half the size of its neighbour, crouches below an outcrop of grey-limestone rocks known as the Pýrgi (Towers). Just below the church the WWF maintains an **information centre**, with worthwhile exhibits on the human and natural history of Pápingo and environs (Mon, Tues, Thurs & Sun 10.30am–5.30pm; Fri, Sat & hols 11am–6pm; free). The village has one main **inn**, Kostas Tsoumanis' *Xenon O Dhias* (Ⓣ26530 41257; ❹; discount for trekkers), its rooms distributed over two buildings bracketing a decent, sometimes lively, **bar-restaurant**.

Bus departures from the two Pápingos back to Ioánnina are all but non-existent. The best exit strategy is to walk west (2hr 30min) to the village of Kalývi Klidhoniás on the Kónitsa–Ioánnina highway, which has regular services, from Megálo Pápingo via the nearly abandoned hamlet of **ÁNO KLIDHONIÁ (Goúliari)**, on a better-than-average marked path, most of it unbulldozed, far quicker and easier than the dreary 23-kilometre haul to the highway along the paved road through Arísti. In Áno Klidhoniá – with more churches remaining than houses – there's a handy **taverna** on the platía, *Filoxenonas Zagori*, with four plain but adequate **rooms** upstairs (Ⓣ26550 24532 or 697 37 01 702; ❸).

The lower Voïdhomátis River valley

For a walk through the lower **Voïdhomátis River gorge**, start (or continue) from Kalývi Klidhoniás, where signposted lanes on either bank take you to the exceptionally graceful, single-arch **Klidhoniávista** bridge – the national park boundary – within twenty minutes. On the south (left) bank stands *Exohiko*

Kendro O Voïdhomatis, fair priced and popular, and the headquarters of **activity outfitter** No Limits (Ⓣ26550 23777, Ⓦwww.nolimits.com.gr). The first bit of the onward walk, on the true right (north) bank, follows a fake *kalderími* laid in garishly inappropriate white fieldstone, but this ends quickly, a more rugged trail bringing you within forty minutes alongside the brief detour up to tiny but vividly frescoed **Áyii Anáryiri** monastic church (unlocked, dated to 1658). The onward, roller-coaster route often permits a close look at the river environment (otters are sighted here); you emerge on a curve of the Arísti–Pápingo road, with the best views possible over the restored, cliff-clinging **monastery of Spiliótissas** (locked).

Just below this point, a **modern bridge** (built 1923) carries the Pápingo-Arísti road across the Voïdhomátis as it exits the Víkos Gorge. The immediate bridge environs are a popular picnic area (no camping), but riverbank trails permit access to more peaceful spots upstream before the gorge blocks further progress. **Kayaking** and **rafting** are the sole way through these narrows; swimming in the Voïdhomátis is done only by trout – anyone defying the ban would probably perish in the icy waters.

With persistence, you can find the old path up from near the river bridge to a point on the Arísti–Víkos asphalt about 2km from the latter, making possible a day-loop taking in the Klidhoniá villages, the lower gorge, Víkos village, the Voïdhomátis springs and back to Pápingo.

Should you need them, there are usually **accommodation** vacancies in relatively unglamorous, 1944-damaged **ARÍSTI** (ex-**Artsísta**), southwest of the Voïdhomátis River. Best of several inns here is the *Zissis* (Ⓣ26530 41147, Ⓕ26530 41088; ④), with small but appealing modern rooms, and a restaurant; it's near the bottom of the village en route to the river-bridge.

Hikes across the Gamíla range

For walkers keen on further, sometimes arduous hiking, there several itineraries beyond the Pápingo villages, across the **Gamíla** range into the central Zagóri. These are provided by the aforementioned O3 long-distance trail, and several of the more ambitious "Z" routes.

Pápingo to Astráka col

All hikes east into Gamíla begin with the steep but straightforward ascent to **Astráka col**. Though the refuge on the col is clearly visible from Megálo Pápingo, the trail essentially starts at Mikró Pápingo, as the resumption of the O3 which has climbed out of the Víkos Gorge. Ten minutes out, you pass Áyios Pandelímon chapel, then traverse forest to Antálki spring (40min from Mikró Pápingo), leaving trees behind as you climb towards Tráfos spring (1hr 40min from Mikró). Twenty minutes beyond Tráfos, a signposted side-trail branches right towards **Astráka summit** (2436m), a three-hour round trip from this point. The main 03 continues, in about 35 minutes, to the **EOS refuge**, perched on the saddle joining Astráka with Mount Lápatos (2hr 45min from Mikró Pápingo). For reservations at the 2005-renovated hut (70 dorm beds; €11; May–Oct), contact warden Yiorgos Rokas on Ⓣ697 32 23 100.

East of Astráka: Dhrakólimni and Gamíla

Northeast of the refuge, on the far side of the boggy Lákka Tsoumáni valley, gleaming **Lake Dhrakólimni**, alive with newts, is tucked away on the very edge of the Gamíla range about an hour's walk from the refuge, along a distinct, waymarked path.

Zagorian bridges

A perennial pleasure as you traverse Zagorian ravine beds is coming upon one of the many fine stone bridges that abound locally. One-, two- or even three-arched, these bridges – and the old cobbled paths serving them – were the only link with the outside world for these remote communities until motor roads were graded in the mid-1950s.

They were erected during the eighteenth and nineteenth centuries by teams of **itinerant craftsmen**, who were away from home between the feasts of Áyios Yeóryios (St George's Day) in late April and Áyios Dhimítrios (St Demetrius) in late October. As in other mountainous regions of Europe, they came from remote, poor communities: Pyrsóyianni and Voúrbiani in the Kónitsa area, and Ágnanda, Prámanda and Houliarádhes southeast of Ioánnina. Closely guarding trade secrets with their own argot, they travelled across Greece and the Balkans until World War II and the Cold War sealed off frontiers.

Surviving bridges mostly span the upper reaches of the Víkos Gorge and its tributaries, and are representative, accessible examples of this vanished craft. Most feature **arkádhes**, either continuous balustrades or more often single stone spikes, the latter used to winch heavily laden pack-animals over slick cobbles on the arch.

Vítsa, Kípi or Koukoúli make convenient bases for visiting the dense **cluster of bridges** in the vicinity, all named after the local worthies who financed them. The Misíou lies below Vítsa; the Kókoros (Noútsos) stands right beside the main valley road; the Kondodhímou (Lazarídhi) nestles between Kípi and Koukoúli; while the remainder are scattered either side of Kípi – the spectacular Plakídha (Kloyerikó) triple span downstream, several more upstream from the village. Remoter, but equally impressive, are the triple span below Kaloutás, the graceful double-arched Petsióni below Frangádhes and the high-arched Kambér Agá 4.5km north of Miliotádhes.

East of the refuge, the O3 route affords a strenuous eight-hour hike to Vryssohóri village via the nastily steep **Karterós pass**. Despite waymarking, this should only be attempted by experienced trekkers equipped with the appropriate map. A more casual, accessible outing is to the **summit of Mount Gamíla** (2497m), an easy two-hour-plus climb from the refuge, with superb June wildflowers en route and unbeatable views into the Aóös valley from up top.

South to central Zagóri: Tsepélovo and around

The most popular onward trek from Astráka col is the five-hour, often faint trail south across the Gamíla uplands, via Mirioúli and the head of the Mégas Lákkos Gorge, to the villages of central Zagóri. Besides water at Mirioúli, there are only two other springs en route, and the scenery consists mostly of forbidding if impressive limestone-dell-scape, but destination **TSEPÉLOVO** merits the effort. With a sawmill at the outskirts, and 180 permanent inhabitants, it has a lived-in feel compared to west-Zagóri villages. The major local attraction is eleventh-century **Rangovoú monastery**, about 1km southwest of the village, just below the main road. Dedicated to Áyios Ioánnis Pródhromos (St John the Baptist), its partly cleaned frescoes are of later vintage but still worth a look. From the perimeter wall of the grounds, two trails (one cobbled) dead-end at different points in the bed of the Vikákis ravine; it is *not* possible for casual walkers to continue downstream to Kípi, though local adventure organizers may organize canyoning expeditions, with swimming involved.

Tsepélovo is the biggest tourist centre in Zagóri after Pápingo. The oldest, least expensive and friendliest **accommodation** is ★ *Hotel Gouris* (☎26530

81214 or ⓣ694 75 61 463, ⓦwww.epirus.com/hotelgouris; B&B ❷), run by Anthoula Gouri, usually at the traditional *Kafenio Gouri* on the platía (where breakfast is served), and daughter Maria; rooms are en suite, with wood floors and restrained decor. A good second choice is *To Arhondiko* (ⓣ26530 81216, ⓦwww.tsavalia.gr; ❸), a gaily painted, arcaded mansion 70m below the platía, with well-kept rooms around an upstairs salon and an attractive courtyard below. On the platía with its giant plane tree are two self-catering options: simple but pine-floored, painted-ceilinged *Deligiannis Rooms* (ⓣ26530 81232; ❸), while *Iy Mikri Arktos* (ⓣ26530 81128 or 697 70 79 871; summer ❹, winter ❺) comprises three comfortable apartments. Tsepélovo's **tavernas**, mostly on the square and the lane leading down to the main road, fluctuate in ownership and quality.

There's a **bus** service three days weekly to and from Ioánnina, with Skamnélli (the next village) the end of the run. But if you don't have a vehicle, the best way of heading down-valley is via a faint path west out of Tsepélovo, across the ravine and then up the palisade, which links up with the paved road serving **Vradhéto** (seasonal café). This is one terminus of an amazing, serpentine *kalderími* – the **Skála Vradhétou** – linking it with Kapésovo village (see below); in the opposite direction, a rehabilitated cobble-path leads forty minutes up to the breathtaking **Belói** lookout over the Víkos Gorge.

Kapésovo, Koukoúli, Kípi and Frangádhes

KAPÉSOVO is a visually attractive place, mostly invisible from the road – and the descending Skála Vradhétou, signposted at the village edge. The gigantic former schoolhouse is now home to an informal ethnographic collection, including wolf-traps. The local **inn**, *To Kapesovo* (ⓣ26530 71724; ❹), though well appointed and featuring historic wall paintings, is neurotically managed, with more rules than a Victorian orphanage; there is no consistently operating place to eat or drink. A conventional trail down to Víkos, though alluringly marked at the outset, is overgrown and ultimately impassable owing to landslips.

Some 4km downhill from Kapésovo, **KOUKOÚLI** is another scarcely commercialized, atmospheric place, with cars banned from the village proper and nightingales audible by day during May and June. The two most reliable **accommodation** options here are Papa-Kosta's simple but clean, seven-room *To Tritoxo* (ⓣ26530 71760, ⓦwww.tritoxo.gr; ❸), and English-run ★ *Roy and Effi's Place* (ⓣ26530 71743 or 694 64 73 276; ❸, discounts for longer stays), consisting of two large pine-trim, white-stucco rooms, overlooking a spacious garden (a rarity in Zagóri) where breakfast is served. For other **meals**, head for the lovingly appointed ★ café-restaurant of the *Tritoxo* inn, with hearty, reasonably priced fare. Koukoúli has direct access to the Víkos Gorge, via an unmarked but still useable path leading from the southwest entrance of the village down to the O3 between Kípi and the Misíou bridge. Alternatively, the **Z31** path heads southeast from a point on the paved, easterly access road near a park bench, with a brief *kalderími* descent to the Kondodhímou bridge, reaching Kípi within 45 minutes.

KÍPI (**Báya**), 2km up a right forking road 6km below Kapésovo, is another handsome village, which until the 1930s served as the administrative centre for the region. Budget **accommodation** includes *Spiti stou Artemi* (ⓣ26530 71644, ⓦwww.epirus.com/spititouartemi; ❸), a wonderfully restored nineteenth-century mansion where several of the seven rooms have fireplaces; *Evangelia Dherva* (ⓣ26530 71658; ❸) is the alternative. Posher lodgings are mushrooming along the roadside; the best is *O Mahalas* (☎26530 71976; ④–⑤), a hotel-apartment complex arrayed around a lawn garden; all 2007-built units have working fireplaces. Opposite stands a co-managed **taverna**, *Stou Mihali*, emphasizing local ingredients (beans, greens) and recipes (various *píttes*), washed down by lovely purple wine – though service can be uneven and prices have rocketed. On the same road, at the east edge of town, is the **Tolis Agapios Folklore Museum** (daily, any reasonable hour), with some 50,000 articles crammed in. **Bus** services to Ioánnina are shared with Tsepélovo's. Other amenities include a small **shop** and **bakery**, and an **activity centre**, Robinson Expeditions (☎26530 71517, Ⓦwww.robinson.gr).

FRANGÁDHES, 20km southeast, justifies the detour for a superb **inn-restaurant**, *Petroto* (☎26530 71107, Ⓦwww.petroto.com; ③), with large balconied, wood-floored rooms, and for access to the **Petsióni bridge**. Two road-bends east of the village, head down a dirt track to a stone *proskynitário,* then walk down a rougher track a few moments to the span; there's also a direct path down from Frangádhes.

North to the Aóös valley and the north Píndhos

Beyond Skamnélli, forest appears, extending north to the **Aóös valley**. Some 14km out of the village, the paved road branches north towards Vryssohóri. You can get there more directly and pleasantly on foot in seven hours from Skamnélli by using a pass between the peaks of **Megála Lithária** (2467m) and **Tsoúka Roússa** (2377m). This is easier hiking than through the Karterós pass previously described, and covered by some organized trekking groups; an added bonus are wild flowers in the **Goúra valley**, directly below Tsoúka Roússa.

VRYSSOHÓRI (**Lesnítsa**) itself is a bit anticlimactic, almost invisible among dense woods at the base of Tsoúka Roússa peak. Tiny and ramshackle (burnt in 1944), the village has two **inns**. The four-room one of the Tsoumani family (☎26530 22687 or 697 45 89 930; April–Oct, otherwise on request; ③) has a communal balcony to hang laundry and from which you can admire the mountains; there's also the slightly larger inn of Marianna Tsiomidhou (☎26530 22785 or 697 30 82 870; ③). If necessary, you can **camp** at the edge of town by one of two springs bracketing the O3 coming down from Karterós. Otherwise, Vryssohóri can offer only a basic *kafenío*-**taverna** dishing out simple fare (sausages, salad and *galotýri* – a yoghurt-like dish).

The O3 across the Aóös from Vryssohóri is now a road, with nothing left of the old trail; engage a taxi in Vryssohóri for the shuttle over to **Paliosélli**, main southerly trailhead for Mount Smólikas (see p.381).

The north Píndhos

The region **north of the Aóös River** is far less visited than Zagóri. Its landscape is equally scenic but its villages are poor relatives – nearly all were burned by the Germans during early 1944, accounting for their present thrown-together appearance. The villagers claim that before this their houses exceeded Zagóri's in splendour, since there was abundant timber for long planks and carved interiors.

Mounts **Smólikas** and Grámmos dominate the area. The former can be approached from **Mount Gamíla** (see p.376) or by vehicle from **Kónitsa**, the county town just off the Ioánnina–Kastoriá highway.

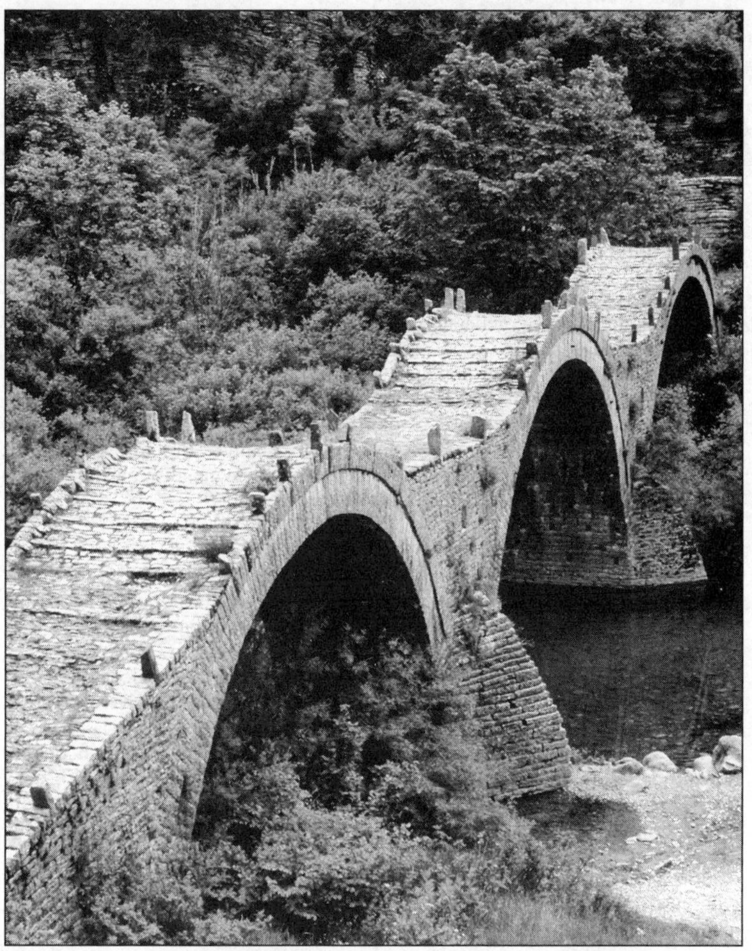

▲ Plakídha bridge, near Kípi

Kónitsa and around

The little market town of **KÓNITSA** takes its Slavic name from the horse-fairs of old; today its most memorable features are a famous bridge and a view. The huge **bridge** over the Aóös was built around 1870 (and repaired after the retreating Ottoman army tried to destroy it in 1913) but looks far older. The **view** comes from the town's amphitheatrical setting on Mount Trapezítsa, above a broad flood plain where the Aóös and Voïdhomátis rivers mingle with the Sarandáporos before flowing through Albania as the Vijöse. The town was besieged by the Communist "Democratic Army" in the week after Christmas 1947, in an unsuccessful bid to establish a provisional capital. Much was destroyed in the fighting, though parts of the old bazaar survive.

The **bus terminal** (frequently to Ioánnina and less regular connections to mountain villages) is on the central platía, while two **ATMS** and the **post office** lie just south. Kónitsa is a recognized **adventure-sports** centre; agencies with bases down by the modern bridge over the main highway include Alpiki Zoni/ Alpine Zone (ⓣ26550 24822, ⓦwww.alpinezone.gr) and En Fysei (ⓣ694 73 33 113). Longest established, and one of the better **rooms** establishments, is *Xenonas To Dhendro* on the hairpin bend of the main access road (ⓣ26550 23982; ❷), whose English-speaking proprietor Yiannis Mourehidhes, one of the characters of Epirus, is a mine of local information. Among other *dhomátia*, calmest, best value and friendliest is *Yerakofolia* (ⓣ26550 22168; ❷), 300m along the road to Paliosélli, occupying a pair of contiguous buildings with great views. As for **hotels**, one mid-range choice is *Gefyri*, down by the old bridge (ⓣ26550 23780, ⓦhttp://gefyri.konitsa.net.gr; rooms ❹, suites ❻); the rooms, one or two with river views, and all with Wi-Fi, are decent enough, and there's a large pool, but the on-site bar may generate noise. Best facilities in the area are offered at the Mourehidhes family's *Grand Hotel Dentro* (ⓣ26550 29365, ⓦwww.grandhoteldentro.gr) 200m down the road from their *xenónas*; standard rooms (❹) have good bathrooms and some balconies, whilst attic suites (❻–❼) feature fireplaces and hydromassage tubs. Cooking at *To Dhendhro*'s attached **restaurant** is decent, featuring baked goat (*gástra*) or lamb, Yiannis's (in)famous *fétta psití*, baked cheese spiked with hot chillies, and Zítsa bulk wine, though the *Kapnismeno Tsoukali* taverna in the centre is also worth trying.

The Aóös Gorge

Beginning at the old bridge over the Aóös, either of two interweaving paths on the south bank leads (90min) to the eighteenth-century **monastery of Stomíou**, perched on a bluff overlooking the narrowest part of the Aóös Gorge. The *katholikón* is minimally interesting, and the premises have been insensitively restored, but the setting is sublime and sporadically resident caretakers are welcoming. There are springs here, so many visitors camp nearby, after bathing in the river below.

The gorge slopes are shaggy with vegetation providing one of the last habitats for lynx, roe deer and raptors. A minimally waymarked path, shown on the recommended map, climbs from the monastery gate up to the **Astráka area** (see p.375). This is five-hours-plus uphill, rather less in reverse – a very useful trekkers' link. Do not, incidentally, be tempted by red-on-yellow metal diamonds marking a supposed direct, riverside trail to Vryssohóri; its middle section has been destroyed by landslides. The only way to Vryssohóri from here goes via Kátsanos meadow below the Karterós pass, on a safe if faintly marked path again shown on the Anavasi map.

Molyvdhosképasti and Molyvdhoskepástou monastery

The tiny hillside village of **MOLYVDHOSKÉPASTI** (**Dhipalítsa**) hugs the Albanian border 23km west of Kónitsa, in an appropriately end-of-the-world setting. The place was once a haunt of seventh-century Emperor Constantine IV Pogonatos, though most of the assiduously signposted churches scattered across the slopes are post-Byzantine; finest is sixteenth-century **Áyii Apóstoli**, right on the frontier. The view from its terrace – into Albania beyond the riverside Mértziani border post, over the Aóös valley, east to Smólikas and Gamíla – is among the best in Epirus. Few **buses** call from Kónitsa, so you really need your own transport to get here. Some 5km below the village stands **Molyvdhoskepástou monastery**, chief among the emperor's surviving monuments. Repopulated in 1991 and attractively restored by its half-dozen monks, it enjoys a bucolic setting on the banks of the Aóös. The curiously long, narrow, thirteenth-century church has badly damaged frescoes and a precariously high Serbian-type dome.

East of Kónitsa: Mount Smólikas

Mount Smólikas (2637m) is the second-highest peak in Greece. It commands a beautiful and very extensive range, covering a hundred square kilometres of mountain territory above 1700m in elevation, including the lake of **Dhrakólimni** (not to be confused with its namesake on Mount Gamíla). The region also retains vestiges of traditional shepherd life, best witnessed at the Vlach village of **Samarína**, though most sheepfolds on the Epirot side of the mountain now lie abandoned. Smólikas saw heavy Greek-Italian fighting during November 1940, and some of the higher ridges still have a rather shell-blasted appearance.

Kónitsa–Dhístrato **buses** (3 afternoons weekly) stop en route at **PALEOSÉLLI** (1100m elevation), the best trailhead on the mountain's southern flank; at the east edge of the village, a placard summarizes the uphill O3. **Accommodation** comprises Dhimitris Grentziou's central inn (☎26550 24626; ❶), as well as more comfortable *dhomátia* at the west outskirts (☎26550 24760 or 26510 79820; ❷). The stone-built former school of **PÁDHES**, 3km further along, has been renovated as a **xenónas** and **taverna** (June–Sept); there's another grill just out of "town".

The paved road continues 20km beyond Pádhes to **DHÍSTRATO**, end of the bus line. This large, relatively thriving village has four **rooms** establishments, thanks partly to the ski centre nearby at the provincial border (see p.382), though few are attended outside peak winter or summer seasons; those of *Elias Svarnas* (☎26650 24841; ❹) on the platía are the plushest. Two **psistariés** work fitfully, as do a few bars. The single **taxi** driver (phone numbers posted on the platía) can prove elusive to find – and uncooperative once you do locate him. From just before Dhístrato those with jeeps or high-clearance vehicles can drive 18km north to Samarína (see p.382) from May until the first snows on a badly rutted forest road.

Hiking from Paleosélli to Ayía Paraskeví

A fine trail leads from Paleosélli up to **Dhrakólimni** (3.5hr), and from there you can climb **Mount Smólikas** (another hour). A recognized variant of the O3 ascends to the lake from Pádhes, but this is heavily damaged by a forestry track – and not worth following.

The Paleosélli–Dhrakólimni route is haphazardly waymarked (with red or green paint dots or arrows besides the standard diamonds) as the main O3; it's mostly trail for 1hr 40min from the village to a pair of **refuges** at **Náne** (1650m). There's water and camping space, but both shelters – an older cabin, and a newer structure (24 beds) just beyond at 1700m – are locked and unstaffed; get the keys if desired from the Paliosélli shop.

Beyond Náne, waymarks lead you up onto a ridge aiming for the summit of Mount Smólikas; the best path keeps a bit to the right (east) side of the ridge. Just under two hours from Náne you emerge into the little depression containing the heart-shaped, fairly shallow **lake** at 2200m. You can camp here, but space is at a premium and you'll need a tent to protect against cold and damp. Owing to global climate change, this former alpine tarn has become a murky brown pond, with noisy frogs.

The classic **ascent of Smólikas** begins from the base of the knoll east of the lake. There's a proper path at first, up to the 2400-metre contour, staked out by "lollipop" markers; after a brief interval over turf, the trail resumes to just below the summit, with a short scramble putting you up top less than an hour from Dhrakólimni (if you're lightly laden). Besides grand views, you'll find a trig point, a solar-power unit, and a granite memorial to a young climber-biologist who fell to his death in 1997.

The easiest way down from Smólikas is along the scenic, well-trodden O3 (2.5hr), starting in the vale between the lake and the summit, to the hamlet of **AYÍA PARASKEVÍ** (**Kerásovo**); should you be reversing this itinerary, a helpful placard at the east edge of "town" details the 3.5hr climb to Dhrakólimni. There are a couple of basic **grill-tavernas** here, including one on the ground floor of the central municipal **xenónas** (☎26550 24215; ❷), as well as infrequent **bus** links to Kónitsa.

Hiking from Dhrakólimni to Samarína

If you don't mind heights, and aren't carrying a heavy pack, the best hiking route from **Dhrakólimni to Samarína** involves tracing the ridge east from the summit, part of a seven-hour walking day. After an hour-plus of cross-country progress, you reach the bleak **Lemós** pass, where you link up with a yellow-paint-marked path coming up from a sheepfold on the Pádhes side. Once through this gap, you descend into the lunar, northwest-facing cirque which drains towards Ayía Paraskeví.

Next you traverse the base of one of Smólikas' secondary peaks before tackling a scree-laden rock "stair". Waymarks change to yellow-and-red blazes or metal "lollipops"; cairns guide you across a flat-topped ridge. The path soon levels out on another neck of land. Way to the right (south) can be glimpsed the other Smólikas **tarn**, as large as Dhrakólimni but difficult to reach. The path becomes more distinct as it snakes down through gullies in eroded rock.

Black pines reappear at the foot of a height capped by a wooden altimeter; the trail threads between this and another peak, at the foot of which lies Samarína. There follows a sharper descent through thick forest, with a spring (**Sopotíra**) gurgling into a log trough amidst a beautiful mountain clearing. Below this, the woods end abruptly as you emerge on a bare slope directly above Samarína's football pitch.

Samarína and the Vassilítsa ski centre

At 1450m, just inside Macedonia's Grevená province, **SAMARÍNA** claims to be the highest village in Greece. It's principally inhabited during summer by Vlachs from the plains of Thessaly, and their sheep – their odour alive or cooked permeating the air (and everything else). The place was burned during both World War II and the civil war, and rebuilt in cheap-and-nasty style; so, while Samarína may seem the Bright Lights after several days' trekking, it's not somewhere you'd detour to visit. This acknowledged, it's a thriving and friendly place, very proud of its traditions. The high point of the year is the August 15 festival, when the place is swamped by nostalgic Vlachs from the lowlands. Yet appearances deceive – pastoral life is vigorous only in comparison to Epirus, with flocks down from the thousands to barely a few hundred.

The interior of the main church of **Megáli Panayía** revels in painted ceilings, an intricately carved *témblon* and frescoes where all the figures are dressed in Greek peasant costume. Though it looks much older, like many local churches it dates from around 1800. Its special hallmark is an adult black pine growing out of the roof of the apse; the keys are with the priest, who lives opposite the main gate.

Samarína is no longer deserted in winter since the inauguration of the **Mount Vassilítsa ski centre** which, with over 20km of mostly north-facing pistes for all ability levels, is the biggest in northwestern Greece. Some 8km from Samarína, the slopes lie a bit further from Dhístrato and Vovoússa, guaranteeing them all winter tourist trade. Two chair-lifts from the lower base at about 1700m get you to the top point of about 2100m; the ski school at the higher (1850m) station is operated by Alpine Zone (see p.366), near four drag-lifts and a small chalet-hotel.

Practicalities

The barracks-like stone building at the top of the village is the municipal **hotel** (☎24620 95216; open most of year; ❹), whose wood-trimmed interior and east-facing terrace are more inviting than first impressions suggest. There are less pricey en-suite **rooms** on or near the stone-paved platía; best are those of Ioannis Parlitsis (☎24620 95279), spread over two premises – older ones, with small kitchens, above the fruit stall (❶), and superior units on a quiet lane towards the church, with fireplaces, balconies and central heating (❸). The platía springs to life by night with a half-dozen **grills**; a single **shop** purveys canned fish, pulses, rice, noodles, cheese and eggs.

Ordinary **cars** can reach Samarína from Ayía Paraskeví along 14km of beautiful but mostly dirt road; this will be paved but until then is no-go from November to May. Leaving Samarína without transport, you have two choices. From June to September there's a bus along the paved road to **Grevená**, 40km away on the Kalambáka–Kastoriá highway, but not daily. Alternatively, follow the E6 route four-and-a-half hours to **Dhístrato** (see p.381) – or keep going to Vovoússa on the east bank of the Aóös (no bus out, however). The E6 crosses good wilderness in parts, but the first hour out of Samarína and the final hour-plus descent to Dhístrato involve dirt and asphalt road-trudging respectively.

The south Píndhos

Most travellers arriving in Epirus have their sights firmly set northwards on the Víkos Gorge and the Zagóri villages. But if you're tolerant of a limited range of places to eat and sleep, the **remote villages** of the south Píndhos provide an interesting, less touristy, alternative. They perch on the flanks of **mounts Tzoumérka** and **Kakardhítsa**, two overlapping ridges of bare mountains linked by a high plateau, plainly visible from Ioánnina. There are few special sights, but you'll get a solid, undiluted experience of Epirot life.

Buses depart Ioánnina's southern station for Ágnanda and Prámanda daily; there is also service from Árta. Buses run in either direction along the secondary road between Árta and Ioánnina, stopping at **Pláka**, which has, amid stunning scenery, a huge eighteenth-century bridge over the Árakhthos; here you can flag down transport further up the mountain.

Ágnanda to Melissourgí

The first significant village, 12km above Pláka, is **ÁGNANDA**, mauled in World War II and not intrinsically attractive, though nearby – closer to Katarráktis village and the slopes of Mount Tzouménka – is the *Dhasiko Horio Kedros* (☎26850 31791, Ⓦwww.guesthousekedros.com; ❻), a self-contained resort of nineteen wooden chalets. Most will continue to **PRÁMANDA**, no more distinguished architecturally than Ágnanda, but strewn appealingly across ridges overlooking the Kallaritikós valley. Just 2km south is the area's major attraction, the **Anemótrypa** (daily dawn to dusk, €6), a cavern discovered in 1960; the first 300m or so, with pools and the usual strange formations, are visitable. Ágnanda's enormous **Ayía Paraskeví** church, an unbeatable example of nineteenth-century kitsch, almost uniquely escaped wartime devastation. The village has a **post office** and *psistariés*, while there's a comfortable **hotel**, the *Tzoumerka* (☎26590 61336; ❹), in tiny Tsópelas hamlet, 2km towards Melissourgí.

MELISSOURGÍ, 5km southeast of Prámanda, is more rewarding. The village escaped destruction during the war, though most buildings – including the historic church – have lost their slate roofs in favour of ugly pantiles. There's a **taverna** and one large **inn** (☎26590 61357; ❸), booked out in midsummer, plus infrequent bus connections with Árta.

Melissourgí to Vourgarélli

Melissourgí is the start-point for rambles on the **Kostelláta plateau**, the upland separating Mount Kakardhítsa (2429m), looming above the village, from Mount Tzouměrka (2393m). Heading south, you can cross these high pastures in a day and a half. The initial stretch of path from Melissourgí is waymarked, and water is available near intermittent summer sheepfolds. You descend to the villages of Theodhóriana and thence **VOURGARÉLLI**, at the edge of the Ahelóös river basin, 57km from Árta, with which there are bus links just two days weekly. Both have **accommodation**, though county town Vourgarélli is better equipped to deal with visitors. There, the most congenial of three inns is well-signed *Hotel Galini* (☎26850 22135; ❷), an attractive chalet with large common areas and easy parking 100m downhill; rooms are plain but quiet, with fridges and balconies. The platía, ringed by several gushing springs, is home to **tavernas**. Some 5km below, by the roadside, stands Byzantine **Kókkini Eklissía**, contemporary with Parigorítissa in Árta (see p.398), a cross-in-square structure with exceptionally fine exterior brickwork, and fragmentary frescoes in the narthex.

Prámanda to Syrráko

With your own transport, you can continue from Prámanda up the Kallaritikós valley to Kallarítes or Syrráko, two handsome villages untouched by war. Public transport, however, means only an occasional minibus to remoter, pastoral Matsoúki (basic **rooms**) from Prámanda, from which it's a two-hour hike (via the eighteenth-century monastery of Vylíza) to Kallarítes. The bus for Syrráko approaches from Ioánnina by the most direct route, a scenic but twisty 52km via Harokópi and Paleohóri (allow at least 90min driving).

The separate turn-off for Kallarítes is at **KIPÍNA** (seasonal taverna). A famous namesake **monastery**, founded in 1212 but uninhabited today, hangs like a martin's nest from the cliff face 1.5km beyond the hamlet. The premises are locked, though the view from its terrace is superb.

Kallarítes

Beyond Kipína monastery, the road continues about 2km upstream to the base of a wonderful *kalderími* climbing to **KALLARÍTES**, perched superbly above the headwaters of the Kallaritikós River (you can also drive the whole way). This Vlach village was a veritable El Dorado throughout the nineteenth century, specializing in gold- and silversmithing; even today Ioánnina craftsmen are mostly of Kallaritiot descent – as is Bulgari, among the most exclusive contemporary jewellers worldwide. Though the village is nearly deserted except during summer, the grand houses of the departed rich are kept in excellent repair by their descendants. The flagstoned platía has remained unchanged since 1881 (when the village was sacked and rebuilt), with its old-fashioned stores and stele commemorating local émigrés who helped finance the War of Independence. Two **kafenío-grills** flank the platía, and the same number of small **inns**: that of Pavlos Patounis (☎26590 62235; ❷) and one kept by Napoleon Zanglis (☎26590 61518; ❷), four simple but serviceable rooms above one of the *kafenía*.

Khroússias Gorge and Syrráko

Just beyond Kallarítes, the awesome **Khroússias Gorge** separates the village from neighbouring Syrráko, visible high up on the west bank but a good hour's walk away. The linking trail is spectacular, including a near-vertical "ladder" hewn out of the rock face. From the river-bridge you glimpse a pair of abandoned water mills upstream. The canyon walls are steep and sun penetrates for only a few hours a day, even in summer.

SYRRÁKO (1120m), hugging a steep-sloped ravine with views towards Kakardhítsa, is even more strikingly set than Kallarítes, with well-preserved stone mansions, archways and churches reminiscent of those in the Zagóri, only built on a far grander scale, right down to the stage-like platía with its huge plane trees. You must leave vehicles at the lower car park and make the final approach on a *kalderími* with two little bridges; despite this, the paving of the direct road west to Ioánnina has made Syrráko a trendy weekend retreat. Not to be outdone by Kallarítes, the village has also erected monuments to various locally born national figures, including the poet Kostas Krystallis. There are two platía **tavernas** (*Galani* and *Stavraetos*) and at least two **inns**, the *Xenonas Galani* off the platía (ⓣ26510 53569; B&B ④) and the *Kasa Kalda* (ⓣ26510 66210 or 697 70 34 517; ③).

The Epirot coast and Étolo-Akarnanía

The **Epirot coast** has some very attractive **beaches** between Igoumenítsa and Préveza, among the best on the mainland outside of Mount Pílio. **Igoumenítsa** itself, the capital of Thesprotía province, is a purely functional ferry port, while the first beaches you'd stop for are at **Sývota**, 23km south. **Párga**, the most established resort on the way to Préveza, is best left for June or September visits. Inland near Párga, there are worthwhile detours from the main route south: the intriguing **Nekromanteion of Acheron** was the legendary gate of Hades; the **gorge of the Ahérondas River** offers fine hiking; and the imposing ruins of **Kassope** and **Nikopolis** break the journey to **Préveza**, a low-key provincial capital at the mouth of the Amvrakikós gulf. **Árta,** surrounded by Byzantine churches, is approached around the gulf from Préveza, past the **Rodhiá Wetland Centre**.

Moving into **Étolo-Akarnanía**, the landscape becomes increasingly desolate, with little to delay progress to Lefkádha island or the Peloponnese. **Páleros** port, south of castle-topped **Vónitsa**, is the one place with any maritime feel, or foreign-tourist trade; committed hermits might retire to **Kálamos** island, reached from the enjoyable little coastal settlement of **Mýtikas**. Walled **Mesolóngi** has Byronic associations, but is otherwise unglamorous, if enjoyable enough for a few hours.

Igoumenítsa and around

IGOUMENÍTSA is Greece's third passenger port after Pireás and Pátra, with frequent ferries to Corfu and Italy. As overland transit through most of ex-Yugoslavia remains dodgy, sea traffic between Greece and Italy has increased significantly. Upon completion of the Vía Egnatía from Grevená to here, this unloved provincial capital will become the country's leading cargo port; a mega-terminal – part of the "Egnatía Port" – for lorries dominates the harbour, and all shipping agencies have branches near this, plus embarkation booths inside it.

Seagoing functions and waterfront apart, Igoumenítsa is pretty unappealing, levelled during World War II and rebuilt in utilitarian style. You should be able to get a ferry out immediately; every day in season there are sailings to Italy in the morning, and throughout the evening (see box, p. 388). If you end up stuck for the day, you're better off taking an excursion from Igoumenítsa than hanging around town.

Practicalities

International ferries depart from the Egnatía Port at the far south end of town, with its own exit from the Vía Egnatía – drivers bound for Italy can skip the town altogether. **Local ferries** to Corfu or Paxí operate from the domestic ferry quay just north of this giant terminal; tickets for these services are purchased at waterside booths. The **KTEL** is inland from the Corfu/Paxí quay on Minermoú, corner Arhilóhou. **Drivers** can use the free car park at the waterfront's north end, near the **post office**, or chance kerbside spaces; Igoumenítsa's **fee-parking** scheme seems to have been abandoned, at least off-season. Numerous **ATMS** line the south end of the front.

The town is not huge but **hotels** are abundant along or behind the waterfront, if often lugubrious and overpriced. Inland, at the southeast corner of the main platía, stands the comfortable, air-conditioned *Egnatia* at Eleftherías 1 (ⓣ26650 23648; ❸); ask for a rear room facing the pine grove, and take advantage of unrestricted street parking out back. The best budget choice is *Stavrodhromi*, Soulíou 14, the street leading diagonally uphill and northeast from the square (ⓣ26650 22343; ❷); this has en-suite, air-conditioned rooms, as well as an in-house restaurant. The closest **campsite** is *Drepano* (ⓣ26650 24442; April–Oct), 5km west.

Restaurants and **cafés** are generally uninspiring, if plentiful on the pedestrian zone one block inland; *Ouzeri To Kohyli* at the south end of Lambráki is

Heading to the coast

For most travellers, the first stage of the journey to the coast – notwithstanding the new Vía Egnatía – will be the old **main highway from Ioánnina to Igoumenítsa**, which mostly follows the valley of the Thiámis (Kálamos) River. This is a dangerous "slaughter alley", especially the curves west of Vrosína, and still infested by long-distance lorries. If you're in your own car or on a bike, a far better (and safer) alternative involves bearing right (north) some 500m east of Vrosína at a disused, concrete sentry post, then crossing the river bridge and veering immediately left towards Ravení, and then through Keramítsa and Dháfni. This route – shown erroneously as a secondary road on some maps – is far more scenic, less stressful, and actually 3km shorter (if not faster) by the time you emerge on the "main" highway between Parapótamos and Mavroúdhi.

fine for seafood, while nearby a few *yirádhika* function all day. After dark, several fish tavernas and ouzerís at the very north end of the front, near the Dhrépano turning, come to life.

Around Igoumenítsa

The best brief escapes are along the coast north of town. The closest beach lies 5km west at **Dhrépano**, a two-kilometre, crescent-shaped sandspit shaded by eucalypts, closing off a lagoon. Near the campsite is a popular municipally run **restaurant**, the *Kendriko*, from whose terrace you can watch the ferries bound for Corfu.

With more time at your disposal, make for **SAYIÁDHA**, the last coastal settlement before Albania. It's reached by a direct road (21km, not shown on some maps) from the north end of Igoumenítsa, passing the hilltop Byzantine **monastery of Ráyio** with its blurred frescoes. Next you cross the Kálamos River and wind through citrus groves to this little fishing/yacht port with exceptionally wide horizons. Among a half-dozen bars and **tavernas** on the flagstoned quay, most popular is *Alekos* – patronized by yachters who know the seafood will be better and cheaper than at Corfu or Sývota. Proper beaches nearby include tiny **Keramídhi** (2.5km north; snack bar), and larger **Strovíli** (4.5km north; no facilities), both along the broad road heading for the **border crossing** towards Albanian Konispol.

Sývota

Sleepy **SÝVOTA**, surrounded by olive groves and oaks 23km south of Igoumenítsa, drapes itself over evocative coastal topography gazing out to Corfu and Paxí. This old fishing anchorage has grown into a resort popular with Brits, Italians and Greeks, but also hosts numerous second-home owners from Ioánnina and Italy. The village proper, bigger than it seems with about a thousand inhabitants, lies several hundred metres inland, while the pedestrianized little port, popular with yachts despite fierce afternoon winds, fronts a line of restaurants and cafés.

West of Sývota there are a couple of sandy patches on **Mávro Óros** islet, joined to the mainland by the sandspit of **Bélla Vráka**. With transport (or a taxi-boat), you can reach a series of other, better beaches off the road to the south (leading to Pérdhika and eventually Párga): tiny but pretty **Závias**, shaded by olives; bigger, sunnier **Méga Ámmos**; **Mikrí Ámmos**, with fee parking; two secluded coves at **Méga Tráfos** (foot or boat access only); **Ayía Paraskeví**, with an islet to swim to; and **Sofás**, with a campsite. Almost all these beaches have tavernas or simple snack-bars.

You may **rent cars or scooters**, or book an excursion, at Isabella Tours (☎26650 93317); a couple of outlets on the quay rent out **dinghies**. Near the harbour there's an **ATM**.

Much of Sývota's **accommodation** is pre-booked, but a few hotels and rooms take walk-in trade. These include the *Hotel Fylakas* (☎26650 93345; Easter & May–Oct; ❹), with pleasant common areas and fair-sized rooms overlooking the harbour; and the well-maintained *Studios Anneta* gallery apartments sleeping four (☎26650 93457 or 694 25 57 584; ❸), set in a peaceful olive grove 200m back from the harbour. At Méga Ámmos, 3km from town, *Mikros Paradisos* (☎26650 93281, Ⓦwww.mikros-paradisos.com; ❺), is scattered across lovely grounds and equipped with bug screens, marble floors and contemporary baths.

Around the harbour, a dozen **eateries** and **bars** vie for your custom. *Apangio* offers quality *mezédhes* and somewhat pricey seafood mains; *Parasole* does

International ferry companies in Igoumenítsa

There's a good spread of **departure times** across the day for Italy-bound ferries, which leave between 7.30am and 10am, with a larger cluster of evening departures between 8pm and 1am (especially 11pm–midnight). During high season, make advance reservations for cabins or vehicles. Services to all destinations remain frequent year-round; even Venice, the remotest, is visited several times weekly in winter.

Companies offer a range of **fares** for cabin and dormitory berths, or "airplane" seats and deck passage, as well as occasional reductions for student-card holders and discounts on return tickets. Brindisi tickets tend to be marginally cheaper than those for Bari, Ancona rather more; Venice is vastly more costly. Peak prices for all Greece–Italy sailings apply between August and early September. Fares and conditions vary significantly between companies, according to boat quality; the introduction of high-speed craft has cut travel times sharply and forced slower, grottier boats out of business. Cars, motorcycles and bicycles (free to transport) are carried on all ferries. Superfast (except July–Aug), Endeavor and Agoudimos allow you to sleep in your camper or van on deck from April to October.

If you have bought tickets from somewhere other than the local central agent – and all agencies promiscuously sell for several companies – you must **check in** with the appropriate *official* agent's embarkation booth in the Egnatía Port at least two hours before departure. Unlike sailings from Pátra, ferries from Igoumenítsa to Italy are not allowed to sell tickets with a **stopover** on Corfu. You can take the domestic ferry to Corfu and pick up many sailings from there, though fares will be the same as from Igoumenítsa.

International ferry companies, central agents and destinations

Agoudimos Nikos Zois, Egnatía Port ☎26650 25682. Bari, daily Aug–Sept (9hr); Brindisi, daily Aug–Sept (7hr 30min).

ANEK Stavros Bakolias, Egnatía Port ☎26650 29063. Ancona, 6–7 weekly all year (15hr 30min); Venice, 4–6 weekly all year (25hr).

Endeavor Eleni Pantazi, Egnatía Port ☎26650 26833. Brindisi, daily May–Christmas, 3–6 weekly March–April (6hr 30min–8hr)

Minoan Ethnikís Andístasis 58A ☎26650 26715. Ancona, 6–7 weekly all year (15hr); Venice, 2–4 weekly all year (22hr).

Superfast/Blue Star Pitoulis, Egnatía Port ☎26650 29200. Bari, daily all year (9hr 30min); Ancona, daily all year (15hr 30min).

Ventouris Milano Travel, Egnatía Port ☎26650 26670. Bari, 3–7 weekly most of year (10hr 30min).

authentic wood-fired, thin-crust pizzas; while *Ostria*, inland under a pergola, is a well-established ouzerí.

Karavostási, Pérdhika, Sarakíniko and Ayiá

About 11km south of Sývota, you reach the edge of Pérdhika village and the poorly marked but paved side road (5km) down to **Karavostási** beach – its hotels are better signposted. It's easier, especially coming from Párga, to use a southerly option going via the Áyios Athanásios monastery and picnic grounds. The 500-metre beach itself – best on the Thesprotian coast – usually has light surf, but the water is clean and brisk, with just a few sunbeds; on the headland above and south are the scanty remains of **ancient Elina** (under excavation). At the river mouth there are two snack and drink bars, and another bar-restaurant above the south end of the beach, but few other facilities besides several **hotels** and a few apartments. Of these, *Karavostasi Beach* is your best-value option (☎26650 91104, www.hotel-karavostasi.gr; B&B ④). Some of the marble-clad rooms have sea views, while the well-designed and landscaped pool-bar area makes an attractive spot for breakfast.

For broader eating options (and an **ATM**), backtrack uphill and across the highway to **PÉRDHIKA**, the closest "real" village; like many spots in Thesprotía province, it was substantially Muslim before its 1940s resettlement by Corfiots, Paxiots and Asia Minor refugees. Pérdhika has a lively after-dark scene at its pedestrianized platía, with a dozen restaurants and cafés used to foreigners but geared up as much to the needs of the sociable locals. The oldest and most characterful **restaurant**, with fare as good as any served here, is *Ta Kavouria*.

Beyond Karavostási, you cross the provincial border into Préveza and just before Ayiá meet the paved, five-kilometre road down to scenic **Sarakíniko**, a short (150m), broad sand-and-pebble cove, with a stream cooling the sea year-round. Descending from the highway, take the left fork on each of two occasions to reach one of the region's best **tavernas**, *Christos* (book peak season on ☎26840 35207 or 697 79 82 207). The fair-priced menu has expanded to creative hot and cold *mezédhes*, building on a track record of select vegetable dishes and fresh seafood; excellent Greek microwinery products and an eclectic soundtrack complete the picture. A garden with swimming pool has been prepared in anticipation of luxury rooms (ready 2009). Among other places to **stay**, try the peaceful, friendly *Periklis' Garden*, 300m south (☎26840 35292; ③), a sideline to the Nanos family farm.

AYIÁ, 10km south of Pérdhika, is more attractive, its amphitheatrically arrayed houses overlooking the Ionian; near the summit of the village, the church of **Áyios Yeóryios** has engaging naive frescoes. Of two **tavernas** along the traditional commercial street, *Oasis* (all year, dinner only) is obviously the favourite, its interior a veritable museum of Greek adverts from the 1920s to the 1960s and an old jukebox; the fare, principally grilled meat, salads, starters and bulk wine, is well-priced, with locals predominating at the terrace seating except in peak season.

Párga and around

PÁRGA, 53km south of Igoumenítsa via Pérdhika, has prospered thanks to its alluring setting on lush coastline with a string of rocky islets offshore. The town itself is less photogenic, concrete construction having completely swamped the outskirts and spread west to Anthoússa village; the old centre, however, an arc of tiered houses set below a Norman-Venetian **kástro** with some fine mansions and mysterious archways in the lower quarter, retains some charm. What saves Párga is the fact that Greeks love it for their own holidays – and that amidst touristic activity, normal life (just) continues, exemplified by older ladies in the traditional garb of black veil, braids and dark blue kerchiefs. Still, in midsummer there are just too many people and cars in such a compact place; you'll have a better time in spring or autumn.

Some history

Párga has an idiosyncratic history, being linked with the Ionian islands as much as with the mainland. From the 1300s to the 1700s the port was a lone **Venetian** toehold in Epirus (the old Slavonic word *prag* indeed means threshold), complementing the Serene Republic's island possessions. Under Venetian rule, a small community of Jews flourished here exporting citrons to western Europe for liturgical use; they, and the citrons, are long gone, but lemon groves remain at Anthoússa, and the Venetian Lion of St Mark still adorns the *kástro* keep.

Later, the Napoleonic **French** briefly took Párga, leaving additional fortifications on the largest islet guarding the harbour. At the start of the nineteenth century, the town enjoyed autonomy under **Russian** protection, and lived from olive export, before being acquired by the **British**, who sold it on to **Ali Pasha**. Ali Pasha rebuilt all the local castles, while the townspeople, knowing his reputation, decamped to the Ionian islands on Good Friday 1819 (though some returned a half-century later to inhabit the lower quarter of town). The area was subsequently resettled by **Muslims** (including Albanian-speaking Tsámidhes); Turks remained until the exchange of populations in 1923, when they were replaced in part by **Orthodox Greek** refugees from the area around Constantinople, while the last Tsámidhes were killed or driven out at the end of World War II. The Muslim quarter lining the upper ridge is still known as Tourkopázaro, and a magnificent mosque and minaret (its base still visible) stood there until razed in the 1950s.

The town, beaches and castles

The blufftop Venetian **kástro** (8am–midnight; free) provides a haven from Párga's bustle; a long stair-street leads up to the crumbled, cypress-tufted ramparts, which offer excellent views. Restored barracks inside the castle boundary house a recommended café (see opposite); you can continue up a cobbled way to one of Ali Pasha's summer palaces, a warren of vaulted rooms and cisterns, with ruined, domed baths at the very summit.

Párga's **beaches** line several consecutive bays, split by various headlands. The small, spring-chilled bay of **Kryonéri** lies opposite the islet studded with a monastery and Napoleonic fortifications, a 200-metre swim or pedalo from the town quay. Tiny but scenic **Gólfo** beach, the next (less clean) cove southeast, is reached by a narrow lane signposted for its eponymous taverna. Immediately northwest beyond the *kástro* (reached on foot by the long ramp from the *kástro* gate, or frequent water-taxis from the town dock) lies **Váltos beach**, more than 1km in length as it arcs around to the eponymous hamlet. **Lýkhnos** beach, 3km in the opposite (southeast) direction, is similarly huge; a shaded path through the olive groves from the far end of Kyronéri short-cuts the winding road in, or again taxi-boats spare you the walk.

A short, five-kilometre excursion (covered several times daily by tourist train from Kyronéri quay) leads to the diminutive hatbox **castle of Ayiá** (actually between Anthoússa and Ayiá), nocturnally illuminated. Head west on the main road through and beyond Anthoússa, then turn off at the side road for Tríkorfo hamlet. The castle is more elaborate and intact than apparent from a distance, having been rebuilt in 1814 by Ali Pasha's Italian engineers. There's unrestricted access to the dungeons, the upper gallery and the roof with its rusty cannons and superb views encompassing Paxí, Váltos beach, Ammoudhiá and Lefkádha.

Practicalities

The **KTEL station** – just a small booth – is up on the bypass road, near the start of Spýrou Livadhá (the way to Váltos); the main **taxi** rank is at the corner of Spýrou Livadhá and Alexándhou Bánga. Established **car rental** outlets include Parga Hire at Spýrou Livadhá 4 (Ⓣ26840 31833, Ⓦwww.pargahire

.com); Synthesis at Alexándhou Bánga 6 (Ⓣ26840 31700) and Budget/National in Kyronéri at Ayíou Athanasíou 4 (Ⓣ26840 32584). Waterfront travel agencies **rent scooters** and sell **excursions** to the Nekromanteio (more easily and cheaply arranged in Ammoudhiá, see p.395), or to Paxí, taking in sea-caves and Andípaxi too. The **post office** is on Alexándhrou Bánga, start of the main market street, which also has two **ATMs** Kanaris Travel on the quay sells a few **maps** and English-language **books/magazines**. Parga.net at the jetty base provides **Internet** access (Wi-Fi signal for laptops); there's no tourist office, though Ⓦwww.parga.gr is a useful source of **information**.

Accommodation

Tour operators and repeat individual clients monopolize most of Párga's **hotels** and quality **apartments** between mid-June and early September. Outside these seasons, however, you'll have ample choice on spec, though **parking** is usually a nightmare – Kryonéri has just one fee lot and a free olive grove – and avoiding scooter or bar noise is paramount. **Rooms**/studios cluster in the lanes inland from Kryonéri, and the ridge of Tourkopázaro (officially Odhós Patatoúka), where premises have unbeatable views over Váltos beach. There are **campsites** 300m behind Kryonéri beach at *Parga Camping* (Ⓣ26840 31161), and unobtrusive *Valtos* (Ⓣ26840 31287; May–Sept), at the far end of Váltos beach by the yacht harbour; enormous *Enjoy Lyhnos Camping* (Ⓣ26840 31171) straddles access to Lýkhnos beach.

Galini edge of town below Váltos road Ⓣ26840 31581, Ⓕ26840 32221. Hotel set in an orchard and as quiet as the name ("Serenity") implies, with large rooms. ❸

Golfo Beach Kryonéri Ⓣ26840 32336, Ⓕ26840 31347. A choice of basic but spotless 1970s rooms, en suite and not, facing a pleasant garden or the sea; s/c kitchen. ❷

Kostas and Martha Christou (Martha's House) Tourkopázaro, near *kástro* Ⓣ26840 31942 or 693 77 96 209. Spartan rooms – some with private bath across hall – in a calm environment, with garden and s/c kitchen. Rates include breakfast in low season. ❸

Lichnos Beach on Lýnknos beach Ⓣ26840 31257, Ⓦwww.lichnosbeach.com. A good-value choice for the car-bound or families, with a mix of standard rooms, studios and bungalows set in lush grounds, big enough that packages don't completely monopolize it. Tennis court, pool and "private" beach with watersport facility. ❺

Magda's Apartments Váltos road just before lane to *kástro* Ⓣ26840 31228, Ⓦwww.magdas-hotel.com. A mix of studios (❺; usually taken by holiday companies), and six superior apartments (❻; let by the week), direct-bookable only, in a hillside garden environment with mountain and partial sea views, plus a terrace pool and two spas. Good breakfasts (extra), easy parking, quality acoustic music sessions and free Internet, plus Wi-Fi in the lobby. English-speaking hosts Kostas and Spyros will do anything for their clients; not surprisingly, three-month advance booking is usually necessary. Greek Easter to late Oct.

Villa Koralli Kryonéri beach Ⓣ26840 31069, Ⓕ26840 32469. Anodyne white-pine-and-tile *dhomátia*, some sea-view, and limited parking. Land-side rooms cheaper. Easter–Nov. ❺

Eating and drinking

There are nearly thirty full-service **tavernas** around town, though quality varies and cooking is usually aimed squarely at the package trade. Most Párga tavernas offer local wine from the barrel; the red is generally excellent. **Nightlife** centres around annually changing, semi-open-air bars on the east quay pumping out 1960s and 1970s sounds to match a thirty-to-fifty-something crowd; there's a more youthful vibe along the steps to the *kástro*, where *Blue Bar* and adjacent *Sail In* get a less sedate, more Greek clientele.

Café Castle/Kastro Restored barracks, *kástro*. The most civilized chill-out place in Párga; a full bar, but the real speciality is 30 kinds of coffee and flavoured Italian chocolate. Live music (Greek) 2 nights weekly in season. Open 9.30am to midnight (high season).

Eden/Edem Bistro Platía Ayíou Dhimitríou, market. Long-running, good-value crêperie and breakfast venue that's diversified to pasta dishes, salads, fresh-squeezed juices, professionally made coffees and a full bar. Open 8am–1am.
Filomela Patatoúka ☎26840 31265. Upmarket Italian eatery that makes a decent fist of risotto or pasta dishes, and a good venue for reliably fresh mussels; usual range of Italian desserts, though many items off-menu in low season. A romantic last-night splurge (allow €45 for 2, more if you crack into the wine list); reserve in summer.
Golfo Beach Kyronéri. Evangelia is heart and soul of one of Párga's oldest tavernas, with a cult following for her sustaining *mayireftá*; three courses and a beer won't much exceed €16; live music some nights. Open 8am–11pm.
Oskar Grigoríou Lambráki (north side of waterfront). Friendly and tiny – thus seasonally packed – Italian/generic Mediterranean place with pizza and pasta, as well as baked *plevrótous* mushrooms and heaping house salads with prosciutto and sun-dried tomatoes. Open all year.
Sakis Turkopázaro, by fountain and plane trees. The place for a cheap-and-cheerful, village-style feed. Good grills and a few *mayireftá*; no seafood.
To Souli Southeast quay. Oldest taverna in town, about the most reliable of several here; internal facelift hasn't changed its *mayireftá* standards plus a few grilled options.
Stefanos Lane between the castle and Váltos. Touting can be off-putting but the fish is reckoned the best in town – and the view is unbeatable.

The Nekromanteion of Acheron

The **Nekromanteion of Acheron** (*Nekromandío* in modern Greek) stands 22km southeast of Párga, just above Mesopótamos village on a rocky hill. Below this, in ancient times, the Acheron (the modern Ahérondas) – associated with the Styx, river of the underworld, the Kokytos, "River of Lamentation", and the Pyriphlegethon, "River of Flaming Fire" – all flowed into marshy Acherousia lake. According to mythology, Charon rowed departed souls across the lake to the gates of Hades, and from Mycenaean to Roman times an elaborate oracle of the dead existed here. The Acheron sanctuary never achieved the stature of Delphi or Dodona, but its fame was sufficient to serve as the Homeric site of Odysseus's visit to Hades. Circe describes it explicitly, when advising Odysseus:

> **You will come to a wild coast and to Persephone's grove, where the hill poplars grow and the willows that so quickly lose their seeds. Beach your boat there by Ocean's swirling stream and march on into Hades' Kingdom of Decay. There the River of Flaming Fire and the River of Lamentation, which is a branch of the Waters of the Styx, unite around a pinnacle of rock to pour their thundering streams into Acheron. This is the spot, my lord, that I bid you seek out . . . then the souls of the dead and departed will come up in their multitudes.**

The sanctuary

Trees still mark the sanctuary (daily 8.30am–3pm, may close later summer; €2), though today they are primarily cypresses, emblems of the dead across the Mediterranean. The ancient Acherousia lake. which once surrounded the island-oracle, has receded to the Ahérondas skirting the marshy plain of Fanári, which still floods in winter; you can pick out its course from a fringe of Homer's willows. All the mythological rivers still flow, though the Pyriphlegethon is the modern Vovós.

The sanctuary **ruins** allow an understanding of the mind-games played by its priestly caste. According to ancient chroniclers, **pilgrims** arriving on the oracle-island were lodged for a night in windowless rooms. Impressed by the atmosphere, and their mission to consult with the souls of the departed, they would be relieved of their votive offerings while awaiting their "day-trip" to the underworld. When their turn came, they were sent groping along labyrinthine corridors into the heart of the sanctuary, where, further disorientated by having ingested psychoactive lupin seeds, they were lowered into the antechamber of "Hades" itself to witness whatever spectral visitation the priests might have devised.

The sanctuary's walls – polygonal masonry standing to head height – allowed excavators to identify the function of each room; there's a rudimentary plan at the entrance. At the summit, visible from a considerable distance, sits a frescoed **medieval chapel** of Ayíou Ioánnou Prodhrómou; just below, *pithária*, **giant storage urns**, have been left in situ. At the centre is a long room with high walls, flanked by chambers used for votive offerings. From here metal steps lead to the damp, vaulted **underground chamber** where the necromantic audiences took place. Originally the descent was by means of a precarious windlass mechanism, which was found on the site.

Practicalities

The Nekromanteion is most easily reached by boat **tour** from Párga or Ammoudhiá (see p.395), or your own transport. **Buses** from Párga stop at Kastrí, 5km from the site, but do not call at Mesopótamos or Ammoudhiá, both on the direct coast road to Préveza, and a different bus line. Mesopótamos has tavernas and a single hotel near the site entrance, though Ammoudhiá (5km distant) is a more amenable base.

East of Párga: Soúli

The highland region four valleys east of Párga was the land of the **Souliots**, an indomitable tribe of Albanian Orthodox Christians, who inhabited eleven villages here. From 1787 until their initial defeat and dispersal in 1803, these 12,000 mountain warriors repeatedly rebelled against Ali Pasha and his Muslim Albanians from their strongholds above the **Ahérondas Gorge**. In 1820 they allied themselves with Ali Pasha and were allowed to return home, but following the sultan's final victory over Ali, the Souliots were exiled permanently as punishment. Today the region remains impoverished and deserted, though celebrated as a linchpin of resistance against Ottoman rule.

Although it's hard to credit the placid Ahérondas near the Nekromanteion as the way to Hell, just a short way inland its swirling waters cut deep into rock strata to form a gorge at the so-called "Gates of Hades", beginning its downstream course between the remote villages of Tríkastro and Serizianá. While not in quite the same league as the Víkos Gorge (see p.369), it's certainly a respectable wilderness, and if you're looking for adventure inland from Párga you won't find better (although it's busy at summer weekends and all of August, mostly with Greeks).

Glykí and the Ahérondas Gorge

Excursions up the Ahérondas start at **GLYKÍ**, 12km from Kanalláki on the inland road between Préveza and Paramythiá, or 18km from Mórfi junction above Párga. The river, still calm here, is flanked by several mediocre eateries near the main road. A side road on the north (true right) bank, signed as "Piyés Ahéronda", dead-ends after passing a few rooms and a handful of **rafting outfitters** (20-minute trips, fun for children). Alternatively, you can wade **upriver** for up to a kilometre through the shady gorge, attended by clouds of butterflies; rivulets feed knee-high water from the side, with occasional deeper, chilly patches to swim in.

On the other (south or true left) riverbank, a "Skála Tzavélenas" sign points up a paved road. Following this, you can bear left after 800m towards the signposted *Piyes Aheronda* **taverna** (1400m from the main road), with grilled fare served on tree-shaded tables on the river sand.

Hiking into Soúliot country

Beyond the *Piyes Aheronda* taverna, serious **walking trails** forge into the hills. Continue along the road parallel to the river, and bear left towards a modern chapel, 1km from the bridge; some 300m further is a flagstoned car park and picnic benches. Here the way dwindles to a track ending 1.9km from Glykí at a laboriously wrought tunnel.

The **Skála Tzavélenas** ("Tzavélena's Stairway") begins just to the tunnel's left; in Souliot days it was a vertiginous corniche path several hundred metres long, named in honour of a local woman who traversed it on a donkey when her menfolk declined to do so. It now has a retaining wall, and the formerly crumbled *skála* down and to the left has been rehabilitated. Below, the canyon walls squeeze together, and upstream a carpet of greenery rolls up to the plainly visible castle of Kiáfa.

Beyond the *skála*, the main trail into Soúli, waymarked sporadically with blue arrows, yellow rectangles and red squares, descends towards the Ahérondas. About twenty minutes along, there's a junction right for the **Pylés Ádhi** ("Gates of Hell") **narrows**, supposedly five hours' hike one-way upstream, waymarked with red diamonds. While it's more like three hours, much of the walk is through deep forest – giving you scant views – and the roller-coaster trail is somewhat neglected; most people visit the "Gates" by road from Préveza, via Loúros and Vrysoúla.

Most walkers continue on the main path, crossing a modern bridge over the Ahérondas and reaching (30min from the tunnel) the tributary Tsangariótiko stream, known locally as the **Piyés Soulíou** (Souliot Springs); the historic Dála bridge over it was swept away in March 2004 and hasn't been rebuilt. Beyond here the marked route climbs out of the Ahérondas valley, arriving at another junction (1hr from tunnel) below a circular gazebo. The right-hand path, waymarked with green triangles, climbs steadily (35min more) to a pass just below **Kiáfa castle**, with goat pens, plane trees and wells on the col. The south gate of the castle, more of a fortified manor built by Ali Pasha to overawe the Souliots, lies another quarter-hour's scramble up a scree slope. The interior is ruined, patrolled by cows, but the climb is justified by fine views west to Paxí and north to the conical hill where the **fortified monastery of Koúngi** once sat until Souliot rebels blew it, and themselves, up rather than surrender – a newer chapel marks the spot.

At the base of Koúngi hill, reached by rough descending track from the col (another 35min), is impoverished **Samoníva** (Samonídha), the only Souliot village still inhabited (no reliable facilities). At a little church below Samoníva's scattered houses, you can pick up the red-rectangle path for the return journey to the tunnel and car park; allow just over an hour for this, for a generous half-day outing.

The coast to Préveza

Approaches to Préveza from the Nekromanteion and Ahérondas area feature a few more resorts and sites before emerging onto the landlocked **Amvrakikós (Ambracian) Gulf**, where in 31 BC Octavian defeated Antony and Cleopatra at the Battle of Actium. The most substantial of the ruins is Octavian's "Victory City" of **Nikopolis**, just south of where the Igoumenítsa–Préveza and the Árta–Préveza highways meet.

Ammoudhiá and the coast road

Two daily local **buses** cover the coastal route to Préveza from **AMMOUDHIÁ**, a little beach resort 5km due west of the Nekromanteion at the mouth of the Ahérondas. By the village entrance is a worthwhile **visitor information centre** (summer only, daily 8.30am–3.30pm; free), whose intelligent, non-jingoistic exhibits highlight the unique ecology of the river and its marshes, as well as the history and ethnology of Soúli. Various informative booklets, both free and for sale, partially offset bouts of Greek-only labelling of the displays.

Tourists equipped with camper vans or caravans occupy the eucalyptus grove separating the rather scrappy village – only founded after the 1950s draining of the malarial Fanári marsh – from the 700-metre sandy **beach**. There's usually washed-up flotsam, the water can be chilly and drownings are reportedly frequent, but it's scenic, with more coastal mountains beyond the headland closing off the funnel-shaped bay.

Bounding the village on the south, the Ahérondas River meets (and cools) the sea here; the paved quay is packed with fishing and **excursion boats** for the jaunt upriver (hourly in season; good birdwatching en route) to the Nekromanteion, and lined with most of Ammoudhiá's **tavernas** and cafés. Easternmost in the series is *Iy Roxani* (*Thanasis Babos*), good for fish, but somewhat overpriced. There are various rooms and apartments, plus several bona-fide **hotels**, including convenient, simple but en-suite *Glaros* (Ⓣ26840 41300; ❷), right behind the river esplanade 200m back from the beach.

There are other sandy coves south across the river, only reachable via the village of Velanidhórahi. The largest is **Keréntza** (aka Órmos Odhysséa; 3.2km from the village), created by a stagnant arm of the Ahérondas, with showers, a *kantína* and views to Paxí and Andípaxi. Postcard-perfect **Alonáki**, 2.8km distant by a different road, is a miniature pine-and-cliff-grit cove opening to the south, again with a shower and seasonal *kantína*. The two are linked by good dirt track, off which a third beach, **Amóni** (drinking water and showers), can be reached by a short, rough drive, though it's exposed and often seaweed-caked.

South of Ammoudhiá the coast road becomes a proper **motorway**, with exits (labelled north to south: Paralía Loútsas, Paralía Vráhou, Paralía Lygiás, Paralía Rizón) to coastal settlements worth breaking a journey at with your own transport. Contiguous **Loútsa** and **Vráhou**, fronted by 2km of clean, golden sand, are accordingly well built up with Greeks' weekend apartments. **LYGIÁ** also has a long if boulder-strewn beach overlooked by a crumbling castle at the south end; **dhomátia** abound, plus there are two beachside **campsites** near the castle (the better being *Corali*, Ⓣ26820 56306, Ⓦwww.camping-corali.gr). Among several local **tavernas**, best by a mile is *To Skaloma* (alias *O Yios tou Foti;* no sign out) at Lygiá's little port, with big portions and small prices for both seafood and vegetarian *mezédhes* attracting a mixed clientele.

Inland: Zálongo and ancient Kassope

Some 28km from Mesopótamos on the inland route, you pass a turning east to **Kamarína** (3km), overlooked by the monastery of Zálongo and the ruins of ancient Kassope. The latter are a steep, shadeless five-kilometre climb from the main highway, so a taxi or your own transport is a good idea. There's also access through **Kryopiyí** village, also 3km off the main road, somewhat quicker if you're approaching from the north.

Zálongo (1km past Kassope) is a staple of Greek schoolbook history, immortalized by the defiant mass suicide of a group of Souliot women. In 1803, troops commanded by Ali Pasha's son Veli cornered in the monastery numerous Souliots who had fled the destruction of Koúngi. As this refuge was overrun, about sixty Souliot women and children fled to the cliff above, where the mothers danced one by one, with their children in their arms, over the edge of the precipice. This act is commemorated by a truly hideous modern cement-and-stone **sculpture**. Both monastery – just below and of no intrinsic interest – and monument attract coach tours of Greek schoolchildren and (at weekends) adults.

Slightly to the west of the monastery, on a natural balcony just below the summit of a similar bluff, lies **ancient Kassope** (daily 8.30am–3pm; €3; side gate often left open), a minor, fortified Thesprotian capital and cult centre today approached via a path through a pine grove. Though founded in the fourth century BC, the city's ruins date mainly from the third century; the place was sacked by the Romans a hundred years later, and definitively abandoned in 31 BC when its citizens were commanded to inhabit Nikopolis (see below). Excellent site placards offer a potted history and help locate highlights on the grid plan, including the central agora, a tiny, eroded *odeion*, a theatre, and (most impressive) a *katagoyeion* (hostelry) for representatives of the Kassopean federation, though revisionist opinion reckons this a larger agora. Principally, though, Kassope is memorable for its superb location – some 600m above sea level, with Lefkádha and the Ionian coastline laid at your feet.

Nikopolis

NIKOPOLIS ("Victory City") was founded by Octavian on the site where his army had camped prior to the Battle of Actium: an ill-considered gesture that made little geographical sense. The settlement was on unstable ground, water had to be transported by aqueduct from the distant Loúros springs, and a population had to be forcibly imported from often distant towns. However, such a *folie de grandeur* was understandable. At **Actium** (modern Áktio), Octavian had first blockaded and then annihilated the combined fleets of Antony and Cleopatra, gathered there for the invasion of Italy. These events culminated in Octavian the general becoming Roman Emperor Augustus.

The subsequent history of Nikopolis is undistinguished, with much of its population drifting back to their homes, and the town suffering barbarian sackings as Rome declined. During the sixth century AD, it flourished briefly as a Byzantine city, but within four centuries it had vanished from the combined effect of earthquakes and Bulgar raids.

The site

The far-flung monuments begin 7km north of Préveza, on either side of the main road. The site is really too scattered to tour by foot or bus (though the latter pass by); hire a taxi in Préveza, or come by car. The ruins look impressive from the road, but the promise of the site is unfulfilled; however a major, ongoing re-excavation and consolidation project – including a new museum – should remedy that.

Nikopolis is bounded on the south by a a formidable stretch of sixth-century Byzantine **walls**, beyond which lie the **Dhométios basilica** (with covered-over mosaics) and the Roman **odeion** dating from the original construction of the city, well restored for use in the local summer festival. From the foundations of the sixth-century **basilica of Alkýsonos** just north of the main **baths**, it's 2km to the main **theatre**, west of which you can discern the sunken outline of the **stadium**, below Smyrtoúna village.

Préveza

At the mouth of the Amvrakikós Gulf, modern **PRÉVEZA** (from the Persian-Turkish *pervaz* or cornice) is the humble successor to Nikopolis, but not without appeal, especially in its bazaar quarter and waterfront below the low-slung fortress of Áyios Andhréas. Since international flights began serving Áktio airport, the town has had a facelift, and more character remains in the old quarter than at Párga. Préveza merits a stopover, not just for Nikopolis, but also for enjoyable evenings at **tavernas** offering the best fare for some distance around.

Practicalities

Charters arriving at nearby Áktio airport generally have transport laid on to the various resorts; otherwise there are only taxis for the seven-kilometre trip to town. The **airport** itself is a cheerless, overcrowded shed at the edge of an air-force base, with two car-rental booths, snacks at the bar, and no banking facilities or anywhere to sit. The **bus station** in Préveza is at the north edge of town, 1km out at the start of the road to Párga; there are sporadic shuttles into the centre and a **taxi** rank on the waterfront. A high-tech **tunnel** under the straits links Préveza and Áktio (3min; €3 cars, €5 camper vans); pedestrians and bicycles are banned and there's no longer a ferry service across the strait. Drivers arriving from Párga or Préveza should follow signposting for "Áktio" to find the "rabbit hole" entrance – you can't get there from the east waterfront.

The **post office** is on Spiliádhou, near the castle. Several banks with **ATMs** are found at the north end of the waterfront, as is a municipal **tourist office** on sidestreet Bálkou (Ⓣ26820 21078; Mon–Fri 8am–2.30pm).

Accommodation

None of the four in-town **hotels** is especially inviting or great value; most tourists will be staying at beachfront resorts to the north, only coming to town after dark for the lively nightlife. The best one is seafront *Avra* at Venizélou 19 (Ⓣ26820 21230, Ⓦwww.epirus.com/hotelavra; ③). Otherwise, there are **rooms** on the shore road towards the far side of the peninsula; follow this south past Venetian **Pandokrátoras** castle (a shell, used as a venue for the summer festival) at the peninsula tip.

The nearest **campsite** is *Kalamitsi* (Ⓣ26820 22192), around 4km north of town on the highway which skims along a few hundred metres back from the coast. Any bus running towards Kanáli (14km out, not to be confused with Kanalláki) will pass the summer-only sites of *Monolithi* (Ⓣ26820 51755) and *Kanali* (Ⓣ26820 22741), on either side of the road at **Monolíthi beach**, a long stretch of sand beginning 10km from Préveza, behind a managed forest (the best bit) – at Kanáli it's less alluring.

Eating, drinking and nightlife

A dozen **tavernas** (many dinner only) are scattered around the inland market lanes in central Préveza, especially on Adhrianopóleos, with cafés and bars mostly along the pedestrianized waterfront esplanade Venizélou. Good inland choices include *Psatha*, Dhardhanellíon 4–6 (one block south of the Venetian clocktower along the main shopping thoroughfare, then west), for standard *mayireftá*, or *Ouzeri Kaixis* at Parthenogoyíou 7; nearby at Niklambá 5, *Dinos* is one of the few places open for lunch. On the lane – officially Grigoríou toú Pémptou – leading seaward (east) from the clocktower, there's a touristy cluster of specialists in grilled sardines and barrelled wine; *Iy Trelli Garidha* just around the corner on Adhrianopóleos is a better alternative. By **night**, these pedestrianized alleys, particularly around the fish-market building and the clocktower, come alive with assorted **bars** and **cafés** (eg *Saïtan Pazar*, on the tiny square west of the tower), patronized by locals, guests from surrounding resorts and denizens of yachts moored at the esplanade. July and August see a range of musical and theatrical events as part of the **Nikopolia festival**, held at various local outdoor venues. There's a summer outdoor **cinema** south of town on the road to Pandokrátoras; the central winter one's on Ethnikís Andístasis.

Árta and around

Some 50km northeast of Préveza lies **ÁRTA**, tucked into a loop of the Árakhthos River as it meanders towards the **Amvrakikós Gulf**. One of the more pleasant mainland provincial capitals, it's a low-key place which retains much of its Ottoman-bazaar aspect (including a covered market on Vassiléos Pýrrou), and some medieval monuments in the centre.

From the west, you enter town within sight of the restored humpbacked **bridge**, subject of a famous folk song recasting a gruesome legend found elsewhere in the Balkans. The bridge-builder, continually thwarted by the current washing his foundations away, took the advice of a talking bird and immured his wife alive in the central pier; the bridge finally held but the woman's voice haunted the place thereafter.

The Town

Árta was known anciently as Ambracia, capital of Pyrrhus, fourth-century BC king of Epirus famous for his hard-won campaigns in Italy – the original Pyrrhic victories. The foundations of a **temple of Apollo** and an **odeion** bracketing Vassiléos Pýrrou recall this period. Northeast of this rises the **Froúrio**, the ancient acropolis and citadel in every subsequent era; there are occasional performances at its open-air theatre.

More substantial monuments date from Árta's second burst of glory, following the 1204 fall of Constantinople, when the town was the seat of the **Despotate of Epirus**, an autonomous Byzantine state. The despotate, which stretched from Corfu to Thessaloníki, was governed by the Angelos dynasty (the imperial family expelled from Constantinople) and survived until 1449.

Most striking and unusual of the Byzantine monuments is **Panayía Parigorítissa** (sometimes rendered Parigorítria; Tues–Sun 8.30am–3pm; €2), a grandiose, five-domed cube at the southwest end of Skoufá. The interior is almost Gothic in appearance, with the main dome supported by a wonky-looking cantilevered-pilaster system. Up top floats a *Pandokrátor* (Christ in Majesty) mosaic in excellent condition, overshadowing much later frescoes below. The church, flanked by two side chapels, was built between 1283 and 1296 by Despot Nikiforos I as part of a monastic complex, of which sixteen cells and the refectory remain east and south of the church, beside foundations of an early shrine.

Two smaller Byzantine churches from the same period also survive in the town. Both are more conventional structures enlivened by intricate brick-and-tile decorations on the outside walls. They're usually locked, but this is no tragedy since the exteriors present the main interest. **Ayía Theódhora**, containing the marble tomb of the wife of Epirot despot Michael II, stands in its own courtyard halfway down Pýrrou. A little further north, opposite the produce market, is thirteenth-century **Áyios Vassilíos**, ornamented with glazed polychrome tiles and bas-reliefs.

Practicalities

Buses arrive at the **KTEL** station on the riverbank at the northeastern outskirts of town. From there it's a ten-minute walk southwest along **Skoufá**, the main commercial street and thoroughfare, to central **Platía Ethnikís Andístasis**. Skoufá, pedestrianized along much of its length, and its parallel streets, Vassiléos Pýrrou and Konstandínou, wind through the oldest part of town. The main **taxi rank** is on Platía Kilkís, at the southwest end of Skoufá. Drivers should beware the **fee-parking scheme** enforced during business hours: a red strip on the sign means parking of one to two hours – get a pay-and-display ticket from kerbside machines – while a green strip denotes resident parking only.

Among several **hotels**, best set and best value is the three-star *Xenia Frourio* (☎26810 27413; ④) inside the *froúrio*, with easy parking, gardens, on-site restaurant and a tennis court. Árta **restaurants**, what few there are, cater for locals; a classic, with all the usual *mayireftá*, is *Papadhakos* at Skoufá 31. Most visitors, however, gravitate towards the old bridge, which you can admire at leisure over a coffee or a meal. *O Protomastoras* and adjacent *Yefira* offer adequate fare to a young crowd, though both are more geared up for drinks than food. In the evenings, people throng the **cafés** around Platía Ethnikís Andístasis; a slightly less central, pleasant one, within sight of Panayía Paregorítissa, is *En Arti*, with seating by a fountain and plane tree.

Monasteries and churches around Árta

Amid the orange groves surrounding Árta, a number of **monasteries and churches** date from the despotate, often built by members of the imperial Angelos dynasty; all are well signposted with yellow-on-brown placards.

Within walking distance (2km south along Komménou, past the hospital turning) stands **Káto Panayía monastery** (daily: May–Sept 7am–1pm & 4.30–7.30pm; Oct–April 8am–1pm & 3–6pm; ring for admission), erected by Michael II between 1231 and 1271 and now occupied by a dozen nuns. The *katholikón* has extravagant exterior decoration, including a graphic *Last Judgement*, but the interior frescoes, showing Christ in three guises, are more compelling. Many are smudged, but not a fine, undamaged Christ Emmanuel in the front vault.

Some 6km north out of Árta by a circuitous route (regular buses; with own transport, turn right 100m past Kostáki turning), the monastic church of **Panayía Vlahernón** in Vlahérna village is engaging inside and out. To the basic three-aisled twelfth-century plan, Michael II added three domes – supported by dissimilar columns – as well as the narthex; one of two tombs inside is probably his. Both north and south narthex portals have finely worked lintels, while high up the south wall is another fine **relief** of the Archangel Michael. Most of the vast marble floor is planked over, but a magnificent, glassed-over tesselated **mosaic** has been left exposed in the middle. This is the most beautiful of Árta's churches, worth contemplating at length from the café just opposite.

Three other churches, apparently never associated with any monastery, lie within easy reach of Árta; most serve today as the graveyard chapels for the nearest village. **Panayía tís Bryónis** lies 800m up the side road towards Megárhi, 6km out of Árta en route to Amfilohía; dating from 1232, it has fine exterior brickwork. By taking the road for Kostáki and Anéza from the historic bridge, and then turning west towards Plisí, you reach partly eleventh-century **Áyios Dhimítrios Katsoúris** after 5km, a high-domed, cross-in-square structure with a later narthex and belfry; it's usually open around dusk. About 1km further north, at the south edge of Kirkizátes village, stands **Áyios Nikólaos tís Rodhiás**, a thirteenth-century, cross-in-square jewelbox with frescoes in heartbreaking condition – though a *Communion of the Apostles* partly survives, and two intricately worked column capitals uphold the dome.

Around the Amvrakikós Gulf

Around the **Amvrakikós Gulf**, there are few stellar attractions aside from Árta. An exceptional bright spot is the **Rodhiá Wetland Centre** (Ⓦwww.rodiawetlands.gr) at Strongylí, reached by a six-kilometre side road 18km west of Árta. This protected environment at the mouth of the Loúros River supports a variety of fauna, from water buffalo to eels by way of a vast assortment of birds. The Centre conducts a worthwhile set **tour** (daily by arrangement, Ⓣ26830 41219) on motorized punts, which includes a stop at the medieval monastery of Panayías Rodhiás (also accessible by trail) and a meal of local dishes at a pavilion in mid-marsh.

At weekends, Ártans head for **seafood meals** at nearby coastal villages, and you should do the same if passing through. The final approach to **KORONISSÍA** (25km southwest of Árta), a former island in the middle of the gulf, lies along a wave-lashed causeway flanked by a seaweedy beach popular with **windsurfers**. Today the village offers a few fish **tavernas**, of which – last in the row – the most notable and consistently open (all year) is *Myrtaria* (*tou Patenda*), with gulf-sourced, fair-priced seafood, and some pleasant **apartments** to rent next door (Ⓣ26810 24021; ❸). Up on the hill, yet another Byzantine church, lopsided, tenth-century **Yénnisis tís Theotókou**, surveys the gulf and lagoons below.

As you head clockwise towards the open sea, **MENÍDHI**, 21km southeast from Árta, lies slightly off the main road, with three **hotels** – the best being the *Sorokos* at mid-quay (Ⓣ26810 88213; ❸) – and several fish **tavernas**. Of these, *Vouliagmeni* (*Pandioras*), the first on the left as you exit the highway, is noted for its fresh gulf shrimps, but prices have climbed with fame – budget €24 minimum per person.

Amfilohía is promisingly situated at the head of the gulf, but proves a dull, small town fronted by stagnant water. If you need to stay the night hereabouts, **VÓNITSA**, 37km west, is more convenient and pleasant. Again, it's not a wildly exciting place, and frustratingly distant from the open sea, but represents a definite improvement with its lively waterside, tree-lined squares and substantial Byzantine **castle** above. Among three surviving **hotels**, quietest is the lightly refurbished *Vonitsa* (Ⓣ26430 22565; ❸) at the east end of the seafront behind the gravelly beach. As at Préveza across the gulf, seafood figures prominently on the menus of a half-dozen waterfront **tavernas**; the pick of these is cheap, cheerful and salubrious *Faros*. The **KTEL** is two blocks inland, on the bypass road.

The Etolo-Akarnanian coast

Heading south towards the Gulf of Kórinthos, there is little of note on the more direct **inland route**. In-your-face ugly **Agrínio** – also the hottest town in Greece during summer – is the regional public transport hub, with buses northwest to Árta/Ioánnina, northeast to Karpeníssi, west to Lefkádha and south to Andírio, for Náfpaktos and Pátra.

The **coast south from Vónitsa** is bleakly impressive, served by a quiet stretch of road skirting the shoreline, with nothing but wilderness inland. By default as much as anything else, the little resorts of **Páleros** and **Mýtikas** are the highlights, approachable also by a more roundabout route taking in the castle and ghost village of **Playiá**.

Páleros and Playiá

Some 18km south of Vónitsa on the direct road, the port-resort of **PÁLEROS** is almost a small town. Traditionally, local men sought their fortunes as seamen; today this is echoed in yacht-based tourism, with UK package companies Sunsail and Mark Warner monopolizing the two local hotels. The district nearest the shore has charm, with its smattering of old houses, yacht anchorages and a decent in-town **beach**; another grittily sandy one, shadeless but popular, extends 2km west of town. A **post office**, one **ATM** and a clutch of **tavernas** and **bars** around the harbour platía constitute the main amenities. Forego the obvious waterfront taverna in favour of *Platanos*, at the back of the square under the namesake plane tree, which dishes up a variety of grills and fresh fish at fair prices, or *Skamnia* a few paces further inland, with tables in an old platía from 1861, under the mulberries of the name.

If approaching Páleros from Lefkádha or Préveza, take the slightly quicker and more scenic route via Néa Playía. On the east side of the channel and its pontoon bridge serving Lefkádha, follow signs towards Peratiá, and then **Néa Playiá**, a modern, post-1953-earthquake village accented by an enormous fourteenth-century **castle** guarding the straits with Lefkádha. The onward road curls under this, then continues 4km east to **old Playiá**, abandoned after the quake and inhabited now by just a few pastoralists; it's a surprisingly large place, looking northwest to the island and the Ionian, a veritable outdoor museum of lovely old tiled houses no longer seen locally. From here it's 11km further through a pass to Stenó hamlet, then 7km to Páleros, paved all the way.

Mýtikas

Beyond Páleros, it's 18km south to sleepy but pleasant **MÝTIKAS**; here, rows of old houses strung along a pebbly shore look out onto the island of Kálamos, with a backdrop inland of sheer, amphitheatric mountainside. Behind the long but decidedly average shingle beach sprawls a steadily expanding, grid-plan modern annexe. But there's nowhere as inviting to stay to the southeast until you reach Náfpaktos (see p.299), and if you're coming northwest from Andírio, it's the first place that prompts thoughts of an overnight.

You'll probably need to stay here to catch the boat across to the island of Kálamos (see below); among three central **hotels**, best is *Kymata* (☎26460 81311; ❸) above a sweet shop, with mosquito screens, air conditioning and fridges in the rooms. *O Glaros* **taverna** on the shore does affordable grilled fish meals; the only alternative, *Taverna stou Thoma* at the far end of the village, is more elaborate but still reasonable. Two **ATMs** and a **post office** complete the list of facilities.

Kálamos island

The island of **Kálamos**, the largest of a mini-archipelago southwest of Mýtikas, is essentially a partly wooded mountain rising abruptly from the sea. Although a dependency of Lefkádha, public utility and transport links are to the mainland opposite. In summer a few yachts anchor below the main village, Hóra, and at

Pórto Leóne in the south, but otherwise the island (permanent population ca. 550) sees few visitors and is ill equipped to host them. The only regular connection is a daily *kaïki* from Mýtikas, which leaves the mainland at about noon and returns from the island at 7.30am the next day; in summer the same craft may do scheduled day-trips, but otherwise you must charter the entire boat at considerable cost. In Hóra there's one **dhomátia** outfit (Ⓣ26460 91238; ❷), but only during July and August, when they fill quickly, so come prepared to camp (though even this is difficult, given the lack of flat ground).

HÓRA, spread out among gardens and olive groves on the south coast, largely survived the 1953 earthquake which devastated many Ionian islands, though there's been no lack of insensitive building since. There are two basic *kafenía*-tavernas and a shop by the harbour, plus a bakery up by a **post office**. The gravelly village **beach** fifteen minutes southwest has no facilities; the better beach of **Merithiá** lies twenty minutes northeast of the port, via a rough scramble along the shore. Your reward will be 500m of sand and fine gravel which could easily host all the tourists Kálamos is ever likely to get; this is also one of the better camping spots, though there's no shade or fresh water.

Kástro, a fortified settlement at the north tip of the island, is linked to the port by a seven-kilometre asphalt road; walking it is drudgery, despite pine-shade and views, so try and hitch the sparse traffic. The small, five-bastioned castle here may be Byzantine, and surveys the straits between here and Mýtikas, as suggested by the name of the road's-end hamlet 2km beyond, **Episkopí** ("Overlook"; no facilities).

Southwest of Hóra, a broad mule-and-tractor track leads across scrub-covered mountainside to **Kefáli (Pórto Leóne)**, its deep, protected bay beloved of yachts. The lower hamlet has been deserted since the 1953 earthquake, except for a single **taverna**, *Panos*. A higher, pirate-proof settlement, nearly invisible now, was abandoned after World War II when the local olive-oil shipping fleet was destroyed. It's a shadeless, two-hour walk from Hóra, with views across to neighbouring Kastós island to compensate; you're best off going by boat.

Astakós, Oeniadae and Etolikó

South of Mýtikas, the coast road offers stunning views west over Kálamos, Kastós, Itháki, Kefaloniá and the Ehinádhes islets – one of the most dramatic seascapes in Greece. After 31km you reach **ASTAKÓS**, ("Lobster"); there's no lobster served, however, at any of the mediocre tavernas lining its quay on the north flank of an all-but-beachless gulf. Though only yacht flotillas now call to take on water, Astakós was once an important port, judging from the two parallel streets of the marketplace, with many Neoclassical buildings from the 1870s.

Arriving by land, the **KTEL** is at one end of the quay, while the single, overpriced hotel, *Stratos* (Ⓣ26460 41911; ❺), sprawls at the other, overlooking the tiny, gravelly town beach; in peak season cheaper **rooms** are available elsewhere. There's just one daily summer **ferry** to Kefaloniá at around noon; ring Ⓣ26460 38020 for current details.

Beyond Astakós the scenery becomes greener as the road winds for 26km over hills covered by the protected **Lesíni ash forest** – remnant of a once-vast habitat – and then down onto the fertile floodplain of the Ahelóös. At Katohí, by the river, there's a five-kilometre, well-signposted detour west to **ancient Oeniadae** (alias Trikardhókastro). In ancient times, when the Ahelóös delta was not so far advanced as today, Oeniadae was the main port of western Greece, and irresistible to any conqueror; accordingly 7km of Hellenistic **walls and gates** loop around to defend it. The American School first excavated it in 1901, after which the city became overgrown again; recently the undergrowth was cleared to re-expose a number of monuments. From the site gate (usually open, free) you can drive most of the way up an access drive to the small **theatre**, backed into an ash-shaded hill with views west over the delta to the Ionian Sea. Closer to the main entrance, a stoutly fenced zone contains ancient **shipyards**, a fortification **tower** and an arched **gateway**.

East of the Ahelóös delta stands **ETOLIKÓ**, built on an island in the stagnant lagoon and reached by two causeways. The place was a Byzantine refuge from assorted raiders, but is today visibly less prosperous than Mesolóngi (see below), of which it seems a miniature version – there's an obvious Roma shantytown. Yet it could make a useful emergency halt, with an acceptable en-suite **hotel** on the west-facing quay: the *Alexandra* (Ⓣ26320 23019; ❷). Next door is the town's fanciest **restaurant**, *To Stafnokari*, featuring local seafood (including eel), though the fare's not quite as good value as in Mesolóngi. There's the usual complement of bars and *kafenía* in the centre, plus an **ATM** and **post office**. Blue-and-white urban buses ply to Mesolóngi, 10km southeast, past the salt factories that today provide the area's living.

Mesolóngi and around

Mesolóngi (Missolongi), for most visitors, is irrevocably associated with **Lord Byron**, who died here to dramatic effect during the War of Independence

Lórdhos Výronos: Byron in Mesolóngi

In January 1824, **Lord Byron** arrived at Mesolóngi, a squalid, inhospitable port amidst lagoons – but also the western centre of **resistance** against the Ottomans. The poet, who had contributed his personal fame and fortune to the war effort, was enthusiastically greeted with a 21-gun salute, and made **commander** of the five-thousand-strong garrison, a role as much political as military. The Greek forces were divided into factions whose brigand-chieftains separately and persistently petitioned him for money. He had already wasted months on Kefaloniá adjudicating such claims before finalizing his own military plan – to march on Náfpaktos and thence take control of the Gulf of Kórinthos – but in Mesolóngi he was again delayed.

Occasionally Byron despaired: "Here we sit in this realm of mud and discord", read one of his journal entries. But while other Philhellenes returned home, disillusioned by the fractious, larcenous Greeks, or worn out by quasi-tropical Mesolóngi, he stayed. Outside his house, he drilled soldiers; he rowed and hunted in the lagoon, where he caught a fever, possibly malaria. On April 19, 1824, Byron **died**; ironically, he became more valuable to the Greek cause dead than alive. News of the poet's demise, embellished to heroic proportions, reverberated across northern Europe; arguably it changed the course of the war in Greece. When Mesolóngi fell again to the Ottomans in spring 1826, there was outcry in the European press, and French and English forces were finally galvanized into sending a naval force that unintentionally engaged an Egyptian fleet at Navarino (see p.254), striking a fatal blow against the Ottoman navy.

Ever since independence, Byron has been a Greek national **hero**. Almost every town in the country has a street – Výronos – named after him; not a few men still answer to "Vyron" as a first name; and there was once an eponymous brand of cigarettes (perhaps the ultimate Greek tribute). Moreover, the respect he inspired was for years generalized to his fellow countrymen – before being dissipated after 1943 by British interference in the Resistance and bungling in Cyprus.

(see box p.403). Mesolóngi can claim some attention for this literary and revolutionary past but it's a fairly shabby and unromantic place: rainy from autumn to spring, and comprised largely of drab, modern buildings between which locals enthusiastically bicycle along a flat grid plan. Amazingly, it, rather than larger Agrínio, is the capital of Étolo-Akarnanía, a decision surely taken more on sentimental than practical grounds. To be fair, the town has been spruced up, especially in the centre, but if you come here on pilgrimage, it's still best to move on the same day. With your own transport, you can get more out of the region by stopping at two underrated nearby archeological sites, **Pleuron** and **Kalydon**, major settlements of the ancient Aetolians.

The Town

You enter the town from the northeast through the **Gate of the Sortie,** named after the April 12, 1826 break-out by nine thousand Greeks, culminating the Ottomans' year-long siege. In one desperate dash they quit Mesolóngi, leaving a group of defenders to destroy it – and some three thousand civilians not capable of leaving – by firing the powder magazines. But those fleeing were betrayed, ambushed on nearby Mount Zygós; less than two thousand evaded massacre or capture and enslavement by an Albanian mercenary force.

Just inside this gate, on the right, partly bounded by the remaining fortifications, is the **Kípos Iróön**, or "Garden of Heroes" (daily: summer 9am–8pm; winter 9am–1.30pm & 4–6pm; free) – signposted in English as "Heroes' Tombs" – where a tumulus covers the bodies of the town's anonymous defenders. Beside the tomb of Souliot commander Markos Botsaris is a **statue of Byron**, erected in 1881, under which – despite apocryphal traditions – is buried neither the poet's heart nor lungs. Byron might conceivably have been offered the throne of an independent Greece: thus the relief of his coat of arms with a royal crown above. Among the palm trees and rusty cannon loom busts, obelisks, cenotaphs to an astonishing range of American, German and French Philhellenes.

Elsewhere in town, Byronic traces are sparse. The **house** in which he lived and died on Levídhou was destroyed during World War II, with only a rather lame memorial garden at the site. Back on central Platía Bótsari, the Neoclassical town hall houses a small **museum** devoted to the revolution (Mon–Fri 9am–1.30pm & 4–7pm, Sat & Sun 9am–1pm & 4–7pm, closes 6pm winter; free), with some emotive paintings on the upper floor (including a copy of Delacroix's *Gate of the Sortie*), reproductions of period lithographs and a rather disparate (and desperate) collection of Byronia on the ground floor. Pride of place, by the entrance, goes to an original edition of Solomos's poem *Hymn to Liberty*, now the words of the national anthem.

Practicalities

KTEL **buses** arrive at Mavrokordhátou 5, by Platía Bótsari, while local blue-and-white ones call just a few paces away. **ATMs** surround the square; the **post office** stands a block east on Spyrídhona Moustaklí.

Hotels in Mesolóngi are cheerless, overpriced and often block-booked by Greek tour groups. If you need or want to stay in town, a budget option is *Avra*, Hariláou Trikoúpi 5 (☎26310 22284; ❷), just off the central platía and close to the best of Mesolóngi's eating and drinking venues. A more upmarket, impersonal choice is *Theoxenia* (☎26310 22493; ❹), a small, landscaped complex just south of town on the lagoon shore – convenient if you're driving, though the 1970s-vintage rooms are ripe for an overhaul.

The prevailing Greek craze for cutting-edge **ouzerís, tavernas** and **bars** has swept Mesolóngi, making at least a lunch stop something to plan on. The place is especially noted for its eels, hunted with tridents in the lagoon and then smoked or grilled fresh; also famous is the local *avgotáraho* or *haviára*, caviar made from grey mullet roe. The main concentration of **tavernas**, interspersed with a few bars, is along and around Athanasíou Razikótsika, a pedestrianized street one block south of similarly car-free Hariláou Trikoúpi. The poshest establishment – worth the extra expense – is *Filoxenos* at no. 7, with exemplary presentation of generous portions and a pleasant interior; also noteworthy are *To Avgo tou Kokora* at no. 15 and *O Aris* at no. 23. In the narrow alleys linking these two broader streets are too many **bars** and **kafenía** to list – you'll find something to suit.

Around Mesolóngi: Tourlídha, Pleuron and Kalydon

More interesting than any town sight is a walk across the **Klísova lagoon**, past two **forts** which were vital defences against the Ottoman navy. The lagoon, with its salt-evaporation ponds and fish farms, attracts a variety of wading birds, especially in spring. A causeway extends 4km to the open sea at **TOURLÍDHA**, a hamlet of wood-plank and prefab summer cottages on stilts, plus a few **tavernas** – most reliable being *Iliovasilema* (rooms upstairs; ⓣ26310 51408, ③). If you can stomach the intermittent stench from the nearby salt-ponds, there's a packed-sand **beach** to swim from, with showers and a few café-bars.

Some 4km northwest of town, on the major road to Etolikó, lies **ancient Pleuron** (signed also as Plévro; variable hours; enclosed but free), which reached its zenith during Hellenistic times. The access road has been paved to facilitate resumed excavations. The most obvious remains are the massive **perimeter wall** of polygonal masonry, a small **theatre** built against one of the towers, and an ingenious **reservoir**; equally impressive are sweeping views over the local saltpans and the lagoon.

About 10km east of Mesolóngi, a hazardous turn off the highway deposits you at the tiny car park and warden's booth of **ancient Kalydon** (unrestricted access; free), excavated by a Danish team each summer. Near the entrance they've uncovered a curious rectangular structure, probably a **bouleuterion**. Follow the signed track to massive foundations of a **heroön**, with an intact subterranean tomb (locked), and then continue west to the equally imposing plinths of a joint **temple to Apollo, Artemis and Laphrias**, atop a fortified, artificially augmented hill. Despite the humming motorway below, it's well worth the detour, and the views are equal to Pleuron's.

Travel details

Buses

Departures cited have similar frequency in each direction, so entries are given just once; check under both starting point and destination.

Agrínio to: Corfu (bus/ferry, 2 daily in season; 4hr); Ioánnina (6 daily; 2hr 20min); Karpeníssi (1 daily; 3hr 30min); Lefkádha (5 daily; 1hr 20min); Mesolóngi–Andírio (12 daily; 40min–1hr 15min).

Árta to: Ioánnina (10 daily Mon–Fri, 6 Sat & Sun; 1hr 30min); Prámanda and Ágnanda (1 daily 2pm; 1hr 30min); Melissourgí (Mon & Fri 2pm; 1hr 40min); Préveza (5 daily Mon–Fri, 2 Sat & Sun; 1hr); Vourgarélli (1 daily Sat & Sun; 1hr).

Igoumenítsa to: Athens (4 daily; 8hr); Párga (4 daily Mon–Fri, 3 Sat, 1 Sun; 1hr); Préveza (1–2 daily; 2hr); Sayiádha (5 daily; 30min); Sývota (Pérdhika bus; 3 daily Mon–Fri, 2 Sat; 30min).
Ioánnina to: Athens (9 daily; 6hr 30min); Igoumenítsa (7 daily; 2hr, or 1hr express on Vía Egnatía); Kastoriá, via Kónitsa (2 daily, change at Neápoli; 5hr); Kónitsa (7 daily Mon–Fri, 5 Sat & Sun; 1hr); Métsovo (4 daily Mon–Fri, 2 Sat, 1 Sun; 1hr 30min); Monodhéndhri (Mon & Thurs 6.15am & 2pm; 45min); Pápingo (Fri only 5.30am/2.30pm; 1hr 15min); Párga (4 daily; 2hr 30min); Pátra (4 daily; 3hr 30min); Prámanda (2 daily Mon–Fri 5.45am & 3pm, Sat & Sun 3pm only; 2hr); Préveza (8 daily Mon–Fri, 6 Sat & Sun; 2hr); Thessaloníki (6 daily; 5hr); Tríkala via Kalambáka (2 daily, 3 Fri & Sun; 3hr); Tsepélovo (2 daily Mon, Wed & Fri 6.15am & 2.15pm; 1hr 15min); Víkos (Tues only 5.30am/2.30pm; 1hr).
Kónitsa to: Dhístrato (Mon & Wed 1.45pm, Fri 2.30pm; 1hr 15min); Kerásovo (Mon & Fri 2pm; 45min); Molydhosképasti (2–3 weekly; 30min).
Mesolóngi to: Athens (8–9 daily; 4hr); Ioánnina (7 daily; 2hr 50min); Náfpaktos (4 daily; 45min); Mýtikas (2 daily; 1hr 15min); Pátra (8 daily; 1hr).
Préveza to: Glykí (1 daily; 1hr); Lefkádha (5 daily; 25min); Párga (4–5 daily Mon–Fri, 3 Sat & Sun; 1hr 30min).
Vónitsa to: Lefkádha (6 daily, last at 5.15pm; 20min); Páleros (3 daily Mon–Fri; 20min); Préveza (3 daily Mon–Fri, 2 Sat & Sun; 25min).

Ferries

Astakós to: Kefaloniá (Sámi; 1 daily around noon, early May to mid-Sept only; Sun also to Itháki; 3hr 30min for full journey).
Igoumenítsa to: Corfu Town (almost hourly in season, 4am–10pm; 1hr "fast" ferry, 1hr 30min "slow"); Lefkími in southern Corfu (6 daily in summer, 7.30am–9pm, 4 daily in winter, 8.45am–6.30pm; 1hr); current info on ⓣ26650 26796; Paxí (Gáïos; 5 weekly, only late May–early Sept; 1hr 40min).

Flights

All are on Olympic unless otherwise specified.
Ioánnina to: Athens (2 daily, plus 1 daily on Aegean; 1hr).
Préveza to: Athens (4–6 weekly; 55min); Corfu (3 weekly; 25min); Kefaloniá (3 weekly; 25min); Sitía, Crete (3 weekly; 1hr 40min); Thessaloníki (2 weekly via Corfu; 1hr 45min); Zákynthos (3 weekly; 1hr 10min).

5

Macedonia and Thrace

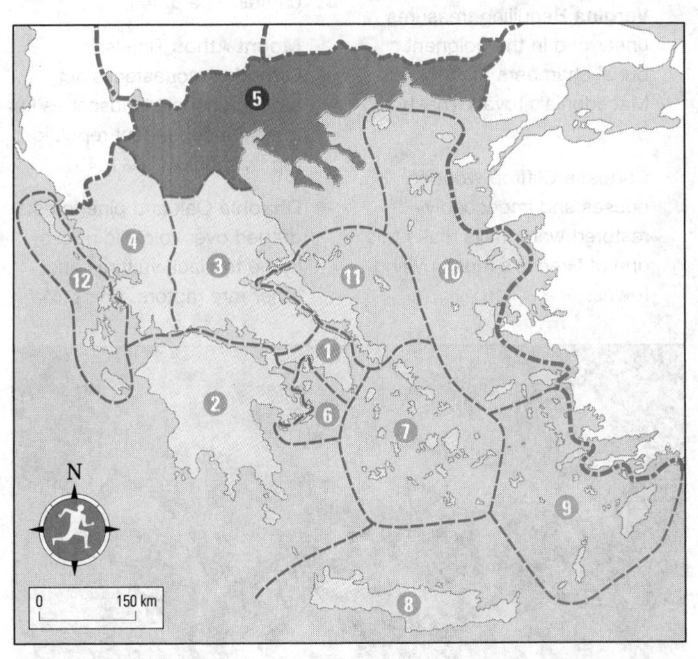

CHAPTER 5 Highlights

* **Thessaloníki** Balkan in atmosphere, Greece's second city offers historic monuments and a vibrant nightlife. See p.411

* **Mount Olympus** The mythical home of the gods; a three-day hike to the summit offers pristine scenery and riots of wild flowers. See p.429

* **Vergina** Beguiling treasures unearthed in the poignant burial chambers of Macedonia's royal dynasty. See p.437

* **Édhessa** Clifftop wooden houses and impeccably restored water mills make this one of Greece's most inviting towns. See p.440

* **The Préspa lakes** Forming the leading ornithological reserve in the region, the reed-fringed shores are a haven for nature lovers. See p.442

* **Kastoriá** Situated on a wooded headland jutting into the pewter-coloured Lake Orestiádha, this unusual resort is the country's fur capital. See p.445

* **Mount Athos** Timeless Orthodox monasteries set among unspoilt landscapes in a semi-independent republic run by monks. See p.457

* **Dhadhiá** Oak and pine forests draped over volcanic ridges, home to black vultures and other rare raptors. See p.477

▲ Mount Olympus

Macedonia and Thrace

The two northern regions of **Macedonia** and **Thrace** have been part of the Greek state for less than a century. Macedonia (Makedhonía) was surrendered by the Turks after the Balkan wars in 1913; Greek sovereignty over western Thrace (Thráki) was not confirmed until 1923 and there is still a sizeable ethnic minority population (see box, p.471). Consequently, they stand slightly apart from the rest of Greece, an impression reinforced for visitors by architecture and scenery, customs and climate that seem more Balkan than typically Mediterranean. The two regions even have their own government ministry, in recognition of their specific nature and needs. In physical terms, they are characterized by densely forested mountains and a clutch of picturesque lakes to the west, and in the east by heavily cultivated flood plains and bird-rich river deltas. Essentially continental in nature, the climate is harsher than in the rest of the country, with steamy summers and bitterly cold winters, especially up in the Rodhópi mountain range that forms the border with Bulgaria. These factors, along with a dearth of good beaches and fewer direct charter flights from abroad, may explain why northern Greece is relatively little known to outsiders.

Only Halkidhikí, a beach-fringed sub-region trailing to the southeast of Thessaloníki, and lofty Mount Olympus, to the southwest, draw large numbers of visitors. While two of **Halkidhikí**'s three mountainous peninsulas serve as a playground for the inhabitants of Greece's second city, more hard-won pleasures – including stunning views – are available on the slopes of **Mount Olympus**, the mythical abode of the gods. If you are male, over 18 and interested enough in monasticism – or Byzantine art, music and architecture – to obtain a pilgrimage permit, **Mount Athos** may prove to be a highlight of a visit to Greece, although women remain firmly barred.

A complete contrast to the serene Mount Athos, the sybaritic capital of Macedonia, **Thessaloníki** (Salonica), and the region's other main city, **Kavála**, just seem to get on with their vigorous day-to-day lives but are, maybe just because of that, interesting places to visit. The region also has some outstandingly beautiful spots, especially the **Préspa National Park** in rugged western Macedonia and the bird-watchers' heaven of the **Kerkíni wetlands** to the east. The lakeside city of **Kastoriá** and the clifftop town of **Édhessa** are among Greece's most beguiling urban centres, thanks to a belated but determined

5 MACEDONIA AND THRACE

attempt to restore some fine old buildings. Admittedly, the region's ancient sites are relatively modest, though there is one notable exception: the awe-inspiring Macedonian tombs discovered at **Vergina** in the 1970s, near the pleasant city of Véria. Not so well known are the Macedonian and Roman sites at **Pella**, with its fabulous mosaics, and at **Philippi**, St Paul's first stop in Greece. Few travellers on their way to Bulgaria or Turkey stray from the dull trunk road through eastern Thrace, but the well-preserved town of **Xánthi**, a trio of minor archeological sites, the waterfowl reserves of the **Évros Delta** and the **Dhadhiá Forest**, with its black vultures, deserve more than just a meal stop. **Alexandhroúpoli** rewards the curious with one of the best ethnological museums in the whole of Greece. Other attractions are two islands just off the coast – popular **Thássos** and alternative, hippyish **Samothráki**, covered in Chapter Ten.

Public **transport** in the north is somewhat limited. A few trains link some of the urban centres, but the railway line east from Thessaloníki curls unhelpfully inland, bypassing Kavála altogether and leaving buses or your own transport as the only alternatives for travelling along the coast. The road system has improved beyond recognition in recent years, however, and the "Via Egnatia" highway – large sections of which are already operational – will by 2010 provide an uninterrupted link between the west coast and the Bulgarian and Turkish borders. The Athens–Thessaloníki motorway should also be finally completed by around the same date.

Thessaloníki (Salonica)

The administrative capital of Macedonia and Thrace, **THESSALONÍKI** – or Salonica, as it is sometimes known to English-speakers – has a distinctly Balkan feel that sets it apart from other Greek cities. Situated at the head of the Gulf of Thessaloníki, a horseshoe-shaped inner recess of the Thermaic Bight, it seems open to the rest of the world, with a wide ethnic mix and an air of general prosperity, stimulated by a major university, an international trade fair and a famously avant-garde live music and entertainment scene. The food is generally better than in the rest of the country, too: there are some very sophisticated restaurants, but also flavoursome traditional fare on offer in a great number of old-fashioned ouzerís and undeniably Turkish-influenced tavernas, not surprising when you consider that Thessaloníki was the main metropolis for the Asia Minor refugees of 1923.

A commercial and industrial centre, rather than a tourist resort, the city has enough to offer the visitor for two or three days, at least. Its many **churches** (see box, p.421) constitute a showcase of Orthodox architecture through the ages, while you can catch glimpses of the Turkish city both in the walled Upper City and in the modern grid of streets on the flatlands below: isolated pockets of **Ottoman buildings**, many of them Islamic monuments, which miraculously survived the 1917 fire (see p.419). Modern Greek architecture is exemplified by Art Deco piles dating from the city's twentieth-century heyday, put up in time for the first International Trade Fair in 1926. Much of the city was restored when it was European Capital of Culture in 1997, while the Byzantine and other buildings that suffered damage in the severe 1978 earthquake are still undergoing painstaking repairs. Thessaloníki's many and often excellent **museums** cover subjects as varied as Byzantine culture, the city's Jewish heritage, folklife, musical instruments, Atatürk (who was born here) and, more recently, modern art and photography. For most visitors, however, the one that stands out is the **Archeological Museum**, albeit depleted since the transfer of most Philip II-related exhibits back to the burial sites at Vergina.

Some history

When King Cassander of Macedonia founded the city in 315 BC, on the site of the ancient Greek settlement of Thermae, he named it after his wife, half-sister of **Alexander the Great**: in turn she had received her name, Thessalonike, after the Macedons' decisive victory (*nike*) over the Thessalians under her father, Philip II. It soon became the region's cultural and trading centre, issuing its own coins.

Macedonia became a **Roman province** in 146 BC, and **Salonica**, with its strategic position allowing both land and sea access, was the natural and immediate choice of capital. Its fortunes and significance were boosted by the building of the Via Egnatia, the great road linking Rome (via Brindisi) with Byzantium and the East, along whose course Amphipolis, Philippi and Neapolis (now Kavála) were also to develop.

Christianity had slow beginnings in the city. St Paul visited twice, being driven out on the first occasion after provoking the local Jewish community. On the second, in the year 56 AD, he stayed long enough to found a church, later writing the two Epistles to the Thessalonians, his congregation there. It was another three centuries, however, before the new religion took full root. **Galerius**, who acceded as eastern emperor upon Byzantium's break with Rome, provided the city with virtually all its surviving late Roman monuments, including the **Rotónda** and the **Arch** named after him – and its patron saint, Demetrius (Dhimítrios), whom he martyred. The first resident Christian emperor was **Theodosius** (reigned 379–95), who after his conversion issued the Edict of Salonica, officially ending paganism.

Under Justinian's rule (527–65) Salonica became the second city of **Byzantium** after Constantinople, which it remained – under constant pressure from Goths and Slavs – until its sacking by Saracens in 904; today the city's Byzantine monuments undoubtedly surpass the Roman ones. The storming and sacking continued under the Normans of Sicily (1185) and with the Fourth Crusade (1204), when the city became for a time capital of the Latin Kingdom of Salonica. It was, however, restored to the Byzantine Empire of Nicea in 1246, reaching a cultural "**golden age**" amidst the theological conflict and political rebellion of the next two centuries, until Turkish conquest and occupation in 1430.

Thessaloníki was the premier **Ottoman Balkan city** when Athens was still a backwater. Its population was as varied as any in the region, with Greek Orthodox Christians in a distinct minority. Besides Ottoman Muslims, who had called the city "Selanik" since their arrival in 1430, a generation before the conquest of Constantinople, there were Slavs (who still know it as "Solun"), Albanians, Armenians and, following the Iberian expulsions after 1492, the largest European **Jewish community** of the age (see box, p.423).

The modern quality of Thessaloníki is due largely to a disastrous **fire** in 1917 which levelled most of the old plaster houses along a labyrinth of Ottoman lanes, including the entire Jewish quarter with its 32 synagogues, rendering 70,000 – nearly half the city's population – homeless. The city was rebuilt, often in a special form of Art Deco style, over the following eight years on a grid plan prepared under the supervision of French architect and archeologist Ernest Hébrard, with long central avenues running parallel to the seafront, and cross-streets densely planted with shade trees. Hébrard's prohibition of high-rises was blithely disregarded, however, within two decades.

The city's opulence has traditionally been epitomized by the locals' sartorial elegance, but since the 1990s an upsurge in **prosperity**, owing to a stable economy and, undoubtedly in part, EU subsidies, has resulted in an upwardly mobile class, whose lifestyles offer a sharp contrast with those of a permanent floating underclass living in shantytowns near the port. There, Pontic or Black Sea Greeks flog substandard goods at the street markets, while unemployed Albanians and eastern European refugees eke out a meagre living by selling contraband cigarettes or cleaning car windscreens. Since around 2000, they have been joined by Africans peddling bootleg CDs.

Arrival, information and city transport

Arriving in Thessaloníki is fairly straightforward. The **train station** on the west side of town, with convenient bus links and a reliable taxi rank, is just a short walk from both the central grid of streets and the harbour. Most **KTEL buses** arrive at the main terminal (predictably called "Makedonia"), located some way to the west of the city centre at Yiannitsón 194 (☎2310 500 111), from where local buses #1 and #78 take you to the train station, while #31 heads along Egnatía. However, all Halkidikí buses leave from the dedicated **KTEL Halkidikís**, well east of the city, just off the Nea Moudhaniá highway. This can be reached on #36 from the Voulgári terminal at the eastern end of the #31 route or from IKEA, the terminal for a number of routes.

"Makedonia" **airport** is located 15km south of the city centre. Facilities include a tourist booth of sorts, operating restricted hours, and ATMs, located near the first-floor café, on departures level. City bus #78 shuttles back and forth from the airport to the KTEL bus terminal once or twice hourly all day and #78N goes once an hour through the night; it makes several central stops, plying Tsimiskí on the way from the airport and Mitropóleos on the way back. A **taxi** ride into town comes to €12, plus extras.

All **ferries** call at the passenger port, within walking distance of the train station, at the western end of the seafront. For all ferry agencies, see "Listings" on p.428; Aegean routes and frequencies are given in the "Travel details" at the end of the chapter.

Information

The city finally has a proper **EOT** office at Tsimiskí 136 (summer daily 9am–9pm, winter Mon–Fri 8am–3pm, Sat 8am–2pm; ☎2310 221 100), which gives away an adequate map of the centre and other brochures. A fairly useful but not always up-to-date **website** is ⓦwww.saloniki.org. If you have any problems, the **tourist police** post (daily 8am–2pm; plus Tues, Thurs & Fri 5–9pm; ☎2310 554 871) is at Dhodhekanissou 4, off Platía Dhimokratías.

For more detailed city **maps**, the one published by Emvelia, which also includes Halkidhikí and the immediate surroundings of the city, is best; they also do a folding map of Thessaloníki if you don't want the indexed atlas.

ACCOMMODATION

- Atlantis — I
- Atlas — J
- Bill — E
- Capsis Bristol — N
- Egnatia Palace — G
- Electra Palace — M
- Kinissi Palace — H
- Le Palace — K
- Les Lazaristes (Domotel) — A
- Macedonia Palace — O
- Nea Mitropolis — F
- Orestias Kastorias — C
- Pella — D
- The Tobacco Hotel (Davitel) — B
- Tourist — L

RESTAURANTS

- Ta Adhelfia tis Pixarias — 23
- Aristotelous — 21
- Ta Bakaliarakia tou Aristou — 28
- Iy Gonia tou Merakli — 12

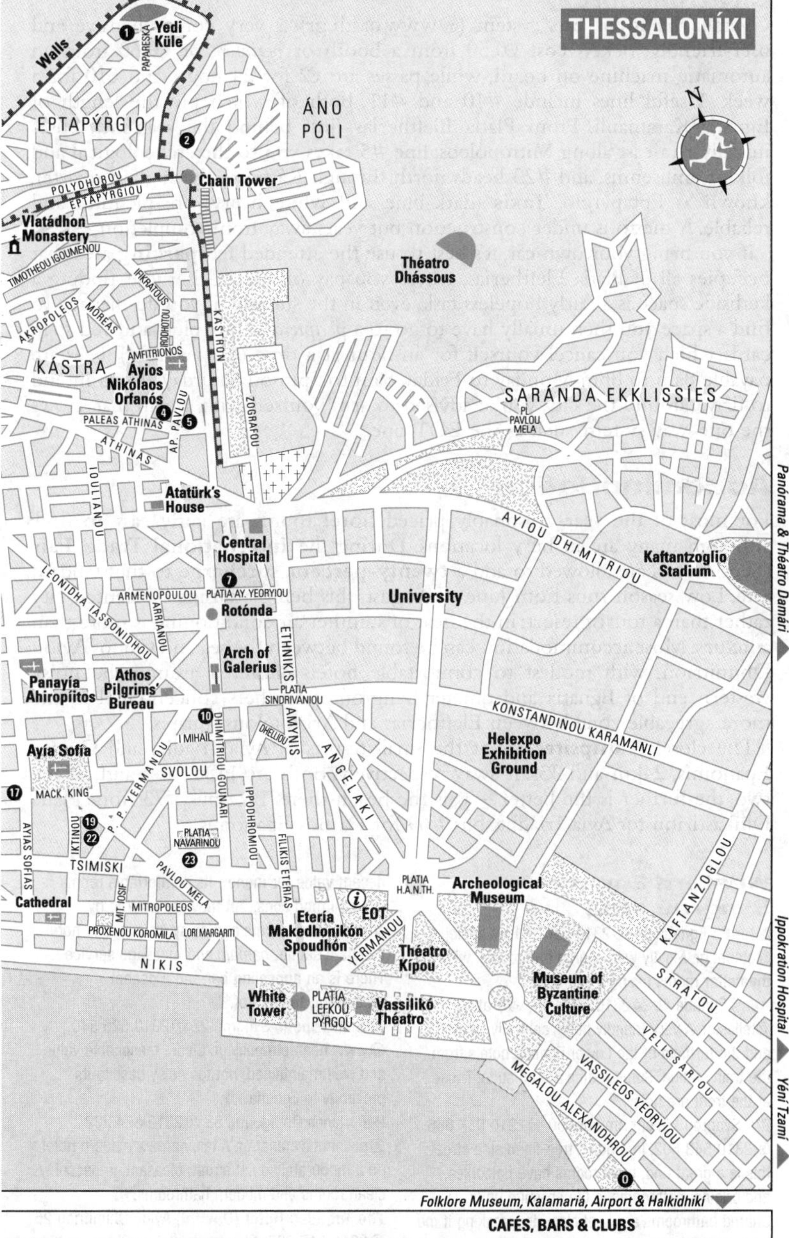

						CAFÉS, BARS & CLUBS			
Hiotis	2	To Makedhoniko	3	Tre Marie	22	Aigli	6	Kourdhisto Gourouni	17
Kamares	7	Molyvos	15	Tsarouhas	8	Cafe Amareion	5	Pasta Flora Darling	19
Koumbarakia	10	Myrovolos Smyrni	18	Vrotos	11	Decadence	29	Santé	14
Krasodhikio	9	Nea Ilyssia	16	To Yendi	1	Dizzy	25		
Louloudhadhika	20	Negroponte	24	Zythos	26	Kissfish	27		
Loutros	13	To Spiti tou Pasa	4			Kitchen Bar	30		

City transport

Overall, the **local bus** system (Ⓦwww.oasth.gr) is very comprehensive and user-friendly; tickets cost €0.50 from a booth or *períptero* or €0.60 from an automatic machine on board, while passes are €2 for 24 hours and €10 for a week. Useful lines include #10 and #11, both of which ply the length of Egnatía/Karamanlí. From Platía Eleftherías (just behind the seafront), buses initially run east along Mitropóleos; line #5 takes you to the archeological and folklore museums, and #23 heads north through Kástra to the highest quarter, known as Eptapýrgio. **Taxis** (dark-blue and white livery) are plentiful and reliable. A metro is under construction but years away from completion.

If you bring your own car, it's best to use the attended fee-**parking** area that occupies all of Platía Eleftherías, where you pay on exit. Otherwise, finding a kerbside space is a fairly hopeless task, even in the suburbs; if you do manage to find a space you then usually have to go to a *períptero* to buy blue-and-red strip cards which you cancel yourself for an hour at a time (€1 per hour). Fees are payable 8am to 8pm Monday to Friday, 8am to 3pm on Saturday. If you intend to drive around the city, you're advised to arm yourself with a map that shows the one-way system, such as the EOT one.

Accommodation

For most of the year, reasonably priced **hotel** rooms are fairly easy to find, although many are in busy locations. During the **International Trade Fair** (Sept) hotels are allowed to add a **twenty-percent surcharge** to the standard rate. Low season runs from June to August, this being a business-oriented city rather than a tourist resort; in the heat of summer air conditioning is more than a luxury. Most accommodation can be found between the sea and Odhós Ayíou Dhimitríou, with modest to comfortable hotels clustered around the noisy western end of Egnatía and quieter Syngroú and others concentrated in the more agreeable zone between Eleftherías and Aristotélous squares.

The closest **campsites** are at the small resorts of Ayía Triádha and Órmos Epanomís, 24km and 33km away respectively. Both are EOT sites and, of the two, the further is the better – as is the beach there. Take bus #73 from Platía Dhikastiríon for Ayía Triádha, bus #69 for Órmos Epanomís.

Western Egnatía & Syngroú area

Atlantis Egnatía 14 Ⓣ2310 540 131, Ⓔatlalej@otenet.gr. Mostly with shared bathrooms, with the better rooms facing a side street. ❶

Atlas Egnatía 40 Ⓣ2310 537 046, Ⓔh-atlas@tellas.gr. A very friendly hotel, centrally located and the furthest of the Lower Egnatía hotels from the train station. Some rooms are en suite. Those at the front are noisy. ❷

Bill Syngroú 29, cnr Amvrossíou Ⓣ2310 537 666, Ⓕ2310 543 602. In a quiet, tree-lined side street, this is a great find; most rooms have balconies, and original bathrooms in the en-suite units. Shared bathrooms are kept clean too, making it the best of the cheapies. ❶

Kinissi Palace Egnatía 41 and Syngroú Ⓣ2310 508 081, Ⓦwww.kinissipalace.gr. By far the smartest in the area, this hotel is decent value for money. Its comfortable rooms have all mod cons, but they are marred by cramped bathrooms and noisy air con. The hotel boasts a sauna, *hamam* and massage service. There is an appealing bar and a decent restaurant, the Averof. ❺

Nea Mitropolis Syngroú 22 Ⓣ2310 525 540, Ⓦwww.neametropolis.gr. Clean, reasonable value and well maintained; not too noisy despite its proximity to Egnatía. ❸

Pella Íonos Dhragoúmi 63 Ⓣ2310 524 222, Ⓔpellahot@otenet.gr. A tall, narrow, modern hotel on a moderately quiet street; pleasant, impeccably clean rooms and modern bathrooms. ❹

The Tobacco Hotel (Davitel) Ayíou Dhimitríou 25 Ⓣ2310 515 002, Ⓦwww.davitel.gr. Sleek double-glazed rooms with contemporary decor verging on the spartan but comfortable; efficient air con, polite staff and healthy breakfasts served in a designer-rustic mezzanine salon. Its origins as a tobacco warehouse explain the name. ⑤

Rest of the city

Capsis Bristol Oplopíou 2 and Katoúni ⓣ2310 506 500, ⓦwww.capsisbristol.gr. Thessaloníki's only boutique hotel to date, with twenty period-furnished rooms in an impeccably restored 1870 building; the Dhipnosofistis restaurant and Medusa bistro are further attractions. Lavish buffet breakfast. ⑧

Egnatia Palace Egnatía 61 ⓣ2310 222 900, ⓦwww.egnatiapalace.gr. A smart hotel in a modern building with some Art Deco flourishes, it has spacious rooms whose modish decor ranges from kitsch to stylish; includes a spa. ⑤

Electra Palace Platía Aristotélous 9 ⓣ2310 294 000, ⓦwww.electrahotels.gr. In one of the town's most prestigious positions – but it can get noisy when there are events in the square. That said, it is as palatial inside as out, with large rooms and a good dining room, albeit with a slightly dated air. ⑦

Les Lazaristes (Domotel) Kolokotróni 16, Stavroúpoli ⓣ2310 647 400, ⓦwww.domotel.gr. Opposite the Moní Lazaristón arts complex (see p.427), this handsome new hotel, in a converted tobacco factory, is a long way from the centre but has free parking for people with a car. Beautiful magazine interiors, with a lot of attention to detail, and a gorgeous pool; the *Fred and Ginger* restaurant draws locals with its gourmet cuisine. ⑧

Macedonia Palace Megálou Aléxandhrou 2 ⓣ2310 897 197, ⓦwww.ellada.net/mac-pal. The smart, elegant and spacious rooms and suites in this city establishment hotel come with the best seafront views and an excellent restaurant, the *Porphyra*, famous for its Sun brunch. ⑦

Orestias Kastorias Agnóstou Stratiótou 14, cnr Olymbou ⓣ2310 276 517, ⓦwww.okhotel.gr. With most rooms in this 1920s building recently converted to en suite, this is a prime, friendly choice and one of the quieter hotels in the city; reservations advised. ③

Le Palace Tsimiskí 12 ⓣ2310 257 400, ⓦwww.lepalace.gr. This Art Deco hotel offers good discounts if booked online: spacious rooms with modern baths and double glazing (still best to ask for a room away from the street). Characterful common areas comprise a mezzanine lounge, a ground-floor café and a restaurant. An outstanding buffet breakfast is included. B&B ⑦

Tourist Mitropóleos 21 ⓣ2310 270 501, ⓦwww.touristhotel.gr. A friendly, rambling *belle époque* palace with parquet-floored lounges, complimentary breakfast salon and a 1920s Swiss lift; 1990s-refurbished rooms all en suite; just two singles. You'll need to book in advance. ④

The City

Once you're within the central grid of streets, **orientation** is made relatively straightforward by frequent sightings of the bay and a series of main commercial avenues: Ayíou Dhimitríou, **Egnatía** (the city's busiest main street), Tsimiskí and Mitropóleos. All run parallel to the quay, but confusingly change their names repeatedly as they head east into the city's post-medieval annexe. Most of central Thessaloníki's principal sights are within easy walking distance of each other, many located on either side of Egnatía. Perpendicular to the avenues, **Aristotélous** is a partly pedestrianized street with Italianate porticos on either side and lined with freshly painted, pale ochre buildings, housing offices, shops and facilities such as the post office and the national railways bureau. It slopes down from Egnatía and opens out at the seaside end into completely pedestrianized **Platía Aristotélous**, where you can enjoy views across to Mount Olympus on clear days. The divide between the older and newer parts of town is marked by the exhibition grounds and the start of the seaside park strip, known locally as Zoo Park and dominated by the **White Tower** (Lefkós Pýrgos).

In the city's best museum, the remarkable **Archeological Museum**, you can admire some of the splendid Vergina treasures, the pride of Macedonia, while minor museums dotted around the centre deal with Byzantine culture, musical instruments, modern art and photography. **Ayía Sofía**, one of the city's most outstanding churches, houses some superb mosaics, as does the converted Roman mausoleum still known by its Latin name, the **Rotónda**. Further highlights include the Turkish **bazaars**, along with other Ottoman monuments – and what remains of the **Jewish city**, now also represented by an interesting museum. Venture into the city's eastern districts and you'll find some fine early-twentieth-century mansions, one of which houses the interesting **Folk & Ethnological Museum**, together with the **Yéni Tzamí**, a beautiful Art Nouveau mosque, now an art gallery.

The Archeological Museum

Although some of its star exhibits have been returned to the original site at Vergina (see p.437), the refurbished **Archeological Museum** at Platía H.A.N.TH. (April–Oct Mon 1–7.30pm, Tues–Sun 8am–7.30pm; Nov–March Mon 10.30am–5pm, Tues–Sun 8am–3pm; €6) is undoubtedly the city's leading museum. The central gallery, opposite as you enter, is devoted to rich grave finds from ancient Sindos, a few kilometres north of the modern city, while the left-hand wing is taken up by Hellenistic and Roman art, in particular some exquisite blown-glass birds, found in the tumuli or *toúmbes* which stud the plain around Thessaloníki. Downstairs is an exhibition of prehistoric finds from the city and region, of limited interest.

But these are all just appetizers for – or anticlimaxes after – the marvellous **Gold of Macedon exhibition** in the south hall, which still displays – and clearly labels in both English and Greek – many of the finds from the royal tombs of Philip II of Macedon (father of Alexander the Great) and others at the ancient Macedonian capital of Aegae, in modern Veryína. They include startling amounts of gold and silver – masks, crowns, necklaces, earrings and bracelets – all of extraordinarily imaginative craftsmanship, both beautiful and practical, as well as pieces in ivory and bronze.

The Museum of Byzantine Culture

The prize-winning **Museum of Byzantine Culture**, in a handsome brick structure at Stratoú 2, just east of the Archeological Museum (and with the same hours; €4), does a fine job of displaying the early Christian tombs and graves excavated in the city, featuring rescued wall paintings depicting, among others, *Susannah and the Elders*, and a naked rower surrounded by sea creatures. Despite this and the faultless lighting and display techniques, most of the displays will appeal more to specialists than to lay visitors.

The White Tower

Close by, at the eastern end of the seafront promenade, Leofóros Níkis, the **White Tower (Lefkós Pýrgos)** is the city's graceful symbol. Originally known as the Lions' Tower and the Fortress of Kalamariá, it formed a corner of the city's Byzantine and Ottoman defences before most of the walls were demolished, late in the nineteenth century. Prior to this, it was the Bloody Tower, a place of imprisonment and, in 1826, execution of the janissaries. In 1890 a Jewish prisoner was given the task of whitewashing the tower, in exchange for his freedom, hence the new name, which stuck, even though it has since been stripped of the white pigment. It was restored in 1985 for the city's 2300th birthday celebrations, and is currently closed for further refurbishment.

Roman remains

The city contains several imposing remains from the Roman era, on or around Egnatía. The **Arch of Galerius** dominates a pedestrianized square just off the eastern end of Egnatía. Along with the nearby Rotónda (see opposite), it originally formed part of a larger Roman complex which included palaces and a hippodrome. The mighty arch is the surviving span of a dome-surmounted arcade that once led towards the palaces. Built to commemorate the emperor's victories over the Persians in 297 AD, its piers contain rather weathered reliefs of the battle scenes interspersed with glorified poses of Galerius himself. The well-displayed remains of **Galerius's palace** can be viewed, below the modern street level, along pedestrianized Dhimitríou Goúnari and into its extension, Platía Navarínou.

A short way up in the opposite direction, across the pedestrianized square dominated by the arch, the **Rotónda**, later converted into the church of **Áyios Yeóryios**, is the most striking single Roman monument in the city. It was designed, but never used, as an imperial mausoleum, possibly for Galerius himself. Consecrated for Christian use in the late fourth century, by the addition of a sanctuary, an apse, a narthex and rich mosaics, it later became one of the city's major mosques, from which period the minaret remains. Áyios Yeóryios is currently still closed for restoration, which is a shame as it contains superb mosaics of various birds and saints, the finest of their era outside Constantinople or Ravenna; check if it has re-opened.

Further west, above leafy Platía Dhikastiríon, the **Roman Forum** (daily summer 8am–7.30pm, winter 8am–3pm; free) has been undergoing gradual excavation for over a decade so access is limited. In many ways, its layout is best observed from the road behind, where the shape of the *stoa*, with several remaining columns, is clear. The restored amphitheatre is used for occasional summer performances.

Atatürk's house

As you head up towards the **Kástra**, as the lower fringes of the Upper Town are known, you will pass the **Turkish consulate** at the corner of Ayíou Dhimitríou and Apostólou Pávlou. In the pink nineteenth-century building immediately behind it, at Apostólou Pávlou 17, **Kemal Atatürk**, creator and first president of the modern secular state of Turkey, was born in 1881. The consulate maintains the house as a small **museum** (daily 10am–5pm; free), with its

Ottoman Thessaloníki

Despite years of neglect, the 1917 fire and the 1978 quake, Thessaloníki has quite a number of vestiges of Ottoman architecture to show, mostly within walking distance of Platía Dhikastiríon. At the eastern corner of the square itself stands the disused but well-preserved Bey Hamam or Parádhisos Baths (Mon–Fri 9am–9pm, Sat & Sun 8.30am–3pm; free), the oldest Turkish bathhouse in the city (1444) and in use until 1968. The doorway is surmounted by elaborate ornamentation, while inside art exhibitions – often paradoxically with Byzantine themes – are held from time to time.

To the south of Platía Dhikastiríon lies the main Turkish bazaar area, bounded roughly by Egnatía, Dhragoúmi, Ayías Sofías and Tsimiskí. Much the most interesting bit, and a quiet midtown oasis, is a grid of lanes between Ayías Sofías and Aristotélous, devoted to selling animals, crafts and cane furniture. Nearby Ottoman monuments include the six-domed Bezesténi or covered valuables market at the corner of Venizélou and Egnatía, now housing jewellery and other shops. Directly opposite, on the north side of Egnatía, rather more modest stores occupy a prominent mosque, the fifteenth-century purpose-built Hamza Bey Tzamí (most mosques in Ottoman Thessaloníki were converted churches), now looking decidedly ramshackle.

Well to the north of Platía Dhikastiríon, beyond Áyios Dhimítrios basilica, is the seventeenth-century Yeni Hamam, now a summer cinema and music venue serving basic food, and better known as the Aigli (see p.426); the fifteenth-century Altaza Imaret, tucked away in a quiet square diagonally opposite, sports a handsome portico and multiple domes.

original fixtures and some Atatürk memorabilia. Security is tight, so to visit you must apply for admission at the consulate itself, with your passport (☎2310 248 452; Mon–Fri 9.30am–12.30pm; ring the bell).

Ayía Sofía

Located between Egnatía and Platía Navarínou, in the lower city, to the west of the Arch of Galerius, the heavily restored eighth-century church of **Ayía Sofía** (daily 7am–1pm & 5–8.30pm; free) is the finest of its kind in the city. Modelled on its more illustrious namesake in Constantinople, it replaced an older basilica, the only trace of which remains a few paces south: the below-street-level holy well of John the Baptist, originally a Roman *nymphaeum* (sacred fountain). Ayía Sofía's dome, 10m in diameter, bears a splendid **mosaic** of the *Ascension*, for which you'll need binoculars. Christ, borne up to the heavens by two angels, sits resplendent on a rainbow throne, right hand extended in blessing; below, a wry inscription quotes Acts 1:11: "Ye men of galilee, why stand ye gazing up into heaven?" The whole is ringed by fifteen figures: the Virgin attended by two angels, and the twelve Apostles reacting to the miracle. The dome was restored late in the 1980s; the rest of the interior decoration was plastered over after the 1917 fire. Another fine mosaic of the *Virgin Enthroned* in the apse apparently replaced a cross, of which traces are visible, dating from the Iconoclast period.

Áyios Dhimítrios

Up at Ayíou Dhimitríou is the massive yet simple church that gives the street its name, **Áyios Dhimítrios** (Mon 12.30–7pm, Tues–Sat 8am–8pm, Sun 10.30am–8pm; free), conceived in the fifth century but heavily restored since.

▲ Áyios Dhimítrios church

Thessaloníki's Byzantine churches

Almost all the Byzantine churches in Thessaloníki are located in the central districts or on the slopes heading up towards the Upper Town. Under the Turks most of the buildings were converted for use as mosques, a process that obscured many of their original features and destroyed (by whitewashing) the majority of their frescoes and mosaics. Further damage came with the 1917 fire and, more recently, with the 1978 earthquake. Restoration seems a glacially slow process, guaranteeing that many of the sanctuaries are locked, or shrouded in scaffolding. Nevertheless, the churches of Thessaloníki remain an impressive group. The main ones are described below, apart from the two most important churches, Ayía Sofía and Áyios Dhimítrios, given their place in the main city account. All are free to enter.

One of the most central is the eleventh-century Panayía Halkéon church (daily 7.30am–noon), a classic though rather unimaginative example of the "cross-in-square" form, nestling on Egnatía at the southwestern corner of Platía Dhikastiríon, amid luxuriant palms, cypress and pines. It is worth popping inside to see the fragmentary frescoes in the cupola and some fine icons. As the Greek name indicates, it served during the Ottoman occupation as the copperworkers' guild mosque; the only remnant of this tradition is the handful of kitsch-copper souvenir shops just across the street.

Several blocks east, and tucked away just out of sight north of the boulevard, the restored, fifth-century, three-aisled basilica of Panayía Ahiropíitos (daily 7am–noon & 4.30–6.30pm) is the oldest in the city, featuring arcades, monolithic columns and often highly elaborate capitals – a popular development begun under Theodosius. Only the mosaics inside the arches survive, depicting birds, fruits and vegetation in a rich Alexandrian style.

Around Áyios Dhimítrios (see opposite) are several more churches, utterly different in feel. To the west along Ayíou Dhimitríou is the church of Dhódheka Apóstoli (daily 8.30am–noon & 5–7pm), built with seven more centuries of experience and the bold Renaissance influence of Mystra. Its five domes rise in perfect symmetry above walls of fine brickwork, while inside are glorious fourteenth-century mosaics, among the last executed in the Byzantine empire. High up in the arches to the south, west and north of the dome respectively are a *Nativity*, an *Entry into Jerusalem*, a *Resurrection* and a *Transfiguration*.

A short climb up Ayías Sofías is Ósios Dhavíd (Mon–Sat 9am–noon & 4–6pm), a tiny fifth-century church on Odhós Timothéou. It doesn't really fit into any architectural progression, since the Ottomans demolished much of the building when converting it to a mosque. However, it has arguably the finest mosaic in the city, depicting a clean-shaven Christ Emmanuel appearing in a vision, surrounded by the Tetramorphs or symbols of the four Gospels. The four Rivers of Paradise, replete with fish, flow from beneath Christ, lapping the feet of the prophets Ezekiel and Habakkuk, who respectively cringe in terror and ponder at the revelation. Ask the curator to switch on the floodlights for a better view; a small donation for a candle will be appreciated.

Farther east in Kástra, to the north of Atatürk's house, on Irodhótou, fourteenth-century Áyios Nikólaos Orfanós (Tues–Sun 8.30am–2.45pm) is a diminutive, much-altered basilica; the imaginative and well-preserved frescoes inside are the most accessible and expressive in the city. In the south aisle, Áyios Yerásimos of Jordan is seen with anthropomorphic lions, while Christ's miracles are set forth in a row above. The naos is devoted to episodes from the Passion, in particular the rarely depicted *Christ Mounting the Cross* and *Pilate Seated in Judgement* at a wooden desk. Above the Virgin Platytera in the apse conch looms the equally unusual *Áyion Mandílion*, an image of Christ's head superimposed on a legendary Turin-style veil sent to an ancient king of Anatolian Edessa. Around the apse is a wonderful *Niptir* (Christ Washing the Disciple's Feet), in which it is thought the painter inserted (in lieu of a signature) an image of himself at the top right above the conch, riding a horse and wearing a white turban.

Far more impressive than the official cathedral down at Mitropóleos, it is the de facto cathedral of the city, with pride of place in Thessalonian hearts, and was almost entirely rebuilt after the 1917 fire. The church is dedicated to the city's patron saint and stands on the site of his martyrdom, and even if you know beforehand that it is the largest basilica in Greece, its immense interior comes as a surprise.

Amid the multicoloured marble columns and vast extents of off-white plaster, six small surviving **mosaics**, mostly on the columns flanking the altar, make an easy focal point; of these, four date back to the church's second reconstruction after the fire of 620. The astonishing seventh-century mosaic of *Áyios Dhimítrios Flanked by the Church's Two Founders*, on the inside of the south (right-hand) pier beside the steps to the crypt, and the adjacent mosaics of *Áyios Sérgios* and *Áyios Dhimítrios with a Deacon*, contrast well with their contemporary on the north column, a warm and humane mosaic of the saint with two young children. The other two mosaics date back to the fifth century. The one on the north pier is a *Deisis* with the Virgin and Áyios Theódhoros, while the other, high on the west wall of the inner south aisle, depicts a child being presented or dedicated to the saint.

The **crypt** (same hours; free) contains the *martyrion* of the saint – probably an adaptation of the Roman baths in which he was imprisoned – and a whole exhibit of beautifully carved column-capitals, labelled in Greek only and arrayed around a seven-columned fountain and collecting basin.

Áno Póli (Upper Town)

Above Odhós Kassándhrou, the street parallel to Ayíou Dhimitríou, rises the Upper Town or **Áno Póli**, the main surviving quarter of Ottoman Thessaloníki. Although the streets here are gradually becoming swamped by new apartment buildings, they remain ramshackle and atmospheric, a labyrinth of timber-framed houses and winding steps. In the past few years the stigma of the district's "Turkishness" has been overcome as the older houses have been bought up and restored – indeed it has become one of its draws – and it is justifiably one of the city's favourite after-dark destinations. Sections of the fourteenth-century **Byzantine ramparts**, constructed with brick and rubble on top of old Roman foundations, crop up all around the northern part of town.

The best-preserved portion begins at a large circular keep, the Trigónion or **Chain Tower** (so called for its encircling ornamental moulding), in the northeast angle where the easterly city walls change direction. A much smaller circuit of walls rambles around the district of **Eptapýrgio** (Seven Towers), enclosing the old eponymous acropolis at the top end. For centuries it served as the city's **prison** until abandoned as too inhumane in 1989; it is described as a sort of Greek Devil's Island in a number of plaintive old songs entitled *Yedi Küle*, the Turkish name for Eptapýrgio. On its south side, the wall is followed by Odhós Eptapyrgíou and edged by a small strip of park – a good place to sit and scan Thessaloníki.

The Jewish Museum

Way down in the Bazaar quarter, an early-twentieth-century house, once belonging to a Jewish family, has been beautifully renovated to accommodate the impressive **Museum of Jewish Presence**, or Museo Djudio de Salonik to give it its Judeo-Spanish name (Tues, Fri & Sun 11am–2pm, Wed & Thurs 11am–2pm & 5–8pm; €3), at Ayíou Miná 13. On the ground floor are a few precious remains and some moving photographic documentation of the city's Jewish cemetery, which contained half a million graves until it was vandalized

Thessaloníki, a former Jewish metropolis

In the early sixteenth century, after virtually all the Jews were expelled from Spain and Portugal, nearly half of the inhabitants of Thessaloníki, over 80,000 people, were Jewish. For them "Salonik" or "Salonicco" ranked as a "Mother of Israel" and the community dominated the city's commercial, social and cultural life for some four hundred years, mostly tolerated by the Ottoman authorities but often resented by the Greeks. The first waves of Jewish emigration to Palestine, western Europe and the United States began after World War I. Numbers had dropped to fewer than 60,000 at the onset of World War II, when all but a tiny fraction were deported from Platía Eleftherías to the concentration camps and immediate gassing. The vast Jewish cemeteries east of the city centre, among the world's largest, were desecrated in 1944; to add insult to injury, the area was later covered over by the new university and expanded trade-fair grounds in 1948. At last, however, the role of the Jewish community in making the city what it is has received some recognition in the form of a new museum, inaugurated in 2001, and a memorial to the victims of the 1943 deportations. Thessaloníki's only surviving pre-Holocaust synagogue is the Monastiriótou at Syngroú 35, with an imposing, if austere, facade; it's usually open for Friday-evening and Saturday-morning worship. At the very heart of the former Jewish district (until 1942 Thessaloníki had no ghetto) sprawls the Modhiáno, the central meat, fish and produce market, named after the wealthy Jewish Modiano family which long owned it. The market has suffered steady decline, with many stalls vacant, but still makes an atmospheric and authentic destination for a meal.

by the Nazis. Outstanding is a marble Roman stele from the third century, recycled as a Jewish tombstone for a member of the post-1492 Sephardic community from Iberia. In the middle of the courtyard is a finely sculpted fountain that once stood in a city synagogue. Upstairs, a well-presented exhibition, clearly labelled in Greek and English, traces the history of the Jewish presence from around 140 BC to the present day, and displays some of the few religious and secular items that miraculously survived the 1917 fire and the Holocaust.

The portside museums

If you cross busy Koundouriótou, the harbour-end extension of Níkis, to the city's **port**, through Gate A you'll find a set of dockside warehouses that have been converted into the city's latest arts complex, complete with bars and, perhaps bizarrely, a kindergarten. Sharing the same warehouse as the hermetic Cinema Museum, only of interest to Greek film buffs, the outstanding **Museum of Photography** (Tues–Fri 11am–7pm, Sat & Sun 11am–9pm; free) stages exhibitions by Greek and international photographers. Across the road in an unprepossessing breeze-block bunker, the **State Museum of Contemporary Art** (daily 10am–2pm & 6–10pm; free) hosts exhibitions of paintings, often related to the city and its history.

The Yéni Tzamí and the Folk & Ethnological Museum of Macedonia

The most enduring civic contribution made to the city by the **Dönme** or **Ma'min,** an odd Islamic sect that followed certain Jewish practices and followed the seventeenth-century false Messiah Sabbatai Zvi, is the orientalized Art Nouveau **Yéni Tzamí** out to the south of the city, at Arheoloyikoú Mousíou 30; dating from 1904, it was the last mosque ever built in the city. Designed by an Italian architect, this engaging folly long served as Thessaloníki's archeological museum from 1923 until the new purpose-built building opened. The interior is nothing other than an Iberian synagogue in disguise, and its elegant decor is likely to overshadow the occasional art exhibitions it houses. It's easy to find, about 0.5km south of the Museum of Byzantine Culture, well signposted off Vasilíssis Ólgas, the southern extension of Vassiléos Yeoryíou.

Still farther out, the **Folk & Ethnological museum** (Fri–Tues 9am–3pm, Wed 10am–10pm; €2) is housed in the elegant early twentieth-century mansion of the **Modiano** family (they of the meat market) – one of several Jewish-built villas in the district – at Vasilíssis Ólgas 68. It is one of the best of its kind in Greece, with well-written commentaries (English and Greek) accompanying temporary exhibitions on housing, costumes, day-to-day work and crafts. The museum is just a half-hour walk (or short bus ride) from the White Tower; catch the #5 bus as it runs east along (Mitropóleos and) Meghálou Aléxandhrou.

Eating

There is a wealth of interesting **places to eat** in Thessaloníki, paralleling the increasing prosperity of the city. The downtown area listings are all within walking distance of Platía Aristotélous; for the others we've given the appropriate transport connections. Quite a few establishments close from mid-July to mid-August – the time when Thessalonians typically take their summer holidays, a bit earlier than the Athenians. Traditionally, the city's ouzerís will provide some sort of sweet on the house, often semolina *halvás* or watermelon. Dozens of prominent bakeries, *zaharoplastía* and *souvladtzídhika*, dotted all across town provide a range of snacks and breakfast possibilities.

Downtown: between the sea and Odhós Ayíou Dhimitríou

The city's central oblong is where you're most likely to be staying, so eating here will save you a taxi fare or a long detour. Mostly clustered in the bazaar area, plus the trendy Ladhádhika district (see p.426), the downtown eateries tend to be no-nonsense ouzerís with the odd taverna dotted here and there.

Ta Adhelfia tis Pixarias Platía Navarínou 7. The best of the good-value places on this archeological site/square, with delicacies such as *tzigerosarmás* (lamb's liver in cabbage) and *mýdhia saganáki* (mussels with cheese), plus real tablecloths – though the service tends to be haphazard and the portions are on the small side. It's often packed, so arrive early.

Aristotelous Aristotélous 8. Tucked discreetly into a courtyard off Odhós Aristotélous behind wrought-iron gates, this stylish, mid-range ouzerí with its fine, arcaded interior and courtyard gets crowded due to its standard but well-executed *mezédhes.* Excellent *tsípouro* is available. Closed mid-July to mid-Aug & Sun afternoon.

Ta Bakaliarakia tou Aristou Koundouriótou 6. Inexpensive heapings of cod and chips, served on greaseproof paper, make this joint in a pedestriani-zed portside alley quite memorable.

Iy Gonia tou Merakli Avyerinoú, alley off Platía Áthonos. Inexpensive seafood, better than average portions, a quality free dessert and highly palatable barrelled wine make this the best of several ouzerís in these atmospheric lanes between Platía Áthonos and Aristotélous.

Kamares Platía Ayíou Yeoryíou 11, by the Rotónda. Excellent, keenly priced seafood, salads and grilled meat at this year-round place, washed down by bulk wine from Límnos. Summer outdoor seating beside the park.

Koumbarakia Egnatía 140. Tucked behind the little Byzantine chapel of the Transfiguration, the outdoor tables of this durable, budget ouzerí groan with Macedonian-style grills, seafood and salads, including *túrsi* (pickled vegetables). Closed Sun and midsummer.

Krasodhikio Filíppou 18 & Venizélou. Another fine ouzerí, serving a range of ample meat and seafood meals and *mezédhes* on the pavement in summer or in the cozy interior when it's cold.

Louloudhadhika Komninón 20. An upmarket eatery, with yellow walls and smart tablecloths, serving extremely good food, especially the fresh fish, and the barrel retsina is wonderfully refreshing. Try and get an outside table in front of the old Jewish baths.

Loutros M. Koundoúra 5. Good fried seafood, simple *orektiká* and excellent retsina, at reasonable prices, next to the Bezesténi. Closed mid-July to mid-Aug.

Molyvos Kapodhistríou 1. Cretan rusks with cheese and salad are among the regional specialities served at this charmingly rustic, moderately priced taverna-ouzerí, with quiet street seating and an Aladdin's cave of a shop selling non-industrial ouzo and olive oils.

Myrovolos Smyrni In arcade in the Modhiáno off Komninón 32 ☎2310 274 170. Friendly, crowded ouzerí, also known as *Tou Thanassi* and reckoned the best of several clustered here. Typical fare includes cheese-stuffed squid, Smyrna-style meatballs, stuffed potatoes and grilled baby fish. Open all year, air conditioned in summer; despite ample seating, reservations are recommended.

Nea Ilyssia Sófou 17. Just below Egnatía, this popular travellers' restaurant maintains especially long hours (8.30am–2am) and serves highly regarded *mayireftá*.

Negroponte Just off Polytechníou, Ladhádhika. One of the few authentic tavernas in an otherwise gentrified zone – witness the strings of garlic, traditional seating and barrelled wine. Delicious taverna fare and low prices compared with most places in this district.

Tre Marie P.P. Yermanoú 13. If any restaurant epitomizes Thessalonian sybaritism then it is this expensive trattoria where the sophisticated menu includes delicacies such as zucchini blooms stuffed with cheese and spearmint in a truffle honey sauce. White-aproned waiters scurry efficiently through a sumptuous decor of marble and dark wood beneath stained-glass ceiling panels and sparkling chandeliers. Small summer terrace in the street.

Tsarouhas Olýmbou 78, near Platía Dhikastiríon. Reputedly the best, and certainly the most famous (and therefore slightly pricier), of the city's *patsatzídhika* – kitchens devoted to tripe-and-trotter soup. Lots of other tasty *mayireftá*, and Anatolian puddings such as *kazandibí* (baked pudding). Closed mid-July to mid-Aug; otherwise open all hours.

Vrotos Mitropolítou Yennadhíou 6, Platía Áthonos ☎2310 223 958. The most imaginative and currently one of the most popular (despite higher prices) of the half-dozen ouzerís in this area, with something for all tastes: elaborate vegetable dishes with or without cheese, meats and seafood recipes. Space is still limited, so it's wise to book ahead. Open daily for lunch and supper except perhaps late July.

Zythos Platía Katoúni 5 ☎2310 540 284. One of the best places in the Ladhádhika district. Very decent, moderately priced food is served at midday and in the evening, along with an excellent selection of wine and several brews of draught and bottled Greek and foreign beers. Reservations recommended at weekends.

Áno Póli (Kástra and Eptapýrgio)

The **Áno Póli** (Upper Town) is home to a variety of eateries, mostly reasonably priced and full of atmosphere; buses #23 or #28 from Platía Eleftherías spare you the climb. Incidentally, the garish, neon-lit joints on either side of the Chain Tower are perfectly fine for a terrace-with-a-view drink, but are not noted for their cuisine.

Hiotis Graviás 2. Just inside the second (eastern) castle gate, near the Chain Tower. Mussels, kebabs and *kokorétsi* served on the terrace under the ramparts, weather permitting. Dinner only in summer, lunch and dinner rest of the year.

To Makedhoniko Sykiés district. To get here, from the main Portára gate, head west, keeping to the walls as much as practicable, passing a second gate, until you reach the west end of the walls, near a third minor gate. You can also get a bus: #28 goes right through this gateway. A limited menu of *tís óras*, dips, salad and retsina is on offer, but it's cheap and popular with the trendy set as well as locals.

To Spiti tou Pasa Apostólou Pávlou 35. As the name (The Pasha's house) suggests, this elegant, two-storey house, stylishly but discreetly decorated, lays emphasis on creature comforts – they include tip-top Límnos wine from the barrel and fresh grilled fish and meats, plus impeccable service, but prices only a little above average. Closed Sun.

To Yendi Paparéska 13, at the very top of Kástra, opposite the Yedi Küle citadel. An ouzerí-type menu that changes daily, dished up in largish portions, and accompanied by *tsípouro*, ouzo or house wine. Ample indoor or terrace seating under trees opposite the gate of Yedi Küle, but service can get overstretched owing to popularity. Evenings only.

Drinking, nightlife and entertainment

It's easy to get the impression that the majority of young people in Thessaloníki spend most of their time lounging in cafés and bars, showing off their designer gear, sipping coffee or beer and chain-smoking. Downtown, the most fashionable nightlife is to be found in **Ladhádhika**, a still partly ramshackle district near the harbour. Another profitable hunting ground for drinking places is **Leofóros Níkis**, the seafront esplanade that is a perennial *vólta* (promenade) favourite owing to its endless row of bar terraces; similar bars can also be found around the more fashionable **Platía Aristotélous**, and along into **Proxénou Koromilá.** A couple of designer bars on the square opposite the **White Tower** are certainly worth checking out, while bustling **Platía Navarínou** and the nearby pedestrianized streets, **Iktínou** and **Zefxídhou**, are lined with some of the trendiest establishments in the city. During the warmer months, action mostly shifts to various glitzy, barn-like establishments lining the coast road out to **Kalamariá**, for which you'll need to take taxis.

Bars, cafés and clubs

Aigli Cnr Ayíou Nikoláou and Kassándhrou, behind Áyios Dhimítrios church. A classy bar-ouzerí, with Anatolian decor, occupies part of this dependency of the nearby Alatza Imaret. A small events hall takes up the double-domed main chamber of the baths, with bar seating outside in summer, when the garden becomes an outdoor cinema.

Cafe Amareion Apostólou Pávlou. This cosy ouzerí-cum-bar with excellent acoustics often puts on good music gigs at weekends.

Decadence A Yeoryíou 21. The most highly rated of the big clubs for cutting edge dance, techno and progressive house music. Near the Mylos centre (see opposite).

Dizzy Eyíptou 5. Full-on rock/goth sounds abound in this lively Ladhádhika bar with motorbikes hanging from sturdy wooden beams and Guinness on tap.

Kissfish Averof and Fokéas. One of a clutch of trendy bars tucked away in these narrow lanes near the up-and-coming portside zone; definitely a place to be seen.

Kitchen Bar Port, next to State Museum of Contemporary Art. A huge harbour warehouse, converted into one of the city's most fashionable hangouts. Head upstairs in the cooler months and out to the seafront terrace in the summer to enjoy sweeping city views as you sip a cocktail, eat a full-blown meal or just tuck into breakfast or an afternoon cheesecake and coffee.

Kourdhisto Gourouni Ayías Sofías 31. Several foreign brews on tap, and a bewildering range of bottled varieties, at this stylish bar with indoor and outdoor seating; expensive food menu also.

Pasta Flora Darling Zefxídhou 6. Garden gnomes and flowery wallpaper, jazzy tables and psychedelic lighting suggest the decor is every bit as eclectic as the clientele at this typical Iktínou-Zefxídhou bar; good for cocktails and vegetarian snacks.

Santé Kapodhistríou 3. Fabulously eccentric bar in a converted Neoclassical silk-factory showroom, with intriguing papier mâché Amerindians and other exotica. There's a Latin flavour to the music, mostly tango, Cuban and Brazilian; the decor is partly inspired by the mind-boggling Santé cigarette pack that gives the place its name.

Events

In **winter**, cultural events, often of high quality, mostly take place in one of the State Theatre of Northern Greece (Kratikó Théatro Voríou Elládhos) venues. Downtown this means either the Etería Makedhonikón Spoudhón or the ultramodern Vassilikó Théatro, within sight of each other behind the White Tower. In **summer**, things move to one of a number of outdoor venues: the Théatro Kípou, near the archeological museum; well up the hill at the Théatro Dhássous, in the pines east of the upper town, with events from late June to mid-September; or the Théatro Damári, above the Kaftantzoglio Stadium in Triandhría district, which hosts big Greek or international stars. Unless your Greek is up to perusing the excellent weekly *About* listings magazine (every Thurs; €1.50), watch for **posters** in the windows of the usual ticket vendors:

the record stores Albandis (Mitropóleos 14–16), Patsis (Tsimiskí 41) and Virgin (shopping mall at Tsimiskí 43), as well as on walls and at bars.

More cutting-edge events are held at Mylos, at Andhréou Yeoryíou 56 (Ⓦwww.mylos.gr), a multifunctional cultural complex housed in an old flour mill some way west of the centre. Here you'll find a couple of bars, a live jazz café, a popular *tsipourádhiko* (open for lunch), a summer cinema, concert halls and exhibition galleries of various sizes, plus a theatre. Another venue of note is the very active Moní Lazaristón in Stavroúpoli at Kolokotróni 25 (Ⓣ2310 652 020; Ⓦwww.monilazariston.gr), a deconsecrated Catholic monastery 2km north of the centre along Langadhá. Officially part of the State Theatre of Northern Greece project (Ⓦwww.ntng.gr), its main and smaller theatres host regular concerts, operas and plays, by top Greek performers and visiting foreign troupes, plus art exhibitions. Buses #34 and #38 go there from Platía Dhikastirión.

Cinema

Central indoor cinemas, closed in summer unless otherwise indicated, have sadly been dying as property values spiral and more suburban multi-plexes are built; the five survivors are Aristotelion, Ethnikís Ámynas 2 (open in summer); Kolosseon, V Olgas 150 (open in summer); Makedhonikon, corner Ethnikís Ámynas and A Svólou; Olympion, Platía Aristotélous 9; and Vakoura, Ioánnou Mihaïl 10. **Open-air cinemas** have all but vanished from the centre; the only ones left are the Aigli, outside the Yeni Hamam; and Natali, at the start of Megálou Alexándhrou, by the *Macedonia Palace* hotel. Listings are given in *About* and the daily Greek papers.

Shopping

Thessaloníki is not really a mecca for consumer therapy but, in addition to its smart clothing and shoe emporia, mostly concentrated along or just off Tsimiskí, you can find some fine shops around the city. Three main possibilities for souvenir hunters would be books, records and a decent bottle of local wine.

Books and newspapers Prometheus/Molho, Tsimiskí 10, and Konstandinidhis, P Melá 11, are far and away the best shops in the city, with excellent stocks of English-language books (in particular related to Thessaloníki). Promitheus, Ermoú 75 and Isavrón, near Platía Navarínou, is good for newspapers and magazines.

Music Best of Thessaloníki's various record stores for Greek music are Studio 52, Dhimitríou Goúnari 46, basement, with lots of out-of-print vinyl and cassettes plus well-sorted CDs; and En Chordais, Ippodhromíou 3–4, a traditional music school and instrument shop, which also has a well-selected stock of folk and innovative CDs. Stereodisc, Aristotélous 4, has a good rock selection, as well as Greek.

Wine Northern Greece nurtures some fine vineyards, and accordingly Thessaloníki has some excellent bottle-shops affordably selling vintages superior to your average taverna plonk: Iy Tsaritsani, Avyerinoú 9, off Platía Áthonos; Aneroto, Dhimitríou Goúnari 42; and Reklos, Ayíou Dhimitríou 118, cnr Ayías Sofías.

Listings

Airlines Aegean, Venizélou 2 Ⓣ2310 280 050; Olympic, Koundouriótou 3 Ⓣ2310 344 444. Most other airlines have offices at the airport.

Airport Ⓣ2310 411 977 for flight information.

Car rental Most central agencies are clustered near the fairgrounds and Archeological Museum on Angeláki, which is a good place to compare prices. The leading multinationals here have kiosks at the airport too, but you will get better deals from local firms, such as Macedonia at no. 9 Ⓣ2310 241 119, Ⓦwww.automotorental.gr; or Vita at no. 17 Ⓣ2310 220 920, Ⓕ2310 254 454.

Consulates Australia, Kifissías 46, Kalamaria Ⓣ2310 482 322; Canada, Tsimiskí 17 Ⓣ2310 256 350; UK/Commonwealth, Aristotélous 21 Ⓣ2310 278 006; US, Tsimiskí 43, 7th floor Ⓣ2310 242 905.

Cultural institutes British Council, Ethnikís Amynis 9, cnr Tsimiskí ⓣ2310 378 300; free library and reading room, plus various events in the winter months.
Exchange For changing notes, use the 24hr automatic exchange machine at the National Bank on Platía Aristotélous 6. Thessaloníki has plenty of reliable ATMs accepting a variety of foreign plastic.
Ferry tickets The most convenient all-round agent, selling tickets for all companies, is Zorpidis, near the port at Salamínas 4 ⓣ2310 555 995, ⓦwww.zorpidis.gr.
Football Thessaloníki's main team is PAOK, whose stadium is in the east of the city at Toúmba. Its two big rivals are Aris, who play in Haríláou, also east of the centre, and Iraklis, whose Kaftantzoglou stadium is both the largest and most central.
Hospitals For minor trauma, use the Yeniko Kendriko at Ethnikís Amynis 41; otherwise, head for the Ippokration at Konstandinopóleos 49, in the eastern part of town.
Internet café There are dozens, but two of the least noisy are *Enterprisse* at Dhimitríou Goúnari 52 and *Planet* at Svólou 55.
Laundries Bianca, Antoniádhou 3, near the Arch of Galerius (quick service and long hours); Freskadha, Filíppou 105, beside the Rotónda; Ion, Karaóli Dhimitríou 52 (good dry cleaning).
Post office Main branch is at Aristotélous 26 (Mon–Fri 7.30am–8pm, Sat 7.30am–2pm, Sun 9am–1.30pm). There are other post offices around the city: the most useful ones are at Koundouriótou (by the port), Ethnikís Amynis 9A and Ayíou Dhimitríou 98.
Train tickets If you want to buy tickets or make reservations in advance, the OSE office at Aristotélous 18 (Mon & Sat 8am–3pm, Tues–Fri 8am–9pm) is far more central and helpful than the station ticket-windows.
Travel agents Most general sales agents and consolidators cluster around Platía Eleftherías, especially on Kalapotháki, Komninón, Níkis and Mitropóleos. Students and under-27s should try Nouvelles Frontières at Kalapotháki 8 (ⓣ2310 237 700) or Sunflight at Tsimiskí 114 (ⓣ2310 280 500). For cheap buses to Turkey, try Bus and Atlantic Tours, Aristotélous 10, 4th Floor ⓣ2310 226 036. Mountain trekking and other outdoor expeditions are offered by Trekking Hellas, Mitropóleos 60 (ⓣ2310 264 082).

Around Thessaloníki

The main **weekend escape** from Thessaloníki is to the Halkidhikí peninsula, but to get to its better beaches requires more than a day-trip. If you just want a respite from the city, or a walk in the hills, consider instead Thessaloníki's

The anastenáridhes: the fire-walkers of Langadhás

On May 21, the feast day of SS Constantine and Helen, villagers at **LANGADHÁS**, 20km north of Thessaloníki, perform a ritual barefoot dance across a bed of burning coals known as the *anastenária*. The festival rites are of unknown and strongly disputed origin. It has been suggested that they are remnants of a Dionysiac cult, though devotees assert a purely Christian tradition. This seems to relate to a fire, around 1250, in the Thracian village of Kostí (now in Bulgaria), from where many of the inhabitants of Langadhás originate. Holy icons were heard groaning from the flames and were rescued by villagers, who emerged miraculously unburnt from the blazing church. The icons, passed down by their families, are believed to ensure protection during the fire walking. Equally important is piety and purity of heart: it is said that no one with any harboured grudges or unconfessed sins can pass through the coals unscathed.

Whatever the origin, the rite is still performed most years – lately as something of a tourist attraction, with an admission charge and repeat performances over the next two days. It is nevertheless eerie and impressive, beginning around 7pm with the lighting of a cone of hardwood logs. A couple of hours later their embers are raked into a circle and, just before complete darkness, a traditional Macedonian *daoúli* drummer and two lyra players precede a group of about sixteen women and men into the arena. These *anastenáridhes* (literally "groaners"), in partial trance, then shuffle across the coals for about a quarter of an hour. Scientific tests have indicated there is no fraud involved.

own local villages and suburbs. Further out, drivers en route to Néa Moudhaniá can take in the extraordinary cave near Petrálona – though half-day trips with a local tour operator make this a possibility for those without their own transport, too.

Panórama

On the hillside 11km southeast of Thessaloniki, **PANÓRAMA**, the closest escape from the city, is exactly what its name suggests: a hillside viewpoint looking down over Thessaloníki and the gulf. Rebuilt after World War II, it is mainly composed of smart villas, coffee shops and a large, modern shopping mall. Of more appeal are a number of traditional cafés, tavernas and *zaharoplastía*, these last selling the premier local speciality, *trígona* (very sweet custard-filled triangular confections) and wonderful *dondurma* (Turkish-style ice cream flavoured with mastic). The village can be reached by #58 bus from Platía Dhikastiríon, or by taxi (around €4 one way).

Petrálona

Fifty kilometres southeast of Thessaloníki, and set among handsome mountain scenery, is the cave of **Kókkines Pétres** (Red Stones), discovered in 1959 by villagers from nearby **PETRÁLONA** looking for water. Besides an impressive display of stalagmites and stalactites, the villagers – and, later, academics – found the fossilized remains of prehistoric animals and, most dramatic of all, a Neanderthal skull, all of which are displayed in a decent museum near the cave entrance.

The cave and museum (daily 9am to sunset; guided tours only €5, no photography), kitted out with dioramas of prehistoric activities and well worth a visit, make an interesting diversion on the way to or from the Kassándhra peninsula; you'll find the village of Petrálona itself roughly 4km north of Eleohória, on the old road running from Thessaloníki to Néa Moudhaniá. There's a small café on site. Doucas Travel Collection in Thessaloníki (K Diehl 20 ⓣ2310 254 450), among other outfits, operate a half-day trip.

Litóhoro and Mount Olympus (Óros Ólymbos)

The highest, most magical and most dramatic of all Greek mountains, **Mount Olympus** – Ólymbos in Greek – rears straight up to 2917m from the shores of the Thermaic Bight and, when pollution allows, is visible from Thessaloníki, some 100km away to the northeast. Its summit was believed by the ancient Greeks to be the home of the gods and it seems that quite a few locals still follow the old religion. Dense forests cover its lower slopes, and its **wild flowers** are without parallel even by Greek standards.

By far the best base for a walk up the mountain, if only part of the way for the views, is the small town of **LITÓHORO** on the eastern side. A fairly pleasant garrison town with two huge army camps on the approach road, its setting, in good weather, affords intoxicating vistas into the heart of the range.

Litóhoro practicalities

Reaching Litóhoro is fairly easy: it has its own motorway turn-off, and buses to the central platía **KTEL** from Thessaloníki or the market town of Kateríni are frequent. The **train station** is 5km away, down by the motorway, where you'll find taxis are sometimes waiting or you can walk 500m and pick up a bus just west of the motorway.

Information sources in Litóhoro are virtually nonexistent, but with this guide you can find your way up the mountain in summer without the need for any other information. For more information see the box on p.432. The **post office** is at 28-Oktovríou 11, and a couple of banks in Litóhoro have **ATMs**.

Accommodation

At the budget end you're best off looking for **rooms** by asking in the cafés and tavernas around the main square. Otherwise, there is a range of moderately priced hostels and hotels.

Enipeas right behind *Xenios Dias* ⓣ23520 84328, ⓕ23520 81328. Newer than most, and spotless, its upper rear rooms have fine views, while attic rooms with skylight only are cheaper. ❸

Myrto Ayíou Nikoláou, just off the main square ⓣ23520 81398, ⓕ23520 82298. Comfortable, extremely clean hotel; you won't find much cheaper but it does get noise from the street and the square. ❶

Olympus Mediterranean Dhionýsou 5 ⓣ23520 81831, ⓦwww.olympusmed.gr. Completely unrecognisable from its previous incarnation as the old *Markesia*. With a smart new lobby and beautifully refurbished rooms, this is the town's poshest option; breakfast included. ❹

Villa Drossos Arheláou 18 ⓣ23520 84561, ⓦwww.villadrossos.gr. Tucked away behind Ayíou Yeoryíou church, two or three streets back from Ayíou Nikoláou, the *Villa* boasts smart rooms, an enticing swimming pool and an open fire in winter, plus parking space; breakfast included. ❸

Xenios Dias On the main square ⓣ23520 81234, ⓦwww.hotel-xeniosdias.gr. With views to equal those of the *Enipeas*, this place has smarter rooms and a cosy bar. ❸

Xenonas Papanikolaou N E Kítrous 1, signposted 100m from square ⓣ23520 81236, ⓦwww.xenonas-papanikolaou.gr. Very central but tucked in a quiet sidestreet, this friendly and excellently appointed hostel offers modernised, yet traditionally decorated en-suite rooms with central a/c/heating and cable TV. Superb value. ❷

Eating

Best of all, both for its central-platía location and commendable culinary endeavours, is the slightly pricey *Gastrodromio en Olymbo*; rabbit and suckling pig stand out from the usual fare, fixed menus are offered and there's a decent wine list. Among the fair selection of alternatives, the *Taverna-Ouzeri Pazari* on Platía 3-Martíou, serves locally caught octopus and squid. At the start of the road towards the mountain (signposted "Olympos"), are a couple of cheap-and-cheerful, sit-down *psistariés* – the *Zeus* in particular passes muster. Out by the start of the path into the canyon, the summer-only *Iy Myli* offers standard taverna fare in the most pastoral surroundings.

The mountain

To reach alpine Olympus, you've a choice of road or foot routes. With your own vehicle, you can **drive** deep into the mountain along a fairly decent road, the first 11km of which is paved. There is an information booth at km3, where (in high season, anyway) your nationality is recorded and you're given some literature advising you of the park rules, but so far there's no admission charge. It is much better, however, to **walk** in from Litóhoro, as far as the monastery of **Ayíou Dhionysíou**, and beyond to the two trailheads following.

As for the final **ascent routes**, there are two main paths: one starting at a spot called **Dhiakládhosi/Gortsiá** (13km up the road from Litóhoro), marked by a signboard displaying a map of the range; and one beginning at **Priónia** – just

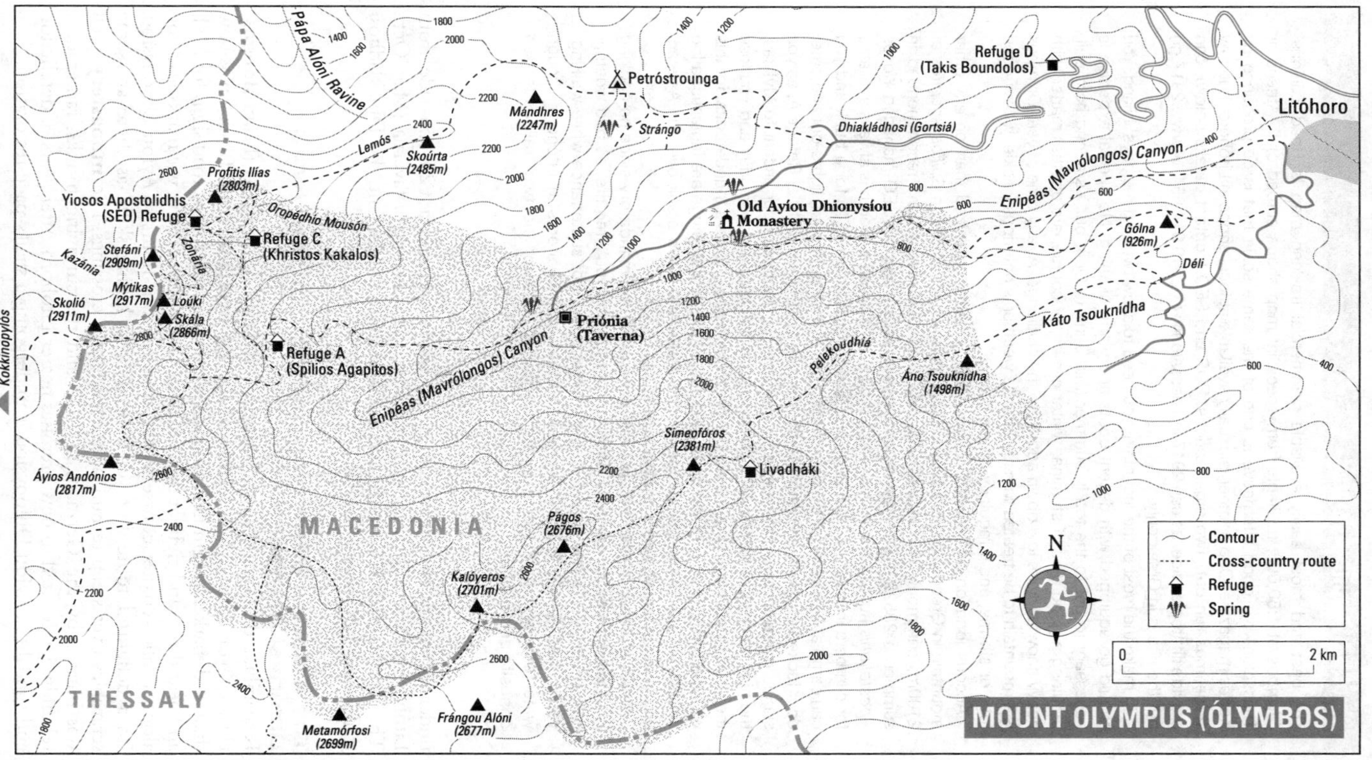
Pápa Alóni Ravine
Petróstrounga
Refuge D (Takis Boundolos)
Litóhoro
Mándhres (2247m)
Strángo
Dhiakládhosi (Gortsiá)
Lemós
Skoúrta (2485m)
Enipéas (Mavrólongos) Canyon
Profitis Ilías (2803m)
Yiosos Apostolidhis (SEO) Refuge
Oropédhio Mousón
Old Ayíou Dhionysíou Monastery
Gólna (926m)
Refuge C (Khristos Kakalos)
Zonária
Stefáni (2909m)
Kazánia
Déli
Mýtikas (2917m)
Loúki
Skolió (2911m)
Skála (2866m)
Kokkinopylós
Priónia (Taverna)
Káto Tsouknídha
Refuge A (Spilios Agapitos)
Enipéas (Mavrólongos) Canyon
Pelekoudhiá
Áno Tsouknídha (1498m)
Simeofóros (2381m)
Livadháki
Áyios Andónios (2817m)
MACEDONIA
Págos (2676m)
Kalóyeros (2701m)
THESSALY
Metamórfosi (2699m)
Frángou Alóni (2677m)
Contour
Cross-country route
Refuge
Spring
N
0
2 km
MOUNT OLYMPUS (ÓLYMBOS)

Climbing Mount Olympus

The best and most easily available commercial trekking map is Road Editions' *Olymbos* at 1:50,000, available from specialist map shops abroad or in Athens or Thessaloníki; a good alternative is one of the same scale that is co-produced by *Korfes* magazine. One or other is usually available at local shops in Litóhoro, but they sometimes run out. Two organizations, EOS and SEO (contact details below), can provide limited advice, as can 2917 in Thessaloniki (Ⓣ2310 914 654, Ⓦwww.2917.gr) but the site is in Greek only.

To make the most of the mountain, you need to allow two to three days' hiking. You should go equipped with decent boots and warm clothing. No special expertise is necessary to get to the top in summer (mid-June to Oct), but it's a long hard pull, requiring a good deal of stamina; winter climbs, of course, are another matter, with heavy snowfall quite low down adding to the challenge. At any time of year Olympus is a mountain to be treated with respect: its weather is notoriously fickle, with sudden fogs or storms, and it regularly claims lives.

Accommodation on Mount Olympus itself is better organized than on any other mountain in Greece. There are two staffed refuges: the EOS-run *Spilios Agapitos* at 2100m, commonly known as Refuge A, (May–Oct, reservations recommended in summer; Ⓣ23520 81800, Ⓦwww.mountolympus.gr), and the SEO-managed *Yiosos Apostolidhis* hut at 2700m (July–Sept, though its glassed-in porch is always available for climbers in need; Ⓣ2310 224 710). Both charge around €10 for a bunk and you can camp at Refuge A for €4.20, including use of their bathroom; lights-out and outer door locked at 10pm, so bring a torch. It's best to stay overnight at Refuge A, as you should make an early start (certainly pre-8am) for the three-hour ascent to Mýtikas, the highest peak at 2917m. The peaks frequently cloud up by midday and you lose the view, to say nothing of the danger of catching one of Zeus's thunderbolts, for this was the mythical seat of the gods. Besides, nights at the refuge are fantastic: a log fire blazes, you watch the sun set on the peaks and dawn break over the Aegean, and you can usually see a multitude of stars.

Meals at either shelter are relatively expensive, and mandatory since no cooking is allowed inside; bring more money than you think you'll require, as bad weather can ground you a day or two longer than planned. For sustenance while walking, you'll need to buy food at the well-stocked grocery stores in Litóhoro, though water can wait until you're in the vicinity of either of the two trailheads (see opposite and p.434).

under 18km up the mountain at the road's end and a €20 taxi ride from Litóhoro – where there's a spring, toilets and a primitive taverna (May–Oct). The Priónia path is more frequented and more convenient, the Dhiakládhosi trail longer but more beautiful.

The Enipéas (Mavrólongos) canyon and Ayíou Dhionysíou monastery

Rehabilitated old paths in the superlatively beautiful **Enipéas (Mavrólongos)** river canyon form a fine section of the **E4 overland trail**. Black-on-yellow diamond markers begin near Litóhoro's central platía; follow road signs for Mýli and bear down and right at the cemetery. Once out of town, waymarks lead you along a roller-coaster course by the river for four hours to Ayíou Dhionysíou. It's a delightful route, but you'll need basic hiking skills, as there are some scrambles over steep terrain, and a few water crossings. The **monastery** itself was burned by the Germans in 1943 and the surviving monks, rather than rebuilding, relocated to new premises nearer Litóhoro. After years of dereliction and vandalism, Ayíou Dhionysíou is undergoing a snail's-pace restoration.

From Ayíou Dhionysíou it's just under an hour more upstream along the riverside E4 to Priónia, or slightly less if you go up the driveway and then east to the Dhiakládhosi trailhead.

The ascent from Priónia

The E4 carries on just uphill by a signpost giving the time to Refuge A as two hours thirty minutes, though it actually takes more like three hours, even at a brisk pace. You cross a stream (last water before Refuge A; purification advisable) and start to climb steeply up through woods of beech and black pine. This path, the continuation of the E4, is well trodden and marked, so there is no danger of getting lost. As you gain height there are majestic views across the Enipéas (Mavrólongos) canyon to your left and to the peaks towering above you. **Refuge A** (see opposite) perches on the edge of an abrupt spur, surrounded by huge storm-beaten trees.

The summit area

The E4 path continues behind the refuge (your last **water source** on the ascent), climbing to the left up a steep spur among the last of the trees. Having ignored an initial right fork towards the usually unstaffed *Khristos Kakalos* hut (Refuge C), within about an hour you reach a signposted **fork** above the tree line. Continuing straight on takes you across the range to Kokkinopylós village with the E4 waymarks, or with a slight deviation right to Mýtikas, via the ridge known as Kakí Skála (1hr 30min–2hr). An immediate right turn leads to the *Yiosos Apostolidhis* hut in one hour along the so-called Zonária trail, with the option after 45 minutes of taking the very steep Loúki couloir left up to Mýtikas; if you do this, be wary of rockfalls.

For the safer **Kakí Skála route**, continue up the right flank of the stony, featureless valley in front of you, with the Áyios Andónios peak up to your left. An hour's dull climb brings you to the summit ridge between the peaks of Skolió on the left and Skála on the right. You know you're there when one more step would tip you over a five-hundred-metre sheer drop into the Kazánia chasm; take great care. The Kakí Skála ("Evil Stairway") begins in a narrow cleft on the right just short of the ridge; paint splashes mark the way. The route keeps just below the ridge, so you are protected from the drop into Kazánia. Even so, it's a tough scramble and those who don't like heights are likely to be reduced to a whimpering crouch.

You start with a slightly descending rightward traverse to a narrow nick in the ridge revealing the drop to Kazánia – easily negotiated. Continue traversing right, skirting the base of the Skála peak, then climb leftwards up a steepish gully made a little awkward by loose rock on sloping footholds. Bear right at the top over steep but reassuringly solid rock, and across a narrow neck. Step left around an awkward corner and there in front of you, scarcely 100m away, is **Mýtikas summit**, an airy, boulder-strewn platform with a trigonometric point, tin Greek flag and visitors' book. In reasonable conditions it's about forty minutes to the summit from the start of Kakí Skála; three hours from the refuge; five and a half hours from Priónia.

A stone's throw to the north of Mýtikas is the **Stefáni peak**, also known as the Throne of Zeus, a bristling hog's back of rock with a couple of nastily exposed moves to scale the last few metres.

Descending from Mýtikas, you can either go back the way you came, with the option of turning left at the signpost for the *Yiosos Apostolidhis* hut (2hr 30min from Mýtikas by this route), or you can step out, apparently into space, in the direction of Stefáni and turn immediately down to the right into the mouth of the Loúki couloir. It takes about forty minutes of vertiginous downward scrambling to reach the main path where you turn left for the hut, skirting the impressive northeast face of Stefáni (1hr), or go right, back to the familiar signpost and down the E4 to *Spilios Agapitos* (2hr altogether).

The ascent from Dhiakládhosi (Gortsiá)

Starting from the small parking area beyond the information placard, take the narrow path going up and left via faint steps – with a wood railing and wooden awning – not the forest track heading down and right. An hour along, you reach the meadow of **Bárba**, and two hours out you'll arrive at a messy junction with a modern water tank and various placards – take left forks en route when given the choice. The signs point hard left to the spring at **Strángo**; right for the direct path to Petróstrounga; and straight on for the old, more scenic way to **Petróstrounga**, passed some two-and-a-half hours along.

Beyond Petróstrounga, there's an indicated right, then the trail wanders up to the base of **Skoúrta** knoll (4hr 15min), above the tree line. After crossing the Lemós (Neck) ridge dividing the Papá Alóni and Enipéas (Mavrólongos) ravines, with spectacular views into both, five-and-a-quarter hours should see you up on the Oropédhio Musón ("Plateau of the Muses"), five-and-a-half hours to the *Apostolidhis* refuge, visible the last fifteen minutes. But you should count on seven hours, including rests, for this route; going down takes about four and a half hours, a highly recommended descent if you've come up from Priónia.

It takes about an hour, losing altitude, to traverse the onward Zonária path linking *Apostolidhis* and the E4, skimming the base of the peaks – about the same time as coming the other way as described above.

Dion

Ancient **DION**, in the foothills of Mount Olympus, was the Macedonians' sacred city. At this site – a harbour before the river mouth silted up – the kingdom maintained its principal sanctuaries: to Zeus (from which the name Dion, or Dios, is derived) above all, but also to Demeter, Artemis, Asklepios and, later, to foreign gods such as the Egyptians Isis and Serapis. Philip II and Alexander both came to sacrifice to Zeus here before their expeditions and battles. Inscriptions found at the sanctuaries referring to boundary disputes, treaties and other affairs of state suggest that the political and social importance of the city's festivals exceeded a purely Macedonian domain.

Most exciting for visitors, however, are the finds of **mosaics, temples and baths** that have been excavated since 1990 – work that remains in progress whenever funds allow. These are not quite on a par with the Vergina tombs (see p.437), but still rank among the major discoveries of ancient Macedonian history and culture. If you're near Mount Olympus, they are certainly worth a detour, and the abundance of water and vegetation makes it cooler and more pleasing on the eye than many sites. The frog ponds and grazing geese in a lush landscape littered with voluptuous statuary lend the place the air of a decadent Roman villa and its gardens.

At the village of **DHÍON** (Malathiriá until the archeological discovery), 7km inland from Litóhoro beach or reached by #14 bus from Kateríni, take a side road 400m east from the defunct *Hotel Dion*, past the remains of a **theatre**, put to good use during the summer Olympus Festival. The main **site** or "park" lies ahead (daily: summer 8am–7.30pm; winter closes 5pm; €6, including the museum). A direct, signposted, paved road links Dion to Litóhoro (see p.429). Recommended for an **overnight** stay is the smart *Safetis Apartments* (Ⓣ23510 46272, Ⓕ23510 46273) in the village, where a few tavernas are firmly pitched at the tourist trade. The nearest campsites are on the beach at Varikó, 11km away: *Stani* (Ⓣ23520 61277) and *Niteas* (Ⓣ23520 61290), both open all year round.

The integrity of the site and its finds is due to the nature of the city's demise. At some point in the fifth century AD, a series of earthquakes prompted an evacuation of Dion, which was then swallowed up by a mudslide from the mountain. The place is still quite waterlogged, and constant pumping against the local aquifer is necessary. The main visible excavations are of the vast **public baths** complex and, outside the city walls, the **sanctuaries** of Demeter and Aphrodite-Isis. In the latter, a small temple has been unearthed, along with its cult statue – a copy of which remains in situ. Two Christian **basilicas** attest to the town's later years as a Byzantine bishopric in the fourth and fifth centuries AD. An observation platform allows you to view the layout of the site more clearly.

In the village, a large but poorly labelled **museum** (same hours as site) houses most of the finds. The sculptures, perfectly preserved by the mud, are impressive, and accompanied by various tombstones and altars. In the basement sprawls a mosaic of Medusa, along with the finest **mosaics** yet discovered at the site: they would have paved the banquet room and depict the god Dionysos on a chariot. Upstairs, along with extensive displays of pottery and coinage, is a collection of everyday items, although pride of place goes to the remains of a first-century BC **pipe organ**.

Véria and Vergina

The broad agricultural plain extending due west from Thessaloníki eventually collides with an abrupt, wooded escarpment, at the panoramic edge of which is a series of towns including Édhessa (see p.440). The largest of these, **Véria** (ancient Berrhoea or Berea) is one of the more interesting northern Greek communities, thanks to its mixed Jewish, Muslim and Christian heritage: in the nineteenth century the town became an important industrial centre, and many of the townsfolk grew prosperous from flour and sesame milling as well as hide tanning. Perhaps most importantly, Véria lies within twenty minutes' drive of the history-changing excavations of ancient Aegae at **Vergina**.

Véria

VÉRIA has few outstanding sites or monuments, with the exception of its excellent new Byzantine Museum and a smattering of appealing religious edifices. The modern town is manageable and pleasant, however, and offers a decent enough range of facilities to make it a reasonable base for the area.

Arrival and information

If you don't have your own transport the best way to get here is by bus, as the train station is very inconvenient, a good 3km from the centre. The **KTEL,** just off Venizélou at the northern end of central Véria, handles the regular services to and from all regional destinations. **Taxis** are lemon-yellow with white roofs. At central Platía Eliás, known locally as the Belvedere, there is an all-but-useless summer-only **EOT** information booth. On or around one-way Mitropóleos, which links Eliás with hub-like Platía Oroloyíou, are the **post office** (on D

Solomoú) and various banks with **ATMs**, plus lots of shops and fast-food joints. The best **Internet** café is along Eliás.

Accommodation

Of the bare handful of **hotels** in Véria, the least expensive is the adequate and clean en-suite *Veroi* at Platía Oroloyíou 1 (ⓣ23310 22866, ⓔeneari@otenet.gr; ④). A slightly smarter, better-value choice is the *Villa Elia*, Elías 16 (ⓣ23310 26800, ⓔeliaver@otenet.gr; ④), but prone to street noise. Much quieter, albeit with rather functional rooms, is the *Makedonia*, Kondoyeorgáki 50 (ⓣ&ⓕ23310 66902, ⓦwww.hotelmakedonia.gr; ④), with a roof garden and substantial breakfasts included. Down on the ring road is the pricey and new *Aiges Melathron* (ⓣ23310 77777, ⓦwww.aigesmelathron.gr; ⑦), really aimed at business travellers, with bright rooms, a good restaurant and a swimming pool.

The Town

Towards the northern end of Leofóros Aníxeos, which snakes along the cliff edge past Véria's most prestigious district, is the town's **Archeological Museum**, although it was closed long term for renovations and extension at the time of writing. Far more impressive is the town's outstanding new **Byzantine Museum**, well signposted along Thomaídhou (Tues–Sun 8.30am–3pm; €2). Housed in a beautifully restored nineteenth-century flour mill, with an austere stone facade, it mostly comprises an exquisite display of icons – Véria was renowned for its painting workshops in the late Middle Ages – along with other treasures mostly from the Byzantine era, including coins. On the ground floor, a highly moving video, with English subtitles, records the history of the mill, its demise and its exemplary refurbishment.

Christianity has a venerable and long history in Véria: St Paul preached here (Acts 17:10–14) on two occasions, between 50 and 60 AD, and a gaudy alcove shrine or "**altar**" of modern mosaics at the base of Mavromiháli marks the supposed spot of his sermons. Four dozen or so small **churches**, some medieval but mostly dating from the sixteenth to eighteenth century, are scattered around the town, earning it the moniker of Little Jerusalem. Under Ottoman rule, many were disguised as barns or warehouses, with little dormer windows rather than domes to admit light; but today, often surrounded by cleared spaces and well labelled, they're not hard to find. The only church regularly open, however, is the well-signposted **Resurrection of Christ, or Anastásseos Christoú** (Tues–Sun 8.30am–3pm; free), with cleaned fourteenth-century frescoes, near the fork end of Mitropóleos. The most striking images here are a *Dormition/Assumption* over the west door and a rare image of Christ mounting the cross on a ladder on the north wall.

Nearby what remains of the old **bazaar** straddles Kendrikís, while downhill and to the west tumbles the riverside Ottoman quarter of **Barboúta** (aka Barboúti). Largely **Jewish** before the 1944 deportations annihilated the one-thousand-strong community, it is today being swiftly gentrified. The disused **synagogue** can be reached via Odhós Dhekátis Merarhías, past the conspicuous officers' club near Platía Oroloyíou. Situated on a plaza with a small amphitheatre, it is a long stone building with an awning over the door, which is sometimes left ajar, allowing you to look at the rambling, arcaded interior. Of the many handsome nineteenth-century mansions hereabouts, the impeccably restored **Arhondikó Béka** currently houses the International Institute of Traditional Architecture.

Survivals of the **Muslim** presence in Véria are more numerous and conspicuous, but less well restored. It is worth hunting down the twin *hamam* complex, **Dhídhymi Loutrónes**, at the end of Loutroú, the small **Ortá**

Tzamí mosque just off Kendrikís, and the splendid **Medresé Tzamí** mosque on Márkou Bótsari, but do not expect to enter them or be impressed by their state of conservation.

Eating and drinking

Along pedestrianized Patriárhou Ioakeím, a lane lined with old Ottoman houses, is a **gastro-taverna**, *Petrino*, serving the usual fare with a twist. An enduring favourite for supper is *Kostalar* in the Papákia district at Afrodhítis 2/D, reached by following Mavromiháli uphill from the St Paul shrine to a plane-tree-shaded square with rivulets; this place specialises in tasty grills and fine *mezédhes*. Just along from the Byzantine Museum at Thomaídhou 2, the respectable *Veryiotiko* serves predictable cuisine, though in winter it comes up with the likes of wild boar with quinces; the summer terrace suffers from road noise but the taverna has the virtue of opening on Mondays when nearly everywhere else seems to shut.

In the daytime, by far the most pleasant place for a **coffee or a beer** is *Elia*, at the edge of the Belvedere, with its shady terrace overlooking the plain. The very sweet-toothed should not leave Véria without trying the local speciality, **revaní**, a syrup-soaked sponge cake. The trendy **bars** along Eliás and around the Belvedere heave with locals sporting tight shirts, bare midriffs and the very latest in mobile phones; for slightly less showing off try the well-located *Kastro*, along towards the archeological museum. If you crave more action after dark, the pedestrianized area around Patriárhou Ioakeím is crammed full with noisy bars and comes into its own.

Vergina: ancient Aegae

The site of **VERGINA**, 16km southeast of Véria, undoubtedly qualifies as one of the most memorable experiences that Greece has to offer. The main finds consist of a series of **chamber tombs** unearthed by Professor Manolis Andronikos in 1977 – the culmination of decades of work on the site – and unequivocally accepted as those of Philip II, the father of Alexander the Great, and other members of the Macedonian royal family. This means that the site itself must be that of **Aegae**, the original Macedonian royal capital before the shift to Pella, and later the sanctuary and royal burial place of the Macedonian kings. It was here that Philip II was assassinated, cremated and buried – and tradition maintained that the dynasty would be destroyed if any king were buried elsewhere, as indeed happened after the death of Alexander the Great in Asia. Until Andronikos's finds, Aegae had long been assumed to be lost beneath modern Édhessa.

To get here, there are buses from Véria every hour or two, taking twenty minutes. The modern village of **Veryína** that now engulfs the site has limited facilities, but does boast an **ATM** and a foreign-note changer. For somewhere to **stay** try the comfortable rooms at the new *Hotel Aigon* (Ⓣ23310 92524, Ⓦwww.hotel-aigon.gr; ③), 200m up the road from the Royal Tombs, or the friendly *Xenonas Evridiki* (Ⓣ23310 92502, Ⓦwww.evridiki.com.gr; ③), just below the Macedonian Tomb. Its plane-shaded **taverna** is a better bet than the tourist joints on the main drag.

The Royal Tombs

Under a tumulus, then just outside modern Veryína, Andronikos discovered several large Macedonian chamber tombs, known simply as the **Royal Tombs** (summer: Mon noon–7.30pm, Tues–Sun 8am–7.30pm; until 3pm in winter; €8; no photography). From outside, all that's visible is a low hillock (the replaced tumulus) with skylights and long ramps leading inside, but once underground in the climate-controlled bunker you can admire the facades and doorways of the tombs in situ, well illuminated behind glass. Finds from the site and tombs, the richest Greek trove since the discovery of Mycenae, are exhibited in the complex along with erudite texts in Greek and English, although some are still on display at Thessaloníki's Archeological Museum (see p.418). It's best to try and get here very early or visit at siesta time in order to avoid crowds.

A clockwise tour takes you round the tombs in the order IV-I-II-III. Tomb IV, the so-called Doric, was looted in antiquity; so too was **Tomb I**, or the **Persephone tomb**, but it retained a delicate and exquisitely crafted **mural** of the rape of Persephone by Hades, the only complete example of an ancient Greek painting that has yet been found. **Tomb II**, that of **Philip II**, is a much grander vaulted tomb with a Doric facade adorned by a sumptuous painted **frieze** of Philip, Alexander and their retinue on a lion hunt. This – incredibly – was discovered intact, having been deliberately disguised with rubble from later tomb pillagings. Among the treasures to emerge – now displayed in the dimly lit but well-labelled hall here – were a marble sarcophagus containing a **gold ossuary** (*larnax*), its cover embossed with the exploding, sixteen-pointed star symbol of the royal line. Still more significantly, five small **ivory heads** were found, among them representations of both Philip II and Alexander. It was this clue, as well as the fact that the skull bore marks of a disfiguring facial wound Philip was known to have sustained, that led to the identification of the tomb as his. Also on view are a fabulous **gold oak-leaf wreath** – so delicate it quivers – and a more modest companion *larnax* found in the antechamber, presumed to contain the carefully wrapped bones and ashes of a legitimate queen or concubine, quite probably a Thracian aristocrat, married for political reasons, and who, according to some sources, stepped into the dead king's pyre of her own accord.

Tomb III is thought to be that of Alexander IV, "the Great's" son, murdered in adolescence – thus the moniker **Prince's Tomb**. His bones were discovered in a silver vase. From the tomb frieze, a superb **miniature of Dionysos and his consort** is highlighted. You should also spare a moment or two to view the excellent **video**, subtitled in English, which brings the archeological finds to life.

Macedonian Tomb

The so-called **Macedonian Tomb**, actually five adjacent tombs, can also be visited after a fashion (same times as Royal; same admission ticket). They are about 500m uphill, above the large parking lot, left of the main road. Like the Royal Tombs, they lie well below ground level, protected by a vast tin roof. Excavated by the French in 1861, the most prominent one, thought to be that of Philip's mother Eurydike, is in the form of a temple, with an Ionic facade of half-columns breached by two successive marble portals opening onto ante- and main chambers. Inside you can just make out an imposing marble throne with sphinxes carved on the sides, armrests and footstool. The neighbouring two pairs of tombs, still undergoing snail-paced excavation, are said to be similar in design.

Palace of Palatítsia

The ruins of the **Palace of Palatítsia** (closed for renovations; date for reopening not known at the time of writing) occupy a low hill 1km southeast of the village. It is reached by continuing along the lane that runs up beside the Macedonian Tomb. The palace complex was probably built during the third century BC as a summer residence for the last great Macedonian king, Antigonus Gonatas. Little more than the foundations remain, but amidst the confusing litter of column drums and capitals you can make out a triple *propylaion* (entrance gate) opening onto a central courtyard. The only substantial items dug up to date are the first two tiers of the **theatre** just below, where Philip II was assassinated in 336 BC, some say at the wedding of his daughter.

Pella

PELLA was the capital of Macedonia throughout its greatest period, and the first capital of Greece after Philip II forcibly unified the country around 338 BC. It was founded some sixty years earlier by King Archelaos, who transferred the royal Macedonian court here from Aegae (see p.437); from its beginnings it was a major centre of culture. The royal palace was decorated by the painter **Zeuxis** and was said to be the greatest artistic showplace since the time of Classical Athens. **Euripides** wrote and produced his last plays at the court, and here, too, **Aristotle** was to tutor the young Alexander the Great – born, like his father Philip II, in the city.

The site today is a worthwhile stopover en route to Édhessa and western Macedonia. Its main treasures are a series of pebble mosaics, some in the museum, others in situ. For an understanding of the context, it is best to visit after looking around the archeological museum at Thessaloníki, from where the site can also be visited comfortably on a rewarding day-trip.

The site

When Archelaos founded Pella, it lay at the head of a broad lake, connected to the Thermaïkós gulf by a navigable river. By the second century BC the river had begun to silt up and the city fell into decline. It was sacked by the Romans in 146 BC and never rebuilt; an earthquake caused further damage around two centuries later. Today its **ruins** (April–Oct Mon 12.30–7pm, Tues–Sun 8am–7.3pm; closes 3pm Nov–March; €6 including museum) stand in the middle of a broad expanse of plain, 40km from Thessaloníki and the sea.

Pella was located by chance finds in 1957; as yet only preliminary digs on the vast site covering over 485 hectares have been made. The **acropolis** at Pella is a low hill to the west of the modern village of Pélla. To the north of the road, at the main site, stand the low remains of a grand official building, probably a government office; it is divided into three large open courts, each enclosed by a *peristyle*, or portico (the columns of the central one have been re-erected), and bordered by wide streets with a sophisticated drainage system.

The three main rooms of the first court have patterned geometric floors, in the centre of which were found intricate **pebble mosaics** depicting scenes of a lion hunt, a griffin attacking a deer and Dionysos riding a panther. These are now in the excellent **museum** across the road (same hours as site), next to the car park. But in the third court three late fourth-century BC mosaics have been left in situ under sheltering canopies; one, a stag hunt, is complete, and astounding in its dynamism and use of perspective. The others represent, respectively, the rape of Helen by Paris and his friends Phorbas and Theseus, and a fight between a Greek and an Amazon.

The mosaics are inevitably a hard act to follow, but the museum merits another half-hour of perusal of its other well-presented exhibits. Highlights

▲ Mosaics at Pella

include rich grave finds from the two local necropolises, delicately worked terracotta figurines from a sanctuary of Aphrodite and Cybele, a large horde of late Classical/early Hellenistic coins, and – on the rarely seen domestic level – metal door fittings: pivots, knocker plates and crude keys.

Practicalities

The nearest **hotels** to the site are at Néa Halkidhóna, a major junction 8km east. Opposite each other on the Véria road, 1km from the junction with the Thessaloníki road, are the decent *Kornelios* (Ⓣ23910 23888; ❷) and the slightly more appealing *Filippos* (Ⓣ23910 22125, Ⓕ23910 22198; ❸). **Buses** from Véria and Veryína to Thessaloníki stop right in front of the *Hotel Kornelios*. The site of Pella lies on the main Thessaloníki–Édhessa road and is served by half-hourly buses, stopping in **Néa Halkidhóna**, in either direction.

Édhessa

The main gateway to the intriguing northwest corner of Macedonia, **ÉDHESSA**, like Véria atop the same escarpment, is a delightful place for a stopover but with rather better accommodation. Its modest fame is attributed to the waters that flow through the town; descending from the mountains to the north, these waters flow swiftly through the middle of town in several courses and then, just to the east, cascade down a dramatic ravine, luxuriant with vegetation, to the plain below. Most of the town's architecture is humdrum, but the various stream-side parks and wide pedestrian pavements are a rare pleasure in a country where the car is tyrant – indeed, Édhessa was the pioneering town in Greece for pedestrianization and is an increasingly important centre for regional tourism.

Arrival and information

Édhessa's **train and bus stations** are both well placed: the main KTEL is on the corner of Filíppou and Pávlou Melá; Flórina/Kastoriá services, however, depart from outside the *Ta Svourakia* snack-bar, 30m north along Filíppou. The train station is in the north of town. The town's excellent new **tourist information office** is in the park at Garéfi and Pérdhika (daily 10am–8pm; Ⓣ23810 20300, Ⓦwww.edessacity.gr) and is far and away the best in the region. English-speaking staff can provide exquisitely produced bilingual leaflets and all manner of information about activities, such as trekking, rafting, kayaking and skiing in the surrounding region. You'll find the **post office** on Pávlou Melá, while several **banks** sport ATMs.

Accommodation

Accommodation at the lower end of the scale is available at the refurbished *Olympia*, towards the train station at 18-Oktovríou 51 (Ⓣ23810 23544; ❸), whose rooms are slightly simpler but also quieter and cheaper than the more central *Alfa*, Egnatía 36 (Ⓣ23810 22221, Ⓦwww.hotel-alfa.gr; ❸). Far more upmarket, the *Xenia* (Ⓣ23810 21898, Ⓦwww.xeniaedessa.gr; ❺), south along Filíppou from KTEL, is the town's most expensive hotel, yet its deluxe facilities and great views make it good value. For some real old-fashioned hospitality, however, try the delightful and popular *Varosi*, in the eponymous district at Arh. Meletíou 45–47 (Ⓣ23810 21865, Ⓔhotelvarosi@yahoo.gr; ❹), run by charming owners, it boasts open fires, cosy en-suite rooms decorated in a vernacular style, and delicious complimentary breakfasts.

The Town

The most interesting neighbourhood in the town is the **Varósi**, tottering atop the cliffs just west of the waterfalls. Its mills and old Balkan-style houses, some decorously decaying, others tastefully renovated, reward aimless wanderings – though everything is well signposted. Some of the **water mills** have been renovated as part of a scheme to create a so-called open-air water museum, which also includes an unusual freshwater **aquarium** (Mon & Wed–Sun 10am–6pm; €2). Several churches and chapels, new and restored, are proudly signposted, but the only real sight as such is a delightful little **folklore museum** (Tues–Sun 10am–6pm; €1.50), on Megálou Alexándhrou, near Ayía Paraskeví church; it displays various household objects and other traditional items of the kind that would once have graced every home in the district.

Eating and drinking

The range of **restaurants** is relatively limited. The best three are *Peri Ousias,* at 18-Oktovríou 20, offering a decent range of starters, *mayireftá* and grills; *Stathmos*, right beside the train station, which has inexpensive meat, seafood and dips; and *Sokaki*, beside the first stream going north from the centre at Thessaloníkis 3, a cosy ouzerí with a fine range of *mezédhes*. Superbly sited among the woods, 2km out of town on the road to Aridhéa, the *Fysiolatrikos Omilos Edhessas*, or *FOE*, puts more effort into its decor than its food, but the latter is appetizingly presented and, with some adventurous Gallic touches, is a welcome change from the norm. Apart from these places, cheap *souvláki* joints abound.

Café and **bar** life is concentrated in the pedestrian zones flanking the rivulets, especially on Angelí Gátsou. Away from here, the municipal café-bar *Psilos Vrahos*, perched atop its namesake vantage point, is worth a visit for a beer or fruit juice. However, Édhessa's – and possibly the whole country's – most unusual entertainment venue is the dramatically sited *To Kanavouryio*, a recently converted hemp factory (complete with intact machinery dating from the early twentieth century) that doubles up as a café-bar-cum-restaurant and **live music** locale (jazz, rock and folk). Located at the foot of the cliffs, it can be reached by two giddying glass lifts accessible from a platform near Áyios Vassílis chapel at the edge of the Varósi district. Anyone whose nerves aren't up to it can reach it by descending the stepped path from the top.

West from Édhessa: Nymféo and the Préspa lakes

The highlights of the area to the west of Édhessa is the handsome mountain village of **Nymféo**, where some of the attractive stone houses have been converted into classy accommodations, and the bird-rich **Préspa lakes**, both of which nestle in a strategic spot where Greece, Albania and the FYROM meet. Flórina, the area's main urban centre, is rather charmless and not worth visiting. Getting around the area is really only viable if you have your own transport – one option might be to rent a car in Édhessa or Kastoriá (see p.445).

Nymféo

Perched at 1300m on the eastern flank of Mount Vítsi, some 85km southwest of Édhessa and 60km northeast of Kastoriá, lies the well-groomed mountain village of **NYMFÉO**, popular of late with prosperous young Greek professionals looking for alternative recreational activities in retreats far from the city. To get there take the poorly marked turn-off at the village of Aetós; you then climb up an incredibly steep side road with hairpin bends.

Facilities fall within the higher budget range. The least expensive **accommodation** is also the least attractive, although its rooms are fine: central *Xenonas Neveska* (Ⓣ23860 31442, Ⓦwww.neveska.gr; ❸). You can also find **rooms** at the *Ederne* which has self-catering facilities (Ⓣ23860 31230 or 23860 31351; ❹) and provides breakfast. The professionally run **inn** at the entrance to the village, *Ta Linouria* (Ⓣ23860 31030, Ⓕ23860 31133; ❻), offers attractively decorated suites and is also a reliable source of decent, if pricey, food; otherwise try one of the cheaper **tavernas** in the village centre. For a special occasion you might consider a night at ★ *La Moara* (Ⓣ2310 287 626, Ⓦwww.lamoara.gr; ❻), a luxurious mansion a short way uphill, where costs rise steeply at weekends. Run by nationally renowned wine-makers, the Boutari family, it offers refined cuisine, to match the cellar, while the rooms are tastefully appointed, with state-of-the-art bathrooms and top-quality linens and accessories.

The Préspa lakes

Climbing west out of the Aliákmonas valley on the serpentine paved side road towards **Préspa**, you have little hint of what's ahead until suddenly you top a pass, and a shimmering expanse of water riven by islets and ridges appears. It is not, at first glance, postcard-pretty, but the basin has an eerie beauty and a back-of-beyond quality that grows on you with further acquaintance. It also has a turbulent history that belies its current role as one of the Balkans' most important wildlife sanctuaries.

During the Byzantine era, Préspa became a prominent place of exile for troublesome noblemen, thus accounting for the surprising number of **ecclesiastical monuments** in this backwater. It was also the scene of vicious local battles during the 1947–49 Greek civil war, which led to mass emigration. It is only since the late 1970s that the villages, still comparatively primitive and neglected, have begun to refill during the summer for the bean and hay season. In 1988, a forest fire on the eastern ridge treated observers to a dangerous fireworks display, as dozens of unexploded artillery shells were touched off by the heat.

Mikrí Préspa, the southerly lake, is mostly shallow (9m maximum depth) and reedy, with a narrow fjord curling west and just penetrating Albanian territory. The borders of Greece, Albania and the FYROM meet in the middle of deeper **Megáli Préspa** and, since the early 1990s, Albanian refugees have used the basin as an exit corridor into Greece. Their presence as illegal agricultural workers is now tolerated, as farms in the area are perennially short-handed. The border here is extremely porous – though unofficial forays into Albania are emphatically not recommended – and a considerable amount of smuggling in duty-free goods goes on.

The core of the **national park**, established in 1971, barely encompasses Mikrí Préspa and its shores, but the peripheral zone extends well into the surrounding mountains, affording protection of sorts to a variety of land mammals. You'll almost certainly see foxes crossing the road, though the wolves and bears up on the ridges are considerably shyer. The lakes have a dozen resident fish species, including *tsiróni* – a sort of freshwater sardine – and *grivádhi*, a kind of carp. But it's **birdlife** for which the Préspa basin, particularly the smaller lake, is most famous. There are few birds of prey, but you should see a fair number of egrets, cormorants, crested grebes and pelicans (this being one of the few breeding sites of both the white and Dalmatian pelican), which nest in the spring, with the chicks out and about by summer. They feed partly on the large numbers of snakes, which include vipers, whip snakes and harmless water snakes which you may encounter while swimming. Observation towers are available at Vromolímni and near Áyios Ahíllios, but dawn spent anywhere at the edge of the reedbeds with a pair of binoculars will be immensely rewarding, though bear in mind that you are not allowed to boat or wade into the reeds. There are **park information centres** in the villages of **Áyios Yermanós** and **Psarádhes** (see p.444).

While you may arrive from Flórina by bus, you really can't hope to tour the area without some means of **transport** – either a mountain bike or a car. Similarly, in view of the area's past underdevelopment, don't expect much in the way of **facilities**: food is adequate and inexpensive, but exceedingly simple; the same might be said of local accommodation, though this has improved in recent years. Préspa is becoming increasingly popular, and you'd be wise to reserve at one of the few accommodations listed during midsummer, especially at weekends.

Mikrolímni

MIKROLÍMNI, 5km up a side road off the main route into the valley, would be your first conceivable stop. The small shop and fish taverna owned by Yiorgos Hassou, on the shoreside square, has a few **rooms** to let (Ⓣ23850 61221; ❶). In the evening, you can look towards sunsets over reedbeds and the snake-infested Vidhronísi (or Vitrinítsi) islet, though swimming isn't good here, or anywhere else on Mikrí Préspa for that matter.

Return to the main road, which reaches a T-junction 16km from the main Flórina–Kastoriá highway, on the spit which separates the larger and smaller lakes. It's probable that at one time there was just one lake here, but now there's a four-metre elevation difference. Bearing right at the junction leads within 4km to Áyios Yermanós; the left option splits again at the west end of the spit, bearing south towards the islet of Áyios Ahíllios or northwest towards the hamlet of Psarádhes.

Áyios Yermanós

ÁYIOS YERMANÓS is a large village of tile-roofed houses, overlooking a patch of Megáli Préspa in the distance. It's worth making the trip up just to see two tiny late-Byzantine churches, whose frescoes, dating from the time when the place belonged to the bishopric of Ohrid, display a marked Macedonian influence. Inside the lower church, **Áyios Athanásios**, seldom open, you can glimpse a dog-faced *St Christopher* among a line of saints opposite the door. Far more impressive, however, is the tiny, eleventh-century parish church of **Áyios Yermanós** up on the square, hidden behind a new monster awkwardly tacked onto it in 1882. The Byzantine structure has its own entrance, and the frescoes, skilfully retouched in 1743, can be lit; the switch is hidden in the narthex. There are more hagiographies and martyrdoms than possible to list here, but there's a complete catalogue of them (in Greek and English) by the door.

In the village is the helpful **Préspa information centre** (daily 9.30am–7.30pm, staff permitting; ⓣ23850 51211, ⓦwww.spp.gr), focusing on the wildlife of the national park; given sufficient warning, the centre can arrange guides for bird-watching trips into the park. It also sells locally farmed organic products. The village has a **post office** – the only one in the Préspa basin – and a few places to **stay**: *Xenonas Iy Paradosi*, opposite the church (ⓣ23850 51266; ❸), and, in the upper part of the village, the slightly better run *To Petrino* (ⓣ23850 51344; ❸). The best **taverna** is *Lefteris*, nearby; when it is closed you can fall back on *To Tzaki*, along from the church.

Koúla beach and Psarádhes

At the far end of the wide causeway dividing the two lakes, 4km from the T-junction, is **Koúla beach**, and a cluster of what passes for tourist development hereabouts: a patch of reed-free sand from where you can swim in Megáli Préspa; a free but basic camping area, now bereft of its water tap; plus an army post. Tents can also be pitched near *Plaz Prespon*, a run-of-the-mill taverna which nonetheless serves better food than *Iy Koula*, by the army post. Just below here, you can see where the waters of Mikrí Préspa trickle into Megáli Préspa.

If you don't intend to camp, it's best to bear right just above the army post, reaching after 6km of panoramic corniche the rickety village of **PSARÁDHES** (Nivitsa in Slav dialect), whose lanes make for a pleasant stroll. Unfortunately, the wonderful old houses lining them are increasingly derelict. Of the two **hotels** set back from the lakeside, *To Arhontiko* (ⓣ23850 46260; ❷) offers marginally better value. There are some **rooms** for rent, such as the spartanly furnished ones above the *Taverna Syndrofia* (ⓣ23850 46107; ❷), a good spot to sample *fassoládha* (bean soup), lake fish and the proprietor's wine. You won't find the fish fried here anywhere else in Greece; similarly, the cows ambling through the lakeside meadows are a locally adapted dwarf variety. Of the other **tavernas**, *Paradhosi* is the best of the bunch and the most reliably open. The *kafenío* on the inland platía has been refurbished as a bar-café, *Mythos*, which does creditable coffees; similarly, the waterfront has been paved and landscaped, with parking provided for tour coaches. It is sometimes possible to take a short **boat excursion** out onto the lake to see some of the lakeside monuments and churches, but this is not the best way to spot birdlife; there is no fixed schedule so ask around.

Áyios Ahíllios

If you keep straight at the end of the causeway, instead of turning right, the road soon brings you to a floating footbridge, 1500m in length, which leads across to the islet of **Áyios Ahíllios** and its impoverished, almost deserted hamlet. A five-minute walk from the footbridge is the ruined Byzantine basilica of **Áyios Ahíllios**, while another ruin, a sixteenth-century monastery, Panayía Porfaras, lies at the southern end of the islet. For unrivalled views of Mikrí Préspa climb up to the summit of the islet's hill. Should you want to **stay** the night or get some refreshment, you'll find **rooms**, a café and decent **taverna** at *Xenonas* (Ⓣ23850 46601; ❷), outwardly rather unprepossessing, but pleasant inside.

Kastoriá

Set on a hilly, wooded peninsula extending deep into a slate-coloured lake, **KASTORIÁ** is one of the most interesting and attractive towns of mainland Greece. It's also wealthy and has been so for centuries as the centre of south-eastern Europe's fur trade; although the local wild beavers (*kastóri* in Greek) had been trapped to extinction by the nineteenth century, Kastoriá still supports a considerable industry of furriers who make up coats, gloves and other items from fur scraps imported from Canada and Scandinavia and, increasingly, from the pelts of locally farmed beavers. Animal-rights activists will find the place heavy going as the industry is well-nigh ubiquitous: you'll see scraps drying on racks, and megastores with profuse Russian signposting line all the approach highways.

For most visitors, however, Kastoriá's main appeal lies in traces of its former prosperity: dozens of splendid *arhondiká* – **mansions** of the old fur families – dating from the seventeenth to nineteenth centuries, plus some fifty Byzantine and medieval **churches**, though only a handful are visitable and of compelling interest. About the only reminder of Muslim settlement is the minaret-less Koursoún Tzamí, marooned in a ridgetop car park; there's also a patch of an originally Byzantine-fortification wall down on the neck of the peninsula.

The town has a strong tradition of **rowing**, and rowers can be seen out on the lake most days. Even the Oxford and Cambridge Blues have been known to practise their strokes here. The less energetic might prefer to take one of the regular **boat trips** on the lake; they leave from the jetty near the fish market on the northern side of town (daily 6pm, plus Fri–Sun noon; €5; Ⓣ24670 26777).

Arrival and information

The **airport** is 10km south of town, and the Olympic Airways office, where airport buses also drop off, is at Megálou Alexándhrou 15. Arriving at the KTEL **bus station**, you'll find yourself at the western edge of the peninsula. Coming by **car**, beware of the fee-parking scheme in effect across much of the city centre, operated by ticket machines; only a couple of the more expensive hotels have free or off-street parking. Kastoriá has a locally based **car-rental** outfit, *Auto Kastoria*, at V Siózou 147 (Ⓣ24670 21440, Ⓦwww.autokastoria.gr). There is a helpful municipal **tourist kiosk** (daily 9am–9pm; Ⓣ24670 26777, Ⓦwww.kastoriacity.gr) in the lakeside park, 150m from KTEL.

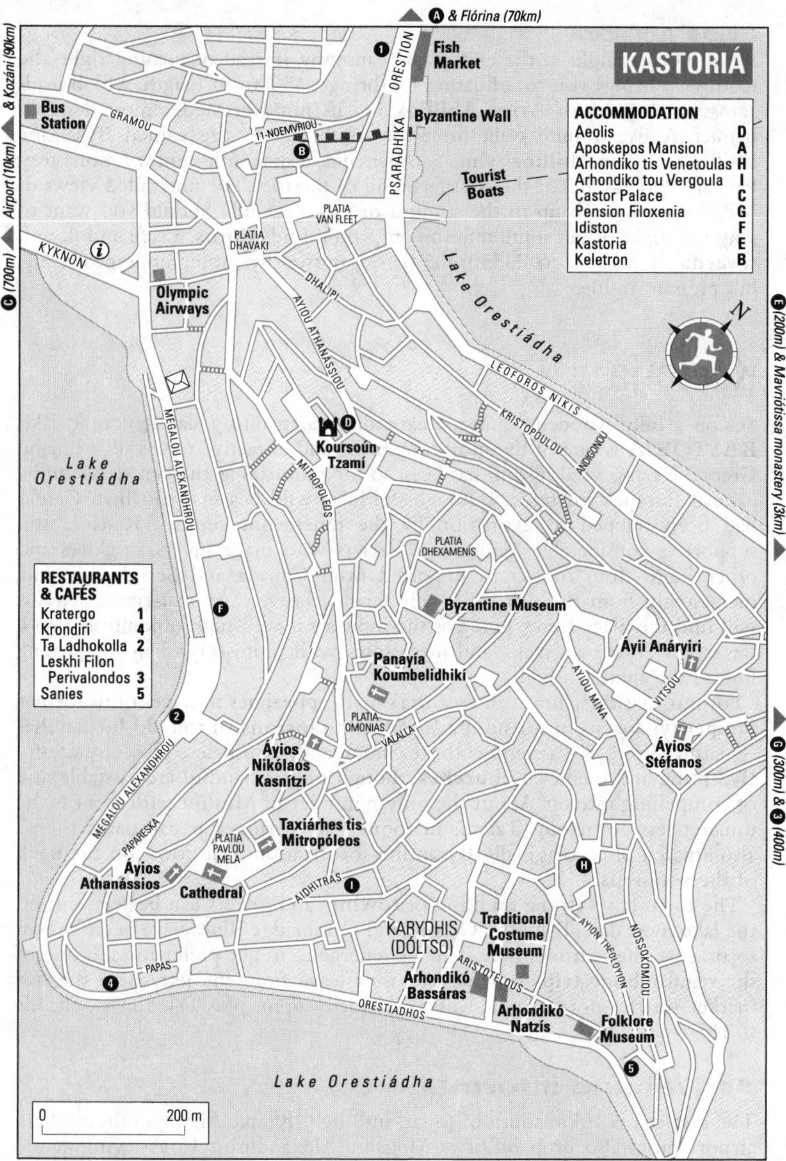

Accommodation

Many of Kastoriá's **hotels**, especially those within easy walking distance of the bus station, are rather noisy with prices above average. Advance booking is a good idea for weekends, although a string of identikit modern business hotels along the airport road takes care of the overspill.

Aeolis Ayíou Athanassíou 30 ⓣ24670 21070. Designer-magazine interiors, tip-top service and every comfort – minibar, hairdryer, hydro-massage – make this 1930s villa one of the town's leading hotels. A full breakfast is served in your room or in the smart dining room. B&B ⑤

Aposkepos Mansion Apóskepos, 4km northeast ⓣ24670 21480, ⓦwww.aposkepos.gr. Lovingly refurbished *arhondikó* in a peaceful mountain village with great views across the lake and city. Don't miss the home-made *tsípouro*. Pick-ups can be arranged. B&B ③

Arhondiko tis Venetoulas Ayíon Theolóyion 6 ⓣ22446, ⓦwww.venetula.gr. A mansion conversion oozing charm. Great location and friendly, attentive service though the rooms are tiny. B&B ④

Arhondiko tou Vergoula Aïdhítras 14 ⓣ24670 23416, Esfinas@otenet.gr. Kastoriá's leading boutique hotel, housed in a handsome mid-nineteenth-century mansion, is in a particularly quiet part of the Dóltso. Rooms with a view are heftily surcharged, but all are faultlessly done out in traditional yet comfortable style, albeit with midget bathrooms. The ground-floor wine bar, serving Greek vintages, is open for patrons and non-residents every Fri and Sat evening. B&B ⑤

Castor Palace Grámmou 237 ⓣ24670 82160, ⓕ24670 82161. The nearest airport road hotel to the town centre, bizarrely located near the lakefront overlooking a military camp. Impeccable rooms and extremely comfortable throughout. B&B ④

Pension Filoxenia Y Paleológou 23 ⓣ24670 22162, ⓦwww.filoxeniakastoria.gr. Beautifully located and decorated, this delightful place offers the best value in town. Rooms of varying sizes, the pricier ones with lake views. Extremely friendly and homely. ③

Idiston Megálou Alexándhrou 91 ⓣ24670 22250, ⓦwww.idiston.gr. Self-catering apartments in a prime location over one of the town's trendy bars, with lake views. Run by a returnee from Canada whose passion for his native town is contagious. Book well ahead. ⑤

Kastoria Leofóros Níkis 122 ⓣ24670 29453, ⓦwww.lake.gr. At the far end of the northern waterfront, the town's smartest hotel offers lake views from its balconied, air-conditioned front rooms, plus free parking. B&B ⑥

Keletron 11-Noemvríou 52 ⓣ24670 22676, ⓦwww.anastassia-hotels.gr. Recently spruced up hotel with its entrance on a side street and some rooms overlooking leafy Platía Van Fleet. B&B ④

The Town

For a sense of what Kastoriá must once have been during its heyday, head for the former lakeside quarter officially called **Karýdhis** but better known as Dóltso. At Kapetán Lázou 10, the splendidly opulent seventeenth-century Aïvazís family mansion has been turned into a **Folklore Museum** (Mon–Sat 9.30am–1pm & 4–7pm, Sun 11am–1pm & 4–7pm; €2). The house was inhabited until 1972 and its furnishings and most of its ceilings are in excellent repair, having miraculously survived German shelling; the Ottoman-style kiosk sports a set of stained-glass windows, three of them original, the others replaced by a local craftsman. Other features are an oriental fireplace in the master bedroom and the kitchen with all the original pots and pans. Other notable mansions nearby are **Bassáras** and **Natzís**, close together on Vyzandíon; the latter was admirably restored in the 1990s. A third, also close by, on Platía Dóltso, now houses the **Traditional Costume Museum** (open by appointment; free; ⓣ24670 22697), a magical display of traditional clothing from western Macedonia and a chance to see another magnificent interior.

The **Byzantine Museum** (Tues–Sun 8.30am–3pm; free), up on Platía Dhexaménís, wisely goes for quality over quantity in this well-lit if unimaginatively displayed collection spanning the twelfth to the sixteenth centuries. Highlights include an unusually expressive thirteenth-century icon of Áyios Nikólaos and a fourteenth-century Ayii Anaryiri, plus a later one depicting the life of St George. There are also a few double-sided icons, including a rare *Deposition*, intended for use in religious processions. Captions are in Greek only.

Kastoriá's churches

The excellent frescoes of the twelfth-century church of **Áyios Nikólaos Kasnítzi** were returned to their former glory during the late 1980s. The unusual epithet stems from the donor, who is shown with his wife on the narthex wall presenting a model of the church to Christ. Lower down are ranks of exclusively female saints, to console the women congregated in the narthex which long served as a women's gallery. High up on the west wall of the nave, the *Dormition* and the *Transfiguration* are in good condition, the former inexplicably backwards (the Virgin's head is usually to the left). **Taxiárhes tís Mitropóleos**, the oldest (ninth-century) church, was built on the foundations of an earlier pagan temple, of which recycled columns and capitals are visible. Its more prominent frescoes, such as that of the *Virgin Platytera and Adoring Archangels* in the conch of the apse, and a conventional *Dormition* on the west wall, are fourteenth century. In the north aisle is the tomb of Greek nationalist Pavlos Melas, assassinated by Bulgarians at a nearby village in 1906, and commemorated by street names across northern Greece; his widow, who survived to the age of 101 (she died in 1974), is interred with him. Lastly, the **Panayía Koumbelidhikí**, so named because of its unusual dome (*kübe* in Turkish), retains one startling and well-illuminated fresco: a portrayal – almost unique in Greece – of God the Father in a ceiling mural of the *Holy Trinity*. The building was constructed in stages, with the apse completed in the tenth century and the narthex in the fifteenth. The cylindrical dome was meticulously restored after being destroyed by Italian bombing in 1940.

If tracking down churches seems too much like hard work, one of the most pleasant things to do in Kastoriá is to follow the narrow road along the tree-lined water's edge all around the **peninsula** to the east of town; at the tip vehicles must circulate anticlockwise, but the route is mainly used by joggers and the odd walker. Although the lake itself is visibly polluted, wildlife still abounds – pelicans, swans, frogs, tortoises and water snakes especially, and on a spring day numerous fish break water. Near the southeastern tip of the peninsula, some 3km along from the *Hotel Kastoria*, stands the **Mavriótissa monastery**, flanked by peacocks and a fair-value restaurant. Two churches are all that remains of the monastery: a smaller fourteenth-century chapel, with fine frescoes of scenes from Christ's life, abutting the larger, wood-roofed eleventh-century *katholikón* on whose outer wall looms a well-preserved *Tree of Jesse*, showing the genealogy of the Saviour.

On the southern shore of the lake, 5km from Kastoriá in the village of Dhispílio, lie the remains of a fascinating **prehistoric lake settlement**, which is thought to date from around 5500–5000 BC during the Neolithic Period. First excavated in 1992, finds include a range of household goods and a wooden tablet, inscribed with an early linear script. A modern recreation of the original huts and eco-museum (daily 9am–2pm & 5–8pm; €3) help bring to life what the area must have looked like in these distant times.

Eating and drinking

Though not renowned for its quality **restaurants**, Kastoriá has enough decent places to eat. *Kratergo*, one road back from the lake at Orestíon 19, is a trendy ouzerí featuring specialities such as aubergines stuffed with bacon and cheese. Lakeside dining is unsurprisingly popular: a couple of stylish tavernas are located on Orestiádhos: the *Krondiri* at no. 13, which serves the town's best food, specializes in fancy *mezédhes*, gratins and "soufflés" in attractive clay pots, and has tables on the lake bank. Further along at no. 79 *Sanies* is somewhat less sophisticated, but still offers tasty fish, such as trout, meat and salads. *Ta Ladhokolla*, which serves meat and fish dishes on greaseproof paper, is the best of the eateries lining the Megálou Aléxandhrou lakefront. **Cafés and bars** are also mostly to be found at the water's edge: there are some near the fish market and more stylish ones on the southwestern side of the promontory. A panoramic alternative is the smart new *Leskhi Filon Perivalondos*, commanding fine views of the northeastern lakeshore from its vantage point up near Profitis Ilías.

Halkidhikí: Kassándhra, Sithonía and Mount Athos

Halkidhikí (Ⓦwww.halkidiki.com) begins at a perforated edge of shallow lakes east of Thessaloníki, then extends into three prongs of land – Kassándhra, Sithonía and Athos – trailing like tentacles into the Aegean Sea. **Kassándhra** and **Sithonía** host some of the busiest holiday resorts in Greece. Large signs at the entrance to both peninsulas remind you that camping outside authorized sites is strictly prohibited. You should have no trouble getting accommodation outside the busy midsummer period, though places start closing down in September and few hotels, rooms or campsites remain open between October and April. The beaches themselves consist of white sand, ranging in consistency from powder to coarse-grained.

Both Kassándhra and Sithonía are connected to Thessaloníki by a four-lane expressway which ends at **Néa Moudhaniá**, a dull town and minor passenger port, from where a network of fast two-lane roads extends around their coastlines. Buses run frequently to all the larger resorts. In spite of this, neither peninsula is that easy to travel around if you are dependent on **public transport**. You really have to pick a place and stay there, perhaps renting a **motorbike** or **car** for excursions.

Mount Athos, the easternmost peninsula, is in all ways separate, a "Holy Mountain", whose monastic population, semi-autonomous within the Greek state, **excludes all females** – even as visitors. The most that women can do is to glimpse the buildings from offshore cruise *kaïkia* sailing from the two small resorts on the periphery of the peninsula – Ierissós and Ouranoúpoli – on the "secular" part of the Athos peninsula.

Kassándhra

Vaguely boot-shaped **Kassándhra**, the nearest of Halkidhikí's three peninsulas to Thessaloníki, is also by far the most developed and its appearance has been done no favours by the extensive 2006 fires that decimated almost the entire forest once covering the central section of its spine. Most of the attractive inland villages date from the mid-nineteenth century, as the earlier ones were left deserted after their inhabitants were massacred during the 1821 War of Independence. On the coast, there were only a few small fishing hamlets here until after 1923, when the peninsula was resettled by refugees from around the Sea of Marmara – these have since burgeoned into holiday venues. Many travellers choose to bypass Kassándhra and keep going to Sithonía or the top end of Athos.

Néa Fókea and Sáni

Bypassing the eyesore of Néa Potídhea, some 6km beyond Néa Moudhaniá and across the ancient canal, the first place you might consider stopping at is **NÉA FÓKEA,** a modest place consisting mostly of holiday apartments for Greeks, rendered picturesque by a Byzantine watchtower on a grassy headland. There are several fish **tavernas**, the best being *Pasarotaverna Seryiani,* in the delightful

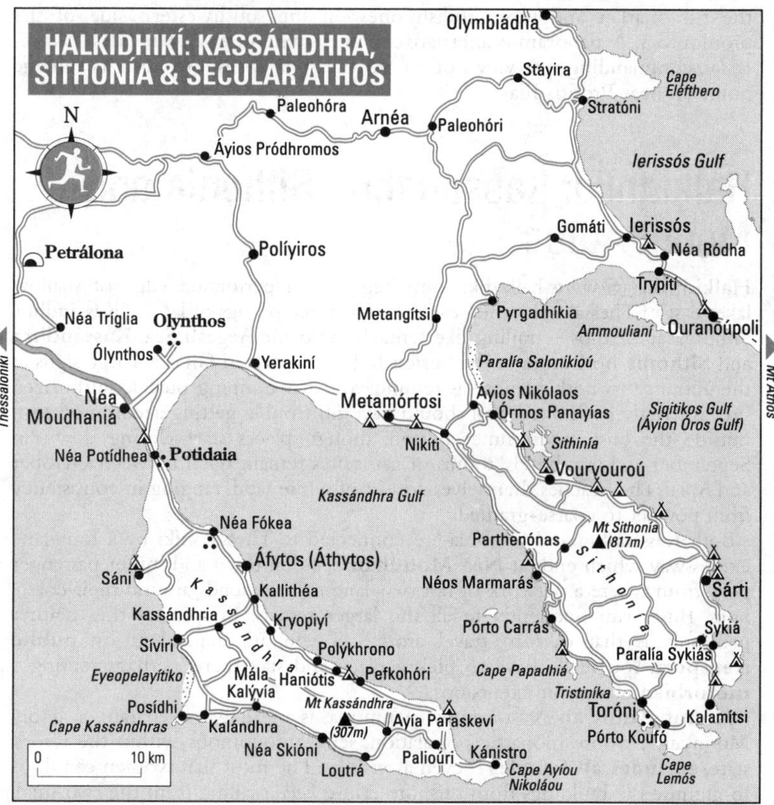

little harbour, from where a long beach heads north under cliffs, improving as you distance yourself from the tower.

Just north of Néa Fókea, an eight-kilometre paved side road takes you westwards through bucolic countryside to **SÁNI** on the west coast, where you'll find the municipally run *Blue Dream* **campsite** (☎23740 31435; May–Sept), plus a British-operated manicured marina, full of boutiques and chic restaurants such as *Domata*, with an expensive but imaginative menu aimed at the yachters who moor their luxury vessels here. Sáni is also noted for its summer **festival**, which boasts a cosmopolitan billing of world music, salsa, jazz and cutting-edge Greek stars. This takes place up by another quaint Byzantine watchtower on the headland.

Áfytos

Some 5km south of Néa Fókea, you reach the turning east for **ÁFYTOS** (or Áthytos), by far the most attractive spot on Kassándhra. This large village of tile-roofed traditional houses spreads over a series of ravines furrowing the bluff here, which ends in a sharp drop to the sea. Near the cliff bottom, a series of springs bubbles from a rock overhang, nurturing a little oasis – doubtless a spur in the founding of Aphytis, the village's ancient predecessor. Both beaches (turn left for Paralía Várkes, right for Paralía Moudhoúnou) are marred by rock sills with lots of sea urchins. On the square, the focus of a mesh of slightly twee cobbled lanes closed to traffic for the nightly promenade, stands a handsome church in post-Byzantine style, dating only from 1850 but seeming much older.

Independent travellers have a choice of **rooms**, set in the lanes towards the cliff edge, such as *Apollo* (Ⓣ23740 91267; ❸). For a bona-fide **hotel**, try the charming *Stamos* (Ⓣ23740 91520, Ⓕ23740 91234; ❺) on the minor road leading to the cliff edge; it has a flowery courtyard and pool, and its studios for three or four make it good for families. Down on Paralía Várkes, the plush *Hotel Afitis* (Ⓣ23740 91233, Ⓦwww.afitis-hotel.gr; ❼) offers splendid facilities but lacks character.

Eating out is best at no-nonsense *To Steki*, just off the main drag, which offers reliable fare and excellent wines. Just further inland, the *Toroneos* ouzerí serves good *mezédhes*. Down at the start of Paralía Várkes, *Anthoula's* is the best seaside eating option. **Nightlife** is fairly lively, with Greek musicians often playing the bars at summer weekends, sometimes under the aegis of the **Kassándhra Festival** which Áfytos shares with Síviri: performances include blues, soul, classical and traditional Greek music.

From Kallithéa to Palioúri

KALLITHÉA, 4km to the south and a complete contrast to Áfytos, is useful only for its **ATMs** and **car, motorbike and windsurfer rental**. At **KRYOPIYÍ**, just under 6km further, most of the development is concentrated along the steep roads that cascade down to the water, where there's a beach, but Kryopiyí has managed to preserve its old village core up the hill, on the land side of the main road. By the somewhat gentrified square are a couple of **tavernas**: the *Iy Platia Tis Anthoulas* has a slight edge over the *Anoyi*.

Beyond Kryopiyí, you head towards the "toe" of the Kassandhrian boot via a trio of tacky and missable coastal resorts – Polýkhrono, Haniótis and Pefkohóri. Just before you reach the scenic and deserted bay of **Khroussoú**, *Paliouri Camping* (Ⓣ23740 92169) is an organised and shady spot for your tent. From here, rather than continuing to the disappointing "toe"-cape at Kánistro, you're better off heading west and inland along the main road to the rambling ridge-top village of **PALIOÚRI**. Although there is not much accommodation, there are a couple of authentic tavernas on the square – try the excellent home cooking at *O Yiannakos*.

Kassándhra's southwestern shore

The southwestern shore of Kassándhra is, in general, developed more for Greek weekenders. Some 6km beyond hilltop Palioúri lies **AYÍA PARASKEVÍ**, a delightful village with sea views and a pair of simple **restaurants**, of which *Khristoforos Psistaria* is the better. A little way beyond it you emerge on the coast at the **Loutrá Ayías Paraskevís**, where a popular **spa** complex (Ⓣ23740 71810) contains a hot sulphurous pool and offers various treatments from €6. **NÉA SKIÓNI**, 4km northwest, can be a decent base, with its good clean beach and appealing seafront. The string of tavernas is supplied by a tiny fleet in the fishing port: seafront *Yiorgos*, opposite the jetty entrance, attracts most foreigners, while Greeks rave about the traditional cuisine at *Iy Mouria*, a couple of blocks inland. Amongst the **places to stay** are the smart *Irida Apartments* (Ⓣ23740 71211; ❸).

Tucked on the cape beyond droll Mála Kalýva is **Posídhi**, whose harbour has a trio of tavernas; *Kyparissis* (Ⓣ23740 42264; ❷), which also has a few rooms, is by far the friendliest and best. At the far end of the **beach**, beyond the lively

Bouda beach bar, the rock reef abates and you can skinny-dip from the tapering sand spit. On the opposite side of the promontory, the splendid beach of **Eyeopelayítiko** is one of the finest on the whole peninsula, with the seasonal *Oramabar* providing refreshments. From here you can return to the main road and complete the clockwise coastal circuit, happily ignoring the unappealing resort of Síviri.

Sithonía

As you move east across Halkidhikí and away from the frontline of tourism, the landscape becomes increasingly green and hilly, culminating in the isolated and spectacular scenery of the Holy Mountain, looming across the gulf. The **Sithonía** peninsula is more rugged but better cultivated than Kassándhra, though here there are even fewer true villages, mostly dating from the 1920s resettlement era. Pine forests cover many of the slopes, particularly in the south, giving way to olive groves on the coast. Small sandy inlets with relatively discreet pockets of campsites and tavernas make a welcome change.

If you're travelling under your own steam, some 6km past the last motorway exit at Néa Moudhaniá en route to Sithonía, it's worth making the slight detour to splendidly located **ancient Olynthos** (daily: summer 8am–7.30pm, winter closes 3pm; €3), atop a hill offering mountain and sea views. This is a rare example of an unmodified Classical town laid out to the geometric grid plan of Hippodamus – the fifth-century BC architect who designed Pireás and Rhodes. There's an initially off-putting walk of 700m, partly up a slope, from the ticket booth, but well-excavated streets, houses and even some mosaics to see once you arrive, most notably one of Bellerophon riding Pegasus and killing the Chimaira. Like the new, informative museum near the entrance, everything is clearly labelled in Greek and English. The modern village of **ÓLYNTHOS**, 1km west across the riverbed here, has **food** and a **hotel**, the central *Olynthos* ⓣ23790 91666, ⓦwww.olynthoshotel.gr; B&B ❸).

Moving on to Sithonía proper, which begins shortly after the unspectacular resort of Metamórfosi, it's best to follow the loop road clockwise around the east coast, so that the peak of Athos is always before you. **Bus services** are sparse: depending on the season, there are up to five daily around the west coast to Sárti, and up to three a day direct to Vourvouroú, but just a single daily KTEL connection, in August only, between these two endpoints. A complete circuit is only really feasible with your own transport.

Órmos Panayías and Vourvouroú

ÓRMOS PANAYÍAS, first of the east-coast resorts, is heavily developed; ranks of villas dwarf the picturesque hamlet and tiny harbour, and the nearest decent beaches lie 4km north en route to Pyrgadhíkia, below the inland village of Áyios Nikólaos, whose square is a traffic-free haven for diners and drinkers. The only real reason to stop at Órmos would be to catch one of the excursion boats that sail around Athos from here, but these are better value from Ouranoúpoli (see p.456).

VOURVOUROÚ, 8km down the coast from Órmos, is not a typical resort, since it's essentially a vacation-villa project for Thessaloníki professors, established in the late 1950s on land expropriated from Vatopedhíou monastery on Athos. Even so, there is a fair amount of short-term **accommodation**: along with a number of rooms, there's the seafront hotel *Diaporos* (ⓣ23750 91313; ❹), with its rooftop restaurant, and the plain but en-suite *Vourvourou* (ⓣ23750 91261; ❸), plus the ecologically minded, high-luxury *Ekies Manor House* (ⓣ2810 300330; ❼), well located on the sea-edge, with its designer rooms, gourmet restaurant and enticing pool. Islets astride the mouth of the bay make for a fine setting, but the beach, while sandy, is extremely narrow, and Vourvouroú is really more of a yachters' haven. **Tavernas** are relatively inexpensive; the *Itamos*, inland from the road, is the best; the *Gorgona/Pullman*, while enjoying the prettiest waterfront location, gets coach tours as the alias implies. There is a **campsite**: *Dionysos* (Ⓣ23750 91214; April–Oct), part of which faces the beach.

Some of Sithonía's best **beaches** lie off the 30km of corniche road between Vourvouroú and the ugly touristic sprawl of Sárti: five signposted sandy coves, each with a **campsite** and little else. The names of the bays, such as Koutloumousíou or Zográfou, reflect the fact that most of the land here belonged to various Athonite monasteries until confiscated by the Greek government to resettle Anatolian refugees. The eponymous campsite (Ⓣ23750 91487; Ⓦwww.armenistis.com.gr) at **Armenistis** is the best developed and a major hangout for ravers from Thessaloníki. A short way beyond, a dirt track leads down to a pair of idyllic coves, almost tropical in appearance.

Paralía Sykiás and Kalamítsi

PARALÍA SYKIÁS, 8km past Sárti, is a well-appointed beach, with just a few tavernas well back from the sea along 2km of coastal highway. At the north end of the beach a **campsite**, *Melissi* (Ⓣ23750 41631), shelters in some trees. The best strategy here is to follow the side road at the south end of the beach towards the more scenic coves and smattering of restaurants at **Pigadháki** or **Paleó Fánaro**, where you can eat fish straight from the nets of the *Koralis* taverna. For a **post office** and shops head for **SYKIÁ**, 2km inland, hemmed in by a bowl of rocky hills; while here, pop into the *Mimosa* taverna for homegrown salads and wild *krítoma* leafs.

KALAMÍTSI, another 8km south of Paralía Sykiás, consists of a beautiful double bay, now sadly becoming commercialized. At the sheltered north bay of Pórto, there are two **campsites**; the highly-developed *Porto Kalamitsi* (Ⓣ23750 41346, Ⓦwww.kalamitsi.com) includes the Dolphin Dive Centre and a decent restaurant. *O Yiorgakis* taverna, next door, offers varied, reasonably priced food, and good **rooms** behind (Ⓣ23750 41338; ❸). The small strand just out front can get cramped in summer, at which time you can easily swim out to the main islet for less company or head over the rocks to the north, where there's an informal nudist beach.

Pórto Koufó, Toróni and Tristiníka

The forest cover gets progressively thinner the further south you go from Sárti, until you reach the recently replanted tip of the peninsula, where the hills spill into the sea to create a handful of deep bays. **PÓRTO KOUFÓ**, just northwest of the cape, is the most dramatic of these, almost completely cut off from the open sea by high cliffs. The name Koufó ("deaf" in Greek) is said to come from one's inability to hear the sea within the confines of this inlet, which served as an Axis submarine shelter during World War II. There's a half-decent beach near where the road drops down from the east, as well as several pricey **hotels** and a few **rooms**. The north end of the inlet, 1km from the beach area, is a yacht and fishing harbour with a string of somewhat expensive seafood **tavernas**.

TORÓNI, 3km north, is the antithesis of this, an exposed, two-kilometre-long crescent of sand with wooded hills behind. It's probably your best Sithonian bet as a base if you just want to flop on a beach for a few days; for more stimulation there is a minimal **archeological site** on the southern cape, sporting the remains of a Byzantine fortress, while nearby is an early Christian basilica. There are lots of apartments here for Greek weekenders and at least half a dozen combination **taverna-studio/rooms** are scattered the length of the beach, among them *Haus Sakis* (Ⓣ23750 51261; ❸), at the northernmost end, with comfortable rooms upstairs and good food plus German beer on tap below.

Just 2km north is the turning for less-developed **Tristiníka**, with another outstanding two-kilometre beach, reached by a recently asphalted road. Two noteworthy tavernas here, *Sotiris* and *Dimitris*, both serve good food but whereas the former's owner is apt to play loud music and dance wildly, the latter is better for tranquility and home-cooking. At the south end of the sand, served by its own access drive, is *Camping Isa* (Ⓣ23750 51235).

Some 5km further north along the coastal route, there's a turning for the recommended, friendly *Camping Areti* (Ⓣ23750 71430, Ⓕ23750 71573), nestled between Cape Papadhiá and Lakithos hamlet, with views of three islets over its private beach. Besides tent space in well-landscaped olive groves, there are also wood chalets (❸) with all amenities.

Pórto Carrás to Nikíti

Beyond Tristiníka, you edge back into high-tech-resort territory, epitomized by Greece's largest planned holiday complex, **Pórto Carrás** (Ⓦwww.portocarras.com), comprising four upmarket hotels that range from mock-Byzantine to futuristic and 3-star to luxury. Established by the Carras wine and shipping dynasty, it features an in-house shopping centre, golf course and vineyards, while from the expansive private beach in front, you can indulge in every imaginable watersport. However, both more affordable and desirable is the *Kelyfos* **hotel** (Ⓣ23750 72833, Ⓕ23750 72247, Ⓦwww.kelyfos.gr; ❻), 1km north of the Pórto Carrás turn-off and impressively located on a hilltop; the smart, new rooms have sea views and all mod cons.

The nearest proper town to all this, with **banks** (ATMs), **tavernas** and a **post office**, is **NÉOS MARMARÁS**, a little fishing port with a small beach. Nowadays, it's popular with Greeks who stay in a score of modest hotels and apartments. Some 3km to the north, there is a decent **campsite**, the *Castello* (Ⓣ23750 71095) – at which point the beach is sandy, and there's tennis, volleyball and a restaurant. Exceptionally good kebabs are carved at *Fast Food O Dhimitris*, between the church and the bus stop.

A visit to **PARTHENÓNAS**, the lone traditional village on Sithonía, will give you some idea of what Sithonía must have looked like before the developers moved in. Crouched at the base of 808-metre Mount Ítamos, it's 5km up from Néos Marmarás and reached via a good road lined with pine and olive groves. Parthenónas was abandoned in the 1960s in favour of the shore, and never even provided with mains electricity; its appealing houses have now largely been restored into chic residences. The *Pension Parthenon* (Ⓣ23750 72225; ❹) in a fine stone house on high ground offers some of the peninsula's most charming accommodation. *To Steki tou Meniou* serves very basic fare in a pleasant hut, but don't go out of your way.

The clockwise loop is completed back at the neck of the peninsula in the pleasant resort of **NIKÍTI**, which can of course be used as a reasonable first base. Although there is nothing too spectacular about the seafront here, the old village on the inland side of the main road is full of venerable old stone houses and contains a couple of local tavernas. Just back from the seafront, the *Ta Tria Skalopatia* taverna has partial sea views from its patio and is better value than the ones right by the sea. If you decide to stay, there is a useful signboard up by the harbour with all the numbers for local **rooms**; it is in Greek only, which attests to the fact that the place is far more popular with holidaying Greeks. For a real pampering, one of the most exclusive hotels in Greece, the *Danai Beach Resort* (Ⓣ23750 20400, Ⓦwww.dbr.gr; ⑧) occupies a secluded patch of coast only 4km northwest. At the opposite end of the tourist spectrum, well-shaded *Camping Mylos* (Ⓣ23750 22041) lies just beyond it.

East to secular Athos

From Órmos Panayías a road winds around the coast and up over a ridge to the head of the Athos peninsula. The principal place you'd think to stop is **PYRGADHÍKIA**, a ravine-set fishing village jutting out into the Sigitikós gulf. It can offer no more than a few basic, unenticingly placed **hotels**, but you still might lunch here at one of the waterfront **tavernas**. There's little beach to speak of, although there are some good ones dotted along the stretch leading towards it. From Pyrgadhíkia the main road heads back inland, while a turn-off via Gomáti takes you through unspoilt moors to Ierissós at the neck of the Athos peninsula. This route has no public transport links, however; to travel between Sithonía and Athos by bus you will have to backtrack via Halkidhikí's inland capital, **Políyiros**.

Ierissós and Néa Ródha

With its good, long beach and a vast, promontory-flanked gulf, **IERISSÓS** is the most Greek-patronized of the secular Athos resorts, although the sizeable town itself, built well back from the shore and with room to expand, is a sterile concrete grid dating from after a devastating 1932 earthquake. The only hint of pre-touristic life is the vast boat-building area on the sand, at the back of the wide beach to the south.

There are a number of inexpensive **hotels** – try the friendly en-suite *Marcos* (Ⓣ23770 22518; ②), overlooking its own garden and car park at the south end of town, as well as numerous **rooms for rent**, such as pleasant *Aliki* (Ⓣ23770 22363; ③), on the northern seafront. A basic municipal **campsite** is situated still further north along the shore, while the more developed *Delfini* (Ⓣ23770 22208) lies en route to Néa Ródha. The beach is surprisingly uncluttered with just a handful of **cafés and tavernas** behind the landscaped promenade, such as the seasonal *To Kolatsi*. The best of several joints on the main drag linking the beach to the town centre is *To Steki Tis Afrodhitis*, which serves decent *mezédhes*. Rounding off the list of amenities, there's a **post office**, two **banks** and a summer **cinema** by the campsite. Ierissós is also the main **port** for the northeast shore of Athos; see p.459 for details.

The road beyond Ierissós passes through mundane **Néa Ródha** before veering inland to follow a boggy depression that is the remaining stretch of **Xerxes' canal**, cut by the Persian invader in 480 BC to spare his fleet the shipwreck at the tip of Athos that had befallen the previous expedition eleven years before.

Ammouliani

You emerge on the southwest-facing coast at **Trypití**, not a settlement but merely the western exit of Xerxes' canal and also the ferry jetty for the small island of **AMMOULIANÍ** (15min; at least 7 daily crossings in summer, fewer off season; €1, car €8). This is Macedonia's only inhabited Aegean island apart from Thássos, and after decades of eking out an existence from fishing, the island's population, originally refugees from the Sea of Marmara, has in recent years had to adjust to an influx of holiday-makers. Like anywhere else in Halkidhikí, it's impossibly oversubscribed in July and August, but in spring or autumn this low-lying, scrub- and olive-covered islet can make an idyllic hideaway.

The only town, where the ferries dock, is another unprepossessing grid of concrete slung over a ridge, with few pre-1960s buildings remaining; it is, however, chock-a-block with **rooms**, many self-catering – try welcoming *Philippos* (Ⓣ23770 51326; ❸) – and there are two **hotels** plainly visible on the left as you sail in. The better of these is the *Sunrise* (Ⓣ23770 51273, Ⓕ23770 51174; ❸), with its own swimming jetty. Of the village's half-dozen **tavernas**, *Glaros* (on the front), *Iy Klimataria* (on the road out) and *Janis* (facing the rear Limanáki port) are all good choices. There are a few shops for self-caterers, but no bank or post office. As for **nightlife**, you've got several bars (one, *Barko*, does breakfasts) and two discos a few hundred metres out of town on the main island road.

Two kilometres southwest of the town is **Alykés**, the islet's most famous beach, named after the salt-marsh just behind it, with the *Afrodite* taverna and *Savana* beach bar, and the rather parched eponymous campsite. Ammouliani's best beaches however, lie in the far southeast, facing the straits with the Athos peninsula. To reach them, bear left onto the newly-paved road 1500m out of town and follow the signs some 2km along this to **Áyios Yeóryios**, whose tiny **chapel** overlooks the excellent beach. Just beyond stands the popular lunchtime-only *Sarandis* taverna, but it's pricier than the exceedingly simple fare warrants, and you might prefer to continue to the far end of the beach to the better-value *Gripos Ouzeri*; this also offers a few rooms of considerable charm (Ⓣ23770 51049; ❸), with copper antiques, beam ceilings, terracotta floor tiles, large balconies and a swimming pool in the garden. The affable owner keeps pheasants and other exotic fowl, whose squawkings vie with those of the gulls nesting on the rock islets of the Dhrénia archipelago just offshore. You can continue a final 500m to the even more enticing **Megáli Ámmos** beach, where the *Island* beach bar has seats in the sand and blaring music, the *Megali Ammos* taverna serves fresh fish and there's a pleasant, olive-shaded campsite. Still other, less accessible, beaches beckon in the northwest of the island, served in season by excursion boats from the town; a popular map-postcard on sale will give necessary hints on how to reach them on foot or by bicycle.

Ouranoúpoli

Fifteen kilometres beyond Ierissós, **OURANOÚPOLI** is the last community before the restricted monastic domains, with a centre that's downright tatty, showing the effects of too much tourism. Somewhat mysteriously, it has become a major resort aside from its function as the main gateway to Mount Athos; local beaches, stretching intermittently for several kilometres to the north, are sandy enough but narrow and cramped. If you're compelled to stay the night while waiting for passage to Athos, the best temporary escape would be either to take a cruise, or to **rent a motor boat**, to the mini-archipelago of **Dhrénia** just opposite, with almost tropical sandy bays and tavernas on the larger islets. Modern craft also offer three-hour **cruises** (from €15 a head, depending on the season; hours vary), which skim along the Athonite coast, keeping their contaminating female presence 500m offshore as required by the monastic authorities. For **ferries** to Mount Athos itself see p.459.

If you need to **stay** – and proprietors are fairly used to one-night stays, en route to or from Athos – there are a fair number of rooms and a similar quantity of hotels, virtually all of them en suite. Less expensive ones include the *Diana* (Ⓣ23770 71052; ❷) on the road leading down from the pilgrims' office. On the southerly seafront there's the *Akroyali* (Ⓣ23770 71201, Ⓕ23770 71395; ❹), while less than 500m north along the beach the totally refurbished *Xenia* (Ⓣ23770 71412, Ⓦwww.papcorp.gr; ❼), is the area's swishest hotel, with decent off-season deals. A **campsite**, better appointed than those in Ierissós, lies 2km north of the village, amidst more luxury hotel complexes. Best value of the half-dozen waterfront **tavernas** is *Sorokadha*, which offers meat dishes for €4. On the south waterfront there are a couple of reasonable alternatives: *T'Apostoli To Koutouki*, which has both grilled and oven dishes, and further on, atop a low-lying cliff, the fancier *Athos*, with a huge menu featuring grilled fish, vegetables, soups and sweets. Ouranoúpoli has a **post office**, but no bank.

Mount Athos: the monks' republic

The population of the **Mount Athos** peninsula has been exclusively male – farm animals included – since the *ávaton* edict banning females, permanent or transient, was promulgated by the Byzantine emperor Constantine Monomachos in 1060. Known in Greek as the **Áyion Óros** (Holy Mountain), it is an administratively autonomous province of the country – a "monks' republic" – on whose slopes are gathered twenty monasteries, plus a number of smaller dependencies and hermitages.

Most of the **monasteries** were founded in the tenth and eleventh centuries; today, all survive in a state of comparative decline but they remain unsurpassed in their general and architectural interest, and for the art treasures they contain. If you are male, over 18 years old and have a genuine interest in monasticism or Greek Orthodoxy, sacred music or simply in Byzantine and medieval architecture, a visit is strongly recommended; this can be easily arranged in Thessaloníki (see box, p.459), but requires advance planning. In addition to the religious and architectural aspects of Athos, it should be added that the peninsula remains one of the most beautiful parts of Greece. For many visitors, this – as much as the experience of monasticism – is the highlight of time spent on the Holy Mountain.

Some history

By a legislative decree of 1926, Athos has the status of **Theocratic Republic**. It is governed from the small town and capital of Karyés by the Ayía Epistasía (Holy Superintendency), a council of twenty representatives elected for one-year terms by each of the monasteries. At the same time Athos remains a part of Greece; all foreign monks must adopt Greek citizenship and the Greek civil government is represented by an appointed governor and a small police force.

The **development of monasticism** on Athos is a matter of some controversy, and foundation legends abound. The most popular asserts that the Virgin Mary was blown ashore here on her way to Cyprus. The earliest historical reference to Athonite monks is to their attendance at a council of the Empress Theodora in 843; probably there were some monks here by the end of the seventh century. The most famous of the **early monks** were Peter the Athonite and St Euthymios of Salonica, both of whom lived in cave-hermitages on the slopes during the mid-ninth century. In 885 an edict of Emperor Basil I recognized Athos as the sole preserve of monks, and gradually hermits came together to form communities known in church Greek as *koinobia* (literally "common life"). The year 963 is the traditional date for the **foundation of the first monastery**, Meyístis Lávras, by Athanasios the Athonite, largely financed by Emperor Nikiforos Fokas. Over the next two centuries foundations were frequent, the monasteries reaching forty in number, alongside many smaller communities.

Troubles for Athos began at the end of the eleventh century. The monasteries suffered sporadically from pirate raids and from the settlement of three hundred Vlach shepherd families on the mountain. After a reputedly scandalous episode between the monks and the shepherdesses, the Vlachs were ejected and a new imperial *chryssobull* (golden edict) was issued, confirming that no female

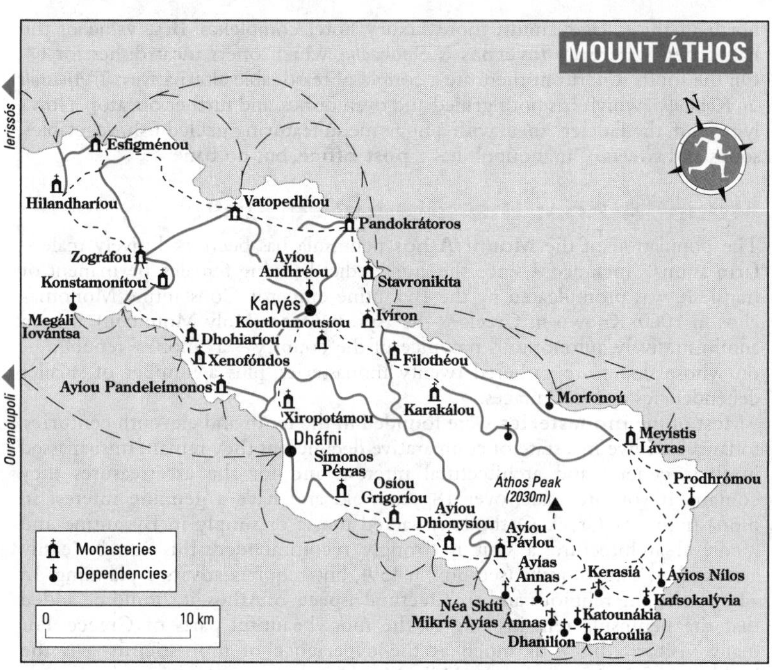

mammal, human or animal, be allowed to set foot on Athos. This edict, called the *ávaton*, remains in force today, excepting various cats to control rodents.

During the twelfth century, the monasteries gained an international – or at least, a **pan-Orthodox** – aspect, as Romanian, Russian and Serbian monks flocked to the mountain in retreat from the turbulence of the age, although the peninsula itself was subject to raids by Franks and Catalans over the next two centuries. After the fall of the Byzantine Empire to the Ottomans, the fathers wisely declined to resist, maintaining good relations with the early sultans, one of whom paid a state visit.

The mountain's real decline came after the early nineteenth-century **War of Independence**, in which many of the monks fought alongside the Greek revolutionary forces but paid the price when Macedonia was easily subdued. This led to a permanent Turkish garrison and the first drastic reduction in the monastic population, which did not increase even when Macedonia returned to Greece in 1912. The Athonite fathers, however, resisted diluting the Greek nature of the Holy Mountain with too many foreign (mainly Russian) monks. By the early 1960s numbers were at their lowest, barely a thousand, compared to 20,000 in Athos's heyday. Today, however, the monastic population has climbed to about two thousand, its average age has dropped significantly and the number of well-educated monks has increased markedly.

Getting there and around

To reach Athos from Thessaloníki, first take a Halkidhikí KTEL bus (see p.455 & 456) to Ouranoúpoli or Ierissós (see p.413). All boats to Athos are run by Ayioríтikes Grammés (☎23770 71149, Ⓦwww.agioreitikes-grammes.com) and if you plan to connect straight onto the *Ayia Anna* (see below), advance booking is advisable. From **Ouranoúpoli** three **boats** sail daily for most of the year: most people take the regular ferry that sails at 9.45am as far as **Dháfni** (90 min; €6), the main port on the southwestern coast of Athos, stopping at each harbour or coastal monastery en route. There are also faster boats at 8.45am and 10.40am (45min; €10) that sail direct to Dháfni. From Dháfni, the small *Ayia Anna* sails round the southern tip of the peninsula as far as Kafsokalývia, stopping at all the major and minor monastic communites en route. From **Ierissós**, a single fast boat leaves at 8.35am daily and travels along the northeast shore as far as the monastery of **Megístis Lavras** (2hr; €15); it may not stop at every harbour on the way but is guaranteed to halt at the Hilandharíou police post for the issue of permits.

Sleek Landrover **minibuses** and less glorious service vehicles usually coincide with the arrival times of the larger ferries at Dháfni and other harbours, to carry people to Karyés and the more inland monasteries accessible by road; they can be expensive and, if they're driven by lay-workers, you should establish a price beforehand. Most foreign visitors, however, prefer to **walk** between monasteries, preferably armed with the excellent map by Road Editions (1:50,000), which includes an informative 48-page booklet. Even with that, you'll still need to be pointed to the start of trails at each monastery, and to confirm walking times and path conditions. New roads are constantly being built, and trails accordingly abandoned; in the humid local climate they become completely overgrown within two years if not used.

Permits, entry and reservations

The first step in acquiring the necessary permit (*dhiamonitírion*) for visiting and staying on Athos is to telephone or email the Mount Athos Pilgrims' Bureau (Grafío Proskynitón Ayíou Órous) in Thessaloníki (Ⓣ2310 252 578, Ⓕ2310 222 424, Ⓔpilgrimsbureau@c-lab.gr). It is located in a fine Neoclassical building at Egnatía 109 (Mon–Fri 9am–2pm, Sat 10am–noon; postcode 54635); staff members speak English. Walk-in visits for reservations and enquiries are not encouraged. Once you have your booking you must reconfirm the reservation closer to the intended date, up to the day before. Your confirmation will be sent directly to the pilgrims' bureau on Athos for you to pick up on the day of entry. Before this, however, you must send them a copy of the ID page of your passport in advance or present it at the office at least the day before entry. As only ten permits per day are issued to non-Orthodox visitors (120 for baptized Greek Orthodox), it is wise to apply as far in advance as possible (five months maximum), especially for summer or Easter visits. Last-minute permits can sometimes be obtained if there's a cancellation but that leaves you with the problem of not having a reservation at any of the monasteries.

You pay for and receive your actual permit either from the pilgrims' bureau in Ouranoúpoli, if sailing from there, or at the police post at Hilandharíou, if sailing from Ierissós. The €30 (students €20) fee entitles you to stay for three nights and four days, during which time board and meals at the monasteries are free. Many visitors wish to arrange for an extension of the basic four-day period. This can theoretically be done at the Ayía Epistasía (Holy Superintendancy) in Karyés; two or three extra days are normally granted, and your chances are much better out of season.

Theoretically, all of the twenty major and four minor monasteries that receive guests require advance reservations, although there are several that do not apply this rule strictly. This is denoted, along with contact details for all the institutions in the boxes on pp.462–465. Just about all the most interesting monasteries do require booking though, and this can be done up to two months in advance. Where hours are denoted, it is best to call during these times on Monday to Saturday, but the phone often goes unanswered even then. Don't even bother trying on Sunday or any major holy day.

Visiting the monasteries

However you move around, you must reach your destination **before dark**, since all monasteries lock their front gates at sunset – which would leave you outside with the wild boars. Upon arrival you should ask for the **guestmaster**, who will proffer the traditional welcome of a *tsípouro, loukoúmi* (Turkish delight) and often a Greek coffee, before showing you to your bed. Most guestmasters speak good English.

Accommodation is typically in dormitories, and fairly spartan, but there's invariably a shower down the hall (often hot) and you're always given sheets and blankets. Athos grows much of its own **food**, and the monastic diet is based on tomatoes, beans, olives, green vegetables, coarse bread, cheese and pasta, with occasional meat dishes or treats like *halvás* and fruit included; a glass of wine is commonly served and fish of some description is standard after Sunday morning service. Only two meals are served daily, the first, more substantial one any time between 8am and 11am, the latter about an hour and a half to two and a half hours before sunset, depending on the time of year. It's a good idea to be partly self-sufficient in provisions – dried fruits, nuts and other energy-rich food are handy – both for the times when you fail to coincide with meals and for the long walks between monasteries. There are a few shops in Karyés and Dháfni, but for a better selection you should stock up before coming to Athos.

You will find the traditional Byzantine **daily schedule** somewhat disorienting, too. On the northeast side of the peninsula the "12 o'clock" position on monastery clocks indicates neither noon nor midnight but sunrise, whereas on the opposite side of Athos it coincides with sunset. Yet Vatopedhíou keeps "worldly" time, as do most monks' wristwatches, and in many monasteries two wall clocks are mounted side-by-side, one showing secular, the other "Byzantine" time. However, the **Julian calendar**, a fortnight behind the outside world, is observed throughout Athos, in particular for the frequent holy days. The advent of electric power from generators has affected the round of life very little; both you and the monks will go to bed early, shortly after sunset. In the small hours your hosts will awake for solitary meditation and study, followed by *órthros*, or matins. Around sunrise there is another quiet period, just before the *akolouthía*, or main liturgy, that precedes the morning meal. The afternoon is devoted to manual labour until the *esperinós*, or vespers, followed immediately by the evening meal and the short *apódhipno*, or compline service.

A few words about **attitudes and behaviour** towards your hosts (and vice versa) are in order, as many misunderstandings arise from mutual perceptions of disrespect, real or imagined. For your part, you should be fully clad at all times, even when going from dormitory to bathroom; shorts should not be worn anywhere on the peninsula, nor hats inside monasteries. Swimming is officially prohibited so if you are tempted, choose a cove where nobody can see you, and certainly don't skinny-dip. Smoking in most foundations is forbidden, though it is often tolerated on the balconies or outside the monastery walls; it would be criminal to smoke on the trail, however, given the chronic fire danger. Singing, whistling and raised voices are taboo; so is standing with your hands behind your back or in your pockets or crossing your legs when seated. If you want to photograph monks you should always ask permission, though photography is forbidden altogether in many monasteries, and video cameras are completely banned from the mountain. Finally, it's best not to go poking around corners of the buildings where you're not specifically invited, even if they seem open to the public.

Monasteries, and their tenants, tend to vary a good deal in their **handling of visitors**; signs at some institutions specifically forbid you from attending services or sharing meals with the monks. Other monasteries put themselves at

Athonite terminology

Arhondáris Guestmaster of a monastery or minor monastic community, responsible for all visitors; similarly, *arhondaríki*, the guest quarters themselves.

Arsanás Harbour annexe of each monastery or minor monastic community, where roll-on-roll-off ferries or *kaïkia* anchor; they can be a considerable distance from the institution in question.

Igoúmenos Abbot, the head of a monastery.

Katholikón Main church of a monastery.

Trápeza Refectory, or dining room.

the disposal of visitors of whatever creed. It is possible to be treated to ferocious bigotry and disarming gentility at the same place within the space of ten minutes. If you are non-Orthodox, and seem to understand enough Greek to get the message, you'll probably be told at some point, subtly or less so, that you ought to convert to the True Faith. It's worth remembering that the monks are expecting religious pilgrims, not tourists.

The monasteries

Obviously you can't hope to visit all twenty monasteries during a short stay, though if you're able to extend the basic four-day period you can fairly easily see the most prominent foundations. Each monastery has a distinct place in the **Athonite hierarchy**: Meyístis Lávras holds the prestigious first place, Konstamonítou ranks twentieth. All other settlements are attached to one or other of the twenty "ruling" monasteries; the dependencies range from a *skíti*, or minor monastic community (either a group of houses, or a cloister-like compound scarcely distinguishable from a monastery), through a *kellí* (a sort of farmhouse) to an *isyhastírio* (a solitary hermitage, often a cave). Numerous laymen – including many Muslim Albanians of late – also live on Athos, mostly employed as agricultural or manual labourers by the monasteries.

For simplicity's sake it is easiest to divide the monasteries according to which coast of the peninsula they belong to, southwestern or northeastern, and the two boxes on p.462 and p.464, which give brief descriptions of the main highlights, reflect this division. The institutions of each coast are described in geographical order, starting with those closest to the mainland. Apart from the four *skítes* that accept overnight visitors and thus merit their own entry, all other dependencies are mentioned in the account of their ruling monastery.

Northeastern Macedonia

Few people ever venture into the arable plains northeast of Thessaloníki, where attractions are sparsely spread among golden fields of corn and tobacco and incredible numbers of storks' nests. Up near the craggy mountains that form the frontier with Bulgaria, artificial **Lake Kerkíni** is home to masses of birds, some of them extremely rare in Europe, making it as interesting to ornithologists as the Préspa lakes much farther west. The tranquil setting and rich flora mean it is not only for avid twitchers.

An alternative way of reaching Kavála (rather than the dull toll motorway) is the busy but scenic route that climbs northeast out of Thessaloníki, first taking you via Sérres before passing **Alistráti**, worth visiting for its memorable caves, and then heading towards Dhráma and ancient **Philippi** along a quieter road that offers majestic panoramas of Mount Meníkio (1963m), Mount Pangéo (1956m) and Mount Falakró (2230m). Regular **buses** from Thessaloníki and between Sérres and Dhráma ply this road.

The Kerkíni Wetlands

Artificial, marsh-fringed **Lake Kerkíni**, tucked up near the mountainous Bulgarian border, enjoys international protected status, thanks to the three-hundred-plus species of **birds** that spend at least part of the year here, some of them on the endangered species list. Huge expanses of water lilies stretch across the large anvil-shaped lake, out of which the River Strymónas flows to the northern Aegean near ancient Amphipolis, while a herd of water buffalo wallows and grazes the eastern banks, and local fishermen compete for eels and roach with every type of heron known to inhabit Europe. Other birds breeding in the Kerkíni wetlands include various species of grebes, terns, egrets, ducks, geese, ibis, spoonbills, avocets and pelicans, plus raptors such as the black kite, the short-toed eagle and the Levant sparrowhawk.

The small town of **Livadhiá**, some 80km north of Thessaloníki on the road from Kilkís to Promahónas, can also be reached by train. From here it is just 7km south to the lake's northern shore and the village of **KERKÍNI**, where you will find the **Kerkíni Wetlands Information Centre** (hours vary; ⓣ23270 28004, ⓔwkerkini@otenet.gr), a few **tavernas** serving fish from the

The southwestern coast monasteries

Zográfou ⓣ&ⓕ23770 23247. Almost an hour from its harbour and within 3hr of the NE coast, the most inland monastery is inhabited by Bulgarian and Macedonian monks. Legend has it the founders left out a wooden panel, upon which, after prayers, a painting of St George appeared, hence the name. Non-Orthodox and believers are segregated but walk-in guests are usually accepted.

Konstamonítou ⓣ&ⓕ23770 23228. Nearly 2hr from Zográfou and 45min from its own harbour. Set amidst thick woodland, it's as humble, bare and poor as you'd expect from the last-ranking monastery; the church nearly fills the quadrangular court with grass growing between the flagstones. Non-Orthodox and believers are segregated but guests are happily taken on spec.

Dhohiaríou ⓣ&ⓕ23770 23245. Nearly 2hr from Konstamonítou. Picturesque monastery with lofty church nearly filling the courtyard. The best frescoes are in the long, narrow refectory, which has sea views. If you're lucky you might be shown the wonder-working icon of *Gorgoipikóöu* ("She who is quick to hear"), housed in a chapel between church and refectory.

Xenofóndos ⓣ23770 23633, ⓕ23770 23631. Only 30min from Dhohiaríou. The enormous, sloping, irregularly shaped court, expanded upwards in the nineteenth century, is unique in possessing two main churches. The small, older one, decorated with exterior frescoes of the Cretan school, was usurped during the 1830s by the huge upper one. Among its many icons are two fine mosaics of SS George and Demetrios.

Ayíou Pandeleïmonos ⓣ&ⓕ23770 23252; 10am–noon. Nearly 2hr from Dháfni and 1hr from Xenofóndos. Also known as "Róssiko", as many of its monks are Russian and its onion-shaped domes underline the tsarist origins of most of its buildings. The main attraction is the enormous bell over the refectory, the second largest in the world. The Slavonic chanting makes it worth trying to get into a service.

Xiropotámou ⓣ23770 23251, ⓕ23770 23733; 10am–12.30pm. Under an hour from Dháfni. Most of its construction and church frescoes date from the eighteenth century.

lake and a couple of **hotels**, including the *Oikoperiigitis* (Ⓣ23270 41450; ❸); in addition to comfortable rooms, a decent restaurant and **camping** facilities, this offers local tours by boat, canoe, bike, jeep or on horseback. You can also negotiate **bird-watching** trips in a *pláva*, a traditional punt-like fishing boat. The surroundings reward exploration with their abundance of flora and fauna, with huge numbers of wildflowers in the spring and early summer.

Alistráti

Just over 20km before you reach the dull market town Dhráma, on the road from Sérres, you come to the village of **ALISTRÁTI**, a pleasant cluster of houses with one or two decent **tavernas**. The only **hotel** is a delightfully restored mansion, *Arhondiko Voziki* (Ⓣ03234 20400, Ⓦwww.hotelboziki.gr; ❹), with beautifully furnished rooms and a swimming pool. The village is well placed for exploring the nearby mountains. The main reason for coming here, though, is to visit the impressive **caves** (daily: Easter–Sept 30 9am–7pm; rest of year 9am–5pm; 1hr guided tours only; €6; Ⓦwww.alistraticave.gr), reached down a scenic side road 6km southeast of the village. First explored in the mid-1970s, these caves easily rival those at Pérama (see p.366), and are claimed to be the most extensive of their kind in Europe not requiring special equipment or training to visit. Dating from the Quaternary period, these gigantic limestone cavities are over two million years old, and bristle with

Like Filothéou, this monastery was at the forefront of the 1980s "renaissance"; here again non-Orthodox are kept segregated from the faithful at meal times.

Símonos Pétras Ⓣ23770 23254, Ⓕ23770 23707; 1–3pm. Best reached by boat. Though entirely rebuilt after a fire at the beginning of the twentieth century, "Simópetra", as it is known, is perhaps the most visually striking monastery on Athos. With its multiple storeys, ringed by wooden balconies overhanging sheer three-hundred-metre drops, it resembles a Tibetan lamasery. Very lively with 60 resident monks but also gets crowded with visitors.

Osíou Grigoríou Ⓣ23770 23668, Ⓕ23770 23671; 11am–1pm. An hour and a half from Símonos Pétras. Of all the monasteries this has the most intimate relation with the sea and is renowned for the quality of its chanting. In the old guest quarters there's an attractive common room/library with literature on Orthodoxy; the guest overflow stays in a wood-trimmed hostel outside the gate, by the boat dock.

Ayíou Dhionysíou Ⓣ23770 23687, Ⓕ23770 23686. Little over an hour from Osíou Grigoríou, this fortified structure, perched spectacularly on a coastal cliff, is among the most richly endowed monasteries. The best icons are in the refectory rather than the dim church and you may be shown round the library with its illuminated gospels. Non-orthodox must eat separately.

Ayíou Pávlou Ⓣ23770 23741, Ⓕ23770 23355; 10am–12.30pm. About an hour from Ayíou Dhionysíou, this edifice actually looks more imposing from afar. Close up it lacks charm; many Cypriot monks in residence.

Néa Skíti Ⓣ23770 23572; 10am–noon. Under an hour from Ayíou Pávlou. Nothing too special about this dependency, except that it serves as another handy base or return point for Athos peak.

Skíti Ayías Ánnas Ⓣ23770 23320. An hour and a half from Ayíou Pávlou. Pleasant location with buildings tumbling down to the shore. With its renovated guest quarters, this is the usual "base camp" for climbing Athos peak (2030m) – best done with a pre-dawn start during the months May–June and September.

a variety of wonderful formations, including the relatively rare eccentrites and helictites, respectively stalactites sticking out at angles, rather than hanging vertically, and twisted forms resembling sticks of barley sugar. The entrance, a long tunnel bored into the hillside, takes you right into the caverns, and a winding path weaves its way through masses of stalagmites, many of them outstandingly beautiful, and some exceeding 15m in length.

Philippi

Some 50km from Alistráti, over halfway along the busy Dhráma-Kavála road, you come to the major site of **PHILIPPI** (Filippoi on some maps and signs). Not surprisingly, the town was named after Philip II of Macedon, who wrested it from the Thracians in 356 BC for the sake of nearby gold mines on Mount Pangéo. However, it owed its later importance and prosperity to the Roman construction of the Via Egnatia. With Kavála/Neapolis as its port, Philippi was essentially the easternmost town of Roman-occupied Europe.

Here, as at Actium, the fate of the Roman Empire was decided at the **Battle of Philippi** in 42 BC. After assassinating Julius Caesar, Brutus and Cassius had fled east of the Adriatic and, against their better judgement, were forced into confrontation on the Philippi plains with the pursuing armies of Antony and Octavian and were comprehensively beaten in two successive battles. As defeat

The northeastern coast monasteries

Hilandharíou ⓣ23770 23797, ⓕ23770 23108. A beacon of Serbian culture since the 13th century, its monks come by rota from the homeland. The fourteenth-century church in the triangular courtyard has attractive but retouched frescoes. Opposite the door of the refectory, look out for the *Ouranóskala* or "Stairway to Heaven". Boasts the most tasteful reception area and most salubrious guest quarters on the mountain.

Esfigménou ⓣ23770 23229. Built fortress-like right on the coast but little visited due to its reputation as the strictest institution on Athos. Has been in dispute with the rest of the monasteries since 2002 for refusing to recognise the authority of Patriarch Bartholemew because of his ecumenical initiatives. Banners proclaim "Orthodoxy or death!"

Vatopedhíou ⓣ23770 41480, ⓕ23770 41462; 9am–1pm. Great 3.5hr walk from Esfigménou. The largest and second most important monastery. The cobbled, slanting courtyard with its freestanding belfry resembles a town plaza, ringed by stairways and stacks of cells for more than three hundred monks, many of them English-speaking. The *katholikón* contains exceptional fourteenth-century frescoes of the Macedonian school and three exquisite mosaics.

Pandokrátoros ⓣ23770 23880, ⓕ23770 23685. Nearly a 3hr walk from Vatopedhíou, its best features are the guestrooms overlooking its own picturesque fishing harbour and the citrus-laden courtyard. In a valley above looms its imposing dependency, Profítis Ilías.

Stavronikíta ⓣ&ⓕ23770 23255; 10am–noon. An hour's walk from both Pandokrátoros and Ivíron, this offers some of the best views of Athos peak and is the most distinct example of an Athonite coastal fortress-monastery. As the narrow church occupies virtually all the gloomy courtyard, the refectory is, unusually, upstairs in the south wing. Orthodox and infidel alike are roused for 3.30am matins, yet it remains popular.

Skíti Ayíou Andhréou ⓣ23770 23810. A former Russian dependency of the great Vatopedhíou monastery, erected in the nineteenth century. Almost deserted today but close to Karyés and may take walk-in overnighters.

became imminent, first Cassius, then Brutus killed himself – the latter running on his comrade's sword with the purported Shakespearean sentiment, "Caesar now be still, I killed thee not with half so good a will."

St Paul landed at Kavála and visited Philippi in 49 AD and so began his religious mission in Europe. Despite being cast into prison, he retained a special affection for the Philippians, his first converts, and the congregation that he established was one of the earliest to flourish in Greece. It has furnished the principal remains of the site: several impressive, although ruined, basilican churches.

Philippi is most easily reached from Kavála, just 14km distant; Kavála-Dhráma **buses** leave every half-hour, and drop you by the road that now splits the site.

The site

The most conspicuous of the churches at the site (Tues–Sun: summer 8am–7pm; winter 8am–3pm; €3) is the **Direkler** (Turkish for "columns" or "piers"), to the south of the modern road which here follows the line of the Via Egnatía. Also known as Basilica B, this was an unsuccessful attempt by its sixth-century architect to improve the basilica design by adding a dome. In this instance the entire east wall collapsed under the weight, leaving only the narthex convertible for worship during the tenth century. The central arch of its west wall and a few pillars of reused antique drums stand amid remains of the Roman **forum**. A line of second-century porticoes spreads outwards in front of the church, and on their east side are the

Koutloumousíou ⓣ23770 23226, ⓕ23770 23731. Small and tidy monastery on the edge of Karyés. Its name is said to derive from a Seljuk chieftain who converted to Christianity.

Ivíron ⓣ23770 23643, ⓕ23770 23248; noon–2pm. Vast place housing around 40 monks. The focus of pilgrimage is the miraculous icon of the *Portaítissa*, the Virgin Guarding the Gate, housed in a special chapel to the left of the entrance. The main church is among the largest on the mountain, with an elaborate mosaic floor dating from 1030 and interesting pagan touches such as ram's-head column capitals. The monastery is also endowed with an immensely rich library and treasury-museum.

Filothéou ⓣ23770 23256, ⓕ23770 23674; noon–3pm. Around 1hr walk uphill from Ivíron. Lively place, which was at the forefront of the monastic revival in the early 1980s but not too attractive apart from the expansive lawn. Non-orthodox visitors are barred from services and dining with the faithful.

Karakálou ⓣ23770 23225, ⓕ23770 23746. Under an hour's walk downhill from Filothéou but a dull six hours on to Meyístis Lavras, so go by boat or vehicle. The lofty keep is typical of the fortress-monasteries built close enough to the shore to be victimized by pirates. Non-orthodox barred from services and dining with the faithful.

Meyístis Lávras ⓣ23770 23754, ⓕ23770 23013. The oldest and foremost of the ruling monasteries, and physically the most imposing establishment on Athos, with no fewer than fifteen chapels within its walls. At mealtimes you can enjoy the frescoes in the refectory, executed by Theophanes the Cretan in 1535. The library contains over 2000 precious manuscripts but is not usually open to visitors. Among its many dependencies, just 10min away by marked path there's the hermitage-cave of Ayios Athanasios, watched over by five skulls.

Skíti Prodhrómou ⓣ23770 23294. A good 2hr walk from Meyístis Lávras, this large dependency is kept spotless by the welcoming young Romanian monks, who may well take you in on spec. Other dependencies further along the southern tip include the *kellí* of Áyios Nílos and the frescoed chapel of Kafsokalývia, from where you can catch a boat round to the southwestern coast.

foundations of a colonnaded octagonal church, which was approached from the Via Egnatía by a great gate. Behind the Direkler and, perversely, the most interesting and best-preserved building of the site, is a huge monumental **public latrine** with nearly fifty of its original marble seats still intact.

Across the road on the northern side, stone steps climb up to a terrace, passing on the right a Roman crypt, reputed to have been the **prison of St Paul** and appropriately frescoed. The terrace flattens out onto a huge paved atrium that extends to the foundations of another extremely large basilica, the so-called Basilica A. Continuing in the same direction around the base of a hill you emerge above a **theatre** cut into its side. Though dating from the same period as the original town, it was heavily remodelled as an amphitheatre by the Romans – the bas-reliefs of Nemesis, Mars and Victory (on the left of the stage) all belong to this period. It is now used for performances during the annual summer Philippi-Thássos Festival. The best general impression of the site – which is extensive despite a lack of obviously notable buildings – and of the battlefield behind it can be gained from the **acropolis**, whose own remains are predominantly medieval. This can be reached by a steep climb along a path from the museum.

Kavála and around

Backing onto the easterly foothills of Mount Sýmvolo, **KAVÁLA** is the second-largest city of Macedonia and the second port for northern Greece; it was an extremely wealthy place in the nineteenth century when the region's tobacco crop was shipped from its docks to the rest of the world. Although its attempt to style itself as the "Azure City", on account of its position at the head of a wide bay, is going a little overboard, it does have a characterful centre, focused on the harbour area and the few remaining tobacco warehouses. A picturesque citadel looks down from a rocky promontory to the east, and an elegant Ottoman aqueduct leaps over modern buildings into the old quarter on the bluff.

Known in ancient times as Neapolis, the town was for two centuries or more a staging post on the Via Egnatía and the first European port of call for merchants and travellers from the Middle East. It was here that St Paul landed en route to Philippi (see p.464), on his initial mission to Europe. In later years, the port and citadel were occupied in turn by the Byzantines, Normans, Franks, Venetians, Ottomans and (during both world wars) Bulgarians. Kavála is also one of the main departure points for Thássos (see p.798) and, to a lesser extent, Samothráki (see p.794) and Límnos (see p.787).

Arrival and information

The main **bus station** is on the corner of Mitropolítou Khryssostómou and Filikís Eterías, near the Thássos ferry and hydrofoil dock. **Taxis** are deep tangerine in colour; if you're **driving** in, you can usually find a space on the quay car park near the Thássos dock. In the main square, Platía Eleftherías, you'll find several banks with **ATMs** and a **municipal tourist office** (daily 8am–9pm; ⓣ2510 231 011), which has a host of brochures and sells tickets for the summer Philippi-Thássos Festival. Kavála's "Megas Alexandhros" **airport**, used by package holiday-makers en route to Thássos and providing domestic flights to and from Athens, lies 29km southeast.

Car ferries sail from Kavála to the port of Skála Prínou in **Thássos** (1hr 15min) almost hourly from 6am to 9pm in season. There is also a regular seasonal **hydrofoil** service to both Skála Prínou and Thassos Town (30–40min

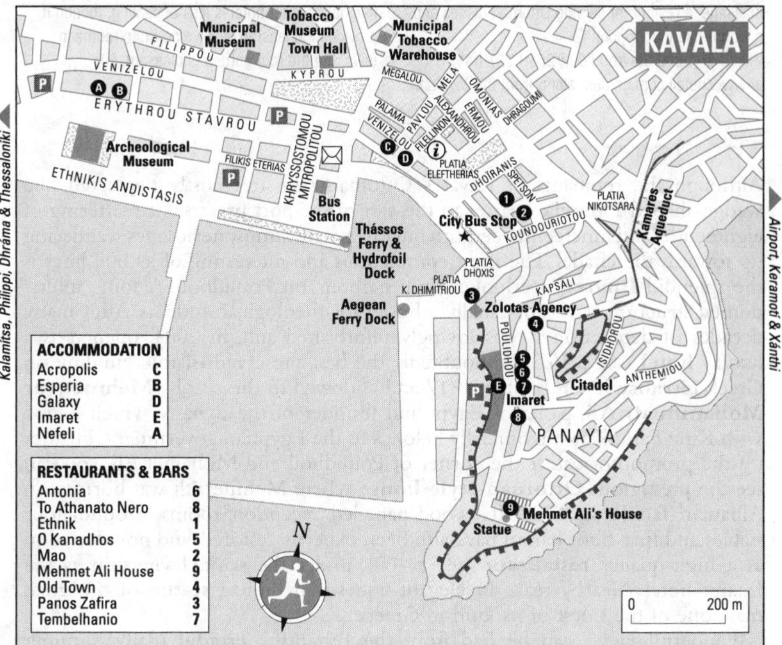

each way). There are also fairly regular ferries to **Samothráki** and **Límnos** with some onward services to, among other places, Áyios Efstrátios, Lésvos, Híos and Lávrio. Details for all services are available from the port authority (☎2510 223 716) and tickets from agencies such as Zolotas (☎2510 835 671), around the harbour front towards the terminal/customs house.

Accommodation

Abundant, good-value **hotel** rooms are not the order of the day in Kavála. Most establishments are overpriced and uninspiring, though proprietors can often be bargained down a category or two in the off-season. The closest **campsite** is *Irini* (☎2510 229 785; open all year), on the shore 3km east of the port and served by city bus #2. Rather better are the *Estella* (☎25920 71465), 9km west, and *Camping Anatoli* (☎25940 21027; May–Sept), with a saltwater swimming pool, at the west end of Néa Péramos, a full 14km west of Kavála.

Acropolis Venizélou 29 ☎2510 223 543, ⓔhotel-acropolis@hotmail.com. The one room with shared bath is the cheapest acceptable place to stay in town, but the en-suite ones are overpriced. ❸

Esperia Erythroú Stavroú 42 ☎2510 229 621, ⓦwww.esperiakavala.gr. A decent hotel offering comfortable rooms with a/c – ask for the quieter side or back ones. Good breakfasts served on a terrace. ❸

Galaxy Venizélou 27 ☎2510 224 811, ⓦwww.hotelgalaxy.gr. Somewhat faded 1960s behemoth offering adequate rooms with fine harbour views. Good off-season reductions. ❹

Imaret Poulídhou 6 ☎2510 620 151, ⓦwww.imaret.gr. This expertly refurbished Ottoman medrasse now functions as a deluxe resort, where every detail has been carefully selected for the discerning traveller. The classy rooms (from €360) and suites have been faultlessly fashioned, whilst keeping the original building intact. Services include a traditional *hamam* with massage, a restaurant serving Ottoman dishes and a womb-like indoor pool. ⑧

Nefeli Erythroú Stavroú 50 ⓣ2510 227 441, ⓦwww.nefeli.com.gr. Just along from the *Esperia*, this nondescript hotel is less appealing, though it provides the least expensive en-suite rooms in town and the roof garden is pleasant. ③

The Town

Although the remnants of Kavála's Ottoman past are mostly neglected, the wedge-shaped **Panayía** quarter to the east of the port preserves a scattering of eighteenth- and nineteenth-century buildings with atmospheric lanes wandering up towards the citadel. The most conspicuous and interesting of its buildings is the splendid **Imaret**, overlooking the harbour on Poulídhou. A long, multi-domed structure, it was originally a hostel for theological students. After many decades of dereliction it was lovingly refurbished and, in 2004, opened as a luxury **hotel** (see p.467). Undoubtedly the best-preserved Islamic building on Greek territory, it was built in 1817 and endowed to the city by **Mehmet (or Mohammed) Ali**, pasha of Egypt and founder of the dynasty which ended with King Farouk; it still officially belongs to the Egyptian government. Further up the promontory, near the corner of Poulídhou and Mohámet Alí, you can see the prestigious **Ottoman-style house** where Mehmet Ali was born to an Albanian family in 1769. Its wood-panelled reception rooms, ground-floor stables and first-floor harem have also been expertly restored, and now function as a high-quality **restaurant** (see p.469), under the same ownership as the Imaret hotel. Nearby rears an elegant equestrian bronze **statue** of the great man, one of the finest of its kind in Greece.

Wonderful views can be had from the Byzantine **citadel** (daily: summer 8am–7pm, sometimes closed for siesta; winter 8am–5pm; free), signposted "castle". You can explore the ramparts, towers, dungeon and cistern, and in season it co-hosts the Philippi-Thássos Festival of drama and music in its main court. From here, sweeping down towards the middle of town, the **Kamáres aqueduct**, built on a Roman model during the reign of Süleyman the Magnificent (1520–66), spans the traffic in Platía Nikotsára.

Finally, on the other side of the harbour from the old town, there are three museums of moderate interest. The **Archeological Museum** (Tues–Sun 8.30am–5pm; €2) on Erythroú Stavroú contains a fine dolphin and lily mosaic upstairs in the Abdera room (when the floor reopens), plus painted sarcophagi in the adjacent section devoted to Thassian colonies. Downstairs there are many terracotta figurines still decorated in their original paint and gold ornaments from tombs at Amphipolis. Just inland, next to some rather dilapidated former tobacco warehouses at Filíppou 4, is the **Municipal Museum** (Mon–Fri 8am–2pm, Sat 9am–1pm; free), closed for refurbishment at the time of writing; along with various collections of stuffed birds, traditional costumes and household utensils, this has a couple of rooms devoted to the Thássos-born sculptor Polygnotos Vayis (see p.802). One more street up, at Paleológou 4, the potentially interesting **Tobacco Museum** (Mon–Sat 9am–1pm; free) falls down on presentation and the lack of explanations in Greek, let alone English, though some of the exhibits, including historic photographs and antique cigarette packets, are worthwhile. The tobacco-led prosperity of nineteenth-century Kavála is perhaps better illustrated by the fabulous facade of the nearby **Municipal Tobacco Warehouse** (Dhimotikí Kapnapothíki), at Platía Kapnergáti; plans to transform this into a shopping centre seem to be on permanent hold.

Eating and drinking

Eating out in Kavála is a better prospect than staying the night; most places on the waterfront, however, are tourist traps, and to find a fish taverna where the locals eat you will need transport to take you along the coast to the east of town. You're far better off walking up into the Panayía district, where a row of moderately priced tavernas and ouzerís tempts you with good and reasonably priced grills and seafood. One of the best **bars,** *Old Town (Glaros)*, is on Poulídhou before you reach the tavernas; back down on pedestrianized Ayíou Nikoláou, behind the eponymous church, *Ethnik* is an imaginatively decorated joint, playing anything from Tom Jones to Jefferson Airplane, while *Mao* draws the leftist student crowd with its murals of the chairman and indie rock. A string of trendy **café-bars** lurks on pedestrianized Palamá, parallel to Venizélou street.

Antonia Poulídhou. Traditional family taverna dishing up platefuls of fried squid accompanied by good bulk wine.

To Athanato Nero Poulídhou. Consistently the best of the Poulídhou establishments, priding itself on a mean mussels *saganáki* and excellent white wine from Limnos.

O Kanadhos Poulídhou. Grilled meat is the speciality at this homely and exceptionally cheap place run by returnees from Toronto – hence the name and the English-speaking management.

Mehmet Ali House Poulídhou. Expensive gourmet restaurant housed in an eighteenth-century monument; Ottoman cuisine.

Panos Zafira Platía Karaolí Dhimitríou. The most reliable of the waterfront eateries, serving decent fish at reasonable prices.

Tembelhanio Poulídhou. Cosy ouzerí serving a tasty range of *mezédhes* to a soundtrack of eclectic Greek and Middle Eastern sounds.

Keramotí

Rather than negotiate the streets of Kavála, many people find it more convenient to take the bus or drive to **KERAMOTÍ**, 46km southeast, and take the car ferry from there to Thássos – especially between September and April, when services from Kavála drop to just a handful of boats daily. Keramotí is a small, rather drab village, 9km beyond the Kavála airport turn-off, with a decent enough beach backed by pines, a few rooms and a half-dozen hotels which you shouldn't have to patronize – the best of a bad bunch is the *Golden Sands* (Ⓣ25910 51509; ❷), tucked away in a quieter part of town.

Xánthi and around

Coming from Kavála, after the turnings to the airport and to Keramotí, you cross the Néstos River which, with the **Rodhópi mountains**, forms the border of Greek Thrace. The Greek/Turkish, Christian/Muslim demographics are almost immediately apparent in the villages: the Turkish settlements, long established, with their tiled, whitewashed houses and pencil-thin minarets; the Greek ones, often adjacent, built in drab modern style for the refugees of the 1920s. The same features are combined in the region's biggest urban centre, the attractive market town of **Xánthi**. Of the mountain villages north of Xánthi, **Stavroúpoli** stands out as the most worth visiting, while to the south and east a trio of **archeological sites** are to be found along the coast near **Komotiní**.

Xánthi

XÁNTHI (Iskeçe for Turkish-speakers), the first town of any size, is definitely the most interesting point to break a journey. There is a busy market area, good food, and – up the hill to the north of the main café-lined square – a very attractive old quarter. The town is also home to the University of Thrace, which lends a lively air to the place, particularly in the area between the bazaar and the campus, where bars, cinemas and bistros are busy in term time. Try, if you can, to visit on Saturday, the day of Xánthi's **street fair** – a huge affair, attended equally by Greeks, Pomaks and Turks, held in an open space near the fire station on the eastern side of the town.

Arrival and information

The **train station** lies just off the Kavála road, 2km south of the centre, while buses draw in at the new **KTEL**, about 300m south of the main square. Taxis, green with white tops, are readily available at both hubs. Note that for Alexandhroúpoli it is better to travel by train, as you will have to change bus in Komotiní. The main south–north thoroughfare is 28-Oktovríou, lined with fast-food outlets and sundry shops. One end is marked by the Kendrikí Platía, recognizable by its distinguished clocktower. Xánthi's pay-and-display **parking** scheme is pretty comprehensive, with fees payable in the centre from 8.30am to 8.30pm, Monday to Saturday. The **post office**, signposted, and Olympic Airways are both very close to the platía, on its uphill side. Several **banks** with **ATMs** line the square.

Accommodation

Downtown **hotel** choices are limited and rather overpriced, and disappointingly there's no official accommodation in the atmospheric old town. Nearest the centre is the refurbished *Democritus*, 28-Oktovríou 41 (Ⓣ25410 25111, Ⓕ25410 25537; ④), where you should insist on a room away from the street.

Thrace: Greece's most ethnically diverse region

Separated from Macedonia to the west by the Néstos River and from the Turkish territory of eastern Thrace by the Évros River and its delta, western Thrace (Thráki) is the Greek state's most recent acquisition, under effective Greek control only since 1920. While the Treaty of Lausanne (1923) sanctioned the forced evacuation of 390,000 Muslims, principally from Macedonia and Epirus, in exchange for more than a million ethnic Greeks from eastern Thrace and Asia Minor (both now part of Turkey), the Muslims of western Thrace were exempt from the exchanges and continue to live in the region in return for a continued Greek presence in and around Constantinople (Istanbul).

Nowadays, out of a total population of 360,000, there are officially around 120,000 Muslims, about half of them Turkish-speakers, while the rest are Pomaks (see p.472) and Roma. Although there are dozens of functioning mosques, some Turkish-language newspapers and a Turkish-language radio station in Komotiní, only graduates from a special Academy in Thessaloníki have been allowed to teach in the Turkish-language schools here – thus isolating Thracian Turks from mainstream Turkish culture. Local Turks and Pomaks claim that they are the victims of discrimination, but despite occasional explosions of intercommunal violence in the past, relationships have improved with each decade and as an outsider you will probably not notice the tensions. In mixed villages Muslims and Greeks appear to coexist quite amicably and this harmony reaches its zenith in Xánthi. All Thracians, both Muslim and Orthodox, have a deserved reputation for hospitality.

More or less around the corner at Mihaïl Karaolí 40, the *Orfeas* (Ⓣ25410 20121, Ⓔorfeasxanthi@yahoo.gr; ❸) has spacious, bright, en-suite rooms and is better value. The town's newest and smartest hotel, offering all-mod-con luxury at relatively low prices, is *Elisso* (Ⓣ25410 84400, Ⓦwww.hotelelisso.gr; ❺), towards the university at Vasilíssis Sofías 9.

The Town

The narrow cobbled streets of the **old town** are home to a number of very fine mansions – some restored, some derelict – with colourful exteriors, bay windows and wrought-iron balconies; most date from the mid-nineteenth century when Xánthi's tobacco merchants made their fortunes. One of them has been turned into an excellent **folk museum** (Tues–Sun 9am–2.30pm; €2), at Odhós Antíka 7, at the bottom of the hill up into the right-bank quarter of the old town. Its home is a beautiful semi-detached pair of mansions, originally built for two tobacco magnate brothers, and worth seeing for their exterior alone; some years ago the interior was lovingly restored with painted wooden panels, decorated plaster and floral designs on the walls and ceilings. The interesting displays include Thracian clothes and jewellery, numerous household objects and historical displays on the tobacco industry and society in general; entry includes an enthusiastic guided tour if requested.

Further up, the roads become increasingly narrow and steep, and the Turkish presence (about fifteen percent of the total urban population) is more noticeable: most of the women have their heads covered, and the more religious ones wear full-length cloaks. Churches and mosques hide behind whitewashed houses with tiled roofs, and orange-brown tobacco leaves are strung along drying frames. Numerous houses, no matter how modest, sport a dish for tuning in to Turkish satellite television.

Eating, drinking and entertainment

Xanthi's **restaurants** are somewhat better than its hotels. Tucked away just to the north of the Kendrikí Platía, at Yeoryíou Stavroú 18, is the eminently reasonable *Ta Fanarakia*, where you can tuck into meat or fish on its pavement seating. A couple of blocks up behind the clocktower at Ayíou Athanasíou 2, *Erodhios* is an all-round quality taverna with a delightful summer garden enclosed by old town walls. At the lower reaches of cobbled Paleológou and Odhós P. Christídhi, you'll find a gaggle of taverna-cum-ouzerís, of which the best is arguably *Myrovolos,* with efficient service and a mix of *mezédhes* and *mayireftá*. For the most genuine Thracian dining experience, however, head a few blocks south of the square to ★ *Erkolos*, hidden in an arcade at Bahtzetzí 18A; here you can wash down inexpensive dishes, such as tenderly fried liver and copious dips, with lashings of *tsípouro*.

Xánthi's buzzing **nightlife** is focused on Vasilíssis Sofías, which forks off Paleológou at the little park sporting a bust of war hero Antíkas, and on the platía itself. Doyen of the various bars on the former is the enormous *Kyverneio*, boasting a huge terrace, while a whole cluster of see-and-be-seen **café-bars** on the platía vies for your custom. You can enjoy genuine Turkish tea, quality coffee and sweets at the delightful trad-style *To Hani*, in the lower reaches of the old town at Venizélou 32. There's a new multi-plex **cinema** in the Cosmos Centre on Mihaïl Karaolí, 200m down from the square.

North of Xánthi

Much of the countryside north of Xánthi, towards the Bulgarian border, is a military controlled area, dotted with signs denoting the fact. If you venture up into the western Rodhópi range here, the main reward is some magnificent scenery; there's not much arable land amidst the wild, forested hills, and what there is – down in the river valleys – is devoted entirely to tobacco, hand-tilled by the Pomaks, who tend to keep themselves to themselves. Owing to the modest increase in material prosperity since the 1980s, the Pomak villages have mostly lost their traditional architecture to concrete multistorey apartments. **SMÍNTHI**, a large and dispersed settlement with a mosque and tall minaret, has a couple of *psistariés* on the through road, the only thing remotely resembling tourist facilities in the immediate area. **ORÉO**, 6km up a side road northwest of Smínthi, is dramatically set on a steep hillside with cloud-covered peaks behind and terraces falling away to the riverbed.

Stavroúpoli

Set among some of the region's most inviting scenery – deep gorges, fir-draped crags and high waterfalls, more like the French Jura than a typically Greek landscape – neat little **STAVROÚPOLI**, 25km west of Smínthi, is doing its very best to attract tourists, so far mainly Greeks. Having suffered a major population drain during the decades of mass emigration, the village, with its immaculate cobbled streets, shady central platía, complete with traditional café, and well-restored Thracian-style houses, is showing sure signs of a revival. Some 30km northwest of Xánthi along the scenic Dhráma road, it is conveniently placed for visiting the most spectacular stretch of the Néstos River, whose meanders and rapids lend themselves to safe rafting and canoeing. With some of the finest hiking in the whole of Greece in its surroundings, Stavroúpoli makes a credible centre for alternative tourism. The town has a delightful little **Folklore Museum**, signposted from the town centre, a proudly displayed collection in a restored house full of local memorabilia donated by residents – everything from embroidered bodices to an ancient still-functioning record player; ask around for the curator as it has no fixed opening hours, nor entry fee.

Stavroúpoli is potentially an excellent alternative to staying in either Xánthi or Komotiní, but for now the only **accommodation** in the town itself is the atmospheric and extremely welcoming *Xenios Zeus* (Ⓣ&Ⓕ 25420 22444; ❸), an old Thracian house with traditional decor just off the main square. Nearby is the excellent **taverna** *Oinos*, which offers not only delicious game and vegetable dishes but also information about kayaking, mountain bikes and horse riding in the region. Just a couple of kilometres south is the hotel *Nemesis* (Ⓣ 25420 21005, Ⓦ www.hotelnemesis.gr; ❹), which looks like a medieval castle and has simple but comfortable rooms and a swimming pool.

South of Xánthi

South of Xánthi, the coastal plain, bright with fields of cotton, tobacco and cereals, stretches to the sea. Heading towards modern Ávdhira, you'll pass through **Yenisséa**, an unspectacular farming village with one of the oldest **mosques** in Thrace, dating from the sixteenth century. Now derelict, it's a low whitewashed building with a tiled roof, crumbled wooden portico and truncated minaret.

Four daily buses serve the village of **ÁVDHIRA**, 10km further on, and, in summer, run on to the **beach** of Paralía Avdhíron, 7km beyond, passing through the site of **ancient Abdera** (daily 8am–7.30pm, winter closes 3pm; free), founded in the seventh century BC by Clazomenians from Asia Minor. The walls of the ancient acropolis are visible on a low headland above the sea, and there are fragmentary traces of Roman baths, a theatre and an ancient acropolis.

The remains are unspectacular, and the setting not particularly attractive, but the **Archeological Museum** (same hours as site; free), located in the village, puts it all into context with a beautifully presented exhibition, accompanied by extensive English texts. A rich collection of ceramics, coins, oil lamps, mosaics and jewellery is dominated by a moving section devoted to burial customs, including some spectacular reconstructions of graves dating from the seventh to fifth centuries BC.

For the most part, the coast east from here is flat and dull. At the southern end of brackish Lake Vistonídha stands **Pórto Lágos**, a semi-derelict harbour partly redeemed by the nearby modern monastery of **Áyios Nikólaos** (closed 1–5pm), built on two islets in the lagoon. The surrounding marshland, a major site for birdlife including herons, spoonbills and pelicans, is more accessible, though less important, than the Évros Delta (see p.477); a few observation towers have been provided along the reedy shoreline. Ornithologists might like to know that this is one of the few wintering habitats in Europe of the endangered white-headed duck.

East of Xánthi

The fertile central plains of Thrace, with their large ethnic Turkish population, are one of the least visited areas of the country, but are not without some appeal. Though outwardly unattractive, the market town of **Komotiní** rewards a brief visit, with its two well-presented museums, one folk, the other archeological. The contents of the latter are complemented by the delightful ancient site of **Maroneia**, on the coast, and **Mesembria**, further east.

Komotiní

Lying 48km east of Xánthi along the direct road skirting the Rodhópi foothills, **KOMOTINÍ** is larger and markedly more Turkish than Xánthi but lacks its charm. Unlike Xánthi, social mixing between the different ethnic groups – roughly at parity population-wise – is almost nonexistent, although Orthodox and Muslims live in the same neighbourhoods. Since the 1990s the town has become even more polyglot, with an influx of Greek, Armenian and Georgian Christians from the Caucasus.

The old **bazaar**, to the north of Platía Irínis, is a little bit of Istanbul, lodged between fine mosques and an elegant Ottoman-era **clocktower**. Alongside shady cafés, tiny shops sell everything from dried apricots to iron buckets; it's especially busy on Tuesdays when the villagers from the surrounding area come into town to sell their wares. Behind this old quarter, you can see the remains of Komotiní's **Byzantine walls**.

Greek influence has been in the ascendant since the waning years of the Ottoman empire, when rich Greeks funded schools in the city. Some of these educational foundations still survive: one, a handsome half-timbered building at Ayíou Yeoryíou 13, has become the **Museum of Folk Life and History** (Mon–Sat 10am–1pm; free), displaying examples of Thracian embroidery, traditional Thracian dress, silverware, copperware and a collection of religious seals, but avoiding any mention of the ethnic Turkish community. The **Archeological Museum** at Simeonídhi 4 (daily 9am–6pm; free) is also worth a visit, giving a lucid overview of Thracian history, by means of plans and finds from local sites, from its beginnings up to the Byzantine era.

Practicalities

The **train station** is over 1km to the southwest of the centre, where **taxis** await arrivals. The **KTEL** is some way to the south of central Platía Irínis, via

Énou. Should you need to stay, be aware that the **hotel** situation is even less promising than Xánthi's. Quaintly basic and friendly, but rather noisy, is the *Hellas* at Dhimokrítou 31 (Ⓣ25310 22055; ❷), with shared showers and toilets. Marginally quieter, but overpriced, is the *Astoria*, a Neoclassical inn restoration at Platía Irínis 28 (Ⓣ25310 35054, Ⓕ25310 22707; ❹); calmer still, but a fair way out, beyond the war memorial at the east end of Platía Irínis, is the *Anatolia*, Anhiálou 53 (Ⓣ25310 36242, Ⓔthessaloniki@anatoliahotel.gr; ❸).

By far the best **eating** is to be found at *Inopion* at Platía Irínis 67, in the form of conventional, impeccably prepared dishes served with considerable style. Tucked away in the narrowest lanes of the bazaar just north of Orféos, two decent ouzerís, *Apolafsis* and the slightly better *Yiaxis*, put out tables under arbours.

Marónia and Mesimvría

Just off the E90 motorway, southeast of Komotiní, lie two archeological sites that make an excellent break in the journey to Alexandhroúpoli. Clearly indicated from the Sápes turn-off is **ancient Maroneia**, a set of ancient and Byzantine ruins scattered among seaside olive groves. It's just below the modern village of **MARÓNIA**, served by six daily buses from Komotiní via the old road. Marónia has held onto a few surviving old Thracian mansions with balconies, and, on the edge of the village, there's an excellent **hotel**, the *Roxani* (Ⓣ25330 21501, Ⓦwww.ecoexplorer.gr; ❹); the spacious rooms look out on fabulous views, and breakfasts are filling, with other meals available. The enthusiastic archeologist who owns the hotel can fix you up with all manner of activities, from bird-watching and astronomy to sea-canoeing and archery, or exploring the nearby caves.

To get to the ruins of ancient Maroneia, attractively situated at the foot of Mount Ísmaros, follow the signs to Marónia's harbour of **Áyios Harálambos**, taking care not to enter the airforce camp nearby. The founder of the city is reckoned to be Maron, the son of the god of wine, Dionysos, and the city became one of the most powerful in all of ancient Thrace. Mostly unexcavated, the remains can be explored at will but are badly signposted. Even so, you should be able to track down traces of a theatre, a sanctuary of Dionysos and various buildings including a house with a well-preserved mosaic floor. The land walls of the city are preserved to a height of 2m, together with a Roman tower above the harbour. Over time, the sea has done its own excavation, eroding the crumbling cliffs and revealing shards of pottery and ancient walls.

A more worthwhile site, **ancient Mesembria**, or **MESIMVRÍA** in modern Greek (daily 8am–7.30pm, winter closes 3pm; €2), is clearly signposted from the motorway and is reached via the nondescript village of Dhíkela. Thanks to its unspoilt seaside location, fruitful recent excavations and a well-thought-out display, it easily qualifies as the most appealing of the three ancient sites on the Thracian coastline. You can stay nearby at the smart, seaview **hotel** *Klio* (Ⓣ25510 71311, Ⓕ25510 71411; ❸), with a decent restaurant at **Ayía Paraskeví**, near Mákri, a fishing village 11km west of Alexandhroúpoli along the old road.

Alexandhroúpoli

Some 120km southeast of Xánthi, the modern city of **ALEXANDHROÚPOLI** (Dedeagaç in Turkish) was designed by Russian military architects during the

Russo-Turkish war of 1878. It does not, on first acquaintance, have much to recommend it: a border town and military garrison, with overland travellers in transit and Greek holiday-makers competing in summer for limited space in the few hotels and the campsite. The town became Greek only in 1920, when it was renamed Alexandhroúpoli after a visit from Greece's King Alexander. There is, however, an excellent **Ethnological Museum** and a lively seafront promenade.

Arrival and information

Arriving by **train**, you'll be deposited next to the port; the **KTEL** is at Venizélou 36, several blocks inland. **Drivers** will find it prudent to enter town from the west along coastal Megálou Alexándhrou, signposted for the ferries and restaurants, since pedestrianization, one-way systems and fee parking effectively block movement between Dhimokratías – local name for the Via Egnatía – and the sea. There is a rudimentary, seasonal **tourist office** in the town hall building at the corner of Dhimokratías and Mitropolítou Kavíri.

Ferries and seasonal hydrofoils will take you to the island of **Samothráki** (see p.794), whose dramatic silhouette looms over 40km off the coast.

Accommodation

Booking ahead is wise in high summer even though there are a number of choices, ranging from some rather third-rate bathless rooms to a string of luxurious resort-cum-conference hotels, well west of town.

Erika K Dhimitríou 110 ⓣ25510 34115, ⓦwww.hotel-erika.gr. Smart seafront hotel near the station with comfortable rooms and a decent breakfast included. ❹

Hera Dhimokratías 179 ⓣ25510 23941–3, ⓕ25510 34222. The entrance, lobby and breakfast room are shiny and modern but the rooms are still on the dowdy side, albeit functional. ❸

Lido Paleológou 15 ⓣ25510 28808, ⓕ25510 34118. A bright and cheerful place, with large en-suite rooms, not far from the bus station. ❸

Majestic Platía Eleftherías 7 ⓣ25510 26444. The closest hotel to the train station, it is a decent, old-fashioned cheapie with shared bathrooms. ❷

Thraki Palace Paleológou 20 ⓣ25510 89100, ⓦwww.thrakipalace.gr. Five kilometres west of town, this sleek, modern five-star establishment has a sea-view swimming pool, a swish restaurant, piano bar, fitness centre and spacious, contemporary rooms, though the surroundings lack any character. ❼

The Town

If you have an hour or so to spare it can be enjoyably spent at the excellent **Ethnological Museum of Thrace** (Tues–Sat 10am–2pm & 6–9pm, Sun 6–9pm; €3), one of the best of its kind in the whole country, at 14-Maïoú 63, several blocks due north of the ferry terminal. Housed in a tastefully restored Neoclassical mansion constructed in 1899 as the country residence of a wealthy tradesman from Edirne, its eye-catching modern displays cover almost every aspect of traditional life in Thrace, for once mentioning every ethnic component of what has always been a multicultural region: Pomaks, Turks, Armenians, Jews and Roma as well as Greeks. Professionally produced videos, with commentaries in Greek only, complement the beautifully lit cabinets on the themes of ritual, music, costume, food, agriculture and crafts. Curiosities include stamps for communion bread, colourful ceremonial brooms, carnival masks, Pomak calendars and colanders, chickpea roasters, ice-cream-making equipment and a *yahanás*, or sesame-oil press, in use until

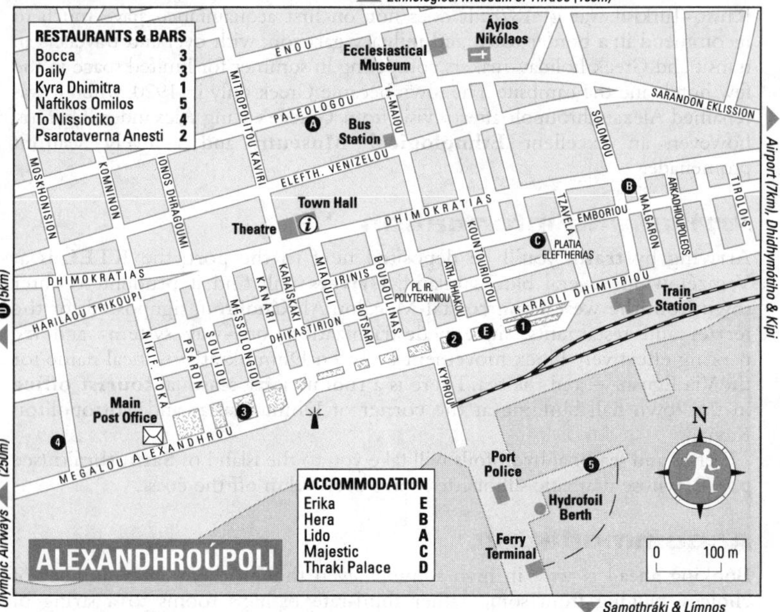

1967. A delightful café, serving local specialities, and a quality museum shop complete the picture.

Otherwise it's the lively seafront that best characterizes the town; dominated by a seventeen-metre-tall 1880 **lighthouse,** the town's symbol, it comes alive at dusk when the locals begin their evening promenade. In summer, café tables spill out onto the road and around the lighthouse; makeshift stalls on the pavements sell pirate cassettes, pumpkin seeds and grilled sweetcorn.

Eating and drinking

For **restaurants** in town, check out the row of good tavernas with terraces, near the train station – the best is *Kyra Dimitra*, where a wide range of vegetable dishes accompanies fried fish. Two other commendable eateries are *To Nissiotiko*, at Zarífi 1, and *Psarotaverna Anesti* at Athanasíou Dhiákou 5; the former, with its picturesque decor, serves a delicious dill-flavoured seafood risotto (*piláfi thalássino*) along with a variety of grilled and fried fish and seafood. Good fish cuisine and an attractive location make the *Naftikos Omilos*, next to the ferry terminal, also worth heading for. Trendy seafront **bars** with popular terraces include adjacent *Bocca* and *Daily*, though a string of **cafés** along Dhimokratías also attracts the crowds.

The Évros Valley and northeastern Thrace

The **Évros Valley**, extending northeast of Alexandhroúpoli, is a prosperous but dull agricultural area. Most towns are ugly, modern concrete affairs full of bored soldiers, with little to delay you; others, such as **Souflí** and **Dhidhymótiho**, retain some character and medieval monuments, and the main route through the valley is well served by public transport. No village is complete without its stork's nest, dominating the landscape like a watchtower. The standout here by some way is the **Dhadhiá Forest** and wildlife reserve, also reachable by bus; you'll need your own transport to head east from Alexandhroúpoli to the **Évros Delta**, one of Europe's most important wetland areas for birds – and one of Greece's most sensitive military areas.

The Évros Delta

To the southeast, the **Évros Delta** is home to more than 250 different species of birds, including sea eagles, pygmy cormorants and the lesser white-fronted goose. Leave Alexandhroúpoli on the main road towards Turkey and Bulgaria; some 10km after the airport, you'll reach the turn-off to **Loutrá Traianópolis**, the site of an ancient Roman spa and its modern continuation Loutrós. Either of the two following hotels in the vicinity would make a good base for exploring the delta: the *Athina* (☎25510 61208; ❷) and the *Plotini* (☎25510 61106; ❷). The delta is best approached by turning right off the main road, opposite the side road to the hotels; the lane is paved only as far as the level crossing but remains good thereafter. The delta is crisscrossed with tracks along the dykes used by farmers taking advantage of the plentiful water supply for growing sweet corn and cotton. The south is the most inspiring part, well away from the army installations to the north; as you go further into the wetlands, the landscape becomes utterly desolate, with decrepit clusters of fishing huts among the sandbars and inlets. At the mouth of the delta sprawls a huge saltwater lake called **Límni Dhrakónda**. Obviously what you see depends on the time of year, but even if birdlife is a bit thin on the ground, the atmosphere of the place is worth experiencing.

Dhadhiá Forest

The **Dhadhiá Forest Reserve** consists of 352 square kilometres of protected oak and pine forest covering a succession of volcanic ridges. The diversity of landscape and vegetation and the proximity of important migration routes make for an extremely diverse flora and fauna, but raptors are the star attraction, and main impetus for this WWF-backed project. The reserve is reached by a clearly marked road off to the left, 1km after passing the second right-hand turn-off to Likófi (Likófos). After a drive of 7km through the rolling, forested hills, you reach the reserve complex (March–May & Sept–Nov daily 9am–7pm; June–Aug daily 8.30am–8.30pm; Dec–Feb Mon–Thurs 10am–4pm, Fri–Sun 9am–6pm), with its information centre and exhibition about the region's wildlife.

All cars – except for a tour van which makes sorties several times daily (€3) – are banned from core areas totalling 72 square kilometres, and foot access is restricted to two marked trails: a two-hour route up to the reserve's highest point, 520-metre **Gíbrena** with its ruined Byzantine castle, and another ninety-minute loop-route to an observation hide overlooking **Mavrórema** canyon. The region is one of two remaining European homes of the majestic **black vulture**, the other being the Extremadura region of Spain. Their numbers have increased from near extinction when protection began in 1980 to some one hundred individuals, and they and griffon vultures make up the bulk of sightings from this post. In all, 36 of Europe's 38 species of diurnal birds of prey, including eagles, falcons, hawks and buzzards, can be sighted at least part of the year.

It's a good idea to stay the night, as the best raptor viewing is in the early morning or evening in summer (but virtually all day Oct–March). Next to the visitors' centre is the comfortable **ecotourism hostel** run by **Dhadhiá** village (25540 32263, www.ecoclub.com/dadia; 2), where the en-suite rooms have been given bird names instead of numbers (keys from the café across the car park, until 11pm). The hostel, which can provide programmes inclusive of **meals**, has a café and restaurant or you could try the inexpensive *Psistaria Pelargos* on the village platía.

Souflí and around

The nearest town to Dhadhiá, 7km north of the side turning and set among lush mulberry groves, is **SOUFLÍ**, renowned for a now all-but-vanished silk industry. The town's history as Greece's silk centre in Byzantine and Ottoman times, and a fascinating explanation of the whole silk-making process, are documented (with English text) in the **Folk and Silk Museum** (Wed–Mon: Easter to mid-Oct 10am–2pm & 5–7pm; rest of year 10am–4pm; €1.50), a little way uphill and west of the main through road. It's lodged in a fine old yellow mansion, one of a number of surviving vernacular houses, including semi-ruined *bitziklíkia*, or *koukoulóspita* in Greek (cocoon-houses), which lend Souflí some distinction. Accommodation is limited to just two **hotels**, both on the noisy main highway: the basic *Egnatia* (25540 24124; 2) at no. 225, with shared bathrooms, or the overpriced *Orfeas/Orpheus* (25540 22922; 3), with air conditioning, almost opposite at no. 172. **Eating** and **drinking** options in town aren't great either, consisting mostly of pizzerias, *souvladzídhika* and *barákia*. If you have your own transport – or if you don't mind taking a taxi – head towards Yiannoúli (signposted) and, 4km away, you'll find the excellent *Lagotrofio* taverna which serves wild boar and other game, plus *mayireftá* standards, at a wonderful hilltop location with panoramic views, under shady trees in summer, when it opens for lunch as well as dinner.

North of Souflí

A pleasant scenic alternative to the trunk road, especially if Bulgaria is your destination, is the labyrinthine, but well-signposted, network of smaller roads that heads inland through isolated villages and beautiful countryside of rolling hills and deciduous woods. It has been a state priority to establish a Greek population in this extremely sensitive and strategic corner of Thrace, hemmed in on three sides by Bulgaria and Turkey; the many signs **forbidding photography** of bridges, rivers and dams should be heeded. Military barracks and traffic police are conspicuous throughout the hinterland and along the eastern border with Turkey.

METAXÁDHES, reached from the village of Mándhra, 5km north of Souflí, is one of the most handsome villages in the area, sited on a steep hill. Once fought over by Bulgars and Turks, Metaxádhes used to support a Turkish community, but now its population is exclusively Greek. Beyond here, you descend north into the vast, fertile **Árdhas river plain** where rich farmland supports a large number of modern villages. One of the most picturesque is hilltop **PENDÁLOFOS**. The nearby **hotel**, *To Evrothirama* (25560 61242; 4), is the sole accommodation in the area and is unusual in that it doubles up as a game reserve. The **restaurant**, open at weekends only outside high season, specializes in delicious venison, wild boar and hare dishes. Accommodation consists of plain but comfortable rooms with traditional furnishing and mod cons, and the hotel's lonely but attractive setting is definitely part of the appeal.

Dhidhymótiho

DHIDHYMÓTIHO, 30km northeast of Souflí, is the last place on the trunk route into Turkey of any interest. The old part of town is still partially enclosed by the remains of double Byzantine fortifications, and some old houses and churches survive, but the area has a feeling of decay despite continuing efforts at restoration. Below the fortified hill, on the central platía, stands the most important surviving monument, a fourteenth-century **mosque**, the oldest and second largest in the Balkans. A great square box of a building with a pyramidal metal roof, its design harks back to Seljuk and other pre-Ottoman prototypes in central Anatolia, and you'll see nothing else like it between here and Divriui or Erzurum in Turkey. Unfortunately, the interior is closed indefinitely for restoration, though you can still admire the ornate west portal.

Staying is slightly problematic, as neither of the town's two **hotels** is wonderful but if you are continuing into Turkey, it's better either to stay here or head straight for Edirne (Adhrianoúpoli in Greek) than overnight in the characterless modern border town of Orestiádha. If you do stay, you'll find the *Plotini* (Ⓣ25530 23400, Ⓕ25530 22251; ❸), a rather gaudy labyrinthine building 1km south of town, set back from the west side of the main road, a better bet than the cheaper and more central but none-too-welcoming *Anessis* (Ⓣ25530 24850; ❸), 250m northwest of the mosque at Vassiléos Alexándhrou 51. For a **meal**, try the *Zythestiatorio Kypselaki* in the central market hall just above the mosque.

Travel details

Trains

Thessaloníki to: Alexandhroúpoli (5 daily; 5–6hr); Athens (11 daily; 4hr 15min–7hr); Édhessa (14 daily; 1hr 15min–1hr 35min); Lárissa (15 daily; 1hr 10min–2hr); Litóhoro (4 daily; 1hr); Véria (14 daily; 1hr); Xánthi (8 daily; 3hr 30min–4hr 20min).

Buses

Alexandhroúpoli to: Dhadhiá (2 daily; 1hr 20min); Dhidhymótiho (every 30min–1hr; 2hr); Komotiní (hourly; 1hr); Thessaloníki (6 daily; 5hr).
Édhessa to: Kastoriá (1 daily; 3hr); Thessaloníki (hourly; 1hr 30min); Véria (3–8 daily; 1hr).
Kastoriá to: Préspes (l daily; 1hr); Thessaloníki (8 daily; 3hr).
Kavála to: Alexandhroúpoli (6 daily; 3hr); Keramotí (hourly; 1hr); Komotiní (half-hourly; 2hr); Philippi (half-hourly; 20min); Thessaloníki (hourly; 2hr 15min); Xánthi (half-hourly; 1hr).
Thessaloníki to: Alexandhroúpoli (6 daily; 5hr); Athens (hourly; 7hr); Édhessa (hourly; 1hr 30min); Ierissós (6–7 daily; 2hr 30min); Ioánnina (5 daily; 7hr); Kalambáka (7 daily; 4hr 30min); Kassándhra (various resorts; 2–12 daily; 2–3hr); Kastoriá (8 daily; 3hr); Kavála (hourly; 2hr 15min); Litóhoro (6 daily; 1hr 30min); Ouranoúpoli (6–7 daily; 2hr 45min); Pélla (hourly; 1hr); Sithonía (various resorts; 3–6 daily; 2hr 30min–3hr 30min); Véria (half-hourly; 1hr 15min); Vólos (4 daily; 4hr).
Véria to: Édhessa (3–8 daily; 1hr); Thessaloníki (half-hourly; 1hr 15min); Vergina (8–10 daily; 20min).
Xánthi to: Kavála (half-hourly; 1hr); Komotiní (every 45min–1hr; 50min–1hr 15min); Thessaloníki (6–7 daily; 3hr 30min).

Ferries

Alexandhroúpoli to: Límnos, Lésvos, Híos, Sámos, Kós or Kálymnos, Rhodes (1 weekly); Samothráki (1–3 daily, 2hr 30min).
Kavála to: Áyios Efstrátios (2–4 weekly; 7hr); Híos (2–3 weekly; 12hr); Lésvos (2–3 weekly; 10hr 30min); Límnos (2–3 weekly; 5hr); Samothráki

(2–5 weekly; 5hr); Thássos (Skála Prínou; 4–8 daily; 1hr 15min).

Keramotí to: Thássos (Liménas) (8–12 daily; 40min).

Thessaloníki to: Iráklion (Crete) via Skiáthos, Tínos, Skýros, Mýkonos, Páros, Náxos and Thíra (1–4 weekly); Límnos, Lésvos and Híos (1–2 weekly); Sámos, Kós, Rhodes (1 weekly).

Flights

Alexandhroúpoli to: Athens (4–5 daily; 1hr); Sitía, Crete (3 weekly; 1hr 45min).

Kastoriá to: Athens (2 weekly; 1hr 15min).

Kavála to: Athens (3–4 daily; 1hr).

Thessaloníki to: Athens (17–20 daily; 50min); Corfu (5 weekly; 1hr); Haniá, Crete (1–2 daily; 1hr 30min); Híos (5 weekly; 1hr 10min–2hr 45min); Iráklion, Crete (3–5 daily; 1hr 15min); Kalámata (3 weekly; 1hr 20min); Kefalonia (3 weekly; 2hr 30min); Kos (summer 1 weekly; 1hr 10min); Lésvos (1–2 daily; 1hr–1hr 50min); Límnos (6 weekly; 50min); Mýkonos (summer 3 weekly; 1hr 20min); Préveza (3 weekly; 1hr 40min); Rhodes (2–4 daily; 50min); Sámos (5 weekly; 1hr 20min); Skýros (3 weekly; 40min); Thíra (summer 1–2 daily; 1hr 30min); Zákynthos (3 weekly; 3hr 15min).

Hydrofoils

Alexandhroúpoli to: Samothráki (1–2 daily April–Sept; 1hr 10min).

Kavála to: Thássos (Liménas) (8–15 daily; 40min); Thássos (Skala Prínou) (2–5 daily; 30min).

The Argo-Saronic

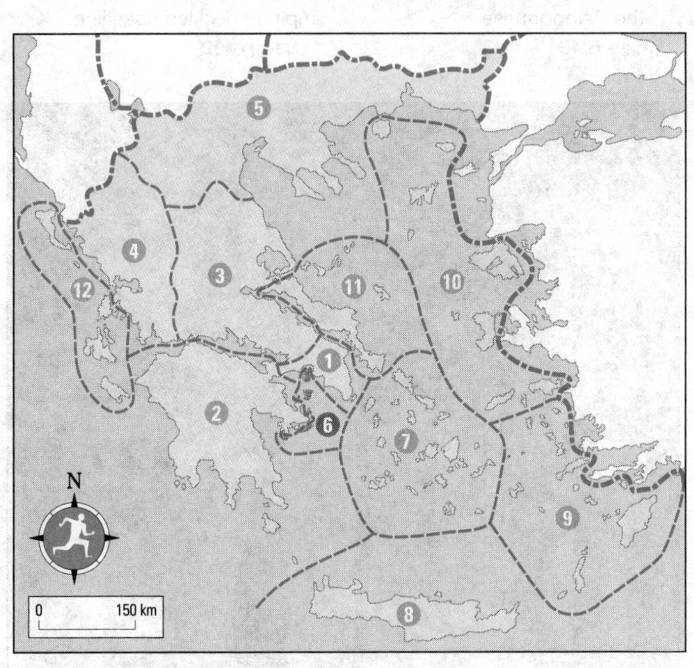

CHAPTER 6 Highlights

✱ **Temple of Aphaea, Égina** The best-preserved Archaic temple on any island, set on a wooded hill with magnificent views.
See p.488

✱ **Póros Town** Climb the clocktower for a view over the Argo-Saronic Gulf and the Peloponnese.
See p.491

✱ **Ýdhra Town** A perfect horseshoe-shaped harbour surrounded by grand eighteenth-century mansions and traffic-free streets.
See p.495

✱ **Spétses** Enjoy some of the most alluring beaches in the Argo-Saronics along Spétses' pine-speckled coastline.
See p.499

▲ Temple of Aphaea, Égina

6

The Argo-Saronic

The rocky, partly volcanic **Argo-Saronic** islands, most of them barely an olive's throw from the mainland, differ to a surprising extent not just from the land they face but also from one another. Less surprising – given their proximity to the mainland and their beauty – is their massive popularity, with Égina (Aegina) almost becoming an Athenian suburb at weekends. Ýdhra (Hydra), Póros and Spétses are scarcely different in summer, though their visitors include a higher proportion of foreign tourists. More than any other group, these islands are best out of season and mid-week, when visiting populations fall dramatically and the port towns return to a quieter, more provincial pace.

The northernmost island of the Argo-Saronic group, **Salamína**, is effectively a suburb of Pireás. The narrow strait, barely a kilometre across (where, in 480 BC, the Greek navy trounced the Persian fleet, see p.900), is crossed by a constant stream of ferries – most from Paloúkia, 5km west of Pireás – but there's little to attract you on the other side and the island isn't covered any further here. **Égina**, important in antiquity and more or less continually inhabited since then, is infinitely preferable: the most fertile of the group, famous for its pistachio nuts and home to one of the finest ancient temples in Greece. The three southerly islands, upmarket **Spétses**, tiny, car-free **Ýdhra** and green **Póros**, are pine-covered to various degrees, comparatively infertile, and rely on water piped or transported in rusting freighters from the mainland. Accordingly, they were not extensively settled until medieval times, when refugees from the mainland established themselves here. In response to the barrenness and dryness of their new homes the islanders adopted seagoing commerce (and piracy) as livelihoods. The seamanship and huge fleets thus acquired were placed at the disposal of the Greek insurgents during the War of Independence. Today, foreigners and Athenians have replaced locals in the depopulated harbour towns; windsurfers, water-taxis and yachts are faint echoes of the massed warships, schooners and *kaïkia* once at anchor.

For all of these islands, **hydrofoil** services are faster and more frequent than ferries, and cost little more. If you hope to bring a vehicle for the weekend, reserve your trip well in advance.

Égina (Aegina)

A substantial and attractive island with a proud history, less than an hour from Pireás, Égina is not surprisingly a popular weekend escape from Athens. Despite

the holiday homes, though, it retains a laid-back, island atmosphere to an extraordinary degree, especially if you visit midweek or out of season. Famous for its **pistachio orchards** – the nuts are hawked from stalls all around the harbour – the island can also boast substantial ancient remains, far and away the finest of which is the beautiful fifth-century BC **Temple of Aphaea**, commanding superb views towards Athens from high above the northeast coast, close to the resort-port of **Ayía Marína**.

Inhabited from the earliest times, ancient **Aegina** was a significant regional power as early as the Bronze Age, and later a rival of Classical Athens. It traded to the limits of the known world, maintained a sophisticated silver coinage system (the first in Greece) and fostered prominent athletes and craftsmen. During the fifth century BC, however, the islanders made the political mistake of siding with the Spartans. Athens used this as a pretext to act on long-standing jealousy; her fleets defeated those of the islanders in two separate sea battles and, after the second, the population was expelled and replaced by more tractable colonists.

Subsequent history was less distinguished, with a familiar pattern of occupation – by Romans, Franks, Venetians, Catalans and Ottomans – before the War of Independence brought a brief period of glory as seat of government for the fledgling Greek nation, from 1826 to 1828. For many decades thereafter Égina was a penal island, and you can still see the **enormous jail** on the edge of town; the building was originally an **orphanage**, founded by first president Kapodhistrias in 1828.

Égina Town

ÉGINA TOWN, the island's capital, makes an attractive base, with some grand old buildings around a large, busy harbour. The Neoclassical architecture is matched by a sophisticated ethos, with a semi-permanent yacht-dwelling contingent, good food and drink, and a well-stocked bazaar which remains lively even at weekends.

Arrival and information

On arrival, you'll find yourself docking pretty much at the heart of town. The **bus station** is on Platía Ethneyersías, immediately north, with excellent services to most villages; buy your tickets beforehand at the little booth. The **taxi** rank is at the base of the jetty, opposite the row of **cabins** selling tickets for the various catamarans, **ferries and hydrofoils**; some hydrofoils from Pireás continue to Angístri, but the most frequent service is the *Angístri Express*, which ties up among the pleasure and fishing boats to the south. The **post office** is at the rear of the platía, and numerous banks have **ATM**s here and around the harbour. Several places on and behind the main waterfront rent cars, scooters, motorbikes and mountain bikes – Égina is large and hilly enough to make a motor worthwhile for anything other than a pedal to the local beaches: try Trust (Ⓣ22970 27010). Aegina Island Holidays (Ⓣ22970 26430), on the waterfront near the church of Panayítsa, offers excursions to the Epidaurus festival, among others (see p.194). **Internet** access is available at Prestige, on Eákou at the corner of Spýrou Ródhi, and at several harbour-front cafés. **Foreign-language papers** are stocked by Kalezis, midway along the waterfront.

Accommodation

As on most of the Argo-Saronics, **accommodation** is at a premium at weekends but midweek and out of season, rates can drop appreciably. With the exceptions noted, most lodgings are subject to a certain amount of traffic noise and facilities, including bathrooms, which can be pretty rudimentary.

Artemis Kanári 20 Ⓣ22970 25195, Ⓦwww.artemishotel-aegina.com. Standard 1960s hotel, but rooms (with fridges and a/c) are adequate and it's probably the quietest location in town; views from the front rooms over a pistachio orchard are second to none. ③

Brown Southern waterfront, past Panayítsa church Ⓣ22970 22271, Ⓦwww.hotelbrown.gr. The town's top offering, this B-class/3-star hotel opposite the southerly town beach, housed in a former sponge factory dating from 1886, earns its rating from its vast common areas (terrace bar, buffet-breakfast salon). The best and calmest units are the garden bungalows; there are also galleried family suites sleeping four. B&B ④

Eginitiko Arhontiko Cnr Thomaïdhou and Ayíou Nikólaou, by the Markellos Tower Ⓣ22970 24968, Ⓦwww.aeginitikoarchontiko.gr. Well-appointed rooms, all with double beds, fridges and a/c, at this spectacular converted ochre-and-orange Neoclassical mansion. The pièce de résistance is the suite (⑤) with painted ceilings; breakfast is served in a pretty conservatory. B&B ④

Elektra Leonárdhou Ladhá 25, northwest of the square Ⓣ22970 26715, Ⓦwww.aegina-electra.gr. Quiet establishment with compact but comfortable rooms with small balconies; near the more easily spotted *Hotel Marmarinos*. ③

Pavlou Behind Panayítsa church at Eyinítou 21 Ⓣ22970 22795. A good budget hotel with a/c and

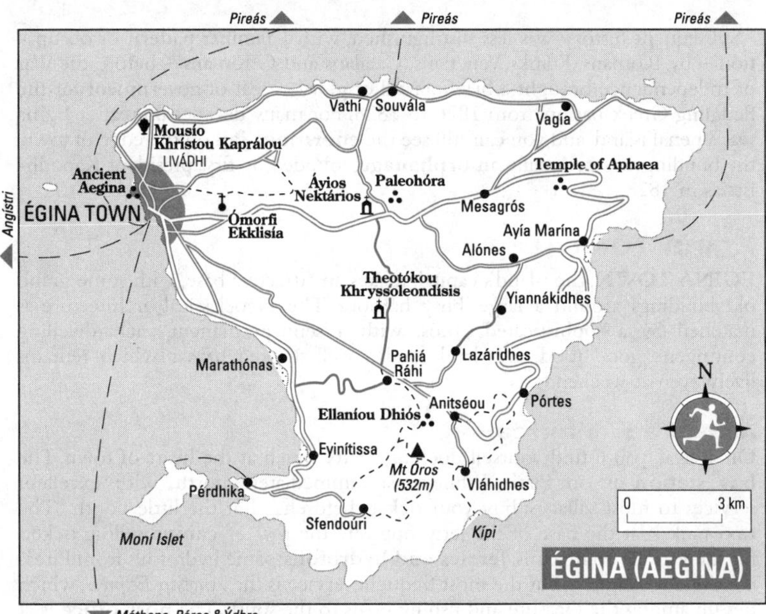

some double beds in the mosaic-floored rooms; some rooms have their baths across the hall. ❸ **Plaza** Kazantzáki 4 ☎22970 25600. One of a series of small waterfront hotels immediately north of Platía Ethneyersías, close to the town beach. En-suite rooms, with fridges and a/c, are pretty basic and can suffer from traffic noise, but there are great sea views from those at the front, and little balconies from which to appreciate them. ❸

The Town

The harbour **waterfront** combines the workaday with the picturesque: fishermen talk and tend their nets, *kaïkia* sell produce from the mainland, and there's one of the finest seascapes in Greece, comprising other Argo-Saronic isles and Peloponnesian mountains. Sights in town are few, but it's well worth seeking out the restored **Pýrgos Markéllou** or Markellos Tower, an extraordinary miniature castle which was the seat of the first Greek government after independence. You can't go inside, but walking there, through the cramped inland streets, is enjoyable in itself.

The site of **Ancient Aegina** (Tues–Sun 8.30am–3pm; €3) lies immediately north of town on a promontory known as **Kolóna** (column), after the lone column that stands there. The extensive remains, centring on a Temple of Apollo at the highest point, are well signed, and some reconstruction makes it easier to make out the various layers of settlement from different eras. Near the entrance, a small but worthwhile **archeological museum** houses finds from the site, along with information on the island's ancient history. Highlights of the display include a room of Minoan-influenced Middle Bronze Age pottery, rescued from a nearby building site.

On the north edge of town, between the port and Kolóna, there's a tiny but popular **beach** with remarkably shallow water. You can also swim to the south of town, but there are more enticing spots further north – immediately beyond Kolóna there's an attractive bay with a small, sandy **beach**, while other small coves lie off the road heading further out of town in this direction. Just one, **Prosínemo**, has any facilities, with loungers and a bar. As you head out this way, a plaque marks the house in the suburb of Livádhi where **Nikos Kazantzakis** lived in the 1940s and 1950s and wrote his most celebrated book, *Zorba the Greek*. Some 3km out of town in the same direction, admirably signposted and marked by a giant bronze sculpture on the seafront outside, is the **Mousío Khrístou Kaprálou/Christos Kapralos Museum** (June–Oct Tues–Sun 10am–2pm & 6–8pm; Nov–May Fri–Sun 10am–2pm; €2), housed in the prominent Greek artist's former studios. The influence of Henry Moore is evident in the hefty wood, terracotta and bronze pieces on display, and there's a replica of his famous frieze *Monument of the Battle of the Pindus*, the original of which now adorns a hall in the Greek Parliament building.

Eating, drinking and entertainment

There are plenty of good places to eat and drink in Égina, particularly at the south end of pedestrianized Panayióti Irióti behind the fish market, and at the far ends of the waterfront – fussy Athenian patronage keeps the standards up (for the most part). The cafés near the ferry jetty and in the centre of the waterfront tend to be less good value. Athenians are also partly responsible for a surprisingly ample choice of **nightlife** given a town of about nine thousand souls. There are three summer open-air **cinemas** – Anesis on Eákou towards the Pýrgos Markéllou, Olympia on Faneroménis opposite the football grounds, and Akroyiali beyond the football grounds on the Pérdhika road; indoor Titina, opposite the Pýrgos Markéllou, is open year-round. **Live music** – mostly Greek – is performed regularly at *En Egini*, Spýrou Ródhi 44 (ⓣ22970 22922); look out for posters to see what's on, and book if you want to secure a table. *Ellinikon* is a big, enjoyable, somewhat touristy club on the southern fringe of town, near the Cine Akroyiali.

Avli Panayióti Irióti 17. Always busy: some of the least expensive breakfasts in town, then later becomes a full-service taverna and into the early hours transforms into a popular bar with Latin/jazz sounds. Summer seating in the *avlí* (courtyard), and a cosy interior with fireplace for winter.

Babis Southern end of the waterfront at cnr of Faneromenis, beyond *Hotel Brown*. Modern, fashionable ouzerí with a seafront terrace and trendy Athenian crowd; excellent food, relatively high prices.

Flisvos North waterfront by town beach. The best spot for grilled fresh fish and a few meat dishes, at fair prices.

Ippokambos Faneromenis 9, a couple of blocks inland from the southern end of the waterfront. An attractive, slightly upmarket *mezedhopolío* run by Lebanese George, with rich fare including dishes such as pork roulade and stuffed squid. Dinner only, 7.30pm–1am.

Lekkas Kazantzáki 4, adjacent to *Flisvos*. Renowned for good vegetable platters and well-sourced meat grills, washed down by excellent sherry-like house wine. Very inexpensive for Égina.

Pelaïsos Waterfront just south of the market. The best value of a cluster of Greek-patronized taverna-ouzerís in this area, with a good mix of platters, but limited seating. Opens 8.15am for breakfast too.

Yeladhakis (also known as tou Steliou or Iy Agora) Rear of fish market. The best, and least expensive, of three rival seafood ouzerís here (though the others are very good too); accordingly it's usually mobbed and you may have to wait for a table. Summer seating in the cobbled lane, winter up in the loft inside.

Paleohóra and the Temple of Aphaea

Two main routes lead east towards Ayía Marína and the Temple of Aphaea: you can head directly inland from Égina Town across the centre of the island, or follow the north coast road via **Souvála**. Along this north coast there are plenty of scruffy beaches and clusters of second-home development, while Souvála itself is something of an Athenian resort (with a direct daily ferry to Pireás) and a number of places to eat on the seafront. On the inland route you'll pass the whitewashed modern convent of **Áyios Nektários,** whose vast church is said to be the largest in Greece.

On the hillside opposite is the ghost-village of **Paleohóra**. Established in early Christian times as a refuge against piracy, it thrived under the Venetians (1451–1540) but was destroyed by Barbarossa in 1537. The Turks took over and rebuilt the town, but it was again destroyed (this time by the Venetians) in 1654, and finally abandoned altogether in the early nineteenth century. The place consists now of some thirty stone chapels dotted across a rocky outcrop, an extraordinary sight from a distance. Little remains of the town itself – when the islanders left, they simply dismantled their houses and moved the masonry to newly founded Égina Town. You can drive right up to the site (unenclosed, free), where a helpful map shows the churches and the paths that lead up the hill between them: most are semi-derelict and locked, but in a couple you can see remains of ancient frescoes.

The Doric **Temple of Aphaea** (summer Tues–Sun 8am–7.15pm, winter Tues–Sun 8am–5pm; €4) stands on a pine-covered hill 12km east of Égina Town, with stunning views all around: Athens, Cape Soúnio, the Peloponnese and Ýdhra are all easily made out. It is one of the most complete and visually complex ancient buildings in Greece, its superimposed arrays of columns and lintels evocative of an Escher drawing. Built between 500 and 480 BC to replace two destroyed sixth-century predecessors, it slightly predates the Parthenon. The dedication is unusual: Aphaea was a Cretan nymph who, fleeing from the lust of King Minos, fell into the sea, was caught by some fishermen and brought to ancient Aegina, the only known locus of her cult, and one observed here since 1300 BC. As recently as two centuries ago, the temple's pediments were intact and essentially in perfect condition, depicting two battles at Troy. However, like the Elgin marbles, they were "purchased" from the Turks – this time by Ludwig I of Bavaria, and they currently reside in Munich's Glyptothek museum. There's excellent, informative signage and a small **museum** (Tues–Sun 8am–2.15pm) with a great deal of information about the history and architecture of the temple as well as numerous statues and architectural features rescued from it.

At least six daily **buses** from Égina Town to Ayía Marína stop at the temple, or you can walk up from Ayía Marína along a well-signed path.

The east: Ayía Marína to Mount Óros

The island's major beach resort, **AYÍA MARÍNA**, lies steeply below the temple on the east coast. It has clearly seen better days, as the number of empty premises and the ugly, half-built hotel overshadowing the beach attest, but package tourism (predominantly Scandinavian) is picking up again, and it can be a lively and enjoyable place, with plenty of hotels and rooms, tavernas, cafés, bars and shops. There's a good, clean beach that shelves very gently, and plenty of places to eat, many of them catering to day-trippers – several direct boats arrive from Pireás daily. *O Faros* taverna, right by the tiny fishing harbour, has a lovely location with ducks and geese wandering through, and good no-nonsense Greek food.

Beyond the resort, the paved road continues south 8km to **PÓRTES**, a tiny hamlet with a distinctly end-of-the-road feel. Three tiny fish **tavernas** overlook the water: *Galinopetra*, by the tiny harbour, is the most basic, *Thanasis* next up is the most ambitious, whilst *Akroyiali* to the south falls somewhere inbetween. All offer fish and *mezédhes*. Beyond *Akroyiali* stretches a partly sandy beach with decent snorkelling and a summer *kantína*.

From here, the road climbs steeply inland, heading back towards Égina Town via the villages of Anitséou (with a taverna), just below a major saddle on the flank of Mount Óros, and **Pahiá Ráhi**. The latter, with fine views eastwards, has been almost entirely rebuilt in traditional style by foreign and Athenian owners.

Marathónas to Pérdhika

The road south of Égina Town, along the west coast of the island, is flat and easy, served by regular buses (8–9 daily). Sprawling **MARATHÓNAS**, 5km from Égina, has the biggest if not the prettiest of the west coast's sandy beaches, along with a scattering of rooms, tavernas and cafés along the shore. The next settlement, **Eyinítissa**, has a popular, sheltered cove backed by eucalypts and a beach bar.

PÉRDHIKA, at the end of the coastal road, scenically set on a little bay packed with yachts, is the most picturesque village on the island. It also has the best range of non-package holiday **accommodation** outside Égina Town: good options include *Hotel Hippocampus* (ⓣ22970 61363, ⓦwww.hippocampus-hotel-greece.com; ❸), *Antzi Studios* (ⓣ22970 61233, ⓦwww.antzistudios.gr; ❸), a large complex with a pool, and pink-painted *Villa Rodanthos* (ⓣ22970 61400, ⓦwww.villarodanthos.gr; ❸).

The pedestrianized waterfront esplanade at the southern edge of Pérdhika, overlooking Moní islet and the Peloponnese, is the heart of tourist life. Half a dozen good **tavernas** compete for your trade: *Saronis* is a little cheaper and gets considerable local patronage; *To Proreon*, with its potted-plant decor, has the most attractive atmosphere; while *Andonis*, an Athenian hangout, is the most popular fish taverna of the bunch. Among several **café-bars**, mostly at the far end, *Hermes* is the main late-night spot.

The only other diversion at Pérdhika is a trip to the pale-limestone offshore islet of **Moní** (10min; several departures daily in summer; €5 return). There are no facilities on the island, most of which is fenced off as a nature conservation area, but it's worth the trip for a swim in wonderfully clear water, since Pérdhika Bay itself is shallow and yacht-tainted.

Angístri

Angístri, fifteen minutes by fast boat from Égina, is a tiny island, obscure enough to be overlooked by most island-hoppers, though the visitors it does have are a diverse mix: Athenian weekenders, retirees who bought and restored property here years ago, plus a few British and Scandinavian package holiday-makers. There's a tiny, not terribly attractive strip of development on the north coast, facing Égina, but the rest of the island is pine-covered, timeless and beautiful – albeit with very few beaches.

Skála, Metóhi and Mýlos

Two small ports just a couple of kilometres apart dominate the north coast. Both are served by the *Angístri Express* from Égina. **SKÁLA** is the main tourist centre, with a sandy beach backed by a straggle of modern development; restaurants, apartments, hotels and cafés. The beach, and most of the new development, lies to the right from the jetty, but there are some far more attractive **places to stay**, looking out over a rocky coastline, if you turn left. Of the places towards the beach, the *Aktaion Hotel* (ⓣ22970 91222, ⓦwww.stayinagistri.gr; ❸), visible from the jetty, is the best option, with a swimming

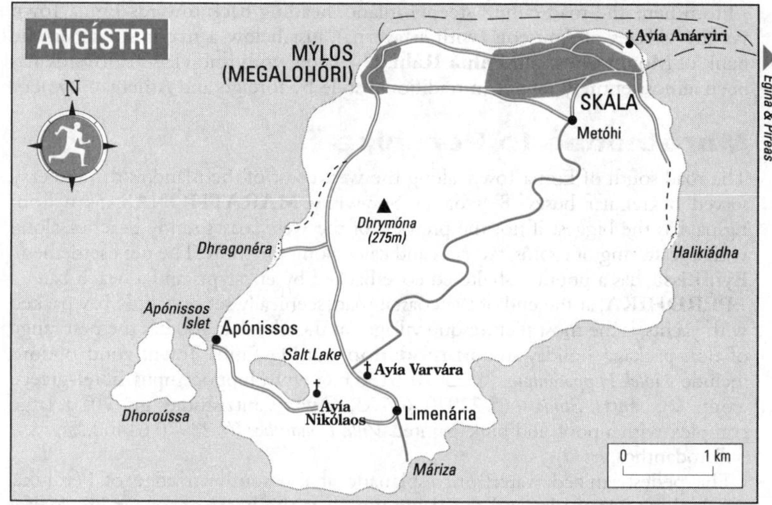

pool, restaurant and well-appointed rooms and apartments. Places to the left (south) offer peace and an unobstructed view of the water: try the *Alkyoni Hotel* (☎22970 91377; ❸), with large stone-floored rooms and a lovely coffee/breakfast bar, or the slightly pricier *Rosy's Little Village* (☎22970 91610, Ⓦwww.rosyslittlevillage.com; ❸), with direct access to its own rocky swimming spot; both offer air conditioning, TV and balconies. *Rosy's* also has a pleasant **restaurant**, and there are plenty more to choose from around the beach: *Yiorgos*, directly above the jetty, and *Gionis*, a short way round to the right, are both recommended. There are lively bars and cafés here too, including a couple with **Internet** access, and even an open-air cinema in summer.

From the paved road's end just beyond the *Alkyoni Hotel*, a marked path leads along the cliff-top to secluded **Halikiádha**, a pebble beach, predominantly nudist, backed by crumbling cliffs. The slightly scary scramble down is rewarded by the island's best swimming.

METÓHI, the hillside hamlet just above Skála, was once the main village, but now consists chiefly of holiday homes. If you can face the steep climb there are wonderful views, though, as well as the excellent *Taverna Parnassos* and comfortable modern studios with kitchen at *Metohi Studios* (☎22970 91382; ❸).

The least attractive aspect of Angístri is the windblown road along the coast to **MÝLOS** (Megalohóri), barely half an hour's walk away, the main port of call for the hydrofoils. Mýlos itself has an attractive, traditional village centre with a church and platía, though lack of a beach means few people stay here. Access to the rest of the island is easy, however, and there are plenty of **rooms** and tavernas.

The rest of the island

Scooters and **mountain bikes** are available for rent from several outlets in Skála and Mýlos; it is less than 10km to the furthest point of the island, so in cooler weather you can comfortably cross Angístri by pedal power, or on foot from Metóhi along a winding dirt track through the pines. In summer only, four daily departures of a box-like **minibus** connect Skála and Mýlos with Limenária. The broad, paved west-coast road takes you past the turning for

Dhragonéra, a beautiful but rocky pine-fringed beach with a dramatic panorama across to the mainland; there's a summer *kantína* here and other small coves accessible across the rocks. Despite the warning signs, people camp in the woods around these beaches.

LIMENÁRIA, a small farming community at the edge of a fertile plateau in the southeast corner of the island, is still largely unaffected by tourism. The single, central **taverna** – *O Tasos* – is popular at weekends, but pricier than you'd expect for the location; they also sell local produce. The closest swimming is a few hundred metres east down a cement drive, then steps, at **Máriza**, where a diminutive concrete lido gives access to deep, crystalline water. A broader paved road leads 2km west, past a shallow salt marsh, to the little anchorage of **Apónissos**, connected via a small causeway to an eponymous islet (private, off limits), with the larger island of **Dhoroússa** looming beyond. The *Aponisos Taverna* here (summer only) has a matchless seaside setting but the only swimming is in a tiny, hot and stagnant area to the right of the harbour.

Póros

Separated from the mainland by a 350-metre strait, **Póros** ("the ford") barely qualifies as an island at all, and more than any other Argo-Saronic island it remains a (mostly Swedish) package-tour venue; proximity to Pireás – and storm-proof access from the Argolid opposite – also guarantees a weekend Athenian invasion. Póros is in fact two islands, **Sferiá** (Póros Town) and the far larger **Kalávria**, separated from each other by a shallow canal, now silting up, spanned by a bridge. The town is a busy place, with constant traffic of shipping and people: if your stay is longer than a couple of nights you may want to base yourself on Kalávria for a little more peace, coming into town for the food, nightlife and shopping.

In addition to regular ferry and hydrofoil connections with Pireás and the other Argo-Saronics, Póros has frequent, almost round-the-clock passenger boats shuttling across from the workaday mainland port of **Galatás** in the Peloponnese (5 min; €0.70, €1 after midnight, pay on the boat), plus a car ferry every half hour. These permit interesting excursions – locally to ancient Troezen and the nearby Dhia voloyéfyro (see p.196), for example, or to Náfplio or Epidaurus. Local travel agents run tours to these places, or simply rent a car in Galatás.

Póros Town

PÓROS TOWN rises steeply across the western half of tiny volcanic Sferiá, a landmark clocktower at its summit offering great views of the tiled rooftops and straits. There's a two-room **archeological museum** on the waterfront (Tues–Sun 8.30am–3pm; €2) whose local finds will fill a spare half-hour, but otherwise few sights. This is a place to eat, drink, shop and watch the world go by. Away from the waterfront you'll quickly get lost in the labyrinth of steep, narrow streets, but nowhere is far away and most of the restaurants reasonably well signed.

In any event, most things are on the waterfront; small passenger boats tie up among the yachts and other small vessels on the southerly side facing Galatás; hydrofoils and ferries further round the promontory to the north, and car ferries from Galatás right at the northern end. Close to the ferry and hydrofoil docking points are several **travel agents**, including Marinos Tours (Ⓣ22980 23423), for Hellenic Seaways hydrofoil tickets and local **maps**; Askeli Travel

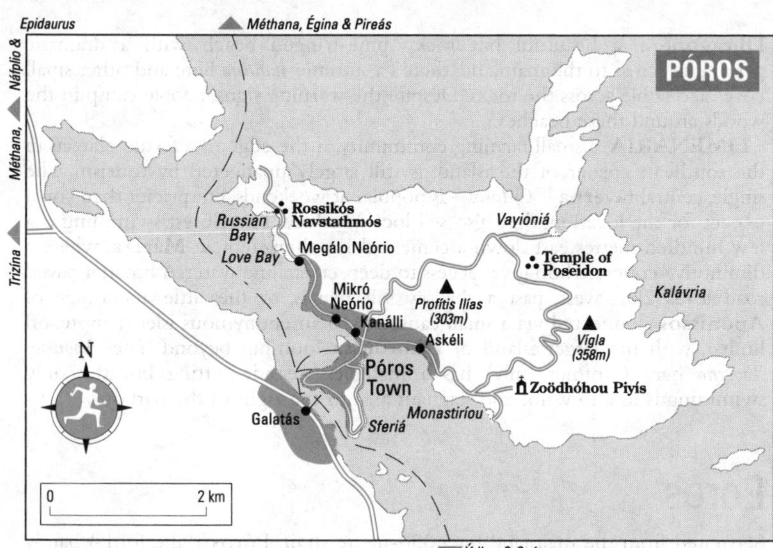

(Ⓣ22980 24900), for conventional ferry tickets; and the Euroseas agent (Ⓣ22980 25902). These and other agencies such as Family Tours (Ⓣ22980 23743) and Saronic Gulf Travel (Ⓣ22980 24555) also offer tours and can find **accommodation** right across the island. Nearby you'll also find **scooter**, **car** and **bicycle** rental outlets, **banks** (with **ATM**s) and a **post office**. **Internet** access and foreign-language newspapers are available at the newsagent/bookshop Kendro Typou, opposite the long-haul ferry berthing, and there are a couple more Internet cafés nearby toward the car ferries. **Buses**, which offer a regular service across to Kalávria and west to Russian Bay or east to the monastery, leave from the central waterfront near the Galatás passenger boats, as do **boat trips** around the island and a little train whose trips include a regular evening haul all the way up to the Temple of Poseidon.

Accommodation

Rooms in Póros Town itself can be in very short supply at weekends and holiday times, when prices are inevitably high (they can be dramatically lower out of season); some noise is always likely too. At busy times it can be worth checking the agencies above, or the extensive listings at Ⓦwww.poros.com.gr. The greatest concentration is found near the Galatás car-ferry dock, where a number of very basic places hang out "rooms" signs. More comfortable hotels around the waterfront include *Dionysos* (Ⓣ22980 23511, Ⓦwww.hoteldionysos.com; ④), a converted mansion immediately opposite the dock, and 7 *Brothers* (Ⓣ22980 23412, Ⓦwww.7brothers.gr; ④), a very friendly place with an unmistakeable pink paint-job, closer to the centre of the waterfront. **Rooms** higher up in town include *Villa Tryfon* (Ⓣ22980 25854, Ⓔvillatryfon@poros.com.gr; ③), small apartments with air conditioning and kitchen, mostly with bay-view balconies and cheerful blue-and-white decor, and *Nikos* rooms at the *Karavolos taverna* (see opposite; Ⓣ693 2160 940; ③).

Over **on Kalávria** there's considerably more choice, with plenty of apartment complexes and small hotels in the touristy enclaves of Askéli – close to good beaches – or less attractive Mikró Neório. Considerably better, more upmarket options include family-run hotel-taverna *Pavlou* (Ⓣ22980 22734, Ⓔ Pavlou@poros.gr; ⑤), right on the beach **in Megálo Neório**, *Sirene* (Ⓣ22980 22741; ⑥), a large hotel with pool and tennis courts spectacularly sited above the beach at Monastiríou, and *Poros Image* (Ⓣ22980 22216, Ⓦ www.porosimage.gr; ⑥), a newly refurbished, elegant designer hotel with great views back across the bay towards Póros Town from the waterfront between Mikró and Megálo Neório.

Eating, drinking and nightlife

The central waterfront is mostly given over to competing cafés, bars and souvenir shops, with just a few full **tavernas**. Of these, the best are near the Town Hall and museum, where the waiters compete furiously for your custom – *Kathestos*, for example, has good seafood. Prices and quality are better up the hill and even, surprisingly, on Kalávria. Beside the open-air Cinema Diana at the northern end of the waterfront, signs point up to *Karavolos* ("snail"; dinner only), which, true to its name, has snails on the menu along with other typical ouzerí fare; portions are large and prices fair. *O Platanos* is one of several evening-only tavernas around the town square by the church of Ayíou Yeoryíou; it's most easily found by following one of the stepped streets up behind the Town Hall.

The southern end of the waterfront is also the place for better-value cafés – two to single out are *Mostra*, at the rear of Platía Dhimarhíou, and *Iy Platia*, next to the archeological museum – and **bars**. These and the **nightlife** get livelier as you head out along the coast road in this direction, with numerous bar/clubs including *Maskes*, *Orion* and *Sirocco*, the latter right round on the uninhabited side of Sferiá. The island's top venue is day-and-night-club *Poseidonio* (1pm until small hours), looking down over town from a Kalávria hillside, with a pool and DJ.

▲ Waterfront, Póros Town

Kalávria: beaches and temples

Crossing the bridge to Kalávria you've a choice of turning left, for beaches at Neório and Russian Bay, or right to Askéli and the road round the island. In either direction, keep going awhile, as the immediate environs of the canal are overdeveloped and unattractive. Heading left (west) the first place worth a stop is **Megálo Neório**, arguably the island's most pleasant resort, small-scale, with a sandy beach, small watersports centre and some excellent beachside tavernas, such as the one attached to the *Hotel Pavlou*. **Love Bay**, next along, has a lovely sandy beach, unfortunately tiny and always packed. End of the road (for the bus at least – paving continues a little further past some more small coves) is the **Rossikós Navstathmós** on Russian Bay, a crumbling Russian naval base dating from the late eighteenth century. There's a hard-packed, mostly shadeless beach here, with lots of small craft anchored offshore.

East of the canal **Askéli**, with its strip of hotels and villas, has some more good places to eat and a long but crowded beach, again with watersports. The bus in this direction terminates at the eighteenth-century **monastery of Zoödhóhou Piyís** (daily sunrise–1.30pm & 4.30pm–sunset) next to the island's only spring. Steps from the bus stop lead down to the pleasant sandy beach of **Monastiríou**, usually one of the island's less crowded, though hardly empty as the two **tavernas** here will testify.

Above the monastery a good paved road winds upward to circle round inland Kalávria and back towards Póros Town. The rest of the island is covered in pine forest and barely inhabited, though there are a couple of fertile plateaus on the northern side with olive terraces, vineyards and magnificent panoramic views. From a saddle between the island's two highest peaks the road descends past the well-signed foundations of a sixth-century BC **Temple of Poseidon** (enclosed but gate always open; free). It was here that Demosthenes, fleeing from the Macedonians after taking part in the last-ditch resistance of the Athenians, took poison rather than surrender. It's an extensive site, though there's not a great deal to see above ground level – many of the stones were carted off to be used as building materials in the seventeenth and eighteenth centuries (much of it ended up on Ýdhra) and some of the more interesting sections are roped off for excavation. Beyond the temple a road leads down to **Vayioniá**, port of the ancient shrine. It's a beautiful spot with a seasonal snack bar, and just about the only accessible beach on the island's north shore, though sand and room for sunbathing are limited.

Ýdhra (Hydra)

The island of Ýdhra is one of the most atmospheric and refreshing destinations in Greece. Its harbour and main town preserved as a national monument, it feels like a Greek island should, entirely traffic-free (even bicycles are banned) with a bustling harbour and narrow stone streets climbing steeply above it. Away from the main settlement the rest of the island is roadless, rugged and barely inhabited. The charm hasn't gone un-noticed of course – Ýdhra became fashionable as early as the 1950s and in the Sixties characters ranging from Greek painter Nikos Hatzikyriakos-Ghikas to Canadian songster Leonard Cohen bought and restored grand old houses here. But even the seasonal and weekend crowds, and a very limited number of good beaches, can't seriously detract from the appeal. When the town is over-run, it's easy enough to leave it all behind on foot or by excursion boat.

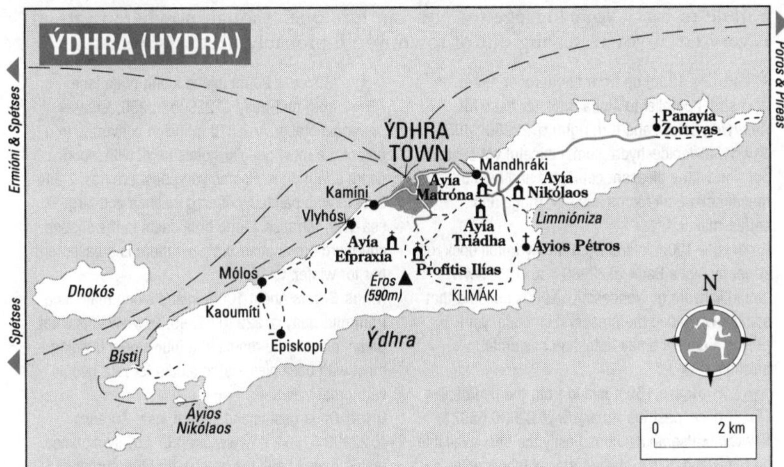

Ýdhra Town

ÝDHRA TOWN and port, with tiers of substantial grey-stone mansions and humbler white-walled, red-tiled houses rising from a perfect horseshoe harbour, form a beautiful spectacle. The waterfront mansions were built mostly during the eighteenth century on the accumulated wealth of a remarkable merchant fleet, which traded as far afield as America and – during the Napoleonic Wars – broke the British blockade to sell grain to France. Fortunes were made and the island also enjoyed a special relationship with the Ottoman Porte, governing itself and paying no tax in return for providing sailors to the sultan's navy. These conditions naturally attracted Greek immigrants from the less privileged mainland, and by the 1820s the town's population was nearly 20,000 – an incredible figure when you reflect that today it is under 3000. During the War of Independence, Ýdhra's merchants provided many of the ships for the Greek forces and consequently many of the commanders.

Arrival and information

The town is fairly compact, but away from the waterfront, streets and alleyways are steep and labyrinthine; the best **map** is that issued by Saitis Tours next to the Alpha Bank (☎22980 52184), also agents for the Euroseas **catamaran**. Tickets for Hellenic Seaways **hydrofoils** and conventional ferries are sold on the eastern front, upstairs right opposite their anchorage (☎22980 54007). Several **banks** with **ATMs** can be found round the waterfront, the **post office** is on the market square just inland, and numerous places offer **Internet** access – closest to the harbour is the shop immediately behind the waterfront Alpha Bank.

Accommodation

Because of the preservation order affecting the entire town, construction of new accommodation is banned, private balconies are rare (though air conditioning is almost universal) and the limited number of beds are in restored premises, all priced accordingly. Addresses and street signs are almost non-existent, so ask for directions when you book. The pricier places may provide a mule to carry your luggage (or you can hire one), though nowhere in town is very far; if you're staying out of town, you'll probably need a water-taxi.

Alkionides 120m up from the harbour street, on next street parallel to Alpha Bank (or head for *Amaryllis*, below, and turn right) ⓣ22980 54055, ⓦwww.alkionideshydra.com. Peaceful yet central pension with a pleasant courtyard and helpful management; all rooms have TV, fridge and coffee-maker. ❹

Amaryllis 100m inland from the hydrofoil dock, up street by Alpha Bank ⓣ22980 53611, ⓦwww.amarillishydra.gr. Nondescript 1960s building that somehow evaded the preservation code, yet it proves a decent small hotel and has small balconies. ❹

Bratsera 150m inland from the hydrofoil dock, past the *Amaryllis* ⓣ22980 53971, ⓦwww.bratserahotel.com. Easily the best available on the island, this A-class/4-star hotel occupies a stylishly renovated former sponge factory, and the extensive common areas (including bar, restaurant, conference room and courtyard pool) serve as a de facto museum of the industry with photos and artefacts. There are five grades of rooms, even the lowest two having flagstone floors and proper shower stalls. Open mid-March to Oct. ❼–❽

Kirki 60m from harbour, close to the market ⓣ22980 52564, ⓦwww.hydrakirki.gr. Unprepossessing entry leads to a delightful old house, with simple, island-style rooms and a small courtyard garden. ❹

Miranda 200m inland along main lane from mid-quay ⓣ22980 52230, ⓦwww.mirandahotel.gr. An 1810 mansion converted into one of the most popular hotels here, with wood floors and fridges. Rooms vary; best are nos. 2 and 3, both with painted, coffered ceilings and large sea-view terraces. Large breakfasts in the shaded courtyard are another big plus; there is a basement bar for winter. ❺–❻

Nikos Botsis About 100m inland along main lane from mid-quay ⓣ22980 52395, ⓦwww.botsis.net. Clean, plain white rooms in a four-storey building, most with balconies – attic studio for four people with great views. ❸

Orloff On largest inland square, near *Miranda* ⓣ22980 52564, ⓦwww.orloff.gr. Lovely mansion restored as a boutique hotel, with blue-curtained and -carpeted, high-ceilinged rooms and suites. High enough in town for partial sea views, with a very secluded courtyard where a superior buffet breakfast is served. ❼

Pityoussa On the southeast edge of town, beyond *Amaryllis*. ⓣ22980 52810, ⓦwww.piteoussa.com. Named after the three giant pines out front, this inn has just five ground-floor, recently refurbished units, with cutting-edge facilities, including CD and DVD players and designer baths. If full, the co-managed, more basic *Theodoros* (❸) is next door. ❺

The Town

At each side of the harbour, cannons facing out to sea and statues of the heroes of independence remind you of Ýdhra's place in history. Between them, the **mansions** of the wealthy eighteenth-century merchant families are still the great monuments of the town; some are labelled at the entrance with "*Oikía*" ("Residence of...") followed by the family name. Among the finest are the two Koundouriotis mansions, one on each side of town. The **Lazaro Koundouriotis Museum** (Tues–Sun 9am–4pm; €4) is the large yellow building high on the western side. It's a hot climb up the stepped alleyways, but you're rewarded with great views down over the town and port, and a lovingly restored interior that looks ready to move into. The red-tiled floors, panelled wooden ceilings and period furnishings outshine the contents of the museum – paintings, folk costume and independence paraphernalia. Across on the eastern waterfront, another of the great houses is now the **Historical Archives Museum** (Tues–Sun 9.30am–5pm; €4), with a small, crowded and enjoyable display of clothing, period engravings, and ships' prows and sidearms from the independence struggle. The **Melina Mercouri Centre**, next door, often has interesting temporary art exhibitions.

The most obvious and important of Ýdhra's many churches is **Kímisis tís Theotókou** by the port, with a distinctive clocktower and a cloistered courtyard housing a small **Ecclesiastical Museum** (Tues–Sun 10am–5pm; €2).

Eating, drinking and nightlife

The many quayside cafés and bars offer an incomparable people- and harbour-watching experience – albeit at a price – but there are few worthwhile restaurants on the harbour. If you want something to take down to the beach with you, there's an excellent **bakery**, with *tyrópittes* and cakes, tucked into the western corner of the harbour by the *Pirate* bar. There's also an open-air **cinema** in summer, on the narrow street leading to the *Alkionides* hotel.

Tavernas, ouzerís, bars and cafés

Amalour near *Bratsera Hotel*. Laid-back bar with an eclectic play list and thirty-to-forty-something crowd; sometimes hosts special events or theme nights.

Barba Dhimas About 125m inland, on the same lane as the summer cinema. A small, well-priced taverna with decent *mezédhes*, small fish and even snail casserole.

Gitoniko (Manolis & Christina's) Inland beyond *Miranda Hotel*, near Áyios Konstandínos church. Very friendly taverna with excellent, well-priced *mayireftá* at lunch – which runs out early – plus grills (including succulent fish) in the evening; extensive roof-terrace in summer.

Hydronetta Tucked under the cannons on the west side of the promontory. The classic sunset-watching bar, where the music carries on into the small hours. Limited seating gives it an exclusive, chill-out vibe.

Iliovasilema (Sunset) Behind the cannons, west promontory above *Hydronetta*. Incomparable setting for an end-of-holiday treat or romantic tryst; delicious modern Greek and Italian cuisine that will set you back about €30 per person including wine.

To Koutouki tis Agoras Rear of market. Rickety-tabled, inexpensive tradesmen's ouzerí whose titbits, ranging from *pastourmás* (cured meat) to octopus, can be exceptional. At its best in the early evening.

Paradhosiako 80m inland on street to *Amaryllis* hotel. All the standard dishes at this heaving, popular ouzerí.

Pirate Corner of waterfront by clocktower. Café by day and an increasingly lively bar as the evening wears on, with a young crowd and Western music.

Zefyros Barely 30m from the harbour, on the lane leading to *Miranda Hotel*. One of several decent options for simple taverna food in this street, with tables in a sheltered courtyard.

The north coast: beaches

There's only one paved road on Ýdhra, leading east from the harbour to the beach at Mandhráki just a couple of kilometres away. Even that's a hot and shadeless walk, so most people rely on the small **boats** that shuttle constantly from the harbour to various beaches around the island, at prices ranging from about €1.50 per person one-way to Mandhráki, to €12 return to Bísti. You can also hire private water-taxis – good value for groups at around €12 per boat to Vlyhós, for example – or even mules for land-based travel.

MANDHRÁKI, to the east, is dominated by the *Miramare Hotel* (Ⓣ22980 52300, Ⓦwww.miramare-hotel.net; ❺), whose beachside bungalows are not

Ýdhra festivals

On the second or third weekend in June, Ýdhra Town celebrates the Miaoulia, in honour of Admiral Andreas Miaoulis whose fire boats, packed with explosives, were set adrift upwind of the Turkish fleet during the War of Independence. The highlight of the celebrations is the burning of a boat at sea as a tribute to the sailors who risked their lives in this dangerous enterprise.

Easter is a particularly colourful and moving experience, especially on Friday evening when the fishermen's parish of Áyios Ioánnis at Kamíni carries its *Epitáfios* or symbolic bier of Christ into the shallows to bless the boats and ensure calm seas. On the second full weekend in October, the town hosts the annual, four-day Rebétiko Conference, with academic seminars by day and rebétika (see p.939) performances at night.

great value. Despite appearances the sandy beach is open to all, and there are watersports here and a decent bar-restaurant occupying the imposing former shipyard of independence war hero Admiral Miaoulis. On a pebbly cove immediately west, *Mandraki 1800* is one of the better rural **tavernas** on the island, with slightly pricey ouzerí fare.

Heading out of town to the west, a paved coastal path leads towards **KAMÍNI**, about a twenty-minute walk. There are several spots en route where you can clamber down to swim from the rocks in crystal clear water, while picturesque Kamíni itself has a shingly beach and a couple of good tavernas and rooms establishments. Of the latter, waterfront *Antonia* (Ⓣ22980 52481; ❸) and *Eleni Petrolekka*, immediately behind (Ⓣ22980 52701; ❸) both offer simple but comfortable accommodation. *Taverna tis Kondylenias*, by the little harbour, is famous for its seafood and wonderful sunset views, while *Christina's*, a short way inland, is plainer and slightly cheaper. There's often interesting art on display at the Verena Foundation (Ⓦwww.verenafoundation.org), the large red building on the far side of the harbour.

If you carry on walking – and again, there are plentiful boats to all these places – you'll pass the popular swimming cove at **Kastéllo** on the way to **VLYHÓS**, a small hamlet with a rebuilt nineteenth-century bridge and a shingle beach with loungers and umbrellas; swimming in the lee of an offshore islet is decent. In peak season there's a taverna and a couple of bar-cafés as well as a single rooms establishment, *Antigone* (Ⓣ22980 53228, Ⓕ22980 53042; ❹).

Beyond Vlyhós the walking gets much tougher as the path tracks high above the bay of Molós, where the beach looks tempting but is hard to reach, and then circles back inland. For the fine coves at the eastern tip, Bísti and Áyios Nikólaos, boat is really your only option. **Bísti** has a smallish, white-pebbled beach surrounded by pine trees that offer shade; **Áyios Nikólaos** is larger and sandier, but with less shade and fewer boats. A path leads over the cape between the two, and both have seasonal snack bars as well as loungers and kayaks to rent.

Interior and south: monasteries

The interior of Ýdhra is mountainous and little-visited, so with a little walking you can find a dramatically different kind of island – one of rural cottages, terraces of grain to feed the donkeys, hilltop monasteries and pine forest.

Following the streets of the town upwards and inland, you reach a path that winds up the mountain for about an hour to either the **monastery of Profítis Ilías** or (slightly lower) the **convent of Ayía Efpraxía**. What must be the longest stairway in Greece (or alternatively a zigzag path) constitutes the final approach to the former (closed noon–4pm, but water and *loukoúm* are hospitably left at the gate). A trail continues left behind Profítis Ilías to a saddle overlooking the south coast (from where a path-less scramble would bring you within twenty minutes to the 590-metre summit of **Mount Éros**, the Argo-Saronic islands' highest point) then down to the sea at Klimáki, before climbing again past Áyios Pétros chapel and some spectacular coast to deserted **Áyios Nikólaos** monastery, 1hr 15min from Profítis Ilías. Alternately there's a well-marked and obvious path from town directly towards Áyios Nikólaos. This continues down to **Limnióniza**, 1hr 15min from town, the best and most scenic cove on the south coast. The pebble beach here is surrounded by pines, and in summer there are watersports, a café-bar and boats back to town.

Spétses

Spétses is probably the best-known of the Argo-Saronic islands, largely thanks to the author John Fowles who lived here in the early 1950s and used the place, thinly disguised, as the setting for his cult novel *The Magus*. A popular, upmarket escape for Athenians, the island had a brief vogue as a package destination but never really developed the mass infrastructure – or the convenient beaches – to match. Today, the town is much the biggest in the Saronic islands, spreading for several kilometres along the northeast coast, but new development is mainly second homes and small apartments and villas; the rest of the island is almost entirely uninhabited, with pine forest inland and numerous excellent small beaches around the coast.

Spétses Town

SPÉTSES TOWN shares with Ýdhra a history of late eighteenth-century mercantile adventure and prosperity, and a leading role in the War of Independence, which made its foremost citizens the aristocrats of the newly independent Greek state. Plenty of fine old homes and public buildings survive, but here there's been little restriction on new building, which spreads along the shore in both directions. And although most cars are banned in town you won't notice it, as they're replaced by thousands of mopeds and scooters that pay little attention to whether a street is pedestrianized or not. In short, it's much less pretty than Ýdhra Town, but also a great deal more lively and earthy; full of pricey shops, bars and restaurants.

Arrival and information

Spétses splits into three main areas. Ferries and hydrofoils will drop you pretty much in the heart of town at the cannon-studded main harbour known as the **Dápia**. To your right is the main town square, with the busy shopping streets of the old town tucked in behind it; left along the seafront lies the **town beach**

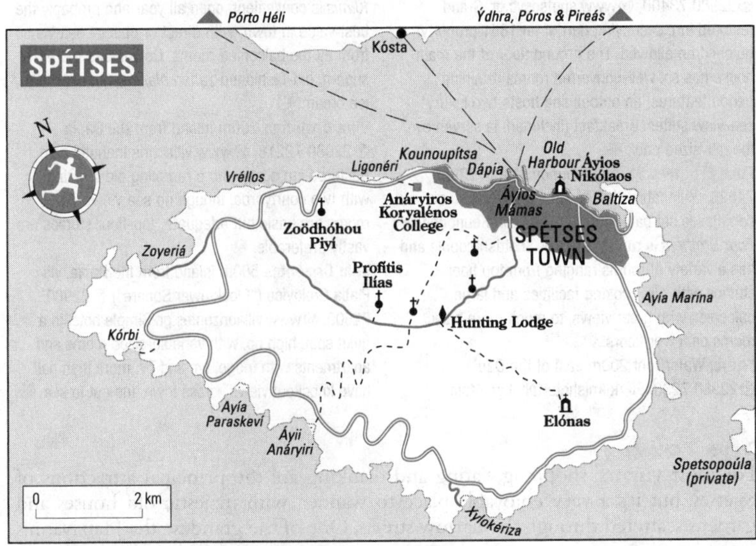

of Áyios Mámas. Continue in this direction (east) around the point and you'll reach the **Old Harbour** area, upmarket focus of the island's nightlife, where private yachts moor up. West of Dápia is **Kounoupítsa**, with more of a suburban feel – much of the simpler accommodation is here, and there are small beaches and waterfront tavernas.

To get around the island there are two **bus** services with frequent departures in summer: from the *Hotel Poseidonion* (the large building undergoing restoration, on the front west of Dápia) to Kounoupítsa and Ligonéri; and from Áyios Mámas to Áyii Anáryiri. Alternatively, dozens of places in town rent **mountain bikes** and **scooters** or, better still, go by **boat**. Self-drive motor boats (€49 per day; information from the Yachting Club, below, or Costas ⓣ22980 75107) give access to plenty of hard-to-reach coves and allow you to circumnavigate the entire island in less than three hours. Also at the harbour are *kaïkia* and private **water-taxis** (€15–60 per boatload depending on destination) for beaches or round-the-island trips; they also shuttle to Kósta and Pórto Héli on the mainland.

Around the harbour you'll see numerous **travel agencies** that can help with accommodation and local maps as well as tickets: Bardakos (ⓣ22980 73141) is the main hydrofoil agent; Mimoza Travel (ⓣ22980 75170) handles the Eurofast catamaran; Alasia Travel (ⓣ22980 74098 ⓦwww.alasiatravel.com) and the Yachting Club (ⓣ22980 73400 ⓦwww.spetsesyc.gr) are good for rooms. There are **banks** with ATMs all around the Dápia and plenty of places with **Internet**, including *Café 1800*, on the waterfront towards Kounoupítsa.

Accommodation

Accommodation, especially at the cheaper end of the range, tends to be widely scattered and, in season at least, in short supply, so it can make life easier to arrange it through one of the agencies above, who will also be able to arrange transport to get you there. In town prices range from high, at comfortable studio complexes, to jaw-droppingly expensive at some of the boutique hotels.

Economou Mansion Kounoupítsa shoreline ⓣ22980 73400, ⓦwww.spetsesyc.gr. Grand restored inn, occupying part of an 1851 property; no children allowed. The ground floor of the main house has six well-converted rooms retaining period features; an outbuilding hosts two luxury sea-view suites. Breakfast (included) is served by the fair-sized pool. ⑦

Four Brothers Studios Kounoupítsa ⓣ22980 74523, ⓔlindabis@hol.gr. One of several studio complexes set back from the water in Kounoupítsa, *Four Brothers* is run by a Greek/Scottish couple and has a variety of rooms ranging from top floor studios with a/c, cooking facilities and large balconies with great views, to much more basic rooms on lower floors. ③

Klimis Waterfront 200m east of the Dápia ⓣ22980 72334, ⓔklimishotel@hol.gr. Most congenial of a number of box-like hotels here, *Klimis* is convenient, open all year and probably the best value in town, with direct or oblique sea views from all the balconied rooms. Downstairs there's a superb, old-fashioned *zaharoplastío* with excellent ice cream. ③

Villa Christina 200m inland from the Dápia ⓣ22980 72218, ⓦwww.villachristinahotel.com. Restored inn occupying a rambling old building with two courtyards, though no sea views. A/c rooms are basic but adequate; top-floor studios are vastly preferable. ③

Villa Orizontes 500m inland from the Dápia, via Platía Oroloyíou ("Clocktower Square") ⓣ22980 72509, ⓦwww.villaorizontes.gr. Simple hotel in a quiet spot, high up, with variable-sized rooms and apartments with fridge, a/c and TV; more than half have knockout views across town and out to sea. ③

The Town

For most visitors, shopping, eating and drinking are the principal attractions of Spétses, but it's a very enjoyable place to wander, with majestic old houses and gardens scattered through the narrow streets. One of the grandest, the Hatziyannis

Mexis family mansion above the east side of town, now houses an enjoyable **local museum** (Tues–Sun 8.30am–2.30pm; €3). Apart from the house itself, highlights include magnificent polychrome-wooden ships' prows from the revolutionary fleet, as well as its flag, plus (out of sight in a plain wooden ossuary) the bones of local heroine Laskarina Bouboulina, a wealthy widow who commanded her own ship (the *Agamemnon*), reputedly seduced her lovers at gunpoint, and was shot in 1825 by the father of a girl her son had eloped with. Her own home, signed not far from the main square, is also a private **museum**. Entertaining guided tours (30min; €5) – the only admission permitted – are given in English up to a dozen times daily.

The twenty-minute walk along the front to the **Old Harbour** is also well worthwhile. There are bars and cafés here where you can sit and admire the visiting yachts, and also relics of an older incarnation as a working port, with rusty tankers and traditional boatyards.

Eating, drinking and nightlife

Brace yourself for some of the steepest **food** and **drink** prices in the Greek islands outside of Mýkonos and Rhodes – especially in the central waterfront cafés and romantic spots around the old harbour. Late-night **nightlife** is mostly centred round Baltíza, the furthest of the inlets at the old harbour – biggest of the clubs are *Privilege*, a vaulted structure on the far side, and *Fortezza*, and there are plenty of quieter bars like *Remezzo*. Closer to town, Áyios Mámas beach also has a couple of lively music bars, including *Mama's Beach Café*. Two open-air cinemas operate in summer, close to the main square – Titania and rooftop Marina.

Exedra Old Harbour. High-quality standard dishes like *moussakás* and *anginares ala políta*, and unbeatable waterside seating, make *Exedra* worth the higher prices.

Kafeneion Dápia, by Alpha Bank. Pebble mosaics underfoot and sepia photos indicate that this was the island's first watering hole; start the day with well-priced English breakfast, and tame sparrows begging for crumbs, progressing later to a full range of *mezédhes*, or just a drink whilst waiting for a hydrofoil.

Lazaros a stiff climb 500m inland from the Dápia, above the dry stream-bed. Cavernous interior with an old jukebox, dangling gourds and wine barrels; it serves a limited but savoury menu of grills, goat in lemon sauce, superior *taramás* and decent barrelled wine – shame about the prefab oven chips. Dinner only, late March–early Oct.

To Liotrivi Old Harbour. The "old olive oil press" serves an upmarket, modern Mediterranean menu to a Latin and jazz soundtrack. Some tables enjoy a stunning position on a jetty that extends right out into the harbour.

Mimoza on the waterfront, west towards Kounoupítsa. Standard taverna fare at somewhat inflated prices, but worth it for the setting, with candle-lit tables set out on the sand and the water lapping almost to your feet as you eat.

Patralis Kounoupítsa waterfront, 300m before the *Spetses Hotel* ☎22980 74441, Ⓦwww.patralis.gr. Upmarket, old-fashioned *psarotaverna*. Very popular with Greek visitors, which can mean slow service and a wait for a table, but excellent fish dishes and good barrelled wine if you don't like the prices on the extensive wine list.

Roussos Áyios Mámas beach. A shrine of unfussy *mayireftá* – courgettes au gratin, *yiouvétsi*, baked fish – and about the least expensive taverna in town; tellingly popular with locals.

Around the island

A single paved road circles Spétses, mostly high above a rocky coast but with access to beaches at various points. **On foot,** you can head up through town and strike directly across the island on marked paths to many of the beaches, with ancient chapels and fine views along the way.

Circling anti-clockwise, the first good beach, just twenty minutes' walk west of town, is **Ligonéri** or College Beach (so called because just inland is the college where John Fowles used to teach), with lots of facilities including loungers, bars and a watersports centre. Next up in this direction is **Vréllos**, also with seasonal sun loungers and bar, in a pretty, wooded bay; some of the Ligonéri buses continue this far, so it can be busy. A couple of rocky coves at the western extremity of the island – **Zoyeriá** and **Kórbi** – are far quieter, but without any facilities or much in the way of sand.

Perhaps the best two beaches on the island occupy adjacent bays on the south coast. **Ayía Paraskeví** has a spectacular 600-metre arc of pebbles backed by a chapel, while **Áyii Anáryiri** is a long, sheltered, mostly sandy bay, with watersports. Both have good tavernas and snack-bars: the bus to the latter brings lots of visitors, though, so by midday both can become very crowded. If it's all too much, carry on a bit to unheralded **Xylokériza** beach, reached by a 500-metre access drive signed merely for its snack bar (June–Sept); the protected bay itself is mixed sand and white pebbles. Finally, **Ayía Marína** or Paradise Beach is back in walking distance of town: a busy beach with watersports, a popular bar and views offshore towards the tempting but off-limits islet of **Spetsopoúla**, the private property of the heirs of shipping magnate Stavros Niarchos.

Travel details

All services from Pireás leave from much the same area of the port – between gates E8 and E9. There are ticket booths here, and rarely any need to book ahead, except on the most popular weekends or if you plan to take a car. The summaries below are for summer weekday services: sailings are more frequent at weekends (Fri–Sun), less so from Oct to June. Hydrofoils or catamarans are twice as fast, and about twice the price of conventional craft. No hydrofoils or catamarans connect Égina with the rest of the islands.

Company contact details for Pireás (local island agencies are given in the island accounts):

Aegean Flying Dolphins (to Égina and Angístri) ⓣ210 41 21 656.

Ayios Nektarios Eginas (ferry to Égina) ⓣ210 42 25 625.

Euroseas (Eurofast catamaran to Ýdhra, Spétses and Pórto Héli) ⓣ210 41 13 108, ⓦwww.euroseas.com.

Hellenic Seaways (ferries, hydrofoils and Flying Cat to all points) ⓣ210 41 99 000, ⓦwww.hellenicseaways.gr.

Nova (ferry to Égina, some to Ýdhra and Spétses) ⓣ210 41 26 181.

Saronic Round (ferry to Ayía Marína, Égina) ⓣ210 41 00 145.

Ferries

Hellenic Seaways ferry unless otherwise stated.

Égina (Égina Town) to: Pireás (9–12 daily with Hellenic Seaways; 3 daily with Ayios Nektarios Eginas; 4 daily with Nova; 1hr–1hr 30min); Angístri (Angístri Express 6 daily Mon–Fri, 3 daily weekends; 15min); Póros (4 daily; 1hr 15min); Ýdhra and Spétses (1 daily; 2hr 15min–3hr 15min).

Égina (Souvála) to: Pireás (2 daily; 1hr 15min).

Égina (Ayía Marína) to: Pireás (Saronic Round 3–4 daily; 1hr).

Póros to: Égina and Pireás (4 daily; 1hr 15min–2hr 30min); Galatás (constant passenger shuttle and roll-on-roll-off car ferry every 30min 6am–10.40pm; 5min).

Ýdhra to: Pireás (1 daily via Égina; 3hr 45min).

Spétses to: Pireás (1 daily via Ýdhra and Égina; 4hr 45min); Kósta (almost hourly roll-on-roll-off barges; 15min).

Hydrofoils and Flying Cat

Égina to: Pireás (Hellenic Seaways and Aegean Flying Dolphins; half-hourly, 7am–8pm; 45min).

Angístri to: Pireás (Hellenic Seaways and Aegean Flying Dolphins; 4 daily; 1hr).

Póros to: Pireás (Hellenic Seaways; 6 daily; 1hr); Ýdhra (6 daily; 30min); Spétses (4–5 daily; 1hr 30min).

Ýdhra to: Pireás (Hellenic Seaways and Euroseas; 9 daily; 1hr 40min); Póros (6 daily; 30min); Spétses (6 daily; 45min).

Spétses to: Pireás (7 daily; 2hr 25min); Ýdhra (6 daily; 30min); Póros (4–5 daily; 1hr 30min).

7

The Cyclades

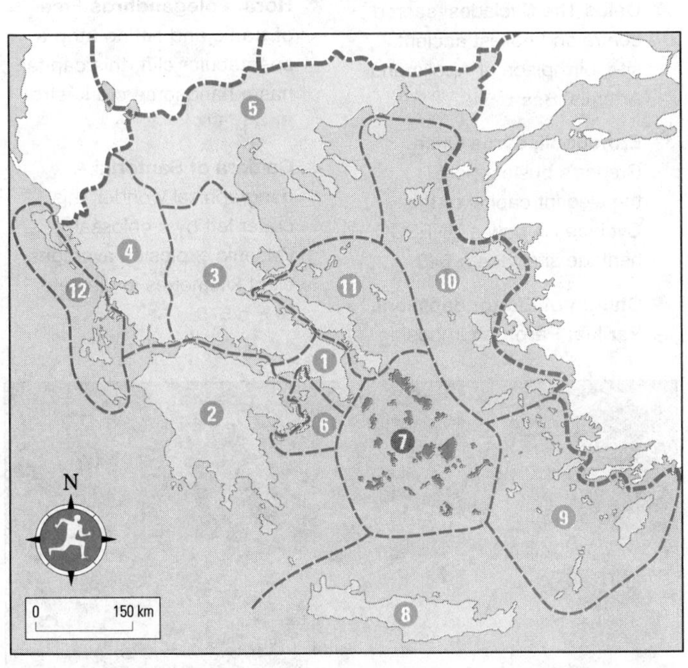

CHAPTER 7 Highlights

* **Beaches of Mílos** Multicoloured rocks and volcanically heated sand. See p.522–523

* **Mýkonos Town** Labyrinthine lanes filled with restaurants, boutiques and nightlife. See p.534

* **Delos** The Cyclades' sacred centre and holiest ancient site, birthplace of Apollo and Artemis. See p.540

* **Ermoúpoli, Sýros** Once Greece's busiest port, the elegant capital of the Cyclades is now a UNESCO heritage site. See p.543

* **Church of Ekatondapylianí, Parikía, Páros** An imposing and ornate Byzantine church incorporating an impressive number of architectural styles. See p.549

* **Zás, Náxos** The Cyclades' highest mountain on the Cyclades' largest island. See p.561

* **Hóra, Folégandhros** Free of traffic and sitting atop a spectacular cliff, this capital has a handsome old kástro. See p.574

* **Caldera of Santoríni** A geographical wonder, this crater left by a colossal volcanic explosion averages eight kilometres in diameter. See p.575

▲ View from Áno Sýros to Ermoúpoli

7

The Cyclades

Named, most probably, after the circle they form around the sacred island of Delos, the **Cyclades** (Kykládhes) is the most satisfying Greek archipelago for island-hopping. On no other group do you get quite such a strong feeling of each island as a microcosm, each with its own distinct traditions, customs and path of modern development. Most of these self-contained realms are compact enough to explore in a few days, giving you a sense of completeness and identity impossible on, say, Crete or most of the Ionian islands.

The islands do share some features, with the majority of them (Ándhros, Kéa, Náxos, Sérifos and Tínos excepted) being arid and rocky; most also share the "Cycladic" style of brilliant-white Cubist architecture, a feature of which is the central **kástro** of the old towns. The typical *kástro* has just one or two entrances, and a continuous outer ring of houses with all their doors and windows on the inner side, so forming a single protective perimeter wall – typically, the two-storey houses have a separate owner for each storey.

The extent and impact of tourism, though, is markedly haphazard, so that although some English is spoken on most islands, a slight detour from the beaten track – from Íos to Síkinos, for example – can have you reaching for your Greek phrasebook. But whatever the level of tourist development, there are only three islands where it completely dominates their character in season: **Íos**, the original hippie-island and still a paradise for hard-drinking backpackers, **Thíra**, the major island in the volcanic cluster of **Santoríni** and a dramatic natural backdrop for luxury cruise liners, and **Mýkonos**, by far the most popular of the group, with its teeming old town, selection of beaches and sophisticated restaurants, clubs and hotels. After these, **Páros**, **Náxos** and **Mílos** are the most popular, with their beaches and main towns packed at the height of the season, which in the Cyclades is late July to late August. The once-tranquil **Minor Cyclades** around Náxos have become fashionable destinations for well-heeled Athenians in recent years, as have nearby **Amorgós**, and **Folégandhros** to the west. To avoid the hordes altogether – except in the Greek summer holidays, when escape is impossible – the most promising islands are **Síkinos**, **Kímolos** or **Anáfi**. For a different view of the Cyclades, visit **Tínos** and its imposing pilgrimage church, a major spiritual centre of Greek Orthodoxy, or **Sýros** with its elegant townscape and (like Tínos) large Catholic minority. Due to their closeness to Athens, adjacent **Ándhros** and **Kéa** are predictably popular – and relatively expensive – weekend havens for Greeks, as are to a lesser extent **Kýthnos** and **Sérifos**, while **Sífnos** remains a popular destination for upmarket tourists of all nationalities. The one major ancient site is **Delos** (Dhílos), certainly worth making time for; the commercial and religious centre of the Classical Greek world, it's visited most

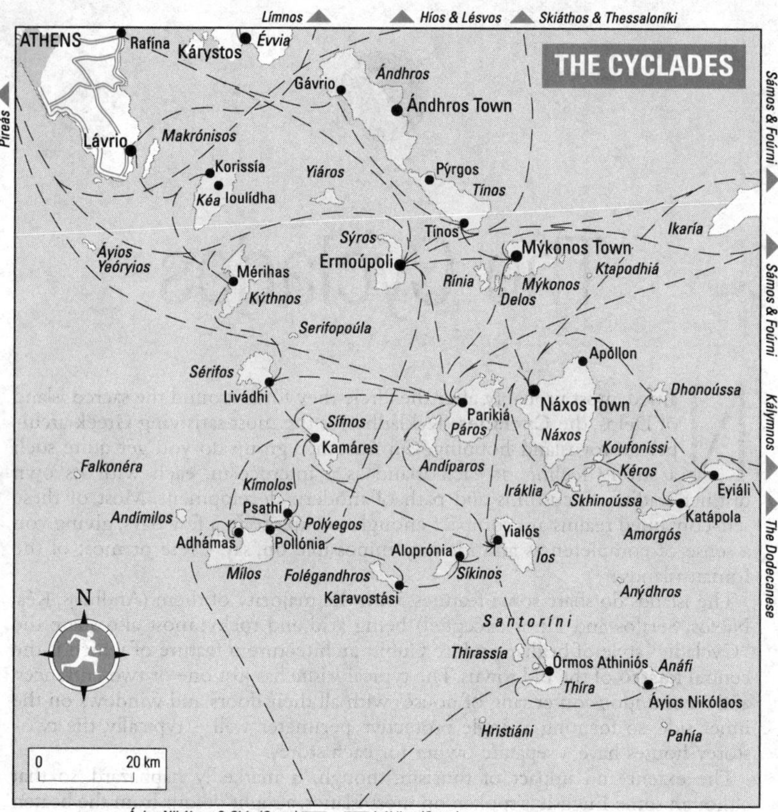

easily on a day-trip by boat from Mýkonos. When it comes to **moving on**, many of the islands – in particular Mílos, Páros, Náxos and Thíra – are handily connected with Crete (easier in late July and August), while from Tínos, Mýkonos, Sýros, Páros, Náxos or Thíra, you can reach many of the Dodecanese by direct boat. Similarly, you can regularly get from Mýkonos, Náxos, Sýros and Páros to Ikaría and Sámos (in the eastern Aegean).

One consideration for the timing of your visit is that the Cyclades often get frustratingly **stormy**, particularly in early spring or late autumn, and it's also the group worst affected by the *meltémi*, which blows sand and tables about with ease throughout much of July and August. Delayed or cancelled ferries (even in the height of tourist season) are not uncommon, so if you're heading back to Athens to catch a flight, leave yourself a day or two's leeway.

Kéa (Tziá)

Kéa, the closest of the Cyclades to the mainland, is extremely popular in August and on weekends year-round with Athenian families. Their impact is now spreading beyond the small resorts, and much of the coastline is peppered with holiday homes and scarred with access roads. There is a preponderance of expensive apartments and villa accommodation and not as many good tavernas as you might expect (and virtually no nightlife) because so many visitors self-cater. Outside August, Kéa, with its rocky, forbidding perimeter and inland oak and almond groves, would be an enticing destination for those who enjoy a rural ramble if the tourist infrastructure were not so poor.

As ancient Keos, the island and its strategic, well-placed harbour supported four cities – a pre-eminence that continued until the nineteenth century when Sýros became the main Greek port. Tourists account for the bulk of the sea traffic with regular (in season) **ferry/speed boat connections** to and from Lávrio on the mainland, plus sporadic catamarans and ferries to and from Sýros and Kýthnos. Frequency of these services should improve as Lávrio port capacity is expanded, but for details you'll have to check directly with its port police as agents in Athens usually won't sell tickets to Kéa.

The northwest coast: Korissía to Otziás

The small northern ferry and hydrofoil port of **KORISSÍA** has fallen victim to uneven expansion, and has become rather dusty and unattractive; if you

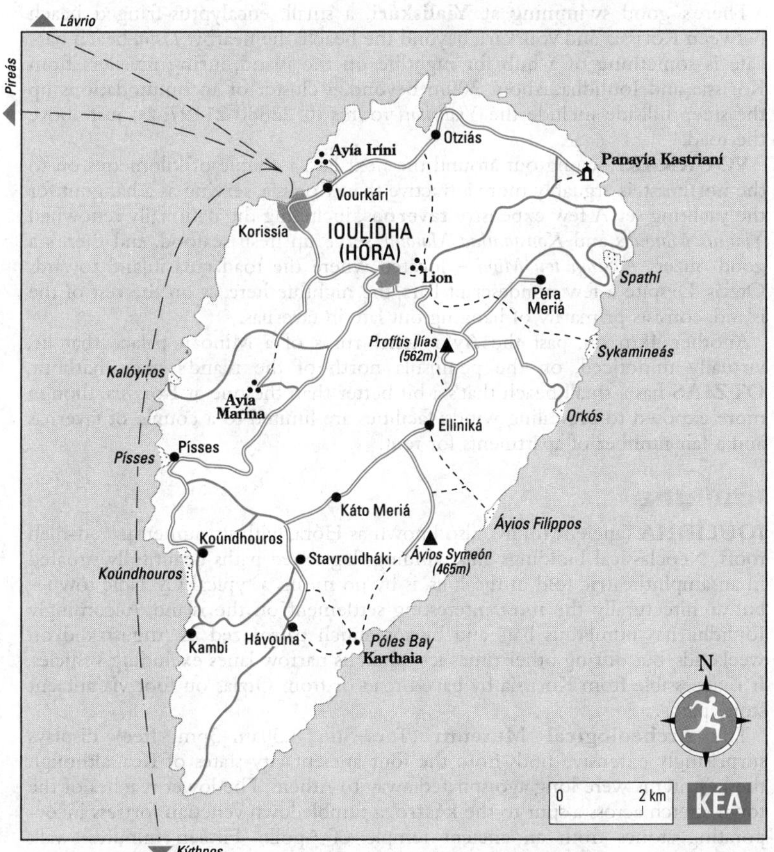

don't like its looks upon disembarking, try to get a bus to Písses (16km), Otziás (6km) or Ioulídha (6km). **Buses** may meet the boats; during July and August there's a regular fixed schedule around the island, but at other times public transport can be very elusive. There are a few **taxis** on Kéa, and one **car-rental** outfit at the port.

The ill-equipped seafront **tourist information** office opens sporadically; next-door, Mouzaki (Ⓣ22880 21428) are agents only for the Marmari Express to Lávrio and unhelpful otherwise. Meltemi (Ⓣ22880 21920), the general ferry agency – including the Goutos Lines' Lávrio ferries *Myrina Express* and *Makedon* – can be more useful. **Accommodation**, in general, is not of a high standard; year-round possibilities near the port are the somewhat noisy *Karthea* (Ⓣ22880 21222; ④) which does, however, have single rooms, or the friendly *Nikitas* pension (Ⓣ22880 21193; ③) with plain, comfortable studios well inland along and to the right of the stream bed. Near the eastern end of the beach, on the road to Vourkári, the comfortable *Hotel Brillante Zoi* (aka *Lamberi Zoi*, Ⓣ22880 22685, Ⓦwww.hotelbrillante.gr ; ⑥) has the quietest rooms at the back, away from the road. A little further along is the cool, contemporary *Keos Katoikies* (Ⓣ22880 84002, Ⓦwww.keos.gr; ⑦) offering a dramatic setting overlooking the bay. For **eating**, a series of nondescript tavernas along the harbour waterfront serves standard, but overpriced Greek fare.

There's good swimming at **Yialiskári**, a small, eucalyptus-fringed beach between Korissía and Vourkári; beyond the beach, the nearby *Tastra* beach bar-café is something of a hub for nightlife on the island, luring revellers from Korissía and Ioulídha. About 300m beyond, a cluster of accommodations up the steep hillside include the *Yialiskari* rooms (Ⓣ22880 21197; ③) just above the road.

VOURKÁRI, strung out around the next bay, a couple of kilometres on to the northeast, is arguably more attractive than Korissía, serving as a hangout for the yachting set. A few expensive **tavernas**, including the nationally renowned *Yiannis Maroulis* and *Konstantina Marouli*, serve up fresh seafood, and there's a good ouzerí – *Strofi tou Mimi* – located where the road cuts inland towards Otziás. Despite a few nondescript bars, the nightlife here, as on the rest of the island, consists primarily of hanging out late in tavernas.

Another 4km on, past the **Ayía Iríni** ruins of a Minoan palace that lie, virtually unnoticed, on the peninsula north of the island's main harbour, **OTZIÁS** has a small beach that's a bit better than the one at Korissía, though more exposed to prevailing winds; facilities are limited to a couple of tavernas and a fair number of apartments for rent.

Ioulídha

IOULÍDHA (ancient Ioulis), also known as Hóra, with its numerous red-tiled roofs, Neoclassical buildings and winding flagstoned paths beautifully situated in an amphitheatric fold in the hills, is by no means a typical Cycladic town – but architecturally the most interesting settlement on the island. Accordingly Ioulídha has numerous bars and bistros, much patronized in August and on weekends, but during other times it's quiet, its narrow lanes excluding vehicles. It is accessible from Korissía by paved road or from Otziás on foot via ancient stone paths.

The **Archeological Museum** (Tues–Sun 8.30am–3pm; free) displays surprisingly extensive finds from the four ancient city-states of Kéa, although the best items were long ago spirited away to Athens. The lower reaches of the town stretch across a spur to the **kástro**, a tumbledown Venetian fortress incorporating stones from an ancient temple of Apollo. Fifteen minutes' walk northeast, on the path toward Otziás, you pass the **Lion of Kéa**, a sixth-century BC sculpture carved out of an outcrop of rock, 6m long and 3m high. There are steps right down to the lion, but the effect is most striking from a distance.

Along with a **post office** and **bank agent**, there are a couple of **accommodations** including the attractive *Hotel Serie* (Ⓣ22880 22355, Ⓦwww.serie.gr; ❺). Choices for **eating** and **drinking** tend to be of a generally higher quality than in Korissía; however, unless you arrive during a busy season, you may find many places closed. *Piatsa*, just as you enter the lower town from the car park, has a variety of tasty dishes, while up on the platía, *Rolando's* serves a full range of fish plates best enjoyed with the ubiquitous ouzo; neighbouring *Kalofagadon* is the best place for a full-blown meat feast. The aptly named *Panorama* serves up pastries and coffee and is a good place to watch the sun set. Once a hub of nightlife, the central town shuts down early these days, though the mayor, Antonakis Zoulos, is one of the most accomplished traditional musicians in Greece, so you could ask at the town hall where he'll be performing next. Full-on *bouzoúki* nights occur regularly at bars, cafés and tavernas in town or back at the port.

Kýthnos (Thermiá)

Though one of the lesser known and most low-key of the larger Cyclades, **Kýthnos** (known as Thermiá from the 13th century until 1827, after its renowned hot springs) is a good antidote to the exploitation that may be encountered elsewhere. Few foreigners visit, and the island is quieter than Kéa, particularly to the south. It's a place where Athenians come to buy land for villas, go spear-fishing and sprawl on sunbed-free beaches without having to jostle for space. You could use it as a first or last island stop; in August there are several **ferry connections** a week with Kéa and Lávrio, and frequent ferry and catamaran services to and from Sérifos, Sífnos, Pireás, Mílos and Kímolos.

Mérihas and around

Boats dock on the west coast at **MÉRIHAS**, an attractive ferry and fishing port with many of the island's facilities. The closest beach of any repute is **Episkopí**, a 500-metre stretch of grey sand with the *Pountaki* beach bar/taverna, thirty minutes' walk north of the town; you can shorten this on coast-hugging trails and tracks below the road. Far better are the popular beaches of **Apókroussi**, which has a canteen, and **Kolóna**, a very picturesque sand spit joining Kýthnos to the islet of Áyios Loukás. About an hour's walk northwest of Episkopí, these are more easily reached by boat trip from Mérihas. Between Episkopí and Apókroussi lie the ruins of the temples, towers, walls and reservoirs of the tenth-century BC fortified town of **Vryókastro** – in 2002 a hoard of some 1500 votive items was discovered here.

Accommodation owners may meet the ferries in high season. The numerous rooms to let tend to be large and equipped for visiting Athenian families, so can be on the expensive side for fewer persons – although with some opportunity for bargaining during the week. Out of season, owners are often not on the premises, but a contact phone number is usually posted. The rooms and studios *Panayiota* (Ⓣ22810 32268; May–Oct; ❸), in several locations, are a popular choice – the owner's shop is just before the small bridge on the seafront. The *Panorama* studios (Ⓣ22810 32184; May–Oct; ❸ slightly more at weekends) up steep steps behind the harbour have panoramic views over the bay. There is

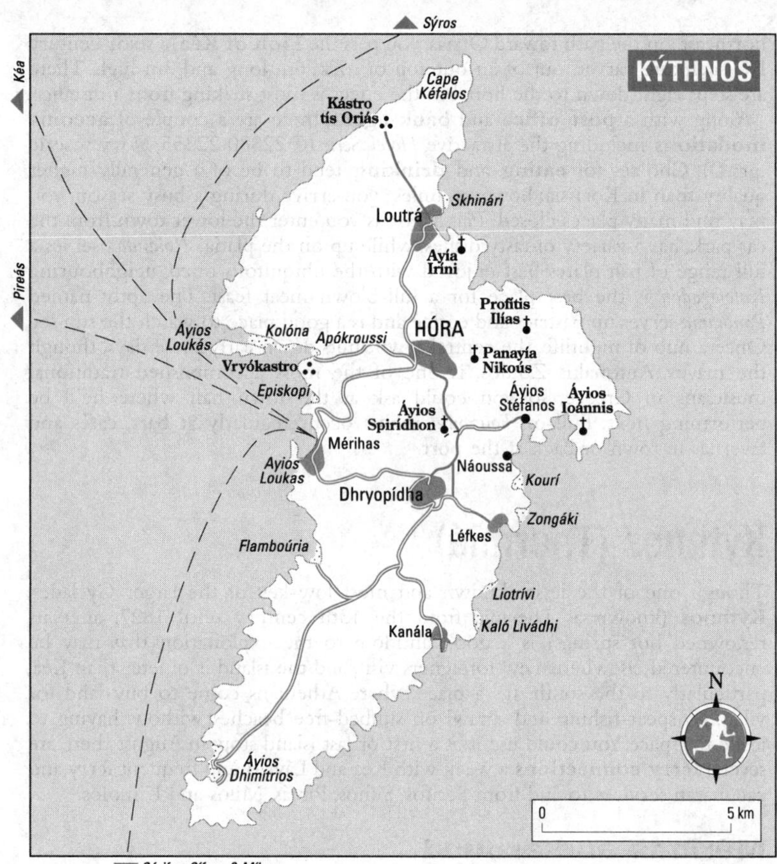

further accommodation opposite the ferry, on the street behind the bridge, and along the Dhryopídha road beyond petrol station and bakery.

The best **restaurants** are *Ostria*, a classic fish taverna by the jetty, *Gialos*, specializing in lamb dishes, behind the central beach, and *To Kandouni*, on the opposite waterfront to the ferry, a tasty grill with specialities such as *sfoungáto* (baked omelette).

The **bus service**, principally to Hóra and Loutrá, Dhryopídha and Kanála, runs around six times daily in summer, less reliably from September to early June; **car** and **motorbike rental** is available through Antonis Lavrentzakis (Ⓣ22810 32104, Ⓔanlarent@otenet.gr), who has the ferry agency above the harbour road, and may be able to help with accommodation (④). There is an Emboriki **bank**, and **ATM**, a short way above the agency, and a second ATM on the harbour road.

Hóra and Loutrá

HÓRA lies 7.5km northeast of Mérihas, in the middle of the island. Though the town is unpromising at first sight, wander into the narrow streets beyond the initial square and you'll find a network of alleyways, painted with white flowers and lined with real ones, weaving their way past shops, churches and through tiny squares with colourful cafés. The only accommodation is the comfortable *Filoxenia* studios (ⓣ22810 31644, ⓦwww.filoxenia-kythnos.gr; ④), arranged around a flowery courtyard next to the A. Kanellopoúlou square. You can **eat** at the friendly *To Kentro* taverna near the small, central square of Ayía Triádha, at *To Steki tou Detzi* (evenings only) grill a few minutes further in, or at *Messaria* (evenings only), next to the *Filoxenia*; a Hóra speciality is rabbit in wine sauce. Hóra had Greece's first wind-farm (now derelict, and replaced by a single, second-generation wind turbine), and its second solar-farm, and these provide part of the island's electricity.

The resort of **LOUTRÁ** (4.5km north of Hóra and named after its sulphur, saline and ferrous thermal baths) is unexciting, its nineteenth-century spa (designed by Schiller, the architect of many of Greece's finest Neoclassical public buildings) long since replaced by a sterile modern construction and its harbour by a marina. The best **taverna**, *Katerini*, is a little out on a limb in the neighbouring bay to the west. Otherwise there are plenty of seafront cafés, bars and tavernas offering facilities to yachting crews, including the PocoLoco **Internet** café, and car and bike rental. Aqua Team (ⓣ22810 31333, ⓦwww.aquakythnos.com) offer PADI, ANDI and IAHD diving courses, plus mountain-bike rental. There is no shortage of places to sleep: **hotels** such as *Meltemi* (ⓣ22810 31271, ⓦwww.meltemihotel-kythnos.gr; ④–⑤), apartments, and the very comfortable *Porto Klaras* (ⓣ22810 31276, ⓦwww.porto-klaras.gr; April–Oct; ⑤), with sea views and beautifully furnished rooms, studios and apartments. Other rooms and studios tend to open only for the brief July–August peak season. You can visit the state-run *Xenia Anagenissis* baths complex (ⓣ22810 31217; July–Aug), where a twenty-minute bath plus basic check-up – blood pressure, heart rate and weight – costs about €5. About a ninety-minute walk from Loutrá, on Cape Kéfalos, lie the picturesque ruins of the medieval capital **Kástro tís Oriás** (aka Kefalikastro or Kástro toú Áï Yióryi), once home to around 5,000 people and 100 churches, but abandoned by the mid-seventeenth century.

Dhryopídha and southern Kýthnos

From Hóra it's possible to **walk** south to **DHRYOPÍDHA** (Sýllaka), mainly on dirt track. It takes about ninety minutes, following a walled lane that leaves Hóra heading due south, crossing a couple of deep valleys. More visually appealing than Hóra by virtue of spanning a well-watered valley, Dhryopídha, with its red-tiled roofs, is reminiscent of Spain or Tuscany. It was once the island's capital, built around one of Greece's largest **caves**, the Katafýki (open evenings). Tucked away behind the cathedral is a tiny **folklore museum** (open evenings, erratically). Beside the cathedral is the *Dryopis,* first of a number of café/snack-bars in the narrow street. Some people let rooms in their houses, but the nearest official accommodation is 6km south at coastal Kanála.

KANÁLA is a relaxed alternative to Loutrá, with the **Panayía Kanála** church set in a tiny but pleasant pine woodland and home to a miracle-working icon by the seventeenth-century Cretan master, Skordhilis. There is **accommodation** in the older settlement up on the promontory, such as the *Nikos Bouritis* (ⓣ22810 32350; ③) studios above a minimarket and with a garden, and a couple of tavernas, including the hospitable *Ofiousa*, with a terrace overlooking the larger western beach, **Megáli Ámmos**. Arranged around a pleasant seafront courtyard at the far end of the beach is the comfortable *Akrogialia* (ⓣ22810 32136; May–Oct; ⑤) studios.

Sérifos

Sérifos has long languished outside the mainstream of history and modern tourism. Little has happened here since the legendary Perseus returned with Medusa's head, in time to save his mother, Danaë, from being ravished by the local king Polydectes – turning him, his court and the green island into stone. Many would-be visitors are deterred by the apparently barren, hilly interior, which, with the stark, rocky coastline, makes Sérifos appear uninhabited until the ferry turns into Livádhi bay. Though newly paved roads have made the interior more accessible in recent years, the island is best recommended for serious **walkers**, who can head for several small villages in the under-explored interior, plus some isolated coves. Many people still keep livestock and produce their own wines, and some gather the wild narcissus for export. A central government proposal to install a large number of giant wind-turbines to provide Athens with electricity has gone down badly with the islanders, who, because of the protected traditional status of Sérifos, are not themselves allowed to install solar heating.

Livádhi and the main beaches

Most visitors stay in the port, **LIVÁDHI**, set in a wide greenery-fringed bay and handy for most of the island's beaches. The usually calm bay here is a magnet for island-hopping yachts, here to take on fresh water which, despite appearances, Sérifos has in abundance. Livádhi and the neighbouring cove of Livadhákia are certainly the easiest places to find rooms and any amenities you might need, which are scarce elsewhere.

Though attractive, the sand of the long, narrow **beach** at Livádhi is hard-packed and sometimes muddy, and the water is probably best at the far northeastern end. Heading away from the dock, turn left up the main business street, or climb over the southerly headland past the cemetery car park, to reach the neighbouring, superior, **Livadhákia**, a golden-sand beach, shaded by tamarisk trees, with a pleasant taverna. Five minutes' stroll across the headland to the south brings you to the smaller **Karávi** beach,

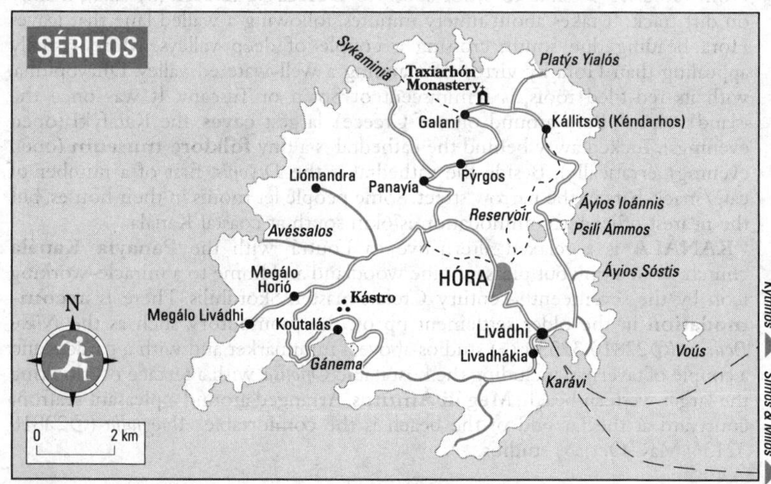

which is cleaner, but has no shade or facilities though there is ongoing development behind.

North of the Livádhi port and accessible by bus in summer – or a 45-minute walk along a surfaced road – is **Psilí Ámmos**, a sheltered, white-sand beach, backed by a large new reservoir, and considered the island's best; accordingly popular, its two rival tavernas tend to be full in high season. It is possible to continue – a ten-minute walk across the headland – towards the larger, often deserted **Áyios Ioánnis** beach, but this is rather exposed, and only the far south end is inviting. Theoretically, both beaches are visited by *kaïkia* from Livádhi, but don't rely on this.

Practicalities

The helpful Krinas Serifos Travel (ⓣ22810 51448, ⓦwww.serifos-travel.com), near the jetty, sells **boat** tickets. The **bus stop** and posted schedule are at the base of the yacht and fishing-boat jetty; **buses** connect Livádhi with Hóra, 2km away, 27–30 times a day in summer, otherwise 7–10 times; in high season buses run a circular route via Panayía, Galaní, Kállitsos, Áyios Ioánnis and Psilí Ámmos, or vice versa (6–7 times), and to Méga Livádhi and Koutalás in the southwest (2 times); outside high season there are just two daily trips to Panayía, Galaní and Kállitsos. You can rent a **bike** or **car** from Blue Bird (ⓣ22810 51511), next to the filling station on the main street, or from Krinas. There are a couple of **ATM**s along the seafront, and **Internet** access is available at the *Malabar* pub, inside the shopping arcade.

Accommodation

Proprietors don't always meet ferries, with the exception of *Coralli Camping* (see below), which often sends a minibus. In high season you'll have to step lively off the boat to get a decent bed; the most rewarding hunting grounds are on the headland above the ferry dock in Livádhi itself, or more peaceful Livadhákia, a ten-minute walk away. Unlike on many islands, most of the accommodation is open year-round.

Livádhi

Anna's Rooms Seafront, near the Hóra road junction ⓣ22810 51263. Comfortable doubles with shared veranda. ❸

Areti Hotel On the headland overlooking the bay ⓣ22810 51479. Attractively positioned. Breakfast €5. ❹

Cristi On the headland overlooking the bay ⓣ22810 51775. Hospitable modern pension in great location. Some rooms have private balconies, others share a veranda; some with sea views. ❹

Naias Hotel On the headland, between Livádhi and Livadhákia; near the ferry dock ⓣ22810 51749, ⓦwww.naiasserifos.gr. A comfortable, good-value hotel. All rooms with balconies, some with sea views. Breakfast €5. ❹

Livadhákia

Alexandros & Vassilia On the beach, behind the taverna of the same name ⓣ22810 51119. Cluster of spotless, balconied doubles and apartments. April–Oct. ❹

Coralli Camping Bungalows Behind the beach ⓣ22810 51500, ⓦwww.coralli.gr. Excellent bungalows (❹) on the campsite, with communal pool, restaurant and bar. Also run the newer 4–6-person *Coralli Studios* (❻) closer to town.

Helios Main road through Livadhákia ⓣ & ⓕ22810 51066. Welcoming bougainvillea-draped pension with homely doubles and all mod cons. ❸

Eating and nightlife

As on most islands, **tavernas** near the quay tend to be slightly pricier; further up the beach meals get less expensive. The bar-restaurant *Passaggio* does some good trans-European fare, although it's not the cheapest spot, and is popular later in the evening, whilst a little further along the bay, the more traditional *Takis* is another good choice, with its tables on the sand. Cheaper options, on the northern half of the beach, include *Stamatis*, a local favourite, and, at the extreme northeast end of the beach, *Margarita*'s with a homely feel and courtyard seating.

Nightlife is surprisingly lively, and mostly clustered in or near a seafront mini-mall just up from the yacht jetty, so you should be able to quickly find something to suit your taste. As well as *Passaggio*, *Karnayio* next door is a popular night-time spot; both play excellent and varied music. One street back, *Metalleio* is a more full-on dance bar that gets into the swing after midnight. For something more Greek, try *Alter Ego* behind the shopping arcade, or the fiercely local *Edem Music Club* on the road up to Hóra.

Hóra

HÓRA is a pleasant if steep forty-minute walk up a cobbled way, with the *kalderími* leading off from a bend in the road about 800m from Livádhi beach. Quiet and atmospheric, it is one of the least spoilt villages of the Cyclades. The best sights are in the precarious upper town: follow signs to the *kástro*, to reach the top via steep and occasionally overgrown stairways. Tiny churches cling to the cliff-edges, and from Áyios Konstandínos on the summit there are breath-taking views across the valleys below.

The central platía, Ayíou Athanasíou, just northwest of the summit, has an attractive church and a small but colourful town hall. It is also home to an ouzerí and atmospheric café, *Stou Stratou,* which offer nice alternatives to eating on the busy seafront down below. A couple of minutes below the square, a circular loop of road has more tavernas, cafés and shops, as well as the main bus stop. There are several windmills in varying states of repair, and a small archeological collection (Tues–Sun, 8.30am–3pm; €2).

Sífnos

Sífnos is a more immediately appealing island than its northern neighbours since it's prettier, more cultivated and has some fine architecture. This means that it's also much more popular; be aware that in July and August, available rooms are in short supply. Take any you can find as you arrive, or come armed with a reservation. In keeping with the island's somewhat upmarket clientele, camping rough is forbidden, while nude sunbathing is not always tolerated.

The island's modest size – no bigger than Kýthnos or Sérifos – makes it eminently explorable. The **bus service** is excellent, most of the roads good, and there's a vast network of paths that are mostly easy to follow. Sífnos has a strong tradition of pottery (as early as the third century BC) and has long been esteemed for its distinctive cuisine, intrinsically linked to the development of pottery, which allowed for the more sophisticated preparation of baked dishes. The island is perhaps best appreciated today, however, for its many beautifully situated **churches** and **monasteries**.

Kamáres

KAMÁRES, the island's port, with a pleasant beach, is tucked away in a long, steep-sided valley that cuts into the cliffs of the island's western side. A still-compact resort, with concrete blocks of villas edging up to the base of the hill-slopes,

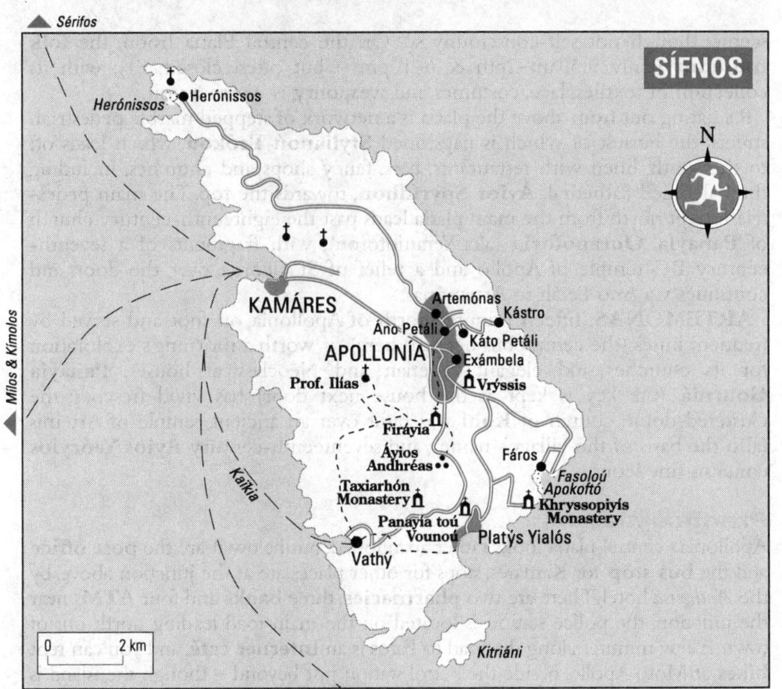

Kamáres' seafront road is crammed with bars, travel agencies, ice-cream shops and restaurants. Proprietors tend not to meet boats; while hunting for a room, you can store luggage at the Aegean Thesaurus **travel agency** (ⓣ22840 33151) right by the ferry dock, who also book accommodation across the island.

Accommodation is relatively expensive, though bargaining can be productive outside peak season. Try the reasonable *Hotel Stavros* (ⓣ22840 33383, ⓦwww.sifnostravel.com; ④), who have a book exchange in their reception, or, further along above the town beach, the friendly *Boulis Hotel* (ⓣ22840 32122, ⓦwww.hotelboulis.gr; ⑤). Behind the *Boulis*, the welcoming *Makis* **campsite** (ⓣ22840 32366, ⓦwww.makiscamping.gr) has good facilities and good-value rooms (③), plus the new *Leonidas* rooms above the main road.

The best **restaurants** are *Meropi Kambourakis*, ideal for a pre-ferry lunch; the *Boulis* on the waterfront with its collection of huge retsina barrels; *Argyris* fish taverna; *Camaron*, serving great pastas and pizzas; the cosy *Kamares* ouzerí and good-value *Kyra Margena* at the far end of the beach in Ayía Marína. Kamáres also has a little **nightlife**; try *Yamas*, good for a sunset cocktail and **Internet** access, and *Follie-Follie*. The best place to **rent a scooter or car** is at No.1 on the road to Apollonía.

Apollonía and Artemónas

A steep twenty-minute bus ride (hourly service until late at night) takes you 5.5km up to **APOLLONÍA**, the centre of Hóra, an amalgam of five hilltop villages which have merged over the years into one continuous community. With white buildings, flower-draped balconies, belfries and pretty squares, it is scenic, though not self-consciously so. On the central Platía Iróön, the **folk museum** (daily 9.30am–2pm & 6–10pm – but often closed; €1), with its collection of textiles, lace, costumes and weaponry, is worth a visit.

Radiating out from above the platía is a network of stepped marble pedestrian streets, the busiest of which is flagstoned **Stylianoú Prókou**, which leads off to the south, lined with restaurants, bars, fancy shops and churches, including the balconied cathedral, **Áyios Spyrídhon**, towards the top. The main pedestrian street north from the main platía leads past the eighteenth-century church of **Panayía Ouranoforía** (aka Yeraniofórou), with fragments of a seventh-century BC temple of Apollo and a relief of St George over the door, and continues via Áno Petáli to Artemónas.

ARTEMÓNAS, fifteen minutes north of Apollonía on foot and served by frequent buses (the central bus depot is here), is worth a morning's exploration for its churches and elegant Venetian and Neoclassical houses. **Panayía Gourniá** (the key is kept at the house next door) has vivid frescoes; the clustered-dome church of **Kohí** was built over an ancient temple of Artemis (also the basis of the village's name); and seventeenth-century **Áyios Yeóryios** contains fine icons.

Practicalities

Apollonía's central platía looks rather abandoned, but below it are the **post office** and the **bus stop** for Kamáres; stops for other places are at the junction above, by the *Anthousa* hotel. There are two **pharmacies**, three **banks** and four **ATMs** near the junction; the police station is located on the main road leading north out of town. A few minutes along the road to Faros is an **Internet café**, and you can rent **bikes** at Moto Apollo, beside the petrol station just beyond – though the island is best explored on foot. **Rooms** are scattered all over the village, making them hard to find; try *Giamaki* rooms (Ⓣ22840 33973, Ⓕ22840 33923; ❸) just off the main pedestrian street at the *Anthousa* end, though your best bet may be on the square at the main branch of the excellent Aegean Thesaurus travel agency (Ⓣ22840 33151, Ⓦwww.thesaurus.gr), or the nearby Room Rental Association (Ⓣ22840 31333). The very friendly *Hotel Sifnos* (Ⓣ22840 31624, Ⓦwww.sifnoshotel.com; ❹), on the main pedestrian street, is the most traditional in its architecture and furnishing, while the *Anthousa* hotel (Ⓣ22840 31431; ❹) at the road junction is a dessert-lovers' paradise with comfortable rooms, and extremely good home-made cakes, chocolates and ice-cream. All the central hotels are sure to be noisy when the nearby clubs are open during the summer and at weekends, but if you want quieter premises with a better view, be prepared to pay more: however, a welcome exception is *Evangelia Kouki* (Ⓣ22840 31894; ❸), on the northern pedestrian street towards Artemónas above the luxurious *Petali Village* (Ⓣ22840 33024, Ⓦwww.hotelpetali.gr; B&B ❼).

There are a number of **restaurants** in Apollonía: on the main pedestrian street, the charmingly decorated *Odos Oneiron* offers eclectic upscale dishes, while the more reasonably priced *Adiexodos* offers great *mezédhes* on its terrace with a view; *Café Sifnos* does something for nearly every taste and is open all day. There are several tavernas up in the backstreets: *To Apostoli to Koutouki* is quite good for standard Greek fare and very reasonable. Probably the most famous place to eat on the island, although not consistently reliable, is *Liotrivi* (*Manganas*) (Ⓣ22840 31246) on the Artemónas main square next to the squat triple-aisled Áyios Konstandínos church; diagonally opposite is the very good *Margerita* ouzerí – but neither are cheap. The *Khryso* taverna in the upper part of the village is hard to find, but well-priced and very popular with the locals at weekends.

Most of the **nightlife** can be found on the main pedestrian street south of the square, at *Botsi*, *Volto* or the long-standing *Argo*. The *Camel Club*, on the road to Fáros, is another popular place for late-night action. For rebétika music there's the *Aloni*, just above the crossroad to Kástro.

The north

Artemónas is the point of departure for **Herónissos**, an isolated hamlet with a few tavernas and rooms, around a small beach in a very deep inlet at the north-western tip of the island. The 14km road is surfaced and there are 3 buses a day – you may find occasional boat trips in season from Kamáres. It is possible to walk back to Artemónas – but the start of the partly-marked path is not obvious – look behind and left of the Áyios Prokópios church. The best taverna is *Ammoudia*, which also does breakfasts (welcome if you've caught the early bus). Rooms include those above the small shop near the church, and – in summer – those above the *Romantza* taverna (Ⓣ22840 33139; ❷) at the bus stop. A dirt track and path from the bus stop car park lead to the small Áyios Yeóryios monastery on the island's northernmost point, from where there are lovely views across to Sérifos.

The east coast

Most of Sífnos's coastal settlements are along the less precipitous eastern shore, within a modest distance of Apollonía and its surrounding cultivated plateau. These all have good bus services, and a certain amount of food and accommodation, **Kástro** being more appealing than the resorts of **Platýs Yialós** and **Fáros** which can get very overcrowded in July and August.

Kástro

KÁSTRO seems the last place on Sífnos to fill up in season, and can be reached on foot from Apollonía in 45 minutes, all but the last ten on a clear path threading its way east via the hamlet of Káto Petáli. Built on a rocky outcrop with a steep drop to the sea on three sides, the ancient capital of the island retains much of its medieval character. There are some fine sixteenth- and seventeenth-century churches with ornamental floors; Venetian coats of arms, ancient wall fragments, and cunningly recycled Classical columns can still be seen on some of the older dwellings, while the occasional ancient sarcophagus perches incongruously on the pavement. In addition, there are the remains of the ancient acropolis, as well as a small **archeological museum** (Tues–Sun, officially 8am–2.30pm; free), installed in a former Catholic church in the higher part of the village; the museum has a small but varied collection of items, mainly from the Hellenistic and Roman periods, including coins, pottery, stelae and other carved marble fragments.

Among the several **rooms**, the modernized *Aris Rafeletos* apartments (Ⓣ & Ⓕ22840 31161; ❼) are open all year – the reception is near the archeological museum. More basic, but boasting gorgeous views, Maximos has a couple of rooms (Ⓣ22840 33692; ❸) next to his jewellery shop. Nationally renowned *Astro (Star)* is an obvious taverna to try, as is *Leonidas*, while the *Kavos Sunrise* café-bar is laid-back and has a fantastic view. On the edge of town, the *Castello* disco-bar is a livelier hangout.

Platýs Yialós

From Apollonía, there are almost hourly buses to the resort of **PLATÝS YIALÓS**, 12km away, near the southern tip of the island. Despite being one of the longest beaches in the Cyclades, the sand can get very crowded. Diversions include a pottery workshop, but many are put off by the continuous row of snack-bars and rooms to rent, which line the entire stretch of beach, and by the strong winds that plague it. **Rooms** are generally expensive; the welcoming *Pension Angeliki* (Ⓣ22840 71288, Ⓦwww.sifnosageliki.com; ❹), near the final #5 bus stop, has reasonably priced doubles however, as well as the stunning *Gerani Suites* apartments (❻–❼). Among several fairly pricey **tavernas** are *Foni*, a friendly fish taverna that hosts live music acts some evenings.

Fáros and around

There are less crowded beaches just to the northeast of Platýs Yialós (though unfortunately not directly accessible along the coast). **FÁROS**, with regular bus links to Apollonía, makes an excellent fall-back base. A small and friendly resort, it has some of the **cheapest accommodation** on the island, such as the new *Sun rooms* (Ⓣ22840 71489; ask at Frangiskos Kakakis' seafront shop-café; ❸) amongst olives behind the beach. *To Kyma* is a pleasant seafront **taverna**, and the smart *On the Rocks*, perched on the small western headland, serves a tasty selection of snacks as well as full meals. The closest beaches are not up to much: the town beach itself is muddy, shadeless and crowded, and Fasolоú to the northeast past the headland is not much better, much of it having been turned into a car park. Head off west through the older part of the village, and the beach improves since it only has pedestrian access, although a new housing development just behind the beach may spell its doom.

Vathý

A fishing village on the shore of an almost circular bay, **VATHÝ** is the most attractive base on the island. Even the surfaced road and the opening of a luxury hotel, frequented by celebrities and politicians, *Elies Resort* (Ⓣ22840 34000, Ⓦwww.eliesresorts.com; B&B ❽), seems not to have changed its remote character. There are regular **buses** (8 daily in high season, 2–4 daily at other times), and *kaïkia* run daily in season from Kamáres. **Rooms** include the attractive new studios at the *Nikos* (Ⓣ22840 71512; Ⓦwww.sifnosrooms.com; April–Nov; ❹) or next door at the *Virginia* (Ⓣ22840 71101; Ⓦwww.vathysifnos.gr; ❹), just before the jetty and the tiny **monastery of the Archangel Gabriel**. For **food**, *Manolis* does excellent grills and has rooms/studios around a garden behind (Ⓣ22840 71111; April–Oct; ❹); *Okeanida* has good *mezédhes* such as chickpea balls and cheesy aubergine patties, while *To Tsikali* on the seafront beyond the monastery has fresh cheese, chunky chips, and rabbit dishes.

Mílos

Volcanic **Mílos** is geologically diverse with weird rock formations, hot springs and good beaches, and offers sensational views. Minoan settlers were attracted by obsidian, and other products of its volcanic soil made the island one of the most important of the Cyclades in the ancient world. Today, the quarrying of bentonite, perlite, kaolin, barite, gypsum, pozzolana, microcrystalline quartz and sulphur has left huge scars on the landscape but given the island a relative prosperity and independence. With some 74 **beaches**, more than any other island in the Cyclades, Mílos hasn't had to tart itself up to court tourism.

You get a good preview of the island's **geological wonders** as your ferry enters Mílos Bay, a striking natural harbour, shaped by a series of explosions in the ancient past. Off the north coast, accessible only by excursion boat, the Glaroníssia (Seagull Isles) are shaped like massed organ pipes, and there are more strange formations round the coast, such as Kléftiko in the southwest, or Sarakiniko and Papafranga in the north. Inland, too, you frequently come across odd, volcanic outcrops, and thermal springs burst forth.

Like most volcanic islands, Mílos is quite fertile; away from the 725m summit of **Profítis Ilías** in the southwest and lower hills in the east, a gently undulating countryside is intensively cultivated to produce grain, hay and orchard fruits.

Adhámas

The main, lively port of **ADHÁMAS** (Adhámandas) was founded by Cretan refugees fleeing a failed rebellion in 1841. Although it boasts a marble-paved esplanade around its natural headland, it is architecturally disappointing compared to some of the Cycladic ports.

On the seafront east of town, about 2km from the centre, the well-organized **Mining Museum of Mílos** (summer daily 9am–2pm & 6–9pm, winter 8am–2.30pm Tues–Sat; free) gives an interesting insight into how mining has shaped the island, with an extensive collection of mining equipment, mineral samples, and geological maps of Mílos, plus informative displays on the extraction, processing and uses of minerals and on reclamation of the exhausted sites. Near the quayside, the small but interesting **Ecclesiastical Museum** (mornings and evenings; free) is housed in the century-old Ayía Triádha church

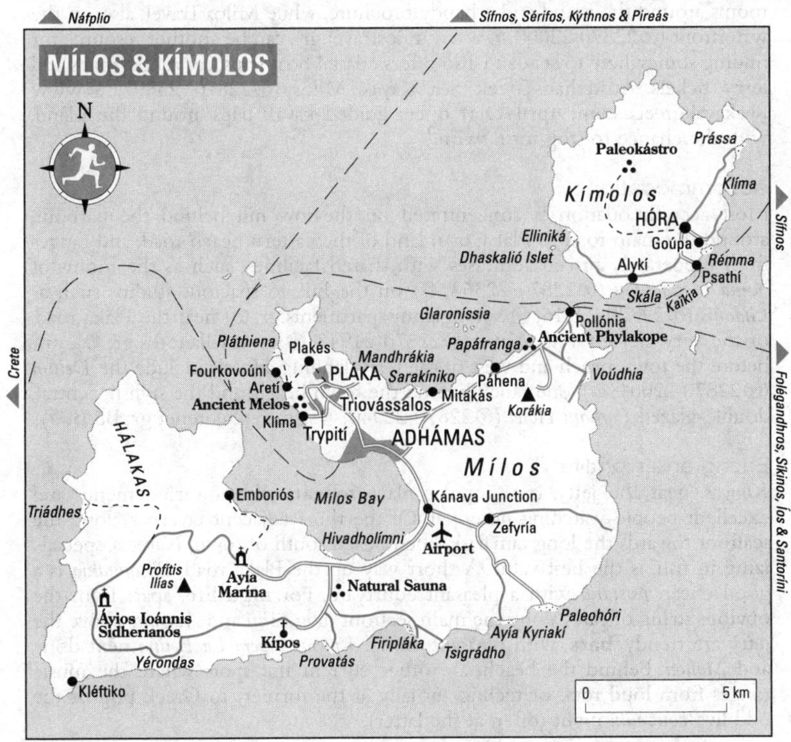

and has a good collection of liturgical paraphernalia and icons. In season there are **boat tours** around the island's bizarre coastline, passing the Glaroníssia and making several stops at otherwise inaccessible swimming spots like the magnificent **Kléftiko**, on the way to Kímolos where they often stop for a late lunch. Weather permitting, the boats normally leave at 9am from the quayside, and return at 6pm. Tickets cost around €30 per person, including lunch.

Practicalities

The ill-defined main square is just inland of the esplanade, at the junction of the Pláka road and the Mílos Bay coastal road: nearby are several **banks**, a **post office** and an **Internet café** (on the right at the start of the Pláka road). **Bus services** start from here – there are few in low season: seven a day to Pláka, and just twice daily (early morning and early afternoon) to Pollónia and Zefyría, and nothing on Sundays. In high season there are daily services to Pláka (17), Pollónia (9), Paleohori via Zefyría (8), the campsite (11, with 8 going on to Hivadhólimni), Provatás (8) and Sarakíniko (2–3). The **taxi** rank is nearby – call ⓣ22870 22219 to book. Some visitors arrive by twice-daily plane from Athens; most seats, however, are reserved by the local mining industry. Olympic Airways is located near the National Bank, near Adhámas port; the tiny **airport** is 5km southeast of the port, on the south side of Mílos Bay. Car rental is available from Tomaso (ⓣ22870 24100, ⓦwww.tomaso.gr) on the waterfront near the jetty.

Open during high season, the **tourist office** opposite the ferry dock (ⓣ22870 22445, ⓦwww.milos-island.gr) has a daily updated list of available rooms around the island and a handy brochure, while Milos Travel, also on the waterfront (ⓣ22870 22000, ⓦwww.milostravel.gr), can be another resource for finding somewhere to stay, and also offers coastal boat trips, car rental, maps and ferry tickets. Australian-Greek Sea Kayak Mílos (ⓣ22870 23597, ⓦwww.seakayakgreece.com; April–Oct) offers guided kayak trips around the island, with the chance to stop for a swim.

Accommodation

Most accommodation is concentrated on the low hill behind the harbour, around the main road to Pláka, or inland of the eastern beach road, and ranges from moderately priced addresses with shared facilities, such as the rooms of *Anna Gozadinou* (ⓣ22870 22364; ❸) on the hill, to spacious studios such as *Giannis* (ⓣ22870 22216, ⓦwww.giannisapartments.gr; ❹) near the Pláka road, or the very elegant *Villa Notos* (ⓣ22870 21943, ⓦwww.villanotos.gr; ❸), just before the town beach and west of the ferry landing. Hotels include the *Delfini* (ⓣ22870 22001; ❹), one block behind the town beach; and the stylish, central, double-glazed *Portiani Hotel* (ⓣ22870 22940, ⓔsirmalen@otenet.gr; B&B ❻).

Eating and nightlife

Kinigos, near the jetty, is a popular place to **eat**, with a varied menu, and excellent people-watching potential. Of the three adjacent tavernas along the seafront towards the long tamarisk-lined beach south of town, *Navagio*, specializing in fish, is the best value. A short way up the Pláka road, *Pitsounakia* is a good cheap *psistariá* with a pleasant courtyard. For **nightlife**, apart from the obvious string of cafés along the main seafront drag, *Akri* and *Aragosta* above the jetty are trendy **bars**, with pleasant views. *Vibera/Vipera La Betina* next door, and *Malion*, behind the beach, are other current hot spots where the music ranges from loud rock or techno (usually at the former) to Greek pop or the odd live *bouzoúki* night (often at the latter).

Greek cuisine

Although clichéd standards like kalamári and moussaka still figure strongly in taverna fare, Greek cuisine is considerably more complex and varied than the ubiquity of these well-loved dishes might suggest. In fact, modern Greeks are busy rediscovering their rich rural culinary heritage, which began as simple and functional, relying on local products, and later expanded under the influence of elaborate, Anatolian-influenced recipes in the 1920s, brought by immigrants from Asia Minor. The result is a wide-ranging cuisine based on fresh, raw ingredients, subtle herbal filips and preparation by charcoal grilling or in wood-burning ovens. You'll find myriad local specialities, all proudly touted: anything from whole pickled caper sprigs to smoked eels, molluscs bottled in brine to soft sheeps' cheese or thyme honey to almond syrup.

Market, Iráklion, Crete ▲

Olives for sale at an Athens street market ▲

Cheese stall, Athens ▼

Eat your greens

Wild and cultivated **vegetables** are the bedrock of Greek cuisine. During the cooler months, street markets overflow with **leafy greens**: purslane, parsley and rocket for salads, or the various chicories, chards and even edible weeds known as *hórta*. These and other garden vegetables find their way into salads, *píttes* (baked pies), fritters and casseroles. *Briám* or *tourloú* is a ratatouille of courgettes, potatoes, aubergines (eggplants) and tomatoes; chickpeas are stewed or formed into *revythokeftédhes* (coarse falafels). Aubergine has numerous uses: fried in slices, baked, stuffed, or even puréed. Any restaurant with an eye to its reputation prepares fresh hand-cut chips daily.

Olives and olive oil

Olive oil is a universal staple; traditionally every family, even city-dwelling, got its own from trees on a remote country property. **Olives** are harvested between November and January depending on locale and variety: beaten off the trees early on, or harvested later, ripe from the ground. There are over a dozen varieties, coloured green to black to purple: some are used mainly for oil, but others are reserved for eating, particularly in the ubiquitous *horiátiki* or "peasant" salad.

Cheeses

Greeks are, perhaps surprisingly, Europe's biggest **cheese** consumers and every region of Greece produces it, feta merely being the most famous. Consistency varies from hard blocks of *kéfalograviéra* suitable for grating over pasta to pyramids of soft cheese, like sweet *manoúri* or *anthótyro* and savoury *dhermatísio*, used for spreading or stuffing. Special treats include the Hiot cow's-milk cheese *mastéllo*, served grilled, or smoked *metsovóne* sheeps' cheese from Epirus.

Meat dishes

Formerly, eating **meat** was reserved for festivals, though it now figures almost daily in local diets. Besides chops and *pansétta* (spare ribs, not belly-bacon), **pork** appears as locally made *loukánika* (sausages), or as the legendary *sto héri* (takeaway snack *souvláki*). Many meat dishes are oven-baked casseroles – standards include the perennial favourites *moussakas* and *stifádho* (stew). **Goat**, whether stewed, baked or grilled, is the healthiest meat around, free-range and redolent of the herby hillside on which it grazed. Those herbs reappear at taverna **grills**, where the proprietor bastes your order, sizzling over olive- or oak-wood coals, with a "broom" of thyme or oregano.

▲ Kebabs

Fish and seafood

As well as premium varieties such as bream and bass, there are more affordable, seasonally available species. Delicacies of the eastern Aegean include **shrimp** and **sole** in springtime, and **anchovies**, *atherína* (silver smelt) and **sardines** in summer, best prepared flash-fried. Everywhere, fried *gópes* (bogue), *soupiá* (cuttlefish) with rice and spinach, and grilled or wine-stewed octopus are good year-round seafood platters. Or, tuck into unusual **shellfish** such as *petalídhes* (limpets), *yialisterés* (smooth Venus), and *petrosolínes* (razor clams), all eaten alive – if they twitch when drizzled with lemon juice, they're alive.

▲ Seafood market, Athens

▼ Restaurant, Pireás, near Athens

Ouzo

Ouzo, the quintessential Greek aperitif, is a spirit produced by boiling, in a copper still, the fermented grape-mash residue left after wine-pressing. The resulting liquid, originally called **rakí**, grew in popularity

Vineyard, Crete ▲

Typical taverna sign ▼

Greek wine

Quality **wine-making** is part of the Greek culinary renaissance; local vintners have a distinguished pedigree going back four thousand years, but still have a relatively small production capacity. If you think that Greek wine begins and ends with retsina, think again – top-drawer vintages are every bit as sophisticated (and pricey) as their French, Australian or South American counterparts. See p.51 for a summary of Greek wine domains.

during the nineteenth century, when distilleries were established in Smyrna, Constantinople and Lésvos. The word ouzo derives from the Italian label *uso Massalia* on *rakí* shipments leaving the Ottoman empire for Marseille. Today it means *rakí* flavoured with various **aromatic spices**, usually star anise or fennel, both containing anethole, which causes ouzo to (harmlessly) turn milky white when water is added. Bottled ouzo's alcohol content varies from 40 to 48 percent, never higher as the risk of exploding glass is too great – home-made ouzo at greater strengths is kept in barrels to avoid this problem.

Greek coffee

Greek coffee (*ellinikós kafés*), despite its name, is essentially the same drink that is prepared across the Middle East and Balkans, with minor variations in each country. It's made with fine-ground robusta coffee beans (rather than the arabica used in filter coffee), sugar to taste and water, combined in a long-handled vessel called a **bríki**. Allowing it to surge – but not boil – twice before decanting produces the prized **kaïmaki** (froth), the test of a properly made coffee, which is always served with a large glass of cold water.

▲ Firopotamos harbour, Mílos

Pláka and Trypití

The main appeal of Mílos is in an area that has been the island's focus of habitation since Classical times, where a cluster of villages huddles in the lee of a crag, 4km northwest of the harbour.

PLÁKA (MÍLOS) is the largest of these communities and the official capital of the island. Behind the lower car park, at the top of the approach boulevard through the newer district, the attractive **Archeological Museum** (Tues–Sun 8.30am–3pm – it does not always look open, even when it is; €3) contains numerous obsidian implements, plus a whole wing of finds from ancient Phylakope (see p.523), whose highlights include a votive lamp in the form of a bull and a rather Minoan-looking terracotta goddess. Labelling is scant, but you'll recognize the plaster-cast copy of the Hellenistic *Venus de Milo*, the original of which was found on the island in 1820. The statue was promptly delivered to the French consul for "safekeeping" from the Turks; her arms were knocked off in the melee surrounding her abduction. This was the last the Greeks saw of *Venus* until a copy was belatedly sent from the Louvre in Paris. Up in a mansion of the old quarter, the recently renovated **Folk Museum** (Tues–Sat 10am–2pm & 6–9pm, Sun 10am–2pm; €3) has a well-presented array of artefacts related to the history of arts, crafts and daily life on Mílos.

A stair-street beginning near the police station leads up to the old Venetian **kástro**, its upper slopes clad in stone and cement to channel precious rainwater into cisterns. From the summit, where the ancient Melians made their last stand against the Athenians before the massacre of 416 BC, are some of the best views in the Aegean, particularly at sunset in clear conditions.

Pláka has a **post office** and a **motorbike-rental** outfit near the Archeological Museum. There are **rooms** available scattered around the village, with those on the west side offering spectacular views. Among the nicest of these are the pretty studios of *Stratis Vourakis* (Ⓣ22870 21702; ④) high on the *kástro*. The *Spiti tis Makhis* (Ⓣ22870 41353; ⑤), below the *Plakiani Gonia* taverna, has newly refurbished rooms in the house where the *Venus de Milo* was allegedly hidden following its discovery; it also has plenty of parking space. There are a number of blocks of modern accommodation overlooking the busy approach road. There are some good places for **eating**: recommended are the *Archontoula* ouzerí serving excellent seafood dishes, and slightly more upscale *Alisachni* restaurant, offering classic Greek dishes with a modern flair.

The attractive village of **TRYPITÍ** (meaning "perforated"), which takes its name from the cliffside tombs nearby and a long ridge 1km south of Pláka, is another good base – and less busy with traffic than lower Pláka. There are **rooms**, including a couple of windmills on the eastern side (Ⓣ22870 22147, Ⓔergonia@otenet.gr; ⑦). The best places to **eat** are rustic *Glaronisia* serving up traditional taverna fare, and *Ergina*, which features oven-roasted goat and cuttlefish; for coffee and evening drinks, the stylish *Remvi Café* just past the bus stop has great views.

Catacombs, Ancient Melos and Klíma

From Pláka's Archeological Museum, signs point you towards the **early Christian catacombs** (Tues–Sun 8am–5pm; free), 1km south of Pláka and just 400m from Trypití village; steps lead down from the road to the inconspicuous entrance. Some 5000 bodies were buried in tomb-lined corridors stretching 200m into the soft volcanic rock, making these the largest catacombs in Greece; however, only the first 50m is illuminated and accessible by boardwalk. Don't miss the ruins of **ancient Melos**, located just above the catacombs, which extend down from Pláka almost to the sea. There are huge Dorian walls, the usual column fragments lying around and, best of all, a well-preserved Roman **amphitheatre** (unrestricted access). Only seven rows of seats remain intact, but these look out evocatively over Klíma to the bay. En route to the theatre from the cement road is the signposted spot where the *Venus de Milo* was found in what may have been the compound's gymnasium.

At the very bottom of the vale, and accessed via a road from the south end of Trypití or steps down from near the catacombs, **KLÍMA** is the most photogenic of the island's several fishing hamlets, with its picturesque boathouses tucked underneath the principal living areas. There's little beach to speak of, and only one place to stay – the impeccably sited *Panorama* (Ⓣ22870 21623, Ⓕ22870 22112; ④), with a balcony taverna.

Southern Mílos

The main road to the south of the island splits at **Kánava junction**, near the large power station. The left (east) fork leads to **Zefyría**, briefly the medieval capital. South of here it's a further 8km down a winding road to **Paleohóri,** one of the island's better beaches, with the sand of the western end of the main strand warmed by underground vulcanism. A little rock tunnel leads west through from here to a second beach, which is backed by extraordinarily coloured cliffs, and where clothing's optional and steam vents heat the shallow water. There are a number of **places to stay**, such as the inland *Paleochori Studios* (Ⓣ22870 31267, Ⓔpaleochori@in.gr; ④) or the purpose-built rooms behind the seafront *Vihos Artemis* restaurant (Ⓣ22870 31222, Ⓕ22870 23386; ④) nearer the beach. There are several **tavernas**, with the *Sirocco* using the hot volcanic sand to cook food. Ayía Kyriakí beach, just to the west of Paleohóri, also has a taverna, plus some tamarisk shade.

The westerly road from Kánava junction leads past the airport entrance to **Hivadholímni**, the best beach on Mílos bay itself. The **campsite** (ⓣ22870 31410, ⓦwww.miloscamping.gr) is just above, so beach camping is frowned upon. The site's minibus meets ferries, and in summer there are frequent buses until late to and from Adhámas.

Just after the campsite, and before Hivadholimni, you can fork south to **Provatás**, a short beach, closed off by multicoloured cliffs to the east. It is easy to get to, and hasn't escaped development: there are two rooms establishments plus, closer to the shore, a newer, luxury complex. The best value for **food and accommodation** is the *Maïstrali* (ⓣ22870 31420, ⓕ22870 31164; ❺), with private rooms and restaurant. Several kilometres before Provatás, an initially-surfaced road forks east to the trendy and popular beach of **Firipláka**, however, the road also runs to a huge quarry and has 24-hour lorry traffic. East of Firipláka, sandy **Tsigrádho** beach is only accessible by boat, or by means of a rope hanging down a crevice in the cliff face, so usually uncrowded, and excellent for swimming.

The north coast

From either Adhámas or the Pláka area, good roads run roughly parallel to the **north coast** which, despite being windswept and little inhabited, is not devoid of at least geological interest. **Sarakíniko**, to the east, is an astonishing sculpted inlet with a sandy sea bed and gleaming white sunbathing rocks popular with local youth. Just east is a shipwreck.

Still heading east, you reach another of Mílos's coastal wonders, **Papáfranga**, a short ravine into which the sea flows under a rock arch – the tiny beach at its inland end is accessed by rock-carved steps. Immediately west and parallel is a second ravine, with at its head a large sea cave inhabited by birds and smelling of volcanic hydrogen sulphide. To the right of the Papáfranga car park, the remains of three superimposed Neolithic settlements – including a large and dramatic section of walling – crown a small knoll at **Fylakopí** (ancient Phylakope); archeological excavation continues.

Pollónia

POLLÓNIA, 12km northeast of Adhámas, is immensely popular with windsurfers, and a diving centre (see below) has further increased its popularity among watersports enthusiasts. Pollónia is essentially a small harbour with a long, curved, tamarisk-lined beach, and the original settlement huddled on – and protected by – a small, northeastern promontory ending in the church of Ayía Paraskeví with its beautiful ceiling paintings.

On the quay are several **tavernas** and a couple of very mediocre café/snack-bars – the *Apanemia* 200m back on the access road is a recommended alternative. To the south is a concentration of **accommodation**, both simple rooms and apartments, most with the slight drawback of occasional noise and dust from quarry trucks. Among the best are the *Kapetan Tasos Studios* (ⓣ22870 41287, ⓦwww.kapetantasos.gr; ❺), with good views of the straits between Mílos and Kímolos, and the nearby *Kostantakis Studios* (ⓣ22870 41357, ⓦwww.kostantakis.gr; ❹), which allows children to help out on its farm. On the northern side of the promontory, the *Apollon* (ⓣ22870 41347/41451, ⓦwww.apollon-diving.com; ❺), has rooms, a restaurant, and a dive centre offering PADI courses and snorkelling trips. To the northwest, *Andreas* (ⓣ22870 41262, ⓔbrigitte-milos@bluewin.ch; ❼) has triple studios with stunning rural views and easy access to the quiet neighbouring bay. Pollónia has no bank or post office. The friendly Axios Rent A Car office (Ⓣ & Ⓕ22870 41234) can advise you on accommodation matters; they also sell second-hand English books.

Taking the ferry to Kímolos may be the main reason you're here. The *Leykas* car ferry makes the trip about four times daily year-round, although it tends not to sail in high winds; call the port authority (Ⓣ22870 28860) to check.

Kímolos

Of the three islands off the coast of Mílos, only **Kímolos** is inhabited. Volcanic like Mílos, it profits from its geology and used to export chalk (*kimolía* in Greek) until the supply was exhausted. Fuller's earth is still extracted locally, and the fine dust of this clay is a familiar sight on the northeast corner of the island, where mining still outstrips fishing and farming as an occupation. Rugged and little cultivated in the scenic interior, it has some fertile land on the southeast coast where wells provide water, and this is where the population of about eight hundred is concentrated. Kímolos is sleepy from September to June, and even in August sees few visitors, just as well since there are fewer than a hundred beds on the whole island, and little in the way of other amenities; those visitors who venture here come for the tranquillity and the walking.

Psathí and Hóra

Whether you arrive by ferry, or by *kaïki* from Pollónia, you'll dock at the tiny port of **PSATHÍ**, which is pretty much a non-event except for the excellent *To Kyma* ("The Wave") **taverna** midway along the beach, specializing in tasty seafood. **Ferry tickets** for onward journeys – unless bought in advance up in Hóra – are only sold outside the expensive café at the end of the jetty, an hour or so before the anticipated arrival of the boat. The *Leykas* comes and goes from Pollónia on Mílos from the base of the jetty four times a day, whilst some larger ferries call briefly on their way to and from Mílos. A summer minibus runs from the port to the capital Hóra, which can also be reached by foot in about fifteen minutes.

Around the bay, there are a few old windmills and dazzlingly white **HÓRA** perched on the ridge above them. The magnificent, two-gated, sixteenth-century **kástro** is one of the best preserved of such fortresses, built against marauding pirates in the Cyclades; the perimeter houses are intact and inhabited, though its heart is a jumble of ruins. Just outside the *kástro* to the north stands the conspicuously unwhitewashed, late sixteenth-century church of **Khryssóstomos**, the oldest and most beautiful on the island. Near the church is the **Archeological Museum** (irregular hours) with pottery from the Geometric to the Roman period. In a restored house near the eastern gateway is the excellent, privately-run **Folk and Maritime Museum** (Ⓣ22870 51118; summer).

There are a few adequate **rooms** near the port, but halfway between the port and town is the hospitable *Villa Maria* (Ⓣ22870 51752, Ⓦwww.hellasislands.gr/kimolos/villa-maria; ❸) rooms and studios, open all year. Other accommodation options include Margaro Petraki's rooms (Ⓣ22870 51314; ❷), tucked away in the rather unglamorous maze of backstreets, or try those of Apostolos Ventouris (Ⓣ22870 51329; ❷) above his *kafenío* nearby. The *Sofia* (Ⓣ22870 51219; ❸) has studios with sea views, close to the church. For **meals**, aside from a couple of basic *psistariés* and a café-bar, the aptly named *Panorama*, near the east gate of the *kástro*, is the most elaborate and consistently open taverna.

Meltemi, to the west of the village, is another good taverna, which also has some rooms (☎22870 51360; ❸). Other facilities include a couple of ship agencies, and a **post office** in the west of the village, as well as an **ATM**.

Around the island

The hamlet of **ALYKÍ** on Kimolos' south coast is about thirty minutes' walk on the paved road that forks left from Psathí; it is named after the saltpan that sprawls between a rather mediocre beach offering no shade, but with rooms and a few simple **tavernas**. You can stroll west one cove to **Bonátsa** for better sand and shallow water, though you won't escape the winds. Passing another cove you come to the even more attractive beach of **Kalamítsi**, with better shade and a decent taverna. Innumerable paths, many well-maintained, invite exploration of the interior of the island; in the northwest, on Kímolos' summit, are the scant ruins of a Venetian fortress known as **Paleókastro**.

Ándhros

Ándhros, the second largest and northernmost of the Cyclades, is also one of the most verdant, making it a great place for serious walkers. Thinly populated but prosperous, its fertile, well-watered valleys and gorges have sprouted scores of Athenian holiday villas – some of the more recent of these have turned villages into scattered settlements with no nucleus, and creating a weekender mentality manifest in noisy Friday- and Sunday-evening traffic jams at the ferry dock. The island doesn't cater extensively for independent travellers, and it can be difficult to find a bed during August, especially at weekends.

On the positive side, the permanent population is distinctly hospitable. Together with some of the more idiosyncratic reminders of the Venetian period, such as the *peristereónes* (dovecote towers) and the *frákhtes* (dry-stone walls, here raised to the status of an art form), this friendliness lends Ándhros its charm. In addition, the island has numerous beaches, including some of Greece's best, with more than sixteen on the northwest and north coast only accessible by boat or long dirt track. For walkers, the island has twelve numbered, waymarked paths, varying from 1.7 to 11.5km, though not all are well-maintained; most are linear and some would need transport arrangements for the return.

Ferries connect the island with Ráfina on the mainland, and in season you can loop back onto the central Cycladic routes via Mýkonos, Tínos or Sýros.

Northern and western Ándhros

All ferries and catamarans arrive at the main port, **GÁVRIO**, a pleasant small town and resort in an oval bay. **Buses** run from the port via Batsí to Hóra at least six times a day in high season, plus some from Gávrio to Órmos Korthíou. However, since buses may wait for delayed ferries, the timetabling in this direction can be very unreliable. A tiny converted dovecote houses a sporadically functioning **tourist office**, and there are half-a-dozen ferry **ticket agents**, **banks** and three **ATMs** at the start of the waterfront, and a **post office** at the other end. There are **Internet** facilities on the side road south of town.

The cheapest **accommodation** is the central *Galaxias* (☎22820 71228; ❸), which serves as a late-arrival fall-back. The pleasant **campsite** (☎22820 71444; May–Oct) is 300m behind the centre of town, has a café and can provide a lift

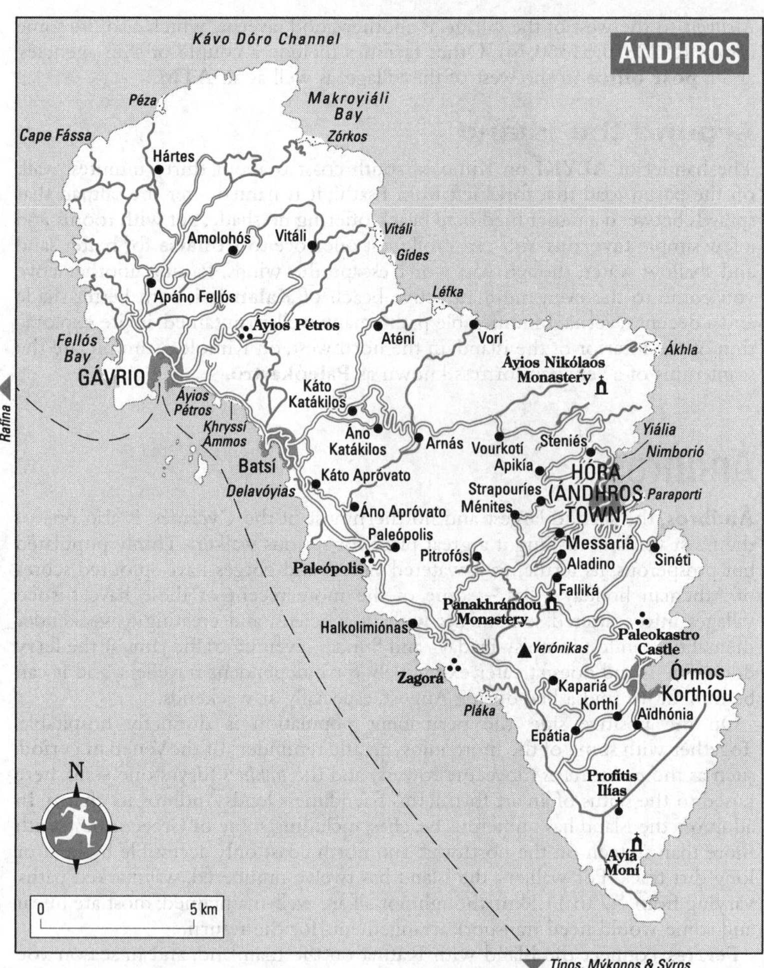

from the port. There is a beach adjacent to town, but there are more attractive alternatives to the southeast, such as **Áyios Pétros**, accessible by a 2km roadside pavement, where you'll also find the area's better accommodation. One of the nearest of these to Gávrio are *Aktio* (Ⓣ22820 71607, Ⓦwww.aktiostudios.gr; ⑤) with large studios, good discounts and some wheelchair access, near the BP station, while the *Andros Holiday Hotel* (Ⓣ22820 71384, Ⓦwww.androstours.com; April–Oct; B&B ⑥) on the headland side road south of town has lovely seaviews. Some 3km south down the coast, between the smaller, pretty Khryssí Ámmos and longer Psilí Ámmos beaches, is the upmarket *Perrakis Hotel* (Ⓣ22820 71456, Ⓦwww.hotelperrakis.gr: ⑦).

Restaurants worth trying include the popular *Konaki*, the *En Gavrio* café-ouzerí, and the *psistariá Smurfs*, near the centre of Gávrio seafront. **Nightlife** revolves around a string of cafés and bars, both along the harbourfront and at Áyios Pétros, where the excellent *Yiannouli* taverna is worth checking out for lunch. Gávrio is the easiest place on the island for **car rental**, with several competing establishments including Colours on the seafront and Escape to Andros (Ⓣ22820 29120) near the BP.

Head northeast and inland from Gávrio on the road to **Áyios Pétros** village, and you will see the remarkable 20m-high, cylindrical **stone tower**, built between 400–300 BC and probably connected with ancient iron mines visible below. Unfortunately the access path to the tower itself is now both overgrown and blocked by beehives.

Most visitors head 8km south to **BATSÍ**, the island's main resort, with hotels, rooms and bars around its fine natural harbour. The beautiful though often crowded beach curves round the bay, and the sea is cold, calm, sandy and clean (except near the jetty). Most facilities cluster around the bend of the seafront road near the fishing jetty. In season it may be possible to hire a boat or join fishing trips locally. Southeast of town, a coastal road leads 1.5km through the Káto Stivári area to the small, picturesque cove at Ayía Marína.

Hotels in Batsí range from the central, comfortable *Chryssi Akti* (Ⓣ22820 41236, Ⓕ22820 41628; ❹) behind the main beach, to the upmarket *Aneroussa Beach Hotel* (Ⓣ22820 41044, Ⓕ22820 41045; ❺), at Ayía Marína. Besides these there are plenty of other rooms, such as the well-equipped and popular *Anemos* (Ⓣ22820 41287, Ⓔanemos@syr.forthnet.gr; ❸) near the start of the Ayía Marína road. **Restaurants** include *Delfinia* near the jetty; the next door *O, Ti Kalo* is run by the same family as the *Anemos*; the well-priced *Corsair* ouzerí is on the upper access road in the south of the village. There are several **café-bars**, such as *Capriccio* and *Nameless* in the centre, plus a half-a-dozen or so loud indoor bars featuring the standard foreign/Greek musical mix, and even an outdoor cinema with a different film every night in the summer. The **bank** has an **ATM**, and there is an Anglican church.

South of Batsí, **Áno Aprováto**, accessed via a winding hill road, has the taverna *Balkoni tou Aigaiou* ("Balcony of the Aegean") with good, well-priced rural food and panoramic views. At **Paleópoli**, 8km from Batsí, there is a small museum (Tue–Sun, 8.30am–3pm; free) containing well-labelled marble statuary/carvings, coins and domestic items from the nearby archeological site. The ancient city of Paleópolis flourished from the sixth century BC to the end of the sixth century AD, covering a large area just northwest of the modern village. A pleasant walk is signed ("beach") from the main road café, via the Káto Paleópoli church, down to the pebble beach, passing fragments of ancient walls and tombs, and with beautiful views back up to the village. You can return via a stony path up from the southeastern end of the beach.

Hóra

A bus service links the west-coast Gávrio and Batsí with east coast **HÓRA** (also known as **ÁNDHROS TOWN**), 35km from Gávrio. Stretched along a rocky spur that divides a huge bay, the capital is the most attractive town on the island. Clad in marble and schist from the still-active local quarries, the buildings near the bus station are grand nineteenth-century affairs, and the squares with their ornate wall fountains and gateways are equally elegant. The old port, Plakoúra, on the west side of the headland has a yacht supply station and a former ferry landing from where occasional boats run to the isolated Ákhla beach in summer. More locally, there are beaches on both sides of the town headland, Nimborió to the north and the better, undeveloped Parapórti to the southeast, though both are exposed to the *meltémi* winds in summer.

From Kaïris square right at the end of Hóra's main street, Embirikoú, you pass through an archway and down through residential area to **Platía Ríva**, with its Soviet-donated statue of an unknown sailor scanning the sea. These replace houses destroyed by German munitions in World War II; also damaged was the now-precarious arched bridge that stretches across to an islet with the remnants of a thirteenth-century Venetian *kástro*. Inside the modern **Archeological Museum** (Tues–Sun 8.30am–3pm; €2), on the main street near Kaïris, are well laid out and labelled displays, with instructive models. Its prize item is the fourth-century *Hermes of Andros*, reclaimed from a prominent position in the Athens archeological museum. Behind it, the **Modern Art Museum** (Mon, Wed–Sun 8am–2.30pm, also 6–8pm in summer; €3) has a sculpture garden and a permanent collection with works by Picasso, Matisse, Kandinsky, Chagall and others, as well as temporary shows. The **Folklore and Christian Art Museum** (April–June Sat 6–8pm, Sun 11am–1pm; July–Sep daily 6–8pm plus Sunday 11am–1pm; €3) is just behind (left) of the *Paradise Hotel*. Near the bus station is an open-air **cinema**.

The few **hotels** in town are on the expensive side and tend to be busy with holidaying Greeks. The *Paradise Hotel* (ⓣ22820 22187, ⓦwww.paradiseandros.gr; B&B ⓻), with its swimming pool and tennis court, is an upmarket choice, but is right beside the main road at the entrance to town. Most rooms are clustered behind the long **Nimborió** beach northwest of town; those towards the far end include the attractive rooms of the *Stella* (ⓣ22820 22471, ⓦwww.pension-stella.gr; ❸) – open all year, and not only with its own café, but next door to a *Dodoni* ice-cream parlour – and studios such as the *Alcioni Inn* (ⓣ22820 24522, ⓦwww.alcioni.gr; ❺).

For **eating**, *Plátanos* at Kaïris has a generous *mezédhes* selection that can be enjoyed with an ouzo under the plane trees, while *Skalakia*, on steps beside a park below the main church, a couple of minutes from the bus station, also does excellent *mezédhes* at reasonable prices. The nicest fish taverna is *Ononas*, tucked away at the town end of Nimborió at the old Plakoúra harbour, next to the wreck of the *Xenia* hotel, while *Cabo del Mar* on the hillside beyond the church at the far end of Nimborió is pricey but good, with an unsurpassed view.

Nimborió beach is the epicentre of the island's **nightlife**, such as it is, with a few thumping discos that start with Western music and shift into Greek pop into the early hours of the morning. Hóra has a **post office**, several **banks** and **ATMs**, a couple of **ferry agents**, and **Internet** facilities at e-Waves, all on the main street, and several **motorbike rentals** behind the beach.

Around Hóra

Hiking is particularly inviting south and west from Hóra, where there are lush little river valleys. The finest monastery on the island is **Panayía Panakhrándou**: founded around 961 and with an icon said to be by St Luke, it's still defended by massive walls but occupied these days by just one monk. From the entrance door, a long passageway leads past gushing springs to the atmospheric church. Panakhrándou clings to the steep hillside below water-seeping cliffs on the ridge southwest of Hóra, to which you can return directly with a healthy two- to three-hour walk down the valley, guided by red dots. It is driveable, from the eastern side of the ridge via Mésa Vouní, however, when nearly at the monastery, you may wish to park then walk down the very steep final section of the road for spectacular views of the building below you.

Southern Ándhros

If you're exploring the south of the island from Hóra, the road runs through the dramatic Dipotámata valley. Beyond the valley, a side road goes 2km (partly surfaced) to **PALEÓKASTRO** (aka Kástro Faneroménis, Kohýlou Epáno Kástro) a ruined Venetian castle perched on a rocky crest at 586m, with amazing views overlooking Kórthi Bay. Legend has it that an old woman, who betrayed the stronghold to the Turks, jumped from the top in remorse, and she remains as a column of rock in the sea off Griás Pídhima beach where she landed.

A short distance further south, the laid-back resort of **ÓRMOS KORTHÍOU** (Kórthi Bay) is a small town with a new seafront esplanade waking up to its tourist potential and is popular with windsurfers. Set on a large bay, isolated from the rest of the island by the high ridge and relatively unspoilt, it is pleasant enough to merit a stay at the austere-looking *Hotel Korthion* (☎22820 61218; ❹) by the bus stop, or at rooms such as the nearby *Villa Korthi* (☎22820 61122; ❹) or at the *Villa Mina* (☎22820 61067, 6944 106234; ❺), apartments with kitchen between the two jetties at the northern end of the harbour. There are also several **tavernas**, including *Galazios Orizontes* (aka *Afoi Paskhali*) at the waterfront. The well-priced *zaharoplastío* near the information kiosk (sporadically open) has good ice cream and cakes, while the friendly *Centro* café near the roundabout is good for people-watching, or relaxing after the beach. Most facilities are on Odhos Yeoryíou Psalti, parallel to the esplanade: **Internet** and pool are available at the Blue Games café; the **bank** opens a couple of mornings a week (Mon, Thurs), but has an **ATM**; the Doropigi travel office is the **ferry agent**. Grias Pídhima beach is accessible via signed road and dirt track from near the northern end of the esplanade, while Kandouni beach covers the southern half of the main bay.

Tínos

Tínos still feels like one of the most Greek of the larger islands in the Cyclades. A few foreigners have discovered its beaches and unspoilt villages, but most visitors are Greek, here to see the church of **Panayía Evangelístria**, a grandiose shrine erected on the spot where a miraculous icon with healing powers was found in 1822. A local nun, now canonized as Ayía Pelayía, was directed in a vision to unearth the relic just as the War of Independence was getting underway, a timely coincidence that served to underscore the links between the Orthodox Church and Greek nationalism. Today, there are two major annual pilgrimages, on March 25 and August 15, when Tínos is inundated by the faithful, and at 11am, the icon bearing the Virgin's image is carried in state down to the harbour.

The Ottoman tenure here was the most fleeting in the Aegean. **Exóbourgo**, the craggy mount dominating southern Tínos and surrounded by most of the island's sixty-odd villages, is studded with the ruins of a Venetian citadel that defied the Turks until 1715, long after the rest of Greece had fallen. An enduring legacy of the long Venetian rule is a persistent **Catholic minority**, which accounts for almost half the population, and a sectarian rivalry said to be responsible for the numerous belltowers scattered throughout the higher parts of the island – Orthodox and Catholic parishes vying to build the tallest. Hills are dotted with some 600 distinctive and ornate **dovecotes**, even more in evidence here than on Ándhros. Aside from all this, the inland village architecture is striking and there's a flourishing folk-art tradition that finds expression

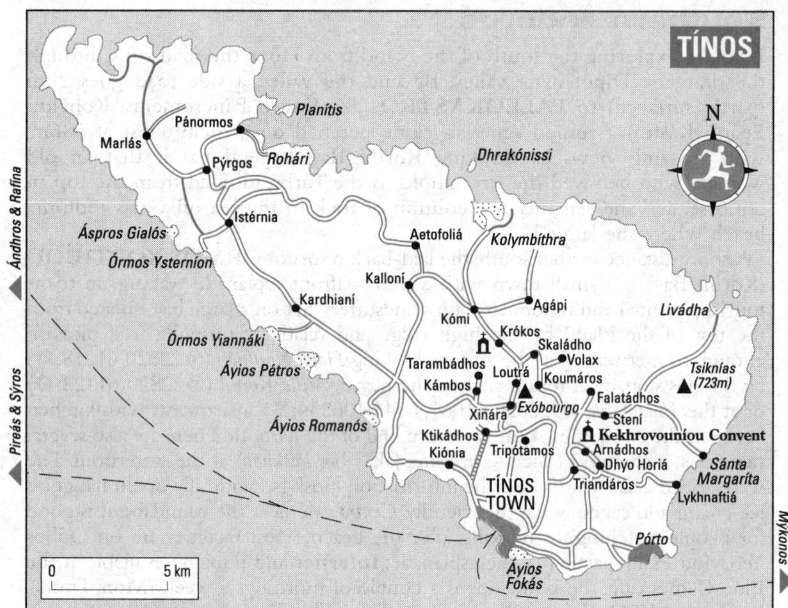

in the abundant local marble. The islanders have remained open and hospitable to the relatively few foreigners and the steady stream of Greek visitors who touch down here, and any mercenary inclinations seem to be satisfied by booming sales in religious paraphernalia to the faithful.

Tínos Town

At **TÍNOS TOWN**, the sale of devotional articles certainly dominates the streets leading up from the busy waterfront to the Neoclassical church **Panayía Evangelístria** (officially daily 8am–8pm) that towers above. Evangelistrías in particular overflows with holy-water vessels, votive candles and plastic icons, while parallel Megalohàris, which points a slightly more direct approach to the church, is relatively clear of shops, making room for the long, thick pad that has been bolted to the street in sympathy for the most religious devotees who crawl to the church uphill on their knees from the harbour. Approached via a massive marble staircase, the famous **icon** inside the church is all but buried under a dazzling array of jewels; below is the crypt (where the icon was discovered) and a mausoleum for the sailors drowned when the Greek warship *Elli*, at anchor off Tínos during a pilgrimage, was torpedoed by an Italian submarine on August 15, 1940. Museums around the courtyard display more objects donated by the faithful, as well as icons, paintings and work by local marble sculptors.

The shrine aside – and all the attendant stalls, shops and bustle – the port is none too exciting, with just scattered inland patches of nineteenth-century buildings. You might make time for the **Archeological Museum** (Tues–Sun 8.30am–3pm; €2) on the way up to the church, whose collection includes a fascinating sundial from the local Roman sanctuary of Poseidon and Amphitrite (see p.532).

Practicalities

Ferries dock at any of three different **jetties**; which one is used may depend on weather conditions. The main "New Jetty" is at the western end of the outer port (Éxo Limáni), below the *Asteria* hotel, while the other jetties are in the eastern inner port (Mesa Limáni), in front of the central, older seafront. When you're leaving, ask your ticket agent which jetty to head for. **Buses** leave from a small parking area in front of a cubbyhole-office on the quay, to Kardhianí-Pýrgos-Pánormos, Kómi-Kalloní-Kolymbíthra, Voláx-Skaládhos, Falatádhos-Stení, Áyios Fokás, Pórto and Kiónia (buses only early morning/ early afternoon outside high season, and no buses after 7.30pm). A **rental-car** or **motorbike** is perhaps a more reliable means of exploring – Vidalis at Zanáki Alavánou 16 and elsewhere (ⓣ22830 23400, ⓦwww.vidalis-rentacar .gr), is a good rental agency.

Windmills Travel (ⓣ & ⓕ22830 23398, ⓦwww.windmillstravel.com), on the front towards the new jetty, can help with information as well as **tour bookings** and hotel bookings both here and on Mýkonos; they sometimes stay open for late ferry arrivals and also have a book exchange. The **tourist police** are located on the road to the west of the new jetty. In season an excursion boat does **day trips** (Tues–Sun; €20 round trip) taking in Delos (see p.540) and Mýkonos (see p.533); this makes it possible to see Delos without the expense of staying overnight in Mýkonos, but only allows you two-and-a-half hours at the site.

Accommodation

To have any chance of securing a reasonably priced **room** around the pilgrimage day of March 25 (August 15 is hopeless), you must arrive several days in advance. At other times, there's plenty of choice, though you'll still be competing with out-of-season pilgrims, Athenian tourists and the ill and disabled seeking a miracle cure. The accommodation listed below is open from mid-April to October only, unless stated otherwise.

Anna's Rooms Stavrós, road to Kiónia ⓣ22830 22877, ⓦwww.tinos.nl. Excellent, Dutch-run apartments set in a large garden just ten minutes' walk out of town. Also separate family apartments on hillside with panoramic seaviews. ❹

Asteria Leoforos Stavrou-Kioniou, behind new jetty ⓣ22830 22132, ⓕ22830 22070. Friendly, older-style hotel with the nearest accommodation to the new jetty and a good fall-back option. March–Oct. B&B ❹

Avra Towards eastern end of waterfront ⓣ22830 22242, ⓔgeorgegerardis@yahoo.co.uk. Neoclassical building with spacious rooms, some with balconies, and attractive plant-filled communal area. B&B ❹

Eleana Ayíou Ioánnou 1, 200m inland from the Commercial bank ⓣ22830 22461. A good, if basic, budget option hotel, with clean rooms. B&B ❺

Tinion Hotel Konstandínou Alavánou 1, on waterfront ⓣ22830 22261, ⓦwww.tinionhotel .gr. Stylish 1920s hotel just back from the waterfront. Spacious rooms, some with balconies. Discount of twelve percent for Rough Guide readers. Breakfast €9. ❹

Tinos Camping Ten-minute walk south of port ⓣ22830 22344, ⓦwww.camping.gr/tinos/. En-suite rooms with a/c and kitchens, set on one of the nicer campsites in the Cyclades. Follow the signs from the port. ❸

Eating and drinking

As usual, most seafront **restaurants** are rather overpriced and indifferent, however about midway along the port, behind the *Leto Hotel*, there is a cluster of excellent tavernas, one of the best being *Epineio* with good-value, tasty Greek dishes and excellent seafood. A small vine-covered alleyway leads from here to Palládha, a public square with a farmers' **market** every morning selling local fruit and vegetables, and lined with yet more choices: *Metaxi Mas*, a pricey *mezedhopolío* that has a remarkably varied menu; and *Palea Palladha*, noted for its grilled *loukániko* (spicy sausage) and sharp local feta. At the end of the alleyway there's a small traditional bakery, *Psomi Horiatiko*. For night-time snacks, try *Edesma* just off Palládha, which stays open late.

There are a few **bars**, mostly in a huddle near the new quay. *Koursaros* on the corner plays rock music at a comfortable volume, *Pyrsos* is pretty lively with a mixture of international hits and Greek music, while *Sivilla* blends Greek and world music in a cosy setting. At 3am all the bars in Tínos Town close, but for those not ready to hit the sack, *Paradise* on the road towards Kiónia stays open later playing mainly Greek music.

Southern beaches

The **Áyios Fokás** beach beyond the headland east of town starts off rocky but improves if you walk 500m further along. **Kiónia**, 3km northwest of Tínos Town (hourly buses in summer), is the site of the **Sanctuary of Poseidon and Amphitrite** (Tues–Sun 8.30am–3pm; free), which was discovered in 1902; the excavations yielded principally columns (*kiónia* in Greek), but also a temple, baths, a fountain and hostels for the ancient pilgrims. The **beach** is functional enough, lined with rooms to rent and snack-bars, but beyond the large, comfortable *Tinos Beach Hotel* (Ⓣ22830 22626, Ⓦwww.tinosbeach.gr; April–Oct; B&B ❺–❻) you can follow an unpaved road to a series of sandy coves. There is further accommodation up the concrete roads in the valley behind the beach, including the well-equipped *Panorama* (Ⓣ22830 24904, Ⓦwww.apartmentspanorama.gr; ❹–❺) studios and apartments.

Northern Tínos

A good beginning to a foray into the interior from Tínos Town is to take the stone stairway – the continuation of Odhós Ayíou Nikoláou – that passes behind and to the left of Evangelistrías. This climbs for ninety minutes through appealing countryside to **KTIKÁDHOS**, a fine village with a good, vine-shaded, seaview taverna, *Drosia*. The lower church, Ypapandís, has even better views. You can either flag down a bus on the main road or stay with the trail until Xinára (see opposite). Heading northwest from the main road junction beyond Ktikádhos, there are some fine **dovecotes** near Tarambádhos – you can follow a signed path through the village if you want to get close, but the best view is from the main road just beyond.

The road stays high, with long descending side-routes to beaches. Beyond Ávdhos, with its weird, eroded giant boulder and square-based ancient tower hidden among modern animal sheds, is **KARDHIANÍ**, 17km from Tínos Town, one of the most strikingly set and beautiful villages on the island, with views across to Sýros from amid a dense oasis. In the lower eastern part is the *Perivoli* café-taverna, and more centrally, a traditional *kafenío*. Just beyond Istérnia village is the turning for **Órmos Isternίon**, a smaller beach, with a lot of holiday homes, and the very pretty little Skhináki beach at the far end. Just over the headland to the northeast is **Áspros Yialós** beach. There are three tavernas and a café, and accommodation includes the *Anemoessa* (Ⓣ22830 31923, Ⓦwww.anemoessa.gr; ❹–❺) with rooms on the seafront and comfortable studios a few minutes inland. The bay is also connected to Istérnia by a broad, partly marble-paved *kalderími*, much of which survives.

Five daily buses along this route finish up at **PÝRGOS**, a few kilometres beyond Istérnia and in the middle of the island's marble-quarrying district. A beautiful village, with local artisans renowned throughout Greece for their skill in producing marble ornamentation; ornate fanlights and bas-relief plaques crafted here adorn houses throughout Tínos. Pýrgos is also home to the School of Arts, and the overpriced **Museum of Tinian Artists** (daily 10.30am–1.30pm & 5.30–7pm; €5) contains numerous representative works from some of the island's finest artists. Nearby, the **Yiannoulis Halepas Museum** (same hours and ticket) is devoted exclusively to the work of the artist who was born in this house in 1851 and is generally recognized as the most important Neoclassical Greek sculptor. There are *kafenía* and **eating** places on the attractive shady platía, including the imaginative *Ta Myronia* taverna and the *Rodaria zaharoplastío*.

Around Exóbourgo

The ring of villages around **Exóbourgo** (Xómbourgo) mountain is another focus of interest on Tínos. The fortified pinnacle itself (570m), with ancient foundations as well as the ruins of three Venetian churches and a fountain, is reached by steep steps from **XINÁRA** (near the island's major road junction), the seat of the island's Roman Catholic bishop for 1350 years. An alternative, shorter access path to the summit is from the Ierás Kardhiás (Sacred Heart) monastery to the east.

At **LOUTRÁ**, the next community north of Xinára, there's an Ursuline convent, and a good **folk art museum** (summer only, daily 10.30am–3.30pm; free) in the old Jesuit monastery. From Krókos, 1km northwest of Loutrá, which has a scenically situated taverna, it's a forty-minute walk via Skaládhos to tiny **VÓLAX**, one of the most remote villages on the island, a windswept oasis surrounded by giant granite boulders. Here, a handful of elderly Catholic basketweavers fashion some of the best examples in Greece – on sale at the central shop, *Petrino*. There is a small **folklore museum** (free, but ask in the village for the key), and the small outdoor Fontaine Theatre which in August hosts visiting theatre groups from all over Greece. There are a couple of places to eat, including the excellent *Rokos* **taverna** which offers local food.

At Kómi, 5km beyond Krókos, in the reed-filled Katomeri valley, you can take a detour for **KOLYMBÍTHRA**, a magnificent double beach: one part wild, huge and windswept (temporary residence to migrating pink flamingos in May), the other sheltered and with a couple of tavernas including *Viktoria*, which also has seaview rooms (Ⓣ22830 51309, Ⓦwww.tinos-victoria.com; Easter–Oct; ③) and **Internet** access. The bus to Kalloní goes on to Kolymbíthra twice a day in season; out of season you'll have to get off at Kómi and walk 4km.

Mýkonos

Originally visited only as a stop en route to ancient Delos, **Mýkonos** has become easily the most popular, most high profile – and most expensive – of the Cyclades. Boosted by direct air links with northern Europe and domestic flights from Athens, it sees more than a million tourists pass through in a good year (half of them in August alone), producing some spectacular overcrowding in summer on Mýkonos's 75 square kilometres. But if you don't mind the crowds, or you come in the shoulder season, the prosperous capital is still one of the more photogenic island towns, its whitewashed houses concealing hundreds of little churches, shrines and chapels.

The sophisticated nightlife is pretty hectic, amply stimulated by Mýkonos's former reputation as *the* gay resort of the Mediterranean – a title that has been surrendered to Sitges in Spain. Today, gay tourists are well in the minority on

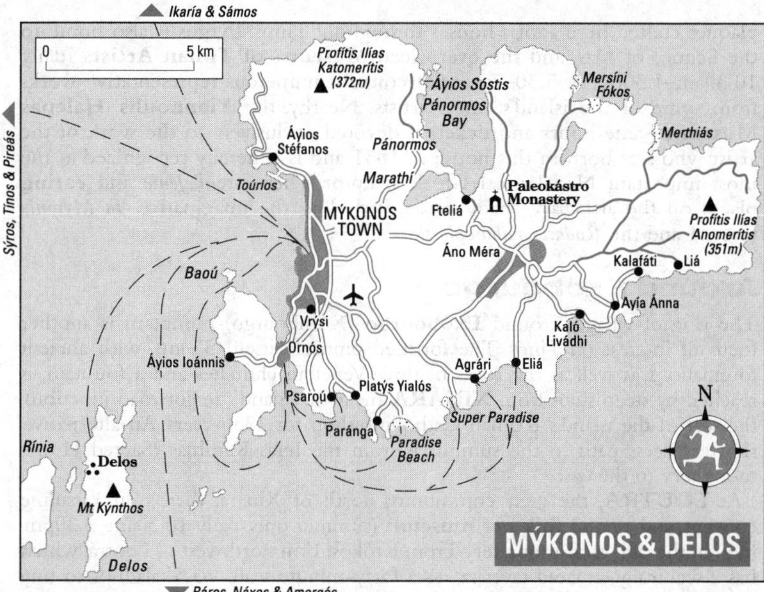

the island until September, when the gay clientele is present in full force. The locals take it all in their stride, ever conscious of the important revenue generated by their laissez-faire attitude. You shouldn't come for scenery, solitude or tradition, but – providing you are gregarious – Mýkonos offers lively beaches and a party lifestyle.

Mýkonos Town and around

Don't let the crowds put you off exploring **MÝKONOS TOWN**, the archetypal postcard image of the Cyclades. In summer most people head out to the beaches during the day, so early morning or late afternoon are the best times to wander the maze of narrow streets. The labyrinthine design was supposedly to confuse the pirates who plagued Mýkonos in the eighteenth and early nineteenth centuries, and it has the same effect on today's visitors.

Arrival, information and accommodation

There is some accommodation information at the small **airport** (3km southeast of town) and at the **new port** where large cruise ships dock (a few kilometres north of town in Toúrlos), but unless you know where you're going it's easier to take a bus or taxi into town, and sort things out there. The vast majority of visitors arrive by ferry at the "old port" **jetty** at the north end of town, where a veritable horde of room-owners pounces on the newly arrived. The scene can be intimidating, so press on 100m further, where a row of offices deals with official hotels, rented rooms and camping information. Alternatively, go into the heart of town to the helpful Mykonos Accommodation Center (Ⓣ22890 23160, Ⓦwww.mykonos-accommodation.com) on Enóplon Dhynaméon near the Maritime Museum.

The **north bus station** for Toúrlos, Áyios Stéfanos, Eliá and Áno Méra is located by the old port; the **south bus station** for the popular southwestern

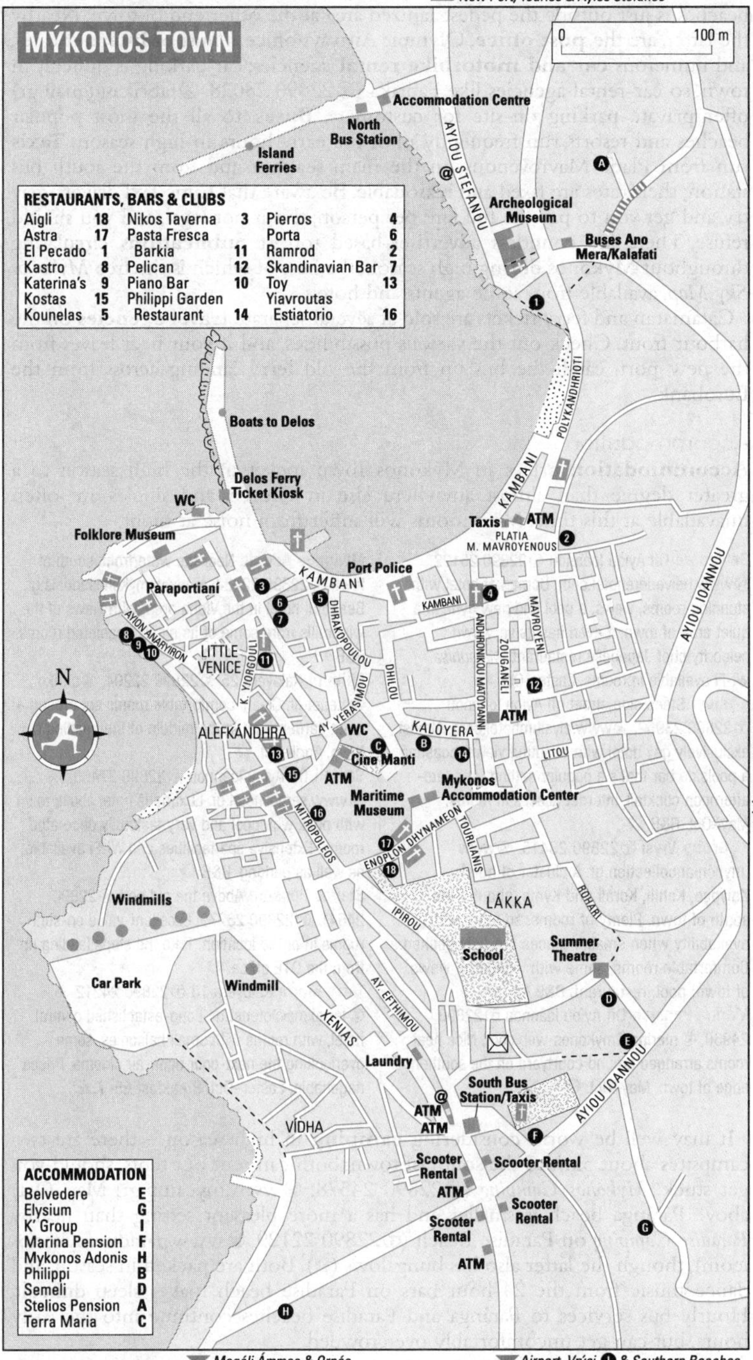
MÝKONOS TOWN
New Port, Toúrlos & Áyios Stéfanos
0 100 m
Accommodation Centre
North Bus Station
Island Ferries
AYIOU STEFANOU
Archeological Museum
Buses Ano Mera/Kalafati
RESTAURANTS, BARS & CLUBS
Aigli 18
Astra 17
El Pecado 1
Kastro 8
Katerina's 9
Kostas 15
Kounelas 5
Nikos Taverna 3
Pasta Fresca Barkia 11
Pelican 12
Piano Bar 10
Philippi Garden Restaurant 14
Pierros 4
Porta 6
Ramrod 2
Skandinavian Bar 7
Toy 13
Yiavroutas Estiatorio 16
POLYKANDHRIOTI
Boats to Delos
KAMBANI
Delos Ferry Ticket Kiosk
WC
Taxis
ATM
PLATIA M. MAVROYENOUS
Folklore Museum
Port Police
Paraportianí
AYION ANARYIRON
LITTLE VENICE
DHRAKOPOULOU
DHILOU
ANDHRONIKOU MATOYIANNI
ZOUGANELI
MAVROYENI
AYIOU IOANNOU
K. YIORGOULI
AY. YERASIMOU
ALEFKÁNDHRA
WC
KALOYERA
LITOU
Cine Manti
ATM
Mykonos Accommodation Center
Maritime Museum
MITROPOLEOS
ENOPLON DHYNAMEON
TOURLIANIS
Áno Méra & By-pass
Windmills
LÁKKA
ROHARI
IPIROU
School
Summer Theatre
Car Park
Windmill
AY. EFTHIMOU
XENIAS
Laundry
South Bus Station/Taxis
ATM
ATM
VÍDHA
AYIOU IOANNOU
Scooter Rental
Scooter Rental
Scooter Rental
Scooter Rental
ATM
ATM
ACCOMMODATION
Belvedere E
Elysium G
K' Group I
Marina Pension F
Mykonos Adonis H
Philippi B
Semeli D
Stelios Pension A
Terra Maria C
Megáli Ámmos & Ornós
Airport, Vrýsi, I & Southern Beaches

beaches is just outside the pedestrianized area at the other end of town. Nearby the latter, are the **post office**, Olympic Airways office, a host of **Internet** cafés, and numerous **car and motorbike rental** agencies; car parking is difficult in town, so car-rental agencies like Fabrika (ⓣ22890 28028, ⓔfabrikas@mail.gr) offer private parking on-site for customers. **Buses** to all the most popular beaches and resorts run frequently until the early hours in high season. **Taxis** run from Platía Mavroyénous on the main seafront and from the south bus station; their rates are fixed and reasonable. Be aware that some taxi drivers may try and get you to pay the full fare per person; this is not legal, and you should refuse. There are countless advertiser-based tourist **publications** circulating throughout Mýkonos during high season, the best of which is the free *Mykonos Sky Map*, available from some agents and hotels.

Catamaran and ferry tickets are sold at several separate **travel agencies** on the harbour front. Check out the various possibilities, and if your boat leaves from the new port, catch the bus up from the old ferry landing across from the Eurobank.

Accommodation

Accommodation prices in Mýkonos Town rocket in the high season to a greater degree than almost anywhere else in Greece, and singles are often unavailable at this time. Most rooms will suffer from noise at night.

Belvedere Off Ayíou Ioánnou ⓣ22890 25122, ⓦwww.belvederehotel.com. Upmarket hotel with stunning rooms, views, a pool and new gym, in a quiet area of town. It even has its very own celebrity chef Japanese restaurant, *Matsuhisa*. Wi-Fi available in rooms. Easter–Oct. ⑧

Elysium Steep side street off Ayíou Ioánnou ⓣ22890 23952, ⓦwww.elysiumhotel.com. Almost exclusively gay hotel with beautiful views, boasting a poolside bar that's a popular setting for a late-afternoon cocktail. Internet access in rooms. May–Oct. B&B ⑧

K' Group Vrýsi ⓣ22890 23415, ⓦwww.myconiancollection.gr. A cluster of hotels, Kalypso, Kohili, Korali and Kyma, about 1 km south of town. Plenty of rooms, so often with availability when smaller places are fully booked. Comfortable rooms, some with wonderful views of town; pool, restaurant. B&B ⑥

Marina Pension Off Ayíou Ioánnou ⓣ22890 24960, ⓔmarina@mykonos-web.com. Nice neat rooms arranged around courtyard on the southern edge of town. May–Oct. ⑤

Mykonos Adonis Near the waterfront, south of town ⓣ22890 22434, ⓦwww.mykonosadonis.gr. Beautiful hotel in the Vídha area, with views of the windmills from some of its nicely appointed rooms. B&B ⑦

Philippi Kaloyéra 25 ⓣ22890 22294, ⓔchriko@otenet.gr. Clean, comfortable rooms set around a quiet garden right in the middle of the bustling old town. April–Oct. ⑤

Semeli Off Ayíou Ioánnou ⓣ22890 27466, ⓦwww.semelihotel.gr. Luxurious hotel above town with pool, whirlpool and very tastefully decorated rooms. Extensive spa facilities and Wi-Fi available, as well as parking. B&B ⑧

Stelios Pension Above the old port ⓣ22890 24641, ⓕ22890 26779. Excellent-value en-suite rooms in prime location. Take the steps leading up from the OTE office. ⑤

Terra Maria Kaloyéra 18 ⓣ22890 24212, ⓔtertaxma@otenet.gr. Long-established central hotel, with rooms with small balconies, some overlooking the next-door open-air cinema. Prices negotiable. Easter–Oct. Breakfast €5–7. ⑤

It may well be worth considering **camping** in high season – there are two campsites about 5km to the south of town; both can rent out tents, should you get stuck. *Mykonos Camping* (ⓣ22890 24578, ⓦwww.mycamp.gr; May–Oct) above Paránga beach is smaller and has a more pleasant setting than nearby *Paradise Camping* on Paradise Beach (ⓣ22890 22129, ⓦwww.paradisemykonos.com), though the latter also has bungalows (⑤). Both are packed in season, and dance music from the 24-hour bars on Paradise beach makes sleep difficult. Hourly bus services to Paránga and Paradise beaches continue into the early hours, but can get uncomfortably overcrowded.

The Town

Getting lost in the convoluted streets and alleys of town is half the fun of exploring Mýkonos, although there are a few places worth seeking out. Coming from the ferry quay you'll pass the **Archeological Museum** (Tues–Sun 8.30am–3pm; €2) on your way into town, which displays some good Delos pottery; the town also boasts a **Maritime Museum** featuring various nautical artefacts, including a lighthouse re-erected in the back garden (Tues–Sun

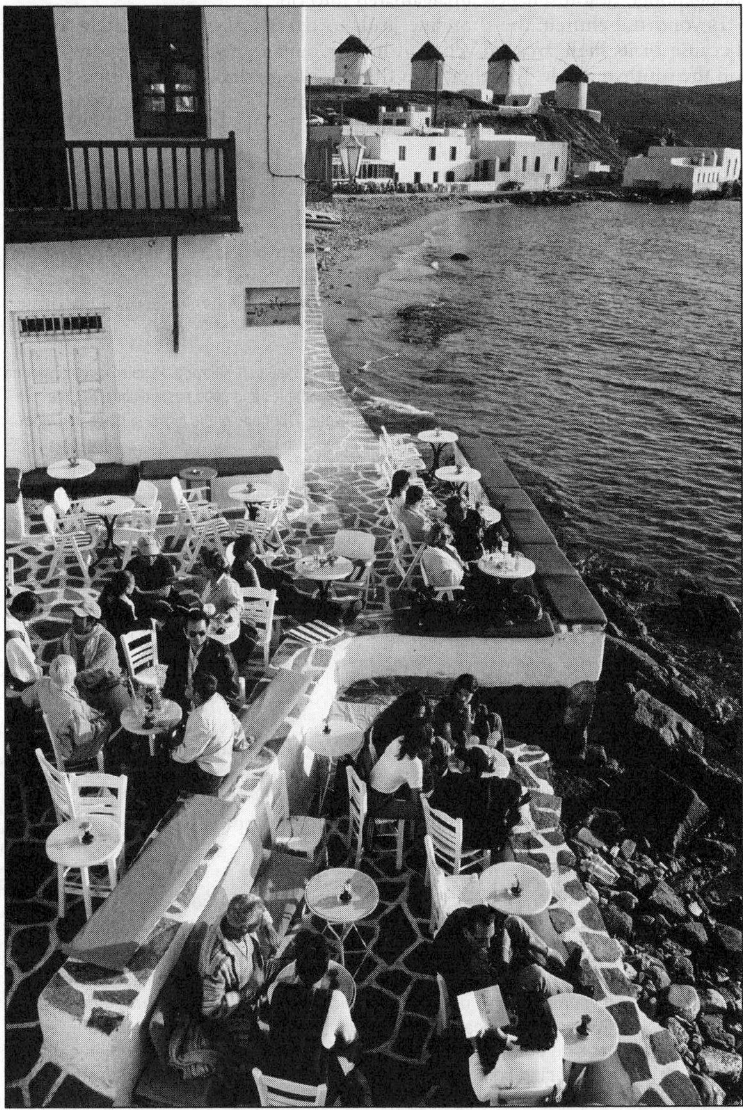

▲ Waterfront café, Mýkonos

10.30am–1pm & 6.30–9pm; €3). Next door is **Lena's House** (Mon–Sat 6–9pm, Sun 5–7pm; free), a completely restored and furnished middle-class home from the nineteenth century. Near the base of the Delos jetty, the **Folklore Museum** (Mon–Sat 5.30–8.30pm, Sun 6.30–8.30pm; free), housed in an eighteenth-century mansion – one of the town's oldest – crams in a larger-than-usual collection of bric-a-brac, with the basement dedicated to Mýkonos's maritime past. The museum sits on the same promontory as Mýkonos's oldest and best-known church, **Paraportianí** (usually closed), which is a fascinating asymmetrical hodgepodge of four chapels amalgamated into one.

Beyond the church, the shoreline leads to the area known as **Little Venice** because of its high, arcaded Venetian houses built right up to the water's edge on the southwest side. Together with the adjoining **Alefkándhra** district, this is a dense area packed with art galleries, trendy bars, shops and clubs. Beyond, the famous **windmills** look over the area, a little shabby but ripe for photo opportunities.

Eating

Even **light meals** and **snacks** can be expensive in Mýkonos, but there are numerous snack-bars, in particular near the south bus station. The area around Alefkándhra is a promising place to head for a full **meal**, whilst if you're looking for late-night coffee, try *Kavos*, right by the town beach. Supermarkets of any size are absent from the centre of town.

Kostas Mitropoléos. Friendly taverna behind Platía Alefkándhra, with competitive prices, and a good wine list including barrelled wine.

Kounelas Svorónou. Seafood taverna, very popular with the locals, tucked away in narrow street near Nikos taverna.

Nikos Taverna inland from the Delos jetty, on Platía Ayías Monís. One of the most famous restaurants on the island. Every inch of its side of the square is packed with customers, which can have a detrimental effect on service.

Pasta Fresca Barkia Yioryoúli. Lively pizza and pasta restaurant.

Pelican Platía off Kaloyéra. Popular taverna serving Greek staples and good pasta dishes. Not the cheapest, but one of the nicest settings in a vine-covered square.

Philippi Garden Restaurant off Kaloyéra. Exclusive restaurant in romantic setting serving home-grown vegetarian food, as well as superb seafood and traditional local dishes.

Yiavroutas Estiatorio off Mitropoléos. Small, unpretentious, family-run place serving excellent-value Greek dishes and good barrelled wine. Also open most of the night, if you're in need of fuel.

Nightlife

Nightlife in town is every bit as good as it's cracked up to be – and every bit as pricey. Those looking for a cheap drink should head for the *Skandinavian Bar* which thumps out dance music and good cocktails until the early hours. For something a bit more sophisticated, try neighbours *Aigli* and *Astra*, two

Gay nightlife

Although there are no huge gay clubs on Mýkonos, there is a good batch of excellent, comparatively laid-back bars in town, both for dancing and drinking, and bar-hopping is definitely the way to go. The **Piano Bar,** with fun cabaret acts, is a very good place to warm up, as is nearby *Toy*, which has great drinks. *Porta*, near *Nikos Taverna*, is a lively place to head to as the evening gets going. Things inevitably end up on the other side of town on Platía Mavroyénous where hundreds of men gather outside, around dancing bars *Ramrod* and the legendary *Pierros* that's thrived since the 1960s.

chic cafés by day that turn clubby by night; or head to the bars that line Andhroníkou and Enóplon Dhynaméon. A slightly more low-key vibe happens in Little Venice's *Katerina's*, *Piano Bar* and *Kastro*; or you could try the stylish lounge-style clubs along the waterfront including *El Pecado* near the Archeological Museum.

The beaches

The closest **beaches** to town are those to the north, at **Toúrlos** (only 2km away but horrid) and **Áyios Stéfanos** (3km, much better), both developed resorts and connected by a very regular bus service to Mýkonos Town. There are tavernas and rooms to let (as well as package hotels) at Áyios Stéfanos, away from the beach; *Mocambo Lido* taverna at the far end of the bay has a pleasant setting and good food.

Other nearby destinations include the southwestern resorts, with undistinguished but popular beaches tucked into pretty bays. The nearest to town, 1km away, is **Megáli Ámmos**, a good beach backed by flat rocks and pricey rooms, but nearby Kórfos bay is unpleasant, thanks to the town dump and machine noise. Buses serve **Ornós**, a package resort on a low-lying area between the rest of the island and the Áyios Ioánnis peninsula. The south side of the resort has a reasonable beach, *kaïkia* to other beaches, a handful of tavernas and numerous accommodations: try the comfortable *Best Western Dionysos* (Ⓣ22890 23313, Ⓦwww.dionysoshotel.com; May–Oct; B&B ❻) with pool. Buses continue a few kilometres west to **Áyios Ioánnis**, the island's westernmost bay, overlooking Delos – the tiny public beach achieved a moment of fame as a location for the film *Shirley Valentine*; there are a few, high-class hotels including the large but friendly *St John* (Ⓣ22890 28752, Ⓦwww.saintjohn.gr; April–Oct; B&B ❽), with private beach, which also has villas with private pools, and the much smaller *Apollonia* (Ⓣ22890 27890, Ⓦwww.apollonia-resort.gr; April–Oct; B&B ❽), set in a very pretty garden.

The western half of the south coast is the island's busiest part. *Kaïkia* ply from Mýkonos Town to all of its beaches, and buses to many of them, and you certainly won't be alone – on any sunny day in season both beaches and transport range from busy to overcrowded. Car drivers will find that parking spaces at most beaches are inadequate, and that turning is difficult. You might begin with **Platýs Yialós**, 4km south of town: one of the longest-established resorts on the island, the sand is monopolized by end-to-end hotels, and almost every room is prebooked between June and September. **Psaroú**, just a steep, hairpin access road away to the west, is much prettier – 150m of white sand backed by foliage and calamus reeds. Here you'll find *N'Ammos*, an elegant fish **restaurant** on the waterfront. Again you'll need to reserve well in advance to secure **rooms** between mid-June and mid-September. Try *Soula* (Ⓣ22890 22006, Ⓦwww.soula-rooms.gr; ❺), pretty studios in a calm garden just behind the beach.

Just over the headland to the east of Platýs Yialós, though accessed by a different, winding road (from near the airport, and off the Paradise beach road) is **Paránga beach**, actually two beaches separated by a smaller headland, the first of which has a decent taverna with some basic rooms and is quieter than its noisier neighbour, which is home to a loud beach bar and *Mykonos Camping* (see p.536).

Next is the golden crescent of **Paradise beach**. Here, as on many of Mýkonos's most popular beaches, it can be difficult to find an opening big enough to fit a towel, and any space clear of people is likely to be taken up by rentable straw umbrellas and loungers. Behind the beach are Dive Adventures

(Ⓣ22890 26539, Ⓦwww.diveadventures.gr; April–Oct. Introductory scuba and full range of PADI), shops, self-service restaurants, and the noisy 24-hour beach bars of *Paradise Camping* (see p.536), while at the far end is *Cavo Paradiso* (Ⓦwww.cavoparadiso.gr), the after-hours club for die-hard party animals of all persuasions, often overseen by world-famous DJs. The next bay east contains **Super Paradise** beach, accessible by *kaïki*, or by a surfaced but extremely steep access road. One of the most fun beaches on the island, it has a decent taverna and two bars at opposite ends of the beach pumping out cheesy summer hits. One half of the beach is very mixed, getting progressively more gay as you walk away from where the *kaïkia* dock towards the beach bar perched in the hills, below which the beach is almost exclusively gay and nudist.

One of the more scenically attractive beaches on Mýkonos is **Eliá**, the last port of call for the *kaïkia* and with a road from Áno Méra (see below) A broad, sandy stretch, with plenty of parking and a mountainous backdrop at the eastern end, it's the longest beach on the island, though divided by a rocky area, and almost exclusively gay and crowded later in the season. Chill-out music is played at the *Elia Pool Bar Restaurant*, while jet-ski, water-ski and parachute boating are available for the more active. The main road southeast from Áno Méra (local bus service) leads to **Kalafáti:** the latter's long sand beach supports an increasing number of hotels and restaurants, and is popular with windsurfers: Planet Windsurfing, (Ⓦwww.planetwindsurfing.com) offer hire and courses.

The **north coast** suffers persistent battering from the *meltémi*, plus tar and litter pollution, and for the most part is bare, brown and exposed. The deep inlet of **Pánormos Bay** is the exception to this, with the lovely, relatively sheltered beaches of **Pánormos** and **Áyios Sóstis** along its northwestern edge beyond the Marathi reservoir; although not served by buses, they are becoming increasingly popular, but remain among the less crowded on the island. Just behind Pánormos is the very attractive *Albatros Club Hotel* (Ⓣ22890 25130, Ⓦwww.albatros-mykonos.com; May–Oct; B&B ❻) with both hotel-style and traditional rooms available; the beach has a bar and restaurant.

Áno Méra

The access point for Eliá and beaches eastward is **ÁNO MÉRA**, the only other major residential settlement on the island, scattered over a large and fertile agricultural plateau. The main sight is the red-roofed sixteenth-century **monastery of Panayía Tourlianí** (closed 1–2pm), next to the main square, where a collection of Cretan icons and the unusual eighteenth-century carved marble belltower are worth seeing.

The square outside the monastery has an air of impermanence, being surrounded by single-storey **restaurants**; more popular for its wide range of Mediterranean dishes is *Daniele,* just outside town on the Hóra road, near the late twelfth-century **Paleókastro monastery** (aka **Dárga**). There are a couple of **hotels** in the area: the new *Anatolia* (Ⓣ22890 71906, Ⓦwww.hotelanatolia.gr; Easter–Oct; ❼), on the Kalafáti road, has a pool, gym, jacuzzi and sauna.

Delos (Dhílos)

The remains of **ancient Delos ("The Brilliant")**, though skeletal and swarming now with lizards and tourists, give some idea of the past grandeur of this small, sacred isle a few sea-miles west of Mýkonos. The ancient town lies on the west coast on flat, sometimes marshy ground that rises in the south to

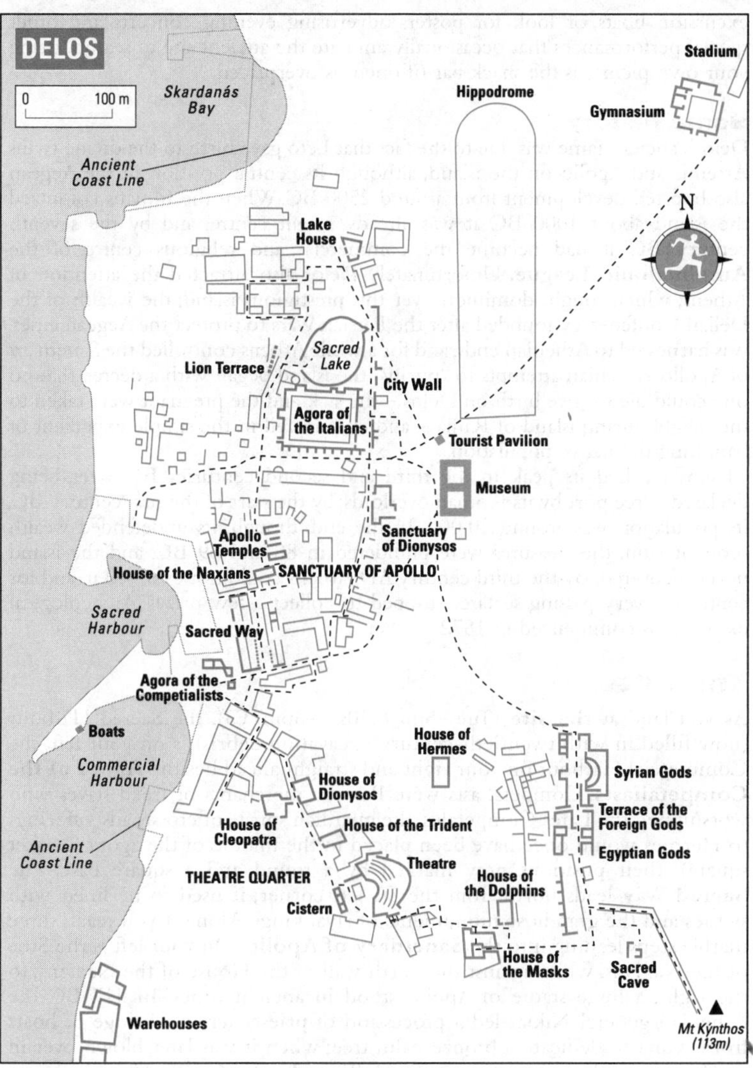

Mount Kýnthos. From the 113m summit there's a magnificent view across the nearby Cyclades.

The first excursion boats to Delos leave the small port near the west end of Mýkonos harbour daily at 8.30 or 9am (€12.50 round trip), except Mondays when the site is closed. You may have to return on the same boat, but in season each does the trip several times and you can choose what time you leave. The last return is usually about 3pm, and you'll need to arrive early if you want to make a thorough tour of the site. In season a daily *kaiki* makes return trips from the Mýkonos beaches (€10) with pick-up points at Platýs Yialós and Ornós, but only allows you three hours on the island. Check ahead with operators of Delos excursion boats or look for posters advertising evening concerts and other special performances that occasionally animate the ancient site in season. Bring your own picnic, as the snack bar (if open) is overpriced.

Some history

Delos's ancient fame was due to the fact that Leto gave birth to the divine twins Artemis and Apollo on the island, although its central position in the Aegean also boosted development from around 2500 BC. When the Ionians colonized the island about 1000 BC it was already a cult centre, and by the seventh century BC it had become the commercial and religious centre of the **Amphictionic League**. Unfortunately Delos also attracted the attention of Athens, which sought dominion over this prestigious island; the wealth of the Delian Confederacy, founded after the Persian Wars to protect the Aegean cities, was harnessed to Athenian ends, and for a while Athens controlled the Sanctuary of Apollo. Athenian attempts to "purify" the island began with a decree that no one could die or give birth on Delos – the sick and the pregnant were taken to the neighbouring island of Rínia – and culminated in the simple expedient of banishing the native population.

Delos reached its peak in the third and second centuries BC, after being declared a free port by its Roman overlords; by the start of the first century BC, its population was around 30,000. In the end, though, its undefended wealth brought ruin: the treasures were plundered in 88 and 69 BC, and the island never recovered. By the third century AD, Athens could not even sell it, and for centuries every passing seafarer stopped to collect a few prizes. Archeological excavations commenced in 1872.

The site

As you land at **the site** (Tues–Sun 8.30am–3pm; €5), the Sacred Harbour (now filled in with twentieth-century excavation debris) is on your left, the Commercial Harbour on your right and straight ahead lies the **Agora of the Competaliasts**. Competaliasts were Roman merchants or freed slaves who worshipped the Lares Competales, the guardian spirits of crossroads; offerings to Hermes would once have been placed in the middle of the agora (market square), their positions now marked by a round and a square base. The **Sacred Way** leads north from the far left corner; it used to be lined with statues and the grandiose monuments of rival kings. Along it you reach three marble steps leading into the **Sanctuary of Apollo**. On your left is the Stoa of the Naxians, while against the north wall of the House of the Naxians, to the right, a huge statue of Apollo stood in ancient times. In 417 BC the Athenian general Nikias led a procession of priests across a bridge of boats from Rínia to dedicate a bronze palm tree; when it was later blown over in a gale it took the statue with it. Three **Temples to Apollo** stand in a row to the right along the Sacred Way: the massive Delian Temple, the Athenian, and the Porinos, the earliest and dating from the sixth century BC. To the east towards the museum you pass the **Sanctuary of Dionysos**, with its marble phalluses on tall pillars.

On the right, behind the small Letoön temple is the huge Agora of the Italians, while on the left loom replicas of the famous lean-bodied **lion statues** put here to ward off intruders who would have been unfamiliar with the fearful creatures. Of the originals, masterfully executed by Naxians in the seventh century BC, at least three have disappeared and one – looted by Venetians in the seventeenth century and ineptly reheaded – adorns the Arsenale in Venice. The remaining ones are in the site **museum** (same hours); otherwise, the best finds from the site have gone to Athens, but the museum is still worth a visit for its marble statuary, mosaic fragments and an extensive collection of phallic artefacts. Opposite the lions, tamarisk trees ring the site of the **Sacred Lake** (now drained) where Leto gave birth, clinging to a palm tree. On the other side of the lake is the City Wall, built in 69 BC – too late to protect the treasures.

Set out in the other direction from the Agora of the Competialists and you enter the residential area, known as the **Theatre Quarter**. The remnants of private mansions such as Dionysos, Trident, Masks and Dolphins are now named after their colourful main **mosaic**; the restoration of some interior walls allows visualization of their magnificence. The theatre itself seated 5500 spectators, and, though much ravaged, offers some fine views, but just below it and structurally almost as spectacular, is a huge underground cistern with arched roof supports. Behind the theatre, a path leads towards the Sanctuaries of the Egyptian and Syrian Gods, then steeply up 113m Mount Kýnthos to a Sanctuary of Zeus and Athena with spectacular views back down over the ruins and out to the surrounding Cyclades. Near the base of the final peak path, a small side path leads to the Antron of Kýnthos or the "Grotto of Hercules", a rock cleft covered with a remarkable roof of giant stone slabs angled against each other.

Sýros

Don't be put off by first impressions of **Sýros**. From the ferry it can seem vaguely industrial, but, away from the Neório shipyard, things improve quickly. Very much a working island with only a relatively recent history of tourism, it is among the most Greek of the Cyclades and the most populous island in the group.

Ermoúpoli

The main town and port of **ERMOÚPOLI** is one of the most striking in the Cyclades. A UNESCO World Heritage Site, it possesses an elegant collection of grand town houses which rise majestically from the bustling, café-lined waterfront. The town was founded during the War of Independence by refugees from Psará and Híos, and grew in importance to become Greece's chief port in the nineteenth century. Although Pireás outstripped it as a port long ago, Ermoúpoli is still the largest town in the Cyclades, and the archipelago's capital. Medieval Sýros was largely a Catholic island, but an influx of Orthodox refugees during the War of Independence created two distinct communities; now almost equal in numbers, the

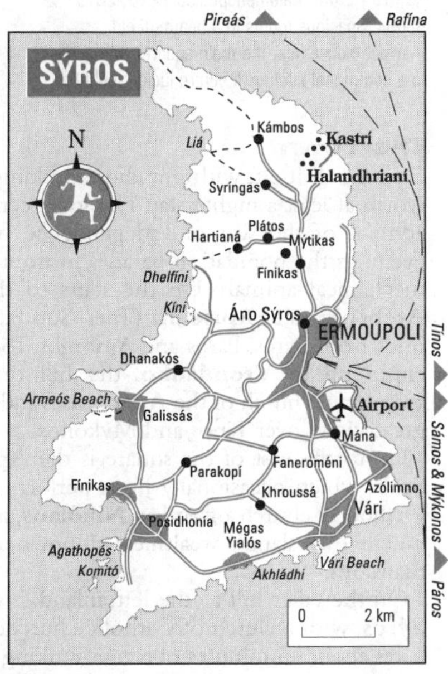

two groups today still live in their respective quarters occupying two hills that rise up from the sea. They do, however, commonly celebrate each others' festivals, lending a vibrant mix of culture that gives the island its colour.

Arrival, information and accommodation

Sýros is a major crossover point on the ferry routes, and most people arrive by boat to be met by the usual horde of locals offering rooms. There is no bus service from the airport, and you will have to take a taxi (ⓣ22810 86222). On the waterfront there are several **travel agencies** that sell boat tickets, and you'll also find the **bus station**, **tourist police** and **banks** here. Of the several **motorbike-rental** places, Apollon on Andipárou, one block behind the seafront, is recommended. There are plenty of **Internet** facilities: inSpot at Aktí Papágou 4 is conveniently near the jetty.

Accommodation

TeamWork agency (ⓣ22810 83400, ⓦwww.teamwork.gr), on the waterfront, is a useful source of information and is able to help with your accommodation needs. In the summer you might try one of the accommodation kiosks on the waterfront. The accommodation listed here is open all year, unless stated otherwise.

Dream Eptanísou 31, off Naxoú ⓣ22810 84356, ⓦwww.dream-rooms.gr. Decent, basic rooms, some with balconies, run by a charming family just back from the waterfront. ③

Hermes Platía Kanári ⓣ22810 88011, ⓦwww.hermes-syros.com. Smart hotel in a prime location, overlooking the port. All rooms have sea views, and the hotel is home to a very popular seafront restaurant. ⑥

Kastro Rooms Kalomenopóulou 12 ⓣ22810 88064. Spacious rooms in a beautiful old mansion house near the main square, with access to a communal kitchen. If you're lucky, you'll be treated to some traditional music from owner Markos. ③

Sea Colours Apartments Athinás (book through TeamWork Agency;). Traditionally decorated apartments for 2–6 people, just above the swimming platforms of Áyios Nikólaos, 5min walk from the main platía. ④

Syrou Melathron Babayiótou ⓣ22810 86495, ⓔsyroumel@otenet.gr. Rather regal hotel set in restored nineteenth-century mansion in a quieter area of town. Has suites as well as spacious rooms, some with sea views. ⑦

The Town

Ermoúpoli itself, with grandiose buildings a relic of its days as a major port, is worth at least a night's stay. The long, central **Platía Miaoúli** is named after an admiral of the War of Independence whose statue stands there, and in the evenings the population parades in front of its arcades, while children ride the mechanical animals. Up the stairs to the left of the town hall is the small **Archeological Museum** (Tues–Sun 8.30am–3pm; free), with three rooms of finds from Sýros, Páros and Amorgós. To the left of the clocktower more stairs climb up to **Vrondádho**, the hill that hosts the Orthodox quarter. The wonderful church of the **Anástasis** stands atop the hill, with its domed roof and great views over Tínos and Mýkonos.

Up to the east of the square is the **Apollon Theatre**, a copy of Milan's La Scala, which occasionally hosts performances. Further on up is the handsome Orthodox church of **Áyios Nikólaos**, and beyond it to the right is **Vapória**, where the island's wealthiest shipowners, merchants and bankers built their mansions.

On the taller hill to the left, inland, is the intricate medieval quarter of **Áno Sýros**, with a clutch of Catholic churches below the cathedral of St George. It takes about 45 minutes of tough walking up Omírou, which becomes Kárga, to

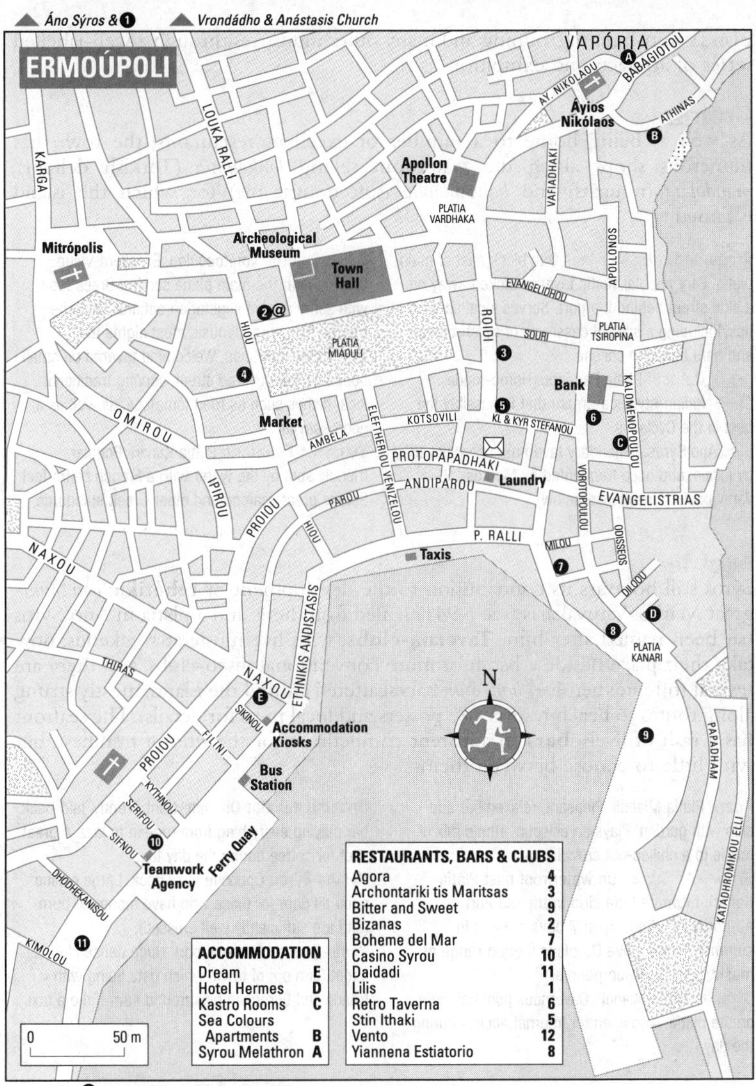

reach this quarter (or a rare bus from the main station), passing the Orthodox and Catholic cemeteries on the way – the former full of grand shipowners' mausoleums, the latter with more modest monuments and French and Italian inscriptions. Once up here it's worth visiting the local art and church exhibitions at the **Markos Vamvakaris Museum** (daily 10.30am–1pm & 7–10pm; €1.50), and the **Byzantine Museum** attached to the monastery.

Heading west from Ermoúpoli, 1.6km along the road leading from the ferry quay to Kíni, accessible by bus, the **Industrial Museum** (Mon & Wed–Sun 10am–2pm, also Thurs–Sun 6–9pm; €2.50, Wed free) traces the history of the island's ship-building, mining and many other industries through a well-labelled series of artefacts and exhibitions.

Eating

As well as being home to a number of excellent restaurants, the town has numerous shops along the waterfront selling *loukoúmia* (Turkish delight), *mandoláta* (nougats) and *halvadhópita* (soft nougat pie) for which the island is famed.

Archontariki tis Maritsas One block east of main platía. Very popular rustic taverna tucked away on a side street behind the port. Serves local specialities, including a special casserole of mushrooms and ham baked in cheese.
Daidadi Platía Papágou. Home-made, Italian-style ice-cream that is possibly the best in the Cyclades.
Lilis Áno Sýros. Legendary taverna much beloved by locals, and once frequented by Markos Vamvakaris himself (see below).
Retro Taverna Vorotopoúlou. Excellent-value taverna near the main platía serving Greek food with some decent vegetarian options. You'll be treated to *bouzoúki* music most nights too.
Stin Ithaki Stefánou. Welcoming taverna on small bougainvillea-covered street, serving traditional local dishes such as fried tomatoes, as well as a good *souvláki*.
Yiannena Estiatorio Platía Kanári. Popular, friendly spot by the water with a French bistro feel. Serves great seafood and other Greek standards.

Nightlife

Sýros still honours its contribution to the development of **rebétika**; *bouzoúki*-great Markos Vamvakaris (see p.941) hailed from here, and a platía in Áno Sýros has been named after him. **Taverna-clubs**, with live music at weekends, now take their place beside a batch of more conventional disco-clubs, and there are several (often expensive) *bouzoúki* bars scattered around the island, mostly strung along routes to beach resorts (see posters and local press for details). The seafront has a rash of lively **bars** in apparent competition for the title of trendiest, but with little to choose between them.

Agora Platía Miaoúli. Pleasant, relaxed bar and club with garden. Plays an eclectic, ethnic mix of music to a chilled-out crowd.
Bitter and Sweet On waterfront past Platía Kanári. Intimate little club in the old Port Authority building. Open 7 days a week in summer, when a live DJ plays a good range of music to dressed-up people.
Bizanas Platía Miaoúli. Cavernous pool hall right on the platía. Also open for Internet access during the day.
Boheme del Mar On waterfront. Trendy, laid-back bar playing everything from reggae to jazz. A great spot for coffee during the day too.
Casino Syrou Opposite ferry dock. Large casino open till 6am for those who have money to burn (and are sufficiently well dressed).
Vento On road to the airport. Huge dance club about 3km out of town, which gets going with trance and European hits around 4am. Take a taxi.

Southern Sýros

Buses ply the main loop road south (to Galissás, Fínikas, Mégas Yialós and Vári) hourly in season, and run until late. First stop, **GALISSÁS**, is fundamentally an agricultural village, but has been taken over since the mid-1980s by backpackers attracted by the island's best **campsite**, *Two Hearts* (ⓣ22810 42052, ⓦwww.twohearts-camping.com). The site has good facilities and sends minibuses to most boats. There is also a surplus of **rooms**, which makes bargaining possible, and a few bona fide hotels, of which the cheapest are *Semiramis* (ⓣ22810 42067, ⓕ22810 43000; ④) and the excellent *Françoise* (ⓣ22810 42000, ⓦwww.francoise-hotel.com; ④), though the *Benois* (ⓣ22810 42833, ⓦwww.benois.gr;

B&B ④) is decent value. Among the many **eating** choices, *To Iliovasilema*, next to *Benois*, is an acceptable fish taverna, and *Cavos*, part of a luxury complex, the *Dolphin Bay Hotel* (Ⓣ22810 42924, Ⓕ22810 42843; ⑦), has impressive views overlooking the bay. *Argo* is a great place for live Greek music. Galissás's identity crisis is exemplified by the proximity of bemused, grazing dairy cattle, a heavy-metal music **pub** and upmarket handicraft shops. Still, the locals are welcoming, and if you feel the urge to escape, you can rent a scooter, or walk ten minutes past the headland to the nudist beach of **Armeós**, where there's fresh spring water. Note that buses out can be erratically routed out of season; to be sure of making your connection you must wait at the high-road stop, not down by the beach.

A pleasant forty-minute walk or a ten-minute bus ride south from Galissás brings you to the more mainstream resort of **FÍNIKAS**, purported to have been settled originally by the Phoenicians (although an alternative derivation could be from *fínikas*, meaning "palm tree" in Greek). The **beach** is narrow and gritty, right next to the road but protected to some extent by a row of tamarisk trees; the pick of the **hotels** is the *Cyclades* (Ⓣ22810 42255, Ⓦwww.hotelcyclades.com; B&B ④), with an acceptable restaurant just in front, while the *Amaryllis* rooms (Ⓣ22810 42894, Ⓕ22810 43681; ④) are slightly cheaper. The fish **taverna** *Barbalias* on the seafront is recommended. Maïstrali Marine, near the bus stop, has **Internet** access.

Fínikas is separated by a tiny headland from its neighbour **POSIDHONÍA** (aka Delagrazzia), a nicer spot with some idiosyncratically ornate mansions and a bright-blue church right on the edge of the village. It's worth walking ten minutes further south, past the naval yacht club and its patrol boat, to **Agathopés**, with a sandy beach and a little islet just offshore. **Accommodation** around Posidhonía ranges from the smart *Possidonion* hotel (Ⓣ22810 42100, Ⓔposidonion@syr.forthnet.gr; ④) on the seafront to basic rooms inland. *Meltemi*, on the road to Agathopés, is a good seafood **taverna**.

Northern Sýros

Closest to the capital, a few kilometres north of Galissás, and reached by bus in fifteen minutes (hourly in season), is the twin-beach coastal settlement of **KÍNI**. Good accommodation can be found at the *Sunset Hotel* (Ⓣ22810 71211, Ⓔenxensyr@otenet.gr; ④), with the excellent *Zalounis* taverna just below. **Dhelfíni**, just to the north, is also a fine pebbly beach, dramatically accessed on coastal footpath or inland road.

Páros and Andíparos

Gently and undramatically furled around the single peak of Profítis Ilías, **Páros** has a little of everything one expects from a Greek island: old villages, monasteries, fishing harbours, a labyrinthine capital, nice beaches and varied nightlife. Parikía, the hóra, is the major hub of inter-island ferry services, so that if you wait long enough you can get to just about any island in the Aegean. However, the island can be touristy and expensive, so it's touch and go when it comes to finding rooms and beach space in August, when the other settlements, the port of **Náoussa**, and the satellite island of **Andíparos** handle the overflow. The August 15 festival here is one of the best such observances in Greece, with a parade of flare-lit fishing boats and fireworks delighting as many Greeks as foreigners, though it's a real feat to secure accommodation around this time.

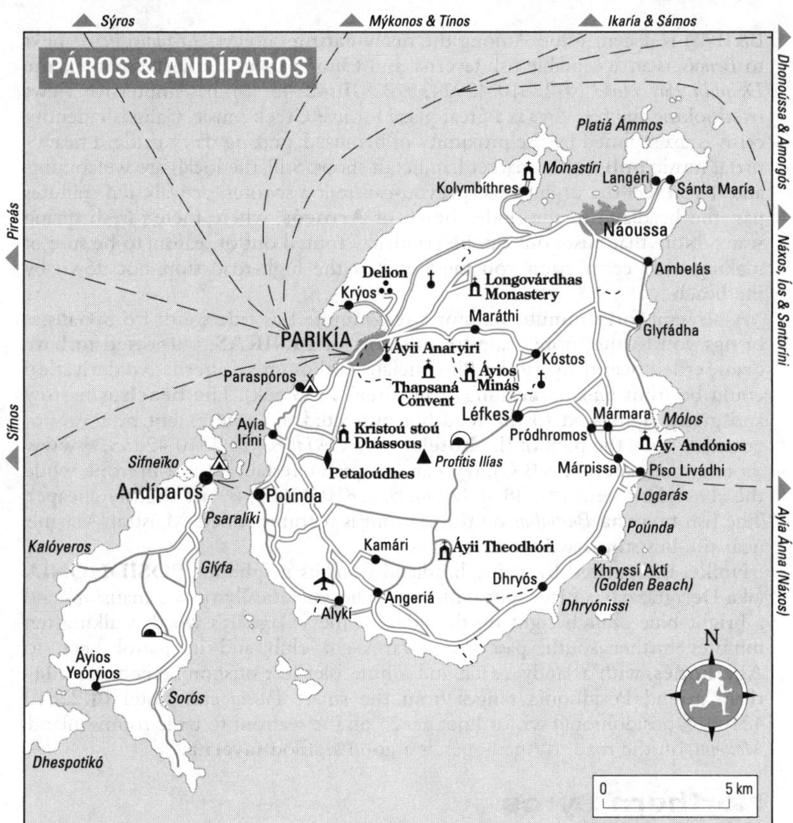

Parikía and around

Bustling **PARIKÍA** sets the tone architecturally for the rest of Páros, with its ranks of typically Cycladic white houses punctuated by the occasional Venetian-style building and church domes.

Arrival, information and accommodation

Ferries dock in Parikía by the windmill; the **bus station** is 100m or so to the right. Bus routes extend to Náoussa in the north, Poúnda (for Andíparos) in the west, Alykí-Angeriá in the south and Dhryós on the island's east coast (with another very useful service between Dhryós and Náoussa). Be aware that there are two places called Poúnda on Páros, one being the west-coast port, the other an east-coast beach on the way to Dhryós. Buses to Náoussa carry on running hourly through the night, while other services stop around midnight. The small **airport**, with domestic flights to Athens, is around 12km south of town, close to Alykí – from where ten daily buses run to Parikía.

Most of the island is flat enough for cycling, though you'll be hard pressed to find any bicycles. **Motorbikes** are more common and are available for rent at several places in town; **car rental** is available from European (☎22840

21771, Ⓦwww.paroscars.de) and Avant Travel (Ⓣ22840 22302, Ⓦwww.europcar-paros.com), on the western and eastern waterfront respectively. Driving and parking rules are enforced: various streets are one way, and the western end of the seafront is closed to traffic during summer evenings.

Polos Tours, left of the windmill, is one of the more together and friendly **travel agencies**, issuing air tickets when Olympic is shut, and acting as agents for virtually all the boats. Luggage can be left at various travel agents (look for the signs) along the waterfront. There are **Internet** cafés on the waterfront: Memphis, where you can also burn digital photos to CD, and Marina, open for more of the season.

Continue inland from the **windmill** past the taxi station to reach **Mandoús Mavroyénou (Ethnikís Andístasis) Platía** around which you'll find a maze of houses and the telephone office, police station (including tourist police), banks and Olympic Airways office.

Accommodation

You'll be met off the ferry by locals offering accommodation, even at the most unlikely hours, although you'll have to be quick to grab a room in summer. Many rooms and hotels are to the left of the windmill, and some can be a long walk. Of the two **campsites** nearest to town, *Koula Camping* (Ⓣ22840 22081, Ⓦwww.campingkoula.gr; April–Oct), 900m along the seafront east of the bus stop, is a reasonable choice for a night or two, with a seasonal café-restaurant and mini-bungalows (❶), whilst *Krios Camping* (Ⓣ22840 21705, Ⓦwww.krios-camping.gr), across the bay to the north, has a nice beach, a pool and a regular minibus into town.

Anna Platanou 800m west of the port Ⓣ22840 21751, Ⓦwww.annaplatanou.gr. Smart, family-run hotel with clean refurbished rooms, with kettles. Ten-percent discount for Rough Guide readers. The family also have larger studios and apartments at the junction of the Alykí–Poúnda roads. Port transfers available. April–Oct. ❹

Argonauta Corner of Platía Mavroyénous near the National Bank Ⓣ22840 21440, Ⓦwww.argonauta.gr. Friendly hotel with smart rooms arranged around a beautiful courtyard. Refurbished 2007. There is a good restaurant underneath. April–Oct. ❹

Dina the old market street, opposite Ayía Triádha church Ⓣ22840 21325, Ⓦwww.hoteldina.com. Pleasant, central little hotel set in a quiet spot. May–Oct. ❸

Mike's Rooms Opposite ferry dock Ⓣ22840 22856. Clean, comfortable studios and hospitable staff. Mike has further accommodation, including very nice studios near Delfíni beach. ❸

Rena Rooms Behind ancient cemetery Ⓣ22840 22220, Ⓦwww.cycladesnet.gr/rena. Spacious doubles and family rooms on a quiet street near the post office, with a courtyard at the rear; a/c extra. Sea views from the top floor. ❷

The Town

Just beyond the central clutter of the ferry port, to the left (southeast) of the windmill, Parikía has one of the most architecturally interesting churches in the Aegean – the **Ekatondapylianí**, or "The One Hundred Gated" (8am–1pm, 4–9pm; free). What's visible today was designed and supervised by Isidore of Miletus in the sixth century, but construction was actually carried out by his pupil Ignatius. Legend tells that it was so beautiful on completion that the master, consumed with jealousy, grappled with his apprentice on the rooftop and both of them fell to their deaths. They are portrayed kneeling at the column bases across the courtyard, the old master tugging at his beard in repentance and his rueful pupil clutching a broken head. The church was substantially altered after a severe earthquake in the eighth century, but its essentially Byzantine aspect remains, its shape an imperfect Greek cross. Enclosed by a great front wall to protect its icons from pirates, it is in fact three interlocking churches; the oldest, the chapel of Áyios Nikólaos to the left of the apse, is an adaptation of a pagan building dating from the early fourth century BC. To the right of the courtyard, the **Byzantine Museum** (daily 9am–9pm; €1.50) displays a collection of icons. Behind Ekatondapylianí, the **Archeological Museum** (Tues–Sun 8am–2.45pm; €2) has a fair collection of antique bits and pieces, its prize exhibits being a fifth-century winged Nike and a piece of the Parian Chronicle, a social and cultural history of Greece up to 264 BC engraved in marble. On the seafront near the marina are the exposed, excavated ruins of an **ancient cemetery** used from the eighth century BC until the second century AD; all around the bay and within 1km of the seafront is a sprinkling of **archeological sites** from the ancient city, including the ruins of a Hellenistic sculpture and pottery workshop, a Delion Apollo sanctuary, and some fragmentary mosaics (at the start of the Áyii Anáryiri road).

These sights apart, the real attraction of Parikía is simply to wander the town itself, especially along the meandering **old market street**, *agorá*, and the adjoining street, Grávari. Arcaded lanes lead past Venetian-influenced villas, traditional island dwellings and ornate wall-fountains. The town culminates in a seaward Venetian **kástro** (1260), whose surviving east wall incorporates a fifth-century BC round tower and was constructed using masonry pillaged from a nearby temple of Athena. Part of the temple's base is still visible next to the beautiful, arcaded church of Áyios Konstandínos and Ayía Eléni which crowns the highest point, from where the fortified hill drops sharply to the quay in a series of hanging gardens.

Eating

Most of the **eating** establishments in Parikía are along the waterfront to the west of the windmill. The Parian Products Farmers' Union, near the police station, is a lovely wine and cheese shop perfect for stocking up for a beach picnic, while the Ragousis Bakery, behind the National Bank, is a good place for sandwiches and pastries. For snacks, there is a cluster of fast-food outlets near the ferry dock, whilst hidden in the backstreets, and along the seafront to the west, there are plenty of small crêperies and cafés.

Apollon Off old market street. Set in a converted 1920s olive press on the tiny backstreets near the market, this is one of the island's best restaurants. Considering its popularity, its prices aren't bad.

Apostolis Livádhia seafront. Well-priced seafood taverna, extremely popular with the Greeks.

Aroma Perifereakos (ring road). Greek and local dishes, expertly prepared and chosen from the kitchen. The Siroco's supermarket next door has a remarkably extensive international selection of alcohol.

Cavo D'Oro Livádhia seafront. Italian restaurant with a large choice of wood-oven pizza and pasta near *Koula Camping*. They also do takeaway.

Happy Green Cow On side street behind National Bank. Remarkably eclectic vegetarian (and chicken) restaurant. Not cheap, but some of the most imaginative vegetarian cooking around.

Hibiscus On waterfront south of windmill. One of the oldest restaurants on the island, it serves generous-sized, wood-oven-baked pizzas in a great spot overlooking the sea.

Trata Behind ancient cemetery. Family-run taverna serving tasty seafood and grilled meats on a vine-covered patio.

Nightlife

Parikía has a wealth of **pubs**, **bars** and low-key **discos**. The most popular cocktail bars extend along the seafront, mostly to the south of the windmill, tucked into a series of open squares and offering staggered "happy hours", so that you can drink cheaply for much of the evening, and there are music clubs along the riverbed street at the western end of the seafront. There's also a thriving cultural centre, Arhilohos (near Ekatondapylianí), which caters mostly to locals, but which has occasional **film** screenings – there are also two open-air cinemas, Neo Rex and Paros, where foreign films are shown in season.

Alexandros Café Southern end of quay. One of the more grown-up choices for a sophisticated evening drink in a fabulously romantic spot around the base of a windmill.
Alga Seafront south of windmill. Hip dance bar further along the bay with outdoor seating and live DJ playing anything from R&B to house to 1970s music.
Dubliner/Paros Rock Just off seafront. Large, brash dance complex set back from the main drag, comprising four loud bars, a snack section, disco and seating area.
Pebbles Seafront south of windmill. Upstairs bar playing classical and lounge music, with good sunset views.
Pirate Bar One block inland from seafront. Popular, established jazz and blues bar near the town hall.
Saloon D'Or Seafront south of windmill. Rowdy but fun spot on the main drag, with cheap drinks and mainstream music.

Southwest from Parikía

If you're staying in Parikía, you'll want to get out into the surroundings at some stage, if only to the beach. There are **beaches** immediately north and south of the harbour, but you might prefer to avoid the northern stretch altogether and head **south** along the asphalt road instead. The first unsurfaced side-track you come to leads to the small, sheltered Delfini beach; fifteen minutes further on is **PARASPÓROS**, with an attractively landscaped and relatively quiet **campsite** (Ⓣ22840 21100) and beach near the remains of an ancient temple to Asklepios, the god of healing and son of Apollo. Continuing for 45 minutes (or a short hop by bus) brings you to arguably the best of the bunch, **AYÍA IRÍNI**, with good sand and a **taverna** next to a farm and shady olive grove.

There's little else to stop for southwest of Parikía until **POÚNDA**, 6km away, and then only to catch the ferry to Andíparos (see p.553), or for the Páros Kite Pro Center (Ⓣ22840 92229, Ⓦwww.paroskite-procenter.com), which offers all levels of kite surfing and equipment rental. The small **airport** is further south, on the road to **ALYKÍ**, a resort on a pretty bay with two sections of beach. Hotels include the friendly, beachfront *Galatis* (Ⓣ22840 91355, Ⓦwww.galatishotel.com; April–Nov; B&B ④) with pool.

Náoussa and around

The second port of Páros, **NÁOUSSA**, is an alternative to Parikía. Although now a sprawling resort town, with modern concrete hotels and attendant trappings, it developed around a charming little port where fishermen still tenderize octopuses by thrashing them against the walls. The local **festivals** – an annual Fish and Wine Festival on July 2, and an August 23 shindig for a naval victory over the Turks – are still celebrated with enthusiasm; the latter may be brought forward to coincide with the August 15 festival of the Panayía. Most people are here for the beaches and the relaxed nightlife; there's really only one attraction, a **museum** (daily 9am–1.30pm & 7–9pm; free) in the monastery of Áyios Athanásios, with an interesting collection of Byzantine and post-Byzantine icons from the churches and monasteries around Náoussa.

Because it's newer and more fashionable than Parikía, accommodation is more expensive. Nissiotissa Tours (Ⓣ22840 51480), off the left side of the main square, can help you find a room, though it specializes in transport. The *Sea House* (Ⓣ22840 52198, Ⓦwww.seahouse.gr; April–Oct; ④) on the rocks above Pipéri beach was the first place in Náoussa to let **rooms** and has one of the best locations. Out of season you should haggle for reduced prices at the basic but well-located *Stella* (Ⓣ22840 51317, Ⓦwww.hotelstella.gr; ④), with rooms arranged around its own garden, several blocks inland from the old harbour. If you don't mind a five-minute climb, the family-run *Katerina* (ⓣ22840 51642, ⓦwww.katerinastudios.gr; ④) has beautiful uninterrupted sea views. A good-value **hostel** is the *Young Inn* (ⓣ694 28 34 911, ⓦwww.young-inn.com; April–Oct; from €8 per bed), which has **Internet** facilities. There are two **campsites** in the vicinity: the relaxed and friendly *Naoussa* (ⓣ22840 51565), west of town towards Kolymbíthres, and the newer *Surfing Beach* complex (ⓣ22840 52491-6, ⓦwww.surfbeach.gr) at Sánta María, northeast of Náoussa, with bungalows (④) as well as a popular beach bar, beach and watersports facilities; both run courtesy minibuses to and from Parikía.

Most of the harbour **tavernas** are decent, specializing in fresh fish and seafood, though there are more interesting places to eat at along the main road leading inland from just beside the little bridge over the canal, such as *Vengera* on the main square or *Open Garden* near the bus stop. There are some excellent **bars** clustered around the old harbour, making bar-hopping easy: *Linardo* and *Agosta* play dance music, whilst *Café del Mar* has one of the best settings with its busy tables stretching out to the edge of the sea. There are several big clubs up from the bus station, including *Vareladikos,* popular with a younger, late-night crowd. Once a week in summer, hordes of people take the 3.30am bus to the *Beach Bar* at Sánta María Camping for a weekly beach party – keep an eye out for flyers.

Local beaches

Pipéri beach is a couple of minutes' walk west of Náoussa's harbour, while **Áyii Anáryiri** is longer and a few minutes to the east; there are other good-to-excellent beaches within walking distance, and a summer *kaïki* service to connect them for about €4 round trip. Northeast of town, the barren headland is spangled with good surfing beaches: **Langéri** is backed by dunes; the best surfing is at **Sánta María**, a trendy beach connected with Náoussa by road, which also has a couple of tavernas, including the pleasant *Aristofanes*. At Sánta María, the Fly Under Diving Club (ⓣ22840 52491), has courses from beginners to advanced and wreck and reef diving; Surfistas (ⓣ697 47 44 499, ⓦwww.surfistas.gr) provides windsurfing training and rental.

The east coast and inland

AMBELÁS hamlet marks the start of a longer trek down the **east coast**. Ambelás itself has a good beach, a small taverna and some rooms and hotels, of which the *Hotel Christiana* (ⓣ22840 51573, ⓕ22840 52503; ③) is good value, with great fresh fish and local wine in the restaurant and extremely friendly proprietors. From here a rough track leads south, passing several undeveloped beaches on the way.

The largest resort on this coast, **PÍSO LIVÁDHI** was once a quiet fishing village, but is now dominated by package-holiday facilities; the main reason to visit is to catch a (seasonal) *kaïki* to Ayía Ánna on Náxos. *Hotel Andromachi* (ⓣ22840 41387, ⓕ22840 41733; ⑤) is a good place behind the beach, or ask at the friendly Perantinos Travel Agency (ⓣ22840 41135) near the bus stop. For a meal try *Vrochas* **taverna**, and head to the *Anchorage* café/bar for afternoon snacks or night-time cocktails.

Between here and Dhryós to the south are several sandy coves including Poúnda (not to be confused with the port of the same name on the opposite coast) – prone to pummelling by the *meltémi*, yet all favoured to varying degrees by campers and windsurfers. Also among these, **KHRYSSÍ AKTÍ** (Golden Beach) now has many tavernas, room complexes and hotels, such as the *Golden Beach Hotel* right on the beach (ⓣ22840 41366, ⓦwww.goldenbeach.gr;

April–Oct; ❺), with large rooms and apartments, watersports, and a restaurant supplied by their own farm.

Andíparos

The secret is definitely out about **Andíparos**. The waterfront is lined with new hotels and apartments, and in high season it can be full, though in recent years families seem to be displacing the young, international crowd. However, the island has managed to hold on to a friendly small-island atmosphere and still has a lot going for it, including good sandy beaches and an impressive cave, and the rooms and hotels are less expensive than on Páros.

Most of the population of eight hundred live in the large low-lying northern **village**, across the narrow straits from Páros, the new development on the outskirts concealing an attractive traditional settlement around the *kástro*. A long, flagstoned pedestrian street forms its backbone, leading from the jetty to the Cycladic houses around the outer wall of the *kástro*, which dates to the 1440s. The only way into the courtyard is through a pointed archway from the platía, where several cafés are shaded by a giant eucalyptus. Inside, more white-washed houses surround two churches and a cistern built into the surviving base of the central tower.

Andíparos's **beaches** begin right outside town: **Psaralíki**, just to the south with golden sand and tamarisks for shade, is much better than Sifnéïko (aka "Sunset") on the island's opposite side. Villa development is starting to follow the paved road down the east coast, but has yet to get out of hand. **Glýfa**, 4km down, is another good beach and, further south, **Sorós** has rooms and tavernas. On the west coast there are some fine small sandy coves at **Áyios Yeóryios**, the end of the road, and another long stretch of sand at **Kalóyeros**. *Kaïkia* make daily trips round the island and, less frequently, to the uninhabited archeological islet of Dhespotikó, opposite Áyios Yeóryios.

The great **cave** (summer daily 10.45am–3.45pm; €3) in the south of the island is the chief attraction for day-trippers. In these eerie chambers the Marquis de Nointel, Louis XIV's ambassador to Constantinople, celebrated Christmas Mass in 1673 while a retinue of five hundred, including painters, pirates, Jesuits and Turks, looked on; at the exact moment of midnight explosives were detonated to emphasize the enormity of the event. Although electric light and cement steps have diminished its mystery and grandeur, the cave remains impressive. Tour buses (€3 round trip) and public buses (€1 one way) run from the port every hour in season; bus services and opening hours are reduced out of season, and in winter you'll have to fetch the key for the cave from the mayor or village council (☎22840 61218).

Practicalities

To get to Andíparos, you have a choice of **boats** from Parikía (hourly in season, weather permitting; 40min), arriving at the jetty opposite the main street, or the car ferry from Poúnda (every 30min; 10min), arriving 150m to the south: the latter, including bus-fare from Parikía, is cheaper.

There are plenty of **hotels** along the waterfront, including *Anargyros* (☎22840 61204; ❸), which has good, basic rooms. More upmarket places to the north of the jetty include *Mantalena* (☎22840 61206, Ⓦwww.hotelmantalena.gr; May–Oct; breakfast €6; ❹) with large rooms and balconies, and *Artemis* (☎22840 61460, Ⓦwww.artemisantiparos.com; April–Oct; breakfast €6; ❸). The popular **campsite** (☎22840 61221) is a ten-minute walk northeast along a track, next to its own nudist beach; the water here is shallow enough for campers to wade across to the neighbouring islet of Dhipló.

The best of the waterfront **tavernas** is *Anargyros*, below the hotel of the same name. The main street leads up beside it; *Klimataria*, 100m inland off to the left, has tables in a pleasant garden, though it's only open at night. *The Internet Café*, also on the main street, has excellent coffee, as does *Romvi's* on the waterfront. There are plenty of **bars** around the eucalyptus-filled platía, where a festive atmosphere prevails at night. *Café Margarita* is a pleasant street-side hangout on the way up to the platía, while the *Nautica* is probably the liveliest of the waterfront spots. A **bank**, a **post office**, a cinema and several **travel agents** cluster around the waterfront, and there's a launderette near the windmill. You can rent scooters and **bicycles** at Europcar near the ferry dock. Blue Island Divers (Ⓣ22840 61493, Ⓦwww.blueisland-divers.gr; April–Oct) on the main street, offer PADI courses around Andíparos.

Náxos

Náxos is the largest and most fertile of the Cyclades, with the second largest (and youngest) population; and with its green and mountainous highland scenery, it seems immediately distinct from many of its neighbours. The difference is accentuated by the **unique architecture** of many of the interior villages: the Venetian Duchy of the Aegean, which ruled from 1204 to 1537, left towers and fortified mansions scattered throughout the island, while medieval Cretan refugees bestowed a singular character upon Náxos's eastern settlements.

Today Náxos could easily support itself without tourists by relying on its production of potatoes, olives, grapes and lemons, but it has thrown in its lot with mass tourism, so that parts of the island are now almost as busy as Páros in season. The island certainly has plenty to see if you know where to look: the highest mountains in the Cyclades, intriguing central valleys, a spectacular north coast and long, marvellously sandy beaches in the southwest. It is also renowned for its wines, cheese – sharp *kefalotýri* and milder *graviéra* – and *kítron*, a sweet liqueur available in green, yellow or clear, distilled from the leaves of this citrus tree.

Náxos Town

A long causeway, built to protect the harbour to the north, connects the town with the islet of Palátia – the place where, according to legend, Theseus was duped by Dionysos into abandoning Ariadne on his way home from Crete. The famous stone **Portára** that has greeted visitors for 2500 years is the portal of a temple of Apollo, built on the orders of the tyrant Lygdamis around 530 BC, but never completed.

Initial impressions suggest that most of the town's life occurs down by the crowded port esplanade or just behind it; a vast network of backstreets and low-arched narrow alleys lead up through the old town, Boúrgos, to the fortified **kástro** from where Marco Sanudo, the thirteenth-century Venetian who established the Duchy of the Aegean, and his successors, ruled over the Cyclades. However, there is a second, more modern, centre of activity to the south, around the main square, **Platía Evripéou**, with more tavernas, shops, car and bike rentals, and numerous Internet cafés.

Arrival, information and accommodation

Náxos is served by a tiny **airport**, located among salt marshes and lagoons just a few minutes' bus ride south from Náxos Town. Large **ferries** dock along the

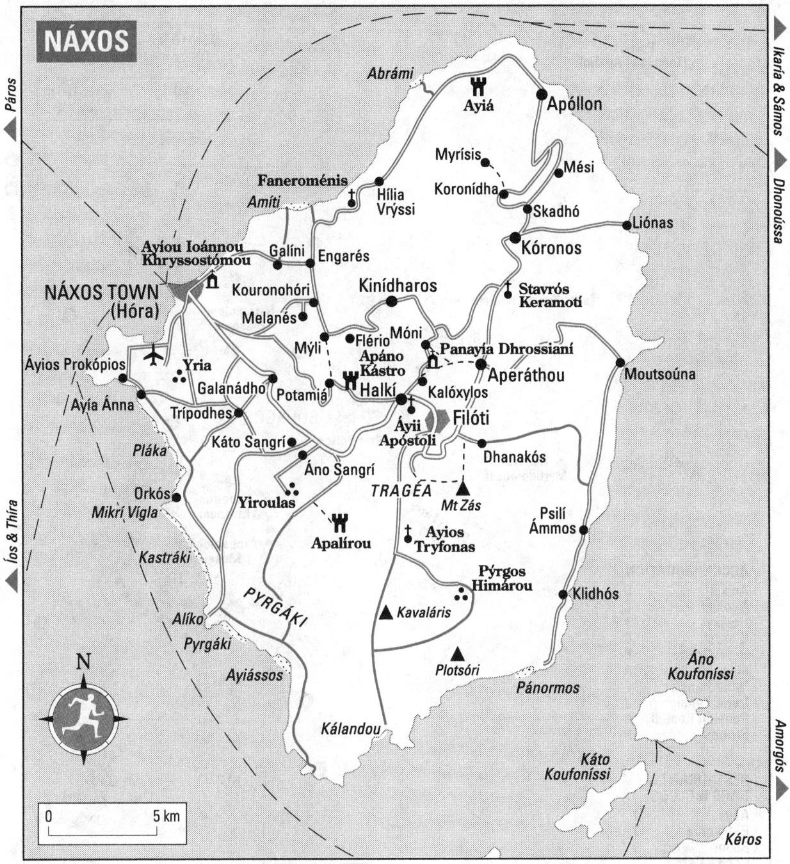

northern harbour pier; all small boats and the useful *Express Skopelitis* ferry use the nearby jetty in the fishing harbour. The **bus station** is at the landward end of the main dock; buses run 2–5 times a day to Apóllon, with one of the morning services going via Engarés and Abrámi, which is much slower. There are 5–6 buses a day to Aperáthou via Filóti, two of these going on to Moutsoúna on the east coast in summer. Buses run (every 30min 7.30am–2am in summer, three times a day in winter) to Áyios Prokópios, Ayía Ánna and (summer only) beyond the Pláka campsite on Pláka beach, and 4–6 times a day (summer only) to Pyrgáki via Kastráki. Printed timetables are available from the bus station; tickets should be bought before you travel, from the station or nominated shops near the stops, and validated in the onboard machine. More convenient are the **day-tours** of Náxos (€20) that can be booked at **Naxos Tourist Information** (Ⓣ22850 25201, Ⓕ22850 25200), on the seafront near the jetty, which offers a wealth of information, and somewhere to leave your bags (€1.50). It's also the best place to book special tours to the Minor Cyclades as well as accommodation, since the proprietor maintains some of the finest properties on the island. **Car, bike** and **cycle rental** companies include Mike's (Ⓣ22850 24975,

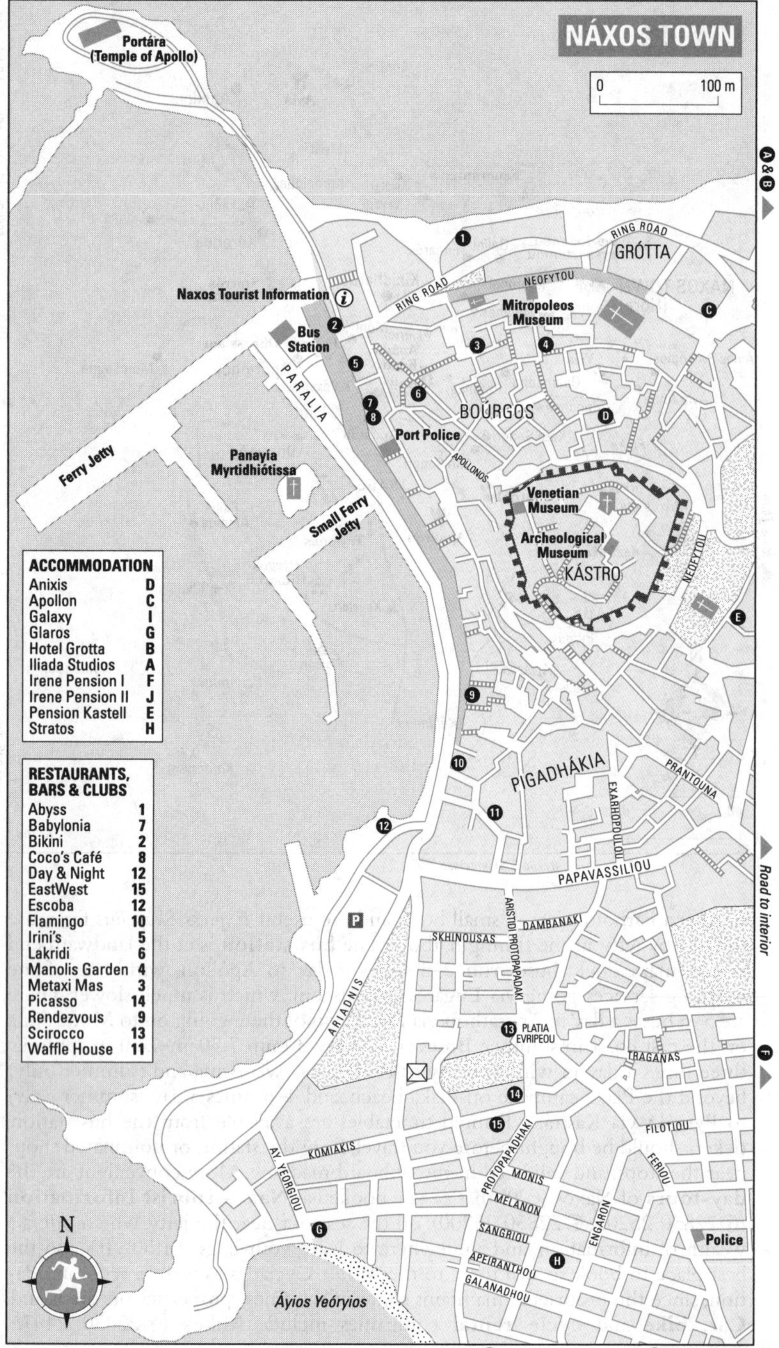

NÁXOS TOWN
0
100 m
Portára (Temple of Apollo)
Naxos Tourist Information
Bus Station
PARALIA
Ferry Jetty
Panayía Myrtidhiótissa
Small Ferry Jetty
RING ROAD
GRÓTTA
NEOFYTOU
Mitropoleos Museum
BOÚRGOS
Port Police
APOLLONOS
Venetian Museum
Archeological Museum
KÁSTRO
PIGADHÁKIA
PRANTOUNA
EXARHOPOULOU
PAPAVASSILIOU
Road to interior
ARISTIDI PROTOPAPADAKI
DAMBANAKI
SKHINOUSAS
ARIADNIS
PLATIA EVRIPEOU
TRAGANAS
FILOTIOU
FERIOU
KOMIAKIS
AY. YEORGIOU
PROTOPAPADAKI
MONIS
MELANON
SANGRIOU
ENGARON
APEIRANTHOU
GALANADHOU
Police
Áyios Yeóryios
A & B
F
I
J & Airport
N
ACCOMMODATION
Anixis D
Apollon C
Galaxy I
Glaros G
Hotel Grotta B
Iliada Studios A
Irene Pension I F
Irene Pension II J
Pension Kastell E
Stratos H
RESTAURANTS, BARS & CLUBS
Abyss 1
Babylonia 7
Bikini 2
Coco's Café 8
Day & Night 12
EastWest 15
Escoba 12
Flamingo 10
Irini's 5
Lakridi 6
Manolis Garden 4
Metaxi Mas 3
Picasso 14
Rendezvous 9
Scirocco 13
Waffle House 11

7 THE CYCLADES

Ⓦwww.naxos-bikes.com) just south of Platía Evripéou. Iris Neubauer at **Naxos Horse Riding** (Ⓣ694 88 09 142) organizes 3hr trips in the area for all levels for around €45 per person.

Accommodation

There's plenty of accommodation in Náxos and you should have no problem finding somewhere to stay. Once you've run the gauntlet of touts on the jetty, you would do well to head straight to Naxos Tourist Information (see p.555) who can book **rooms** for you, including at the owner's two hotels. There are three areas in town to look: the old quarter near the *kástro*, where they are hard to find and relatively expensive; up to the northeast of town in Grótta (which can be exposed to the wind); and southern part of town between the main square, Evripéou, and Áyios Yeóryios beach, where they are most abundant and less expensive, but sometimes with significant night-time noise from clubs and discos. Parking immediately next to the accommodations is not always possible.

Anixis Boúrgos Ⓣ22850 22932, Ⓦwww.hotel-anixis.gr. Pleasant, smart rooms set around a garden near the *kástro*, with wonderful views. Two larger studio apartments are also available here, and they have more studio accommodation at Áyios Yeóryios. April–Oct. Breakfast €5. ③

Apollon South of Grótta Ⓣ22850 22468, Ⓦwww.naxostownhotels.com. Comfortable, modern doubles, all with balconies, near the Mitropoleos Museum. ⑥

Galaxy Just south of town, near Áyios Yeóryios Ⓣ22850 22422, Ⓦwww.hotel-galaxy.com. Upmarket hotel with pool and large modern rooms and studios with sea views and balconies. B&B ⑥

Glaros Áyios Yeóryios Ⓣ22850 23101, Ⓦwww.hotelglaros.com. Comfortable, stylish hotel at the quieter western end of the beach. Most rooms come with sea views, and have Wi-Fi (there is also an Internet room). March–Oct. ④

Grotta Kampanélli 7, Grótta Ⓣ22850 22215, Ⓦwww.hotelgrotta.gr. Welcoming hotel in good location, only a 5min walk from the waterfront. Offers comfortable rooms, an indoor Jacuzzi, a generous breakfast and free Wi-Fi. B&B ④

Iliada Studios Grótta Ⓣ22850 23303, Ⓔiliada@otenet.gr. Quiet studio complex in Grótta on the cliff beyond town, with fabulous views out to sea. Parking. Easter–Oct. ④

Irene Pension I & II East and southeast of the main square Ⓣ22850 23169 or 697 33 37 782, Ⓦwww.irenepension-naxos.com. Clean, spacious studios in two locations, the second with a nice pool and sundeck near Áyios Yeóryios. The friendly English-speaking proprietor, Stavros, will meet guests at the port and is an excellent source of information on the island. ③

Pension Kastell Just south of the *kástro* Ⓣ22850 23082, Ⓦwww.kastell.gr. Friendly pension offering pleasant rooms with balconies and a nice roof garden. Access to the port in 5 minutes around the eastern side of the *kástro*. Hearty breakfast €5. March–Oct. ③

Stratos Sangrioú Ⓣ22850 25898, Ⓦwww.studios-stratos.com. Comfortable studios in two units near Áyios Yeóryios. ④

The Town

Only two of the *kástro*'s original seven towers remain, though the **north gate** (approached from Apóllonos and known as the Traní Portá or "Great Gate"), by the Kríspi (Glezos) tower, survives as a splendid example of a medieval fort entrance. A few of the Venetians' Catholic descendants still live in the old mansions that encircle the site, many with ancient coats of arms above the doorways. One mansion next to the Traní, the **Venetian Museum** (Domus Della-Rocca-Barozzi; daily 10am–3pm & 7–10pm (to 11pm in July–Aug); €5, student €3), is open to the public and offers the best views from the *kástro*; the guided tour includes a tasting from the family's wine cellar; live classical and Naxian evening concerts take place all year in the building or adjoining courtyard. They also offer a two-hour tour of the *kástro* at 11am Tues–Sun in season; €15 includes entrance to all the *kástro* museums.

Catholic buildings in the *kástro* include a seventeenth-century Ursuline convent, and the cathedral, unsubtly restored but still displaying a thirteenth-century crest inside. Nearby was what was to become one of Ottoman Greece's first schools, the French Commercial School; opened by Jesuits in 1627 for Catholic and Orthodox students alike, its pupils included, briefly, Nikos Kazantzakis (see p.487). The school building now houses an excellent **archeological museum** (Tues–Sun 8.30am–3pm; €3), with finds from Náxos, Koufoníssi, Kéros and Dhonoússa, including an important collection of Early Cycladic figurines. Archaic and Classical sculpture and pottery dating from Neolithic to Roman times, as well as obsidian knives, spectacular gold rosettes from a tomb, and a large collection of Roman glass, are also on display, though labelling is sparse. On the outdoor terrace, a Hellenistic mosaic floor shows a nereid (sea nymph) surrounded by deer and peacocks. In the centre of the *kástro* are the plain stone remains of a rectangular tower, said to be the residence of Sanudo.

More archeology is accessible a few minutes' walk east from the harbour, at the remains of the Mycenaean city. In front of the Orthodox cathedral, the **Mitropoleos Museum** (Tues–Sun 8.30am–3pm; free) has walkways over a recently excavated tumulus cemetery, from the thirteenth to the eleventh century BC, with various funerary remnants including a *hermax*, a pile of the stones that were traditionally thrown behind on leaving a cemetery. In the general area, items dating from the early Cycladic period (3200 BC) right through to late Roman (500 AD) have been found.

Eating

The waterfront is crammed with places to eat, most of them decent. For picnics, there's a good bakery towards the southern end of the harbour front.

Bikini Opposite ferry dock. This popular crêperie also serves good breakfasts and snacks. Ideal if you're waiting for a ferry.

EastWest just off A. Protopapadháki, below Platía Evripéou. Indian and Thai food.

Flamingo Paralía. Upstairs taverna, with huge, well-priced menu, and live music several times a week (and subsequent extra cover charge).

Irini's Paralía. One of the best of the *mezedhopolia/* oven-food tavernas on the waterfront, with some imaginative salads.

Manolis Garden Boúrgos. Popular taverna with small but excellent menu both in taste and value for money. Located in a large garden in the old town.

Metaxi Mas Boúrgos. Friendly ouzerí serving excellent, well-priced food on a little street heading up to the *kástro*.

Picasso A. Protopapadháki, southwest corner of Evripéou square. Popular Mexican restaurant, with some good vegetarian options, and another branch on Pláka beach. Evenings only.

Rendezvous Paralía. Busy waterfront café serving excellent cakes and coffee.

Scirocco Platía Evripéou. Well-known restaurant popular with locals and tourists alike for its good-value traditional meals, hence the occasional long queue to get in.

Waffle House Excellent, home-made, Italian-style ice-cream, to eat in or take away. There is a summer branch at Pláka beach.

Nightlife

Much of the evening action goes on at the south end of the waterfront, where you'll find **café-bars** and **clubs** jostling for business, luring people in with staggeringly huge menus of cheap cocktails. Should that fail to tempt, there's also an open-air **cinema**, the Cine Astra, on the road to the airport at the southern end of town; it's a fair walk out, but the Ayía Ánna bus stops here.

Abyss road to Grótta. The town's biggest club, with dancing to European hits split over two floors.
Babylonia Náxos's first gay bar, discreetly situated on the upper-level of a building on the waterfront.
Coco's Café Good little cocktail spot on the waterfront, playing South American music and serving breakfast through the day.
Day & Night Popular bar turning out European, and later on Greek, music every weekend on its packed veranda.
Escoba Just behind *Day & Night*, this place serves yet more great cocktails, and is a little larger, so less of a crush.
Lakridi A tiny jazz bar, which sometimes plays classical music, tucked away on a street behind the port police.

The southwestern beaches

Of the **beaches** around Náxos Town, **Grótta**, just to the north, is easiest to reach; not ideal for sunbathing but the remains of submerged Cycladic buildings are visible to swimmers. The finest spots, though, are all **south** of town, with the entire southwestern coastline boasting a series of excellent **beaches** accessible in summer by regular bus. **ÁYIOS YEÓRYIOS**, a long sandy bay fringed by the town's southern accommodation area, is within walking distance. There's a line of cafés and tavernas at the northern end of the beach, and a windsurfing school, Flisvos Sportsclub (Ⓣ22850 24308, Ⓦwww.flisvos-sportclub.com) which offers kitesurfing, windsurfing, catamarans and mountain biking. There is a campsite further south, although there are far more attractive places to camp on Pláka beach (see below).

Buses take you to **ÁYIOS PROKÓPIOS** beach, a long line of sand with lagoons behind; the village has a southeastern part on the beach, main road and bus route, and a separate western annex 1.5km away (at the base of the distinct double cone of Stelídha hill) which is itself approximately 1km from a separate section of the beach. There are plenty of basic tavernas, reasonably priced hotels, and rooms, such as the *Adriana* (Ⓣ22850 42804; ④) with pool along the road towards Stelídha, as well as the very attractive *Hotel Lianos Village* (Ⓣ22850 26366, Ⓦwww.lianosvillage.com; B&B ⑦), with pool and Internet facilities, nearer to Stelídha. Two excellent, traditional restaurants in the beachfront area are *Anessio* and *Colosseo*, while the younger, funkier *Kahlua* and *Splash* are good cafés.

Rapid development along this stretch means that this resort has blended into the next one, **AYÍA ÁNNA**, further along the busy road, with accommodation of a similar price and quality. The seaview *Iria Beach Hotel* (Ⓣ22850 42600, Ⓦwww.iriabeach-naxos.com; ⑤) studios are a comfortable option. Some of the best food in Ayía Ánna is at the *Gorgona* taverna, family run and with excellent prices. *Gorgona* also offers rooms, studios and apartments, all newly refurbished with en-suite bathrooms and air conditioning (Ⓣ 22850 41007; ③). Further along the coast, away from the built-up area, the beach is sheltered by juniper trees and is naturist.

Beyond the headland, **PLÁKA** beach, a vegetation-fringed expanse of white sand, stretches for 5km with the best sections towards the middle and south and accessed by a flat unsurfaced road from the north. Buildings are much more scattered and some parts of the beach are naturist where shielded from the road by dunes past *Plaka* campsite, although they are being edged out by beach umbrellas and sun-loungers. There are two suitably laid-back **campsites** here: *Maragas* (Ⓣ22850 24552, Ⓦwww.maragascamping.gr), which also has double rooms and studios (④), and the friendly *Plaka* (Ⓣ22850 42700, Ⓦwww.plakacamping.gr), about 700m further south, which is smaller and quiet with a comfortable and spacious new studio hotel (April–Oct; breakfast €5; ④). Good **tavernas** in the vicinity of Pláka include *Paradiso* near the Ayía Ánna end, *Manolis* at *Maragas*, and *Petrino*. Naxos Diving (Ⓣ22850 42072, Ⓦwww.naxosdiving.com; all year) offer PADI courses or wreck, reef, cave and exploration diving on Náxos and elsewhere in the Cyclades.

Central Náxos and the Tragéa

Although buses bound for Apóllon (in the north) link up the central Naxian villages, the core of the island, between Náxos Town and Aperáthou, is best explored with your own transport or on foot. Much of the region is well off the beaten track, and a rewarding excursion if you've had your fill of beaches; Christian Ucke and Dieter Graf's *Walking The Greek Islands: Naxos and the Small Cyclades*, published by Graf Editions and available from bookshops such as Zoom in Náxos Town, is a useful guide for hikers. Drivers should note that there are no **petrol stations** beyond Engarés when heading northeast, nor beyond the two at Halkí when heading into the mountains.

To the east of Náxos Town is **FLÉRIO**, the most interesting of the ancient Naxian marble quarries of the seventh- to sixth-century BC and home to two famous **kouri**, that were left recumbent and unfinished because of flaws in the material. Even so, they're finely detailed figures, over 5m in length. The Koúros Flerioú (Koúros Melánon), from around 570 BC, is a short walk along the stream valley, next to the *Paradise* garden café; the Koúros Farangioú (Koúros Potamiás) is a steeper walk up the hillside. Just above the car park is a compact, recently excavated and well-labelled **Sanctuary**, contemporary with the marble quarries. The bus from Náxos town is signed "Melanes Kouros".

On the road leading southeast of Náxos Town, the twin villages of Sangrí are on a plateau at the head of a long valley. Thirty minutes' stroll away from **Áno Sangrí**, on a path leading south out of the village, or 3km by surfaced lane, are the partially rebuilt remains of a **Classical temple of Demeter** (Tues–Sun 8.30am–3pm; free) from 530 BC, over which was constructed an early Christian basilica. The attractively laid out site, also known as Yiroulas, is on a low hill overlooking an appropriately agricultural valley, and has an award-winning museum with further reconstructions.

The Tragéa

From Sangrí, the road twists northeast into the **Tragéa** region, scattered with olive trees and occupying a vast highland valley. The area is the only part of the Cyclades to have a regular winter snowfall, and the only part with traditional songs about snow. It's a good jumping-off point for all sorts of exploratory rambling, and **HALKÍ** is a fine introduction to what is to come. Set high up, 16km from Náxos Town, it's a quiet town with some lovely churches, including the **Panayía Protóthronis**, with its eleventh- to thirteenth-century frescoes; it only opens to visitors in the morning. Just behind is the restored seventeenth-century Venetian **Grazia-Barozzi Tower**. ★ *Yiannis* **taverna** is the focal point of village activity and has a good selection of well-prepared local food. Nearby is the distillery (1896) and shop of Vallindras Naxos Citron, whose charming proprietors explain the process of producing *kítron* followed by a little tasting session. The olive plantations surrounding Halkí are criss-crossed by paths and tracks, the groves dotted with numerous Byzantine chapels – Áyios Yeóryios Dhiasorítis and Panayía Dhamiótissa (theoretically both open Mon–Fri 10am–2.30pm) are well-signed from Halkí and the Moní road respectively.

At the far end of the gorgeous Tragéa valley, **FILÓTI**, the largest village in the region, lies on the slopes of Mount Zás (or Zeus) which, at just over 1000m, is the highest point in the Cyclades. Under the shade of the plane trees on the main platía are several pleasant *kafenía*, as well as *Babulas Grill-Restaurant*, which has the best rooms (Ⓣ22850 31426; ❷) in the village. To get an idea of the old village, climb the steps up the hill starting at the platía.

From Filóti, it's a round-trip walk of three to four hours on partly marked trails to the summit of **Zás**, a climb which rewards you with an even more astounding panorama of virtually the whole of Náxos and its Cycladic neighbours. The initial path out of the village climbs up to rejoin the Apóllon road. Take the Dhanakós turning, to the waymarked final approach trail which begins beside small Ayía Marína chapel. There is also a marked turn-off steeply down to the 150m-deep Zás Cave, but this is more easily accessed by a separate route (1hr) from Filóti.

A turning at the southern end of Filóti is signposted to the **Pýrgos Himárrou** (12.5km, paved), a remote twenty-metre Hellenistic watchtower – swathed in scaffolding for the foreseeable future, but impressive nonetheless – and onward (11km, unpaved) to **Kalandoú** beach on the south coast. En route to the tower, at the Áyios Trýfonas pass, there are some of the best views on Náxos, including seventeen other Cycladic islands. There are no villages in the south-central part of the island, so bring supplies if you're planning to camp.

Aperáthou

APERÁTHOU (officially Apíranthos), a hilly, winding 8km beyond Filóti, shows the most Cretan influence of all the interior villages. Being high in the mountains, it is noticeably cooler and greener in summer than the coastal areas. There are two Venetian fortified mansions, Bardáni and Zevgóli, an **ATM**, and several small **museums**: the Natural History (April–Oct, 10.30am–1.30pm, €1.50) and Geological (April–Oct, 10.30am–2pm, €2) are on the main road, the Folklore is further inside town. **Cafés** and **tavernas** on the main street look out over a terraced valley below; the nationally renowned taverna *Leftheri*, here, is generally regarded as one of the best restaurants on the island, serving up carefully prepared local dishes. **Rooms** are available but are not obvious – ask in the cafés or shops – the exception being the *Zorbas Studios* (Ⓣ22850 61339 or 694 41 01 566; ❸) at the northern end of town.

Northern Náxos

The route through the mountains from Aperáthou to Apóllon is very scenic, and the road surface is in reasonable condition all the way. At the Stavrós Keramotís col there are dramatic views down to both sides of the island. Jagged ranges and hairpin bends confront you after Kóronos village, past Skadhó, to the remote, emery-miners' village of **KORONÍDHA** – the highest on the island and the original home of *kítron* liqueur. Alternatively, avoid over 5km of bends by diverting right after Skadhó, through Mési.

Back on the main road, a further series of bends leads down a long valley to **APÓLLON** (Apóllonas), a small resort with two beaches: a tiny and crowded stretch of sand backed by a line of cafés and restaurants, and a longer, quieter stretch of shingle. The main **hotels** are the central *Adonis* (Ⓣ22850 67060, Ⓦwww.adonis-hotel.com; ❹) and the *Kouros* behind the long beach (Ⓣ22850 67000; ❹). There are studios and rooms available, such as *Flora* (Ⓣ22850 67070; ❸), one of the few open outside high season. The only major attraction is a **kouros**, approached by a path from the main road just above the village. Lying in situ at a former marble quarry, this largest of Náxos's abandoned stone figures is just over 10m long, but less detailed than those at Flério. Here since 600 BC and probably intended for the Dionysian temple at Ýria, it serves as a reminder of the Naxians' traditional skill; the famous Delian lions (see p.542) are also made of Apollonian marble. Not surprisingly, bus tours descend upon the village during the day, and Apóllon is quite a popular little place. The local festival, celebrated on August 28–29, is one of Náxos's best.

Minor Cyclades

Four of the six small islands in the patch of the Aegean between Náxos and Amorgós have slid from obscurity into fashion in recent years. The group is known commonly as the Minor Cyclades and includes **Áno Koufoníssi**, **Skhinoússa**, **Iráklia** and **Dhonoússa**. The islands' new popularity is hastening the development of better facilities and higher prices, but with little room for expansion and only limited ferry services, they've managed to avoid the mass tourism of the rest of the Cyclades. The Pireás-based Blue Star **ferries** call at the islands, often during the night – linking them with Náxos, Amorgós and (sometimes) Páros. However, the small, local *Express Skopelitis* is a more frequent fixture, leaving the smaller ferry quay in Náxos from Mondays to Saturdays to head to most of the islets (Dhonoússa has fewer connections).

Iráklia

Iráklia (locally Iraklía), the westernmost of the Minor Cyclades, and with the least spoiled scenery, has just over 100 permanent residents. As the first stop on the ferry service from Náxos, the island is hardly undiscovered by tourists, but with fewer amenities than some of its neighbours it retains the feel of a more secluded retreat.

Ferries call at **ÁYIOS YEÓRYIOS**, a small, sprawling settlement behind a sandy tamarisk-backed beach. *Anna's Place* (Ⓣ & Ⓕ22850 71145; ❸–❹) on the hill-slope at the back of the village has great views, rooms with shared cooking facilities in the gardens above, and some luxurious studios. Another accommodation option is the *Maïstrali* taverna (Ⓣ22850 71807, Ⓔnickmaistrali@in.gr; ❸),

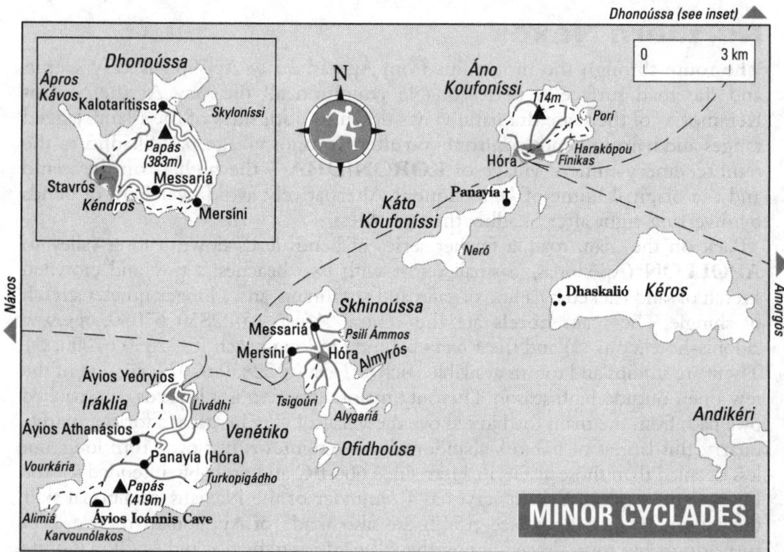

on the way to *Anna's*, which has studios near the *Alexandra*. Details of these and other accommodations can be found on the island website Ⓦwww.iraklia.gr. For eating, there are several good **tavernas**, including the laid-back *Maïstrali,* and the *Perigiali* near the harbour, which also has a small shop. The post office, a short distance above the *Perigiali*, is also the agency for **ferry tickets**, but there is no bank/ATM in town, nor is there public transport.

Livádhi, the biggest beach on the island, is a 1.5-kilometre walk southeast of the port, and rather disappointing on closer inspection. The *Makuba* taverna, halfway there, has a rather scruffy, seasonal campsite in the valley behind the beach. The village of Livádhi, deserted since 1940, stands on the hilltop just behind the beach, its houses ruined; among the remains are Hellenistic walls incorporated into a later building, and Venetian fortifications from the time of Marco Sanudo.

PANAYÍA (HÓRA), an undistinguished hamlet at the foot of Mount Papás, is an hour's walk (4km) inland along the paved road, with an en-route short-cut possible up a brief, remaining section of the old *kalderími* path. It has no rooms, but the small taverna *Tou Steki* also functions as a shop with a few basic supplies.

The **cave of Áyios Ioánnis** lies behind the mountain, at the head of a valley leading to Vourkária bay. From behind the main church in Áyios Yeóryios, follow a signposted dirt track up to the near-deserted hamlet of **Áyios Athanásios** from where a faint path continues up to a col northwest of Mount Papás. It is met here by an alternative, more obvious, signed path coming up from Panayía. The combined route then descends as a narrow, sometimes steep, stony path, around to the southeast side of the mountain. Go left, at a well-marked junction, to the cave, just over 90 minutes from the port or 50 minutes from Panayía. There is a larger cave entrance on the left, but a church bell hangs from a cypress tree above the whitewashed entrance to the right; inside there's a shrine, and the cave opens up into a large chamber with stalactites and stalagmites. With a good torch – and some care – it can be explored to a depth of 120m and is thought to be part of a much larger cave system, yet to be opened up; a festival is held here every year on August 28.

The main trail continues beyond the cave to a small sandy beach at **Alimiá** but this can be reached more easily with the beach-boat from Áyios Yeóryios. In season, the boat – owned by the *Anna's Place* family – sails daily to either Skhinoússa, Alimiá or the nearby pebble beach of Karvounólakos.

Skhinoússa

A little to the east, the island of **Skhinoússa** (locally sometimes Skinoússa) is just beginning to awaken to its tourist potential. Its indented outline, sweeping valleys and partly submerged headlands provide some of the most dramatic views in the group. Boats dock at the small port of Mersíni, which has a taverna; a road leads up to **HÓRA** (also called Panayía), with the shadeless walk taking about fifteen minutes, with some stony shortcuts for the upper bends. As you enter the village, the agent for ferries, except the *Skopelitis*, is on the right, and there are three small supermarkets before the road junction for the tiny settlement of Messariá. There is also another tourist office, Central Travel Agency, at the Almyrós-Lióliou/Livádhi junction at the other end of town, next to the laundry.

Accommodation is mostly comfortable rather than luxurious. Just east of the main square, the *Anna* rooms and studios (Ⓣ22850 71161; May–Oct; ②) are quiet and comfortable, whilst the nearby *Iliovasilema Hotel* (Ⓣ22850 71948, Ⓔiliovasilema@schinousa.gr; May–Oct; breakfast €4; ③), under the same management, is well-priced and enjoys stunning views of the harbour. At the southern end are the hospitable *Meltemi* (Ⓣ22850 71947, Ⓦwww.cyclades-tourism.gr/meltemi.htm; Easter–Oct; ③) rooms and studios, beside the family taverna, and, just out of town, the pleasant *Pension Galini* (Ⓣ22850 71983; May–Oct; ❸). All offer transport to and from the port, and the *Iliovasilema* runs beach excursions by minibus in the summer.

The main concentration of **restaurants** and cafés is along the central thoroughfare. Traditional *Panorama* and more trendy *Margarita* offer diners some of the best views on the island. There is a tiny folk museum (uncertain opening hours), near the Tsigoúri beach track.

There are no fewer than sixteen **beaches** dotted around the island, accessible by a network of dirt tracks. **Tsigoúri** is a ten-minute track walk downhill from northwest Hóra and gradually being developed. The *Grispos Villas* (Ⓣ22850 71930, Ⓦwww.grisposvillas.com; B&B ❹), perched above at the northwest end, have a good taverna, and new rooms and studios with great views; they also sell ferry tickets in season. On the beach itself is the *Ostria* taverna. The locals' preferred choice of beaches are Alygariá to the south, Psilí Ámmos to the northeast, and **Almyrós**, half an hour southeast, which has a canteen.

Áno Koufoníssi and Káto Koufoníssi

Áno Koufoníssi (usually referred to simply as Koufoníssi) is the most populous and developed island of the group. With some of the least-spoilt beaches in the Cyclades, the island is attracting increasing numbers of Greek and foreign holidaymakers. Small enough to walk round in a morning, the island can feel overcrowded in July and August.

The old, single street (now pedestrianized) of **HÓRA**, crossing a low hill behind the ferry harbour, has been engulfed by new room and hotel development, but the town still has a friendly, small-island atmosphere. To the west (left) of the jetty a dirt road leads to a small bay with fishing boats, to the right is the town and town beach, from where the short main street has several supermarkets and the well-stocked *Yioryioula* bakery-café. The Koufonissia Tours ticket agency is on the pedestrian street of Hóra, and there is a **post office** (limited hours) up a side street by the *Hotel Roussetos*, with an **ATM**. At the eastern end of the beach is a further cluster of accommodations, and the road to the eastern beaches. A map by the jetty shows the layout of town, and where to find the island's **rooms** providing you know the name of the owner rather than that of the accommodation. The hospitable Katerina Prassinos has a variety of rooms, including the upmarket studios and apartments at the *Hotel Roussetos* (Ⓣ22850 74176, Ⓕ22850 71844; ❹), at the corner of the town beach and start of the main street. Her mother, Maria Prassinou (Ⓣ22850 71436, Ⓕ22850 71369; ❸), has a variety of rooms just east of the beach, as well as a couple of old houses (❻) to rent. On the pedestrian street of Hóra, the pension *Melissa* (Ⓣ22850 71454, Ⓕ22850 71732; May–Oct; ❸), behind a popular taverna, is a good, family-run choice, just inland from the beach – they have further studios near Fínikas beach. The *Yioryioula* bakery has comfortable rooms at *Hondros Kavos* (Ⓣ22850 71707, Ⓕ22850 71441; May–Oct; ❸), located over a popular seafood taverna about 10–15 minutes' walk to the east, near Fínikas beach – they have a transfer minibus for the ferry.

Koufoníssi is noted for its fish **tavernas**; *Neo Remezzo*, in the little street directly above the ferry jetty, has excellent food and a cosy atmosphere, while *Capetan Nicolas*, at the bay to the west, is cheaper than most and has a fine array of seafood. The most popular nightspot is *Soroccos*, a lively **café-bar** on the eastern seafront with views of Kéros, while *Ta Kalamia* on the main street has a quieter choice of music.

All the good beaches are in the southeast of the island, getting better as you go east along a semi-paved road that skirts the gradually developing coastline along the edge of low cliffs. **Fínikas**, a fifteen-minute walk from the town, is the first of four wide coves with gently shelving golden sand, where there are an increasing number of rooms, and the *Hondros Kavos* taverna. Further east is **Harakópou**, which has a windswept **campsite** (ⓣ22850 71683) with cane shade and a minibus, but limited facilities, situated on the headland before the next beach **Thános**, where thumping music plays at the beach bar *Fanos*. Next is **Platiá Poúnda**, where caves have been hollowed out of the cliffs. Further east, the path rounds a rocky headland to **Porí**, a much longer and wilder beach, backed by dunes and set in a deep bay. It can be reached more easily from the town by following a dirt road heading inland through the low scrub-covered hills.

Dhonoússa

Dhonoússa is a little out on a limb compared with the other Minor Cyclades, and ferries call less frequently. Island life centres on the pleasant port settlement of **STAVRÓS**, spread out behind the harbour and the village beach.

Rooms, most without signs, tend to be booked up by Greek holiday-makers in August; beyond the beach try the rooms and studios at *Iliovasilema* (ⓣ22850 51570, ⓔxsigalas@yahoo.gr; breakfast €4; ❷), which also has a good restaurant, and is agent for the Blue Star ferries; or nearby *Prasinou* (ⓣ22850 51579; ❸–❹), with studios and some beautifully furnished apartments. Next to the *Aposperides* taverna are the *Skopelitis* studios (ⓣ22850 52296, ⓔskopelitis@gmx.net; May–Oct; ❷), set around a flowery garden.

There are a few **tavernas** in town; one of the best for *mezédhes* is *Captain George*, with lovely sea views. The **ticket agency** above the harbour changes money at unfavourable rates, so you would be wise to bring enough with you.

The hills around Stavrós are low and barren and scarred by bulldozed tracks, but a little walking is repaid with dramatic scenery and a couple of fine beaches. Sunbathers head for **Kéndros**, a long and attractive stretch of sand fifteen minutes over the ridge to the east, although shade is limited; there is a family taverna and a small area for camping. **Mersíni** (population 13) is an hour's walk from Stavrós and has a new café/taverna at the lower end of the village, the *Tsitsi*, which uses locally sourced products. A nearby path leads down to Livádhi, an idyllic white-sand beach with tamarisks for shade. In July and August, there's a beach-boat from the port to Kéndros and, weather permitting, Livádhi.

Amorgós

Amorgós, with its dramatic mountain scenery and laid-back atmosphere, is attracting visitors in increasing numbers; most ferries and catamarans call at both Katápola in the southwest and Eyiáli (Aegiali) in the north – with these destinations, rather than Amorgós, on schedules – and there is a bus service (2–6 daily) between both ports. The island can get extremely crowded in midsummer, the numbers swollen by French people paying their respects to the film location of Luc Besson's *The Big Blue*, although few actually venture out to Líveros at the island's west end to see the wreck of the *Olympia* which figured so prominently in the movie. In general it's a low-key, escapist clientele, happy to have found a relatively large, interesting, uncommercialized and hospitable island with excellent walking.

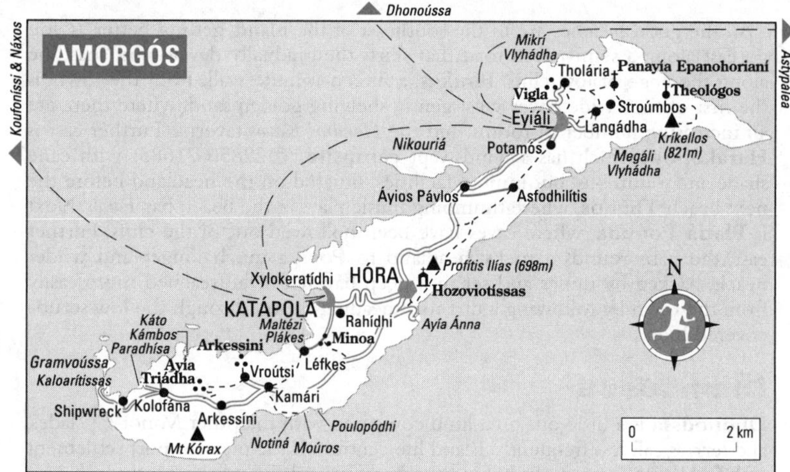

Katápola and around

KATÁPOLA, set at the head of a deep inlet, is actually three separate villages: **Katápola** proper on the south side, **Xylokeratídhi** on the north shore, and **Rahídhi** on the central ridge. There is a beach in front of Rahídhi, but Káto Krotíri beach to the west of Katápola is better, though not up to the standards of Eyiáli in the northeast. In season there is also a regular *kaïki* to nearby beaches at **Maltézi** and **Plákes** (€3 return) and a daily *kaïki* to the islet of **Gramvoússa** off the western end of Amorgós (€6–8 return).

Prekas in Katápola, just along from the ferry dock, is the one-stop **boat-ticket agency**. There are several **car/bike-rental outfits**, such as Thomas (Ⓣ22850 71777, Ⓦwww.thomas-rental.gr); the Eko petrol station is partway up the road to Hóra, below a large supermarket. Alternatively, in high season, the local bus service is more than adequate and the walking trails delightful. There are several walking maps on sale throughout the island, that published by Anavasi being the most useful. The **bus** shuttles regularly between Katápola and Hóra, the island capital; several times daily it continues to Ayía Ánna via Hozoviótissas monastery, and 2–7 times weekly out to the "Káto Meriá", made up of the hamlets of Kamári-Vroútsi, Arkessíni and Kolofána.

There are plenty of small **hotels** and **pensions** and, except in high summer when rooms are almost impossible to find, proprietors tend to meet those boats arriving around sunset – though not necessarily those that show up in the small hours. On the waterfront square, the neighbouring smart *Hotel Minoa* and *Landeris* (Ⓣ22850 71480, Ⓔhotelminoalanderis@yahoo.com; breakfast €3; ③), have some very comfortable, large new rooms, as well as **Internet** access. A good place next to the small beach at the western end of Katápola is *Eleni* rooms and studios (Ⓣ22850 71628, Ⓔroomseleni@hack-box.net; ③). Well-signed south of the port you'll find the hospitable *Anna Studios* (Ⓣ22850 71218, Ⓕ22850 71084; ③), in a spacious garden setting, with basic cooking facilities and mosquito nets. The town **campsite** (Ⓣ & Ⓕ22850 71257) is well signed, just off the beach between Rahídhi and Xylokeratídhi. There's also a newer one, *Camping Kastanis* (Ⓣ22850 71277, Ⓦwww.kastanis.com), a ten-minute walk uphill towards Hóra.

In Katápola proper, *Mourayio* is the most popular **taverna** in town; alternatively, try the *Psaropoula* or *Minos*. There are four tavernas close to the campsite near Xylokeratídhi, of which the nearest is a friendly fish taverna, and of the others around the corner *Vitzentzos* is by far the best. What **nightlife** there is focuses on a handful of cafés and pubs. The bar *Le Grand Bleu* in Xylokeratídhi regularly shows *The Big Blue* on video, but there are other less obvious and less expensive places to drink, such as the popular *Moon Bar* nearby. **Internet** access is available at the *Teloneio* café, near the laundry.

A signed surfaced road runs past the church in Rahídhi and south out of Katápola to the remains of **ancient Minoa**, about a half-hour's walk uphill. The site is in the process of being excavated, and is impressive for its size, and the views it commands over the bay, Hóra and ancient Arkessíni, as much as anything else. Your walk is rewarded by fragments of polygonal wall, four or five courses high, the foundations of an Apollo temple, a crumbled Roman structure and bushels of unsorted pottery shards.

Hóra and around

HÓRA, accessible by an hour-long walk along the path beginning from behind the Rahídhi campsite, is one of the better-preserved settlements in the Cyclades, with a scattering of tourist shops, cafés, tavernas and rooms. Dominated by an upright volcanic rock plug, wrapped with a chapel or two, the thirteenth-century Venetian fortifications look down on nearly thirty other churches, some domed, and a line of decapitated windmills beyond. Of the half-dozen or so **places to stay**, the *Politimi* rooms (Ⓣ22850 71542; ❸), belonging to the *Leonidas* café, are a possibility, as is the stunning *Traditional Guest House Embrostiada* (Ⓣ22850 71814, Ⓦwww.amorgos-studios.amorgos.net; ❻), one of the most beautiful designer hotels in the Cyclades. Hóra is littered with atmospheric little places to **eat** and **drink**: *Liotrivi* restaurant, down the steps from the bus stop, and with a roof terrace, is very popular. Of the several café-bars, *Lodza* and *Kallisto* is good, whilst *Bayoko*, by the bus stop, does a hearty breakfast. Also in the upper square is the island's main **post office**.

From the top of Hóra, near the upper telecoms tower, a wide cobbled *kalderími* drops down to two major attractions, effectively short-cutting the road and taking little longer than the bus to reach them. For the **monastery of Hozoviótissas** (daily 8am–1pm, 5–7pm; donation expected), bear left at an inconspicuous fork, and you'll join the monastery/Ayía Ánna road near the bus stop junction: the small monastery car park is about 300m along to the left. From the car park, a path leads rather steeply upwards, for about 700m to the spectacular monastery which appears suddenly as you round a bend, its vast wall gleaming white at the base of a towering orange cliff. Modest dress is required of visitors; the sign advises that trousers are not suitable for women, but you will find that most female Greek visitors wear them. If you arrive during a service, you will need to wait until it finishes before you can see anything beyond the church. Only three monks occupy the fifty rooms now, but they are quite welcoming considering the number of visitors who file through; you can see the eleventh-century icon around which the monastery was founded, along with other treasures. Legend has it that during the Iconoclastic period, a precious icon of the Virgin was committed to the sea by beleaguered monks at Hózova, in the Middle East, and it washed up safely at the base of the palisade here.

The right-hand trail leads down, within forty minutes, to the pebble **beaches** at **Ayía Ánna**. Skip the first tiny coves, where the car park is larger than the sand, in favour of the path to Kambí bay, where naturists cavort, almost in scandalous sight of the monastery far above: bring food and water for the day.

Southwestern Amorgós

For alternatives to Ayía Ánna, head west to **Kamári** hamlet for the twenty-minute walk (road and path) down to the adjacent beaches of **Notiná**, **Moúros** and **Poulopódhi**. Like most of Amorgós's south-facing beaches, they're clean, with calm water. The westward road from Kamári goes through the rural hamlet of modern **Arkessíni** where rooms and studios are available. The main path from Minoa ends next to the well-preserved Hellenistic fort ("Pýrgos"), just outside the hamlet. The next settlement, 2.5km further west, is **Kolofána**, with a minimarket, a *kafenío*, and the *T'Apanemo* and *Delfini* tavernas – the latter (Ⓣ22850 72244; May–Oct; ❷) has newly refurbished rooms and studios arranged around a garden at the back, with rural field and mountain views. From here the surfaced road leads towards the far western tip of the island, to the spectacular **Kalotarítissas** bay with a tiny fishing jetty, and small sand and pebble beach, partly enclosed and sheltered by a rocky headland and opposite the islet of Gramvoússa. About 1.8km before Kalotarítissas, the **wreck of the Olympia** is visible down to the right, in Líveros bay.

Northeastern Amorgós

The energetically inclined can walk the four to five hours from Hóra to Eyiáli, continuing on the faint trail just beyond Hozoviótissas; remember to take water, as there is nowhere to fill up on the way

EYIÁLI (AEGIALI) is smaller and more picturesque than Katápola, and so tends to be more popular; the main **beach** is more than serviceable, getting less weedy and reefy as you stroll further north. For **boat tickets** try Nautilus, just back from the water; there's no bank, but an **ATM** near the ferry dock. **Car and bike rental** is available from Thomas (Ⓣ22850 73444, Ⓦwww.thomas-rental.gr); the Elin petrol station is 500m behind the beach, off the Tholária road. **Accommodation** is scattered around the backstreets on the hill behind and is easy to find; above the jetty is the well-priced and very comfortable hotel *Karkisia* (Ⓣ22850 73180, Ⓦhttp://karkisia.amorgos.net, or contact through nearby bakery; Easter–Oct; ❹), and behind it the friendly *Pension Christina* (Ⓣ22850 73236, Ⓦwww.christina-pension.amorgos.net; ❸) with bright, cheerful rooms. In the Lakkí area, behind the beach and on the road to Tholária, is the friendly official **campsite**, *Aegiali Camping* (Ⓣ22850 73500, Ⓦwww.aegiali-camping.gr), usually busier than the one in Katápola. For **eating out**, *Asteria* on the platía has good food at excellent prices, while *Limani* in a narrow street beyond is very popular and has both traditional Amorgan food as well as occasional Thai nights. *To Steki tou Kritikou* at the start of the beach sometimes has live music.

There is a **bus service** up to each of the two villages east of and 200m above Eyiáli bay, with 3–8 departures daily up and down (a timetable is posted by the harbour bus stop), but it would be a shame to miss out on the beautiful **loop walk** linking them with the port (2–3hrs). Head northeast out of Eyiáli and take the first right after the Tholária turning. Join a well-made *kalderími* path that climbs up, below the cliff-hung tiny cave-church of Ayía Triádha, to **LANGÁDHA** village. The *Artemis Pension* (Ⓣ22850 73315, Ⓦwww.artemis-pension.gr; ❸), just before the upper car park, is a friendly place to stay, and owns the good *Loza* taverna in a small nearby square. Beyond Langádha, turn left off the main onward path towards the pretty, monastery-like Panayía Epanohorianí, then continue around the hillside to Tholária.

THOLÁRIA is named after vaulted Roman tombs found around Vígla, the site of ancient Aegiale on a hill opposite the village, but there is little to see beyond the bases of statues and traces of city walls incorporated into later terracing. Tholária has several good **taverna-cafés** including, near the church, the *Kali Kardia,* and next door *Thalassino Oneiro* (Ⓣ22850 73345; ❷) with basic rooms, plus the hospitable *Vigla* hotel (Ⓣ22850 73288, Ⓕ22850 73332; B&B ❺) by the car park.

Íos

Though not terribly different – geographically or architecturally – from its immediate neighbours, no other island attracts the same vast crowds of young people as **Íos**. However, it is has worked hard to shake off its late-twentieth-century reputation for alcohol and drug excesses and to move the island's tourism upmarket; buildings are now painted white with blue trim, instead of garish psychedelic hues, camping rough is discouraged, and Greece's early closing laws are enforced, so bars no longer stay open all night, though dancing clubs do. The island is still extremely popular with the young backpacker set, who take over the island with a vengeance in July and August, although at other times a large number of young families are choosing to holiday here.

The only real villages are clustered in a western corner of the island, and development elsewhere is somewhat restricted by poor roads. As a result there are still some very quiet beaches with just a few rooms to rent. Yialós itself has one of the best and safest natural harbours in the Cyclades. Most visitors stay along the arc delineated by the port – at Yialós, where you'll arrive (there's no airport), in Hóra above it, or at the beach at Mylopótamos. **Buses** constantly shuttle between Koumbára, Yialós, Hóra and Mylopótamos, with a daily service running roughly from 8am to midnight; you should never have to wait more than twenty minutes during high season, but at least once try the short walk up (or down) the stepped path between Yialós and Hóra. There are public and private buses running to the beaches at Manganári and Ayía Theodhóti; they sell return tickets only and are a bit expensive (€6). To rent your **own transport**, try Jacob's Car and Bike Rental (Ⓣ22860 91047) in Yialós or Vangelis Bike Rental (Ⓣ22860 91919) in Hóra. For a motorboat, head to Mylopótamos where Ios Boat Rental (Ⓣ22860 91301, Ⓦwww.iosboat.com) requires no licence, just a credit card. For a quick escape from the party atmosphere at the height of the season, try one of the daily excursions around quiet nearby beaches on the wooden *Leigh Browne* sailing vessel moored in the harbour (€20).

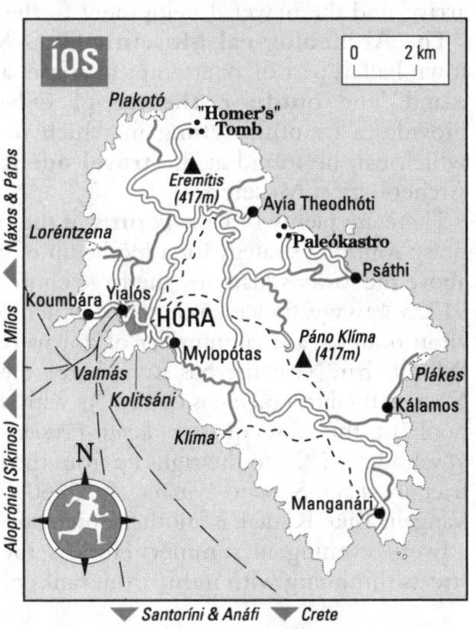

Despite its past popularity, **sleeping on the beach** on Íos is discouraged these days; given the problem of theft, it's best to stick to the official campsites.

Yialós

From **YIALÓS** quayside, **buses** start just along to the right (east), while Yialós **beach** – surprisingly peaceful and uncrowded – is five minutes' walk in the same direction. You might be tempted to grab a room in Yialós as you arrive: owners meet the ferries, touting the town's **accommodation**, and there are also a couple of kiosks by the jetty that will book rooms for you. In shoulder season you can bargain for prices considerably lower than those listed below. *Hotel Mare Monte* (Ⓣ22860 91585, Ⓔmaremonte@otenet.gr; B&B ❹), about halfway down the beach, has clean spacious rooms, studios and a small pool. One of the best choices is the family-owned *Golden Sun* (Ⓣ22860 91110, Ⓦwww.goldensun.gr; ❹), about 300m up the road to Hóra, which has nice views and a pool, and the newly revamped *Yialos Beach* (Ⓣ22860 91421, Ⓦwww.yialosbeach.gr; ❺) with smart doubles and studios set around a pool, just behind the hospital. There are more rooms on the stepped path from Yialós to Hóra, although they can be noisy at night. *Ios Camping* (Ⓣ22860 91329), at the far south end of the waterfront, is friendly and clean and has a rather luxurious swimming pool. Yialós has other essentials, including an **ATM** near the quay, the large Marinopoulos supermarket and **tavernas**. The *Octopus Tree*, a small *kafenío* by the fishing boats, serves cheap fresh seafood caught by the owner; nearby *Enigma* is a warm, intimate space serving Cypriot cuisine.

Hóra

HÓRA (also called Íos Town, but often just "Village"), a twenty-minute walk up behind the port, is one of the more accessible picturesque towns in the Cyclades, filled with meandering arcaded lanes and whitewashed chapels, though it's pretty lively when the younger crowd moves in for the high season, and the laddish logos and inscriptions available on T-shirts and at tattoo parlours are not entirely in keeping with its upmarket aspirations. The main road divides it naturally into two parts: the old town climbing the hillside to the left as you arrive, and the newer development to the right.

The **Archeological Museum** (Tues–Sun 8.30am–3pm; €2), in the yellow town hall, is part of an attempt to attract a more diverse range of visitors to the island. The **outdoor theatre** of Odyssevs Elytis, behind the windmills, provides a beautiful setting in which to enjoy concerts and plays, details of which can be found at the **travel agent** and information booth next to the Archeological Museum.

There are plenty of basic **rooms** in the old part, although the bars can make it noisy. Your best strategy for a modicum of quiet is to wend your way up from just above the lower square (by the large church) to the excellent *Francesco's* (Ⓣ22860 91223, Ⓦwww.francescos.net/; ❸) which offers the best value on the island, with clean doubles, a small number of dorms (€12 per person) and spectacular views from its bar. Near the bus stop, there's the newer *Mediterraneo* (Ⓣ22860 91521, Ⓦwww.mediterraneo-ios.com; ❺), with nice balconied rooms overlooking a pool. In the new quarter *Lofos Pension* (Ⓣ22860 91481, Ⓔlofosvillagehotel @yahoo.com; ❹), to the right up from the Rollan supermarket, is a good bet. The friendly *Four Seasons Pension* (Ⓣ22860 91308, Ⓕ22860 91136; ❷), up from Vangelis Bike Rental, is another quiet, but still central, choice.

Every evening in summer, Hóra is the centre of the island's **nightlife**, its streets throbbing with music from ranks of competing discos and clubs – mostly free, or with a nominal entrance charge, and inexpensive drinks. (Do, however, be wary of drinks that are overly cheap, as a few unscrupulous bars still resort to selling *bomba*, a cheap local drink that gets you drunk fast and makes you sick. If in doubt, ask for spirits by brand name.) Most of the smaller **bars** and pubs are tucked into the thronging narrow streets of the old village on the hill, offering something for everyone, and you'll have no trouble finding them. Evenings tend to start out lower down in places like the *Fun Pub*, which also plays free films and has a pool table, and then progress around midnight to the bars up in the old town where *Rehab*, *Flames, Skorpion* and the *Red Bull Bar* are popular choices. Those looking to carry on, eventually stagger down to the main road, where the larger **dance clubs** such as *Scorpion* and *Sweet Irish Dreams* are clustered near the bus stop.

Eating is a secondary consideration, but there are plenty of cheap and cheerful *psistariés* and takeaway joints: sound choices include the Italian restaurant *Pinocchio*, *The Nest* taverna, and the *Lord Byron mezedhopolío* off the large church square – it's open year round and tries hard to recreate a traditional atmosphere, with old rebétika music and some good, unusual Greek food.

Around the island

The most popular stop on the island's bus routes is **MYLOPÓTAS (officially** Mylopótamas), the site of a magnificent beach with watersport facilities. Meltemi Extreme Watersports (Ⓣ22860 91680, Ⓦwww.meltemiwatersports.com), who also operate at Manganári beach, offer a variety of activities and hire, with a ten percent discount for Rough Guide readers.

Due to the large number of young travellers in Íos, **camping** is a popular option. *Far Out Beach Club* (Ⓣ22860 91468, Ⓦwww.faroutclub.com) is the larger of the campsites, with well-organized facilities, including a pool, laundry, Internet, ATM, good-value cafeteria. It is, however, very popular and can get noisy and crowded in August. They also have the adjacent hotel, *Far Out Village* (❺). *Purple Pig Stars* (Ⓣ22860 91302, Ⓦwww.purplepigstars.com) is a friendly, laid-back complex by the road up to Hóra, with clean bungalows (❷) and good camping facilities, including its own club and poolside bar. Nearby is the attractive and luxurious *Dionysos* hotel (Ⓣ22860 91301, Ⓦwww.dionysos-ios.gr; June–Sept; B&B ❼). Up the road at the far end of the beach, the French-run *Hotel Ios Plage* (Ⓣ22860 91301, Ⓦwww.iosplage.com; June–Sept; B&B ❹) have reasonable rooms, recently refurbished, with an excellent French cuisine restaurant on its terrace.

From Yialós, daily boats depart at around 10am (returning in the late afternoon; €12 return) to **Manganári** on the south coast, where there's a beach and a swanky hotel. Most people go from Yialós to Manganári by buses (€6 return), which leave Yialós about 1am and 1pm, calling at Hóra and Mylopótas and returning later in the afternoon.

Síkinos

Síkinos has so small a population that the mule ride or walk up from the port to the village was only replaced by a bus late in the 1980s and, until the new jetty was completed at roughly the same time, it was the last major Greek island where ferry passengers were still taken ashore in launches. With no dramatic characteristics, nor any nightlife to speak of, few foreigners make the short trip over here from neighbouring Íos and Folégandhros. There is now a **bank** with

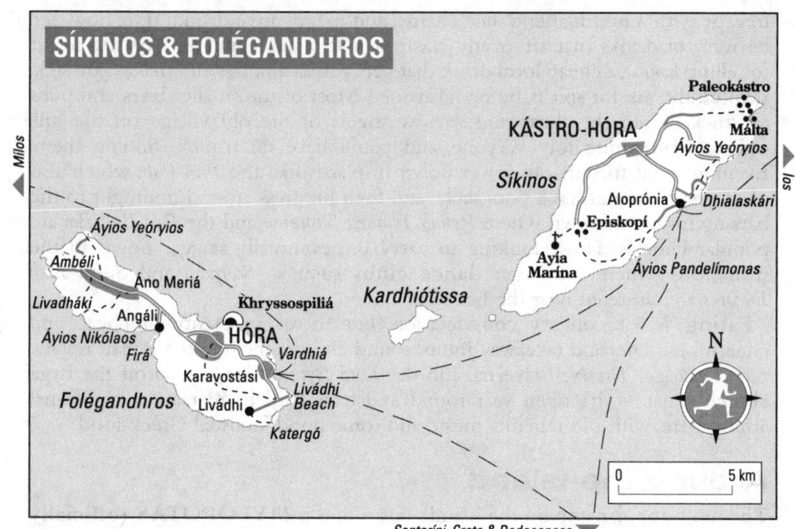

an **ATM**, and a **post office**, up in Kástro-Hóra, and you can sometimes change cash at the store in Alopronía.

Alopronía and Kástro-Hóra

Such tourist facilities as exist are concentrated in the little harbour of **ALOPRÓNIA**, with its long sandy beach, breakwaters and jetty. Many of the houses are summer holiday homes owned by ex-patriot Sikiniotes now resident in Athens or beyond. **Accommodation** owners such as Lucas meet the ferries; he has waters' edge studios (Ⓣ22860 51076; Ⓔlucassikinos@in.gr; ❸) on the opposite side of the bay, as well as rooms and studios among a cluster of buildings by the Eko petrol station (and nearby bus stop), at the back of the village, 700m from the harbour along the road to Kástro-Hóra. Nearer to the Eko is the comfortable and hospitable *Hotel Kamares* (Ⓣ22860 51234, Ⓣ22860 51281; ❸) and the smaller *Flora* (Ⓣ22860 51214, Ⓕ22860 51100, info at the harbour shop; ❷). The much pricier but luxurious *Porto Sikinos* complex (Ⓣ22860 51220, Ⓦwww.portosikinos.gr; June–Sept; ❻) is tucked into the hillside, just beyond the Flora shop and *Lucas* taverna. On the jetty side of the bay are two **tavernas** and two **café-bars**: the *Meltemi* has a small menu but well-prepared food; the laid-back *Rock* café, perched above the jetty, has great views.

The double village of **KÁSTRO-HÓRA** is served by the single island bus, which shuttles regularly (from around 7.15am–11.45pm) between the harbour and here, with a single evening extension (around sunset) out to Episkopí and its Roman Monument. On the ride up, the scenery turns out to be less desolate than initial views from the ferry suggest. Draped across a ridge overlooking the sea, the village is a delightfully unspoiled settlement, with most of the facilities being in the larger, northeastern Kástro, whereas Hóra (officially Apáno Horió) is mainly residential. The oil-press **museum** (summer 5–7pm; free), run privately by a Greek-American, is highly recommended. A partly ruined fortress-monastery, **Zoödhóhou Piyís** ("Life-giving Spring"), crowns the cliff-edged hill above, and is accessed by a stepped path out of the top of Kástro; the warden opens the church for a couple of hours in the evening from around 6pm – entrance is free, but donations to the restoration fund are very welcome. The architectural highlight of the place is the actual **Kástro**, a quadrangle of eighteenth-century mansions arrayed defensively around a blue-domed church. There are only a few **rooms** in town, including a beautiful room and some family apartments at the *Iliovasilema* café/*zaharoplastío* (Ⓣ22860 51173; ❷–❸) at the upper bus stop, between the two villages. The café also makes its own sweets including *pastélli*, a mixture of honey, sesame and orange, traditionally given as wedding and baptismal gifts. A good selection of **food** is available, along with fine local wine, at the central *Klimataria* and *To Steki tou Garbi* next door.

Folégandhros

The cliffs of **Folégandhros** rise sheer over 300m from the sea in places, and until the early 1980s they were as effective a deterrent to tourists as they always were to pirates. Folégandhros was used as an island of political exile right up until 1974, but life in the high, barren interior has been eased since the junta years by the arrival of electricity and the construction of a road running lengthways from the harbour to Hóra and beyond. Development has been given further impetus by the recent increase in tourism and the mild commercialization this has brought. An expansion in accommodation for most budgets, and improvement in ferry arrival times, means there is no longer much local tolerance of sleeping rough on the beaches – although in high summer there may be no accommodation left for late arrivals. The increased wealth and trendiness of the heterogeneous clientele are reflected in fancy jewellery and clothes shops. Yet away from showcase Hóra and the beaches, the countryside remains mostly pristine, and is largely devoted to the cultivation of barley, the mainstay of many of the Cyclades before the advent of tourism. Donkeys and their paths are also still very much in evidence, since the terrain on much of the island is too steep for vehicle roads.

Karavostási and around

KARAVOSTÁSI, the port whose name simply means "ferry stop", serves as a last-resort base; it has several **hotels** and plenty of rooms but little atmosphere. Best value is *Hotel Aeolos* (Ⓣ22860 41205, Ⓦwww.aeolos-folegandros.gr; June–Sept; ❹) at mid-beach, while *Vardia Bay* (Ⓣ22860 41277, Ⓦwww.vardiabay.com; B&B ❻) has rooms and studios in a great location above the jetty. The modern *Vrahos Hotel* (Ⓣ22860 41450, Ⓦwww.hotel-vrahos.gr; May–Sept; ❺) has nice rooms on the far side of the bay. *Kali Kardhia* **taverna** above the harbour has an excellent traditional menu, and there are a couple of pleasant beach **bars** including the *Syrma* ouzerí, housed in a converted boathouse. There are many buses a day in summer to Hóra, from where further buses run to Áno Meriá or Angáli beach; Spyros's **motorbike rental** (Ⓣ22860 41448) is cheaper than its counterparts in Hóra. Ferry tickets are available at the Makrati agency.

The closest **beach**, other than the narrow main shingle strip, is the smallish, sand-and-pebble **Vardhiá**, signposted just north over the tiny headland. Some fifteen minutes' walk south lies **Livádhi**, a rather average beach with tamarisk trees and the island's official **campsite**, *Livadhi Camping* (Ⓣ & Ⓕ22860 41204; June–Sept), which is good and friendly, with a café-restaurant, although the hot water supply can be erratic.

Touted as the island's most scenic beach, **Katergó** is a 300-metre stretch of pea-gravel with two offshore islets, on the southeastern tip of the island. Most visitors come on a boat excursion from Karavostási or Angáli, but you can also get there on foot (20min) from the hamlet of Livádhi, itself a 15-minute dirt road walk inland from Livádhi beach. Be warned, though, that it's a rather arduous and stony trek, with a final 80m descent on loose-surfaced paths; there is no shade on the walk or the beach.

Hóra

The island's real character and appeal are to be found in the spectacular **HÓRA**, perched on a cliff-edge plateau some 35 minutes' walk from the dock; an hourly high-season **bus** service (6 daily spring & autumn) runs from morning until late at night, with additional services for ferries. Locals and foreigners – hundreds of them in high season – mingle at the cafés and tavernas under the trees of the two adjacent central squares, passing the time undisturbed by traffic, which is banned from the village centre. Towards the northern cliff-edge, and entered through two arcades, the defensive core of the medieval **kástro** is marked by ranks of two-storey residential houses, with repetitive stairways and slightly recessed doors.

From the cliff-edge Platía Poúnda, where the bus stops, a path with views down the northern coastline zigzags up to the wedding-cake church of **Kímisis Theotókou**, whose unusual design includes two little fake chapels mounted astride the roof. The church, formerly part of a nunnery, is on the gentlest slope of a pyramidal hill and is a favourite spot for watching some of the Aegean's most spectacular sunsets.

Practicalities

Accommodation around Hóra includes both hotels and rooms, with concentrations around the Platía Poúnda bus stop near the eastern entrance to the village and around the southern ring road which becomes the road to Áno Meriá. Of the hotels, the *Polikandia* (ⓣ22860 41322, ⓕ22860 41323; ④–⑤), around a garden just before the bus stop square, is a good choice, with some new studios. The only hotel actually within old Hóra is the traditional *Castro* (ⓣ22860 41230, ⓦwww.hotel-castro.com; breakfast €11; ④–⑥), with three rather dramatic rooms looking directly out to a precipitous drop to the sea. Near the southern ring-road, the *Aigio* hotel (ⓣ22860 41468; April–Sept; ④) has **Internet** facilities and a minibus to meet ferries; the family also has the immaculate *Evgenia/Embati* rooms (April–Oct) near the bus stop. At the western edge of Hóra, below the road to Áno Meriá, the *Anemoussa* (ⓣ22860 41077; May–Oct; ④) has some of the most spectacular views out over the northern sea.

Hóra's dozen or so **restaurants** are surprisingly varied. The *Folegandhros* ouzerí-snack bar in the first plaza, Platía Dounávi, is a popular hangout with information, board games and **Internet** connection. In the adjacent Platía Kondaríni are the very popular *Melissa*, *Piatsa*, *Kritikos* and *Chic*. *Pounda*, near the bus stop, has a pleasant shady garden.

Hóra is inevitably beginning to sprawl at the edges, and the burgeoning **nightlife** – a few dance bars along with a number of music pubs and ouzerís – is to the south, and away from most accommodation. *Patitiri* and *Greco* are two lively bars, while *Kellari* is a rustic and charming wine bar with a more relaxed atmosphere. A **post office**, **ATM** (Platía Dounávi), and **Internet** access in the Diaplous and Makrati travel agencies between Dounávi and Poúnda squares, complete the list of amenities.

The rest of the island

West of Hóra, a paved road threads its way along the spine of the island towards **ÁNO MERIÁ**, the other main settlement and winter residence for many of Hóra's inhabitants. After 4km you pass its first houses, and then the small **folk museum** (daily 5–8 pm, mid-June–mid-Sept; donation requested), on a nineteenth-century farm *(themoniá)* giving an insight into past rural life and with wonderful views of Hóra and its cliffs in the evening sunlight. Many of the features such as *alónia*, circular threshing floors for winnowing barley and legumes, and *dhendhrospítia*, high walls enclosing individual lemon or fruit trees, are still in use today. About 1.5km beyond the museum are a couple of grocery shops and *Mimis*, the best of the settlement's three tavernas, using locally produced food and open all year.

Up to seven times a day in high season, a **bus** trundles out here to drop people off at the long footpaths down to the various beaches on the southwest shore of the island; the end of the line is at **Taxiárhis**, near the *Iliovasilema* taverna. Muleteers await the buses here and will, for a fee, transport tourists down dirt roads to beaches at **Ambéli** and **Áyios Yeóryios**; the former is small, and can get crowded, the latter is a much better beach but faces north and is only comfortable when the wind blows from the south. **Livádhaki** beach, accessed by signed path from just beyond Taxiárhis, is an attractive beach with dunes and some tree shade.

A separate bus line starts from Hóra towards Áno Meriá, but turns steeply down to the attractive and popular, sheltered south coast beach of **Angáli**, where there are a few tavernas – the *Angali* is very well-priced, with good food. There are few **rooms** in the western part of the island, but the majority are around Angáli: they include *Pano to Kyma* (Ⓣ22860 41190; ❸) and *Panagiotis* (Ⓣ22860 41301; ❸).

Santoríni (Thíra)

As the ferry manoeuvres into the great caldera of **Santoríni**, the land seems to rise up and clamp around it. Gaunt, sheer cliffs loom hundreds of metres above, nothing grows or grazes to soften the awesome view, and the only colours are the reddish-brown, black and grey pumice striations layering the cliff face of **Thíra**, the largest island in this mini-archipelago, and the location of all but the smallest of its modern settlements. The landscape tells of a history so dramatic and turbulent that legend hangs as fact upon it.

From as early as 3000 BC, the island developed as a sophisticated outpost of Minoan civilization, until sometime between 1647 and 1628 BC when catastrophe struck: the volcano-island erupted, the second largest in human history and ejecting some 60 cubic km of magma. The island's heart sank below the sea, leaving a crater (**caldera**) 10km in diameter. Earthquakes and tsunami reverberated across the Aegean, Thíra was destroyed, and the great Minoan civilization on Crete was dealt a severe blow by the ensuing ash fallout; Thíra's history became linked with legends of Atlantis, the "Happy Isles Submerged by Sea". Modern tourists come here to take in the spectacular views of the crater, stretch out on the island's dark-sand beaches and absorb the peculiar, infernal geographic features. The tourism industry has changed traditional island life, creating a rather expensive playground. There is one time-honoured local industry, however, that has benefited from all the outside attention: **wine**. Santoríni is one of Greece's most important producers, and the fresh, dry white

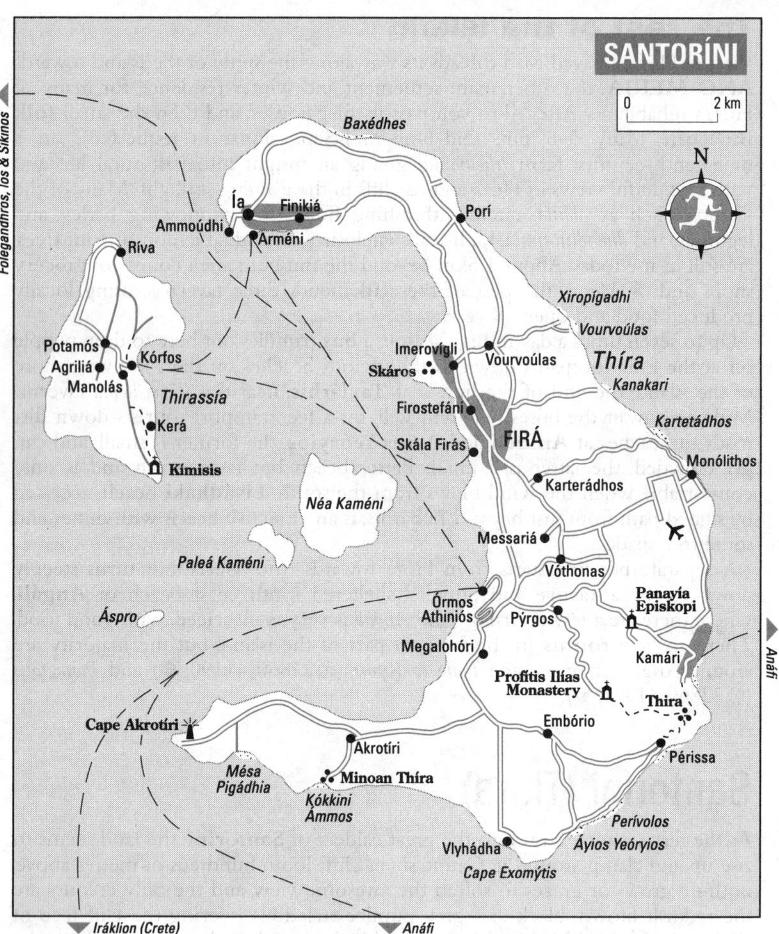

wines it is known for (most from the *assýrtiko* grape for which the region is known) are the perfect accompaniment to the seafood served in the many restaurants and tavernas that hug the island's cliffs.

Arrival

Ferries dock at the functional port of **Órmos Athiniós**, where infamously the cruise ship *Sea Diamond* sank while trying to moor in 2007. **Skála Firás** and **Ía** in the north are reserved for local ferries, excursion *kaïkia* and cruise ships. **Buses**, astonishingly crammed, connect Athiniós with the island capital Firá, and, less frequently, with Ía and the main beaches at Kamári and Périssa. Disembark quickly and take whatever bus is going, if you want to avoid a long wait or a tedious hike up. You'll be accosted at Athiniós by people offering rooms all over the island; in the summer it might be a good idea to pay attention to them, given the scramble for beds, in Firá especially. There are, however, various scams involving the promise of beds in Firá which turn out to be elsewhere; keep your wits about you, and if in doubt, ask someone else. From Skála Firás, you have the traditional route of 580 steps (about 45 minutes) up to Firá – not too difficult a walk, if you don't mind mule manure (avoid sandals) – or you can go by mule (€3.50, negotiable off-season) or cable car (summer only 6.30am–10pm, every 20min; €3.50, luggage €1.50 extra), so exhilarating a ride that you may want to take it for fun. The overstretched **airport** is on the east side of the island, near Monólithos; check Ⓦ www.ktel-santorini.gr for details of buses.

Firá

Half-rebuilt after a devastating earthquake in 1956, **FIRÁ** (also known as Thíra or Hóra) clings precariously to the edge of the enormous caldera. The rising and setting of the sun are especially beautiful when seen here against the Cycladic buildings lining the clifftop, and are even enough to make battling through the high-season crowds worthwhile.

Arrival, information and accommodation

Buses leave Firá from just south of Platía Theotokopoúlou to Périssa, Perívolos, Kamári, Monólithos, Akrotíri, Órmos Athiniós and the airport. The island's **taxi** base (Ⓣ 22860 22555) is near the bus station, within steps of the main square. If you want to see the whole island in a couple of days, a rented **motorbike** might do; try Moto Chris at the top of the road that leads down to *Santorini Camping*, while Ancient Thira Tours (Ⓣ 22860 23915) on the main street in Firá, hire out **mountain bikes** and quads. The Firá branch of Nomikos Travel, opposite the OTE, is friendly and organizes **excursions** and trips to ancient Thíra and Thirassía in conjunction with Kamari Tours (Ⓣ 22860 31390). The tiny state-run **tourist office** (daily 9am–midnight in season; Ⓣ 22860 25490), on the main street between the bus station and the main square, may also be able to help you out. There are several **Internet cafés** gathered on the main square, and a number of **launderettes** dotted around town, the best being We do Laundry, just above the road to the campsite.

Accommodation

Santoríni certainly isn't cheap, and properties in Firá with a view of the caldera tend to be expensive. **Firostefáni**, between Firá and Imerovígli, has slightly less expensive rooms with equally stunning views, though as the area gets trendier by the minute, it's hardly a bargain destination. Another good location, where you don't have to pay as much for the view, is **Karterádhos**, a small village about twenty minutes' walk southeast of Firá. The only other option for budget accommodation is *Santorini Camping* (Ⓣ 22860 22944, Ⓦ www.santorinicamping.gr), the nearest **campsite** to town. (The best campsite on the island is near Akrotíri village; see p.582.) Considering Santoríni's popularity, it's definitely worth phoning for accommodation in advance.

Firá

Archontiko Apartments By Áyios Minás church, below the cathedral Ⓣ 22860 24376, Ⓔ archontikoapartments@hotmail.com. Stunning antique-furnished apartments in a 350-year old stone house perched in a quiet spot over the caldera. May–Oct. ❺

Pelican On road to *Santorini Camping* Ⓣ 22860 23113, Ⓦ www.pelican.gr. Large hotel with spacious rooms near the centre with free Wi-Fi. B&B ❻

San Giorgio Tucked away to left of parking below main square Ⓣ 22860 23516, Ⓦ www.sangiorgiovilla.gr. Hospitable, excellent value, clean rooms, all with balconies (ten percent discount for Rough Guide readers); small pool at rear. Free transfers. March–Nov. ❹

Theoxenia Ypapandís Ⓣ 22860 22740, Ⓦ www.theoxenia.net. Stylish boutique hotel with large rooms right in the old town. Guests can also use the caldera-side pool at the nearby *Aresanna* hotel. B&B 7

Villa Rena 10 minutes' walk from town towards the folklore museum ⓣ22860 28130, ⓦwww.renasplace.gr. Comfortable hotel with a large pool in a quiet spot near the open-air cinema (ten percent discount for Rough Guide readers). Free transfers. May–Oct. 5

Firostefáni

Galini On waterfront ⓣ22860 22095, ⓦwww.hotelgalini.gr. Good-value, friendly hotel carved into the cliff face in a relatively quiet spot 10 minutes' walk from Firá. March–Nov. 6

Manos Apartments On waterfront ⓣ22860 23202, ⓦwww.manos-apartments.gr. Large, cool studios and apartments with large verandas and great views. April–Oct. Breakfast €5. 6

Mylos On main street ⓣ22860 23884. One of the cheaper hotel options in Firostefáni; rooms come with all mod cons and balconies. April–Oct. 5

Karterádhos

Pension George ⓣ22860 22351, ⓦwww.pensiongeorge.com. Comfortable rooms and studios, pool, and a good welcome, just fifteen minutes' walk from Firá. 4

The Town

Along with the views, Firá also has several museums. Between the cathedral and bus station, the **Museum of Prehistoric Thira** (Tues–Sun 8.30am–7.30pm; €3 includes entrance to the Archeological Museum), has informative displays of fossils, Cycladic art and astonishing finds from Akrotíri. The **Archeological Museum** (Tues–Sun 8am–5pm; €3 includes entrance to the above), near the cable car to the north of town, is less well presented, but has a collection which includes a curious set of erotic Dionysiac figures. The handsome **Megaro Ghyzi** (Mon–Sat 10.30am–1.30pm & 5–8pm, Sun 10.30am–4.30pm; €3), just north of the Archeological Museum in an old mansion owned by the Catholic diocese of Santoríni, has been restored as a cultural centre, and has a good collection of old prints and maps as well as photographs of the town before and after the 1956 earthquake. Further north along the caldera, the **Thíra Foundation** (signed "Wall-paintings of Thera", daily 10am–8pm; €3), housed in the galleries carved into the cliffside, contains superb life-size colour photo reproductions of the frescoes of Akrotíri. Towards the back of the town, north of the main square, is the extensive **Lignos Folklore Museum** (daily 10am–2pm & 6–8pm; €3), which features a completely furnished nineteenth-century house with period winery, cavern, garden and workshops, as well as a gallery and historical archive.

Eating and nightlife

Firá's **restaurants** are primarily aimed at the tourist market, but for dependably good food with a sensational view (and prices to match) find *Aris*, below the *Loucas* hotel, or try the *Flame of the Volcano*, the last of the caldera-side restaurants north past the cable-car station (towards Firostefáni). *Mama's House*, just north of the main square on the road to Ía, is an excellent, backpacker-friendly spot with cheap, filling dishes and views from its balcony. On Erythroú Stavroú, the first street up from the main square, *Nikolas* is an old and defiantly traditional taverna, but it can be hard to get a table; the best moderately priced choice is *Naoussa*, further north on the same street, upstairs on the right. Opposite the cathedral, *Sphinx* offers exotic pasta dishes with a Greek twist at a price, while *Calderimi* nearby serves excellent Italian and Mediterranean food.

Most of the **nightlife** is northwest of the central square on Erythroú Stavroú, often not starting much before midnight and busiest between 1–6am: *Murphy's Bar* is a well-priced Irish pub with all the obligatory hilarity, while above there's the pricier, slightly cooler *Enigma* and *Koo* with chilled-out music and candles to set the scene. The best bars from which to admire the caldera are *Franco's* and

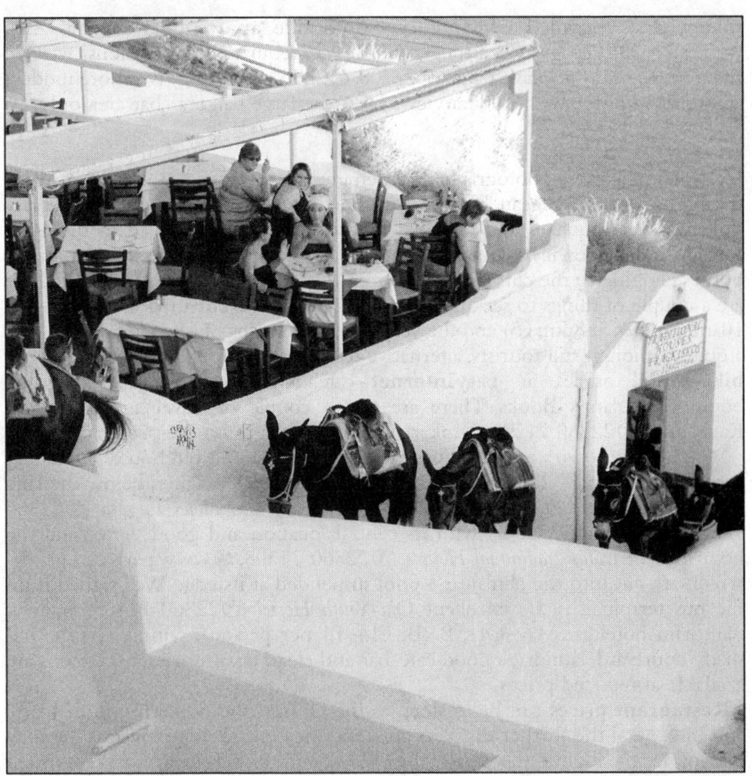

▲ Sea-view restaurant, Santoríni

Palia Kameni, two rather exclusive and pricey cocktail bars with unbeatable locations. More laid-back, but set back from the caldera, is the *Kira Thira* bar, which also offers a wine-tasting package. There is an open-air **cinema** near the folklore museum.

Northern Santoríni

Once outside Firá, the rest of Thíra comes as a surprise. The volcanic soil is highly fertile, with most of the more level areas terraced and cultivated: mainly grapes, but some tomatoes, pistachios and wheat, all still harvested and planted by hand. However, the advent of tourism has led to much unsightly ribbon development along the roads, and away from the caldera Santoríni is undoubtedly one of the less attractive Cycladic islands.

A satisfying – if demanding – approach to **Ía**, 12km from Firá in the northwest of the island, is to walk the stretch from **IMEROVÍGLI** (Merovígli), 3km out of Firá, using a spectacular footpath along the lip of the caldera; the walk takes around two hours. Jutting up from the side of the cliff is the conspicuous conical rock of **Skáros**, a Venetian fortress from 1207 and until the eighteenth century the site of an important settlement, although now almost all the structures have succumbed to earthquakes. It can be mounted along a steep but obvious trail for unsurpassed views over the caldera and back to Thíra.

Imerovígli is crowded with luxury, caldera-side **apartments** such as *Astra* (Ⓣ22860 23641, Ⓦwww.astra.gr; B&B ❽), requiring reservations well in advance; *Kastro Katerinas* (Ⓣ22860 22708, Ⓕ22860 23398; ❺) is a more moderately priced hotel, with caldera views from the large balcony/bar area only.

Ía and around

ÍA (Oía), the most photographed settlement on the island, was once a major fishing port of the Aegean, but it has declined in the wake of economic depression, wars, earthquakes and depleted fish stocks. Partly destroyed in the 1956 earthquake, the town has been sympathetically reconstructed, its multicoloured houses clinging to the cliff face. Apart from the caldera and the town itself, there are a couple of things to see, including the **Naval Museum** (Mon & Wed–Sun 10am–2pm & 5–8pm; €3) and the very modest remains of a Venetian castle. Ía is a quieter, though still touristy, alternative to Firá, with a **post office** and several **bike-rental** offices, an **easyInternet** café, and a good foreign-language bookshop, Atlantis Books. There are also a couple of travel agencies – try Karvounis (Ⓣ22860 71290, Ⓔmkarvounis@otenet.gr), on the pedestrian street.

Much of the town's **accommodation** is in its restored old houses, including the *Hotel Laouda* (Ⓣ22860 71204, Ⓕ22860 71274; ❺), perched below the rim, the popular *Hotel Anemones* (Ⓣ22860 71220; ❺), the *Hotel Fregata* (Ⓣ22860 71221, Ⓕ22860 71333; ❺) with its central location and good views; and the luxurious *Perivolas Traditional Houses* (Ⓣ22860 71308, Ⓦwww.perivolas.gr; ❼), which are cut into the cliff near a pool suspended at its edge. Well signed from the bus terminal, is the excellent *Oia Youth Hostel* (Ⓣ22860 71465, Ⓦwww.santorini-hotel.gr; May–Oct; B&B; €14–16 per person), with a terrace and shady courtyard, laundry, a good café-bar and clean dormitories; excursions are available at reduced prices.

Restaurant prices can be as steep as the cliffs at the western end of town, and in general the further east you go along the central ridge towards the new end of Ía, the better the value: the *Anemomilos* and *Laokastri* are two such examples. Slightly removed from the sunset tourist stampede, the pleasant *Karma*, serving Eastern cuisine, is on the road leading down to the youth hostel, while, for a splurge, *1800* is often regarded as the finest restaurant on the island, serving a highly refined Mediterranean cuisine. **Nightlife** revolves around sunset-gazing, for which people are coached in from all over the island, creating traffic chaos and driving up prices, though the sunset is little different seen from Ía than from Firá.

Below the town, two sets of 220-odd steps switchback hundreds of metres down to two small harbours: one to **Ammoúdhi**, for the fishermen, and the other to **Arméni**, where the excursion boats dock. Both have decent fish tavernas, the one in Arméni specializing in grilled octopus lunches.

The east coast

Beaches on Thíra, to the east and south, are long black stretches of volcanic sand which get blisteringly hot in the afternoon sun. They're no secret, and in the summer the crowds can be a bit overpowering.

In the southeast, **KAMÁRI** is popular with package-tour operators, and hence more touristy. Nonetheless it's quieter (apart from airport noise) and cleaner than most, with a well-maintained seafront promenade, and is home to a decent diving centre. There's a range of beachfront **accommodation**, including *Hotel Nikolina* (Ⓣ22860 32363, Ⓔnikolina-htl@hol.gr; ❸), with basic but cheap rooms towards the southern end of the beach, as well as the *White House* (Ⓣ699 70 91 488; ❹) and further north along the beach, the friendly *Sea Side Hotel*

(Ⓣ22860 33403, Ⓦwww.seaside.gr; May–Oct; ④), above the recommended *Giorgio's* restaurant. *Rose Bay Hotel* (Ⓣ22860 33650, Ⓦwww.rosebay.gr; April–Oct; B&B ⑦) is a much pricier option, with a pleasant pool setting, set back from the beach amongst other luxurious hotels in the north part of town. At the foot of Mount Profitis Ilías, a good choice is the *Villa Ostria* (Ⓣ22860 31727, Ⓦwww.villaostria.gr; ④), a friendly, family-run oasis of studios and apartments in pleasant contrast to the resort's many large hotel blocks.

Psistaria Kritikos, a taverna-grill frequented by locals, is one of the better places to **eat** on the island. It's a long way out of Kamári on the road up to Messariá, and too far to walk, but the bus stops outside. There are plenty of cafés and restaurants behind the beach, though many are expensive or uninspiring. *Saliveros*, in front of the *Hotel Nikolina*, has taverna food at reasonable prices, and *Almira*, next to *Sea Side Rooms*, is a smarter restaurant and only a little more expensive. For a seafood splurge, try *Skaramangas*. Kamári is a family resort with little in the way of clubs and nightlife, but there is a good open-air **cinema** near the campsite. On the seafront, Navy's Diving Centre (Ⓣ22860 31006, Ⓦwww.navys.gr) offers courses for beginners and volcanic reef diving for certified divers. West of Kamári is **Panayía Episkopí**, the most important Byzantine monument on the island. Built in the eleventh century, it was for centuries the setting of conflict between Orthodox Greeks and Catholics, but is most notable today for its carved iconostasis of light blue marble with a white grain. A visit can be combined with the **Canava Roussos winery** (May–Sept daily 11am–7pm; free), 1km away, and the abandoned village of Exogoniá.

Things are considerably scruffier at **PÉRISSA**, around the cape. Because of its beach and abundance of cheap rooms, it's crowded with backpackers. *Camping Perissa Beach* (Ⓣ22860 81343) is right behind the beach and has plenty of shade but is also next to a couple of noisy late-night bars. There is also a basic youth hostel on the road into Périssa: *Anna* (Ⓣ22860 82182, Ⓔannayh@otenet.gr; €8 per person). There are plenty of cheap rooms in the same area and some upmarket hotels behind the beach; the modern *Meltemi Hotel* (Ⓣ22860 81325, Ⓦwww.meltemivillage.gr; B&B ⑤) on the main road, which also runs the nearby water park, is a good choice. The beach itself extends several kilometres to the west, through Perívolos to Áyios Yeóryios, sheltered by the occasional tamarisk tree and with beach bars dotted along at intervals. *Dichtia* ("Nets") and *Aquarius* are two excellent restaurants here.

Kamári and Périssa are separated by the Mésa Vounó headland, on which stood **ancient Thira** (Tues–Sun 8.30am–2.30pm; free), the post-eruption settlement dating from 915 BC through to the Venetian period. Excursion buses go up from Kamári (€8), staying two hours at the site (ask at Ancient Thira Tours, Ⓣ22860 31827, at the foot of the Kamári hill), but you can also ride a donkey up (€15) or walk the interminably looping cobbled road, Archaias Thiras, starting from Ancient Thira Tours. A more interesting route is the zigzag path that starts beside the *Antinea* hotel and goes via the whitewashed cliff-set Zoödhóhou Piyís church where a cave contains one of Thíra's few freshwater springs. The path meets the road at a saddle between Mésa Vounó and Profitis Ilías, where a refreshments van sells drinks. The site can also be reached by a stony, shadeless path from Périssa; from either it's less than an hour's walk. From here, the path to the site passes a chapel dating back to the fourth century AD before skirting round to the Temenos of Artemidoros with bas-relief carvings of a dolphin, eagle and lion representing Poseidon, Zeus and Apollo. Next, the trail follows the sacred way of the ancient city through the remains of the agora and past the theatre. Most of the ruins (dating mainly from Hellenistic and Roman times) are difficult to place, but the site is impressively large and the views are awesome.

Inland Santoríni

By way of contrast to the coast, **MESSARIÁ,** northwest of Kamári, has a skyline consisting solely of massive church domes that lord it over the houses huddled in a ravine. The **Arhondikó Aryírou** (daily 9am–2pm & 4.30–7pm; €4) is a fully restored nineteenth-century mansion combining Neoclassical elements with island architecture. South of Pýrgos and towards Megalohóri, are scattered a few of Santoríni's most important **wineries**, the largest of which, Boutari (just out of Megalohóri, Ⓦwww.boutari.gr), and Santo (near Pýrgos, Ⓦwww.santowines.gr) offer the most comprehensive tours (€2–3), complete with multi-media presentations. Slightly more hidden on the road to Kamári are smaller wineries, such as the welcoming Canava Roussos, Antoniou and Koutsoyianopoulos – the last is also home to the **Wine Museum** (daily noon–8pm; €4 includes tasting) – which offer a more intimate glimpse at the wine-making process. Whatever the scale of the tour, none is complete without a taste of Santoríni's prized dessert wine, **visánto** (reminiscent of the Tuscan *vin santo*), among the finest wines produced in Greece. Tour prices at the smaller wineries (€2–5) usually include tastings, while samples are available from the larger wineries for a nominal fee.

Akrotíri and the south coast

Evidence of the Minoan colony that once thrived here has been uncovered at the ancient site of Minoan Thira at **Akrotíri** (closed at the time of writing, for safety work, but check with the prehistoric museum in Firá, see p.578), at the southwestern tip of the island. The site was inhabited from the Late Neolithic period, through to the seventeenth century BC. Tunnels through the volcanic ash uncovered structures, two and three storeys high, first damaged by earthquake, then buried by eruption. Only a small part of what was the largest Minoan city outside of Crete has been excavated thus far, but progress is being made. Many of the lavish frescoes that once adorned the walls are currently exhibited in Athens, though you can see excellent reproductions at the Thíra Foundation in Firá (see p.578).

Akrotíri itself can be reached by bus from Firá or Périssa. The newest and best **campsite** on the island, *Caldera View Camping* (Ⓣ22860 82010, Ⓕ22860 81889), is situated here, as is the excellent *Glaros* **taverna**, on the way to **Kókkini Ámmos** (Red Beach), which has fine food, though the equally good *Dolphins Taverna* is better situated on the water. Kókkini Ámmos is about 500m from the site and is quite spectacular, with high reddish-brown cliffs above sand of the same colour. There's a drinks stall in a cave hollowed into the base of the cliff. It's a better beach than the one below the site, but gets crowded in season.

The Kaméni islets and Thirassía

From either Firá or Ía, boat excursions and local ferries run to the charred volcanic islets of **Paleá Kaméni** (formed 46–1458 AD) and **Néa Kaméni** (formed 1707–1950). At Paleá Kaméni you can swim from the boat to hot springs with sulphurous mud, and Néa Kaméni, with its own mud-clouded hot springs, features a demanding hike to a smouldering, volcanically active crater. Prices range from €10 for transport on a large ferry to about €30 for a more intimate guided tour on a traditional *kaïki*. The glass-bottom *Calypso* makes the same excursion for €20 and hovers over the volcanic reefs at the end of each journey to allow passengers a peek at the depths of Santoríni's flooded crater.

Moving on

When it comes to **leaving** Santoríni, especially for summer evening ferry departures, it's best to buy your ticket in advance. Note, too, that although the bus service stops around midnight, a taxi isn't expensive (about €6 from Firá to Athiniós). Incidentally, **ferry information** from any source is notoriously unreliable on Thíra and rival agencies don't inform you of alternatives – Nomikos Travel (Ⓣ22860 23660), with seven branches, is the largest, though Pelikan (Ⓣ22860 22220) is also recommended. In any case, it's wise to enquire about your options at several agencies and triple-check departure times before working your way back to the port. If you do get stranded in Athiniós, there's no place to stay, and the tavernas are mediocre, though there is **Internet** access at @thinios.com café. With time on your hands, it's probably worth calling for a taxi (Ⓣ22860 22555) or zigzagging the 3.5km up to the closest village, **Megalohóri**.

The boat excursions and local ferries also continue to the relatively unspoilt islet of **Thirassía**, which was once part of Thíra until shorn off by an eruption in the third century BC. It's an excellent destination, except during the lunch-hour, tour-boat rush. At other times, the island is one of the quietest in the Cyclades, with views as dramatic as any on Thíra. The downside is that there is no sandy beach, no nightlife and nowhere to change money, though there is an **ATM**.

Most tour boats head for the village of **Kórfos**, a stretch of shingle backed by fishermen's houses and high cliffs. It has a few tavernas, including *Tonio* which stays open when the day-trippers have gone, but no rooms. From Kórfos a stepped path climbs up to **MANOLÁS**, nearly 200m above and where donkeys are still used for transport. Manolás straggles along the edge of the caldera, an untidy but attractive small village that gives an idea of what Thíra was like before tourism arrived there. It has a bakery, a couple of shops and the friendly *Panorama* and *Candouni* tavernas which both do a great octopus *souvláki*, and open for the midday rush. Dhimitrios Nomikos has **rooms** (Ⓣ22860 29102; ❷) overlooking the village from the south.

The best **excursion** from Manolás is to follow the unmade road heading south; about halfway along you pass the church of Profitis Ilías on a hilltop to the left. From here an old and overgrown trail descends through the deserted caldera-side village of **Kerá**, before running parallel with the road to the **monastery of the Kímisis** above the southern tip of the island. Minoan remains were excavated in a pumice quarry to the west of here in 1867, several years before the first discoveries at Akrotíri, but there is nothing to be seen today.

Ferries run to Thirassía from Órmos Athiniós five times a week; ask at Santo Star (Ⓣ22860 23082, Ⓦwww.santostar.gr) in Firá for details. There is no problem taking a car or rental bike over, but fill up with petrol first.

Anáfi

A ninety-minute boat ride to the east of Santoríni, **Anáfi** is the last stop for ferries and is something of a travellers' dead end, with no high-season ferries on to Crete or the Dodecanese, and no bank or ATM. Not that this is likely to bother most of the visitors, who come here for weeks in midsummer to enjoy the island's beaches.

Although idyllic geographically, Anáfi is a harsh place, its mixed granite and limestone core overlaid by volcanic rock spewed out by Thíra's eruptions. Apart

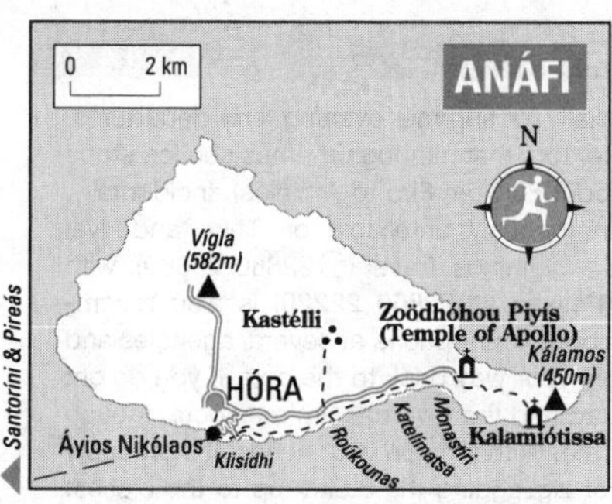

from the few olive trees and vines grown in the valleys, the only plants that seem to thrive are prickly pears.

The harbour and Hóra

The tiny harbour hamlet of **ÁYIOS NIKÓLAOS** has a taverna, *Akroyiali Popi's*, with a few rooms (Ⓣ22860 61218; ❸), and a travel agent selling boat tickets next door, plus a café/snack bar at the inland end. In August there are enough Greek visitors to fill all the rooms on the island, so it's a good idea to book ahead. In season a bus runs from the harbour up to Hóra every two hours or so, 9am to 11pm, to stops at both ends of the village.

HÓRA itself, adorning a conical hill, is a stiff 25-minute climb up the obvious broad concrete path which short-cuts the modern road. Exposed and blustery when the *meltémi* is blowing, Hóra can initially seem a rather forbidding ghost town. This impression is slowly dispelled as you discover the hospitable islanders taking their coffee in sheltered, south-facing terraces, or under the barrel vaulting that features in domestic architecture here and in Santoríni, partly due to the lack of timber for making normal roofs.

For accommodation, try the *Ta Plagia* (Ⓣ22860 61308, Ⓦwww.taplagia.gr; B&B ❷–❸) with rooms, studios and family houses, plus good home-made breakfasts and Internet facilities, or *Panorama* (Ⓣ & Ⓕ22860 61292; May–Oct; ❷), at the east edge of the village, with stunning views south. Also recommended are the rooms of *Illiovasilema* (Ⓣ22860 61280, Ⓕ22860 61238; ❸) on the other side of the village (ask at *To Steki* restaurant if you can't find them). Evening **diners** seem to divide their custom between the simple, welcoming *To Steki*, with good food and barrel wine served on its terrace, and the more upmarket *Alexandhra's* on the central walkway. Nightlife takes place in *Mylos*, in a converted windmill in the village, and *Argo*, which is also a good spot for breakfast. For exploring Anáfi's roads by **bike**, you can rent one at either *Panorama* (see above) or Rent Moto-Bikes (Ⓣ22860 61280) at the other side of the village. There is also a **travel agency**, Jeyzed Travel (Ⓣ22860 61253), who sell boat tickets and arrange excursions around the island. Several tiny shops, a bakery and a **post office** round up the list of amenities.

East along the coast: beaches and monasteries

The glory of Anáfi is a string of south-facing beaches starting under the cliffs at Áyios Nikólaos, and accessible by road; four buses a day ply the route from Hóra, although walking is still an option. Head for **Klisídhi**, east of the harbour, which has 200m of gently shelving sand. Above the reed-and-tamarisk oasis backing the beach there are two cafés, a taverna, *Margaritas*, which has rooms (Ⓣ22860 61237, Ⓔanafi1@hol.gr; ❷), and the comfortable *Villa Apollon* (Ⓣ22860 61348; ❹) on the hillside above. Klisídhi can be reached by road but it's quicker to take the short clifftop path starting behind the power station at the harbour.

From a point on the paved road just east of Hóra, the **main path** skirting the south flank of the island roller-coasters in and out of several agricultural valleys that provide most of Anáfi's produce and fresh water. Just under an hour along, you veer down a side trail to **Roúkounas**, with some 500m of broad sand rising to tamarisk-stabilized dunes; unfortunately much of the area behind is used as a toilet by the many rough campers. A single indifferent taverna operates up by the main trail in season. Beyond Roúkounas, it's another half-hour on foot to the first of the exquisite half-dozen **Katelímatsa** coves, of all shapes and sizes, and 45 minutes to **Monastíri** beach, where the bus stops – all without facilities, so come prepared. Nudism is banned on Monastíri, because of its proximity to the monastery.

The monasteries

Between Katelímatsa and Kálamos, the main route keeps inland, to arrive at the **monastery of Zoödhóhou Piyís**, (two hours' walk from Hóra). The bus stops at a patch of bare ground a few hundred metres before the building. A ruined temple of Apollo is incorporated into the monastery buildings to the side of the main gate, while the courtyard, with a welcome cistern, is the venue for the island's major festival, celebrated eleven days after Easter. Go left immediately before the monastery to join the spectacular onward path to **Kalamiótissa**, a little monastery perched atop the abrupt limestone pinnacle at the extreme southeast of the island. It takes another hour to reach, but is eminently worthwhile for the stunning scenery and views over the entire south coast – there is no accessible water up here, so bring enough with you.

Travel details

Ferries

Most of the Cyclades are served by main-line ferries from **Pireás**. Boats for Kéa, and seasonally elsewhere, depart from **Lávrio**. There are regular services from **Ráfina** to Ándhros, Tínos and Mýkonos, with seasonal sailings elsewhere. All three ports are easily reached by bus from Athens. Between May to Sept there are also a few weekly sailings, to the most popular islands, from **Crete** and the **Eastern Aegean**.

The frequency of Pireás, Lávrio and Ráfina sailings given below is from Jan to Dec, and the timings are for both direct and indirect services. For other islands the listings are intended to give an idea of services from late June to early Sept, when most visitors tour the islands. During other months, expect departures to be at or below the minimum level listed, with some routes cancelled entirely. The *Blue Star* ships are usually the fastest for only slightly more than the price of standard tickets and much less than the cost of catamaran services.

All agents are required to issue computerized tickets, to conform to EU regulations and prevent the ferry overcrowding so common in the past. In high season (particularly Aug, Spring Break and elections), popular routes will be booked up well in advance, so it is important to check availability on arrival in Greece and book your outward and final inbound pre-flight tickets well ahead (particularly those returning to Pireás from the most popular islands). That said, agents are notoriously ill-equipped with advance information on ferry schedules, and purchasing a ticket too far in advance can lead to problems with delayed or cancelled boats. There is usually more space on ferries sailing between islands than to and from Pireás. For catamaran details see p.587.

Pireás to: Amorgós (3–7 weekly; 8–14hr); Dhonoússa (2–4 weekly; 8–13hr); Folégandhros (2–6 weekly; 12hr); Íos (4–9 weekly; 9–13hr); Iráklia (2–3 weekly; 8–10hr); Kímolos (0–4 weekly; 7–8hr); Koufoníssi (2–3 weekly; 8–11hr); Kýthnos (5–9 weekly; 3–4hr); Mílos (7–11 weekly; 5–10hr); Mýkonos (10–11 weekly; 5–6hr); Náxos (14–18 weekly; 5–8hr); Páros (18–25 weekly; 4–7hr); Sérifos (5–9 weekly; 4–6hr); Sífnos (5–9 weekly; 5–7hr); Síkinos (2 weekly; 11–13hr); Skhinoússa

(2–3 weekly; 8–10hr); Sýros (14–18 weekly; 4–5hr); Thíra (12–15 weekly; 8–16hr); Tínos (7 weekly; 5hr).

Lávrio to: Ándhros (0–1 weekly; 10hr); Folégandhros (0–1 weekly; 14hr); Íos (0–1 weekly; 13hr); Kéa (14–31 weekly; 50min); Kímolos (0–1 weekly; 16hr); Kýthnos (0–12 weekly; 2hr); Mílos (0–1 weekly; 17hr); Mýkonos (0–1 weekly; 7hr); Náxos (0–1 weekly; 10hr); Páros (0–1 weekly; 9hr); Síkinos (0–1 weekly; 13hr); Sýros (0–3 weekly; 5–7hr); Tínos (0–1 weekly; 6hr).

Ráfina to: Ándhros (15–40 weekly; 2hr); Folégandhros (0–1 weekly; 14hr); Íos (0–1 weekly; 9hr); Kímolos (0–1 weekly; 16hr); Mílos (0–1 weekly; 17hr); Mýkonos (13–28 weekly; 5hr); Náxos (0–2 weekly; 6hr); Síkinos (0–1 weekly; 13hr); Sýros (0–1 weekly; 3hr); Tínos (13–29 weekly; 4hr).

Amorgós to: Ándhros (2–3 weekly; 8hr); Astypálea (3 weekly; 1hr 30min); Dhonoússa (2–3 weekly; 1hr 30min); Iráklia (2–3 weekly; 1hr); Koufoníssi (2–3 weekly; 1hr); Mýkonos (2–3 weekly; 6hr); Náxos (6–8 weekly; 4hr); Páros (6–8 weekly; 5hr 30min); Skhinoússa (2–3 weekly; 1hr); Sýros (3–4 weekly; 7hr); Tínos (2–3 weekly; 7hr).

Anáfi to: Folégandhros (1 weekly; 4hr 30min); Íos (6–8 weekly; 2hr 30min); Náxos (6–8 weekly; 3hr 30min), Páros (6–8 weekly; 4hr); Síkinos (1 weekly; 4hr); Sýros (1 weekly; 10hr); Thíra (6–8 weekly; 1hr 30min & 2 weekly mail boats; 2hr).

Ándhros to: Amorgós (2 weekly; 8hr); Mýkonos (3 daily; 2hr 30min); Náxos (2 weekly; 7hr); Páros (1–4 weekly; 7hr); Sýros (4 weekly; 3hr); Tínos (3 daily; 2hr).

Dhonoússa to: Amorgós (3 weekly; 1hr 15min); Mýkonos (2–3 weekly; 6hr); Náxos (2–3 weekly; 5hr); Páros (2–3 weekly; 5hr 30min); Sýros (2–3 weekly; 7hr 30min); Tínos (2–3 weekly; 6hr 30min).

Folégandhros to: Íos (3–6 weekly; 1hr 30min); Kímolos (2 weekly; 2hr 30 min); Kýthnos (2 weekly; 8hr); Mílos (2 weekly; 2hr 30min); Náxos (3–6 weekly; 2hr 30min); Páros (3–6 weekly; 4hr); Sérifos (2 weekly; 5hr 30min), Sífnos (2 weekly; 5hr); Síkinos (6 weekly; 30min); Sýros (2 weekly; 5hr 30min).

Íos to: Anáfi (4 weekly; 4hr); Crete, Iráklioh (1 weekly; 10hr); Folégandhros (4–5 weekly; 1hr); Kímolos (1 weekly; 4hr); Mílos (1 weekly; 4hr); Mýkonos (1 daily; 2hr); Náxos (3 daily; 3hr); Páros (3 daily; 5hr); Sérifos (1 weekly; 5hr); Sífnos (1 weekly; 5hr 30min); Síkinos (4–5 weekly; 30min); Sýros (2–3 weekly; 6hr); Thíra (3 daily; 1hr).

Iráklia, Koufoníssi, Skhinoússa to: Amorgós (1 weekly; 40min–1hr 45min); Náxos (1 weekly; 1 hr); Páros (1 weekly; 2hr 15min).

Kéa to: Folégandhros (1 weekly: 13hr); Kýthnos (1 weekly; 1hr 20min); Mílos (1 weekly; 15hr); Náxos (1 weekly; 9hr); Páros (1 weekly; 8 hr); Sýros (1 weekly; 4hr).

Kímolos to: Folégandhros (2 weekly; 1hr); Kýthnos (2–5 weekly; 3hr 30min); Mílos, Adhámas (2–8 weekly; 1hr); Mílos, Pollónia (4 daily; 30min); Pireás (1–3 weekly; 6–9hr); Sérifos (2–5 weekly; 2hr 30min); Sífnos (2–5 weekly; 2hr); Síkinos (2 weekly; 90min); Thíra (2 weekly; 3hr).

Kýthnos to: Folégandhros (3–4 weekly; 8hr 30min); Íos (1–2 weekly; 8hr); Kéa (1–2 weekly; 1hr 30min); Kímolos (4–8 weekly; 3hr 30min); Mílos (4–8 weekly; 4hr); Sérifos (4–8 weekly; 1hr); Sífnos (4–8 weekly; 1hr 30min); Síkinos (1–2 weekly; 8hr), Sýros (1–2 weekly; 3hr); Thíra (3–4 weekly; 10hr).

Mílos to: Crete (Áyios Nikólaos, Iráklion, Sitía; 1–2 weekly; 8–12hr); Folégandhros (2–3 weekly; 1hr); Íos (2–3 weekly; 2hr); Kárpathos and Kássos (2 weekly; 14–17hr); Kímolos (2–5 daily *kaïkia* & 4–6 weekly ferries; 30min); Kýthnos (1 daily; 3hr); Rhodes and Hálki (2 weekly; 19–22hr); Sérifos (1 daily; 1hr 30min); Sífnos (1 daily; 2hr); Síkinos (2–3 weekly; 1hr 30min); Sýros (2 weekly; 6hr); Thíra (2–3 weekly; 3hr).

Mýkonos to: Ándhros (13–23 weekly; 2hr 30min); Ikaría (7 weekly; 1hr 15min); Íos (1 daily; 2hr); Kós (1 weekly; 8hr); Léros (1 weekly; 6 hr); Náxos (1 daily; 3hr); Páros (daily; 1hr 30min); Pátmos (1 weekly; 4hr); Rhodes (1 weekly; 10hr); Sámos (7 weekly; 3hr 40min); Sýros (1 daily; 1hr 15min); Tínos (13–22 weekly; 40min).

Náxos to: Amorgós (5–7 weekly; 2–6hr); Anáfi (3 weekly; 7hr); Ándhros (2 weekly; 4hr); Astypálea (1 weekly; 3hr 30min); Crete, Iráklion (1 weekly; 12hr); Dhonoússa (3–6 weekly; 5hr); Folégandhros (2 weekly; 4hr); Ikaría (1 weekly; 3hr 20min); Íos (2–8 weekly; 2hr); Iráklia (2–3 weekly; 1hr 30min); Kárpathos and Kássos (1 weekly; 9–11hr); Koufoníssi (2–3 weekly; 2hr 30min); Páros (15 weekly; 45min–1hr 30min); Síkinos (5 weekly; 3hr); Sámos (1–2 weekly; 6hr); Skhinoússa (2–3 weekly; 2hr); Sýros (6–8 weekly; 3hr); Thíra (at least 3 daily; 2hr 30min); Tínos (4–5 weekly; 4hr).

Páros to: Amorgós (4–6 weekly; 4hr); Anáfi (4–6 weekly; 9hr); Ándhros (4 weekly; 5hr); Andíparos (hourly from Parikía, 40min; hourly car ferry from Poúnda, 20min); Astypálea (1–2 weekly; 4hr 30min); Crete, Iráklion (1 weekly; 14hr); Folégandhros (4–6 weekly; 4hr 30min); Íos (2 weekly; 3hr 10min); Kárpathos and Kássos (1 weekly; 22–24hr); Mýkonos (1 weekly; 2hr 40min); Náxos (16 weekly; 40min–1hr 20min); Rhodes (1 weekly; 30hr); Síkinos (4–6 weekly; 4hr); Sýros (6–8 weekly; 2hr); Thíra (6 weekly; 3–8hr); Tínos (6–8 weekly; 1hr 30min).

Sérifos to: Folégandhros (2–3 weekly; 2hr 30min); Íos (1 weekly; 6hr 30min); Kímolos (2–5 weekly;

1hr 30min); Kýthnos (5–12 weekly; 30min); Mílos (5–10 weekly; 1hr 30min); Sífnos (5–12 weekly; 30min); Síkinos (2–3 weekly; 3hr); Sýros (2 weekly; 6hr); Thíra (1 weekly; 7hr).

Sífnos to: Folégandhros (2–3 weekly; 2hr); Íos (1 weekly; 6hr 30min); Kímolos (2–5 weekly; 1hr); Kýthnos (5–12 weekly; 1hr); Mílos (5–10 weekly; 1hr); Páros (2 weekly; 5hr); Sérifos (5–12 weekly; 30min); Síkinos (2–3 weekly; 2hr 30min); Sýros (2 weekly; 6hr 30min); Thíra (2–3 weekly; 7hr).

Síkinos to: Folégandhros (6 weekly; 30min); Íos (3–6 weekly; 2hr); Kímolos (2 weekly; 2hr); Kýthnos (2 weekly; 7hr 30min); Mílos (2 weekly; 2hr); Náxos (3–6 weekly; 3hr); Páros (3–6 weekly; 4hr 30min); Sérifos (2 weekly; 5hr), Sífnos (2 weekly; 4hr 30min); Sýros (2 weekly; 5hr); Thíra (3–6 weekly; 2hr).

Sýros to: Amorgós (3 weekly; 7hr); Ándhros (at least 2 weekly; 3hr 30min); Astypálea (2–3 weekly; 5hr); Folégandhros (1 weekly; 4hr 30min); Ikaría (7 weekly; 3hr 15min); Íos (2–4 weekly; 7hr); Iráklia (3 weekly; 7hr); Kéa (2–3 weekly; 4hr); Koufoníssi (3 weekly, 7hr 30min); Kýthnos (2 weekly; 3hr); Mílos (2 weekly; 5hr); Kímolos (2 weekly; 5hr); Mýkonos (at least 2 daily; 2hr); Náxos (at least 2 daily; 3hr); Páros (at least 2 daily; 2hr); Pátmos (1 weekly; 5hr 20min); Sámos (7 weekly; 6hr 40min); Sérifos (2 weekly; 4hr); Sífnos (2 weekly; 3hr 30min); Síkinos (1 weekly; 6hr); Skhinoússa (3 weekly; 8hr); Thíra (2–4 weekly; 8hr 30min); Tínos (at least 2 daily; 1hr).

Thíra to: Anáfi (4–6 weekly; 2hr; 2 weekly mail boats); Crete (Áyios Nikólaos, Iráklion, Sitía; 1–2 weekly; 4–7hr); Folégandhros (6–8 weekly; 1hr 30min); Íos (at least 3 daily; 1hr); Kárpathos and Kássos (2 weekly; 10–12hr); Mílos and Kímolos (2–4 weekly; 2hr); Mýkonos (daily; 2hr 30min); Náxos (at least 3 daily; 2hr); Páros (at least 3 daily; 3hr); Rhodes and Hálki (2 weekly; 15–18hr); Sérifos (1–2 weekly; 7hr); Sífnos (4–6 weekly; 7hr); Síkinos (6–8 weekly; 2hr); Sýros (6–8 weekly; 8hr); Thirassía (1–6 weekly; 30min); Tínos (3–5 weekly; 5hr).

Tínos to: Ándhros (at least 2 daily; 1hr); Íos (1 weekly; 8hr); Mýkonos (at least 2 daily; 30min); Náxos (3–4 weekly; 2hr); Páros (3–4 weekly; 1hr 30min); Sýros (at least 2 daily; 1hr); Thíra (3 weekly; 5hr).

Catamaran and small-boat services

Catamaran services operate during the summer season from Pireás and Ráfina, replacing winter ferries on some routes. The Cycladic routes are covered by Aegean Speed Lines (ⓦwww.aegeanspeedlines.gr), Hellenic Seaways (ⓦwww.hsw.gr), SeaJets (ⓦwww.seajets.gr), and NEL (ⓦwww.nel.gr). Catamaran travel is expensive; however, when time is an issue, these handy high-speed craft are a welcome addition to the conventional fleet. The slower *Express Skopelitis* plies daily in season between Náxos and Amorgós, overnighting at the latter and connecting Iráklia, Skhinoússa, Koufoníssi and Dhonoússa – for current info call ⓣ22850 71256.

Pireás to: Amorgós (1 weekly); Folégandhros (10 weekly; 3hr 35min); Íos (13 weekly; 3hr 30min); Kímolos (4 weekly; 2hr 45min); Mílos (17 weekly); Mýkonos (26 weekly); Náxos (21 weekly); Páros (25 weekly; 3hr 15min); Ráfina (12 weekly); Sérifos (14 weekly; 2hr 40min); Sífnos (22 weekly; 2hr 30min); Sýros (21 weekly; 2hr 55min); Thíra (27 weekly; 4hr 15min); Tínos (17 weekly).

Ráfina to: Mýkonos (13 weekly); Náxos (13 weekly); Páros (13 weekly); Pireás (12 weekly); Tínos (13 weekly; 2hr 15min).

Amorgós to: Folégandhros (daily); Náxos (daily; 70min); Páros (daily); Pireás (daily); Sífnos (daily); Sýros (daily); Thíra (daily; 80min);

Folégandhros to: Amorgós (daily); Náxos (daily); Páros (daily); Pireás (9 weekly; 3hr 40min); Sífnos (9 weekly; 55min); Thíra (10 weekly; 55min).

Íos to: Crete, Iráklion (6 weekly); Mýkonos (6 weekly); Páros (6 weekly; 70min); Pireás (13 weekly; 2hr 15min); Thíra (13 weekly; 65min).

Kímolos to: Folégandhros (1 weekly; 50min); Mílos (3 weekly; 55min); Pireás (4 weekly); Sérifos (1 weekly); Sífnos (3 weekly).

Mílos to: Pireás (14 weekly); Sérifos (12 weekly); Sífnos (12 weekly; 1hr).

Mýkonos to: Crete, Iráklion (20 weekly); Íos (6 weekly); Náxos (13 weekly; 1hr); Páros (19 weekly; 1hr); Pireás (25 weekly); Ráfina (6 weekly); Sýros (13 weekly; 45min); Thíra (6 weekly); Tínos (13 weekly; 30min).

Náxos: Amorgós (daily; 70min); Crete, Iráklion (2 weekly); Folégandhros (daily); Mýkonos (12 weekly; 1hr); Páros (22 weekly; 40min); Pireás (19 weekly); Ráfina (6 weekly); Sífnos (daily); Sýros (daily); Thíra (daily); Tínos (12 weekly).

Páros to: Amorgós (daily); Crete, Iráklion (6 weekly); Folégandhros (daily); Íos (6 weekly; 65min); Mýkonos (19 weekly); Náxos (21 weekly; 40min); Pireás (26 weekly; 3hr 15min); Ráfina (6 weekly); Sífnos (daily); Sýros (daily; 45min); Thíra (16 weekly; 90min); Tínos (13 weekly; 55min).

Sérifos to: Mílos (11 weekly; 1hr); Pireás (13 weekly; 2hr 35min); Sífnos (13 weekly; 35min).

Sífnos to: Amorgós (1 weekly); Folégandhros (8 weekly; 55min); Mílos (13 weekly; 55min); Náxos (daily); Páros (8 weekly; 1hr); Pireás (21 weekly; 2hr 25min); Sérifos (12 weekly; 35min); Thíra (8 weekly).

Sýros to: Amorgós (daily); Folégandhros (daily); Mýkonos (14 weekly); Náxos (daily); Páros (daily;

50min); Pireás (27 weekly; 2hr 40min); Sífnos (daily); Thíra (daily); Tínos (14 weekly; 35min).
Thíra to: Amorgós (daily; 1hr 10min); Crete, Iráklion (8 weekly; 1hr 50min); Folégandhros (10 weekly; 55min); Íos (13 weekly; 50min); Mýkonos (6 weekly); Náxos (daily); Páros (16 weekly; 1hr 30min); Pireás (25 weekly; 4hr 15min); Sífnos (8 weekly); Sýros (daily).
Tínos to: Crete, Iráklion (2 weekly); Mýkonos (20 weekly; 35min); Náxos (13 weekly); Páros (13 weekly); Pireás (20 weekly); Ráfina (6 weekly; 2hr 10min); Sýros (8 weekly).

Flights

There are **airports** on **Páros**, **Mýkonos**, **Thíra**, **Sýros**, **Mílos** and **Náxos**. In season, or during storms when ferries are idle, you have little chance of getting a seat on any flight at less than three days' notice, and tickets are predictably expensive. Expect off-season (Oct–April) frequencies to drop by at least eighty percent. Flights are on Olympic unless otherwise stated. Airsea Lines (Ⓣ210 94 02 012; Ⓦwww.airsealines.com) briefly pioneered seaplane flights in summer 2007 from **Lávrio** to Íos–Santoríni, to Mýkonos–Kálymnos–Kós and to Páros – they intend eventually to have harbour landings on all these islands; however, seaplanes are more vulnerable to adverse weather conditions than ordinary flights.
Athens to: Mílos (1–2 daily; 45min); Mýkonos (4–5 daily on Olympic; 3–4 daily on Aegean; 40min); Náxos (6 weekly; 45min); Páros (2–3 daily; 40min); Sýros (3–6 weekly; 35min); Thíra (5–6 daily on Olympic; 3–5 daily on Aegean; 45min).
Mýkonos to: Rhodes (2 weekly; 55min); Thessaloníki (2 weekly on Olympic, 3 weekly on Aegean; 1hr 10min); Thíra (4 weekly; 30min).
Thíra to: Rhodes (2–5 weekly; 50min); Thessaloníki (2 weekly on Olympic, 1 daily on Aegean; 1hr 10min).

8

Crete

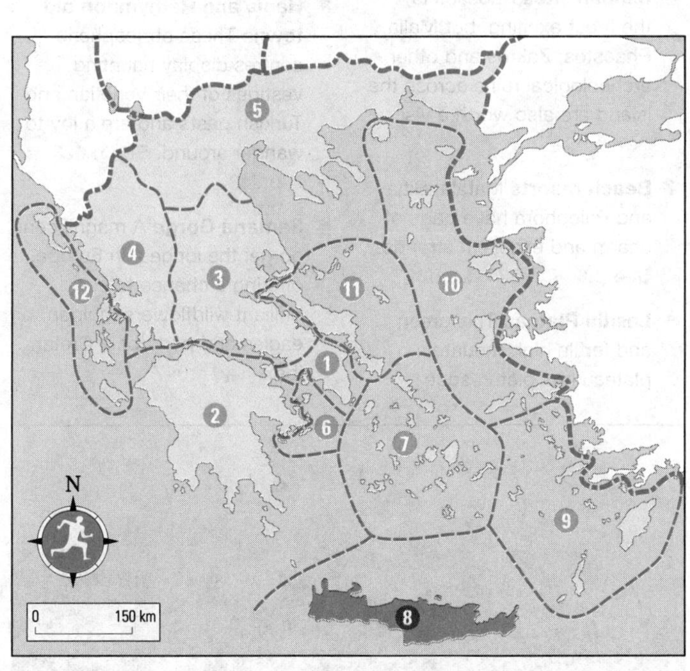

CHAPTER 8 Highlights

* **Archeological Museum, Iráklion** The world's foremost Minoan museum. Following a substantial renovation the museum is set to partially reopen in July 2008 and fully reopen in 2009. See p.598
* **Minoan sites** Knossos is the most exciting, but Malia, Phaestos, Zakros and other archeological ruins across the island are also worth a visit. See p.602
* **Beach resorts** Mátala, Sitía and Paleohóra have bags of charm and excellent strands. See p.608, p.624 & p.652
* **Lasíthi Plateau** This green and fertile high mountain plateau has picturesque agricultural villages and unique white cloth-sailed windmills. See p.616
* **The Dhiktean cave** Mythological birthplace of Zeus, the Dhiktean cave is stunningly situated on the Lasíthi Plateau. See p.617
* **Haniá and Réthymnon old towns** These atmospheric centres display haunting vestiges of their Venetian and Turkish pasts and are a joy to wander around. See p.633 & p.643
* **Samariá Gorge** A magnificent gorge: the longest in Europe, offering a chance to see brilliant wildflowers, golden eagles and perhaps a Cretan ibex. See p.647

▲ Windmill, Lasíthi Plateau

8

Crete

Crete (Kríti) is a great deal more than just another Greek island. In many places, especially in the cities or along the developed north coast, it doesn't feel like an island at all, but rather a substantial land in its own right. Which of course it is – a precipitous, wealthy and at times a surprisingly cosmopolitan one with a tremendous and unique history. But when you lose yourself among the mountains, or on the lesser-known coastal reaches of the south, it has everything you could want of a Greek island and more: great beaches, remote hinterlands and hospitable people.

In history, Crete is distinguished above all as the home of Europe's earliest civilization. It was only at the beginning of the twentieth century that the legends of King Minos and of a Cretan society that ruled the Greek world in prehistory were confirmed by excavations at Knossos and Phaestos. Yet the Minoans had a remarkably advanced society, the centre of a maritime trading empire as early as 2000 BC. The artworks produced on Crete at this time are unsurpassed anywhere in the ancient world, and it seems clear that life on Crete in those days was good. This apparently peaceful culture survived at least three major natural disasters; each time the palaces were destroyed, and each time they were rebuilt on a grander scale. Only after the last destruction, probably the result of an eruption of Santoríni and subsequent tidal waves and earthquakes, do significant numbers of weapons begin to appear in the ruins. This, together with the appearance of the Greek language, has been interpreted to mean that Mycenaean Greeks had taken control of the island. Nevertheless, for nearly 500 years, by far the longest period of peace the island has seen, Crete was home to a culture well ahead of its time.

The Minoans of Crete probably originally came from Anatolia; at their height they maintained strong links with Egypt and with the people of Asia Minor, and this position as meeting point and strategic fulcrum between east and west has played a major role in Crete's subsequent history. Control of the island passed from Greeks to Romans to Saracens, through the Byzantine empire to Venice, and finally to Turkey for more than two centuries. During World War II, the island was occupied by the Germans and attained the dubious distinction of being the first place to be successfully invaded by paratroops.

Today, with a flourishing agricultural economy, Crete is one of the few Greek islands that could probably support itself without tourists. Nevertheless, tourism is heavily promoted and is making inroads everywhere. The northeast coast in particular is overdeveloped, and though there are parts of the south and west coasts that have not been spoilt, they are getting harder to find. By contrast, the high mountains of the interior are still barely

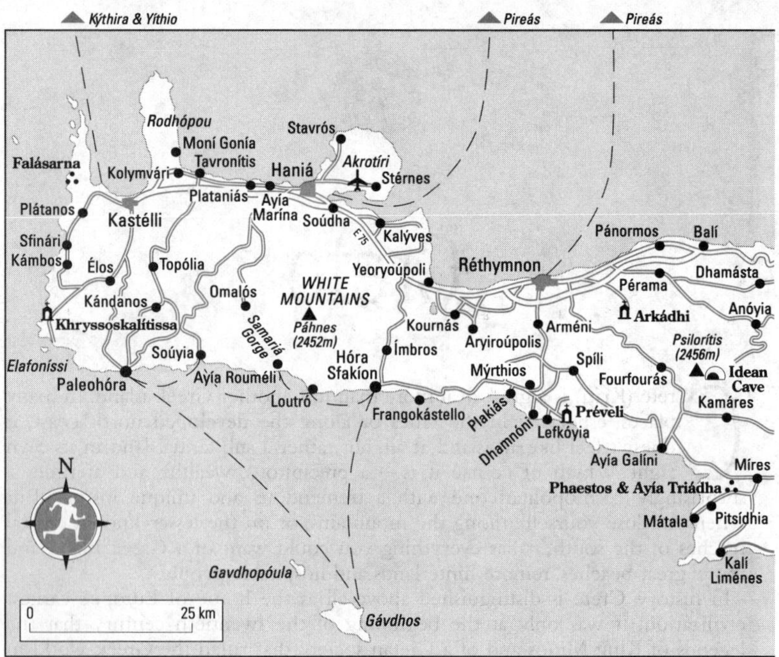

touched, and one of the best things to do on Crete is to rent a vehicle and explore the remoter villages.

Every part of Crete has its loyal devotees and it's hard to pick out highlights, but generally if you want to get away from it all you should head west, towards Haniá and the smaller, less well-connected places along the south and west coasts. It is in this part of the island that the White Mountains rise, while below them yawns the famous Samariá Gorge. The far east, around Sitía, is also relatively unscathed, with a string of isolated beaches worth seeking out to the south of the over-popular Väï beach, which lures crowds attracted by its famous palm grove. Whatever you do, your first priority will probably be to leave Iráklion (Heraklion) as quickly as possible, having paid the obligatory, and rewarding, visit to the archeological museum (reopens July 2008; see p.598) and nearby Knossos. The other great Minoan sites cluster around the middle of the island: Phaestos and Ayía Triádha to the south (with Roman Gortys to provide contrast), and Malia on the north coast. Almost wherever you go you'll find a reminder of the island's history, whether it's the superbly preserved Minoan town of Gourniá near the cosmopolitan resort of Áyios Nikólaos, the exquisitely sited palace of Zakros in the far east, or the lesser sites scattered around the west. Unexpected highlights include Crete's Venetian forts at Réthymnon and Frangokástello; its hundreds of frescoed Byzantine churches, most famously at Kritsá; and, at Réthymnon and Haniá, the cluttered old Venetian and Turkish quarters.

Crete has by far the longest summers in Greece, and you can get a decent tan here right into October and swim at least from May until November. The one seasonal blight is the *meltémi*, a northerly wind, which regularly blows harder here and more continuously than anywhere else in Greece – the best of several reasons for avoiding an August visit if you can. It's far from an ill wind, however,

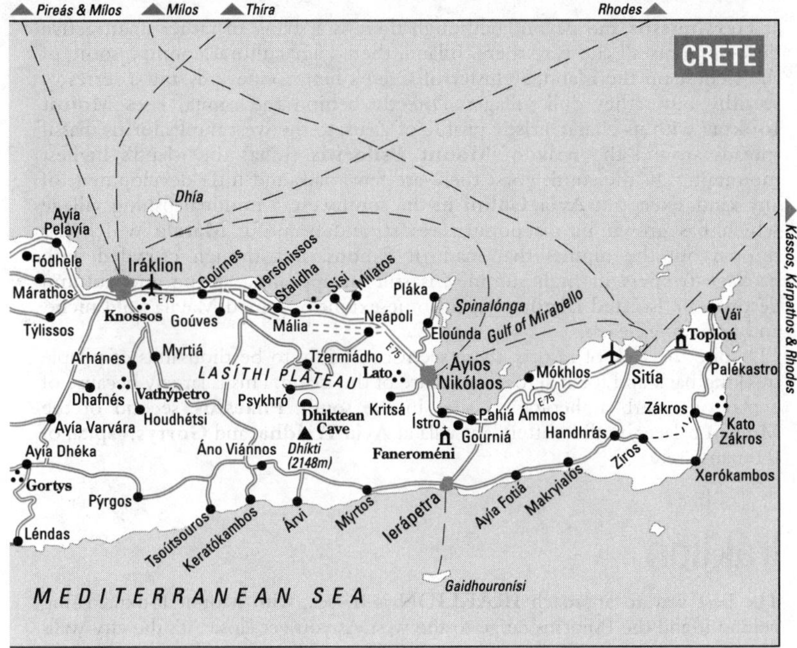

as it also lowers humidity and makes the island's higher summer temperatures more bearable.

Iráklion, Knossos and central Crete

Many visitors to Crete arrive in the island's capital, **Iráklion** (Heraklion), but it's not an outstandingly beautiful city, and its central zones are often a maelstrom of traffic-congested thoroughfares. However, it does provide a convenient base for visits to an outstanding **archeological museum** and nearby **Knossos**. On the positive side, the city does have quite a few plus points – superb fortifications, a fine market, atmospheric old alleys and some interesting lesser museums added to a recent makeover of central areas by the city hall that has improved things considerably.

The area immediately around the city is less touristy than you might expect, mainly because there are few decent beaches of any size on this central part of the coast. To the west, mountains drop straight into the sea virtually all the way to Réthymnon, while eastwards the main resorts are at least 30km away, at **Hersónissos** and beyond, although there is a string of rather unattractive developments all the way there. Inland, there's agricultural country, some of the richest on the island, a cluster of Crete's better vineyards and a series of wealthy but rather dull villages. Directly behind the capital rises **Mount Ioúktas** with its characteristic profile of Zeus; to the west the Psiloritis massif spreads around the peak of **Mount Psiloritis** (Ídha) the island's highest mountain. On the south coast there are few roads and little development of any kind, except at **Ayía Galíni** in the southwest, a nominal fishing village which has grown into a popular resort, and beautiful **Mátala** which has thrown out the hippies that made it famous, and, though crowded with package-trippers in high summer, is still an appealing spring and autumn destination. Isolated **Léndas** has to some extent occupied Mátala's old niche, and has a fine beach.

Despite the lack of resorts, there seem constantly to be thousands of people trekking back and forth across the centre of the island. This is largely because of a trio of superb archeological sites in the south: **Phaestos**, second of the Minoan palaces, with its attendant villa at **Ayía Triádha**, and **Gortys**, capital of Roman Crete.

Iráklion

The best way to approach **IRÁKLION** is by sea, with Mount Ioúktas rising behind it and the Psiloritis range to the west. As you get closer, it's the city walls that first stand out, still dominating and fully encircling the oldest part of town; finally you sail in past the great **Venetian fortress** defending the harbour entrance. Unfortunately, big ships no longer dock in the old port but at great modern concrete wharves alongside, which neatly sums up Iráklion itself. Many of the old parts have been restored and are attractive, but these are offset by the bustle and noise that characterize much of the city today. In more recent times, however, Iráklion's administrators have been giving belated attention to dealing with some of the city's image problems, and large tracts of the centre – particularly the focal Platía Eleftherías – have been landscaped and refurbished with the aim of presenting a less daunting prospect to the visitor.

Orientation, arrival and information

Virtually everything you're likely to want to see in Iráklion lies within the northeastern corner of the walled city. The most vital thoroughfare, the recently pedestrianized **25-Avgoústou**, links the harbour with the commercial city centre. Its southern end is lined with shipping and travel agencies, rental outlets and a few restaurants, but further up the hill these give way to banks and stores. **Platía Venizélou** (or Fountain Square), off to the right, is crowded with cafés and restaurants; behind Venizélou lies **El Greco Park** (actually a rather cramped garden), with a few stylish bars, while on the opposite side of 25-Avgoústou are some of the more interesting of Iráklion's older buildings. Further up 25-Avgoústou, **Kalokerinoú** leads down to Haniá Gate and westwards out of the city; straight ahead, **Odhós-1821** is a major shopping street, and adjacent 1866 is given over to the animated street **market**, perhaps the best on the island. To the left, Dhikeosínis heads for the city's main square, **Platía Eleftherías**, paralleled by the pedestrian alley, Dedhálou, lined with many of the city's swankier fashion stores and the direct link between the two squares. The revamped Eleftherías is very much the traditional centre of the city, both for

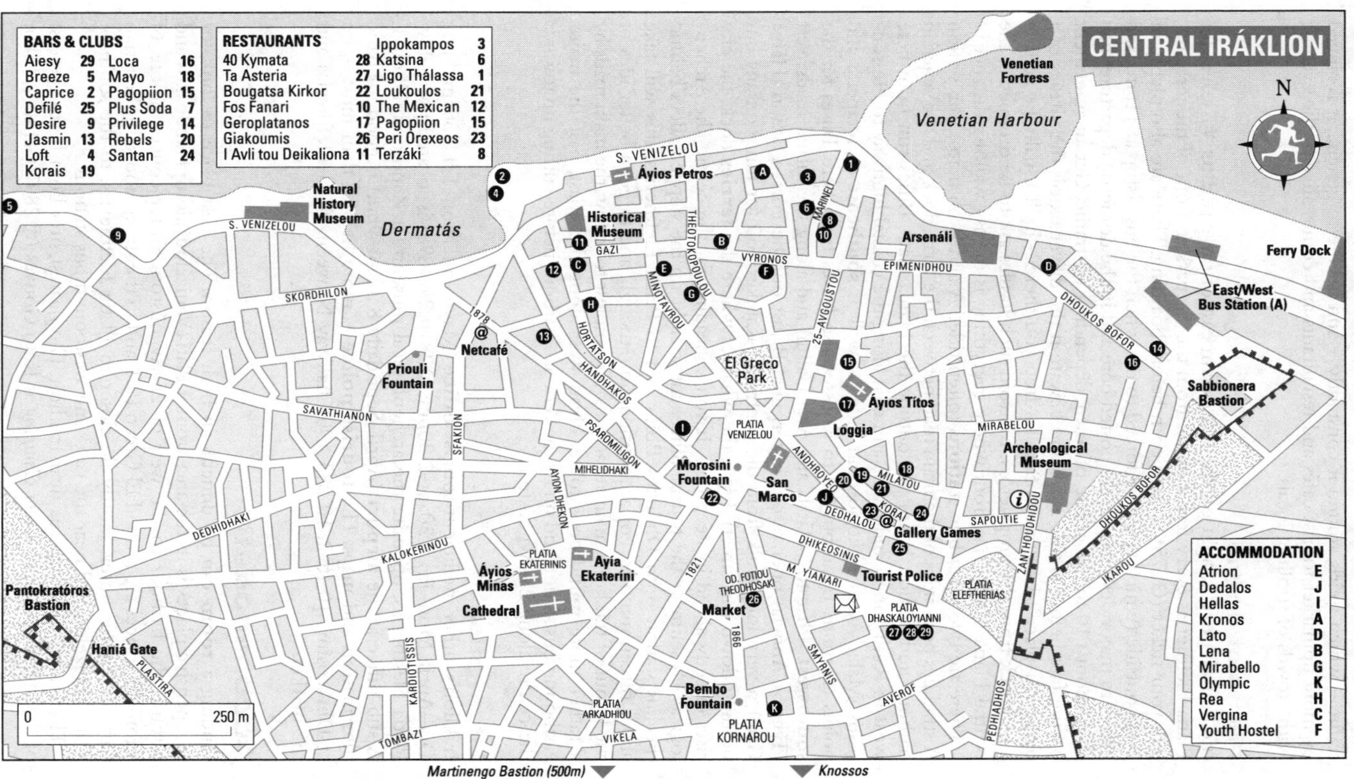
CENTRAL IRÁKLION
N
BARS & CLUBS
Aiesy 29
Breeze 5
Caprice 2
Defilé 25
Desire 9
Jasmin 13
Loft 4
Korais 19
Loca 16
Mayo 18
Pagopiion 15
Plus Soda 7
Privilege 14
Rebels 20
Santan 24
RESTAURANTS
40 Kymata 28
Ta Asteria 27
Bougatsa Kirkor 22
Fos Fanari 10
Geroplatanos 17
Giakoumis 26
I Avli tou Deikaliona 11
Ippokampos 3
Katsina 6
Ligo Thálassa 1
Loukoulos 21
The Mexican 12
Pagopiion 15
Peri Orexeos 23
Terzáki 8
ACCOMMODATION
Atrion E
Dedalos J
Hellas I
Kronos A
Lato D
Lena B
Mirabello G
Olympic K
Rea H
Vergina C
Youth Hostel F
Venetian Fortress
Venetian Harbour
Dermatás
Natural History Museum
Historical Museum
Áyios Petros
Arsenáli
Ferry Dock
East/West Bus Station (A)
Sabbionera Bastion
El Greco Park
Áyios Títos
Loggia
Archeological Museum
Netcafé
Priouli Fountain
Morosini Fountain
San Marco
Gallery Games
Tourist Police
Market
Áyios Minas
Ayía Ekateríni
Cathedral
Bembo Fountain
Pantokratóros Bastion
Haniá Gate
PLATIA VENIZELOU
PLATIA EKATERINIS
PLATIA ELEFTHERIAS
PLATIA DHASKALOYIANNI
PLATIA ARKADHIOU
PLATIA KORNAROU
S. VENIZELOU
GAZI
THEOTOKOPOULOU
MINOTAVROU
VYRONOS
MARINELI
EPIMENIDHOU
25-AVGOUSTOU
DHOUKOS BOFOR
MIRABELOU
SKORDHILON
HORTATSON
HANDHAKOS
1878
SAVATHIANON
SFAKION
PSAROMILIGON
MIHELIDHAKI
AYION DHEKON
ANDHROYEO
MILATOU
KORAI
DEDHALOU
SAPOUTIE
ZANTHOUDHIDOU
IKAROU
DHIKEOSINIS
M. YIANARI
OD. FOTIOU THEODHOSAKI
1821
1866
SMYRNIS
AVEROF
PEDHIADHOS
DEDHIDHAKI
KALOKERINOU
KARDIOTISSIS
TOMBAZI
VIKELA
PLASTIRA
0
250 m
Áyios Andhréas Bastion (100m) & 7
Bus Station B (50m)
Martinengo Bastion (500m)
Knossos

traffic – which swirls around it constantly – and for life in general; it is ringed by more upmarket tourist cafés and restaurants and comes alive in the evening with crowds of strolling locals.

Points of arrival

Iráklion **airport** is right on the coast, 4km east of the city. **Bus** #1 leaves for Platía Eleftherías every few minutes from the car park in front of the terminal; buy your ticket (€0.75) at the booth before boarding. There are also plenty of **taxis** outside (which you'll be forced to use when the buses stop at 11pm), and prices to major destinations are posted here and in the domestic departures hall – it's about €10 to the centre of town, depending on traffic. Get an agreement on the fare before taking a cab and beware if the driver extols the virtues of a particular place to stay and offers to drop you there – he'll usually be getting a kickback from the proprietors. To avoid such hassles ask to be dropped at the central Platía Eleftherías, from where everything is in easy walking distance.

There are two main **bus stations** (often titled A and B on maps). Bus station A straddles both sides of the main road between the ferry dock and the Venetian harbour, and Station B lies just outside the Haniá Gate. Buses run from here **west** to Réthymnon and Haniá and **east** along the coastal highway to Hersónsissos, Mália, Áyios Nikólaos and Sitía, as well as **southeast** to Ierápetra and points en route. Local bus #2 to Knossos also leaves from here. Buses for the **southwest** (Phaestos, Mátala and Ayía Galíni) and along the inland roads west (Týlissos, Anóyia) operate out of terminal B just outside Pórta Haníon (Hánia Gate), a very long walk from the centre up Kalokerinoú (or jump on any bus heading down this street). From the wharves where the **ferries** dock, the city rises directly ahead in steep tiers. If you're heading for the centre, the Archeological Museum or the tourist office, cut straight up the stepped alleys behind the bus station onto Dhoúkos Bofór and to Platía Eleftherías; this will take about fifteen minutes. For accommodation, though, and to get a better idea of the layout of Iráklion's main attractions, it's simplest to follow the main roads by a rather more roundabout route. Head west along the coast, past the major eastbound bus station and on by the Venetian harbour before cutting up towards the centre along 25-Avgoústou.

Information

Iráklion's rather inefficient **tourist office** (May–Sept: Mon–Fri 8.30am–9pm; Oct–April: Mon–Fri 8.30am–2.30pm; ⓣ2810 246 298) is located just below Platía Eleftherías, opposite the archeological museum at Zanthoudhídhou 1. A sub-office at the **airport** (April–Sept daily 8.30am–9pm) is good for basic information and maps. The **tourist police** – more helpful than most – are at Dhikeosínis 10 (ⓣ2810 283 190), halfway between Platía Eleftherías and the market.

Accommodation

Finding a **room** can be difficult in high season. The best place to look for inexpensive places is in the area around Platía Venizélou, along Hándhakos and towards the harbour to the west of 25-Avgoústou. Other concentrations of affordable places are around El Greco Park and in the streets above the Venetian harbour. Better hotels mostly lie closer to Platía Eleftherías, to the south of Platía Venizélou and near the east- and westbound bus stations.

There are no **campsites** near Iráklion. The nearest sites both lie to the east of the city: first comes *Creta Camping* at Káto Goúves (ⓣ28970 41400), 16km out, followed by *Caravan Camping* (☎28970 22901) at Hersónissos, 28km from the city.

Atrion Hronaki 9 ☎2810 246 000, ⓦwww.atrion.gr. Attractive, newish central hotel with well-equipped balcony rooms, satellite TV and free Internet connection. ❺

Dedalos Dedhálou 15 ☎2810 244 812, ⓔinfo@daedalos.gr. Recently refurbished hotel with balcony rooms overlooking a pedestrianized shopping street which is tranquil at night. All rooms are en suite and equipped with TV and a/c. ❸

Hellas Hándhakos 24 ☎2810 288 851, ⓕ2810 284 442. Hostel-style place with simple doubles, and dorms (€7 per person) favoured by younger travellers. Also has a roof garden and snack-bar. ❷

Kronos Agaráthou 2, west of 25-Avgoústou ☎2810 282 240, ⓦwww.kronoshotel.gr. Pleasant, friendly hotel with en-suite, sea-view balcony rooms. ❸

Lato Epomenídhou 15 ☎2810 228 103, ⓦwww.lato.gr. Stylish and luxurious hotel whose a/c rooms have minibar, TV and fine balcony views over the Venetian harbour (the higher floors have the better views). B&B ❻

Lena Lahana 10 ☎2810 223 280, ⓦwww.lena-hotel.gr. Quiet and efficient small hotel offering a/c en-suite rooms with balcony and TV. ❸

Mirabello Theotokopoúlou 20 ☎2810 285 052, ⓦwww.mirabello-hotel.gr. Good-value, family-run hotel featuring en-suite balcony rooms, some with a/c and TV and others sharing bath. In a quiet street just north of El Greco Park. ❸–❹

Olympic Platía Kornárou ☎2810 288 861, ⓕ2810 222 512. Overlooking the busy platía (hence double-glazed windows) and the famous Bembo fountain. One of the many hotels built in the 1960s, but one of the few that has been refurbished; facilities include minibar and safe. B&B ❻

Rea Kalimeráki 1 ☎2810 223 638, ⓕ2810 242 189. A friendly, comfortable and clean *pension* in a tranquil location. Some rooms with washbasin, others en suite. ❶–❷

Vergina Hortátson 32 ☎2810 242 739. Basic but pleasant rooms with washbasins and shared bath in a quiet street and set around a courtyard with banana trees. ❶–❷

Youth Hostel Vkronos 5 ☎2810 286 281, ⓔheraklioyouthhostel@yahoo.gr. Formerly Iráklion's official youth hostel, now privately operated by the friendly and helpful proprietors. There's plenty of space and some beds (albeit illegal) on the roof if you fancy sleeping under the stars. Private rooms (❷) as well as dorm beds (€10 per person); hot showers, breakfast and other meals available.

The Town

A good place to start your explorations of the town is the focal **Platía Venizélou**, crowded most of the day with locals patronizing its café terraces, and with travellers who've arranged to meet in "Fountain Square". The **Morosini Fountain**, which gives the square its popular name, is not particularly spectacular at first glance, but on closer inspection is really a very beautiful work; it was built by Venetian governor Francesco Morosini in the seventeenth century, incorporating four lions which were some three hundred years old even then. From the platía you can strike up Dedhálou, a pedestrianized street full of fashion and tourist shops, or continue on 25-Avgoústou to a major traffic junction at Platía Nikifoúrou Foka. To the right, Kalokerinoú leads west out of the city, the market lies straight ahead along Odhós-1866, and Platía Eleftherías is a short walk to the left up Dhikeosínis.

Platía Eleftherías and the Archeological Museum

Platía Eleftherías, with seats shaded by palms and eucalyptuses, is very much the traditional heart of the city and the focus for political demonstrations and occasional free concerts; on summer evenings strolling crowds come to fill its café terraces. Most of Iráklion's more expensive shops are in the streets leading off the platía.

Just off the north side of Platía Eleftherías lies the **archeological museum** (April–Sept Mon 1–7.30pm, Tues–Sun 8.30am–7.30pm; Oct–March daily

Renovation of the Archeological Museum

The long-overdue **renovation** of the Archeological Museum began in 2007, since which time it has been closed to visitors. It is scheduled to partly reopen in July 2008 with two galleries displaying the main items from the collection; the complete reopening is planned for the summer of 2009.

8am–5pm; confirm times with the adjacent tourist office). Almost every important prehistoric and Minoan find on Crete is included in this fabulous, if bewilderingly large and unimaginatively presented, collection. Hopefully, the current refurbishment will improve matters; note that upon reopening some of the items mentioned below may not be in the rooms indicated. The museum tends to be crowded, especially when a guided tour stampedes through, but it's worth taking time over. You can't hope to see everything, nor can we attempt to describe it all (several good museum guides are sold here, the best probably being the glossy ones by J.A. Sakellarakis or Andonis Vasilakis), but highlights include the "**Town Mosaic**" from Knossos in Room 2 (the galleries are arranged basically in chronological order), the famous **inscribed disc** from Phaestos in Room 3 (itself the subject of several books), most of Room 4, especially the magnificent bull's-head **rhyton** (drinking vessel), the **jewellery** in Room 6 (and elsewhere) and the engraved steatite **black vases** in Room 7. Save some of your time and energy for upstairs, where the **Hall of the Frescoes**, with intricately reconstructed fragments of the wall paintings from Knossos and other sites, is especially wonderful.

Walls and fortifications

The massive **Venetian walls**, in places up to 15m thick, are the most obvious evidence of Iráklion's later history. Though their fabric is incredibly well preserved, access is virtually nonexistent. It is possible, just, to walk along them from Áyios Andhréas Bastion over the sea in the west, as far as the Martinengo Bastion where lies the **tomb of Nikos Kazantzakis**, Cretan author of *Zorba the Greek*, whose epitaph reads: "I believe in nothing, I hope for nothing, I am free." At weekends, Iraklians gather here to pay their respects and enjoy a free view of the soccer matches played by one of the city's two teams in the stadium below. If the walls seem altogether too much effort, the **port fortifications** are much easier to see. Stroll out along the jetty (crowded with courting couples at dusk) and you can get inside the sixteenth-century **Venetian fortress** (Tues–Sun 8.30am–3pm; €2) at the harbour entrance, emblazoned with the Venetian Lion of St Mark. Standing atop this, you begin to understand how Iráklion (or Candia as both the city and the island were known to the Venetians) withstood a 22-year siege before finally falling to the Ottomans. On the landward side of the port, the Venetian **arsenáli** (arsenals) can also be seen, their arches rather lost amid the concrete road system all around.

Churches and other museums

From the harbour, 25-Avgoústou will take you up past most of the town's other highlights. The **church of Áyios Títos**, on the left as you approach Platía Venizélou, borders a pleasant little platía. Byzantine in origin but substantially rebuilt by the Venetians, it looks magnificent principally because, like most of the churches here, it was adapted by the Turks as a mosque and only reconsecrated in 1925; consequently it has been renovated on numerous occasions. On the south side of this platía, abutting 25-Avgoústou, is the Venetian **city hall** with its famous loggia, again almost entirely rebuilt. Just above this, facing Platía Venizélou, is the **church of San Marco**, its steps usually crowded with sightseers spilling over from the nearby platía. Neither of these last two buildings has found a permanent role in its refurbished state, but both are generally open to house some kind of exhibition or craft show.

Slightly away from the obvious city-centre circuit, but still within the bounds of the walls, there is a clutch of lesser museums worth seeing if you have the time. First of these are the excellent collection of **icons** in the **church of Ayía Ekateríni** (Mon–Sat 9.30am–7.30pm; €2), an ancient building just below the undistinguished cathedral, off Kalokerinoú. The finest here are six large scenes by Mihaïl Damaskinos (a near-contemporary of El Greco) who fused Byzantine and Renaissance influences. Supposedly both Damaskinos and El Greco studied at Ayía Ekateríni in the sixteenth century, when it functioned as a sort of monastic art school.

The **Historical Museum** (Mon–Sat 9am–5pm; €5; ⓦ www.historical-museum.gr) lies some 300m north of here, on the waterfront. Its display of folk costumes and jumble of local memorabilia include the reconstructed studies of both Nikos Kazantzakis and Emanuel Tsouderos (the latter both Cretan statesman and former Greek prime minister). There's enough variety to satisfy just about anyone, including the only El Greco painting on Crete, the uncharacteristic *View of Mount Sinai and the Monastery of St Catherine*.

To the west, rehoused in a converted old power plant overlooking the bay of Dermatás, is the **Natural History Museum** (Sun & Mon 10am–3pm €3; ⓦ www.nhmc.uoc.gr), definitely worth a visit. Currently only two floors of the building have been completed, housing displays on the ecosystems of the eastern Mediterranean as well as a child-oriented Discovery Centre. As the renovation progresses the building's remaining three floors will include flora and fauna displays, exhibits detailing the island's geological evolution, the arrival of man, and the environment as it would have appeared to the Minoans.

Eating

Big city though it is, Iráklion disappoints when it comes to eating, and not many of the central restaurants and tavernas provide good value. The cafés and tavernas of platíes Venizélou and Eleftherías are essential places to sit and watch the world pass, but their food is expensive and mediocre. One striking exception is *Bougatsa Kirkor*, by the Morosini Fountain in Venizélou, where you can sample authentic Cretan *bougátsa* – a creamy cheese pie sprinkled with sugar and cinnamon. For **snacks** and **takeaways**, there's a group of *souvláki* and other fast-food stalls clustering around the top of 25-Avgoústou near the entrance to El Greco Park, which is handy if you need somewhere to sit and eat. For *tyrópita* and *spanakópita* (cheese or spinach pies) and other pastries, sweet or savoury, there is no shortage of *zaharoplastía* and places such as *Everest* – just north of the Morosini Fountain – which does takeaways of these as well as lots of other savouries. On and around Platía Dhaskaloyiánni (near the Archeological Museum) are some authentic and inexpensive ouzerís: try *Ta Asteria* or *40 Kymata* on the platía itself for atmosphere and tasty *mezédhes*.

I Avli tou Deikaliona Kalokairinoú 8 at the rear of the Historical Museum ⓣ2810 244 215. Popular taverna with a great little terrace fronting the Idomeneus fountain, serving up well-prepared meat and fish dishes. In high summer you may need to book to ensure an outdoor table. Should you despair of getting one, nearby Paraskevas, with similar fare and terrace, is a good substitute.

Fos Fanari Marinélli 1, opposite the tiny church of Ayios Dimítrios. The first in a row of ouzerís that line this alley off Vironos, sloping down to the harbour. Good fish dishes and *mezédhes*. The similar neighbouring (and pricier) *Terzáki* is also worth a try.

Geroplatanos in the leafy square fronting the church of Ayios. Títos. Taking its name from the great old plane tree beneath which its tables are set out, this is one of the most tranquil lunch spots in town and provides the usual taverna staples.

Giakoumis Fotiou Theodhośaki 5, in the market ⓣ2810 284 039. Established in 1935, this is the city's oldest taverna and locals claim it serves up the best *païdhákia* (lamb chops) on the island – some tribute given the competition. You can wash them down with the *hýma* (house) wine produced by Lyrarakis, a noted Pezá vineyard.

Ippokampos Sófoklí Venizélou, west of 25-Avgoústou. The best and least expensive fish to be had in Iráklion, served in unpretentious surroundings. Deservedly popular with locals for lunch *mezédhes* as well as dinner, this place is often crowded late into the evening, and you may have to queue or turn up earlier than the Greeks eat. Has a pleasant shaded terrace over the road on the seafront.

Katsina Marinélli 12. A simple and friendly ouzerí at the opposite (seaward) end of the alley from *Fos Fanari* (above). Tasty and economical seafood *mezédhes* served at outdoor tables.

Ligo Thálassa at the foot of Marinélli near the Venetian fort. This pleasant new ouzerí serves up a good selection of seafood *mezédhes* and has a small terrace facing the harbour.

Loukoulos on the alley off Koraí. With a leafy courtyard terrace and an Italian slant to its international menu, this is one of the better tavernas in Iráklion. However, the pricey food and expensive wine list seem aimed more at luring Iráklion's smart set than the casual visitor.

The Mexican Hándhakos 71. Inexpensive Mexican tacos and beers, complemented by salads and bean dishes.

Pagopiion Platía Ayíou Títou. This is the mid-priced restaurant of Iráklion's most original bar serving Cretan and international dishes to a high standard. There's also a recommended *mezedhákia* buffet (Sat 12.30–4.30pm) which allows you to fill a plate for €6. A pleasant terrace is also good for lazy breakfasts and snacks.

Peri Orexeos Koraí 10, almost opposite *Loukoulos* (above). This popular small taverna is a good bet for traditional Cretan cooking at reasonable prices.

Nightlife and entertainment

Because it's a university town, Iráklion has plenty of **clubs** and bars where you can let your hair down. As with the island generally, young Cretans tend to be more into sitting and chatting with background sounds rather than hitting the dance floor; consequently large areas of Koraí and the surrounding streets have been turned into outdoor lounges with lines of expansive sofas and armchairs. In addition to the central nightlife, venues are also to be found in the suburbs or out along the hotel strip to the west at Amoudhára. A phenomenon emerging in Iráklion over recent years has been the arrival of a new breed of **kafenío**, aimed at a younger crowd: the drinks are cocktails rather than *raki*, the music is modern Greek or Western, and there are prices to match. The city's most animated **bars** are located around **Platía Koraí** behind Dedhálou (up from *Taverna Loukoulos* listed above), along the alley of the same name to the west and its parallel Milatou, slightly to the north.

Bars

Aiesy Platía Dhaskalyiánnis. This laid-back café-bar casts off its daytime serenity after dark when locals gather to sink into the canvas chairs on the square, to listen to soft rock and sip long drinks.

Defilé Platía Koraí. Trendy little bar frequented by students, on a pleasant square just to the north of Dedhálou.

Santan Platía Koraí. This bar has outdoor tables and serves a wide variety of exotic (and expensive) beers and cocktails. Those on a tight budget can nurse a *frappé* for hours.

Jasmin Ayiostefanitón 6, tucked in an alley on the left midway down Hándhakos. Another good night-time rendezvous, with jazz, soul and Latin music and an outdoor terrace. Also serves 45 different types of tea.

Korais on the alley Koraí. Glitzy open-air café with spacious plant-festooned terraces, overhead movie screens and music – highly popular with Iráklion's stylish set.

Mayo Millátou 11. This new extravaganza of a bar with spotlights, screens and music under a big canopy terrace is one of the places to be seen for Iráklion's student set. Its arrival has spawned a whole new set of bars and cafés along the same street.

Pagopiion (Ice Factory) Platía Ayíou Títou. Stunningly elegant bar created by photographic artist Chryssy Karelli inside Iráklion's former ice factory. She has preserved much of the old building including a lift for hauling the ice from the basement freezer and a fascistic call to duty in German Gothic script on one wall – a remnant of Nazi occupation of the factory in World War II. Make sure to visit the toilets – in an artistic league of their own.

Rebels Perdhikári 3. A stylish bar which has cloned numerous similar places nearby. On summer weekends this area is the trendiest place to be if you're under 30.

Clubs

Iráklion has a large selection of **discos** and **clubs**, playing Western music, interspersed with Greek tunes (not the type played for tourists). *Privilege* is the most popular, down towards the harbour at the bottom of Dhoúkos Bofór, below the archeological museum; the nearby *Loca* provides competition. Two pleasant and popular music bars with a seafront location are *Loft* and *Caprice* overlooking the western end of Dermatás bay near the Natural History Museum. *Desire* and *Breeze* are similar seafront places further west along the coast road, while *Plus Soda*, further out still in Amoudhára, is one of the biggest and best of the many clubs in this western beach suburb.

Listings

Airlines Aegean, Dhimokratias 11 (Ⓣ2810 330 475, Ⓦwww.aegeanair.com), and Olympic, 25-Avgoústou 27 (Ⓣ2810 237 203, Ⓦwww.olympic-airways.com), are the main scheduled airlines with connecting flights to Athens and other parts of Greece. Charter airlines flying into Iráklion mostly use local travel agents as their representatives.

Airport For airport information call Ⓣ2810 229 191. Bus #1 runs from the eastern side of Platía Eleftherías to the airport every few minutes; buy a ticket (€0.75) from a kiosk near the bus stop.

Banks There are ATMs all over town, but the main bank branches are on 25-Avgoústou.

Car and bike rental The upper end of 25-Avgoústou is lined with rental companies, but you'll often find good deals on the backstreets nearby; it's always worth asking for discounts. For cars and bikes, good places to start include: Blue Sea, Kosmá Zótou 7, just off the bottom of 25-Avgoústou (Ⓣ2810 241 097, Ⓦwww.bluesearentals.com), which gives a twenty percent discount to Rough Guide readers, and Sun Rise, 25-Avgoústou 46 (Ⓣ2810 221 609, Ⓦwww.crete-web.gr/rentacar/sunrise). For cars try: Kosmos, 25-Avgoústou 15 (Ⓣ2810 241 357, Ⓦwww.cosmos-sa.gr) or Ritz in the Hotel Rea, Kalimeráki 1 (Ⓣ2810 223 638). All offer free delivery to hotels and airport.

Ferry tickets Available from Minoan Lines, 25-Avgoústou 78 (Ⓣ2810 229 646, Ⓦwww.minoan.gr), which handles the islands and Athens; and ANEK Lines, 25-Avgoústou 33 (Ⓣ2810 222 481, Ⓦwww.anek.gr), for Athens only; also try any of the travel agents listed below. Another source for tickets and ferry information is the long-established Paleologus Travel, 25-Avgoústou 5 (Ⓣ2810 346 185); their comprehensive websites (Ⓦwww.ferries.gr, Ⓦwww.greekislands.gr) are excellent.

Hospital The closest is the Venizelou Hospital, on the Knossós road south out of town (Ⓣ2810 368 000).

Internet There are a number of Internet cafés in and around the centre, including Netcafé, Odhós-1878 4 (daily 10am–2am) and Gallery Games, Koraí 14.

Laundry Washsalon, Hándhakos 18 (Mon–Sat 8.30am–9pm), is reliable and also does service washes (€7 for 6kg). The slightly cheaper (€5.80 for 6kg) Laundry Perfect at Malikoúti 32, north of the Archeological Museum, is also good (Mon–Sat 9am–9pm).

Left luggage Offices in (bus) Station A (daily 6.30am–8pm; €1 per bag per day), but not Station B, as well as a commercial agency at Hándhakos 18 (daily 24hr; €1.50 per large locker per day). Blue Sea, Kotzia 3 off Epimenidhou near the Venetian harbour (daily 7am–11pm) is a reliable and similar outfit and stores bags for €1 per day. You can also leave bags at the youth hostel (even if you don't stay there) for €2 per bag per day. If you want to leave your bag while you go off on a bike for a day or two, the rental company should be prepared to store it.

Newspapers and books For English-language newspapers and novels, Bibliopoleio, almost opposite the Morosini Fountain on Platía Venizélou, is the most central. The excellent Planet International Bookstore, near the seafront at Hándhakos 73, has the island's biggest stock of English-language titles and is a great place to browse.

Pharmacies Plentiful on the main shopping streets – at least one is open 24hr on a rota basis; the others will have a sign on the door indicating which it is. There are traditional herbalists in the market.

Post office Main office in Platía Dhaskaloyiánnis, off Platía Eleftherías (Mon–Fri 7.30am–8pm).

Taxis Major taxi ranks are in Platía Eleftherías, Platía Kornarou and at the bus stations, or call ⓣ2810 210 102/168. Prices displayed on boards at the taxi stands.

Toilets In Platía Kornarou (at the southern end of the market) and the public gardens near the cathedral, or at the bus stations.

Travel agencies Budget operators and student specialists include the extremely helpful Blavakis Travel, Platía Kallergón 8, just off 25-Avgoústou by the entrance to El Greco Park (ⓣ2810 282 541). For excursions around the island, villa rentals and so on, the bigger operators are probably easier: Creta Travel Bureau, Dhikeosínis 49 (ⓣ2810 300 610), or Hilouris Travel, 25-Avgoústou 76 (ⓣ2810 343 400).

Knossos

KNOSSOS, the largest of the **Minoan palaces**, reached its cultural peak more than three thousand years ago, though a town of some importance persisted here well into the Roman era. It lies on a low, largely man-made hill some 5km southeast of Iráklion; the surrounding hillsides are rich in lesser remains spanning 25 centuries, starting at the beginning of the second millennium BC.

Just over a century ago the palace existed only in mythology. Knossos was the court of the legendary King Minos, whose wife Pasiphae bore the Minotaur, half-bull, half-man. Here the labyrinth was constructed by Daedalus to contain the monster, and youths were brought from Athens as human sacrifice until Theseus arrived to slay the beast and, with Ariadne's help, escape its lair. The discovery of the palace, and the interplay of these legends with fact, is among the most amazing tales of modern archeology. Heinrich Schliemann, the German excavator of Troy, suspected that a major Minoan palace lay under the various tumuli here, but was denied the necessary permission to dig by the local Ottoman authorities at the end of the nineteenth century. It was left for Sir Arthur Evans, whose name is indelibly associated with Knossos, to excavate the site, from 1900 onwards.

Local **buses** #2 and #4 set off every ten minutes from Iráklion's city bus stands (adjacent to the eastbound bus station), proceed up 25-Avgoústou (with a stop just south of Platía Venizélou) and out of town on Odhós-1821 and Evans. This is also the route you should take if **driving** (follow the signs from Platía Eleftherías); there's a large **free car park** downhill on the left, immediately before the site entrance, which will enable you to avoid paying exorbitant rates for the private car parks dotting the road immediately before this (and whose touts will attempt to wave you in). A **taxi** from the centre will cost around €7. At Knossos, outside the fenced site, stands a partly restored Minoan caravanserai where ancient wayfarers would rest and water their animals. Head out onto the road and you'll find no lack of watering holes for modern travellers either – a string of rather pricey tavernas and tacky souvenir stands.

The British School at Athens has a useful website (ⓦhttp://www.bsa.ac.uk/knosos/index.htm?vrtour) dedicated to Knossos, with detail on the history of the site and excavations in addition to a virtual tour.

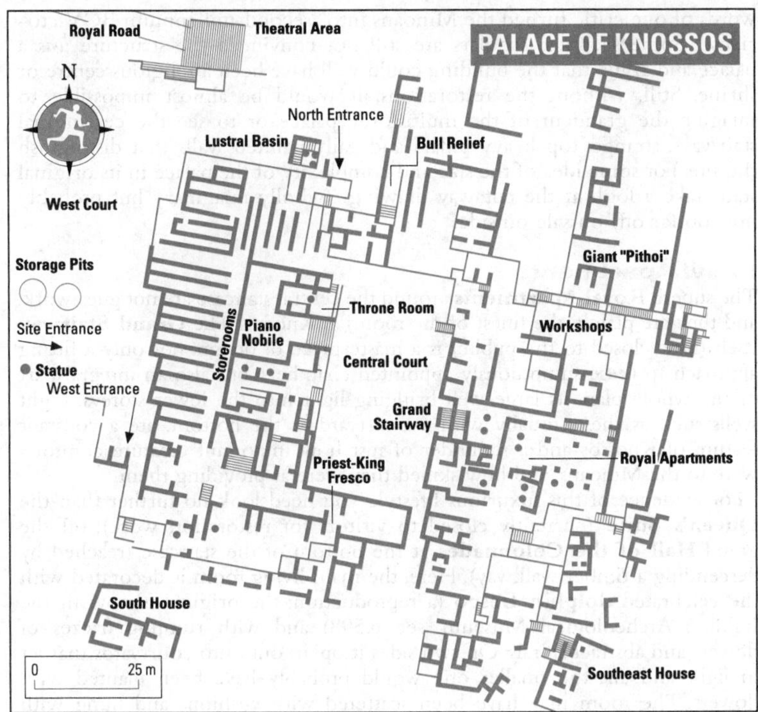

The site

As soon as you enter the **Palace of Knossos** (daily: April–Sept 8am–7.30pm; Oct–March 8.30am–3pm; €6) through the West Court, the ancient ceremonial entrance, it is clear how the legends of the labyrinth grew up around it. Even with a detailed plan, it's almost impossible to find your way around the complex with any success, although a series of **timber walkways** – whose purpose is to protect the monument from the feet of its hundreds of thousands of visitors – now channels visitors around the site, severely restricting the scope for independent exploration. If you're worried about missing the highlights, you can always tag along with one of the constant guided tours for a while, catching the patter and then backtracking to absorb the detail when the crowd has moved on. Outside the period December to February you won't get the place to yourself, whenever you come, but exploring on your own does give you the opportunity to appreciate individual parts of the palace in the brief lulls between groups.

Knossos was liberally "restored" by Evans, and these restorations have been the source of furious controversy among archeologists ever since. It has become clear that much of Evans' upper level – the so-called *piano nobile* – is pure conjecture. Even so, and putting archeological ethics to one side, his guess as to what the palace might have looked like is certainly as good as anyone's, and it makes the other sites infinitely more meaningful if you have seen Knossos first. Almost as controversial are Evans' designations of the various parts of the palace: he fantasized a royal family living here and in the words of one critic turned the Minoans into "second-millennium BC Victorians". Some sceptical scholars are still not convinced the structure *was* a palace and argue that the building could well have been a religious centre or shrine. Still, without the restorations, it would be almost impossible to imagine the grandeur of the multistorey palace or to see the ceremonial stairways, strange, top-heavy pillars and gaily painted walls that distinguish the site. For some idea of the size and complexity of the palace in its original state, take a look at the cutaway drawings (wholly imaginary but probably not too far off) on sale outside.

Royal Apartments

The superb **Royal Apartments** around the central staircase are not guesswork, and they are plainly the finest of the rooms at Knossos. The **Grand Stairway** itself (now closed to the public) is a masterpiece of design: not only a fitting approach to these sumptuously appointed chambers, but also an integral part of the whole plan, its large well bringing light into the lower storeys. Light wells such as these, usually with a courtyard at the bottom, are a constant feature of Knossos and a reminder of just how important creature comforts were to the Minoans, and how skilled they were at providing them.

For evidence of this luxurious lifestyle you need look no further than the **Queen's Suite** (currently closed to visitors for restoration work), off the grand **Hall of the Colonnades** at the bottom of the staircase (reached by descending a timber walkway). Here, the main living room is decorated with the celebrated **dolphin fresco** (a reproduction; the original is now in the Iráklion Archeological Museum, see p.598) and with running friezes of flowers and abstract spirals. On two sides it opens out onto courtyards that let in light and air; the smaller one would probably have been planted with flowers. The room may have been scattered with cushions and hung with plush drapes, while doors and further curtains between the pillars would have allowed for privacy, and provided cool shade in the heat of the day. Remember, though, that all this is speculation and some of it is pure hype; the dolphin fresco, for example, was found on the courtyard floor, not in the room itself, and would have been viewed from an upper balcony as a sort of trompe l'oeil, like looking through a glass-bottomed boat. Whatever the truth, this is an impressive example of Minoan architecture, the more so when you follow the dark passage around to the queen's **bathroom** (now only partially visible behind a screen). Here is a clay tub, protected behind a low wall (and again probably screened by curtains when in use), and the famous "flushing" toilet (a hole in the ground with drains to take the waste away – it was flushed by throwing a bucket of water down).

The much-perused **drainage system** was a series of interconnecting terracotta pipes running underneath most of the palace. Guides to the site never fail to point these out as evidence of the advanced state of Minoan civilization, and they are indeed quite an achievement, in particular the system of baffles and overflows to slow down the runoff and avoid any danger of flooding. Just how much running water there would have been, however, is another matter. Although the water supply was, and is, at the bottom of the hill, the combined efforts of collecting the rainwater and hauling it up to the palace can hardly have been sufficient to supply the needs of more than a small elite. The recent discovery of remnants of an aqueduct system carrying water to the palace from springs on nearby Mount Ioúktas (the same source that today provides water for the Morosini Fountain in Iráklion) could mean that this was not the only water supply.

The Grand Stairway ascends to the floor above the queen's domain, and a set of rooms generally regarded as the **King's Quarters** (currently not on view). These are chambers in a considerably sterner vein; the staircase opens into a grandiose reception chamber known as the **Hall of the Royal Guard** (or Hall of the Colonnades), its walls decorated in repeated shield patterns. Immediately off here is the **Hall of the Double Axes** (or the King's Room), believed to have been the ruler's personal chamber, a double room that would allow for privacy in one portion while audiences were held in the more public section. Its name comes from the double-axe symbol carved into every block of masonry.

The Throne Room and the rest of the palace

At the top of the Grand Stairway (you will need to retrace your steps up the timber staircase), you emerge onto the broad **Central Court**, a feature of all the Minoan palaces. Open now, this would once have been enclosed by the walls of the buildings all around. On the far side, in the northwestern corner of the courtyard, is the entrance to another of Knossos's most atmospheric survivals, the **Throne Room**. Here, a worn stone throne – with its hollowed shaping for the posterior – sits against the wall of a surprisingly small chamber; along the walls around it are ranged stone benches, suggesting a king ruling in council, and behind there's a reconstructed fresco of two griffins. Just how much rebuilding took place here can be gauged from the fact that when the throne was unearthed the surrounding ruins cleared its back by only a few centimetres: the ceiling and rooms above are all the creation of Evans' "reconstitution", as he preferred to describe his imaginative reconstructions. Anyway, in all probability in Minoan times this was the seat of a priestess rather than a ruler (there's nothing like it in any other Minoan palace), and its conversion into a throne room seems to have been a late innovation wrought by the invading Mycenaeans, during their short-lived domination prior to the palace's final destruction in the fourteenth century BC. The Throne Room is now closed off with a wooden gate, but you can lean over this for a good view, and in the antechamber there's a wooden copy of the throne on which everyone used to perch to have their picture taken, but this is now also off limits.

The rest you'll see as you wander, contemplating the legends of the place which blur with reality. Try not to miss the giant *pithoi* in the northeast quadrant of the site, an area known as the palace workshops; the storage chambers which you see from behind the Throne Room, and the reproduced frescoes in the reconstructed room above it; the fresco of the Priest-King looking down on the south side of the central court, and the relief of a charging bull on its north side. This last would have greeted you if you entered the palace through its north door; you can see evidence here of some kind of gatehouse and a lustral bath, a sunken area perhaps used for ceremonial bathing and purification. Just outside this gate is the **theatral area** (another Evans designation), an open space a little like a stepped amphitheatre, which may have been used for ritual performances or dances. From here the **Royal Road**, claimed as the oldest road in Europe, sets out. At one time, this probably ran right across the island; nowadays it ends after about 100m in a brick wall beneath the modern road. Circling back around the outside of the palace, you can get an idea of its scale by looking up at it; on the south side are a couple of small reconstructed Minoan houses which are worth exploring.

Southwest from Iráklion: sites and beaches

If you take a **tour** from Iráklion (or one of the resorts), you'll probably visit the **Gortys**, **Phaestos** and **Ayía Triádha** sites in a day, with a lunchtime swim at **Mátala** thrown in. Doing it by public transport, you'll be forced into a rather more leisurely pace, but there's still no reason why you shouldn't get to all three and reach Mátala within the day; if necessary, it's easy enough to hitch the final stretch. **Bus services** to the Phaestos site are excellent, with some nine a day to and from Iráklion (fewer Sun), five of which continue to or come from Mátala; there are also services direct to Ayía Galíni. If you're arriving in the afternoon, plan to visit Ayía Triádha first, as it closes early.

The route to Áyii Dhéka

The road from Iráklion towards Phaestos is a pretty good one by the standards of Cretan mountain roads, albeit rather dull. The country you're heading towards is the richest agricultural land on the island and, right from the start, the villages en route are large and businesslike. In the biggest of them, **Ayía Varvára**, there's a great rock outcrop known as the **Omphalos** (Navel) of Crete, supposedly the very centre of the island.

Past here, you descend rapidly to the fertile fields of the Messará plain, where the road joins the main route across the south near the village of **ÁYII DHÉKA**, for religious Cretans something of a place of pilgrimage; its name, "The Ten Saints", refers to ten early Christians martyred here under the Romans. The old Byzantine church in the centre of the village preserves the stone block on which they are supposed to have been decapitated and in a crypt below the modern church on the village's western edge you can see the martyrs' (now empty) tombs. It's an attractive village to wander around, with several places to eat and even some **rooms** – try *Dimitris Taverna* (☎28920 31560; ❷), where you can both stay and eat, which has excellent-value en-suite, air-conditioned rooms with views above its **restaurant** with an attractive terrace at the rear below.

Gortys and around

Within easy walking distance of Áyii Dhéka, either through the fields or along the main road, sprawls the site of **Gortys** (daily 8am–7.30pm; €4), ruined capital of the Roman province that included not only Crete but also much of North Africa. After a look at the plan of the extensive site at the entrance, cutting across the fields to the south of the road will give you some idea of the scale of this city, at its zenith in approximately the third century AD. An enormous variety of remains, including an impressive **theatre** and a couple of **temples,** are strewn across your route, and more spectacular discoveries are being unearthed by the archeologists who return to dig each summer. Even in Áyii Dhéka you'll see Roman pillars and statues lying around in people's yards or propping up their walls.

There was a settlement here from the earliest times and evidence of a Minoan site has been unearthed on the acropolis, but the extant ruins date almost entirely from the Roman era. Only now is the site being systematically excavated by the Italian Archeological School. At the main entrance to the **fenced site**, to the north of the road, are the ruins of the still impressive **basilica of Áyios Títos**; the eponymous saint converted the island to Christianity and was its first bishop.

Beyond this is the **odeion** which houses the most important discovery on the site, the **Law Code**. These great inscribed blocks of stone were incorporated by the Romans from a much earlier stage of the city's development; they're written in an obscure early Greek-Cretan dialect, and in a style known as *boustrophedon* (ox-ploughed), with the lines reading alternately in opposite directions like the furrows of a ploughed field. At 10m by 3m, this is reputedly the largest Greek inscription ever found. The laws set forth reflect a strictly hierarchical society: five witnesses were needed to convict a free man of a crime, only one for a slave; raping a free man or woman carried a fine of a hundred *staters*, violating a serf only five. A small **museum** in a loggia (also within the fenced area) holds a number of large and finely worked sculptures found at Gortys, more evidence of the city's importance. Next to the museum is a **café** (same hours as site).

Míres

Some 20km west of Gortys, **MÍRES** is an important market town and focal point of transport for the fertile Messará plain: if you're switching buses to get from the beaches on the south coast to the archeological sites or the west, this is where you'll do it. There are good facilities including a **bank**, a few **restaurants** and a couple of **rooms**, though there's no particular reason to stay unless you are waiting for a bus or looking for work (it's one of the better places for agricultural jobs). A useful **Internet** café, Net Escape, near the bus stop will allow you to send a few emails while awaiting onward connections. Heading straight for Phaestos, there's usually no need to stop.

Phaestos (Festós)

The **Palace of Phaestos** (daily 8am–7.30pm; €4, joint ticket with **Ayía Triádha** €6) was excavated by the Italian Federico Halbherr (also responsible for the early work at Gortys) at almost exactly the same time as Evans was working at Knossos. The style of the excavations, however, could hardly have been more different. Here, to the approval of most traditional archeologists, reconstruction was kept to an absolute minimum – it's all bare foundations, and walls which rise at most 1m above ground level. This means that, despite a magnificent setting overlooking the plain of Messará, the palace at Phaestos is not as immediately arresting as those at Knossos or Malia, but no less fascinating.

It's interesting to speculate why the palace was built halfway up a hill rather than on the plain below – certainly not for defence, for this is in no way a good defensive position. Psychological superiority over the peasants or reasons of health are both possible, but it seems quite likely that it was simply the magnificent view that finally swayed the decision. The site looks over Psilorítis to the north and the huge plain, with the Lasíthi mountains beyond it, to the east. Towards the top of Psilorítis you should be able to make out a small black smudge to the right of a saddle between two peaks. This marks the entrance to the Kamáres Cave, a shrine sacred to the Minoans and the source of a great hoard of elaborate pottery now in the Iráklion Archeological Museum.

On the ground closer at hand, you can hardly fail to notice the strong similarities between Phaestos and the other palaces: the same huge rows of storage jars, the great courtyard with its monumental stairway, and the theatre area. Unique to Phaestos, however, is the third courtyard, in the middle of which are the remains of a **furnace** used for metalworking. Indeed, this eastern corner of the palace seems to have been home to a number of craftsmen, including potters and carpenters. Oddly enough, Phaestos was much less ornately decorated than Knossos; there is no evidence, for example, of any of the dramatic Minoan wall-paintings.

The **tourist pavilion** near the entrance serves drinks and **food**, as well as the usual postcards, books and souvenirs. The nearby village of **ÁYIOS IOÁNNIS**, along the road towards Mátala, has economical **rooms**, including some basic ones at *Taverna Ayios Ioannis* (Ⓣ28920 42006; ❶), which is also a good place to eat charcoal-grilled *kounélli* (rabbit) and lamb on a leafy terrace.

Ayía Triádha

Some of the finest artworks in the museum at Iráklion came from **Ayía Triádha** (daily: May–Sept 10am–4pm; Oct–April 8.30am–3pm; €4, joint ticket with Phaestos €6), about a 45-minute walk (or short drive) from Phaestos. No one is quite sure what this site is, but the most common theory has it as some kind of royal summer villa. It's smaller than the palaces but, if anything, even more lavishly appointed and beautifully situated. In any event, it's an attractive place to visit, far less crowded than Phaestos, with a wealth of interesting little details. Look out in particular for the row of **stores** in front of what was apparently a marketplace, although recent thinking tends towards the idea that these were constructed after the villa had declined, possibly in the Mycenaean period. The remains of a **paved road** that probably led down to a harbour on the Gulf of Messará can also be seen running alongside the royal villa. The sea itself looks invitingly close, separated from the base of the hill only by Timbáki airfield (mainly used for motor racing these days), but if you try to drive down there, it's almost impossible to find your way around the unmarked dust tracks. There's a fourteenth-century **chapel** – dedicated to Áyios Yeóryios – at the site, worth visiting in its own right for the remains of ancient frescoes (key available from the ticket office).

Mátala and around

MÁTALA has by far the best-known beach in Iráklion province, widely promoted and included in tours mainly because of the famous caves cut into the cliffs above its beautiful sands. These are believed to be ancient tombs first used by Romans or early Christians, but more recently inhabited by a sizeable hippie community (including some famous names such as Bob Dylan and Joni Mitchell) in the 1960s and 1970s. You'll still meet people who will assure you that this is *the* travellers' beach on Crete, although today in high season the town is full of package tourists and tries hard to present a more respectable image. The caves have long since been cleared and cleaned and are now a fenced-off archeological site (April–Sept daily 10am–7pm; €2), locked up every evening.

The years since the early 1980s have seen the arrival of crowds and the development of hotels, restaurants and even a disco to service them; early afternoon, when the tour buses pull in for their swimming stop, sees the beach packed to overflowing. If you're prepared to accept Mátala for what it is – a resort of some size – you'll find the place more than bearable. The town beach is beautiful, and if the crowds get excessive, you can climb over the rocks in about twenty minutes (past more caves, many of which are inhabited through the summer) to another excellent stretch of sand, known locally as "Red Beach". In the evening, when the day-trippers have gone, there are waterside bars and restaurants looking out over invariably spectacular sunsets. If you are arriving **by car**, park either on the road leading into the town or at the beach car park (€1 per day), on the right as you reach the town proper.

The chief problems with staying in Mátala concern prices and crowds: rooms are relatively expensive and oversubscribed, and food is good but not cheap. If you want **accommodation**, a cluster of places lies near to the *Zafiria* hotel (Ⓣ28920 45112, Ⓦwww.zafiria-matala.com; ❸), just beyond the car park turn-off. Here rooms come with air conditioning but no TV, and there's a pool. For more economical options try looking in the little street to the left just beyond the *Zafiria* signed "Hotels and Rent Rooms". Here you'll find several rooms for rent, such as *Matala View* (Ⓣ28920 45114, Ⓦwww.matala-apartments.com; ❷), which also rents studios and apartments sleeping two (❸) or up to four (❹). Nearby, the pleasant, modern and good-value *Fantastik* (Ⓣ28920 45362, Ⓕ28920 45492; ❷) has airy air-conditioned en suites with fridge, and the equally good and very friendly *Hotel Nikos* (Ⓣ28920 45375, Ⓦwww.interkriti.net/hotel/matala/nikos/; ❷) has pleasant air conditioning rooms off a plant-filled patio. If these are full, then everywhere closer in is likely to be as well, so head back out along the main road where places tend to fill up last, or try the **campsite**, *Camping of Matala* (Ⓣ28920 45720), next to the beach above the car park; *Kommos Camping* (Ⓣ28920 45596) is a nicer site, but a few kilometres out of Mátala and reached by heading back towards Pitsídhia and turning left along a signed track.

There are places to **eat and drink** all over the main part of town. It's worth seeking out the *Skala* fish taverna on the south side of the bay for fresh seafood and a great view, while *Taverna Eleni* is another reliable choice overlooking the beach. **Nightlife** is generally low-key; there are numerous bars which gradually turn up the music volume as the evening wears on. Most of the livelier places are at the southern end of the bay including *Port Side*, a cocktail bar with an enviable beachside location, and *Marinero* and *Tommy's Music Bar* which get lively later on. *Kafe Kantari*, on the main square, is another place where people gather after dark. **Internet** access is available inside the stylish *Kafeneio* bar on the same square or at the *Zafiria Café* opposite (and owned by) the hotel of the same name. Other facilities, including various stores and a good **bookshop** (with international press), are next to *Kafeneio*. Currency exchange and **ATMs**, car and bike rental and travel agents are located on or around the square too, just off which there's also a covered market where tourist tat has almost

▲ View of the beach from one of Mátala's caves

squeezed out the fruit and veg stalls. The small **post office** lies 50m to the east of the *Zafiria* hotel, facing the entrance to the car park.

Around Mátala: Pitsídhia and Kalamáki

A more peaceful place to stay is **PITSÍDHIA**, about 5km inland. This has long been an alternative inland option to staying in Mátala, so it's not quite as cheap as you might expect, but there are plenty of rooms, lively places to eat and even music bars. If you decide to stay here, the beach at **KALAMÁKI** is an alternative to Mátala. Both beaches are approximately the same distance to walk, though there is a much better chance of a bus or a lift to Mátala. Kalamáki has developed somewhat, with a number of **rooms** – *Psiloritis* (Ⓣ28920 45693, Ⓕ28920 45249; ❶–❷) is a good bet – and a couple of tavernas, but it's still a rather unfinished, soulless little place. The beach stretches for miles, surprisingly wild and windswept, lashed by sometimes dangerously rough surf. At the southern end (more easily reached by a path off the Pitsídhia–Mátala road) lies **Kommos**, once a Minoan port serving Phaestos and now the site of a major archeological excavation. It's not yet open to the public, but you can peer into the fenced-off area to see what's been revealed so far, which is pretty impressive: dwellings, streets, hefty stonework and even the ship sheds where repairs on the Minoan fleet were carried out.

Iráklion's south coast

South of the Messará plain are two more beach resorts, **Kalí Liménes** and **Léndas**, with numerous other little beaches along the coast in between, but nothing spectacular. **Public transport** is very limited indeed; you'll almost always have to travel via Míres (see p.607). If you have your own transport, the roads in these parts are all passable and newly sealed, but most are very slow going; the Kófinas hills, which divide the plain from the coast, are surprisingly precipitous.

Kalí Liménes and Léndas

While Mátala itself was an important port under the Romans, the chief harbour for Gortys lay on the other side of Cape Líthinon at **KALÍ LIMÉNES**. Nowadays, this is once again a significant port – for oil tankers. This has rather spoilt its chances of becoming a major resort, and there are few proper facilities, but some people like Kalí Liménes: it's certainly off the beaten track and the constant procession of tankers gives you something to look at while beach lounging. **LÉNDAS**, further east along the coast, is far more popular, with a couple of buses daily from Iráklion and a partly justified reputation for being peaceful (sullied by considerable summer crowds). Many people who arrive think they've come to the wrong place, as at first sight the village looks shabby, the beach is small, rocky and dirty, and the rooms are frequently all booked. A number of visitors leave without ever correcting that initial impression; the attraction of Léndas is not the village at all but the beach on the other (west) side of the headland. Here lies a vast, excellent sandy strand named **Dhytikós** (or Dhiskós) **Beach**, part of it usually taken over by nudists, with a number of taverna/bars overlooking it from the roadside. The beach is a couple of kilometres from Léndas, along a rough track; if you're walking, you can save time by cutting across the headland. A considerably more attractive prospect than staying in Léndas itself is **camping** on the beach to the west of the village or, with luck, getting a **room** at one of the few beach tavernas – try *Villa Tsapakis* (Ⓣ28920 95378, Ⓦwww.villa-tsapakis.gr; ❷), with sea-view rooms and reductions for longer stays. They will also change money on a credit card here (a useful service in this part of Crete where banks and ATMs are nonexistent) and have their own decent **taverna**, *Odysseas*, nearby. After you've discovered the beach, even Léndas begins to look more welcoming, and at least it has most of the facilities you'll need, including a couple of **minimarkets**, both of which will change money, phone box, and an **Internet** café (enterprisingly named Café Internet) on the main square. **Car rental** is available at the *Villa Tsapakis* (see p.610). Léndas also has numerous places to **eat and drink**: the outstanding *Taverna El Greco* (☎28920 95322) with a leafy terrace above the beach on the east side of the village is one of the best restaurants on the whole south coast – their *oktapódhi* (octopus), *kolikythákia* (fried zucchini) or prime Messará beef pepper steak are all recommended. Its popularity means that you may need to book in high season; *Akti* and *Elpida* on the main square are reasonable substitutes.

Once you've come to terms with the place, you can also explore some deserted beaches eastwards, and the scrappy remains of **ancient Lebena** on a hilltop overlooking them. There was an important Asklepion (temple of the god Asklepios) here around some now-diverted warm springs, but only the odd broken column and fragments of mosaic survive in a fenced-off area on the village's northern edge.

East of Iráklion: the package-tour coast

East of Iráklion, the startling pace of **tourist development** in Crete is all too plain to see. The merest hint of a beach is an excuse to build at least one hotel, and these are outnumbered by the concrete shells of resorts-to-be. It's hard to find a room in this monument to the package-tour industry, and it can be expensive if you do. That said, there are one or two highlights amidst the dross, which are well worth a visit. On the eastern fringe of Hersónissos there's a superb folk museum and, beyond the teenage-package resort of Mália, a fine **Minoan palace** will transport you back three and a half millennia.

Goúrnes and Goúves

As a general rule, the further east you go, the better things get: when the road detours all too briefly inland, the more alluring Crete of olive groves and stark mountains asserts itself. You certainly won't see much of it at **GOÚRNES**, where an abandoned former US Air Force base still dominates much of the coastline, awaiting a plan for its redevelopment, or at nearby Káto Goúves, where there's a **campsite**, *Camping Creta* (☎28970 41400), sharing a boundary with the former base. From here, however, you can head inland to the old village of **GOÚVES**, a refreshing contrast, and just beyond to the **Skotinó cave**, one of the largest and most spectacular on the island (about an hour's walk from the coast; open all hours; free).

Hersónissos (Límin Hersoníssou)

Heading east from Goúves you'll pass the turn-off for the new E75 Hersónissos bypass (avoiding the beach resort's bottleneck), which cuts inland to rejoin the coast road just before Stalídha. Shortly beyond this junction, there's the turning for the direct route up to the Lasíthi Plateau. Carry straight on, though, and you'll roll into the first of the really big resorts, **HERSÓNISSOS** or, more correctly, Límin Hersoníssou; Hersónissos is the village in the hills just behind, also overrun by tourists. Once just a small fishing village, today Hersónissos is the most popular of Crete's package resorts. If what you want is plenty of video-bars, tavernas, restaurants and Eurodisco nightlife, then this is the place to come. The resort has numerous small patches of sand beach between rocky outcrops, but a shortage of places to stay in peak season.

The focal main street, two-kilometre-long Odhós Eleftheriou Venizélou, is a seemingly endless ribbon of bars, travel agents, tacky jewellery and beachwear shops, amusement arcades and – during the daytime at least – nose-to-tail traffic jams. North of here, along the modern seafront, a solid line of restaurants and bars is broken only by the occasional souvenir shop; in their midst you'll find a small pyramidal Roman **fountain** with broken mosaics of fishing scenes, the only real relic of the ancient town of Chersonesos. Around the headland above the harbour and in odd places along the seafront, you can see remains of Roman harbour installations, mostly submerged.

Beach and clubs excepted, the distractions of Hersónissos comprise **Lychnostatis Open-Air Museum** (Mon–Fri & Sun 9.30am–2pm; €5), a surprisingly rewarding "museum" of traditional Crete, on the coast at the eastern edge of the town; a small aquarium, **Aqua World** (April–Oct daily 10am–6pm; €8 adults, €5 under-12s), just off the main road at the west end of town, up the road almost opposite the stylish *Vibe* style bar. To cool down, there's the watersports paradise **Star Beach Water Park** (daily: April & May 10am–6pm; June–Sept 10am–7pm; free entry but charges for most activities) near the beach at the eastern end of the resort or, 3km inland, the competing and more elaborate **Aqua Splash Water Park** (€18 full day, under-12s €12; cut-price late-entry deals).

A short distance inland are the three **hill villages** of Koutoulafári, Piskopianó and "old" Hersónissos, which all have a good selection of tavernas, and are worth searching out for accommodation.

Practicalities

Finding somewhere to **stay** in Hersónissos can verge on the impossible in July and August. Much of the **accommodation** is allocated to package-tour operators and what remains for casual visitors is among the priciest on the island. To check for general availability of accommodation, the quickest and best option is to enquire at one of the many travel agencies along Venizélou such as KTEL Tours next to the bus stop and opposite the petrol station in the centre of town. The town's most reasonably priced central options include *Zorba's Hotel*, Beach Road (Ⓣ28970 22134, Ⓦwww.hersonissos.com/zorbas; ❸), and *Selena*, Maragáki 13 (Ⓣ & Ⓕ28970 25180; ❸) near the sea-front action, which can be noisy at night. One place to try on the western edge as you enter the town is *Hotel Ilios* (Ⓣ28970 22500, Ⓕ28970 22582; ❸–❹), just back from the main road, which has a rooftop pool. There are two good **campsites**: one at the eastern end of town, *Caravan Camping* (Ⓣ28970 24718), which also has several reed-roofed bungalows, and *Camping Hersonissos* (Ⓣ28970 22902), just to the west of town.

Despite the vast number of **eating places**, there are few worth recommending, and the tavernas down on the harbourfront should be avoided. One of the few Greek tavernas that stands out is *Kavouri* along Arhéou Theátrou, but it's fairly expensive; a cheaper in-town alternative for some delicious and inexpensive Cretan cooking is *Taverna Creta Giannis*, Kaniadhakí 4, just off the south side of Venizélou slightly east of the church (closes 10pm). Nearby, and also definitely worth a try, is *Passage to India*, an authentic and extremely good Indian restaurant; it lies on Petrákis, another side street just off the main street near the church. For an evening stroll you could head a couple of kilometres up the hill to Hersónissos village where *Tria Adelphi* (The Three Brothers) is one of the more authentic tavernas clustered around its main square. Both here and in the neighbouring hill village of Koutoulafári, you can have a relaxed evening amongst the narrow streets and small platíes.

Hersónissos is renowned for its **nightlife**, and there's certainly no shortage of it. A night's partying kicks off in the **bars** along and around Venizélou. After 10pm the crowds start to head down the main pedestrianized street leading to the harbour area which is soon packed with promenaders and the overspill from countless noisy music bars through to the early hours. *Camelot* is currently one of the most popular clubs here with the nearby music bars *Cameo*, *Status* (which opens at 4.30am), *TNT* and the *Copa Cabana Club* also attracting plenty of custom.

There is an open-air **cinema** showing original-version films at the *Creta Maris* hotel at the west end of the town and close to the beach.

Services such as **banks**, **bike and car rental** and a **post office** are all on or just off Venizélou, as are the **taxi ranks**. There are a number of **Internet** cafés: Easy Internet Café is one of several on the waterfront near the harbour, while CNet, Papadoyiorgi 10, alongside the church, is a more central option. **Buses** running east and west leave from the main bus stop on Venizélou every thirty minutes.

Mália

Some 8km east of Hersónissos and similar to the other resorts along this stretch of coast, much of **MÁLIA** is carved up by the package industry, so in peak season finding a place to stay is not always easy. The town's focus is a T-junction (where the **bus** drops you) and from where the beach road – a kilometre-long strip lined with bars, clubs, games arcades, tavernas and souvenir shops – heads north to the sea and beaches. South of this junction the older village presents a slightly saner image of what Mália used to be, but even here rampant commercialism is making inroads.

Practicalities

The best **accommodation** options, especially if you want any sleep, are among the numerous **rooms** and *pensions* signposted in the old town, such as *Esperia* (Ⓣ28970 31086; ③), up a side road slightly east of the T-junction. Backtracking from the junction, along the main Iráklion road (Elefthériou Venizélou), there are a number of reasonably priced **pensions** on the left and right, including *Hibiscus* (Ⓣ28970 31313, Ⓕ28970 32042; ③), which has rooms and studios with kitchenette and fridge around a pool in a garden behind, or the nearby *Apartments Kipseli* (②) for simple studios with kitchenette, fridge and balcony. Otherwise, on arrival visit one of the travel companies along the main road – such as the reliable SK-Travel, Elefthériou Venizélou 200 (Ⓣ28970 31481) – to enquire about accommodation availability. All the other things you're likely to need – banks with **ATMs**, **post office** and food shops – are strung out along the main street near the junction. **Internet** access is widely available too: one of the cheaper and faster places is Citynet, at Elefthériou Venizélou 176.

Eating in Mália is unlikely to be a problem as **restaurants** jostle for your custom at every step, especially along the beach road. None is particularly good here, and a few are diabolical. The best places for a meal are around Platía Ayíou Dhimitríou, a pleasant square beside the church in the centre of the old village to the south of the main road. Here, you could try *Kalimera* or *Petros*, or the very pleasant *Kalesma* with a delightful terrace, perhaps after an aperitif at *Bar Yiannis* just north of the church or *Ouzeri Elizabeth* alongside it, where they serve local wine from the barrel. A little harder to find, and to the west of the square, *Apolafsi* is a good-quality small family taverna which is slightly less pricey than the others.

The beach road comes into its own at night, when the profusion of **bars** and **clubs** erupts into a pulsating cacophony. The aptly named *Zoo* is one of the most frenetic, and once past midnight the internal walls part to reveal an even larger dance area. Other popular venues (many British-owned and -run) along the strip include *Cloud Nine*, *Malibu*, *Zig-Zag*, *Apollo* and *Camelot Castle*. There is also a clutch of "English pubs" with names like *Newcastle*, *Red Lion* and *Brit's Bar*. Unfortunately, a good night's clubbing is frequently spoilt by groups pouring out of these places and getting into drink-fuelled brawls. Recent years have seen a police clampdown on such activities, and the situation has improved considerably.

The Palace of Malia

Much less imposing than either Knossos or Phaestos, the **Palace of Malia** (Tues–Sun 8.30am–3pm; €4), 2km east of Mália town, in some ways surpasses both. For a start, it's a great deal emptier and you can wander among the remains in relative peace. While no reconstruction has been attempted, the palace was never reoccupied after its second destruction in the fifteenth century BC, so the ground plan is virtually intact. It's much easier to comprehend than Knossos and, if you've seen the reconstructions there, it's easy to envisage this seaside palace in its days of glory. There's a real feeling of an ancient civilization with a taste for the good life, basking on the rich agricultural plain between the Lasíthi mountains and the sea.

From this site came the famous **gold pendant** of two bees (which can be seen in the Iráklion Archeological Museum or on any postcard stand), allegedly part of a hoard that was plundered and whose other treasures can now be found in the British Museum in London. The beautiful leopard-head axe, also in the museum at Iráklion, was another of the treasures found here. At the site, look out for the strange indented stone in the central court (which probably held ritual offerings), the remains of ceremonial stairways and the giant *pithoi*, which stand like sentinels around the palace. To the north and west of the main site, archeological digs are still going on as the **large town** which surrounded the palace comes slowly to light, and part of this can now be viewed via an overhead walkway.

Any passing **bus** should stop at the site, or you could even rent a **bike** for a couple of hours as it's a pleasant, flat ride from Mália town. Leaving the archeological zone and turning immediately right, you can follow the road down to a lovely stretch of clean and relatively peaceful **beach**, backed by fields, scrubland and a single makeshift **taverna**, which serves good fresh fish. From here you can walk back along the shore to Mália or take a bus (every 30min in either direction) from the stop on the main road.

Inland towards Mount Psiloritis

Of the **inland routes**, the old main road (via Márathos and Dhamásta) is not the most interesting. This, too, was something of a bypass in its day and there are few places of any size or appeal, though it's a very scenic drive. If you want to dawdle, you're better off on the road which cuts up to **Týlissos** and then goes via **Anóyia**. It's a pleasant ride through fertile valleys filled with olive groves and vineyards, a district (the Malevísi) renowned from Venetian times for the strong, sweet Malmsey wine.

Týlissos and Anóyia

TÝLISSOS has a significant archeological site (daily 8.30am–3pm; €2) where three Minoan houses were excavated; unfortunately, its reputation is based more on what was found here (many pieces in the Iráklion Archeological Museum) and on its significance for archeologists than on anything which remains to be seen. Still, it's worth a look, if you're passing, for a glimpse of Minoan life away from the big palaces, and for the tranquillity of the pine-shaded remains.

ANÓYIA is a much more tempting place to stay, especially if the summer heat is becoming oppressive. Spilling prettily down a hillside close below the highest peaks of the mountains, it looks traditional, but closer inspection shows that most of the buildings are actually concrete; the village was destroyed during World War II and the local men rounded up and shot – one of the German reprisals for the abduction of General Kreipe by the Cretan resistance. The town has a reputation as a centre of **lyra playing** (many famous exponents were born here) and also as a **handicrafts** centre (especially for woven and woollen goods), skills acquired both through bitter necessity after most of the men had been killed, and in a conscious attempt to revive the town. At any rate it worked, for the place is thriving today – thanks, it seems, to a buoyant agricultural sector made rich by stockbreeding, and the number of elderly widows keen to subject any visitor to their terrifyingly aggressive sales techniques.

Quite a few people pass through Anóyia during the day, but not many of them **stay**, even though there are some good *pensions* and rented **rooms** in the upper half of the town, including the flower-bedecked *Rooms Aris* (Ⓣ28340 31817, Ⓕ28340 31058; ❷) and the nearby *Aristea* (Ⓣ28340 31459; B&B ❷), which has an ebullient female proprietor and en-suite rooms with spectacular terrace views.

The town has a very different, more traditional ambience at night, and the only problem is likely to be finding a **place to eat**: although there are plenty of snack-bars and so-called tavernas, most have extremely basic menus, more or less limited to spit-barbecued lamb, which is the tasty local speciality served up by the grill places on the lower square. Options in the upper town include *Aetos* for spit-roasted lamb, on the main street, or a steep hike beyond this to the top of the village will bring you to *Taverna Skalomata* offering well-prepared taverna standards, good barbecued lamb, plus a fine view. Opposite this taverna is Anóyia's solitary **Internet** café, Infocost@.

Mount Psiloritis and its caves

Heading for the mountains, a smooth road ascends the 21km from Anóyia to an altitude of 1400m on the **Nídha plateau** at the base of Mount Psiloritis. Here, the *Taverna Nida* (Ⓣ28340 31141; April–Sept daily; Oct–March Sat & Sun only) serves up hearty mountain dishes featuring lamb, pork and chicken, and has a couple of simple **rooms** (B&B ❶), which makes it a good base for hikes in the surrounding mountains. A short path leads from the taverna to the celebrated **Idean cave** (Idhéon Ándhron), a rival of that on Mount Dhíkti (see p.617) for the title of Zeus's birthplace, and certainly associated from the earliest of times with the cult of Zeus. The remnants of a major archeological dig carried out inside – including a miniature railway used by archeologists to remove tonnes of rock and rubble – still litter the site, giving the place a rather unattractive prospect. When you enter the cave down concrete steps into the depths, it turns out to be a rather shallow affair, devoid even of natural wonders, with little to see.

The taverna also marks the start of the way to the top of **Mount Psiloritis** (2456m), Crete's highest mountain, a climb that for experienced, properly shod hikers is not at all arduous. The route (now forming a stretch of the E4 Pan-European footpath) is well marked with the usual red dots and paint splashes, and it should be a six- to seven-hour return journey to the **chapel of Tímios Stavrós** ("Holy Cross") at the summit, although in spring, thick snow may slow you down.

Eastern Crete

Eastern Crete is dominated by **Áyios Nikólaos**, and while it is a highly developed resort, by no means all of the east is like this. Far fewer people venture beyond the road south to **Ierápetra** and into the eastern isthmus, where only **Sitía** and the famous beach at **Váï** ever see anything approaching a crowd. Inland, too, there's interest, especially on the extraordinary **Lasíthi Plateau**, which is worth a night's stay if only to observe its abidingly rural life.

Inland to the Lasíthi Plateau

Leaving the palace at Malia, the highway cuts inland towards **NEÁPOLI**, soon beginning a spectacular climb into the mountains. Set in a high valley, Neápoli is a market town little touched by tourism. Just off a leafy main square there's an excellent **hotel**, *Neapolis* (☎28410 33967, www.neapolis-hotel.gr; ③), with air-conditioned rooms, some with fine views. On the main square there's a superb little **folk museum** (Mon 9am–2pm, Wed–Sun 9.30am–4.30pm; €1.50) displaying some fascinating photos, utensils and farming equipment from Neápoli's past, as well as reconstructions of a bar, schoolroom, cobbler's workshop and domestic kitchen from a bygone age. On the square – and 50m from the museum entrance – *Taverna Yeúseis* is a good place to **eat** and has a pleasant shady terrace. Beyond the town, it's about twenty minutes before the bus suddenly emerges high above the Gulf of Mirabéllo and Áyios Nikólaos, the island's biggest resort. If you're stopping, Neápoli also marks the second point of access to the **Lasíthi Plateau**.

Scores of bus tours drive up here daily to view the "thousands of white-cloth-sailed windmills" which irrigate the high plain ringed by mountains, and most groups will be disappointed. There are very few working windmills left, and these operate only for limited periods (mainly in June), although most roadside tavernas seem to have adopted many of those made redundant as marketing features. The drive alone is worthwhile, however, and the plain is a fine example of rural Crete at work, every inch devoted to the cultivation of potatoes, apples, pears, figs, olives and a host of other crops; stay in one of the villages for a night or two and you'll see real life return as the tourists leave. There are plenty of easy rambles around the villages as well, through orchards and past the rusting remains of derelict windmills.

You'll find **rooms** in the main village of **TZERMIÁDHO**, where the *Hotel Kourites* (☎28440 22194; ②) is to be found on the eastern edge, in **ÁYIOS YEÓRYIOS**, where there's a **folk museum and crafts centre**, as well as the economical and friendly *Hotel Dias* (☎28440 31207; ❶); in **MAGOULÁS** where rooms and fine food are on offer at *Taverna Dionysos* (☎28440 31672; ❷) and in **PSYKHRÓ**, where the *Hotel Zeus* (☎697 29 81 782 or enquire at *Taverna Halavro* close to the cave car park; ❷) lies close to the Dhiktean cave.

The Dhiktean cave

Psykhró is the most visited village on the plateau, as it's the base for visiting Lasíthi's other chief attraction: the birthplace of Zeus, the **Dhiktean cave** (daily 8am–7pm; €4; ask for the free information leaflet on the cave). In legend, Zeus's father, the Titan Kronos, was warned that he would be overthrown by a son, and accordingly ate all his offspring; however, when Rhea gave birth to Zeus in the cave, she fed Kronos a stone and left the child concealed, protected by the Kouretes, who beat their shields outside to disguise his cries. The rest, as they say, is history (or at least myth). There's an obvious path running up to the cave from Psykhró, near the start of which (beyond the car park) the mule handlers will attempt to persuade you the ascent is better done on one of their steeds (costing a hefty €10 one way). In reality, it's hardly a particularly long or dauntingly steep hike to the cave entrance.

The cave has been made more "visitor friendly" in recent years, with the introduction of concrete steps in place of slippery stones, and electric lighting instead of flashlamps and candles. Inevitably some of the magic and mystery has been lost, and the guides, who used to make the visit much more interesting with their hilarious and preposterous tales, have now been banned, presumably in the interests of accuracy and decorum. Thus you will now have to pick out for yourself the stalactites and stalagmites formed in the image of the breasts of Rhea where the infant Zeus was suckled, as well as the baby Zeus himself – a feat verging on the impossible for someone lacking a Cretan imagination.

One of the cave guardians, Petros Zarvakis, is also a wildlife expert and leads **guided wild-flower and bird-spotting hikes** (April–Sept) into the mountains surrounding the plain, and also to the summit of Mount Dhíkti; if he is not on duty at the cave entrance or at the taverna (*Taverna Petros* run by his family) in the car park, he can be contacted on ☎28440 31600 or 694 56 16 074. **Buses** run around the plateau to Psykhró direct from Iráklion and from Áyios Nikólaos via Neápoli. Both roads offer spectacular views, coiling through a succession of passes guarded by lines of ruined windmills.

Áyios Nikólaos and around

ÁYIOS NIKÓLAOS ("Ag Nik" to the majority of its British visitors) is set around a supposedly bottomless salt lake, now connected to the sea to form an inner harbour. It is supremely picturesque and has some style and charm, which it exploits to the full. There are no sights as such, but the excellent **Archeological Museum** (Tues–Sun 8am–5pm; €3) on Paleológou north of the lake, and an interesting **Folk Museum** (Tues–Sun 10am–2pm; €3) near the tourist office are both worth seeking out. The lake and port are surrounded by restaurants and bars, which charge above the odds, and whilst the resort is still very popular, some tourists are distinctly surprised to find themselves in a place with no decent beach at all.

There are swimming opportunities further north, however, where the pleasant low-key resort of **Eloúnda** is the gateway to the mysterious islet of **Spinalónga**, and some great backcountry inland – perfect to explore on a scooter. Inland

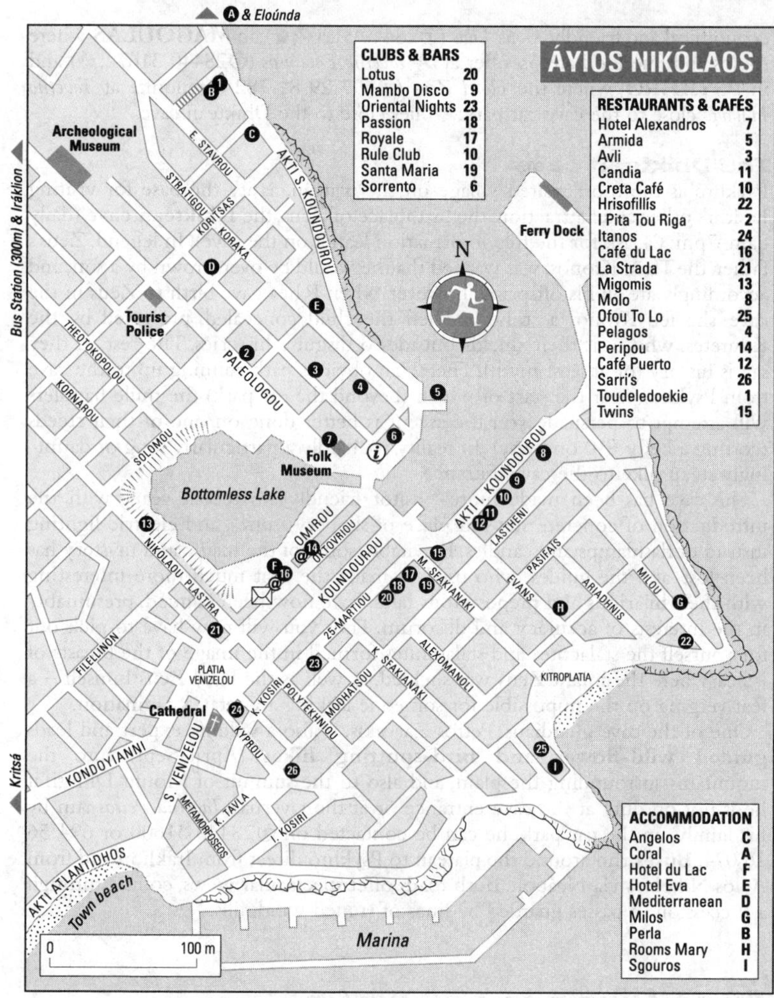

from Áyios Nikólaos, **Kritsá** with its famous frescoed church and textile sellers is a tour-bus haven, but just a couple of kilometres away, the imposing ruins of **ancient Lato** are usually deserted.

Áyios Nikólaos practicalities

The **tourist office** (daily: May–Oct 8am–9.30pm; ⓣ28410 22357, ⓔinfoagn@otenet.gr), situated between the lake and the port, is one of the best on the island for information about accommodation. The **bus station** is situated to the northwest end of town near the Archeological Museum. You'll find the greatest concentration of **shops** and **travel agents** on the hill between the bridge and Platía Venizélou (along the streets 25-Martíou, Koundoúrou and pedestrianized 28-Oktovríou), and the main **ferry agent**, Plora Travel (ⓣ28410 82804) on the corner of 28-Oktovríou and K. Sfakianáki. The **post**

office (Mon–Sat 7.30am–2pm) is halfway up 28-Oktovríou on the right. For **motorbike**, **scooter** or **mountain bike rental,** try the reliable Mike Manolis (Ⓣ28410 24940), who has a pitch along Modhátsou near the junction with K. Sfakianáki. Good **car rental** deals are available at Club Cars, 28-Oktovríou 24 (Ⓣ28410 25868), near the post office. Various **boat trips** to points around the gulf (such as Spinalónga and Eloúnda; about €12–17) leave from the west side of the harbour. **Internet** access is available at Peripou, 28-Oktovríou 25 (daily 9.30am–2am), and at Café du Lac (similar opening times) at no. 17 on the same street.

Accommodation

Since many of the package companies have pulled out in recent years the town is no longer jammed solid as it once was, though in the peak season you won't have so much choice. One thing in your favour is that there are literally thousands of **rooms**, scattered all around town. The tourist office normally has a couple of boards with cards and brochures about hotels and rooms, including their prices; if these seem very reasonable it is because many are for the low season. The nearest **campsite** is *Gournia Moon*, 17km away (see p.623).

Angelos Aktí S. Koundoúrou 16 Ⓣ28410 23501, Ⓕ28410 25692. Welcoming small hotel offering excellent a/c balconied rooms with TV and fridge, plus fine balcony views over the Gulf. ②

Coral Aktí S. Koundoúrou 17 Ⓣ28410 28363, Ⓦwww.mhotels.gr. One of Áyios Nikólaos' leading in-town hotels offering a/c rooms with sea view, fridge, balcony and satellite TV, plus a rooftop pool and bar. Out of high season, prices can fall by up to 50 percent. In July & Aug ask for the room-only price as they will quote you half board. B&B. ⑤

Hotel du Lac 28 Octovríou 17 Ⓣ28410 22711, Ⓦwww.dulachotel.gr. Perhaps the most unexpected bargain in town, with classily renovated rooms and studios in designer style with all facilities including a/c, TV and (in studios) kitchen in a prime location overlooking the lake. However, it's also in the heart of things – night-time noise from revellers is the only downside. ③

Hotel Eva Stratigoú Kóraka 20 Ⓣ28410 22587. Decent en-suite a/c rooms with TV and sea view in a misnamed *pension* close to the centre. ②

Mediterranean S. Dhávaki 27 Ⓣ28410 23611. Clean, en-suite rooms with fridges and fans, close to the lake. ②

Milos Sarolídi 2 Ⓣ28410 23783. Sweet little *pension* east of the Kitroplatía beach, with some of the best rooms in town for the price. Spotless, en-suite balcony rooms (number 2 is a dream) with spectacular sea views over the Gulf. ②

Perla Salaminos 4, Ⓣ28410 23379. Decent budget option close to the sea, on a hill to the north of the harbour. En-suite rooms with fans and fridges, and front rooms have sea-view balconies. ②

Rooms Mary Evans 13, near the Kitroplatía Ⓣ28410 23760. Very friendly place with a/c (€5 extra), en-suite balcony rooms (some with sea view), access to fridge and use of kitchen. Some apartments also available nearby costing only slightly more. ②

Sgouros Kitroplatía Ⓣ28410 28931, Ⓦwww.sgourosgrouphotels.com. Good-value modern hotel with a/c balcony rooms overlooking one of the town's beaches, and close to plenty of tavernas. ③

Eating

At least when it comes to eating there's no chance of missing out, even if some of the prices are fancier than the restaurants. There are tourist-oriented **tavernas** all around the lake and harbour and little to choose between them, apart from the different perspectives you get on the passing fashion show. Have a drink here perhaps, or a mid-morning coffee, and choose somewhere else to eat. The places around the Kitroplatía are generally fairer value, but again you are paying for the location.

Avlí Odhós P. Georgíou 12, two blocks behind the tourist office. Delightful garden ouzerí offering a wide *mezédhes* selection as well as more elaborate dishes. Open dinner only.

Hrisofillís Aktí Themistokleous. Attractive, stylish and creative *mezedhopolío* with reasonably priced fish, meat and veggie *mezédhes* served on a pleasant sea-facing terrace fronting the east side of the Kitroplatía beach.

I Pita Tou Riga Paleológou 24, close to the lake. Excellent Lilliputian snack-bar/restaurant serving imaginative fare – salads, filled pitta breads and some Asian dishes; has a small terrace up steps across the road. They'll let you bring your own bottle of wine.

Itanos Kýprou 1, off the east side of Platía Venizélou. Popular with locals, this traditional taverna serves Cretan food and wine and has a terrace across the road.

La Strada Nikoláou Plastíra 5. Authentic Italian fare in swish surroundings serving up good-value pizza and pasta (meat dishes are pricier), should you fancy a change of cuisine.

Café/Restaurant Migomis Nikoláou Plastíra 22 (☎28410 24353). Pleasant café high above the bottomless lake with a stunning view. Perfect (if pricey) place for breakfast, afternoon or evening drinks. Their next-door restaurant enjoys the same vista and is pricier than the norm, but perhaps worth it if you've booked a frontline table to feast on that view.

Ofou To Lo Kitroplatía. Best of the moderately priced places on the seafront here: the food is consistently good. Try their *loukánika me tirí* (sausages with cheese) starter.

Pelagos Stratigoú Kóraka 10 ☎28410 25737. Housed in an elegant mansion, this stylish fish taverna has an attractive, leafy garden terrace which complements the excellent food. Pricey, but worth it.

Sarri's Kýprou 15. Great little economical neighbourhood café-diner especially good for breakfast fare and *souvláki*, all served on a leafy terrace.

Toudeledoekie Café Aktí S. Koundoúrou 24. Friendly, low-key Dutch-run café with international press to read; great sandwiches and milkshakes by day, chilled bar at night.

Twins Fronting the harbour. Handy pizzeria, fast-food outlet and coffee bar, open all hours. Their "small" pizzas are big enough for two.

Drinking and nightlife

After you've eaten you can get into the one thing which Áyios Nikólaos undeniably does well: **bars and nightlife**. Not that you really need a guide to this – the bars are hard to avoid, and you can just follow the crowds to the most popular places centred around the harbour and 25-Martíou. For a more relaxed drink you could try *Hotel Alexandros* on Paleológou (behind the tourist office), with a rooftop cocktail bar overlooking the lake, which after dark metamorphoses into a 1960s-to-1980s music bar. One curiosity worth a look in the harbour itself is *Armida* (April–Oct), a bar inside a beautifully restored century-old wooden trading vessel, serving cocktails and simple *mezédhes*.

Music bars with terraces filled with easy chairs and even sofas spread along Aktí I Koundoúrou from the harbour where *Café Puerto*, *Candia* and *Creta Café* play cool sounds to their lounging clientele. Further along, a bunch of fashionable new café-bars look out over the ferry dock; *Molo* is a good choice here. There are bars on the opposite side of the harbour too, though fewer of them: *Sorrento* is a long-established haunt of ex-pats and tour reps, loud and fun; *Moritz* could hardly be more different, fashionable and ultra-cool.

Later on it's an easy move to go **dancing** at places like *Rule Club* (above the *Creta Café*) and the nearby *Mambo Disco* – the only genuine dance venues. The more raucous music bars and clubs crowd the bottom of 25-Martiou (known as "Soho Street") as it heads up the hill. *Royale*, *Passion* and *Lotus* all go on into the small hours, as does *Santa Maria* around the corner on M. Sfakianáki. Further up 25-Martíou at no. 19, *Oriental Nights* is a big, Middle Eastern-themed club.

The coast north of Áyios Nikólaos

North of Áyios Nikólaos, the swankier hotels are strung out along the coast road, with upmarket restaurants, discos and cocktail bars scattered between them. **ELOÚNDA**, a resort on a more acceptable scale, is about 8km out along this road. **Buses** run regularly, but if you feel like renting a **scooter** it's a spectacular ride, with impeccable views over a gulf dotted with islands and moored supertankers. Ask at the bookshop near the post office, on the central square facing the sea, about the attractive *Milos* and *Delfinia* **rooms**, studios and apartments (Ⓣ28410 41641, Ⓦwww.pediaditis.gr; ❷–❸), which come with sea views and, at the more modern *Milos*, a pool. You could also try the friendly *Pension Oasis* (Ⓣ28410 41076, Ⓦwww.pensionoasis.gr; ❷), which has en-suite rooms with kitchenette and is just off the square, behind the church. There are more options along the same road with similar prices and facilities. The seafront *Akti Olous Hotel* on the Olous road (Ⓣ28410 41270, Ⓦwww.greekhotels.net /aktiolous; ❹) is one of the better options. If you're having trouble finding a room or apartment (which only happens in high summer), ask at one of the many travel agents around the main square for help; try the friendly Olous Travel (Ⓣ28410 41324, Ⓕ28410 41132), which also gives out **information** and changes money and travellers' cheques. For **eating**, *Britomares*, in a plum spot in the centre of the harbour, the nearby *Poulis* and the ultra-chic *Ferryman* (tellingly with a menu in English only) are the town's best (and priciest) tavernas, but more economical fish and *mezédhes* are to be had at the simple *Ouzeri Maritsa* below the church tower at the north end of the square. Almost next door to the *Akti Olous Hotel*, *Melissa* is a very pleasant garden taverna with less inflated prices than most and a pontoon terrace on the water. **Nightlife** tends to be generally low-key, and centres on café terraces and cocktail bars around the main square; *Babel* and *Aligos* are among the biggest and loudest. *Katafigio*, right at the start of the Olous road, has live Greek music.

Just before the centre of the village, a road (signposted) leads downhill to a natural causeway leading to the ancient "sunken city" of **Olous**. Here you'll find restored windmills, a short length of canal, Venetian salt pans and a well-preserved

▲ Spinalónga island

dolphin **mosaic**, inside a former Roman basilica, but nothing of the sunken city itself beyond a couple of walls in about 70cm of water. Swimming here is good, however – but watch out for sea urchins.

From Eloúnda, boats run half-hourly in high season (€10 return) to the fortress-rock of **Spinalónga**. As a bastion of the Venetian defence, this tiny islet withstood the Turkish invaders for 45 years after the mainland had fallen; in more recent decades and until 1957 it served as a leper colony. As you look around at the roofless shells of houses once inhabited by the unfortunate lepers, and the boat which brought you disappears to pick up another group, an unnervingly real sense of the desolation of those years descends. **PLÁKA**, back on the mainland, and 5km north of Eloúnda, used to be the colony's supply point; now it is a haven from the crowds, with a small pebble beach and a clutch of fish **tavernas**, one of which, *Taverna Spinalonga*, can arrange a boat to take you across to Spinalónga (April–Sept) for about €7 return. This taverna also rents **rooms** (❷) and good-value apartments for the same price for stays of at least two nights. There are **boat trips** daily from Áyios Nikólaos to Olous, Eloúnda and Spinalónga (costing around €12–17), usually visiting at least one other island along the way.

Inland to Kritsá and Lato

The other excursion everyone takes from Áyios Nikólaos is to **KRITSÁ**, a "traditional" village about 10km inland. Buses run at least every hour from the bus station, and despite the commercialization it's still a good trip: the local **crafts** (weaving, ceramics and embroidery basically, though they sell almost everything here) are fair value and Michalis Apostolakis's olive woodcarving workshop on the main street is especially worth a look: some of his carvings are worked from wood 500 to 1500 years old. A trip out to Kritsá is also a welcome break from living in the fast lane at "Ag Nik". In fact, if you're looking for somewhere to stay around here, the village has a number of advantages: chiefly availability of **rooms**, better prices and something at least approaching a genuinely Cretan atmosphere; try *Argyro* (ⓣ28410 51174, ⓦwww.argyrorentrooms.gr; ❷), with pleasant rooms – some en suite – around a courtyard on your way into the village. *Pension Kera* (ⓣ28410 51045; ❶), up the main street from where the bus drops you, has the cheapest rooms but although clean, they're pretty basic. The small platía at the centre of the village is the focus of life and there are a number of decent **places to eat** here, too: the central *Kafenío Saridhakis* is a wonderfully old-fashioned throwback to a Crete fast disappearing, with tables under a shady plane tree, or you could head to the baker's for tempting *tyrópita* (cheese pies) or currant breads. One of the best-situated tavernas is *Castello*, also in the centre, and there are a few others near where the bus stops.

On the approach road, some 2km before Kritsá, is the lovely Byzantine **church of Panayía Kyrá** (daily 8.30am–5.30pm; €3), inside which survives perhaps the most complete set of Byzantine frescoes in Crete. The fourteenth- and fifteenth-century works have been much retouched, but they're still worth the visit. Excellent (and expensive) reproductions are sold from a shop alongside. Just beyond the church, a surfaced road leads off for 3km to the archeological site of **Lato** (Tues–Sun 8.30am–2.30pm; €2), where the substantial remains of a Doric city are coupled with a grand hilltop setting. The city itself is extensive, but largely neglected, presumably because visitors and archeologists on Crete are more concerned with the Minoan era; an informative booklet is on sale at the ticket office. Ruins aside, you could come here just for the views: west over

Áyios Nikólaos and beyond to the bay and Olous (which was Lato's port), and inland to the Lasíthi mountains.

The eastern isthmus

The main road south and then east from Áyios Nikólaos is not a wildly exciting one, essentially a drive through barren hills sprinkled with villas and skirting above the occasional sandy cove. The stretch of the E75 northern highway beyond Ístro is undergoing major **engineering works** intended to by-pass the archeological site of Gourniá and the coastal town of Pahía Ámmos, making the route to Ierápetra more direct as well as upgrading the route to Sitía. Some 5km east of Ístro, along a newly completed stretch of the E75, an exit on the left is signed for the **monastery of Faneroméni**. The way bends around to cross the E75 on a viaduct before heading inland along a track (partly asphalted in its early stage) that climbs dizzily skywards for 6km, giving spectacular views over the Gulf of Mirabéllo along the way. The **view** from the monastery over the gulf is one of the finest in Crete. To get into the rather bleak-looking monastery buildings, knock loudly. You will be shown up to the chapel, built into a cave sanctuary, and the frescoes – although late – are quite brilliant.

Gourniá, Pahiá Ámmos and Mókhlos

Back on the coast road, it's another 2km to the site of **Gourniá** (Tues–Sun 8.30am–3pm; €2), slumped in the saddle between two low peaks. The most completely preserved **Minoan town**, its narrow alleys and stairways intersect a throng of one-roomed houses (of which only the ground-floor walls survive – they would have had at least one upper floor) centred on a main square, and the rather grand house of what may have been a local ruler or governor. Although less impressive than the great palaces, the site is strong on revelations about the lives of the ordinary people – many of the dwellings housed craftsmen, who worked with wood, metal and clay, and left behind their tools and materials to be found by the excavators. Its desolation today (you are likely to be alone save for a dozing guardian) only serves to heighten the contrast with what must have been a cramped and raucous community 3500 years ago.

It is tempting to cross the road here and take one of the paths through the wild thyme to the sea for a swim. Don't bother – the bay and others along this part of the coastline act as a magnet for every piece of floating detritus dumped off Crete's north coast. There is a larger beach (though with similar problems), and rooms to rent, in the next bay along at **PAHIÁ ÁMMOS**, about twenty minutes' walk, where there is also an excellent seafront fish taverna, *Aiolus*; the fish (caught with their own boat), *kolokithokéftedes* (courgette balls) and *achinosalata* (sea urchin's eggs) are outstanding. In the other direction, there's the **campsite** of *Gournia Moon* (Ⓣ28420 93243; May–Sept), with its own small cove and a swimming pool.

This is the narrowest part of the island, and from here a fast road cuts across the isthmus to Ierápetra (see p.629) in the south. In the north, the route on towards Sitía is one of the most exhilarating in Crete. Carved into cliffs and mountainsides, the road teeters above the coast before plunging inland at Kavoúsi. Of the beaches you, only the one at **MÓKHLOS** is at all accessible, some 5km below the main road. This sleepy seaside village has a few rooms, a hotel or two and a number of **tavernas** – *To Bogazi* is good – squatting along its tiny harbour; if you find yourself needing a **place to stay**, you could try the rooms at the clean and simple *Pension Hermes* (ⓣ28430 94074; ❷) behind the waterfront, which are the cheapest in the village, or there's *Hotel Sofia* (ⓣ28430 94738, ⓕ28430 94238; ❸) on the harbour itself for a bit more en-suite comfort. Nearer Sitía the familiar olive groves are interspersed with vineyards used for creating wine and sultanas, and in late summer the grapes, spread to dry in the fields and on rooftops, make an extraordinary sight in the varying stages of their slow change from green to gold to brown.

Sitía

SITÍA is the port and main town of the relatively unexploited eastern edge of Crete. It's a pleasantly scenic if unremarkable place, offering a plethora of waterside restaurants, a long sandy beach and a lazy lifestyle little affected even by the thousands of visitors in peak season. There's an almost Latin feel to the town, reflected in (or perhaps caused by) the number of French and Italian tourists, and it's one of those places that tends to grow on you, perhaps inviting a longer stay than intended. For entertainment there's the **beach**, providing good swimming and windsurfing, and in town a mildly interesting **folklore museum** (Mon–Sat 10am–1pm; €2), a Venetian fort and Roman fish tanks to explore, plus an excellent **Archeological Museum** (Tues–Sun 8.30am–3pm; €2). As part of a government push to increase tourism at this end of the island, a new **international airport** (set to open to international flights in 2008) has been constructed on a plateau above the town, and is likely to have a big impact on Sitía itself as well as the surrounding area.

Arrival and information

The bus drops you at the **bus station** (actually an office on the street; ⓣ28430 22272) on the southwest fringe of the centre and close to the town's main **supermarket**, useful for stocking up on provisions. **Internet** access is available at Enter Café, Venizélou 95, to the west of Platía Iroón Polytekhniou (daily 8am–midnight) and at Billy's Internet (daily 10am–10pm), Papandreou 16, near the tourist office.

Should you have problems finding somewhere to stay, the **tourist office** (Mon–Fri 9.30am–2.30pm & 5.30–9pm, Sat 9.30am–2.30pm; ⓣ28430 28300), on the seafront at the start of the beach road, should be able to help, or there's the **tourist police** at Therisou 31 (daily 7.30am–2.30pm; ⓣ28430 24200), who also provide limited tourist information; both can supply a good town map. A colourful weekly **market** takes place on Tuesdays between 7am and 2pm along Itanou near the Archeological Museum.

Accommodation

There are plenty of cheap *pensions* and **rooms** within easy walking distance, especially in the streets around the folklore museum and beyond here towards the ferry port. For economical rooms, try the friendly *Pension Venus*, I. Kondhiláki 60 (ⓣ28430 24307; ❶) for rooms sharing bath, or *Arhontiko*, I. Kondhiláki 16 (ⓣ28430 28172; ❷) with attractive rooms in a house with a pleasant garden terrace. En-suite accommodation is available at *Rooms Apostolis*, N. Kazantzákis 27 (ⓣ28430 22993; ❷), where balcony rooms come with fridges and fans, or *Nora*, Rouseláki 31 (ⓣ28430 23017, ⓔnorahotel@yahoo.gr; ❷), near the ferry port with excellent en-suite balcony rooms featuring harbour views. An upmarket option in the centre is *Itanos*, Platía Iróön Polytekhníou (ⓣ28430 22900, ⓦwww.itanoshotel.com; ❸), with balconied sea-view rooms on the town's main square.

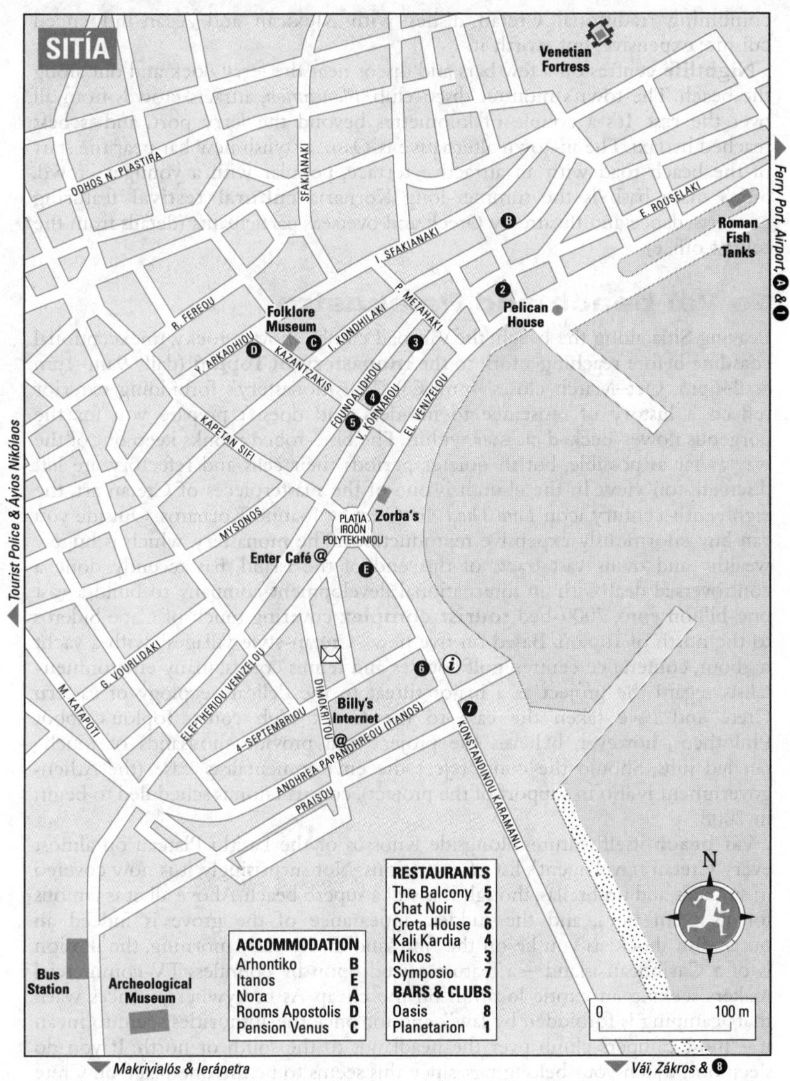

Eating, drinking and nightlife

For **food**, the waterside places are relatively expensive; the best-value choices near here are *Kali Kardia*, Foundalídhou 28, two blocks in from the waterfront, for tasty snail, fish and cheese *mezédhes* served on a pleasant terrace, and *Creta House*, at the start of the beach road (Konstandínou Karamanlí), serving traditional island dishes. Just behind the seafront, the popular *Mikos*, V. Kornárou 117, serves up charcoal-grilled meat and a potent local wine, and has a seafront terrace around the corner, whilst *The Balcony*, Foundalídhou 19 behind the seafront, is perhaps Sitía's most stylish restaurant with a menu combining traditional Cretan dishes with Mexican and Asian-influenced cuisine; expensive, but worth it.

Nightlife centres on a few bars and discos near the ferry dock and out along the beach. The town's monster disco-club, *Planetarion*, attracts crowds from all over the east. It's a couple of kilometres beyond the ferry port, and is best reached by taxi. The in-town alternative is *Oasis*, a stylish new bar near the start of the beach road with an attractive terrace, popular with a younger crowd. Sitía's main bash is the summer-long Kornaria **cultural festival** featuring concerts, dance and theatre by Greek and overseas participants (details from the tourist office).

To Váï beach and Palékastro

Leaving Sitía along the beach, the Váï road climbs above a rocky, unexceptional coastline before reaching a fork to the **monastery of Toploú** (daily 9am–1pm & 2–6pm, Oct–March closes 4pm; €3). The monastery's forbidding exterior reflects a history of resistance to invaders, and doesn't prepare you for the gorgeous flower-decked cloister within. The blue-robed monks keep out of the way as far as possible, but in quieter periods their cells and refectory are left discreetly on view. In the church is one of the masterpieces of Cretan art, the eighteenth-century icon *Lord Thou Art Great* by Ioannis Kornaros. Outside you can buy enormously expensive reproductions. The monastery, which is hugely wealthy and owns vast tracts of this end of the island, has recently done a controversial deal with an international development company to build a vast one-billion euro, 7000-bed **tourist complex** covering much of Cape Sideros to the north of Toploú. Based on five new "Cretan-style villages" with a yacht harbour, conference centres, golf courses and tennis courts, many environmentalists regard the project as a major threat to the delicate ecology of eastern Crete and have taken the case to the Greek high court. Toploú's abbot Philotheos, however, believes the project will provide thousands of much-needed jobs. Should the court reject the environmentalists' case (the Athens government is also in support of the project), construction is scheduled to begin in 2008.

Váï beach itself features alongside Knossos or the Lasíthi Plateau on almost every Cretan travel agent's list of excursions. Not surprisingly, it is now covered in sunbeds and umbrellas, though it is still a superb beach. Above all, it is famous for its palm trees, and the sudden appearance of the grove is indeed an outlandish shock; as you lie on the fine sand in the early morning, the illusion is of a Caribbean island – a feature seized upon by countless TV-commercial makers seeking an exotic location on the cheap. As everywhere, notices warn that "camping is forbidden by law", and for once the authorities seem to mean it – most campers climb over the headlands to the south or north. If you do sleep out, watch your belongings, since this seems to be the one place on Crete with crime on any scale. There's a compulsory car park (€2.50), a café and an expensive taverna at the beach, plus toilets and showers. Because of its status as a nature reserve there is **no accommodation** here whatsoever; the nearest place offering a bed for the night is Palékastro. By day you can find a bit more solitude by climbing the rocks or swimming to one of the smaller beaches which surround Váï. **Ítanos**, twenty minutes' walk north by an obvious trail, has a couple of tiny beaches and some modest ruins from the Classical era.

PALÉKASTRO, an attractive farming village some 9km south, makes a good place to stop over. Although its beaches can't begin to compare with those at Váï, you'll find several modest places with **rooms** – among them *Hotel Hellas* (Ⓣ28430 61240, Ⓦwww.palaikastro.com; ❷), which offers comfortable en-suite rooms with balcony, TV and fridge and reductions for longer stays. The good-value *Vaï* (☎28430 61414; ❶), with rooms above a taverna at the west end of the village on the Sitía road is another possibility. There are some attractive rooms and apartment options a little further out on the roads leading to the beaches; information is available from the tourist office. The extensive **beaches** provide plenty of space to **camp** out without the crowds, but you should respect local sensitivities, keeping away from the main strands and disposing of any rubbish responsibly.

When it comes to **eating**, there are plenty of tavernas both in the village – that of *Hotel Hellas* is particularly recommended – and out at the beaches. Add a **tourist office** (April–Oct daily 9am–10pm; ☎28430 61546) on the main street, a small **folk museum** (May–Oct Tues–Sun 10am–1pm & 5–8.30pm; €1.50), an **Internet** café inside the *Hotel Hellas*, a few **bars** and even a **club**, *Design*, just outside the village on the Váï road, and the place begins to seem positively throbbing. The sea is a couple of kilometres down a dirt track, effortlessly reached with a **scooter** rented from Moto Kastri (☎28430 61477), on the eastern edge of the village along the Váï road. Palékastro is also the crossroads for the road south to Zákros, and your own transport presents all kinds of exploration possibilities.

Zákros

ÁNO ZÁKROS (Upper Zákros) lies a little under 20km from Palékastro. There are several **tavernas** and a simple **hotel**, the *Zakros* (☎ & ℻28430 93379; ❷), which has some en-suite rooms and great views from its rear rooms; it also offers guests a free minibus service to the Minoan palace and beach. The Minoan palace is actually at Káto ("lower") Zákros, 8km further down towards the sea. Most buses run only to the upper village, but in summer a couple do run every day all the way to the site; it's usually not difficult to hitch if your bus does leave you in the village. Some 2km along the road you can, if on foot, take a short cut through an impressive **gorge** (the "Valley of the Dead", named for ancient Minoan tombs in its sides). The gorge entrance is signed "Dead's Gorge" next to an information board and car park area with a steep path leading down to the trail, which then follows a stream bed for 4km to reach the sea near the Minoan palace. It's a solitary but magnificent hike, brightened especially in spring with plenty of plant life.

The **Palace of Zakros** (daily July–Oct 8.30am–5pm, Nov–June 8am–3pm; €3) was an important find for archeologists; it had been occupied only once, between 1600 and 1450 BC, and was abandoned hurriedly and completely. Later, it was forgotten almost entirely and as a result was never plundered or even discovered by archeologists until very recently. The first major excavation began only in 1960; all sorts of everyday objects, such as tools, raw materials, food and pottery, were thus discovered intact among the ruins, and a great deal was learned from being able to apply modern techniques (and knowledge of the Minoans) to a major dig from the very beginning. None of this is especially evident when you're at the palace, except perhaps in a particularly simple ground plan, so it's as well that it is also a rewarding visit in terms of the setting. Although the site is set back from the sea, in places it is often marshy and waterlogged – partly the result of eastern Crete's slow subsidence, partly the fault of a spring which once supplied fresh water to a cistern beside the royal apartments, and whose outflow is now silted up. In wetter periods, among the remains of narrow streets and small houses of the town outside the palace and higher up, you can keep your feet dry and get an excellent view down over the central court and royal apartments. If you want a more detailed overview of the remains, buy the guide to the site on sale at the entrance.

The delightful village of **KÁTO ZÁKROS** is little more than a collection of tavernas, some of which rent out rooms around a peaceful beach and minuscule fishing anchorage. It's a wonderfully restful place, but is often unable to cope with the volume of visitors seeking accommodation in high season; you'd be wise to ring ahead. You should also be aware that villagers are far more hostile these days to wild camping after years of problems, and you should be sensitive to their concerns. Reliable **rooms** (en suite and not) can be found at the simple *Poseidon* (Ⓣ28430 26896; ❶–❷), which has stunning sea views, and the friendly *George Villas* (Ⓣ & Ⓕ28430 26883; ❸), 600m behind the archeological site along a driveable track. *Zakros Palace Apartments* (Ⓣ28430 29550, Ⓦwww.palaikastro.com/katozakrospalace/welcome/indexeng.htm; ❸–❹) is an attractive new option on the hill overlooking the bay offering air-conditioned rooms, studios and apartments, all with terraces. Otherwise ask at the *Taverna Akrogiali* (Ⓣ28430 26893, Ⓦwww.katozakros.sitiarealestate.com; ❶–❸) on the seafront, which acts as a rooms agent.

Ierápetra and the southeast coast

The main road from Sitía to the south coast is a cross-country, roller-coaster ride between the east and west ranges of the **Sitía mountains**. One of the first places it hits on the south coast is the sprawling resort of **Makryialós**, soon followed by the bustling farming town and resort of **Ierápetra**. More tranquil hideaways lie further west at the charming, pint-sized resorts of **Mýrtos** and **Keratókambos**.

Makryialós

Although originally comprised of two distinct villages, the larger **MAKRYIALÓS** (Ⓦwww.makrigialos.gr) has gobbled up its neighbour Análipsi to form a single and unfocused resort, whose only real plus point is a long strand with fine sand which shelves so gently you feel you could walk the two hundred nautical miles to Africa. Unfortunately, since the early 1990s it has been heavily developed, so while still a very pleasant place to stop for a swim or a bite, it's not overflowing with cheap **rooms**. The first budget option is *María Tsanakalioti* (Ⓣ28430 51557, Ⓔdtsanakalioti@hotmail.com; ❷) on the seaward side as you enter the resort from the east; the friendly proprietor offers pleasant studio rooms – some with sea view and terrace – with kitchenette, air conditioning and TV. Nearby and up a track inland signed "*María Apartments*" lies *Stefanos Rooms* (Ⓣ28430 52062; ❷) offering decent en-suite rooms with fans. A little before these two and signed up a side road (that soon degenerates into a track) 1km inland is the more upmarket *White River Cottages* (Ⓣ28430 51120; Ⓔwriver@otenet.gr; ❹), where an abandoned hamlet of traditional stone dwellings (originally Áspro Pótamos or "White River") has been restored as a warren of charming air-conditioned studios and apartments with a focal pool. At the western end of town beyond a steep hill (topped with a sign on the left for a Roman villa), *Taverna-Rooms Oasis* (Ⓣ28430 51918; ❸) fronts the sea at the end of a short track. Offering sea-view en-suite rooms with air conditioning and fridge, downstairs there's an outstanding **taverna** which has based its reputation on using only fresh (never frozen) fish, meat and vegetables, and they claim with some justification that their *moussakás* is the best on the island. Other places to eat include *Faros* and *To Limani*, with great positions overlooking the harbour.

From here to Ierápetra there's little reason to stop; the few beaches are rocky and the coastal plain submerged under ranks of polythene-covered greenhouses. Beside the road leading into Ierápetra are long but exposed stretches of sand, including the appropriately named Long Beach, where you'll find a **campsite**, *Camping Koutsounari* (Ⓣ28420 61213), which offers plenty of shade and has a taverna and minimarket.

Ierápetra and beyond

IERÁPETRA itself is a bustling modern supply centre for the region's farmers. It also attracts a fair number of package tourists but nowhere near as many as in its heyday of twenty or so years ago. The tavernas along the tree-lined seafront are scenic enough and the EU blue-flagged beach stretches a couple of miles east. But as a town, most people find it pretty uninspiring, despite an ongoing modernization programme, which has cleaned up the centre and revamped the seafront. Although there has been a port here since Roman times, only the **Venetian fort** guarding the harbour and a crumbling Turkish minaret remain as reminders of its glory days. What little else has been salvaged is in the fusty one-room **Archeological Museum** (Tues–Sun 8.30am–3.30pm; €2) near the post office.

One way to escape the urban hubbub for a few hours is to take a boat to the **island of Gaidhouronísi** (aka Chrissi or Donkey Island) some 10km out to sea. It's a real uninhabited desert island 4km long with a cedar forest, fabulous "**Shell beach**" covered with millions of multicoloured mollusc shells, some good beaches and a couple of tavernas. **Boats** (daily 10.30am & 12.30pm out, 4pm & 7pm return; €20, under-12s €10) leave from the harbour, and you can buy tickets on the boat or in advance from Iris Travel (Ⓣ28420 25423) at the north end of the seafront. The voyage to the island takes 50 minutes and the boats have an on-board bar.

Heading **west** from Ierápetra, the first stretch of coast is grey and dusty, the road jammed with trucks and lined with drab ribbon development and plastic greenhouses. There are a number of small resorts along the beach, though little in the way of public transport. If travelling under your own steam, there is a scenic detour worth taking at Gría Lygiá: the road on the right for Anatolí climbs to Máles, a village clinging to the lower slopes of the **Dhíkti range**. Here would be a good starting point for **walking** through some stunning mountain terrain (the E4 Pan-European footpath which crosses the island from east to west passes just 3km north of here). Otherwise, the dirt road back down towards the coast (signposted Míthi) has spectacular views over the Libyan Sea, and eventually follows the Mýrtos river valley down to Mýrtos itself.

Mýrtos, Keratókambos and Tsoútsouros

MÝRTOS, 18km west of Ierápetra, is the first resort that might actually tempt you to stop, and it's certainly the most accessible, just off the main road with numerous daily **buses** from Ierápetra and a couple direct to Iráklion. Although developed to a degree, it nonetheless remains a tranquil and charming white-walled village kept clean as a whistle by its house-proud inhabitants. There are plenty of **rooms** possibilities, amongst which you could try the central, friendly and good-value *Hotel Mirtos* (Ⓣ28420 51227, Ⓦwww.mirtoshotel.com; ❷), with comfortable en-suite rooms above an excellent taverna. Nearby, *Rooms Angelos* (Ⓣ28420 51091; ❷) and *Nikos House* (Ⓣ28420 51116, Ⓦwww.nikoshouse.cz in Czech only; ❷) are slightly cheaper options, or there's the basic and friendly *Rooms Despina* (☎28420 51524; ❶) at the back of the village near the bus stop. A useful travel agent, Magic Tours (☎28420 51203, Ⓦwww.magictours.gr) on the central main street, is a good source of **information**, and also **changes money**, rents **cars**, sells boat and plane tickets and operates a taxi service to Iráklion and Haniá airports. Prima Tours (☎28420 51035; Ⓦwww.sunbudget.net), near the beach towards the eastern end of the village, is also good. Just off the road from Ierápetra a couple of kilometres east of the village (and signed) are a couple of excavated hilltop **Minoan villas**: Néa Mýrtos (aka Fournoú Korifí) and Mýrtos Pýrgos. Some of the finds from these sites – in addition to a folklore section with tools, kitchen and farming implements once used by the villagers – are displayed in a superb village **museum** (April–Oct Mon–Fri 9am–1pm; €1.50), located to the side of the church. A recent and highly popular addition to the museum is a wonderfully detailed **scale model** of the Fournoú Korifí site as it would have looked in Minoan days by resident English potter, John Atkinson.

After Mýrtos the main road turns inland towards Áno Viánnos, then continues across the island towards Iráklion; several places on the coast are reached by a series of recently asphalted roads replacing the former rough tracks. **KERATÓKAMBOS**, reached on a side road 4km from Áno Viánnos, has a rather stony beach and, although popular with Cretan day-trippers, is a great place to escape the tourist grind for a spell. It has a range of **rooms**, though they're not easy to come by in August. Try the *Morning Star* taverna (☎28950 51209; ❷) which has air-conditioned rooms with and without bath, or the comparable *Taverna Kriti* (☎28950 51231, Ⓕ28950 51456; ❸) next door; the **food** at both places is tasty, too.

TSOÚTSOUROS (Ⓦwww.tsoutsouros.com), 10km west as the crow flies and now linked by an eleven-kilometre-long asphalted road to the major highway further north, is similar to its neighbour with a line of tavernas, hotels and rooms places arching behind a seafront and yacht harbour, to the east and west of which are a couple of decent, if pebbly, grey-sand **beaches**. **Accommodation** may be available here when the other resorts are full: *Rooms Mihalis* (☎28910 92250; ❶) or the good-value *San Georgio Hotel* (May–Sept ☎28910 92322; ❷) further east are both worth trying. There are no facilities for changing money at either place, although both have a couple of **supermarkets**, handy for gathering picnic ingredients.

If you hope to continue across the **south** of the island, be warned that there are no buses, despite completion of the road towards Míres after years of work. It's an enjoyable rural drive, but progress can be slow.

Réthymnon and around

The relatively low, narrow section of Crete which separates the Psiloritis range from the White Mountains in the west seems at first a nondescript, even dull, part of the island. Certainly in scenic terms it has few of the excitements that the west can offer; there are no major archeological sites and many of the villages seem modern and ugly. On the other hand,

Réthymnon itself is an attractive and lively city, with some excellent beaches nearby. And on the south coast, in particular around **Plakiás**, there are beaches as fine as any Crete can offer and, as you drive towards them, the scenery and villages improve.

Réthymnon

Since the early 1980s, **Réthymnon** has seen a greater influx of tourists than perhaps anywhere else on Crete, with the development of a whole series of large hotels extending almost 10km along the beach to the east. For once, though, the middle of town has been spared, so that at its heart Réthymnon remains one of the most beautiful of Crete's major cities (only Haniá is a serious rival) with an enduringly provincial air. A wide sandy beach and palm-lined promenade border a labyrinthine tangle of Venetian and Turkish houses lining streets where ancient minarets lend an exotic air to the skyline. Dominating everything from the west is the superbly preserved outline of the **fortress** built by the Venetians after a series of pirate raids had devastated the town.

Arrival and information

The **bus station** in Réthymnon is by the sea to the west of the town centre just off Periferiakós, the road which skirts the waterfront around the fortress. If you arrive by **ferry**, you'll be more conveniently placed, over at the western edge of the harbour. The **tourist office** (Mon–Fri 8am–2.30pm, Sat 10am–4pm; ⓣ28310 29148, ⓦwww.rethymnon.com) is located in the Delfini Building at the eastern end of the town beach and provides maps, timetables and accommodation lists. For **Internet** access, head for the Galero Internet Café (daily 9am–midnight), beside the Rimóndi fountain in the old town. Réthymnon is served by a daily **ferry** (currently sailing at 8pm) to Athens; tickets and latest timetable information on this and travel on the island generally is available from the helpful Ellotia Tours, Arkhadíou 155, behind the seafront (ⓣ28310 51981).

Accommodation

There's a great number of places to stay in Réthymnon, and only at the height of the season are you likely to have difficulty finding somewhere, though you may get weary looking. The greatest concentration of **rooms** is in the tangled streets west of the inner harbour, between the Rimóndi fountain and the museums; there are also quite a few places on and around Arkadhíou and Platía Plastíra.

The nearest **campsite**, *Camping Elizabeth* (ⓣ28310 28694), lies 4km east of town; take the bus for the out-of-town hotels (marked *Scaleta/El Greco*) from the bus station to get there. It's a pleasant, large site on the beach, with all facilities.

Atelier Himáras 32 ⓣ28310 24440, ⓔatelier@ret.forthnet.gr. Pleasant en-suite rooms run by a talented potter, who has her studio in the basement and sells her wares in a shop on the other side of the building. ❷

Barbara Dokimaki Platía Plastíra 14 ⓣ28310 24581 ⓔalicedokk@yahoo.gr. Strange warren of a place, with one entrance at the above address, just off the seafront behind the *Ideon*, and another on Dambérgi; ask for the newly refurbished top-floor studio rooms, which have balconies and kitchenettes. ❷–❹

Byzantine Vospórou 26, near the Porta Guora ⓣ28310 55609, ⓦwww.byzantineret.gr. Pleasant en-suite rooms with fans in a renovated Byzantine palace with elegant interior courtyard. ❸

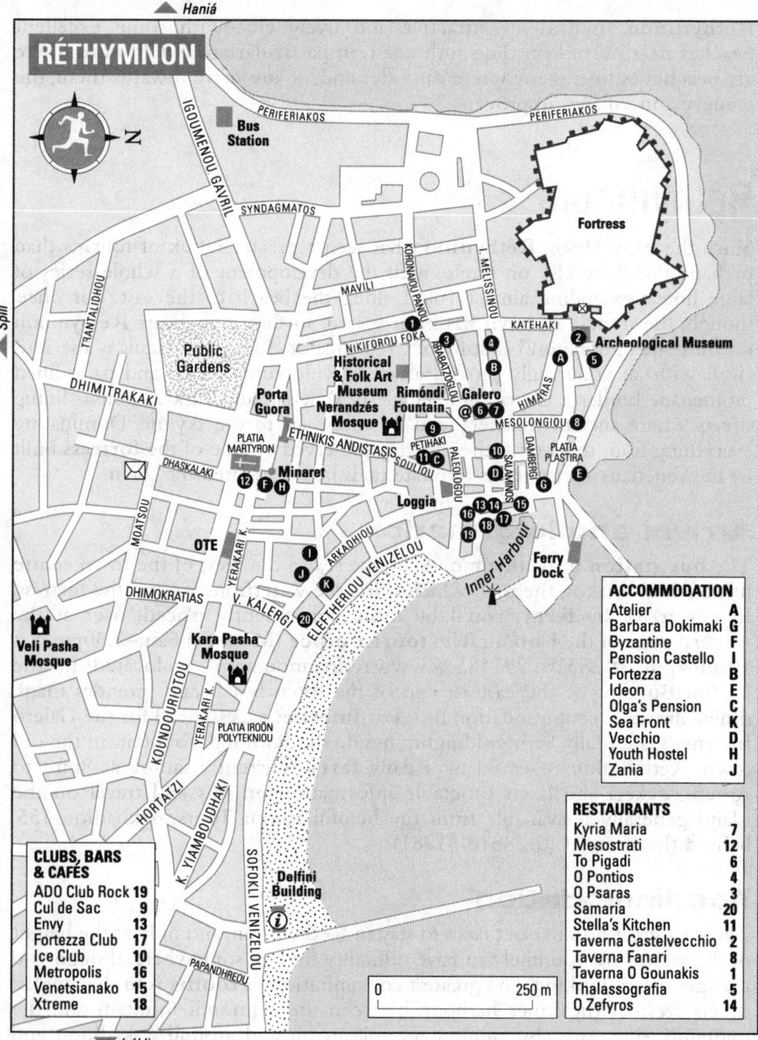

Pension Castello Karaoli 10 ⓣ28310 23570, ⓔcastelo2@otenet.gr. A very pleasant small *pension* in a 300-year-old Venetian-Turkish mansion; a/c en-suite rooms with fridge and a delightful patio garden. ❸

Fortezza Melissinoú 16, near the fortress ⓣ28310 55551, ⓦwww.fortezza.gr. Stylish, top-of-the-range but great value hotel with a/c rooms, pool and restaurant. B&B ❹

Ideon Platía Plastíra 10 ⓣ28310 28667, ⓦwww.hotelideon.gr. High-class hotel with a brilliant position just north of the ferry dock; little chance of getting one of their balconied, sea-view en-suites without pre-booking in high season, though. B&B ❺

Olga's Pension Soulíou 57 ⓣ28310 54896, ⓕ28310 29851. The star attraction at this very friendly *pension* on one of Réthymnon's most touristy streets is the resplendent flower-filled roof garden. Offers a variety of rooms (some en suite), as well as studios with sea view. ❶–❸

Sea Front Arkadhíou 159 ⓣ28310 51981, ⓔseafront@rethymno.crete.com. En-suite rooms with sea views and balconies in an attractively

refurbished mansion with ceiling fans. The welcoming owners also have a number of good value apartments (❸) nearby. Ten percent discount for *Rough Guide* readers. ❷–❸
Vecchio Daliani 4, near the Rimondi fountain. ⓣ28310 54985, ⓦwww.vecchio.gr. Elegant Venetian mansion tastefully transformed into an enchanting small hotel with a/c rooms (some with balcony) set around a pool. B&B ❸
Youth Hostel Tombázi 41 ⓣ28310 22848, ⓦwww.yhrethymno.com. The cheapest beds (€8) in town. Large, clean, very friendly and popular, it has food, showers, clothes-washing facilities, internet access and a multilingual library.
Zania Pávlou Vlástou 3 ⓣ28310 28169. *Pension* right on the corner of Arkadhíou in a well-adapted and atmospheric Venetian mansion, but with only a few airy, high-ceilinged, rooms with a/c and fridge; bathrooms are shared. ❷

The Town

With a **beach** right in the heart of town, it's tempting not to stir at all from the sands, but Réthymnon repays at least some gentle exploration. For a start, you could try checking out the further reaches of the beach itself. The waters protected by the breakwaters in front of town have their disadvantages – notably crowds and dubious hygiene – but less sheltered sands stretch for miles to the east, crowded at first but progressively less so if you're prepared to walk a bit.

Away from the beach, you don't have far to go for the most atmospheric part of town, immediately behind the **inner harbour**. Almost anywhere here, you'll find unexpected old buildings, wall fountains, overhanging wooden balconies, heavy, carved doors and rickety shops, many still with local craftsmen sitting out front, gossiping as they ply their trades. Many of these workshops house *lyra* makers, the "national" instrument of Crete, and they will be only too pleased to show you their beautiful creations should you show an interest. Look out also for the **Venetian loggia**, which houses a shop selling high-quality and expensive reproductions of Classical art; the **Rimóndi fountain**, another of the more elegant Venetian survivals; and the **Nerandzés mosque**, the best preserved in Réthymnon but currently serving as a music school and closed to the public. When (seemingly endless) repairs are completed it should again be possible to climb the spiral staircase to the top of the **minaret** for a stunning view over the town. Simply by walking past these three, you'll have seen many of the liveliest parts of Réthymnon. Ethnikís Andístasis, the street leading straight up from the fountain, is the town's **market** area.

The old city ends at the Porta Guora at the top of Ethnikís Andístasis, the only surviving remnant of the city walls. Almost opposite are the quiet and shady **public gardens**. These are a soothing place to stroll, and in the latter half of July the **Réthymnon Wine Festival** is staged here. Though touristy, it's a thoroughly enjoyable event, with spectacular local dancing as the evening progresses and the barrels empty. The entrance fee includes all the wine you can drink, though you'll need to bring your own cup or buy one of the souvenir glasses and carafes on sale outside the gardens.

The museums and fortress

A little further up the street from the Nerandzés mosque at M. Vernárdhou 28, a beautifully restored seventeenth-century Venetian mansion is the home of the small but tremendously enjoyable **Historical and Folk Art Museum** (Mon–Sat 9am–2pm; €3). Gathered within four, cool, airy rooms are musical instruments, old photos, basketry, farm implements, an explanation of traditional ceramic and breadmaking techniques, smiths' tools, traditional costumes and jewellery, lace, weaving and embroidery (look out for a traditional-style tapestry made in 1941 depicting German parachutists landing at Máleme), pottery, knives and old wooden chests. It makes for a fascinating insight into a fast-disappearing rural (and urban) lifestyle, which survived virtually unchanged from Venetian times to the 1960s.

Heading in the other direction from the fountain you'll come to the fortress and **Archeological Museum** (Tues–Sun 8.30am–3pm; €3), which occupies a building almost directly opposite the entrance to the fortress. This was built by the Turks as an extra defence, and later served as a prison; it's now entirely modern inside: cool, spacious and airy. Unfortunately, the collection is not particularly exciting, and really only worth seeing if you're going to miss the bigger museums elsewhere on the island.

The massive **Venetian fortress** (daily 8am–8pm; closes 6pm Nov–March €3.10) is a must, however. Said to be the largest Venetian castle ever built, this was a response, in the last quarter of the sixteenth century, to a series of **pirate raids** (by Barbarossa among others) that had devastated the town. Inside is now a vast open space dotted with the remains of all sorts of barracks, arsenals, officers' houses, earthworks and deep shafts, and at the centre a large domed building that was once a church and later a **mosque** complete with surviving *mihrab* (a niche indicating the direction of Mecca). The fortress was designed to be large enough for the entire population to take shelter within the walls. Although much is ruined, it remains thoroughly atmospheric, and you can look out from the walls over the town and harbour, or in the other direction along the coast to the west. It's also worth walking around the outside of the fortress, preferably at sunset, to get an impression of its fearsome defences, plus great views along the coast; there's a pleasant resting point around the far side at the *Sunset* taverna.

Eating and drinking

Immediately behind the town beach are arrayed the most touristy **restaurants**, the vast majority being overpriced and of dubious quality. Around the inner **harbour** there's a second, rather more expensive, group of tavernas, specializing in fish, though occasionally the intimate atmosphere in these places is spoilt by the stench from the harbour itself.

If you want takeaway food, there are numerous **souvláki** stalls, including a couple on Arkadhíou and Paleológou and another at Petikháki 52, or you can buy your own ingredients at the **market** stalls set up daily on Ethnikís Andistásis below the Porta Guora. The **bakery** *Iy Gaspari* on Mesolongíou, just behind the Rimóndi fountain, sells the usual cheese pies, cakes and the like, and it also bakes excellent brown, black and rye bread. There's a good *zaharoplastío*, *N.A. Skartsilakos*, at Paleológou 36, just north of the fountain, and several more small cafés which are good for **breakfast** or a quick coffee. The *Cul de Sac* and *Galero* cafés overlooking the fountain are relatively expensive, but great for people-watching.

Taverna Castelvecchio Himáras 29. A long-established family taverna next to the fortress which has a pleasant terrace with views over the town and offers some vegetarian choices.

Taverna Fanari Makedhonías 5. A good-value little seafront taverna serving up tasty lamb and chicken dishes.

Taverna O Gounakis Koronéou 6. Hearty, no-frills traditional cooking by a family who leave the stove to perform *lyra* every night, and when things get really lively the dancing starts.

Kyria Maria at Moskhovítou 20, tucked down an alley behind the Rimóndi fountain. Pleasant, unassuming little taverna for good-value fish and meat dishes; after the meal, everyone gets a couple of Maria's delicious *tyropitákia* with honey on the house.

Mesostrati Yerakári 1. Tucked behind the church on Platía Martíron, this is a pleasant little neighbourhood ouzerí/taverna serving well-prepared Cretan country dishes on a small terrace. It's a haunt frequented by some of Réthymnon's (and Crete's) top *lyra* and *lauto* (lute) players and with a bit of luck you may just hit on one of their jam sessions.

To Pigadi Xanthoúdhidhou 31. In a street containing a cluster of upmarket restaurants with overinflated prices and pretensions, this place stands out for its excellent, reasonably priced food and efficient service; the attractive terrace's main feature – an ancient well (*pigádi*) – has also inspired its name.

O Pontios Melissinoú 34. A good lunchtime stop close to the Archeological Museum, this is a simple place with surprisingly good food, outdoor tables and an enthusiastic female proprietor.

O Psaras cnr Nikiforou Foka and Kironéou. An economical and unpretentious fish taverna (although less fish and more meat is served in summer) with tables on a terrace beside a church.

Samaria Venizélou, on the seafront facing the town beach. One of the few seafront tavernas that maintains some integrity (and reasonable prices) and is patronized by locals.

Stella's Kitchen Great-value little diner serving healthy, home-baked food and six daily specials (at least two of which are vegetarian); there's a leafy terrace roof garden and they also do breakfasts. Closes 9pm.

Thalassografia Kefaloyanídhon 33 ⓣ28310 52569. Best approached from the car park fronting the fortress entrance (although there are steps up from the coast road below), this is a superb "new style" taverna perched on a cliff overlooking the sea and currently one of the "in" places for *rethimniotes* to dine out (making booking advisable). Tables have sensational views and service is slick; recommended dishes include *arní sti stamna* (jugged lamb) and *loukánika krasata* (sausages in wine).

O Zefyros at the inner harbour. One of the less outrageously pricey fish places here, and maintains reasonable standards.

Nightlife

Nightlife is concentrated in the same general areas as the tavernas. At the west end of Venizélou, in the streets behind the inner harbour, the overflow from a small cluster of noisy music bars – *Venetsianako*, *Envy* and *Xtreme* – begins to spill out onto the pavement as partygoers gather for the nightly opening of the *Fortezza Club* in the inner harbour itself, which is the glitziest in town, flanked by its competitors *Metropolis*, *ADO Club Rock* and the nearby *Ice Club* a little way down Salamínos. A relatively new bar scene popular with the local student community has taken root around Platía Plastíra, above the inner harbour, where music bars include *Art*, *Da Cappo*, *Coz*, *Kenzo* and *Aroma*, all with expansive terraces.

Around Réthymnon

While some of Crete's most drastic resort development spreads ever eastwards out of Réthymnon, to the west a sandy coastline, not yet greatly exploited, runs all the way to the borders of Haniá province. But of all the short trips that can be made, the best-known and still the most worthwhile is to the **monastery of Arkádhi**.

Southeast to Arkádhi

The **monastery of Arkádhi** (daily 9am–8pm; €2), some 25km southeast of the city and immaculately situated in the foothills of the Psiloritis range, is also something of a national Cretan shrine. During the 1866 rebellion against the Turks, the monastery became a rebel strongpoint in which, as the Turks gained the upper hand, hundreds of Cretan independence fighters and their families took refuge. Surrounded and on the point of defeat, the defenders ignited a powder magazine just as the Turks entered. Hundreds (some sources claim thousands) were killed, Cretan and Turk alike, and the tragedy did much to promote international sympathy for the cause of Cretan independence.

Nowadays, you can peer into the roofless vault where the explosion occurred and wander about the rest of the well-restored grounds. Outside the entrance a modern monument displays the skulls of many of the victims. The sixteenth-century **church** survived, and is one of the finest Venetian structures left on Crete; other buildings house a small **museum** devoted to the exploits of the defenders of the (Orthodox) faith. The monastery is easy to visit by public bus or on a tour.

West to Aryiroúpolis and Yeoryoúpoli

Leaving Réthymnon to the west, the main road climbs for a while above a rocky coastline before descending (after some 5km) to the sea, where it runs alongside sandy **beaches** for perhaps another 7km. An occasional hotel offers accommodation, but on the whole there's nothing but a line of straggly bushes between the road and the windswept sands. If you have your own vehicle, there are plenty of places to stop for a swim, with rarely anyone else around – but beware of some very strong currents.

One worthwhile detour inland is to **ARYIROÚPOLIS**, a picturesque village perched above the Mousselás river valley and the seat of ancient Lappa, a Greek and Roman town of some repute. The village is famous for its **springs**, which gush dramatically from the hillside and provide most of the city of Réthymnon's water supply. Among a number of **places to stay** near the springs in the lower village, *Rooms Argiroupolis* (ⓣ28310 81148, ⓔmrom@mia.gr; B&B ❷) has en-suite rooms in a garden setting. In the livelier upper village there's *Rooms Zografakis* (ⓣ28310 81269, ⓦwww.ezogrofakis.gr; B&B ❷), or – with great views from its air-conditioned rooms and taverna terrace – the friendly and excellent-value *Agnantema* (ⓣ28310 81172; ❷). Information on a number of attractive and good-value **apartments** around the village (available for stays of two nights or more) is available from Lappa Avocado (see below). For **places to eat**, you're spoilt for choice, with five tavernas at the springs (try *Vieux Moulin* with an attractive terrace) and three bars (serving *mezédhes*) in the upper village, together with tavernas attached to the *Zografakis* and *Agnantema pensions*, the latter enjoying a spectacular terrace view down the river valley. The best taverna by far in these parts lies 4km north of the village on the road to Episkopí: O *Kipos Tis Arkoúdainas* (ⓣ28310 61607) serves up creative lamb and pork dishes and has a delightful tree-shaded garden. A shop under the arch in the main square, named Lappa Avocado (ⓣ28310 81070) and selling local products of the region including olive oil and avocado-based skin products, can provide a free **map** detailing a surprising number of churches, caves and ancient remains to see in and around the village, including an outstanding third-century **Roman mosaic**. An interesting **folklore museum** (daily 10am–7pm; free) – signed from the main square – is worth a look for its collection of tapestries, farm implements, photos and ephemera collected by the Zografakis family who have lived here for countless generations. There are numerous fine **walks** in the surrounding hills, on which the proprietor of Lappa Avocado, who speaks English, will advise. Although little over 20km from Réthymnon and easy to get to with your own transport, Aryiroúpolis is also served by **buses** from Réthymnon's bus station (Mon–Fri only), currently leaving at 11.30am and 2.30pm, and in the reverse direction (from the upper village) at 7am, 12.30pm and 3.30pm.

Back on the coastal route, **YEORYOÚPOLI**, just across the provincial border in Haniá, is the best choice if you are looking for a place to stop. Here the beach is cleaner, wider and further from the road, and though Yeoryoúpoli is very much a resort, packed with rooms to rent, small hotels, apartment buildings, tavernas and travel agencies, everything remains on a small scale. As long as you don't expect to find too many vestiges of traditional Crete, it's a very pleasant place to pass a few days. **Kournás**, the island's only freshwater lake, is easily accessible, as are the traditional villages of the **Dhrapáno peninsula**. For **accommodation**, most of the beachfront places are exclusively for package tourists, so it's best to head along the roads down towards the beach from the central platía. Here, you'll find *Andy's Rooms* (ⓣ28250 61394; ❷) and *Zorbas* (ⓣ 28250 61381, ⓦwww.zorbas-geo.com; ❷), more or less opposite each other, both with comfortable air-conditioned rooms and small apartments, most with balconies; *Zorbas* also has a good taverna and tiny courtyard swimming pool. In the other direction, on the far side of the bridge across the river, *Anna* (ⓣ28250 61556, ⓦwww.annashouse.gr; ❷/❹) offers some of the best-value rooms in town – simple places in a garden setting – as well as a new complex of stylish studios and apartments (sleeping up to 7) around a large pool. *Taverna Paradise* (ⓣ28250 61313; ❷), towards the river from the square, has more rooms, studios and apartments, as well as a good taverna set in lush gardens; *Taverna Babis*, down towards the beach, is also good for plain Greek **food**, as is *Sirtaki*, near the bridge. *East Garden*, between the square and the bridge, is a pleasantly laid-back courtyard bar/café, with **Internet** access and occasional live acoustic music.

South from Réthymnon

There are a couple of alternative routes south from Réthymnon, but the main one heads straight out from the centre of town, an initially featureless road due south across the middle of the island towards **Ayía Galíni**. About 23km out, a turning cuts off to the right for **Plakiás** and **Mýrthios**, following the course of the spectacular Kourtaliótiko ravine.

Plakiás and the south coast

PLAKIÁS has undergone something of a boom in recent years and is no longer the pristine village all too many people arriving here expect. That said, it's still quite low-key, with a satisfactory beach and a string of good tavernas around the dock. There are hundreds of **rooms**, but at the height of summer you'll need to arrive early if you hope to find one; the last to fill are generally those furthest inland, heading towards the youth hostel. Good places to try include *Gio-ma Taverna* (ⓣ28320 32003, ⓦwww.gioma.gr; ❷–❸), on the seafront by the harbour with sea-view rooms and studios, or the excellent balcony rooms at *Ippokambos* (ⓣ28320 31525, ⓔamoutsos@otenet.gr; ❷), slightly inland on the road to the enjoyably relaxed **youth hostel** (ⓣ28320 32118, ⓦwww.yhplakias.com; €9 for dorm bed), which is 500m inland and signed from the seafront. The bougainvillea-draped *Pension Afrodite* (ⓣ28320 31266, ⓔkasel@hol.gr; ❷) is a quiet spot with pleasant apartments, off the road to the hostel. More accommodation options can be found online at ⓦwww.plakias-filoxenia.gr.

Once you've found a room there's not a lot else to discover here. Every facility you're likely to need is strung out along the waterfront or on the few short streets off it, including a **post office** (Mon–Fri 7.30am–2pm), **bike rental**, **ATMs** and **money exchange**, several **supermarkets** and even a **laundry**. Places to eat are plentiful too. The attractive **tavernas** on the waterfront in the centre are a little expensive; the pick of them – with inviting terraces – are *Sofia* near the bus stop and *Gio-ma*, overlooking the harbour at the western end of the seafront, for fish. You'll eat more cheaply further inland: seek out the splendid, traditional *Taverna Medousa* at the east end of town, reached up the road inland past the post office and then right. On the way here you'll pass *Nikos Souvlaki* which dishes up the least expensive meals in town – excellent *souvláki* or even fish and chips – often accompanied by live *bouzoúki* music in the evenings. Beyond the harbour at the west end of town *Psarotaverna Tassomanolis* is one of a line of waterfront places enjoying spectacular sunsets and specializes in fish caught by the proprietor from his own boat.

Mýrthios

For a stay of more than a day or two, **MÝRTHIOS**, in the hills behind Plakiás, also deserves consideration. Originally put on the map for legions of younger travellers by a legendary youth hostel (now closed), these days it's distinctly pricey, but there are some great apartments and wonderful views and you'll generally find locals still outnumbering the tourists. To **stay**, check out the classy *Anna Apartments* (Ⓣ697 33 24 775, Ⓦwww.annaview.com; ❷–❹), while for **food** the long-established *Taverna Plateia* on the square in the centre of the village has had a complete makeover but still serves up excellent traditional Cretan cooking, great wines, and has arguably the most spectacular terrace **view** of any taverna on the island. A car is an advantage here, although the Plakiás bus will usually loop through Mýrthios (be sure to check – otherwise, it's less than five minutes' walk uphill from the junction). It takes twenty minutes to walk down to the beach at Plakiás, or a little longer to reach a fine beach further east at Dhamnóni.

Préveli and Palm Beach

Next in line along the coast is **PRÉVELI**, some 6km southeast of Lefkóyia, served by two daily **buses** from Réthymnon (check current times with any tourist office). It takes its name from a **monastery** (April & May daily 8am–7pm; June–Oct Mon–Sat 8am–1.30pm & 3.30–7.30pm, Sun 8am–7.30pm; in winter, knock for admission; Ⓦwww.preveli.org; €2.50) set high above the sea which, like every other in Crete, has a proud history of resistance, in this case accentuated by its role in World War II as a shelter for marooned Allied soldiers awaiting evacuation. There are fine views and a new monument – to the left as you approach – commemorating the rescue operations and depicting a startling life-size, rifle-toting abbot and an allied soldier cast in bronze. The evacuations took place from **Palm Beach**, a sandy cove with a small date-palm grove and a solitary drink stand where a stream (actually the Megapótamos River) feeds a little oasis. The beach usually attracts a summer camping community (now officially discouraged by the authorities due to litter and sanitation problems) and is also the target of day-trip boats from Plakiás and Ayía Galíni. Sadly, these groups between them deposit heaps of rubbish, often leaving this lovely place filthy, and despite an ongoing clean-up campaign it seems barely worth the effort. The easiest way to get to "Palm Beach" from the monastery is to follow a newly asphalted road that leaves the main road 1km before the monastery itself. This leads, after a further kilometre, to a **pay car park** (€1.50) where you'll need to leave any transport. From here, a marked path clambers steeply down over the rocks – about a ten-minute descent to the beach (but a sweaty twenty-minute haul back up). Should you not wish to return this way (although you'll have little option if you've brought transport), you can avoid the arduous, steep climb by taking a track on the east side of the beach which follows the river valley 2km back to a stone bridge, where there are cafés. You should be able to get one of the two daily buses to drop you at this bridge. All this said, **boat trips** from Plakiás and Ayía Galíni will get you here with a great deal less fuss.

Spíli and Ayía Galíni

Back on the main road south, the pleasant country town of **SPÍLI** lies about 30km from Réthymnon. A popular coffee break for coach tours passing this way, Spíli warrants time if you can spare it. Sheltered under a cliff are narrow alleys of ancient houses, all leading up from a platía with a famous 24-spouted **fountain** that replaced a Venetian original. If you have your own transport, it's a worthwhile place to stay, peacefully rural at night but with several good **rooms** for rent. Try the *Green Hotel* (Ⓣ28320 22225, Ⓦwww.greenhotel.gr; ❷), on the main road, or the charming *Rooms Herakles* (Ⓣ28320 22111, Ⓔheraclespapadakis@hotmail.com; ❷, reductions for more than one night) with air-conditioned en-suite rooms with balconies just behind; the genial proprietor will provide **information** on the town to non-guests, can advise on some superb **walks** in the surrounding hills and also rents out **mountain bikes**. There are two **banks** along the main street (with **ATMs**) and **Internet** access is possible at *Café Babis*, close to the fountain.

The ultimate destination for most people on this road is **AYÍA GALÍNI**, but this picturesque "fishing village" is so busy in high season that you can't see it for the tour buses, hotel billboards and package tourists. It also has a beach that is much too small for the crowds that congregate here. Even so, there are a few saving graces – mainly some excellent restaurants and bars, a lively nightlife scene, plenty of rooms and a friendly atmosphere that survives and even thrives on all the visitors. Out of season, when the climate is mild, it can be quite enjoyable too, and from November to April, despite competition from immigrant workers, a number of long-term travellers spend the winter packing tomatoes or polishing cucumbers here. If you want somewhere **to stay**, start looking at the top end of town, around the main road: the economical and great value *Hotel Minos* (Ⓣ28320 91292; ❶), with en-suite rooms with superb views, is a good place to start, with the nearby *Hotel Idi* (Ⓣ & Ⓕ28320 91152; ❷) and *Hotel Hariklia* (Ⓣ & Ⓕ28320 91257, Ⓦwww.agia-galini.com; ❷) as back-ups, and close to the foot of the hill leading to the harbour, *Neos Ikaros* (Ⓣ28320 91447, Ⓦwww.neosikaros.gr; ❸) is a more upmarket option with superb garden pool. There are dozens of other possibilities, and usually something to be found even at the height of summer. A **campsite,** *Camping Agia Galini* (April–Oct Ⓣ28320 91386), is sited to the east, near the mouth of the Plátis River. There are plenty of **places to eat** – although of fairly indifferent quality – lining the central "Taverna Street" and along the harbourfront; *Onar* is perhaps the most reliable among the former and *Bozos* of the places nearer the water. **Internet** access is available at the *Café Zanzibar* next to the bus stop.

The coastal plain east of Ayía Galíni, hidden under acres of polythene greenhouses and burgeoning concrete sprawl, must be among the ugliest regions in Crete, and **Timbáki** the dreariest town. Since this is the way to Phaestos and back to Iráklion, you may have no choice but to grin and bear it.

Haniá and the west

The substantial attractions of Crete's westernmost quarter are enhanced by its relative lack of visitors, and despite the now-rapid spread of tourist development,

the west is likely to remain one of the emptier parts of the island. This is partly because there are no big sandy beaches to accommodate resort hotels, and partly because it's so far from the great archeological sites. But for mountains and empty (if often pebbly) beaches, it's unrivalled.

Haniá itself is an excellent reason to come here, but the immediately adjacent coast, especially to the west of the city, is overdeveloped and not particularly exciting; if you want beaches head for the south coast or the far west. Here, **Paleohóra** is the only place which could really be described as a resort, and even this is on a thoroughly human scale; others are emptier still. Elsewhere on the south coast, **Ayía Rouméli** and **Loutró** can be reached only on foot or by boat; **Hóra Sfakíon** sees hordes passing through but few who stay; **Frangokástello**, nearby, has a beautiful castle and the first stirrings of development. Behind these lie the **White Mountains** (Lefká Óri) and, above all, the famed walk through the **Samariá Gorge**. In the far-west, great beaches at Falásarna and Elafoníssi are mostly visited only as day trips.

Haniá

HANIÁ, as any of its residents will tell you, is spiritually the capital of Crete, even if the official title was passed back (in 1971) to Iráklion. For many, it is also by far the island's most attractive city, especially if you can catch it in spring, when the White Mountains' snowcapped peaks seem to hover above the roofs. Although it is for the most part a modern city, you might never know it as a tourist. Surrounding the small outer harbour is a wonderful jumble of half-derelict **Venetian streets** that survived the wartime bombardments, and it is here that life for the visitor is concentrated. Restoration and gentrification, consequences of the tourist boom, have made inroads of late, but it remains an atmospheric place.

Arrival, information and orientation

Large as it is, Haniá is easy to handle once you've reached the centre; you may get lost wandering among the narrow alleys of the old city but that's a relatively small area, and you're never far from the sea or from some other obvious landmark. The **bus station** is on Kydhonías, within easy walking distance from the centre – turn right out of the station, then left down the side of Platía 1866, and you'll emerge at a major road junction opposite the top of Halídhon, the main street of the old quarter leading straight down to the Venetian harbour. Arriving by **ferry**, you'll anchor about 10km east of Haniá at the port of Soúdha: there are frequent buses from here which will drop you by the **market** on the fringes of the old town, or you can take a taxi (around €8); there are also KTEL buses to Réthymnon and Kastélli meeting most ferries. From the **airport** (15km east of town on the Akrotíri peninsula), taxis (around €12) will almost certainly be your only option, though it's worth a quick check to see if any sort of bus is meeting your flight. The very helpful **tourist office** is in the *dhimarhío* (town hall) at Kydhonías 29 (Mon–Fri 8am–2.30pm ⓣ28210 36155, ⓦwww.chania.gr), four blocks east of the bus station; in summer they run two handy information booths, one on the harbour just behind the Mosque of the Janissaries, the other in front of the market (both open June–Sept daily 10am–2pm & 6–10pm).

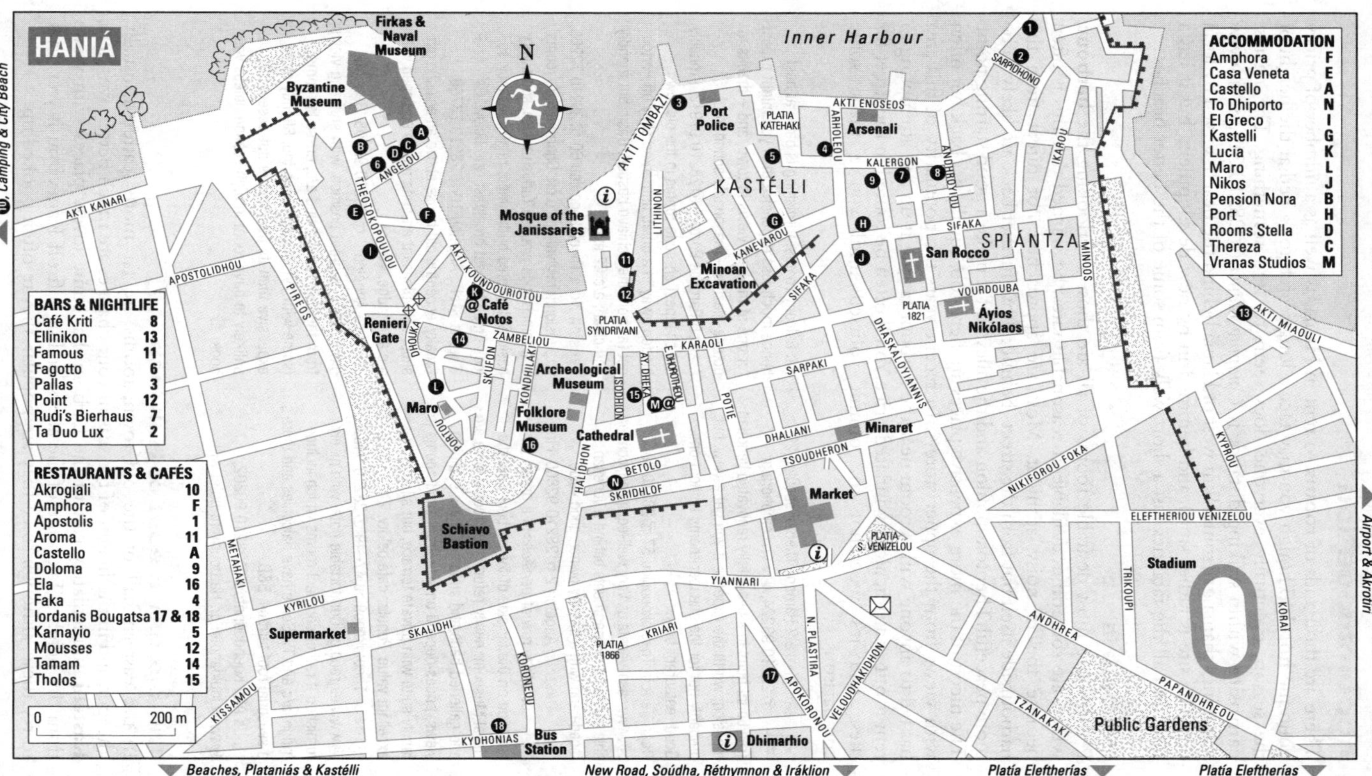

HANIÁ
Inner Harbour
N
ACCOMMODATION
Amphora F
Casa Veneta E
Castello A
To Dhiporto N
El Greco I
Kastelli G
Lucia K
Maro L
Nikos J
Pension Nora B
Port H
Rooms Stella D
Thereza C
Vranas Studios M
BARS & NIGHTLIFE
Café Kriti 8
Ellinikon 13
Famous 11
Fagotto 6
Pallas 3
Point 12
Rudi's Bierhaus 7
Ta Duo Lux 2
RESTAURANTS & CAFÉS
Akrogiali 10
Amphora F
Apostolis 1
Aroma 11
Castello A
Doloma 9
Ela 16
Faka 4
Iordanis Bougatsa 17 & 18
Karnayio 5
Mousses 12
Tamam 14
Tholos 15
0 200 m
Firkas & Naval Museum
Byzantine Museum
Mosque of the Janissaries
Port Police
Arsenali
KASTÉLLI
SPIÁNTZA
San Rocco
Áyios Nikólaos
Minoan Excavation
Renieri Gate
Café Notos
Archeological Museum
Folklore Museum
Cathedral
Maro
Minaret
Market
Schiavo Bastion
Supermarket
Bus Station
Dhimarhío
Stadium
Public Gardens
AKTI KANARI
APOSTOLIDHOU
PIREOS
THEOTOKOPOULOU
ANGELOU
AKTI KOUNDOURIOTOU
AKTI TOMBAZI
LITHINON
PLATIA KATEHAKI
ARHOLEOU
AKTI ENOSEOS
KALERGON
ANDHROYIOU
SARPIDHONO
IKAROU
SIFAKA
KANEVAROU
MINOOS
VOURDOUBA
PLATIA 1821
AKTI MIAOULI
PLATIA SYNDRIVANI
ZAMBELIOU
DHOUKA
SKUFON
KONDHILAKI
ISODHION
AY. DHEKA
E. DHOROTHEOU
KARAOLI
SARPAKI
DHASKALOYIANNIS
POTIE
PORTOU
DHALIANI
TSOUDHERON
BETOLO
SKRIDHLOF
HALIDHON
NIKIFOROU FOKA
KYPROU
ELEFTHERIOU VENIZELOU
PLATIA S. VENIZELOU
YIANNARI
TRIKOUPI
KORAÏ
ANDHREA
PAPANDHREOU
TZANAKAKI
METAHAKI
KYRILOU
SKALIDHI
KISSAMOU
KORONEOU
KYDHONIAS
PLATIA 1866
KRIARI
N. PLASTIRA
VELOUDHAKIDHON
APOKORONOU
10, Camping & City Beach
Airport & Akrotiri
Beaches, Plataniás & Kastélli
New Road, Soúdha, Réthymnon & Iráklion
Platía Eleftherías
Platía Eleftherías

Accommodation

There are thousands of **rooms** to rent in Haniá, as well as a number of pricey boutique **hotels**. Though you may face a long search for a bed at the height of the season, eventually everyone does seem to find something. The nearest **campsite** within striking distance is *Camping Hania* (Ⓣ28210 31138, Ⓦwww.camping-chania.gr), some 4km west of Haniá behind the beach, served by local bus. The site is rather small, and hemmed in by new development, but it has a pool and all the facilities just a short walk from some of the better beaches.

Harbour area

Perhaps the most desirable rooms of all are those overlooking the **harbour**, which are sometimes available at reasonable rates: be warned that this is often because they're noisy at night. Most are approached not direct from the harbourside itself but from the streets behind; those further back are likely to be more peaceful. Theotokopoúlou and the alleys off it make a good starting point. The nicest of the more expensive places are here, too, equally set back but often with views from the upper storeys. In recent years the popularity of this area has led to anyone with a room near the harbour tarting it up and attempting to rent it out at a ridiculously inflated price. You'll often be touted in the street for these and it's wise not to commit yourself until you've made some comparisons.

Amphora 2 Párodos Theotokopoúlou 20 Ⓣ28210 93224, Ⓦwww.amphora.gr. Traditional hotel in a beautifully renovated Venetian mansion; worth the expense if you get a view, but probably not for the cheaper rooms without one. Good restaurant below. ⑤–⑥

Casa Veneta Theotokopoúlou 57 Ⓣ28210 90007, Ⓦwww.casa-veneta.gr. Very well-equipped, comfortable studios and apartments behind a Venetian facade and with a friendly owner; good value. ④

Castello Angélou 2 Ⓣ28210 92800. First of a little row of *pensions* in a great situation on the far side of the harbour near the Naval Museum; newly refurbished rooms have a/c and galleried beds and almost all have stunning views; prices depend on size, from small rooms to family suite with private terrace, but all are excellent value. Popular café below. ③

El Greco Theotokopoúlou 47–49 Ⓣ28210 94030, Ⓦwww.elgreco.gr. Comfortable hotel with nicely furnished if rather compact rooms which include fridge, a/c and TV. Some have balconies and there's a seasonal roof terrace. B&B ④

Lucia Aktí Koundouriótou Ⓣ28210 90302, Ⓦwww.loukiahotel.gr. Harbourfront hotel with a/c balcony rooms; furnishing is basic at best, hence much less expensive than you might expect for one of the best views in town, and – thanks to double-glazing – reasonably soundproof. ③

Maro B Párodos Porto 5 Ⓣ28210 97913. Probably the cheapest en-suite rooms in the old town, hidden away in a quiet, unmarked alley off Portou not far from the Schiavo bastion. Basic but friendly and clean; a/c €2 extra. ②

Pension Nora Theotokopoúlou 60 Ⓣ28210 72265, Ⓔpensionnora@yahoo.co.uk. Charming a/c rooms in a ramshackle wooden Turkish house, some very basic with shared bath, others relatively fancy, so look first. Pleasant breakfast café below. ②

Rooms Stella Angélou 10 Ⓣ28210 73756. Creaky, eccentric old house above an eclectic gift shop, with pleasant en-suite rooms equipped with a/c and fridge. ③

Thereza Angélou 8 Ⓣ28210 92798. Beautiful old house in a great position, with stunning views from the roof terrace and a/c, en-suite rooms (some with TV); classy decor, too. Slightly more expensive than its neighbours but deservedly so; unlikely to have room in high season unless you book. ④

The old town: east of Halídhon

In the eastern half of the old town, rooms are far more scattered, usually cheaper, and in the height of the season your chances are much better over here. **Kastélli**, immediately east of the harbour, has some lovely places with views from the heights. Take one of the alleys leading left off Kanevárou if you want to try these, although since they are popular, they're often booked up.

To Dhiporto Betólo 41 ⓣ28210 40570 ⓦwww.todiporto.gr. Pleasant, good-value en-suite rooms, all with a/c, TV and fridge; some triples and singles too. ❸

Kastelli Kanevárou 39 ⓣ28210 57057, ⓦwww.kastelistudios.gr. A comfortable, modern, reasonably priced *pension* that's very quiet at the back. All rooms come with fans or a/c and plug-in mosquito repellents. The owner is exceptionally helpful and also has a few apartments and a beautiful house (for up to five people) to rent. ❷

Nikos Dhaskaloyiánnis 58 ⓣ28210 54783. Built on top of a Minoan ruin (visible through a basement window), this is one of several rooms places along this street near the inner harbour; good-value, relatively modern rooms, all with a/c, shower and fridge. The same owner has economical studios nearby with fully-equipped kitchens. ❷–❸

Port Sífaka 73, just off Dhaskaloyiánnis ⓣ28210 59484. Clean, quiet, modern place with good-size, en-suite rooms with a/c. ❸

Vranas Studios Ayíon Dhéka, cnr Sarpáki ⓣ28210 58618, ⓦwww.vranas.gr. Pleasant, spacious, studio-style rooms with TV, a/c, fridge and kitchenette. ❹

The City

Haniá has been occupied almost continuously since Neolithic times, so in some ways it is surprising that there's so little specifically to see or do. It is, however, fascinating simply to amble around, stumbling upon surviving fragments of city wall, the remains of **ancient Kydonia**, which are being excavated, and odd segments of Venetian or Turkish masonry. A few small museums help add focus to your wanderings.

Kastélli and the harbour

The **port** area is, as ever, the place to start, the oldest and the most interesting part of town. It's at its busiest and most attractive at night, when the lights from bars and restaurants reflect in the water and crowds of visitors and locals turn out to promenade. By day, things are quieter. Straight ahead from Platía Syndriváni (also known as Harbour Square) lies the curious domed shape of the **Mosque of the Janissaries**, built in 1645 (though heavily restored since) and the oldest Ottoman building on the island. It is occasionally open as a gallery, housing temporary exhibitions.

The little hill that rises behind the mosque is **Kastélli**, site of the earliest habitation and core of the Minoan, Venetian and Turkish towns. There's not a great deal left, but archeologists believe that they may have found the remains of a Minoan palace (logically, there must have been one at this end of the island), and the "lost" city of Kydonia, in the **excavations** being carried out – and open to view – along Kanevárou. It's also here that you'll find traces of the oldest **walls**; there were two rings, one defending Kastélli alone, a later set encompassing the whole of the medieval city. Beneath the hill, on the inner (eastern) harbour, the arches of sixteenth-century **Venetian arsenals**, a couple of them beautifully restored (and one housing a reconstructed Minoan ship), survive alongside remains of the outer walls.

Following the esplanade around in the other direction leads to a hefty bastion which now houses Crete's **Naval Museum** (April–Oct daily 9am–4pm, Nov–March daily 9am–2pm; €3). The collection consists of model ships and other naval ephemera tracing the history of Greek navigation, plus a section on the 1941 **Battle of Crete** with fascinating artefacts, and poignant photos depicting the suffering here under the Nazis. From the **Fírkas**, the fortress behind the museum, the modern Greek flag was first flown on Crete (in 1913). Walk around the back of these restored bulwarks to a street heading inland and you'll find the best-preserved stretch of the outer walls. Just behind the Naval Museum at the top of Theotokopoúlou lies the **Byzantine Museum** (Tues–Sun 8.30am–7.30pm; €2, combined ticket with Archeological Museum €3), with a small but interesting collection of mosaics, icons and jewellery from the various periods of Byzantine rule. Continue up Theotokopoúlou and explore the alleys off it to discover some of the most attractive parts of the old town, with widespread restoration and plenty of fascinating small shops.

Halídhon and beyond

Behind the harbour lie the less picturesque but more lively sections of the old city. First, a short way up Halídhon on the right, is Haniá's **Archeological Museum** (Mon 1–7.30pm, Tues–Sun 8am–7.30pm; €2, combined ticket with Byzantine Museum €3), housed in the Venetian-built church of San Francesco. Damaged as it is, especially from the outside, this remains a beautiful building and it contains a fine little display, covering the local area from Minoan through to Roman times. In the garden, a huge fountain and the base of a minaret survive from the period when the Ottomans converted the church into a mosque; around them are scattered various other sculptures and architectural remnants. The nearby **Folklore Museum** (Mon–Sat 9.30am–3pm & 6–9pm; €2) is worth a look as much for its setting, on a fine courtyard that is also home to Haniá's Roman Catholic church, as for its contents.

The **cathedral**, ordinary and relatively modern, is just a few steps further up Halídhon on the left. Around the cathedral square are busy cafés and some of the more animated shopping areas, leading up to the back of the market: **Odhós Skrídhlof** ("Leather Street") still has numerous traditional leathermakers plying their trade among the tackier souvenirs. In the direction of the Spiántza quarter further east are ancient alleys with tumbledown Venetian stonework and overhanging wooden balconies; though gentrification is spreading apace, much of the quarter has yet to feel the effect of the city's modern popularity. There are a couple more **minarets** too, one on Dhaliáni, and the other attached to the church of Áyios Nikólaos, currently undergoing restoration. Nearby Platía 1821 is a fine traditional square to stop for a coffee.

The beaches

Haniá's beaches all lie to the west of the city. For the crowded but clean **city beach** this means no more than a ten-minute walk, following the shoreline from the Naval Museum, but for more extensive spaces you're better off taking the local bus (#21) out along the coast road. This leaves from the east side of Platía 1866 and runs along the coast as far as **Kalamáki beach**. Kalamáki and the previous stop, **Oásis beach**, are again pretty crowded but they're a considerable improvement over the beach in Haniá itself. In between, you'll find plenty of alternatives, though some of these are quite a walk from the bus stop. Further afield there are even finer beaches at **Ayía Marína** (see p.647) to the west, or **Kalathás** and **Stavrós** (p.647) out on the Akrotíri peninsula, all of which can be reached by KTEL buses from the main station.

Eating

You're never far from something to **eat** in Haniá: in a circle around the harbour is one restaurant, taverna or café after another. These tend to be pricey, though, and the quality at many leaves a lot to be desired. Away from the water, there are plenty of slightly cheaper possibilities on Kondhiláki, Kanevárou and most of the streets off Halídhon. For snacks or lighter meals, the cafés around the harbour generally serve cocktails and fresh juices at exorbitant prices, though breakfast can be good value. For more traditional places, try around the market and along Dhaskaloyiánnis (*Synganaki* here is a good traditional bakery serving *tyrópita* and the like, with a cake shop next door). Fast food is also increasingly widespread.

Akrogiali Aktí Papanikolí 19, behind the city beach ☎28210 73110. Worth the walk, or short taxi ride, to this excellent, reasonably priced seafront fish taverna with a summer terrace. Always packed with locals, so may be worth booking – though there are plenty of alternatives along the same street.

Amphora Aktí Koundouriótou, under the *Hotel Amphora*. One of the most reliable places on the outer harbour, with good, simple Greek food.

Apostolis Aktí Enóseos 6 & 10, inner harbour. The fish tavernas at the inner end of the harbour are rated much more highly by locals than those further round – some locals claim *Apostolis 2*, practically the last, and just a couple of doors down from its seemingly identical sister restaurant, is the best of all. The fish is excellent, but pricey.

Aroma Aktí Tombázi 4. Pleasant café with great harbour view to savour over lazy breakfasts or late drinks. *Mousses*, nearby at the corner of Kanevárou, is equally good, and open 24 hours.

Castello Angélou 2. Slow, relaxed terrace bar beneath the rooms place of the same name; good for breakfast, and where locals (especially expats) sit whiling the day away or playing *tavli*.

Doloma Karsokályvon 5, near the Arsenali. Excellent little taverna with a nice terrace serving well-prepared and economical Cretan dishes.

Ela Top of Kondhiláki. Standard taverna food with live Greek music accompaniment to enliven your meal in a romantically semi-ruinous old mansion.

Faka Arholéon 15. Set back from the harbour, so significantly less touristy and less expensive than many near neighbours, *Faka* serves excellent traditional local food, often with live Greek music. Check out the daily specials, made using local seasonal ingredients.

Iordanis Bougatsa branches at Kydhonías 96 and Apokorónou 24. Specializes in traditional creamy *bougátsa*, a sugar-coated cream-cheese pie to eat in or take away.

Karnayio Platía Kateháki 8 ☎28210 53366. Not right on the water, but one of the best harbour restaurants nonetheless. Excellent fish, traditional Cretan cooking and a fine selection of wines – all served on an inviting terrace – make this a winner.

Tamam Zambelíou. Excellent, fashionable place with adventurous Greek menu including much vegetarian food. Unfortunately only a few cramped tables in the alley outside, and inside it can get very hot. Service can be slow.

Tholos Ayíon Dhéka 36. Slightly north of the cathedral, *Tholos* is another "restaurant in a ruin", this time Venetian/Turkish, with a wide selection of Cretan specialities.

Bars and nightlife

To start your evening, there are dozens of **bars** in the area around the harbour. This is an incomparable setting, but generally somewhat touristy: locals head east, to the scores of bars and cafés lining Aktí Miaoúli, the seafront outside the walls – these are heaving by 11pm. Sometime after midnight, action will move on to the **clubs**, and where these are depends on the time of year. In summer, many of the downtown venues close down and the action moves to the vibrant club scene on the coast west of town. The top places here include *Destijl* and *Vareladiko* in Ayía Marína and the huge *Porto Kali*, just beyond Plataniás. Over winter, *Vareladiko* operates from a waterfront warehouse by the Port Police.

For other events, such as **Greek music** concerts, look out for posters, especially in front of the market: some of these take place in the open-air auditorium in the public gardens, but most – and the most authentic – are at out-of-town restaurants. The hoardings in front of the market also have **movie** posters: there are open-air screenings at Attikon, on Venizélou out towards Akrotíri, about 1km from the centre, and occasionally in the public gardens.

Ta Duo Lux Sarpidhónos. Comfy bar-café in a street full of similar places that attract a slightly older crowd than nearby Aktí Miaoúli.

Ellinikon Aktí Miaoúli. One of the more popular and consistent of the bars on this coastal strip, packed nightly with young locals: if this doesn't appeal, take your pick from its dozens of neighbours.

Famous Aktí Tombázi, above *Aroma*. Live Greek-music venue, occasionally with big-name performers.

Fagotto Angélou 16. Pleasant, laid-back jazz bar off the quieter end of the harbour, often with live performances.
Café Kriti Kalergón 22, corner of Andhroyíou. Greek music and dancing virtually every night at what is basically an old-fashioned *kafenío*.
Pallas Aktí Tombázi 15, near Port Police. Quiet upstairs café/cocktail bar with a roof terrace that's ideally placed to admire the sunset over the harbour.
Point Platía Syndriváni, above *Mousses* café. Chilled bar that gets wilder as the night goes on.
Rudi's Bierhaus Kalergón 16. Haniá's beer shrine: Austrian – and long-time Haniá resident – Rudi Riegler's bar stocks more than a hundred of Europe's finest. Excellent *mezédhes* to accompany them.

Listings

Airlines Olympic, with scheduled daily flights between Haniá and Athens, plus frequent flights to Thessaloníki, has an office at Tzanakáki 88 (Mon–Fri 9am–4pm; ⓣ28210 57701, airport ⓣ28210 63264). Aegean at the airport (ⓣ28210 63366).
Banks and exchange The main branch of the National Bank of Greece is directly opposite the market with two ATMs, and there's a cluster of banks with more ATMs around the top of Halídhon. You'll also find plenty of out-of-hours exchange places on Halídhon, in the travel agencies.
Bike and car rental For bikes, Summertime, Dhaskaloyiánnis 7, slightly northeast of the market (ⓣ28210 45797, ⓦwww.strentals.gr) has a huge range, including mountain bikes. For cars, two reliable local companies are Hermes, Tzanakáki 52 (ⓣ28210 54418) and Tellus Rent a Car, Halídhon 108, opposite Platía 1866 (ⓣ28210 91500). Good deals for *Rough Guide* readers (25 percent off normal rates) are available from El Greco Cars at the *El Greco* hotel (ⓣ28210 60883, ⓦwww.elgreco.gr; see "Accommodation").
Boat trips A number of boats run trips from the harbour (around €10 for two hours), mainly to the nearby islands of Áyii Theódori and Lazarétta, for swimming and *krí-krí* (ibex) spotting: you're unlikely to escape the attentions of their stalls around the harbour. Alternatives include sunset cruises and all-day trips to the Rodhópou peninsula.
Diving Blue Adventures Diving, Arholéon 11, near the inner harbour (ⓣ28210 40608, ⓦwww.blueadventuresdiving.gr), runs daily diving and snorkelling trips.
Ferry tickets From any travel agent, or the ANEK line office is on Venizélou, right opposite the market (ⓣ28210 27500); Hellenic Seaways at Platía 1866 14 (ⓣ28210 75444).
Internet There are plenty of Internet cafés including Vranas, Ayíon Dhéka beneath *Vranas Studios* (see p.643) and Café Notos, on the outer harbour under the *Hotel Lucia*.
Laundry Try Speedy Laundry (ⓣ28210 88411; 9am–2pm & 6–9pm), junction of Koronéou and Korkídhi, just west of Platía 1866, who will collect and deliver your load if you call, the Old Town Laundromat, Karaóli 40, or Oscar, Kanevárou, just off Platía Syndriváni.
Left luggage The bus station has a left-luggage office (6am–8.30pm; €1–2 per item per day depending on size).
Market and supermarkets To buy food, head for the entertaining market which has fresh fruit and vegetables, meat and fish, bakers, dairy stalls and general stores for cooked meats, tins, etc; on Saturday mornings there's a wonderful line of stalls along Minöos, inside the eastern city wall, where local farmers sell their produce. Several small stores by the harbour platía sell cold drinks and food; they are expensive but open late. Small supermarkets can be found on Platía 1866, and the larger Champion supermarket is at the top of Pireos, outside the western wall, close to the Schiavo bastion.
Post office The main post office is on Tzanakáki (Mon–Fri 7.30am–8pm, Sat 9am–1pm).
Taxis The main taxi ranks are on Platía 1866. For radio taxis try ⓣ28210 18300, ⓣ28210 94300 or ⓣ28210 98700.
Travel agencies Plenty, concentrated around the top of Halídhon and on Platía 1866, as well as around the bus station. Try El Greco Travel, on Kydhonías near the bus station (ⓣ28210 86015), or Tellus Travel, Halídhon 108 (ⓣ28210 91500).

Around Haniá: the Akrotíri and Rodhópou peninsulas

North of Haniá, the **Akrotíri peninsula** loops around to protect the Bay of Soúdha and a NATO military base and missile-testing area. The peninsula's northwestern coastline is fast developing into a luxury suburb; the excellent beach of **Kalathás**, near Horafákia, is surrounded by villas and apartments. **STAVRÓS**, further out, has not yet suffered this fate, and its **beach** is absolutely superb if you like the calm, shallow water of an almost completely enclosed lagoon. It's not very large, so it does get crowded, but rarely overpoweringly so. There's a makeshift taverna/*souvláki* stand on the beach, and a couple of tavernas across the road, but for accommodation you need to search slightly south of here, in the area around **Blue Beach**, where there are plenty of apartment buildings but very little availability in summer: one to try is *Zorba's Apartments* (Ⓣ28210 39010, Ⓦwww.hotel-zorbas.gr; ❸), for slightly dated studios and apartments round a pool very near Blue Beach.

Inland are the **monasteries** of **Ayía Triádha** (daily 7.30am–2pm & 5–7pm; €2) and **Gouvernétou** (Easter–Sept Mon, Tues & Thurs 9am–noon & 5–8pm, Sat & Sun 5–11am & 5–8pm; Oct–Easter afternoon hours are 4–7pm; free). Ayía Triádha is much more accessible and has a beautiful seventeenth-century church inside its pink-and-ochre cloister. It is also a thriving and commercial place, producing and selling its own organic olive oil, for example. Gouvernétou, by contrast, is isolated, contemplative and strict; visitors are expected to respect this. There are fine frescoes in the ancient church, and from just beyond the monastery you can clamber down a craggy path to the amazing and abandoned ruins of the **monastery of Katholikó**, built into a craggy ravine, and the remains of its narrow harbour.

West to Rodhópou

The coast to the west of Haniá was the scene of most of the fighting during the German invasion in 1941, and at Máleme there's a big German cemetery; the Allied cemetery is in the other direction, on the coast just outside Soúdha. There are also beaches and considerable tourist development along much of this shore. At **Ayía Marína** there's a fine sandy beach and an island offshore said to be a sea monster petrified by Zeus before it could swallow Crete. Seen from the west, its "mouth" still gapes open.

Between **Plataniás** and **Kolymvári** an almost unbroken strand unfurls, exposed when the wind blows and by no means all sandy, but deserted for long stretches between villages. The road here runs through mixed groves of calamus reed (Crete's bamboo) and oranges; the windbreaks fashioned from the reeds protect the ripening oranges from the *meltémi*. At Kolymvári, the road to Kastélli cuts across the base of another mountainous peninsula, **Rodhópou**. Just off the main road here is a monastery, **Goniá** (summer Mon–Fri & Sun 8am–12.30pm & 4.30–8pm, Sat 4–8pm; winter afternoon hours 3.30–5.30pm; free; respectable dress required), with a view most luxury hotels would envy. Every monk in Crete can tell tales of his proud ancestry of resistance to invaders, but here the Turkish cannon balls are still lodged in the walls to prove it, a relic of which the good fathers are far more proud than any of the icons.

South to the Samariá Gorge

From Haniá the spectacular **Samariá Gorge**, which, at 16km, claims to be Europe's longest, can be visited as a day-trip or as part of a longer excursion to the south. The **gorge** begins at the *xylóskalo*, or "wooden staircase", a stepped path plunging steeply down from the southern lip of the Omalós plain. Here, at the head of the track, opposite the sheer rock face of Mount Gíngilos, the crowds pouring out of buses disperse rapidly as keen walkers march purposefully down while others dally over breakfast, contemplating the sunrise. The descent is at first through almost alpine scenery: pine forest, wildflowers and greenery – a verdant shock in the spring, when the stream is at its liveliest. Small churches and viewpoints dot the route, and about halfway down you pass the abandoned village of **Samariá**, now home to a wardens' station, with picnic facilities and filthy toilets. Further down, the path levels out and the gorge walls close in until, at the narrowest point (the *sidherespórtes* or "iron gates"), one can practically touch both tortured rock faces at once and, looking up, see them rising sheer for almost a thousand feet.

At an average pace, with regular stops, the walk down takes five or six hours (though you can do it far quicker), and the upward trek considerably longer. It's strenuous – you'll know all about it next day – the path is rough, and walking boots or solid shoes are vital. On the way down there is plenty of water from springs and streams (except some years in Sept and Oct), but nothing to eat. The park that surrounds the gorge is a refuge of the Cretan wild ibex, the *krí-krí*, but don't expect to see one; there are usually far too many people around.

Gorge practicalities

The National Park that houses the gorge (€5 entry) is open from May to October, though in the first and last few weeks of that period it may close if there's a danger of flash floods. **Buses** leave Haniá bus station for the top at 6.15am, 7.30am, 8.30am and 2pm (this latter service changes to 4.30pm outside school holidays), depositing you at the gorge entrance and then collecting you at the port of Hóra Sfakíon for the return trip to Haniá. You can also get the boat and bus back via Soúyia or Paleohóra, and if this is your intention you should specify when you buy your ticket: otherwise, for the three early buses, you'll normally be sold a return trip (valid from Hóra Sfakíon at any time). Should you take the last bus you will need to spend a night at Ayía Rouméli (the end of the gorge), as you will not get through in time for the last boat, and if you arrive after 4pm you will only be allowed into the first couple of kilometres from either end. The wardens ensure that no one remains in the gorge overnight, where camping is strictly forbidden.

It's well worth catching the earliest bus to avoid the full heat of the day while walking through the gorge, though be warned that you will not be alone – there are often as many as five coachloads setting off before dawn for the nail-biting climb into the White Mountains. There are also direct early-morning buses from Iráklion, Réthymnon, Soúyia and Paleohóra as well as bus **tours** from virtually everywhere on the island, adding up to a thousand-plus walkers on most days during high season.

Omalós

One way to avoid an early start from the north coast would be to stay at the elevated village of **OMALÓS**, in the middle of the mountain plain from which the gorge descends. The climate is cooler here all year round and the many paths into the hills surrounding the plateau are a welcome bonus; in season a profusion of wildflowers and birdlife is to be seen. There are plenty of **tavernas** and some surprisingly fancy **rooms** with all facilities; the *Hotel Neos Omalos* (Ⓣ28210 67269, Ⓦwww.neos-omalos.gr; ❷) is perhaps the best, but the slightly cheaper neighbouring *Hotel Gingilos* (Ⓣ28210 67181; ❷) is also very friendly. Both have tavernas and offer lifts to the top of the gorge in the morning if you stay overnight. However, since the village is some way from the start of the path, and the first buses arrive as the sun rises, it's almost impossible to get a head start on the crowds. Some people sleep out at the top (where there's a bar-restaurant in the *Tourist Lodge* and kiosks serving drinks and sandwiches), but a night under the stars here can be a bitterly cold experience. The one significant advantage to staying up here would be if you wanted to undertake some other **climbs** in the White Mountains, in which case the **Kallérgi mountain hut** (Ⓣ28210 33199 or Ⓣ693 66 57 954; €12 per person) is about ninety minutes' hike (signed) from Omalós or the top of the gorge.

Villages of the southwest coast

When you finally emerge from the gorge, it's not long before you reach the singularly unattractive village of **AYÍA ROUMÉLI**, which is all but abandoned until you come to the beach, a mirage of iced drinks and a cluster of tavernas with **rooms** for rent. *Livikon* (Ⓣ28250 91363; ❷), at the back of the village, is one of the more tranquil places. On arrival, it's best to buy your boat tickets straightaway to be sure of getting the sailing you want (though in theory they guarantee that no one will be left behind, and that the buses will wait for the boat). If you plan to stay on the south coast, you should get going as soon as possible for the best chance of finding a room somewhere more attractive than Ayía Rouméli. From May to October there are three boats daily to Loutró and Hóra Sfakíon (11.30am, 3.45pm and 6pm, plus 9am mid-June to mid-Sept), plus a daily sailing to Soúyia and Paleohóra (Mon–Thurs 4.45pm, Fri–Sun 5.30pm).

Loutró

For tranquillity, it's hard to beat **LOUTRÓ**, two-thirds of the way to Hóra Sfakíon, and accessible only by boat or on foot. The chief disadvantage of Loutró is its lack of a real beach; most people swim from the rocks around its small bay. If you're prepared to walk, however, there are plenty of lovely **beaches** along the coast in each direction; these can also be reached by hired **canoe**, and some (particularly Sweetwater to the east and Mármara to the west) by regular excursion boats. For walkers, the **coastal trail** through Loutró covers the entire distance between Ayía Rouméli and Hóra Sfakíon (now part of the E4 Pan-European footpath), and there's also a daunting zigzag path up the cliff behind to the mountain village of **Anópoli**. Loutró itself has a number of **tavernas** and **rooms**, though not always enough of the latter in peak season. You'll find links to much of the accommodation at Ⓦwww.loutro.net, or call the *Blue House* (Ⓣ28250 91127; ❸–❹), where there are comfortable, sea-front en-suite rooms and a wonderful (slightly pricier) top-floor extension as well as a great taverna. *Rooms Manousoudaki* (Ⓣ28250 91348 ❷–❸), set further back in the village, behind the church, is simpler and cheaper, and its air-conditioned en-suite rooms with fridge may be available when seafront places have all sold out.

Hóra Sfakíon and beyond

HÓRA SFAKÍON is the main terminus for walkers traversing the gorge, with a regular boat service along the coast to and from Ayía Rouméli, and buses back to Haniá and elsewhere. Be warned that the sole ATM is notoriously unreliable. There are plenty of **rooms** here and some excellent **tavernas**. For a place to stay try the *Hotel Stavris* (Ⓣ28250 91220, Ⓦwww.hotel-stavris-chora-sfakion.com; ❶) for plain but comfortable en-suite rooms (and smarter apartments on the edge of town) or the *Hotel Xenia* (Ⓣ28250 91202; ❸), with the best rooms and the best location in town.

What is missing in Hóra Sfakíon is a decent beach; if this is what you're after you should jump straight on a bus (currently running at 11am and 6pm April–Sept) heading toward Plakiás (see p.637). Plenty of opportunities for a dip present themselves en route, one of the most memorable at **FRANGOKÁSTELLO**, named after a crumbling Venetian attempt to bring law and order to a district that went on to defy both Turks and Germans. The four-square, crenellated and imposing thirteenth-century **castle**, isolated a few kilometres below a chiselled wall of mountains, looks as though it's been spirited out of the High Atlas or Tibet. The place is said to be haunted by ghosts of Greek rebels massacred here in 1829: every May, these *dhrossoulítes* ("dewy ones") march at dawn across the coastal plain and disappear into the sea near the fort. The rest of the time Frangokástello is peaceful enough, with a superb beach and a number of tavernas and rooms scattered for some distance along the coast. The greatest concentration is immediately below the castle – try *Maria's Studios* (Ⓣ28250 92159, Ⓦwww.marias-studios.com; ❷) or the more basic *Kali Kardia* (Ⓣ28250 92123; ❶).

Kastélli and the western tip

Apart from being Crete's most westerly town, and the end of the main coastal highway, **KASTÉLLI** (Kíssamos, or Kastélli Kissámou as it's variously known) has little obvious attraction. It's a busy town with a rocky central **beach** (there's also a small sandy beach to the west) visited mainly by people using the boat that runs twice weekly to the island of Kýthira and the Peloponnese. The very ordinariness of Kastélli, however, can be attractive: life goes on pretty much regardless of outsiders, and there's every facility you might need. The town was important in antiquity, when the Greco-Roman city-state of **Kísamos** was a major regional power. The most important remnants of this have been gathered into a superb new **museum** (Tues–Sun 8.30am–3pm; free), on the main square, Platía Kastellíou. The highlights are the stunning Roman-era **mosaics** on the upper floor. Mosaic production was a local speciality, and many more are being excavated around town, where it is hoped that some of them will be put on display *in situ*.

As regards **practicalities**, almost everything you need is also on or near Platía Kastellíou. The bus station is here, as are a couple of cafés; banks, shops and travel agencies (for ferry tickets or car rental) lie east of the square along Skalídhi; another group can be found around nearby Platía Venizélou, on the main road through town. The **ferry port** is some 3km west of town – a significant walk if you're heavily laden, or a cheap taxi ride; there are daily boat trips from here to beautiful beaches at Gramvoússa and Bállos Bay, at the far northwestern tip of Crete. For **rooms**, *Vergerakis* (aka *Jimmy's*; Ⓣ28220 22663; ❶) is right by Platía Kastellíou, but you'll find better facilities and location if you head downhill to the shore. Here the excellent *Galini Beach Hotel* (Ⓣ28220 23288, Ⓦwww.galinibeach.com; B&B ❸), whose sparkling air conditioned, sea-view rooms come with balconies and bountiful breakfasts, lies at the pebbly, eastern end of the seafront near the sports stadium. Behind the central seafront, *Argo* (Ⓣ28220 23322, Ⓦwww.papadaki.biz; ❷) has plainer rooms with air conditioned, TV, fridge and balcony.

Here on the beach promenade are a number of **tavernas** – *Papadakis* and *Aretousa* are both recommended. Around them are numerous cafés and **bars**, popular with young locals and hence livelier than you might expect, particularly at weekends.

Falásarna to Elafoníssi

To the west of Kastélli lies some of Crete's loneliest and, for many visitors, finest coastline. The first place of note is **FALÁSARNA**, where the scant ruins of an ancient city are ignored by most visitors in favour of some of the best beaches on Crete, wide and sandy with clean water, though far from undiscovered. There's a handful of **tavernas** and an increasing number of **rooms** for rent:

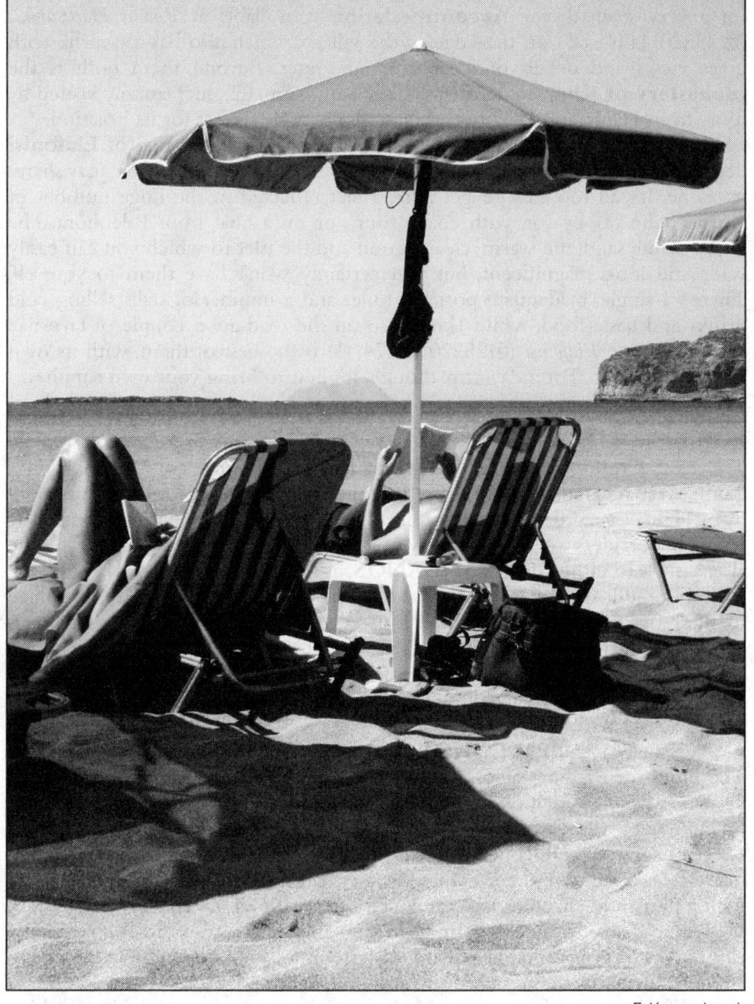

▲ Falásarna beach

Sunset (☎28220 41204; ❶), at the end of the paved road near the archeological site, is among the better choices for both. Plenty of people **camp** out here too; if you join them, be sure to take any litter away with you. Rubbish, occasional tar and crowds of locals on summer weekends can always be escaped if you're prepared to walk, and the beaches are worth it. The nearest real town is **Plátanos**, 5km up a paved road, where you'll find supermarkets and a bank with **ATM**.

Further south, the western coastline is far less discovered. **SFINÁRI** is a quiet village with a number of rooms to rent on the road down to a quiet beach, sandy in patches. At the bottom are a couple of tavernas; try *Captain Fidias,* which offers free camping and sunloungers to clients.

KÁMBOS is similar, but even less visited, its beach a good hour's walk down a well-marked gorge path – a branch of the E4 – starting from the village square (or a very steep drive). **Accommodation** is available at *Rooms Hartzulakis* (☎28220 44445; ❶) on the edge of the village, which also has a taverna with great views and details of local walking routes. Beyond them both is the **monastery of Khryssoskalítissa** (daily 8am–8pm, €2), increasingly visited by tours from Haniá and Paleohóra, but well worth the effort for its isolation.

Some 5km beyond Khryssoskalítissa, the tiny uninhabited islet of **Elafonísi** lies marooned on the edge of a gloriously scenic turquoise lagoon that shares its name. It's all too easy to get here, a fact reflected in the huge number of visitors who do, by car, with coach tours, or on a boat from Paleohóra. The pinky-white sand, the warm, clear lagoon and the islet to which you can easily wade still look magnificent, but you certainly won't have them to yourself. There's a single, inadequate portable toilet and a number of stalls selling cold drinks and basic food, while 1km or so up the road are a couple of taverna/rooms places – *Elafonisi* (☎28220 61274; ❷) is the best of them, with its own excellent taverna. For a day-trip, though, it's best to bring your own supplies.

Paleohóra

The easiest route to the far southwest leaves the north coast at Tavronítis, 22km west of Haniá, heading for Paleohóra; several buses follow this route from Haniá every day, and although this road also has to wind through the western outriders of the White Mountains, it lacks the excitement of the alternatives to either side. **KÁNDANOS**, at the 58-kilometre mark, has been entirely rebuilt since it was destroyed by the Germans for its fierce resistance to their occupation. The original sign erected when the deed was done is preserved on the war memorial in the central square: "Here stood Kándanos, destroyed in retribution for the murder of 25 German soldiers, and never to be rebuilt again." The pleasantly easy-going and once-again substantial village had the last laugh.

When the beach at **PALEOHÓRA** finally appears below, it is a welcome sight. The little town is built across the base of a peninsula, its harbour and a beach known as Pebble Beach on the eastern side, the wide sands (Sandy Beach) on the other. Above, on the outcrop, ruined Venetian ramparts stand sentinel. Though a resort of some size, Paleohóra remains thoroughly enjoyable, with a main street that closes to traffic in the evenings so diners can spill out of the restaurants, and with a pleasantly chaotic social life. You'll find a helpful **tourist office** (Mon & Wed–Sun 10am–1pm & 6–9pm; ☎28230 41507) in a cabin on Pebble Beach, close to the ferry harbour. They have full accommodation lists and provide a **map** which is useful for finding food and accommodation locations. When you tire of beach life there are plenty of alternative entertainments, from dolphin-watching trips to excursions into the hills to Azoyirés, or a five-to-six-hour hike along the coastal path to Soúyia.

There are hundreds of **places to stay** (though not always many vacancies in high season) – try the friendly *Castello Rooms* (ⓣ28230 41143; ❷), at the southern end of Sandy Beach; the alleys behind here, beneath the castle, have many more simple rooms places. Just north of here the *Sandy Beach Hotel* (ⓣ28230 42138, ⓕ28230 42139; ❸) is the town's chicest hotel option for air-conditioned balcony rooms with fridge, TV and sea view. *Villa Marise* and *Europa Studios* (ⓣ28230 41162, ⓦwww.villamarise.com; ❸–❹) enjoy one of the best locations in town, right on the sandy beach more or less opposite the post office; they share a pool and have a variety of well-equipped rooms, apartments and studios. Probably the least expensive rooms in town are at *Anonymous* (ⓣ28230 41509; ❶), in a backstreet behind the main street (Odhós Venizélos), with shared bathrooms and kitchen, and a very friendly atmosphere. There's also a fair-sized **campsite**, *Camping Paleohora* (ⓣ28230 41120), 2km north of Pebble Beach.

For **eating** and **drinking**, tavernas, bars and cafés are to be found throughout the resort, particularly along the roads behind the two beaches. The summer of love still lives at *The Third Eye*, where the excellent **vegetarian** food includes plenty of Asian spices and ingredients you won't find anywhere else on the island (plus inexpensive rooms; ⓣ28230 41234, ⓦwww.thethirdeye-paleochora.info; ❷). Other decent in-town eating places include *Pizzeria Niki*, off the south side of Kontekáki (the road running from east to west at the south end of Venizélou), and *The Wave* at the south end of Pebble Beach, serving good fish on a seaside terrace. Paleohóra's flagship seafood restaurant, however, is the outstanding *Caravella*, overlooking the harbour; the cooking and service are excellent, as is their chilled *hýma* (barrelled wine) from a vineyard in the Kastélli Kissámou area.

Nightlife in Paleohóra is enjoyable but distinctly tame – there are plenty of bars and even small clubs, but on the whole they adapt to the local mood and keep the noise levels low. The greatest concentration of bars is around the junction of Kontekáki and Venizélou. *Nostos*, on Pebble Beach by the tourist office, is open as a café and bar throughout the day, with a chilled club atmosphere at night. The one real dance place is *Paleohora Club*, at the extreme north end of Pebble Beach close to the campsite. A great little open-air **cinema**, Cine Attikon, is tucked away in the northern backstreets; most of their films are in English and programmes (which change daily) are posted outside the town hall and on fliers around town.

Almost everything else you're likely to need is located in the centre of town along and around Odhós Venizélos. **Banks** (with ATMs), **travel agents**, a **laundry**, **mountain bike** and **car-rental** companies and **Internet** access (at Er@to Cafe or Notos Travel) are all along Venizélou, while the **post office** is on the road behind Sandy Beach. There are three **pharmacies** on Kontekáki and there's a **health centre** in the street parallel to Venizélos to the west. When the tourist office is closed, Notos Travel (ⓣ28230 42110), on Venizélou, is a friendly source of information on almost everything to do in Paleohóra and has lots of information on renting apartments, cars, mountain bikes and lots more; there are plenty of other travel agents nearby. PADI-certificated courses in **scuba diving** are on offer at Aquacreta, Kontekáki 4, close to Venizélos (ⓣ28230 41393, ⓦwww.aquacreta.gr).

Boats run from Paleohóra to Elafoníssi and along the coast to Soúyia and Ayía Rouméli; they also run to the island of **Gávdhos**, some 50km south, which is only in the infancy of tourist development – truly isolated except in August when thousands of Greek visitors descend. Notos Travel (see p.653), on Venizélos, and E-Motion (Ⓣ28230 41755), on Kontekáki by the harbour, are good sources of information and tickets for all boats. They also have information about other trips – to walk the **Samariá Gorge**, for example, although you can also do that independently by catching the bus leaving daily at 6am throughout the summer, and a boat back from Ayía Rouméli.

Soúyia

It's a long, winding, spectacular and lonely drive from Paleohóra to **SOÚYIA**, which can also be approached directly from the north coast, or by boat. A small village slowly on its way to becoming a resort, Soúyia is not, in all honesty, a particularly attractive place. The exceptionally slow pace of life here does help it grow on you however, and there's an enormous swathe of bay with a long, grey pebble beach and sparkling water. At the far end of this bay most summers there's something of a nudist and camping community – known locally as the Bay of Pigs. Otherwise, sights are few – the local church has a sixth-century Byzantine mosaic as the foundation – but there are a couple of fabulous walks down the beautiful **Ayía Iríni Gorge** or a wonderful hour-long hike over to the nearby ancient site of **Lissós** with temples and mosaics.

Surprisingly few facilities are on offer apart from food and accommodation – no fuel for example – though there is an ATM, a couple of minimarkets and the occasional organised excursion. **Rooms** are scattered around the road on the way in and along the seafront: the latter tend to be both pricier and noisier. There are links to many, and a handy map, at Ⓦwww.sougia.info. One of the many places on the road as it comes into Soúyia is *Captain George* (Ⓣ28230 51133; ③), where there are some larger apartments, or the peaceful *El Greco*, set further back (Ⓣ28230 51186; ②); both offer balcony rooms with fridge and (some) kitchenette. On the seafront, *Hotel Santa Irene* (Ⓣ28230 51342; ③) is the fanciest place in town with air-conditioned balcony rooms with marble floors and fridges.

Bus tickets are sold at the beachfront booth opposite the *Hotel Santa Irene*, where you can also book taxis: there's an early morning bus to Omalós for the Samariá Gorge. **Boats** depart from the little harbour at the west end of the bay, where a kiosk opens to sell tickets about ten minutes before departure. **Taxi boats** to local beaches (get one to bring you home from Lissós, for example) can be arranged through one of the minimarkets or at *Captain George*. For **food**, *Rembetiko* has a pleasant garden terrace just off the main street, while the seafront is packed with possibilities. The German-run *Omikron* taverna has a more northern-European ambience and offers some vegetarian choices; *Café Lotos* provides **Internet** access.

Travel details

Buses

The following are the main routes only. For the latest timetables and complete route and fare information for the west of the island, visit the website at Ⓦwww.bus-service-crete-ktel.com.

Áyios Nikólaos to: Iráklion (at least 20 daily, 6 via Iráklion Airport 6.15am–9.30pm; 1hr 30min); Kritsá (10 daily 7am–8pm; 20min); Lasíthi Plateau (2 daily; 2hr); Sitía (7 daily 6.15am–8.30pm; 1hr 45min).

Haniá to: Falásarna (3 daily 8.30am–3.30pm; 2hr); Hóra Sfakíon (3 daily 8.30am–2pm; 2hr); Iráklion via Réthymnon (18 daily, 2 via old road 5.30am–9pm; 3hr); Kastélli (16 daily 6.30am–10pm; 1hr 15min); Omalós (Samariá Gorge; 4 daily 6.15am–2pm; 1hr 15min); Paleohóra (5 daily

5am–4pm; 2hr); Soúyia (2 daily 5am–2pm; 2hr); Stavrós (5 daily 6.50am–8.15pm; 1hr).
Iráklion to: Ayía Galíni (8 daily 6.30am–4.30pm; 2hr 15min); Áyios Nikólaos (26 daily 6.30am–10pm; 1hr 30min); Haniá (18 daily 5.30am–9pm; 3hr); Ierápetra (8 daily 7am–7.30pm; 2hr 30min) Phaestos (10 daily 7.30am–5.30pm; 1hr 30min).
Réthymnon to: Ayía Galíni via Spíli (6 daily 5.30am–5pm; 45min–1hr 30min); Haniá (19 daily 6.15am–10.30pm; 1hr 30min–3hr); Iráklion (20 daily 6.30am–10.15pm; 1hr 30min–2hr); Plakiás (7 daily 6.15am–7.30pm; 45min).

Ferries

For the latest timetables for domestic and international ferries to and from Crete visit Ⓦwww.cretetravel.com, Ⓦwww.ferries.gr, Ⓦwww.greekislands.gr, or Ⓦwww.openseas.gr.
Áyios Nikólaos and Sitía 2–3 sailings a week to Pireás (12hr–15hr); 2–3 ferries a week to Kássos (4hr), Kárpathos (6hr), Hálki (9hr 30min) Mílos (8hr) and Rhodes (11hr).
Haniá 2 fast ferries daily overnight to Pireás (6hr 30min).
Iráklion 2 ferries daily to Pireás (9hr); 1 daily fast catamaran to Thíra (2hr), also fast boats and hydrofoils (2hr 30min); 4–5 weekly ferries to Páros, Mýkonos, Íos and Náxos in season; twice weekly to Tínos & weekly to Skiáthos.
Kastélli 2 ferries weekly to Kýthira/Pireás (3hr 30min/12hr), one of them via Yíthio (6hr).
Réthymnon Daily ferries to Pireás (10hr); seasonal day-trips to Thíra.
South Coast summer: 4 daily Hóra Sfakíon, Loutró, Ayía Rouméli; 2 daily Paleohóra, Soúyia, Ayía Rouméli; 4 weekly Hóra Sfakíon to Gávdhos; 2 weekly Paleohóra and Soúyia to Gávdhos.

Flights

Haniá to: Athens (5 daily on Olympic; 3 daily on Aegean; 50min); Thessaloníki (1 daily on Olympic, 3 weekly on Aegean; 1hr 30min).
Iráklion to: Athens (14 daily with Olympic and Aegean; 50min); Rhodes (at least 2 daily on Olympic and Sky Express; 1hr); Thessaloníki (at least 2 daily on Olympic, Aegean or Sky Express; 1hr 15min).
Sitía to: Alexandhroúpoli in Thrace (3 weekly on Olympic); Athens (3 weekly on Olympic); Préveza in northwest Greece (3 weekly on Olympic). Ipsuscili-quis augue mincincilla augiat. Rilit lore min ulla feu facil utat, sum vel ute dolut praesed magnis non eliscip et, quat lor sustie exerit aliquis doloborAm

9

The Dodecanese

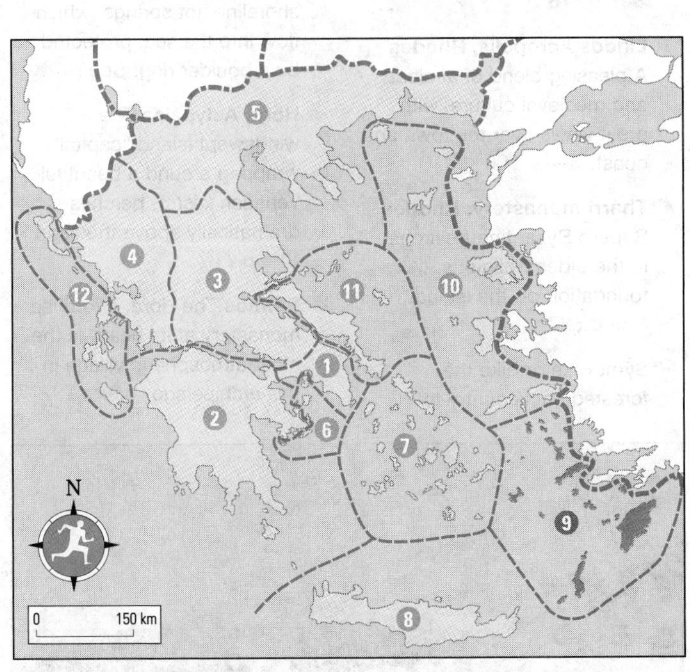

CHAPTER 9 Highlights

* **Northern Kárpathos** Old walking trails take you between isolated villages. See p.667

* **Ródhos Old Town** Superbly preserved medieval streets, inextricably linked with the Knights of Saint John. See p.673

* **Lindos Acropolis, Rhodes** A pleasing blend of ancient and medieval culture, with great views over the town and coast. See p.680

* **Thárri monastery, Rhodes** Superb Byzantine frescoes in the oldest religious foundation on the island. See p.683

* **Sými** Hike or bike the forested backcountry to frescoed medieval chapels. See p.690

* **Volcano at Níssyros** The craters of the dormant volcano still hiccup, with the most recent activity in 1933. See p.703

* **Brós Thermá, Kós** Relax in shoreline hot springs, which flow into the sea, protected by a boulder ring. See p.710

* **Hóra, Astypálea** The windswept island "capital", wrapped around a beautiful Venetian *kástro*, perches dramatically above the sea. See p.716

* **Pátmos** The Hóra, a fortified monastery at its heart, is the most atmospheric village in this archipelago. See p.732

▲ Hot springs, Kós

9

The Dodecanese

The furthest island group from the Greek mainland, the **Dodecanese** (Dhodhekánisos) lie against the Turkish coast – some almost within hailing distance of Anatolia. Because of their strategic position, these islands have a turbulent history: they were the scene of ferocious battles between German and British forces in 1943–44, and were only finally included in the modern Greek state in 1948 after centuries of rule by Crusaders, Ottomans and Italians. Although relations between Greece and Turkey are currently at their best ever, the Greek military retains numerous military bases and smaller watch-points that multiplied after the 1996 incident over the disputed double islet of Ímia.

Whatever the rigours of the various occupations, their legacy includes a wonderful blend of **architectural styles** and cultures; almost every island has Classical remains, a Crusaders' castle, a clutch of vernacular villages and whimsical or grandiose public buildings. For these last the Italians, who held the Dodecanese from 1912 to 1943, are responsible. In their determination to turn them into a showplace for Fascism they undertook ambitious public works, excavations and reconstruction; if historical accuracy was often sacrificed on the altar of visual propaganda, only an expert is likely to complain. A more sinister aspect of the Italian administration was the attempted forcible Latinization of the populace: the Greek language and Orthodox observance were banned in progressively stricter phases between the mid-1920s and 1936. The most tangible reminder of this policy is the (rapidly dwindling) number of older people who can still converse – and write – as fluently in Italian as in Greek.

Aside from this bilingualism, the islands themselves display a marked topographic and economic schizophrenia. The dry limestone outcrops of **Kastellórizo**, **Sými**, **Hálki**, **Kássos** and **Kálymnos** have always relied on the sea for their livelihoods, and the wealth generated by maritime culture – especially during the nineteenth century – resulted in attractive port towns. The relatively fertile giants **Rhodes** (Ródhos) and **Kós** have recently seen their traditional agricultural economies almost totally displaced by a tourist industry focused on good beaches and nightlife, as well as some of the more compelling monuments in the Aegean. **Kárpathos** falls somewhere in between, with a forested north grafted on to a rocky limestone south; **Tílos**, despite its lack of trees, has ample water, though the green volcano-island of **Níssyros** does not. **Léros** shelters softer contours and more amenable terrain than its map outline would suggest, while **Pátmos** and **Astypálea** at the fringes of the archipelago offer architecture and landscapes reminiscent of the Cyclades.

The largest islands in the group are connected by regular **ferries and catamarans**, as well as flights; only Kastellórizo and Tílos are hard to reach. Rhodes is the main **transport** hub, with connections for Crete, the north-eastern Aegean, the Cyclades and the mainland also. Kálymnos, with a useful small ferry based there, is an important secondary terminus, as is Kós, the fulcrum for various hydrofoil services, and Pátmos, home base for one of two local catamarans, which conveniently supplement the larger ferries calling at uncivil hours.

Kássos

Like Psará in the northeast Aegean, **Kássos** contributed its large fleet to the Greek revolution, and likewise suffered appalling consequences. In May 1824, an Ottoman army sent by Egyptian governor Ibrahim Pasha besieged the island; on June 7, aided perhaps by a traitor's fingering the weak point in Kássos's defences, the invaders descended on the populated north-coastal plain, slaughtered most of the inhabitants and put houses, farms and trees to the torch.

Barren and depopulated since then, Kássos attracts few visitors, despite air links with Rhodes and Kárpathos, and being a stop on ferry lines from those isles to Crete. Sheer gorges slash through lunar terrain relieved only by fenced smallholdings of midget olive trees; spring grain crops briefly soften the usually empty terraces, and livestock somehow survives on a thin furze of scrub. The remaining population occupies five **villages** facing Kárpathos, leaving most of the island uninhabited and uncultivated. There's little sign here of the wealth bestowed on other islands by diaspora Greeks or – since Kássos hasn't much to offer them – tourists; amid the occasional new concrete monster, crumbling old houses poignantly recall better days. A history of serving as roving captains, or residence in Egypt (Kassiots were instrumental in digging the Suez Canal), has been eclipsed by subsequent **emigration to the US**.

Kássos can be tricky to reach, since in extreme wind conditions, **ferries** are unable to dock at the jetty in Frý (pronounced "free"). In such cases, you disembark at Kárpathos and fly the remaining distance in a 38-seater aircraft, or use one of the Finíki (Kárpathos)-based excursion **kaïkia** which can manoeuvre into Boúka port in most weathers. The **airport** lies 1km west of Frý, an easy enough walk, otherwise a cheap ride in one of the island's three taxis. Except during summer – when a single **scooter/quad rental** outfit operates, a Mercedes van provides a regular bus service and boat excursions are offered – the only way to explore the island is by some fairly arduous **hiking**. Place-name signposting tends to be in Greek only, and in Kassiot dialect at that – clearly nobody's expecting many non-Kassiot-diaspora visitors.

Frý

Most of the appeal of the capital, **FRÝ**, is confined to the wedge-shaped **Boúka** fishing port, protected from the sea by two crab-claws of breakwater and overlooked by Áyios Spyrídhon cathedral. Inland, Frý is engagingly unpretentious, even down-at-heel in spots; there are no concessions to tourism, though some attempts have been made to prettify a little town that's quite desolate out of season. There's just one overpriced seafront **hotel**, the *Anagenissis* (Ⓣ22450 41495, Ⓦwww.kassos-island.gr; ❸), run by the eponymous travel agency just below. Better-value, quieter lodgings include the basic, seaside *Flisvos* (Ⓣ22450 41284; ❷), 150m east of the new harbour, with a shared kitchen; *Captain's House* (Ⓣ22450 41801, Ⓔhpetros@otenet.gr; ❹), galleried trad-style studios above Kassian Travel, near the police station; or best of all, *Angelica's* (Ⓣ22450 41268, Ⓦwww.angelicas.gr), four apartments in a converted mansion overlooking Boúka. There are two stand-alone **ATMs**, plus an **Internet** café by the police station.

Outside peak season, Frý supports just one full-service **taverna**: *O Mylos*, overlooking the ferry port; luckily it's excellent, with *mayireftá* at lunch and grills by night. From late June to early September tavernas at **Boúka** include *Iy Orea Bouka* for Kassiot dishes and lamb specialists *To Koutouki*. Several **bar-kafenía-ouzerí** perched above Boúka are the focus of low-key **nightlife**.

Local beaches

Frý's **town beach**, if you can call it that, is at **Ammouá**, a thirty-minute walk beyond the airstrip along the coastal track. This sandy cove, just before Áyios Konstandínos chapel, is often caked with seaweed and tar, but persevere five minutes more and you'll find cleaner pea-gravel coves. The determined swim off the little patch of sand at **Emboriós**, fifteen minutes from Frý, along with the resident ducks, and there's a more private pebble stretch off to the right. Continue ten minutes along the shore, first along an old track, then on a path past the last house, for a final scramble to the base of the **Pouthená ravine**, where there's another secluded pebble cove. In high season, boats sail to the far better beaches on two islets visible to the northwest, **Armathiá** and **Makrá**.

The villages and Áyios Mámas

At the edges of the agricultural plain inland from Frý cluster several villages, linked to each other by road; all can be toured on foot in a single day. Larger and yet more rural than Frý, **AYÍA MARÍNA**, 1500m inland and uphill, is most attractive seen from the south, arrayed above olive groves; its two belfried churches are the focus of the island's liveliest **festivals**, on July 16–17 and September 13–14. Fifteen minutes beyond the hamlet of **Kathístres**, a further 500m southwest, the cave of **Ellinokamára** has a late Classical, polygonal wall blocking the entrance; its ancient function is uncertain, perhaps a cult shrine or tomb complex.

Generally Kássos **trails** are limited and unmarked, with no shade and few reliable water sources. An exception is the path from **Arvanitohóri to Póli** (40min), which is clearly walled in and enjoyable, shortcutting the road effectively – it starts at the base of the village, where two trees occupy planter-wells. **PÓLI**, impoverished and agricultural, is the site of a badly deteriorated ancient and medieval acropolis – a few stretches of fortification remain – and marks the start of a four-kilometre paved-road southeast to **Áyios Mámas**, signposted as "**Áï Mámas**", one of two important rural monasteries, perched spectacularly overlooking the sea. Alternatively, from Póli you descend – again on walled-in path for the first twenty minutes, then dirt track – to **PANAYÍA**, famous for its now-neglected sea-captains' mansions and for the oldest surviving church on the island, the eighteenth-century **Panayía tou Yióryi**, focus of an August 14–15 festival to rival Ayía Marína's.

Áyios Yeóryios Hadhión and Hélatros

Between Ayía Marína and Arvanitohóri, another paved road veers southwest towards the rural monastery of **Áyios Yeóryios Hadhión**. There's not much joy to be had in walking this, so take a taxi, rent a scooter or hitch a lift in at least one direction. The start of the route skirts the narrows of a dramatic gorge, beyond which you're unlikely to see another living thing aside from goats, sheep or an occasional Eleonora's falcon. Soon the Mediterranean appears; when you reach a fork, take the upper, right-hand turning, following phone lines and signs for "**Áï Yeóryi**", 12km from Frý. Cistern water is available.

From the monastery it's another 2.5km on a paved road to **Hélatros**, a lonely cove at the mouth of one of the larger, more forbidding Kassiot canyons. Only the right-hand 80m of this sand-and-pea-gravel beach is usable, but the water is pristine and – except for the occasional fishing boat or yacht – you'll probably be alone. The lower, left-hand option at the fork is the direct, dirt-surface track to Hélatros; this is only 700m shorter but perfectly passable by a scooter, and varies the return to town.

Kárpathos

A long, narrow island between Rhodes and Crete, wild **Kárpathos** has always been an underpopulated backwater, although it's the third largest of the Dodecanese. A habitually cloud-capped **mountainous spine** rises to over 1200m, dividing the lower-lying south from an exceptionally rugged north. A magnificent, windswept **coastline** of cliffs and promontories attracts significant numbers of package tourists, who pretty well monopolize several resorts in the southern part of the island, pushing independent travellers up to the remote **north**. Most visitors come for a glimpse of traditional village life in the far north, and for the numerous superb, secluded **beaches** lapped by proverbial crystalline water. Note, however, that food prices (in the south especially) have soared to beyond-Rhodes levels, offsetting reasonable room rates.

Kárpathos' **interior** isn't always alluring: the central and northern uplands have been scorched by repeated forest fires, while agriculture plays a slighter role than on any other Greek island of this size. The Karpathians are too well off to engage in much farming; emigration to North America and the resulting remittance economy has transformed the islands into one of the wealthiest parts of Greece.

Four local Classical **cities** figure little in ancient **history**. Kárpathos was held by the Genoese and Venetians after the Byzantine collapse and so has no castle of the crusading Knights of St John, nor any surviving medieval fortresses of note. The Ottomans couldn't be bothered to settle or even garrison it; instead they left a single judge or *kadi* at the main town, making the Greek population responsible for his safety during the many pirate attacks.

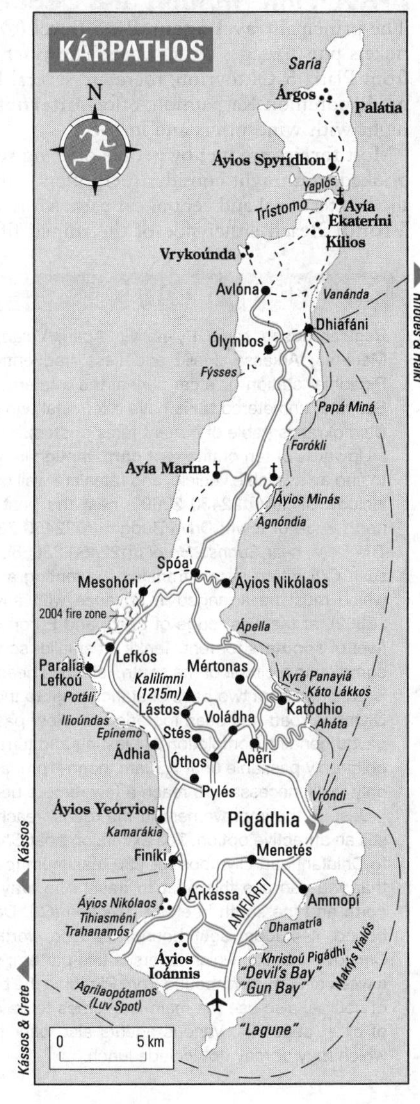

Pigádhia (Kárpathos Town)

The island capital of **PIGÁDHIA** (or Kárpathos) nestles at the south end of scenic **Vróndi Bay**, whose sickle of sand extends 3km northwest. The town itself, curling around the jetty and quay where ferries and excursion boats dock, is as drab as its setting is beautiful; an ever-increasing number of concrete blocks leave the impression of a vast building site, making the Italian-era port police and county-government buildings heirlooms by comparison. While there's nothing special to see, Pigádhia does offer most facilities you might need, albeit with a definite package-tourism slant. The name of the main commercial street – Apodhímon Karpathíon ("**Karpathians Overseas**") – speaks volumes about the pivotal role of emigrants and emigration here.

Arrival, information and accommodation

The principal **travel agent**, Possi Travel (☎22450 22235) on the front, sells air tickets plus passages on all boats. The **post office** is on Ethnikís Andístasis up from Platía 5-Oktovríou; there are several bank **ATMs**. *Café Galileo* (all year), on Apodhímon Karpathíon, offers **Internet** and Wi-Fi access; it's very lively at night with windsurfers and locals.

Most **ferries** are met by people offering **self-catering studios**. Unless you've booked, you might consider such offers – the best location is the hillside above the bus terminal and central car park. More comfortable places lie north, behind **Vróndi** Beach either side of the ruined fifth-century basilica of **Ayía Fotiní**,

Getting around Kárpathos

Regular **buses** serve Pylés, via Apérí, Voládha and Óthos, as well as Ammopí, Menetés, Arkássa, Finíki and (less frequently) Mesohóri via Paralía Lefkoú; the Pigádhia "station" is a car park at the western edge of town, beyond the post office. Set-rate, unmetered **taxis** have a terminal two blocks inland from the fountain along Dhimokratías (table of current fares posted).

Upwards of ten outfits **rent cars**, though in season you may have to try every one to find an available vehicle, and rates are well over the norm. Tried-and-true agencies include Circle (☎22450 22690) near the post office; Avis (☎22450 22702), at the north edge of town; Drive/Budget (☎22450 23873), 2km out behind Vróndi Beach; The Best, near *Sunrise Hotel* (☎22450 23655); and Billy's (☎22450 22921). You can save €25 return in taxi transfers by renting a car from/to the **airport** (17km away) which must be arranged in advance with any agency. Moto Carpathos (☎22450 22382), at the west edge of town, and Euromoto (☎22450 23238) have the largest fleet of **scooters** for rent. Tanks on smaller scooters are barely big enough to permit completing a circuit of the south, let alone head up north; the only **fuel** on Kárpathos is obtained from two pairs of stations just to the north and south of town. The Spóa–Ólymbos road has been regraded to allow passage of ordinary cars, but is not yet paved pending completion of blasting and terracing works 8km south of Ólymbos, a point only passable until 7.30am, noon–1pm, and 5–6pm daily until 2009. **Jeeps** are only really necessary to reach a few remote beaches served by atrocious tracks.

Despite the improvement in the roads, reaching **Northern Kárpathos by boat** is still an attractive option. The excursion boat *Chrisovalandou III* offers all-in **day-tours** to Dhiafáni and Ólymbos for €20 maximum (pay on board); unpublicized is the fact that you can use this boat to travel **one way** (1hr 20min–1hr 30min) between the north and the south in either direction (€8). Departures are typically 8.30am northbound, 4–4.30pm southbound. It's also worth knowing about the tiny **mail kaïki** *Chrisovalandou I*, which reverses this pattern: southbound from Dhiafáni three days a week at 8am, northbound from Pigádhia the previous day at 3pm (€8; 1hr). You can, of course, also use the main-line ferries to travel between the two ports – cheapest of all at about €4. Various agents also offer trips to isolated east coast beaches, which may or may not include lunch.

but tend to be occupied by package clients. Better hillside premises include *Amarillis Studios* (Ⓣ22450 22375, Ⓔjohnvolada@in.gr; ③), with enormous, air-conditioned units, and the helpful *Elias Rooms* (Ⓣ22450 22446 or 697 85 87 924, Ⓦwww.eliasrooms.com; ③; mid-May to Sept) just above the *Hotel Karpathos*, with variable, mostly en-suite rooms in a converted older house. Up an alley beyond Avis at the start of Vróndi, *Paradise Studios* (Ⓣ22450 22949; ③) offers seven simple but practical, good sized air-conditioned studios in a quiet, aesthetic orchard setting. The only comfortable hotel catering to independent travellers is helpful *Atlantis*, opposite the Italian "palace" – rates include breakfast (Ⓣ22450 22777, Ⓦwww.atlantishotelkarpathos.gr; ④).

Eating, drinking and nightlife

Many Pigádhia-waterfront **tavernas**, where tacky photo-menus and defrosted *yíros* and chips reign supreme, are undistinguished and overpriced; quality and value improve significantly as you head east towards the ferry dock. Near the end of the strip stand characterful *Anna*, good for fair-priced, non-farmed fish with heaping salads; and the best all-rounder next door, *Iy Orea Karpathos*, with palatable local bulk wine, *trahanádhes* soup, spicy sausages, marinated artichokes and great spinach pie – locals use it as an ouzerí and just order *mezédhes*. They have competition from *To Spitikon*, the first place in from the seafront fountain, with a large range of salads, island specialities and *mayireftá*, though portion sizes are erratic. Also a block inland, *Mezedhopolio To Ellinikon* (all year), caters to a local clientele with hot and cold *orektiká*, meat and good desserts. If *yíros* and chips it must be, then the best place for it – the fresh kind, own-sourced – is *Ovelistirio tis Erasmias*, inland on Dhimokratías opposite the taxi rank. *Enigma* offers taped **music** from a perch overlooking the bay, while *Oxygen* is the longest-standing indoor midnight-to-dawn **dance club**.

Southern and western Kárpathos

The southern extremity of Kárpathos, near the airport, is desolate and windswept. There are a few undeveloped sandy beaches along the southeast coast in **Amfiárti** district, but most are only attractive to foreign **windsurfers** who come to take advantage of the prevailing northwesterlies, especially during the late-June European championships. The most established surf school here is Pro Center Kárpathos (Ⓣ22450 91063 or 697 78 86 289, Ⓦwww.Chris-Schill.com), which has the advantage of three separate bays near the airport, catering to different ability levels, though smaller, more personal Soultravels (Ⓣ694 29 42 090, Ⓦwww.soultravels.ch) occupies an adjacent cove. The most comfortable **hotel** in the region, though sometimes full with surf packages, is *Poseidon* (Ⓣ22450 91066; B&B; ③) above sheltered **Dhamatría** beach.

Most people go no further than **AMMOPÍ** (alias "Amoopi"), 7km south of Pigádhia, the biggest of Kárpathos' three purpose-built resorts (the others being Arkássa and Paralía Lefkoú). Three sand-and-gravel, tree- or cliff-fringed coves are fringed by half a dozen tavernas and numbers of **hotels** and **studios**. Quietest of these are the well-designed *Vardes Studios* (Ⓣ22450 81111 or 697 21 52 901, Ⓦwww.hotelvardes.com; ③), with distant sea views and orchard setting. Of the **tavernas**, much the best is *Esperida,* about halfway along the approach road, coping efficiently with crowds scoffing local cheese, wine and sausage, roast eggplant, and pickled wild vegetables.

West out of Pigádhia the road climbs steeply 9km to **MENETÉS**, draped in the lee of a ridge, with some handsome old houses and a spectacularly sited – if hideous – church. The most distinctive local **taverna**, east beyond the World War II resistance monument memorial, is *Pelayia* (all year) in Kritháres district, offering local marinated "sardines" (really the larger *ménoula*), cheese, wild greens and live music some nights.

Arkássa, Iníki and Ádhia

Beyond Menetés, you descend to **ARKÁSSA**, on the slopes of a ravine, with excellent views to Kássos en route. A few hundred metres south of where the ravine meets the sea, a signposted cement side road leads briefly to the whitewashed chapel of **Ayía Sofía**. Remains of a much larger, surrounding Byzantine basilica feature several mosaic floors with geometric patterns, the best one inside a vaulted cistern at one corner. The Paleókastro headland beyond was the site of Mycenaean Arkessia; the walk up is scarcely worth it for the sake of a few stretches of polygonal wall and a couple of tumbled columns.

Despite just one good nearby beach, Arkássa has been heavily developed, with **hotels** and often mediocre **tavernas** aimed at the package tour market sprouting along the rocky coastline. Independent travellers could try **Áyios Nikólaos beach**, a rare 100-metre stretch of sand signposted just south. Here you'll find *Montemar Studios* (Ⓣ22450 61394; ④) with units in two grades, and – right behind the beach – the *Glaros* (Ⓣ22450 61015, Ⓕ22450 61016; ④), with five studios and an attached **taverna**.

The tiny fishing port of **FINÍKI**, 2km north, offers a minuscule beach, and four weekly excursions in season to Kássos. Comfortable **accommodation** is provided by the well-designed and -built *Arhontiko Studios* on the main bypass road (Ⓣ22450 61473, Ⓦwww.hotelarhontiko.com; ③). Best of three port **tavernas** is locally attended *Marina*, good for fish.

Some 7km north of Finíki along the coast road, Karpathian forest resumes at **ÁDHIA** hamlet, where the appropriately named *Pine Tree Restaurant* offers home-baked bread, lentil soup and octopus *makaronádha* (plus other *mayireftá*) washed down by sweet Óthos wine. They also have **accommodation** overlooking the orchard and the sea (Ⓣ697 73 69 948, Ⓔpinetree_adia@hotmail.com). Easy paths lead twenty minutes west to tiny **Epínemo beach** (and 10min further to larger **Ilioúndas**), while a meatier **hike** up the **Flaskiá gorge** up towards Mount Kallílímni starts from the main-road bridge (signposted for Lastós; 2hr 20min one way).

Paralía Lefkoú and Mesohóri

Dense forest continues much of the way to the turning for the attractive resort of **PARALÍA LEFKOÚ**. Three **car rental** outfits – Lefkos (Ⓣ22450 71057), Hot Wheels (Ⓣ22450 71085) or Drive (Ⓣ22450 71415) – make this a feasible touring base, and it's also perfect for flopping on one of the three local beaches – **Yialoú Horáfi**, **Panayiás tó Limáni**, **Frangolimniónas** – separated by a striking topography of cliffs, islets and sandspits. There are more than two dozen places to stay, and perhaps half as many tavernas, but package companies monopolize the better **accommodation** from June to September. About the only exception is spartan but en-suite *Sunweek Studios* (Ⓣ22450 71025; ②), on the promontory dividing Yialoú Horáfi from Panayiás tó Limáni. You'll have better luck at **Potáli**, the stonier, fourth bay just south of the access road; go here for quiet and spacious *Akroyiali Studios* (Ⓣ22450 71263, Ⓕ22450 71178; ③), with balconies overlooking the beach, or the smaller *Lefkosia Studios* near the road (Ⓣ22450 71176 or 22450 71148; ③). **Tavernas** at Yialoú Horáfi can disappoint: best options are *Mihalis* at the base of the promontory, with lots of vegetarian platters, or the kindly *Blue Sea* with its pizzas, meat-rich *mayireftá* and pancake breakfasts.

Back on the main road, you climb northeast through severely fire-damaged pine forest to **MESOHÓRI**. The village tumbles towards the sea around narrow, stepped alleys, coming to a halt at the edge of a bluff dotted with three tiny, ancient chapels and separated from the village proper by extensive orchards. These are nurtured by the fountain (the best water on the island) beneath the church of **Panayía Vryssianí**, wedged against the mountainside just east. On the stair-street leading to this church is an excellent, reasonably priced **taverna**, the *Dhramoundana*, featuring local capers, sausages and the local marinated "sardines". The paved main road continues over the island's watershed to Spóa, overlooking the east coast.

Central Kárpathos

Central Kárpathos supports a group of villages blessed with commanding hillside settings, ample running water – and a cool climate, even in August. Nearly everyone here has "done time" in North America, then returned home with their nest eggs; the area has the highest per capita income in Greece. West-facing **PYLÉS** is the most attractive, set above another spring-fed oasis, while **ÓTHOS**, noted for its sweet, tawny-amber wine, is the highest (around 400m) and chilliest, on the flanks of 1215-metre Mount Kalilímni. On the east side of the ridge nestles **VOLÁDHA** with its tiny Venetian citadel and two nocturnal tavernas. From the smart track-and-soccer stadium below **APÉRI**, the largest, lowest and wealthiest settlement, a paved five-kilometre road leads to **Aháta** pebble beach (which has a shower and a pricey taverna).

Beyond Apéri, the road up the **east coast** passes above **beaches** often visited by boat trips from Pigádhia. A paved, twisty side road via Katódhio hamlet leads first to a further turning (2km of rough, steep dirt track; jeep required) to **Káto Lákkos**, 150m of scenic sand and gravel favoured by naturists, and then after 4km on the main pavement to **Kyrá Panayiá**. Numerous villas and rooms huddle in the ravine behind 150m of fine gravel and sheltered, turquoise water; the beach taverna is mediocre. **Ápella** is the best of the beaches you can reach by road, though there's a final short path from the single, good-value **taverna-rooms** to the scenic 300-metre gravel strand. The route ends at **SPÓA**, high above the shore just east of the island's spine, with a **snack-bar** and *kafenío* at the edge of the village, which might make better meal stops than the overpriced *Votsalo* down at **Áyios Nikólaos**, 5km below, with an average beach.

Northern Kárpathos

Although it's now far easier to reach **northern Kárpathos** from Spóa, arrival **by sea** is the cheapest option, as taxis are exorbitant. Inter-island ferries call at Dhiafáni two or three times a week in season, while foot passengers can use the smaller boat services from **Pigádhia** (see p.664). Excursion-boat arrivals are met at Dhiafáni for an eight-kilometre bus transfer up to the traditional village of **Ólymbos**, the main local attraction, along with good walking opportunities. The imminent paving of the road in from Spóa will probably, however, pull the rug out from under the day-trip industry, and should encourage a more thoughtful type of tourism. Coastal **Dhiafáni** makes a better base for those who want to be by the sea, with excellent **beaches** either side.

Ólymbos and hiking

Founded as a pirate-safe refuge during Byzantine times, windswept **ÓLYMBOS** straddles a long ridge below slopes studded with ruined windmills. Two restored ones, beyond the main church, grind wheat and barley in late summer only, though one is kept under sail during any tourist season. The village has long attracted foreign and Greek ethnologists for the sake of its **traditional dress**, crafts, dialect and music long since vanished elsewhere in Greece – and dwindling by the year here too. Nowadays it's only older women and those working in several tourist shops who wear striking, colourful apparel – while assiduously flogging trinkets mostly imported from China, India or Bulgaria. Women play a prominent role in daily life: tending gardens, carrying goods on their shoulders or herding goats. Nearly all Ólymbos men emigrate to Baltimore or work outside the village, sending money home and returning only on holidays. The long-isolated villagers speak a unique dialect, said to maintain traces of its Doric and Phrygian origins – "Ólymbos" is pronounced "Élymbos" locally. Live vernacular music is still played regularly, especially at **festival** times (Easter and August 15), when visitors have little hope of finding a bed.

From the village, the superb west coast beach at **Fýsses** is a sharp drop below, served by jeep track. **Local hikes**, however, head more gently north or east, many on waymarked paths, though you'll have to stay overnight locally to partake. Easiest is the ninety-minute walk back down to Dhiafáni, beginning just below the two working windmills. The way is well marked, with water en route, eventually dropping to a ravine amid extensive forest. You could also tackle the trail north (just under 3hr one way) via sparsely inhabited **AVLÓNA**, set on a high upland devoted to grain, to the ruins and beach at **Vrykoúnda** ("Vrougoúnda" in dialect), which offers traces of Hellenistic/Roman Brykous, the remote cave-shrine of John the Baptist on the promontory and good swimming. **Trístomo**, a Byzantine anchorage in the far northeast of Kárpathos, can also be reached on a magnificent cobbled way beginning above Avlóna (2hr 30min); you could return by a spectacular coastal path back to **Vanánda** (4hr). There's also a fine ninety-minute marked path from Avlóna down to Vanánda beach (see below).

The best **accommodation** in Ólymbos is ★ *Anemos* (contact Minas on ⓣ693 28 58 901 or ⓦwww.geocities.com/escape2olympos/; ③), a traditional house beyond the church divided into studios with knockout views. Honourable mentions go to friendly *Rooms Olymbos* (ⓣ22450 51009; ②), near the village entrance, which has modern units with bath and unplumbed ones with traditional furnishings (and an excellent, inexpensive ★ **restaurant**), plus the eight-room, en-suite *Hotel Astro* (ⓣ22450 51421; B&B; ③) managed by the two sisters who run *Café-Restaurant Zefiros*, near the centre; breakfast is taken in the **restaurant**. *Restaurant Olymbos* has an annexe at Ávlona, central *Restaurant Avlona*, on the through road; with four en-suite rooms (ⓣ694 60 18 521; ②), it makes an ideal base for walkers.

Dhiafáni and beaches

The pace of life in **DHIAFÁNI** is slow outside high summer; the only attraction is a small **monk seal information office** just inland from the quay. Seasonal boat trips are offered to remoter local **beaches**, as well as to uninhabited **Saría islet** (most reliably Thurs, 10am out, 4.30pm back; €24 with lunch); passengers hike the trans-island path to the Byzantine site of Palátia, where you swim and have barbecued lunch before returning. Among coves within walking distance, closest is stony **Vanánda**; follow the pleasant signposted path north through the pines for thirty minutes, shortcutting the more recent road. Naturist **Papá Miná**, with a few trees and cliff-shade, lies an hour's walk distant via the cairned trail taking off from the road to the ferry dock. An ordinary car can drive the 4km there, with the last 300m on foot; with more caution you can just about get a car to 250-metre long, naturist **Forókli** (5.5km below the Spóa–Ólymbos road). But you really need a jeep to reach **Áyios Minás** (seasonal taverna; bear left at fork partway along) or equally pristine **Agnóndia** (bear right).

There's a small **travel agency** where you buy ferry tickets and can change money if the **ATM** by the waterfront fountain isn't working. Dhiafáni has abundant sleeping and eating opportunities, though aggressive touts on the quay are worth avoiding. In terms of **accommodation**, top of the heap in all senses is hospitable George and Anna Niotis' *Hotel Studios Glaros* (Ⓣ22450 51501 or 694 79 44 601, Ⓦwww.hotel-glaros.gr; ❸) up the south slope, with sixteen huge, tiered units, some of which sleep four. Worthy alternatives, 300m along the road west, more or less opposite each other, are the pleasant, ground-floor *Dolphins/Dhelfinia Studios* (Ⓣ22450 51354; ❷) under the eponymous restaurant, or the (uniquely here) air-conditioned *Hotel Nikos* (Ⓣ22450 51410, Ⓦwww.nikoshotel.gr; ❷). Among **tavernas**, *Dolphins/Dhelfinia* does good fish, and vegetables from the garden below, while vine-shrouded, backstreet *Iy Anixi* offers a few inexpensive, homestyle *mayireftá* daily. Behind the fountain, favourite meeting places are the Italian-run *Iy Gorgona/L'Angolo*, featuring light dishes, wonderful desserts, proper coffees, and *limoncello* digestif, and *Koral (Mihalis & Popi's)* across the lane, which serves good grills, fish, salads, Cretan *tsikoudhiá* and doubles as the liveliest **nightspot**.

Rhodes (Ródhos)

It's understandable that **Rhodes** is among the most visited Greek islands. Not only is its southeast coast adorned with numerous sandy **beaches**, but the capital's nucleus is a beautiful **medieval city**, legacy of the crusading Knights of St John who used the island as their main base from 1309 until 1522. Unfortunately this showpiece is jammed to capacity with over a million tourists in a good season, versus about 120,000 permanent inhabitants (including many foreigners).

Ródhos Town's medieval **Old Town** is very much the main event, but **Líndhos**, with its ancient acropolis and (occasionally) atmospheric village, ranks second. The southeastern **beaches** – particularly near **Afándou** and **Yennádhi** – and isolated monuments of the interior, such as castles near **Monólithos** and **Kritinía**, and frescoed churches at **Thárri** and **Asklipió**, are also worth pointing a car towards. Adrenalin junkies go to extremes at the far south cape, **Prassoníssi**, one of the best windsurfing spots in Europe.

Some history

Blessed with an equable climate and strategic position, Rhodes was important from earliest times despite a lack of good harbours. The best natural port served the ancient town of **Lindos** which, together with the other Dorian city-states **Kameiros** and **Ialyssos**, united in 408 BC to found a new capital, **Rodos** (Rhodes), at the windswept northern tip of the island. At various moments the cities allied themselves with Alexander, the Persians, Athenians or Spartans as conditions suited them, generally escaping retribution for backing the wrong side by a combination of seafaring audacity, sycophancy and burgeoning wealth as a trade centre. Following the failed siege of Demetrios Polyorketes in 305 BC, Rhodes prospered even further, displacing Athens as the major venue for rhetoric and the arts in the east Mediterranean.

Decline set in when the island became involved in the Roman civil wars, and was sacked by Cassius; by late imperial times, it was a backwater, and victim of numerous barbarian raids during the Byzantine period. The Byzantines ceded Rhodes to the Genoese, who in turn surrendered it to the Knights of St John.

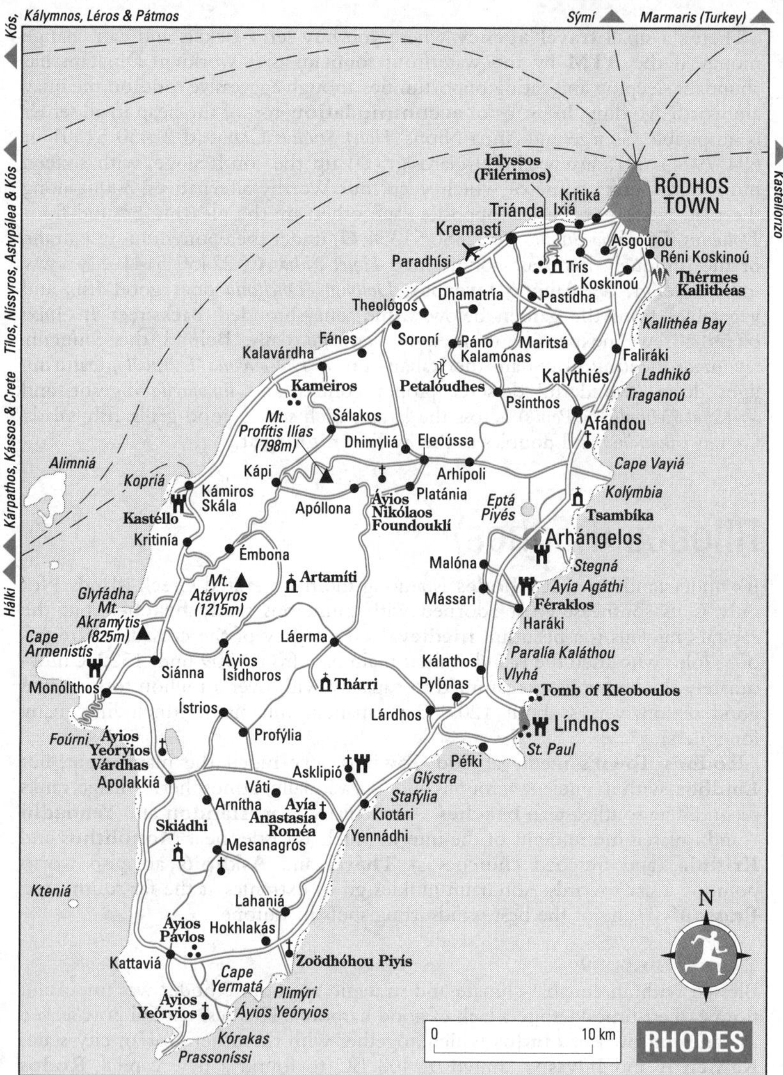

The second great siege of Rhodes, during 1522–23, saw Ottoman Sultan Süleyman the Magnificent oust the stubborn knights; Rhodes once again lapsed into relative obscurity, though heavily colonized and garrisoned, until its seizure by the Italians in 1912.

Arrival, information and transport

All international and inter-island **ferries and catamarans** dock at the middle of Rhodes' three ports, **Kolóna harbour**; excursion craft, the small *Sea Star* catamaran and **hydrofoils** use the yacht harbour of **Mandhráki**. Its entrance was supposedly once straddled by the Colossus, an ancient statue of Apollo commemorating the end of the 305 BC siege; today two columns surmounted by bronze deer serve as replacements.

The **airport** lies 14km southwest of town, by Paradhísi village; there's a bus stop outside Arrivals (into town infrequently 6.45am–11.20pm); public buses returning from Kalavárdha, Theológos or Sálakos also pass the stop on the main road opposite the northerly car-park entrance more frequently. A **taxi** into town will cost €15–23, depending on time of day. Rhodian taxi drivers have a poor reputation – overcharging of new arrivals is routine, as is refusing to take you to your chosen hotel, while steering you to accommodation giving them kickbacks. Most won't enter the Old Town either. **Buses** for the west and east coasts leave from two almost adjacent terminals on Papágou and Avérof, just outside the Italian-built **New Market** (a tourist trap, eminently missable except for the wonderful rotunda of the old fish market inside).

Between the lower eastern station and the **taxi** rank at Platía Rimínis there's a **municipal tourist office** (June–Sept Mon–Sat 8am–9.30pm, Sun 9am–3pm), while some way up Papágou on the corner of Makaríou the **EOT office** (Mon–Fri 8.30am–2.45pm) dispenses bus and ferry schedules, plus a list of standard taxi fares, complete with complaint form (see warning above).

Ródhos Town

Ancient Rodos, which lies beneath most of the modern city, was laid out by Hippodamos of Miletos in the grid pattern in vogue at the time, with planned residential and commercial quarters. Its perimeter walls totalled almost 15km, enclosing nearly double the area of the present town, and the Hellenistic population was over 100,000 – a staggering figure for late antiquity, as against 50,631 at the 2001 census.

The contemporary town divides into two unequal parts: the compact **walled Old Town**, and the **New Town**, which sprawls around it in three directions. The latter dates from the Ottoman occupation, when Greek Orthodox residents – forbidden to dwell in the old city – founded several suburb villages or *marásia* in the environs, long since merged. Commercialization is predictably rampant in the walled town, and in the modern district of **Neohóri** ("Niohóri" in dialect), west of Mandhráki yacht harbour: a cantonment of hotels, souvenir shops, designer outlets, mediocre restaurants, car rental or travel agencies and bars – easily thirty in every category.

Accommodation

Hotels and pensions at all price levels abound in the Old Town; there are also some possibilities in Neohóri, especially useful if you're off to the airport early. During busy seasons, or late at night, it's prudent to **reserve** well in advance – only the worst unlicensed accommodation is touted by desperate proprietors at the ferry and catamaran quays.

Old Town

Andreas Omírou 28D ⓣ22410 34156, ⓦwww.hotelandreas.com. Perennially popular (reservations with credit card deposit mandatory) place under the dynamic management of Patrick (Belgian) and Constance (American), this is one of the more imaginative old-Turkish-mansion restoration-pensions. Rooms (some a/c) in various formats (including family-size and a spectacular "penthouse") all have baths, though some are across a corridor. Terrace bar with views for excellent breakfasts (extra) and evening drinks; two-night minimum stay. Open all year. ❸–❺

Apollo Tourist House Omírou 28C ⓣ22410 32003, ⓦwww.apollo-touristhouse.com. Six unique, wood-trimmed, centrally heated, en-suite rooms; rates include breakfast. Under new

RÓDHOS TOWN

BARS & CLUBS

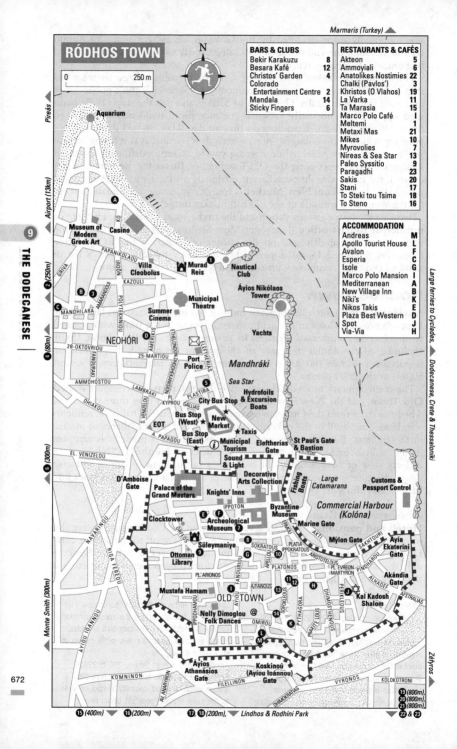

Bekir Karakuzu	8
Besara Kafé	12
Christos' Garden	4
Colorado Entertainment Centre	2
Mandala	14
Sticky Fingers	6

RESTAURANTS & CAFÉS

Akteon	5
Ammoyiali	6
Anatolikes Nostimies	22
Chalki (Pavlos')	3
Khristos (O Vlahos)	19
La Varka	11
Ta Marasia	15
Marco Polo Café	I
Meltemi	1
Metaxi Mas	21
Mikes	10
Myrovolies	7
Nireas & Sea Star	13
Paleo Syssitio	9
Paragadhi	23
Sakis	20
Stani	17
To Steki tou Tsima	18
To Steno	16

ACCOMMODATION

Andreas	M
Apollo Tourist House	L
Avalon	F
Esperia	C
Isole	G
Marco Polo Mansion	I
Mediterranean	A
New Village Inn	B
Niki's	K
Nikos Takis	E
Plaza Best Western	D
Spot	J
Via-Via	H

0 250 m

N

Marmaris (Turkey)
Pireás
Airport (13km)
2 (250m)
4 (80m)
6 (300m)
Monte Smith (300m)
Large ferries to Cyclades, Dodecanese, Crete & Thessaloniki
Zéfyros
19 (800m), 20 (800m), 21 (800m), 22 & 23
15 (400m)
16 (200m)
17, 18 (200m), Líndhos & Rodhíni Park

Aquarium
Élli
Museum of Modern Greek Art
Casino
Papanikolaou
Iroón
Koú
Villa Cleobolus
Murad Reis
Nautical Club
Griva
Kazouli
Amarandou
Polytekhniou
Mandhilara
Áyios Nikólaos Tower
Municipal Theatre
Summer Cinema
Yachts
Neohóri
Amerikis
Ethelondon Dhodhekanision
Eleftherias
28-Oktovriou
25-Martiou
Fanouraki
Port Police
Mandhráki
Ammohostou
Sea Star
Lambraki
Pl. Kyprou
Plastira
Gallias
Dhiakou
S. Venizelou
City Bus Stop
Hydrofoils & Excursion Boats
Bus Stop (West)
New Market
EOT
Taxis
A. Papagou
Bus Stop (East)
Municipal Tourism
Eleftherías Gate
St Paul's Gate & Bastion
El. Venizelou
Sound & Light
D'Amboise Gate
Decorative Arts Collection
Fishing Boats
Large Catamarans
Customs & Passport Control
Palace of the Grand Masters
Knights' Inns
Ippoton
Commercial Harbour (Kolóna)
Byzantine Museum
Clocktower
Archeological Museum
Marine Gate
Ermou
Akti
Orfeos
Navarinou
Mýlon Gate
Sakhtouri
Ayía Ekateríni Gate
Süleymaniye
Sokratous
Platia Ippokratous
Aristotelous
Riga Fereou
Ottoman Library
Apellou
Platonos
Pl. Evreon Martyron
Pindharou
Pl. Arionos
Fanouriou
Alhadef
Akándia Gate
A/Fanous
Mustafa Hamam
Old Town
Ayiou
Sofokleous
Dhimosthenous
Perikleous
Kal Kadosh Shalom
Afstralias
Ippodhamou
Pythagora
Nelly Dimoglou Folk Dances
Omirou
Praxitelous
Ayiou Ioannou
Áyios Athanásios Gate
Koskinoú (Ayíou Ioánnou) Gate
Komninon
Av. Anaryiron
Fillellinon
Vyronos
Kolokotroni
Dhimokratias

management from 2007. April–Oct; also by the month in winter. 4

Avalon Háritos 9 ⓣ22410 31438, ⓦwww.avalonrhodes.gr. Converted in 2007, this fourteenth-century manor house offers six unique luxury suites (some quads, four with fireplaces) with plasma TV and Internet. Breakfast in your unit or down in the vaulted bar. Rack rates are high – €350–500 – but Internet specials or booking through the recommended agent (see p.678) can be more affordable. 8

Isole Evdhóxou 75 ⓣ22410 20682, ⓦwww.hotelisole.com. Simple, salubrious B&B rooms with Hellenic-blue decor in a converted Ottoman house, run by a welcoming, multilingual Italian couple. Pleasant breakfast area and superb roof terrace. March to mid-Nov. 3 standard rooms (one with fireplace), 4 tower suite.

Marco Polo Mansion Ayíou Fanouríou 42 ⓣ22410 25562, ⓦwww.marcopolomansion.gr. Superb conversion of another old Turkish mansion, with a *hamam* on site; all rooms are en suite and exquisitely furnished with antiques from the nearby gallery of the same name, plus cotton pillows and handmade mattresses. Large buffet breakfasts are provided in the garden snack bar, open to all later in the day (see p.676). One-week minimum stay, reservations and credit card deposit mandatory. April–Oct. Garden rooms are a little cheaper. 6

Niki's Sofokléous 39 ⓣ22410 25115, ⓦwww.nikishotel.gr. Some rooms can be on the small side, but all are en suite, most have a/c, and upper-storey ones (three with private balconies) have fine views. There's a washing machine, two common terraces and friendly, helpful management. Someone will wait up for late-night arrivals. All year. 3 B&B

Nikos Takis Panetíou 26 ⓣ22410 70773, ⓦwww.nikostakishotel.com. Miniature "fashion hotel" in a restored mansion with just seven, somewhat gaudy units (including painted ceilings), from junior suites with CD players to "honeymoon" suites with fridge, DVD and TV. Pebble-mosaic courtyard, with views over town, for breakfast and drinks. 7–8

Spot Perikléous 21 ⓣ & ⓕ22410 34737, ⓦwww.spothotelrhodes.com. In a modern building, various cheerfully painted a/c en-suite rooms with textiles on the walls offer excellent value (including unlimited buffet breakfast in rear patio). Internet and free luggage storage. Open March–Nov. 3

Via-Via Lysipoú 2, alley off Pythagóra ⓣ & ⓕ22410 77027, ⓦwww.hotel-via-via.com. Efficient, congenially run hotel; most one-to-four-person rooms, all a/c, are en suite but two have baths across the hall. All are simply and tastefully furnished. Roof terrace with pergola and divans for three grades of breakfast and an eyeful of the Ibrahim Pasha mosque opposite. All year. 4–5

Neohóri

Esperia Yeoryíou Gríva 7 ⓣ22410 23941, ⓦwww.esperia-hotels.gr. Well-priced 3-star in a quiet spot overlooking a little plaza. Small-to-medium size, but salubrious and tasteful rooms with showers in the baths. All year. 4

Mediterranean Kó 35 ⓣ22410 24661, ⓦwww.mediterranean.gr. Beachfront 4-star hotel in a prime location; less expensive than you'd think, especially if booked through the recommended travel agent (see p.678). The street-level snack-bar/café is very popular around the clock with nonresidents. 6–8

New Village Inn Konstandopédhos 10 ⓣ22410 34937, ⓦwww.newvillageinn.gr. Whitewashed, somewhat grotto-like en-suite rooms (upper-floor units have balconies), arrayed around a courtyard breakfast-bar. Friendly Greek and American management; singles available at a good rate. Open April–Oct. 3

Plaza Best Western Ieroú Lóhou 7, ⓣ22410 22501, ⓦwww.rhodes-plaza.com. One of the better 4-stars within Rhodes city limits, convenient for Mandhráki. Pool garden, sauna, Jacuzzi, buffet English breakfast, restaurant. All year; good discounts Nov–April. 6

The Old Town

Merely cataloguing its principal monuments and attractions cannot do justice to the **medieval city**. There's ample gratification to be derived from slipping through the eleven surviving gates and strolling the streets, under flying archways built for earthquake resistance, past warm-toned sandstone and limestone walls painted ochre or blue, and over the *votsalotó* (pebble-mosaic) pavements.

Dominating the northernmost sector of the fourteenth-century fortifications is the **Palace of the Grand Masters** (summer Mon 12.30–7pm, Tues–Sun 8am–7.30pm; winter Mon 12.30–3pm, Tues–Sun 8.30am–3pm; €6, or €10 for

▲Rhodes Old Town

a joint ticket for all museums in this section). Destroyed by an 1856 ammunition depot explosion set off by lightning, it was reconstructed by the Italians as a summer home for Mussolini and Vittore Emmanuele III ("King of Italy and Albania, Emperor of Ethiopia") – neither of whom ever visited Rhodes. The exterior, based on medieval engravings and accounts, is passably authentic, but inside, free rein was given to Fascist delusions of grandeur: a marble staircase leads up to rooms paved with Hellenistic mosaics from Kós, and the clunky period furnishings rival many a northern European palace. The ground floor contains splendid galleries entitled **Rhodes from the 4th century until the Turkish Conquest** and **Ancient Rhodes, 2400 Years** (same hours and admission), jointly the best museums in town. The medieval collection highlights the importance of Christian Rhodes as a trade centre, placing the island in a trans-Mediterranean context. The Knights are represented with a display on their sugar-refining industry and a gravestone of a Grand Master; precious manuscripts and books precede a wing of post-Byzantine icons. Across the courtyard, "Ancient Rhodes" overshadows the official archeological museum by covering everyday life around 250 BC; highlights include a Hellenistic floor mosaic of a comedic mask and a household idol of Hecate, goddess of the occult.

The heavily restored **Gothic Street of the Knights** (Odhós Ippotón) leads east from Platía Kleovoúlou in front of the palace; the "Inns" lining it lodged the Knights of St John, according to linguistic and ethnic affiliation, until the Ottoman Turks compelled them to leave for Malta after a six-month siege in which the defenders were outnumbered thirty to one. Today the Inns house government offices, foreign consulates or cultural institutions vaguely appropriate to their past, with occasional exhibitions, but the overall effect of the Italian renovation is sterile and stagey (indeed, nearby streets were used to film both *Pascali's Island* and *El Greco*).

At the bottom of the hill, the Knights' Hospital has been refurbished as the **Archeological Museum** (Tues–Sun 8.30am–2.45pm; €3 or joint ticket), though the arches and echoing halls of the building somewhat overshadow its contents – largely painted pottery dating from the ninth through the fifth centuries BC.

Behind the second-storey sculpture garden, the Hellenistic statue gallery is more accessible; in a rear corner stands *Aphrodite Adioumene* or the so-called "Marine Venus", beloved of Lawrence Durrell, but lent a rather sinister aspect by her sea-dissolved face – in contrast to the friendlier *Aphrodite Bathing*. Virtually next door is the **Decorative Arts Collection** (Tues–Sun 8.30am–2.45pm; €2 or joint ticket), gleaned from old houses across the Dodecanese; the most compelling artefacts are carved cupboard doors and chest lids painted with mythological or historical episodes.

Across the way stands the **Byzantine Museum** (Tues–Sun 8.30am–2.45pm; €2 or joint ticket), housed in the old cathedral of the Knights, adapted from the Byzantine shrine of Panayía toú Kástrou. Medieval icons and frescoes lifted from crumbling chapels on Rhodes and Hálki, as well as photos of art still *in* situ, constitute the exhibits. Highlight of the permanent collection is a complete fresco cycle from the domes and squinches of Thárri monastery (see p.683) from 1624, removed in 1967 to reveal much older work beneath.

Turkish and Jewish Rhodes

If you head south from the Palace of the Grand Masters, it's hard to miss the most conspicuous Turkish monument in Rhodes, the rust-coloured, candy-striped **Süleymaniye Mosque**. Rebuilt in the nineteenth century on foundations three hundred years older, it's currently shut like many local Ottoman monuments, though thoroughly refurbished in anticipation of opening. The Old Town is in fact well sown with mosques and *mescids* (the Islamic equivalent of a chapel), many converted from Byzantine churches after the 1522 conquest, when the Christians were expelled from the medieval precinct. A few, such as the **Ibrahim Pasha Mosque** on Plátonos, are still used by the sizeable **Turkish-speaking minority** here. Their most enduring civic contributions are, opposite the Süleymaniye, the **Ottoman Library** (Mon–Sat 9.30am–4pm; tip custodian), with a rich collection of early medieval manuscripts and Korans; an **imaret** (mess-hall) at Sokrátous 179, now an exceptionally pleasant café (*Palio Syssitio*), with temporary exhibits across the courtyard; and the imposing, still-functioning **Mustafa Hamam**, or Turkish bath, on Platía Aríonos (Mon–Fri 10am–5pm, Sat 8am–5pm, last admission 3.30pm; €1.50). Bring everything you need – soap, shampoo, towel, loofah – to enjoy separate men's and women's sections. Heading downhill from the Süleymaniye Mosque, you reach **Odhós Sokrátous**, since time immemorial the main commercial thoroughfare, and now the "Via Turista", packed with fur and jewellery stores pitched at cruise-ship tourists. Beyond the tiled central fountain in Platía Ippokrátous, Odhós Aristotélous leads to **Platía tón Evréon Martýron** ("Square of the Jewish Martyrs"), named in memory of the large local community almost totally annihilated during the summer of 1944; a black granite column in the centre honours them. Of the four synagogues that once graced the nearby Jewish quarter, only the ornate, arcaded **Kal Kadosh Shalom** (daily except Sat 10am–3pm; donation) on Odhós Simíou, just to the south, survives. It's maintained essentially as another memorial to the approximately 2100 Jews of Rhodes and Kós sent to the concentration camps; plaques in French commemorate the dead. To one side, a well-labelled, three-room **museum**, set up by a Los Angeles attorney of Jewish Rhodian descent, thematically chronicles the community's life on Rhodes and its far-flung diaspora in the Americas and Africa.

Neohóri

Kumburnú, the pointy bit of **Neohóri,** is surrounded by a continuous **beach** (loungers, parasols and showers), particularly at **Élli**, the more sheltered east-facing section. At the northernmost point of the island the **Aquarium** (daily: April–Sept 9am–8.30pm; Oct–March 9am–4.30pm; €4.50) offers displays on the history and function of the building, a monk seal buried as an ancient family's pet, a stuffed Cuvier's beaked whale and a subterranean maze of fish tanks. Immediately south, on Ekatón Hourmadhiés ("100 Palms") Square, in the Nestorídhio Mélathro, is housed the **Museum of Modern Greek Art** (Tues–Sat 8am–2pm & Fri 5–8pm; €3), the most important collection of twentieth-century Greek painting outside of Athens: all the heavy hitters – Ghikas, Spyros Vassiliou, Yiannis Tsarouhis, surrealist Nikos Engonopoulos, naïve artist Theophilos, neo-Byzantinist Fotis Kontoglou – are amply represented. East of "100 Palms", the Italian-built Albergo delle Rose (*Hotel Rodon*) has become the **Rhodes Casino**, Greece's third largest. Continue in the same direction to the **Murad Reis mosque** and its atmospherically neglected Muslim cemetery, just past the **Villa Cleobolus**, where Lawrence Durrell lived from 1945 to 1947.

About 2km southwest of Mandhráki, sparse, unenclosed remains of **Hellenistic Rhodes** – a restored theatre and stadium, plus three columns of an Apollo temple – perch atop Monte Smith, the hill of Áyios Stéfanos renamed for a British admiral during the Napoleonic Wars.

Eating and drinking

Eating well for a reasonable price in and around Ródhos Town is a challenge, but not an insurmountable one. As a general rule, the further south towards Zéfyros you go, the better value you'll find – so touristy, alas, has most of the Old Town (and Neohóri) become. Unless otherwise stated, establishments operate year round.

Old Town

Marco Polo Café Ayíou Fanouríou 42. What started as the breakfast venue for the eponymous hotel (see p.673) has become the sleeper of the Old Town. Traditional adapted recipes, adeptly blending subtle flavours, include pilaf with lamb and raisins, *kaltsoúnia*, and *psaronéfri* with *manoúri* cheese, fig and red peppercorn sauce. Excellent wine list and desserts of the day; last orders 11pm. April–Oct.

Myrovolies Láhitos 13. Popular if pricey ouzerí featuring hearty pork and mushroom dishes, with patio and indoor seating. Live music three nights a week; budget €80 for three with modest tippling.

Mikes (pronounced "mee-kess") Nameless alley behind Sokrátous 17. Inexpensive but salubrious hole-in-the-wall, serving only grilled fish, a few shellfish appetizers, salads and wine; outdoor tables, galley-like kitchen. April–Nov.

Nireas Sofokléous 22, www.nireas-rhodes.gr. A kindly managing family, fair prices for the Old Town and atmospheric indoor/outdoor seating make this a good choice for a treat. Food is all-fresh fish and shellfish, with, unusually, a range of Italian desserts too. Around €70 for two including dessert and wine.

Sea Star Sofokléous 24. The least expensive quality seafood outlet after *Mikes* serves a limited but delicious menu of scaly fish, shellfish and *mezédhes* like *kápari* and salt-cured mackerel. Indoor seating in winter, otherwise outside on the little square.

La Varka Sofokléous 5. Hole-in-the-wall ouzerí with sought-after outside seating (and erratic service); good salads, grilled *thrápsalo*, fried or salt-cured seafood titbits, cheapish ouzo and *soúma* by the carafe. Daily 11.30am–2am.

Neohóri

Akteon Platía Eleftherías. Café in a graceful Italian building by the law courts; moderate prices for Rhodes, and great people-watching under the trees.

Ammoyiali Voríou Ipírou 17, cnr Kennedy. High-end bistro purveying salads, pasta dishes, accomplished desserts and a decent wine list. Moderately expensive; dinner only.

Chalki (Pavlos') Kathopoúli 30. Ancient bottles of who-knows-what provide the decor in this little ouzerí doing good vegetarian *mezédhes* and a limited range of mains (including seafood), washed down by ouzo and CAÏR wine. Average portions, but quite cheap. Evenings only.

Ta Marasia Platía Ayíou Ioánni 155. Ouzerí operating out of a 1923-vintage house, with plenty for vegetarians – eggplant *bourekákia*, grilled oyster mushrooms, stuffed squash blossoms – plus seafood platters like urchins and *rengosaláta*, and a full meat list, with decent bulk wine.

Meltemi Platía Koundourióti 8 Élli. Classy beachside ouzerí offering *karavidhópsyha* (crayfish nuggets), octopus croquettes and grilled peppers in balsamic to a local crowd; pleasant winter salon inside. Open all day.

Stani Ayías Anastasías 28, cnr Paleón Patrón Yermanoú, out the Koskinoú Gate. Central outlet of a Rhodian Turkish confectioners' chain, scooping two dozen flavours of Rhodes' best ice cream – queues all day (until 1am) tell you this is the place.

To Steki tou Tsima Peloponnísou 22, around the corner from *Stani*. Seafood ouzerí, featuring titbits like *foúskes* (fresh marine invertebrates), *spiniálo* (pickled version of same) and small fish not prone to farming. No airs or graces, just patently fresh ingredients. Daily eves only.

To Steno Ayíon Anaryíron 29, 400m southwest of Ayíou Athanasíou Gate. Traditional "cult" taverna with indoor/outdoor seating by season. The menu encompasses sausages, chick pea soup, *pitaroú-dhia* (courgette croquettes) and fried little fish; "discovery" means it's oilier and pricier than formerly, but still worth showing up.

Zéfyros and around

Anatolikes Nostimies Klavdhíou Pépper 109, Zéfyros Beach. The name means "Anatolian Delicacies": Thracian Pomak/Middle Eastern dips and starters, plus more strictly beef-based kebabs than the usual lamb or pork. Beach-hut atmosphere, but friendly and reasonable; post-prandial hubble-bubble on request. 1pm–midnight.

Khristos (O Vlahos) Klavdhíou Pépper 165, bend before Zéfyros Beach. Enduringly popular *estiatório* where civil servants from the nearby tax office habitually lunch at outdoor seating. Great tzatzíki, plus vegetable-strong *mayireftá* (cuttlefish with spinach, pork stew, fish soup, eggplant *imam*) that sell out quickly.

Metaxi Mas Klavdhíou Pépper 113–115, Zéfyros Beach. No English sign – look for the elevated boat – at this ouzerí purveying marinated red mullet, a few shellfish, lobster on occasion, veggie starters and some meat. You can eat well at a fraction of Old Town costs, with a sea view (and winter fireplace) to boot. Mon–Sat lunch and supper, Sun lunch only.

Paragadhi Cnr Klavdhíou Pépper and Avstralías. Seafood/fish restaurant (as opposed to ouzerí) that's the haunt of the Rhodian *beau monde*. Reasonable *mezédhes* and wine prices are offset by somewhat bumped-up fish rates; their *risótto thalassinoú* is excellent if not absolutely authentic. Large parties must book weekend nights (ⓣ 22410 37775); closed Sun eve & Mon noon.

Sakis Kanadhá 95, cnr Apostólou Papaïoánnou; ⓦ www.tavernasakis.gr. A friendly old favourite with pleasant patio and indoor seating, equally popular with Rhodians and foreigners. Known for its shellfish (such as limpets and snails), meat (chops, Cypriot *seftaliés*) and the usual starters. Supper daily, also Sun lunch.

Nightlife and entertainment

In the Old Town, an entire alley (Miltiádhou) off Apelloú is home to a dozen loud, annually changing **music bars** and **clubs**, extending into Plátonos and Platía Dhamayítou, and frequented mostly by Greeks (especially off-season). Another nucleus of activity is around Platía Aríonos and Menekléous, with at least six clubs catering to a slightly older, mixed-nationality crowd. These have now rather eclipsed the forty or so surviving bars and clubs in Neohóri, where theme nights and various other gimmicks predominate. They are found mostly in the area bounded by Alexándhrou Dhiákou, Orfanídhou, Lohagoú Fanouráki and Nikifórou Mandhilará.

Sedate by comparison, **folk dances** (June 15–Oct 1 Mon, Wed & Fri 9.20pm; €12) are presented with live accompaniment by the Nelly Dimoglou Company in the landscaped Old Town Theatre off Andhroníkou, near Platía Aríonos. The **Sound and Light** show spotlights sections of the city walls, staged in a garden just off Platía Rimínis. There's English-language narration nightly except Sunday, its screening time varying from 8.15pm to 10.15pm (€7).

Two air-conditioned **cinemas** showing first-run caper-and-action movies operate year round: the Metropol multi-plex, at the corner of Venetokléon and Výronos, southeast of the Old Town opposite the stadium, and the nearby Pallas multi-plex on Dhimokratías. The Rodon open-air cinema behind the town hall is only used for special events, such as the excellent mid-to-late-June **film festival** (Ⓦ www.ecofilms.gr).

Bekir Karakuzu Sokrátous 76. Bags of atmosphere in this last traditional Turkish *kafenío* in the Old Town, with an Oriental-fantasy interior with ornate *votsalotó* floor. Yoghurt, *loukoúmi, alisfakiá* tea and coffees are on the expensive side – consider it admission to an informal museum. 11am–midnight.

Besara Kafé Sofokléous 11–13, Old Town. Congenial breakfast café/low-key bar run by Australian-Texan Besara Harris, with interesting mixed clientele and live Greek acoustic music Thurs–Sat nights Oct–May.

Christos' Garden Dhilberáki 59, Neohóri. This combination art gallery/bar/café occupies a carefully restored old house and courtyard with pebble-mosaic floors throughout.

Colorado Entertainment Centre Orfanídhou 57, cnr Aktí Miaouli, Neohóri. Triple venue: "Colorado Live" with in-house band, "Studio Fame" with recorded sounds, and club, plus chill-out "Heaven" bar upstairs.

Mandala Sofokléous 38, Old Town. Part-Swedish-run, popular snack café/garden bar where the generic Med-lite salads and pasta dishes are overpriced and incidental to good beer, the crowd, and live Greek acoustic music on Sat eve. Open all year 2pm–3am; inside by the fireplace in winter.

Sticky Fingers Anthoúla Zérvou 6, Neohóri. Durable music bar with live rock several nights a week from 10.30pm onwards, Fri & Sat only off-season. Typical admission €15.

Listings

Car rental Rack rates weigh in at €45–55 per day, but can be bargained down to €25–35 a day, all-inclusive, out of peak season and/or for long periods. Especially recommended is Drive/Budget (Ⓦ www.driverentacar.gr), who change their cars every 12–18 months; they have several premises across the island, including at the airport (Ⓣ 22410 81011); their central, long-hours reservation number is Ⓣ 22410 68243. Other flexible outfits in Neohóri include Ansa, Mandhilará 70 (Ⓣ 22410 31811) and Kosmos, Papaloúka 31 (Ⓣ 22410 74374). Major international chains include Alamo/National, Iraklídhon 41, Ixiá (Ⓣ 22410 91117) and at the airport (Ⓣ 22410 81600); Avis, Theodhoráki 3, Neohóri (Ⓣ 22410 91700) and the airport (Ⓣ 22410 82896); plus Sixt, Iraklídhon 141, Ixiá (Ⓣ 22410 90802) and at the airport (Ⓣ 22410 81995).

Exchange Conventional banks (Alpha is open Sat morning & evenings) with ATMs are grouped around Platía Kýprou in Neohóri; plus there are exchange bureaux keeping longer hours. In the Old Town, there are bank ATMs near the museums, and along Sokrátous.

Ferry agents ANES (Ⓣ 22410 37769), for catamarans and hydrofoil to Sými; Kydon (Ⓣ 22410 23000), for Agoudimos Lines; Dodhekanisos Navtiliaki (Ⓣ 22410 70590), for the *Dodekanisos Express/Dodekanisos Pride* catamarans; Inspiration (Ⓣ 22410 36170) for GA boats; Skevos (Ⓣ 22410 22461), for Blue Star; Zorpidhis (Ⓣ 22410 20625), for LANE; *Sea Star* catamaran (Ⓣ 22410 78052). Any changes should be shown on the EOT office's (semi-) reliable handouts.

Hospital/clinic The state hospital, on the hillside just south of Neohóri, has a deservedly poor reputation; especially if you're insured, head for the well-signed Euromedica clinic in Koskinoú, 6.5km south (24hr; Ⓣ 22410 45000)

Internet cafés The most central and competitive of several are On the Spot Net (inside the *Spot Hotel*; 8am–midnight), and *Mango Bar (same hours)* at Platía Dhoriéos 3, Old Town.

Motorbike rental Low-displacement scooters will make little impact on Rhodes; sturdier Yamaha 125s, suitable for two people, start at €25 a day. Recommended outlets in Neohóri include Margaritis, Ioánni Kazoúli 23, with a wide range of models up to 500cc, plus mountain bikes; or Kiriakos, Apodhímon Amerikís 16, which will deliver to the old town and shuttle you back once you've finished.

Travel agencies In Neohóri, conveniently located Triton Holidays at Plastíra 9 (Ⓣ 22410 21690, Ⓦ www.tritondmc.gr) is excellent for all local travel arrangements, including Drive/Budget car rental, domestic catamaran, ferry and air tickets for every company, plus the catamaran to Turkey or charters to the UK. They also have accommodation affiliates across the Dodecanese, bookable at attractive rates. French-run Passion Sailing Cruises (Ⓣ 22410 73006, Ⓦ www.aegeanpassion.com) offers a bespoke service for skippered cruises, as well as bareboat charter.

The east coast

Heading down the east coast from the capital, the first tempting stop – 7km along – is the former spa at **Piyés Kallithéas**, a prize example of orientalized Art Deco from 1928–29, the work of a young Pietro Lombardi who, in his old age, designed Strasbourg's European Parliament building. Accessed via a short side road through pines, the complex (daily 8am–8pm; €2) has an upscale bar serving from inside artificial grottoes at the swimming lido, just below the dome of the Mikrí Rotónda in a clump of palms. The main Megáli Rotónda higher up is now a small **museum**, with changing modern art exhibits and a permanent collection of stills from 1961's *The Guns of Navarone* (partly filmed here) and the spa in its postwar heyday. Southwest of the spa complex, several well-signed coves, furnished with sunbeds and snack bars (*Oasis* is the best), are framed by rock formations that often interpose themselves between the water and the sand.

Once past **Faliráki** – a monstrous resort of high-rise hotels on the north juxtaposed uneasily with the cheap-and-nasty southern zone, notorious for its drink-fueled brawls, rapes, public lewdness and the odd murder – the next stop of interest is the cape just south, **Ladhikó**. On its north flank nestles the scenic bay of "**Anthony Quinn**", named in honour of the late actor whom Greeks took to their hearts following his roles in *Zorba the Greek* and *The Guns of Navarone*. The main cove, south of the promotory, has better swimming and a reasonable full-service taverna.

South of Ladhikó extends the pebble-and-sand expanse of **Afándou Bay**, the least developed large beach on the east coast, with just a few stretches of sunbeds and showers. Spare a moment, heading down the main access road to mid-bay, for the atmospheric sixteenth-century **church of Panayía Katholikí**, paved with a *votsalotó* floor throughout and incorporating fragments of a much older basilica; recently cleaned frescoes include an almond-eyed *Virgin Enthroned* on the left of the *témblon*. Immediately opposite is a very popular **taverna**, doing grills, salad and dips: *Estiatorio Katholiki* (Mon–Sat supper, Sun lunch also). For more exalted cuisine, head for pricey but excellent fish specialists *Reni Afandou* (*Avandis*) on the beach.

The enormous promontory of **Tsambíka**, 26km south of town, offers unrivalled views from up top along some 50km of coastline. From the main highway, a steep, 1500-metre cement drive leads to a small car park from where steps mount to the summit. On its September 8 festival childless women climb up – on their hands and knees in the final stretches – to the otherwise unremarkable monastery here to be cured of infertility; any children born afterwards are dedicated to the Virgin with the names Tsambikos or Tsambika, particular to the Dodecanese. Shallow **Tsambíka Bay** south of the headland (2km access road) has an excellent if packed beach, protected by its owners, the Orthodox Church, from permanent development – there are just eight *kantínas*. For a proper **taverna**, try the polite *Panorama Tsambikas*, up the main highway south of the beach turning, with good grills and *mezédhes*.

The next beach south is gravelly **Stegná** with its mix of summer cottages for locals and German-monopolized **accommodation**. The best of its few **tavernas** is *To Periyiali* down by the fish anchorage, where Greeks go for seafood, hand-cut chips and home-made *yaprákia*. Stegná is reached by a steep road east from the comparatively nondescript inland village of **ARHÁNGELOS**, overlooked by a crumbling castle. Another overnight base on this coast, English-dominated this time, is **HARÁKI**, a pleasant if undistinguished two-street fishing port with mostly self-catering **accommodation** (generally ③) overlooked by the stubby ruins of **Feraklós Castle**, the last Knights' citadel to fall to the Turks. You can swim off the town beach in front of the waterfront cafés and **tavernas** (best of these is *Maria's*), but most people head northwest to sunbed-carpeted **Ayía Agáthi beach**, or down the coast 8km to **Paralía Kaláthou**, with its attractive, less claustrophobic stretch of sand and fine gravel.

Líndhos

LÍNDHOS, the island's number-two tourist attraction, erupts from barren surroundings 12km south of Haráki. Like Ródhos Old Town, its charm is heavily undermined by commercialism and crowds. At noon dozens of tour coaches barricade the outskirts; in the village itself, those few vernacular houses not snapped up by package operators have, since the 1960s, been bought up and refurbished by British, Germans and Italians. The old *agorá* or serpentine high street presents a series of fairly indistinguishable bars, crêperies, mediocre restaurants and travel agents. Although high-rise hotels and all vehicular traffic are banned, the result is a theme park – hot and airless from June to August, but eerily deserted in winter.

Nonetheless, if you arrive outside peak season, when the lanes between the immaculately whitewashed houses are relatively empty, you can still appreciate the village's beautiful, atmospheric setting. The belfried, post-Byzantine **Panayía church** (Mon–Sat 9am–3pm & 6.30–8pm, Sun 9am–3pm) is covered inside with well-preserved eighteenth-century frescoes. The most imposing **medieval captains' residences** are built around *votsalotó* courtyards, their monumental doorways often fringed by intricate stone braids or cables supposedly corresponding in number to the fleet owned.

On the bluff looming above the town, the ancient **acropolis** with its Doric **Temple of Athena** and imposing **Hellenistic stoa** is found inside the **Knights' castle** (mid-June to mid-Sept Mon 12.30–6.45pm, Tues–Sun 8am–6.45pm; spring/autumn closes 5.45pm; winter Tues–Sun 8.30am–2.45pm; €6) – a surprisingly felicitous blend of ancient and medieval. Though the ancient city of **Lindos** and its original temple dated from at least 1100 BC, the present structure was begun by local ruler Kleoboulos in the sixth century BC.

Líndhos's north **beach**, once the principal ancient harbour, is overcrowded; quieter **options** lie one cove beyond at **Pállas** beach (nudist annexe around the headland), or 5km north at **Vlyhá Bay**. South of the acropolis huddles the small, perfectly sheltered **St Paul's harbour**, with excellent swimming; the apostle purportedly landed here in 58 AD on a mission to evangelize the island.

Practicalities

If you're not met at the bus stop under the giant fig tree by proprietors touting **accommodation**, Pallas Travel (Ⓣ22440 31494) or Lindos Suntours (Ⓣ22440 31333) can arrange a room or even a villa for a small fee; just watch that you're not shoved into a windowless cell – ventilation is paramount. The only real **hotel** in Líndhos, the most exclusive on the island, is *Melenos* (Ⓣ22440 32222, Ⓦwww.melenoslindos.com; Easter–Oct; ⑧), discreetly sited on the second lane above the north beach, by the school. No expense has been spared in laying out the twelve luxurious suites – which go for €350–800 – with semi-private, *votsalotó* terraces and tasteful furnishings; there's also a swanky garden-bar and restaurant.

Most local **restaurants** tend to be poor. You may as well plump for *Mavrikos* on the fig-tree square, founded in 1933 and in the same family ever since. Starters such as *yígandes* in carob syrup, sweet marinated sardines, or beets in goat-cheese sauce, are accomplished, as are fish mains such as skate timbale with sweetened balsamic, or superior traditional recipes like *dolmádhes* and *tyrokafterí*; choosing from the excellent (and expensive) Greek wine list will add €18 minimum a bottle to the typical food charge of €23–28 per person. For **snacks** and desserts, try *Il Forno*, an Italian-run bakery, and *Gelo Blu*, best of several gelaterie, also serving decadent cakes and juices. The better-equipped of two **Internet cafés** is helpful Lindianet; The Link is a unique combination of **laundry** and secondhand **bookshop** (Mon–Sat 9am–8pm); and there are four bank **ATMs**. Líndhos also has a **spa** (Mon–Sat 1pm–9pm), offering the usual range of services.

The west coast

Rhodes' windward **west coast** is damper, more fertile and more forested than the rest of the island; beaches, however, are exposed and often rocky. None of this has deterred development and, as on the east coast, the first few kilometres of the busy main road have been surrendered entirely to tourism. From Rhodes town limits down to the airport, the shore is lined with generic Mediterranean-*costa* hotels, though **Triánda**, **Kremastí** and **Paradhísi** are still nominally villages, with real centres.

There's little inducement to stop until you reach the site of ancient **KAMEIROS**, which together with Lindos and Ialyssos united to found the powerful city-state of Rhodes; soon eclipsed by the new capital, Kameiros was abandoned and only rediscovered in 1859. Thus it's a particularly well-preserved Doric townscape in a beautiful hillside setting (Tues–Sun: summer 8am–6.40pm; winter 8.30am–3pm; €4). You can make out the foundations of two small temples, the re-erected pillars of a Hellenistic house, a Classical fountain, and the *stoa* of the upper agora, complete with a water cistern. Because of the gentle slope of the site, there were no fortifications, nor was there an acropolis.

At the tiny anchorage of **KÁMIROS SKÁLA** (aka Skála Kamírou) 15km south, there are five touristy **restaurants**, the best being *Loukas* nearest the quay, with big salads and no hype or picture-menus. Less heralded is the weekday *kaïki* which leaves for the island of **Hálki** (see p.685) at 2.30pm, weather permitting; on Sundays there are two journeys at 9am and 6pm. With transport, proceed 400m southwest to off-puttingly named **Paralía Kopriá** ("Manure Beach"), where *Psarotaverna Johnny's* has good fish and *mezédhes*.

Some 2km south of Skála, **Kástro Kritinías** is – from afar – the most impressive of the Knights' rural strongholds, and the paved access road is too narrow and steep for tour buses. Close up it proves to be no more than a shell, but a glorious shell, with fine views west to Hálki, Alimniá, Tílos and Níssyros. The castle is being restored, with a small museum in the old church, a café, and formal admission tickets foreseen.

Beyond the quiet hillside village of Kritinía itself, the main road winds south through dense forests below mounts Akramýtis and Atávyros to **SIÁNNA**, famous for its aromatic honey and *soúma*, similar to Italian *grappa* but far smoother. The tiered, flat-roofed houses of **MONÓLITHOS**, 4km southwest at the end of the bus line, don't themselves justify the long trip out, but the view over the Aegean is striking and you could base yourself at the *Hotel Thomas* (Ⓣ22460 61291; ❷), whose fair-sized rooms belie a grim exterior. Best of several **tavernas** is welcoming *O Palios Monolithos*, opposite the church: not a bargain, but tops for grilled meat and dishes of the day, accompanied by good bread and non-CAÏR bulk wine. Local diversions include yet another **Knights' castle**, 2km west of town, photogenically perched on its own pinnacle but enclosing very little, and the sand-and-gravel beaches at **Foúrni**, five paved but curvy kilometres below the castle.

The interior

Inland Rhodes is hilly and still partly wooded, despite the depredations of arsonists. You'll need a vehicle to tour its highlights; no single site justifies the expense of a taxi or the inconvenience of trying to make the best of sparse bus schedules.

Ialyssos and Petaloúdhes

Starting from the west-coast highway, turn inland at the central junction in Trianda for the side road (5km) up to the scanty acropolis of ancient **Ialyssos** (Tues–Sun 8.30am–2.45pm; €3) on flat-topped, strategic Filérimos hill; from here Süleyman the Magnificent directed the 1522 siege of Rhodes. Filérimos means "lover of solitude", after tenth-century Byzantine hermits who dwelt here; **Filérimos monastery**, restored successively by Italians and British, is the most substantial structure. Directly in front of the church sprawl foundations of third-century **temples to Zeus and Athena**, built atop a far older Phoenician shrine; below this lies the partly subterranean church of **Aï-Yeórgis Hostós**, a vaulted structure with faint fourteenth- and fifteenth-century frescoes. Southwest of all this, a **Via Crucis**, with the fourteen stations marked out in copper plaques during the Italian era, leads to an enormous concrete nocturnally illuminated crucifix, a 1995 replacement of an Italian-built one; you're allowed to climb out onto the cross-arms as a supplement to the already amazing view.

The only much-promoted tourist "attraction" in the island's interior, **Petaloúdhes** ("Butterfly Valley") (daily: May–Sept 8am–dusk; April & Oct 9am–3pm; €3–5 by season), is reached by a seven-kilometre side road bearing inland between Paradhísi and Theológos. It's actually a rest stop for Jersey tiger moths; only in summer do they congregate here, attracted for unknown reasons by the abundant *Liquidambar orientalis* trees growing abundantly in this stream canyon. The moths roosting in droves on the tree trunks cannot eat during this final phase of their life cycle, rest to conserve energy, and die of starvation soon after mating. When stationary, the moths are a well-camouflaged black and yellow, but flash cherry-red overwings in flight.

Some 2km before Petaloúdhes, the **microwinery** (15,000–20,000 bottles annually) of Anastasia Triandafyllou merits a stop for its ten varieties, including Athiri whites, Muscat rosé, sweet dessert wine and Cabernet or Mandhilari reds (daily 8.30am–7pm). The best nearby **taverna** is at the edge of **PSÍNTHOS** village, where friendly *Piyi Fasouli* serves excellent grills and appetizers as well as a few tasty *mayireftá* at tables overlooking the namesake spring.

Eptá Piyés to Profítis Ilías

Heading inland from Kolýmbia junction on the main east-coast highway, it's 4km to **Eptá Piyés** ("Seven Springs"), an oasis with a tiny irrigation dam created by the Italians. A trail, or a rather claustrophobic Italian aqueduct-tunnel, both lead from the vicinity of the springs to the reservoir. Continuing on the same road, you reach neglected Italian structures at **Eleoússa** (built as the planned agricultural colony of Campochiaro in 1935–36) after another 9km, in the shade of dense forest. From the vast Art Deco pool just west of the village, stocked with the endangered local *gizáni* fish, keep straight 3km further to the late Byzantine church of **Áyios Nikólaos Foundouklí** ("St Nicholas of the Hazelnuts"). Interior frescoes, dating from the thirteenth to the fifteenth centuries, could use a good cleaning, but scenes from the life of Christ are recognizable.

Continuing west from the church brings you to **Profítis Ilías hamlet**, where the Italian-vintage chalet-hotel *Elafos Hotel* (☎ *22460 22402*, Ⓦ www.elafoshotel.gr; ❹ doubles, ❻ suites) has high-ceilinged rooms with retro charm, and arcaded ground-floor common areas including a restaurant. It looks out from deep woods just north of the 780-metre peak, Rhodes' third-highest point but off-limits as a military area; however, there's good, gentle strolling below and around the summit. There are more facilities just downhill in **SÁLAKOS**: for example the simpler but again Italian-era *Hotel-Café Nymph* (☎ 22460 22206, Ⓦ www.nymph.gr; ❸) at the top of the village.

Atávyros villages

All tracks and roads west across Profítis Ilías converge on the road from Kalavárdha bound for **ÉMBONA**, a large, architecturally nondescript village backed up against the north slope of 1215-metre **Mount Atávyros**. Émbona lies at the heart of the island's most important wine-producing districts, and CAÏR – the Italian-founded vintners' co-operative – produces a choice of acceptable mid-range varieties. However, products of the smaller, family-run **Emery winery** (daily 9am–4.30pm) at the northern outskirts are more esteemed. You can carry on clockwise around the peak to less visited **ÁYIOS ISÍDHOROS**, with nearly as many vines, a more open feel and the **trailhead** for the five-hour return **ascent of Atávyros**. This placard-documented path, beginning at the northeast edge of the village and well marked with paint splodges, is the safest and easiest way up the mountain, though the slopes are sullied by a wind-power farm, a radar "golf ball" up top and the tracks built to install these.

Thárri monastery

The perennially rough road from Áyios Isídhoros 12km east to Láerma is worth enduring if you've any interest in Byzantine monuments. The **monastery of Thárri**, lost in pine forests 5km south of Láerma, is the oldest religious foundation on the island, re-established as a vital community in 1990 by charismatic abbot Amfilohios. In the striking *katholikón* (daily, all day), successive cleanings have restored damp-smudged frescoes dated 1300–1450 to their former exquisite glory. The most distinct, in the transept, depict the Evangelists Mark and Matthew, plus the Archangel Gabriel, while the nave has various acts of Christ, including the *Storm on the Sea of Galilee*, *Meeting the Samaritan Woman at the Well* and *Healing the Cripple*.

The far south

South of a line connecting Monólithos and Lárdhos, you might think you'd strayed onto another island; gone are most mega-hotels, with second-home villa developments more a feature of the landscape. Only a few weekly buses serve the depopulated villages here (Yennádhi has much better frequencies); tavernas dot the village centres and popular beaches, but aside from the package enclaves of Lárdhos, Péfki and Kiotári, there's scant accommodation.

Dense beachfront development flanks **LÁRDHOS**, solidly on the tourist circuit despite the village's inland position. The beach 2km away is gravelly and exposed; **Glýstra** cove, 3km south, proves a small, more sheltered crescent that gets crowded in season. Best **accommodation** hereabouts is *Lindian Village* (☎ 22440 35900, Ⓦ www.lindianvillage.gr; ❽), an attractive bungalow complex with two gourmet restaurants, a spa/gym and private beach; rack rates start at €500 for a double room (contact recommended agent Triton, p.678). Four kilometres east of Lárdhos, **PÉFKI** (Péfkos) began life as the garden annexe and overflow of Líndhos, but is now a burgeoning resort in its own right; the sea is clearer than at Lárdhos, with small, secluded beaches tucked at the base of low cliffs (the biggest, in western Péfki, is **Lothiáriko**). Among **tavernas**, *Kavos* at the east edge of town has the Greekest menu and the nicest setting.

Asklipió

Nine kilometres beyond Lárdhos, a side road heads 3.5km inland to **ASKLIPIÓ**, a sleepy village enlivened by a crumbling Knights' castle and the Byzantine **Kímisis Theotókou church** (daily: summer 9am–6pm, spring/autumn 9am–5pm; €1). This dates from 1060, with a pebble-floored ground plan similar to Thárri's, though two apses were added during the eighteenth century. Frescoes inside are in better condition owing to the drier local climate, and also a bit later, though the final work at Thárri and the earliest here were possibly executed by the same hand.

The format and themes of the **frescoes** are unusual in Greece: didactic "cartoon strips" often extending completely around the church, featuring Old Testament stories alongside the more usual lives of Christ and the Virgin. There's a complete Genesis sequence, from the *Creation* to the *Expulsion from Eden*; note the comically menacing octopus among the fishes in the panel of the Fifth Day, and Eve being fashioned from Adam's rib. An *Apocalypse* takes up most of the south transept, while an enormous Archangel Michael dominates the north transept, with sword in right hand and a small soul to be judged in his left. Two adjacent buildings house an ecclesiastical exhibit, and a more interesting folklore gallery in an ex-olive mill, full of rural craft tools and antiquated, belt-driven machinery.

Kiotári, Yennádhi. Váti and Profýlia

Back on the coast road, **KIOTÁRI** beachfront district has mushroomed as a package venue for Germans and Italians since the Orthodox Church sold its vast holdings here. You could stop for a **meal** at bistro-bar *Mourella* on the beachfront road, or **stay** at superior *Paraktio Apartments* (Ⓣ22440 47278, Ⓦwww.paraktio.com; ❸) on the main highway, with direct beach access and a café. But you'll likely continue 4km to **YENNÁDHI**, the only sizeable settlement on this coast, whose rather drab outskirts mask the attractive older village core inland. Amenities include an **ATM**, **post office**, **car rental** and some **accommodation** – pick of this being *Effie's Dreams* at the northern end of things (Ⓣ22440 43410, Ⓦwww.effiesdreams.com; ❸), overlooking a fountain-fed oasis. There's a bar and **Internet** café downstairs from the serviceable studios. The Greek-Australian owners can help locate the key-keeper for sixth-to-fifteenth-century **Ayía Anastasía Roméa**, the village cemetery-church 300m northwest through the oasis, covered inside with naïve post-Byzantine frescoes. Most local **tavernas** stand just behind the dark-sand-and-gravel beach extending kilometres in either direction, clean and with the usual amenities laid on.

From Yennádhi, a good road heads 7km inland, past baby pines slowly greening up a fire-blasted landscape, to **VÁTI**, where you can **eat** at *O Petrinos Kafenes*, doubling as the central *kafenío*. It's pricey for the location, partly justified by the quality of country-style offerings like spicy *revíthia* soup, good bread, *hórta* and roast suckling. If this doesn't suit, the nearby village of **PROFÝLIA** – accessed by the best, newest road on the island – offers *To Limeri tou Listi* (closed Mon low season), though the food isn't quite up to the setting and friendly service. Its tables share a terrace with the little sixteenth-century **chapel of Áyios Yeóryios and Arhángelos** (always open), its humane contemporary frescoes with protagonists in period dress.

The southern tip

Some 10km south of Yennádhi, then 2km inland, **LAHANIÁ** village has a smattering of **rooms**. Abandoned after a postwar earthquake, since the 1980s its older houses have been mostly occupied and renovated by foreigners. On the main platía at the lower, eastern end of the village, *Platanos* **taverna** has superb *mezédhes* platters like hummus and *dolmadhákia*, and seating between the church and two wonderful Ottoman fountains.

From Lahaniá a good road heads 9km northwest to picturesque hilltop **MESANAGRÓS**, which already existed by the fifth century AD, judging from a ruined basilica at the village outskirts. A smaller thirteenth-century chapel sits amid foundations of the larger, earlier church, with a *votsalotó* floor and barrel arches (key from the nearby *kafenío*). You can also go directly from Lahaniá to **Plimýri**, an attractive sandy bay backed by dunes, with swimming marred only by strong afternoon winds; the sole facility is a popular, mainly fish **taverna** next to the **church of Zoödhóhou Piyís** (May–Oct Sun noon–5pm), with ancient columns upholding its vaulted porch.

Beyond **Plimýri** the road curves inland to **KATTAVIÁ**, nearly 90km from the capital, lost amid grain fields; the village, like so many hereabouts, is at best seasonally occupied by returning immigrants from Australia or North America. There are some **rooms** to rent, a vital **filling station** and several **tavernas** at the junction that doubles as the platía.

From Kattaviá a road goes to **Prassoníssi** ("Leek Island"), Rhodes' southernmost extremity and a European **windsurfing** mecca. The sandspit tethering Prassoníssi to Rhodes was breached by currents to form a channel in 1996, but enough remains to create flat water on the east side and up to two-metre waves on the west, ideal for all levels. Of two **windsurfing schools** operating here, Polish-run Prasonisi Center (late April–Oct; ⓣ 22440 91044, ⓦ www.prasoniscenter.com) is keener and friendlier. They're geared up for one-week packages, lodging their clients in Yennádhi and Kattaviá rather than at the two indifferent **taverna-rooms** outfits here (*Oasis* is marginally better).

Beyond Kattaviá, the highway loops to emerge onto the deserted, sandy southwest coast just below workaday, agricultural **APOLAKKIÁ**, equipped with nondescript **tavernas** but no accommodation. Northwest, the road leads to Monólithos, while the northeasterly bearing leads quickly and pleasantly back to Yennádhi via Váti. Due north, near an irrigation reservoir, the tiny frescoed Byzantine chapel of **Áyios Yeóryios Várdhas** (unlocked) deserves a four-kilometre detour (with your own transport).

Hálki

Hálki, a waterless, limestone speck just west of Rhodes, is a fully fledged member of the Dodecanese, though all but a few hundred of the three-thousand-strong population emigrated (mostly to Rhodes or Florida) following Italian restrictions on sponge-fishing in 1916. Despite a renaissance through tourism, the island is tranquil compared to its neighbour, albeit with an artificial, stage-set atmosphere; foreigners vastly outnumber the 400–800 locals depending on the season. The big event of the day is the arrival of the *kaïki* from Kámiros Skála on Rhodes.

Hálki first attracted postwar foreign attention in 1983, when **UNESCO** designated it the "isle of peace and friendship" and the seat of regular international conferences. Some 150 derelict houses were to be restored at UNESCO's expense as accommodation for delegates, but by 1987 just one hotel had been completed, and the only sign of "peace and friendship" were UNESCO and Athenian bureaucrats staging periodic musical binges disguised as "ecological seminars". Confronted with an apparent scam, the islanders sent UNESCO packing and engaged two UK package operators to complete restorations and bring in paying guests. There are now six tour companies present, and most of the ruins have been refurbished to host their clients.

Emborió

The skyline of **EMBORIÓ**, **Hálki**'s port and sole habitation, is pierced by the tallest freestanding clocktower in the Dodecanese and – a bit further north – by the belfry of Áyios Nikólaos. Emborió's restored houses are largely block-booked from May to late September by tour companies; independent travellers will be lucky to find anything on spec, though matters have improved slightly since one tour company folded. Recommended **accommodation**, requiring advance reservations, includes the delightful, en-suite *Captain's House* (T 22460 45201, E captainshouse@ath.forthnet.gr; 2), with a shady garden and the feel of an old French country hotel; Frances Mayes' *Mouthouria House* (F 22460 45061, E francesm@otenet.gr; €210–500 per week, sleeps 4); the two luxury apartments at *Villa Praxithea* (T 697 24 27 272, W www.villapraxithea.com; sleeps 6–8; 6 for 2; minimum 1-week stay), with private lido; and the municipally owned *Hotel Halki* (T 694 62 12 836; 4) in the old sponge factory on the south side of the bay. Among six full-service **tavernas** along the field-stoned, pedestrianized waterfront, *Remezzo* is excellent for *mayireftá* and pizzas, *Maria* behind the post office is the cheap-and-cheerful option (quality varies), while *Avra* is conscientiously run by Greeks from Caucasian Georgia. Among a similar number of quayside **bars** and **cafés**, *Theodosia's* (or "The Parrot Bar" after its resident bird), at the base of the jetty, has puddings and home-made ice cream to die for, as well as good breakfasts, while *To Steki* is usually the most musically active. In September the **Hálki Festival** has performances by top Greek musical names. There's a **post office**, a stand-alone **ATM**, four well-stocked stores, a bakery, plus a sixteen-seat **bus** that shuttles between the waterfront, Póndamos and Ftenáya. The more useful of two **travel agencies**, Zifos (T 22460 45028, E zifos-travel@rho.forthnet.gr) sells boat tickets and also has a selection of apartments unfilled by tour companies (€90 for 4).

The rest of the island

Three kilometres west looms the old pirate-safe village of **HORIÓ**, abandoned in the 1950s but still crowned by its Knights' castle. Except during the major August 14–15 festival, the church here is kept locked to protect its frescoes. Across the valley, little **Stavrós monastery** hosts another big bash on September 14. There's not much else inland, though you can cross the island on an eight-kilometre road, the extension of the cement Tarpon Springs Boulevard donated by the expat community in Florida. At the end (1 bus daily; €10 return) you'll reach the monastery of **Ayíou Ioánnou Prodhrómou** (festival Aug 28–29 *kantína* otherwise), with some charm in its array of cells (you can stay the night) around a courtyard dominated by a huge juniper. The terrain en route is bleak, but compensated by views over half the Dodecanese and Turkey.

Longish but narrow **Póndamos**, fifteen minutes' walk west of Emborió, is the only sandy beach on Hálki, subject to scouring by storms. The lone facility is somewhat pricey; *Nick's Pondamos Taverna*, serving lunch daily, plus supper two random evenings weekly; they also offer four basic, terrazo-floored, sea-view rooms (Ⓣ&Ⓕ22460 45295; ❷). A few minutes' well-signposted path-walk behind the *Hotel Halki*, a tiny pebble cove and the gravel sunbed-lido at **Ftenáya** are also heavily subscribed; a paved lane also leads to its decent **taverna-bar** (*Tou Vangeli*) with good seafood and *ouzomezédhes*. Small, pebbly **Yialí**, west of and considerably below Horió via jeep track, lies an hour's hike away from Póndamos.

Better swimming can be had by signing on at Emborió quay for **boat excursions** to remoter beaches. More or less at the centre of Hálki's southern shore, directly below Horió's castle, **Trahiá** consists of two coves to either side of an isthmus; you can (just) reach this overland by rough path from Yialí. North-coast beaches figuring as excursion-boat destinations include the pretty fjord of **Aréta**, **Áyios Yeóryios** just beyond and the remote double bay of **Dhýo Yialí**. Of these, Aréta is the most attractive, and the only one accessible overland (90min one way) by experienced hillwalkers equipped with the *Chalki, Island of Peace and Friendship* **map** based on the old Italian topographical survey sheet. **Alimniá (Alimiá) islet**, roughly halfway between Hálki and Rhodes, is another potential (€15–20) target, though beach space is very limited, there's little to see other than a castle (45min climb) and it's probably not somewhere you'd want to be stuck all day.

Kastellórizo (Meyísti)

Despite Kastellórizo's official name, Meyísti ("Biggest" – of a local archipelago of islets), it's actually the smallest of the Dodecanese, more than 100km from Rhodes but barely more than a nautical mile off the Turkish coast. At night its lights are quite outnumbered by those of Turkish Kaş opposite, with which Kastellórizo has excellent relations.

During the island's **heyday** (1860–1910) 10,000 people lived here, supported by schooners transporting timber from the Anatolian mainland. But events during the next two decades – a French 1915–21 occupation, attracting destructive shelling from Ottoman territory, the subsequent Italian occupation, and the post-1923 frontier between Kastellórizo and republican Turkey, combined with the expulsion of all Anatolian Greeks – dealt the local fleet a fatal blow. In the 1930s Kastellórizo enjoyed a brief role as a major stopover point for French and British seaplanes, but World War II events ended any hopes of the island's continued viability.

When Italy capitulated to the Allies in September 1943, about 1500 Commonwealth commandos occupied Kastellórizo, departing in November after the German capture of the other Dodecanese – and leaving the island vulnerable to looters. In early July 1944, a harbour fuel dump caught (or was set on) fire and an adjacent arsenal **exploded**, demolishing half of the thousand houses on Kastellórizo. Most islanders had already left for Rhodes, Australia and North America. Today there are just 342 registered inhabitants (about 250 of them permanent), maintained by remittances from more than 30,000 emigrants and subsidies from the Greek government to prevent the island reverting to Turkey should numbers diminish further.

Yet Kastellórizo has a future of sorts, thanks partly to repatriating "Kassies" returning each summer to renovate their crumbling ancestral houses as second homes. The harbour has been improved, and the island will soon become an **official Greek port of entry**, eliminating problems for yachties and travellers crossing from Turkey.

The biggest boost in Kastellórizo's fortunes, however, was providing the location for the Italian film **Mediterraneo**, winner of the 1992 Best Foreign Film Oscar, resulting in numerous Italian visitors (though the island in fact gets a variety of tourists). They either love Kastellórizo and stay a week, or crave escape after a day; detractors dismiss it as a human zoo maintained by the Greek government to placate nationalists, while partisans celebrate an atmospheric, barely commercialized outpost of Hellenism.

Kastellórizo Town

The population is concentrated in the northern settlement of **KASTELLÓRIZO** – supposedly the finest natural harbour between Beirut and Fethiye on the Turkish coast – and its "suburb" of **Mandhráki**, just over the fire-blasted hill with a half-ruined Knights' castle. Most of the town's surviving original mansions are ranged along the waterfront, sporting tiled roofs, wooden balconies and blue or green shutters on long, narrow windows. Derelict houses in the backstreets are now being attended to, and even the hillside is sprouting new constructions in unlikely colours, though the cumulative effect of World War I shelling, a 1926 earthquake, 1943 air-raids and the 1944 explosions will never be reversed. Black-and-white posters and postcards for sale of the town in its prime are poignant evidence of its later decline.

The castle's outer bulwark houses the worthwhile **archeological museum** (Tues–Sun 8.30am–3pm; free), its displays including Byzantine plates, frescoes rescued from decaying rural churches and a reconstruction of an ancient basilica on the site of today's gaudy, crumbling Áyios Yeóryios Santrapé church at Horáfia. Just below and beyond the museum, in the cliff-face opposite Psorádhia islet, is Greece's only **Lycian house-tomb**; it's well signposted from the shoreline walkway. The 1755-vintage **mosque**, also below the castle in waterfront Kávos district, is home to the **Historical Collection** (Tues–Sun 8.30am–3pm; free), with ethnographic items, local costumes, and a good photographic archive marred only by a tendentious video blaming British and Italian bombing for the town's destruction.

Arrival, information and transport

A single **ATM** stands on the east quay; the **post office** is on the far side of the bay. The sole **travel agency** is Papoutsis (☎22410 70630 or 693 72 12 530), selling all sea and air tickets. A **minibus** shuttles once between town and airstrip at flight times (€1.50); excess passengers are accommodated in the lone **taxi**, which may make multiple journeys at €5 per passenger.

It is possible to arrange a ride over **to Turkey** on one of four local boats, most reliably on Monday or Friday (8am departure). The standard day-return fee is €15, plus any required visa costs on the Turkish side (if you stay overnight); leave your passport with the authorities the day before. Although Kastellórizo is not yet a legal port of entry to Greece – a border "post" is being built – police cannot legally deny disembarkation to EU/EEA nationals arriving **from Kaş**, an official entry/exit point for Turkey. In theory, non-EU nationals cannot even make day-trips; in practice, there are few checks.

Accommodation

Kastellórizo is not really equipped for large numbers of visitors, though **accommodation** has gentrified and become pricier of late. Budget options include the large-roomed if basic *Pension Caretta* (ⓣ22460 49056, ⓦwww.kastellorizo.de; ②), which also has a fine restored apartment (④) for two, and *Pension Asimina*, with wood-trimmed rooms behind the arcaded Italian market (ⓣ22460 49361; ②). An excellent mid-range choice is *Karnayo* off the platía at the west end of the south quay (ⓣ22460 49266, ⓔkarnayo@otenet.gr); air-conditioned rooms or studios (③) and an apartment sleeping four spread over two quiet, sensitively restored buildings. At the end of the northwest quay, *Pension Mediterraneo* (ⓣ22460 49007 or 697 36 76 038, ⓦwww.mediterraneo-kastelorizo.com) has simple rooms (④ B&B), furnished with mosquito nets and wall art, and some with sea view, plus an arcaded, waterside basement suite (⑥ B&B). Best of the bunch, in the middle of the west quay, is friendly *Kastellorizo Hotel* (ⓣ22460 49044, ⓦwww.kastellorizohotel.gr; March–Nov), with its own lido, a thalasso-spa-pool and suites in two sizes (⑤–⑥).

Eating, drinking and nightlife

Apart from fish, goat meat and wild-fig preserves, plus produce smuggled over from Kaş, Kastellórizo has to import food and drinking water from Rhodes; add to this the island's celebrity status and taverna **prices** are higher than elsewhere. Incidentally, the mains **water** is not safe to drink. Recommendable waterfront **tavernas** include cheap, cheerful and popular *Iy Ypomoni* (dinner only), two doors to the left of the arcaded market, with a limited seafood menu; and inexpensive *Akrothalassi*, purveying large grills and salads near the west end of the quay – popular at lunch too, as they've the only shaded quayside seating. Inland, *Ta Platania* (June to mid-Oct), on the Horáfia platía, is good for daily-changing *mayireftá* and desserts. It served as the *Mediterraneo* production canteen, and it is now adorned with film posters. There are more puddings and good breakfasts at *Zaharoplastio Iy Meyisti*, back on the waterfront.

Nightlife spills out of the half-dozen *barákia* lining the quay. *Faros* near the mosque is a cool place with a roof terrace and noise levels kept under control; it's also a "day-bar" with sunbeds on the quay. *Mythos,* towards the ferry jetty, also has an extensive menu – handy when all bona-fide tavernas are booked in mid-summer – while *Radio Café* next door offers **Internet** access and ouzo-*mezédhes*.

The rest of the island

Kastellórizo's austere **hinterland** is predominantly bare rock, flecked with stunted vegetation; incredibly, a century ago this was carefully tended, producing abundant wine of some quality. A rudimentary paved road system links points between Mandhráki and the airport, plus there's a dirt track towards Áyios Stéfanos, but there aren't many specific attractions and no scooters for rent. Karstic cliffs drop sheer to the sea, offering no anchorage for boats except at the main town, Mandhráki and Návlakas fjord.

Rural monasteries and ruins

Heat permitting, hike up the obvious, zigzag stair-path from town, then south through scrub to the sadly dilapidated **monastery of Ayíou Yeoryíou toú Vounioú**, thirty minutes from Horáfia's platía. The sixteenth-to-eighteenth-century church (obtain key from the keeper in town) has fine rib-vaulting, an ancient *votsalotó* floor and a carved *témblon*, as well as a rare fresco of Christ emerging from the tomb in the left of the *ierón*. But the most unusual feature is a crypt incorporating the subterranean chapel of **Áyios Harálambos**, with a dark niche-fresco of the saint; access is via a steep, narrow passage descending from the church floor – bring a torch. Just beyond, east of the old path (not the new track), there's a sixth-century BC **wine press** carved into the rock; another, even better one can be seen by varying the return to town and using a secondary path from the monastery to Horáfia via Avlónia – only five minutes longer.

Alternatively, a fifteen-minute track-walk west of the port leads to peaceful **Ayías Triádhas monastery**, perched on the saddle with the telecom tower, and an army base. After twenty minutes, the onward path reaches ancient **Paleókastro** citadel, with a warren of vaulted chambers, tunnels and cisterns plus another little monastery with a *votsalotó* courtyard. From any of the heights above town there are tremendous views over sixty kilometres of Anatolian coast.

The shoreline

Swimming is complicated by a total absence of beaches and an abundance of sea urchins and razor-sharp limestone reefs; the safest entries near town lie beyond the graveyard at Mandhráki and the cement jetty below the power plant at road's end – or people just dive from the lidos on the northwest quay. Once clear of the shore, you're rewarded by clear waters with a rich variety of marine life. **Taxi-boats** can take you to remote coves, like Plákes, accessible only by sea.

From Ayíou Yeoryíou toú Vounioú, you can continue forty minutes further on foot, first on a modern bulldozer track, then on the original, French-built *kalderími*, to **Návlakas fjord**, a favourite mooring spot for yachts and fishing boats. Uniquely on Kastellórizo, this bay is sea-urchin-free, with freshwater seeps keeping the temperature brisk; there's superb snorkelling to 25-metre depths off the south wall.

Further along the southeast coast, accessible by a 45-minute boat excursion (€8–10) from town, **Perastá grotto** (Galázio Spílio) deserves a look for its stalactites and strange blue-light effects; the low entrance, negotiable only by inflatable raft, gives little hint of the enormous chamber within, with monk seals occasionally sheltering in another adjacent cave.

Sými

Sými's most pressing problem, lack of fresh water, is in some ways also its saving grace. As with other dry, rocky Dodecanese islands, **water** must be imported from Rhodes, pending completion of a reservoir in the distant future. Consequently, the island can't support more than a few large hotels; instead, hundreds of people are shipped in for seasonal day-trips from Rhodes. This arrangement suits both the Symiots and those visitors lucky enough to stay longer; many foreigners return regularly, or even own houses here. The island, long fashionable among Italians, Brits and Danes, entered domestic Greek consciousness in a big way after 2005 when it featured in the Turkish TV serial *The Frontiers of Love*. With fame has come fortune – it's an expensive resort, with restaurant meals and bar drinks at Rhodian prices.

Once beyond the inhabited areas, you'll find an attractive island that has retained some **forest** of junipers, valonea oaks and even a few pines – ideal walking country in spring or autumn (though not midsummer, when temperatures are

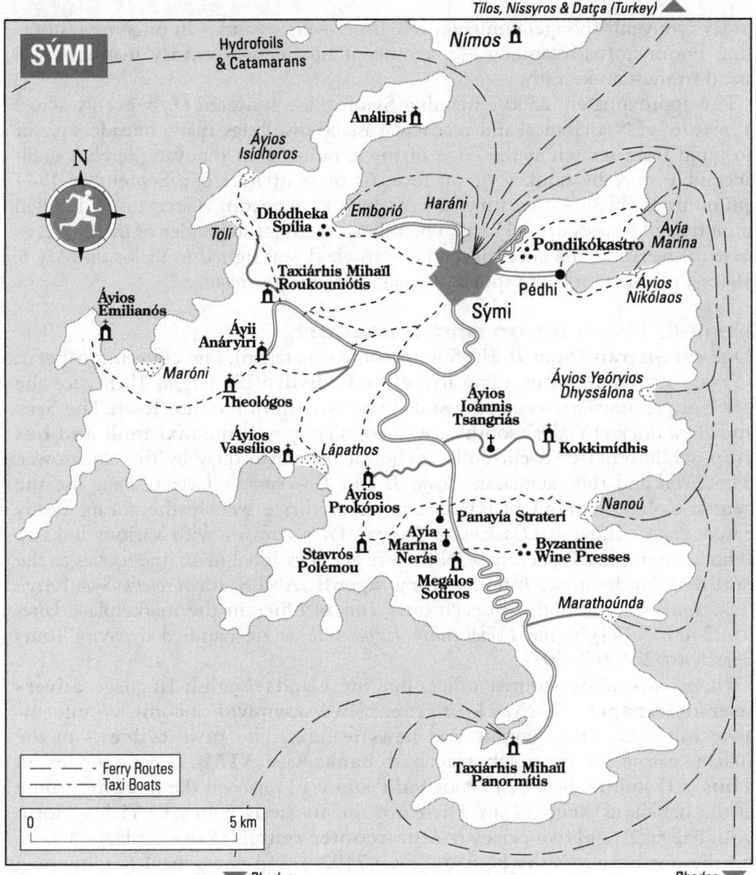

among the highest in Greece). Dozens of privately owned tiny **monasteries** dot the landscape; though generally locked except on their patron saint's day, their freshwater cisterns are usually accessible.

Sými Town

SÝMI, the capital and only town, comprises **Yialós**, the excellent natural port, linked to **Horió**, the "Old Town", on the hillside above, by two massive stair-paths, the **Kalí Stráta** and **Katarráktes**. Arriving by sea, the town's exquisite Neoclassical mansions slowly reveal themselves as your vessel rounds the promontories guarding the deeply inset harbour. Incredibly, around 1895 the place was more populous (25,000) than Ródhos Town, its wealth generated by shipbuilding and sponge-diving, skills nurtured since ancient times. Under the Ottomans, Sými enjoyed considerable autonomy, in exchange for a yearly tribute in sponges to the sultan; but the 1913 Italian-imposed frontier, the 1919–22 Greco-Turkish war, the advent of synthetic sponges and the gradual replacement of crews by Kalymniots shattered the local economy. Vestiges of past nautical glories remain in still-active boatyards at Pédhi and Haráni, but today's souvenir sponges come entirely from overseas and – an ongoing restoration boom notwithstanding – magnificent nineteenth-century mansions still stand roofless and empty.

The approximately 2500 remaining Symiots are scattered fairly evenly across a mixture of Neoclassical and vernacular island dwellings; many outsiders prefer to build from scratch at the edge of town, rather than renovate derelict shells accessible only by donkey or on foot. As on Kastellórizo, a September 1944 ammunition blast – this time set off by the retreating Germans – levelled hundreds of houses up in Horió. The official German surrender of the Dodecanese to the Allies, the last Axis territory to yield, was signed in Yialós on May 8, 1945: a plaque marks the spot at *Restaurant Les Catherinettes*.

Arrival, information and transport

One **catamaran** (*Symi II*, 1hr 50min; some cars taken), one conventional craft (*Symi*, 1hr 50min; many cars carried) and a **hydrofoil** (*Aegli*, 1hr; twice the price of previous) each run at least daily to Sými from Ródhos Town. The *Symi* and *Aegli* dock at Yialós's south quay, conveniently near the **taxi rank and bus stop**, while other craft currently anchor at the north quay by the clocktower. The *Symi* and the catamarans *Symi II* and *Dodekanisos Express/Pride* use the central Kolóna harbour of Rhodes; twice or thrice weekly, the cheap, locally based *Protevs* and the *Dodekanisos Express/Pride* chip in with various links to Rhodes and other Dodecanese, plus there are occasional main line ferries to the northern Dodecanese. Among **ferry agents**, ANES, for *Protevs/Symi/Aegli* tickets, maintains booths on each quay and an office in the marketplace lanes (Ⓣ22460 71444), while *Dodekanisos Express/Pride* are handled by Symi Tours nearby (Ⓣ22460 71307).

There's no official tourist office, but the island's English-language **advertiser-newspaper**, *The Symi Visitor* (free; Ⓦwww.symivisitor.com), has informative historical, ethnographic and news features. The **post office** is in the Italian "palace" on the north quay; both **banks** have **ATMs**. During the season a **bus** (€1) shuttles between Yialós and Pédhi via Horió on the hour (returning at the half-hour) until 11pm. There are also six **taxis** (allow €4 Yialós–Horió with baggage), and two pricey **motor-scooter rentals** (€18–25/day) – Glaros on the north quay is the best (Ⓣ22460 71926), and **car rental** (a whopping €58–70/day). **Taxi-boat** fares (€7–10, no one ways) make a scooter – or walking – that much more attractive.

Accommodation

Sými has a reasonable choice of accommodation for independent travellers, especially since a major package operator left the island. Studios and apartments, rather than simple rooms, predominate; curiously you may find vacancies more easily in July/August than during spring and autumn, the most pleasant seasons here. The asphyxiating summer heat and non-universality of air conditioning mean you should go for north-facing and/or balconied units if possible.

Albatros Marketplace Ⓣ22460 71707, Ⓦwww.albatrosymi.gr. Partial sea views from this exquisite small hotel with a/c; pleasant second-floor breakfast salon. ❸

Les Catherinettes Above eponymous restaurant, north quay Ⓣ22460 71671, Ⓔmarina-epe@rho.forthnet.gr. Spotless en-suite pension in a historic building with painted ceilings, fridges, fans and sea-view balconies in most rooms (❸). They also offer three studios in Haráni, plus a family apartment (❹)

Fiona At the top of the Kalí Stráta Ⓣ22460 72088. Mock-traditional hotel whose large airy rooms have double beds and stunning views; breakfast is taken on a common balcony. Also 3 studios next door. ❹

Niriides Apartments On Haráni–Emborió road, 2km from Yialós Ⓣ22460 71784,

ⓦ www.niriideshotel.com Spacious, quiet, plain units sleeping four, spread over four hillside buildings. All have phone, TV and optional a/c. Friendly father-and-son management, on-site "lounge-café"; discount for Internet bookings. ⑤

Symi Villas ⓣ 22460 71819, ⓦ www.symi-villas.gr. Jean manages four traditional houses in Horió, suitable for two to six people, with stunning views. ③–⑤

Symi Visitor Accommodation ⓣ 22460 72755, ⓦ www.symivisitor.com. Managed by returned Greek-Australian Nikos Halkitis and partner Wendy Wilcox, who offer a variety of restored properties, mostly double-occupancy studios, in prime Horió locations. The pricier units can sleep up to five. ⑤–⑥

Villa Agapi Behind Yialós platía; enquire at *Kandrimi* bar ⓣ 22460 71381, ⓣ 693 64 21 215 or ⓦ www.symigreece.com/agapi.htm. Exceptionally well-appointed 3-bedroom, 2-bath house sleeping 6. €175 a night for the entire 2-storey house; weekly rates.

Villa Symeria Halfway up Kalí Stráta. Contact *Hotel Albatros*. Old mansion divided into two apartments accommodating 5 (€175/day) or 4 people (€135/day). ⑦–⑧

The Town

At the architecturally protected **port**, spice and sponge and souvenir stalls on the north quay throng with Rhodes-based trippers between 10am and 3pm, when the excursion craft disgorging them envelop the quay with exhaust fumes. But just uphill, away from the water, the pace of village life takes over, with livestock and chickens roaming free. The **Kalí Stráta** and **Katarráktes** effectively deter most day-trippers and are especially dramatic towards sunset; owl-haunted ruins along the lower Kalí Stráta are lonely and sinister after dark, though these too are now being renovated.

A series of arrows through Horió leads to the excellent local **museum** (Tues–Sun 8.30am–2.30pm; €2). Housed in a fine old mansion at the back of the village, the collection highlights Byzantine and medieval Sými, with exhibits on frescoes in isolated, often locked churches. The nearby **Hatziagapitos mansion** serves as an annexe; here, wonderful carved wooden chests are the main displays, along with allegorical wall-paintings. At the very pinnacle of things, a **Knights' castle** occupies the site of Sými's ancient acropolis, so you glimpse a stretch of Classical polygonal wall on one side. The **church of the Assumption**, inside the fortifications, replaces one blown to bits when the Germans detonated the munitions cached there. One of the bells in the new belfry is the nose-cone of a thousand-pound bomb, hung as a memorial.

Eating and drinking

At most places on the north and west quays of the port, ingredients, prices and attitudes have been warped by the day-trip trade. Elsewhere, you've a fair range of choice among *koultouriárika* **tavernas**, old-style *mayireftá* places, genuine ouzerís and cafés both traditional and modern.

Dhimitris South quay, heading out of Yialós. Excellent, family-run ouzerí with exotic seafood items like *hokhlióalo* (sea snails), *foúskes*, *spinóalo* and the miniature local shrimps, along with sausages, chops and vegetarian starters.

Evoi Evan North side, Yialós square. The big attraction at this café/breakfast venue, and at similar *Kandrimi* next door is the shade of huge spreading ficus trees.

Filos Top of Kalí Stráta, Horió. New outfit off to a good start with *mezédhes* such as *bákla* (broad beans) and *taboúli*, meat grills and *mayireftá* like *hirinó me sélino* at friendly prices; good bulk wine and home-made *galaktoboúriko* for dessert. Ground-level plus (somewhat windy) roof-terrace seating.

George & Maria's (ex-Yiorgos) Top of Kalí Stráta, Horió. Jolly, much-loved Sými institution, with summer seating on a pebble-mosaic courtyard. Service can be slipshod and food quality fluctuates, but perennial dishes include feta-stuffed peppers, beans with sausage, chicken in mushroom-wine sauce, and a full range of grills. Open random lunch-times in season, supper all year (winter indoors).

Lefteris Top of the Kalí Stráta, second shopfront on Platía Syllógou, Horió. The local characters' *kafenío*, attended by all. Coffee or ice cream at any hour; also simple *mezédhes.*

O Meraklis Rear of the bazaar. Polite service and fair portions of *mayireftá*, fresh fish and *mezédhes* make this a reliable year-round bet. Sample meal: beans, beets, dips, and roast lamb with potatoes as a tender main course.

Mythos Meze South quay, Yialós. Roof-terrace supper venue (late May to late September) in the former summer cinema, serving among the best, and best-value, cooking on the island. Chef-owner Stavros's tasting menu (€25 a head plus drink) of six or seven platters might comprise *poungí* (seafood parcel in fyllo), squid, lamb stifádho, moussaka, *psaronéfri*, feta *saganáki* in fig sauce, plus dessert. The original premises, at the traffic barrier, is now *Mythos* Fish, stressing à la carte seafood, open a longer season and some lunches too. Current menus and reservations on www.mythos-symi.com.

Syllogos Just south of Platía Syllógou, Horió. Vast but not impersonal place with indoor/outdoor seating, great for taverna standards like *skordhaliá*, *saganáki*, fried fish and eggplant recipes.

Nightlife and events

Nightlife continues into the early hours and is biased towards Yialós. Convivial *Jean & Tonic* is heart and soul of the bar scene in Horió, catering to a mixed clientele (visitors and expats until 3am, Greeks 3am until dawn) with 1960s music; *Kali Strata* at the top of said stairs has the best views, jazz/ethnic soundtrack and stiff drink prices. Down at Yialós, *Harani Club* offers Greek or international music depending on the crowd; in the same alley, *Vapori* offers free newspapers, breakfasts and **Internet** access with Wi-Fi . Elsewhere, *Astarti* on the east quay towards the filling station often hosts special events like belly dancing nights. There's are also year-round Friday-night **movie screenings** in various venues, while the July-to-early-September **Sými Festival** has become one of Greece's more interesting small summer bashes, with a mix of classical and popular Greek performances.

Around the island

Sými has no large sandy **beaches**, but instead various pebbly stretches at the heads of deep, protected bays that indent the coastline. **PÉDHI**, 1km beyond Horió, retains some of its past as a fishing hamlet, with the plain behind – the island's largest – supporting a few vegetable gardens. The beach is medicore, though, and patronage from yachts and the *Pedhi Beach* hotel has bumped up prices at local **tavernas**, of which the most reasonable and authentic is fish specialist *Tolis* (no sign), tucked away by the boatyard at the north corner of the bay. Many will opt for either a sporadic taxi-boat or a fifteen-minute path walk from the brackish springs by the church, along the south shore of the almost landlocked bay, to **Áyios Nikólaos**. The only all-sand cove on Sými, this offers sheltered swimming, shady tamarisks, a bar, beach volleyball and an overpriced taverna. Alternatively, a paint-splodge-marked path on the north side of the inlet leads in half an hour to **Ayía Marína**, where there's a minuscule beach, a shingle lido with sunbeds, an uneven taverna-bar and a monastery-capped islet to which you can easily swim.

Around Yialós, you'll find the tiny, man-made *Symi Paradise* "beach" (still called **NOS** or Navtikós Ómilos Sýmis by most) ten minutes beyond the Haráni boatyards, with an eponymous restaurant, coarse-shingle shore (in shade all afternoon) and frankly poor swimming. You can continue along the cement-paved coast road, or cut inland from the Yialós platía past the abandoned desalination plant, to quiet **Emborió** (Nimborió) Bay, with a good taverna, a coarse-shingle beach, and tranquil swimmiing. Inland from here lie Byzantine mosaic fragments (follow signs to "Early Christian Basilica"), and, nearby, the **Dhódheka Spília** catacomb complex.

Remoter bays and monasteries

Plenty of other, more **secluded coves** are accessible to energetic walkers, or those prepared to pay for taxi-boats (daily outbound 10am–1pm, returning 4–6pm). These are the most popular method of reaching the large southern bay of Nanoú, and the only method of getting to the spectacular fjord of **Áyios Yeóryios Dhyssálona**. Dhyssálona lacks a taverna and lies in afternoon shade, while **Marathoúnda** (usually reached overland) is fringed by coarse, often slimy pebbles, though it has a fairly priced **taverna**, popular at weekends. **Nanoú** is the most popular destination for day-trips, its 200-metre beach consisting of gravel, sand and small pebbles, with a scenic backdrop of pines and a reasonable, seafood-strong **taverna** just behind. It's also possible to reach Nanoú overland, via Panayía Straterí chapel on the main trans-island road, descending a scenic, forested gorge for 45 minutes; most of the old path from Horió to Panayía Straterí still exists, making a marvellous traverse of about three hours in total, leaving time for a meal and swim before the boat trip back to Yialós.

Other meaty hikes cross the island from Horió in ninety minutes to scenic **Áyios Vassílios** gulf (or 40min from road's end along a paint-splodge-marked path), with a namesake little monastery above **Lápathos** beach; or in three hours, partly through forest, from Yialós to **Áyios Emilianós** at the island's extreme west end, where another tiny monastery is tethered to the body of Sými by a causeway. On the way to the latter you'll pass **Taxiárhis Mihaïl Roukouniótis** monastery (ring inner doorbell), Sými's oldest, with naïve eighteenth-century frescoes and the current *katholikón* superimposed on a lower, abandoned thirteenth-century structure, with an intriguing fresco of St Lawrence. More and better frescoes are scattered across the island – especially at hilltop, 1697-vintage **Kokkimídhis monastery** (usually open), reached by steep track off the Panormítis road, with a complete cycle showing the acts of the Archangel and the risen Christ; at **Ayía Marína Nerás** church (always open) further along the same trunk road, with naïve if damaged fifteenth-century images of the Crucifixion, the Angel at the Tomb and a Nativity with the Virgin nursing; and at nearby **Megálos Sotíros** (often locked, key from Kalodoukas Tours), just before the drop down the escarpment, with fine frescoes from 1727 including a *Deposition*, with Joseph of Arimathaea holding a winding sheet to receive the dead Christ, and a *Resurrection* with Jesus seemingly doing a jig on the sepulchre. Across the road, a signposted trail leads to some worthwhile, reconstructed Byzantine **wine presses**.

Panormítis monastery

The Archangel is most honoured at giant **Taxiárhis Mihaïl Panormítis monastery** in the far south, the first port of call for some excursion boats from Rhodes. These allow only a thirty-minute tour; for more time, come from Yialós by scooter (the road down from the central escarpment is steep, with nine hairpin bends) or bus (4–5 daily). You can stay at the **inn** (☎22460 72414; ❶) meant for pilgrims, who fill it all summer – Mihaïl is the Dodecanese patron of sailors.

Panormítis was thoroughly pillaged during World War II, so – except for its lofty belfry – don't expect much of the building or its contents. An appealing *votsalotó* courtyard surrounds the central *katholikón*, lit by an improbable number of oil lamps. It's also graced by a fine *témblon* and of course the cult icon, though frescoes are mediocre. One of two small **museums** (€1.50 each) contains a strange mix of precious antiques, exotic junk, votive offerings, models of ships and a chair piled with messages-in-bottles brought here by Aegean currents

– supposedly if the bottle or toy boat arrived, the sender got their prayer answered. There's a **shop/kafenío**, a **bakery** and a **taverna** popular with passengers on the many yachts calling here. A memorial commemorates three Greeks, including the monastery's abbot, executed on February 11, 1944 by the Germans for aiding British commandos.

Tílos

The small, usually quiet island of **Tílos**, with an official population of about five hundred (dwindling to 100 in winter), is among the least frequented and most unpredictably connected of the Dodecanese. While it's a great place to rest on the beach or go walking, there's nothing very striking at first glance. After a few days, however, you may have stumbled on several small **castles** of the Knights of St John studding the crags, or found some of the inconspicuous, often frescoed **medieval chapels** (ring Pandelis Yiannourakis on ⓣ22460 44240 for admission), clinging to the hillsides.

Tílos shares the characteristics of its closest neighbours: limestone **mountains** like those of Hálki, plus volcanic lowlands, pumice beds and red-lava sand as on Níssyros. Though rugged and scrubby on its heights, the island has ample **water** – from springs or pumped up from the agricultural plains – and clusters of oak and terebinth near the cultivated areas. From many points you've startling views across to Kós, Sými, Turkey, Níssyros, Hálki, Rhodes and even (weather permitting) Kárpathos.

Recent changes on Tílos, however, threaten the things that many visitors value; besides burgeoning **development** at Livádhia, a hyperactive bulldozing programme has scarred nearly every mountain in the east of the island. Thankfully, the remotest beaches are located in too steep terrain to be approached by road without prohibitive expense, and a project exists to protect much of coastal and mountain Tílos as a **national park** (check ⓦwww.tilos-park.org, or visit the "Tilos Information Centre" by the church in Livádhia).

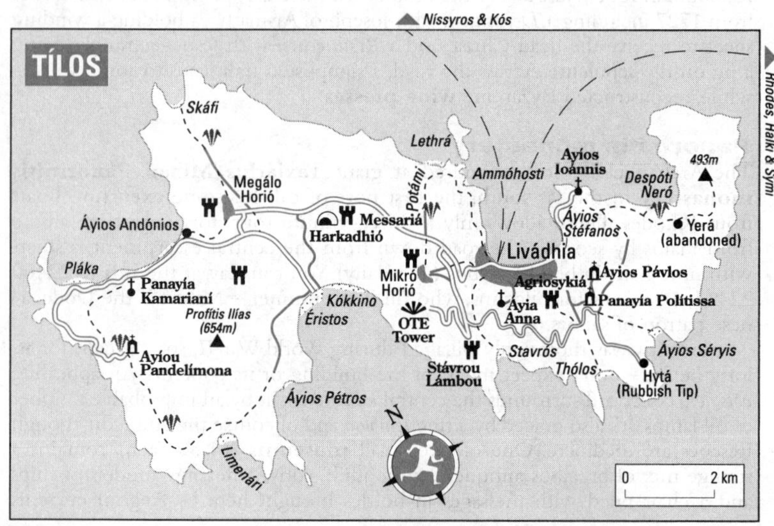

Getting around and information

Tílos's main road runs 7km from **Livádhia**, the port village, to **Megálo Horió**, the capital and only other significant habitation. A blue-and-white **bus** links the two, theoretically coinciding with seaborne arrivals; otherwise it makes up to five runs daily between Livádhia and Éristos. There is just one **taxi**; you could **rent a car** from Livádhia outlets such as Drive (Ⓣ22460 44173) and Tilos Travel (see below). Stefanakis, also in Livádhia (Ⓣ22460 44310), has a monopoly on **ferry** and **hydrofoil tickets**; Tilos Travel is arguably more helpful (Ⓣ22460 44294 or 694 65 59 697, Ⓦwww.tilostravel.co.uk), offering a good accommodation booking service, used-book swap and scooter- as well as car-rental. The unreliable *Sea Star* **catamaran** has its own office by the church (Ⓣ22460 44000); the single **filling station** lies between Livádhia and Megálo Horió.

Many visitors come specifically to **walk**, assisted by the accurate **map** prepared originally by Baz Ward and sold locally – or by certified walking **guides** Iain and Lyn Fulton (Ⓣ22460 44128 or Ⓦwww.tilostrails.com), who may take you on itineraries not described or mapped in existing literature. A half-dozen sections of deteriorating trail or *kalderími* have been surveyed in preparation for consolidation.

There's a **post office** in Livádhia, a single **ATM**, **Internet** cafés (try Balthazar or Croma Bar) and two well-stocked **supermarkets**.

Livádhia

Despite ambitious waterfront improvement programmes – flagstoned terraces, shoreline walkway, a playground – **LIVÁDHIA** with its unfinished building sites, higgledy-piggledy layout and overdrawn (therefore brackish) water supply makes a poor introduction to the island. Yet it remains the best-equipped settlement to deal with tourists, and is closest to the majority of path-hikes.

Accommodation

Simple doubles are the rule when it comes to **accommodation**; apartments and houses are still rare. There are generally enough beds to go around, but at peak season it's worth phoning ahead or consulting the Tilos Travel website. Budget options are dwindling in favour of newer, better-appointed, **sea-view** choices like galleried ★ *Blue Sky Apartments* above the ferry dock (apply to Tilos Travel; ❹); *Marina's Studios* (Ⓣ22460 44023; ❸), up on the hillside; the tranquil and hospitable *Faros Hotel* (Ⓣ22460 44068, Ⓔdimkouk@otenet.gr; ❸) at the far end of Livádhia bay; and ★ *Eleni Beach Hotel* (Ⓣ22460 44062, Ⓦwww.elenihoteltilos.gr; ❸), offering the highest standard and best value on the shore, with bug screens and Wi-Fi throughout.

Inland, go for the *Hotel Irini* (Ⓣ22410 44293, Ⓦwww.tilosholidays.gr; ❸), 200m inland from mid-beach, with its large pool, good breakfasts, Wi-Fi and pleasant gardens making up for somewhat small, mock-antique-furnished rooms. The same family keeps state-of-the-art ★ *Ilidi Rock* on the west hillside (❹–❺), with Wi-Fi , a conference centre, gym, private beach, some apartments sleeping four and one wing with disabled access.

Eating, drinking and nightlife

Less than half of Livádhia's dozen or so peak-season **tavernas** merit consideration, and in spring or fall, you must book timed seatings at the more Anglophilic restaurants – unheard of on other islands. Among the more authentic spots are *Mihalis*, with no-nonsense roast goat and fish as well as good vegetable platters and non-CAÏR bulk wine served at garden tables; *To Armenon* (alias *Nikos'*) on the shore road, a professionally run and salubrious beach-taverna-cum-ouzerí, with large portions of octopus salad, white beans, meaty mains and fish platters washed down by Alfa beer on tap; and nearby *Oneiro/Dream*, with a limited menu of excellent grills but overpriced bulk wine.

Among **cafés**, *Iy Omonia* (aka *Tou Mihali*), under trees strung with light bulbs overlooking the park, is the enduringly popular traditional venue for a sundowner, breakfast or a tipple while waiting for a ferry; its inexpensive, tasty, generous *mezédhes* will stand in for a formal meal. The jetty-café *Remezzo* also does excellent, reasonable ouzo-*mezédhes*.

Organized **nightlife** in or near Livádhia is limited to *Bozi* at the far east end of the bay (nightly in summer, weekends otherwise) and musical bars *To Mikro Café* and *Café Ino*, two restored shoreline cottages.

Around Livádhia

From Livádhia you can walk an hour north along an obvious trail to the pebble bay of **Lethrá**, or in about the same time south on separate itineraries to the secluded coves of **Stavrós** or **Thólos**. The track to the former, soon a trail, begins between the *Tilos Mare Hotel* and the *Castellania Apartments*; once up to the saddle with its paved road, you've a sharp drop to the beach. Ignore over-eager cairning in the ravine bed; the true path is up on the right bank, indicated by red-painted surveyor's marks. The route to Thólos begins by the cemetery and the chapel of **Áyios Pandelímon**, then curls under the seemingly impregnable castle of **Agriosykiá**; from the saddle on the paved road overlooking the descent to Thólos (25min; also red-marked), a cairned route leads northwest to the citadel in twenty minutes. Head east a couple of curves along that paved road to the trailhead for **Áyios Séryis** bay, the most pristine of Tílos' beaches but the hardest to reach (30min one way).

It's less than an hour's walk west, with some surviving path sections short-cutting the road curves, to the ghost village of **Mikró Horió**, whose 1200 inhabitants left for Livádhia during the 1950s. The only intact structures are churches (locked to protect frescoes) and an old house restored as a small-hours **music pub** (July & Aug).

Megálo Horió and Éristos

The rest of Tílos's inhabitants live in or near **MEGÁLO HORIÓ**, which enjoys sweeping views over the vast agricultural plain stretching down to Éristos (see opposite), and is overlooked in turn by a prominent **Knights' castle**, built atop ancient Tílos, whose recycled masonry remains evident. You reach it by a stiff, thirty-minute climb that begins on the lane behind the Ikonomou supermarket before threading its way through a vast jumble of cisterns, house foundations and derelict chapels – the remains of much larger medieval Megálo Horió. Towards the northeast end of the village is one of Tílos' few unlocked churches: **Áyios Ioánnis Thelógos**, with engaging sixteenth-to-seventeenth-century frescoes. Two more nearby fortresses stare out across the plain: the easterly one of **Messariá** marks the location of the **Harkadhió cave** (closed), where Pleiocene midget-elephant bones were discovered in 1971. The bones themselves will soon be displayed in a purpose-built museum near the cave.

Accommodation in the village comprises the central *Milios Apartments* (Ⓣ22460 44204, Ⓕ22460 442665; ❷–❸) and *Studios Ta Elefandakia* (Ⓣ22460 44213; ❷), set among attractive gardens by the car park; a more comfortable choice is British-run *Eden Villas* just beyond (Ⓣ22460 44094, Ⓦwww.eden-villas.com), with two well-sited three-bedroom villas with pool and

Wi-Fi (€1300/week peak season). The lone **taverna**, *Kastro*, is somewhat glum but serves own-raised meat, goat cheese and home-made *dolmádhes*; above historic Taxiárhis church, Athenian-run *Kafenio Ilakati* (July–Sept eves only) does desserts and drinks.

Below Megálo Horió, signs direct you 3km south to long, pink-grey-sand **Éristos beach**, allegedly the island's best (and home to summer colonies of campers), though a reef must be crossed entering the water. The far south end, where the reef recedes, is nudist, as are the two secluded, attractive coves at **Kókkino** beyond the headland (accessible by path from obvious military pillbox). On the secondary, parallel road down to Éristos, *En Plo* is the best nearby venue for a **snack**, while the *Eristos Beach Hotel* (☎22460 44025; ❸) offers big balconies, a pleasant pool and larger apartments for four.

The far northwest

The main road beyond Megálo Horió hits the coast again at somewhat grim **ÁYIOS ANDÓNIOS** with an exposed, truncated beach; the best of two **tavernas** is *Dhelfini*, packed at weekends but frequented otherwise mainly by local fishermen. There's better, warm-water swimming at isolated, sandy **Pláka beach**, 2km west of Áyios Andónios, where people camp rough despite a total lack of facilities.

The paved road ends 8km west of Megálo Horió at fortified **Ayíou Pandelímona monastery** (daily: May–Sept 10am–7pm, may close briefly at noon; Oct–April 10am–4pm), founded in the fifteenth century for the sake of its miraculous spring, still the best water on the island. A fitfully operating drinks café hosts the island's major **festival** of July 25–27. The monastery's tower-gate and oasis setting, high above the forbidding west coast, are its most memorable features, though a photogenic inner courtyard boasts a *votsalotó* surface, and the church a fine tesselated mosaic floor. On the south *katholikón* wall, an early eighteenth-century fresco shows the founder-builder holding a model of the monastery, while behind the ornate altar screen hides another rare fresco of the Holy Trinity.

The public bus calls at the monastery only on Sunday as part of a tour, so you'll need transport to get here. To vary the return to Megálo Horió, take a taxi out then walk back much of the way on a signposted path; it's shown on Baz Ward's map (see p.697).

Níssyros

Volcanic **Níssyros** is noticeably greener than its neighbours Tílos and Hálki, and unlike them has proven wealthy enough to retain more than eight hundred of its population year-round. While remittances from abroad (particularly New York) are significant, most of the island's income is derived from the offshore islet of **Yialí**, a vast lump of **pumice** slowly being quarried away by Lava Ltd. The concession fee collected from Lava by the municipality has engendered a huge public payroll and vast per-capita income. Accordingly, the Nissyrians bother little with agriculture other than keeping cows and pigs; the hillside terraces carved out for grain and grapes mostly lie fallow, though a small amount of wine and *koukouzína* (distilled spirit) is made.

The island's peculiar geology is potentially a source of other benefits: the Greek power company sunk exploratory **geothermal** wells between 1988 and 1992, attempting to convince the islanders of the benefits of cheap electricity.

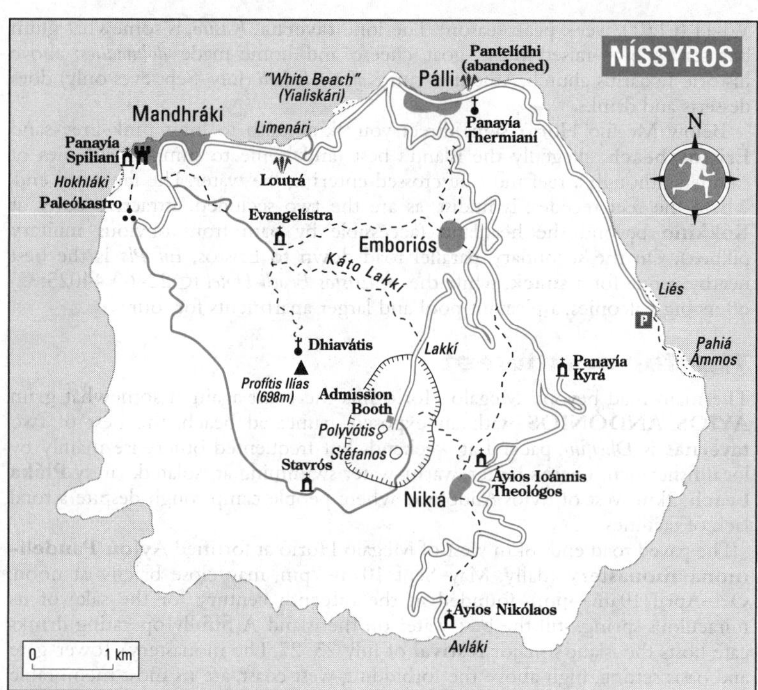

In 1993, a local referendum went massively against the project, as did (by a closer margin) a 1997 poll, after which DEI and its Italian contractor took the hint and packed up. A desalination plant scarcely provides enough fresh water; the relatively few tourists (mostly German) who stay the night, as opposed to day-trippers from Kós, still find peaceful villages with few concrete eyesores and a friendly if rather tight-knit population.

Níssyros also offers good **walking** opportunities through a countryside studded with oak and terebinth, on a network of trails fitfully marked and maintained; the pigs gorge themselves on the abundant acorns, and pork figures prominently on local menus. Autumn is a wonderful time to visit, especially for the sake of the wonderful local figs (the Turks knew the island as *Incirli*.

Mandhráki

MANDHRÁKI is the deceptively large port and capital, with blue patches of sea visible at the end of narrow stone-paved lanes lined with whitewashed houses, whose brightly painted balconies and shutters are mandated by law. Except for the tattier fringes near the ferry dock, where multiple souvenir shops and bad tavernas pitched at day-trippers leave a poor first impression, the town is attractive and village-like – a fact not lost on the many engaged in restorations – arrayed around the *kámbos* (community orchard) and overlooked by two fortresses.

Into a corner of the nearer, fourteenth-century **Knights' castle**, is wedged the little monastery of **Panayía Spilianí** (daylight hours), built here in accordance with an islander's vision of the Virgin; raiding Saracens overlooked vast quantities of silver sheathing a collection of Byzantine icons. During 1996–97, the Langadháki district just below was rocked by several **earthquakes**, damaging a score of venerable houses (mostly repaired now); the seismic threat is ever present, quite literally cutting the ground out from under those who erroneously dub the volcano "extinct".

As a defensive bastion, the seventh-century-BC Doric **Paleókastro** (unrestricted access), twenty minutes' well-signposted walk out of Langadháki, is infinitely more impressive, ranking as one of the more underrated ancient sites in Greece. You can clamber up onto the massive, polygonal-block walls by means of a broad staircase beside the still-intact gateway.

Information and transport

The most useful of Mandhráki's four **travel agencies** are Kendris (Ⓣ22420 31227), near the town hall, handling ANES and Blue Star ferries, and Dhiakomihalis (Ⓣ22420 31459), which represents ANES and the *Panayia Spiliani*, and rents cars; both sell air tickets. There's a **post office** near the pharmacy, a stand-alone **ATM** at the harbour and high-speed/Wi-Fi **Internet** access at *Proveza* café-bar, in Lefkandió district. Also at the jetty-base is the **bus stop**, with up to five daily departures to the hill villages and six to Pálli. Otherwise, there are two set-rate **taxis** and two outlets for **scooter rental**, the more economical being Manos K (Ⓣ22420 31029) on the harbour, also renting **cars**.

Accommodation

With few exceptions, **lodging** is of a basic, 1980s-vintage standard. Among a handful of port **hotels** on your left as you disembark, the best value and most comfortable are the well-kept *Romantzo* (Ⓣ22420 31340; ❷), whose best, air conditioned rooms are on the top floor; the municipal *Xenon Polyvotis* (Ⓣ22420 31011; ❷), whose biggish, neutral rooms mostly have knockout sea views; and the slightly overpriced *Haritos* (Ⓣ22420 31322, Ⓦwww.haritoshotel.gr; all year; ❸), with a seaside hot-spring pool (11am–4pm & 7–10pm; €3 non-guests). In the town centre, Mandhráki's best amenities are to be found at the *Porfyris* (Ⓣ22420 31376; ❹), with a large swimming pool and breakfast terrace; most rooms, with air conditioning and fridges, overlook the sea and *kámbos*. Otherwise, splurge on a restoration project making some use of Níssyros's considerable architectural heritage: on the shore lane near the windmill, the two comfortable suites at *Ta Liotridia* (Ⓣ22420 31580, Ⓔliotridia@nisyrosnet.gr; ❼) host up to four, with fine sea views and volcanic-stone-and-wood decor.

Eating and nightlife

Culinary **specialities** include *pittiá* (chickpea croquettes), pickled caper greens, honey and *soumádha*, almond syrup sold in recycled wine bottles (dilute 4:1 to drink, consume within 3 months). When eating out, give most of the shoddy shoreline **tavernas** a miss in favour of more genuine haunts. Evenings-only *Mezedhopolio Ankyrovoli*, at Áyios Sávvas quay, has indoor and outdoor seating, rebétika soundtrack and well-priced, hearty food including rich, pork-based *boukouniés* and plenty for vegetarians, along with Attica bulk wine. Runners-up include *Kleanthis* in Lefkandió district, best for fish, or *Taverna Nissiros* inland, the oldest eatery in town, always busy despite its average grills.

Several cafés on ficus-shaded Platía Ilikioméni act as **nightlife** venues – most characterful is *Antrikos*, while *Rendezvous* does sweets. There are also a few *barákia* on the shore at Lefkandió district: try the musical *Enallax* or the striking, ex-olive-press bar of the *Liotridia* inn.

The coast

Beaches on Níssyros are in even shorter supply than water, so much so that excursions are offered to a sandy cove on **Áyios Andónios islet** opposite. Closer to hand, the short, black-rock beach of **Hokhláki**, behind the Knights' castle, is unusable if the wind is up. It's best to head east along the main road, passing the old-fashioned spa of **Loutrá** (hot baths 6–7am, 9am–noon & 6–8pm; bring own towel; €3/20min). For excellent **meals**, continue east to *Limenari* (aka *Makis & Ourania*; lunch & supper), perched scenically in a terraced valley above the namesake bay, with fair prices for big portions of homestyle food.

A kilometre or so further, 4km from Mandhráki, the fishing village of **PÁLLI** makes a good retreat when the port fills with trippers. **Tavernas** have multiplied, but some are overpriced, so best stick with long-running *Ellinis*, with spit-roasted meat by night, grilled fish in season and simple rooms upstairs (☎22420 31453; ❷). An economical **scooter-rental** outlet (*Captains*) and an excellent **bakery** cranking out brown bread and pies (branch in Mandhráki) make Pálli also worth considering as a base. There's more **accommodation** at *Frantzis Studios* by the bakery (☎22420 31240; ❷), with well-kept units in slightly scruffy grounds. A tamarisk-shaded, dark-sand **beach**, kept well groomed, extends east to the abandoned Pantelídhi spa, behind which the little grotto-chapel of **Panayía Thermianí** is tucked inside the vaulted remains of a Roman baths complex.

To reach Níssyros's **best beaches**, continue in this direction, along an initially bleak shoreline, to the delightful cove of **Liés**, with a snack-bar (July–Aug only). Just past here the paved road ends at a car park 5km beyond Pálli; in summer taxi-boats from Mandhráki call here too. Another fifteen minutes by trail over the headland brings you to the idyllic, 300-metre expanse of **Pahiá Ámmos**, with grey-pink sand heaped in dunes, limited shade at the far end and a large colony of rough campers and naturists in summer.

The interior

Níssyros's central, dormant **volcano** lends the island its special character and nurtures its abundant vegetation – no stay would be complete without a visit. Tours from Kós tend to monopolize the crater floor between 11am and 2pm, so if you want solitude, use early-morning or late-afternoon scheduled buses to Nikiá (a few continue to the crater floor), a scooter or your own two feet to get there.

The road up from Pálli winds first past the all-but-abandoned village of **EMBORIÓS**, where pigs and free-ranging cattle (a major driving hazard) far outnumber people (winter population 5), though the place is being bought up and restored by Athenians and foreigners. New owners often discover natural volcanic saunas in the basements of the crumbling houses; at the outskirts of the village there's a signposted public **steam bath** in a grotto, its entrance outlined in white paint. If you're descending to Pálli from here, an old cobbled way starting at the sharp bend below the sauna offers an attractive short cut of the four-kilometre road, while another *kalderími* drops from behind the little platía to within a quarter-hour's walk of the craters. Also just off the platía, by the church, is the better of two **tavernas**: *Apyria/Triandafyllos* (all year, supper only; book on ☎22420 31377), with spit-roasted suckling pig in summer – otherwise grills and *mezédhes*.

Some 3km past Emboriós, a paved drive leads down to **Panayía Kyrá**, the island's oldest and most venerable monastery, worth a stop for its enchanting, arcaded festival courtyard as much as its church. **NIKIÁ**, the larger village on

▲Volcano of Níssyros

the east side of the caldera, is – with thirty year-round inhabitants – more of a going concern, and its spectacular situation 14km from Mandhráki offers views out to Tílos as well as across the volcano. The sole **taverna**, at the village entrance, is pricey *Andriotis* (Easter–Oct), with a good if limited menu and chocolatey desserts. On the engagingly round platía called Pórta, ringed by stone seating and marked out in white paint for folk dances, are two cafés. From the bus turnaround area, a 45-minute **trail** descends to the crater floor; a few minutes downhill, detour briefly to the eyrie-like **monastery of Áyios Ioánnis Theológos**, whose festival grounds come to life at the September 25–26 evening festival. To **drive** directly to the volcanic area you must use the road that veers off just past Emboriós.

The volcano

However you approach the **volcano**, a sulphurous stench drifts out to meet you as trees and pasture, then clumps of oregano, gradually give way to lifeless, caked powder. The sunken main crater of **Stéfanos** presents a striated moonscape of grey, white, brown and pale yellow; there is another, less-visited double crater (dubbed **Polyvótis**) to the west, arguably more dramatic, with a clear trail leading up to it from the snack-bar. The perimeters of both are punctuated with tiny blowholes from which steam puffs and around which form little pincushions of sulphur crystals. Since the millennium, boiling mud-pots have surfaced towards the eastern side of Stéfanos (danger of falling through the crater-floor at their edges); anywhere nearby it sounds like a huge cauldron bubbling away below you. In legend this is the groaning of Polyvotis, a titan crushed here by Poseidon under a huge rock torn from Kós. When tour groups appear, a small, tree-shaded **snack-bar** operates in the centre of the wasteland, and a booth on the access road charges admission (€1.50) to the volcanic zone.

Since DEI's 1991 destruction of the ancient *kalderími* between the volcano and Mandhráki, finding pleasant **walks** back to town requires a bit of imagination – though surviving paths are marked with red paint-dots and wooden signposts – and possession of Beate and Jürgen Franke's GPS-drawn topographical **map** (download from ⓦwww.bjfranke.privat.t-online.de/).

Kós

After Rhodes, **Kós** is the second largest and second most visited Dodecanese, with superficial similarities between the two. Here also the harbour is guarded by an imposing castle of the Knights of St John; the streets are lined with Italian-built public buildings; minarets and palm trees punctuate extensive Hellenistic and Roman remains. Although its hinterland mostly lacks the wild beauty of Rhodes' interior, Kós is the most fertile of this archipelago, blessed with rich soil and abundant ground water.

Mass **tourism** has largely displaced the old agrarian way of life; all-inclusive complexes comprising tens of thousands of beds are a blight that contribute little to the local economy, and have forced many restaurants and more modest hotels to close. Except in Kós Town and Mastihári, there are few independent travellers, and from mid-July to mid-September you'll be lucky to find a room without reserving far in advance. The tourist industry is juxtaposed rather bizarrely with cows munching amid baled hay, and Greek Army tanks exercising in the volcanic badlands around the airport. All these peculiarities acknowledged, Kós is still worth a few days' time while island-hopping: its few **mountain villages** are appealing, the tourist infrastructure excellent and **swimming** opportunities limitless – about half the island's perimeter is fringed by **beaches** of various sizes, colours and consistencies.

Kós Town

KÓS TOWN, home to more than half of the island's population of just over 28,000, radiates out from the harbour, with most of its charm residing in scattered ancient and medieval antiquities. Apart from the Knights' castle, the first thing you see on arrival, there's a wealth of Hellenistic and Roman remains, many only revealed by an earthquake in 1933, and excavated subsequently by the Italians, who also laid out the "garden suburbs" extending either side of the central grid. Elsewhere, extents of open space alternate with a hotchpotch of Ottoman monuments and later mock-medieval or 1930s Modernist buildings.

Arrival, transport and information

Large **ferries and catamarans** anchor at a dock by one corner of the castle; **excursion boats** to neighbouring islands sail right in and berth all along Aktí Koundouriótou; **hydrofoils** tie up south of the castle at their own jetty, on Aktí Miaoúli. Virtually all ferry, catamaran and *kaïki* agents sit within 50m of each other at the waterfront end of pedestrianized **Vassiléos Pávlou**. Among those representative of ferries and hydrofoils, not just expensive excursions, are Kentriko (for Blue Star and Agoudimos) by the DEAS terminal (ⓣ22420 28914); Exas (for almost everyone else) opposite the National Bank at Andóni Ioannídhi 4 (ⓣ22420 29900); and Hermes at Vasiléos Pávlou 2 (ⓣ22420 26607) for the *Panayia Spiliani* to Níssyros, catamarans, hydrofoils and boats to Turkey.

The **airport** is 24km southwest of Kós Town in the centre of the island; Aegean Airways operates a shuttle bus to the town terminal by the Casa Romana, but other flight arrivals may have to either take a taxi, or flag down an orange-and-cream-coloured KTEL bus at the giant roundabout outside the

KÓS & PSÉRIMOS

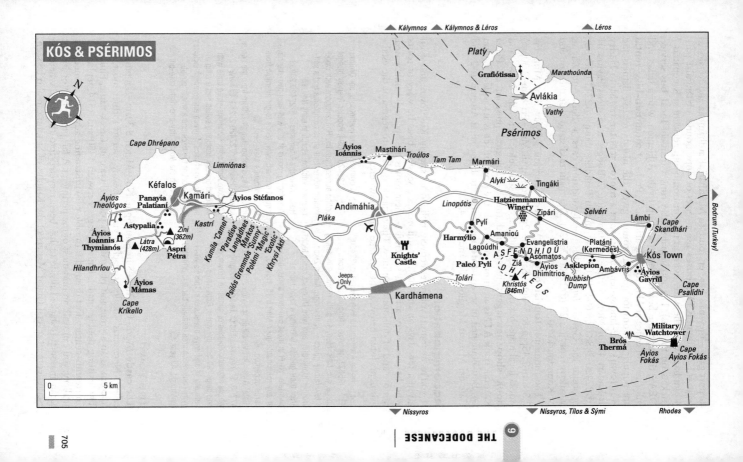

airport gate – they pass here en route to Mastihári, Kardhámena and Kéfalos as well as Kós Town. **KTEL buses** use a series of stops around a triangular park 400m back from the water, with an information booth adjacent at Kleopátras 7 (tickets on the bus). The municipality also runs a frequent **local bus** service, DEAS, through the beach suburbs and up to the Asklepion, with a ticket and information office at Aktí Koundouriótou 7. Push- or **mountain-bike rental** are popular options for getting around, given the island's relative flatness and Kós Town's bike-lane system; if you want a **motor scooter**, try Moto Harley at Kanári 42, or Moto Service at Harmylíou 7. Budget at Vassiléos Pávlou 31 (ⓣ22420 28882 or 694 45 00 062) and in Psalídhi suburb (ⓣ22420 28882), opposite the *Grecotel Imperial*, has good-condition **cars**, as does AutoWay at Vassiléos Yeoryíou 22 (ⓣ22420 25326). The main **taxi** stand is at the east end of Koundouriótou.

The municipal **tourist office** at Vassiléos Yeoryíou 3 (May–Sept Mon–Fri 7.30am–2.45pm & 5–8pm, Sat 9am–2pm; Oct–April Mon–Fri 8am–2.30pm) stocks local maps, bus timetables and seagoing schedules; there's also Newsstand **book shop/newsagent** just behind the archeological museum on Platía Kazoúli. Bank **ATMs** are numerous, while the **post office** is at Vassiléos Pávlou 14. Best-equipped of several **Internet cafés** are E-global at Artemisías 2, and Cafe del Mare at Megálou Alexándhrou 4a.

Accommodation

If you're in transit, you're effectively obliged to **stay** in Kós Town, and even given a few days on the island, it still makes a sensible base. Be wary of **touts** who besiege every arriving sea-craft – their rooms are apt to be unlicensed, remote and of dubious cleanliness. They may also claim to represent the establishments listed below, and then take you elsewhere.

Hotel Afendoulis Evrypýlou 1 ⓣ22420 25321, ⓦwww.afendoulishotel.com. Large, a/c, balconied, en-suite rooms – including a few family quads – with fridge. Alexis Zikas, brother Ippokrates and wife Dionysia really look after their guests, winning a loyal repeat clientele. Wi-Fi in most common areas; breakfast at any reasonable hour. March 15–Nov 15; credit cards accepted. ❸

Hotel Aktis Art Vassiléos Yeoryíou 7 ⓣ22420 47200, ⓦwww.kosaktis.gr. Designer lodgings whose futuristic doubles or suites, in brown, grey and beige, all face the water. Bathrooms are naturally lit and have butler sinks. There's Wi-Fi, gym, conference area, seaside bar and affiliated restaurant. All year. ❽

Pension Alexis Irodhótou 9, cnr Omírou ⓣ22420 25594. Popular, friendly budget option across from the Roman agora with wood-floored rooms that share bathrooms and a self-catering kitchen. March to early Nov. ❷

Hotel Kamelia Artemisías 3 ⓣ22420 28983. Rear-facing rooms at this well-kept two-star have a quiet orchard view; tends to get overflow from the *Afendoulis*. May–Sept. ❸

Hotel Theodhorou Beach 1200m from the centre, towards Psalídhi ⓣ22420 22280, ⓦwww.theodorouhotel.com. Generous-sized units with disabled access, including suites and a wing of self-catering studios. A green environment includes a lawn-pool at the back and a small "private" beach with the *Nostos* day-and-night café-bar. ❹

The Town

The **castle** (April–Oct Tues–Sun 8am–6pm, Nov–March 8.30am–2.30pm; €3), called "Nerantziás" locally, is reached via a causeway over its former moat, now filled in as an avenue and planted with palms (hence its Greek name, Finíkon). The existing double citadel, built in stages between 1450 and 1514, replaced a fourteenth-century fort deemed incapable of withstanding advances in medieval artillery; you can walk around most of the perimeter. A fair proportion of ancient Koan masonry is stacked inside or has been recycled into the walls, where the escutcheons of several Grand Masters of the Knights of St John can also be seen.

▲ 1, Aktí Zouroúdhi (800m) & Lámbi (2km)

KÓS TOWN

PLATÍAS

Ayías Paraskevís	D
Dhiagóras	F
'Dolphin'	A
Eleftherías	C
Kazoúli	B
K. Paleológou	E

0 — 200 m

ACCOMMODATION

Hotel Afendoulis	D
Art Aktis	B
Pension Alexis	A
Hotel Kamelia	C
Hotel Theodhorou Beach	E

RESTAURANTS & CAFÉS

Aenaos	5
Ambavris	12
Barbas	8
Kanadheza	10
Koakon	11
Pote tin Kyriaki	7
Psaropoula	2
Swedco	9

BARS & CLUBS

Fashion Club	3
Four Roses	6
Hamam Club	4
Mylos	1

N

Ferry & Catamaran Dock
Knights' Castle
Hippocrates Park
Hellenistic Baths
Excursion Boats
Port Police
Loggia
Hippocrates' Plane Tree
Turkish Bath
Hydrofoil Jetty
★"Train" to Asklepion
DEAS Terminal
PUB LANES
Museum
Old Synagogue
Pórta toú Fórou
Agora
Defterdar
Winter Cinema
Market
Ancient Stadium
Atik
Turkish Fountain
Nymphaion
Western Excavations
Roman Odeion
Casa Romana
Airport Coach Stop
KTEL
Olympic Airways
Summer Cinema
Yacht Marina
ITALIAN QUARTER
ITALIAN QUARTER

ETHNIKIS ANDISTASIS
PAMFYLON
PIXIOTON
MANDHILARA
NAVARINOU
AMERIKIS
ALIKARNASSOU
KANARI
SPETSON
THEMISTOKLEOUS
AVEROF
SALAMINOS
PSARON
BOUBOULINAS
VERIOPOULOU
IRODHOTOU
OMIROU
KYPROU
25. MARTIOU
PINDHOU
ZERVOU
ELEFTHERIOU VENIZELOU
KLEOVOULOU
THEOFRASTOU
MEGALOU ALEXANDHROU
ARYIROKASTROU
KORITSAS
EYILION
ZARAFTOU
VORIOU IPIROU
THEOKRITOU
HRISTODHOULOU
THEOLOGOU
NISSIRIOU
KOLOKOTRONI
APELLOU
PISSANDHROU
METSOVOU
GRIGORIOU TOU PEMPTOU
TSALDHARI
GALIAS
MAKARIOU
KREKOUKIA
FILITA
IFESTOU
25 MARTIOU
RIGA FEREOU
AKTI KOUNDOURIOTOU
FINIKON
PLESSA
DHIAKOU
NAFKLIROU
XANTHOU
IPPOKRATOUS
ANDONI IOANNIDHI
KLEOPATRAS
VASSILEOS PAVLOU
MEROPIDHOS
VYRONOS
KAVAKOPOULOU
AYIOU NIKOLAOU
MITROPOLEOS
AKTI MIAOULI
KORAI
EPIHARMOU
ARSENIOU
VASSILEOS YEORYIOU
ARTEMISIAS
KOUROUKLI
G. IOANNIDHI
THIMAKANI
FILIMONOS
THESSALOU
XENOFONDOS
HALKONOS
EVRYPYLOU
FENARETIS
ARTEMISIAS
KARAISKAKI
MAKRIYIANNI
HARMYLOU
YEORYIOU PAPANDHREOU

E (200m), Psalídhi, Áyios Fokás & Brós Thermá ▶
◀ Villages, Airport & Asklepion
Catholic Cemetery ▼
▼ 12, Ambávris & Platáni

Immediately opposite the causeway stands the riven trunk of **Hippocrates' plane tree**, its branches propped up by scaffolding; at seven hundred years of age, it's not really elderly enough to have seen the great healer, though it's certainly one of the oldest trees in Europe. Adjacent are two **Ottoman fountains** (a dry hexagonal one and a working one feeding an ancient sarcophagus) and the eighteenth-century **Hassan Pasha mosque**, also known as the Loggia Mosque; its ground floor – like that of the **Defterdar mosque** on central Platía Eleftherías – is taken up by rows of shops.

Also on Platía Eleftherías stands the Italian-built **Archeological Museum** (Tues–Sun 8.30am–2.30pm; €3), with a predictable Latin bias. Four statue galleries surround an atrium with a mosaic of Hippocrates welcoming Asklepios to Kós; the most famous item, purportedly a statue of Hippocrates, is indeed Hellenistic, but most of the other famous works (such as Hermes seated with a lamb) are Roman.

The largest single section of ancient Kós is the **agora** (closed for works), a confusing jumble of ruins owing to repeated earthquakes between the second and sixth centuries AD. More comprehensible are the so-called **western excavations**, lent definition by two intersecting marble-paved streets and the **Xystos** or colonnade of a covered running track. In the same area lie several interesting **floor mosaics** (most famous is Europa being abducted by Zeus-as-a-bull), all viewable under protective canopies. To the south, across Grigoríou toú Pémptou, are a Roman-era **odeion**, garishly restored both during the 1930s and again in 2000, and the **Casa Romana** (shut for works indefinitely), a third-century AD house whose surviving patches of mosaic floors show panthers, tigers and assorted sea creatures.

Kós also retains a thoroughly commercialized **old town**, lining the pedestrianized street between the Italian market hall on Platía Eleftherías and Platía Dhiagóras with its isolated minaret overlooking the western archeological zone. One of the few areas to survive the 1933 earthquake, today it's crammed with expensive tourist boutiques, cafés and snack-bars. About the only genuinely old thing remaining is a capped **Turkish fountain** with a calligraphic inscription, where Apéllou meets Odhós Venizélou.

Eating and drinking

Despite an overwhelming first impression of Euro-stodge cuisine, it's easy to **eat** well and even reasonably in Kós Town, as long as you search inland, away from the harbour. Koan **wine-making** has been revived recently; the Hatziemmanouil label is particularly worth sampling.

Aenaos Platía Eleftherías. Join the largely local crowd at this café under the Defterdar mosque, and people-watch while refilling your Greek coffee from the traditional *bríki* used to brew it. Also a variety of teas and flavoured hot chocolates.

Ambavris 500m south of the edge of town along the road from near Casa Romana, in the eponymous suburb village. Skip the English-only à la carte menu, take the hint about "Mezedes" and let the house bring on their best. This changes seasonally but won't much exceed €25 (drink extra) for six plates – typically *pinigoúri* (bulgur pilaf), *pikhtí* (brawn), little fish, spicy *loukánika*, stuffed squash flowers and *fáva*. May–Oct eves only.

Barbas Evrypýlou 6, opposite *Hotel Afendoulis*. Excellent grills as well as the odd seafood choice like octopus salad, at cozy outdoor seating. April–Oct.

Kanadheza Evrypýlou, cnr Artemisías. Creditable pizzas as well as grills and some *mayireftá*, served at indoor/outdoor tables. All year.

Koakon (aka *Andonis*) Artemisías 56. Versatile all-rounder purveying grilled meat and fish, *mezédhes* and a few daily *mayireftá* with equal aplomb, without the usual multinational flags and photo-menus. All year.

Pote tin Kyriaki Pissándhrou 9. Kós's sole genuine ouzerí, whose creatively assembled menu (in school copy-books) has delights such as shrimps, fried mussels or *gávros*, *monastiriakí* (Cretan "monk's" salad), as well as grilled chops and *loukánika*. Summer Mon–Sat eves only, winter Thurs–Sat eves plus lunch.

Psaropoula Avérof 17. Long the town's best-value fish/seafood specialist, with many Greeks in attendance; open all year.

Special (Arvanitakis) Vassiléos Yeoryíou. Hole-in-the-wall *zaharoplastío* with dynamite gelato.

Swedco Vassiléos Pávlou 20. Ultra-sleek outlet of the Rhodes café chain, with (pricey) sandwiches, hot drinks and decadent desserts.

Nightlife and entertainment

The most durable dance-floor **clubs** are *Four Roses* on the corner of Arseníou and Vassiléos Yeoryíou, and *Fashion Club* on the west side of the inner port. The "**Pub Lanes**", officially Nafklírou and Dhiákou, are the place for techno and house; bar identities change each season, however, and it's become listless. The most stable and classy venue here is *Hamam Club*, installed in an ex-Turkish bath, with its original oriental decor, chill-out sofas and outdoor seating before a midnight "curfew" moves everyone indoors. There are **newer, better nightlife areas** near Platía Dhiagóra (mostly Greeks) and out at Aktí Zouroúdhi, where *Mylos* – built around an old windmill on the beach – is currently the top day-and-night-bar, with both live music and DJ evenings. Otherwise there is one active **cinema**, the Orfeas, with summer and winter (Oct–May) premises as shown on the map on p.707; the indoor premises also host special events.

The Asklepion and Plateáni

Native son **Hippocrates** is justly celebrated on Kós; not only does he have a tree, a street, a park, a statue and an international medical institute named after him, but his purported **Asklepion** (May–Oct Tues–Sun 8am–6pm, Nov–April 8.30am–2.30pm; €3), 4km south of town, one of three in Greece, is a major attraction. A little fake green-and-white train shuttles to the site regularly; otherwise take a DEAS bus to Platáni (see p.710), from where the ruins are a further fifteen-minute walk.

The Asklepion was actually founded just after Hippocrates' death, but the methods used and taught here were probably his. Both a sanctuary of Asklepios (god of healing, son of Apollo) and a renowned curative centre, its magnificent setting on three artificial terraces overlooking Anatolia reflects early concern with the therapeutic environment. Until recently, springs provided the site with a constant supply of pure water, and stretches of clay piping are still visible, embedded in the ground.

Hippocrates

Hippocrates (ca. 460–370 BC) is generally regarded as the father of scientific medicine, though the Hippocratic oath, anyway much altered from its original form, probably has nothing to do with him. Hippocrates was certainly born on Kós, probably at Astypalia near present-day Kéfalos, but otherwise confirmed details of his life are few; probably he was a great physician who travelled throughout the Classical Greek world, but spent at least part of his career teaching and practising on his native island. Numerous medical writings have been attributed to Hippocrates, only a few of which he could have actually written; *Airs, Waters and Places*, a treatise on the importance of environment on health, is generally thought to be his, but others are reckoned a compilation from a medical library in Alexandria during the second century BC. This emphasis on good air and water, and the holistic approach of ancient Greek medicine, now seems positively contemporary.

Today, very little remains standing, owing to periodic earthquakes and the Knights' use of the site as a quarry. The lower terrace never had many buildings, being instead the venue for the observance of the Asklepieia – quadrennial celebrations and athletic/musical competitions in honour of the god. Sacrifices to Asklepios were conducted at an **altar**, the oldest structure here, whose foundations are found near the middle of the second terrace. Just east, the Corinthian columns of a second-century AD **Roman temple** were partially re-erected by nationalistically minded Italians. A monumental **staircase** leads from the altar to a second-century BC **Doric temple** of Asklepios on the highest terrace, last and grandest of a succession of the deity's local shrines.

About halfway to the Asklepion, the village of **PLATÁNI** (also Kermedés, from the Turkish Germe) is, along with Kós Town, home to the island's dwindling community of ethnic Turks. Until 1964 there were nearly three thousand of them, but successive Cyprus crises and the worsening of relations between Greece and Turkey prompted mass emigration to Anatolia, and a drop in the Muslim population to well below a thousand. Several excellent, Turkish-run **tavernas** are found at and around the main crossroads junction, with a working Ottoman fountain: *Arap* (summer only); *Asklipios* (aka *Ali's*) and *Sherif*, adjacent across the way (also summer only); and *Gin's Place* (all year), each offering Anatolian-style *mezédhes* and kebabs better than most in Kós Town. Afterwards, retire across from *Arap* to *Zaharoplastio Iy Paradhosi* for the best ice cream on the island.

Just outside Platáni on the road back to the port, the island's neglected **Jewish cemetery** lies in a dark conifer grove, 300m beyond the well-kept Muslim graveyard. Dates on the Hebrew-Italian-script headstones stop after 1940, after which none of the local Jews were allowed a natural death prior to their deportation in summer 1944. Their former **synagogue**, a wonderfully orientalized Art Deco specimen from 1934, at Alexándhrou Dhiákou 4, is now a municipal events hall; a plaque commemorates its former use.

Eastern Kós

To reach anything resembling a deserted **beach** near the capital, you'll need to use the DEAS bus line connecting the various resorts to either side of town, or else rent a vehicle; designated cycle-paths extend as far east as Cape Psalídhi.

The easterly bus line usually terminates at **Áyios Fokás**, 8km southeast of Kós Town, but sometimes continues an extra 4km almost to remote **Brós Thermá** (last service around 6pm); with your own transport you negotiate a dirt track for the final kilometre. Brós Thermá is celebrated for its massively popular **hot springs** – best experienced at sunset or after – which issue from a grotto and flow through a trench into a shoreline pool formed by boulders, heating the seawater to an enjoyable temperature. Winter storms disrupt the boulder wall, rebuilt every April, so that the pool changes from year to year. Just uphill, long-running *Psarotaverna Therma* does pricey fish and a few *mezédhes*.

Tingáki and Marmári

The two neighbouring beach resorts of Tingáki and Marmári are separated by the **Alykí** salt marsh, which retains water – and throngs of migratory birds, including flamingoes – until June after a wet winter. There's almost always a breeze along this coast, attracting windsurfers; the profiles of Kálymnos, Psérimos and Turkey's Bodrum peninsula all make for spectacular offshore scenery. If you're aiming for either resort from town, especially on a two-wheeler, it's safest and most pleasant to go via the **minor road** from the southwest corner of town (follow initial signage for the Vassiliadhi supermarket);

the entire way to Tingáki is paved, and involves the same distance as using the main trunk road and marked turn-off. Similarly, a grid of paved rural lanes links the inland portions of Tingáki and Marmári.

TINGÁKI, popular with Brits, lies 12km west of the harbour. Oddly, there's little **accommodation** near the beach; most surviving mid-sized hotels and more numerous studios are scattered inland through fields and cow pastures. Much the best local **taverna** here, with pleasant seating indoors and out, is ✱ *Ambeli* (May–Oct daily; Nov–April Fri/Sat eve, Sun lunch; book peak season on ⓣ22420 69682), well signposted 2.5km east of the main beachfront crossroads; featured dishes include *pinigoúri* (cracked wheat), *bekrí mezé*, *pykhtí* (brawn), *yaprákia* (the local *dolmádhes*) and *arnáki ambelourgoú*, washed down with wine from their own vineyard. Among **car rental** outfits, Sevi (ⓣ22420 68299) can be recommended. The beach itself is white sand, long and narrow – improving, and veering away from frontage road, as you head southwest.

MARMÁRI, 15km from town, has a smaller built-up area than Tingáki, and the beach itself is broader, especially to the west where it forms little dunes. Most German-slanted hotels here are all-inclusive; an exception, on the main access road down from the island trunk road, is *Esperia* (ⓣ22420 42010, ⓦwww.hotelesperiakos.gr; ❹).

The Asfendhioú villages

The inland villages of **Mount Dhíkeos**, a handful of settlements collectively referred to as **Asfendhioú**, nestle amid the island's only natural forest. Together these communities give a good idea of what Kós looked like before tourism and ready-mix concrete arrived, and all have been severely depopulated by the mad rush to the coast. They are accessible via the curvy side road from Zipári, 8km from Kós Town; an inconspicuously marked minor road to Lagoúdhi; or by the shorter access road for Pylí.

The first Asfendhioú village you reach up the Zipári road is **Evangelístria**, where a major crossroads by the eponymous parish church leads to Lagoúdhi and Amanioú (west), Asómatos (east) and Ziá (uphill). **ZIÁ**'s spectacular sunsets make it the target of up to six evening tour buses daily, though the village has barely a dozen resident families, and its tattiness increases annually. Best of the dozen **tavernas** here, one of the few not relying on photo-menus, is Greek-patronized ✱ *Oromedon* (all year), serving good *pinigoúri*, mushrooms and local sausage on a roof terrace. Secluded *Kefalovrissi*, near the top of the village, is good for *mezédhes* plus selected daily mains like *pantsétta* or *bakaliáros*. Ziá is also the trailhead for the ascent of 846-metre **Dhíkeos peak**, a minimum two-and-a-half-hour round trip, initially on track but mostly by path. The route is fairly obvious, and the views from the pillbox-like summit chapel of **Metamórfosis** amply reward the effort. Up top, you can also ponder the symbolism of a giant crucifix fashioned out of PVC sewer pipe and filled with concrete.

East of Ziá or Evangelístria, roads converge at **ASÓMATOS**, home to about twenty villagers and various outsiders restoring abandoned houses; the evening view from the gaily painted church of **Arhángelos** with its *votsalotó* courtyard rivals that of Zía, though there are no amenities. **ÁYIOS DHIMÍTRIOS (**aka **Haïhoútes)**, 2km beyond along a paved road, is ruined except for a few restored houses next to the attractive church; in its narthex, a small photo display documents a much larger population until World War II, when the village was a centre of resistance to the occupation. You can continue 3.5km further to the junction with the road descending from the rubbish tip to Platáni.

Pylí

Pylí can be reached via the road through Lagoúdhi and Amanioú, or from beside the duck-patrolled Linopótis pond on the main island trunk road, across from which indoor-outdoor *Ouzeri Limni* (aka *Karamolengos;* noon–11pm except Tues, all year) is well worth a nocturnal drive from elsewhere (at lunchtime road-noise is offputting). They've got the broadest variety of ouzo, *tsikoudhiá* and *tsípouro* in the islands, platters in three sizes, and a broad range of dishes from *atherína* and fresh *bakaliáros* to baked chickpeas and grills.

In the upper of **PYLÍ**'s two neighbourhoods, 100m west of the partly pedestrianized square and church, *Iy Palia Piyi* taverna serves inexpensive *soutzoukákia* grilled with onions, home-made tzatzíki, fried-vegetable *mezédhes* and local sweet wine in a superb setting, beside a giant, lion-spouted cistern-fountain (*piyí*). Pylí's other attraction is the **Harmýlio** ("Tomb of Harmylos"), signposted near the top of the village as "Heroon of Charmylos". This fenced-off, subterranean, niched vault was probably a Hellenistic family tomb; immediately above, traces of an ancient temple have been incorporated into the medieval chapel of Stavrós.

Paleó (medieval) **Pylí**, 3km southeast of its modern descendant, was the Byzantine capital of Kós. Head there via Amanioú, keeping straight at the junction where signs point left to Ziá and Lagoúdhi. In any case, the castle is obvious on its rock, straight ahead; the paved road ends next to a spring, opposite which a stair-path leads within fifteen minutes to the roof of the fort. En route you pass the remains of the abandoned town tumbling southwards down the slope, as well as two fourteenth-to-fifteenth-century chapels (and an earlier locked one) with fresco fragments; the lowest church, **Arhángelos**, has the best-preserved ones, mostly scenes from the Life of Christ.

Western Kós

Near the desolate centre of the island, well sown with military installations, a pair of giant, adjacent roundabouts by the airport funnels traffic northwest towards **Mastihári**, northeast back towards town, southwest towards **Kéfalos**, and southeast to **Kardhámena**. Most visitors are after the south coast **beaches**, reached from the Kéfalos-bound turning.

Mastihári, Andimáhia and Kardhámena

The least "packaged" and least expensive of the north shore resorts, **MASTIHÁRI** has a shortish, broad beach extending west. Quiet **accommodation** overlooking it includes simple *Hotel Kyma* (Ⓣ22420 59045; ❷) or *Hotel Fenareti* (Ⓣ22420 59024) further up the slope, with rooms (❷) and studios (❸) in a peaceful garden. *O Makis*, one street inland from the quay, and *Kali Kardia*, at the base of the jetty, are the best of a half-dozen **tavernas**, well regarded for fresh fish, *mezédhes* and (at *Kali Kardia*) *mayireftá* and desserts. Mastihári is also the port for roll-on-roll-off **ferries** (current information on Ⓣ22420 59124) and smaller **jet boats** to Kálymnos; there are three and five well-spaced daily departures respectively in each direction most of the year, the jet boats timed more or less to coincide with flight arrivals from Athens.

The workaday village of **ANDIMÁHIA**, 5km southeast of Mastihári, straggles over several ridges; the only concession to tourism, besides a single **windmill** kitted out as a museum (sporadic hours; €1.50) is a line of snack-bars at the southwestern edge, easily accessible from the airport (across the road and car park) if your outbound flight is delayed. East of Andimáhia, reached via a marked, 2.8-kilometre side road, an enormous, triangular **Knights' castle** (unrestricted access) overlooks the straits to Níssyros. Its **Áyios Nikólaos** chapel features an interesting fresco of Áyios Khristóforos (St Christopher) carrying the Christ child.

KARDHÁMENA, 31km from Kós Town, is the island's largest package resort after the capital environs itself, with locals outnumbered twenty to one in a busy season by boozing-and-bonking visitors (mostly heavily tattooed young Brits). A beach stretches to either side of the town – sandier to the southwest, but intermittently reefy and hemmed in by a road going northeast towards Tolári and Kós's largest all-inclusive complex – but runaway local development has banished any redeeming qualities the place might have had.

The resort is most useful as a place to catch a **boat to Níssyros**. There are two daily sailings in season: the morning excursion *kaïki* at 9.30am, and another, less expensive, unpublicized one – either the *Ayios Konstandinos* or the *Nissyros* – at anywhere from 2.30 to 7pm depending on the day.

South coast beaches

The portion of Kós southwest of the airport and Andimáhia boasts the most scenic and secluded beaches on the island, plus a number of minor ancient sites. Though given fanciful English names and shown separately on tourist maps, these **south-facing beaches** form essentially one long stretch at the base of a cliff, most with sunbeds and a jet ski franchise. "**Magic**", officially Polémi, is the longest, broadest and wildest, with a proper taverna above the car park, no jet skis and a nudist zone ("**Exotic**") at the east end. "**Sunny**", signposted as Psilós Gremmós and easily walkable from "Magic", has another taverna and jet skis; **Langádhes** is the cleanest and most picturesque, with junipers tumbling off its dunes and more jet skis. "**Paradise**", alias "**Bubble Beach**" because of volcanic gas-vents in the tidal zone, is small and oversubscribed, with wall-to-wall sunbeds. Jet-ski-free "**Camel**" (Kamíla) is the shortest and loneliest, protected somewhat by the steep, unpaved drive in past its hillside taverna; the shore here is pure, fine sand, with good snorkelling either side of the cove.

Uninterrupted beach resumes past **Áyios Stéfanos** headland, overshadowed by a *Club Med* complex, and extends 5km west to Kamári (see below). A marked public access road leads down to beaches either side of a small peninsula, crowned with the remains of two triple-aisled, sixth-century **basilicas**. Though the best preserved of several on the island, most columns have been toppled, and wonderful bird mosaics languish under a permanent layer of protective gravel. The basilicas overlook tiny, striking **Kastrí** islet with its little chapel; in theory it's an easy swim (sometimes wading) across from the westerly beach, with decent snorkelling around the rock formations, but you must run a gauntlet of boats from the local water-sports outfit.

The far west

Essentially the shore annexe of Kéfalos, **KAMÁRI** is a sprawling package resort and watersports venue of scattered breeze-blocks, with more families and oldies than at Kardhámena. **KÉFALOS** itself, 43km from Kós Town and terminus for buses, covers a bluff looking down the length of the island. Aside from some lively cafés at the south end, it's a dull village mainly of note as a staging point for expeditions into the rugged **peninsula** terminating dramatically at **Cape Kríkello**.

Main highlights of a visit there, beginning along the ridge road south, include a Byzantine church, **Panayía Palatianí**, amid the ruins of a much larger ancient temple, 1km beyond the village; and the Classical theatre (unrestricted access) – with two rows of seats remaining – and Hellenistic temple of **ancient Astypalia**, 500m further at the side-path starting from an unmarked but unlocked gate. A paved road west just beyond Astypalia leads to an often windy beach at **Áyios Theológos**, 7km from Kéfalos; the *Ayios Theologos* **taverna** here is popular locally at weekends, despite ruthlessly exploiting its monopoly and a snacky menu (fish on request). Keeping to the main paved road to its end brings you to the appealing (but usually locked) monastery of **Áyios Ioánnis Thymianós**, also 7km from the village; from here, an unmarked dirt track leads just under 4km to clothing-optional **Hilandhríou** beach, 300m-plus of fine sand with no reliable facilities.

Psérimos

Psérimos could be an idyllic little island were it not so close to Kós and Kálymnos. Throughout the season, both of these larger neighbours dispatch so many daily excursion boats that a second jetty has been built to accommodate them at little **AVLÁKIA** port. In midsummer, day-trippers blanket the main sandy beach which curves in front of Avlákia's thirty-odd houses and huge communal olive grove; even during May or late September you're guaranteed at least eighty outsiders daily (versus a permanent population of 25). There are three other, variably attractive beaches to hide away on: clean **Vathý** (sand and gravel), a well-marked, thirty-minute path-walk east, starting from behind the *Taverna Iy Pserimos*; grubbier **Marathoúnda** (pebble), a 45-minute walk north on the main trans-island track; and best of all **Grafiótissa**, a 300-metre-long beach of near-Caribbean quality at the base of low cliffs. This lies half an hour's walk west of town, more or less following the coast; the way is cross-country around illegally fenced hillside plots, until a trail kicks in at a large, lone tree by a stone corral.

Even during high season there won't be many other overnighters, since there's a limited number of beds. Pick of several small **rooms** establishments is *Tripolitis* (☎22430 23196; May–Oct; ❶), upstairs from English-speaking *Anna's* café/snack-bar, or the rooms above *Taverna Manola* on the opposite end of the beach (☎22430 51540; ❶). Next door are the slightly better *Studios Kalliston* (no phone; ❸). There's just one limited-stock **shop**, since most of the island's supplies are brought in from Kálymnos. **Eating out**, though, won't break the bank, and there's often fresh fish in the handful of **tavernas**; many have contracts with the tour boats, but *Taverna Manola* doesn't, and despite its bar-like appearance (it provides the main **nightlife**) proves adept at ouzerí fare and seafood.

Most **boats based** at Kós harbour operate triangle tours to Platý islet and somewhere on Kálymnos as well as Psérimos, with only a brief stop at the latter. If you want to spend the entire day here, you'll have to depart Póthia (Kálymnos) at 9.30am daily on the roll-on/roll-off *Maniaï*, returning at 5–6pm (€6.60 round trip); there's also one daily service at noon on the *Kalymnos Star/Kalymnos Dolphin*.

Astypálea

Geographically, historically and architecturally, **Astypálea** (alias Astropália) really belongs to the Cyclades – on a clear day you can see Anáfi or Amorgós far more easily than any of the other Dodecanese. Its inhabitants are descendants of medieval colonists from the Cyclades, and the island looks and feels more like one of these than its neighbours to the east.

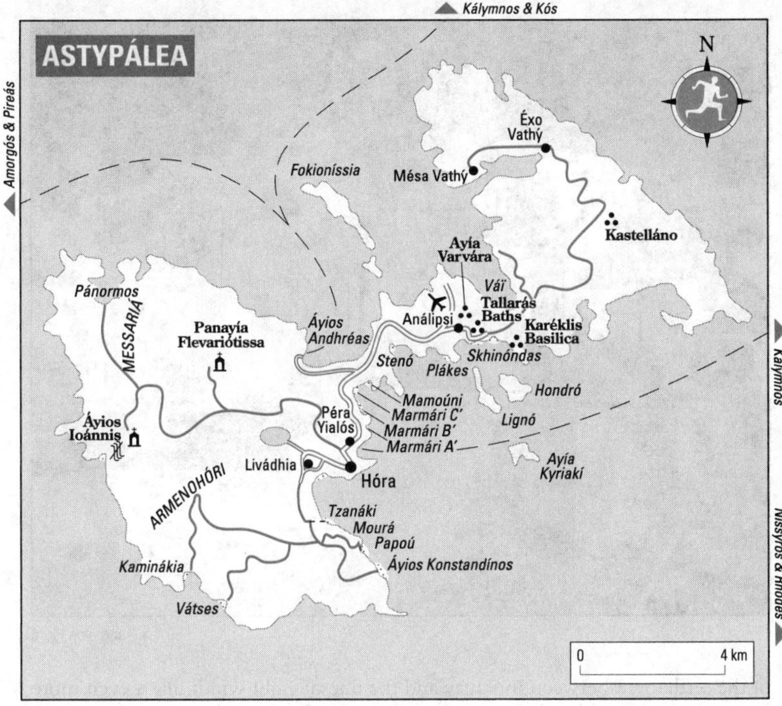

Despite an evocative butterfly shape, Astypálea may not immediately seem especially beautiful. Many **beaches** along the bleak, heavily indented coastline have reef underfoot and periodic dumpings of seaweed. Windswept heights are covered in thornbush or dwarf juniper, yet the sage *alisfakiá*, brewed as a tea, flourishes too, and hundreds of sheep and goats (source of the excellent local **cheese**) manage to survive – as opposed to snakes, which are (uniquely in the Aegean) entirely absent. Citrus groves and vegetable patches in the valleys signal a relative abundance of water, hoarded in a reservoir. Besides cheese, Astypálea is renowned for its **honey**, **fish and lobster**.

Ferry links with Pireás and the Cyclades have improved, though arrival/departure times remain grim (typically 3am/5am) and service to the Dodecanese other than Kálymnos is spotty. Thus you may need or want to take advantage of **flights** to Léros, Kós or Rhodes. There is no conventional **package tourism** on Astypálea, and its remoteness discourages casual trade, but motivated people descend during the short, intense **midsummer season** (mid-July to early Sept), when 1500 permanent inhabitants are vastly outnumbered by visitors. Most arrivals are Athenians, French or Italians, supplemented by large numbers of yachties and foreign second-home owners in picturesque Hóra. At such times you won't find a bed without reserving well in advance, and camping rough is expressly frowned upon.

Péra Yialós and Hóra

The main harbour of **PÉRA YIALÓS** or Skála dates from the Italian era (Astypálea was the first Dodecanese island occupied by the Italians) and most

▲ Astypálea Hóra

of the settlement between the quay and the line of eight windmills is even more recent. Its only real bright spot is a small **archeological museum** (June–Sept Tues–Sun 10am–1pm & 6.30–10pm; Oct–May Tues–Sun 8.30am–2.30pm; free), its single gallery crammed with local finds spanning the Bronze Age to medieval times.

As you climb up towards **HÓRA**, however, the neighbourhoods get progressively older and more attractive, their steep streets enlivened by photogenic *poúndia*, or colourful wooden balconies-with-stairways attached to whitewashed houses. Building styles here owe much to colonists from Mýkonos and Tínos who were brought over to repopulate the island in 1413. The whole culminates in the thirteenth-century **kástro** (always open; free), one of the finest in the Aegean, erected not by the Knights but by the Venetian Quirini clan and subsequently modified by the Ottomans after 1537. Until well into the twentieth century more than three hundred people dwelt inside, but depopulation and a severe 1956 earthquake combined to leave only a desolate shell. The fine rib vaulting over the main west gate supports the church of **Evangelístria Kastrianí**, one of two here, the other being **Áyios Yeóryios** (both usually locked). The *kástro* interior is in the throes of a major consolidation and restoration project, so about half of it is off-limits at any given time.

Arrival, information and transport

All **ferries** except the *Nissos Kalymnos* call at northerly Áyios Andhréas port, 7km away (in summer there's a shuttle bus); otherwise the two **buses** ply the paved road between Hóra, Péra Yialós, Livádhia and Análipsi (July & Aug frequently 8am–11pm; out of season 3–4 daily). Análipsi-bound buses usually don't dovetail well with arriving/departing flights, so ask your chosen accommodation or car-rental outfit to fetch you. The one set-rate **taxi** can't cope with passenger numbers in season; fares are reasonable, for example €7 from Skála to the airport. Various places offer **scooters** (cheap), **cars and jeeps** (expensive), the most reliable being Lakis and Manolis (☎22430 61263), at Skála dock, Tomaso next door (☎22430 61000), and Vergoulis (☎22430 61351) near the museum. Also near the museum, Astypalea Tours (☎22430 61571) represents the *Nissos Kalymnos* and Olympic Airways; Paradisos under the namesake hotel (☎22430 61224) handles Blue Star. Road Editions publishes the best island **map**, worth snagging in advance; others sold locally are grossly inaccurate, even by Greek island standards, though rural junctions are adequately signposted. The **post office** and most shops are in Hóra, though the island's only **ATM** is down in Péra Yialós.

Accommodation

Accommodation in Péra Yialós, and to a lesser extent Hóra, ranges from spartan, 1970s-vintage rooms to new luxury complexes. Somewhere in between are atmospheric restored studios or entire houses (❸–❹) up **in Hóra**; enquire at Kostas Vaïkousis' antique shop on Skála's quay or reserve on ☎22430 61430 or 697 74 77 800. Rather plusher are ★ *Studios Kilindra* on the quiet west slope of Hóra (☎22430 61966, ⓦwww.astipalea.com.gr; April–Dec; ❺–❻), with a swimming pool and good breakfasts – units accommodate two to three people. About halfway along the road from Hóra to Livádhia, non-air-conditioned *Provarma Studios* (☎22430 61096; June to early Sept; ❸), comprise southwest-facing galleried studios with large balconies.

The best accommodation **in Péra Yialós** is the *Hotel Thalassa* (☎22430 59840; ⓦwww.stampalia.gr; all year; ❼), one of the last buildings on the way to Análipsi, consisting entirely of suites and studios. The less remote *Akti Rooms* (☎22430 61114, ⓦwww.aktirooms.gr; ❹) is better value, with on-site car rental and a popular restaurant. The en-suite *Rooms Australia,* above the eponymous restaurant (☎22430 61275 or 22430 61067; ❸) have fans or air conditioning; the same family offers compact studios closer to the water, with heating and double glazing (❹). A basic **campsite** (☎22430 61900; July–Aug) operates amongst calamus reeds and tamarisks behind Dhéftero Marmári Bay, about 4km along the road to Análipsi, but (like much of the island) it can be mosquito-plagued after a wet winter.

Eating, drinking and nightlife

During August, nearly thirty **tavernas** and **beach snack-bars** operate across the island, few of them memorable. Among the more reliable **Péra Yialós** options, *Akroyiali* has only slightly better-than-average food but fills nightly due to its fair prices and unbeatable setting with tables on the sand. The *Astropalia* (closes end Sept), just off the road to Hóra, does good, if somewhat pricey, fish and little else. Best of the lot, with even better seafood, and superbly prepared home-grown vegetable dishes, is homey ★ *Australia* (April–Nov), just inland from the head of the bay. On the far (west) side of the bay, you'll find more polished presentation and higher prices at *Maïstrali* (*Tou Penindara*; all year), the place for lobster, scaly fish or *mayireftá* from a broad menu. Under *Hotel Astynea*, the *Dapia Café* is good for full **breakfasts**, crêpes and novelty teas; a few steps down, on the corner, *Iy Vouli* (*O Mihalis)* is tops for inexpensive home-made desserts and warm *píttes* plus morning coffees. The only serious taverna up in **Hóra** is *Barbarossa* (all year) near the *dhimarhío*, popular for its pleasant interior, desserts and dishes of the day (though the salads are a disappointment).

Except for the *Yialos* music café near *Akroyiali*, most **nightlife** happens up in Hóra, where the esplanade between the windmills and the base of the *kástro* forms one solid café-bar. Of these, favourites are unsigned *Tou Nikola* (*Iy Myli*) on a corner, with the island's characters in residence, and music bar *Notos* tucked in by the triple chapel, with desserts as well. These are joined in season by *Kastro*, good for conversation-level music.

Southwestern Astypálea

A twenty-minute walk (or short bus journey) from Hóra brings you to **LIVÁDHIA**, a fertile valley draining to a popular, serviceable **beach** with a collection of restaurants and cafés immediately behind. You can rent a **studio** just inland – for example at *Studios O Manganas* (ⓣ22430 61468; ❹), on the frontage road (they've even tiny washing machines in the units), or *Venetos Studios* (ⓣ22430 61490 or 694 43 01 381; May–Sept; ❸), at the base of the westerly hillside, comprising several buildings scattered in a pleasant orchard. Better than either, however, is the 2007-built *Kalderimi* complex on the road bend just above (ⓣ22430 59843; ❼), a cluster of eleven impeccably appointed mock-trad air-conditioned cottages with CD players, Internet and satellite TV. Among the half-dozen **tavernas**, *To Yerani* (until early Oct) is renowned for its excellent *mayireftá*; they also offer quality rooms, with modern furnishings and marble floors (ⓣ22430 61484; ❸).

If the busy beach here doesn't suit, continue southwest fifteen minutes on foot to three small fine-pebble coves at **Tzanáki**, packed with naturists in midsummer. The third large bay beyond Livádhia, more usually reached by motorbike, is **Áyios Konstandínos**, a partly shaded, sand-and-gravel cove with a good seasonal taverna. Beyond, the lonely beaches of Vátses and **Kaminákia** are visited by seasonal excursion boats from Péra Yialós. By land, Vátses has the easier dirt road in, some 25 minutes by scooter from Livádhia; it's one of the sandier island beaches, with a basic *kantína*, but often windy. The track to Kaminákia, 8.5km from Livádhia, is rough and steep for the final 2km – best to go in a jeep – but the sheltered, clean and scenic cove, Astypálea's best, repays the effort. A good **taverna** (*Linda*, July–Sept) oversees a handful of sunbeds and offers honest, rustic fresh fish, salads and dishes of the day.

Northeastern Astypálea

Northeast of the harbour are the three coves known as **Próto** (First), **Dhéftero** (Second) and **Títo** (Third) **Marmári**. The first is home to the power plant and boatyards; the next hosts the campsite, while the third, relatively attractive, also marks the start of the path east to the decent but unfortunately named **Mamoúni** ("bug" or "critter" in Greek) coves. Beyond Títo Marmári, the main beach at **Stenó** ("narrow", after the isthmus here), with sandy shore and shallows, a few tamarisks and a seasonal *kantína*, is the best.

ANÁLIPSI, widely known as **Maltezána** after medieval Maltese pirates, is 9km from Péra Yialós. Although the second-largest settlement on Astypálea, there's surprisingly little for visitors save a narrow, exposed, packed-sand beach (there are better ones east of the main bay at **Skhinóndas**, and west at **Plákes**) and a nice view south to islets. Despite this, blocks of **rooms/studios** (July–Aug) sprout in ranks well back from the sea, spurred by the proximity of the airport. A more reliable exception, the island's largest **hotel**, is the 48-unit *Maltezana Beach* (ⓣ22430 61558, ⓦwww.maltezanabeach.gr; Easter to mid-Sept; ❸–❺), with large, well-appointed bungalow-rooms, pool and on-site restaurant. Among several **tavernas** here, the most consistently open (Feb–Christmas) is *Analipsi* (aka *Ilias and Irini's*) by the jetty, which doubles as the fishermen's *kafenío*. The food – fried squid, bean soup – is simple but wholesome; confirm prices and portion size of the often frozen seafood. Behind calamus reeds and eucalyptus near the fishing jetty lie well-preserved mosaic floors at the Byzantine **Tallarás baths**, though sadly they're now under a layer of protective gravel (photos in Skála's museum); view exposed ones at the **Karéklis basilica** 1km east (geometric and animal designs) or at fifth-century **Ayía Varvára** basilica, an equal distance north (abstract and vegetal motifs) – easiest access is past the last house and windmill.

Kálymnos

Most of **Kálymnos'** 17,000-strong population lives in or around the large port of **Póthia**, whose historical prosperity was based on its **sponge industry**. Unfortunately, almost all of the eastern Mediterranean's sponges were devastated by a mysterious disease in 1986, and only a few boats of the thirty-strong fleet are still in use. Most of the sponges processed and sold in the warehouses behind the harbour are imported from Asia and the Caribbean. You will see numbers of elderly (and middle-aged) men with severe mobility problems, stark evidence of the havoc wrought in their youth by nitrogen embolism (the "bends") before divers understood its crippling effects.

In response to the sponge blight (and a repeat outbreak in 1999), the island established a **tourist industry** – confined to one series of beach resorts – and also adapted most sponge boats for deep-sea fishing. But **mass tourism** proved as fickle as sponges, and has essentially **collapsed** since the millennium. The then-unfinished airport near Árgos village (not built for jets anyway), and thus the ongoing need for tedious transfers from Kós, was the main excuse for a mass pull-out by most package companies. Subsequently, the island re-invented itself as an off-season **hiking** and **rock-climbing** destination – it has some of the best cliffs in Greece, and a respectable surviving path network – and began promoting **scuba-diving** and sea-kayaking through a late-summer festival.

Kálymnos essentially consists of two cultivated, inhabited valleys sandwiched between three limestone ridges, harsh in the full glare of noon but magically tinted towards dusk. The climate is purported to be drier and healthier than that of neighbouring Kós or Léros, since the quick-draining limestone strata, riddled with many caves, doesn't retain as much moisture. This rock does, however, admit seawater, which has tainted Póthia's wells; drinking **water** must be trucked in from the Vathýs valley, and there are also potable springs at Kamári, Potamí district of Póthia and Hóra.

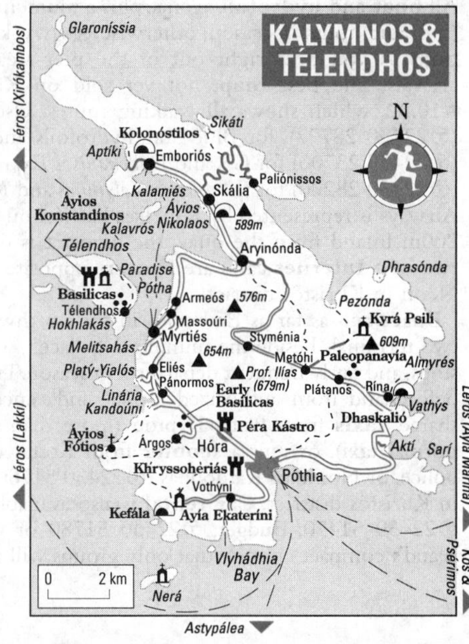

Póthia

PÓTHIA, without being conventionally picturesque, is colourful and authentically Greek, its houses marching up the valley inland or arrayed in tiers along the hillsides framing it. With nearly 16,000 inhabitants, it has overtaken Kós Town as the second-largest Dodecanesian municipality after Ródhos Town, and your first impression may be of phenomenal noise engendered by motorbike traffic and the cranked-up sound systems of the half-dozen waterfront cafés. Things get even louder on **Easter Sunday** evening, when teams stationed on the heights engage in an organized dynamite-throwing contest, with feasting and general merriment after the inevitable casualties are taken to hospital.

Perhaps the most rewarding way to explore Póthia is by wandering the **backstreets**, where elegant Neoclassical houses, painted the traditional pink or ochre, are surrounded by surprisingly large gardens, and craftsmen ply their trade in a genuine workaday bazaar. They particularly excel in iron-working, and all but the humblest dwellings in eastern Evangelístria district are adorned by splendidly ornate banisters, balcony railings and fanlights.

The best of two local museums is the **Municipal Nautical and Folklore Museum** (daily 10am–1pm; €1.50), on the seaward side of Khristós cathedral. A large photo shows Póthia in the 1880s, with no quay, jetty, roads or sumptuous mansions, and with most of the population still up in Hóra, while other images document sponge fishing and the Allied liberation of 1945. You can also see horribly primitive divers' breathing apparatus, and "cages" designed to keep propellers from cutting air lines, a constant danger. Eventually (nobody knows when), a new annexe to the soporific existing **archeological museum** in Evangelístria (Tues–Sun 9am–2pm) will open, featuring a dazzling array of Roman and Byzantine finds.

Information and transport

All **boat** and **hydrofoil** agents, plus a municipal **tourist information** booth (sporadic hours in season; otherwise Ⓦwww.kalymnos-isl.gr), line the waterfront as you bear right out of the pier-area gate, where **taxis** also await arrivals. The best **map**, not yet sold on Kálymnos, is Anavasi's 1:25,000 #10.32, which shows all walking routes. Useful **agencies** include Mangos (Ⓣ22430 28777), for Blue Star, hydrofoils and Agoudimos; Sofia Kouremeti (Ⓣ22430 23700) for GA and *Dodekanisos Express/Pride*; and Kalymna Yachting (Ⓣ22430 28200) for the *Nissos Kalymnos* and *Kalymnos Star/Dolphin*. Olympic Airways is represented by Kapellas, Patriárhou Maxímou 12 (Ⓣ22430 29265), 200m inland from the quay; the **airport** is 6km west by Árgos village. The two best **Internet** cafés are Heaven, opposite the yacht anchorage, and giant Neon in Khristós district.

Buses run as far as Emboriós in the northwest and Vathýs in the east, from two terminals beside the municipal "palace", with schedules posted near many stops, and fairly frequent departures in season. Tickets (€0.80–2) must be bought beforehand from authorized kiosks, and cancelled on board. Otherwise, use shared **taxis** from Platía Kýprou (more than KTEL buses, less costly than a normal taxi), or rent a **scooter** from Kostas (Ⓣ22430 50110) near the port police, or Nomikos Kardoulias (Ⓣ22430 51780), just back from the waterfront in Khristós disttrict. **Car rental** is also available on the quay (Spiros Kypraios, Ⓣ22430 51470; Budget, Ⓣ22430 51780 or Ⓣ697 28 34 628), though the island's compact enough that only groups will need one.

Accommodation

Accommodation is rarely a problem, with a high-season booking office on the quay; as on Kós, beware of *dhomátia* touts as you disembark, flogging substandard, unlicensed or remote premises. The town's most elegant, and quietest **hotel**, near the archeological museum, is garden-set ⚑ *Villa The-Melina* (Ⓣ22430 22682; all year; B&B; ❸), an early-twentieth-century mansion with high-ceilinged, bug-screened, wood-floored rooms, a modern annexe of studios and apartments (❸), plus breakfast patio and a large salt-water swimming pool. Less characterful alternatives include, on Áyios Nikólaos's southwest quay, *Arhondiko* (Ⓣ22430 24051; all year; ❷), another refurbished mansion whose plain rooms have TV and fridge, or – high up in Amoudhára district west of the harbour – the well-kept *Hotel Panorama* (Ⓣ22430 22917, Ⓦwww.panorama.kalymnos-hotels.com; April–Oct; ❸), with balconied rooms with a view and a pleasant breakfast salon.

Eating and drinking

The most obvious place to eat is the line of seafood **tavernas** northeast along the waterfront past the Italian-built municipal "palace", but most are much of a muchness. An exception is friendly, family-run *To Steki ton Navtikon*, with good fresh and cured seafood. Much the best-value meals, however, are scoffed at ⚑ *Kafenes*, on Khristós esplanade opposite the county "palace", always packed thanks to generous, tasty salads, seafood, local cheese and bulk wine. *Taverna Pandelis*, tucked inconspicuously into a cul-de-sac behind the waterfront *Olympic Hotel*, is tops for meat grills and *mezédhes*, with wild scaly fish and shellfish off-menu – ask for the daily catch. Wood-fired pizzas are served at *Pizza Porto* and *Pizza Imia* at mid-quay. *Dhodhoni*, in "restaurant row", is the ice cream outlet; Greek sweetmeat fans should make for the traditional *Zaharoplastio O Mihalaras* two steps away, or their more modern annexe near the ferry jetty. **Nightlife**, except for *Blue Note* bar near *Pandelis*, is resolutely quayside café/*frappádhika*-based; for more ambitious seasonal venues outside town, watch for posters. Adjacent summer (Oasis) and winter (Splendid) **cinemas** function behind the traditional, column-facaded café-tearoom *Ai Musai*, on the front.

Medieval monuments around Póthia

In the suburb of Mýli, 1.2km northwest of Póthia, stands the Knights' **Kástro Khryssoheriás** (unrestricted access), whose whitewashed battlements offer wonderful views southeast over town to Kós and north towards Hóra and Péra Kástro. The former Kalymnian capital of **HÓRA** (aka Horió), 1.5km further along the main road, is still a large, busy village, guarding a critical pass in local geography. Steep steps lead up from its eastern edge to the nocturnally illuminated Byzantine citadel-town of **Péra Kástro** (Mon–Fri 9am–1pm; free), appropriated by the Knights of St John and inhabited until the late 1700s. Inside the massive gate and perimeter walls you'll find nine **medieval chapels**, several – Áyios Nikólaos, Ayía Ánna, Timíou Stavroú and Metamórfosis – containing fifteenth-to-sixteenth-century fresco fragments.

Some 200m beyond the turning for Árgos en route to the northwest coast, you can visit two early Byzantine **basilicas** that are among the biggest, and easiest to find, of a vast number on Kálymnos. The more impressive of the two, accessed by steps on the left just as the highway begins to descend, is **Khristós tís Ierousalím**, probably dating from the late fourth century, with a fully preserved apse.

West coast resorts: Brostá

From the basilicas, the main road leads to the half-dozen consecutive **beach resorts** collectively referred to as "Brostá" by islanders. **KANDOÚNI**, some 200m of brown, hard-packed sand favoured by the locals, is the shore annexe of the agricultural villages of **Pánormos** and **Eliés**. **Accommodation** includes the *Kalydna Island Hotel* (Ⓣ22430 47880, Ⓦwww.kalydnaislandhotel.gr; ④), and the **nightlife** (try *Café del Mar* and *Domus* on the beach) is fairly active, but most will prefer **LINÁRIA**, the north end of the same bay. A smaller cove set apart from Kandoúni proper by the Patélla outcrop, this has better sand, and lodging at *Skopellos Studios* (Ⓣ22430 47155; ③), below the hillside church. Of two shoreline full-service **tavernas** here, seafood-strong *Mamouzelos* (alias *Yiorgos*; supper only) offers big portions of excellent food let down by high prices and rude service.

The next beach north, **PLATÝ-YIALÓS**, again a bit shorter than Kandoúni, is arguably Kálymnos's best: cleaner than its neighbours, more secluded, and placed scenically at the base of a cliff, opposite Ayía Kyriakí islet. A lone **taverna** (*Kyma/Wave*) at road's end purveys simple, inexpensive lunches and sunset drinks (it closes shortly after). **Staying** locally, the blue-and-white *Mousselis Studios* (Ⓣ22430 48307, Ⓔmousellis_studios@yahoo.gr; ③), just up the road from the beach, accommodate two to six people, with half board available.

The main road climbs from Pánormos up to Kamári pass, before descending in zigzags to seaside **MYRTIÉS**, 8km from Póthia. Together with **MASSOÚRI** (1km north) and **ARMEÓS** (2km north and terminus for most buses), Myrtiés was hardest hit by the Kalymnian tourism slump, so vacant and for-sale premises abound. Thriving exceptions include *Akroyiali* (Ⓣ22430 47521 or 693 89 13 210; ③), beachside apartments in Massoúri sleeping two adults and two kids which require advance booking; *Bar Babis* on the square in Myrtiés, an Anglophile institution; jointly operated Avis/Alfa (Ⓣ22430 47430, Ⓦwww.kalymnosrent.com) **renting cars and bikes** and a daily early-afternoon *kaïki* from Myrtiés to Xirókambos on Léros. The best surviving **taverna**, in Armeós, is the friendly if pricey meat specialist *Tsopanakos* (all year), serving fresh meat and cheese dishes from island-grazed goats. Armeós is also the local mecca for **rock-climbers**, with many of the most popular cliffs overhead and a small equipment shop (Climber's Nest) catering to them. There's also some Greek-pitched **nightlife**, with live music at *Kastelli Club*.

The **beach** at Myrtiés is narrow, pebbly and cramped by development, though it does improve as you approach Massoúri, where *Stavedo Beach Bar* (Ⓦwww.stavedo.com) offers a range of **water sports**. The closest all-sand beach to Myrtiés lies 500m south, at **MELITSÁHAS** cove, where one of three **tavernas**, *Iy Dhrossia* (aka *O Andonis*; all year), is noted for seafood and scaly fish. On-spec **accommodation** is easy to find; try spacious *Maria's Studios* (Ⓣ22430 48135 or 22430 28528; ②) on the hillside, or attractively tiered *Vassilis Studios* opposite (Ⓣ22430 47751; ③). Possibly this coast's most appealing feature is its setting, opposite evocatively shaped Télendhos islet (see opposite), which frames some of the most dramatic **sunsets** in Greece.

Some 5km beyond Massoúri, **ARYINÓNDA** has a clean pebble beach, two **tavernas** (*Katerina* has **rooms**; Ⓣ22430 40036; ②) and sunbeds. It's also the trailhead for the spectacular two-and-a-half-hour traverse **walk** over two gentle passes to Metóhi in the Vathýs valley. From the bus stop and paved car-park area and cistern-spring, head southeast on a path between rock walls which soon climbs the south flank of the ravine here, sporadically marked by paint dots; the route is shown correctly on the Anavasi map. Walkers need a sun hat, stout boots and a litre or two of water, as the next source is in Plátanos hamlet (opposite a small, good

taverna), beyond Metóhi; **drivers** can use the road, all but the 4.2km up from Aryinónda now paved, to complete a 42-kilometre loop around Kálymnos.

The end of the bus line, **EMBORIÓS**, 20km from the port, offers a gravel-and-sand beach, **accommodation** and several **tavernas**, including *Harry's Paradise*, with garden apartments (Ⓣ22430 40061; air conditioning; ❸). If the twice-daily **bus** service fails you, there is a **shuttle boat** back to Myrtiés at 4pm (leaving the latter at 10am). There are also better, if unamenitied **beaches** between here and Skália, such as **Kalamiés** (more attractive than Emboriós, with a taverna) and **Áyios Nikólaos**.

Télendhos

The trip across the straits to the striking islet of **TÉLENDHOS** is arguably the best reason to come to Myrtiés; little boat-buses shuttle to and fro regularly (every 30min each direction 8am–midnight; €1.50), occasionally dodging numerous sea-kayaks. According to local legend, Télendhos is a petrified princess, gazing out to sea in the wake of her ill-starred affair with the prince of Kastélli in Armeós; the woman's-head profile is most evident at dusk. The hardly less pedestrian geological explanation has the islet sundered from Kálymnos by a cataclysmic earthquake in 554 AD; traces of a submerged town are said to lie at the bottom of the straits.

Home to about fifteen permanent inhabitants, Télendhos is car-free and blissfully tranquil, even more so since certain package operators gave up allotments here. For cultural edification you'll find the ruined thirteenth-century **monastery of Áyios Vassílios** and an enormous **basilica of Ayía Triádha** up on the ridge, part way along the flagstoned, ten-minute path to **Hokhlakás** pebble **beach**, small but very scenic, with sunbeds for rent and a **restaurant**, *Chochlaka Sunset*, by Ayía Triádha. **Pótha** and nudist "**Paradise**" on the other side of the islet are preferred by some: sandy and with calm water, but no afternoon sun.

There are nine places to eat and a roughly equal number of **places to stay**, many linked to the tavernas. Best bets include *Pension Studios Rita* (Ⓣ22430 47914, Ⓕ22430 47927; April to late Oct), its rooms (❶) and renovated-house studios (❷) managed by *Rita's Café*; the simple en-suite rooms above *Zorba's* (Ⓣ22430 48660; ❶); the high-standard *Rinio Studios* (Ⓣ22430 23851; ❷), set a bit inland; or, north beyond Áyios Vassílios, Greek-Australian-run *On the Rocks* (Ⓣ22430 48260, Ⓦwww.otr.telendos.com; April–Nov; ❸), three superbly appointed rooms and a more remote studio with double glazing, satellite TV, bug screens, fridges and Internet, as well as kayaks on the beach out front. It's fairly easy to get a room at the large, friendly *Hotel Porto Potha* (Ⓣ22430 47321, Ⓦwww.telendoshotel.gr; April to late Oct; ❸), at the edge of things but with a large pool, "private" beach, eight self-catering studios. Recommended **tavernas** include *Barba Stathis* (aka *Tassia's*), en route to Hokhlakás, with a few hot dishes each day; *Zorba's*, doing excellent goat or fresh squid; *Plaka*, next to *On the Rocks*, good for inexpensive meat; and the slightly pricey, full-service taverna at *On the Rocks* itself, with lovely home-made desserts, and a bar that's the heart of local **nightlife**. At one corner of the premises the chapel of Áyios Harálambos occupies a former Byzantine bathhouse; energetic types can walk just under an hour on a waymarked path up to the chapel of **Áyios Konstandínos** inside Byzantine fortifications, with fine views.

Vathýs and around

The first 4km east from Póthia seem vastly unpromising (power plant, rubbish tip, gasworks, cement quarries, fish farms), until you round a bend and the ten-kilometre ride ends dramatically at **VATHÝS**, a long, fertile valley whose orange and tangerine groves provide a startling contrast to the mineral greys and ochres higher up on Kálymnos. At the fjord port of **RÍNA**, some of the five **tavernas** are overpriced, geared toward the yachtie crowd; best are *The Harbors*, the first place on the right at road's end, with shambolic service but good fish, and the more upmarket but good-value *To Limanaki tou Vathy* near the lido, with tasty octopus and eggplant dishes.

The steep-sided inlet is beachless; the closest pebble-coves reachable overland are **Aktí**, 3km back towards Póthia, a functional pebble strand with sunbeds and a snack-bar; secluded **Mikrés Almyrés**, forty minutes away by rough path as traced on the Anávasi map (where the cove is unlabelled); and **Pezónda**, a little further north, reached by steep track (and then a 45-minute walk northwest) starting from Metóhi hamlet. At track's end another path heads east in fifteen minutes to the amazingly set little **monastery of Kyrá Psilí**. Most of Vathýs' historic **Byzantine churches** are locked; one exception, north of the road before Plátanos, is ruined **Paleopanayía**, with vivid sixth-century floor mosaics.

It's possible to **walk** back to Póthia along the old direct *kalderími* that existed before the coastal highway – a two-hour jaunt beginning in Plátanos hamlet. Without the Anavasi map, the route is tricky to find in this direction, so many people start in Póthia at the church of Ayía Triádha behind the *Villa The-Melina* hotel – look for red paint splodges at the start. In theory – and in possession of the Anavasi map – one can do a **day-long circuit**, returning from Áyios Nikólaos chapel west of Metóhi, via Profítis Ilías and a gorge, to Horío.

The southwest

As you climb southwest out of Póthia towards Áyios Sávvas monastery, the most worthwhile halt is the **Folklore Museum-Traditional House of Kalymnos** (daily 9am–9pm; €1.50), a treasure trove of old-time furnishings and costumes. Some 6km southwest of Póthia, small **Vlyhádhia** bay is reached via the nondescript village of Vothýni. The sand-and-pebble **beach** here isn't really worth a trip, since the bay is apt to be stagnant and reliable amenities are limited to a single beachside **snack bar** (*Paradise*). A local diver has assembled an impressive **Museum of Submarine Finds** (Mon–Sat 9am–7pm, Sun 10am–2pm; free), which besides sponges and shells displays a reconstructed ancient wreck with amphorae and World War II debris. Most of the Kalymnian coast is now legal for **scuba diving**; the most reputable local dive operator, Pegasus Diving Club (ⓣ694 41 80 746, ⓦwww.kalymnosdiving.com), works out of Póthia.

From Vothýni a different road leads west past Ayía Ekateríni convent to within a few minutes' trail walk of the **Kefála cave** (daily 9am–dusk), the most impressive of half a dozen caverns around the island. The cavern was inhabited in pre-history, and later served as a sanctuary of Zeus (fancifully identified with an imposing stalagmite in the biggest of six vividly coloured chambers).

Léros

Léros is so indented with deep, sheltered anchorages that between 1928 and 1948 it harboured, in turn, much of the Italian, German and British Mediterranean fleets. Unfortunately, these magnificent bays seem to absorb rather than reflect light, and the island's **fertility** – with orchards and vegetable gardens a-plenty – can make Léros seem scruffy compared to the crisp lines of its more barren neighbours. Such characteristics, plus a lack of spectacular beaches, meant that until the late 1980s just a few hundred Italians who grew up on Léros, and not many more Greeks, visited each summer. Since then the tourist profile has broadened to include Scandanavians and Brits, and the season lengthened, but numbers have levelled off as the present airport can't accommodate jets.

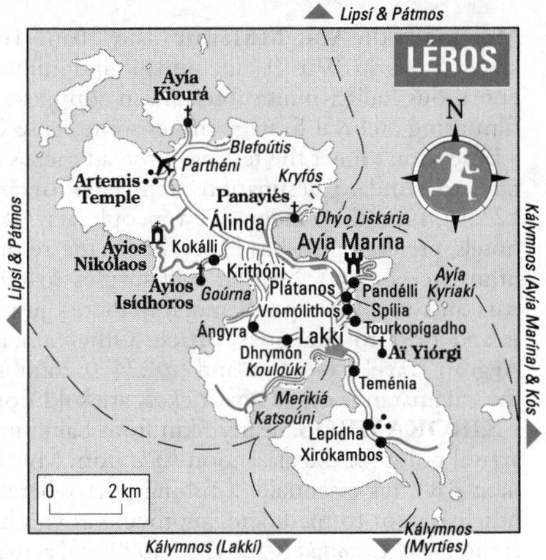

For decades, Léros relied not on mass tourism but on prisons and sanatoria, built in former Italian military constructions. During the civil war and the later junta, leftists were confined to a notorious **detention centre** at Parthéni, and from 1948 on several **hospitals** essentially warehoused many of Greece's intractable psychiatric cases and mentally handicapped children. In 1989, a major scandal erupted concerning the asylums, with EU funds found to have been embezzled, and inmates kept in degrading conditions. Most wards were eventually closed, with patients dispersed to sheltered housing and seven hundred carers (who can't be made redundant) left idle. Some of the slack was taken up by tourism, some by the opening of a major nursing college.

More obvious today is the legacy of the **Battle of Léros** on November 12–16, 1943, when German forces displaced a Commonwealth division that had occupied the island following the Italian capitulation. Bomb nose-cones and shell casings turn up as gaily painted garden ornaments in the courtyards of churches and tavernas, or do duty as gateposts. Each year for three days following September 26, memorial services and a naval festival commemorate the sinking of the Greek battleship *Queen Olga* and the British *Intrepid* during German air-raids in the weeks prior to their November landing.

Unusually for a small island, Léros has abundant ground **water**, channelled into several cisterns (only the two on the Plátanos upper bypass are potable). These, plus damp ground staked with avenues of Italian-planted eucalyptus, make for horrendously active mosquitoes.

Léros has a reasonably reliable **bus** service, plus several **motor-** and **mountain-bike** rental outlets; Motoland (Pandélli, ⓣ22470 24103; Álinda, ⓣ22470 24584) also offers **cars**. If you rent a **scooter**, take care – Lerian roads are particularly narrow, potholed and gravel-strewn, and the low-slung, fat-tyred bikes on offer don't cope well.

Lakkí and Xirókambos

All large **ferries**, the *Nissos Kalymnos* and the *Dodekanisos Pride* catamaran arrive at **LAKKÍ** port, built in 1935–38 as a model town to house 7500 civilian dependants of an adjacent Italian naval base. Boulevards, generous even for today's traffic, are lined with Rationalist edifices, including the round-fronted cinema, the church, the primary school, a shopping centre and the derelict *Leros Palace Hotel*. A restoration programme should see most of these marvellous buildings refurbished by 2009. The only other attraction, 1500m west at

Merikiá, is the **War Museum** (daily 10am–1pm; €3), a huge quantity of barely labelled World War II documents and military hardware crammed into an enormous Italian-built subterranean complex; at the end a somewhat histrionic film using archival footage makes some sense of it all.

Buses don't meet the ferries – instead there's a **taxi squadron** that charges set fares to standard destinations; rent **cars or bikes** from Koumoulis (Ⓣ22470 22330), near the cinema. Few people stay at any of Lakkí's handful of drab hotels, preferring to head straight for the resorts of Pandélli, Álinda or Vromólithos (see below). Neither will surplus-to-requirements pizza parlours, snack bars and *yirádhika* appeal much – there's just one proper **taverna**, *To Petrino*, inland next to the **post office**. Other amenities include three **ATMs**, and Aegean Travel a block inland (Ⓣ22470 26000), agent for Blue Star Ferries and the catamaran – other boat tickets are sold from a booth on the jetty.

XIRÓKAMBOS, nearly 5km from Lakkí in the far south of the island, is the arrival point for the afternoon *kaïki* from Myrtiés on Kálymnos (returns 7.30am next day). It's essentially a fishing port where folk also happen to swim – the beach is poor to mediocre, improving as you head west. Top **accommodation** is the *Hotel Efstathia* (Ⓣ22470 24099; ❸), actually studio apartments with huge, well-furnished doubles (though baths are basic) as well as family four-plexes, plus a large pool. *To Aloni* is the best of three **tavernas** along the shore road. The island's **campsite** (Ⓣ22470 23372; mid-May to early Oct), with an in-house **scuba-diving** centre (Ⓣ694 42 38 490; Ⓦwww.lerosdiving.com), occupies an olive grove at the village of **LEPÍDHA**, 750m back up the road to Lakkí. Just north of the campsite, an access drive (signposted "Ancient Fort") leads up to a tiny acropolis with stretches of ancient masonry behind the modern summit chapel.

Pandélli and Vromólithos

Just under 3km north of Lakkí, Pandélli and Vromólithos together form an attractive and scenic resort. **PANDÉLLI** is a working port, the cement jetty benefiting local fishermen rather than yachts, which in high season must anchor offshore. A small but reef-free, pea-gravel **beach** is complemented by a relative abundance of non-package **accommodation**, such as *Pension Happiness* (Ⓣ22470 23498; ❷), where the road down from Plátanos meets the sea. For a higher standard, try Australian-Greek-run *Niki Studios* (Ⓣ22470 25600; ❸) at the base of the road up to the castle – double units and quad apartments (both a/c, and with partial sea views) – or, further up the castle road, the ✱ *Windmills/Anemomyli* (Ⓣ22470 25549; May–Oct; ❹), two galleried windmill apartments and a long cottage, all with stone floors and great views from rear terraces. Up on the ridge dividing Pandélli from Vromólithos in **Spília** district, the *Hotel Rodon* (Ⓣ22470 23524, Ⓦwww.leros.travel; ❸) comprises studios and larger apartments, with knock-out views. On summer nights there may be a faint strain of **music** from *Café del Mar*, perched on a rock terrace below; the other long-standing local **bar** is the civilized, English-Danish-run *Savana*, at the opposite end of Pandélli, with excellent music (you can request your favourites). It stands beyond a row of decidedly patchy waterfront **tavernas**, the best of which are *Psaropoula* (all year), with good, non-farmed fish and *mayireftá*, and *Tou Mihali*, a corner *kafenío* where expertly fried *gópes* or *sargoudháki*, mixed salads and good wine are scoffed by a largely local crowd. Up in Spília, next to the *Hotel Rodon*, ✱ *Mezedhopolio O Dimitris O Karaflas* (all year) is one of the best-sited ouzerís on the island, and scores high for its ample portions of delicacies such as chunky local sausages, onion rings and *floyéres*, or dairy-based dips like *galotýri and batíris*.

VROMÓLITHOS has the best easily accessible **beach** on the island, car-free and hemmed in by oak-studded hills. The shore is gravel and coarse sand, and the sea is clean, but you have to cross a rock pavement at most points before reaching deeper water; there's a more secluded, sandier cove southeast towards **Tourkopígadho**, and an even better duo at the end of the sideroad to Aï Yiórgi. Two **tavernas** behind Vromólithos beach trade more on their location than their cuisine but **accommodation** here is better than at Pandélli. Prime choices are *Tony's Beach*, spacious studio units set in extensive waterside grounds (Ⓣ22470 24742, Ⓦwww.tonysbeachstudios.gr; June–Sept; ❹), and the stone-floored *Glaros*, just inland (Ⓣ22470 24358, Ⓕ22470 23683; May–Oct; ❹).

Plátanos and Ayía Marína

The Neoclassical and vernacular houses of **PLÁTANOS**, 1km west of Pandélli, are draped gracefully along a saddle between two heights, one of them crowned by the inevitable Knights' castle or **Kástro** (daily 8.30am–12.30pm, also May–Oct Wed, Sat & Sun 3.30–6.30pm). This is reached either by a zigzagging road peeling off the Pandélli-bound road, or via a stair-path from the central square; the views from the top of the caper-festooned battlements, recently restored, are especially dramatic at sunset. The medieval church of **Panayía tou Kástrou** inside the gate houses a small ecclesiastical museum, though its carved *témblon* and naïve oratory are more remarkable than the sparse exhibits. The **archeological museum** (Tues–Sun 8am–2.30pm; free), down the road to Ayía Marína, is more interesting, compensating for a dearth of artefacts with a comprehensible gallop through Lerian history. Plátanos is not really a place to stay or eat, although it's well sown with amenities, including a **post office** down the road towards Ayía Marína and a few **ATMs**. A single **bus** (schedule posted at stop opposite the island's main **taxi** rank) runs several times daily between Parthéni and Xirókambos.

Plátanos merges seamlessly with **AYÍA MARÍNA**, 1km north on the shore of a fine bay, still graced by a small, Italian-built public market building and customs house. Travelling to Léros on an excursion boat from Lipsí, the *Dodekanisos Express*, or a hydrofoil, this will be your port of entry – unless high winds force a diversion to Lakkí. At the western edge of things the superior ✱ *Ouzeri (Nero-) Mylos*, out by the wave-lapped windmill, has the most romantic setting on the island (March–Nov; reservations mandatory July–Aug; Ⓣ22470 24894), the best music, and some of the tastiest **food**. Specialities include expertly homemade *garidhopílafo* (shrimp-rice), grilled *mastéllo* cheese, seasonal fresh fish, and *kolokythokeftédhes* (courgette patties). Lively (for Léros) **nightlife** is provided by several bars between the police station and the customs house, such as ultra-sleek *Thalassa*; *Enallaktiko*, with a few **Internet** terminals; and *Glaros* which also does snacks. Kastis Travel nearby (Ⓣ22470 22140) handles all ticket sales for hydrofoils and the *Dodekanisos Express*, and there are two **ATMs**.

Álinda and Krithóni

ÁLINDA, 3km northwest of Ayía Marína, ranks as the longest-established resort on Léros, with development just across the road from a long, narrow strip of pea-gravel beach. It's also the first area to open in spring, and the last to shut in autumn. Worthwhile **accommodation** not dominated by tour-company allotments includes, just back from mid-beach, *Hotel Alinda* (*Xenonas Mavrakis*; Ⓣ22470 23266, Ⓦwww.alindahotel.gr; ❸), with well-kept air-conditioned rooms with fridges plus the very good *Taverna Alinda* and sunken Byzantine mosaic out front, and the marvellously atmospheric ✱ *Archontiko Angelou* well inland

(Ⓣ22470 22749, Ⓦwww.hotel-angelou-leros.com; ❻), with Victorian bath fittings, beamed ceilings and antique furnishings. The other reliable beachfront **restaurant** is somewhat pricey *Giusi e Marcello* (supper only), with pasta, meat and Italian wines. At **KRITHÓNI**, 1.5km south, luxury is available at the island's top accommodation: *Crithoni's Paradise* (Ⓣ22470 25120, Ⓦwww.crithonisparadise-hotel.com; all year; ❻–❽), a low-rise complex whose vast common areas include a large pool, gym, sauna and Wi-Fi corner; rooms and baths are fair-sized.

The **Allied War Graves Cemetery**, mostly containing casualties of the November 1943 battle, occupies a walled enclosure at the south end of the beach; immaculately maintained, it serves as a moving counterpoint to beachside life outside. The other principal sight at Álinda is the **Historical and Ethnographic Museum** (May–Sept Tues–Sun 9am–1pm & 6–8pm; €3) housed in the castle-like mansion of Paris Bellenis (1871–1957). Most of the top floor is devoted to the Battle of Léros: relics from the sunken *Queen Olga*, a wheel from a Junkers bomber, a stove made from a bomb casing. There's also a grisly mocked-up clinic (mostly gynaecological tools), assorted rural implements, costumes and antiques. One room is devoted to Communist artist Kyriakos Tsakiris (1915–98), interned here by the junta, with works executed on stones, shells and wood, plus pen-and-ink studies for the Ayía Kiourá frescoes (see below) and daily life at Parthéni camp.

Other **beaches** near Álinda include **Dhýo Liskária**, a series of gravel coves at the far northeast of the bay (snack-bar/café), and **Goúrna**, the turning for which lies 1km or so off the trans-island road. The latter, Léros's longest sandy beach, is hard-packed and gently shelving, if wind-buffeted; a few sunbeds are provided by the hospitable *Gourna* **taverna**, which has grills, wild fish and good *mezédhes*.

The far north

Seven kilometres from Álinda along the main route north, a side-track leads left to the purported **Temple of Artemis**, on a slight rise west of the airport runway. In ancient times, Léros was sacred to the goddess, and the temple here was supposedly inhabited by guinea fowl – the grief-stricken sisters of Meleager, metamorphosed thus by Artemis following their brother's death. All that remains now are some jumbled, knee-high walls, almost certainly (as signposted) an ancient fortress, but the view is superb.

The tiny **airport** terminal is no place to be stuck a minute longer than necessary; if your midday flight to Astypálea or Rhodes is delayed, the only diversion lies across the road at overpriced *Taverna To Arhondiko* – eat elsewhere beforehand and just have a coffee here.

The onward route skims the shores of sumpy, reed-fringed **Parthéni Bay**, with its yacht dry-dock and dreary, Italian-built army base (the 1946–51 and 1967–74 political prison). The camp, however, left one outstanding cultural legacy: the chapel of **Ayía Kiourá** (always open), reached by a one-kilometre marked access road. During the junta era, Kyriakos Tsakiris and two other prisoners decorated this otherwise unremarkable church with striking murals – squarely in the tradition of Diego Rivera's 1930s Leftist art – rather than conventional frescoes. The Orthodox Church has always abhorred these images – a local monk obliterated several in the 1980s – but Ayía Kiourá is now a protected monument. The paved road ends 11km from Álinda at **Blefoútis** and its huge, almost landlocked bay. The small **beach** (the rough Lerian norm) has tamarisks to shelter under and an adequate **taverna**, *Iy Thea Artemi*.

Wild Greece

Read the holiday brochures and you might think Greece is all sunbed-packed beaches, luxury hotels and watersports. However, venture inland and the country reveals extraordinary wilderness landscapes ranging from cloud-grazing craggy peaks to bird-filled coastal wetlands. These wilderness areas are some of Europe's most dramatic and act as home to a range of wildlife – including populations of large carnivores such as bears and wolves that have survived despite centuries of persecution.

Samariá Gorge, Crete ▲

Wild flowers, Lésvos ▼

Mountains and gorges

Today, at the start of the twenty-first century, Greece's **mountain peaks** are still resolutely remote; the rocky slopes, though often slashed and cicatrized by dirt roads, conceal places from which even an all-terrain vehicle would not return. The **White Mountains** above Samariá and the **North Píndhos** of Víkos are genuine wildernesses; the first a waterless lunar desert of grey and white rocks over which lammergeier vultures fly, the latter a mixture of densely wooded valleys (home to many of Greece's largest mammals, as well golden jackals), abrupt escarpments, alpine meadows and scree-covered peaks. Different as they are, snow can lie on the high ground in both regions until well into July.

At the base of these mountains, huge **gorges** cut the landscape formed by the native karst limestone and frequent earthquake activity. Crete's famous **Samariá Gorge** (see p.647) is a stark geological masterclass and at 18km, one of Europe's longest ravines. The cliffs, partly due to their inaccessibility to grazing animals, are home to a number of **rare plants**, unique to Crete: perfectly adapted to this precarious habitat of severe drought and extreme temperatures, but unable to survive away from it. In the northeast of

There are a number of categories of wildlife and habitat reserves, with varying degrees of protection. While reserves often have restrictions on the times and place of entry, much of Greece's wild country is still wide open to anyone prepared to make the effort to get there. Visitors to these areas – particularly the mountains – need to be well prepared, competent and self-sufficient, as these are lands without the benefit of search and rescue. However, for those willing to explore, the rewards are unlimited.

the mainland, the **Víkos Gorge** (see p.369) of the River Voïdhomátis is the equal of Samariá in majesty, but is softer and more verdant with native 25m horse chestnut trees, spectacular when in flower.

Marshes and wetlands

Belying the popular image – carefully nurtured by the tourist industry – of a Greece with perpetual summer-holiday temperatures and a lack of rain, the mainland does have significant amounts of freshwater, particularly in the north. The ancient **Prespá lakes** (see p.443) on the northwestern border constitute one of the most substantial bodies of water in the Balkans, with large breeding colonies of spoonbills and two species of pelican. Another significant northern wetland is the complex of brackish and freshwater lakes around **Vistonídha** and **Pórto Lágos** (see p.473), near Xánthi. Here there is a large population of flamingoes, as well as rarities such as the pygmy cormorant and the globally endangered white-headed duck. Emblematic of a healthy aquatic environment are the storks that nest on nearby churches and telegraph poles, bringing up their young on the plentiful supply of marsh frogs.

More accessibly, the Peloponnese's humid western coast also has some remarkable and stunningly beautiful **coastal wetlands**, including the salty, reed-fringed lagoons behind the fabulous perfect crescent of **Voïdokiliá beach** (see p.255), which shelter migrating cranes and flamingoes and a small resident population of chameleons. Further north, near Kalogriá, are the sandy woods and multi-coloured swamps of **Strofyliá** (see p.266) where the aptly named umbrella pines have their easternmost outpost, and rare birds such as collared pratincoles nest on muddy gravel.

▲ Storks nesting

▼ Piyés Aöóu reservoir, Píndhos mountains

▼ Voïdokiliá bay, the Peloponnese

Mount Athos, Halkidikí peninsula ▲

Woodlands near the Metéora, Thessaly ▼

Woodlands

Woodlands have, since ancient times, been under pressure as a source of fuel and building materials; however, in the northeastern corner of Greece, squeezed between the Bulgarian and Turkish borders, the **Dhadhiá Forest Reserve** (see p.478) shelters fine virgin forest. Reaching towards the Rodhópi mountains, this is some of the best woodland in the country, sheltering a remarkable variety of **raptors** – hawks, eagles and particularly vultures.

On the gentle slopes of **Mount Ménalo** (see p.240), in the dead centre of the Peloponnese, there are still – despite recent fire damage – forests of densely green and symmetrical fir trees. Usually visited during the skiing season when everything lies under deep snow and wildlife is dormant, this high altitude area is verdant in summer when the groves shelter a plethora of **woodland flowers** and orchids, interspersed with alpine meadows bright blue with larkspur.

Mountain of the Gods

At 2917m, **Mount Olympus** (see p.429) is the second-highest point in the entire Balkans, and its summit is the fabled home of the ancient Greek deities. It's almost unique in mainland Europe for its combination of height, isolation and proximity to the sea. The resultant ecosystem is home to over 1600 species of wild plant in just forty square kilometres – a similar number to that found in the entire United Kingdom; around 32 types of plant are confined to this mountain alone – the most famous being Jankaea, a small relative of the African violet. First climbed less than a century ago, Olympus's highest summits still demand respect from those who enter into their dominion; the mountain and its swiftly changing weather regularly claim the lives of hikers and climbers.

Pátmos

Arguably the most beautiful, certainly the best known of the smaller Dodecanese, **Pátmos** has a distinctive, palpable atmosphere. In a cave here St John the Divine (in Greek, *O Theológos* or "The Theologian") set down the New Testament's Book of Revelation and shaped the island's destiny. The **monastery** honouring him, founded in 1088, dominates Pátmos both physically – its fortified bulk towering over everything else – and, to a considerable extent, socially. While its monks no longer run the island unchallenged as they did for centuries, their influence has stopped it going the way of Rhodes or Kós – though Pátmos now has several nudist beaches, something unthinkable a decade or so ago.

Despite the island's firm presence on the cruise and yachting circuits, **day-trippers** still exceed overnighters, and Pátmos feels an altogether different place once the last cruise-ship or excursion-boat has left after sunset. While there are several music bars around the main port and up in **Hóra**, drunken rowdiness is all but unknown. Package clients never outnumber **independent visitors**, and are pretty much confined to Gríkou and a few larger hotels at Skála and Kámbos. Away from Skála, touristic development is subdued if not deliberately retarded, thanks to the absence of an airport. On outlying beaches, little has superficially changed since the 1980s, though "for sale" signs on every field or farmhouse, plus villa developments at coves closer to Skála, suggest such days are strictly numbered.

Skála and around

SKÁLA, where most of the island's three thousand people live, seems initially to contradict any solemn, otherworldly image of Pátmos; the commercial district with its gift boutiques is incongruously sophisticated for such a small town. During peak season, the quay and inland lanes throng by day with trippers souvenir-hunting or being shepherded onto coaches for the short ride up to the monastery; after dark there's considerable traffic in cliques of visitors on furlough from the huge, humming cruisers that weigh anchor around midnight. In winter (which here means by early October), Skála becomes a ghost town as most shops and restaurants close, their owners and staff returning to Rhodes or Athens.

Hóra, overhead up the mountain, would be a more attractive base, but has relatively little accommodation. And given time, 1820s-built Skála reveals more enticing corners

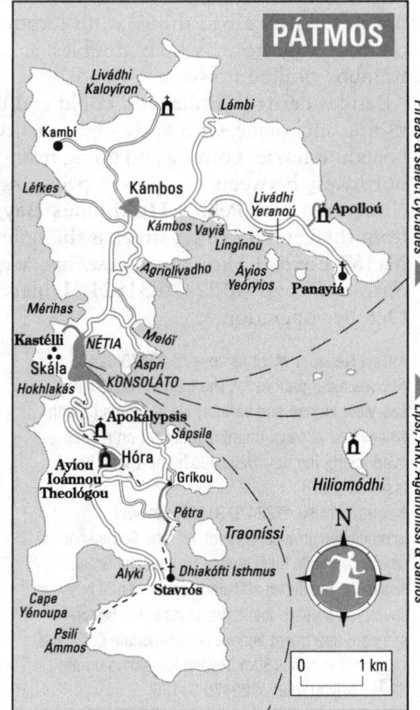

in the residential fringes to the east and west, where vernacular mansions hem in pedestrian lanes creeping up the hillsides. At the summit of the westerly rise, **Kastélli**, lie extensive foundations of the island's ancient acropolis.

Information and transport

Almost everything of note can be found within, or within sight of, the Italian-built municipal "palace": all arriving sea-craft anchor opposite, the **port police** occupy the east end, the **post office** one of its corners, the main **bus stop**, with a posted timetable, and **taxi rank** are in front, and three **ATMs** stand nearby. There's no **tourist office**, but ⓦwww.patmos-island.com is useful. **Scooter rental** outfits such as Billis (ⓣ22470 32218) and Aris (ⓣ22470 32542) are numerous, as are car-rental outlets (Aris; Stratas, ⓣ22470 32580); **drivers** must use **car parks** at Hókhlakas, behind the town beach or off the road to Hóra. **Excursion boats** to Psilí Ámmos and Arkí/Maráthi leave at about 10am (7.30–8am to Léros and Lipsí) from in front of Astoria Travel and Apollon Travel, the two **agencies** handling hydrofoil tickets; Apollon (ⓣ22470 31324) is also the central rep for Blue Star Ferries. GA Ferries (ⓣ22470 31217) and the *Nissos Kalymnos* (ⓣ22470 31314) have separate agencies on, or just off, the central waterfront square; several outlets sell tickets for the *Dodekanisos Express/Pride* catamarans. Best of three **Internet cafés is** Millennium, upstairs in a fine old building just behind the little park inland from the port.

Accommodation

Pátmos's vernacular architecture is quite distinctive, but you wouldn't know it from the island's bland, often overpriced **accommodation**. Touts meet all arriving sea-craft; their offerings tend to be a long walk distant and/or inland – not necessarily a bad thing, as no location is hopelessly remote, and anywhere on the waterfront, which doubles as the main road between Gríkou and Kámbos, will be noisy.

Besides **central Skála**, you could end up in **Konsoláto** district, east near the fishing anchorage, with fairly high-quality digs, but the worst noise from fishing boats and ferries coming and going from 1 to 4am. **Nétia**, the unglamorous area northwest between the power plant and Mérihas cove, is actually not a bad choice as a base. Pebbly **Hokhlakás Bay**, a ten-minute walk southwest starting from the central market street, is the quietest area, with wonderful sunset views. **Melóï cove**, 1.5km northwest, has a good beach and hosts the **campsite**, *Stefanos-Flowers* (ⓣ22470 31821). Unless otherwise stated, assume late-April to October operation.

Asteri Nétia, nr Mérihas cove ⓣ22470 32465, ⓦwww.asteripatmos.gr. The best in Nétia: large sea-view lounge and variably sized rooms (2 with wheelchair access) unimprovably set on a knoll overlooking the bay. Delicious home-made breakfasts. ❹ B&B

Australis Nétia ⓣ22470 31576, ⓦwww.patmosweb.gr/australishotel_en.htm. Somewhat spartan en-suite hotel owned by a helpful Greek-Australian family; an affiliated scooter-rental business saves you traipses into town. Units in the better-standard apartment annexe accommodate 6. ❸ B&B

Blue Bay 150m beyond Konsoláto on the Gríkou road ⓣ22470 31165, ⓦwww.bluebay.50g.com. Probably the best-value, quietest choice for this area, with helpful Australian-Greek management, a/c, sea-view rooms with fridges, plus a small Internet café. Credit cards accepted for stays of over 2 days. ❻ B&B

Captain's House Konsoláto ⓣ22470 31793, ⓦwww.patmos-island.com/captainshouse.html. The rear wing, with quiet rooms, overlooks a fair-sized pool and shady terrace. Friendly management, nice furnishings and on-site car rental. ❺

Doriza Bay Hokhlakás, south hillside ⓣ22470 33123, ⓦwww.dorizabay.com. This hillside annexe of *Porto Scoutari* has the best sunsets in Skála, bar none. There's a wing of standard rooms with a breakfast salon, and galleried maisonettes (including some two-bedroom apartments) across the way. Off-street scooter parking. ❺–❼

Effie On hillside above the beach car park, centre ☎22470 32500, ⓦwww.effiehotel.gr. Two-wing hotel with ordinary heated/a/c rooms and private parking. Open all year. ❹

Maria Hokhlakás flatlands, 150m from sea ☎22470 31201. Quietly set small hotel where the pleasant front garden, a/c and big sea-view balconies make up for tiny bathrooms. ❺

Porto Scoutari Melóï ☎22470 33124, ⓦwww.portoscoutari.com. Pátmos's premier hotel, this hospitable bungalow complex overlooks the beach from a hillside setting. Common areas and spacious a/c units, with TV and phone, are furnished with mock antiques and original art, arrayed around a large pool. ❼ B&B, by the week ❻

Yvonni Studios Hokhlakás, north hillside ☎22470 33066, ⓦwww.12net.gr/yvonni. Basic but salubrious mid-sized pine-and-tile units with fridges, a/c and oblique sea views over a hillside garden. Walk-ins should call at the gift shop next to the Nissos Kalymnos agency. ❸

Eating, drinking and nightlife

Among the all-too-numerous **snack stalls** and *souvláki/yíros* joints in Skála are a handful of full-service, sit-down **restaurants**. Cheap, sometimes cheerful, and crowded *Ouzeri To Hiliomodhi* (all year), at the start of the Hóra road, offers vegetarian *mezédhes* and seafood delicacies such as limpets (served live) or grilled octopus with summer seating in a pedestrian lane. The best all-rounder (Easter to early Sept; reserve on ☎22470 32988) is *Vegghera*, opposite the yacht marina, with flawlessly presented stuffed scorpion fish, vegetarian or seafood salads, superb desserts, and per-head bills of about €40. At *Pandelis* (all year), one lane inland behind Astoria Travel, a wide-ranging menu of reliably good *mayireftá* makes up for famously dour – if efficient – service.

Otherwise, you're best off heading slightly out of town; **beach tavernas** excel on Pátmos. **Melóï** has a decent, reasonably priced *mayireftá* taverna, *Melloi (Stefanos)*, best for lunch (though it gets coach tours), with a long season. Just over the hill at **Áspri** cove are *Aspri* and *Kyma*: the former, just inland, has a broader menu, but the latter (mid-June to Aug 31), a waterside fish specialist, scores for its romantic setting though presentation is basic and service slipshod. At **Sápsila** cove, 2km southeast of Skála, *Benetos* (June–early Oct Tues–Sun supper only; reserve in summer ☎22470 33089) serves creative Mediterranean and Pacific-Rim fusion dishes stressing seafood. Budget a minimum of €36 for drink and three courses, which might include baked fish fillet with risotto and Hubbard squash, *barboúni* sashimi and lemon sorbet.

Back in town, the focus of *frappádhika* life is the square in from the Italian "palace", but the biggest, most durable **café-bar** is wood-panelled, barn-like *Café Arion* further along, where all sorts sit outside, dance inside, or prop up the long bar. Other **nightlife** venues include pricey, inland *Isalos*, occasionally hosting live music, and, the northernmost building in Nétia, *Anemos*, a restored old house with music and beer. More perhaps in sync with the island's tone is the annual, open-air **Festival of Religious Music** (late Aug/early Sept) featuring performers from Russia, Turkey and the entire Balkans.

The monasteries and Hóra

Top of your sightseeing agenda is likely to be **Ayíou Ioánnou Theológou** (St John) **monastery** in hilltop Hóra. Coach tours pack the place around noon, so go early or late. The best **dates** to visit, besides the famous Easter observances, are September 25–26 (Feast of John the Theologian) and October 20–21 (Feast of Khristodhoulos), both featuring solemn liturgies and processions of the appropriate icon. About eight KTEL **buses** serve Hóra daily, or you can take a forty-minute **walk** along a beautiful old cobbled path. Proceed through Skála

towards Hokhlakás, and once past the telecoms building bear left onto a lane starting opposite the ironmonger's; follow this uphill to its end on the main road – immediately opposite you'll see the cobbles. Just over halfway, pause at the **Apokálypsis monastery** (daily 8am–1.30pm, also Tues, Thurs & Sun 4–6pm; free) built around the cave where St John heard the voice of God issuing from a cleft in the rock, and where he sat dictating to his disciple Prohoros. In the cave wall, the presumed nightly resting place of the saint's head is fenced off and outlined in beaten silver.

This is merely a foretaste of **Ayíou Ioánnou Theológou monastery** (same hours and admission). In 1088, the soldier-cleric **Ioannis "The Blessed" Khristodhoulos** (1021–93) was granted title to Pátmos by Byzantine emperor Alexios Komnenos; within three years he and his followers had completed most of the existing monastery, the threats of piracy and the Selçuk Turks dictating a heavily fortified style. A warren of courtyards, chapels, stairways, arcades, and roof terraces, it offers a rare glimpse of a Patmian interior. Off to one side, the **treasury** (same hours; €6) doesn't quite justify its entrance fee with its admittedly magnificent array of religious treasure, mostly medieval icons of the Cretan school. Pride of place goes to an unusual mosaic icon of Áyios Nikólaos, and the eleventh-century parchment chrysobull (edict) of Emperor Alexios Komnenos, granting the island to Khristodhoulos.

Hóra

The reassurance provided by St John's stout walls spurred the growth of **HÓRA** immediately outside the fortifications. It remains architecturally homogeneous, with cobbled lanes sheltering dozens of shipowners' mansions from the island's seventeenth-to-eighteenth-century heyday. High, windowless walls and imposing wooden doors betray nothing of the painted ceilings, *votsalotó* terraces, flagstone kitchens and carved furniture inside. Inevitably, touristic tattiness disfigures the main approaches to the monastery, but elsewhere are lanes that rarely see traffic, and by night, when the ramparts are startlingly floodlit, it's hard to think of a more beautiful Dodecanesian village. Neither should you miss the **view** from **Platía Lótza**, particularly at dawn or dusk. Landmasses to the north, going clockwise, include Ikaría, Thýmena, Foúrni, Sámos, Arkí and double-humped Samsun Dağ (ancient Mount Mykale) in Turkey.

The best of Hóra's few **tavernas** is *Pantheon* (all year; good *ouzomezédhes*), at the start of the monastery ramp; *Lotza*, just below the eponymous platía, offers snacks, crêpes and desserts as well as hot and alcoholic drinks. There are, however, few places to **stay** if you're not one of the lucky outsiders who've bought up and restored almost half of the mansions since the 1960s. Even in spring or autumn, book well ahead at the *dhomátia* of Yeoryia Triandafyllou (Ⓣ22470 31963; ③) on the south flank of the village, en suite with a communal terrace and self-catering kitchen, or the more comfortable *Epavli Apartments* at the east edge of Hóra, on the ring road (Ⓣ22470 31261, Ⓦwww.12net.gr/epavli; ⑥), a restored building with superb views, good bathrooms and raised bed-platforms.

The rest of the island

Pátmos, as a local guidebook once proclaimed, "is immense for those who know how to wander in space and time"; lesser mortals get around on foot or by bus, if not a scooter. Unfortunately, most paths have been destroyed by road-building and property development; the single **bus** offers a reliable service between Skála, Hóra, Kámbos and Gríkou.

After its extraordinary atmosphere and striking scenery, **beaches** are Patmos's principal attraction. From Konsoláto, a principal road heads east to uninspiring **Sápsila** beach, home not only to *Benetos* taverna (see p.731) but also to the welcoming *Studios Mathios* (ⓣ22470 32119, ⓦwww.mathiosapartment.gr; ④), superior rural **accommodation** with creative decor and extensive gardens. The onward road, and another from Hóra, converge at the sandiest part of overdeveloped and cheerless **GRÍKOU** – shut tight as a drum come mid-September. The beach itself, far from the island's best, forms a narrow strip of hard-packed sand, giving way to sand and gravel, then large pebbles at **Pétra** immediately south, whose far end is colonized by nudists. Its near side features about the best rural **taverna** on Pátmos, *Ktima Petra* (Easter–Oct 15), with brown bread, lush salads, good bulk retsina, carefully cooked *mayireftá*, plus grills after dark. En route to Pétra, you pass hillside *Flisvos* (*Floros*), now rather eclipsed by nearby *Ktima Petra* but known for its limited choice of inexpensive, savoury *mayireftá*. They also have basic **rooms** (ⓣ22470 31380; ③) and fancier apartments (④).

From Hóra – but *not* Pétra – you can ride a scooter as far as the car park just past the Dhiakoftí isthmus, beyond which a 25-minute walk southwest on a bona fide path leads to **Psilí Ámmos** beach. This is the only pure-sand cove on the island, with shade lent by tamarisks, nudism at the far south end and a good lunchtime **taverna** that occasionally does fresh roast goat. A summer *kaïki* service to here from Skála departs by 10am and returns at 4 or 5pm.

Northern Pátmos

There are more good beaches in **the north**, tucked into the startling eastern shoreline (west-facing bays are unusable owing to the prevailing wind and washed-up debris); most are accessible from side roads off the main route north from Skála. **Melóï** is handy and quite appealing, with tamarisks behind the slender belt of sand, and good snorkelling offshore. The first beach beyond Méloï, **Agriolívadho (Agriolivádhi)**, has mostly sand at its broad centre, kayak rental, and a good fish **taverna**, *O Glaros*, on the south hillside. Hilltop **KÁMBOS** is the island's only other real village, the focus of scattered farms in little surrounding oases; Pátmos is lucky enough to be able to tap a vein of water from Turkey, with a public fountain just before Kámbos. Best of two **tavernas** at the crossroads is *Panagos* (all year), superb for traditional *mayireftá*; don't miss the archival photos inside. **Kámbos beach**, 600m downhill, is the most developed remote bay on the island, with non-motorized watersports facilities and two tavernas, though its appeal is diminished by the road just inland.

East of Kámbos, several less-frequented coves include pebble/coarse-sand **Vayiá**; nudist, double-bay **Lingínou** (shore *kantína*) and long, sand-and-gravel **Livádhi Yeranoú**, the latter with tamarisks, an islet to swim out to and an excellent **taverna** for simple seafood, chops, roast goat, *hórta* and salads. Another road from Kámbos leads north to **Lámbi bay**, best for swimming when the prevailing wind is from the south, and renowned for its multicoloured volcanic stones. A good **taverna**, *Leonidas* (May–Oct), up at Koumariá pass overlooking the bay, has terrace seating and massive portions of grilled chops; down on the shore, *Lambi* is better for fish.

Lipsí

Of the various islets north and east of Pátmos, **LIPSÍ** is the largest, most interesting, most populated and the one with the most significant summer tourist trade. Returning clients of a now-vanished British package company, on-spec Italian and French travellers, and the island's appearance on minor ferry routes and catamaran/hydrofoil lines mean that it's unwise to show up in peak season without reservations.

During quiet months, however, Lipsí still provides an idyllic halt, its sleepy pace almost making plausible a spurious link with **Calypso**, the nymph who legendarily held Odysseus in thrall. Deep wells water many small farms, but there is only one flowing spring, and pastoral appearances are deceptive – four times the full-time population of about six hundred live overseas (many in Hobart, Tasmania).

Recently, however, Lipsí acquired a definite – and unwanted – link with **Dhekaeftá Noemvríou/17 November**, Greece's (and Europe's) longest-lived terrorist organization. In July 2002, the national anti-terrorist squad swooped on the island and apprehended the group's supremo, Alexandhros Yiotopoulos (alias Mihalis Ikonomou), in the act of leaving for Sámos on the way to Turkey. He had been living quietly here for 17 years in a faded-pink hilltop villa, now abandoned following his December 2003 conviction and life sentencing; ironically Yiotopoulos was much liked by the islanders for his generosity, sociability and willingness to help with bureaucratic problems.

The port settlement

Arriving craft use the dock at the far west end of the port settlement; boat tickets are sold from a booth before departures in the jetty café *Okeanis*, while further along the quay there's a stand-alone **ATM**. The **post office** is up a stairway on the attractive cathedral platía, opposite a hilariously eclectic **ecclesiastical museum** (daily 9am–2.30pm; free) featuring such "relics" as earth collected from Mount Tabor and water from the River Jordan, as well as archeological finds, medieval glazed ware and two letters from Greek revolutionary hero Admiral Miaoulis.

Accommodation

A prime **accommodation** choice is Nikos' and Anna's welcoming *Apartments Galini* (☎22470 41212; ❸), the first building above the ferry jetty; Nikos may take guests fishing on request. Equally popular, though less airy, are *Studios Kalymnos* (☎22470 41141, ⓦwww.lipsi-island.gr; ❸) in a garden on the road north out of town. Other good options include *Rena's Rooms* (☎22470 41110 or 697 93 16 512; ❸) – nos. 3 and 4 overlook Liendoú beach – and *Glaros* (☎22470 41360; ❷) on the north hillside, with *terrazzo*-floored 1980s rooms sharing cooking facilities. Top of the heap is the *Aphrodite Hotel* (☎22470 41000; ❹), a studio-bungalow complex just in from Liendoú.

Eating and drinking

Of the nine full-service **tavernas**, mostly on or just behind the quay, the best are *O Yiannis* (early May to early Oct), an excellent all-rounder with meat/seafood grills and *mayireftá*; *To Pefko* (May to late Sept) nearby, with creative oven dishes and *mezédhes*, plus efficient service; and good-value *Karnayio* on the far side of the bay, serving big portions. On the waterfront, *kafenía* and **ouzerís** with idiosyncratic decor (especially *Asprakis*) offer al fresco twilight drinks and *mezédhes* – an atmospheric and almost obligatory pre-supper ritual – or even a full meal; rivals *Nikos* and *Sofoklis* operate all year. Winners among the handful of **bars** are *The Rock*, with a congenial crowd and good taped music, and livelier *Meltemi*, next to *Karnayio*; *To Limani* (*Stratos*) is the place for **breakfast** and coffees.

Around the island

None of Lipsí's **beaches** is more than an hour's walk from the port. Closest to town, and sandiest, are **Liendoú** and **Kámbos**, but many prefer attractive **Katsadhiá** and **Papandhriá**, adjacent sand-and-pebble coves 2km south of the port by paved road. A musical **taverna-café**, ✱ *Dilaila* (June–Sept), which overlooks the left-hand bay here, serves such delights as rosemary fish, saffron rice, *fáva* and salad with balsamic dressing. You can **stay** locally at Scottish-run, hillside *Katsadia Studios* (☎22470 41317 or 697 87 09 558; ❸), well designed and with sweeping views.

Another paved road leads 4km west from town to protected **Platýs Yialós**, a shallow, sandy bay with a single **taverna** (mid-June to late Sept). In summer, two white vans provide a **minibus** service from the port to all points cited above (there's also a single **taxi**); otherwise rent a **scooter** from one of two outlets and point them towards isolated east coast beaches without facilities. Of these, **Hokhlakoúra** consists of rather coarse shingle (finer pebbles at mid-strand); nearby **Turkómnima** is much sandier and shadier, if windy, while **Xirókambos** is calmer but treeless. A final ten-minute path scramble gets you from a rough track's end to **Monodhéndhri** on the northeast coast, notable only for its lone juniper tree and nudist practice – there's a superior, nameless cove just to the right.

The road network, paved or otherwise, limits opportunities for genuine path **walks** through the undulating countryside, dotted with blue-domed churches. The most challenging route heads west, high above the coast, from the far end of Kámbos bay to **Kímisi** bay (3hr round trip), where the religious **hermit Filippos**, long a cult figure among foreign visitors, once lived in a tiny monastery above the shore, next to the single island spring. A particularly steep, ugly road was bulldozed in from the north and later paved, disturbing his solitude; Filippos moved to town and died, aged 85, in 2002, though a small memorial at the monastery commemorates him.

Arkí and Maráthi

About two-thirds the size of Lipsí, **Arkí** is considerably more primitive, lacking properly stocked shops or much in the way of a coherent village. Just 45 permanent inhabitants eke out a living here, mostly engaged in fishing or goat/sheep-herding, though catering for yacht parties attracted by the superb anchorage is also important. Arkí is a stop on the *Nissos Kalymnos*, which people use to make cheap day-trips from Pátmos; post *kaïkia* (4 weekly) or excursion boats sail right into the main harbour to dock at the inner quay. Among three **tavernas** on the harbourside platía, the more frequented – *Nikolas* (☎22470 32477; B&B; ❸) and *O Trypas* (aka *Tou Manoli*; ☎22470 32230; ❷) – provide **accommodation**; *O Trypas* is perhaps better value. *Nikolas* has home-made puddings, while *O Trypas* does very decent fish meals and doubles as the happening **music pub**. The most accomplished seafood grills are had at ✱ *Apolavsi*, one inlet southeast at **Dhídhymi Ormí**; yachties (and land-lubbers) in the know come here for garden vegetables, slow-cooked fish, octopus and other *mezédhes* at attractive prices.

You can swim at the "Blue Lagoon" of **Tiganákia** at the southeast tip of the island, but other **beaches** on Arkí take some resourcefulness to find. The more obvious ones are the artificially augmented sandy cove at **Pateliá** by the ferry jetty, or tiny **Limnári** bay on the northeast coast which fits four or five bathers at a pinch, a 25-minute walk away via the highest house in the settlement.

The nearest large, sandy, tamarisk-shaded beach lies just offshore on the islet of **Maráthi**, where **tavernas** cater to day-trippers from Pátmos or Lipsí.

Marathi (☎22470 31580; all year; ❷) is the more traditional, cosy outfit, with waterside seating and simple, adequate rooms; *Pantelis* (☎22470 32609; June–Oct; ❸) is plusher but more commercially minded – and apt to lock the gate at 11pm if you drink at his rival's bar.

Agathoníssi

The small, steep-sided, waterless islet of **Agathoníssi (Gaïdharo)** is too remote – much closer to Turkey than Pátmos, in fact – to be a popular day-trip target, though a few are half-heartedly offered from Sámos. Intrepid Greeks and Italians form its main clientele, along with a steady trickle of yachts. Even though the *Nissos Kalymnos* (and one or two weekly hydrofoils) appear regularly, you should count on staying for at least two days, especially if the wind's up. Despite the lack of springs (cisterns are ubiquitous, topped up by tankers from Rhodes), the island is greener and more fertile than apparent from the sea; mastic, carob and scrub oak on the heights overlook two arable plains in the west. Just 146 people live here, down from several hundred before World War II, but those who've remained seem determined to make a go of raising goats or fishing (or rather, fish-farming), and there are almost no abandoned or neglected dwellings.

Most of the population lives in **Megálo Horió hamlet**, just visible on the ridge above the harbour of **ÁYIOS YEÓRYIOS**, and eye-level with tiny **Mikró Horió**. Except for two sporadically open café-restaurants in Megálo Horió, all amenities are in the port. Among five **accommodation** choices, preferred are *Rooms Theoloyia Yiameou* (☎22470 29005; ❷), the vine-patioed *Hotel Maria Kamitsi* (☎22470 29003; ❷), or *Aganandi* above the *Limanaki* taverna (☎22470 29019; ❷). Eating out, you'll almost certainly try all three full-service **tavernas**: *George's* for fish, *Seagull/Glaros* for meat, *Limanaki* as the cheap-and-cheerful Greeks' hangout. There's no **post office** or **ATM**; ferry and hydrofoil **tickets** must be bought in advance at a little booth opposite the *Café Yetoussa*, the best **bar** and also a good source of breakfast.

With no wheeled transport for rent, exploring involves **walking** along the cement-road network, or following a limited number of tracks and paths. If you won't swim at the port, which has the largest **beach**, walk ten minutes southwest along a track to shingle-gravel **Spiliás**, or continue another quarter-hour along a faint path over the ridge to **Gaïdhourávlakos**, a finer gravel cove. Bays in the east of the island, all served by the paved road system (occasionally supplemented by trails), include **Thóli** in the far southeast, with good snorkelling and some morning shade, and **Pálli** on the opposite shore of the same bay, a small but pristine fine-pebble cove reached by fifteen-minute walk down from the trans-island road. Also at **Thóli**, an hour-plus trek away, stands an arcaded **Byzantine structure**, probably a combination granary and trading post, and by far the most venerable sight on Agathoníssi.

Travel details

To simplify the lists below, some companies' offerings are summarized first. Agoudimos provides a weekly link between Rhodes, Kós, Kálymnos, Sámos and Thessaloníki in each direction, plus another weekly link from Rhodes to Alexandhroúpoli via Kós, Kálymnos, Sámos, Híos, Lésvos and Límnos.

Nissos Kalymnos

The small, slow but reliable **Nissos Kalymnos** (cars carried) is the lifeline of the islands between Kálymnos and Sámos, visiting them all several times weekly between mid-March and mid-Jan:
Mon, Wed, Fri & Sun Leaves Kálymnos 7am for Léros (Lakkí), Lipsí, Pátmos, Arkí, Agathoníssi, Sámos (Pythagório; arrives 2.30pm). Turns around immediately and retraces steps through the same islands in reverse order, arriving Kálymnos 10pm.
Tues, Thurs & Sat Leaves Kálymnos 7am, arrives Astypálea 10.15am, turns around immediately to arrive Kálymnos at 1.30pm.

Protevs (Proteus)

From March to Oct, the small, slow but reliable **Protevs** serves as a counterpart to the *Nissos Kalymnos* in the southern Dodecanese. Its schedule (confirm on ⓦwww.anes.gr) is:
Tues Leaves Rhodes in morning, arrives Kastellórizo noon, returns to Rhodes, evening trip to Sými.
Wed & Fri Noon departure from Sými to Tílos, Níssyros and Kós; on Wed a morning roundtrip Sými–Rhodes–Sými as well.
Thurs & Sat Early morning departure from Kós to Níssyros, Tílos, Sými and Rhodes, from where there's a noon trip out to Kastellórizo and back, returning near midnight.
Sun Morning departure from Rhodes to Tílos, returning evening, via Hálki each direction.

Large ferries and local kaïkia

Astypálea 3 weekly to Amorgós, Náxos, Dhonoússa, Páros and Pireás on Blue Star; 1 weekly to Kálymnos, Kós, Níssyros, Tílos, Rhodes and Pireás on Blue Star.
Hálki 2–3 weekly to Ródhos Town, Kárpathos (both ports), Kássos, Crete (Sitía & Áyios Nikólaos), Santoríni and Mílos on LANE. Daily *kaïki* (daily 6 or 8am, also Wed/Sun afternoon departures) to Rhodes (Kámiros Skála).
Kálymnos Similar frequencies to Kós, plus 3 daily roll-on-roll-off ferries, well-spaced, to Mastihári; 5 passenger-only speedboats (*Kalymmos Star* or *Kalymnos Dolphin*) daily to Mastihári; daily morning *kaïki* to Psérimos, plus 1 noon speedboat; and a daily *kaïki* (1pm) from Myrtiés to Xirókambos on Léros.
Kárpathos (both ports) and **Kássos** 2–3 weekly with each other, Hálki, Crete (Áyios Nikólaos & Sitía), Mílos, Santoríni and Ródhos Town, on LANE; 1 weekly to Rhodes, Kós, Sýros and Pireás on Blue Star; 1–2 weekly to Rhodes, Kássos, Iráklio, select Cyclades and Sporades and Thessaloníki on GA.
Kós At least daily to Rhodes, Kálymnos, Léros, Pátmos and Pireás on GA or Blue Star; 3 weekly to Sýros on Blue Star; 1 weekly to Kós, Tílos, Níssyros and Astypálea on Blue Star; 5 weekly on *Panayia Spiliani* mid-afternoon to Níssyros; daily afternoon small *kaïki* from Kardhámena to Níssyros.
Léros At least daily to Pireás, Pátmos, Kálymnos, Kós and Rhodes on GA or Blue Star; 2–3 weekly to Sýros on Blue Star; daily excursion boats from Ayía Marína to Lipsí and Léros (2pm), and from Xirókambos to Myrtiés on Kálymnos (7.30am).
Níssyros and Tílos 1 weekly with each other, Rhodes, Kós, Kálymnos, Astypálea and Pireás on Blue Star. Excursion boats between Níssyros and Kós as follows: to Kardhámena and Kós Town nearly daily at 3.30–4pm (these are seasonal); Níssyros-based *Panayia Spiliani* (2–3 cars carried) leaves 5 days weekly at 7.30am (Sat 9am) for Kós Town, while the *Ayios Konstandinos* and/or *Nisyros* (foot pax only) goes 4–6 times weekly at 7am to Kardhámena; 2 weekly on *Panayia Spiliani* from Níssryos to Tílos, Hálki, Rhodes and back the same day.
Pátmos Near-identical ferry service as Léros, plus additional tourist *kaïkia* to Sámos (Pythagório), Lipsí and Léros on a daily basis; to Arkí and Maráthi 4 weekly.
Rhodes At least daily to Kós and Pireás on GA or Blue Star; 4–5 weekly to Kálymnos, Léros and Pátmos on GA or Blue Star; 2–3 weekly to Hálki, Kárpathos, Kássos, Crete (Sitía & Áyios Nikólaos), Santoríni and Mílos on LANE; 1 weekly to Tílos, Níssyros, Astypálea on Blue Star; 2–3 weekly to Sýros on Blue Star; 1 weekly to Santoríni on Blue Star; 1–2 weekly to Kárpathos, Kássos, Iráklio, select Cyclades and Sporades and Thessaloníki on GA.
Sými 2–3 daily run by ANES (ⓦwww.anes.gr) to Rhodes; 2 weekly on 6-A to Kós, Kálymnos, Léros, Lipsi, Patmos, & Pireás.

Catamarans

Three long-distance **catamarans** ply the Dodecanese: *The Dodekanisos Express*, the co-owned *Dodekanisos Pride* (ⓦwww.12ne.gr for both) and the *Sea Star*.

Dodekanisos Express

The *Dodekanisos Express*, based on Rhodes, carries 4–5 cars and a slightly higher number of two-wheelers; it's a sleek Norwegian-built craft, with a limited amount of aft deck space. High-season schedules are as follows: Tues–Sun, 8.30am departure from Rhodes to Sými, Kós, Kálymnos, Léros and Pátmos; it returns from Pátmos at 1.30pm via the same islands, arriving at Rhodes 6.30pm. On Thurs & Sat it stops at Lipsí, heading south; on Mon it makes a single journey to Kastellórizo, arriving 11am, returning at 4pm. In spring or autumn there is no Kastellórizo service, and services to Pátmos are just 3 weekly.

Dodekanisos Pride

The *Express's* sister ship, *Dodekanisos Pride*, is based on Pátmos during high season but nearly identical in all other respects. Schedule patterns are as follows: Mon–Sat departure from Pátmos daily at 6am, arriving at Rhodes via Léros, Kálymnos, Kós and Sými (Panormítis, not Yialós, on Sun), at 10.40am, leaving northbound via the same islands at 3pm. But on Sat it swings via Níssyros and overnights at Kálymnos, from where it returns to Rhodes next day, again including Níssyros, before relocating to Pátmos on Sun evening. In spring and autumn it's based on Kálymnos, departing there Mon–Sat 7.40am to Rhodes via Kós and Sými, returning at 3pm.

Sea Star

The deeply unreliable *Sea Star* does not carry vehicles and serves mainly the route Rhodes–Tílos–Rhodes, with occasional (2–3 weekly) diversions via Sými. Schedules are so unpredictable that it's impossible to generalize, other than saying it does at least a daily trip in each direction (1hr 20min), with multiple trips Thurs and Sun.

Hydrofoils

Currently just one scheduled **hydrofoil**, based at Pythagório, Sámos and run by Aegean Flying Dolphins, serves the northern Dodecanese between mid-May and mid-Oct, providing an 8am service out of Pythagório as far as Kós, arriving at 11.30am and returning at 2.30pm. It calls daily at Pátmos, Lipsí, Léros and Kálymnos en route in both directions, adding Agathoníssi 2 days weekly. In 2008, Dinoris Hydrofoils on Kós should begin a complementary service through the same islands, departing Kós at 8.30am and returning from Pythagório in the afternoon.

International ferries

NB: In all cases port taxes are included but cost of Turkish visas, required by most nationals, is not.
Kálymnos to Bodrum, Turkey (1hr 45min), departing at 7–8am; €30 day-return, though €20 "specials" 2 days weekly.
Kós At least daily April–Nov to Bodrum, Turkey (30–45min). Greek boat or hydrofoil leaves 9am & 4pm; additional out-and-back 10am/5pm Fri & Sun, 3 extra departures Tues (market day) and Sat 9.30am/4.30pm to Turgut Reis. Fares €20–25 day return/one way, €50 open return. Only the Turkish boat (*Fahri Kaptan*) carries cars (€100) and is pricier for foot passengers, but provides sole service (3 weekly, Tues guaranteed) Dec–March.
Kastellórizo 2 weekly (Mon & Fri) to Kaş, Turkey; €15 one way/day return; €32 maximum (bargain with boatman if necessary) if you begin travel from the Turkish side.
Rhodes Daily April–Nov to Marmaris, Turkey (1hr) by Greek catamaran or hydrofoil at 8–9.30am, Turkish catamaran at 5pm (50min); prices same at €57 day return, open return, €50 one way. one weekly car ferry, usually Thurs at 3pm; Sea Dreams at Grigoríou Lambráki 46 in Neohóri (☎22410 76535) is the central agent, though other agencies (such as Triton Travel) will readily sell you passage.
Sými Up to 3 weekly *kaïkia* (80min, €40 return plus $12 Turkish tax) and 1 hydrofoil or catamaran (40min, €30 return plus Turkish tax) to Datça; Sat most reliable day.

Flights

NB: All are on Olympic Aviation/Olympic Airways unless stated otherwise.
Astypálea 4–5 weekly to Athens; 3 weekly to Léros, Kós and Rhodes on the same plane.
Kálymnos 1 daily to Athens.
Kárpathos 2 daily to Rhodes; 9 weekly to Kássos and Sitía (Crete); daily to Athens.
Kássos 9 weekly to Kárpathos, Sitía (Crete) and Rhodes.
Kastellórizo (Meyísti) 6 weekly to Rhodes.
Kós 3 daily to Athens on Olympic, 2–3 daily on Aegean; 3 weekly to Astypálea, Léros and Rhodes; 3 weekly on Sky Express to Iráklio, Crete.
Léros 1 daily to Athens; 3 weekly to Astypálea, Kós and Rhodes.
Rhodes Olympic: 4–5 daily to Athens; 1–2 daily to Iráklio; 3 weekly to Kós, Léros and Astypálea on same plane; 2 weekly to Sámos and Híos; 5 weekly to Lésvos and Límnos; 8–9 weekly to Thessaloníki; 9 weekly to Kárpathos, Kássos & Sitía on same plane. Aegean: 5 daily to Athens; 2–3 daily to Thessaloníki. Sky Express: daily to Iráklio; 2 weekly to Haniá; daily to Santoríni.

10

The East and North Aegean

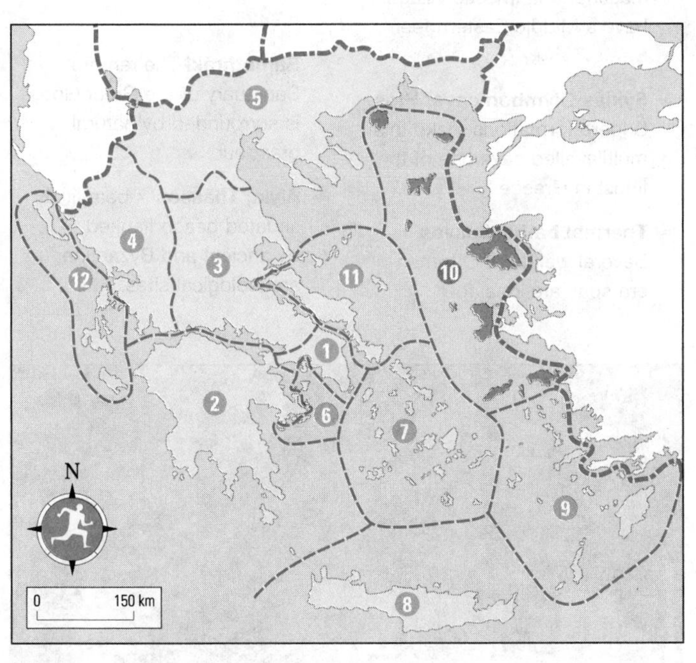

CHAPTER 10 **Highlights**

* **Vathý, Sámos** The two-wing archeological museum is among the best in Greece. See p.745

* **Ikaría** Western Ikaría has superb beaches and an idiosyncratic lifestyle. See p.757

* **Southern Híos** The architecturally unique *mastihohoriá* (mastic villages) have a Middle Eastern feel. See p.765

* **Sykiás Olýmbon cave, Híos** Superb formations make this multilevelled cave one of the finest in Greece. See p.767

* **Thermal baths, Lésvos** Several well-kept Ottoman-era spas are ideal for relaxing in. See p.777, p.780, p.786

* **Mólyvos, northern Lésvos** This castle-crowned resort village is arguably the most beautiful on the island. See p.784

* **Límnos villages** Characterful, basalt-built villages with lively central tavernas and great wines to sample. See p.791, p.742

* **Samothráki** The remote Sanctuary of the Great Gods is surrounded by natural grandeur. See p.796

* **Alykí, Thássos** A beautifully situated beach flanked by ancient and Byzantine archeological sites. See p.803

▲ Byzantine castle, Mýrina, Límnos

10

The East and North Aegean

The seven substantial islands and four minor islets scattered off the Aegean coast of Asia Minor form a rather arbitrary archipelago. While there are similarities in architecture and landscape, the strong individual character of each island is far more striking. Despite their proximity to modern Turkey, only Lésvos, Límnos and Híos bear significant signs of an **Ottoman** heritage in the form of old mosques, *hamams* and fountains, but by and large the enduring Greekness of these islands is testimony to a four-millennium-long **Hellenic** presence in Asia Minor, which ended only in 1923. This heritage has been regularly referred to by Greece in an intermittent propaganda war with Turkey over the sovereignty of these far-flung outposts. Tensions here have occasionally been worse than in the Dodecanese, aggravated by suspected undersea oil deposits in the straits between the islands and Anatolia. The Turks have also persistently demanded that Límnos, astride the sea lanes to and from the Dardanelles, be demilitarized, and only since 2001 has Greece shown signs of complying, with garrisons also much reduced on Sámos and Lésvos.

As in the Dodecanese, local agencies do a thriving business shuttling passengers between the easternmost islands and the **Turkish coast** with its archeological sites and busy resorts. Most main **port-towns** are urbanized capitals and far from picturesque; suppress any initial impulse to take the next boat out, and discover their worthwhile interiors. Also bear in mind that the **tourist season** this far north is short – late June to early September – with many restaurants and lodgings shut outside this period.

Sámos ranks as the most visited island of the group but, once you leave its crowded resorts behind, is still arguably the most beautiful, even after a devastating 2000 fire. **Ikaría** to the west remains relatively unspoilt, if a minority choice, and nearby **Foúrni** is (except in summer) a haven for determined solitaries, as are the Híos satellites **Psará** and **Inoússes**, neither of which has any package tourism. **Híos** proper offers far more cultural interest than its neighbours to the south, but far fewer tourist facilities. **Lésvos** may not impress initially, though once you get a feel for its old-fashioned Anatolian ambience you may find it hard to leave. By contrast, few foreigners visit **Áyios Efstrátios**, for good reason. **Límnos** to the north is much livelier, its most popular villages and beaches – and attractive harbour capital – residing in its western half. To the

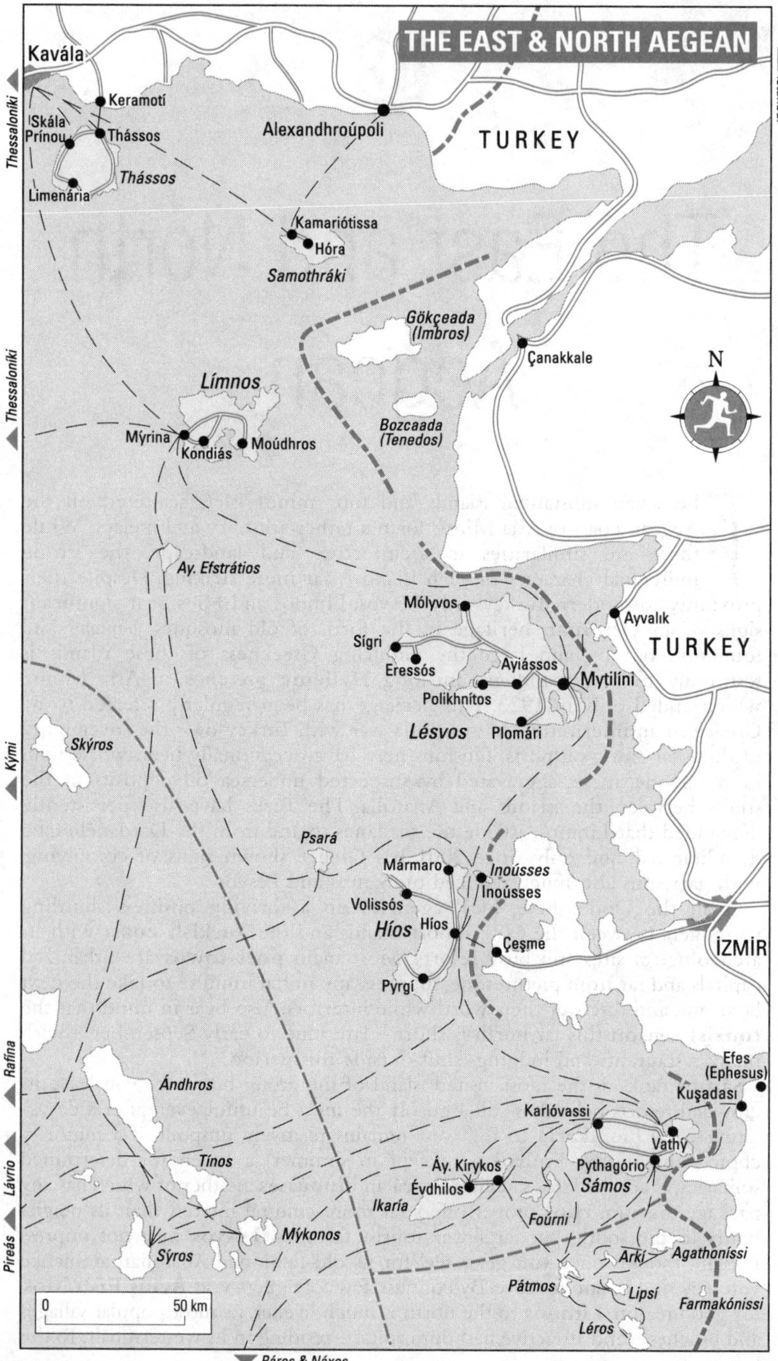
THE EAST & NORTH AEGEAN
Kavála
Keramotí
Skála Prínou
Thássos
Thássos
Limenária
Alexandhroúpoli
TURKEY
Kamariótissa
Hóra
Samothráki
Gökçeada (Imbros)
Çanakkale
N
Límnos
Mýrina
Kondiás
Moúdhros
Bozcaada (Tenedos)
Ay. Efstrátios
Mólyvos
Ayvalık
TURKEY
Sígri
Eressós
Ayiássos
Mytilíni
Polikhnítos
Lésvos
Plomári
Skýros
Psará
Mármaro
Inoússes
Inoússes
Volissós
Híos
Híos
Çeşme
İZMİR
Pyrgí
Efes (Ephesus)
Kuşadası
Ándhros
Karlóvassi
Vathý
Pythagório
Sámos
Tínos
Áy. Kírykos
Évdhilos
Ikaría
Foúrni
Mýkonos
Arkí
Agathoníssi
Sýros
Pátmos
Lipsí
Farmakónissi
Léros
0
50 km
Thessaloniki
Thessaloniki
Kými
Rafína
Lávrio
Pireás
İstanbul
Páros & Náxos

north, Samothráki and Thássos are relatively isolated, and remain easier to visit from northern Greece, which administers them. **Samothráki** (officially in Thrace) has one of the most dramatic seaward approaches of any Greek island, and one of the more important ancient sites. **Thássos** (technically part of eastern Macedonia) is more varied, with sandy beaches, mountain villages and minor archeological sites.

Sámos

The lush, seductive island of **Sámos** was formerly joined to Asia Minor's Mount Mykale until sundered by Ice Age cataclysms; the resulting 2500-metre strait provides the narrowest maritime distance between Greece and Turkey, except at Kastellórizo. Sámos was also once the **wealthiest island** in the Aegean and, under the patronage of tyrant Polykrates, home to a thriving intellectual community that included Epicurus, Pythagoras, Aristarkhos and Aesop. Decline set in as Classical Athens was on the rise, though Sámos's status improved in Byzantine times when it formed its own imperial administrative district. Late in the fifteenth century, the Genoese **abandoned** the island to the mercies of pirates, and Sámos remained **almost uninhabited** until 1562, when repopulated with Greek Orthodox settlers recruited from various corners of the empire.

The new Samians **fought** fiercely for independence during the **1820s**, but despite their sinking a Turkish fleet in the narrow strait and annihilating a landing army, the Great Powers handed the island back to the Ottomans in 1830, with the consoling proviso that it be **semi-autonomous**, ruled by an appointed Christian prince. This period, referred to as the **Iyimonía** (Hegemony), was marked by a renaissance in fortunes, courtesy of the hemp and (especially) tobacco trades. However, union with Greece in 1912, the ravages of a bitter World War II occupation and mass emigration effectively reversed this recovery until tourism appeared on the horizon during the 1980s.

The heterogeneous descent of today's islanders largely explains an enduring identity crisis and a rather thin topsoil of **indigenous culture**. Most village names are either clan surnames, or adjectives indicating origins elsewhere. There is no distinctly Samian music, dance or dress, and little that's original in the cuisine and architecture. The economy relies on **package tourism**, with Kokkári – and the southeastern and southwestern coasts – pretty much surrendered to holiday-makers, although the more rugged west and northwest has retained its undeveloped grandeur. The absence of a campsite, low-key nightlife a world away from that in the Dodecanese and Cyclades, and phalanxes of self-catering villas hint at the sedate, thirty-to-fifty-something, couples-orientated (Scandanavian, Brit, central European) custom expected.

Heavily developed areas have been the most afflicted by **repeated wildfires**, most recently in July 2000, which destroyed a quarter of the island's forest and orchards, and more than ninety dwellings; taking into account other areas torched since 1987, Sámos is now about half denuded. Volunteer-staffed fire-lookouts have since sprouted, but as ever the trees will be a half-century in returning.

Arrival and getting around

Sámos' **airport** (five car rental booths, one ATM) lies 14km southwest of Vathý and 3km west of Pythagório. There is no airport bus; **taxi** fares to all points are posted on placards, and in summer taxis to the airport or ferry docks must be

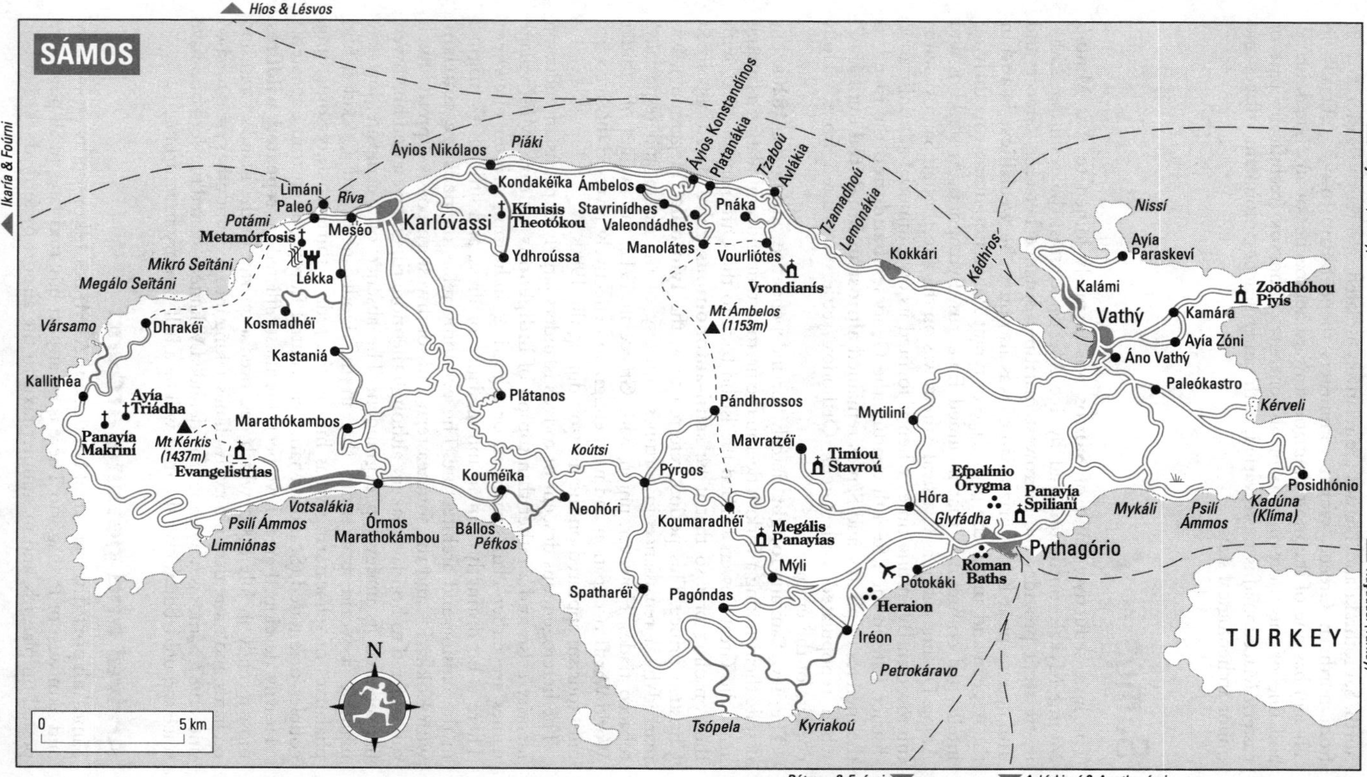
SÁMOS
Híos & Lésvos
Ikaría & Foúrni
Kuşadası (Turkey)
Kuşadası (Turkey)
Pátmos & Foúrni
Arkí, Lipsí & Agathoníssi
TURKEY
Áyios Nikólaos
Piáki
Limáni
Paleó
Ríva
Potámi
Metamórfosis
Meséo
Karlóvassi
Kondakéïka
Kímisis Theotókou
Ámbelos
Stavrinídhes
Valeondádhes
Ydhroússa
Áyios Konstandínos
Platanákia
Tzaboú
Avlákia
Pnáka
Manolátes
Vourliótes
Vrondianís
Tzamadhoú
Lemonákia
Kokkári
Kédhros
Nissí
Ayía Paraskeví
Kalámi
Vathý
Kamára
Zoödhóhou Piyís
Ayía Zóni
Áno Vathý
Paleókastro
Kérveli
Mikró Seïtáni
Megálo Seïtáni
Lékka
Kosmadhéï
Várasamo
Dhrakéï
Kastaniá
Mt Ámbelos (1153m)
Kallithéa
Ayía Triádha
Panayía Makriní
Mt Kérkis (1437m)
Evangelistrías
Marathókambos
Plátanos
Pándhrossos
Mytiliní
Mavratzéï
Timíou Stavroú
Koútsi
Pýrgos
Kouméïka
Neohóri
Votsalákia
Psilí Ámmos
Limniónas
Órmos Marathokámbou
Bállos
Péfkos
Koumaradhéï
Megális Panayías
Hóra
Efpalínio Órygma
Panayía Spilianí
Glyfádha
Mykáli
Psilí Ámmos
Kadúna (Klíma)
Posidhónio
Pythagório
Roman Baths
Potokáki
Mýli
Heraion
Spatharéï
Pagóndas
Iréon
Petrokáravo
Tsópela
Kyriakoú
N
0
5 km

booked in advance. There are three **ferry ports**: Karlóvassi in the west, plus Vathý and Pythagório in the east, making the island a major travel hub. All ferries between Pireás and Sámos call at both Karlóvassi and Vathý, as does the small, locally based *Samos Spirit*, linking the island with Foúrni and Ikaría. Vathý also receives most sailings between northern Greece and the Dodecanese, via major intervening islands, the weekly ferry between Thessaloníki and Rhodes, plus small boats from Kusadasi. Pythagório sees four regular weekly ferry connections from Kálymnos in the Dodecanese (and intervening islands), as well as a **hydrofoil service** to all Dodecanese down to Kós.

The **bus terminals** in Pythagório and Vathý lie (just) within walking distance of the ferry dock; at Karlóvassi, you can take a taxi or an occasional shuttle bus the 3km into town. The weekday KTEL service is adequate along the Pythagório–Vathý and Vathý–Kokkári–Karlóvassi routes, but poor at weekends or for other destinations; it's easy to find a good deal year round at numerous car- and motorbike-rental outlets.

Vathý

Lining the steep northeastern shore of a deep bay, beachless **VATHÝ** (often referred to as "Sámos") is a busy provincial town which grew from a minor anchorage after 1830, when it replaced Hóra as the island's capital. It's an unlikely, rather ungraceful resort, where numerous hotels have closed or become apartments since the 1990s, and holds little of interest aside from some Neoclassical mansions and the hill suburb of **Áno Vathý**, a separate community of tottering, tile-roofed houses.

The only real must is the excellent **archeological museum** (Tues–Sun 8.30am–3pm; €3), set behind the small central park beside the nineteenth-century town hall. The collections are housed in both the old Paskhallion building and a modern wing across the way, specially constructed to house the star exhibit: a majestic, five-metre-tall *kouros* discovered out at the Heraion sanctuary. The largest free-standing effigy surviving from ancient Greece, the *kouros* was dedicated to Apollo, but found next to a devotional mirror to Mut (the Egyptian equivalent of Hera) from a Nile workshop.

In the Paskhallion, more votive offerings of **Egyptian** design prove trade and pilgrimage links between Sámos and the Nile valley going back to the eighth century BC. Mesopotamian and Anatolian origins of other artwork confirm an exotic trend, most tellingly in a case full of ivory miniatures: Perseus and Medusa in relief, a kneeling, perfectly formed mini-*kouros*, a pouncing lion and a bulls-head drinking horn. The most famous local artefacts are numerous bronze griffin-heads, for which Sámos was the major centre of production in the seventh century BC; they were mounted on the edge of cauldrons to ward off evil spirits.

Arrival, information and transport

From the **ferry dock** the shore boulevard – Themistoklí Sofoúli – describes a 1300-metre arc around the bay. About 400m along is pedestrianized **Platía Pythagóra**, distinguished by its lion statue; about 800m along there's a major turning inland to the **KTEL** terminal, a perennially bus-cluttered intersection by the ticket office. If you've arrived with your own vehicle, use the free **parking lots** on the shoreline near the KTEL turning – there's never any street parking to be had.

The most comprehensive waterfront **ferry/travel agent** is By Ship, with one branch at the base of the jetty (☎22730 80445), another about 300m southeast (☎22730 25065). Helpful ITSA (☎22730 23605), also at the jetty base, are main agents for the Kallisti Ferries catamaran. Among about ten **scooter- and car-rental** agencies, three to try are Aramis (ⓣ22730 23253) at Themistoklí Sofoúli 7, Avis/Reliable (ⓣ22730 80445), both with branches island-wide, and Auto Union at Themistoklí Sofoúli 79 (ⓣ22730 27444), which negotiates good long-term rates and will deliver cars to the airport. Other amenities include the **post office**, remote on Themistoklí Sofoúli; six waterfront **ATMs**; and various **Internet cafés,** the best equipped being Dhiarlos on the front near the KTEL, serving Czech beer.

Accommodation

Abundant **accommodation** clusters in the hillside district of **Katsoúni**, above the ferry dock; except in August, you'll have little trouble finding vacancies. Budget choices include *Pension Dreams*, up a stair-lane at Áreos 9 (ⓣ22730 24350; all year; ❷), its well-kept en-suite rooms with fridges and double beds, or *Pension Avli* (ⓣ22730 22939; June–Sept; ❷), at Áreos 2, inside an atmospheric former convent school; affable manager Spyros can advise on local places to eat and drink.

For more comfort, proper hotels include the surprisingly affordable B-class *Ino Village* (ⓣ22730 23241, ⓦwww.inovillagehotel.com; ❸–❹), beyond the hospital in **Kalámi** district, with views, a big pool and a decent on-site restaurant. The *Samos Hotel* (ⓣ22730 28377, ⓦwww.hotelsamos.gr; all year; ❹), right by the ferry dock but with double glazing against noise, has a plunge-pool on the roof garden.

Eating, drinking and nightlife

Top **tavernas**, open all year, are *T'Ostrako* at Themistoklí Sofoúli 141, doing shellfish, a few scaly fish of the day and an ample selection of *orektiká*; family-run *To Steki* in the shopping centre behind the Catholic church, tops for *mayireftá* like bean soup at lunch; and *Artemis,* near the dock at Kefalopoúlou 4, busiest with locals at lunch, doing excellent, affordable seafood and starters. Up in Áno Vathý, *Iy Nostimies tou Tassou* (closed Sun, dinner all year, plus lunch Oct–May) by the school and community office is esteemed for its elaborate vegetarian dishes, seafood and the odd meat platter.

Vathý's most reliable **nightlife** occupies a "strip" at the start of Kefalopoúlou north of the jetty, where bars with seaside terraces include *Selini* and *Escape*. The best sundowner ouzo-*mezédhes* are had at *Kafenio Neon*, on Themistoklí Sofoúli near the Bank of Greece. The plushly fitted Cine Olympia, inland on Yimnasiárhou Katevéni, offers a variable programme of **films** for most of the year.

Beaches around Vathý

Some modest **beaches** around Vathý compensate for lack of the same in the capital, though you'll need your own transport to visit them. As you head southeast from Vathý along the main island loop road, the triple chapel at **Trís Ekklisíes** marks an important junction, with another fork 100m along. Bearing left twice takes you through the hilltop village of **Paleókastro**, 3km beyond which is another junction; forking left yet again brings you after another 3km to striking **Kérveli bay**, with a small but popular beach, a pair of **tavernas** – of which friendly *Sea and Dolphin* has good *mezédhes* and *soúma*, the local spirit, as well as mains. Another durable, inexpensive favourite with roast goat by pre-order and the best lamb chops on Sámos is *Iy Kryfi Folia*, about 500m uphill along the access road. Bearing right at the junction before Paleókastro leads to the beaches of Mykáli and Psilí Ámmos. **Mykáli**, a kilometre of windswept sand and gravel, has only all-inclusive hotels for Italians, and no outstanding tavernas.

Psilí Ámmos, further east around the headland, is a crowded, sandy cove backed by several **tavernas**, the best being *Psili Ammos*, on the far right as you face the sea, with good seafood, salads and meat grills. If you swim to the islet, beware strong eastbound currents in the narrow straits.

Pythagório and around

Most traffic south of Vathý heads for **PYTHAGÓRIO**, the island's premier resort, renamed in 1955 to honour Pythagoras, ancient mathematician, philosopher and initiater of a rather subversive cult. Until then it was known as Tigáni (Frying Pan) – in midsummer you'll learn why. Sixth-century BC tyrant Polykrates had his capital here, now subject to sporadic excavations which have made modern Pythagório expand northeast and uphill. The village core of cobbled lanes and stone-walled mansions abuts a cozy **harbour**, fitting almost perfectly into the confines of Polykrates' ancient jetty (traces still visible), but today devoted almost entirely to pleasure craft and overpriced café-bars.

Sámos's most complete **castle**, the nineteenth-century *pýrgos* of local chieftain Lykourgos Logothetis, overlooks both town and shoreline. A 2005-built **archeological museum** at the start of the Vathý road, featuring finds from the ancient city, seems destined never to open. Other antiquities include **Roman baths**, signposted as "Thermai", 400m west of town (Tues–Sun 8.45am–2.30pm; free); considerably more interesting is the well-signposted **Efpalínio Órygma** (Tues–Sun 8.45am–2.15pm; €4), a 1040-metre aqueduct bored through the mountain just north of Pythagório at the behest of Polykrates. Visits consist of traversing a hewn rock ledge used to transport the spoil from the water channel far below; there are guard-grilles over the worst drops, and lighting for the first 650m. Although slave-labour crews started digging from opposite sides of the mountain, the eight-metre horizontal deviation from true, about halfway along, is remarkably slight, and the vertical error nil: a tribute to the competence of ancient surveyors.

Practicalities

The **bus stop** lies just west of the intersection of the main thoroughfare, Lykoúrgou Logothéti, and the road to Vathý; the **taxi** rank is at the harbour end of Lykoúrgou Logothéti. A few **ATM**s line the same street; the **post office** is in a lane up from the quay, right from the taxi stand facing the water. The flattish country just west is ideal for **cycling**; if instead you want to rent a **motorbike**, several outfits on Logothéti will oblige you. These are interspersed with numerous **car rental** outlets, though **parking** in Pythagório is impossible – use the pricey fee lot near the main T-junction, or the free one just west behind the town beach.

Accommodation proprietors meet all arriving ferries and hydrofoils, even in peak season – some touted prices seem too good to be true, but it's free to look, and no location is that inconvenient. The **tourist information booth** (June–Sept daily 8.30am–9.30pm; ⓣ22730 62274), on Lykoúrgou Logothéti can also help find rooms. Quietly located at the seaward end of Pythagóra, south of Lykoúrgou Logothéti, the modest *Tsambika* (ⓣ22730 61642; ❷) or the more comfortable *Dora*, a block west (ⓣ22730 61456; ❸), are worth contacting in advance. A peaceful area is the hillside north of Platía Irínis, where *Studios Galini* (ⓣ22730 61167 or 210 98 42 248 in winter; ❹) has high-quality self-catering units with ceiling fans, balconies and kind English-speaking management.

Eating out can be frustrating in Pythagório, with good value and sound ingredients often completely alien concepts. Bright spots include, at the far north end of the quay, then inland, *Dolichi* (supper only), serving upscale Greek/

Mediterranean fusion cuisine in a space doubling as an art gallery; *Remataki* just beyond, having undergone a complete decor and menu makeover in 2007; cheap (for Pythagório) and cheerful *Maritsa* on a lane near Metamórfosis church; *Viva* at the base of the jetty for well-priced pizza and pasta; and best of all, just inland from the west car park, *Lemonies*, with home-style *mayireftá* and roasts at friendly prices (they're planning to move to Vathý in 2008). In terms of **nightlife**, while bunker-clubs like *Mythos* on the main square and *La Nuit* or *Sail In* exist on the quay, the top outing is to *Amadeus* (closed Mon) near the post office, with quality live Greek acts at bearable amplification. Aficionados will love the Rex, one of the best-maintained outdoor **cinemas** in the islands, on the outskirts of Mytiliní village, 7km northwest; they screen quality first-run **films**, with free *loukoumádhes* (sweet fritters) and cheap pizza at intermission.

Around Pythagório

The local, variable beach stretches several kilometres west of the Logothetis castle, punctuated about halfway along by the end of the airport runway, and the cluster of nondescript hotels known as **POTOKÁKI**. Just before the turn-off to the heart of the beach sprawls the luxury *Doryssa Bay* complex (Ⓣ22730 61360, Ⓦwww.doryssa-bay.gr; ⑦–⑧), which includes a meticulously concocted fake village; no two of its units are alike, and there's even a platía with a (pricey) café. Although you'll have to contend with the hotel crowds and low-flying jets, the sand-and-pebble **beach** here is well groomed, the water clean and sport facilities available.

Under layers of alluvial mud, plus today's runway, lies the processional Sacred Way joining ancient Samos with the **Heraion**, a massive shrine of the **Mother Goddess** (daily June–Sept 8am–7.30pm; Oct–May 8.30am–3pm; €3). Much touted in tourist literature, this assumes humbler dimensions – one surviving column and low foundations – upon approach. Yet once inside the precinct you sense the former grandeur of the temple, never completed owing to Polykrates' untimely death at the hands of the Persians. The site chosen, near the mouth of the still-active Imvrassós stream, was Hera's legendary birthplace and site of her trysts with Zeus; in the far corner of the fenced-in zone you tread a large, exposed patch of the Sacred Way.

Modern **IRÉON** nearby is a nondescript, grid-plan resort behind a coarse-shingle beach, where the water can be cold owing to the outflow of the Imvrassós; nonetheless the place has fanatical devotees who patronize studios and small hotels, mostly within sight of the more characterful waterfront. Seaside **tavernas** are tempting, but the best eating here lies inland, either at corner premises *Angyra*, a welcoming, super-hygienic, seafood-strong ouzerí, or nearby *Ioannis O Psaras* on a perpendicular to the shore, more shambolic but serving only fresh, own-caught fish – which sells out quickly.

Southern Sámos

Since the circum-island bus only passes through or near the places below once or twice weekly, you really need your own vehicle to explore them. Three Samian "**pottery villages**", in addition to the usual wares, specialize in the *Koúpa toú Pythagóra* or "Pythagorean cup", supposedly designed by the sage to leak over the user's lap if they were overfilled. The biggest concentration of retail outlets is at **KOUMARADHÉÏ**, about 7km west of Hóra. From here you can descend to the sixteenth-century monastery of **Megális Panayías** (Wed–Mon 10am–1pm & 5.30–8pm), containing very damp-smudged frescoes, then carry on via **Mýli** to **PAGÓNDAS**, a large hillside community with a splendid main square (venue for a lively Pentecost Sunday-evening festival) and an unusual communal fountain house on the southerly hillside. From there, a scenic road curls 15km around deforested hillside to **PÝRGOS**, at the head of a ravine draining southwest and the centre of Samian honey production; best **taverna** here is central *Koutouki tou Barba Dhimitri* (all year, supper only) with a good range of vegetarian *mezédhes* and grills.

The rugged coast south of the Pagóndas–Pýrgos route is largely inaccessible and fire-scarred, glimpsed by most visitors for the first and last time from the descending plane bringing them to Sámos. **Tsópela**, a scenic sand-and-gravel cove at a gorge mouth, is the only **beach** here with marked track access and a good rustic **taverna** in a surviving pine grove, with fish and a dish or two of the day; with care, ordinary cars regularly make the six-kilometre descent. The western reaches of this shoreline are approached via handsome **KOUMÉÏKA**, with a massive inscribed marble fountain and a pair of *kafenía*-snack bars on its square. Below extends the long pebbly bay at **Bállos**, with sand, rock overhangs and a naturist area at the far east end. Bállos itself is merely a collection of summer houses, several places to stay (some contracted to package operators) and a few **tavernas**, all on the shore road. The best **accommodation** for walk-ins is *Hotel Amfilissos* (Ⓣ22730 31669; ❹), while good-value grills and a few seafood items are served at simple *Paralia* (May–early Oct). From Kouméïka, the paved side road going west just before the village is a very useful short cut for travelling towards Órmos Marathokámbou (see p.752) and beyond.

Kokkári and around

Leaving Vathý on the north-coast section of the island loop road, you've little to stop for until **KOKKÁRI**, Sámos's second major tourist centre. The town's profile, covering two knolls behind twin headlands, remains unchanged, and one or two fishermen still doggedly untangle nets on the quay, but its identity has been altered beyond recognition by inland expansion across old vineyards. Since the exposed, coarse-pebble **beaches** here are buffeted by near-constant winds, locals have made a virtue of necessity by developing the place as a successful **windsurfing** resort – just west of town a **school** (Ⓣ22730 92102, Ⓦwww.samoswindsurfing.gr) thrives all season long.

Practicalities

Buses stop on the through road, by the church. Other amenities on the same road include a municipal **tourist office** (Mon–Fri 8.30am–1.15pm; Ⓣ22730 92217), a few **ATMs**, branches of all major Samian **travel agents**, and a **newsstand/bookstore**, Lexis; on a seaward lane stands a **post office** in a Portakabin.

As at Pythagório, a fair proportion of Kokkári's **accommodation** is booked solid by tour companies; exceptions include *Lemos* (Ⓣ22730 92250; ❹), near the north end of the west beach, *Pension Angela* (Ⓣ22730 92052; ❸) and (for a guaranteed view of the fishing port), *Pension Alkyonis* (Ⓣ22730 92225; ❸). If money's no object, then plump for A-class *Arion* (Ⓣ22370 92020, Ⓦwww.arion-hotel.gr; ❼), a well-designed bungalow/hotel-wing complex on an unburnt patch of hillside 2km west.

Tavernas lining the north waterfront have a nice view and little else to recommend; an exception is *Piccolo Porto* (supper only), serving wood-oven pizzas. The area is better for **nightlife**, with **bars** on the little square where the concreted stream meets the sea. By far the best eating is either at *Iy Byra*, opposite the main church, packed every night for its limited but superbly executed range of light *mezédhes*, or *Ammos Plaz* on the west beach, one of the oldest establishments in town, offering fair-priced *mayireftá* and fish – they've a loyal repeat clientele, and you must book days in advance (☎22730 92463) for seaside tables.

West of Kokkári: the coast

The closest sheltered **beaches** are twenty to thirty minutes' walk west, all with sunbeds and permanently anchored umbrellas. The first, **Lemonákia**, is a bit close to the road, though *Arion* patrons favour it and there's an adequate, if not brilliant **taverna**. The graceful crescent of **Tzamadhoú**, 1km beyond, has path-only access, with the eastern third of the beach (saucer-shaped pebbles) a well-established nudist zone. There's one more pebble bay, 7km west beyond Avlákia, called **Tzaboú**, with a snack-bar, but it's not worth a special trip when the prevailing northwest wind is up.

At **Platanákia**, essentially a handful of buildings at a bridge by the turning for Manolátes (see below), *Iy Apolavsis* **taverna** has a limited choice of good *mayireftá*. Platanákia is actually the eastern quarter of **ÁYIOS KONSTANDÍNOS**, whose surf-pounded esplanade has been prettified. However, there are no usable beaches within walking distance, so the collection of warm-toned stone buildings, with few modern intrusions, constitutes a peaceful alternative to Kokkári, only seeing much trade in spring when Dutch hikers frequent the place. For **accommodation**, try *Hotel Iro* (☎22730 94013; ❸), or *Hotel Apartments Agios Konstantinos* (☎22730 94000; ❹), both on the road down to the sea. **Eating** out, you're spoilt for choice; besides *Iy Apolavsis*, there's cheap-and-cheerful *Akroyiali* at mid-quay, open all day, or superior *Aeolos* (May–Sept) at the far west end of the esplanade (June–Sept), with terrific fish or grilled meat and a few daily baked dishes, served at tables adjoining a tiny pebble beach.

Beyond this point, the mountains hem the road in against the sea, and the terrain doesn't relent until **Kondakéïka**; its diminutive shore annexe of **Áyios Nikólaos** has a good venue for fish meals in *Iy Psaradhes* (☎22730 32489; Easter–Oct), with a terrace lapped by the waves – you'll need to book in season as it's appeared (deservedly) in so many guides. A reasonable pebble beach, **Piáki**, lies ten minutes' walk east past the last studio units.

From Kondakéïka, a road – first paved, then good dirt – leads inland 2.5km to the signposted Byzantine **church of Kímisis Theotókou**. The oldest and most artistically noteworthy on Sámos, it has extensive frescoes contemporaneous with the building (late twelfth or early thirteenth century). The deceptively simple exterior gives little hint of the glorious barrel-vaulted interior (unlocked) covered with saints, the Archangel and Christ in various guises, still vivid except where ceiling damp has blurred the images.

Hill villages

Inland between Kokkári and Kondakéïka, an idyllic landscape of pine, cypress and orchards is overawed by dramatic mountains; except for streaks of damage reaching the sea between Lemonákia and Tzaboú, it miraculously escaped the 2000 fire. Despite bulldozer vandalism, some of the trail system linking the various **hill villages** is still intact, and walkers can return to the main highway to catch a bus back to base.

VOURLIÓTES, closest to Kokkári, has beaked chimneys and brightly painted shutters sprouting from its typical tile-roofed houses. But by cutting down all the shade trees and packing tables into every available space local restaurateurs have ruined the formerly photogenic central square; it's best to pass over the **tavernas** there in favour of *Iy Pera Vrysi*, at the village entrance, or *Piyi Pnaka*, in the idyllic eponymous hamlet just off the ascending Vourliótes road. **MANOLÁTES**, further uphill and an hour-plus walk away via a deep river canyon, also has several simple **tavernas** (the pick of these being *Iy Filia*), and is the most popular trailhead for the five-hour round-trip up **Mount Ámbelos** (Karvoúnis), the island's second-highest summit. From Manolátes you can no longer easily continue on foot to Stavrinídhes, the next village, but should plunge straight down, partly on a cobbled path, through the shady valley known as **Aïdhónia** (Nightingales), towards Platanákia.

Karlóvassi

KARLÓVASSI, 31km west of Vathý and Sámos's second town, is sleepier and more old-fashioned than the capital, despite having roughly the same population. It's a useful base for enjoying western Sámos's excellent **beaches** or taking a number of rewarding **walks**. The name, despite a vehement denial of Ottoman legacy elsewhere on Sámos, appears to be a corruption of the Turkish for "snowy plain" – the plain in question being the conspicuous saddle of Mount Kérkis overhead. The town divides into five straggly neighbourhoods: Néo, well inland, whose growth was spurred by the influx of post-1923 refugees; Meséo, across the usually dry riverbed, tilting appealingly off a knoll and then blending with the shoreline district of Ríva; and picturesque Paleó (or Áno), above Limáni, the small harbour district.

Most tourists stay at or near **Limáni**, which has most tourist facilities. Hotels here tend to have road noise and not much view; **rooms**, all on the inland pedestrian lane behind the through road, are quieter – try *Vangelis Feloukatzis* (Ⓣ22730 33293; ❷). The port itself is an appealing place with a working boatyard at the west end and **ferry-ticket agencies** along the approach road. *Frappádhika* and bars line the pedestrianized quay, interrupted only by two overpriced **tavernas** (Meséo, below, is preferable for eating); *Semifredo* at the east end is a better bet for sweets and ice cream in swish surroundings.

Immediately overhead is the partly hidden hamlet of **Paleó**, its hundred or so houses draped either side of a leafy ravine, but with no reliable facilities. **Meséo**, just east, has three **tavernas** on the central platía, of which the most ambitious is *Dionysos* (all year), with creative dishes, pleasant indoor/outdoor tables and a wine list aspiring to Athenian sophistication. Quick-serving *Iy Platia* across the way is perhaps better value, popular with locals at lunchtime for traditional *mayireftá* and a few grills. Following the street linking this square to **Ríva**, you pass one of the huge, early twentieth-century **churches**, topped with twin belfries and a blue-and-white dome, that dot the coastal plain here. Just at the intersection with the shore road, you'll find the very popular, sunset-view ouzerí *To Kyma* (April–Oct), where Ethiopian proprietress Berhane adds a welcome Middle Eastern/East African touch (try *alí saláta*, with sun-dried tomatoes, cashews and courgettes) to the range of seafood and vegetarian dishes – expect a wait for tables. Otherwise, Ríva has little of interest besides derelict stone-built warehouses, tanneries and mansions, reminders of the defunct leather industry that flourished here until the 1960s. As for **Néo**, you'll almost certainly visit one of several **ATMs**, the **post office** or the **bus stop/taxi rank** on the main lower square. The local university students keep **nightlife** lively enough; besides *Popcorn* on Limáni's quay, there's *Café-Bar Toxotis* and local **cinema** Gorgyra on the same street in the east of town.

Western Sámos

The closest **beach** to Karlóvassi is **Potámi**, forty minutes' walk away via the coast road from Limáni or an hour by a more scenic, high trail from Paleó. This broad arc of sand and pebbles gets crowded at summer weekends, when effectively the entire town descends on the place. There are a few **rooms east of the beach**, though many folk camp rough along the lower reaches of the river that gives the beach its name. A streamside path leads twenty minutes inland, past the eleventh-century church of **Metamórfosis** – oldest on Sámos – to a point where the river disappears into a small gorge (a guard-railed but still vertiginous stairway takes you up and left here). Otherwise, you must swim and wade 100m in heart-stoppingly cold water through a series of fern-tufted rock pools before reaching a low but vigorous waterfall; bring shoes with good tread and perhaps even rope if you want to explore above the first cascade. Just above the Metamórfosis church, a clear if precipitous path leads up to a small, contemporaneous **Byzantine fortress**. There's little to see inside other than a subterranean cistern and badly crumbled lower curtain wall, but the views in all directions are terrific; in October the place is carpeted with pink autumn crocuses.

The **coast beyond Potámi** ranks among the most beautiful and unspoilt on Sámos; since the early 1980s it has served as a protected refuge for the rare **monk seal**, still glimpsed occasionally by lucky hikers or bathers. The dirt track at the west end of Potámi bay ends after twenty minutes on foot, from which you backtrack 100m or so to find the well-cairned side trail running parallel to the water. After twenty minutes you'll arrive at **Mikró Seïtáni**, a small pebble cove guarded by sculpted rock walls. A full hour's walk from the trailhead, through olive terraces, brings you to **Megálo Seïtáni**, the island's finest beach, at the mouth of the intimidating Kakopérato Gorge. Bring food and water, though not necessarily a swimsuit – there's no dress code at either of the Seïtáni bays. During peak season, there are a couple of daily **water-taxi** services from Karlóvassi port (€10 return) for non-walkers.

Southwestern beach resorts

The first substantial place you reach on the island loop road south of Karlóvassi is **Marathókambos**, an amphitheatrical village overlooking the eponymous gulf; there are no tourist facilities, and by taking the bypass road you'll avoid the village's traffic bottlenecks – and save about 4km. Its port, **ÓRMOS MARATHOKÁMBOU**, 18km from Karlóvassi, has become something of a resort, though with ample character in its backstreets. The harbour is the starting point for several weekly *kaïki* **day-trips** to the nearby islet of Samiopoúla, inaccessible parts of the south coast and sometimes Foúrni. Otherwise, the main focus of attention is the pedestrianized quay, home to several **tavernas**, of which the best is *Iy Trata* at the far east end of things, just off the pedestrian zone. **Accommodation** includes *Studios Avra* (Ⓣ22730 37221; ③), unimprovably perched above the jetty, or *Hotel Kerkis Bay* (Ⓣ 22730 37202, Ⓦwww.kerkis-bay.com; ③), one block inland from mid-quay.

The **beach** immediately east of Órmos is hardly the best; for better ones continue 2km west to **VOTSALÁKIA** (signposted as "Kámbos"), Sámos's most family-pitched resort, straggling a further 2km behind the island's longest (if not its most beautiful) beach. But for many, Votsalákia is still an improvement on the Pythagório area, and Mount Kérkis looming overhead rarely fails to impress (see opposite). For **accommodation**, try *Elsa Hiou*'s rooms behind her *Evoinos* taverna near mid-strand (Ⓣ22730 37791 or 694 67 92 923; ③); *Emmanuil Dhespotakis* has numerous premises towards the quieter, more scenic western end of things (Ⓣ22730 31258; ③–④). Also nearby are two **tavernas** employing wood-fired ovens: *Loukoullos*, overlooking the sea, best at night, and *Akroyialia* (*Anna's*), about the oldest (1979) eatery here, where tasty recipes offset small portions and bumped-up prices. Branches of nearly all the main Vathý **travel**

agencies offer **vehicle rental** and there are two stand-alone **ATMs**; during summer a **bus** calls several times daily from Karlóvassi.

Loukoullos marks the start of the access track to **Fournáki**, a series of sand-and-pebble **nudist coves** backed by low cliffs – sun traps in spring or autumn. Alternatively, continue 3km further to 600-metre-long **Psilí Ámmos**, not to be confused with its namesake beach in southeastern Sámos. The sea shelves ridiculously gently here, and more cliffs shelter clusters of naturists at the east end. Development comprises just three **studio complexes** in the pines at mid-beach, and two **tavernas** up on the approach road. Access to **Limniónas**, a smaller cove 2km further west, passes the *Limnionas Bay Hotel* (Ⓣ22730 37057; ❺), the best local **accommodation**, with tiered units arrayed around a garden and pool. Yachts and *kaïkia* occasionally call at the protected bay, which offers decent swimming at the east end, away from a rock shelf in the middle.

Mount Kérkis and around

Gazing up from a supine seaside position, you may be inspired to **climb Mount Kérkis**. The classic route begins from Votsalákia, along the paved but narrow lane leading inland towards Evangelistrías convent. After a 45-minute walk through olive groves, the path begins, more or less following power lines up to the convent. A friendly nun may proffer an ouzo and point you up the paint-marked trail, continuing even more steeply up to the peak. The views are tremendous, though the climb itself is humdrum once you're out of the trees. About an hour before the top there's a chapel with an attached cottage for sheltering in emergencies, and just beyond, a welcome spring. All told, it's a seven-hour return outing from Votsalákia, not counting rest stops.

Less ambitious walkers might want to circle the mountain, first by vehicle and then by foot. The road beyond Limniónas to Kallithéa and Dhrakéï, back-of-beyond villages with views across to Ikaría, is paved to Dhrakéï, making arrival possible on an ordinary motorbike. The bus service is better during term time, when a vehicle leaves Karlóvassi (Mon–Fri 1.20pm) bound for these remote spots; during summer it only operates two days a week at best (most reliably Mon).

From **DHRAKÉÏ**, a lovely trail – minimally disrupted by a track – descends ninety minutes through forest to Megálo Seïtáni, from where it's easy to continue on to Karlóvassi within another two-and-a-half hours. People climbing up from Seïtáni discover that the bus (if any) returns from Dhrakéï at dawn or 2.45pm, compelling them either to retrace their steps, summon a taxi or stay at a few unofficial **rooms** establishments (summer only) in Dhrakéi, and dine at one of four **taverna-kafenía**. In **KALLITHÉA**, there's only a simple *psistariá* on the tiny square. From Kallithéa, a newer track (from beside the cemetery) and an older trail both lead up within 45 minutes to a spring, rural chapel and plane tree on the west flank of Kérkis, with path-only continuation for another thirty minutes to a pair of faintly frescoed cave-churches. **Panayía Makriní** stands at the mouth of a high, wide but shallow grotto, whose balcony affords terrific views. By contrast, **Ayía Triádha**, a ten-minute scramble overhead, has most of its structure made up of cave wall; just adjacent, another long, narrow, volcanic cavern can be explored with a torch some hundred metres into the mountain.

After these subterranean exertions, the closest spot for a swim is **Vársamo** (Válsamo) cove, 4km below Kallithéa and reached via a well-signposted if rough dirt road. The **beach** consists of multicoloured volcanic pebbles, with two caves to shelter in, and a basic but not especially cheap **taverna** just inland, which also offers **rooms** (Ⓣ22730 37847; ❶).

Ikaría

Ikaría, a narrow, windswept landmass between Sámos and Mýkonos, is comparatively little visited and invariably underestimated by travel writers who haven't even shown up. The name supposedly derives from Icarus, who in legend fell into the sea just offshore after the wax bindings on his wings melted. For years the only substantial tourism was generated by a few **hot springs** on the south coast; since the early 1990s, however, tourist facilities of some quantity and quality have sprung up in and around Armenistís, the only resort of note. Overseas flights still don't land, as the airport at the northeast tip can't accommodate jets.

Ikaría, along with Thessaly, Lésvos and the Ionian islands, has traditionally been one of the **Greek Left**'s strongholds. This dates from long periods of right-wing domination in Greece, when (as in Byzantine times) the island was used as a place of **exile** for political dissidents, particularly Communists, who from 1946 to 1949 outnumbered native islanders. The strategy backfired, with the transportees (including Mikis Theodhorakis – see p.944 – in 1946–47) favourably impressing and proselytizing their hosts. But early in the twentieth century, many Ikarians had emigrated to North America and ironically their capitalist remittances kept the island going for decades. Nowadays posters urge you to attend anti-racist summer camps on Páros or help fund a Zapatista teacher-training school in Chiapas. Athens has always reacted to such contrarian stances with punitive neglect, which only made the islanders more self-sufficient and idiosyncratic. Local pride dictates that outside opinion matters little, and many Ikarians exhibit a lack of obsequiousness, and a studied **eccentricity**, which some visitors mistake for hostility.

For many the place is an acquired taste, contrasting strongly (for better or worse) with Sámos; heaps of construction waste, rusting machinery and automobile carcasses lend the place a scruffy air. Except for forested portions in the northwest (now fire-denuded near the shore), it's not a strikingly beautiful island. The mostly desolate south coast is overawed by steep cliffs, while the less sheer north face is furrowed by deep canyons creating hairpin road-bends extreme even by Greek-island standards. Neither are there many picturesque villages, since houses are scattered so as to be next to their vineyards and famous apricot orchards.

Áyios Kírykos and around

Ferries on the Pireás–Cyclades–Sámos line call at the south-coast port and capital of **ÁYIOS KÍRYKOS**, about 1km southwest of the main thermal resort. Because of the spa trade, beds are at a premium in late summer; arriving in the evening from Sámos, accept any reasonable offers of rooms, or – if in a group – offers of a taxi-ride to the north coast, which shouldn't cost more than €50 to Armenistís. A **bus** crosses the island from the seafront (July–Sept 10; Mon–Fri noon) to Évdhilos, usually changing vehicles there for the onward trip to Armenistís.

The spa of **Thérma**, 1km northeast of the port, saw its heyday in the 1960s, and now relies on a mostly elderly, government-subsidized clientele. Of more general interest is the *spílio* or **natural sauna** on the shore (7.30am–noon & 5.30–8pm; €3). Other good bets for informal soaks are the seaside, open-air pool of the **Asklipioú hot springs**, reached by steps down from the courthouse, or (better) the natural, shoreline hot springs at **Thérma Lefkádhos**, 2km southwest of Áyios Kírykos, where scalding water mixes

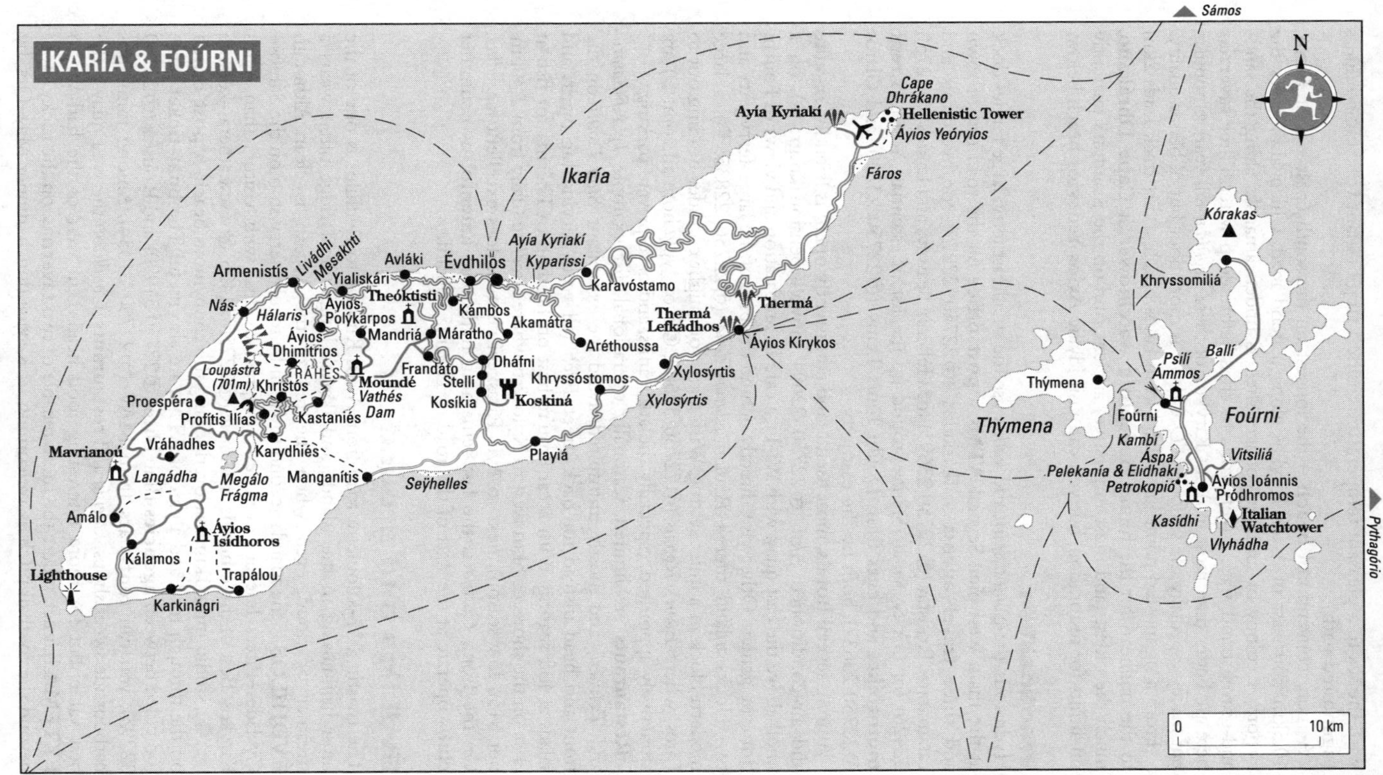

IKARÍA & FOÚRNI
Sámos
N
Cape Dhrákano
Ayía Kyriakí
Hellenistic Tower
Áyios Yeóryios
Fáros
Ikaría
Ayía Kyriakí
Kyparíssi
Armenistís
Livádhi
Mesakhtí
Avláki
Évdhilos
Yialiskári
Karavóstamo
Nás
Theóktisti
Háloris
Áyios Polýkarpos
Kámbos
Thermá
Thermá Lefkádhos
Akamátra
Áyios Dhimítrios
Mandriá
Máratho
Aréthoussa
Áyios Kírykos
Loupástra (701m)
RAHES
Frandáto
Dháfni
Khristós
Moundé
Stellí
Xylosýrtis
Proespéra
Vathés Dam
Kosíkia
Koskiná
Khryssóstomos
Xylosýrtis
Profítis Ilías
Kastaniés
Vráhadhes
Karydhiés
Playiá
Mavrianoú
Langádha
Megálo Frágma
Manganítis
Seÿhelles
Amálo
Áyios Isídhoros
Kálamos
Lighthouse
Trapálou
Karkinágri
Kórakas
Khryssomiliá
Ballí
Psilí Ámmos
Thýmena
Foúrni
Thýmena
Foúrni
Kambí
Áspa
Vitsiliá
Pelekanía & Elidhaki
Petrokopió
Áyios Ioánnis Pródhromos
Italian Watchtower
Kasídhi
Vlyhádha
Pythagório
0
10 km
Náxos, Páros, Sýros & Mýkonos
Pátmos

with the sea to a pleasant temperature inside a ring of giant volcanic boulders (signposted path).

A more conventional **beach** – the longest on the south coast – is at **Fáros**, 10.5km northeast of Áyios Kírykos along a good road, which also serves the airport. A colony of summer cottages shelters under tamarisks along the sand-and-gravel strand, with a reefy zone to cross before deep water. Three **tavernas** here are better than most in Áyios Kírykos; of these *Leonidas* (all year) is popular, but pricey, especially the seafood – *O Grigoris* is more dour but of better quality.

From a signposted point just inland from Fáros beach, a dirt track leads 2km to the trailhead for the round **Hellenistic watchtower** at **Cape Dhrákano**, much the oldest (and most impressive) ancient ruin on the island; it's currently off-limits for restoration, but you can visit idyllic **Áyios Yeóryios** beach below.

Practicalities

Hydrofoils, the *Samos Spirit* and *kaïkia* use the small east jetty; large ferries dock at the main west pier. Several **ATMs**, a **post office** on the road out of town and three **travel agents** – Ikariadha (Ⓣ22750 22277) for hydrofoils and catamarans, Roustas (Ⓣ22750 23691) for Hellenic Seaways and Lakios (Ⓣ22750 22426) for GA & *Samos Spirit* – round up the list of essentials. You can **rent motorbikes** and **cars** from Dolihi Tours/Lemy (Ⓣ22750 23230) and Glaros Ⓣ22750 23637), both by the east jetty.

Among several **hotels**, most useful (and consistently open) is friendly, en-suite and air-conditioned *Akti* (Ⓣ22750 22694, Ⓦwww.pensionakti.gr; ❸), on a knoll above the east quay, with Wi-Fi, a café in preparation and views of Foúrni from the garden. Otherwise, directly behind the base of the large-ferry jetty and two blocks inland there's *Pension Maria-Elena* (Ⓣ22750 22835; ❸), a large modern block in a quiet setting. With a car you might consider heading out to Fáros, where *Evon's Rooms* (Ⓣ22750 32580, Ⓔevon_yp@hotmail.com; ❸) are attractively appointed, especially the attic units, and have private parking.

Restaurants are limited, seasonally operational (for example *Iy Klimataria* and *Tzivaeri*) and mostly uninspired; avoid the exorbitant *Stou Tsouri* on the front and head instead for back-street *Filoti* (all year), serving big pizzas and salads at loft seating. With a car, you're best off heading to Thérma for fish at *Avra* on the shore, or 5km west to Xylosýrti where *Arodhou* (daily from 2.30pm, not Mon low season), next to Ayía Paraskeví church, does excellent *mezédhes*. On the front, *Casino* is the last remaining traditional **kafenío**; two summer **clubs** operate at the start of the road to Thermá Lefkádhos.

Évdhilos and around

The twisting, 37-kilometre road from Áyios Kírykos to Évdhilos is one of the most hair-raising in the islands, and Ikaría's longitudinal ridge often wears a streamer of cloud, even when the rest of the Aegean is clear. Although **ÉVDHILOS** is the island's second town and a regular ferry stop on the Sámos–Cyclades–Pireás line, it's even less equipped to deal with visitors than Áyios Kírykos. Best of three **hotels** is *Kerame* (Ⓣ22750 31426, Ⓦwww.atheras-kerame.gr; ❹), studio units 1km east overlooking the eponymous beach. A **post office** on the through road and a pair of **ATMs** are also useful. The **boat-ticket** trade is divided between **agencies** Blue Nice (Ⓣ22750 31990) and Roustas (Ⓣ22750 32293); you can **rent cars** from MAV (Ⓣ22750 31354). Among numerous harbourside sweet shops, *kafenía* and **restaurants**, *Coralli* on the west quay is the best value, but for more interesting food head 1km west of the harbour to **FÝTEMA** hamlet, where the more reliable of two **tavernas**, on the rocky shore beyond the football pitch, is welcoming *Kalypso* (lunch/dinner May–Oct, by arrangement otherwise on ⓣ22750 31387), with excellent, reasonable vegetable dishes and fish.

KÁMBOS, 1.5km west of Fýtema, offers a small hilltop **museum** with finds from nearby **ancient Oinoe**; the twelfth-century church of **Ayía Iríni** stands adjacent, with column stumps and mosaic patches of a fourth-century basilica defining the entry courtyard. Lower down still are the sparse ruins of a **Byzantine palace** used to house exiled nobles, signposted as "odeion", which earlier structure it encloses. An unmarked track below the palace leads to a 250-metre-long sandy **beach** with a *kantína* and sunbeds. *Rooms Dhionysos* (ⓣ22750 31300 or 22750 31688; ❷), on the paved drive to the west end of the beach, are available from the green-doored store run by Vassilis Kambouris, who also acts as the unofficial and enthusiastic tourism officer for this part of Ikaría.

From Kámbos, a twisty road leads up 4km – as does an easier road from Avláki, in 3km – to Ikaría's outstanding medieval monument, the **monastery of Theóktisti**, looking over pines to the coast from its perch under a chaos of slanted granite slabs (under one of which is tucked the much-photographed chapel of **Theoskepastí**). The *katholikón* features damaged but worthwhile naïve frescoes dated to 1688; there's also a pleasant *kafenío* on site.

By following the road heading south and inland from Évdhilos' main church, signposted for Manganítis, you pass after 15km the marked side-track to the Byzantine **castle of Koskiná** (Nikariás). Any vehicle can cover the 2km to the start of a short walk up to the tenth-century fort, perched on a distinctive conical hill, with an arched gateway and vaulted chapel.

Beyond this turning, the paved road creeps over the island watershed before dropping steadily towards the south coast; with your own vehicle this is a quicker and much less curvy way back to Áyios Kírykos compared to going via Karavóstomo. The principal potential detour, 2km past the castle turning, is the road right (west) to the secluded pebble beach of **Seyhélles** ("Seychelles"), the best on this generally inhospitable coast, with the final approach by ten-minute hike.

Armenistís and around

Most visitors congregate at **ARMENISTÍS**, 51km from Áyios Kírykos via Évdhilos, and for good reason: this little resort lies below Ikaría's greatest (if slightly diminished) forest, with two enormous, sandy **beaches** battered by seasonal surf – **Livádhi** and **Mesaktí** – five and fifteen minutes' walk east respectively, the latter with several seasonal reed-roofed *kantínas*. The waves are complicated by strong lateral currents, and regular summer drownings have (at Livádhi) prompted the institution of a lifeguard service and installation of a string of safety buoys. Armenistís itself is spectacularly set, facing northeast along the length of Ikaría towards sun- and moonrise, with Mount Kérkis on Sámos visible on a clear day. Boats hauled up in a central sandy cove lend the place the air of a Cornish fishing village, though in fact it started out as a smuggler's depot, with no dwellings. Despite an ongoing building boom just west, it remains manageable, even if gentrification (and a package presence) set in some time ago.

Accommodation

There are easily a score of *dhomátia* in the Armenistís area, as well as four **hotels**, mostly working a May-to-September season. Among the latter, the *Erofili Beach*, at the entrance to town (ⓣ22750 71058, ⓦwww.erofili.gr; ❻), is considered the best on the island, though the common area and pool perched dramatically over Livádhi beach impress more than the rooms. Runners-up include the *Messakti Village* complex (ⓣ22750 71331, ⓦwww.messakti-village.com; ❻) just above Mesaktí beach, with a bigger pool, its common areas and private terraces complementing large, minimally furnished self-catering units suitable for three to six, or – on the western edge of Armenistís – the good-value ★ *Daidalos* (ⓣ22750 71390, ⓦwww.daidaloshotel.gr; ④), with another eyrie-pool, unusually appointed rooms and a shady breakfast terrace. Among **rooms**, the *Kirki* by the *Erofili Beach* (ⓣ22750 71254 or ask at *Dhefini* taverna; ③) is spartan but en suite, with large private balconies and sea views; along the shore lane, *Paskhalia Rooms* (ⓣ22750 71302; Easter–Oct; ②) are on the small side but with air-conditioning, TV and fridge, while at the far end of Livádhi beach, ★ *Valeta Apartments* (ⓣ22750 71252, ⓦwww.valeta.gr, May–Oct; ④) offer the best standard and setting outside of the hotels, with both studios and quads.

Eating, drinking and nightlife

There are five full-service **tavernas** in Armenistís, of which two have a consistently good reputation. *Dhelfini*, its terrace hovering above the fishing-boat cove, is a cheap-ish-and-cheerful favourite – come early or very late for a table, and a mix of grills or *mayireftá*. *Paskhalia* (aka *Vlahos* after the helpful managing family), under the eponymous rooms, serves more elaborate food at its sea-view terrace, and is a reliable venue for both breakfast and during off-season. At the far end of Livádhi, *Atsahas* is acceptable as a beach taverna, with generous, slightly oily vegetarian platters. Of two *zaharoplastía*, go for ★ *Paradhosiaka Glyka* (*Kioulanis*), featuring addictive *karydhópita* with goats'-milk ice cream. Just east of Mesaktí in the fishing settlement of **YIALISKÁRI**, looking out past pines to a picturesque jetty church, there's another pair of tavernas above the boat-launching slips: ★ *Kelaris* (aka *tis Eleftherias*) tops for well-executed *mayireftá* and the freshest fish locally, and nearby *Symposio*, good for non-stodgy *mayireftá* and meat grills. Small **summer-clubs** like *Casmir* and *Pleiades* operate in the river reeds behind Livádhi, though most **nightlife** involves extended sessions in a few **café-bars** at the north end of Armenistís quay – or up in Ráhes (see below).

Information, transport - and getting away

The only **Internet café** is Internet Point, at the west edge of the resort. There are at least three **scooter/mountain-bike rental** agencies; among five **car-rental** outlets, Aventura (ⓣ22750 71117) and Dolihi Tours/Lemy (ⓣ22750 71122) are the most prominent, with branches for drop-offs in Évdhilos and Áyios Kírykos respectively, handy for ferry departures towards Sámos at an ungodly hour. Indeed, getting away when you need to is problematic, since taxis and buses can prove elusive – with the exception of the fairly frequent (late June to early Sept) shuttle linking Armenistís with Yialiskári, Nás and Ráhes. Theoretically, long-distance **buses** head for Évdhilos twice daily (once Sat/Sun) mid-July to early September; Áyios Kírykos has only one through service year-round in the morning, though this fills with school kids in term-time. If you've a ferry to catch, it's more sensible to prebook a **taxi**: a list of numbers is posted at the entrance to Armenistís.

The Ráhes villages

Armenistís was originally the port of four inland hamlets – Áyios Dhimítrios, Áyios Polýkarpos, Kastaniés and Khristós – collectively known as **Ráhes**. Despite the modern, paved access roads through the pines, the settlements retain a certain Shangri-La quality, with older residents speaking a positively Homeric dialect. On an island not short of foibles, **KHRISTÓS** (Khristós Rahón in full) is particularly strange inasmuch as most locals sleep until 11am or so, shop until about 4pm, then have another nap until 8pm, whereupon they rise and spend most of the night shopping, eating and drinking, in particular excellent home-brewed **wine** traditionally kept in goatskins. In fact most villages west of Évdhilos adhere to this schedule, defying edicts to bring them into line with the rest of Greece. The local **festival** is August 6, though better ones take place the same day at Stávlos; further southwest in the woods at Langádha valley (August 14–15); or at Áyios Isídhoros monastery (May 14).

On or near the pedestrianized *agorá* of Khristós, there's a **post office**, plenty of rustic **bars** (4pm–3am) and a few sweet shops. In accordance with the prevailing nocturnalism, **eating** lunch here is a non-starter; *Kapilio* on the pedestrian zone is a good carniverous supper option, though *Platanos* just downhill in **ÁYIOS DHIMÍTRIOS** is reckoned the best locally, while *Aoratos* bar-restaurant is the place to be in **ÁYIOS POLÝKARPOS**.

Walking between Ráhes and the coastal resorts on old paths is a favourite visitor activity, and a locally produced, accurate map-guide is available: *The Round of Ráhes on Foot* shows most asphalt roads, tracks and trails in the west of the island, as well as a loop-hike taking in the best the Ráhes villages have to offer. The marked route sticks partly to surviving paths; the authors suggest a full day for the circuit, though total walking time won't exceed six hours. More advanced outings involve descending the Hálaris canyon – with its historic Loupástra bridge – to Nás, or crossing the island to Manganítis via Ráhes.

Nás

Following altercations with locals, hippies and beachside naturists have shifted themselves 3km west of Armenistís by paved road to **NÁS**, a tree-clogged river canyon ending at a deceptively sheltered sand-and-pebble beach. This little bay is almost completely enclosed by weirdly sculpted rock formations, but for the same reasons as at Mesaktí it's unwise to swim outside the cove's natural limits – marked here also with a line of buoys. The crumbling foundations of the fifth-century BC temple of **Artemis Tavropoleio** (Artemis in Bull-Headress) overlook the permanent deep pool at the mouth of the river. Back at the top of the stone-paved stairs leading down to the beach from the road are several **tavernas**, most of them offering rooms. Among **accommodation**, the rambling *Artemis* (☎22750 71485; ❷ rooms, ❸ studios) overlooks the river canyon, while ★ *Thea* (☎22750 71491; ❷) faces out to sea. The latter offers the most accomplished **cooking** in the area, working weekends October to May as well, with lots of vegetarian options like *soufikó* (the local ratatouille) and pumpkin-filled pítta.

Satellite islands: Thýmena and Foúrni

The straits between Sámos and Ikaría are speckled with a mini-archipelago of several islets – once the lair of pirates from various corners of the Mediterranean – of which Thýmena and Foúrni are inhabited. Most westerly **Thýmena** has one tiny hillside settlement; *kaïkia* call regularly at the quay below on their way between Ikaría or Sámos and Foúrni, but there are no tourist facilities or attractions, save one large beach south of "town". **FOÚRNI** is home to a huge fishing fleet and one of the more thriving boatyards in the Aegean; thanks in part to these its population is stable, unlike so many small Greek islands.

The small **ferry** *Samos Spirit* and **kaïki** *Samos Sun* are based much of the week at Foúrni, making morning shopping-and-post departures to Sámos, returning the same day. Larger main-line ferries that call every few days in either direction are likewise run for the benefit of the islanders. The only way to visit Foúrni on a **day-trip** is by using one of the several weekly morning departures of the *Samos Sun* from Áyios Kírykos.

Apart from remote **Khryssomiliá** hamlet in the north, reached by the island's longest (18km) and worst road, Foúrni's inhabitants are concentrated in the **port** and **Kambí** hamlet just to the south. The harbour community is larger than it seems from the sea, with a friendly ambience reminiscent of 1970s Greece.

Foúrni port practicalities

The central "high street", fieldstoned and mulberry-shaded, ends well inland at a little **platía** with two giant plane trees, a bakery and a café; between them stands a Hellenistic sarcophagus found in a nearby field. Nearby there's a **post office** and stand-alone **ATM**, plus several well-stocked shops.

Manolis and Patra Markakis (Ⓣ22750 51268, Ⓦwww.fourni-patrasrooms.gr), immediately left of the *kaïki* quay, manage three popular **accommodation** options, ranging from wood-floored, antique-bed rooms, some with balconies (❶), to fourteen superb hillside apartments, most sleeping up to four, in a tiered complex (❸). When they're full, plump for *Bilios Resort*, apartments high up the south hillside (Ⓣ22750 51113, Ⓔbilioshotel@axiotis-group.com; ❸), or the 2007-built *Archipelagos Hotel* by the fishing port (Ⓣ22750 51250, Ⓦwww.archipelagoshotel.gr; ❹–❺), with designer fittings in its doubles and suites.

Among waterfront **tavernas**, local favourite is *Nikos'*, where *astakós* may be on the menu (except Sept–Jan); on the high street, *To Koutouki tou Psarakou* is good for grilled meat. For breakfast and desserts, repair to the tamarisk terrace of *To Arhondiko tis Kyras Kokonas*, under the *Markakis* inn. There's surprisingly lively **nightlife** at a half-dozen music cafés, clubs and ouzerís, often until 5am.

Around Foúrni

A fifteen-minute walk south from the primary school on a flagstone lane, skirting the cemetery and then slipping over the windmill ridge, brings you to **KAMBÍ**, a scattered community overlooking a pair of sandy, tamarisk-shaded coves. There are two cheap and sustaining **tavernas**: *Kambi*, with tables on the sand, and slightly more accomplished *O Yiorgos*, just up a valley inland. A path continues south around the headland to other, more secluded bays of varying sizes and beach consistencies which, like Kambí cove, are favourite anchorages for passing yachts, but unlike Kambí host summer communities of rough campers and naturists. One, **Elidháki**, has paved-road access, and (like Kambí) seasonal taxi-boat service from the port.

The main paved road ends at the southerly hamlet and monastery of **Áyios Ioánnis Pródhromos**. Just before arrival, paved drives lead to isolated **Vlyhádha** and **Vitsiliá**, which like most local beaches have no facilities. Overall, southern Foúrni is the most rewarding part; two beaches immediately north of the harbour have been spoilt in various ways and, in the extreme north of the island, remote **KHRYSSOMILIÁ**, is still most easily approached by taxi-boat or on the *Samos Sun* rather than along the atrocious road. The village, divided into a shore district and a hillside settlement, has a decent main beach flanked by better, less accessible ones. There are two **tavernas** near the jetty and a few **rooms**, though the locals can be less than forthcoming with outsiders.

Híos

"Craggy Híos", as **Homer** aptly described his putative birthplace, has a turbulent history and a strong identity. This large island has always been prosperous: in medieval times through the export of **mastic resin** – a trade controlled by Genoese overlords between 1346 and 1566 – and later by the

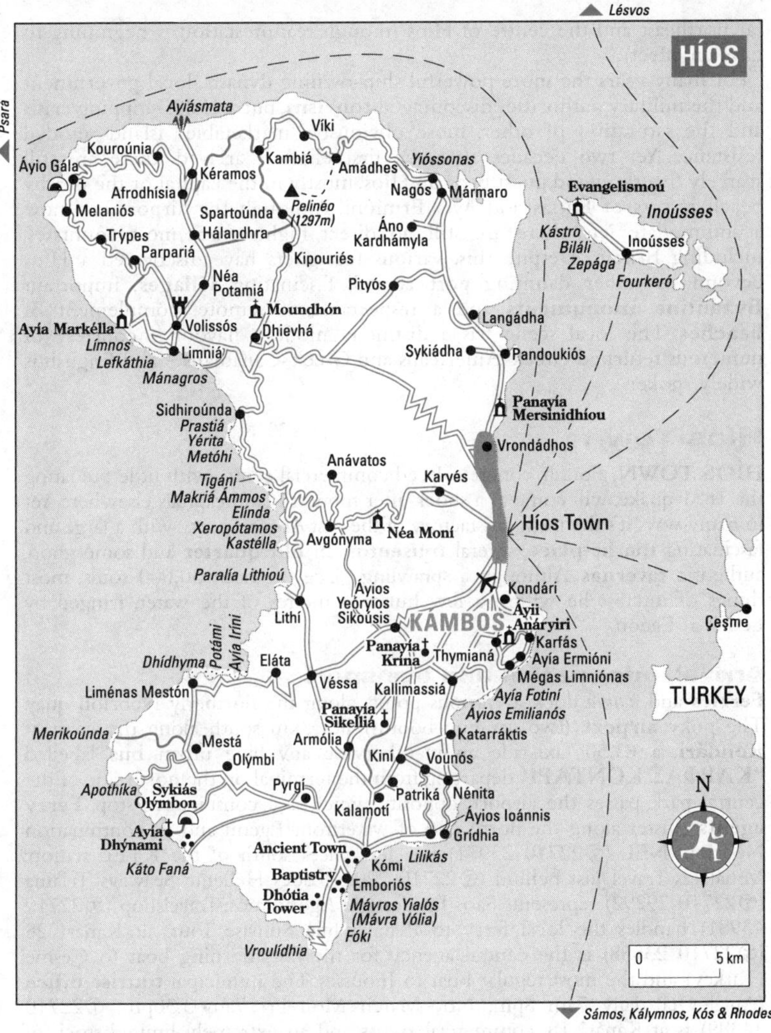

Ottomans, who dubbed the place Sakız Adası ("Resin Island"). Since union with Greece in 1912, several shipping dynasties have emerged here, continuing to generate wealth. Participation in maritime life is widespread, with someone in almost every family spending time in the merchant navy.

Unfortunately, the island has suffered more than its share of **catastrophes** during the past two centuries. The Ottomans perpetrated their most infamous, if not their worst, anti-revolutionary atrocity here in March 1822, massacring 30,000 Hiots and enslaving or exiling even more. In 1881, much of Híos was destroyed by a violent earthquake, and throughout the 1980s the island's natural beauty was compromised by devastating forest fires, compounding the effect of generations of tree-felling by boat-builders. Over half of the majestic pines are now gone, with substantial patches of woods persisting only in the far northeast and the centre of Híos (though reafforestation is beginning to have an effect).

For many years the more powerful ship-owning dynasts, local government and the military authorities discouraged **tourism**, but a 1980s shipping crisis and the saturation of other, more obviously "marketable" islands eroded resistance. Yet two decades after the first charters arrived, there are still scarcely five thousand guest beds on Híos, mostly in the capital or the nearby beach resorts of Karfás and Ayía Ermióni. Although the airport can now accommodate jets, there are still no direct flights from most countries, including Britain. Despite this, various foreigners have discovered a Híos beyond its rather daunting port capital: fascinating **villages**, important **Byzantine monuments** and a respectable, if remote, complement of **beaches**. The local scene has a distinctly modern flavour – courtesy of numerous returned Greek-Americans and Greek-Canadians – and English is widely spoken.

Híos Town

HÍOS TOWN, a brash, concrete-laced commercial centre with little predating the 1881 quake, will come as a shock after modest island capitals elsewhere. Yet in many ways it's the most satisfactory of the east Aegean ports, with a large and fascinating **marketplace**, several **museums**, an **old quarter** and some good, authentic **tavernas**. Although a sprawling place of about 30,000 souls, most things of interest lie within a few hundred metres of the water, fringed by Leofóros Egéou.

Arrival, information and transport

Ferries and *kaïkia* dock at various points along the northerly Neoríon quay. The poky **airport** (two car-hire booths) lies 3km south along the coast at **Kondári**, a €3.50 taxi-ride away; otherwise any blue urban **bus** labelled "ΚΑΡΦΑΣ ΚΟΝΤΑΡΙ" departing from the terminal on the north side of the central park passes the airport, opposite which is a conspicuous stop. **Ferry agents** cluster along the north end of waterfront Egéou and its continuation Neoríon: NEL (Ⓣ22710 23971) is a few paces south of the KTEL station; Mihalakis Travel just behind (Ⓣ22710 22034) does Hellenic Seaways; Triaina (Ⓣ22710 29292) represents Saos Ferries and Agoudimos; Travelshop (Ⓣ22710 43981) handles the local ferry to Psará; while Sunrise Tours at Kanári 28 (Ⓣ22710 23558) is the central agency for the fast morning boat to Çeşme (Turkey) and the most regular boat to Inoússes. The municipal **tourist office** (April–Oct daily 7am–8pm; Nov–March Mon–Fri 7am–3.30pm; Ⓣ22710 44389) is at Kanári 18; commercial **maps** and an extremely limited stock of English-language **books** are found at Newsstand, at the first "kink" in Egéou. The most reliable **Internet** café is Enter, just seaward of the *Fedra Hotel*. The **post office** is on Omírou; **ATM**s are legion.

Long-distance **KTEL buses** leave from just behind the passenger waiting-room on Egéou. While services to the south of Híos are adequate, those bound elsewhere are almost nonexistent, and to explore properly you'll need to rent a powerful **motorbike** or a car, or share a **taxi** (bright red here, not grey as in most of Greece; main rank on central platía). Two independent or small-chain **car-rental** agencies sit at Evyenías Handhrí 5–7, behind the eyesore *Chandris Hotel*; of these, Vassilakis/Reliable Rent a Car (Ⓣ22710 29300 or 694 43 34 898), with a branch at Mégas Limniónas (Ⓣ22710 31728), is recommended.

Accommodation

Híos Town has a fair quantity of affordable **accommodation**, rarely completely full. Most places line the water or the perpendicular alleys and parallel streets behind, and almost all are plagued by traffic noise to some degree – listed are the more peaceful establishments.

Chios Rooms Egéou 110, cnr Kokáli ⓣ22710 20198 or 697 28 33 841, ⓦwww.chiosrooms.gr. Don and Dina's lovingly restored tile- or wood-floored, high-ceilinged rooms, some en suite and relatively quiet for a seafront location. Best is the penthouse "suite" with private terrace. ❷

Fedra Mihaïl Livanoú 13 ⓣ22710 41130. Well-appointed *pension* in a nineteenth-century mansion, with stone arches in the downstairs winter bar; in summer the bar operates outside, so get a rear room to avoid nocturnal noise. ❹

Filoxenia Roïdhou 2, cnr Voupálou 8 ⓣ22710 22813. Better than it looks from outside, this rambling, early 1900s building is wrapped around an atrium-airshaft. Room furnishings – including round double beds, TV, and a/c – are part updated; breakfast is offered at the mezzanine level. ❸

Grecian Castle Bella Vista shore avenue, en route to airport ⓣ22710 44740, ⓦwww.greciancastle.gr. Occupying the shell of an old factory, this is Híos Town's top-rated (4-star) digs. Lovely grounds and a sea-view pool, but the smallish main-wing rooms, despite their marble floors, wood ceilings and bug screens, don't justify the rates; the rear "villa" suites are more pleasant. ❻–❽

Kyma East end of Evyenías Handhrí ⓣ22710 44500, ⓔkyma@chi.forthnet.gr. Variable hotel rooms in a Neoclassical mansion or a modern extension, with huge terraces on the sea-facing side; most of the units have new handmade wood-and-leather furniture. Theo's splendid service and big breakfasts really make the place. The old wing saw a critical moment in modern Greek history in Sept 1922, when Colonel Nikolaos Plastiras commandeered it as his HQ after the Greek defeat in Asia Minor, and announced the deposition of King Constantine I. B&B ❹

The Town

South and east of the **main platía**, officially Plastíra but known universally as **Vounakíou**, extends the marvellously lively tradesmen's **bazaar**, where you can find everything from parrots to cast-iron woodstoves. Opposite the Vounakíou **taxi rank**, the **"Byzantine Museum"**, occupying the old **Mecidiye Mosque** with its leaning minaret (closed for renovation), is little more than an archeological warehouse.

Until the 1881 earthquake, the Byzantine-Genoese **Kástro** stood completely intact; thereafter developers razed the seaward walls, filled in the moat to the south and sold off the real estate thus created along the waterfront. The most dramatic entry to the citadel is via the **Porta Maggiora** behind the town hall. The top floor of a medieval mansion just inside is home to the **Giustiniani Museum** (Tues–Sun 8.30am–3pm; €2), with a satisfying collection of unusual icons and twelve fourteenth-century frescoes of Old Testament prophets rescued from Panayía Krína church. The old residential quarter inside the surviving castle walls, formerly the Muslim and Jewish neighbourhoods (now home to Albanians and refugees), is worth a brief wander, less for the sake of the main street's dilapidated wood-and plaster-houses than for assorted **Ottoman monuments**. These include a Muslim cemetery, the minaretless Bayraklı mosque, two ruined *hamams* – one being restored – a *medresse* in the courtyard of Áyios Yeóryios church and several inscribed **fountains**, the most ornate of which – with four facets – stands outside opposite the central park.

Further afield, three other museums beckon. The **Maritime Museum** at Stefánou Tsoúri 20 (Mon–Sat 10am–1pm; free) consists principally of model ships and nautical oil paintings, all rather overshadowed by the mansion containing them. In the foyer are enshrined the knife and glass-globe grenade of Admiral Kanaris, who partly avenged the 1822 massacre by ramming and sinking the Ottoman fleet's flagship. The central **Argenti Folklore Museum** (Mon–Thurs 8am–2pm, Fri 8am–2pm & 5–7.30pm, Sat 8am–12.30pm; €2), on the top floor of the Koráï Library at Koráï 2, features ponderous genealogical portraits of the endowing family, an adjoining wing of costumes and rural impedimenta, plus multiple replicas of Delacroix's *Massacre at Hios*, a painting which did much to arouse sympathy for the cause of Greek independence.

The **archeological museum** on Mihálon (June–Aug daily 8am–7pm; Sept–May Tues–Sun 8.30am–3pm; €3) has a wide-ranging, well-lit collection from Neolithic to Roman times. Highlights include limestone column bases from the Apollo temple at Faná in the shape of lions' claws; numerous statuettes and reliefs of Cybele (an Asiatic goddess especially honoured here); Archaic faïence miniatures from Emborió in the shape of a cat, a hawk and a flautist; a terracotta dwarf riding a boar; and figurines (some with articulated limbs) of *hierodouloi* or sacred prostitutes, presumably from an Aphrodite shrine. Most famous is an inscribed edict of Alexander the Great from 322 BC, setting out relations between himself and the Hiots.

Eating

Eating out in Híos Town can be better than the fast-food joints, touristy fake ouzerís and multiple *barákia* on the waterfront would initially suggest. Brusque service, however, is near-universal – brace yourself.

O Hotzas Yeoryíou Kondhýli 3, cnr Stefánou Tsoúri. Oldest and most popular taverna in town, with fourth-generation chef Ioannis Linos presiding. Menu (and quality) varies seasonally, but expect a mix of vegetarian dishes and *lahanodolmádhes*, sausages, baby fish and *mydhopílafo* (rice and mussels) washed down with own-brand ouzo or retsina. Dinner only, capacious garden in summer; closed Sun.

Kronos Filíppou Aryéndi 2, cnr Aplotariás. The island's best, and own-made ice cream, purveyed since 1929. Limited seating or takeaway. Noon–midnight.

Ta Mylarakia At the four restored windmills in Tambákika district, just before the hospital ⓣ22710 40412. A large if erratically priced seafood selection, every kind of Hiot ouzo (Tetteri Penindari is the best) and limited seating at the island's most romantic waterside setting. Reservations advisable in summer. Dinner daily all year, lunch also Oct–April.

Tavernaki tou Tassou Stávrou Livanoú 8, Bella Vista district. Superb all-rounder with creative salads, better-than-average bean dishes, *dolmádhes*, snails, good chips, a strong line in seafood, good barrel wine, and maybe a *mastíha* digestif on the house. Open lunch and supper most of the year, with good service, sea-view garden seating in warmer months and a heated gazebo in winter.

Theodhosiou Ouzeri Neoríon 33. The oldest of three ouzerís on this quay, occupying a domed, arcaded building. A fair amount of meat grills for this type of place, plus various seafood standards. Generally, avoid fried platters in favour of grilled or boiled ones. Dinner only; closed Sun.

Drinking, nightlife and entertainment

Some 1400 local university students help keep things lively, especially along the waterfront between the two "kinks" in Egéou. Shooting **pool** is big here; many bars have several tables. One, *Bowling Club* at the east end of Egéou, has seven **bowling** alleys as well. **Film** fans are well served by Cine Kipos (late June to early Sept), in one corner of the central park, with quality/art-house first-run screenings; from October the action shifts to Cine Diana, under the eponymous hotel. On the south side of the park, the Omirio cultural centre and events hall hosts changing exhibitions; name (foreign) acts often come here after Athens concerts.

Beaches near Híos Town

The locals swim at tiny pebble coves near **Vrondádhos**, north of Híos Town, or from the grubby town beach in **Bélla Vísta** district, but really the closest decent option is at **Karfás**, 7km south beyond the airport and served by frequent blue buses. Most large Hiot resort **hotels** are planted here, to the considerable detriment of the 500-metre-long beach itself, sandy only at the south end. The main bright spot is a unique **pension**, *Markos' Place* (℡22710 31990 or 697 32 39 706, www.marcos-place.gr; April–Nov; ❷), occupying the disestablished **monastery of Áyios Yeóryios and Áyios Pandelímon**, on the hillside south of the bay. Markos Kostalas has created a peaceful, leafy environment much loved by special-activity groups. Guests are lodged in the former pilgrims' cells, with a kitchen available or superior breakfasts provided by arrangement; individuals are more than welcome, as are families (in two quads), though reservations are advisable and the minimum stay is four days.

Shoreline **restaurants** aren't brilliant; it's better to strike inland for eating opportunities. The closest venue is attractive **THYMIANÁ** village, where central, family-run *To Talimi* purveys excellent home-style *mayireftá* like *yiouvarlákia, kókoras krasáto* or bean-and-artichoke salad at friendly prices; an honourable mention goes to nearby *Roussiko* despite its kitsch decor. *Ouzeri To Apomero* (daily all year), in hillside **Spiládhia** district west of the airport (bear off the Pyrgí road towards Áyios Theodhósios and follow luminous green signs) has terrace seating with an eyeful of the Çeşme peninsula and unusual dishes such as Cretan sausages and battered artichoke hearts. Between Thymianá and Neohóri, *Fakiris Taverna* (all year; weekends only in winter) offers home-marinated aubergine and artichokes, goat baked in tomato sauce and excellent wood-fired pizzas along with well-executed seafood and large pork-based *bekrí mezé*. To find it, head south on the road to Kalimassiá, then turn west onto the Ayíou Trýfonos road, just before Neohóri, and proceed about 1km.

Some 2km further along the coast from Karfás, **AYÍA ERMIÓNI** is a fishing anchorage surrounded by a handful of tavernas (none stands out) and apartments to rent. The nearest proper **beach** is at **Mégas Limniónas**, a few hundred metres further, smaller than Karfás but more scenic, with low cliffs as a backdrop; here *Ankyra* is a reliable **taverna**. Both Ayía Ermióni and Mégas Limniónas are served by extensions of blue-bus routes to either Karfás or Thymianá. From the latter, you can (with your own transport) continue 3km south towards Kalimassiá to the turning for **Ayía Fotiní**, a 600-metre pebble **beach** with exceptionally clean water. Cars are excluded from the shore area; the pedestrian esplanade is lined with various rooms, plus there's car rental locally. A few **tavernas** cluster where the side road meets the sea, but there's far better food, especially fish, at **KATARRÁKTIS** (return to the Kalimassiá road), where *O Tsambos* is the best and cheapest of several contenders.

Southern Híos

Besides olive groves, southern Híos's gently rolling countryside is home to the **mastic bush** (*Pistacia lentisca*), found across much of Aegean Greece but only here producing aromatic resin of any quality or quantity. For centuries it was used as a base for paints, cosmetics and the chewable jelly beans that became an addictive staple in Ottoman harems. Indeed, the interruption of the flow of mastic from Híos to Istanbul by the revolt of spring 1822 was a main cause of the brutal Ottoman reaction.

The wealth engendered by the mastic trade supported twenty **mastihohoriá** (mastic villages) from the time the Genoese set up a monopoly in the substance during the fourteenth century, but the demise of imperial Turkey and the development of petroleum-based products knocked the bottom out of the mastic market. Now it's just a curiosity, to be chewed – try the sweetened Elma-brand gum – or drunk as *mastíha* liqueur. It has also had medicinal applications since ancient times, and high-end cosmetics, toothpaste and mouthwash are now purveyed at the Mastiha Shop at Egéou 36 in Híos Town.

These days, however, the *mastihohoriá* live mainly off their tangerines, apricots and olives. The villages, the only settlements on Híos spared by the Ottomans in 1822, are architecturally unique, designed by the Genoese but retaining a distinctly Middle Eastern feel. The basic plan involves a rectangular warren of tall houses, with the outer row doubling as perimeter fortification, and breached by a limited number of gateways.

The mastic villages

ARMÓLIA, 20km from town, is the smallest and least imposing of the mastic villages; its main virtue is its pottery industry. **PYRGÍ**, 5km further south, is the most colourful, its houses elaborately embossed with *xystá*, patterns cut into whitewash to reveal a layer of black volcanic sand underneath; in autumn, strings of sun-drying tomatoes add a further splash of colour. On the northeast corner of the central square the twelfth-century Byzantine church of **Áyii Apóstoli** (erratic hours), embellished with much later frescoes, is tucked under an arcade. In the medieval core you'll find an **ATM**, a **post office** and an array of **cafés** and *souvláki* stalls on the central platía. **OLÝMBI**, 7km further west along the same bus route, is one of the less visited mastic villages, but not devoid of interest. The characteristic **tower-keep**, which at Pyrgí stands half-inhabited away from the modernized main square, here looms bang in the middle of the platía, its ground floor occupied by the community *kafenío* on one side, and a **taverna-bar** on the other.

Sombre, monochrome **MESTÁ**, 4km west of Olýmbi, is considered the finest of the villages; despite more snack-bars and trinket shops than strictly necessary, it remains just the right side of twee, since most people here still work the land. From its main square, dominated by the **church of the Taxiárhis** with its two icons of the Archangel – one dressed in Byzantine robes, the other in Genoese armour – a maze of dim lanes, with anti-seismic

▲ Pyrgí, Híos

tunnels, leads off in all directions. Most streets end in blind alleys, except those leading to the six portals; the northeast one still has its original iron gate. Top-drawer **accommodation** is provided by the scattered *Medieval Castle Suites* (Ⓣ22710 76345, Ⓦwww.medievalcastlesuites.com; ❹–❻), with the reception in a lane just off the square. Humbler **rooms** in other restored traditional houses are managed by Dhimitris Pipidhis (Ⓣ22710 76029; ❸); alternatively, three separate studio apartments managed by Anna Floradhi's gift shop (Ⓣ22710 76455; ❸) are more modernized. Of two **taverna-cafés** sharing table-space on the main platía, *Mesaionas (Kyra Dhespina)* is better value and has the more helpful proprietor (she also has rooms: Ⓣ22710 76494; ❸).

The mastic coast – and the Sykiás Olýmbon cave

The closest good, protected **beach** to Mestá lies 4.7km southwest by paved, narrow road at **Apothíka**. Others, east of unused Liménas Mestón port, include **Dhídhyma** (4km away), a double cove with an islet protecting it; **Potámi**, with a namesake stream feeding it; and less scenic **Ayía Iríni** (8km), with a reliable **taverna**. All these little bays will catch surf and flotsam when the north wind is up.

From Olýmbi, a paved road heads 6km to the well-signed **cave of Sykiás Olýmbon** (June–Aug Tues–Sun 10am–8pm, Sept 11am–6pm; admission in groups of 25 or less every 30min; €5). For years it was just a hole in the ground where villagers disposed of dead animals; after 1985, speleologists began to explore it properly. The cavern, with a constant temperature of 18°C, evolved in two phases between 150 million and 50 million years ago, and has a maximum depth of 57m (though tours only visit the top 30m). Its formations, with fanciful names like Chinese Forest, Medusa and Organ Pipes, are among the most beautiful in the Mediterranean. Before or after your subterranean tour, you can continue another 1500m on a dirt track to the little cape-top monastery of **Ayía Dhýnami** and two sheltered swimming **coves**.

Pyrgí is closest to the two major beach resorts in this corner of the island. The nearest, 6km distant, is **EMBORIÓS**, an almost landlocked harbour with four passable **tavernas**; *Porto Emborios* has the edge with almost year-round operation, fair prices, home-made desserts and good seafood. **Ancient Emboreios** on the hill to the northeast has been rehabilitated as an "archeological park" (summer daily 9am–3pm, winter closed Mon; €2). Down in modern Emboriós a cruciform **early Christian baptistry** is signposted in a field just inland; it's protected by a later, round structure (locked but everything's visible through the grating).

For **swimming**, follow the road to an oversubscribed car park and the beach of **Mávros Yialós** (Mávra Vólia), then continue by flagstoned walkway over the headland to the more dramatic pebble strand (part nudist) of purple-grey volcanic stones, **Fóki**, twice as long and backed by impressive cliffs. If you want sand (and amenities) go to **KÓMI**, 3km northeast, also accessible from Armólia via Kalamotí; there are a few **tavernas** (most reliably open *Bella Mare* and *Nostalgia*, both offering sunbeds for patrons), café-bars and seasonal apartments behind the pedestrianized beachfront.

Central Híos

The portion of Híos extending west and southwest from Híos Town matches the south in terms of interesting **monuments**, and good roads make touring under your own steam an easy matter. There are also several **beaches** on the far shore of the island which, though not necessarily the best on Híos, are fine for a dip en route.

The Kámbos

The **Kámbos**, a vast fertile plain carpeted with citrus groves, extends southwest from Híos Town almost as far as the village of Halkió. The district was originally settled by the Genoese during the fourteenth century, and remained a preserve of the local aristocracy until 1822. Exploring by two-wheeler may be less frustrating than going by car, since the web of narrow, poorly marked lanes sandwiched between high walls guarantees disorientation and frequent backtracking. Behind the walls you catch fleeting glimpses of ornate old mansions built from locally quarried sandstone; courtyards are paved in pebbles or alternating light and dark tiles, and most still contain a pergola-shaded irrigation pond filled by a *mánganos* or donkey-powered waterwheel, used before the advent of electric pumps to draw water from wells up to 30m deep.

Many of the sumptuous dwellings, constructed in a hybrid Italo-Turco-Greek style, have languished derelict since 1881, but several have been converted for use as private estates or unique **accommodation**. The best of these are *Mavrokordatiko* (Ⓣ22710 32900, Ⓦwww.mavrokordatiko.com; B&B; ❺), about 1.5km south of the airport, with enormous heated, wood-panelled rooms, and *Arhondiko Perleas* (Ⓣ22710 32217, Ⓦwww.perleas.gr; B&B ❻) on the Vitiádhou road, set in a huge organic citrus ranch, with a well-regarded in-house restaurant.

Not strictly speaking in Kámbos, but most easily reached from it en route to the *mastihohoriá*, is an outstanding rural Byzantine monument. The eleventh-century hillside **church of Panayía Krína** is worth the challenge of negotiating a maze of paved but poorly marked lanes beyond Vavýli village, 9km from town. It's being comprehensively restored and should open as a tourist attraction in 2009; all of the late-medieval frescoes have been removed, some displayed in Híos Town's Giustiniani Museum (see p.763). The remaining twelfth-century layer includes some fine saints, a *Resurrection* and a *Communion of the Apostles*, originally lit only by a twelve-windowed drum, echoed somewhat clumsily by the lantern added later over the narthex.

Néa Moní

Almost exactly in the middle of the island, the **monastery of Néa Moní** was founded by the Byzantine Emperor Constantine Monomahos ("The Dueller") IX in 1042 on the spot where a wonder-working icon had been discovered. It ranks among the most important monuments on any of the Greek islands; the mosaics, together with those of Dháfni and Ósios Loukás on the mainland, are the finest surviving art of their era in Greece, and the setting – high in partly forested mountains 15km west of the port – is equally memorable.

However, EU part-funded **restoration** work proceeds at a snail's pace, with no end date in sight; the *katholikón* exterior is cocooned in scaffolding, while the interior is regrettably off-limits indefinitely. Accordingly it's not worth shelling out especially for a taxi at the moment, but do stop in briefly if you're touring with a bike or car.

Once a powerful community of six hundred monks, Néa Moní was pillaged in 1822 and most of its residents (including 3500 civilians sheltering here) put to the sword. The 1881 tremor caused comprehensive damage, wrecking many of its outbuildings (though sparing the refectory and vaulted cisterns), while exactly a century later a forest fire threatened to engulf the place until the resident icon was paraded along the perimeter wall, miraculously repelling the flames.

Just inside the **main gate** (daily 8am–1pm & 4–8pm, 5–8pm in summer) stands a **chapel/ossuary** containing some of the bones of the 1822 victims; axe-clefts in children's skulls attest to the savagery of the attackers. The *katholikón*, its cupola resting on an octagonal drum, is of a design seen elsewhere only in Cyprus; once restoration is complete, the famous **mosaics** should reappear in all their glory. The narthex contains portrayals of various local saints sandwiched between *Christ Washing the Disciples' Feet* and the *Betrayal*, in which Judas's kiss has unfortunately been obliterated, but Peter is clearly visible lopping off the ear of the high priest's servant. In the dome, which once contained a complete life cycle of Christ, only the *Baptism*, part of the *Crucifixion*, the *Descent from the Cross*, the *Resurrection* and the evangelists Mark and John survived the earthquake.

The west coast

Some 5km west of Néa Moní sits **AVGÓNYMA**, a cluster of dwellings on a knoll overlooking the coast; the name means "Clutch of Eggs", an apt description when it's viewed from the ridge above. Since the 1980s, the place has been restored as a summer haven by descendants of the original villagers, though the permanent population is just seven. A returned Greek-American family runs a reasonable, simple **taverna**, *O Pyrgos* (all year), in an arcaded mansion on the main square. The classiest **accommodation** option is *Spitakia*, a cluster of small restored houses sleeping up to five people (Ⓣ22710 20513 or 22710 81200, Ⓦwww.spitakia.gr; ❹–❺), though *O Pyrgos* also keeps more modernized units in the village (Ⓣ22710 42175; ❸).

A side road continues another 4km north to **ANÁVATOS**, whose empty, dun-coloured dwellings, soaring above pistachio orchards, are almost indistinguishable from the 300-metre-high bluff on which they're built. During the 1822 insurrection, some four hundred islanders threw themselves over this cliff rather than surrender to the besieging Ottomans. Anávatos can now only muster two permanent inhabitants; given a lack of accommodation, one mediocre snack-bar, plus an eerie, traumatized atmosphere, it's no place to linger.

West of Avgónyma, the main road descends 6km to the sea in well-graded loops. Turning right (north) at the junction leads first to the beach at **Elínda**, alluring from afar but rocky and often murky up close; it's better to continue towards more secluded, mixed sand-and-gravel coves to either side of Metóhi – best of these are **Tigáni** and **Makriá Ámmos**, the latter nudist. Semi-fortified **SIDHIROÚNDA**, the only village hereabouts, enjoys a spectacular hilltop setting overlooking the sea; both view and architecture – including gates and towers – surpass Avgónyma's. There's a competent **taverna**, *Mylos*, at the village entrance, while you can enjoy Sidhiroúnda's famous sunsets from the imaginatively named *Sunset Cafe*.

All along this coast stand round **watchtowers** erected by the Genoese to look out for pirates – the second swimmable cove you reach after turning left from the junction bears the name **Kastélla** (officially Trahíli), again mixed sand and gravel. The first cove, more protected and popular, is **Xeropótamos**. Friendly **LITHÍ** village perches on a forested ledge overlooking the sea 9km south of the junction. There are **tavernas** and *kafenía* in the centre, but most visitors head 2km downhill to **Paralía Lithioú**, a popular weekend target of Hiot townies thanks to its large but hard-packed, windswept beach. The better of two adjacent, pricey fish **tavernas** is *Ta Tria Adherfia*.

South of Lithí some 5km, valley-bottom **VÉSSA** is, like Sidhiroúnda, an unsung gem: more open and less casbah-like than Mestá or Pyrgí, but still homogeneous, its tawny buildings arrayed in a vast grid punctuated by numerous belfries and arcaded passages. There's a *kafenío* installed on the ground floor of the tower-mansion on the main through road, while across the square *Kostas* (aka *Froso's*) does excellent *yíros*, *loukániko* and *souvláki*.

Northern Híos

Northern Híos never really recovered from the 1822 massacre, and between Pityós and Volissós the forest's recovery from 1980s **fires** has been partly reversed by a bad 2007 blaze north ofVolissós. Most villages usually lie deserted, with about a third of the former population living in Híos Town, returning occasionally for major festivals or to tend smallholdings; others, based in Athens or North America, visit their ancestral homes for just a few midsummer weeks.

The road to Kardhámyla

Blue urban buses from Híos Town serve **VRONDÁDHOS**, an elongated coastal suburb that's a favourite residence of the many local seafarers. Homer is alleged to have lived and taught here, and in terraced parkland just above the little fishing port and pebble beach you can visit his purported lectern, probably an ancient altar of Cybele. Accordingly most buses heading here are labelled ΔΑΣΚΑΛΟΠΕΤΡΑ, "the Teacher's Rock".

Some 14km out of town, the tiny bayside hamlet of **PANDOUKIÓS** has an excellent if pricey waterside **taverna**, *Kourtesis*, where lobster can often be had. But **LANGÁDHA**, 2.5km beyond, is probably the first point on the eastern coast road you'd be tempted to stop, though there is no proper beach nearby. Set at the mouth of a deep valley, this attractive little harbour settlement looks across its bay to a pine grove, and beyond to Turkey. Night-time/weekend visitors come for the sustaining, reasonable **seafood** at the best of three quayside **tavernas**: *Tou Kopelou*, better known as *Stelios'*.

Just beyond Langádha a side road leads 5km up and inland to **PITYÓS**, an oasis in a mountain pass presided over by a small, round castle; people come here from some distance to **eat** at *Makellos*, a shrine of local cuisine on the southwest edge of the village (late June to early Sept daily lunch/dinner; rest of year Fri–Sun evenings only). Continuing 4km further brings you to a junction that allows quick access to the west of the island.

Kardhámyla and around

Most traffic proceeds to **ÁNO KARDHÁMYLA** and **KÁTO KARDHÁMYLA**, the latter 37km out of Híos Town. Positioned at opposite edges of a fertile plain rimmed by mountains, they initially come as welcome relief from Homer's crags. Káto, better known as **MÁRMARO**, is larger – indeed, the island's second town – with a bank, post office and filling station. However, there is little to attract casual visitors other than some Neoclassical architecture; the mercilessly exposed port is strictly businesslike, and there are few tourist facilities. A sterling exception is *Hotel Kardamyla* (Ⓣ22720 23353, Ⓕ22720 23354; ❺ Aug, ❹ otherwise), co-managed with Híos Town's *Hotel Kyma*, offering spacious, fan-equipped **rooms** and a few suites. The in-house restaurant is a reliable lunch venue (July & Aug); worthwhile independent **tavernas** include *Ouzeri Barba Yiannis* (all year), beside the port authority, and newer *Thalasses*, upmarket but good value.

For better swimming head west 5km to **Nagós**, a pebble bay at the foot of an oasis, end of the summer bus line. The place name is a corruption of *naos*, after a Poseidon temple that once stood near uphill springs enclosed in a rock overhang, but no trace of it survives today. Down at the shore the swimming is good, though the water's chilly; there are mediocre **tavernas** (there's a better one inland, by the spring) and a few **dhomátia**. Your only chance of relative solitude in mid-summer lies 1km west at **Yióssonas,** a much longer if less sheltered and rockier beach, with no facilities.

Volissós and around

VOLISSÓS, 42km from Híos Town by the most direct road (but just 44km by the much easier route via Avgónyma), was once the market town for a dozen remote hill villages beyond. Its old stone houses still curl appealingly beneath a crumbling hilltop Byzantine-Genoese **fort**. Volissós can seem depressing at first, with the bulk of its 250 mostly elderly permanent inhabitants living in newer buildings around the main square, but impressions improve with time. This backwater ethos may not last; the upper quarters are in the grip of a restoration mania, most in good taste, with ruins changing hands for stratospheric prices.

Grouped around the platía you'll find a **post office**, an **ATM** and three mediocre **tavernas**. A pair of **filling stations** operate 2.5km out of town, the only ones hereabouts; if reliant on public transport, plan on overnighting since the bus only ventures out here on Sundays on a day-trip basis, plus on three weekly workdays in the early afternoon (unless you care to travel at 4.30am). This should cause no dismay, since the area has some of the best beaches and most interesting **accommodation** on Híos. The most reasonable and longest established of a few restoration projects are sixteen old houses, mostly in Pýrgos district, available through *Volissos Travel* (Ⓣ22740 21413 or 693 69 75 470, Ⓦwww.volissostravel.gr; May–Sept; ④). Units usually accommodate two people – all have terraces, fully equipped kitchens, air conditioning and features such as tree trunks upholding sleeping lofts, reflecting proprietress Stella's background as a sculptor.

LIMNIÁ (or Limiá), the port of Volissós, lies 2km south, bracketed by the local beaches, though *kaïki* service from here to Psará is suspended. The most consistent **taverna** here is *O Zikos* (all year) at the far end of the quay, with good grills and a fine house salad featuring sun-dried tomatoes, plus occasional seafood. A 1.5-kilometre drive or walk southeast over the headland brings you to **Mánagros**, a seemingly endless sand-and-pebble beach. More intimate, sandy **Lefkáthia** lies just a ten-minute stroll along the cement drive over the headland north of the harbour; amenities are limited to a seasonal snack shack on the sand, and Ioannis Zorbas's garden-set **apartments** (Ⓣ22740 21436, Ⓦwww.chioszorbas.gr; ④), where the concrete drive joins an asphalt road down from Volissós. This is bound for **Límnos**, the next protected cove 400m east of Lefkáthia, where *Taverna Iy Limnos* features fish grills and specials like *kokorás krasáto*, and the spruce *Latini Apartments* (Ⓣ22740 21461, Ⓕ22740 21871; ③) are graced with multiple stone terraces. **Ayía Markélla**, 5km further northwest of Límnos, has a long **beach** (with mediocre taverna) fronting the eponymous, barracks-like pilgrimage **monastery** of Híos's patron saint (festival July 22).

The dirt road beyond Ayía Markélla is passable with care by any vehicle, and emerges on the paved road running high above the northwest coast. Turn left for remote **ÁYIO GÁLA**, notable for a **grotto-church** complex built into a stream-lapped palisade at the bottom of the village. Signs ("Panayía Ayiogaloúsena") point the way, but for off-season access you'll need to find the key-keeper (ask at the central *kafenío*), and descend via a flight of stairs starting beside a eucalyptus tree. Of two churches inside the cavern, the larger one is fifteenth-century but seems newer owing to a 1993 external renovation. Beyond, however, a fantastically intricate *témblon* vies for your attention with a tinier, older chapel, built entirely within the cavern. Its frescoes are badly smudged, except for a wonderfully mysterious and mournful Virgin, surely the saddest in Christendom, holding a knowing Child. Still further inside, a **cave system** with all the usual formations has limited admission hours (June–Aug Fri–Sun 11am–6pm; €5).

Satellite islands: Psará and Inoússes

There's a single settlement, with beaches and an isolated rural monastery, on both of Híos's satellite islets, but each is surprisingly different from the other, and of course from their large neighbour. **Inoússes**, the nearer and smaller, has a daily *kaïki* service from Híos Town in season, sometimes permitting day-trips; **Psará** has equally regular small-ferry services, plus occasional mainline services on the Lávrio–Límnos route, but is too remote for day-trips.

Psará

The birthplace of revolutionary war hero Admiral Konstandinos Kanaris, **Psará** devoted its merchant fleets – the third largest in 1820s Greece – to the cause of independence, and paid dearly for it. Vexed beyond endurance, the Turks landed overwhelming forces in 1824 to stamp out this nest of resistance. Perhaps 3000 of the 30,000 inhabitants escaped in small boats to be rescued by a French fleet, but the majority retreated to a hilltop powder magazine and blew it (and themselves) up rather than surrender. The nationalist poet Dhionysios Solomos immortalized the incident in famous stanzas:

On the Black Ridge of Psará,
Glory walks alone.
She meditates on her heroes
And wears in her hair a wreath
Made from a few dry weeds
Left on the barren ground.

Today, it's a sad, bleak place fully living up to its name ("the mottled things" in ancient Greek), and never really recovered from the holocaust. The Turks burned whatever houses and vegetation the blast had missed, and the official population now barely exceeds four hundred. A 1980s revitalization project instigated by a French-Greek descendant of Kanaris saw the port improved, mains electricity and potable water provided, a secondary school opened, and cultural links between France and the island established, though this never resulted in a tourist boom.

Since few buildings in the east-facing harbour community predate the twentieth century, you face a strange hotchpotch of ecclesiastical and secular architecture on disembarking. There's a distinctly southern feel, more like the Dodecanese or the Cyclades, and some peculiar churches, no two alike in style. **Accommodation** ranges from a handful of fairly basic rooms to three more professional outfits: *Psara Studios* (Ⓣ22740 61233; ④) and *Apartments Restalia* (Ⓣ22740 61201, Ⓕ22740 61000; ②–④), both a bit stark but with balconies and kitchens, or the *EOT xenónas* (Ⓣ22740 61293; ④), multi-bedded rooms in a restored prison. A few **tavernas**, a **post office**, bakery and shop complete the amenities; there's no full-service bank.

Psará's **beaches** are decent, improving the further northeast you walk from the port. You quickly pass **Káto Yialós**, **Katsoúni** and **Lazarétto** with its off-putting power station, before reaching **Lákka** ("narrow ravine"), fifteen minutes along, apparently named after its grooved rock formations in which you may have to shelter – much of this coast is windswept, with a heavy swell offshore. **Límnos**, 25 minutes from the port along the coastal path, is big and attractive, but there's no reliable **taverna** here, or indeed at any of the beaches. The only other thing to do on Psará is to follow the paved road north across the island to **Kímisis (Assumption) monastery**; uninhabited since the 1970s, this comes to life only during the first week of August, when its revered icon is carried in ceremonial procession to town and back on the eve of August 5.

Inoússes

Inoússes has a permanent population of about three hundred – less than half its prewar figure – and a very different history from Psará. For generations this medium-sized islet, first settled around 1750 by Hiot shepherds, has provided Greece with many of her wealthiest shipping families: various members of the Livanos, Lemos and Pateras clans were born here. This helps explain the large villas and visiting summer gin-palaces in an otherwise sleepy Greek backwater – as well as a **maritime museum** (daily 10am–1pm; €2) near the quay, endowed by various shipping magnates. At the west end of the quay, the bigwigs have also funded a large nautical academy, which trains future members of the merchant navy.

On Mondays, Fridays and Sundays you can make an inexpensive **day-trip** to Inoússes from Híos with the locals' ferry *Inousses II*; on most other days of the week this arrives at 1 or 3pm, returning 8am the next day. Otherwise, during the tourist season you must take one of the pricier excursions offered from Híos, with return tickets running more than double the cost of the regular ferry.

Two church-tipped islets, each privately owned, guard the unusually well-protected harbour; the **town** of Inoússes is surprisingly large, draped over hillsides enclosing a ravine. Despite the wealthy reputation, its appearance is unpretentious, the houses displaying a mix of vernacular and modest Neoclassical style. There is just one, fairly comfortable, **hotel**, the *Thalassoporos* (Ⓣ22720 55475; ❹), on the main easterly hillside lane, but no licensed *dhomátia*. **Restaurants** are similarly limited; the most reliable option is *Taverna Pateronisso*, at the base of the disembarkation jetty, though every season a few simple ouzerís off towards the nautical academy try their luck. **Café-bars** such as *Naftikos Omilos* provide a semblance of **nightlife**. Beside the museum you'll find a **post office** and a **bank**.

The southern slope of this tranquil island is surprisingly green and well tended; there are no springs, so water comes from a mix of fresh and brackish wells, as well as a reservoir. The sea is extremely clean and calm on the sheltered southerly shore; among its beaches, choose from **Zepága**, **Biláli** or **Kástro**, respectively five, twenty and thirty minutes' walk west of the port. More secluded **Fourkeró** (or Farkeró) lies 25 minutes east: first along a cement drive ending at a seaside chapel, then by path past pine groves and over a ridge. As on Psará, there are no reliable facilities at any of the beaches.

At the end of the westerly road stands the rather macabre convent of **Evangelismoú**, endowed by a branch of the Pateras family. Inside reposes the mummified body of the recently canonized daughter, Irini, whose prayers to die in place of her terminally ill father were answered early in the 1960s; he's entombed here also, having outlived Irini by some years. The abbess is none other than the widowed Mrs Pateras; only women are admitted, and casual visits are not encouraged.

Lésvos (Mytilíni)

Lésvos, the third-largest Greek island after Crete and Évvia, is the birthplace of ancient bards Sappho, Aesop, Arion and – more recently – the Greek primitive artist Theophilos, the Nobel laureate poet Odysseus Elytis and the novelist Stratis Myrivilis. Despite these **artistic associations**, the island may not initially strike the visitor as particularly beautiful or interesting; much of the landscape is rocky, volcanic terrain, encompassing vast grain fields, salt pans or

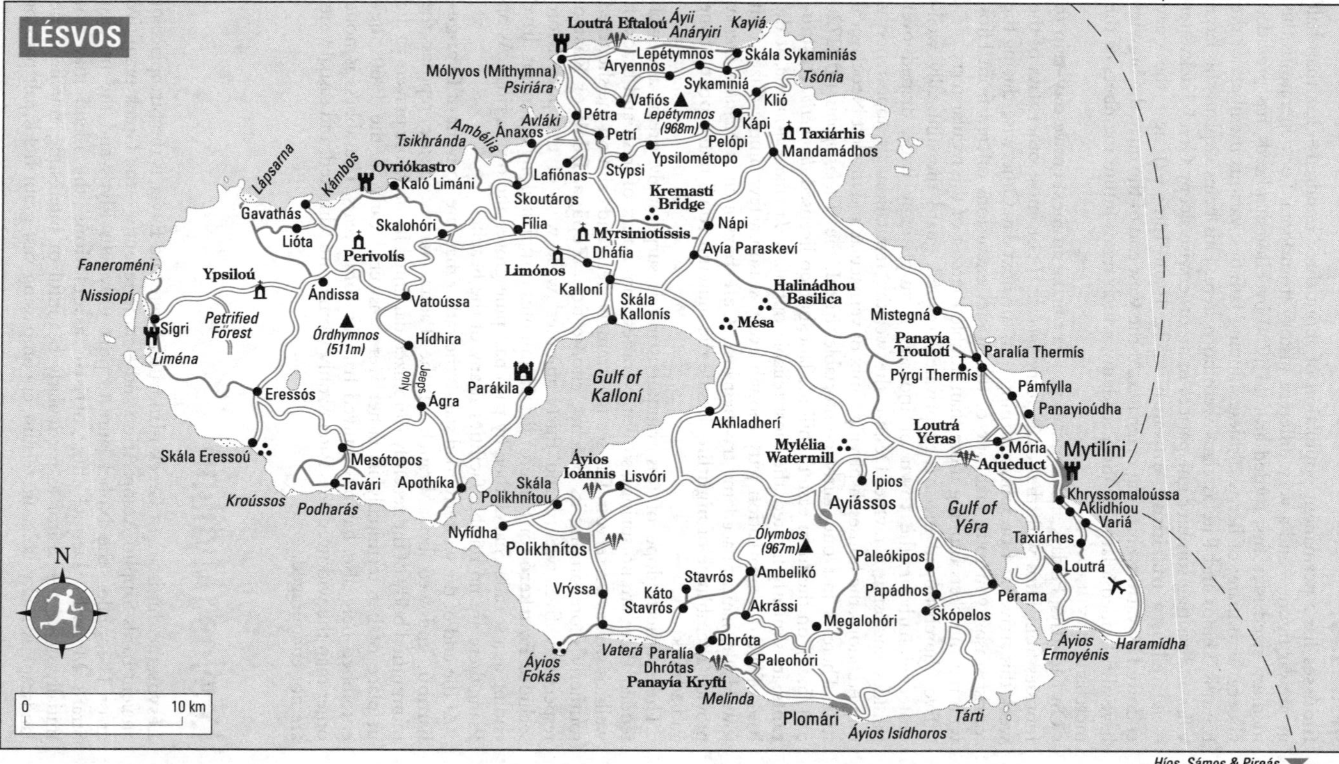
LÉSVOS
Límnos, Thessaloníki, Alexandhroúpoli & Kavála
Híos, Sámos & Pireás
Loutrá Eftaloú
Áyii Anáryiri
Kayiá
Lepétymnos
Skála Sykaminiás
Mólyvos (Míthymna)
Áryennos
Sykaminiá
Tsónia
Psiriára
Vafiós
Klió
Pétra
Lepétymnos (968m)
Kápi
Taxiárhis
Avláki
Ánaxos
Petrí
Pelópi
Ambélia
Tsikhránda
Mandamádhos
Ypsilométopo
Lápsarna
Kámbos
Ovriókastro
Kaló Limáni
Lafiónas
Stýpsi
Skoutáros
Kremastí Bridge
Gavathás
Skalohóri
Fília
Nápi
Liótá
Perivolís
Myrsiniotíssis
Dháfia
Ayía Paraskeví
Faneroméni
Limónos
Ypsiloú
Kalloní
Halinádhou Basilica
Nissiopí
Ándissa
Vatoússa
Skála Kallonís
Mistegná
Sígri
Petrified Forest
Órdhymnos (511m)
Mésa
Liména
Hídhira
Panayía Troulotí
Paralía Thermís
Pýrgi Thermís
Jeeps only
Gulf of Kalloní
Parákila
Pámfylla
Eressós
Ágra
Panayioúdha
Akhladherí
Loutrá Yéras
Skála Eressoú
Mesótopos
Mylélia Watermill
Mória
Mytilíni
Áyios Ioánnis
Aqueduct
Tavári
Apothíka
Lisvóri
Ípios
Khryssomaloússa
Kroússos
Podharás
Skála Polikhnítou
Ayiássos
Gulf of Yéra
Aklidhíou
Variá
Nyfídha
Taxiárhes
Polikhnítos
Ólymbos (967m)
N
Paleókipos
Loutrá
Stavrós
Ambelikó
Vrýssa
Káto Stavrós
Papádhos
Pérama
Akrássi
Skópelos
Megalohóri
Dhróta
Áyios Ermoyénis
Haramídha
Vaterá
Paralía Dhrótas
Paleohóri
Áyios Fokás
Panayía Kryftí
Melínda
0
10 km
Plomári
Tárti
Áyios Isídhoros

even near-desert. But there are also oak and pine forests as well as endless olive groves, some more than five hundred years old. Lésvos tends to grow on you with prolonged exposure.

Lovers of medieval and Ottoman **architecture** certainly won't be disappointed. Castles survive at Mytilíni Town, Mólyvos, Eressós, Sígri and near Ándissa; most date from the late fourteenth century, when Lésvos was given as a dowry to a Genoese prince of the Gattilusi clan following his marriage to the sister of one of the last Byzantine emperors. Apart from Crete and Évvia, Lésvos was the only Greek island where Turks settled significantly in rural villages (they usually stuck to the safety of towns), which explains the occasional Ottoman bridge, box-like mosque or crumbling minaret in the middle of nowhere. Again unusually for the Aegean islands, eighteenth-century Ottoman reforms encouraged the emergence of a Greek Orthodox land- and industry-owning aristocracy, who built imposing mansions and tower-houses, a few of which survive. The worthies in Mytilíni Town erected Belle Époque townhouses to French Second Empire models; many have been pressed into service as government buildings or even restored as hotels.

Social **idiosyncrasies** persist: anyone who has attended one of the village *paniyíria*, with hours of music and tables groaning with food and drink, will not be surprised to learn that Lésvos has the highest alcoholism rate (and some of the worst driving habits) in Greece. Breeding livestock, especially horses, remains important, and signs reading "Forbidden to Tether Animals Here" are still common, as are herds of apparently unattended donkeys wandering about. Much of the olive acreage is still inaccessible to vehicles, and the harvest can only be hauled out by those donkeys – who are loaded en masse onto the back of trucks to be transported to the point where the road fizzles out. Organic production has been embraced enthusiastically as a way of making Lésvos agricultural products more competitive – *Violoyikó Ktíma* (Organic Plot) or *Violoyikí Kaliéryia* (Organic Cultivation) signs abound.

Historically, the olive plantations, ouzo distilleries, animal husbandry and fishing industry supported those who chose not to emigrate, but when these enterprises stalled in the 1980s, **tourism** made appreciable inroads. However, it still accounts for less than ten percent of the local economy: there are few large hotels outside the capital, Skála Kalloní or Mólyvos, and visitor numbers have levelled off since the late 1990s.

Public **buses** observe schedules for the benefit of villagers coming to the capital on errands, not day-tripping tourists. Accomplishing such excursions from Mytilíni is impossible anyway, owing to Lésvos's **size** – about 70km by 45km at its widest points – though the road network is now mostly improved, along with its signposting. Moreover, the topography is complicated by the two deeply indented gulfs of Kalloní and Yéra, with no bridges across their mouths, which means that both bus and car journeys will involve a change or transit at Kalloní, near the middle of the island. It's best to pick a resort and stay there for a few days, exploring its immediate surroundings on foot or by rented vehicle.

Mytilíni Town

MYTILÍNI, the port and capital, sprawls between and around two bays divided by a fortified promontory, and in Greek fashion often doubles as the name of the island. Many visitors are put off by the combination of urban bustle and (in the traditionally humbler northern districts) slight seediness, and contrive to leave as soon as possible; the town returns the compliment by being a fairly impractical and occasionally expensive base.

Arrival, transport and information

There's no bus link with the **airport** (one **ATM** in arrivals, three car rental booths), so you'll need to take a **taxi** the 7km into Mytilíni Town. As on Híos, there are two **bus terminals**: the iperastykó (standard KTEL) buses leave from a small station near Platía Konstandinopóleos at the southern end of the harbour, while the astykó (blue bus) service departs from a stand at the top of the harbour. Drivers should use the enormous free public **car park** a few blocks south of the KTEL, or the oval plaza near the new archeological museum – there are no other easily available spaces. If you're intent on getting over to Ayvalik in **Turkey**, you've a choice of two boats (*Jale* or *Konstandinos I*); most likely **agencies** are at Koundouriótou 78 (Ⓣ22510 46668) or Dimakis Tours at Koundouriótou 73 (Ⓣ22510 27865). Agoudhimos is represented by Picolo Travel at no. 73a (Ⓣ22510 27000), while Saos Ferries are handled by Pan Tours at no. 87 (Ⓣ22510 46595). NEL Lines has a booth in the harbour zone (Ⓣ22510 42239), though nearly everyone sells their tickets.

Car rental is arrangeable through reputable franchises like Payless/Auto Moto at Koundouriótou 49 (Ⓣ22510 43555, Ⓔautomoto@otenet.gr), Budget/Sixt at no. 47 (Ⓣ22510 29600, Ⓦwww.lesvosholidays.com), or Best at no. 87–89 (Ⓣ22510 37337, Ⓦwww.best-rentacar.com) – though it may be cheaper to rent at the resort of your choice. Other amenities include the **post office** behind the central park, and numerous **ATMs** starting just outside the port gate. Before leaving town, you might visit **EOT regional headquarters** at James Aristárhou 6 (Mon–Fri 8am–2.30pm) to get hold of their excellent town and island **maps**, plus other brochures, or the Newsstand **bookshop** at Vostáni 6 for a limited selection of English literature.

Accommodation

Finding **accommodation** can be frustrating: waterfront hotels are noisy and overpriced; supply usually exceeds demand for the better-value rooms in the backstreets. *New Life* at the end of Olýmbou, a cul-de-sac off Ermoú (Ⓣ22510 42650 or 693 22 79 057; ❸), offers wood-floored, en-suite rooms in an old mansion, or similarly priced ones, with modern murals in the halls, at co-managed *Arion* down the street at Aríonos 4. The most distinctive hotel is pricey *Pyrgos*, Eleftheríou Venizélou 49 (Ⓣ22510 25069, Ⓦwww.pyrgoshotel.gr; ❻), a converted mansion with over-the-top kitsch decor in the common areas. However, the rooms – most with a balcony – are perfectly acceptable; the three round units in the tower are nicest. Especially with transport, the best local base is *Votsala* (Ⓣ22510 71231, Ⓦwww.votsalahotel.com; ❸), a sophisticated beachfront hotel with well-tended gardens but no TV in the rooms, 12km north in Paralía Thermís.

The Town

Despite its potential logistical difficulties, Mytilíni justifies a few hours' stopover. On the promontory sits the Byzantine-Genoese-Ottoman **fortress** (Tues–Sun 8.30am–2.30pm; €2), comprising ruined structures from all these eras and an Ottoman inscription above a Byzantine double-headed eagle at the south gate. Further inland, the town skyline is dominated in turn by the Germanic-Gothic belfry spire of **Áyios Athanásios cathedral** and the mammary dome of **Áyios Therápon**, both expressions of the (post)-Baroque taste of the nineteenth-century Ottoman Greek bourgeoisie. They stand more or less at opposite ends of the **bazaar**, whose main street, Ermoú, links the town centre with the little-used north harbour of **Epáno Skála**. On its way there Ermoú passes various expensive antique shops near the roofless, derelict **Yéni Tzamí** at the heart of the old Muslim quarter, just a few steps east of a superb Turkish **hamam**, restored to its former glory but – like the mosque – closed unless a special exhibit is being held. Between Ermoú and the castle lies a maze of atmospheric lanes lined with Belle Epoque mansions and humbler vernacular dwellings; more ornate townhouses are found in the southerly districts of **Sourádha** and **Kióski**, towards the airport.

Mytilíni's excellent **archeological collection** is housed in **two separate galleries** (Tues–Sun 8.30am–3pm; €3), a few hundred metres apart. The newer, upper museum, at the base of 8-Noemvríou, is devoted to finds from wealthy Roman Mytilene, in particular three rooms of well-displayed mosaics from second/third-century AD villas. Highlights include a crude but engaging scene of Orpheus charming all manner of beasts and birds, two fishermen surrounded by clearly recognizable (and edible) sea creatures, and the arrival of baby Telephos, son of Auge and Hercules, in a seaborne box, again with amazed fishermen presiding. Earlier eras are represented in the older wing (same hours, same ticket), located in a former mansion just behind the ferry dock. The star, late-Classical exhibits upstairs include minutely detailed terracotta figurines: a pair of acrobats, two *kourotrophoi* figures (goddesses suckling infants, predecessors of all Byzantine Galaktotrofoússa icons), children playing with a ball or dogs, and Aphrodite riding a dolphin.

There's also a worthwhile **Byzantine Art Museum** (Mon–Sat 9am–1pm; €2) just behind Áyios Therápon, containing various icons rescued from rural churches, plus a canvas of the *Assumption* by Theophilos (see p.778).

Eating, drinking and nightlife

The obvious, if touristy, venue for a seafood blowout is the cluster of **tavernas** on southerly Fanári quay; *Stratos* at the end is marginally the best, and doesn't tout aggressively. For *mayireftá* (including early-morning *patsás*), look no further than the *Averoff* on the west quay, popular for lunch before an afternoon ferry departure. Two traditional **ouzerís** mark opposite ends of the bazaar. *Kalderimi* (closed Sun) occupies three premises around Thássou 2, with seating under the shade of vines; the food is abundant if a bit plainly presented. For less outlay (and friendlier service), make for *Ermis* (daily), the best of a few ouzerís up at Epáno Skála; a 1999 refit didn't much affect its century-old decor (panelled ceiling, giant mirrors, faded oil paintings), or its claimed two centuries of purveying titbits to a jolly, varied crowd in the pleasant courtyard.

For **snacks and drinks**, *Navayio* at the head of the harbour is the favourite, with an unbeatable combo **breakfast** at a fair price. Mytilíni can offer decent **nightlife and entertainment**, especially along the trendy northeast quay, ground zero for *frappádhika*-cum-bars. Most durable are *Marush* and *Hott Spott*, interspersed with other annually changing outfits (one the former premises of the Banque Ottomane Imperiale). Otherwise, watch as usual for flybills advertising out-of-town happenings in summer. The summer **cinema** Pallas is on Vournázon near the park; the winter cinema, Arion, is near the KTEL.

Around Mytilíni

Beyond the airport and Krátigos village, the paved road loops around to **Haramídha**, 14km from town and the closest decent (pebble) **beach**; the eastern bay has a few **tavernas**, best of these being *Theodhora Klava* (*Grioules*). The double cove at **Áyios Ermoyénis**, 3km west and directly accessible from Mytilíni via Loutrá village, is more scenic and sandy, with a single adequate **taverna**, but small and crowded at weekends. For other pleasant immersions near Mytilíni, make for **Loutrá Yéras**, 8km along the main road to Kalloní.

These **public baths** (daily: June–Sept 8am–7pm; April–May & Oct 8am–6pm; Nov–March 9am–5pm; €2.50) are just the thing if you've spent a sleepless night on a ferry, with two ornate spouts that feed 38°C water to marble-lined pools in vaulted chambers; there are separate facilities for men and women.

The Variá museums

The most rewarding single targets near Mytilíni are a pair of museums at **VARIÁ**, 5km south of town (hourly buses). The **Theophilos Museum** (daily 10am–4pm; €2) honours the painter, born here in 1873, with four rooms of wonderful, little-known compositions commissioned by his patron Thériade (see below) during the years leading up to Theophilos' death in 1934. A wealth of detail is evident in elegiac scenes of fishing, reaping, olive-picking and baking from the pastoral Lésvos which Theophilos obviously knew best; there are droll touches also, such as a cat slinking off with a fish in *The Fishmongers*. In classical scenes – Sappho and Alkaeos, a landscape series of Egypt, Asia Minor and the Holy Land, and episodes from wars historical and contemporary – Theophilos was on shakier ground; *Abyssinians Hunting an Italian Horseman* has clearly been conflated with New World Indians chasing down a conquistador.

The adjacent, imposing **Thériade Museum** (Tues–Sun 9am–2pm & 5–8pm; €2) is the legacy of another native son, Stratis Eleftheriades (1897–1983). Leaving the island in his youth for Paris, he Gallicized his name to Thériade and eventually became a renowned avant-garde art publisher, enlisting some of the leading artists of the twentieth century in his ventures. The displays consist of lithographs, engravings, ink drawings, wood-block prints and watercolours by the likes of Miró, Chagall, Picasso, Giacometti, Matisse, Le Corbusier, Léger, Rouault and Villon, either annotated by the painters themselves or commissioned as illustrations for the works of prominent poets and authors (for example Alfred Jarry's *Ubu Roi*): an astonishing collection for a relatively remote Aegean island.

Southern Lésvos

Southern Lésvos is indented by two great inlets, the gulfs of **Kalloní** and **Yéra**: the first curving in a northeasterly direction, the latter northwesterly, creating a fan-shaped peninsula at the heart of which looms 967-metre **Mount Ólymbos**. Both shallow gulfs are landlocked by very narrow outlets to the open sea, which don't – and probably never will – have bridges spanning them. This is the most verdant and productive olive-oil territory on Lésvos, and stacks of pressing-mills stab the skyline.

PÉRAMA, its oddly atttractive townscape dotted with disused olive-oil warehouses, is one of the larger places on the Gulf of Yéra, and has a regular *kaïki* service (no cars carried) linking it with Koundoroudhiá and blue city buses to/from Mytilíni on the far side. The most likely reason to show up is for one of the better **taverna-ouzerís** in the region: *Balouhanas* (all year; lunch and dinner), the northernmost establishment on the front, with a wooden, cane-roofed conservatory jutting out over the water plus outdoor tables. The name's a corruption of *balıkhane* or "fish-market" in Turkish, and seafood is a strong point, whether grilled or made into croquettes, as are regional starters and own-made desserts.

Plomári and around

Due south of Mount Ólymbos, at the edge of the "fan", **PLOMÁRI** is the only sizeable coastal settlement hereabouts, and indeed the second-largest municipality on Lésvos. It presents an unlikely juxtaposition of scenic appeal and its famous ouzo industry, courtesy of several local **distilleries**; the largest and oldest, *Varvayianni* (Ⓦwww.barbayanni-ouzo.com), offers free tours (and tasting) during working hours. Despite a resounding lack of good **beaches** within walking distance, Plomári is popular with Scandinavian tourists, but you can usually find a **room** (prominently signposted) at the edge of the old, charmingly dilapidated town, or 1km west in **Ammoudhélli** suburb, which has a small pea-gravel beach. A good on-spec bet is *Pension Lida* above the inland Platía Beniamín (Ⓣ22520 32507; ③), a restoration inn occupying two old mansions, with sea-view balconies for most units (some not en suite). Rustling up a decent meal presents more difficulties; the line of obvious **tavernas** on the shore either side of the **post office** (**ATM**s too) are all much of a muchness. Imperial (Ⓣ22520 32896) is the most ubiquitous local **car-rental** outlet.

Áyios Isídhoros, 3km east, is where most tourists actually stay; best of the **hotels** here, at the highest point in the settlement, is *Sandy Bay* (Ⓣ22520 32825, Ⓦwww.sandybay.br; B&B ④), with well-appointed rooms (though no balcony partitions) and a pleasant lawn around the pool. For a shoreline location, try *Pebble Beach* (Ⓣ22520 31651, Ⓕ22520 31566; B&B ④), where many rooms overlook a slightly reefy section of beach – though avoid those near the bar if you value sleep. **Eating out** locally, the clear winner is *Taverna tou Panaï* (all year) in an olive grove just by the northerly town limits sign; here you'll find salubrious meat, seafood and *mayireftá* dishes, and mostly Greeks in attendance.

Melínda, a 700-metre sand-and-shingle beach at the mouth of a canyon, lies 6km west of Plomári by paved road. Of the several inexpensive **taverna-rooms** outfits, ramshackle *Maria's* (Ⓣ22520 93239; ②) offers basic **lodging** and more elaborate **meals**. The Gannosis family's *Melinda Studios* (Ⓣ22520 93282 or 694 95 50 629; ②) two doors along, has better accommodation (though no meals), as does *Melinda* (aka *Dhimitris Psaros*; Ⓣ22520 93234; ②) at the west end of the strand.

Ayiássos and around

AYIÁSSOS, nestled in a remote, wooded valley under the crest of Mount Ólymbos, is the most beautiful hill town on Lésvos, its narrow cobbled streets lined by ranks of tiled-roof houses. On the usual, northerly approach, there's no hint of the enormous village until you see huge knots of parked cars at the southern edge of town, 26km from Mytilíni. From this point, keen walkers can follow marked paths/tracks three hours to the **Ólymbos summit**.

Most visitors proceed past endless ranks of kitsch wooden and ceramic souvenirs or carved "Byzantine" furniture, aimed mostly at Greeks, and the central **church of the Panayía Vrefokratoússa** – built in the twelfth century to house an icon supposedly painted by the Evangelist Luke – to the **old bazaar**, with its *kafenía*, yoghurt/cheese shops and butchers' stalls. With such a venerable icon as a focus, the local August 15 *paniyíri* is one of the liveliest in Greece, let alone Lésvos. **Restaurants** include *Dhouladhelli*, on the right at the Y-junction as you enter the village from its south end, or idiosyncratic *Ouzerí To Stavri*, at the extreme north end of the village in Stavrí district.

Headed for Ayiássos with your own transport, you might visit the **Mylélia water mill** (daily 9am–6pm; Ⓦwww.mylelia.gr), whose inconspicuously signposted access track takes off 1km west of the turning for Ípios village. The name means "place of the mills", and there were once several hereabouts. The last survivor, restored to working order, has not been made twee in the least; the keeper will show you the mill race and paddle-wheel, as well as the flour making its spasmodic exit, after which you're free to buy gourmet pastas and other products at the shop. Since its 1990s restoration, Mylélia has branched out into cheeses, jams, vinegar, salted fish, even cooking courses – and their products are sold in every Lésvos resort as well as overseas.

Vaterá, Skála Polikhnítou – and spas en route

A different bus route from Mytilíni leads to Vaterá beach via the inland villages of Polikhnítos and Vrýssa. **VRÝSSA** itself has a **natural history museum** (daily 9.30am–5pm; €1.50) documenting local paleontological finds – though it's not exactly required viewing until the gallery is expanded. Until 20,000 years ago, Lésvos (like all other east Aegean islands) was joined to the Asian mainland, the gulf of Vaterá was a subtropical lake, and all manner of creatures flourished here, their fossilized bones constituting the star exhibits, such as they are.

If you're after a hot bath, head for the vaulted, well-restored **spa complex** 1.5km east of **Polikhnítos** (daily: April–Oct 9am–8pm, Nov–March 2–7pm; €3); there are separate, warm-hued chambers for each sex. These are preferable to the erratically managed, indifferently maintained **hot springs** at **Áyios Ioánnis**, 3km below the village of Lisvóri (daily 8.30–midnight; €3), where the better Ottoman bath-house is often booked by groups.

VATERÁ, 9km south of Polikhnítos, is a huge, seven-kilometre-long sand beach, backed by vegetated hills; the sea here is delightfully calm and clean, the strand itself among the best on Lésvos. Development, mostly seasonal villas and apartments for locals, straggles for several kilometres to either side of the central T-junction; at the west end of the strip is one of the few consistently attended and professionally run **hotels**, *Vatera Beach* (ⓣ22520 61212, ⓦwww.vaterabeach.gr; ④ but 20 percent web discount), with air conditioning and fridges in the rooms. It also has a good **restaurant** with own-grown produce and shoreline tables looking 3km west to the cape of **Áyios Fokás**, where only foundations remain of a temple of Dionysos and a superimposed early Christian basilica. The little tamarisk-shaded anchorage here has a fair-priced fish **taverna**, *Akrotiri/Angelerou* (April–Oct), better than most at Vaterá, and as good as those at **SKÁLA POLIKHNÍTOU**, 4km northwest of Polikhnítos itself, where *T'Asteria*, *Iliovasilema* and *Akroyiali* can all be recommended. Skála itself is pleasantly workaday, with only a short, narrow beach that morphs into a better one at **Nyfídha**, 3km west.

East from Vaterá, a mostly paved road leads via Stavrós and Akrássi to either Ayiássos or Plomári within ninety minutes, making day-trips feasible. When going north towards Kalloní, use the completely paved, fast short-cut via the naval base and seashore hamlet (with a good eponymous **taverna**) at **Akhladherí**.

Western Lésvos

The main road west of Loutrá Yéras is surprisingly devoid of habitation, with little to stop for before Kalloní other than an ancient **Aphrodite temple** at **Mésa** (Méson), 1km north of the main road, and signposted just east of the Akhladherí turn-off. At the **site** (which may be closed for excavation), just eleventh-century BC foundations and a few column stumps remain, plus the ruins of a fourteenth-century Genoese basilica wedged inside; it was once by the sea, but a nearby stream has silted things up in the intervening millennia. It doesn't merit a special trip, merely a short detour if passing by with your own transport.

More rewardingly, you can turn northeast towards **AYÍA PARASKEVÍ** village, midway between two more important (and photogenic) monuments from diverse eras: the Paleo-Christian **basilica of Halinádhou**, and the large

medieval bridge of Kremastí. Ayía Paraskeví itself can offer, at the southern outskirts, the eminently worthwhile **Mousío Viomihanikís Elaeouryías Lésvou/Lesvos Museum of the Olive-Pressing Industry** (daily except Tues 10am–6pm, closes 5pm Oct 16–Feb 28; €3), housed in the restored communal olive mill. This, built by public subscription in the 1920s, only ceased working under the junta; the industrial machinery has been lovingly refurbished and its function explained, while former outbuildings and warehouses are used as venues for secondary exhibits and short explanatory films.

KALLONÍ is a lively agricultural and market town in the middle of the island, with various shops and services (including a **post office** and three **ATMs**). Some 3km south lies **SKÁLA KALLONÍS**, an unlikely package resort backing a long, sandy but absurdly shallow beach on the lake-like gulf whose water can be turbid. It's mainly distinguished as a **bird-watching** centre during the March–May nesting season in the adjacent salt marshes. Pick of a half-dozen **hotels** west of town is the garden-set *Aegeon* (Ⓣ22530 22398, Ⓦwww.aegeon-lesvos.gr; ④), with above-average furnishings for its class, a large pool and friendly owners. **The local speciality is** the gulf's celebrated, plankton-fed **sardines**, best eaten fresh-grilled from August to October (though they're available salt-cured all year round); **tavernas** near the in-town fishing jetty are pretty indistinguishable, though *Omiros* is a decent, inexpensive option conveniently behind the west beach.

Inland monasteries and villages

West of Kalloní, the road winds 4km uphill to **Limónos monastery**, founded in 1527 by the monk Ignatios, whose cell is maintained in the surviving medieval north wing. It's a huge, rambling, three-storeyed complex around a vast, plant-filled courtyard, home to just a handful of monks and lay workers. The *katholikón*, with its ornate carved-wood ceiling and archways, is traditionally off-limits to women; a sacred spring flows from below the south foundation wall. Only a ground-floor **ecclesiastical museum** (daily 9.30am–6.30pm, may close 3pm off-season; €1.50) currently functions, with the more interesting ethnographic gallery upstairs closed, though you can see an overflow of farm implements in a storeroom below, next to a chamber where giant *pithária* (urns) for grain and olive oil are embedded in the floor.

The main road beyond passes through **VATOÚSSA**, a beautiful landlocked settlement with a **folklore/historical museum** in the ancestral mansion of Grigorios Gogos. Just beyond Vatoússa a paved side road leads 7km to the outskirts of **HÍDHIRA**, where the **Methymneos Winery** (daily July–Sept 30 9am–6pm, otherwise by appointment on Ⓣ22530 51518; Ⓦwww.methymneos.gr) has successfully revived the local ancient grape variety, decimated by phylloxera some decades ago. Because of the altitude (300m) and sulphur-rich soil (you're in a volcanic caldera), their velvety, high-alcohol, oak-aged red can be produced organically; 2007 saw the introduction of bottled white wines. Proprietor Ioannis Lambrou gives a highly worthwhile twenty-minute tour of the state-of-the-art premises, in English.

Some 8km beyond Vatoússa, a short track leads down to the thirteenth-century **monastery of Perivolís** (daily 10am–1pm & 5–6pm; donation, no photos), built amid a riverside orchard (*perivóli*), with fine if damp-damaged sixteenth-century frescoes in the narthex. An apocalyptic panel worthy of Bosch (*The Earth and Sea Yield up their Dead*) shows the Whore of Babylon riding her chimera and assorted sea monsters disgorging their victims; just to the right, towards the main door, the Three Magi approach the Virgin enthroned with the Christ Child. On the north side there's a highly unusual iconography of *Abraham, the Virgin, and the Penitent Thief of Calvary in Paradise*, with the Four Rivers of Paradise gushing forth under their feet; just right are assembled the Hebrew kings of the Old Testament.

ÁNDISSA, 3km further on, nestles under the arid west's only substantial pine grove; at the western edge of the village a sign implores you to "Come Visit Our Square", not a bad idea for the sake of a handful of **tavernas** and *kafenía* sheltering under three sizeable plane trees. Directly below Ándissa a paved road leads 6km north to the fishing village of **GAVATHÁS**, with a shortish, partly protected **beach** (there's a bigger, often surf-buffeted one at **Kámbos** just east) and a few places to **eat** and **stay** – among these *Pension Restaurant Paradise* (Ⓣ22530 56376; ②), serving good fish and locally grown vegetables.

Just west of Ándissa there's an important junction. Keeping straight leads you past the still-functioning, double-gated **monastery of Ypsiloú**, founded in 1101 atop an outrider of the extinct volcano of Órdhymnos. The *katholikón*, tucked in one corner of a large, irregular courtyard, has a fine wood-lattice ceiling but has had its frescoes repainted to detrimental effect. Exhibits in the upstairs **museum** (donation) encompass a fine collection of *epitáfios* (Good Friday) shrouds, ancient manuscripts, portable icons and – oddest of all – a *Deposition* painted in Renaissance style by a sixteenth-century Turk. Ypsiloú's patron saint is John the Divine, a frequent dedication for monasteries overlooking apocalyptic landscapes like the surrounding parched, boulder-strewn hills.

Just west begins the five-kilometre side road to the main concentration of Lésvos's rather overrated **petrified forest** (daily: June–Sept 8am–sunset, Oct–May 8am–4pm; €2), a fenced-in "reserve" toured along 3km of walkways. For once, contemporary Greek arsonists cannot be blamed for the state of the trees, created by the combined action of volcanic ash from Órdhymnos and hot springs some fifteen to twenty million years ago. The mostly horizontal sequoia trunks average 1m or less in length, save for a few poster-worthy exceptions; another more accessible (and free) cluster is found south of Sígri.

Sígri

SÍGRI, near the western tip of Lésvos, has an appropriately end-of-the-line feel; its bay is guarded both by an Ottoman castle and the long island of **Nissiopí**, which protects the place somewhat from prevailing winds. Until the early 1990s Sígri was an important NATO naval base; then civilian ferries called here fitfully for some years before ceasing entirely. The eighteenth-century **castle** (built atop an earlier one) sports the reigning sultan's monogram over the entrance, something rarely seen outside Istanbul, evidence of the high regard in which this strategic port with a good water supply was held. The odd-looking **church of Ayía Triádha** is in fact a converted **mosque**, with a huge water cistern taking up the ground floor; this supplied, among other things, the half-ruined *hamam* just south. At the top of town stands the well-executed but overpriced **Natural History Museum of the Lésvos Petrified Forest** (daily: May 15–Oct 15 8.30am–8pm, Oct 16–May 14 8.30am–4.30pm; €5), which covers pan-Aegean geology with samples and maps (including, ominously, seismic patterns), as well as the expected quota of petrified logs and plant fossils from when the surrounding hills were far more vegetated. Sígri itself presents an odd mix of vernacular and concrete dwellings, while the town **beach**, south of the castle headland, is long, narrow and protected, with a **taverna**. There are much better beaches at **Faneroméni**, 3.5km north by coastal dirt track from the northern outskirts of town, or at **Liména** (part naturist), 2km south, just below the fifteen-kilometre dirt track to Eressós (passable with care in 35min); neither has any facilities.

Package companies have vanished along with the ferries, so **accommodation** is fairly easy to find; one of the best is *Evangelia* (ⓣ694 49 43 063, ⓦhttp://sigri-lesvos.co.uk/evan2.html; ❷–❸), with studios and apartments and some units looking across the bay. Among a half-dozen **tavernas**, the *Cavo d'Oro/Blue Wave* (no sign) by the harbour is a classic for lobster and scaly fish; most of the restaurants around the platía are run-of-the-mill in comparison. **Nightlife** is provided by *Notia* (June–Sept), with frequent live jazz sessions.

Skála Eressoú

Most visitors to western Lésvos park themselves at **SKÁLA ERESSOÚ**, reached via a southerly turning between Ándissa and Ypsiloú. Its three-kilometre **beach** rivals Vaterá's, and consequently the resort just trails Mólyvos, Pétra and Plomári for visitor numbers. Behind stretches the largest and most attractive agricultural plain on Lésvos, a welcome green contrast to the volcanic ridges above.

There's not much to central Skála – just a roughly rectangular grid of perhaps five streets by twelve, angling up to the oldest cottages on the slope of **Vígla hill** above the east end of the beach. The waterfront pedestrian lane is divided midway by a café-lined, circular platía with a bust of **Theophrastos**. This renowned botanist hailed from **ancient Eressós** atop Vígla hill – the remaining citadel wall is still visible from a distance. The ruins themselves prove scanty, but it's worth the scramble up for the views – you can spy the ancient jetty submerged beyond the modern fishing anchorage.

Another famous native of ancient Eressós, honoured by a stylized statue on the platía, was **Sappho** (ca. 615–562 BC), poetess and reputed lesbian. There are thus always conspicuous numbers of gay women about, particularly in the clothing-optional zone of the **beach** west of the river mouth, home to a small community of terrapins. Ancient Eressós lasted into the Byzantine era, whose main legacy is the **Áyios Andhréas basilica** behind the modern church – foundations and a fragmentary, if restored, floor mosaic remain. The **tomb** of the saint, an early Cretan bishop (not the patron of Scotland), huddles just beyond.

Practicalities

Skála has countless **rooms and apartments** (❷–❹), but those near the sea fill quickly and can be noisy; in peak season you should aim for something quiet and inland, overlooking a garden or fields. Most package companies have recently dropped the resort, usually citing a lack of commitment to "family values" – that is, the lesbian contingent was tricky for their clients to handle – so vacancies are now easier to find. Still, it's wise to entrust the search to Sappho Travel (ⓣ22530 52202 or 22530 52140, ⓦwww.lesvos.co.uk), which also serves as a car-rental station, ferry agent and air-ticket source. Otherwise, there are few bona fide **hotels** in the village, some of which – for example the seafront *Sappho the Eressia* (ⓣ22530 53233, ⓦwww.sappho-hotel.com; ❸), with Wi-Fi and a pleasant ground-floor snack-bar, and *Mascot* (book through Sappho Travel; ❹), three blocks inland – are **women-only**. A straight alternative is the popular if basic *Kyma* (ⓣ22530 53555, ⓕ22530 53556; ❹), at the east end of the front, with seven of ten rooms facing the sea, and Wi-Fi in the lobby.

Most **tavernas**, with elevated wooden dining platforms, crowd the beach; in the wake of the tourism slump, they've been subjected to harsh winnowing. Worthy survivors include *Kyani Sardhini/Blue Sardine*, a creditable seafood ouzerí at the far west end of the front, or nearby *Soulatsos*, one of the more reliable and popular grill-and-*mezédhes* outfits. With about seven clubs/bars to choose from in peak season, local **nightlife** is the best on the island. Gay women favour *Sappho Garden of the Arts* inland, often with live events; *Parasol* and *Cooya Caribu* are straighter café-bars on the east esplanade, while well-established *Primitive*, west of town past the bridge over the terrapin-filled river, is unbeatable for theme parties. There's also a central, open-air **cinema** (July to early Sept), called (predictably) Sappho. Skála has a **post office**, an **ATM**, and a seafront **Internet café** on the east walkway and two bars with Wi-Fi. An alternative local **car rental agency** is Igfa (Alamo/National reps; ⓣ22530 53001).

If you're **returning to the main island crossroads** at Kalloní, you can loop back from Eressós along the western shore of the Gulf of Kalloní via Mesótopos and Ágra villages, much quicker than returning via Ándissa and Skalohóri. Just off this paved road there's an excellent **beach** at **Kroússos**, with a cult **taverna** in an immobilized bus at the east end; here Kyra-Maria lays on home-style food (good white bulk wine, snails, chickpea soup, *dolmádhes*, beans, maybe sea urchin roe) a world away from resort platters, at attractive prices.

Northern Lésvos

The road **north from Kalloní** curls up a piney ridge and then down the other side into countryside stippled with poplars and blanketed by olive groves. Long before you can discern any other architectural detail, the cockscomb silhouette of **Mólyvos castle** indicates your approach to the oldest-established destination on Lésvos.

Mólyvos (Míthymna)

MÓLYVOS (officially Míthymna after its ancient predecessor), 61km from Mytilíni, is arguably the island's most beautiful village, with tiers of sturdy, red-tiled houses, some standing with their rear walls defensively towards the sea, mounting the slopes between the picturesque harbour and the **Byzantine-Genoese castle** (closed for restoration). A score of weathered Turkish fountains, a mosque and *hamam* grace flower-fragrant, cobbled alleyways, reflecting the fact that before 1923 Muslims constituted more than a third of the local population and owned many of the finest dwellings. The **Komninaki Kralli mansion**, high up in the town, is particularly worth a look (daily 9am–5pm; free); the lower floor houses a well-signposted **"School of Fine Arts"**, but the wall- and ceiling-murals on the upper storey (dated 1833) compare with those of the Vareltzídena mansion in Pétra (see p.786). Panels in the smallest room portray dervish musicians and women dancing to *shaum* and drum, while other murals depict stylized versions of Constantinople and Mytilíni Town; you can tell the men's and women's quarters apart by the wider recessed "throne" provided for the latter.

Modern dwellings and hotels have been banned from the old core, but this hasn't prevented a steady drain of all authentic life from the upper **bazaar**; just one lonely tailor still plies his trade amongst souvenir shops vastly surplus to requirements. Once an exclusive resort, Mólyvos is now firmly middle of the road, with the usual silly T-shirts and other trinkets carpeting every vertical surface of a stage-set, albeit an attractive one, for package tourism. The shingly **town beach** is mediocre, improving considerably as you head towards the sandy southern end of the bay, called **Psiriára**, with its clothing-optional zone. Advertised **boat excursions** to Pétra and remoter bays seem a frank admission of this failing; there are also frequent shuttle buses in season, linking all points between Ánaxos and Eftaloú.

Arrival and information

The municipal **tourist office** (summer Mon–Sat 10am–3pm, Sun 10am–2.30pm; ⓣ22530 71347, ⓦwww.mithymna.gr) by the **bus stop**, **taxi rank** and main **car**

▲ Byzantine-Genoese castle, Mólyvos

park at the southeast edge of town (a big new lot has opened above the port) keeps lists of rented **rooms**. Adjacent you'll find three **ATMs**, plus numerous **motorbike and car-rental** places, including Kosmos (Ⓣ22530 71710), Best (Ⓣ22530 72145) and Avis (Ⓣ22530 71797), the latter two offering the option of pick up here and drop off in Mytilíni or the airport. The main **post office** is near the top of the upper commercial street; Centraal, down near the harbour, is the principal **Internet** café (no high-speed or Wi-Fi).

Accommodation

The main sea-level thoroughfare of Mihaïl Goútou links the tourist office with the harbour; just seaward stand a number of bona fide **hotels** or **pensions** not completely taken over by packages. These include the *Hermes* on the beach (Ⓣ22530 71250, Ⓦwww.hermeshotel-molivos.com; ❸), with variable, marble-floored rooms, and the *Molyvos I* next door (Ⓣ22530 71496, Ⓦwww.molyvos-hotels.com; ❹), with large balconied rooms, and breakfast served on the flagstoned terrace under the palms. For more comfort, head 1km south of town to the friendly *Delfinia* (Ⓣ22530 71315, Ⓦwww.hoteldelfinia.com; all year; ❺–❼, Internet discounts), with rooms and bungalows set in 87 acres of greenery, a castle-view pool, tennis courts and direct access to Psiriára beach.

Rooms are scattered along the lanes leading uphill from the upper market thoroughfare. Best of these are *Studios Voula* below the castle car park (Ⓣ22530 71719 or 694 52 41 994), which has studios (❸) and a restored four-person house (❺), both with knockout views. Families should consider the restored *Captain's House* offered by Theo and Melinda (Ⓣ22530 71241, Ⓦwww.lesvosvacations.com), up by the Komninaki Kralli mansion; it sleeps up to six, with seasonal rates of €90–140 for the entire premises. The municipal **campsite**, *Camping Methymna* (late June–Sept), lies 2km northeast of town on the Eftaloú road.

Eating, drinking and nightlife

The sea-view **tavernas** on both lower and upper market lanes are all much of a muchness, where you pay primarily for the view; best head for the fishing port, where ⭑ *The Captain's Table* (supper only) offers squirmingly fresh seafood, meat grills and vegetarian *mezédhes*, washed down by their very palatable, own-label wine. *To Ouzadhiko tou Baboukou* (all year), around the corner on the south quay, has an impressive array of ouzos, a bohemian atmosphere and competent, well-priced (for the location) renditions of the usual *mezédhes*. *Babis*, at the town approaches with semi-rural seating, is the place to head for good grills and a few *mayireftá* of the day. For **snacks**, municipally run *Iy Agora* (*To Dhimotiko Kafenio*), just downhill from the converted mosque/conference centre, has a lovely wood interior, a panoramic balcony, inexpensive ouzo-*mezédhes* combos and larger platters from a limited menu.

Nightlife revolves around several music bars: most durable is youth-orientated, tropical-themed *Congas* (May–Sept) down by the shore, with DJ events, sunset snacks and theme nights; the partly outdoor *Café del Mar*, just up from the harbour, hosts live music some nights (closed Mon). Nearby *Molly's Bar* is the thirty-somethings' preferred hangout, with taped music at a conversational level and a cozy balcony, while *Bazaar* opposite is the main indoor dance hall. There's also a well-regarded outdoor **cinema** (June–Sept) next to the taxi rank.

Pétra and Ánaxos

Given political and practical limits to expansion in Mólyvos, many package companies have shifted emphasis to **PÉTRA**, 5km due south. Modern outskirts sprawl untidily behind its broad sand beach, but two attractive nuclei of old stone houses, some with Levantine-style balconies overhanging the street, extend back from the seafront square. Pétra takes its name from the giant, unmissable **rock monolith** inland, enhanced by the eighteenth-century **church of the Panayía Glykofiloússa**, reached via 114 rock-hewn steps. Other local attractions include the sixteenth-century **church of Áyios Nikólaos**, with three phases of well-preserved frescoes, and the intricately decorated **Vareltzídhena mansion** (Tues–Sun 8am–2.30pm; free), with naive wall paintings of courting couples and a stylized view of a naval engagement at Constantinople.

Most small **hotels** and studios are block-booked, so on-spec arrivals might contact the **Women's Agricultural Tourism Cooperative** on the south side of the seafront square (Ⓣ22530 41238, Ⓔwomes@otenet.gr), which arranges rooms or studios (❷–❸) in scattered premises. For more comfort, try the *Hotel Michaelia* behind the south waterfront (Ⓣ22530 41730, Ⓕ22530 22067; ❹), with decent buffet breakfasts. The excellent, well-priced Women's Coop **restaurant**, under separate management, serves grills and *mayireftá* at rooftop seating. Alternatives include cheap-and-cheerful grill *Kostas*, on a little square east of the monolith; characterful *Rigas* (evenings only), Pétra's oldest ouzerí, further inland; and *Tsalikis Café* on the square for excellent own-made ice cream. You may prefer to leave town – either to ⭑ *Taverna Petri* (all day May to mid-Oct) in **PETRÍ** village 3km inland, with superb home-recipe *mayireftá*, meat grills and a view-terrace, or to tiny **Avláki** beach and its competent, signposted **taverna/ouzerí**, 1.5km southwest en route to Ánaxos.

ÁNAXOS, 3km south of Pétra, is a higgledy-piggledy package resort fringing by far the cleanest **beach** and seawater in the area: 1km of sand well sown with sunbeds and a handful of **tavernas**. From anywhere along here you enjoy beautiful sunsets between and beyond three offshore islets.

Around Mount Lepétymnos

East of Mólyvos, the villages of 968-metre, poplar-tufted **Mount Lepétymnos** provide a day's rewarding exploration. The first stop, though not exactly up the hill, might be **Loutrá Eftaloú thermal baths** 5km east of Mólyvos. Patronize the hot pool under the Ottoman-era domed structure, not the sterile modern tub-rooms (daily: Dec–April variable access; May & Oct 9am–1pm & 3–7pm; June–Sept 10am–2pm & 4–8pm; €3.50 for group pool). The spa is well looked after, with the water mixed up to a toasty 43°C, so you'll need to cool down regularly; outside stretches the long, good pebble beach of **Áyii Anáryiri**, broken up by little headlands, with the two remotest coves nudist. There's a fetchingly positioned **taverna** here, the *Khrysi Akti*, which also lets small en-suite **rooms** (Ⓣ22530 71879; ❷) in the old spa-patrons' inn, built around a church.

EFTALOÚ itself has numerous fancy **hotels** and bungalow complexes, the friendliest and best value (though tour-dominated like the others) being the *Eftalou* (Ⓣ22530 71584, Ⓦwww.eftalouhotel.com; ❹), with a pool, well-tended garden and loyal repeat clientele. Two worthwile **tavernas** within sight of the spa are *Iy Anatoli* (all year, weekends only in winter) with good salt-cured and fresh fish, or nearby *Iy Eftalou*, with a shady courtyard, large meat grills, fish and *mayireftá*, if sometimes glum service.

The main paved road around Lepétymnos first heads 5km east to **VAFIÓS**, with its clutch of three fairly comparable **tavernas** with views (*Vafios*, *Ilias*, *Petrino*) – *Petrino* is the cheapest, and open winter weekends too – before curling north around the base of the mountain. The exquisite hill village of **SYKAMINIÁ** (**Sykamiá, Skamniá**) was the 1892 birthplace of the novelist Stratis Myrivilis; below the platía, with its two *kafenía* and views north to Turkey, one of the imposing basalt-built houses is marked as his childhood home.

A marked trail shortcuts the twisting road down to **SKÁLA SYKAMINIÁS**, easily the most picturesque fishing port on Lésvos. Myrivilis used it as the setting for his best-known work, *The Mermaid Madonna*, and the tiny rock-top chapel at the end of the jetty will be instantly recognizable to anyone who has read the book. Skála has ample **accommodation**, including the central, partly air-conditioned *Gorgona* (Ⓣ22530 55301; ❸), with a shaded breakfast terrace, and several **tavernas**. *Iy Skamnia* (*Iy Mouria tou Myrivili*) has seating under the mulberry tree in which Myrivilis used to sleep on hot summer nights, though *Anemoessa* (by the chapel, open winter weekends too) has the edge quality-wise, with good stuffed squash blossoms complementing fresh seafood. The only local **beach** is the pebble-on-sand-base one of **Kayiá** 1.5km east, where the *Poseidon* **taverna** operates in season.

Some 5km east from upper Sykaminiá, you reach **KLIÓ**, whose single main street leads down to a platía with a plane tree, fountain, *kafenía* and more views across to Turkey. The village is set attractively on a slope, down which a six-kilometre road, widened and repaved in 2008, descends to **Tsónia** beach, 600m of beautiful pink volcanic sand. *Oniro* at the more protected north end is by far the more popular of two **tavernas**.

Just south of Klió, a right (west) fork toward Kápi allows you to complete a loop of the mountain. **PELÓPI** is the ancestral village of unsuccessful 1988 US presidential candidate Michael Dukakis (who finally visited the island in 2000); the main street is now named after him. Garden-lush **YPSILOMÉTOPO**, 5km further along, is punctuated by a minaret (but no mosque) and hosts revels on July 16–17, the feast of Ayía Marína.

Límnos

Límnos is a sizeable agricultural and military island whose remoteness and peculiar ferry schedules protected it until the 1990s from most aspects of the

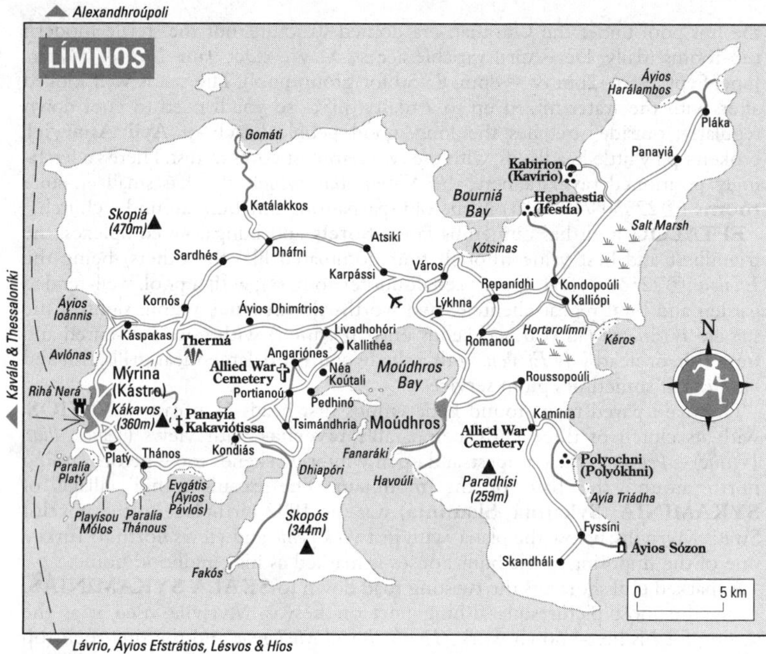

holiday trade. Conventional tourism was late in coming because hoteliers lived primarily off the visiting relatives of the numerous soldiers stationed here; most summer visitors are still Greek, particularly from Thessaloníki, though Danes, Brits, Austrians, Czechs and Italians now arrive by charter flights. Bucolic Límnos has become positively trendy of late: there are upscale souvenir shops, old village houses restored by mainlanders (and foreigners) as seasonal retreats, and a noon-to-small-hours music bar during summer at nearly every beach.

The island has long been the focus of **disputes** between the Greek and Turkish governments; Turkey has a perennial demand that Límnos be demilitarized, and Turkish aircraft regularly intrude Greek air space overhead, prompting immediate responses from the Greek Air Force squadron here. Límnos's **garrison** ran to 25,000 soldiers at the nadir of Greco-Turkish relations during the 1970s and 1980s, though it is now down to about 6000, and set to fall further if/when Greece abolishes conscription and most of the remaining army camps (but not the air base) close.

The **bays** of **Bourniá** and **Moúdhros**, the latter one of the largest natural harbours in the Aegean, divide Límnos almost in two. The west of the island is dramatically hilly, with abundant basalt put to good use as street cobbles and house masonry. The east is low-lying and speckled with seasonal salt marshes, where it's not occupied by cattle, combine harvesters and vast corn fields. Like most volcanic islands, Límnos produces excellent wine – good dry white, rosé and retsina – plus ouzo.

Despite off-islander slander, Límnos is not flat, barren or treeless; the rolling hills are well vegetated except on their heights, with substantial clumps of almond, jujube, myrtle, oak, poplar and mulberry trees. This far north, snow falls annually and stays on the ground, responsible for both novelty postcards of a white Límnos and a healthy hydrology, with irrigation water pumped from deep wells, and a few potable springs in the western half. Various streambeds bring sand to long, **sandy beaches** around the coast, where it's easy to find a stretch to yourself. Most bays shelve gently, making them ideal for children and quick to warm up in spring, with no cool currents except near the river mouths.

Mýrina

MÝRINA (aka Kástro), the port-capital on the west coast, has the ethos of a provincial market town rather than of a resort. With about five thousand inhabitants, it's pleasantly low-key, if not especially picturesque.

Arrival, information and transport

The civilian **airport** lies 18km east of Mýrina, almost at the geographic centre of the island, sharing a runway with an enormous air-force base; there are three **car rental** booths, a bank **ATM**, a few **taxis** outside – and no shuttle bus into town. **Ferries** dock at the southern edge of Mýrina, in the shadow of the castle; the newer jetty on the far side of the bay serves commercial lorries only. There are separate **agencies** for the sailings of NEL and Agoudimos ferries (Pravlis Travel, ⓣ22540 24617) and Saos Ferries (ⓣ22540 29571). The **bus station** is on Platía Eleftheríou Venizélou, at the north end of Kydhá. One look at the sparse schedules (a single daily afternoon departure to most points) will convince you of the need to **rent a vehicle** from outlets clustered around the harbour area. **Cars, motorbikes** and **bicycles** can be rented from Limnos Car Rental (ⓣ22540 23777, airport ⓣ694 54 95 104), Myrina Rent a Car (ⓣ22540 24476), Petrides Travel (ⓣ22540 22039, airport ⓣ22540 24787) and Holiday (ⓣ22540 23280, airport 693 24 81 056); rates for bikes are only slightly above the island norm, but cars are exorbitant. A motorbike (most obviously from Moto Lemnos, ⓣ22540 25002, in from the jetty clock tower) is generally enough to explore the coast and the interior of the closer villages, as there are few steep gradients but many perilously narrow streets. A 2006-built **bypass road** via Néa Mádhitos district and the commercial port has relieved most of Mýrina's **traffic** bottlenecks; **parking**, however, remains nightmarish, with spaces possible only at the outskirts.

Most **ATMs** cluster around a platía about halfway along Kydhá; the main **taxi** rank is here too, while the **post office** is around the corner on Garoufalídhi. Among three **Internet** cafés, most convenient and pleasant is *Excite* just back from the harbour roundabout.

Accommodation

Despite Límnos's steady gentrification, and explicit discouragement of backpackers, one may still be met off the boat with offers of a **room or studio**; there are officially two dozen or so licensed establishments in Mýrina, especially in the northern districts of **Rihá Nerá** and **Áyios Pandelímonas**. Otherwise there are adequate in-town **hotels** plus upmarket complexes at nearby beaches. At **Romeïkós Yialós** a few restored old buildings serve as small inns, though most are affected by noise from the seafront bars. There's **no official campsite**, though a few tents sprout furtively at Kéros (see p.792).

Apollo Pavilion On Frýnis ⓣ22540 23712, ⓦwww.apollopavilion.com. Hidden away in a peaceful cul-de-sac about halfway along Garoufalídhou, this offers three-bed a/c studios with TV and mini-kitchen. Most units have balconies, with views of either the castle or the mountains. Open all year. ❸

Arhondiko Cnr Sakhtoúri and Filellínon, Romeïkós Yialós ⓣ22540 29800, ⓦwww.guestinn.com. Límnos's first hotel, this 1851-built mansion was reopened in 2003 as three floors of small-to-medium-sized, wood-trimmed rooms with all mod cons (but no balconies). There's a pleasant ground-floor bar/breakfast lounge, though bathrooms are already dated and a major overhaul is set for late 2007. ④

Ifestos Ethnikís Andístasis 17, Andhróni district, inland from Rihá Nerá ⓣ22540 24960, ⓕ22540 23623. Quiet, professionally run C-class hotel, with pleasant common areas. Slightly small rooms have a/c, fridges, balconies and a mix of sea or hill views. ④

Nefeli Suites Castle approach, Romeïkós Yialós ⓣ22540 23551, ⓔinfo@nefeli-lemnos.gr. These apartments include four-plexes suitable for families, though no balconies. Enjoy the view instead from the terrace-café on the west side of the building. Limited parking. ④

Porto Myrina Avlónas beach, 1.5km north of Rihá Nerá ⓣ22540 24805. The island's best beachfront lodging, though its five stars are one too many. Standard rooms and free-standing bungalows surround an Artemis temple found during construction; vast common areas include tennis courts, a football pitch, one of the largest (salt-water) pools in Greece, and summer watersports on the beach. Open May–Oct 15; ⑥–⑦

The Town

Mýrina's main attraction is its **Byzantine castle** (unrestricted access), perched on a craggy headland between the ferry dock and Romeïkós Yialós, the town's beach-lined esplanade backed by ornate Neoclassical mansions. Ruinous despite later Genoese and Ottoman additions, the fortress is flatteringly lit at night and warrants a climb towards sunset for views over the town, the entire west coast and – in clear conditions – Mount Áthos, 35 nautical miles west. Miniature, skittish deer imported from Rhodes, and fed by the municipality, patrol the castle grounds to the amusement of visitors. Also worth exploring is the town's core neighbourhood of old stone houses dating from the Ottoman era. Few explicitly Islamic monuments have survived, though an unassuming **fountain** at the harbour end of the main drag, Kydhá, retains its calligraphic inscription and is still highly prized for drinking water.

Shops and amenities are mostly found along **Kydhá** and its continuation **Karatzá** – which meanders north from the harbour to Romeïkós Yialós – or **Garoufalídhi**, its perpendicular offshoot, roughly halfway along. As town **beaches** go, **Romeïkós Yialós** and **Néa Mádhitos** (ex-Toúrkikos Yialós), its counterpart to the southeast of the harbour, are not bad; **Rihá Nerá**, the next bay north of Romeïkós Yialós, is even better, shallow as the name suggests and popular with families, with watersports on offer.

The **archeological museum** (Tues–Sun 8.30am–3pm; €2) occupies the former Ottoman governor's mansion right behind Romeïkós Yialós, not far from the site of Bronze Age Myrina. Finds from all of the island's major sites are assiduously labelled in Greek, Italian and English, and the entire premises exemplary in terms of presentation – the obvious drawback being that the best items have been spirited away to Athens, leaving a collection of specialist interest. The star upper-storey exhibits are votive lamps in the shape of sirens, found in an Archaic sanctuary at Hephaestia (Ifestía), much imitated in modern local jewellery. Rather less vicious than Homer's creatures, they are identified more invitingly as the "muses of the underworld, creatures of superhuman wisdom, incarnations of nostalgia for paradise". An entire room is devoted to metalwork, of which the most impressive items are gold jewellery and bronze objects, both practical (cheese graters, door-knockers) and whimsical-naturalistic (a snail, a vulture).

Eating, drinking and nightlife

Seafood is excellent on Límnos, owing to the island's proximity to the Dardanelles and seasonal fish migrations. For waterside dining, *To Limanaki* is among the most popular of several establishments around the little fishing harbour, with strong ouzo in bulk and big portions, but also lax service and tricky fish pricing

– *O Glaros* nearby is more professional and accomplished. About halfway along Kydhá, *O Platanos* serves traditional *mayireftá* to big crowds on an atmospheric little square beneath two plane trees. Most restaurants along Romeïkós Yialós offer poor value; the tree-shaded tables of *Iy Tzitzifies* (May–Oct) at Rihá Nerá are a far better option for daily-changing *mayireftá* and a few fish dishes. Romeïkós Yialós is, however, the hub of *frappádhika* action and where **nightlife** kicks off with a sunset drink in the shadow of the castle; the two are combined nicely at *Karagiozis* at no. 32, by the bridge (11am–late). Choices elsewhere are limited, for example to stunningly appointed *Alexandros* at the base of the jetty; the closest after-hours beach bar is *Kioski* (July–Aug) on the sand at Avlónas. There's also the Maroula **cinema-theatre** on Garoufalídhi.

Western Límnos

Beyond Mýrina's respectable town beaches, the closest good sand lies 3km north at **Avlónas**, unspoilt except for the local power plant just inland. Just beyond, the road splits: the right-hand turning wends its way through **Káspakas**, its north-facing houses in neat tiers and a potable spring (but no taverna) on its platía, before plunging down to **Áyios Ioánnis**, also reached directly by the left-hand bypass. There are **studios** here, plus a few **tavernas**, most distinctive the one (late June to late Aug) featuring seating in the shade of piled-up volcanic boulders, but nearby **beaches** – buffeted by southwesterly winds – are not the best and the shore is densely built-up.

Just east, the old Ottoman baths at **Thérma** have been restored as an eye-wateringly expensive contemporary health spa, with all conceivable treatments available – or you can just have a hydromassage soak (daily 10am–2pm & 5–9pm; €12). Some 7km north of here, **SARDHÉS** is the highest village on the island, with a celebrated central **taverna**, *Man-Tella* (all year, lunch and dinner). Portions are large and the food rich, so arrive hungry; book for summertime dinner (Ⓣ22540 61349) in the pleasant courtyard.

Beyond Sardhés, 5km below Katálakkos, lies the spectacular, well-signposted **dune environment at Gomáti**, one of the largest such in Greece. There are two zones reached by separate dirt tracks: one at a river mouth, with a bird-rich marsh, and the other to the northwest, with a beach bar and sunbeds. Despite wind exposure, the latter portion especially is a popular outing locally.

Platý to Paleó Pedhinó

PLATÝ, 2km southeast of Mýrina, has had its profile spoilt by the modern villa construction that is blighting many Limnian villages, but it does have two nocturnal **tavernas**. The better of these is *O Sozos*, just off the main platía (groups reserve in season on Ⓣ22540 25085), featuring huge, well-priced grills, salads and a few *mayireftá* like *dolmádhes*, washed down by *tsípouro* and local bulk wine. The long sandy **beach**, 700m below, is popular, with non-motorized watersports available at the south end through Babis, below the unsightly *Lemnos Village* complex. Near mid-strand, *Grigoris* proves a reliable, popular beachside **taverna**, with fish occasionally. The highest standard **hotel** in the area, if not the whole island, is *Villa Afroditi* (Ⓣ22540 23141, Ⓦwww.afroditivillasa.gr; mid-May to early Oct; ⑤–⑥), with its spectacular topiary, pleasant pool bar, and one of the best buffet breakfasts in the islands. Completely refurbished in 2007, with a new wing added, it comprises standard doubles and two-room apartments.

THÁNOS, 2km further southeast, proves bigger and more architecturally characterful, with Nikos Dhimou's high-standard mock-trad **bungalows** at the east edge (Ⓣ22540 25284; ④). **Paralía Thánous**, 1.5km below, is among the most scenic of southwestern beaches, flanked by volcanic crags and looking out to Áyios Efstrátios island. There's good-value **accommodation** at *Villa Thanos Beach* (☎22540 23496 or 697 37 10 543; ❸), with a lush front garden, plus good food (if surly service) at *Yiannakaros* **taverna**. Beyond Thános, the road curls over to the enormous beach at **Evgátis** (**Áyios Pávlos**), reckoned the island's best, with more igneous pinnacles for definition and Áyios Efstrátios still on the horizon. Three music bar/*kantínas* offer sunbeds, while *Evgatis Hotel* across the road (☎22540 51700; ❹) has a full-service **taverna**.

Some 3km further along (11km from Mýrina), **KONDIÁS** is the island's third-largest settlement, cradled between hills tufted with Límnos's biggest pine forest. Stone-built, often elaborate houses combine with the setting to make Kondiás an attractive inland village, a fact not lost on the Greeks and foreigners restoring those houses with varying degrees of taste. Cultural interest is lent by the central **Pinakothíki Valkanikís Tékhnis/Balkan Art Gallery** (daily except Fri 10am–2pm & 7.30–9.30pm; €2), the result of a 2005 residential programme whereby prominent painters from across the Balkans – especially Bulgarian Svetlin Rusev – donated works as the core collection; a repeat event is planned. Short-term facilities are limited to *Iy Galini* **taverna**, where seating under mulberries makes up for average food; you'll eat better 2.5km away at **TSIMÁNDHRIA**, where *Iy Kali Kardhia* on the central square purveys cheap, salubrious grills and a few seafood dishes; at **PALEÓ PEDHINÓ** 5km northeast, where *Petrino Horio* (dinner only, June–Aug) offers fine meat and an enchanting setting on the flagstoned platía of this mostly abandoned village; or 1km further at **NÉA KOÚTALI**, where *Iy Glaroupoula* (lunch too), despite a position three blocks inland, is the place for a seafood blowout.

Eastern Límnos

The shores of **Moúdhros Bay**, glimpsed south of the trans-island road, are muddy and best avoided by serious bathers. The bay itself enjoyed strategic importance during World War I, culminating in the Ottoman surrender aboard British warship *HMS Agamemnon* here on October 30, 1918. **MOÚDHROS**, the second-largest town on Límnos, is a dreary place, with only the wonderfully kitsch, two-belfried **Evangelismós church**, and perhaps the two restaurants attached to the overpriced hotels, to recommend it. The closest decent **beaches** are at **Havoúli**, 4km south by dirt track, and **Fanaráki** 4km west, but both have muddy sand and don't really face open sea; far superior is **Ayía Triádha,** accessed off the Polyókhni (see opposite) road, with blonde sand heaped in dunes and a *kantína*.

About 800m along the Roussopoúli road, you pass an **Allied military cemetery** (unlocked) maintained by the Commonwealth War Graves Commission; its neat lawns and rows of white headstones seem incongruous in such parched surroundings. In 1915, Moúdhros Bay was the principal staging area for the disastrous Gallipoli campaign. Of approximately 36,000 Allied dead, 887 are buried here, with 348 more at another signposted, immaculately maintained graveyard behind the hilltop church in **Portianoú**.

KALLIÓPI, 8km northeast of Moúdhros via **Kondopoúli**, has smart **rooms** (*Keros*, ☎22540 41059; ❹) at the start of the road down to **Kéros beach**, popular despite being exposed and often dirty. A 1500-metre stretch of sand with dunes and a small pine grove, plus shallow water, it attracts foreigners with camper vans and windsurfers as well as Greeks; a small *kantína* keeps sunbeds during July and August only.

On the other side of Kondopoúli, reached via Repanídhi, the hard-packed beach at **Kótsinas** is set in the protected western limb of Bourniá Bay.

The nearby anchorage (follow signs to "Kótsinas Fortress") offers two busy, seafood-strong **tavernas**, of which pricier *To Mourayio* is worth the difference for more careful cooking and better service compared to rival *To Koralli*. On a knoll overlooking the jetty stands a corroded, sword-brandishing statue of **Maroula**, a Genoese-era heroine who briefly delayed the Ottoman conquest, and a large **church of Zoödhóhou Piyís** (the Life-Giving Spring), with intriguing kitsch icons, a vaulted wooden ceiling and antique floor tiles. Out front 63 steps lead down through an illuminated tunnel in the rock to the potable (if slightly mineral) spring in question, oozing into a cool, vaulted chamber.

Ancient sites

Indications of the most advanced Neolithic Aegean civilization have been unearthed at **Polyochni** (**Polyókhni**), 10km east of Moúdhros, on a bluff overlooking a long, narrow beach flanked by stream valleys. Since the 1930s, Italian excavations have uncovered five layers of settlement, the oldest from late in the fourth millennium BC, predating Troy on the Turkish coast opposite. The town met a sudden, violent end from war or earthquake in about 2100 BC. The **ruins** (Tues–Sun 8.30am–3pm; free) are well labelled but mostly of specialist interest, though a small, well-presented museum behind the entrance helps bring the place to life.

Hephaestia and Kabirion, Límnos's other significant ancient sites, are remote and only reachable with your own transport. **Hephaestia** (present-day Ifestía; Tues–Sun 8.30am–3pm), 4.5km from Kondopoúli by rough, signposted track, offers an admirably reconstructed theatre, overlooking its former harbour. **Kabirion**, also signposted as "Kabeiroi" (modern Kavírion), on the opposite shore of Tigáni Bay and accessed by a paved road, remains more evocative. The **ruins** (Tues–Sun 8.30am–3pm; free) are of a sanctuary connected with the cult of the Samothracian Kabiroi (see p.796), though the site here is probably older. Little survives other than eleven column stumps staking out a *stoa*, behind the *telestirio* or shrine where the cult mysteries took place. A nearby sea grotto has been identified as the Homeric **Spiliá toú Filoktíti**, where Trojan war hero Philoktetes was abandoned by his comrades-in-arms until his stinking, gangrenous leg had healed by application of *límnia yí*, a poultice of volcanic mud. Landward access to the cave is via steps leading down from the caretaker's shelter, though final access (from a little passage on the right as you face the sea) involves some wading.

Áyios Efstrátios (Aï Strátis)

Áyios Efstrátios is one of the quietest and loneliest islands in the Aegean, with a registered population of around 350 (but just 200 full-time residents); it was only permanently settled during the sixteenth century, and land is still largely owned by three monasteries on Mount Áthos. Historically, the only outsiders to visit were those compelled to do so – political prisoners exiled here both during the 1930s and the civil war years.

ÁYIOS EFSTRÁTIOS village – the island's only habitation – must be one of the ugliest in Greece. Devastation caused by an earthquake on February 20, 1968, which killed 22 and injured hundreds, was compounded by the reconstruction plan: the contract went to a junta-linked company, who prevented survivors from returning to their old homes and used army bulldozers to raze even those structures – comprising one of the more beautiful ports in these islands – that could have been repaired. From the hillside, some two dozen surviving houses of the old village overlook grim rows of prefabs, a sad monument to the corruption of the junta years.

Architecture apart, Áyios Efstrátios still functions as a traditional fishing and farming community, with the prefabs set at the mouth of a wooded stream valley draining to the sandy harbour beach. Tourist amenities consist of just two basic **tavernas** (one operating July–Aug only), plus four **pensions**. Best of these, in one of the surviving old houses, is *Xenonas Aï-Stratis* (☎22540 93329; ④); *Andonis Paneras* (☎22540 93209; ③), *Stavros Katakouzinos* (☎22540 93362; ③) and *Apostolos Paneras* (☎22540 93343; ③) have more conventional **rooms** in prefabs. Stiff prices for such an out-of-the-way place reflect Áyios Efstrátios's trendiness with Greeks, and you may not find a vacancy in mid-summer.

Beyond the village – there are few vehicles and no paved roads – the **landscape**, arid slopes dotted with a surprising number of oak trees, is deserted apart from rabbits, sheep, an occasional shepherd, and some good **beaches**. **Alonítsi**, on the north coast – a ninety-minute walk from the village following a track due east out of the port and over a low ridge – is a 1500-metre stretch of sand with rolling breakers and views across to Límnos. South of the harbour, there's a series of grey-sand beaches, most with wells and drinkable water, accessible by roundabout tracks. **Áyios Dhimítrios**, an hour-plus distant, and **Lidharió**, ninety minutes away at the end of an attractive wooded valley, are the most popular.

Ferries on the Kavála/Alexandhroúpoli–Límnos–Lávrio line call at Áyios Efstrátios several times weekly much of the year; in summer a small Límnos-based ferry, the *Aiolis*, sails every weekday at 2.30pm from Límnos, returning the next day at 6.30am. Despite improvements, Áyios Efstrátios still has a very exposed mooring, and in bad weather you could end up stranded here far longer than you bargained for. If an indefinite stay does not appeal, visit from Límnos on the admittedly overpriced **day-trips** (€30 return; Wed, Sun & often Fri).

Samothráki (Samothrace)

Samothráki boasts one of the most dramatic profiles of all the Greek islands, second only to Thíra (Santoríni): its dark mass of granite rises abruptly from the sea, culminating in the 1611-metre **Mount Fengári**. Seafarers have always been guided by its imposing outline, clearly visible from the mainland, and, in legend, Poseidon watched over the siege of Troy from its summit. Landing is notoriously subject to the unpredictable weather, but that did not deter the pilgrims in antiquity, who for centuries journeyed here to be initiated into the mysteries of the **Sanctuary of the Great Gods**. Now the island's main archeological attraction, the sanctuary combines earthy simplicity with natural grandeur, and draws many New Age types, as evidenced by ubiquitous Om symbols and an annual World Music Festival. The tourist season, however, is relatively short-lived, though some facilities are open by Easter, and one or two remain open year round.

Kamariótissa

Ferries and hydrofoils dock at the dull village of **KAMARIÓTISSA**. While you're unlikely to want to spend much time here, it does make a convenient base, as some of Samothráki's best **hotels** lie along or just behind the tree-lined seafront and various **rooms** for rent can be found in the maze of streets behind; owners often meet incoming vessels. Accommodation can be pricey for what

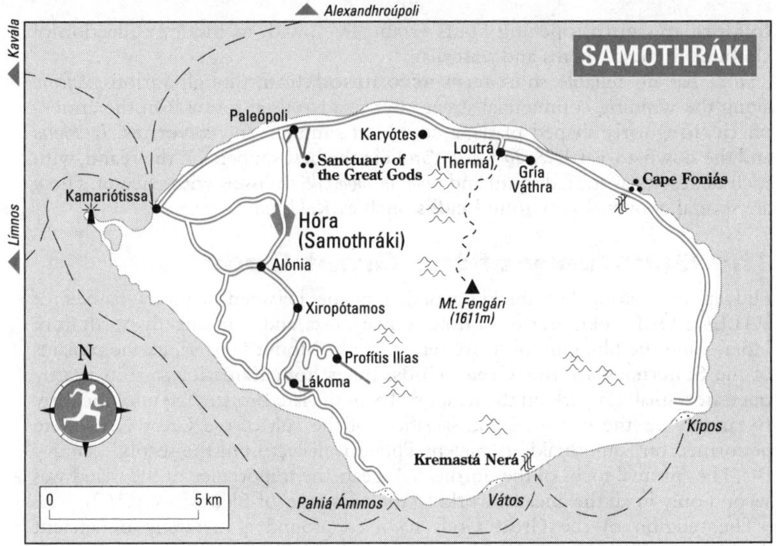

you get, and bargaining is not always productive, especially in midsummer. Along the shore, some way east of where you arrive, is *Kyma* (☎25510 41263; ❷), where rooms overlooking the pebbly beach can get noise from the establishments below. Occupying a bluff to the northeast, the slightly impersonal *Aeolos* (☎25510 41595, Ⓕ25510 41810; ❹) has a large pool and quiet, spacious rooms; Samothráki's most comfortable accommodation, it offers good half-board deals out of season. The spacious new *Kyrkos* apartments (☎25510 41620; ❸), 500m from the port, just off the road to Hóra, can also be booked through their car rental agency (see below). Bars and cafés on the harbour front serve snacks and breakfasts – lively *Aktaion* also has Internet – while the best of the **tavernas** is the *Iy Klimataria*, towards the northeast end, serving fresh fish and meat.

Motorbikes and **cars** are in short supply in season; reserve a bike in advance from Hanou Brothers (☎25510 41511) or a car from Niki Tours (☎25510 41465), or either one from Kyrkos car rental (☎25510 69728). A car is preferable, as Samothracian roads are often dangerously windswept for bikes. The only fuelling station on the entire island is 1km above the port, en route to Hóra. A fairly reliable timetable for island **buses** is also posted at the port; these travel up to eight times daily in season (twice weekly in winter) along the north coast to Loutrá (Thermá) via Paleópoli, near the site of the Sanctuary, or Karyótes, or directly inland seven times daily to the largest village, Hóra. A converted container opposite the docks acts as a ticket and information offices for **ferries and hydrofoils**. Kamariótissa also hag two **banks** with **ATM**s, and the island's only **post office**.

Hóra

HÓRA, also known as **Samothráki**, is the island's capital. Far larger than it looks from out at sea, it's an attractive town of Thracian-style stone houses, some whitewashed, clustered around a hollow in the western flanks of Mount Fengári. It is dominated by the Genoese Gateluzzi fort, of which little survives other than the gateway. Half an hour or so can be whiled away at the charming

folklore museum (opening hours erratic; free), with its motley collection of clothing, domestic items and miscellany.

Hóra has no reliable short-term **accommodation**, though various *kafenía* along the winding commercial street offer unadvertised rooms. On the atmospheric, irregularly shaped platía, a couple of summer-only **tavernas**, *Iy Platia* and the down-to-earth *To Kastro*, provide the best suppers on the island, with such delicacies as stuffed squid and *mýdhia saganáki* (mussels with cheese). There are several convivial year-round **cafés**, such as *Kalderimi*.

The Sanctuary of the Great Gods

Hidden in a stony but thickly wooded ravine between the tiny hamlet of **PALEÓPOLI** – 6km northeast from Kamariótissa, and 3km directly north from Hóra – and the plunging northwestern ridge of Mount Fengári, lie the remains of the **Sanctuary of the Great Gods**. Buses from Kamariótissa stop nearby, opposite a small car park on the seashore. From the late Bronze Age until the early Byzantine era, the mysteries and sacrifices of the cult of the Great Gods were performed on Samothráki, in ancient Thracian dialect until the second century BC. The spiritual focus of the northern Aegean, the importance of the island was second only in all the ancient world to the Mysteries of Eleusis (see p.162).

The religion of the Great Gods revolved around a hierarchy of ancient Thracian fertility figures: the Great Mother Axieros, a subordinate male deity known as Kadmilos, and the potent and ominous twin demons the Kabiroi, originally the local heroes Dardanos and Aeton. When the Aeolian colonists arrived (ca. 700 BC) they simply syncretized the resident deities with their own – the Great Mother became Cybele, while her consort Hermes and the Kabiroi were fused interchangeably with the *Dioskouroi* Castor and Pollux, patrons of seafarers. Around the nucleus of a sacred precinct the newcomers started what became the sanctuary.

Ancient writers feared the wrath of the Kabiroi, so despite their long observance, the mysteries of the cult were never explicitly recorded, but it's known that two levels of initiation were involved. Both ceremonies, in direct opposition to the elitism of Eleusis, were open to all, including women and slaves. The lower level of initiation, or *myesis*, may, as is speculated at Eleusis, have involved a ritual simulation of the life, death and rebirth cycle and certainly ended with joyous feasting. The higher level of initiation, or *epopteia*, carried the unusual requirement of a moral standard. This second level probably involved a full confession followed by absolution and baptism in bull's blood.

The only **accommodation** nearby is in Paleópoli, where the old, basic *Xenia Hotel* (Ⓣ25510 41166 or 25510 41230; ❹) offers a downmarket alternative to the smart but overpriced *Kastro Hotel* (Ⓣ25510 89400, Ⓦwww.kastrohotel.gr; ❺), which comes with pool, restaurant and sea views. Basic but en-suite rooms (❸) are also available on the seashore below the *Kastro*.

The site

The well-labelled **site** (daily 8am–7.30pm, closes 3pm in winter; €3 combined ticket with museum) strongly evokes its proud past while commanding views of the mountains and the sea. For an explanatory introduction, you might like first to visit the **archeological museum** (Tues–Sun 8am–7.30pm, closes 3pm in winter), where exhibits span all eras of habitation, from the Archaic to the Byzantine. Highlights include a **frieze** of dancing girls from the propylon of the Temenos, entablatures from different buildings, and Roman votive offerings such as coloured glass vials from the necropolis of the ancient town east of the sanctuary. You can also see a reproduction of the exquisitely sculpted marble statue, the *Winged Victory of Samothrace*, which once stood breasting the wind at the prow of a marble ship in the Nymphaeum; the original is in the Louvre.

The **Anaktoron**, or hall of initiation for the first level of the mysteries, dates in its present form from Roman times. Its inner sanctum was marked by stele, now in the museum. In the **Priestly Quarters**, an antechamber at the southeast corner, candidates for initiation donned white gowns. Alongside, the **Arsinoeion**, the largest circular ancient building known in Greece, was used for libations and sacrifices. A little further south, you come to the **Temenos**, a rectangular area open to the sky where the feasting probably took place, and, edging its rear corner, the conspicuous **Hieron**, the site's most immediately impressive structure, heavily restored in Roman times. Five columns and an architrave of this large Doric edifice, which hosted the higher level of initiation, have been re-erected. Roman benches for spectators remain in situ, along with the sacred stones where confession was heard. West of the path you can just discern the outline of the theatre, while just above it, tucked under the ridge, is the **Nymphaeum (Fountain) of Nike**, over which the *Winged Victory* used to preside. West of the theatre, occupying a high terrace, are remains of the main *stoa*; the elaborate medieval fortification immediately north of this is made entirely of antique material.

Loutrá and further east

With its running streams, giant plane trees and namesake hot springs, **LOUTRÁ (THERMÁ)**, 6km east of Paleópoli, is a pleasant place to stay, packed in late July and August with an incongruous mixture of foreign hippies and elderly Greeks here to take the sulphurous waters. Even more appealing than the baths themselves, the low waterfalls and rock pools of **Gría Váthra** are signposted 1.5km up the paved side road east of the main Thermá access road.

Loutrá is the prime base for the tough, six-hour climb up the 1611-metre **Mount Fengári** (known to the ancients as **Sáos**, a name found on some maps to this day), the highest peak in the Aegean islands; the path starts at the top of the village, beside a concrete water tank and a huge plane tree. Tell your accommodation proprietors that you're going, as a precaution against the mountain's unforgiving nature. Fengári is Greek for "moon" and, according to legend, if you reach the top on the night of a full moon your wish will come true – most of those foolhardy enough to attempt this will just hope to get back down safely.

Loutrá is a rather dispersed place, with its winding dead-end streets, all ghostly quiet in winter, and its miniharbour – built as an alternative to Kamariótissa, but never used. **Accommodation** includes the B&B *Kaviros Hotel* (Ⓣ25510 98277, Ⓕ25510 98278; ❸), just east of the "centre", and, further downhill, 700m from the beach, the slightly cheaper *Mariva Bungalows* (Ⓣ25510 98258; ❸). Of the **tavernas**, *Paradhisos* has the best setting, up under the trees. A few seasonal eateries, like leafy *To Perivoli T'ouranou,* are dotted along the side road to Gría Váthra.

Beyond Loutrá the wooded coastline holds two municipal **campsites**. *Platia* (Ⓣ25510 98244), 1.5km from the village, is large but has no facilities except toilets, while *Voradhes* (Ⓣ25510 98258), 3km out, has hot water, electricity, a small shop, restaurant and bar. The Loutrá bus may go to either site if you ask nicely.

Though **beaches** on Samothráki's north shore are uniformly pebbly and exposed, albeit mostly clean, it's still worth continuing along the road east from Loutrá. At **Cape Foniás** you'll find a ruined Gateluzzi watchtower and, 45 minutes' walk inland along the stream, much more impressive **waterfalls** and cold pools than those at Gría Váthra. Some 15km from Loutrá along a fine corniche road, **Kípos beach** is a shelving mass of pebbles, backed by open pasture and picturesque crags facing the Turkish-held island of Gökçeada (Ímvros to the Greeks). The water is clean and there's a rock overhang for shelter at one end, a spring, shower and seasonal *kantína*, serving basic food.

The south coast

The warmer south flank of the island, with its fertile farmland dotted with olive groves, offers fine views out to sea – as far as Gökçeada on a clear day. Up to three daily buses go from Kamariótissa via the sleepy village of Lákoma as far as **PROFÍTIS ILÍAS**, an attractive hill village. The best of its good **tavernas**, *Paradhisos*, has a wonderful terrace, and there's also some basic **accommodation**.

From Lákoma itself, which has an admirable ouzerí, *O Mavros*, it's less than 2km down to the eponymous beach, where *To Akroyiali* fish taverna (☎25510 95123; ❸) has some **rooms**. A further 6km east lies **Pahiá Ámmos**, a long, clean beach with the *Delfini* taverna-rooms outfit (☎25510 94235; ❸) at the west end. The nearest (meagre) supplies are in Lákoma, but this doesn't deter big summer crowds who also arrive by excursion *kaïkia*. These continue east to **Vátos**, a secluded beach (nudity tolerated) that's also accessible by land, the **Kremastá Nerá** coastal waterfalls, and finally round to Kípos beach (see above).

Thássos

Just 12km from the mainland, **Thássos** has long been popular with northern Greeks. Since the 1980s, it has also attracted a cosmopolitan range of tourists from all over Europe. All are entertained by two or three *bouzoúkia* (music halls) and tavernas that lay on music at weekends (and during the week in July and August), while nature lovers can enjoy areas of outstanding beauty, especially inland. Moreover, the island's traditional industries remain thriving. The elite of Thássos still make a substantial living from the pure-white **marble** that constitutes two-thirds of the land mass, found only here and quarried at dozens of sites in the hills between Liménas and Panayía. Olives – especially the oil – honey, fruit and nuts provide valuable income to a wider range of people. The spirit *tsípouro*, rather than wine, is the main local tipple; pear extract, onions or spices like cinnamon and anise are added to home-made batches.

Inhabited since the Stone Age, Thássos was settled by Parians in the seventh century BC, attracted by **gold** deposits between modern Liménas and Kínyra. Buoyed by revenues from these, and from **silver** mines under Thassian control on the mainland opposite, the ancient city-state here became the seat of a medium-sized seafaring empire. Commercial acumen did not spell military invincibility, however; the Persians under Darius swept the Thassian fleets from the seas in 492 BC, and in 462 BC Athens permanently deprived Thássos of its autonomy after a three-year siege. The main port continued to thrive into Roman times, but lapsed into Byzantine and medieval obscurity.

Sadly, recent history has been dominated by the devastating, deliberately set **fires** of the 1980s and 1990s. Only the northeastern quadrant of the island, plus the area around Astrís and Alykí, escaped, though the surviving forest is still home to numerous pine martens.

Thássos is small enough to circumnavigate in one full day by rented motorbike or car. KTEL will do the driving for you – albeit with little chance for stopping

– with their complete circuit four times daily. **Car rental** is offered by the major international chains and local Potos Car Rental (ⓣ25930 23969), with branches in all main resorts; it's worth bargaining in the shoulder seasons. On the other hand, don't bother showing up in Thássos between early October and late April, as the weather can be dodgy and most facilities, including hotels, will be shut.

Liménas

The largely modern town of **LIMÉNAS** (also signposted as Limín or Thássos) is the island's capital, though not the only port. At first glance plagued with vehicle traffic and often noisy bars, Liménas seems an unlikely resort, but it's partly redeemed by its picturesque fishing harbour and the substantial remains of the ancient city.

Arrival, transport and information

Kavála-based **ferries** stop down the coast at Skála Prínou, with a KTEL bus on hand to meet most arrivals except the last. The KTEL office is on the front, opposite the ferry mooring; the service is good, with several daily **buses** to

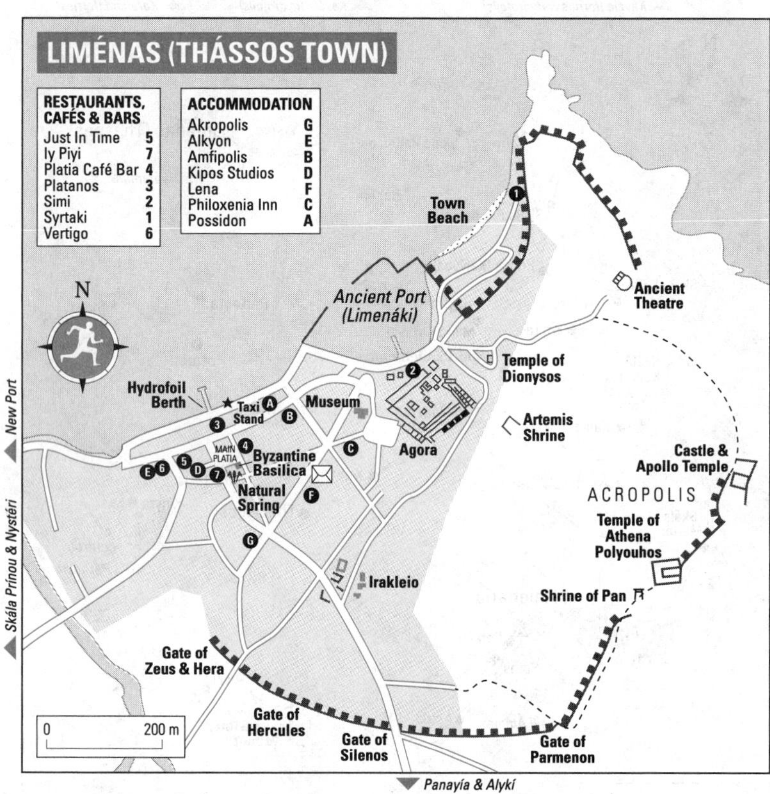

Panayía and Skála Potamiás, Limenária via Potós, Theológos, Kínyra and Alykí. The **taxi** rank is just in front of the bus stop. **Bikes** can be rented from Thomai Tsipou (ⓣ25930 22815), back from the front. Thassos Tours (ⓣ25930 23250) and Indispensible Holiday Services (ⓣ25930 22041; (ⓔihs@kav.forthnet.gr) provide various services. Several banks have **ATMs**.

Accommodation

While few **hotels enjoy** any tranquillity or decent views (and most are shut Oct–April), some are reasonable enough, and relatively quiet **rooms** are available just behind the town beach. The closest **campsite** is the pretty basic one at Nystéri cove, 2.5km west.

Akropolis ⓣ25930 22488, ⓕ25930 22441. Occupying a fine traditional house with flagstone floors and a rear garden-bar, but subject to traffic noise. ❸

Alkyon ⓣ25930 22148, ⓕ25930 23662. Certainly the most pleasant harbour hotel; English tea and breakfast plus friendly, voluble management make it a home away from home for independent British travellers. Open most of the year; ask also about their cottage in Sotíras and beach villa at Astrís. B&B ❸

Amfipolis ⓣ25930 23101, ⓕ25930 22110. Housed in a folly, this atmospheric hotel is the most exclusive accommodation outfit – and guests pay dearly for the privilege. It also has a stylish drinks terrace. ❺

Kipos Studios ⓣ25930 22469, ⓦwww.kipos-apartments.gr. In a quiet cul-de-sac next to

Iy Piyi taverna, this has cool lower-ground-floor doubles and four-person galleried apartments, plus a pool in the garden. ❸

Lena ⓣ25930 23565, ⓔhotellena@hotmail.com. The best-value hotel in town, with compact but comfy rooms near the post office; run by a welcoming American ex-pat. ❷

Philoxenia Inn ⓣ25930 23331, ⓦwww.philoxeniainn.gr. Quietly situated behind the archeological museum, this has immaculate rooms with fridges, designated breakfast areas and a garden with a small pool. ❹

Possidon ⓣ25930 22690, ⓦwww.thassos-possidon.com. Unattractive concrete block on the seafront with nicely refurbished rooms. Somewhat overpriced but the only place guaranteed to be open all year. ❹

The Town

Thanks to its mineral wealth and safe harbour, **ancient Thassos** prospered from Classical to Roman times. The largest excavated area is the agora, a little way back from the fishing harbour. Fenced but usually unlocked, the site (free) is most enjoyably seen towards dusk. Two Roman *stoas* are prominent, but you can also make out shops, monuments, passageways and sanctuaries from the remodelled Classical city. At the far end, a fifth-century BC passageway leads through to an elaborate sanctuary of Artemis, a substantial stretch of Roman road and a few seats of the odeion. The nearby **archeological museum** (Tues–Sun 9am–3pm; €2) contains small but absorbing displays on prehistoric finds, archeological methods and ancient games. Pride of place goes to the four-metre-tall, seventh-century BC *kouros* carrying a ram, found on the acropolis.

From a **temple of Dionysos** behind the fishing port, a path curls up to a **Hellenistic theatre**, fabulously positioned above a broad sweep of sea. Sadly, it's only open for performances of the **summer festival** (ⓦwww.thassos-festival.gr). From just before the theatre, the trail winds on the right up to the **acropolis**, where a Venetian-Byzantine-Genoese fort arose between the thirteenth and fifteenth centuries, constructed from recycled masonry of an Apollo temple. You can continue, following the remains of a massive circuit of fifth-century walls, to a high terrace supporting the foundations of the Athena Polyouhos (Athena Patroness of the City) temple, with Cyclopean walls. From the temple's southern end, a short path leads to a cavity in the rock outcrop that was a shrine of Pan, shown in faint relief playing his pipes. Following the path to the left, a track, then a paved lane, descend through the southerly neighbourhoods of the modern town, completing a satisfying one-hour circuit.

Eating, drinking and nightlife

Given the cheap-and-cheerful-package ethos, cuisine is not Liménas's strong point. The picturesque **tavernas** around the old harbour are predictably touristy – sophisticated *Simi* is by far the best, open all year, and serves memorably good wine. Another good option is *Syrtaki*, at the far eastern end of the crowded town beach. In the town centre, a dependable favourite for *mayireftá* is *Iy Piyi*, at the south corner of the main square, while *Platanos*, with a pleasant terrace opposite the ferry docks, is the place to head for breakfast. By contrast, there's plenty of choice in local **bars**: *Vertigo* near the *Hotel Alkyon* is popular with Greeks and tourists alike for its rocky ambience; across the road, *Just In Time* is another lively café-bar; *Platia Café Bar*, back on the square, also has a decent atmosphere.

Around the coast

Whichever way you plan to circumnavigate the island, plan on a lunch stop at photogenic **Alykí**, roughly a third of the way along in the clockwise circuit described below.

Panayía, Potamiá and Mount Ypsárion

Bypass the first beach east of Liménas, touristic **Makrýammos**, and carry on to **PANAYÍA**, the attractive hillside village overlooking Potamiá Bay. Life here life revolves around the central square with its large plane trees, fountain and slate-roofed houses. Top **accommodation** choice in both senses is the *Hotel Thassos Inn* (Ⓣ25930 61612, Ⓕ25930 61027; ④), up in the Tris Piyés district near the Kímisis church, with fine views over the rooftops. Down on the main road, beside the municipal car park, the clean *Pension Stathmos* (Ⓣ25930 61666; ③) is the quietest of several nearby, with more stunning views. Avoid the tout-infested competing **tavernas** on the square; for a lower-key approach, try *Iy Thea*, a view-terrace *psistariá* at the southeast edge of town en route to Potamiá.

POTAMIÁ, much lower down in the river valley, is far less prepossessing – with modern red tiles instead of slates on the roofs – and thus little visited, though it has a lively winter carnival. It also offers the **Polygnotos Vayis Museum** (Tues–Sat 9.30am–12.30pm, summer also 6–9pm, Sun 10am–1pm; free), devoted to the locally born sculptor; Vayis emigrated to America when young, but bequeathed most of his works to the Greek state. Potamiá also marks the start of the preferred route up to the 1204-metre summit of **Mount Ypsárion**. Follow the bulldozer track to the big spring near the head of the valley west of the village (the last source of water), where you'll see red-painted arrows on trees. Beyond this point, cairns mark the correct turnings in a modern track system; forty minutes above the spring, take an older, wide track, which ends ten minutes later at a narrow ravine with a stream and the current trailhead. The path is steep, strenuous and unmaintained, so watch for the cairns and arrows. Go early in the day or season, allowing four hours up from Potamiá, and nearly as much for the descent.

Skála Potamiás and Khryssí Ammoudhiá

The onward road from Potamiá is lined with rooms and apartment-type accommodation. A side road some 12km from Liménas takes you down to **SKÁLA POTAMIÁS**, at the southern end of the bay, where uninspired **tavernas** line the harbour front; honourable exceptions include *Krambousas*, which serves tasty grills and oven dishes, and *Afrodite* with its *mayireftá*. A road to the left brings you to sand dunes extending right to the far northern end of the bay. At *Eric's Bar*, on the main road just outside the village, Stratos Papafilippou has made a career of his uncanny resemblance to footballer Eric Cantona; full English breakfast is available, as well as Premier League football, of course.

The best places to **stay** are either above the plane-shaded traffic turnaround area by the port, beyond the tavernas – where the *Hera* (Ⓣ25930 61467; ②), just on the left looking inland, or the *Delfini* (Ⓣ&Ⓕ25930 61275; ②), 200m straight back, are peaceful but basic – or, for almost double the price, the *Miramare* further up the same lane (Ⓣ25930 77209, Ⓦwww.hotelmiramare.gr; ④), has a swimming pool and well-manicured gardens.

The north end of this beach – **Khryssí Ammoudhiá**, better known as **"Golden Beach"** – is chaotic and very built-up; a direct road (plied by infrequent buses) spirals for 5km down from Panayía. Once there, choose between the self-catering *Villa Emerald* (Ⓣ25930 61979, Ⓕ25930 61886; ④) or the *Golden Sand* (Ⓣ25930 61771; ③), nearer the sands. The *Golden Beach* **campsite** (Ⓣ25930 61472) is the only official one on this side of the island. **Water taxis** come here from Liménas twice daily in summer, at 10am and 4.30pm (€7).

Kínyra and Alykí

The dispersed hamlet of **KÍNYRA**, 24km south of Liménas, marks the start of the burnt zone, though recovery is underway; it's endowed with a poor beach, a couple of grocery stores and several small **hotels**. Those not block-booked include the northerly *Villa Athina* (☎25930 41214; ❷), whose top-floor rooms view the water over the olive trees, and the welcoming *Pension Marina* (☎25930 31384; ❷). *Yiorgos* and *Faros* are the best **tavernas**. Kínyra is convenient for the superior **beaches** of Loutroú (1km south) and partly nudist Paradise (3km along), both reachable down poorly signed dirt tracks. Officially called Makrýammos Kinýron, Paradise is the most scenic Thassian beach, with still-forested cliffs inland and a namesake islet offshore beyond the extensive shallows, but a couple of mediocre snack-bars provide the only refreshment.

The south-facing coast of Thássos has the balance of the island's best beaches. **ALYKÍ** hamlet, just below the main road 35km from Liménas, faces a perfect double bay, which almost pinches off a headland. Uniquely, it retains its original whitewashed, slate-roofed architecture, as all construction is banned thanks to the presence of extensive antiquities. Those ruins include an ancient temple to an unknown deity, and two exquisite early Christian basilicas out on the headland. The sand-and-pebble west bay gets oversubscribed in peak season; head instead for the less crowded, rocky east cove, or snorkel in the crystal-clear waters off the marble formations on the headland's far side. A lively bar and a row of water-edge **tavernas** compete for your custom, with *To Limanaki/The Little Mole* winning, if only for its more varied menu. At secluded **Kékes** beach, in a pine grove 1km further along the coast, traditional taverna *Skidhia* offers en-suite, air-conditioned **rooms** in plain but comfortable bungalows (☎25930 31528; ❸).

Arhangélou Mihaïl to Potós

The hideously renovated twelfth-century **convent of Arhangélou Mihaïl** (open dawn to dusk) clings spectacularly to a cliff on the seaward side of the road, 5km west of Alykí. A dependency of Filothéou on Mount Áthos (see p.465), its prize relic is a purported nail from the Crucifixion.

At the extreme south tip of Thássos, 9km further west, **ASTRÍS** (Astrídha) can muster two uninspiring medium-sized hotels, a few rooms and a good beach. Just 1km west is another better but crowded beach, **Psilí Ámmos**, with watersports on offer. A few kilometres further, **POTÓS** is the island's prime Germanophone package venue, its centre claustrophobically dense, with the few non-block-booked rooms overlooking cramped alleys. However, the kilometre-long beach is still unspoilt. For a less touristy place to eat, the **taverna** *Piatsa* is tucked away at the southern end of the seafront, in a semi-pedestrianized street; next door, *Michael's Place* has great ice cream and breakfasts. Along the harbour front a string & **bars and cafés** offers viable alternatives. There are plenty of rental outlets for **cars**, scooters and mountain bikes, including the headquarters of Potos Rent a Car. **Pefkári**, with its manicured beach and namesake pine grove, 1km west, is essentially an annexe of Potós, with a few mid-range **accommodation** options such as *Prasino Veloudho* (☎25930 52001, Ⓔnikolis7@hol.gr; ❸) and the more upmarket *Thassos* (☎25930 51596, Ⓔthassoshotel@msn.com; ❹). The *Pefkári* **campsite** (☎25930 51190; June–Sept) has an attractive wooded location and clean facilities.

Limenária and the west coast

LIMENÁRIA, the island's second town, was built to house German mining executives brought in by the Ottomans between 1890 and 1905. Their remaining mansions, scattered on the slopes above the harbour, lend some character, but despite attempts at embellishing the waterfront, it's not the most attractive place on Thássos, though it is handy for its **ATM**s and **post office**. The best **accommodation** is the *Hotel George* (Ⓣ&Ⓕ25930 51413; ❹), with bright and modern rooms at the lower end of the main street down to the harbour front. At the east end of the quay, some 1960s blocks hold a cluster of very basic hotels such as the *Sgouridis* (Ⓣ&Ⓕ25930 51241; ❸). Plenty of **rooms** are also on offer. Of the many bars and eateries along the front, only *Mouragio* comes close to having some charm.

The nearest good beach is **Trypití**, a couple of kilometres west – turn left into the pines at the start of a curve right. All development – mostly package villas – is well inland from the broad, 800-metre-long strand, which has umbrellas and sun loungers for rent. The cleft to which the name refers (literally "pierced" in Greek) is a slender tunnel at the west end of the beach, leading to a tiny three-boat anchorage.

Continuing clockwise from Limenária to Liménas, the western coast is exposed and scenically unimpressive, so there's progressively less reason to stop. Most of the *skáles* (harbours) along the way are bleak, straggly and windy. Only **Skála Marión**, 13km from Limenária, is an exception: an attractive little bay, with fishing boats hauled up on the sandy foreshore, and the admittedly modern low-rise village arrayed in a U-shape all around. It has **rooms**, a few tavernas and, most importantly, two fine beaches on either side. There's little to recommend **Skála Prínou**, other than ferries to Kavála, which usually coincide with buses. If you want to stay, there are several hotels, numerous rooms, and a selection of quayside tavernas. Finally, **Pahýs beach**, 9km short of Liménas, is by far the best strand on the northwest coast. Narrow dirt tracks lead past various tavernas through surviving pines to the sand, partly shaded in the morning.

The interior

While few visitors explore inland Thássos – with the post-fire scrub still struggling to revive, it's not always rewarding – but there are several worthwhile excursions to or around the **hill villages**, besides the aforementioned trek up Mount Ypsárion from Potamiá (see p.802).

From Potós you can head 10km along a well-surfaced but poorly signed road to **THEOLÓGOS**, founded by sixteenth-century refugees from Constantinople and the island's capital under the Ottomans. Its single high street holds a couple of *kafenía* and some traditional shops, while houses, most with oversized chimneys and slate roofs, straggle in long tiers to either side, surrounded by generous kitchen gardens or walled courtyards. Two good local **tavernas** are the long-running *Psistaria Lambiris*, at the entrance into town, and *Kleoniki/Tou Iatrou*, in the very centre. They're at their best in the evening when the roasting spits gyrate with goat or suckling pig.

From Skála Marión an unmarked but paved road (slipping under the main highway bridge to the north) proceeds 11km inland through gnarled old olive trees to well-preserved **MARIÉS** at the top of a wooded stream valley; the well-signed *Bethel* is the better of its two **tavernas**. From Skála Sotíros, a very steep road heads 3.5km up to **SOTÍRAS**, the only interior village to offer unobstructed views of sunset over the Aegean, which is therefore popular with foreigners, who've restored half of its houses. On the plane-shaded square below the old fountain, the congenial *O Platanos* **taverna** offers grills plus one *mayireftá* dish-of-the-day, good bulk wine and sometimes potent, home-made *tsípouro*, but only in July and August.

From Prínos (Kalýves) on the coast road, a six-kilometre journey inland leads to the Kazavíti villages, shrouded in greenery that escaped the fires; they're poorly signposted and mapped officially as Megálo and Mikró Prínos but still universally known by their Ottoman name. **MIKRÓ KAZAVÍTI** marks the start of the track south for **MEGÁLO KAZAVÍTI**, where the magnificent platía, one of the prettiest spots on the whole island, is home to a couple of decent **tavernas**. *Vassilis*, below in a beautifully restored house, is regarded as a cut above.

Travel details

Conventional ferries

To simplify the following lists we've excluded certain peripheral services on north-to-south routes. These are the weekly Saos Ferries sailing between Sámos, Híos, Lésvos, Límnos and Thessaloníki, and back (23hr 30min each way), the 2 weekly Saos departures from Sámos (Vathý or Karlóvassi), Híos, Lésvos, Límnos and Kavála, and back (19–20hr), the weekly Agoudimos sailing between Rhodes and Thessaloníki via Kós, Kálymnos, Sámos, and back (27hr each way); and the weekly Agoudimos sailing between Rhodes and Alexandhroúpoli via the same islands, and back (28hr each way).

Áyios Efstrátios 4 weekly on Saos Ferries to Límnos, Kavála and Lávrio; 5 weekly, early morning, by small local ferry to Límnos.

Foúrni 3 weekly to Sámos (northern ports) and Pireás, on GA; daily 7.30am except Mon & Fri on the *kaïki Samos Sun* or the small ferry *Samos Spirit* to Karlóvassi, returning 2.15–3.30pm; 5 weekly on the *Samos Spirit* (7.30am) to Vathý, returning 2.15pm.

Híos 6 weekly on NEL Lines to Pireás (10hr) and Lésvos (3hr 30min), daily to same destinations on Hellenic Seaways (5hr/2hr); 1 weekly to Límnos on NEL, 1 weekly on Saos. Daily 1pm or 3pm *kaïki* to Inoússes except Sun morning, and Tues in off-season; 6 weekly on *Nisos Thira* – usually at 3pm or 7.30pm – from Híos Town to Psará (3hr).

Ikaría At least daily from either Áyios Kírykos or Évdhilos to Sámos (both northern ports) and Pireás, on Hellenic Seaways or GA; 2 weekly to Foúrni from Áyios Kírykos on GA; 3 weekly to Mýkonos and Sýros from Áyios Kírykos on GA, 1 weekly to same from Évdhilos on Hellenic Seaways; 2 weekly to Náxos and Páros from Áyios Kírykos on GA; daily *kaïki* (*Samos Sun*) or small ferry (*Samos Spirit*) from Áyios Kírykos to Foúrni, at either 10am or 5.20pm; 3 weekly *kaïkia*, typically Mon, Wed & Fri mornings, from Manganítis to Áyios Kírykos.

Lésvos (Mytilíni Town) 6 weekly on NEL Lines to Pireás (13hr), daily on Hellenic Seaways (8hr 30min); 6 weekly to Híos (3hr 30min), daily on Hellenic Seaways (2hr); 1 weekly on NEL to Límnos (5hr 30min); 1 weekly to Thessaloníki on NEL (13hr 30min).

Límnos 3 weekly on NEL Lines to Lésvos (Mytilíni) & Híos, 2–4 weekly on Saos Ferries; 4 weekly to Áyios Efstrátios and Lávrio on Saos Ferries; 4–5 weekly to Kavála on Saos; 1 weekly to Thessaloníki on NEL; 2 weekly to Alexandhroúpoli on Saos; 1 weekly to Pireás on NEL; 1 weekly to Kými (Évvia), Alónissos, Skópelos, Skiáthos and Áyios Konstandínos on Saos.

Sámos (Pythagório) 4 weekly (Mon, Wed, Fri & Sun afternoon) on *Nissos Kalymnos* to Agathónissi, Arkí, Lipsí, Pátmos, Léros and Kálymnos, with onward connections to southern Dodecanese (see p.737 for the full schedule).

Sámos (Vathý & Karlóvassi) 1–2 daily on GA or Hellenic Seaways, to Ikaría (Áyios Kírykos or Évdhilos) and Pireás (11–14hr); 2 weekly to Páros and Náxos, on GA; 3 weekly to Foúrni on GA; 3–5 weekly to Mýkonos and Sýros on GA or Hellenic Seaways.

Samothráki 2–3 daily to Alexandhroúpoli (2hr 30min) in season, dropping to 5–6 weekly in winter; 2 weekly late spring and early autumn, up to 3 weekly in July and Aug, to Kavála; 1 weekly direct to Límnos during July and Aug.

Thássos At least 7 daily in summer (2–4 daily Oct–May), from Skála Prínou to Kavála (1hr 15min); 8–12 daily year round from Liménas to Keramotí (40min).

Hydrofoils and catamarans

Aegean Flying Dolphins operates daily out of Pythagório (Sámos) once daily at 8am to Pátmos, Lipsí, Léros (Ayía Marína), Kálymnos and Kós, arriving 11.30am and returning at 2pm. Agathoníssi is included 1–2 times weekly. Advertised midsummer detours to Foúrni and Ikaría (Áyios Kírykos) rarely run owing to weather conditions.

Kallisti Ferries' *Corsica Express* plies 3–6 days weekly, usually at 8am, on the route Vathý–Karlóvassi–Ikaría (either port)–Piréas, with Foúrni added once weekly (7–8hr total journey time).
Hellenic Seaways' *Nisos Mykonos* provides a competing service 5–6 days weekly via the same ports, leaving towards Pireás 10pm except Sun at 2pm.
Samothráki to: Alexandhroúpoli (April–Sept 1–2 daily; 1hr 10min).
Thássos (Liménas) to: Kavála (April–Oct 8–15 times daily; 40min).
Thássos (Skála Prinou) to: Kavála (April–Oct 2–4 daily; 30min).

International ferries

Híos–Çeşme (Turkey) 2–13 boats weekly at 8.30am and/or 4.30–5pm, depending on season. Passenger fares on the Greek boat (*San Nicholas*, Sunrise Tours) or Turkish vessel (*Ertürk II*) are nominally about €40 return, including Greek taxes (no Turkish tax), but "special offers" of €30 are frequent, plus €10 coach transfer to izmir; one way €25. Small cars €65–70 one way, €110 return, plus small Greek tax. Journey time 30min (*San Nicholas*) or 45min (*Ertürk II*).
Mytilíni (Lésvos)–Ayvalık/Dikili (Turkey) Daily May–Oct; winter link sporadic. Two Mytilíni-based craft, the Turkish *Jale* and the Greek Costar Line's *Konstandinos I*, depart Mytilíni 8.30–9am most days. Passenger rates €25 one way or round trip, all taxes inclusive. Dikili services run Tues, Thurs and Sat, for €35 return. Small cars (each boat carries two) €60 one way, €90 return. Journey time 1hr 20min to Ayvalik, 1hr 30min to Dikili.
Mytilíni (Lésvos)–Foça (Turkey) Mid-May to Oct, Tues/Thurs 9am, Fri/Sun eve on the Turyol speedboat; no cars carried, €38 return, €25 one-way.
Vathý (Sámos)–Kuýadası (Turkey) 2 daily, early May to late Oct (maximum 1 weekly in winter). Greek boat at 8.30am; afternoon (4.45pm) Turkish boats (usually 2 craft in season). Rates are €43 one way including taxes, €47 day return including taxes, €65 open return including taxes. Cars are ferried only on the Greek craft Mon and Fri (€100 one way, €150 return for a small car). Journey time 1hr 30min.

Flights

NB: All flights on Olympic Airlines/Aviation unless otherwise specified. Frequencies are for June–Oct.
Híos to: Athens (2–3 daily on Olympic, 2 daily on Aegean; 50min); Límnos (2 weekly, both via Lésvos; 1hr 35min); Rhodes (2 weekly, 1 via Sámos; 55min–1hr 45min); Thessaloníki (5 weekly, 2 via Lésvos/Límnos; 1hr 10min–2hr 45min).
Ikaría to: Athens (4–6 weekly; 50 min); Iráklio (Crete), 1 weekly on Sky Express; 1hr).
Lésvos to: Athens (2–4 daily on Olympic, 2–3 daily on Aegean; 50min–1hr); Híos (2 weekly, 30min); Límnos (5 weekly; 40min); Rhodes (2 weekly, via Sámos; 1hr 40min); Sámos (2 weekly, 1 direct; 45min–1hr 30min); Thessaloníki (1–2 daily, 5 weekly via Límnos, on Olympic; 3–6 weekly direct on Aegean; 55min–1hr 50min).
Límnos to: Athens (2 daily; 55min); Lésvos (5 weekly; 40min); Rhodes (5 weekly; 2hr 5min–3hr 40min); Thessaloníki (6 weekly; 45min).
Sámos to: Athens (4–5 daily on Olympic, 2 daily on Aegean; 50–60min); Iráklio, Crete (2 weekly on Sky Express; 1hr 15min); Lésvos (2 weekly, 1 via Híos; 50min–1hr 30min); Límnos (2 weekly, via Lésvos/Híos; 1hr 35min–1hr 55min); Rhodes (2 weekly; 45min); Thessaloníki (3 weekly direct, 2 via intervening islands; 1hr 20min–3hr 45min).

11

The Sporades and Évvia

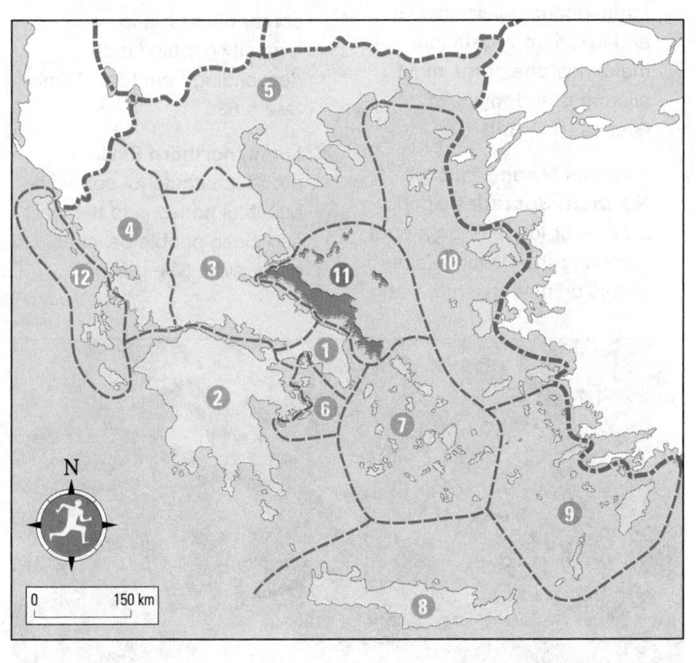

CHAPTER 11

Highlights

Lalária beach, Skiáthos White oval stones and turquoise waters, backed by steep cliffs and a natural rock arch, form a photogenic contrast to the island's other, mostly sandy, bays. See p.813

Skópelos Town Wooden shutters, ornate balconies, domed churches, atmospheric passageways and luxuriant vegetation make this one of the most alluring island towns in Greece. See p.815

National Marine Park of Northern Sporades Spend a day – or longer – on a boat exploring the visitable islets of this pristine reserve, with their wildlife, monasteries and secluded bays. See p.823

Skýros An outrageously pagan carnival, a striking hillside Hóra and traditional interiors are all found on one of the least spoiled islands in the Aegean. See p.824

Dhimosári Gorge, southern Évvia Traverse the wildest corner of the island on a mostly cobbled path descending from Mount Óhi. See p.833

Límni, northern Évvia A proud, characterful port with beautiful horizons to the west and clean pebble beaches either side. See p.834

▲ Goat dancers at the Skýros carnival

11

The Sporades and Évvia

The three northern **Sporades**, as their name suggests, are scattered off the central mainland, their hilly terrain betraying their status as extensions of Mount Pílio (see p.314); they're also culturally, historically and administratively very much part of Magnisía province, centred on Vólos. Archetypal Aegean-holiday islands, with fine beaches, lush vegetation and transparent sea, they're all packed out in mid-summer. **Skiáthos**, nearest to Pílio, is the busiest of the trio thanks to excellent sandy beaches, nightlife and an airport, but **Skópelos**, with a healthy pine forest and idyllic pebble bays, is catching up fast. The quietest, remotest and least developed, **Alónissos**, is part of a National Marine Park, and attracts more nature lovers than night-owls.

Skýros, the fourth inhabited Sporade, lies well southeast, having little historical (or logistical) connection with the others. It has best succeeded in retaining its traditional culture, though tourism (and real estate sales) are accelerating. While the dramatically set *hóra* remains a "normal" village, its main street is well used to visitors, and popular beach resorts await nearby.

Between Skýros and central Greece, enormous **Évvia** (classical "Euboea") extends for nearly 200km alongside the mainland. Although in spots one of the most dramatic Greek islands, with forested mountains and rugged stretches of little-developed coast, it attracts fewer foreign tourists, perhaps because it lacks that certain mid-Aegean island feel. Nonetheless, mainlanders throng the island, erecting holiday homes around several seaside resorts.

The northern Sporades are well connected by **bus** and **ferry** with Athens (via Áyios Konstandínos or Vólos), and less often by boat from Thessaloníki; it's easy to island-hop between them. The only reliable connection to Skýros is from Kými on Évvia via ferry. Évvia is linked to central Greece by two bridges at Halkídha, and by local ferries from half a dozen strategic points on the mainland. Only Skiáthos and Skýros have **airports**. Many people come to the forested Sporades to hike; the best **maps** are those published for each island by Anavasi, available in Athens, Vólos and on the islands themselves, for €5–7.50.

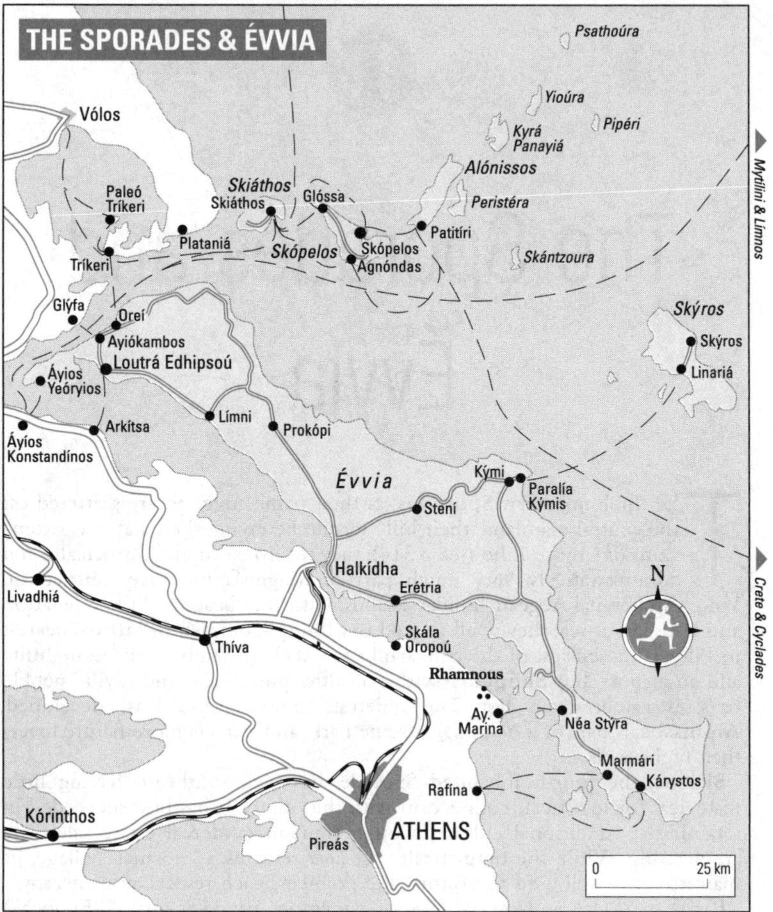

Skiáthos

Well-watered green countryside, some fine rural monasteries and the main town's labyrinthine old quarter certainly rate, but the real business of **Skiáthos** is **beaches**: the best, if most oversubscribed, in the Sporades. There are supposedly over sixty, still not enough to absorb hordes of visitors; the island's five thousand inhabitants are vastly outnumbered all season – in spring and autumn by Brits, during summer by Italians and Greeks. The main road along the south and southeast coasts serves an almost unbroken line of villas, hotels, minimarkets and restaurants; although they've not impinged much on Skiáthos's natural beauty, they make it difficult to find anything particularly Greek here. But by either **hiking** or using a **4WD vehicle**, you can find relative solitude, refreshing vistas and charming medieval monuments in the north of the island.

Skiáthos Town

SKIÁTHOS TOWN, the main habitation and harbour, clambers over two small promontories, one of them dividing the picturesque fishing port from the workaday ferry quay and yacht marina. The southwesterly old quarter, with its fine old gardened houses, maze-like lanes, shady platíes and the graceful belfries of Trís Ierárhes and Ayía Triádha churches, rewards random strolling, though tourist development has scarred the northeast side of town around main drag Alexándhrou Papadhiamándi, where most services, tackier shops, and "English" pubs are found.

There aren't many sights, but the **Alexandros Papadiamantis Museum** (Tues–Sun 9.30am–1.30pm & 5–8pm; €1) on Mitropolítou Ananíou, housed in the nineteenth-century home of one of Greece's best-known writers, is worth a look. The upper storey has been maintained as it was while the writer lived (and died) here, while the ground floor operates as a bookshop-cum-exhibition-area. **Galerie Varsakis antique shop** (open long hours) on Platía Trión Ierarhón, just inland from the old port, has one of the best **folklore displays** in Greece, and many of the older items would do Athens' Benáki Museum (see p.132) proud; the proprietor neither wants nor – given his stratospheric prices – expects to sell most of these, which include textiles, handicrafts, copperware, rural tools and jewellery.

Arrival, transport and information

As you exit the **ferry harbour**, the main **taxi** rank is 50m right of the gate; the **bus** stop is at the yacht end of the quay, by the landscaped platía. In between are numerous **rental outlets** offering bicycles, motorbikes, cars and motorboats; for an honest approach, try *Heliotropio* (Ⓣ24270 22430, Ⓦwww.heliotropio.gr) under their *Akti Hotel*. Small cars cost €30 per day, based on a week's high-season rental; scooters cost €15–20 per day. You can also get your bearings on a **boat trip** around the island (€20 per person; 5–6hr), departing at 10am from in front of the bus terminal. A shorter seagoing jaunt heads for **Tsougriá** islet (opposite Skiáthos Town; beach and taverna); boats leave from the old port beyond the Boúrtzi ex-islet and its causeway linking it to the quay.

Most other facilities are on Alexándhrou Papadhiamándi, including the **post office** and several **ATMs**. One block in from the old port on Nífonos, Enter has both Wi-Fi signal and high-speed **Internet** terminals. The Hellenic Seaways **ferry agent** (Ⓣ24270 22209) is at the base of Papadhiamándi; GA/Saos is handled by Dhioyenis Theodhorou (Ⓣ24270 22204), 100m further right.

Accommodation

Town **accommodation** is heavily booked during summer, though you can usually find a pension-room, albeit pricier (minimum ④) than elsewhere; at other times, supply exceeds demand and rates dip. The quayside room-owners' association kiosk operates long hours in high season; otherwise bookings can be made through several tourist agencies.

Good, small **hotels** include the jointly run *Bourtzi* (Ⓣ24270 21304, Ⓦwww.hotelbourtzi.gr; ④) at Moraïtou 8, and *Pothos* (Ⓣ24270 22694; ④), on Evangelistrías, both immaculate with delightful gardens; the former has a swimming pool, the latter a shady patio. Noisier, though with sea views, are waterfront *Meltemi* (Ⓣ24270 22493, Ⓔmeltemi@skiathos.gr; ④), with breakfast available in the eponymous snack-bar out front, or the nearby *Akti* (Ⓣ24270 21736, Ⓦwww.heliotropio.gr; ⑤), with a top-floor penthouse, sleeping four.

Eating and drinking

Most full-service **tavernas** (as opposed to fast-food joints) cluster around Platía Trión Ierarhón or line the old harbour. Live *bouzoúki* or guitar serenades with

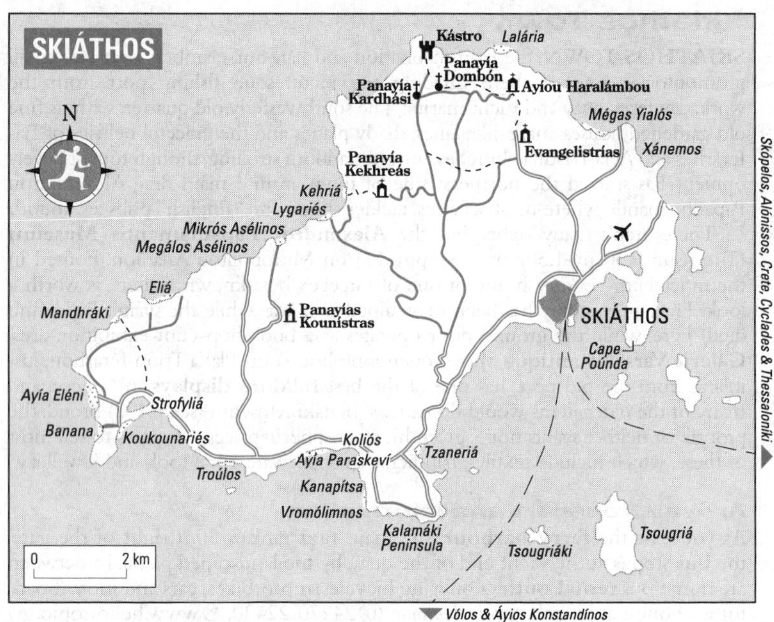

your meal are the norm. The best fish restaurants – priced accordingly (€55-plus/kilo) – line the far end of the old port.

Alexandhros Kapodhistríou, well signposted from Platía Trión Ierarhón. Decent *mezédhes*, excellent lamb chops (or *mayireftá*), home-made creme caramel, all at reasonable prices, and Greek sing-alongs with the ad hoc musicians make this a winner, let down only by poor bulk wine. Summer tables under the mulberry tree; winter seating indoors in an old stone-built salon.

Amfiliki Opposite the hospital, southwest shore of old town. All the standard taverna recipes, salubriously prepared – as tempting aromas wafting from the kitchen up front tell you. Just twelve rear tables overlooking the sea, so reserve in season on ☎24270 22839.

Kambourelias Old port, opposite excursion boats. The best moderately priced seafood venue here, with such platters as squid and sardines; open all year.

Maria's Syngroú 6, behind old port. Specialists in pizza, pasta and creative salads, but the riotous interior decor – like Gallerie Varsakis (see p.811) updated on hallucinogens – is worth it alone. One of the cheaper places, at about €25 for two people with salad, pizza and wine. Dinner only.

Mesoyia Beyond and northwest of Platía Trión Ierarhón. Cheap-and-cheerful outfit, with some Greek diners, featuring the usual grilled and *mayireftá* suspects, plus daily changing seafood. Some corners – such as tinned *dolmádhes* – may be sharply cut, but overall it's still worth showing up. Tables in the lane in summer; indoors during the cooler months.

Nightlife

Three trendy, consecutive **bars** – *Slip Inn*, *7 Steps* and *Rock & Roll* – nearly identical with their scatter cushions and young clientele, line the stairway from the fishing port. Otherwise, **nightlife** centres on shoreline clubs at the yacht marina, where long-running *Borzoi* plays a mix of Latin, blues, rock and Greek sounds, while nearby *Kahlua* and *BBC* rely on designer decor and decks jutting over the water. Exceptions include *Kentavros*, near the Papadiamantis Museum, an evergreen, much-loved jazz and blues bar. The summer **cinema**, Attikon, is next door, but entered from Papadhiamándi. Another seasonal venue is the Boúrtzi islet, whose fortress grounds host occasional **theatrical** and **musical** performances.

Around the island

With two dozen numbered stops along the way, the island **bus** shuttles at least hourly in summer (every fifteen minutes at peak times) until late between town and Koukounariés, a major resort 12km west. You'll need your own transport to explore the rewarding hinterland, overgrown with pine, lentisc, holm oak and arbutus – all second-growth **forest** because it's so frequently **burned** by arsonists (most recently in a huge July 2007 blaze between Koliós and Troúlos). Thanks to the humid climate and springs fed from the mainland, it regenerates quickly, but camping rough is strictly forbidden (as it is throughout the Sporades).

The beaches

Many northeast-coast **beaches** aren't accessible unless you take an excursion *kaïki*, hire a jeep, or embark on fairly long treks. In any case, the south coast is better protected from the prevailing northerly *meltémi*, and its beaches are just a few steps from the bus stops. The more popular coves have a drinks/snacks stall, while Vromólimnos, Megálos Asélinos and Troúlos support proper tavernas.

Famous **Lalária** beach, appearing on all postcard-stands, nestles near the northernmost point of Skiáthos, only reachable by taxi-boat from town. Covered in white pebbles, with steep cliffs rising behind and an artistic natural arch, it's undeniably beautiful, but beware the undertow when swimming. Three **sea-grottoes** just east feature in many of the "round-the-island" trips. About 3.5km north of Skiáthos Town, reached by vehicle followed by a steep ten-minute path down, **Mégas Yialós** – 250m of coarse sand and gravel – is a lovely naturist beach, though a lack of shade and facilities (a taverna is 400m up the access road) discourages casual visits. You can drive a similar distance right up to **Xánemos**, at the end of the airport runway, if you don't mind being buzzed by occasional aircraft.

On the southeast coast, beaches before the **Kalamáki peninsula** are no great shakes, but on the promontory itself are excellent **Tzaneriá** on the east and west-facing **Vromólimnos**. At Tzaneriá, PADI-affiliated Dolphin Diving Centre (Ⓣ24270 21599, Ⓦwww.ddiving.gr) at the *Nostos* hotel offers **scuba diving** around Tsougriáki islet. Vromólimnos offers **windsurfing** and **water-skiing** facilities, with two lively bar-restaurants in peak season.

Mega-hotels dominate the beaches between Vromólimnos and Troúlos; just before the latter, a side road leads 3.5km north through a lush valley to **Megálos Asélinos**, an exposed, coarse-sand beach with a bar, reasonable taverna and showers. The fork in the paved road leading to Panayías Kounístras continues to **Mikrós Asélinos**, east of its larger neighbour and quieter.

Beaches around **KOUKOUNARIÉS**, the island's third settlement after Troúlos, are excellent if you don't mind sharing them. The 1200-metre-long main bay of clear, gradually deepening water is backed by acres of stone pines; wooden walkways traverse the sand to a series of *kantínas*. The approach road runs behind a small lake, **Strofyliá**, behind the grove – all of it a protected reserve – past a line of **hotels**, **apartments** and **restaurants**, as well as a decent **campsite**, *Koukounaries* (Ⓣ24270 49250; May 15–Sept 15). The two-bedroomed, garden-set *Strofilia Apartments* (Ⓣ24270 49251, Ⓔstrophilia@skiathos.gr; ⑥) are particularly nicely furnished. All usual **water sports** are available at the beach, plus **horse riding** at the Skiathos Riding Centre.

Signposted across the headland, "**Banana beach**" (officially Krassás) is among the island's trendiest, with **watersports**, two bars and naturism; a headland separates the yellow-sand crescent of "Big Banana" from partly gay "Small Banana". The side road for neighbouring **Ayía Eléni** leads 1km to a more family-oriented scene with a snack-bar. Further north, an appallingly rough track system (walk from the lake, or drive from Ayía Eléni) leads to excellent **Mandhráki** (aka **Limáni tou Xérxi**) and **Eliá** (alias **Gournés)**, each with sunbeds and a snack bar.

The monasteries and Kástro

From town, you arrive at eighteenth-century **Evangelistrías monastery** (daily 10.30am–2.30pm & 5–8pm) by motorized transport in ten minutes or on foot in just over an hour, using the path short-cut shown on the Anavasi map. Founded by Athonite monks, it's exceptionally beautifully set; inside there's an eclectic **museum** (same hours, €3) comprising ecclesiastical and rural-folklore galleries, a display of world music instruments, and a vast collection of documents and photos from the Balkan Wars donated by the Potamianos family.

Beyond Evangelistrías, another **path** starting beside a watermill, then rough track, continue to restored **Ayíou Haralámbous** monastery, full of cats and chickens kept by the caretaker. Out the back gate, a faint trail heads west up to a pass, where a broader path drops to **Panayía Dombón** chapel and then to **Panayía Kardhási** on the way to Kástro (see below). Motorists can reach Kástro from Evangelístria by heading southwest to Stavrós junction and then turning north; foot passengers can disembark one of the tour *kaïkia* at the beach below it, or – if already at Evangelistrías – use the *kalderími* indicated on the recommended map from a point just southwest to emerge on the main Kástro-bound road. Another path shortcut, not shown on any commercial map, is possible from Kardhási to **Áyios Ioánnis**, the last chapel before Kástro proper.

Kástro, 8km from the south-coast road (final approach from a car park by broad, ten-minute path), straggles over a windswept headland, reached by stone steps replacing the former drawbridge leading to the gatehouse. This sixteenth-century fortified settlement, established for security from pirate raids, was abandoned after 1830, when the new Greek state stamped hard on piracy and the population left to build the modern town on the site of ancient Skiáthos. The crumbled ruins are overgrown, and only four **churches** survive, the largest (Yénnisi tou Khristoú) retaining original frescoes. From both the gatehouse and car park, paths descend east to a good sandy **beach**; a wooden bridge crosses the stream here to a friendly, not too overpriced, limited-menu **taverna**. As so often, the beach is wonderful in June or September, but fairly overrun in summer despite its remoteness.

Returning from Kástro, about 3km south, is the rough, steep track down to seventeenth-century **Panayía Kekhreás (Kehriás)** monastery, oldest on the island, with superb frescoes from 1745 under its pink-and-blue cupola. The track continues a bit further down the canyon, past watermills, towards sand-and-pebble **Kehriá** beach, but the final approach is on path; this beach, and its neighbour **Lygariés**, are usually reached by a better, separate track from the south-coast highway.

Skópelos

Its extensive pine forests mostly still unburnt, **Skópelos** is bigger and more rugged than Skiáthos and almost as popular, but its concessions to tourism are lower key and in better taste. Besides conifers there are olive groves, and orchards of plums (**prunes** are a local speciality), pears and almonds. **Skópelos (Hóra)** and **Glóssa**, the two main towns, are the prettiest in the Sporades, their hillside houses distinguished by painted wooden trim and grey slate roofs. The island has sufficient ground water, if less than Skiáthos and not really enough to support villa projects burgeoning across the bay from the hóra.

Foreign **occupiers** at various stages of the island's history have included Romans, Venetians, French and, of course, the Ottomans. The Ottoman pirate-admiral Barbarossa – actually a Greek renegade from Lésvos – slaughtered the entire population during the sixteenth century. Today, Greek visitor numbers match foreign (mostly British, Scandinavian, Italian and French) ones, owing to the lack of an airport.

Skópelos should offer better **walking** than it does, with the trail network becoming overgrown or bulldozed into tracks. Long-time Skópelos resident Heather Parsons battles to maintain paths and leads walks along what remains (Ⓣ694 52 49 328, Ⓦwww.skopelos-walks.com), as well as publishing a hiking guide. That said, the **countryside** – especially the southwest coast – remains spectacular, and served as the location for the **film** version of *Mamma Mia!* (starring Pierce Brosnan and Meryl Streep) during September 2007.

Skópelos Town and around

SKÓPELOS TOWN (Hóra) pours off a hill on the west flank of a wide, oval bay; a cascade of handsome mansions and slate-domed churches below the ruined Venetian **kástro** is revealed slowly as the boat rounds the north headland with its postcard-fixture Panayítsa toú Pýrgou. This is just one of a reputed 123 **churches** and chapels scattered across town, most locked except on their saint's day. Away from the requisite waterside commercial strip, the *hóra* is endearingly time-warped – indeed among the most unspoilt in the islands – with wonderfully idiosyncratic shops of a sort long vanished elsewhere, and vernacular domestic architecture unadulterated with tasteless monstrosities.

Arrival, transport and information

The **new port** is toward the east end of the tree-lined quay, with two ticket **agencies** (Lemonis for Saos and GA, Ⓣ24240 22363; Hellenic Seaways, straight out of the gate, Ⓣ24240 22767). Both the **taxi** stand and **KTEL stop** are 100m to the left of the port as you exit; **buses** (4–8 daily by season) ply the main paved road between here and Loutráki via Glóssa and all the main beaches. Drivers should use the free municipal **car park** beside the KTEL terminal. Several **car and scooter rental** outlets, such as Magic (Ⓣ22420 23250, Ⓦwww.skopeloscars.com), cluster near the start of the road towards Glóssa. **Boat cruises** cost €20 for a trip around the island, or €45–50 to the Sporades National Marine Park (see p.823) – a very long day at sea, better done from Alónissos. Quayside **ATM**s abound, while the **post office** is on Dhoulídhi, a lane east of the platía ("Souvlaki Square") graced with plane trees, in from the port; nearby Click and Surf is the best **Internet** café (Wi-Fi and high-speed terminals). There's no tourist office, but Ⓦwww.skopelos.net is a very useful **website**.

Accommodation

There are numerous **rooms** (❸–❹) for rent in the backstreets, as well as entire houses; these – plus apartments and hotels – are best arranged through helpful Madro Travel, by the old port (Ⓣ24240 22145, Ⓦwww.madrotravel.com), also good for boat excursions. Unless you've booked through them or an overseas operator, you're unlikely to find high-season space in the comfortable hillside **hotels** with pools.

Georgios L. Northwest promenade, by Panayítsa toú Pýrgou Ⓣ24240 22308. Bland, 1970s-vintage hotel, but all sea-view rooms (some a/c), parking nearby and Internet terminals in the ground-floor café. ❹

Kapetanios Up from ferry jetty Ⓣ24240 22110. Just a short walk inland, but very quiet, garden-set, 1970s-built hotel over two wings. ❸

Kyr Sotos Just in from mid-quay Ⓣ24240 22549. A rambling, restored old-house *pension* with wood-floored, a/c, en-suite rooms that's justifiably a favourite budget option. Best are the quieter rear units in general, facing the courtyard, and specifically no. 4, with its fireplace. Open all year. ❷

Mando Ⓣ24240 23917, Ⓦwww.skopelos.net/mando/. Easily the best accommodation at Stáfylos (see below), very friendly and quiet with stone-floored, a/c rooms set among manicured lawns, a short way up from its own lido. Also a family suite with fireplace. ❺

Skopelos Village 600m around bay from ferry dock Ⓣ24240 22517, Ⓦwww.skopelosvillage.gr. Studio and apartment complex set among landscaped grounds; the plushest local option, popular with families and package companies. April to mid-Oct. Studios ❼ suites ❽

Thea Home On ring road Ⓣ24240 22859, Ⓦwww.skopelosweb.gr/theahome/. Studios and larger apartments with white-tile-and-pine decor, fridges, phones and TV, most with balconies with sweeping sea views; easy street parking. Breakfast (extra) offered on a pleasant patio. April–Oct. ❹

The Town and around

The disorganized **folklore museum** (daily 10am–2.30pm & 6–10pm; €2) musters a motley collection of weaving, embroidery and costumes; informative panels explaining local customs and the religious calendar redeem it. The "Photographic Centre" has dissolved, reopened only for temporary exhibits, though there's a permanent display of 1950s photos in the municipal quayside *kafenío*.

On the slopes of Mount Paloúki east of the bay stand three historic monasteries: **Evangelistrías (Evangelismós;** daily 8am–1pm & 5–8pm), visible from town; more secluded **Prodhrómou** (same hours), occupied by five nuns; and, at the top of a verdant ravine, sixteenth-century **Metamórfosis**, an Athonite dependency with one summer-resident monk. Without transport, access is simplest via a track from Áyios Andónios chapel behind the football pitch, which goes first to Metamórfosis; from there what's left of the old *kalderími* system effectively shortcuts the roads to Evangelistrías and Prodhrómou.

Some 4km south of town, **Stáfylos** is the closest decent beach, though small and seasonally crowded, with a spring and a mediocre taverna. You're best off walking five minutes east over the headland to larger, more scenic, sand-and-fine-gravel **Velanió**, with an official naturist zone and a *kantína* renting sunbeds.

Northwest of Skópelos Town, reached by taxi-boats and a paved road, **Glystéri** is a small sand-and-pebble beach with sunbeds, its *Palio Karnayio* **taverna** much frequented at weekends. A side-turning, 1km out of town, from the Glystéri road leads west via the lush, well-watered Karyá valley to the east flank of 681-metre **Mount Dhélfi** and a major junction just below Áyios Riyínos pass; bear right for the trailhead to the **Sendoúkia** (four ancient rock-cut tombs, probably Roman).

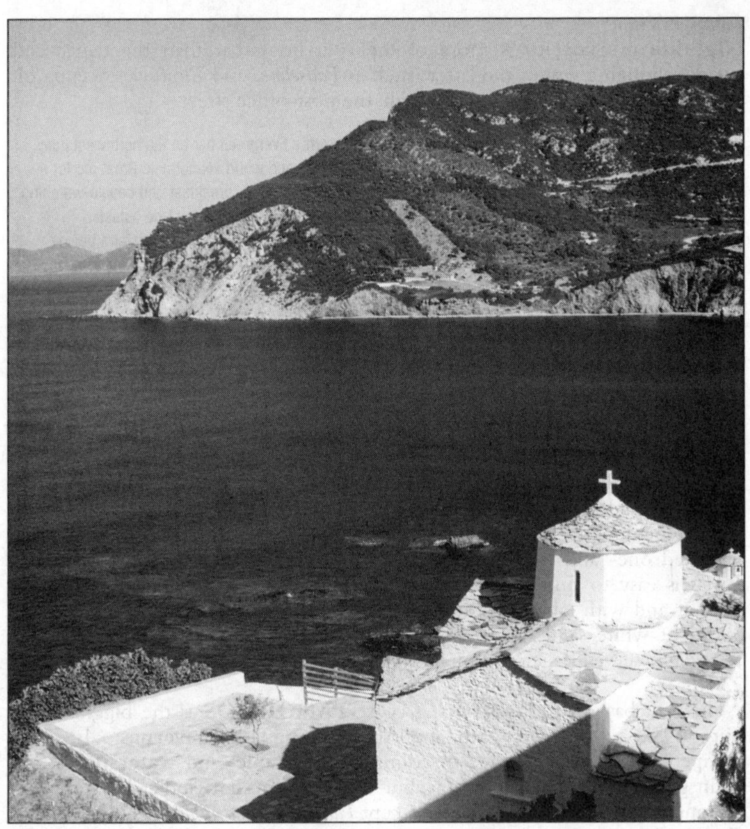

▲ Coastline, Skópelos Town

Eating and drinking

There's a range of in-town **tavernas**, from acceptable *yirádhika* on the plane-tree platía to excellent, photo-menu-free eateries on the northwest quay or near the T-junction on the road out, by way of forgettable tourist traps at mid-quay and *koultouriárika* outfits inland.

Le Bistro Just above the ferry dock. High-end, Mediterranean "fusion" eatery with a wine-bar annexe and mostly terrace seating. Budget €35 a head with modest drink intake. Dinner only.

Englezos Northwest quay. 2007-opened all-rounder that's worth the 15 percent extra for Greek island standards with a slightly nouvelle twist: eggplant and cheese roulade, samphire, creative salads, and lamb joint with cubed potatoes, accompanied by good bulk wine.

Klimataria Next to the *dhimarhío*. Reasonable (for Skópelos) fish by the kilo like *mousmoúlia*, scorpion fish and stewed grouper; a few *mayireftá* and *mezédhes* too.

Ta Kymata (Angelos) Last building, northwest quay. About the oldest taverna on Skópelos, a shrine of quality *mayireftá* such as *exohikó* (lamb and vegetables in a phyllo triangle) and *mezédhes* like fresh beets with greens.

Nastas Near T-junction on Glóssa road. Greek-patronized ouzerí that's really more seafood taverna, strong on fish and lobster. Portions aren't huge but quality is high and service assiduous. All year; out under the mulberries in summer, in the wood-floored salon during winter.

Perivoli Up a lane from the plane-tree platía with its *yirádhika*. Courtyard taverna preparing Greek recipes with a cordon bleu twist; wine by the glass.

Nightlife

Nightlife in Skópelos is more of the after-hours-bar than the dance-club variety, though a few of the latter (such as *Panselinos* and *Eleotrivio*) occupy old olive mills or warehouses on Dhoulídi, the post-office street.

Anatoli Veteran rebétika musician Yiorgos Xintaris performs (and sells a worthwhile CD) at this unsigned outfit on top of the *kástro*. Daily July & Aug, weekends only June & Sept.

Merkourio (Mercurius) Mixed musical offerings at this Greek-favoured bar by Áyios Merkoúrios church.

Oionos Old-house bar inland from mid-quay with a jazz, blues and world playlist, plus a staggering variety of imported beers and whiskies.

Platanos Evergreen bar on the northwest quay, with jazz and world soundtrack. Great too for a morning coffee or breakfast and people-watching under the namesake plane tree outside.

Vengera Another old-house upstairs bar on a backstreet corner; mellow ambience and good music.

The south and west coast

About 7km due south of town lies the elephant's-foot-shaped bay of **AGNÓNDAS**, the island's back-up harbour when the main port is storm-shut, and port of call for boats to the Cyclades, Thessaloníki and Crete. **Accommodation** includes *Pavlina Apartments* (ⓣ24240 23272, ⓔpavlinaskopelos@mail.gr; ❸) behind the short pebble beach, offering four high-ceilinged, wood-trimmed one- and two-bedroomed units. Among three **tavernas**, waterfront *Pavlos* is easy to find and reliable for fish, though *Fotini* opposite is cheaper, homier and with tables on the beach. The next cove west is **LIMNONÁRI**, 300m of white sand bracketed by the steep-sided bay. The *Limnonari Beach Restaurant* serves delicious spiral *striftés tyrópittes* and rents **rooms** (ⓣ24240 23046; ❹).

The first bay on the west-facing coast, **PÁNORMOS** is the biggest resort outside Skópelos Town, with abundant lodging, four **tavernas** (*Asterias* is competent), yacht anchorage in contiguous **Bló** inlet and **watersports**. The main gravel beach shelves steeply, but there are smaller, sandier bays close by. Among **accommodation**, the well-kept *Panormos Beach Hotel* (ⓣ24240 22711, ⓦwww.skopelosweb.gr/panormosbeach; ❺) has fine views and a huge lawn studded with fruit trees; 1km beyond it, isolated ✱ *Adrina Beach* (ⓣ24240 24250, ⓦwww.adrina.gr; late May to Sept; ❼) comprises ivy-clad bungalows, a sea-water pool, on-site taverna and private beach.

Just around the corner, **Miliá** is a 600-metre sweep of tiny pebbles opposite Dhassía islet. The **taverna** here is decidedly average, and the beach bar can get noisy; many will prefer **Kastáni**, 150m of fine sand and indisputably the island's best beach, immediately north.

Élios (Néo Klíma), 4km north of the Kastáni turning, was established by the junta to house residents of the earthquake-damaged villages above it; it's a dreary place, redeemed mainly by adjacent **Hóvolo** Beach. Overhead, the renovated village of **Palió Klíma** marks the start of a beautiful 45-minute **trail** to Glóssa, via the foreigner-owned hamlet of **Áyii Anáryiri** and the island's oldest settlement, **Athéato** (Mahalás).

Glóssa, Loutráki and around

Skopelos's second town, **GLÓSSA**, 26km from Hóra near the northwest tip of the island, is much more countrified, with lush gardens amidst a mix of vernacular houses and unfortunate modern additions arrayed in stepped tiers on the hillside. Along narrow, mostly car-free lanes are several *psistariés*, an **ATM** and a few (sometimes substandard) **dhomátia**; an exception, *Kostas and Nina's Place* (☎24240 33686; ❸) has simple, clean rooms, and studios rented out longer term. The well-signposted central *koultourárika* **taverna**, *To Agnandi*, serves upscale (and pricey) takes on traditional recipes – pork with prunes or *hortokeftédhes* (vegetable croquettes) – at both indoor and roof-terrace seating, though locals patronize *To Steki tou Mastora* at the outskirts, by the church.

Hydrofoils, catamarans and some ferries call at diminutive **LOUTRÁKI port** ("Glóssa" on ferry and hydrofoil schedules; the harbour **agent** is Triandafyllou, ☎24240 33435), 3km from Glóssa proper down a serpentine road (or a much shorter *kalderími*). There's not much here aside from some ruined **Roman baths** and a narrow pebble beach. If you need to **stay**, there are various **rooms** (❸) signposted just inland, or the more comfortable *Selinounda Hotel* (☎24240 34073; ❹) up the road. Quayside **tavernas** aren't really worth a special drive but will do for a meal before a boat ride; *Orea Ellas* is cheap and cheerful but culinarily undistinguished, while *Akrotiri* at the jetty base gets a Greek clientele.

Beaches near Glóssa are all on the northeast-facing coast, reached by partly paved roads. **Perivolioú**, 7km away and about 100m long, is the best: scenic, coarsely sandy and with rock overhangs for shade, though prone to surf. A good motorable track continues 1.5km east to **Hondroyiórgis** beach, similar though marred by rocks in the water, before looping back to Glóssa. From 250m east of where this track returns, a paved, narrow road leads around 5km to photogenic **Áyios Ioánnis Kastrí** church, perched on a rock monolith (steps lead up). A brief, steep path leads southeast to a small sandy cove.

Alónissos

Thanks to remoteness, lack of airport and seasonally sparse ferry/catamaran connections, **Alónissos** attracts fewer casual foreign visitors than Skópelos or Skiáthos. There are, however, numerous British and Italian tourists (the latter mostly in all-inclusive club hotels); Greeks descend in force all summer; whilst second-home owners fill a broad spectrum of nationalities. The resulting scene is trendy in a low-key way, with art exhibits, a homeopathic academy, and resident herbalists.

Alónissos is the largest and only permanently inhabited member of a mini-archipelago (of which more below) at the east end of the Sporades. It's more **rugged** and **wild** than its neighbours, but no less green, and has spring water; pine forest, olive groves and fruit orchards cover the southern half, while a dense maquis of arbutus, heather, kermes oak and lentisc cloaks the north. A salubriously dry climate once made the island's **wine** notable, until 1950s phylloxera wiped out the vineyards (resistant vines now support a modest revival); the famous local June **apricots** were unaffected. Some of Greece's cleanest sea surrounds Alónissos, though **beaches** tend to be functional rather than picturesque.

Known in ancient times as Ikos, and during the medieval period as Hiliadhrómia (both names exploited by local businesses), Alónissos was, like its neighbours, a Byzantine and Ottoman backwater, with a Venetian tenure during the fifteenth and sixteenth centuries. The most significant event in recent **history** was the March 9, 1965 earthquake, which shattered the hilltop *hóra*.

Patitíri

The port and de-facto capital, **PATITÍRI**, occupies a sheltered, piney bay flanked by steep cliffs, and ringed by bars, cafés and tavernas. It's inevitably a bit

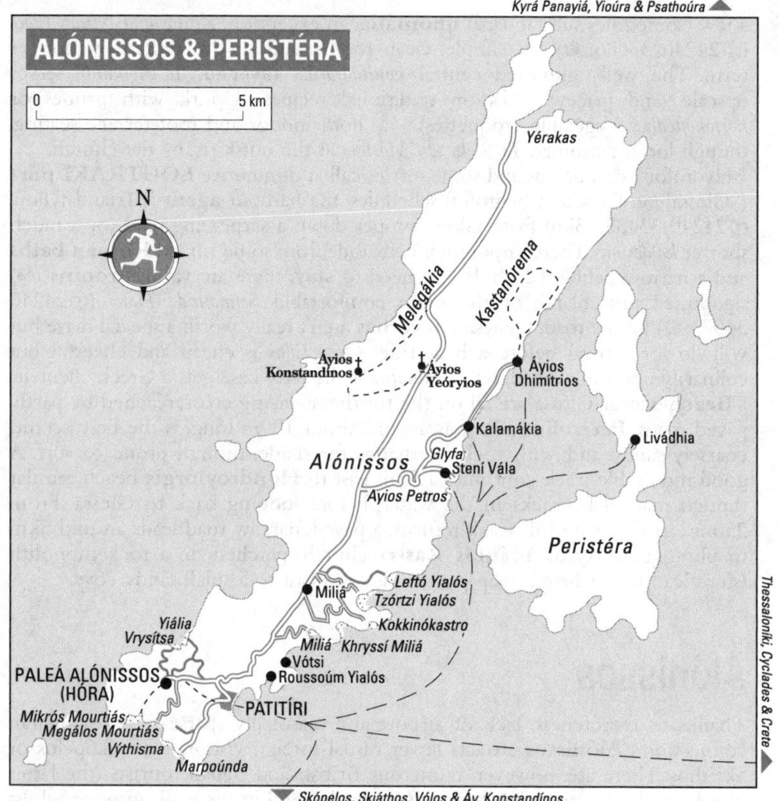

soulless – some "shoebox" prefab earthquake housing still lurks in the backstreets – but it has tried to compensate with a stone-paved waterfront (strictly no parking) and general tidy-up. The waterfront **MOM Information Centre** (daily 10am–4pm & 6–10pm; free; Ⓦwww.mom.gr), just above the Alkyon ticket agency, has models and multimedia displays about the endangered **monk seal** (see box p.823). In an unmissable stone building on the southern side of the cove, the **Costas and Angela Mavrikis Museum** (daily 11am–7pm; €3 includes drink at café) is crammed with local artwork, traditional costumes, reconstructed island interiors, war memorabilia, wine-making equipment, and exhibits on piracy and seafaring.

Practicalities

Orientation is straightforward, with two shopping streets forging inland from the quay (the rightmost straight, the left-hand one in roundabout fashion) to unite as the road to **Hóra**. **Buses** and four **taxis** stop adjacent on the waterfront end of the right-hand shopping street, which hosts the single **ATM** and the **post office**. There are many outlets for hiring **scooters and cars** along the quay and up either commercial street; online booking is possible with National/Alamo (Ⓣ24240 66242). Waterfront offices also rent **motorboats and dinghies**. Two **agencies** divide the shipping trade: Alonissos Travel (Ⓣ24240

65188) for GA or Saos ferries/catamarans, Alkyon Travel (Ⓣ24240 65220) for all Hellenic Seaways ferries, catamarans and hydrofoils.

Most Alónissos **accommodation** is in Patitíri or immediately around; you may be approached with offers as you disembark at the port. Albedo Travel (Ⓣ24240 65804, Ⓦwww.albedotravel.com) handles hotels, studios and villas, while the local room-owners' association booth (Ⓣ24240 66188) on the waterfront can also find you a room (mostly ❸) in Patitíri or nearby Vótsi. The best budget option is *Pension Pleiades* (Ⓣ24240 65235; ❸) up behind Albedo Travel, with rooms and two apartments. Fully fledged hotels include *Haravyi* (Ⓣ24240 65090, Ⓕ24240 65189; ❹) above mid-bay, again with mixed rooms and studios, and *Liadromia* (Ⓣ24240 65521, Ⓔliadromia@alonissos.com; doubles ❹ suites ❺), with pastel-tinted, engagingly furnished units, reached by steps near the post office.

Waterfront **restaurants** are reasonably priced, but nothing special; an exception is *Archipelagos*, the only place locals will be caught in. A recommended ouzerí is friendly ✱ *To Kamaki*, 150m up towards the post office from the waterfront; portions are not huge but the menu encompasses unusual dishes like crab croquettes, skate and *tsitsíravla* shoots. **Nightlife** is low-key, mostly confined to the seafront cafés; Hóra (see below) is livelier after dark, especially in summer.

Hóra (Paleá Alónissos)

Hóra (PALEÁ ALÓNISSOS) was damaged by the Sporades-wide March 1965 quake, after which most of the population was compulsorily moved to Patitíri, with considerable reluctance; the issue was essentially forced in 1977 by the closure of the school and cutting off of electricity. Outsiders, mostly Germans (now selling up), plus Brits and Athenians, bought up the abandoned houses for a song and restored them in variable taste; only a few locals still live here, which gives the village a very un-Greek atmosphere, but it is picturesque, with great views. Much of the year, though, there are far more hedgehogs than people about; the place only really comes to life – noisily so – in mid-summer.

Hóra can be **reached** from Patitíri by a fine, signposted *kalderími* (45min uphill, 30min down); alternatively, there's a frequent bus service (10 min; €1.30) most of the day. For **accommodation**, *Konstantina's Studios* (Ⓣ&Ⓕ24240 66165; ❹) is a renovated building with eight studios and one apartment, all enjoying exceptional views, while the beam-ceilinged *Fantasia House* (Ⓣ24240

Hiking on Alónissos

Although its often harsh, rugged landscape might suggest otherwise, of all the Sporades Alónissos caters best to **hikers**. Fourteen routes have been surveyed and numbered, with path-starts admirably signposted and all itineraries figuring prominently on the Anavasi **map**. In 2007, an EU grant helped clean and refurbish certain trails. Many admittedly provide just short walks from a beach to a village or the main road, but some can be combined to make meaty circular treks. The best in that category are trail #11 from Áyios Dhimítrios, up the Kastanórema and then back along the coast (2hr 30min), or trails #13 plus #12, Melegákia to Áyios Konstandínos and Áyios Yeóryios (just over 2hr, including some road-walking to return to start). Consult also the **website** (Ⓦwww.alonnisoswalks.co.uk) of island resident Chris Browne, who has written a comprehensive walking guide to Alónissos and several neighbouring islets (obtainable through Ⓦwww.travelleur.com).

65186; ③) just up from the bus stop has a pleasant view-terrace. The most obvious, sea-view **restaurants** are stratospherically priced; you'll get better value in the old central square at either cheap-and-cheerful *Rocks* (May–Oct) or *Kastro* (late June to early Sept). At the far end of the main street, *Hayiati* is unbeatable for coffees and traditional sweets like *kazandibí*, not overpriced considering the incomparable view to Skópelos. *Arhondostasi* at the *agora's* near end is a classy **nightlife** venue with occasional live Greek acoustic music; *Panselinos* bar on the bus-stop platía also serves creditable snacks.

The rest of the island

The **roads** between Patitíri, most beaches, Stení Vála and Áyios Dhimítrios are paved, and other dirt roads down to minor beaches – with some exceptions – are in good condition. There's infrequent (3–4 daily) **bus service** along the Paleá Alónissos–Patitíri–Stení Vála route; a few pricey morning **water-taxis** ply in high season from near the hydrofoil berth in Patitíri north to the remoter east-coast beaches, returning late afternoon.

In southern Alónissos, the beach at **Marpoúnda**, sandwiched between a defunct hotel and an all-inclusive Italian complex, does not appeal; turn right instead before Marpoúnda on a rough but passable dirt track towards **Výthisma**. Use the secondary path descending from the power pole by the parking area, not the broad main track which is washed out at the bottom. The 200-metre sand-and-pebble stretch is pretty, but without facilities or shade. Further along the coast, pebbly and crowded **Megálos Mourtiás** (two tavernas) is reached by paved road (2km) from Paleá Alónissos; **Mikrós Mourtiás** just west, served by marked path and a dirt track, is more secluded. Immediately north of Paleá Alónissos, visibly tucked into their respective finger-like inlets, compact **Vrysítsa** and **Yiália** (with a picturesque windmill) both have more sand than pebbles, but no facilities and are prone to *meltémi*-borne debris.

The next two bays northwest of Patitíri are auxilliary fishing ports more than beaches; **ROUSSOÚM YIALÓS** does have a small pebbly strand, a few **dhomátia** and a **taverna**, *Remezzo*. Bigger **VÓTSI** beyond – almost a proper village – can offer three **tavernas**, homiest, most reasonable and best being *Iy Mouria*, dishing up big salads, squid and *mayireftá* washed down with bulk retsina and red wine; they have simple **rooms** (ⓣ24240 65273; ③) too. Neither **Miliá** nor **Khryssí Miliá** are memorable as beaches, though on the slopes just before Miliá is top-standard **accommodation**: *Milia Bay Hotel Apartments* (ⓣ24240 66032, ⓦwww.milia-bay.gr; April–Oct; studios ⑥ apartments ⑦–⑧), whose units offer sea views over lovingly landscaped grounds and a pool area. The first indisputably good – and most scenic – east-coast **beach** is **Kokkinókastro**, whose flanking headland is the site of ancient Ikos (inaccessible by land). Pebbles on a red-sand base (without facilities) extend both sides of the promontory; access to the northerly one is allowed through an unfenced private estate. There are **tavernas** at each of the next two pebble coves along, **Tzórtzi Yialós** and **Leftó Yialós**.

STENÍ VÁLA attracts many of the yacht flotillas combing the Sporades; facilities include a shop, a couple of café-bars, a few **rooms** (such as *Dhrosoula Dhrosaki*, ⓣ24240 65776; ③) and three **tavernas**, of which *Steni Vala* (aka *Tassia;* open most of year) is noted for *mayireftá*. Locally based, Greek/South-African-run Ikion Diving (ⓣ24240 65158, ⓦwww.ikiondiving.gr) offers **scuba expeditions** around the nearby islets. There's also a **campsite**, *Ikaros* (ⓣ24240 65258) in a nearby olive grove; a long pebble beach – **Glýfa** – just north; and a better one, **Áyios Pétros**, a ten-minute path-walk south.

KALAMÁKIA, the next hamlet north along the coast road, hasn't a beach but it does have a fishing-port feel and a reliable **taverna/rooms**, *Margarita* (☎24240 65738; May–Oct; ❸), with good fish and *mezédhes*. The sealed road ends at **Áyios Dhimítrios,** where boats anchor off a curving pebbly, unshaded beach (there's no proper harbour) with a snack-bar and sunbed rental.

The National Marine Park of Alónissos-Northern Sporades

The 1992-founded **National Marine Park** protects monk seals, dolphins, wild goats and rare seabirds in an area encompassing Alónissos plus a dozen tiny **islets** speckling the Aegean to the east. None of these (save one) have any permanent population, but a few can be visited by summer-only excursion boats, weather permitting; the 25-metre wooden *kaïki Planitis* run by Alonissos Travel (see p.820) is recommended. **Pipéri** islet forms the core zone of the park – an off-limits seabird and monk seal refuge, approachable only by scientists authorized by the appropriate government ministry. **Peristéra**, right opposite Alónissos, is uninhabited, though some Alonissans cross to tend olive groves in the south; since a park-wide ban on campfires was imposed, it's little visited by excursion craft. Fertile **Kyrá Panayiá,** the next islet out, belongs to Meyístis Lávras monastery on Mount Áthos; there's a monastery here too, restored in the 1990s and inhabited. Boats are allowed to anchor at two bays, southerly Áyios Pétros and northerly Planítis, for

The Mediterranean monk seal

The **Mediterranean monk seal** (*Monachus monachus*) has the dubious distinction of being the most endangered European mammal – fewer than 350 survive, the majority around the Portuguese Atlantic island of Madeira but also off North Africa and Croatia. A small population occupies the Ionian and Aegean seas of Greece; the largest community, of fifty to sixty, lives and breeds around the islets of the Sporades marine park.

Females have one **pup** about every two years, which (according to skeletal dentition analysis) can live for 45 years, attaining 2m in length and over 200 kilos in weight as **adults**. Formerly pups were reared in the open, but disturbance by man led to whelping seals retreating to isolated sea caves with partly submerged entrances.

Monk seals can swim 200km a day in search of food – and compete with fishermen in the overfished Aegean, often destroying nets. Until recently fishermen routinely killed seals; this occasionally still happens, but the establishment of the **National Marine Park of Alónissos-Northern Sporades** has helped by banning September–November fishing northeast of Alónissos and prohibiting it altogether within 1.5 nautical miles of Pipéri. These measures have won local support through the efforts of the **Hellenic Society for the Protection of the Monk Seal** (HSPMS), based at Stení Vála, even among Sporadean fishermen who realize that the restrictions should (in theory – violations continue) exclude industrial-scale trawlers from elsewhere and help restore local fish stocks. The HSPMS has reared several abandoned seal pups (bad weather often separates them from their mothers), all subsequently released in the sea around Alónissos.

Without spending some weeks on a local boat, your chances of seeing a seal are slim. It's best not to approach sea caves potentially used for nesting; if seals are spotted (usually dozing on the shore or swimming in the open sea), keep a deferential distance.

passengers to walk up to the monastery. Nearby **Yioúra** has a Neolithically inhabited stalactite cave which legendarily sheltered the Homeric Polyphemus, plus the main wild-goat population, but you won't see either as *kaïkia* must keep 400m clear of the shore. Tiny, northernmost **Psathoúra** is dominated by its powerful lighthouse, tallest in the Aegean; excursions call for a swim at a pristine, white sand beach. Flat, green **Skántzoura**, off southeast towards Skýros and too remote for tours to visit, has a single empty monastery and populations of Eleonora's falcon and Audoin's gull.

Skýros

Despite its airport and natural beauty, **Skýros** until recently had a low touristic profile, thanks to few major sites or resorts, problematic land-and-sea access from Athens, plus its ability to rely economically on about nine hundred naval and air force personnel. Times have changed, with Italians and French especially showing up overland, the Dutch flying in on once-weekly charters, and trendy Athenians and Thessalonians taking advantage of domestic flights. The vaguely New Age Skyros Centre, pitched mostly at Brits, has also effectively publicized the place, though the tourist season is still relatively brief.

The popular theory that Skýros was originally two islands seems debatable, but certainly the character of its two parts differs. The fertile **north, Merói,** has a gentler landscape, retaining much of its original pine forest, while the more barren, rocky **south, Vounó,** is mountainous (though it has most of the island's springs), quarried for marble and home to semi-wild herds of the local pony (see p.828). Voúno belongs mostly to Athonite monastery Meyístis Lávras, which has sharply polarized the population with its proposal to erect 111, enormously tall power-generating **wind turbines**, which would be the largest such installation in the world.

Local **beaches** are generally serviceable rather than film-set-worthy like Skópelos, if a bit better than Alónissos. Those along the west coast attract seaborne rubbish so that, while the scenery can be spectacular, the swimming isn't. East-coast beaches cluster around Skýros Town, which makes staying there or immediately nearby the most attractive choice. Good, isolated beaches in the north of the island are under threat of being expropriated by the air force, which otherwise keeps a low profile (except off-season when pilots and their families keep many tavernas and bars open).

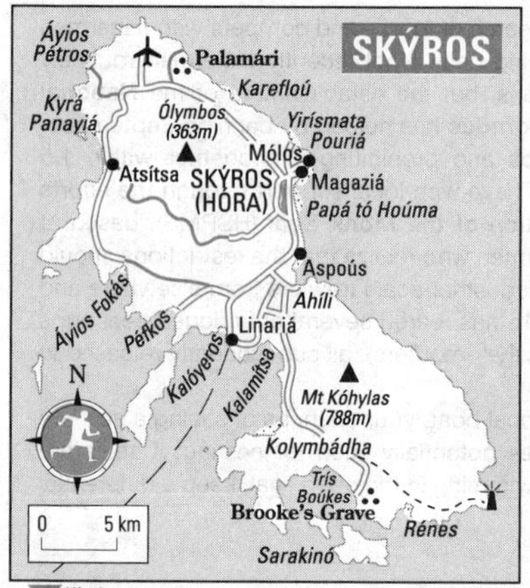

All this notwithstanding, Skýros still ranks as one of the most interesting places in the Aegean. It has a long history of **woodcarving** in mulberry, its apotheosis the *salonáki skyrianó* (a set of sitting-room furniture), as well as **pottery**, originally not local but obtained through collaboration with passing pirates. A very few old men still wear the traditional cap, vest, baggy trousers and *trohádhia* (sandals), while some

Carnival on Skýros

Skýros has a particularly outrageous *apokriátika* (pre-Lenten) **carnival**, featuring its famous **goat dance**, performed by grouped masked revellers in the streets of **Paleá Alónissos**. The leaders of each troupe are the **yéri**, menacing figures (usually men but sometimes sturdy women) dressed in goat-pelt capes, weighed down by huge garlands of sheep bells, their faces concealed by kid-skin masks, and brandishing shepherd's crooks. Accompanying them are their "brides", men in drag known as **korélles** (maidens), and **frángi** (maskers in assorted "Western" garb). When two such groups meet, the *yéri* compete to see who can ring their bells longest and loudest with arduous body movements, or even get into brawls using their crooks as cudgels. For the full story, see Joy Coulentianou's *The Goat Dance of Skyros*, available in Athens from Ekdotiki Ermis (Ⓦwww.ermis-ekdotiki.gr).

These rites take place on each of the four **weekends** before Clean Monday (see "Basics" p.58), but the final one is more for the benefit of tourists, both Greek and foreign. The Skyrians are less exhausted and really let their (goat) hair down for each other during the preceding three weeks. Most local hotels open for the duration, and you have to book rooms around Christmas.

elderly women still wear the requisite yellow scarves and embroidered skirts, but this is dying out. And then there's the **Carnival** (see box above).

Linariá

Ferries dock at **LINARIÁ** port, a functional place on the southwest-facing coast, tolerable enough for an hour or two while waiting for a boat. **Taxis** and the **KTEL** bus meet arrivals for the trip to Skýros Town (10km), and buses continue to Magaziá and Mólos in high season. If you need to **stay** (convenient for the occasional morning departure), choose between *King Lykomides* (Ⓣ22220 93249, ❸), spotless, air-conditioned *dhomátia* with little balconies above the harbour, or – behind this – *Linaria Bay Hotel* (Ⓣ22220 93274; ❹), a mixture of rooms and apartments. The best of four quayside **tavernas** is *O Maïstros*, hidden behind a plane tree, with good vegetarian *mezédhes* and fresh fish that you'll wait a bit for. **Nightlife** means hillside *Kavos Bar*, a short walk up the hóra-bound road, which does light snacks by day too and greets the evening ferry with a rousing musical fanfare. In high season, **excursion kaïkia** (€25 including lunch) offer trips from Linariá to the islet of **Sarakinó**, with its white-sand beach at Glyfádha, also stopping at various sea caves.

Skýros Town

SKÝROS Town (**Hóra**), with its somewhat Cycladic, flat-roofed architecture, covers the leeward, southwest slope of a pinnacle rising precipitously from the coast; in legend, King Lykomede raised the young Achilles in his palace here, and also pushed Theseus to his death from the summit. Given its workaday atmosphere, the town doesn't feel like a resort, but away from the scruffier outskirts it's decidedly picturesque, with covered passageways, churches and distinct historical quarters (the higher neighbourhoods having more social status). On the climb up, you may glimpse traditional house interiors with gleaming copperware, painted pottery and antique embroideries decorating chimney hoods, a matter of intense pride for residents. Arrival at the **kástro**, enclosing an originally Byzantine **monastery of Áyios Yeóryios** erected atop the ancient **acropolis**, will be sadly anticlimactic, as it's all closed due to 2001 earthquake damage, with no re-opening foreseen.

Taking the descending, left-hand fork in Hóra's central lane brings you to a round platía at the north edge of town with its nude bronze statue of "Immortal Poetry"; this is actually a **memorial to Rupert Brooke**, the British poet adopted as the paragon of patriotic youth by Kitchener and later Churchill, despite his socialist and internationalist views. Brooke arrived as a naval officer off the south of the island on April 17, 1915, dying six days later of blood poisoning on a French hospital ship. He's become a local hero despite his limited acquaintance with Skýros, and lies buried in an olive grove above the bay of Trís Boúkes (see p.828).

Just below the Brooke statue, the **archeological museum** (Tues–Sun 8.30am–3pm; €2) has a modest collection from local excavations, especially Palamári (see opposite); highlights include a Geometric-era ceramic rhyton in the form of a Skyrian pony (see p.828) and a vase-rim with eight birds being beset by snakes. Nearby, in an early nineteenth-century mansion built over a bastion in the ancient walls, the private **Manos Faltaïts Museum** (daily 10am–noon & 5.30–8pm/6–9pm in summer; €2 admission, €5 includes guided tour; Ⓦwww.faltaits.gr) is more compelling. It's an Aladdin's cave of curious industrial and household items like a Kavála tobacco press and collapsible furniture, a mocked-up typical Skyrian house interior, traditional costumes of each social class, rare documents including the excommunication of the Greek revolutionaries by Patriarch Grigorios V and Skyrian pottery – covetable examples, by Faltaïts himself, are sold in the gift shop.

Practicalities

The **bus** (2–3 services daily) leaves you by the school, 200m below the main square, beyond which only rogue scooterists drive; other drivers must use the signposted **car park** on the far side of the village. The **post office** and **lone ATM** are each on or near the platía; the most reliable **Internet** café is Mano.com, on the *agorá* (high street). There's no tourist office, but municipal **website** Ⓦwww.skyros.gr is useful. Skyros Travel (Ⓣ22220 91600, Ⓦwww.skyrostravel.com), on the same commercial lane, **rents cars and scooters** trading as Pegasus Rentals (though there are three other outlets for bikes), does excursions and has limited accommodation, but the ferry **boat agency** is across the way (Ⓣ22220 91790). If you arrive by plane (the **airport** is 11km distant), only Pegasus has a booth at arrivals, though competitors like Theseus-Yiannakakis (Ⓣ22220 91459) will bring a car to meet you – otherwise budget €15 for a taxi transfer.

You may be met off the bus with offers of **rooms,** perhaps in a traditional Skyrian house like those of Anna Stergiou (Ⓣ22220 91657) and Maria Mavroyiorgi (Ⓣ22220 91440), both clean, cosy and ❸. The island's plushest hotel, *Nefeli* (Ⓣ22220 91964, Ⓦwww.skyros-nefeli.gr; ❻–❼), on the main road before the square, offers cutting-edge designer rooms in various grades, or traditional studios in the "Petrino" wing, arrayed around a large salt-water pool. Alternatively, a bit further south out of town are the *Atherinis Apartments* (Ⓣ22220 93510, Ⓦwww.simplelifeskyros.com; ❸), a mix of self-catering rooms and larger units in a garden setting, with half-board available.

The platía and the *agorá* lane climbing north from it host a wide choice of *kafenía* and *yirádhika*, though only a few outstanding full-service, all-year **tavernas**. Top of the heap in all senses – it's the highest establishment – is *O Pappous ki Ego* (dinner only), an atmospheric ouzerí in a former pharmacy with a good range of *mezédhes* and quality Greek music on the stereo (but live rebétika Fri/Sat off-season, €5 extra; book on ⓣ22220 93200); specialities include wild mushrooms and cuttlefish in anise sauce. Popular *Maryetis* slightly down the same lane is tops for grilled fish and good bulk wine from Thessaly, though *mayireftá* can be uneven. *To Konaki* ("*Konatsi*" in dialect), just downhill from the platía, is another, slightly cheaper ouzerí, off to a good start under new management in 2007.

Nightlife is bar-based until very late, when the few clubs get going. Besides the obvious, loud, Greek-rock **bars** (such as *Iroön* and *Nostos*) overlooking the platía, further up the *agorá* there's summer-only *Kalypso* (jazz and blues); *Akamatra*, a versatile place with conversational-level music; and *Kalitekhnikon/Artistiko* near *Maryetis*, a veritable sardine tin of a pub, with quality recorded Greek sounds. The most durable summer-only **clubs** are *Skyropoula*, south of Magaziá on the coast road, and Stone further south at Basáles cove.

Magaziá, Mólos, Pouriá and Yirísmata

A direct stairway and a roundabout road descend from the Brooke platía to the small coastal village of **MAGAZIÁ**. From Magaziá, an 800-metre-long sandy beach – rather sullied at the start by an artificial reef offshore – stretches to the adjacent settlement of **MÓLOS**; since the 1990s, though, a real-estate boom between the inland road and the beach has amalgamated the two. Magaziá is livelier, with a better selection of rooms; more scattered Mólos has a good range of studios and better sand.

The narrow lane down to Magaziá beach's south end holds a clutch of **rooms** for rent; best and most helpful of these is ★ *Perigiali* (ⓣ22220 92075, Ⓦwww.perigiali.com; all year), a mix of studios (❺) and well-furnished air-conditioned rooms (❹) with phone, overlooking a large garden where breakfast is offered. Other top choices include spacious *Paliopyrgos Studios* (ⓣ22220 91014; ❹), up on the road between Magaziá and the *kástro*, or bungalow complex *Angela* (ⓣ22220 91764; ❹) near the supermarket in Mólos, just behind the beach.

Local beachfront **tavernas** often compare favourably with those in town. In Magaziá, popular *Stefanos* (April–Oct) is reliable for *mayireftá*, while at the south end of Mólos, *Tsipouradhiko Iy Istories tou Barba* (all year), installed in a restored rural cottage, purveys good grilled seafood and chunky *mezédhes* at slightly bumped-up prices, accompanied by good recorded Greek music. Twenty four-hour *Juicy Beach Bar*, hosting beach volleyball, stands halfway between Magaziá and Mólos.

Beyond Mólos, the beach becomes punctuated by weirdly eroded rock outcrops as you approach **Pouriá**, opposite several offshore islets, one (**Áyios Ermoláos**) serving as the venue for a lively festival on July 25–26. Much of the erosion is man-made, as the **rocks** were **quarried** by the Romans; one squared-off monolith, by the cape with its snack-bar/windmill, shelters a chapel of **Áyios Nikólaos** tucked into a corner. Roads north through Mólos end at **Yirísmata**, a long, sandy if exposed beach with a popular **taverna**, *Stelios* (all year, winter weekends only).

Around the rest of the island

In **Merói**, the first point of interest – heading anticlockwise from Hóra along its mostly paved loop road – is **Palamári** (Mon–Fri 7.30am–2.30pm; free), an early Bronze Age settlement overlooking its sandy harbour **beach**; walkways have been prepared, and much of the landward fortification walls exposed. The closest amenity is an excellent, reasonable **taverna** at the airport turning, ★ *To Perasma* (all year), where half the local air force tucks

Skyrian ponies

Skýros has a race of **native pony**, related to Exmoor or Dartmoor ones. They are thought to be the diminutive steeds depicted in the Parthenon frieze; in legend Achilles went off to fight at Troy mounted on a chestnut specimen. In more recent times they were used for summer threshing; communally owned, they were left to graze wild ten months of the year on Vounó, from where each family in turn rounded up the ponies they needed. Currently only about 150 individuals survive, and the breed is **threatened** by the decline of local agriculture, indifference and cross-breeding; this figure includes about twenty sterile mules fathered by donkeys, who can prevent pure-blood stallions from mating. To be classed as a true Skyrian pony, the animal must be 98–115cm in height, and 130cm maximum from shoulder to tail. The largest concentration of the appealing beasts can be seen at Amanda and Stathis' **Skyrian Horse Project** (Ⓣ22220 92918; daily 11am–1pm & 6.30–8pm), behind the Mólos supermarket. Donations are gratefully accepted as they get no official support for their efforts to maintain a healthy and genetically viable pony population.

into the family's own meat and cheese dishes. West, then north of here – the last 2.5km on track – **Áyios Pétros** is among the most scenic of the remoter beaches, though without facilities and a reef to cross into deeper water. The paved circular route hits the coast again at **Kyrá Panayiá** beach (summer taverna) before continuing to **Atsítsa**, home of the Skyros Centre. It's an attractively pine-fringed bay with a seafood **taverna** (*Andonis*) and a few inland **dhomátia**, but only a small rocky beach. From here, you can either head back to town on a good dirt road through the woods, or carry on along asphalt to **Áyios Fokás,** a poor beach with a good taverna-rooms establishment, *Kali* (Ⓣ693 70 90 848; ③). Roadworks are ongoing between here and deeply indented **Péfkos**, best of the southwest coast bays; there's a **taverna**, *Stamatia*, by the jetty, and simple **rooms** run by Makis Mavromihalis (Ⓣ693 88 18 886; ②) at one end of the long, sandy beach.

South from Hóra and Magaziá, on the coastal bypass road, there's an undeveloped nudist beach, **Papá tó Hoúma**, directly below the *kástro*, though reaching it requires acrobatics as the path down is washed out. Some 4km further, the next consequential beach is 200-metre, sandy **Aspoús**, where roadside facilities include the *Ahillion* **hotel** (Ⓣ22220 93300; all year; ⑤) and an excellent, all-year **taverna**, ★ *Lambros*, grilled fish and chops specialists, with an inviting interior and efficient, polite service. From Aspoús, a minor paved road heads southeast – past **Ahíli** (its beach ruined by a fishing port) and **Fléa** hamlet with its **taverna** *Mouries* (May–Oct & Carnival), serving local lamb and wine under the namesake mulberries – to Kalamítsa beach, a narrow pebble strand. At Kalamítsa there's *O Pappous ke Ego stin Thalassa*, summer annexe of the Hóra premises, with weekend music, and the possibility of continuing into **Vounó**, where the only paved roads lead eventually to military facilities – and Rupert Brooke's grave at **Trís Boúkes**.

Évvia (Euboea)

Looming across a narrow gulf from central Greece, **Évvia** – the second-largest Greek island after Crete – seems more like an extension of the mainland to which it was once joined. At **Halkídha**, the old drawbridge link spans a forty-metre channel, Évvia having been mythically split from Attica and Thessaly by a blow from Poseidon's trident (earthquakes and subsidence being more pedestrian explanations). Besides a newer suspension bridge bypassing Halkídha, there are ferry crossings at six points along its length, and the south of the island is far closer to Athens than it is to the northern part. In midsummer, Évvia can seem merely a beach annexe for Athens and the mainland towns across the Gulf.

Nevertheless, Évvia *is* an island, often a very beautiful one. But it has an idiosyncratic history, and has largely remained out of the mainstream of tourism. A marked **Albanian influence** in the south, and scattered **Frankish** watchtowers across the island, lend a distinctive flavour. The **Ottomans** had a keen appreciation of the island's wealth; their last garrison was not evicted until 1833, hanging on in defiance of the treaty awarding Évvia to the new Greek state. Substantial Turkish communities remained in the northwest half of the island until 1923. Évvia has always been prized for its exceptional **fertility**, producing grain, corn, cotton, kitchen vegetables and livestock. The classical name, Euboea, means "rich in cattle", but nowadays goat and lamb are more common, and highly rated, as is the local retsina (though wine in northern Évvia is flavoured with herbs, not resin).

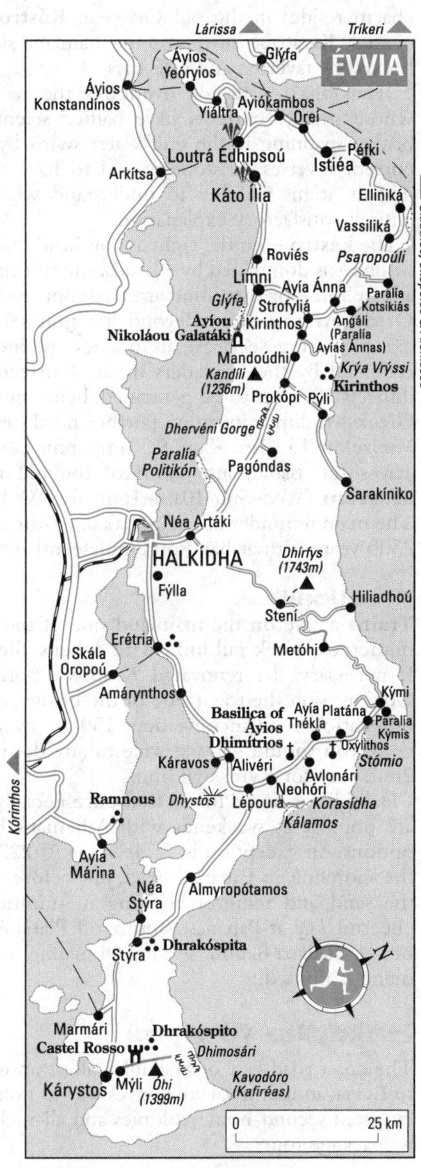

The rolling countryside of the **north** is the most conventionally scenic part of the island, with combines whirling on sloping grain fields between olive groves and pine forest. The **northeast coast** is rugged and sometimes inaccessible, its few sandy beaches surf-pounded and often debris-strewn; the **southwest shore** is gentler and more sheltered, though much disfigured by heavy industry. The **centre** of the island, between Halkídha and the easterly port of Kými, is mountainous and dramatic, while the far **southeast** is more arid and isolated. There are **bus** services to Kárystos in the southeast, and Límni and Loutrá Edhipsoú in the northwest, but explorations are best conducted by car.

Halkídha

Évvia's capital, **HALKÍDHA** (ancient Chalkis) has a population of over 50,000. A shipyard, rail-sidings and cement works hardly make it attractive, but some charm resides in the old Ottoman **Kástro** district, around the seventeenth-century Karababá fortress on the mainland side and along waterfront Voudhoúri, backed by tavernas and café-bars.

Halkídha's waterside overlooks the narrow **Évripos** (Euripus) channel, whose strange currents have baffled scientists for centuries. Below the old bridge spanning it, the gulf water swirls by like a river; every few hours the current reverses. Aristotle is said to have thrown himself into the waters in despair at his inability to understand what was happening; there is still no entirely satisfactory explanation.

The **kástro** – on the right as you head inland along Kótsou from the Euripos bridge – is dominated by a handsome fifteenth-century **mosque** (locked), now a warehouse of Byzantine artefacts; out front is an exceptionally ornate carved **Ottoman fountain**. Beyond lies unusual **Ayía Paraskeví basilica** (shut except during services); its oddness is due to its conversion into a Gothic cathedral by the Crusaders in the fourteenth century. The *kástro*'s residential districts have yet to be gentrified, being in part a shanty town for gypsies and Greek Muslim minorities. Further northeast, the **archeological museum** at Venizélou 13 (Tues–Sun 8.30am–3pm; €2) has a good display of finds from across the island. Just south of the old market, a 2006-opened **Folklore Museum** (Wed–Sun 10am–1pm, also Wed 6–8pm; €3) occupies the old jail. The main reminder of Halkídha's once-thriving Jewish community, dating back 2500 years, is their handsome nineteenth-century **synagogue** at Kótsou 27.

Practicalities

Trains arrive on the mainland side of the channel, beneath Karababá; given numerous, quick rail links with Athens, there's little reason to stay overnight. If necessary, the renovated *Kentrikon* hotel (Ⓣ22210 22375; ❹), at Angéli Govíou 5 on the town side of the bridge, offers reasonable value. The **KTEL** bus station is an inconvenient 1500m away at the east edge of town (take a taxi); you should get a service to any destination as long as you show up by 2pm, later for Kými or Límni.

Halkídha is noted for its seafood, especially **shellfish**; waterfront **restaurants** are popular at weekends with Athenians but not necessarily the best-value options. An exception is *Apanemo* (Ⓣ22210 22614), at the far north end of the shoreline, in Fanári district, just before the lighthouse, which has tables on the sand and requires booking in summer. Inland you might try durable, cheerful *Tsaf* at Papanastasíou 3, off Platía Agorás, or less expensive *O Yiannis*, nearby at Frízi 8, both serving all manner of seafood, though *Yiannis' mezédhes* menu is limited.

Halkídha to Kými

The coast road east of Halkídha offers an exceptionally libellous introduction to Évvia; an industrial zone gives way to nondescript suburb-villages, succeeded by gated second-home colonies and all-inclusive hotel compounds frequented by package tours.

Erétria and Amáranthos

The first substantial town is modern **ERÉTRIA**, a dull resort on a grid plan; for most travellers its main asset is **ferry** service across to Skála Oropoú in Attica. **Ancient Eretria** is more distinguished, though town-centre remains are confined to an **agora** and a **temple of Apollo**. More interesting are the northwest excavations, behind the excellent small **museum** (Tues–Sun 8.30am–3pm; €2), run in collaboration with the Swiss School of Archeology. At the **theatre**, steps from the orchestra descend to an underground vault used for sudden entrances and exits. Beyond the theatre and museum are the **House of Mosaics** and a **gymnasium**. One of the more interesting **hotels** is *Island of Dreams* (Ⓣ22290 61224, Ⓦwww.dreamsisland.com.gr; ❻), comprising bungalows and standard rooms on a landscaped islet linked by causeway to the end of the bay.

AMÁRYNTHOS, 10km further, is a smaller and more pleasant resort with an ample selection of **tavernas**, such as *Ouzeri di Stefano* or *Theodoros* on the waterfront, and *To Limanaki* 300m further west on the shore. Sound **accommodation** options include *Iliaktidhes Hotel Apartments* (Ⓣ22290 37215; all year; ❹), just off the main road, and the low-key, beachfront *Artemis Hotel* (Ⓣ22290 36168, Ⓦwww.artemis-hotel.gr; all year; ❺), with an indoor/outdoor café and Wi-Fi signal.

Beyond Amárynthos an exceptionally bleak landscape, made worse by a 2007 fire and enlivened only by some medieval towers, unfolds past Alivéri to Lépoura, with its strategic fork in the road system.

Lépoura to Kými

Heading north from Lépoura towards Kými, the first potential detour, after 5km at Neohóri, is east to secluded beaches at **Kálamos** (7km) and **Korasídha** (11km); **accommodation** at Kálamos includes the pleasant *To Egeon* (Ⓣ22230 41865; ❸), which has a downstairs **restaurant**.

At **Háni Avlonaríou**, 6km past Neohóri, stands the thirteenth-century **Áyios Dhimítrios basilica**, Évvia's largest and finest (key at the café next door). This region is in fact well endowed with Byzantine chapels. The best one is shed-like **Ayía Thékla**, tucked in a vale below the modern church near the eponymous hamlet; slightly later than Áyios Dhimítrios, its interior fresco fragments depict large-eyed faces.

The inland road passing Ayía Thékla continues to upper **KÝMI**, built on a green ridge overlooking the sea, while Paralía Kýmis, the ferry port, lies 4km below, via a winding road. All buses from Halkídha leave you in the upper town, except for those connecting with Skýros ferries. Just below town, on the harbour-bound road, a **folklore museum** (daily 10am–1pm and 6–8.30pm; €2) houses a vast collection of costumes, rural implements and old photos recording the doings of Kymians both locally and in the US, home to a huge emigrant community. Among them was Dr George Papanikolaou, deviser of the "Pap" cervical smear test, and a statue honours him up on the platía, with its **post office** and **ATM**s. Kými's only **taverna**, just below the museum, is *Tou Hari*.

The coast road forks right north of Háni Avlonaríou, meeting the sea at **Stómio,** a rivermouth beach beside straggly seaside **PLATÁNA** (tavernas). The functional port of **PARALÍA KÝMIS** awaits 3km further; despite the name it has no real beach, and isn't a congenial place to stay, which you shouldn't need to do as there's always a late-afternoon ferry to Skýros. For a lunch **taverna**, head to *Ouzeri Iy Skyros*, 150m north of the jetty with its **ticket agency** (Ⓣ22220 22020).

Southeastern Évvia

So narrow that you sometimes spot the sea on both sides, lightly populated **southeastern Évvia** is often bleak and windswept, geologically resembling Ándhros with its slates and marble. Also like Ándhros, it was settled by Albanian migrants from the early fifteenth century onwards, and **Arvanítika – medieval Albanian** – was long the first language of remoter villages here.

Just southeast of Lépoura, **Lake Dhýstos** has been largely reclaimed as farmland, but **migratory birds** still frequent its shallow marshes – about 7km along the trunk road, a sign points to the observation area. Atop conical Kastrí hill on the east shore are sparse fifth-century-BC ruins of **ancient Dystos** and a subsequent medieval citadel.

With your own transport, it's worth stopping at the north edge of **STÝRA** (35km from Lépoura), where three **dhrakóspita** ("dragon houses") are signposted and reachable by track. So named because only such mythical beings were thought capable of installing the enormous masonry blocks, their origins and purpose remain obscure. One cogent theory suggests that they are sixth-century BC temples built by immigrants or slaves from Asia Minor working in nearby quarries.

The shore annexe of **NÉA STÝRA**, 3.5km downhill, is a Greek-frequented resort, worth knowing about only for its handy ferry connection to Ayía Marína. Much the same is true of **MARMÁRI**, 20km south, except here the link is with Rafína. The road between upper Stýra and Marmári is under (re)construction, slowing progress until 2009.

Kárystos and around

First impressions of **KÁRYSTOS** are of a boring grid (courtesy of an 1843 Bavarian town-planner), ending fairly abruptly to east and west, studded with modern construction. After a short while you'll notice graceful, nineteenth-century Neoclassical buildings in the centre, some endearingly old-fashioned shops and tavernas, and its magnificent setting on a wide bay, with good (if often windy) beaches flanking it. The town feels bigger and livelier than the official population of about three thousand, and it grows on many visitors, who stay longer than intended. Only a fenced-in **Roman heroön** in the bazaar bears out Kárystos' ancient provenance; the oldest obvious structure is the fourteenth-century, waterfront **Boúrtzi** (locked except for special events), all that's left of once-extensive fortifications. Opposite this small Venetian tower, in the Yiokálio Centre, a small but interesting **archeological museum** (Tues–Sun 8.30am–3pm; €2) displays statues, temple carvings and votive objects from the region.

Practicalities

No **ferries** serve Kárystos directly; Marmári, 13km west, acts as its passenger port. There's also no bus shuttle between them – the car-less should arrange to share a taxi. The **KTEL** station is at the west end of Kriezótou, a block in from the water; the **post office** and **ATMs** lie within sight of central, waterfront Platía Amalías. There's no tourist office, but helpful South Evia Tours at Platía Amalías 7 (☎22240 26200) sells ferry tickets, rents cars and bikes, finds lodging and arranges excursions.

There's ever-increasing **accommodation** at outlying beaches and inland, but central hotels are confined to rambling *Galaxy* (☎22240 22600; all year; ③) at the west end of waterfront Kriezótou, a veritable 1970s time capsule with its naugahide sofas, lino floors and floral bath tiles, but friendly and with lobby Wi-Fi signal; or quieter *Karystion* (☎22240 22391, Ⓦwww.karystion.gr;

March–Oct; B&B; ⑤), 150m east of the Boúrtzi, with filling breakfasts, renovated sea-view rooms and direct access to the adjacent beach.

There's far more choice when eating out; central **tavernas** include *Kavo Doro*, in a lane between Kriezótou and parallel Sakhtoúri one block west of the square, for *mayireftá*; or a line of *psistariés* on Theohári Kotsíka, of which *Panouryias* at no. 9 and *Karystaki* at no. 3 are popular. But much the best hereabouts is *To Koutouki* (*Hondhronastos*) at Sakhtoúri 75 (Oct–May), a terrazzo-floored *inomayerío* mustering just six tables laden with bean soup, *lahanodolmádhes*, chops and *fáva*, plus *halvás* on the house. Further afield (May–Oct only), *Ta Kalamia*, at the start of the westerly beach, is a popular lunchtime option, while 2km east at **Káto Aetós**, seaside *To Kyma* is favoured for an evening meal or Sunday lunch. Local bulk **wines** are well worth sampling, especially at the late-August Wine Festival.

Mount Óhi and the Dhimosári Gorge

Just inland from Kárystos, **Mount Óhi** (1399m) is Évvia's third highest peak and the focus of trekking trails of sufficient quality as to attract overseas expeditioneers. Some 3km north, **MÝLI**, a fair-sized village around a spring-fed oasis with a few tavernas, is a natural first stop. Medieval **Castello Rosso (Kokkinókastro)** lies a twenty-minute climb from the main church; inside, the castle is ruinous, except for an Orthodox **chapel** built over the water cistern, but sweeping views make the trip worthwhile.

From Mýli, it's a three-hour-plus **hike** up the bare slopes of Óhi, mostly by a good path shortcutting the road; about forty minutes along are various finished and half-finished cipollino marble **columns**, abandoned almost two thousand years ago. The path reaches an alpine club shelter (springwater outside; ⓣ22240 24414 to get the keys) and another schist-slab **dhrakóspito**, more impressive than the Stýra trio (see opposite), seemingly sprouting from the mountain.

Once over the west shoulder of Óhi to Petrokánalo ridge, you're poised to tackle the one unmissable excursion of southeastern Évvia: the three-hour **traverse of the Dhimosári Gorge**. The descent northeast, mostly in deep shade past various springs and watermills, is on path (often *kalderími*) as far as the farming hamlet of Lenoséi, then track to **Kallianós** village, with another path just before the latter down to a beach. You'll have to arrange a taxi beforehand, or trust to hitching back to Kárystos, as there's no bus.

Northwestern Évvia

At bustling Néa Artáki, 5km north of Halkídha, a side road (daily bus) leads east to **STENÍ**, a village-cum-hill-station at the foot of Mount Dhírfys. Of two **hotels**, the *Steni* (ⓣ22280 51221; ③) – with newer bathrooms and sumptuous common areas – is preferable. Eight **tavernas** specializing in meaty fare line the roadside and two adorn the village-centre platía, where *O Vrahos* is the most atmospheric, with seating under a mulberry. There are track-damaged hiking trails up Dhírfys, Évvia's highest summit, but they can't compare to trekking around Mount Óhi. Of more interest is the very useful, scenic **road link to Kými**, all paved except for 8km just before Metóhi; it's 51km or 95 minutes' drive (follow signposting for Metóhi if starting from Kými).

Beyond Psahná, the main road snakes steeply over a forested ridge and then down through the **Dhervéni Gorge**, gateway to **Évvia's northwest**. **PROKÓPI** just beyond, in a broad wooded upland, is famous for its hideous 1960s pilgrimage **church of St John the Russian**, actually a Ukrainian soldier captured by the Ottomans early in the eighteenth century and taken to central Anatolia, where he died. His mummified body began to promote miracles; the saint's relics were brought here from Cappadocian Prokópi (today Ürgüp) in the 1923 population exchange.

Evvian Prokópi was part of **Ahmétaga**, the Turkish fiefdom bought in 1832 by English Philhellene nobleman Edward Noel, a relative of Lady Byron. His direct descendant Philip Noel-Baker now lives in the manor house of the estate (Ⓣ694 42 02 112, Ⓦwww.candili.gr) overlooking the village, with the tastefully converted outbuildings operating as **accommodation** and a course centre (yoga, ceramics, etc); with space for 25, groups and families may rent the entire premises.

From Mandoúdhi, 8km north of Prokópi, the closest decent – if shortish – **beach** is **Paralía Kírinthos**, better known as **KRÝA VRÝSSI** (accessed from **Kírinthos** hamlet, 3km beyond Mandoúdhi), where a tiny landscaped platía supports seasonal tavernas and cafés. Dutch-run **hotel** *Kirinthos* (Ⓣ22270 23660; ③), some of whose impeccable rooms enjoy sea views, primarily operates as a craft centre.

At **Strofyliá**, 8km beyond Mandoúdhi, the left fork leads west to Límni (see below). The right-hand turning arrives after 7.5km at **AYÍA ÁNNA,** its worthwhile **Folklore Museum** (Wed–Sun 10am–1pm & 5–7pm; €3) well signposted at the southeast edge of the village; displays include exquisite local weavings, rural impedimenta and photographic documentation of festivals which ceased after the 1920s. Most travellers are interested in the turn-off for **Angáli beach**, a long and dark swath of sand 4km below. For **accommodation**, the *Agali Hotel* (Ⓣ22270 97103; ④) is congenial, at the protected north end of the pedestrianized esplanade lined with cafés, bars and tavernas. **Horseriding** is offered by Atio stables (Ⓣ694 52 91 110), hidden in the pines inland.

Towards the northernmost cape of Évvia, the next appealing – if small – beach is **Elliniká**, with a picturesque, church-capped islet offshore; the final approach road has **studios** and a few **tavernas**. Beyond Elliniká, the main road (and bus line) curl southwest towards **PÉFKI**, a seaside resort with multinational clientele now leavening the historical Greek contingent; it straggles 2km along a mediocre beach, behind which are **hotels** such as 2006-renovated *Galini* (Ⓣ22260 41208; all year; ⑤) and more modest *Myrtia* (Ⓣ22260 41202; April–Sept; ④).

The next resort, 14km southwest, **Oreí**, faces the sunset; in a quayside glass case is a fine Hellenistic statue of a bull, recovered from the sea in 1965. Nearby **Néos Pýrgos** beach has a better selection of **rooms** and restaurants, though Oreí sees a regular summer jet-boat bound for Tríkeri and Vólos (see p.349). Some 7km west, **AYIÓKAMBOS** has regular **ferry** connections to Glýfa on the mainland, and proves surprisingly pleasant, with a patch of beach, two or three **tavernas** and **dhomátia**.

Límni and around

Límni, a well-preserved Neoclassical town built from nineteenth-century shipping-based wealth, is the most appealing on Évvia, with congenial beach suburbs just northwest and a remarkable convent nearby. Further along the scenic coast road, Loutrá Edhipsoú is one of Greece's most popular **spa** towns, its thermal springs exploited since antiquity. Both Límni and Loutrá Edhipsoú are termini of separate Halkídha-based KTEL services, though the bus also links them.

Límni

Some 13km southwest of Strofyliá, tile-roofed **LÍMNI** (ancient Elymnia) is a delightful, sheltered port, with magnificent views west to the mainland. The worthwhile **museum** (Mon–Sat 9am–1pm, Sun 10.30am–1pm; €2) has archeological finds, including a late Roman mosaic on the ground floor, and a rich historical/ethnographic collection upstairs: a mocked-up rural kitchen, photos of events and personalities and costumed mannequins.

Buses stop in front of quayside *Tsambanis Kafenio* (the ticket office), one of eight waterfront **cafés** and **bars**; the **post office** and two **ATM**s are found inland. In-town **rooms** and **hotels** can disappoint; a 2007-opened exception, on a calmer junction near the east end of the front, is the heated, air conditioned *Graegos Studios* (Ⓣ22270 31117, Ⓦwww.graegos.com; all year; ❸). Other possibilities lie 2km northwest at **SPIÁDHA**, the hamlet behind the good pebble strand of **Kohýli**, where *Livadhitis Studios* (Ⓣ22270 31640; ❸) has a prime location on a quiet beachfront cul-de-sac; on the inland side of the main road, *Ostria* (Ⓣ22270 32247, Ⓦwww.ostria-apartments.gr; all year; B&B; ❺) is overpriced, though its pool-bar across the road abuts the best stretch of beach. Adjacent is the purpose-built theatre hosting the annual summer **Elymnia Festival**. **KHRÓNIA**, the next village 1km along, has another possibility in *Dennis House* (Ⓣ22270 31787 or 694 52 94 040; all year; ❸), down on the shore, good value for ample parking, sweeping balcony views and large (if rather well-worn) studios. Some 4.5km separate Khrónia from **ROVIÉS**, famous for its olives and a medieval tower but now a busy resort; much the best choice here is unsigned, family-friendly *Eleonas* (Ⓣ22270 71619, Ⓦwww.eleonashotel.com; most of year; ❺), secluded up in its namesake olive ranch – besides tasteful doubles, there's a wing of quad apartments (€170) and an on-site restaurant.

Back in Límni itself, forego obvious central-waterfront **tavernas and ouzerís** in favour of *To Pyrofani* (*Livadhitis*) at the west end, a bit pricey for mains portion sizes but high quality and with big salads and nice touches like sides of sweet cabbage; or at the opposite end, always crowded *To Pikandiko*, a *yirádhiko* with daily specials like *kebáb*, *splinándero* (innards) and *provatína* in addition to the usual fare, with seating indoors and out. Inland favourites include cheap-and-cheerful *Lithostroto* one lane up from the platía, with seafood platters, meat grills and even *patsás*; or local *koultouriárika* entrant *Stous Efta Anemous* (dinner only; closed Tues low season), with generic Mediterranean fare like pizza, pasta with salmon, salads and a few grills served in a garden or (in cooler months) inside by a roaring fire.

Ayíou Nikoláou Galatáki

Nearly 9km south of Límni, **Ayíou Nikoláou Galatáki** (daily winter 8am–noon & 2–5pm, summer 8am–noon & 4–8pm; no photos) perches superbly on the wooded slopes of Mount Kandíli, overlooking the Evvian Gulf. Though much rebuilt since its original Byzantine foundation atop a Poseidon temple, the convent retains a thirteenth-century, anti-pirate tower, and a crypt. One of just six nuns will show you narthex **frescoes** dating from the principal sixteenth-century renovation. Especially vivid, on the right, is the *Entry of the Righteous into Paradise*: the virtuous ascend a perilous ladder to be crowned by angels and received by Christ, while the wicked miss the rungs and fall into the maw of Leviathan. Further to the right is a chapel portraying grisly martyrdoms.

Below Ayíou Nikoláou Galatáki are pebble-and-sand beaches at **Glýfa**, the most secluded on this coast. Several in succession lead up to the very base of Mount Kandíli: some reachable by paths, the last few only by boat. The shore is remarkably clean, considering the number of campers defying prohibitions against the practice; there's a single roadside spring, 800m before the road turns inland to the monastery.

Loutrá Edhipsoú

It's 22km from Roviés to **LOUTRÁ EDHIPSOÚ**, one of Greece's most popular **spa** towns (**ferry** links with Arkítsa). If your wallet doesn't stretch to services at the *Thermae Sylla Spa* (such as a 45min "oriental bath" for €123) – you can bathe **for free** at the adjacent public **beach**, where geothermal water pours into an artificial set of cascades. There are more free, open-air **hot springs** at **Káto Ília**, 8km east, where sulphurous water boils up at 65 degrees on the pebble beach, then channelled at more bearable temperatures into ad hoc pits by shovel-wielding locals.

Numerous seafront **hotels** stand to the right as you leave the ferry port; outside peak season, good deals can be had, and all have some sort of spa facility on site. The Art Deco-Internationalist *Aegli* (ⓣ22260 22215; May–Oct; ④), with a restaurant opposite, is one good choice, while the *Avra* next door (ⓣ22260 22226; ⓦwww.avraspahotel.gr; all year; ⑥), also 1920s-vintage, proves considerably more luxurious, with a historically VIP clientele. The only plusher option is 1897-built, 1998-overhauled *Thermae Sylla* (ⓣ22260 60100, ⓦwww.thermaesylla.gr; all year; ⑧) all the way along the promenade, an elegant French-style pentagonal complex; non-guests can use their 34°C indoor pool for €25. For affordable, relative elegance, try 1908-inaugurated *Istiaia* between the preceding two (ⓣ22260 22309; April to early Nov; ④), with high-ceiling, laminate-floored rooms (if basic baths), and a pleasant ground-floor wine bar. About the best independent **taverna** is *Smpanios* right opposite the ferry dock, specializing in reasonable grilled sardines, the usual *mezédhes* and local rosé wine.

Travel details

Conventional car ferries between the northern Sporades and Vólos run year-round (see p.349 in Chapter 3 for full details). Hydrofoils/catamarans between Vólos or Áyios Konstandínos to the Sporades ply reliably only between late June and early September; again see p.349 for details.

Skiáthos, Skópelos and Alónissos

Long-distance ferries

Skiáthos/Skópelos/Alónissos to: Iráklion, Thessaloníki and select Cyclades – typically Tínos, Mýkonos, Páros, Náxos, Íos and Thíra (1–2 weekly June–Sept on GA Ferries); Áyios Konstandínos (4 weekly June–Sept on Saos Ferries; Lésvos/Límnos and Kavála (1 weekly July & Aug on Saos Ferries).

Flights

Skiáthos to: Athens (April–Oct 1 daily, otherwise 2 weekly; 45min).

Skýros

Local ferries

The car ferry *Achilleas* between Kými (Évvia) and Linariá (Skýros) takes 1hr 45min. Services are twice daily from mid-June to early Sept from Kými (around noon and also early evening), and once daily (late afternoon) the rest of the year; from Linariá summer departures are at mid-morning and mid-afternoon. Download current timetables from ⓦwww.sne.gr. There is a connecting bus service for the later boat out of Kými from Athens' Liossíon 260 terminal.

Flights

Skýros to: Athens (2–3 weekly; 40 min); Thessaloníki (2–3 weekly; 40min).

Évvia

Buses

Athens (Liossíon 260 terminal) to: Halkídha (every 30min 5.30am–9pm; 1hr 15min); Kými (5 daily; 3hr 15min).
Halkídha to: Kárystos (2–3 daily; 3hr); Kými (8 daily; 2hr); Límni (3–4 daily; 2hr); Loutrá Edhipsoú (3–4 daily; 2hr 30min).

Trains

Athens (Laríssis station) to: Halkídha (20 daily 6am–11pm; 1hr 30min).

Ferries

Loutrá Edhipsoú to: Arkítsa (at least hourly mid-June to mid-Sept, every 1–2hr otherwise; 45min; information ⓣ22260 23800/330).
Néa Stýra to: Ayía Marína (5–9 daily; 45min; information ⓣ22240 41533).
Ayiókambos to: Glýfa (11 daily summer, 5 daily winter; 25min; information ⓣ22260 31245).
Marmári to: Rafína (5–6 daily April–Oct, 3–4 Nov–March; 1hr; information ⓣ22240 32341).
Erétria to: Skála Oropoú (June–Sept hourly all day, much less often Oct–May; 30min; information ⓣ22290 62201).
NB: Connecting buses link Athens with Rafína (every 30min; 1hr), Ayía Marína (5–6 daily; 1hr 15min) and Skála Oropoú (hourly; 1hr), using the Mavromatéon terminal, and with Arkítsa and Glýfa from the Liossíon 260 terminal.

12

The Ionian Islands

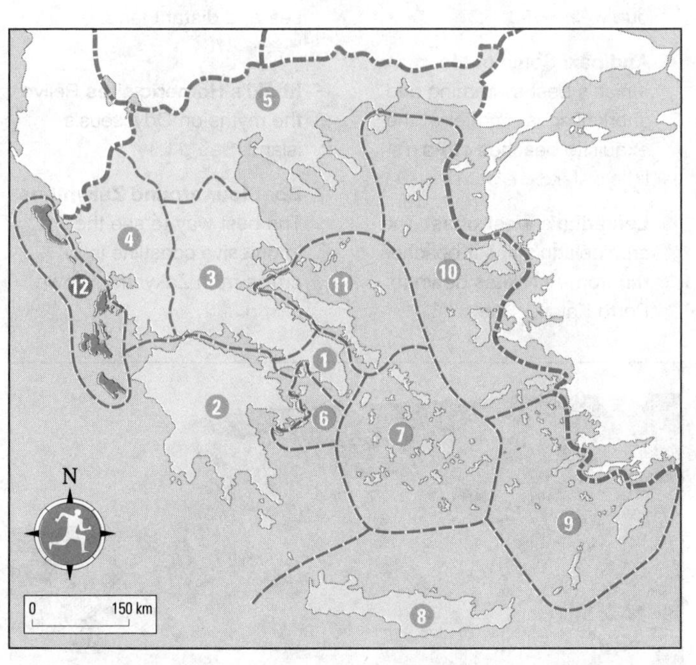

CHAPTER 12

Highlights

* **Kérkyra (Corfu) Town** Venetian fortresses, beautiful churches, fine museums and appealing architecture. See p.843

* **Perouládhes, Corfu** Shaded till early afternoon and backed by sheer vertical cliffs, this beach is an excellent hang-out. See p.853

* **Andípaxi** Some of the Ionian's best swimming and snorkelling is on offer at the exquisite beaches of Paxí's little sister. See p.861

* **Lefkádha's west coast** The archipelago's finest beaches run from Áï Nikítas down to Pórto Katsíki. See p.867

* **Melissáni Cave, Kefaloniá** See dappled sunlight on the water amid rock formations on a boat trip inside this once-enclosed underwater cave. See p.869

* **Mount Énos, Kefaloniá** The highest point in the Ionians has stunning vistas of sea and distant land. See p.876

* **Itháki's Homeric sites** Relive the myths on Odysseus's island. See p.878

* **Boat tour around Zákynthos** The best way to see the impressive coastline is to cruise from Zákynthos Town. See p.883

△ Pórto Katsíki, Lefkádha

12

The Ionian Islands

The six Ionian islands, shepherding their satellites down the west coast of the mainland, float on the haze of the Ionian sea, their green, even lush, silhouettes coming as a shock to those more used to the stark outlines of the Aegean. The fertility of the land is a direct result of the heavy rains that sweep over the archipelago – and especially Corfu – from October to May, so if you visit at this time, come prepared.

The islands were the Homeric realm of Odysseus, centred on Ithaca, (modern Itháki) and here alone of all modern Greek territory (except for Lefkádha) the Ottomans never held sway. After the fall of Byzantium, possession passed to the **Venetians** and the islands became a keystone in Venice's maritime empire from 1386 until its collapse in 1797. Most of the population remained immune to the establishment of Italian as the official language and the arrival of Roman Catholicism, but Venetian influence remains evident in the architecture of the island capitals, despite damage from a series of earthquakes.

On Corfu, the Venetian legacy is mixed with that of the **British**, who imposed a military "protectorate" over the Ionian islands at the close of the Napoleonic Wars, before ceding the archipelago to Greece in 1864. There is, however, no question of the islanders' essential Greekness: the poet Dhionyssios Solomos, author of the national anthem, hailed from the Ionians, as did Nikos Mantzelos, who provided the music, and the first Greek president, Ioannis Kapodhistrias.

Today, **tourism** is the dominating influence, especially on **Corfu** (Kérkyra), which was one of the first Greek islands established on the package-holiday circuit, though it does not get as swamped as in the past. Despite parts of its coastline sporting development to match the Spanish costas, the island is large enough to contain parts as beautiful as anywhere in the group. The southern half of **Zákynthos** (Zante) – which with Corfu has the Ionians' most oversubscribed beaches – has also gone down the same tourist path, but elsewhere the island's

Kýthira and Andikýthira

The islands of **Kýthira** and **Andikýthira**, isolated at the foot of the Peloponnese, are historically part of the Ionian islands. However, at some 200km from the nearest other Ionians, and with no ferry connections to the northerly Ionians, they are most easily reached from **Yíthio** or **Neápoli** and are thus covered in Chapter Two.

Similarly, the island of **Kálamos**, Lefkádha's most distant satellite, is inaccessible from the Ionian group and covered therefore in Chapter Four.

pace and scale of development is a lot less intense. Little **Paxí** lacks the water to support large-scale hotels and has limited facilities tucked into just three villages, meaning it gets totally packed in season, when connections to Corfu and the mainland peak. Perhaps the most rewarding trio for island-hopping are **Kefaloniá**, **Itháki** and **Lefkádha**. The latter is connected to the mainland by a causeway and iron bridge but still has quite a low-key straggle of tourist centres and only two major resorts, despite boasting some excellent beaches, strung along its stunning west coast. Kefaloniá offers a series of "real towns" and a life in large part independent of tourism, as well as a selection of worthwhile attractions. Finally Itháki, Odysseus's rugged capital, is protected from a tourist influx by an absence of sand. The Ionian islands' claims to Homeric significance are manifested in the countless bars, restaurants and streets named after characters in the *Odyssey,* especially the "nimble-witted" hero himself.

Corfu (Kérkyra)

Dangling between the heel of Italy and the west coast of mainland Greece, green, mountainous **Corfu (Kérkyra)** was one of the first Greek islands to attract mass tourism in the 1960s. Indiscriminate exploitation turned parts into eyesores, but much of the island still consists of olive groves, mountain or woodland. The majority of package holidays are based in the most developed resorts, but unspoiled terrain is often only a few minutes' walk away.

Corfu is thought to have been the model for Prospero and Miranda's place of exile in Shakespeare's *The Tempest*, and was certainly known to writers such as Spenser and Milton and – more recently – Edward Lear and Henry Miller, plus Gerald and Lawrence Durrell. Lawrence Durrell's *Prospero's Cell* evokes the island's "delectable landscape", still evident in some of its beaches, among the best in the whole archipelago.

The staggering amount of accommodation (over 5000 places) on the island means that competition keeps prices down even in high season, at least in many resorts outside of Kérkyra Town. Prices at restaurants and in shops also tend to be a little lower than average for the Ionians.

Kérkyra (Corfu) Town

The capital, **KÉRKYRA (CORFU) TOWN**, has been one of the most elegant island capitals in the whole of Greece since it was spruced up for the EU summit in 1994. Although many of its finest buildings were destroyed in World War II, two massive forts, the sixteenth-century church of Áyios Spyrídhon and buildings dating from French and British administrations remain intact. As the island's major port of entry by ferry or plane, Kérkyra Town can get packed in summer.

Arrival, information and services

Ferries and hydrofoils to and from Italy, the mainland (Igoumenítsa and Pátra) and Paxí dock at the New Port (Néo Limáni) west of the Néo Froúrio (New Fort). The Old Port (Paleó Limáni), east of the New Port, is used only for day excursions. Most of the ferry offices are on the main road opposite the New Port; ferries to Italy or Pátra become very busy in summer and booking is advisable. The port authority (domestic ⓣ26610 32655, international ⓣ26610 30481) can advise on services.

The **airport** is 2km south of the city centre. There are no airport buses, although local **blue buses** #5 and #6 can be flagged at the junction where the airport approach drive meets the main road (500m from terminal). It's a thirty-minute walk on flat terrain into town (follow the road running beside the *Hotel Bretagne* opposite the junction for the shortest route or turn right then follow the sea road). **Taxis** charge a whopping €10 for this and can be summoned on ⓣ26610 33811 anywhere in town.

The new **tourist office** (Easter–Oct daily 9am–9pm, winter daily 8am–2pm; ⓣ26610 37520, ⓔeotcorfu@otenet.gr) was due to be operating opposite the town hall at Evangelístrias by 2008. The **post office** is on the corner of Alexándhras and Zafirópoulou (Mon–Fri 7.30am–8pm). Of the town's several **Internet** cafés, the best value is X-plore, N. Lefteriti 4, a couple of blocks north

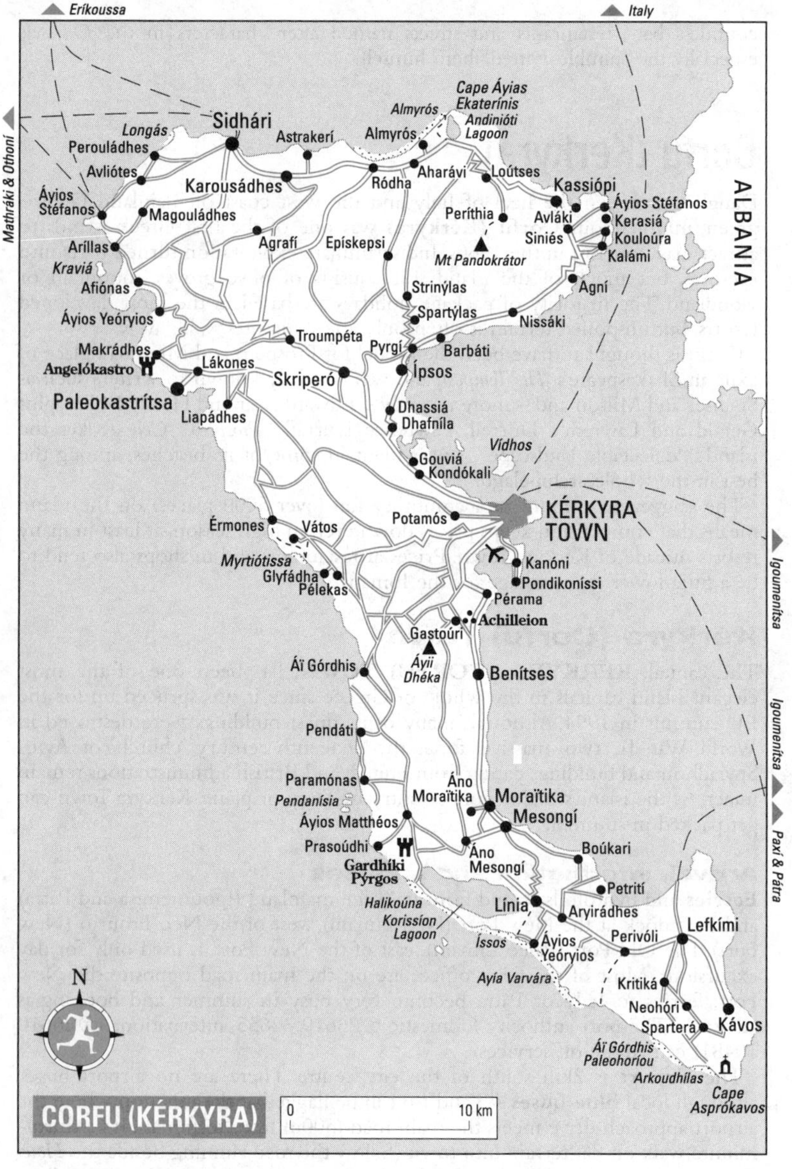

of Platía Saróko (often anglicized to San Rocco, though it is officially named Platía Yeoryíou Theotóki).

Accommodation

Accommodation in Kérkyra Town is fairly busy all year round, and not good value at all when compared to the rest of the island. For rooms you can try the Room Owners' Association at D. Theotóki 2A (Mon–Fri 9am–1.30pm, plus summer Tues, Thurs & Fri 6–8pm; ⓣ26610 26133, ⓔoitkcrf@otenet.gr). Budget travellers might best head straight for the nearest **campsite** at Dhassiá (see p.850).

Astron Dónzelot 15 ⓣ26610 39505, ⓔhotel_astron@hol.gr. Tastefully renovated hotel in the Old Port. Good deals available outside the short peak season. All rooms with fan and optional a/c. ❹

Atlantis Xenofóndos Stratigoú 48 ⓣ26610 35560, ⓦwww.atlantis-hotel-corfu.gr. Large and spacious a/c hotel in the New Port; its functional 1960s ambience rather lacks character. ❺

Bella Venezia Zambéli 4 ⓣ26610 46500, ⓦwwwbellaveneziahotel.com. Smart, yellow Neoclassical building just behind the Cavalieri, with all the Cavalieri's comforts, but cheaper, and an elegant atmosphere. ❺

Cavalieri Kapodhistríou 4 ⓣ26610 39041, ⓦwww.cavalieri-hotel.com. Smart and friendly, with all mod cons, great views and a roof bar open to the public. ❻

Corfu Palace Hotel Leofóros Dhimokratías 2 ⓣ26610 39485, ⓦwww.corfupalace.com. Luxury hotel with pools, landscaped gardens and excellent rooms, each with a marble bath. The smartest place on the island. ❽

Konstantinoupolis Zavitsiánou 1 ⓣ26610 48716, ⓦwww.konstantinoupolis.com.gr. Classy hotel in the Old Port with tasteful decoration and comfortable rooms. Good discounts out of high season. ❺

Royal Kanóni ⓣ26610 39915, ⓕ26610 44690. Splendidly located on a hill 3km south of town and extremely good value. There's a pool and all rooms have balconies with bay views. Buffet breakfast included. ❹

The Town

Kérkyra Town comprises a number of distinct areas. The **Historic Centre**, the area enclosed by the Old Port and the two forts, consists of several smaller districts: **Campiello**, the oldest, sits on the hill above the harbour; **Kofinéta** stretches towards the Spianádha (Esplanade); **Áyii Apóstoli** runs west of the Mitrópolis (orthodox cathedral); while tucked in beside the Néo Froúrio are **Ténedhos** and what remains of the old **Jewish quarter**. These districts form the core of the old town, and their tall, narrow alleys conceal some of Corfu's most beautiful architecture. **Mandoúki**, beyond the Old Port, is the commercial and dormitory area for the port, and is worth exploring as a living quarter of the city, away from the tourism racket. The town's **commercial area** lies inland from the Spianádha, roughly between Yeoryíou Theotóki, Alexándhras and Kapodhistríou streets, with the most shops and boutiques around Voulgaréos, Yeoryíou Theotóki and off Platía Saróko. Tucked below the southern ramparts of the Néo Froúrio is the old morning **market**, which sells fish and farm produce.

The most obvious sights are the forts, the **Paleó Froúrio** and **Néo Froúrio**, whose designations (*paleó* – "old", *néo* – "new") are a little misleading, since what you see of the older structure was begun by the Byzantines in the mid-twelfth century, just a hundred years before the Venetians began work on the newer citadel. They have both been damaged and modified by various occupiers and besiegers, the last contribution being the Neoclassical shrine of **St George**, built by the British in the middle of Paleó Froúrio during the 1840s. Looming above the Old Port, the Néo Froúrio (daily summer 8am–7.30pm, winter closes 3pm; €2) is the more interesting of the two architecturally. The entrance, at the back of the fort, gives onto cellars, dungeons and battlements, with excellent views over the town and bay; there's a small gallery and café at the summit. The Paleó Froúrio (same hours as Néo Froúrio; €4) is not as well preserved and contains some incongruous modern structures, but has an interesting Byzantine museum just inside the gate, and even more stunning views from the central Land Tower. It also hosts daily son et lumière shows.

Just west of the Paleó Froúrio, the **Listón**, an arcaded street built during the French occupation by the architect of the Rue de Rivoli in Paris, and the green

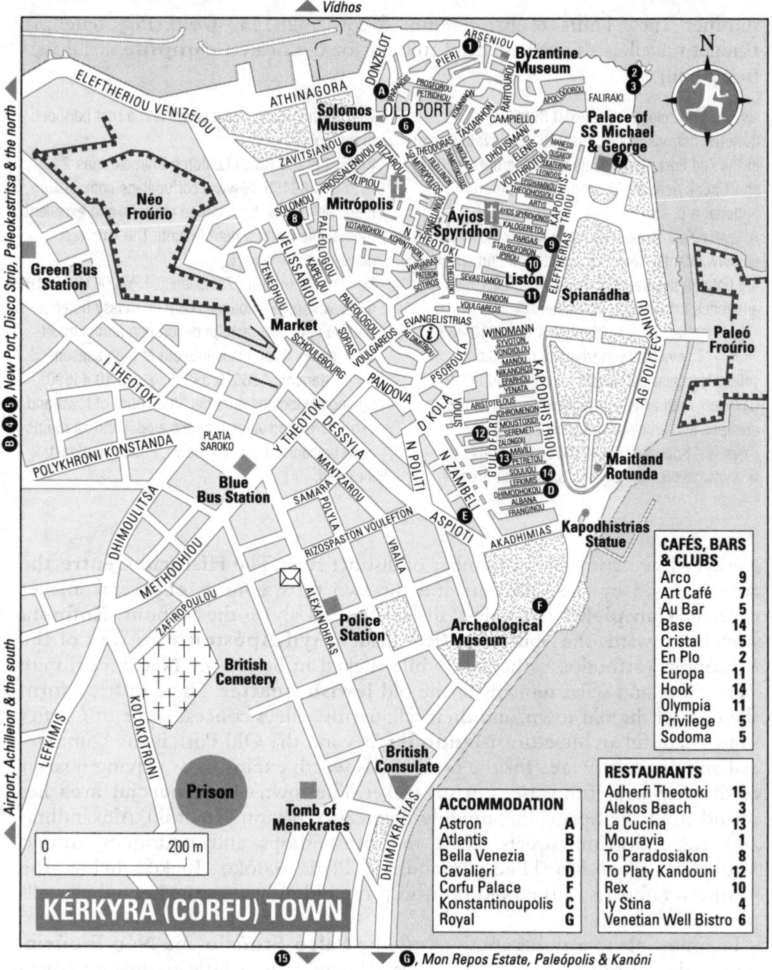

Spianádha (Esplanade) it overlooks, are the focus of town life. The cricket pitch, still in use at the northern end of the Spianádha, is another British legacy, while at the southern end the **Maitland Rotunda** was built to honour the first British High Commissioner of Corfu and the Ionian islands. The neighbouring statue of Ioannis Kapodhistrias celebrates the local hero and statesman (1776–1831) who led the diplomatic efforts for independence and was made Greece's first president in 1827. At the far northern end of the Listón, stands the nineteenth-century **Palace of SS Michael and George**, a solidly British edifice built as the residence of their High Commissioner, and later used as a palace by the Greek monarchy. The former state rooms house the **Asiatic Museum** (Tues–Sun 8am–7.30pm; €3) which is a must for aficionados of Oriental culture. Amassed by Corfiot diplomat Gregorios Manos (1850–1929) and others, it includes Noh theatre masks, woodcuts, wood and brass statuettes, samurai weapons and art works from Thailand, Korea and Tibet. The adjoining

Modern Art Gallery (daily 9am–5pm; €1.50) holds a small collection of contemporary Greek art. It's an interesting diversion, as are the gardens and café-bar secreted behind the palace.

In a nearby backstreet off Arseníou, five minutes from the palace, is the museum dedicated to modern Greece's most famous nineteenth-century poet, **Dhionysios Solomos** (Mon–Sat 9.30am–2pm; €1). Born on Zákynthos, Solomos was author of the poem *Ýmnos stín Eleftheria* (*Hymn to Liberty*), which was to become the Greek national anthem. He studied at Corfu's Ionian Academy, and lived in a house on this site for much of his life.

Up a short flight of steps on Arseníou, the **Byzantine Museum** (Tues–Sun 9am–3pm; €2) is housed in the restored church of the Panayía Andivouniótissa. It houses church frescoes and sculptures and sections of mosaic floors from the ancient site of Paleópolis, just south of Kérkyra Town. There are also some pre-Christian artefacts, and a collection of icons dating from the fifteenth to nineteenth centuries.

A block behind the Listón, down Spyrídhonos, is the sixteenth-century **church of Áyios Spyrídhon** (daily 8am–9pm), whose maroon-domed campanile dominates the town. Here you will find the silver-encrusted coffin of the island's patron saint, **Spyridhon** – Spyros in the diminutive – after whom seemingly half the male population is named. Four times a year (Palm Sunday and the following Sat, Aug 11 and the first Sun in Nov), to the accompaniment of much celebration and feasting, the relics are paraded through the streets of Kérkyra Town. Each of the days commemorates a miraculous deliverance of the island credited to the saint.

The next most important of the town's many churches, the **Mitrópolis** (orthodox cathedral), perched at the top of its own square opposite the Old Port, also houses the remains of a saint, in this case St Theodora, the ninth-century wife of Emperor Theophilos. The building dates from 1577 and the plain exterior conceals a splendid iconostasis, as well as some fine icons, including a fine sixteenth-century image of *Saint George Slaying the Dragon* by the Cretan artist Mihaïl Dhamaskinos, and three dark, atmospheric Italianate paintings.

Kérkyra Town's **Archeological Museum** (Tues–Sun 8.30am–3pm; €3), just south round the coast, is the best in the archipelago. The most impressive exhibit is a massive (17m) gorgon pediment excavated from the Doric temple of Artemis at Paleópolis, just south of Kérkyra Town; this dominates an entire room, the gorgon flanked by panthers and mythical battle scenes. The museum also has fragments of Neolithic weapons and cookware, and coins and pots from the period when the island was a colony of ancient Corinth.

Just south of Platía Saróko and signposted on the corner of Methodhíou and Kolokotróni, the well-maintained **British cemetery** features some elaborate civic and military memorials. It's a quiet green space away from the madness of Saróko and, in spring and early summer, it comes alive with dozens of species of orchids and other exotic blooms.

The outskirts

Each of the following sights on the outskirts of the city is easily seen in a morning or afternoon, and you can conceivably cover several in one day.

Around the bay from the Rotunda and Archeological Museum, tucked behind Mon Repos beach, the area centered around the **Mon Repos** estate (8am–7.30pm; free) contains the most accessible archeological remains on the island, collectively known as **Paleópolis**. Within the estate, thick woodland conceals two **Doric temples**, dedicated to Hera and Poseidon. The Neoclassical **Mon**

Repos villa, built by British High Commissioner Frederic Adam in 1824 and handed over to Greece in 1864, is the birthplace of Britain's Prince Philip and has been converted into the **Paleópolis Museum** (daily 8.30am–7.30pm; €3). As well as various archeological finds from the vicinity, including some fine sculpture, it contains period furniture in situ, and temporary modern art exhibitions. Other remains worth a peek outside the confines of the estate include the **Early Christian Basilica** (Tues–Sun 8.30am–3pm; free) opposite the entrance, the **Temple of Artemis**, a few hundred metres west, and the eleventh-century church of **Áyii Iáson and Sosípater**, back towards the seafront on Náfsikas.

The most famous excursion from Kérkyra Town is to the islets of **Vlahérna** and **Pondikoníssi**, 3km south of town below the hill of Kanóni, named after the single cannon trained out to sea atop it. A dedicated bus (#2) leaves Platía Saróko every half-hour, or it's a pleasant walk of under an hour. Reached by a short causeway, the tiny white convent of Vlahérna is one of the most visited sights on Corfu. Pondikoníssi (Mouse Island) can be reached by a short boat trip from the dock at Vlahérna (€2.50 return). Tufted with greenery and the small chapel of Panayía Vlahernón, Vlahérna is identified in legend with a ship from Odysseus's fleet, petrified by Poseidon in revenge for the blinding of his son Polyphemus. A quieter destination is **Vídhos**, the wooded island visible from the Old Port, reached from there by an hourly shuttle *kaïki* (€1 return, last boat back 1.30am). It makes a particularly pleasant summer evening excursion, when there is live music at the municipal restaurant near the jetty.

Four kilometres further to the south, past the resort sprawl of Pérama, is a rather more bizarre attraction: the **Achilleion** (daily 8am–7pm, winter closes 4pm; €7), a palace built in a unique blend of Teutonic and Neoclassical styles in 1890 by Elizabeth, Empress of Austria. Henry Miller considered it "the worst piece of gimcrackery" that he'd ever laid eyes on and thought it "would make an excellent museum for surrealistic art". The house is predictably grandiose, but the gardens are pleasant to walk around and afford splendid views in all directions. Finally, 6km inland, served by its own dedicated blue bus, is one of Greece's busiest and most high-tech water parks, **Aqualand** (summer daily 10am–6pm; €22).

Eating and drinking

Although there are the inevitable tourist traps, Kérkyra Town offers some excellent, quality restaurants. As usual, be wary of the fish prices at the *psarotavérnes* on the Garítsa seafront.

Adherfi Theotoki M. Athanassíou, Garítsa. By far the best of the several *psarotavérnes* tucked behind the seafront park, this popular family taverna serves excellent *mezédhes*, meat and good-value fish dishes.

Alekos Beach Faliráki jetty. Set in the tiny harbour below the Palace of SS Michael & George, with great views, this place offers simple, mostly grilled meat and fish dishes at good prices.

La Cucina Guildford 15. The town's most authentic Italian food, including fine antipasti, seafood or meat spaghetti dishes at a little above taverna prices.

Mourayia Arseníou 15–17. This unassuming, good-value ouzerí near the Byzantine Museum does a range of tasty *mezédhes*, including sausage and seafood such as mussels and shrimp in exquisite sauces. One of the best establishments in town, with views of passing ferries and Vídhos island.

To Paradosiakon Solomoú 20. Behind the Old Port, this friendly place serves good fresh food, especially home-style oven dishes such as *stifádho* and *kokkinistó*.

To Platy Kandouni Guildford 14. Convivial *mezedhopolío*, serving small but fairly priced portions of dishes like *soupiés* and lamb, which you can wash down with *tsípouro*.

Rex Kapodhistríou 66 (the Listón). Pricey owing to its location, but some of the best food in the centre, especially the delicious oven food, mixing Greek with north European.

Iy Stina Xenofóndos Stratigoú 78, Mandoúki. Quaint traditional taverna one block back from the seafront, serving a fine range of *mezédhes* and main courses, including tasty meat from the oven.

Venetian Well Bistro Platía Kremastí. A well-kept secret, tucked away in a tiny square a few alleys to the south of the cathedral, this is the nearest you're likely to get to Greek nouvelle cuisine, with large portions, and exotica such as Iraqi lamb and Albanian calves' livers in ouzo. Very expensive.

Cafés and nightlife

Kérkyra Town has a plethora of **cafés**, most noticeably lining Listón, the main pedestrianized cruising street. None of these popular establishments is cheap, but among the more reasonable are the *Europa*, *Olympia* or rockier *Arco*, all guaranteed to be packed from morning till late at night. *En Plo* on Faliráki jetty, however, has an unbeatably brilliant and breezy setting and is much quieter, as is the leafy *Art Café*, behind the Palace of SS Michael and George.

The hippest youth **bars** in town are the trio on Kapodhistríou adjacent to the *Cavalieri* hotel, of which *Hook* is the rockiest and *Base* offers a mixture of pop, rock and dance sounds. The rooftop bar at the *Cavalieri* itself is more middle-of-the-road musically but can be heaven at night.

Club action takes place at Corfu's self-proclaimed **disco** strip, a couple of kilometres north of town, past the New Port. This only revs up after midnight, when it becomes classic *kamáki* territory, although in summer many of its

Moving on from Kérkyra (Corfu) Town

Corfu's **bus** service radiates from the capital. There are **two** terminals: the islandwide green bus service is based on Avramíou (also for Athens and Thessaloníki), and the suburban blue bus system, which also serves nearby resorts such as Benítses and Dhassiá, is based in Platía Saróko. Islandwide services stop between 6 and 9pm, suburban ones at between 9 and 10.30pm. Printed English timetables are available for both and can be picked up at the tourist office or the respective terminals.

Frequent **ferries** run throughout the day from the New Port to Igoumenítsa on the mainland, as well as regular services to Pátra and several Italian ports. All the major lines have franchises on the seafront opposite the port: Agoudimos (☎26610 80030, ⓦwww.agoudimos-lines.com), Anek (☎26610 24503, ⓦwww.anek.gr), Fragline (☎26610 38089, ⓦwww.fragline.gr), Minoan (☎26610 25000, ⓦwww.minoan.gr), Superfast (☎26610 32467, ⓦwww.superfast.com), Ventouris (☎26610 21212, ⓦwww.ventouris.gr) and Snav (☎26610 36439, ⓦwww.snav.it). **Hydrofoil** services to Paxí are run by Ionian Cruises through the Petrakis agency (☎26610 25155, ⓦwww.ionian-cruises.com), who also operate tours to Albania, Párga and other Ionian islands at much cheaper rates than the travel agents in the resorts.

In late 2004 the much-fanfared **seaplane** service (ⓦwww.airsealines.com) to Paxí finally got off the ground. There are daily flights to Paxí and varying numbers weekly to Ioánnina, Kefaloniá, Lefkádha, Itháki and Pátra. It actually takes off from Gouviá marina (see overleaf). For further details on all public transportation see "Travel details" p.849.

Increasing numbers of visitors rent their own vehicles to get round the sizeable island. **Cars** can be rented from international agencies at the airport or in town; try Avis, Ethnikís Andístasis 42 (☎26610 24404, airport 26610 42007), behind the new port, Budget, Venizélou 22 (☎26610 28590; airport 26610 44017) or Hertz, Ethnikí Lefkímis (☎26610 38388, airport 26610 35547). Among local companies, Sunrise, Ethnikís Andístasis 14 (☎26610 44325) is reliable and many agents listed throughout the resorts offer competitive deals. **Motorbikes** and **scooters** can be rented from Easy Rider, Venizélou 4 (☎26610 43026) or Atlantis, Xenofóndos Stratigoú 48 (☎26610 40580) both in the New Port.

macho regulars forsake it for the resorts in order to hunt foreign females. The currently "in" joints are *Privelege*, a standard disco, *Au Bar*, a large indoor club which mixes in some Latin, *Sodoma*, which boasts an impressive lightshow, and *Cristal*, whose DJs favour trance and ethnic.

Kérkyra Town's two **cinemas** – the winter Orfeus on the corner of Akadhimías and Aspióti and the open-air summer Phoenix down the side street opposite – both show mostly English-language films.

The northeast and the north coast

The **northeast**, at least beyond the immediate suburbs, is the most typically Greek part of Corfu – it's mountainous, with a rocky coastline chopped into pebbly bays and coves, above wonderfully clear seas. Green **buses** between Kérkyra Town and Kassiópi serve all resorts, along with some blue suburban buses as far as Dhassiá.

Kérkyra Town to Áyios Stéfanos

The landscape just north of Kérkyra Town is an industrial wasteland, and things don't improve much before **DHAFNÍLA** and **DHASSIÁ**, set in adjacent wooded bays with pebbly beaches, around 6km from town. The latter is much larger and contains nearly all the area's facilities, including a trio of **water-sports** enterprises. It is also home to the most respected UK-qualified doctor on the island, Dr John Yannopapas (ⓣ26610 97811), whose surgery is on the main road. Two luxury sister **hotels**, the *Dassia Chandris* and *Corfu Chandris* (both ⓣ26610 97100–3, ⓦwww.chandris.gr; ⓻), dominate the resort, with extensive grounds, pools and beach facilities. Down at the beach the twin *Dassia Beach/Dassia Margarita* (ⓣ26610 93224, ⓦwww.dassiahotels.gr; ⓸) is the best bet. Independent **rooms** can be scarce, the most reliable source being Helga Holiday Services (ⓣ26610 97505, ⓔhelga@otenet.gr). Dhafníla does, however, have the best **campsite** on the island, *Dionysus Camping Village* (ⓣ26610 91417, ⓦwww.dionysuscamping.com); tents are pitched under terraced olive trees. Friendly *Dionysus* also has simple bungalow huts, a pool, shop, bar and restaurant, and Rough Guide readers can get a ten percent discount. Two of the best eateries in Dhassiá are *Nikos*, a pleasant fish taverna on the beach, and *Karydia*, a multi-cuisine restaurant at the north end of the main road.

Just beyond the tasteless party strip of Ýpsos, the hamlet of Pyrgí is the main point of access for the villages and routes leading up to **Mount Pandokrátor** from the south; the road, signposted Spartýlas, is 200km beyond the junction in Pyrgí. A popular base for walkers is the village of **STRINÝLAS**, 16km from Pyrgí. Accommodation is basic but easy to come by: the *Elm Tree* taverna, a long-time favourite with walkers, can direct you to rooms. In summer the main routes are busy, but there are quieter walks taking in the handsome Venetian village of Epískepsi, 5km northwest of Strinýlas – anyone interested in walking the Pandokrátor paths is advised to get the **map** of the mountain by island-based cartographer Stephan Jaskulowski or one of Hilary Whitton-Paipeti's walking books, available locally.

The coast road beyond Ýpsos mounts the slopes of Pandokrátor towards **BARBÁTI**, 4km further on. Here you'll find the best beach on this coast, though its charm has been somewhat diminished recently by the construction of the gargantuan *Riviera Barbati* apartment complex. The beach is a favourite with families, and much **accommodation** is prebooked in advance. However, there are some rooms available on spec – try *Paradise* (ⓣ26630 91320, ⓕ26630 91479; ⓷) or King Travel Agency (ⓣ26630 91719, ⓦwww.corfu-holiday-rentals.com), both up on the main road. For **eating**, *Akrogiali* has good food and great views from a terrace just below the main road, while *Akti Barbati* is a decent beach taverna with a lawn and watersport facilities.

The mountainside becomes steeper and the road higher beyond Barbáti, and the population thins drastically. **NISSÁKI** is a sprawling roadside settlement rather than a village, with a number of coves, the first and last accessible by road, the rest only by track – the furthest dominated by the gigantic and rather soulless *Nissaki Beach Hotel* (Ⓣ26630 91232, Ⓦwww.nissakibeach.gr; ⑤ half-board). There are a couple of shops and a bakery, and a couple of travel and **accommodation agencies**, most notably the Nissaki Holiday Center (Ⓣ26630 91166, Ⓦwww.nissakiholidays), up by the first junction. The white-pebble cove below boasts three very good tavernas – try the quayside *Mitsos*.

Three more pebbly coves no one visiting this coast should miss are Agní, not far past the *Nissaki Beach Hotel*, Kalámi and neighbouring Kouloúra: the first for its trio of fine tavernas, the second for its Durrell connection, the third for its exquisite bay. Crowds flock to **AGNÍ** for the fine eating – *Nikolas* is the oldest taverna and just pips *Toula* and *Agni* for quality; it also runs the peaceful *Nikolas Apartments* (Ⓣ26630 91243, Ⓦwww.agnibay.com; ④). **KALÁMI** is on the way to being spoilt, but the village is still small and you can imagine how it would have looked when Lawrence Durrell lived here on the eve of World War II. The **White House**, where Durrell wrote *Prospero's Cell*, is now split in two: the lower half is an excellent **restaurant**, a cut above the standard *Kalami Beach* at the back of the strand. Meanwhile the posh upper floor of the White House is let through CV Travel (see Basics, p.32), while Kalami Tourist Services (Ⓣ26630 91062, Ⓦwww.kalamits.com) has a range of rooms on its books. Two cocktail bars compete for the happy-hour trade. The tiny harbour of **KOULOÚRA** nearby has managed to keep its charm intact, set at the edge of an unspoilt bay with nothing to distract from the pine trees and *kaïkia*. The fine sole **taverna** here is one of the most idyllic settings for a meal in the whole of Corfu.

The most attractive resort on this stretch of coast, however, 3km down a lane from Siniés on the main road, is **ÁYIOS STÉFANOS** (officially Áyios Stéfanos Sinión to distinguish it from a namesake in northwestern Corfu). Most **accommodation** here is of the upmarket prebooked villa sort, and the village has yet to succumb to any serious development; the only independent rooms and apartments are managed by the *Cochili* taverna (Ⓣ26630 81522; ③). For **food**, as well as the friendly *Kochili* itself, try the *Galini* and *Eucalyptus* tavernas; the latter, over by the village's small beach, is pricier but serves more adventurous fare such as pork with artichokes. The *Damianos* cocktail bar is the main spot to idle with a drink.

Kassiópi to Avliótes: the north coast

Just around the northeastern tip is **KASSIÓPI**, a fishing village that's been transformed into a major party resort. The Roman emperor Tiberius had a villa here, and the village's sixteenth-century Panayía Kassópitra church is said to stand on the site of a temple of Zeus once visited by Nero. Little evidence of Kassiópi's past survives, apart from an abandoned Angevin *kástro* on the headland – most visitors come for the nightlife and the five pebbly beaches. Most nonpackage **accommodation** in Kassiópi is rented through village agencies; the largest, Travel Corner (Ⓣ26630 81220, Ⓦwww.kassiopi.com), with offices near the square and the harbour, is a good place to start. An independent alternative, the great-value *Kastro* restaurant-cum-pension (Ⓣ26630 81045, Ⓔkyrosai@hol.gr; ③), overlooks the beach behind the castle, while *Panayiota*

Apartments (Ⓣ26630 81063, Ⓦwww.panayotakassiopi.com; ❷) offers bargain studios one block behind Kalamíones beach on the west side. The most popular **restaurants** are multi-cuisine tavernas, which supplement a traditional Greek diet with various international dishes, such as *Janis*, by the corner of Kalamíones beach. Other options include the *Porto* fish restaurant at the harbour and *Sze Chuan* Chinese on the main road.

At night, Kassiópi rocks to the cacophony of its **music and video bars**: the flashiest is the gleaming high-tech *Eclipse*, which also shows DVDs, closely followed by *Angelos* and *Visions*, all within falling-over distance of the small town square. The *Passion Club* is the liveliest spot down at the otherwise laid-back harbour. The village is also home to one of the most reliable diving operations, Corfu Divers (Ⓣ26630 81218, Ⓦwww.corfudivers.com), which is partly British-run. You can get online at Photonet.

The coastline west of Kassiópi is overgrown and marshy until you get to little-developed **Almyrós** beach, one of the longest on the island, with only a few apartment buildings and one huge new resort dotted sporadically behind it. For a peaceful stay you could try *Villa Maria* (Ⓣ26630 63359; ❸) and eat at *Avra*, a pleasant taverna further along the beach. The **Andinióti lagoon**, smaller than Korissíon in the south but still a haven for birds and twitchers, backs Cape Ayías Ekaterínis to the east, which marks the northern end of the Corfu Trail (see p.859). The beach extends east all the way to **AHARÁVI**, whose initial impression is not great due to the ugly main road bisecting it. The village proper is tucked on the inland side of the road in a quiet crescent of old tavernas, bars and shops. Aharávi makes a quieter beach alternative to the southerly strands, and should also be considered by those seeking alternative routes up onto **Mount Pandokrátor**. Roads to small hamlets such as Áyios Martínos and Láfki continue onto the mountain, and even a stroll up from the back of Aharávi will find you on the upper slopes in under an hour. Those with children might also appreciate the proximity of **Hydropolis** water park (summer daily 10.30am–6.30pm; €15), just to the east, a less manic version of Aqualand.

Accommodation isn't always easy to find in Arahávi, but a good place to start is Castaway Travel (Ⓣ26630 63541, Ⓦwww.corfucastaway.com). One independent hotel is *Dandolo* (Ⓣ26630 63557, Ⓔdandolo@otenet.gr; ❸), set in lush grounds towards the old village. Of the many **restaurants** on Aharávi's main drag the *Pump House* steak and pasta joint and *To Ellinikon psistariá*-taverna are the best. Meanwhile *Neraïda*, which specializes in meat dishes with mushroom or pepper sauces and trout salad, takes the prizes on the beach and the excellent *Theritas* taverna in the old village wins the authenticity award. The main drag's bar-restaurants tend to get quite rowdy at night, although the light and airy *Captain Aris* is a pleasant watering hole. For a quieter drink, head for the friendly *Iy Paskhalia kafenío* or cosy *Harry's Bar*, both in the old village.

Continuing further west, **RÓDHA** has tipped over into overdevelopment, and can't be wholeheartedly recommended for those in search of a quiet time. Its central crossroads have all the charm of a service station, and the beach is rocky in parts and swampy to the west. "Old Ródha" is a small warren of alleys between the main road and the seafront, where you'll find the best **restaurants** and **bars**. Sunriders good-rate motorbike rental (Ⓣ26630 63626) and Costas horse-riding (Ⓣ694 41 60 011; €20 for 2hr) are based here. Several kilometres inland from Ródha, just east of Agrafí, the relatively undiscovered *Angonari mezedhopolío* serves an excellent range of dishes and great barrelled wine in a relaxed garden with subtle live music.

The next notable resort, **SIDHÁRI**, is constantly expanding and totally dominated by British-package tourists; its small but pretty town square, with a bandstand set in a small garden, is lost in a welter of bars, shops and joints. The beach is sandy but not terribly clean, and many people tend to head just west to the curious coves, walled by wind-carved sandstone cliffs, around the vaunted Canal d'Amour. The biggest accommodation agency is run by young tycoon Philip Vlasseros, whose Vlasseros Travel (Ⓣ26630 95695, Ⓕ26630 95969) also handles car rental, horse-riding and excursions, including day-trips to the Dhiapóndia islands (see below). Sidhári's **campsite**, *Dolphin Camping* (Ⓣ26630 31846), is over 1km inland from the junction at the western end of town. Most **restaurants** are pitched at those looking for a great night out rather than a quiet meal in a taverna. The best value is to be found at *Bournis,* which also does Mexican, or at *Kavvadias*, on the eastern stretch of beach. Asian cuisine, such as the Indian food at *Kohenoor* or Chinese at *Hong Kong*, and cheap full-on English breakfasts are also readily available. There are no quiet bars in Sidhári, and several **nightclubs** vie for late custom, such as *IQ*, *Mojo* and *Ice Club*. Sidhári also has its own waterpark with free entry, a good place to keep the kids happy.

The Sidhári bus usually continues to **AVLIÓTES**, a handsome hill town with the odd *kafeníο* and tavernas but few concessions to tourism. The town is noteworthy for two reasons: its accessibility to quiet **Perouládhes** in the very northwest and **Áyios Stéfanos** (see p.855) to the southeast, both only a few kilometres away. Stunning **Longás beach**, bordered by vertical reddish layer-cake cliffs that make for shady mornings, lies below Perouládhes. You can stay 200m back from the beach at *Logas Beach Studios* (Ⓣ26630 95412, Ⓔgiorkou@mailbox.gr; ❸) or enjoy a splendid sunset dinner at the clifftop *Panorama* taverna.

Corfu's satellite islands

Only three of Corfu's quintet of **Dhiapóndia islands**, scattered up to 20km off the northwest coast are inhabited: **Eríkoussa**, **Othoní** and **Mathráki**. Some travel agencies in the northern resorts offer **day-trips** for sunbathing on Eríkoussa only, while a trip taking in all three islands from Sidhári or Áyios Stéfanos is excellent value. You can also travel independently between the islands on regular *kaïkia*. The thrice-weekly **ferry** from Kérkyra Town is the least efficient way to get there. Each of the islands supports a tiny year-round community but only really comes alive in summer.

Flattish **ERÍKOUSSA** is the sandiest and most visited of the trio. There is an excellent golden sandy beach right by the harbour and quieter **Bragíni** beach, reached by a path across the wooded island interior. The island's cult following keeps its one **hotel**, the *Erikousa* (Ⓣ26630 71110, Ⓦwww.hotelerikousa.gr; ❹), busy throughout the season; the hotel also boasts the only bona fide taverna. **OTHONÍ** is the largestof the islands and has a handful of places to stay and eat in its port, **Ámmos**, which has two pebbly beaches. The sizeable *Hotel Calypso* (Ⓣ26630 72162, Ⓕ26630 71578; ❸), 200m east of the jetty, has relieved pressure on **accommodation**, while the one smart **restaurant**, *La Locanda dei Sogni* also has **rooms** (Ⓣ26630 71640; ❸). Two tavernas, *New York* and tiny *Lakis*, offer decent but fairly limited menus. The village of **Horió** in the island's centre and sandy but deserted **Fýki Bay** are worth visiting if you stay. Hilly, densely forested and with long empty **Portéllo beach**, beautiful **MATHRÁKI** has the fewest inhabitants of the three islands. However, the island is gradually gearing up towards visitors, and locals Tassos Kassimis (Ⓣ26630 71700; ❷) and Khristos Aryiros (Ⓣ26630 71652; ❸) rent **rooms** and **studios** on Portéllo beach. At the harbour, **Plákes**, the *Port Centre* restaurant specializes in freshly caught fish.

Paleokastrítsa and the northwest coast

The northwest part of Corfu conceals some of the island's most dramatic coastal scenery, the violent interior mountainscapes jutting out of the verdant countryside. The area's honeypot attraction is **Paleokastrítsa**, the single most picturesque resort on Corfu, which suffers from its popularity. Further north, the densely olive-clad hills conceal better, sandier beaches, such as **Áyios Yeóryios** and **Áyios Stéfanos**. Public **transport** all along the west coast is difficult: virtually all buses ply routes from Kérkyra Town to single destinations, and rarely link resorts.

Paleokastrítsa

PALEOKASTRÍTSA, a small village surrounded by dramatic hills and cliffs, has been identified as the Homeric city of Scheria, where Odysseus was washed ashore and escorted by Nausicaa to the palace of her father Alkinous, king of the Phaeacians. It's a stunning location, as you would expect, though one that's long been engulfed by tourism. The focal point of the village is the car park on the seafront, which backs onto the largest and least attractive of three **beaches**, home to sea taxis and *kaïkia*. The second beach, to the right, is stony with clear water, and the best of the three is a small unspoilt strand reached along the path by the *Astakos Taverna*. Protected by cliffs, it's undeveloped apart from the German-run Korfu-Diving Centre (ⓣ26630 41604) at the end of the cove. From the first beach you can get a **boat trip** to some nearby seawater caves, known as the "blue grottoes" (€2–3 for a half-hour trip), which is worth taking for the spectacular coastal views. Boats also serve as a taxi service to three neighbouring beaches, Áyia Triánda, Palatákia and Alípa, which all have snack-bars.

On the rocky bluff above the village, the **Theotókou monastery** (7am–1pm & 3–8pm; free, donations welcome) was probably established in the thirteenth century. It has a museum, resplendent with icons, jewelled bibles and other impedimenta of Greek Orthodox ritual, though the highlight is the gardens, with spectacular coastal views. Paleokastrítsa's ruined castle, the **Angelókastro**, is around 6km up the coast but was closed for renovations at the time of writing; only approachable by path from the hamlet of Kríni, it has stunning, almost circular views of the surrounding sea and land. For a drink or snack with tremendous views on the way up, it's worth stopping at the excellent *O Boulis* taverna in Lákones or the *Bella Vista* or *Golden Fox* tavernas, between there and Makrádhes.

Accommodation is not too hard to find but sprawls a long way back from central Paleokastrítsa, often leaving quite a walk to the beach. A good **hotel** is the family-run *Odysseus* (ⓣ26630 41209, ⓦwww.odysseushotel.gr; half-board ④), on the road into town. Along the first turning back from the centre on the north side of the main road, the friendly family-run *Villa Korina* (ⓣ26630 44064; ②) has great value **rooms**, as does the *Dolphin Snackbar* (ⓣ26630 41035; ②), further back above Alípa beach. Michalas Tourist Bureau (ⓣ26630 41113, ⓔmichalastravel @ker.forthnet.gr) is another source, as well as offering all the usual services. *Paleokastritsa Camping* (ⓣ26630 41204, ⓕ26630 41104) is just off the main road, almost a half-hour walk from the centre. There isn't a huge choice of **restaurants** in the centre of Paleokastrítsa. The *Astakos Taverna* and *Corner Grill* are two traditional places, while the seafront *Smurfs* has a good seafood menu despite the dreadful name. Also recommended is the very smart *Vrahos*, which offers pricey fish and some unusual dishes like artichokes. **Nightlife** hangouts include the restaurant-bars in the centre, and those straggling back up the hill, such as the relaxing *Petrino* bar.

Áyios Yeóryios to Áyios Stéfanos

Like many of the west-coast resorts, **ÁYIOS YEÓRYIOS**, 6km north of Paleokastrítsa, isn't actually based around a village, though it is sometimes referred to as Áyios Yeóryios Pagón after the inland village of Payí to avoid confusion with its southern namesake. The resort has developed in response to the popularity of the large sandy bay, and it's a major **windsurfing** centre, busy even in low season. Contrary to the general trend, more **accommodation** is now block-booked here than in the past but independent rooms are available in the cute walled-garden complex of Kóstas Bardhís (ⓣ26630 96219; ❷), towards the north end of the beach, and at the Arista supermarket (ⓣ26630 96350; ❸) or *Studio Eleana* (ⓣ & ⓕ26630 96366; ❸), both behind the central section of beach. The *San George* campsite (ⓣ26630 51759) is nearly 1km back from the beach towards Kavvadhádhes. *To Vrahos* at the northern end and *Spiros* halfway along are among the better **restaurants**, both serving Greek and international cuisine, while gaily-painted *Ostrako* is unbeatable for seafood in the far south. Nearby *Noa Noa* is one of the liveliest nightspots.

On the way north towards Áyios Stéfanos, the pleasant sandy beach of **Aríllas** has given rise to gradual development, including several **tavernas** – try *Kostas on the Beach* or the *Brouklis psistariá*, 200m back inland. **Accommodation** can be arranged through Arillas Travel (ⓣ26630 51280, ⓦwww.arillastravel.gr), which is very friendly and has a couple of quality hotels on its books, or there is the smart B&B *Akti Arilla* hotel (ⓣ26630 51201, ⓔaktiaril@otenet.gr; ❹).

The northernmost of the west coast's resorts, **ÁYIOS STÉFANOS** is low-key, popular with families and a quiet base from which to explore the northwest and the Dhiapóndia islands (see p.853), visible on the horizon. Day-trips to these run several times a week in season (€15–20 per person), as well as cheaper passenger services (€8–10 return) most days on the Aspiotis lines *kaïki*. Áyios Stéfanos's oldest **hotel**, the *Nafsika* (ⓣ26630 51051, ⓦwww.nafsikahotel.com; ❸), has a large restaurant, a favourite with villagers, and gardens with a pool and bar. Also behind the main southern beach is the great-value *Hotel San Stefano* (ⓣ26630 51053, ⓕ26630 51202; ❷), while the *Restaurant Evinos* (ⓣ & ⓕ26630 51766; ❸) has small apartments above the northern end of the village. For those on a budget, Peli and Maria's gift shop offers bargain **rooms** (ⓣ26630 51424, ⓦwww.pelimaria.gr; ❷) and a number of travel agencies handle accommodation, among them San Stefanos (ⓣ26630 51910, ⓦwww.san-stefano.gr; ❷) in the centre. Besides the above-mentioned establishments, good options for **eating** include the *Waves* taverna above the beach, while *O Manthos* serves Corfiot specialities such as *sofríto* and *pastitsádha*. For **nightlife**, lively *Condor* and more laid-back *Summer Dreams* stand out among the handful of music bars.

Central and southern Corfu

Two natural features divide the centre and south of Corfu. The first is the **plain of Rópa**, whose fertile landscape backs on to some of the best beaches on the west coast, such as delightful **Myrtiótissa**. Settlements and development stop a little to the south of Paleokastrítsa and only resume around **Érmones** and **Pélekas** – a quick bus ride across the island from Kérkyra Town. Down to the south, a second dividing point is the **Korissíon lagoon**, the sandy plains and dunes that skirt this natural feature being great places for botanists and ornithologists. Beyond, a single road trails the interior, with sporadic side roads to resorts on either coast. The landscape here is flat, an undistinguished backdrop for a series of increasingly developed beaches and, in the far south, **Kávos**, Corfu's big youth resort.

Érmones to the Korissíon lagoon: the west coast

ÉRMONES, around 15km south of Paleokastrítsa by road, is one of the busiest resorts on the island, its lush green bay backed by the mountains above the Rópa River. The resort is dominated by the luxury *Ermones Beach* **hotel** (Ⓣ26610 94241, Ⓦwww.sunmarotel.com; ❼), which provides guests with obligatory full board and a funicular railway down to the beach. Of the two mid-range hotels on the other side of the river, the *Philoxenia* (Ⓣ26610 94091, Ⓦwww.hotelphiloxenia.gr; ❹) is better value, while cheaper rooms can be found at *Georgio's Villas* (Ⓣ26610 94950; ❷), further back on the hillside above the road that leads to the beach. Both the *Maria* and *Nafsica* **tavernas** above the beach provide good, filling *mezédhes* and main dishes. Just inland is the Corfu Golf and Country Club (Ⓣ26610 94220), the only golf club in the archipelago, and said to be one of the finest in the Mediterranean.

Far preferable to the gravelly sand of Érmones, are the sandy beaches just south of the resort at Myrtiótissa and Glyfádha. In *Prospero's Cell*, Lawrence Durrell described **Myrtiótissa** as "perhaps the loveliest beach in the world"; for years a well-guarded secret, it is now a firm favourite, especially with nudists, busy enough to support three seasonal *kantínes*, so it's at its best well out of high season. Above the north end of beach is the tiny, whitewashed **Myrtiótissa monastery**, dedicated to Our Lady of the Myrtles. There are a few **rooms**, just off the approach road at the friendly *Myrtia* taverna (Ⓣ26610 94113, Ⓔsks_mirtia@hotmail.com; ❸), which serves tasty home-style cooking.

The sandy bay of **GLYFÁDHA**, walled in by cliffs, is dominated by the huge and overpriced *Louis Grand* hotel. Far more reasonable **accommodation** is available at the extreme north end of the beach at two good adjacent tavernas; *Glyfada Beach* (Ⓣ26610 94258, Ⓕ26610 94257; ❷) and *Glyfada* (Ⓣ26610 94224; ❶), whose simple rooms are a real bargain. Nightlife centres on two music bars, the *Kikiriko* and *Aloha*, which pump out heavy-duty sounds all day, as the beach is popular with young Greek and Italian trendies.

PÉLEKAS, inland and 2km south of Glyfádha, has long been popular for its views – the **Kaiser's Throne** viewing tower, just above the town, was Wilhelm II's favourite spot on the island. As the only inland resort, it has some good **room** deals, including the friendly *Pension Paradise* (Ⓣ26610 94530; ❶), on the way in from Vátos, the *Alexandros* pension (Ⓣ26610 94215, Ⓦwww.alexandrospelekas.com; ❷) and *Thomas* (Ⓣ26610 94441; ❸), both on the way towards Kaiser's Throne. Among the **tavernas**, *Alexandros*, *Pink Panther* and *Roula's Grill House*, the latter especially good for simple succulent meat, are all highly recommended. Colourful *Zanzibar* is a pleasant spot for a drink by the diminutive square, whose Odhiyítria church, renovated in 1884, is worth a peek.

Around 7km south of Pélekas, **ÁÏ GÓRDHIS** is one of the key play beaches on the island, largely because of the activities organized by the startling **Pink Palace** complex (Ⓣ26610 53103, Ⓦwww.thepinkpalace.com), which dominates the resort. It has pools, games courts, Internet access, restaurants, a shop and a disco. Backpackers cram into communal rooms for up to ten (smaller rooms and singles are also available) for €18–26 a night, including breakfast and an evening buffet. Other accommodation is available on the beach, notably at *Michalis Place* taverna (Ⓣ26610 53041; ❸); the neighbouring *Alex in the Garden* **restaurant** is also a favourite, as is the beachside *Alobar*.

Inland from the resort is the south's largest prominence, the humpback of **Áyii Dhéka** (576m), reached by path from the hamlet of Áno Garoúna; it is the island's second-largest mountain after Pandokrátor. The lower slopes are wooded, and it's possible to glimpse buzzards wheeling on thermals over the higher slopes. The monks at the tiny monastery just below the summit lovingly tend a bountiful orchard.

Under 10km south by road from Áï Górdhis, the inland town of **Áyios Matthéos**, is still chiefly an agricultural centre, although a number of *kafenía* and tavernas offer a warm if slightly bemused welcome to passers-by. On the other side of Mount Prasoúdhi from here, 2km by road, is the **Gardhíki Pýrgos**, the ruins of a thirteenth-century castle built in this unlikely lowland setting by the despots of Epirus. The road continues on to the northernmost tip of splendid and deserted **Halikoúna** beach on the sea edge of the **Korissíon lagoon**, which, if you don't have your own transport, is most easily reached by walking from the village of Línia (on the Kávos bus route) via **Íssos** beach (see p.858). Over 5km long and 1km wide at its centre, Korissíon is home to turtles, tortoises, lizards and numerous indigenous and migratory birds. For one of the quietest stays on the island, try *Marin Christel Apartments* (Ⓣ26610 75947; ❸), just north of Halikoúna beach, or *Logara Apartments* (Ⓣ26610 76477; ❹), 500m inland. *Spiros* has the slightly better selection of the two tavernas on this stretch of road. The beach is an idyllic spot for rough camping but only a seasonal canteen operates in the immediate vicinity.

Benítses to Petrití: the east coast

South of Kérkyra Town, there's nothing to recommend before **BENÍTSES**, a once-notorious bonking-and-boozing resort, whose old town at the north end has long since reverted to a quiet bougainvillea-splashed Greek village. There are a couple of minor attractions, namely the modest ruins of a Roman bathhouse at the back of the village and the impressive **Shell Museum** (March–Oct daily 9am–7pm, closes later in high season; €4). **Rooms** are plentiful, as visitor numbers have never returned to heyday levels: try Best Travel (Ⓣ26610 72037, Ⓕ26610 71036). Among **hotels** offering good deals, the central *Hotel Potamaki* (Ⓣ26610 71140, Ⓦwww.potamakibeachhotel.gr; ❹), is a gigantic 1960s throwback, while smaller modern *Benitses Arches* (Ⓣ26610 72113; ❷) offers quiet rooms set back from the main road. Benítses has its fair share of decent **tavernas**, notably English-run *Hawaii* and the Corfiot specialist *O Paxinos*, as well as the plush Italian *Avra*. Lively **bars** such as *Lacey's* and *Sunshine* are concentrated behind the crescent-shaped park that separates the old village from the coast road, while larger **nightclubs** like *Casanovas 2000* or *Stadium* are at the southern end of the main strip.

MORAÏTIKA's main street is an ugly strip of bars, restaurants and shops, but its beach is the best between Kérkyra Town and Kávos. Confusingly, the biggest touristic landmark in the area, the *Messonghi Beach* **hotel** complex (Ⓣ26610 75830, Ⓦwww.messonghibeach.gr; ❺), set in lush landscaped gardens and home to the Nautilus diving centre (daily 5–7pm; Ⓣ26610 83295), actually lies just within the limits of Moraïtika, which is separated from neighbouring Mesongí by the Mesongís River. Other reasonable beachside **hotels** include the *Margarita Beach* (Ⓣ26610 75267, Ⓦwww.corfu-hotel-margarita.com; ❹), while Budget Ways Travel (Ⓣ26610 76768, Ⓕ26610 76769; ❸) offers a range of **rooms**. Much of the main drag is dominated by souvenir shops and minimarkets, as well as a range of **bars**, including 1939 vintage *Charlie's* and the lively *Very Coco* nightclub. The *Rose Garden* **restaurant** is just off the main road and has a fair mix of vegetarian, Greek and international food, as does the beach restaurant *Kavouria*, where the seafood and special salads are excellent The village proper, **ÁNO MORAÏTIKA**, is signposted a few minutes' hike up the steep lanes inland, and is virtually unspoilt. Its tiny houses and alleys are practically drowning in bougainvillea, among which you'll find two **tavernas**:

the *Village Taverna* and the *Bella Vista*; the latter has a basic menu but justifies its name with a lovely garden, sea views and breezes.

Commencing barely a hundred metres on from the Moraïtika seafront, **MESONGÍ** continues this stretch of package-tour-oriented coast but is noticeably quieter and has a range of **accommodation** deals. Both the *Hotel Gemini* (Ⓣ26610 75221, Ⓦgeminihotel.gr; ④) and far better value, British-run *Pantheon Hall* (Ⓣ26610 75802, Ⓦwww.corfu-summer.com; ②) have pools and gardens, and en-suite rooms with balconies. Mesongí has a number of good **restaurants**: notably the beachside *Dionysos* taverna, which offers Corfiot dishes and its own barrel wine, and *Marilena,* back in the village. Try the *Oasis* pub for a relaxed drink.

The quiet road from Mesongí to Boúkari follows the seashore for about 3km, often only a few feet above it. **BOÚKARI** itself comprises little more than a handful of tavernas, a shop and a few small, family-run hotels; the *Boukari Beach,* 1km north of the tiny harbour, is the best of the **tavernas**, offering fresh fish and live lobster. The very friendly Vlahopoulos family who run the taverna also offer rooms and own two small hotels nearby, the fully renovated *Penelopi* and *Villa Alexandra* (Ⓣ26620 51269, Ⓦwww.boukaribeach.com; ③). Boúkari is out of the way, but an idyllic little strip of unspoilt coast for anyone fleeing the crowds elsewhere on the island, and inland from here is the unspoiled wooded region around **Aryirádhes**, rarely visited by tourists and a perfect place for quiet walks.

Back on the coastline, the village of **PETRITÍ**, only created in the 1970s when geologists discovered the hill village of Korakádhes was sliding downhill, fronts onto a small but busy harbour. It is mercifully free of noise and commerce, with a beach of rock, mud and sand, set among low olive-covered hills. The *Pension Egrypos* (Ⓣ26620 51949, Ⓦwww.egrypos.gr; ③) has B&B **rooms** and a restaurant. At the harbour, a few **tavernas** serve the trickle of sea traffic: the smart *Limnopoula* and the more basic but friendly *Leonidas* and *Stamatis* are all fine. Barely 2km south of Petrití, the rocky coves of **Nótos** beach are little visited and conceal a wonderful and friendly place to stay in the shape of half-board *Panorama Apartments* (Ⓣ26620 51707, Ⓦwww.panoramacorfu.gr; ③), which also has a fine shady restaurant.

Southern Corfu

Across the island on the west coast, the beach at **Áyios Yeóryios** spreads as far south as Ayía Varvára, and north to encircle the edge of the Korissíon lagoon, around 12km of uninterrupted sand. The resort itself, however, is an unprepossessing seafront sprawl and tourism here has the most mercenary air of anywhere on the island so it is best avoided. Ten minutes' walk north, however, **ÍSSOS** is a far better and quieter beach; the dunes north of Íssos towards the Korissíon lagoon are an unofficial nude bathing area. Facilities around Íssos are sparse: one **taverna**, the *Rousellis Grill*, a few hundred metres from the beach on the lane leading to Línia on the main road; the smart new yellow-and-maroon *Vicky's Apartments* (Ⓣ26620 53161; ④), above a bend in the lane; and the *Friends* snack-bar in Línia itself. The highly professional CWC **windsurfing school** (Ⓦwww.corfu-windsurfing-centre.com) operates on the beach.

Anyone interested in how a Greek town works away from the bustle of tourism shouldn't miss **LEFKÍMI**, towards the island's southern tip. The second-largest settlement after Kérkyra Town, it's the administrative centre for the south of the island as well as the alternative ferry port to or from Igoumenítsa, with half a dozen daily crossings in summer. The town has some fine architecture, including several striking churches: **Áyii Anáryiri** with a huge double belfry, **Áyios Theódhoros**, on a mound above a small square, and **Áyios Arsénios**, with a vast orange dome that can be seen from afar. There are some **rooms** at the *Cheeky Face* taverna (Ⓣ26620 22627; ①), by the bridge over the canal that carries the Himáros River through the lower part of town, and even cheaper ones at *Maria Madalena* apartments (Ⓣ26620 22386; ①) further up. For **food** look no further than the home-cooking at the tiny *Maria estiatório*, on the opposite side of the canal to *Cheeky Face*. A few local **bars** are tucked in corners of the upper town, such as *Mersedes* and *Esperos*, which has a leafy garden, or you can sip a coffee at trendy new *Central* café.

There are no ambiguities in **KÁVOS**, 6km south of Lefkími: either you like 24-hour drinking, clubbing, bungee-jumping, go-karts, video bars named after British sitcoms and chips with almost everything, or you should avoid the resort altogether. Kávos stretches over 2km of decent sandy beach, with watersports galore. This is still Club 18–30 territory, although numbers have dropped of late so unbelievable bargains can be had; look around for signs offering **rooms** for as little as €10 per night or ask at Pandis Travel (Ⓣ26620 61400, Ⓔpandisnikos@hotmail.com). The nearest to genuine Greek **food** you'll find is at the *Two Brothers psistariá*, at the south end of town. Fast food and British-style Asian cuisine are much easier to come by. *Future* is the most happening **club**, with imported north European DJs, followed by *42nd St* and *Sex*. Favourite **bars** include *Rolling Stone*, *The London Pub*, *The Face*, *SOS* and *Bonkers*, and at night the main drag is one unbroken mass of young revellers.

Beyond the limits of Kávos, where few visitors stray, a path leaving the road south to the hamlet of Sparterá heads through unspoilt countryside; after around thirty minutes of walking it reaches the cliffs of **Cape Asprókavos** and the crumbling **monastery of Arkoudhílas**. The cape looks out over the straits to Paxí, and down over deserted **Arkoudhílas** beach, which can be reached from Sparterá, a pleasant village 5km by road but only 3km by the signed path from Kávos; its *Fantasia* and *Paradise* tavernas are far more appealing and authentic than any in the resort. Even wilder is **Áï Górdhis Paleohoríou** beach, 3km further on from Sparterá, one of the least visited on the island and not to be confused with the eponymous beach further north; a municipal café provides the only refreshment. The Cape is also the southern starting point for the **Corfu Trail**, inaugurated in 2001, after years of planning by local walkers. Signposted by yellow waymarkers the trail meanders back and forth over 200km of varying terrain all the way to Cape Ayías Ekaterínis on the north coast and is designed to take at least ten days. Those interested should get a copy of Hilary Whitton Paipeti's *Walking the Corfu Trail* or check out Ⓦwww.travelling.gr/corfutrail for more details.

Paxí (Paxos) and Andípaxi

Verdant, hilly and still largely unspoilt, **Paxí (Paxos)** is the smallest of the main Ionian islands. Barely 12km by 4km, it has no sandy beaches, no historical sites, only three hotels and a serious water shortage, yet is so popular it is best avoided in high season. It's a particular favourite of yachting flotillas, whose spending habits have brought the island an upmarket reputation, making it just about the most expensive place to visit in the Ionian islands and lending it a rather cliquey air. Most accommodation is block-booked by travel companies, though there are local tour operators whose holiday deals are often a fraction of the price. The capital, **Gáïos**, is quite cosmopolitan, with delis and boutiques, but northerly **Lákka** and tiny **Longós** are where hardcore Paxophiles head.

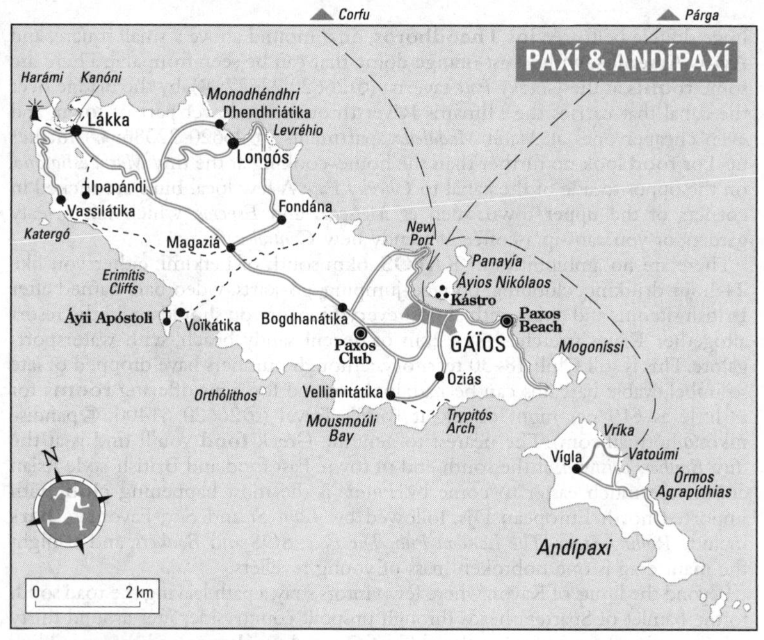

Gáïos and around

Most visitors arrive at the new port, 1km north of **GÁÏOS**, a pleasant town built around a small square on the seafront overlooking two islets. Given the shortage of rooms, it's advisable to phone ahead: try Gaïos Travel (Ⓣ26620 32033, Ⓦwww.gaiostravel.com) or Bouas Tours (Ⓣ26620 32401, Ⓦwww.bouastours.gr), both situated on the seafront. Paxí's two most established seasonal **hotels** are both near Gáïos: the *Paxos Beach Hotel* (Ⓣ26620 32211, Ⓦwww.paxosbeachhotel.gr; ❺ half-board) which has smart en-suite bungalows on a hillside above a pebbly beach 2km south of town, and the fairly luxurious *Paxos Club* (Ⓣ26620 32450, Ⓦwww.paxosclub.gr; ❻), nearly 2km inland from Gáïos.

Gáïos boasts a number of decent **tavernas**, most of which are on the pricey side. The best of the bunch are *Dodo's*, set in a garden inland from the Anemoyiannis statue, which has a full range of *mezédhes* and main courses; *Genesis*, most reasonable of the seafront establishments; and *Vassilis*, which has the best selection and prices of the trio to the left of the road up towards the bus stop. *The Cellar* at the top of the square is the best place for a tasty *souvláki*. *Gonia*, by the Párga *kaïki* mooring, is the better of the two remaining *kafenía*. Trendier **bars** include *Remego* on the southern seafront and *Alter Ego* round the quay towards the new port. The *Castello Music Club*, beyond the bus stop, is the most established summer disco.

Inland are some of the island's oldest settlements, such as Oziás and Vellianitátika, in prime walking country, but with few, if any, facilities. Noel Rochford's book, *Landscapes of Paxos*, lists dozens of walks, and cartographers Elizabeth and Ian Bleasdale's *Paxos Walking Map* is on sale in most travel agencies. The **coast south** of Gáïos is punctuated by the odd shingly cove, none ideal for swimming, until matters improve towards the tip at **Mogoníssi** beach, which shares some of Andípaxi's sandier geology and has an eponymous taverna.

The north of the island

Paxí's one main road runs along the spine of the island, with a turning at the former capital **Magaziá**, leading down to the tiny port of Longós. The main road continues to Lákka, the island's most hip resort, set in a breathtaking horseshoe bay. Buses ply the road between Gáïos and Lákka four or five times a day, most diverting to swing through Longós. The Gáïos–Lákka bus (30min) affords panoramic views, and the route is an excellent walk of under three hours (one way). A taxi between the two costs around €9.

Approached from the south, **LÁKKA** is an unprepossessing jumble of buildings, but once in its maze of alleys and neo-Venetian buildings, or on the quay with views of distant Corfu, you do get a sense of its charm. Lákka's two rather stony **beaches**, Harámi and Kanóni, are none too brilliant for swimming or sunbathing, however. Apart from high season, **accommodation** is plentiful from the area's two biggest agencies: local Routsis (ⓣ26620 31807, ⓦwww.routsis-holidays.com) or the British-owned Planos Holidays (ⓣ26620 31744 or UK 01373 814200, ⓦwww.planos.co.uk), both on the seafront. Paxí's third bona-fide hotel is the snooty and overpriced *Amfitriti Hotel* (ⓣ26620 30011, ⓦwww.amfitriti-hotel.gr; ❼). Mercifully, the practice of low-key, freelance camping behind Kanóni has not been affected. There's a wealth of fine **tavernas**, such as the friendly *Nionios* and neighbouring *Stasinos Garden*, both serving a fine range of Hellenic favourites on the square, the secluded *Alexandros*, great for *gourounópoulo* and fresh fish, and more upmarket seafront *La Rosa di Paxos*, which does risottos and ravioli. There's a similar wealth of **bars**: the seafront *Romantica* cocktail bar and *Harbour Lights*, *Fanis* in the square, or the friendly *kafenío* of Spyros Petrou – the hub of village life. Lákka is also well situated for **walking**: up onto either promontory, to the lighthouse or Vassilátika, or to Longós and beyond. One of the finest walks is an early evening visit to the **Erimítis cliffs**, near the hamlet of Voïkátika: on clear afternoons, the cliffs change colour at twilight like a seafacing Uluru (Ayers Rock), while full moons see the odd party at the sole bar, *Sunset*.

LONGÓS is the prettiest village on the island, and perfectly sited for morning sun and idyllic alfresco breakfasts. The village is dominated by the upmarket villa crowd, making the Planos office here (ⓣ26620 31530) the best place to look for accommodation. Longós also has a set of great **restaurants**: the seafront *Vassilis*, which does terrific fish dishes and tasty starters, *Nassos*, also with a wide variety of fish and seafood, and *O Gios*, a much simpler and cheaper taverna. *To Taxidhi* on the quay is a nice spot for coffee or an early drink, while *Roxi Bar* and *Ores* pander to the night-owls. Longós has a small, scruffy beach, with sulphur springs favoured by local grannies, but most people swim off **Levrehió** beach in the next bay south, which gets the occasional camper.

Andípaxi

Under 2km south, Paxí's tiny sibling **Andípaxi** has scarcely any accommodation and no facilities beyond several beach tavernas open during the day in season. It is most easily reached by the frequent shuttle *kaïkia* from Gáïos (€6 return). The glass-bottomed boat (€15 return) also takes you to its sea stacks and caves, the most dramatic in the Ionians. Andípaxi's sandy, blue-water coves have been compared with the Caribbean, but you'll have to share them with *kaïkia* and sea taxis from all of Paxos' villages, plus larger craft from Corfu and the mainland resorts.

Boats basically deposit you either at the sandy **Vríka** beach or the longer pebble beach of **Vatoúmi**. Vríka has a taverna at each end, of which *Spiros* (ⓣ26620 31172) has great grilled and oven food and can arrange self-catering accommodation up in **Vígla**, the island's hilltop settlement, on a weekly basis. Vatoúmi also has two restaurants, the justifiably named *Bella Vista* restaurant, perched on a cliff high above the beach, and the newer *Vatoumi*, a little way back from the beach. For a swim in quieter surroundings the trick is to head south, away from the pleasure-craft moorings, although path widening has made even the quieter bays more accessible.

Lefkádha (Lefkas)

Lefkádha is an oddity. Connected to the mainland by a long causeway through lagoons and a metal bridge, historically it isn't an island. It is separated from the mainland by a canal cut by Corinthian colonists in the seventh century BC. Lefkádha was long an important strategic base, and approaching the causeway you pass a series of fortresses, climaxing in the fourteenth-century castle of **Santa Maura** – the Venetian name for the island. These defences were too close to the mainland to avoid an Ottoman tenure, which began in 1479, but the Venetians wrested back control a couple of centuries later. They were in turn overthrown by Napoleon in 1797 and then the British took over as Ionian protectors in 1810 until 1864, when Lefkádha was reunited with Greece, along with the other islands.

The island immediately creates a more positive impression than the mainland just opposite. The whiteness of its rock strata – *lefkás* has the same root as *lefkós*, "white" – is apparent on its partly bare ridges, the highest of which is sadly marred by military and telecom installations. While the marshes and boggy inlets on the east coast can lead to mosquito problems, the island is a fertile place, supporting cypresses, olive groves and vineyards, particularly on the western slopes, and life in the mountain villages remains relatively untouched. The rugged **west coast**, however, is the island's star attraction, boasting some of the finest beaches in the Ionians and attractive **Áï Nikítas**. Lefkádha remains relatively undeveloped, with just two major resorts, both on the east coast: the windsurfing mecca of **Vassilikí**, and **Nydhrí**, which overlooks the island's satellites, including delightful **Meganíssi**. Meanwhile, **Lefkádha Town** is a pleasant place to spend some time, an admirable mixture of venerable churches and modern facilities, such as the superb new marina.

Lefkádha Town and around

LEFKÁDHA TOWN sits at the island's northernmost tip, hard by the causeway. Like other capitals in the southern Ionian, it was hit by the earthquakes of 1948 and 1953, and the town was mostly destroyed. As a precaution against further quakes, little was rebuilt above two storeys, and most houses acquired second storeys of wood, giving the western dormitory area an unintentionally quaint look. The town is small and still very attractive, especially the largely pedestrianized area around the main square, Platía Ayíou Spyridhónos, and the arcaded high street of Ioánnou Méla. The centre boasts over half a dozen richly decorated private family **churches** in the Italianate style, which were mercifully spared by the earthquake. Many contain rare works from the Ionian School of painting, including work by its founder, Zakynthian Panayiotis Doxaras.

The town has also been home to various literati, including two prominent Greek poets, Angelos Sikelianos and Aristotelis Valaoritis, and the British writer Lafcadio Hearn. Support for the arts continues in the form of a well-attended

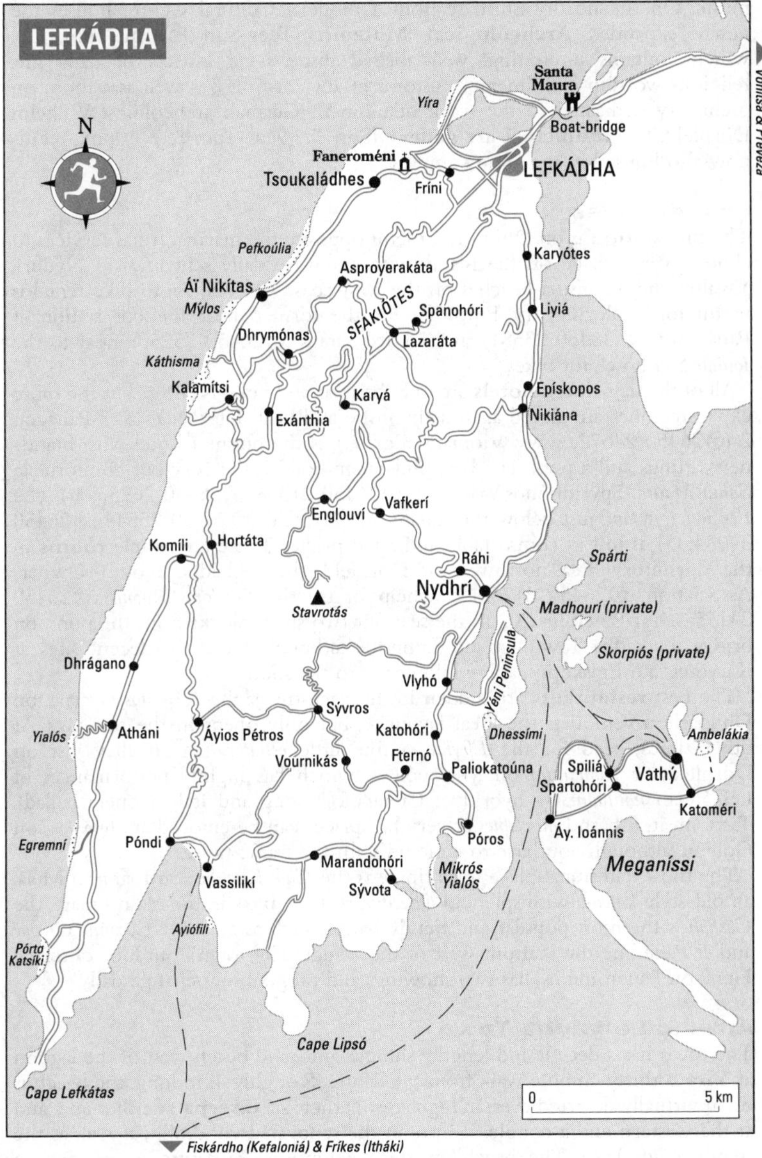

international **festival** of theatre and folk-dancing, now extended throughout the summer, with most events staged in the Santa Maura castle.

The folklore museum has been closed for a number of years but you can catch a glimpse of the old way of life at the quaint little **Phonograph Museum** (daily 10am–2pm & 7–midnight, high summer only; free), which is dedicated to antique phonographs and bric-a-brac, and sells cassettes of rare traditional music. On the northwestern seafront a modern Cultural Centre houses the newly expanded **Archeological Museum** (Tues–Sun 8.30am–3pm; €2), which contains interesting, well-labelled displays on aspects of daily life, religious worship and funerary customs in ancient times, as well as a room on prehistory dedicated to the work of eminent German archeologist Wilhelm Dörpfeld. The **municipal art gallery** (Sun–Fri 9am–1pm & 7–10pm; free) is now also housed in the same complex.

Practicalities

The **bus station** is on Dhimítri Golémi opposite the marina. It has services to almost every village on the island, with extensive daily schedules to Nydhrí, Vassilikí and Káthisma beaches on the west coast. Car and motorbike rental is useful for exploring; try EuroHire for the former, near the bus station at Panágou 6 (Ⓣ26450 23581), and I Love Santas (Ⓣ26450 25250), next to the *Ionian Star* hotel, for bikes.

All of the half-dozen **hotels** are in busy areas and none is cheap, but the more expensive ones are glazed against the noise and heat. The *Ionian Star*, Panágou 2 (Ⓣ26450 24672, Ⓦwww.ionianstar.gr; ➎), is the plushest hotel with brand-new fittings and a pool. The best mid-range hotel is the cosy but comfortable *Santa Maura*, Spyridhónos Viánda 2 (Ⓣ26450 21308, Ⓕ26450 26253; ➍). The *Pension Pyrofani*, just below the square on Dörpfeld (Ⓣ26450 25844, Ⓕ26450 24084; ➍), is just as comfortable and a tad pricier. There are simple **rooms** in the dormitory area northwest of Dörpfeld: the Lefkádha Room Owners Association (Ⓣ26450 21266) can help, or try the *Pinelopis Rooms* (Ⓣ26450 24175; ➋) at Pinelópis 20, off the seafront two short blocks from the pontoon bridge. Lefkádha Town has no campsite, although there are decent sites at Karyótes and Epískopos, a few kilometres to the south.

The best **restaurants** are hidden in the backstreets: the *Regantos* taverna, on Dhimárhou Venióti is the local favourite, but only opens in the evenings. At other times, head for the *Eftyhia*, a fine little *estiatório* in an alley just off Dörpfeld, or *Romantica* on Mitropóleos, which has nightly performances of Lefkádhan *kantádhes* (a hybrid of Cretan folk song and Italian opera ballad). Tasty meat, fish and *mezédhes* at very fair prices can be enjoyed at *Agirovoli*, on Golémi, although you have to contend with the traffic noise.

The most traditional place for a tipple is the *Cafe Karfakis*, on Ioánnou Méla, an old-style *kafenío* with splendid *mezédhes*. Of the **bars** in the main square, the *Cäsbäh* is the most popular and trendy haunts such as adjacent *Coconut Groove* and *Il Posto* line the seafront west of the bridge. The town's outdoor **cinema**, Eleni, on Faneroménis, has two showings and programmes change daily.

Around Lefkádha Town

The town has a decent and lengthy shingle-and-sand beach west of the lagoon at **Yíra**, a thirty-minute walk from the centre. Roughly 4km long, the beach is often virtually deserted even in high season; there's a **taverna** at either end, and at the western end a couple of **bars** in the renovated windmills, as well as the trendy *Club Milos*. The beach's western extension, **Aïyánnis**, is growing in popularity and now has several restaurants, including *Tilegraphos* (Ⓣ26450 24881; ➌), which also lets out some **rooms**.

The uninhabited **Faneroméni monastery** (daily 8am–2pm & 4–8pm; free) is reached by any of the west-coast buses, or by a steep 45-minute hike from town through the hamlet of Fríni. There's a small museum and chapel, and an ox's yoke and hammer, used when Nazi occupiers forbade the use of bells. There are wonderful views over the town and lagoon from the Fríni road.

The island's **interior**, most accessible from Lefkádha Town, offers imposing mountainscapes and excellent walking between villages only a few kilometres apart. **KARYÁ** is its centre, and offers some **rooms**: try the Kakiousis family (Ⓣ26450 61136; ❷) or Haritini Vlahou (Ⓣ26450 41634; ❶). The leafy town square has a popular taverna, *Iy Klimataria*, just below it and two *psistariés* on it, *Ta Platania* and the smarter *O Rousos*. Karyá is the centre of the island's lace and weaving industry, with a small but fascinating **folklore museum** set in a lacemaker's home (April–Oct daily 9am–9pm; €2.50). The historic and scenic villages of **Vafkerí** and **Englouví** are within striking distance, with the west-coast hamlets of **Dhrymónas** and **Exánthia** a hike over the hills.

The east coast to Vassilikí

Lefkádha's east coast is the most accessible and most developed part of the island. Apart from the campsite at Karyótes, *Kariotes Beach* (Ⓣ & Ⓕ26450 71103), there's little point stopping before the small fishing port of **LIYIÁ**, which has some rooms and the smart hotel *Konaki* (Ⓣ26450 71127, Ⓦwww.hotelkonaki.gr; ❺), as well as some restaurants such as *O Xouras psarotavérna* and, as you head south, the inexpensive and excellent garden taverna *Iy Limni*, which features unique dishes such as *spartiátiko*, a delicious concoction of pork, peppers, mushroom, cheese, wine and cognac. Further on, beyond the *Episcopos Beach* campsite (Ⓣ26450 71388), lies **Nikiana**, another fishing village where you'll find the *Christina* pension (Ⓣ26450 25194; ❷) and *Villa Katapodi* (Ⓣ26450 29134; ❸). In addition, Nikiána has a selection of fine tavernas, notably *Pantazis psistariá*, which also has rooms to let (Ⓣ26450 71211; ❸), and *Lefko Akroyiali*, a good fish restaurant further south. Beaches here tend to be pebbly and small.

Most package travellers will find themselves in **NYDHRÍ**, the island's biggest resort by far, with ferry connections to Meganíssi and myriad **boat trips** around the nearby satellite islands. The German archeologist Wilhelm Dörpfeld believed Nydhrí, rather than Itháki, to be the site of Odysseus's capital, and did indeed find Bronze Age tombs on the plain nearby. His theory fell into disfavour after his death in 1940, although his obsessive efforts have been rewarded by a statue on Nydhrí's quay and impressive tomb at Ayia Kyriakí on the opposite side of the bay.

Nydhrí is an average resort, with some good pebble beaches and a lovely setting, but the centre is an ugly strip with heavy traffic. The best **place to stay** is the refurbished *Ionian Paradise* (Ⓣ26450 92268, Ⓦwww.ionianparadise.gr; ❸), set in a lush garden away from the traffic a minute along the Ráhi road, which leads to Nydhrí's very own **waterfall**, a 45-minute walk inland. Rooms are best arranged through any of the resort's many travel agencies – try All Seasons Holidays (Ⓣ26450 92623, Ⓔallseasons@aias.gr). The town's focus is the Aktí Aristotéli Onássi quay, where most of the rather ritzy **restaurants** and **bars** are found. Well established places like the *Barrel* taverna offers dishes of reliable quality, whereas the *Titanic* on the beach is both quieter and a little cheaper. The most economical places to eat are predictably on the noisy main drag – try *Agrabeli* or *To Liotrivi*. Nightlife centres around bars like *Iguana* and *The Old Saloon*, and later on the *Sail Inn Club*, which claims to be open for 22 hours of the day.

Nydhrí sits at the mouth of a deep inlet stretching to the next village, somnolent **VLYHÓ**, with a few good tavernas and mooring for yachts. Over the Yéni peninsula across the inlet is the large **Dhessími Bay**, home to two campsites: *Santa Maura Camping* (Ⓣ26450 95007, Ⓕ26450 26087) and *Dessimi Beach Camping* (Ⓣ26450 95374, Ⓕ26450 95190), one at each end of the beach but often packed with outsized mobile homes. The *Pirofani* beach taverna in between them is excellent.

The coast road beyond Vlyhó turns inland and climbs the foothills of Mount Stavrotás, through the hamlets of Katohóri and Paliokatoúna to **Póros**, a quiet village with few facilities. Just south of here is the increasingly busy beach resort of **MIKRÓS YIALÓS**, more widely known as Póros beach. It boasts a handful of **tavernas**, a few rooms at *Oceanis Studios* (Ⓣ & Ⓕ26450 95095; ③), plus the posh *Poros Beach Camping* (Ⓣ26450 95452, Ⓦwww.porosbeach.com.gr), which has bungalows (③), shops and a pool. For food, try the *Rouda Bay* taverna opposite the beach, which also has smart rooms (Ⓣ26450 95634, Ⓦwww.roudabay.com; ④).

A panoramic detour off the main road to quiet **Vournikás** and **Sývros** is recommended to walkers and drivers (the Lefkádha–Vassilikí bus also visits); both places have tavernas and some private rooms. It's around 14km to the next resort, the fjord-like inlet of **SÝVOTA**, 2km down a steep hill (bus twice daily). There's no beach except for a remote cove, but some fine tavernas, mostly specializing in fish: the excellent *Palia Apothiki* is the most attractive and serves giant shrimps wrapped in bacon, but the *Delfinia* and *Ionion* also draw numerous customers. Just above the middle of the harbour there are **rooms** of varying sizes at *Sivota Apartments* (Ⓣ26450 31347, Ⓕ26450 31151; ③) or you can ask at any of the seafront supermarkets.

Beyond the Sývota turning, the mountain road dips down towards Kondárena, almost a suburb of **Vassilikí**, the island's premier watersports resort. Winds in the huge bay draw vast numbers of windsurfers, with light morning breezes for learners and tough afternoon blasts for advanced surfers. Booking your **accommodation** ahead is advisable in high season: *Pension Hollidays* (Ⓣ26450 31011, Ⓕ26450 31426; ③), round the corner from the ferry dock, is a reasonable option with air conditioning and TV in all rooms. In the centre of town you'll find the good-value *Vassiliki Bay Hotel* (Ⓣ26450 31077, Ⓦwww.vassilikibay.gr; ③), with full amenities. Rooms and apartments are available along the beach road to Póndi: try the smart and purpose-built *Billy's House* (Ⓣ26450 39363; ③) or ask at the central Samba Tours (Ⓣ26450 31520, Ⓦwww.sambatours.gr). The largest of the three beach windsurf centres, British-based *Club Vassiliki* (Ⓣ26450 31588, Ⓦwww.clubvass.com; ③), offers all-in **windsurf tuition** and accommodation deals. Vassilikí's only **campsite**, the large *Camping Vassiliki Beach* (Ⓣ26450 31308, Ⓕ26450 31458), is about 500m along the beach road; it has its own restaurant, bar and shop.

Vassilikí's pretty quayside is lined with **tavernas** and bars: the most popular eateries are *Penguins*, specializing in fish and seafood dishes like *marinara*, and *Alexander*, which has pizza as well as Greek cuisine. Quieter spots round the headland include the *Jasmine Garden* Chinese and the leafy *Apollo* taverna. The best place for a **drink** is *Livanakis kafenío* (next to the bakery), now modernized but still genuine and cheap.

The beach at Vassilikí is stony and poor, but improves 1km on at tiny **Póndi**; most non-windsurfers, however, use the daily *kaïki* trips to nearby Ayiófili or around Cape Lefkátas to the superior beaches at Pórto Katsíki and Egremní on the sandy west coast (see opposite). There's a gradually increasing number of **places to stay** at Póndi, some with great views of the bay and plain behind. One fine spot is the terrace of the *Ponti Beach Hotel* (Ⓣ26450 31572, Ⓕ26450 31576; ⑤), which is very popular with holidaying Greeks, and has a decent restaurant and bar. The *Nefeli* (Ⓣ26450 31378, Ⓔclubnefeli@hotmail.com; ③), right on the beach, is much better value though. The *Panorama* **taverna** serves delights such as garlic prawns and steak Diana.

The west coast

Although **Pefkoúlia beach** makes a worthy stop, Lefkádha's splendid west coast kicks off in earnest at **ÁÏ NIKÍTAS**, the prettiest resort on Lefkádha. A jumble of lanes and small wooden buildings, the village itself is now a pedestrian zone. The most attractive **accommodation** is in the *Pension Ostria* (ⓣ26450 97300, ⓔagnikitasostria@e-lefkas.gr; ④), a beautiful blue-and-white building above the village, decorated in a mix of beachcomber and ecclesiastical styles. The *Villa Milia* (ⓣ26450 97475; ③), by the junction, offers comfy rooms at reasonable rates. Other options line the main drag or hide in the alleys running off it; the best bets are the inexpensive *Aphrodite* (ⓣ26450 97372; ②) and quieter *Olive Tree* (ⓣ26450 97463, ⓦwww.olivetreelefkada.com; ④), which is also signposted from the main road. The best **tavernas** include the *Sapfo* fish taverna by the sea, the *T'Agnantio*, just above the main street, which serves excellent traditional cuisine, and *O Lefteris*, a good inexpensive restaurant on the main street. *Captain's Corner* near the beach is the liveliest drinking venue.

Sea taxis (€2 one way) ply between Áï Nikítas and **Mýlos** beach, cut off by the sheer headland, or it's a 45-minute walk (or take the bus) to the most popular beach on the coast, **Káthisma**, a shadeless kilometre of fine sand, which becomes much quieter, nudist-friendly and a haven for freelance camping beyond the rocks halfway along. Of the two tavernas on the beach choose the barn-like *Kathisma* (ⓣ26450 97050, ⓦwww.kathisma.com; ④), which also has smart apartments. The new *Club Copla* attracts the night-time crowd with house parties. Above the beach the upgraded *Sunset* has **rooms** (ⓣ26450 97488, ⓦwww.sunsetstudios.gr; ⑤), while the nearby *Hotel Sirius* (ⓣ26450 97025, ⓦwww.hotelsirios.gr; ④) also commands fine views. Back on the main road, *Kathisma Camping* (ⓣ26450 97015) is the only official site on this coast.

From here the road winds up through **Kalamítsi**, which has some places to stay if the coast is full, and on to **Hortáta**, home to the excellent *Lygos* taverna with rooms (ⓣ26450 33395, ⓔaglakost@freemail.gr; ②). Beyond Komíli, the landscape becomes almost primeval. At 38km from Lefkádha Town, **Atháni** is the island's most remote spot to stay, with a couple of good tavernas both offering great-value rooms: the *Panorama* (ⓣ26450 33291, ⓕ26450 33476; ②) and *O Alekos* (ⓣ26450 33484; ②), the latter only open in high season. Three of the Ionian's choicest **beaches**, where azure and milky turquoise waves buffet strands enclosed by dramatic cliffs, are accessible from Atháni: the nearest, reached by a 4km paved road, is **Yialós**, followed by **Egremní**, down a steep incline unpaved for the last 2km; the former has the *Yialos* café-restaurant and a couple of *kantínes*, the latter just one *kantína*. Further south an asphalted road leads to the dramatic and popular twin beach of **Pórto Katsíki**, where there are several better-stocked *kantínes* on the cliff above.

Keeping to the main road for 14km from Atháni will bring you to barren **Cape Lefkátas**, which drops abruptly 75m into the sea. Byron's Childe Harold sailed past this point, and "saw the evening star above, Leucadia's far projecting rock of woe: And hail'd the last resort of fruitless love". The fruitless love is a reference to Sappho, who in accordance with the ancient legend that you could cure yourself of unrequited love by leaping into these waters, leapt – and died. This act was imitated by the lovelorn youths of Lefkádha for centuries afterwards, as well as in an annual ritual, whereby unwilling scapegoats were selected for the plunge by priests from the Apollo temple, whose sparse ruins lie close by.

Lefkádha's satellites

Lefkádha has four satellite islands clustered off its east coast, although only one, **Meganíssi**, the largest and most interesting, is accessible. **Skorpiós**, owned by the Onassis family, fields armed guards to deter visitors. **Madhourí**, owned by the family of poet Nanos Valaoritis, is private and similarly off-limits, while tiny **Spárti** is a large scrub-covered rock. Day-trips from Nydhrí skirt all three islands, and some stop to allow swimming in coves.

Meganíssi

Meganíssi, twenty minutes by frequent daily ferries from Nydhrí, is a large island with limited facilities but a magical, if bleak landscape. Ferries stop first at **Spiliá**, ten minutes by foot below **SPARTOHÓRI**, an immaculate village with whitewashed buildings and an abundance of bougainvillea. The locals – many returned émigrés from Australia – live by farming and fishing and are genuinely welcoming. You arrive at a jetty on a pebble beach with a few **tavernas** such as the excellent *Stars*. The village proper boasts three restaurants: a pizza place called the *Tropicana*, which can direct you to **rooms** (Ⓣ26450 51486; ❷), as can the simple *Gakias* (Ⓣ26450 51050; ❸); the trio is completed by the fine traditional taverna *Lakis*. Further west round the coast at Áyios Ioánnis there is a good beach with the *Il Paradiso* taverna and a makeshift campsite, a great spot to unwind in.

The attractive inland village of **Katoméri** is an hour's walk through magnificent country. It has the island's one **hotel**, the *Meganissi*, a comfortable place with a restaurant and pool (Ⓣ26450 51240, Ⓕ26450 51639; ❸), and a few café-bars. Ten minutes' walk downhill is the main port of **VATHÝ**, with some accommodation such as *Different Studios* (Ⓣ26450 22170; ❸) and several highly rated **restaurants**, notably the waterside taverna, *Porto Vathi*, which Lefkadans flock to on ferries for a Sunday fish lunch, and the *Rose Garden*. The *Twins Bar* by the ferry dock is a friendly spot for a drink. After the high-season madness of Nydhrí, Meganíssi's unspoilt landscape is a tonic and easy to take in as a **day trip** from Nydhrí, by getting off at Spiliá, then walking via Spartohóri and Katoméri to Vathý for the ferry back.

Kefaloniá

Kefaloniá is the largest of the Ionian islands – a place that has real towns as well as resorts. Like its neighbours, Kefaloniá was overrun by Italians and Germans in World War II; the "handover" after Italy's capitulation in 1943 led to the massacre of over five thousand Italian troops on the island by invading German forces, as chronicled by Louis de Bernières in his novel, *Captain Corelli's Mandolin*. Virtually all of its towns and villages were levelled in the 1953 earthquake, and these masterpieces of Venetian architecture had been the one touch of elegance in a severe, mountainous landscape. Whether it was due to a feeling the island was thus difficult to market or due to their notorious insularity and eccentricity, the Kefalonians paid scant regard to tourism until the late 1980s.

There are definite attractions here, however, with some **beaches** as good as any in the Ionian islands, and a fine (if pricey) local wine, the dry white Robola. Mercifully, the anticipated "Corelli factor" did not lead to the island becoming either oversubscribed or over-expensive, despite some predictable theming. Moreover, the island seems able to soak up a lot of people without feeling at all crowded, and the magnificent scenery speaks for itself, the escarpments culminating in the 1632-metre bulk of **Mount Énos**, a national park.

For **airport** arrival see the Argostóli section on p.874. Kefaloniá's **bus** system is basic but reliable, and with a little legwork it can be used to get you almost anywhere on the island. Key routes connect Argostóli with the main tourist centres of **Sámi**, **Fiskárdho**, **Skála** and **Póros**. There's a useful connection from Sámi to the tiny resort of **Ayía Efimía**, which also attracts many package travellers. If you're using a motorbike, take care: a few of the more remote roads are still very rough and gradients sometimes rather challenging for underpowered machines. The island has a plethora of **ferry** connections (see p.889) to neighbouring islands and several mainland towns, while direct sailings between Sámi and one of the Italian ports – usually Brindisi – are offered most years in peak season.

Sámi and around

Most boats dock at the large and functional port town of **SÁMI**, near the south end of the Itháki straits, more or less on the site of ancient Sami. This was the capital of the island in Homeric times, when Kefaloniá was part of Ithaca's maritime kingdom: today the administrative hierarchy is reversed, Itháki being considered the backwater. With the only ferry link to Pátra, frequent connections to Itháki and direct (albeit erratic) links to Italy, the town is clearly preparing itself for a burgeoning future. The long sandy beach that stretches round the bay is quite adequate; 2km beyond ancient Sami lies a fine pebble beach, **Andísamis**, with the lively *Mojito Beach Bar* providing refreshments.

The town has three big **hotels**: the friendly *Athina Beach* (Ⓣ26740 23067, Ⓦwww.athina-beach-hotel.com; ⑤), is the better of the two at the far end of the beach, actually in Karavómylos, while the *Pericles* (Ⓣ26740 22780, Ⓕ26740 22787; ④), which has extensive grounds, two pools and sports facilities, lies over 1km along the Argostóli road. The best place in town is the comfortable seafront *Kastro* (Ⓣ26740 22282, Ⓦwww.kastrohotel.com; ④). Sámi's **campsite**, *Camping Karavomilos Beach* (Ⓣ26740 22480, Ⓔvalettas@hol.gr), has over 300 well-shaded spaces, a taverna, shop and bar, and opens onto the beach – it is by far the better of the island's two official sites.

Sámi's only **tavernas** are dotted along the seafront; *Mermaid* and *Faros*, both with a decent selection of veg and meat dishes, including the famous local meat pie, are the best of the central bunch. Better still, head further along the beach to *Dionysos*, where you can sample fresh seafood at low prices and hear live music at weekends. The inevitably renamed *Captain Corelli's* and *Aqua Marina* are the favourite **bars** in the evenings, while the *Asteria bouzoúki* club on the road to Karavómylos can make for an entertaining night out. The seafront Sami Center (Ⓣ26740 22254) rents out **motorbikes** at fair rates and Island (Ⓣ26740 23084, Ⓔislecars@otenet.gr) is a reliable local **car rental** company.

The Dhrogaráti and Melissáni caves

The main reason to stay in Sámi is its proximity to the Dhrogaráti and Melissáni caves; the former is 5km out of town towards Argostóli, the latter 3km north towards Ayía Efimía. A very impressive stalagmite-bedecked chamber, **Dhrogaráti** (April–Oct daily 9am–8pm; €4) is occasionally used for concerts thanks to its marvellous acoustics. **Melissáni** (daily 8am–7pm; €6) is partly submerged in brackish water, which, amazingly, emerges from an underground fault extending the whole way underground from Katavóthres (see p.875) near Argostóli, where the sea gushes endlessly into a subterranean channel; this fact has been proven by

KEFALONIÁ & ITHÁKI

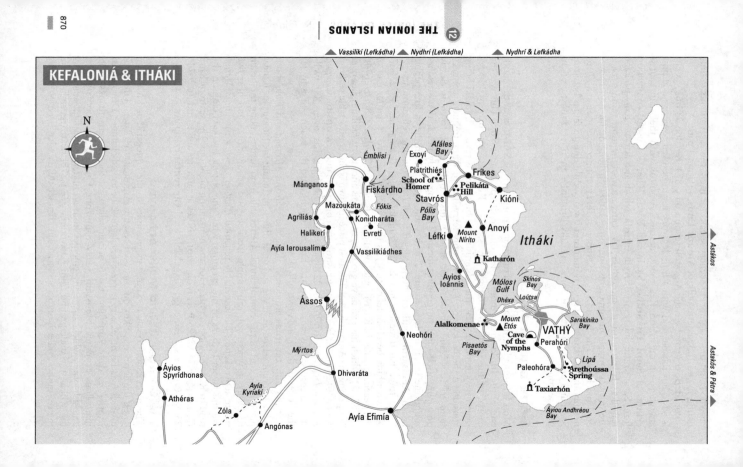

Kefaloniá

Petaní
Ayía Thékli
Kipouréon
Lixoúri
Katavóthres
Mantzavináta
Lépedha
Kounópetra
Cape Akrotíri
Xí
Mégas Lákkos
Fársa
Dhavgáta
Dhilináta
Mount Evmorfía (846m)
ARGOSTÓLI
Dhrápano Causeway
Lássi
Makrýs Yialós
Platýs Yialós
Melissáni Cave
Karavómylos
Ayía Paraskeví
Andísamis
SÁMI
Dhrogaráti Cave
Frangáta
Áyios Elefthérios
Áyios Yerásimos
Áyios Yeóryios Fortress
Peratáta
Mount Énos (1632m)
Lakíthra
Metaxáta
Kourkomeláta
Keramiés
Trapezáki
Pessádha
Spartiá
Koriána
Ávythos
Moussáta
Vlaháta
Lourdháta
Sissiá
Póros
Tzanáta
Pástra
Markópoulo
Skála
Ratzaklí
Káto Kateliós
Kyllíni
Kyllíni
Áyios Nikólaos (Zákynthos)
0 5 km

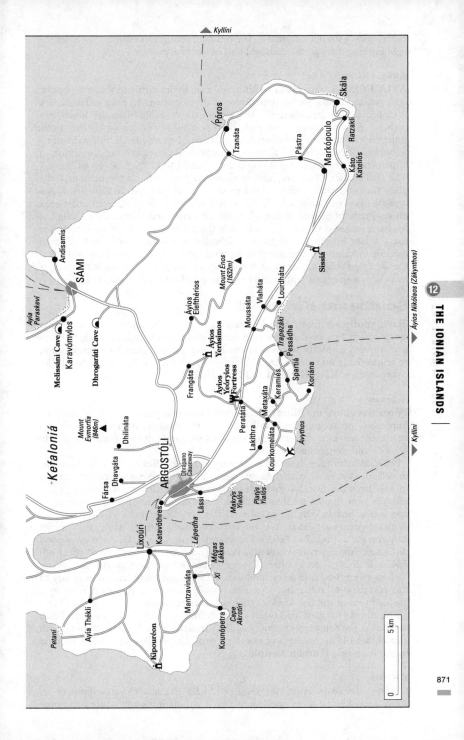

experiments with fluorescent dye. The beautiful textures and shades created by the light pouring through the collapsed roof of the cave make it a must.

Ayía Efimía

AYÍA EFIMÍA, 9km north of Sámi, is a friendly little fishing harbour popular with package operators, yet with no major developments. Its principal drawback is its beaches, or lack thereof – the largest, risibly named Paradise beach, is a pathetic 20m of shingle, although there are other tiny coves to the south. Independent **accommodation** here is confined to one hotel, the welcoming *Moustakis* (Ⓣ26740 61030, Ⓦwww.moustakishotel.com; ④); and a selection of apartments – try Yerasimos Raftopoulos (Ⓣ26740 61233, Ⓕ26740 61216; ②). The *Paradise Beach* **taverna**, furthest round the headland past the harbour, is the place for moderately priced island cuisine; the *Pergola* and *To Steki Ton Kalofagadhon* also both offer a wide range of island specialities and standard Greek dishes. Predictably, the café-bar where the film crew and actors used to hang out has been renamed *Captain Corelli's*, while the *Strawberry zaharoplastío* is the place for a filling breakfast. The town's nightclub is *Paranoia*, 700m out of town towards Fiskárdho. If you are making your own way between here and Sámi, the *Ayía Paraskeví* taverna, at the tiny cove of the same name, is famous for its delicious spaghetti with mussel marinade and boasts a great setting.

Southeast Kefaloniá

Travel **southeast from Sámi** is easy enough on the asphalt road to **Póros** along which a twice-daily bus runs between the two. Continuing south, Póros is connected to **Skála** by another coastal route, which then loops back round to rejoin the main road to Argostóli, from which there is easy access to smaller resorts such as **Káto Kateliós** and **Lourdháta**.

Póros

Póros was one of the island's earliest developed resorts, and definitely gives the impression of having seen better days. The town's small huddle of hotels and apartment blocks is almost unique on Kefaloniá, and not enhanced by a scruffy seafront and thin, pebbly beach.

Póros does, however, have a regular ferry link to **Kyllíni** on the Peloponnesian mainland, a viable alternative to the Sámi–Pátra route. Póros is actually made up of two bays: the first, where most tourists stay, and the actual harbour, a few minutes over the intervening headland. There are plenty of rooms, apartments and a few **hotels**. The best deal is at the cosy *Santa Irena* (Ⓣ26740 72017, Ⓔmaki@otenet.gr; B&B; ②), by the crossroads inland, while the nearby *Odysseus Palace* (Ⓣ26740 72036, Ⓦwww.odysseuspalace.eu; ⑤) often gives good discounts. Among **travel agents**, Poros Travel by the ferry dock (Ⓣ26740 72476, Ⓕ26740 72069) offers a range of accommodation, as well as services such as **car rental** and ferry bookings. The main seafront has the majority of the **restaurants** and **bars**. The *Fotis Family* taverna serves good food in a pleasant setting and the *Mythos* café has **Internet** access.

The aforementioned road twists 12km around the rocky coastline from Póros to Skála at the southern extremity of the island. It's a lovely, isolated route, with scarcely a building on the way, save for a small chapel, 3km short of Skála, next to the ruins of a **Roman temple**.

Skála

In total contrast to Póros, the resort of **Skála** is a low-rise development set above a few kilometres of good sandy beach, although the area's once handsome pines have suffered from fire damage. A **Roman villa** (daily 10am–2pm & 5–8pm, longer hours in summer; free) and some mosaics were excavated here in the 1950s, near the site of the *Golden Beach Palace*.

A faithful return crowd keeps Skála busy until beyond high season, when **accommodation** can be hard to find. There are studios and apartments at *Dionysus Rooms* (Ⓣ26710 83283; ❷), a block south of the main street, or a range is available through Etam Travel Service (Ⓣ26710 83101, Ⓦetam-carhire.gr), whose main speciality is vehicle rental. Of hotels, the cosy *Captain's Hotel* (Ⓣ26710 83389, Ⓦwww.captainshouse.net; ❸), on the road parallel to the main street to the east, is comfortable and friendly, while the more upmarket *Tara Beach Hotel* (Ⓣ26710 83250, Ⓦwww.tarabeach.gr; ❹) has rooms and individual bungalows in lush gardens on the edge of the beach. Skála boasts a number of **tavernas**: *The Old Village* and the *Flamingo* are both good spots in the village, with a standard range of Greek and continental cuisine, while, on the beach, *Paspalis* serves fish and home-cooking and *Sunrise* offers pizza as well as Greek food. Drinkers head for *Veto* **bar** and the beachside *Stavento* restaurant-bar, which plays the coolest sounds.

Skála to Lourdháta

Some of the finest sandy beaches on the island are just beyond Skála below the village of Ratzaklí, and around the growing micro-resort of **KÁTO KATELIÓS**, which already has a couple of hotels: the smart *Odyssia* (Ⓣ26710 81615, Ⓕ26710 81614; ❹) and the mostly German-occupied *Galini Resort* (Ⓣ26710 81582, Ⓦwww.galini.de; ❹), which has good deals on **apartments** for four. There are also some rooms and apartments available through the local branch of CBR Travel (Ⓣ26710 22770, Ⓦwww.cbr-rentacar.com). Of the half a dozen restaurants and cafés at the seafront, the *Blue Sea* taverna is renowned for the freshness and quality of its fish, the *Ostria* offers a wide selection of inexpensive dishes, while the *Cozy* bar is the prime drinking location. The coast around Káto Keteliós is also Kefaloniá's key breeding ground for the loggerhead **turtle** (see box, p.885). Camping on the nearby beaches is therefore discouraged.

The inland village of **MARKÓPOULO**, claimed by some to be the birthplace of homophonous explorer Marco Polo, witnesses a bizarre snake-handling ritual every year on August 15, the **Assumption of the Virgin festival**. The church where this ritual is enacted stands on the site of an old convent. The story goes that when the convent was attacked by pirates, the nuns prayed to be transformed into snakes to avoid being taken prisoners. Their prayers were supposedly answered, and each year the "miraculous return" of a swarm of small, harmless snakes is meant to bring the villagers good luck.

The coastline is largely inaccessible until the village of **Vlaháta**, which has some rooms and restaurants, but there's little point in staying up here, when you can turn 2km down to **Lourdháta**, which has a kilometre-long shingle beach, mixed with imported sand. *Adonis* (Ⓣ26710 31206; ❸) and *Ramona* (Ⓣ26710 31032, Ⓦwww.dionaramona.com; ❸) have **rooms** just outside the village on the approach road, while behind the beach the smart new *Christina Studios* (Ⓣ26710 31130, Ⓔchristinastudio@in.gr) and *Thomatos Apartments* (Ⓣ26710 31656, Ⓔcritithomatos@yahoo.com; ❹) both offer fully equipped kitchen-studios. Of the smattering of **tavernas**, the *Diamond*, on the tiny plane-shaded village square, does a good range of vegetarian items and further up the hill towards Vlaháta *Dionysus* serves good taverna standards. At the beach itself *Patritsia* is good for inexpensive fish and *Lorraine's Magic Hill* has good food and a laid back feel to it. The *Platanos* café back in the village is a friendly watering hole. An even better beach, reached by a turning from

Moussáta, west of Vlaháta, is **Trapezáki**, an attractive strand with just one restaurant by the small jetty.

Argostóli and around

ARGOSTÓLI, Kefaloniá's capital, is a large and thriving town – virtually a city – with a marvellous site on a bay within a bay. The stone bridge, connecting the two sides of the inner bay, was initially constructed by the British in 1813. The bridge, known as Dhrápano owing to its sickle shape, was closed to traffic indefinitely in 2005, rendering it a far more pleasant walk. The town was totally rebuilt after the 1953 earthquake, but has an enjoyable atmosphere that remains defiantly Greek, especially during the evening *vólta* around **Platía Valiánou** (formerly Platía Metaxá) – the nerve centre of town – and along the pedestrianized Lithóstroto, which runs parallel to the seafront.

Arrival and information

Argostóli's modern **Kefaloniá airport** lies 7km south of town. There are no airport buses, and suburban bus services are so infrequent or remote from the terminal that a taxi (at an inflated flat rate of at least €10) is the only dependable connection. Those arriving in Argostóli by bus will wind up at the KTEL **bus station**, a minute from the Dhrápano causeway and ten minutes' walk south of Platía Valianoú. Argostóli's friendly **tourist office** (Mon–Fri 7.30am–2.30pm; ⓣ26710 22248, ⓕ26710 24466), next to the port authority on Andoníou Trítsi, has information about rooms, piles of printed material, and gives reliable advice on the entire island. The island-wide Sunbird agency (ⓣ26710 23723, ⓦwww.sunbird.gr) is a reliable outlet for car or motorbike rental. Excelixis at Minoös 3, behind the church on Lithóstrotou, has **Internet** facilities.

Accommodation

Hotels in Argostóli open all year and are mostly mid-range, the best value of these being the snazzy *Ionian Plaza* (ⓣ26710 25581, ⓦwww.ionianplaza.gr; ❺), right on the main square. A substantially cheaper option in the opposite corner of the square is the *Mirabel* (ⓣ26710 23454, ⓦwww.mirabel.gr; ❹); the best budget deal, if you don't mind sharing a bathroom, is the friendly *Chara* (ⓣ26710 22427; ❶), set in a lovely shady courtyard at the corner of Vergóti and Dhevossétou near Dhrápano bridge. Back near the port, *Kyknos Studios* (ⓣ26710 23398; ❸) is good value, with TV in all the air-conditioned kitchenettes. In a working town with a large permanent population, **private rooms** are scarce, but you can call the Room Owners Association (ⓣ26710 29109) or ask at an agency like Ainos Travel (ⓣ26710 22333, ⓦwww.ainostravel.gr; from ❷), opposite the Archeological Museum. The town's basic and rather shadeless **campsite**, *Argostoli Camping* (ⓣ26710 23487), is a good 2km walk north of the centre, just beyond the Katovóthres sea mills.

The town

The **Korgialenio History and Folklore Museum** (Mon–Sat 9am–2pm; €4), on Ilía Zervoú behind the Municipal Theatre, has a rich collection of local religious and cultural artefacts, including photographs taken before and after the earthquake. Insight into how the island's nobility used to live can be gained from a visit to the **Focas-Cosmetatos Foundation** (May–Oct Mon–Sat 9.30am–1pm, plus Tues–Sat 7–10pm; €3), on Valiánou opposite the provincial government building. It contains elegant furniture and a collection of lithographs and paintings, including works by nineteenth-century British artists Joseph Cartwright and Edward Lear. The excellent **Archeological**

Museum (Tues–Sun 8.30am–3pm; €3), on nearby Vergóti, has a sizeable collection of pottery, jewellery, funerary relics and statuary from prehistoric, through Mycenaean to late Classical times. It is well laid out and labelled, rivalling Kérkyra Town's (see p.847) as the best such museum in the Ionians. At the northern tip of the town's peninsula a small rotunda stands beside the peculiar **Katavóthres**, swirling sinkholes that until the 1953 earthquake were strong enough to drive mills. Nearby there is a moving **memorial** to the soldiers of the Italian Acqui Division who were executed by the Germans in World War II.

Eating, drinking and nightlife

The *Tzivras estiatório* (only open until 5pm), down a sidestreet opposite the seafront fruit market, is one of the best places to try Kefalonian cuisine; the upmarket *Captain's Table* **taverna** just off the main square offers nightly live *kantádhes*, though they are just about as easily heard from the patio of the adjacent *Arhontiko,* which has better food at much lower prices. Of the seafront eateries, the friendly ✱ *Kiani Akti*, perfectly located beyond the Lixoúri ferry, has a great, high-quality selection of seafood and *mezédhes*, which can be enjoyed from the wooden deck that juts out above the water. For a change of diet, try *Kohenoor*, 50m towards the front from the square, which dishes up good, authentic Indian food.

Local posers hang out at the café-bars lining the square, while more discerning drinkers head for *Pub Old House*, a relaxed hangout behind the playground 150m north of the square, or the more modern *Bodega* en route to it. *Bass*, by the museum, is the town's big late-night indoor club. The quayside bars, particularly the *Aristofanis kafenío* by the Dhrápano bridge, are quiet, cheap and have the best views.

South of Argostóli: beaches and Áyios Yeóryios

Many package travellers will find themselves staying in **LÁSSI**, a short bus ride or twenty-minute walk from town. Lássi sprawls unattractively along a busy main road and it cannot be recommended to the independent traveller, although the *Ionio* family-run taverna is worth a stop for its delicious wrapped snapper. There are also a couple of good sandy beaches, namely **Makrýs Yialós** and **Platýs Yialós**, although they're right under the airport flight path. Further on, **beaches** such as **Ávythos** are well worth seeking out, although if you're walking beyond **Kourkomeláta** there is a real, if occasional, risk of being attacked by farm dogs, particularly during the hunting season (Sept 25–Feb 28). There is very little accommodation in the region, and precious few shops or bars. **Pessádha** has a twice-daily ferry link with Zákynthos in summer, but little else, and be warned that the pathetic bus service from Argostóli is no good for connecting with the boats. You'll have to hitch or take an expensive taxi in most cases.

With a vehicle, the best inland excursion is to **ÁYIOS YEÓRYIOS**, the medieval Venetian capital of the island. The old town here supported a population of 15,000 until its destruction by an earthquake in the seventeenth century: substantial ruins of its **castle** (Tues–Sun 8.30am–3pm; free) can be visited on the hill above the modern village of Peratáta. Byron lived for a few months in the nearby village of Metaxáta and was impressed by the view from the summit in 1823. The *Castle* **café-bar** provides refreshments and great views from near the castle gates. Two kilometres south of Áyios Yeóryios is a fine collection of religious icons and frescoes kept in a restored church that was part of the nunnery of Áyios Andhréas.

Mount Énos and around

At 15km from a point halfway along the Argostóli–Sámi road, **Mount Énos** isn't really a walking option, but roads nearly reach the official 1632-metre summit. The mountain has been declared a national park, to protect the *Abies cephalonica* firs (named after the island), which clothe the slopes. There are absolutely no facilities on or up to the mountain, but the views from the highest point in the Ionians out over its neighbours and the mainland are wonderful. Out of summer, watch the weather, which can deteriorate with terrifying speed. Not far before the mountain turning, taking a detour towards Frangáta is doubly rewarded, firstly by the huge and lively **Áyios Yerásimos monastery** (daily 9am–1pm & 4–8pm), which hosts two of the island's most important festivals (Aug 15 and Oct 20); its most interesting feature is the double cave beneath the back of the sanctuary, where St Yerásimos meditated for lengthy periods. Right behind the monastery, the **Robola winery** (April–Oct daily 7am–8.30pm; Nov–March Mon–Fri 7am–3pm; Ⓦwww.robola.gr) offers a free self-guided tour and generous wine-tasting.

Lixoúri and its peninsula

Half-hourly ferries (hourly in winter) ply between the capital and **LIXOÚRI** throughout the day until after midnight. The town was flattened by earthquakes, and hasn't risen much above two storeys since. It's a little drab, but has good restaurants, quiet hotels and is favoured by those who want to explore the eerie quake-scapes left in the south and the barren north of the peninsula. **Hotels** are not especially plentiful or cheap, but two comfortable air-conditioned options are the *La Cité* (Ⓣ26710 92701, Ⓕ26710 92702; ④), four blocks back from the front, and the seafront *Summery* (Ⓣ26710 91771, Ⓦwww.hotelsummery.gr; ⑤), just south of town. Two agencies offer cheaper accommodation: A. D. Travel (Ⓣ26710 93142, Ⓦwww.adtravel.gr), on the main road through town, and Perdikis Travel (Ⓣ & Ⓕ26710 92503) on the quay. Among the tavernas, *Akrogiali* on the seafront is excellent and cheap for fish and homecooking, drawing admirers from all over the island. *Iy Avli*, on the block behind, serves a variety of dishes in a leafy garden, while *Adonis* is a good basic *psistariá* at the back of the square. *Overdose* is the trendy place to drink on the square, while the old seafront *kafenía* have also been replaced by youth-orientated cafés such as *Club Vamos*.

Lixoúri's nearest beach is **Lépedha**, a two-kilometre walk south. Like the **Xí** and **Mégas Lákkos** beaches, served by bus from Lixoúri and both with restaurants and accommodation, it has rich-red sand and is backed by low cliffs. Those with transport can also strike out for the monastery at **Kipouréon**, and north to the spectacular beach at **Petaní**. Here there are two restaurants, the better being the further of the two, *Xougras*, whose friendly Greek-American owner Dina has rooms (Ⓣ26710 97128, Ⓔpetani@in.gr; ④) or you can stay up the access road at the *Niforo* apartments (Ⓣ26710 97350; ④).

The west coast and the road north

The journey between Argostóli and Fiskárdho is the most spectacular ride in the archipelago. Leaving town, the road rises into the Evmorfía foothills, where you can detour a short way inland to visit the modest **Museum of Natural History** (summer daily 9am–1pm, plus Mon–Fri 6–8pm, rest of year Sun–Fri 9am–1pm; €1.50) at **Dhavgáta**. Continuing to rise beyond Agónas, the coast road clings to near-sheer cliffs as it heads for Dhivaráta, which has a smattering of rooms, such as *Mina Studios* (Ⓣ26740 61716, Ⓔmarkela1@hol.gr; ③), and a couple of restaurants. This is the access point for dramatically photogenic

Mýrtos beach, 4km down a motorable road; there is just one snack-bar on this splendid strip of pure-white sand and pebbles, which offers no natural shade and gets mighty crowded in high season.

Six kilometres on is the turning for the atmospheric village of **Ássos**, clinging to a small isthmus between the island and a huge hill crowned by a ruined fort. Accommodation is scarce so it's wise to book: try the neat and friendly *Cosi's Inn* (Ⓣ26740 51420, Ⓦwww.cosisinn.gr; ③), the posher *Kanakis Apartments* (Ⓣ26740 51631, Ⓦwww.kanakisapartments.gr; ④) or, more standard, Andhreas Rokos' rooms (Ⓣ26740 51523; ②); all three are on the approach road. Ássos has a small pebble beach, and three **tavernas**, notably the *Nefeli* and the *Platanos Grill*, on a plane-shaded village square backed by mansions, mostly now restored after being ruined in the quake. It can get a little claustrophobic, but there's nowhere else quite like it in the Ionians.

Fiskárdho

Fiskárdho, on the northernmost tip of the island, sits on a bed of limestone that buffered it against the worst of the quakes. Two **lighthouses**, Venetian and Victorian, guard the bay, and the ruins on the headland are believed to be from a twelfth-century chapel begun by Norman invader Robert Guiscard, who gave the place its name. The nineteenth-century harbour frontage is intact, nowadays occupied by smart restaurants and chic boutiques. There is an **Environmental and Nautical Museum** (summer Mon–Fri 10am–6pm, Sun 10am–2pm; donations), housed in a renovated Neoclassical mansion on the hill behind the village. The volunteers who curate it conduct valuable ecological research and also run a **scuba diving operation** (Ⓣ26740 41182, Ⓦwww.fnec.gr). There are two good pebble beaches nearby – **Émblisi,** over 1km back out of town, and **Fókis,** almost the same distance south – and a nature trail on the northern headland. Daily **ferries** connect Fiskárdho to Lefkádha year-round and Itháki in season.

The island's premier resort, Fiskárdho remains busy through to the end of October, with **accommodation** at a premium. The cheapest rooms are at welcoming *Regina's* (Ⓣ & Ⓕ26740 41125; ③), up by the car park, and those of Sotiria Tselenti (Ⓣ26740 41204, Ⓦwww.fiskardo-ellis.gr; ③), arranged through the bakery 50m back from the tiny square. A splendid if pricey option is the beautifully converted mansion *Archontiko* (Ⓣ & Ⓕ 26740 41342; ⑥), above and behind a harbourfront minimarket. Pama Travel (Ⓣ26740 41033, Ⓦwww.pamatravel.com), on the seafront furthest away from the ferry quay, is another source of rooms and costlier apartments. There's a wealth of good but mostly expensive harbourside **restaurants**: *Tassia* is famous for a vast range of seafood but check the price of any fish you order carefully, likewise at the *Captain's Table*. Just round the headland past Pama Travel, *Panormos* has much lower prices and a great location. Just off the only square, *Lagoudera*, specializes in tasty oven food and now has a second seafront location. *Irida's* and the *Yacht Inn* are two of the most popular harbourside **bars**. The dance spot is *Kastro Club* up at the back of the village.

Itháki

Rugged **Itháki**, Odysseus's legendary homeland, has yielded no substantial archeological discoveries, but it fits Homer's description to perfection: "There are no tracks, nor grasslands . . . it is a rocky severe island, unsuited for horses, but not so wretched, despite its small size. It is good for goats." In Constantine Cavafy's splendid poem *Ithaca*, the island is symbolized as a journey to life:

When you set out on the voyage to Ithaca
Pray that your journey may be long
Full of adventures, full of knowledge.

Despite the romance of its name, and its proximity to Kefaloniá, very little tourist development has arrived to spoil the place. This is doubtless accounted for in part by a dearth of beaches beyond a few pebbly coves, though the island is good walking country and indeed the interior with its sites from the **Odyssey** is the real attraction. Most visitors will arrive at **Vathý**, the capital, which enjoys a splendid location, although some arrivees from Kefaloniá will dock at laid back **Fríkes** or the small port of Pisaetós.

Vathý

Ferries from Pátra, Astakós and a minority of those from Kefaloniá land at the main port and capital of **VATHÝ**, a bay within a bay so deep that few realize the mountains out "at sea" are actually the north of the island. This snug town is compact, relatively traffic-free and boasts the most idyllic seafront setting of all the Ionian capitals. Like its southerly neighbours, it was heavily damaged by the 1953 earthquake, but some fine examples of pre-quake architecture remain here and in the northern resort of **Kióni**. Vathý has a small **Archeological Museum** on Kalliníkou (Tues–Sun 8.30am–3pm; free), a short block back from the quay. Down an alley beside the ATEbank **ATM**, there is also the moderately interesting **Folklore & Cultural Museum** (summer Mon–Sat 10am–2pm; €1). There are more banks, a post office, police and a medical centre in town.

The oldest of Vathý's **hotels** is the refurbished and air-conditioned *Mentor* (Ⓣ26740 32433, Ⓦwww.hotelmentor.gr; ❺) in the southeast corner of the harbour. Further on round the bay are the posh *Omirikon* (Ⓣ26740 33598, Ⓕ26740 33596; ❻), and, just beyond it, the much better-value *Captain Yiannis* (Ⓣ26740 33419, Ⓕ26740 32849; ❸), complete with tennis court and pool. The best source of rooms, studios or villas is the town's two main quayside travel agents, Polyctor Tours (Ⓣ26740 33120, Ⓦwww.ithakiholidays.com) and Delas Tours (Ⓣ26740 32104, Ⓦwww.ithaca.com.gr). A wealth of advice on accommodation and the island in general can also be found at the excellent website Ⓦwww.ithacagreece.com.

Even though it's tiny, Vathý has a wealth of **tavernas** and **bars**. Many locals head off south around the bay towards the friendly, family-run *Paliocaravo* (aka *Gregory's*), popular for its lamb and fish and best of the three fine eateries in that direction. In town, the excellent *O Nikos*, just off the square, fills early, while *To Kohili* is by far the best of the half-dozen harbourside tavernas. As usual, the town's ancient *kafenio* one street back from the front is the best spot for a quiet and inexpensive tipple with the locals.

There are two reasonable pebble **beaches** within fifteen minutes' walk of Vathý: **Dhéxa**, over the hill above the ferry quay, and tiny **Loútsa**, opposite it around the bay. Better beaches out on the east coast are **Sarakíniko** and **Skínos**, an hour's trek from Vathý along recently improved roads. In season, daily *kaïkia* ply between the quay and remote coves.

Odysseus sights around Vathý

Three of the main **Odysseus sights** are just within walking distance of Vathý: the Arethoússa Spring, the Cave of the Nymphs and ancient Alalkomenae, although the last is best reached by vehicle. The walk to the **Arethoússa Spring** – allegedly the place where Eumaeus, Odysseus's faithful swineherd, brought his pigs to drink – is a three-hour round trip along a track signposted next to the seafront telecoms office. The unspoilt but shadeless landscape and sea views are magnificent, but the walk crosses slippery inclines and is not for those nervous of heights. Near the top of the lane leading to the spring path, a signpost points up to what is said to have been the **cave of Eumaeus**. The route to the spring continues for a few hundred metres, and then branches off onto a narrow footpath through gorse-covered steep cliffs. Parts of the final downhill track involve scrambling across rock fields (follow the splashes of green paint), and care should be taken around the small but vertiginous ravine that houses the **spring**, a trickle of water above which a crag known as **Kórax** (the raven) matches Homer's description. There is a small cove a short scramble down from the spring.

The **Cave of the Nymphs** (Marmarospíli) is about 2.5km up a rough but navigable road signposted on the brow of the hill above Dhéxa beach. The cave is atmospheric but underwhelming compared to the caverns of neighbouring Kefaloniá. The claim that this is the actual Homeric cave where the returning Odysseus concealed the gifts given to him by King Alkinous is enhanced by the proximity of Dhéxa beach, although there is some evidence that the "true" cave was much closer to the beach and unwittingly demolished during quarrying many years ago.

Alalkomenae, Heinrich Schliemann's much-vaunted "Castle of Odysseus", is signposted some 300m uphill from the Vathý–Pisaetós road, on the saddle between Dhéxa and Pisaetós, with views over both sides of the island. The actual site, however, is little more than foundations spread about in the gorse. Schliemann's excavations unearthed a Mycenaean burial chamber and domestic items such as vases, figurines and utensils (displayed in the archeological museum), but the ruins actually date from three centuries after Homer. In fact, the most likely contender for the site of Odysseus's castle is above the village of Stavrós (see below).

The sight is most easily approached by **moped** or **taxi** (no more than €15 round trip), as is the harbour of **Pisaetós**, about 2km below, with a large pebble beach that's good for swimming and popular with local rod-and-line fishermen. There is just one *kantína* here, serving those awaiting the regular ferries from Sámi on Kefaloniá.

Northern Itháki

The main road out of Vathý continues across the isthmus and takes a spectacular route to the northern half of Itháki, serving the villages of **Léfki**, **Stavrós**, **Fríkes** and **Kióni**. There is no regular bus service but it is excellent scooter country; the close proximity of the settlements, small coves and Homeric interest also make it good rambling terrain. Occasional summer *kaïkia* also visit the last two of those communities when there is demand. As with the rest of Itháki there is only a limited amount of accommodation.

Stavrós and around

STAVRÓS, the second-largest town on the island, is a steep two kilometres above the nearest beach (Pólis Bay). It's a pleasant enough town nonetheless, with *kafenía* edging a small square dominated by a rather fierce statue of Odysseus. There is even a tiny **museum** (Tues–Sun 8.30am–3pm; free) off the road to Platrithriés, displaying local archeological finds. Stavrós's Homeric site is on the side of **Pelikáta Hill**, where remains of roads, walls and other structures have been suggested as the possible site of Odysseus's castle. Stavrós is useful as a base if both Fríkes and Kióni are full up, and for exploring the northern interior hamlets. Both Polyctor and Delas handle **accommodation** in Stavrós and the traditional *Petra* taverna (ⓣ26740 31596; ③) offers rooms. The oldest and best **taverna** is *Fatouros*, and the *Margarita zaharoplastío* is a good place for a drink or to sample the local sweet *rovaní* (syrupy rice cakes).

A scenic mountain road leads 5km southeast from Stavrós to **ANOYÍ**, which translates roughly as "upper ground". Once the second-most important settlement on the island, it is almost deserted today. The centre of the village is dominated by a free-standing Venetian campanile, built to serve the (usually locked) church of the **Panayía**, which comes alive for the annual *paniyíri* on August 14, the eve of the Virgin's Assumption. On the outskirts of the village are the foundations of a ruined **medieval prison**, and in the surrounding countryside are some extremely strange rock formations, the biggest being the eight-metre-high Iraklis (Hercules) rock, just east of the village.

Two roads push north of Stavrós: one, to the right, heads 2km down to Fríkes, while the main road, to the left, loops below the hill village of **Exoyí**, and on to **Platrithiés**, where the new *Yefiri* taverna serves a wide range of tasty fare. Just off the start of the road up to Exoyí a signpost points about 1km along a rough track to the supposed **School of Homer**, where excavations still in progress have revealed extensive foundations, a well and ancient steps. The site is unfenced and well worth a detour for its views of **Afáles Bay** as much as the remains. On the outskirts of Platrithiés a track leads down to the bay, the largest on the entire island, with an unspoiled and little-visited pebble-and-sand beach.

Fríkes

At first sight, tiny **FRÍKES** doesn't appear to have much going for it. Wedged in a valley between two steep hills, it was only settled in the sixteenth century, and emigration in the nineteenth century almost emptied the place but the protected harbour is a natural year-round port. There are no beaches in the village, but plenty of good, if small, pebble strands a short walk away towards Kióni. When the ferries and their cargoes have departed, Fríkes falls quiet and this is its real charm: a downbeat but cool place to lie low.

Fríkes's one **hotel** is the upmarket *Nostos* (ⓣ26740 31644, ⓦwww.hotelnostos-ithaki.gr; ⑤), which has a pool, or you can try the equally comfy *Aristotelis Apartments* (ⓣ26740 31079, ⓦwww.aristotelis-ithaca.gr; ④). The Gods souvenir shop (ⓣ & ⓕ26740 31021) can help find **rooms**, though in peak season chances are slim. Fríkes has a quartet of good seafront **tavernas**, of which *Rementzo*, with its fresh fish, salads and pizza, and *Ulysses,* specializing in succulent homestyle cuisine, stand out. Tucked in the corner of the harbour, *Café Bemenis* is the established watering hole but adjacent *Isalos* café-bar offers more ambience, to-die-for cakes and an eclectic taste in music.

Kióni

KIÓNI sits at a dead end 5km southeast of Fríkes. On the same geological base as the northern tip of Kefaloniá, it avoided the very worst of the 1953 earthquakes, and so retains some fine examples of pre-twentieth-century architecture. It's an extremely pretty village, wrapped around a tiny harbour, and tourism here is dominated by British blue-chip travel companies and visiting yachts. The bay has a small sand and pebble **beach**, 1km along its south side, with a summer-only snack-bar.

While the best **accommodation** has been snaffled by the Brits, some local businesses have rooms and apartments to let, among them *Captain's Apartments* (ⓣ26740 31481, ⓦwww.captains-apartments.gr; ④), set up above the village, and *Maroudas Apartments* (ⓣ26740 31691, ⓔmaroudas@greek-tourism.gr; ❹), closer to the harbour. Another option, a short walk uphill on the main road in the hamlet of Ráhi, are the studios of Captain Theofilos Karatzis (ⓣ26740 31679; ❸), which have panoramic views. Kióni's **restaurants** are dotted around the picturesque harbour, but compare unfavourably with those in Fríkes; *Oasis* has a wide selection and is the best of the bunch, the *Avra* fish taverna is adequate, while *Mythos* specializes in *mayireftá* and the upmarket *Calypso* taverna has imaginative dishes like pork with artichokes. Other facilities include two well-stocked shops, a post office and a couple of bars and cafés, of which *Spavento* is marginally the best.

Zákynthos (Zante)

Zákynthos, southernmost of the six core Ionian islands, is somewhat schizophrenically divided between unspoilt natural beauty and indiscriminate commercialization. The island has three distinct zones: the barren, mountainous northwest; the fertile central plain; and the eastern and southern resort-filled coasts. The biggest resort – rivalling the busiest on Corfu – is **Laganás**, on Laganás Bay in the south. There are smaller, quieter resorts north and south of the capital, **Zákynthos Town**, and the southerly Vassilikós peninsula has some of the best countryside and beaches, including exquisite **Yérakas**.

Although half-built apartment blocks and a few factories are spreading into the central plain, this is where the quieter island begins: farms and vineyards, ancient villages and the ruins of Venetian buildings levelled in the 1948 and 1953 earthquakes. Zákynthos still produces fine wines, such as the white Popolaro, as well as sugar-shock-inducing *mandoláto* nougat. The island is the birthplace of *kantádhes*, which can be heard in tavernas in Zákynthos Town and elsewhere. It also harbours some of the key breeding sites of the endangered **loggerhead sea turtle** (see box, p.885).

Zákynthos Town

The town, like the island, is known as both **ZÁKYNTHOS** and Zante. This former "Venice of the East" (*Zante, Fior di Levante*, "Flower of the Levant", in an Italian jingle), rebuilt on the old plan after the 1953 earthquake, has bravely tried to re-create some of its style, though reinforced concrete can only do so much.

Arrival and information

Zákynthos is a working town with limited concessions to tourism, although there are hotels and restaurants aplenty, and it's the only place to stay if you want to see the island by public transport. The **bus** station is one block back from the seafront, about halfway along it. **Cars** and **mopeds** can be rented from Eurosky (ⓣ26950 26278, ⓦwww.eurosky.gr) at Makrí 6, two blocks south of the main square. Halfway along the front, the **tourist police** have a fairly welcoming office (May–Oct daily 8am–10pm; ⓣ26950 24482) in the main police station, which can supply basic information and help people find accommodation. There are a couple of **Internet** cafés on pedestrianized Alexándhrou Romá, parallel to the seafront but several blocks back.

Accommodation

The Room Owners Association (ⓣ26950 49498) can be contacted for accommodation around town and all over the island. Of the central seafront

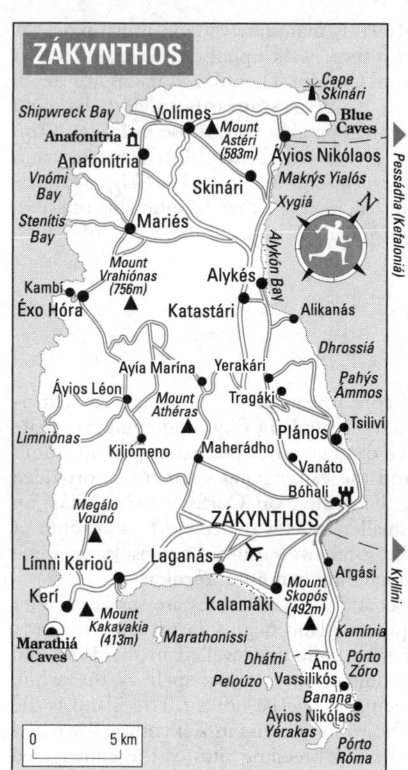

hotels, the *Egli*, on Loútzi (Ⓣ26950 28317; ④) is the best bet, tucked in beside the gargantuan eyesore of the *Strada Marina*. There are quieter hotels in the Repára district beyond Platía Solomoú: try either the *Plaza*, Kolokotróni 2 (Ⓣ26950 45733, Ⓕ26950 48909; ③), or the classy and surprisingly inexpensive *Palatino*, Kolokotróni 10 (Ⓣ26950 27780, Ⓦwww.palatinohotel.gr; ④), both near the municipal lido.

The town

The town stretches beyond the length of the wide and busy harbour, its main section bookended by the grand **Platía Solomoú** at the north, and the church of **Áyios Dhionýsios** (daily 8am–1pm & 5–10pm), patron saint of the island, at the south. The church is well worth a visit for the dazzling giltwork and fine modern murals inside, and a new **museum**, which has some fine paintings and icons (daily summer 8am–10pm, winter 9am–1pm & 5–9pm; €2). The vestments of St Dhionysios are kept in the restored church of **Áyios Nikólaos tou Mólou** on Platía Solomoú. The **square** is named after the island's most famous son, the poet Dhionysios Solomos, a champion of modernism in Greek literature, the movement that established demotic Greek over elitist *katharévousa* (see Language, p.968) as a literary idiom. He is best known as the author of the lyrics to the national anthem, an excerpt from which adorns the statue of Liberty in the square. There's an impressive **museum** (daily 9am–2pm; €3) devoted to the life and work of **Solomos** and other Zakynthian luminaries in nearby Platía Ayíou Márkou. It shares its collection with an eponymous museum on Corfu (see p.847), where Solomos spent most of his life.

Platía Solomoú is home to the town's **library**, which has a small collection of pre- and post-quake photography, and the massive **Byzantine Museum** (Tues–Sun 8am–3pm; €3), sometimes referred to as the Zákynthos Museum, most notable for its collection of artworks from the Ionian School, the region's post-Renaissance art movement, spearheaded by Zakynthian painter Panayiotis Doxaras. The movement was given impetus by Cretan refugees, unable to practise their art under Turkish rule. It also houses some secular painting and a fine model of the town before the earthquake.

Zákynthos's other main attraction is its massive **kástro**, brooding over the hamlet of Bóhali on its bluff above the town. The ruined Venetian fort (daily 8am–7.30pm in summer, 8am–2pm in winter; €1.50) has vestiges of dungeons, armouries and fortifications, plus stunning views in all directions. Its shady carpet of fallen pine needles makes it a great spot to relax or picnic. Below the *kástro* walls, **Bóhali** has a good though expensive taverna with panoramic views. The ugly new **amphitheatre** on the road up from town sometimes hosts concerts. Further towards the *kástro* the **Maritime Museum** (daily 9am–2pm & 6–9pm; €2.50) contains plenty of naval paraphernalia and presents an interesting chronological history of Hellenic seafaring.

Eating, drinking and nightlife

Most of the **restaurants** and bars on the seafront and Platía Ayíou Márkou are bedevilled by traffic, although the seafront *Psaropoula* does fine meat and fish, and the pricey but elegant *Komis*, across the quay from Áyios Dhionýsios, serves unusual seafood dishes and is far enough away from the bustle. First stop though, should be the friendly *Arekia* beyond the lido, which offers a succulent range of dishes and the best nightly *kantádhes* to be heard anywhere. The *Green Boat*, further along, serves up quality fare in a romantic waterside setting. When the bored teens get off their bikes, they go **clubbing** in bars like *Base* on Ayíou Márkou, which plays an eclectic dance mix, or the *Jazz Café*, on Tertséti which, despite the name, is actually a house/techno bar.

The south and west

The busy southern end of the island comprises the **Vassilikós Peninsula**, headed by the package resort of **Argási**, and the large sweep of **Laganás Bay**, whose resort of the same name is a major party destination. At the far southwest end of the bay, the landscape ascends into the mountains around **Kerí**, the first of a series of villages along the sparsely inhabited **west coast**.

Argási

The road heading southeast from Zákynthos passes through **ARGÁSI**, the busiest resort on this coast, but with a beach barely a couple of metres wide in parts. Although independent travellers would be better off basing themselves at one of the places further down, it could be used as a jumping-off point for the Vassilikós peninsula; there are rooms at the *Pension Vaso* (Ⓣ26950 44599; ❸) and *Soula* (Ⓣ26950 44864; ❷), both just off the main road entering the village, and some smart hotels on the seafront, such as the B&B *Locanda* (Ⓣ26950 45386, Ⓦwww.locanda.gr; ❹) and the *Iliessa Beach* (Ⓣ26950 27800, Ⓦwww.iliessa.com; ❹). Taverna culture is mainly low-brow with set-piece "Greek nights", one notable exception being the *Venetsiana*, which accompanies traditional food with nightly *kantádhes*. Argási is also home to some of the island's biggest and most popular discos on the town side, such as *Byblos* and *Manhattan*, and a host of cheap and cheerful bars in the village.

Boat trips from Zákynthos

At least ten pleasure craft offer **day-trips** around the island from the quay in Zákynthos Town for around €15. All take in sights such as the **Blue Caves** at Cape Skinári, and moor in **To Naváyio** (**Shipwreck Bay**) and the **Cape Kerí** caves. You might want to shop around for the trip with the most stops, as eight hours bobbing round the coast can become a bore. Check also that the operators actually take you into the caves.

The Vassilikós peninsula

The peninsula that stretches southeast of Argási is one of the most attractive parts of the island, with a happy blend of development and natural beauty. The real interest lies in the series of small beach resorts, mainly situated on the east coast. The first two are **Kamínia**, with the comfortable *Levantino* rooms (Ⓣ26950 35366, Ⓦwww.levantino.gr; ❹), and the more established **Pórto Zóro**, a better strand with the good-value eponymous hotel (Ⓣ26950 35304, Ⓦwww.portozorro.gr; ❸) and restaurant. The only real facilities away from the coast are to be found at the sprawling village of **Áno Vassilikós**, which serves the nearby beaches of **Iónio** and **Banana**. Among accommodation possibilities are the *Vassilikos Apartments* (Ⓣ26950 35280; ❸), on the main road, and *Angelika* (Ⓣ26950 35201; ❷), by the church just off it. Among the **tavernas**, on the main road, *Kostas' Brother* is well worth a try, as is *O Gallos*, which has French tinges; the *Logos* **bar** is fine for a drink too. Isolated **Áyios Nikólaos** has a good beach and lures day-trippers from Argási, Kalamáki and Laganás with a **free bus** service in season. Its expanding *Vasilikos Beach* (Ⓣ26950 35325, Ⓦwww.hotelvasilikosbeach.gr; ❺) complex is the focal point of a fast-emerging hamlet with a few restaurants and rooms – the neat white *Christina's* (Ⓣ26950 39474, Ⓕ26950 35421; ❸) is friendly and good value.

At the very tip of the peninsula is its star: **Yérakas**, a sublime crescent of golden sand. It's also a key loggerhead turtle breeding ground, and is therefore off-limits between dusk and dawn; the number of bathers allowed on the beach at one time during the day is also restricted but that only becomes a real issue in high season. The excellent open-air **Turtle Information Centre** (Ⓦwww.earthseasky.org) provides interesting background on these and other sea creatures, as well as eco boat cruises. **Accommodation** in the vicinity is best booked through British-based Ⓦwww.ionian-eco-villagers.co.uk. Otherwise, there's little here beyond three tavernas back from the beach – try *To Triodi* for fresh fish or well-prepared meat dishes. The only beach on the west coast of the peninsula really worth visiting, especially in the quieter months, is **Dháfni**; the road to it is now paved and there are a couple of tavernas, such as the fine *Mela Beach*.

Laganás and Kalamáki

The majority of the hundreds of thousands of people who visit Zákynthos each year find themselves in **LAGANÁS**. The nine-kilometre beach in the bay is good, if trampled, and there are entertainments from watersports to ballooning, and even an occasional funfair. Beachfront hotels, bars and restaurants stretch a couple of kilometres and establishments on the main drag over a kilometre inland. The competing video and music bars can make Laganás at night resemble the set of *Bladerunner*, but that's how its predominantly English visitors like it. **Accommodation** is mostly block-booked by package companies. There's a basic campsite (Ⓣ26950 51585) on the southern edge of town, where there are also quietish private rooms, or you can contact the Union of Room Owners (daily 8.30am–2pm & 5–8pm; Ⓣ26950 51590). As for hotels, try the old-fashioned *Byzantio* (Ⓣ26950 51136; ❸), near the crossroads, *Pension Tasoula* (Ⓣ26950 51560; ❷), between the beach and the campsite, or the larger *Ionis* (Ⓣ26950 51141, Ⓦwww.hotelionis.com; ❹), on the main drag towards the beach. *Dionysos*, halfway along the main drag, and *Zougras*, just before the river along the Kalamáki road, are among the more authentic **tavernas**, the latter hosting *kantádhes* most nights, while cheap and filling Chinese and Indian buffets can be had at *Butterfly* or *Estia*, both well back along the main drag. Favourite **bars** include *Kamikazi* and *Potters Bar;* popular clubs like *Zeros* and *End* carry on till dawn.

Neighbouring **KALAMÁKI** has a better beach than Laganás, and is altogether quieter, although it does suffer from some airport noise. There are several sizeable, mostly package-oriented hotels, but the upmarket *Crystal Beach* (Ⓣ26950 42788, Ⓕ26950 42917; ⑤) keeps some rooms aside and the islandwide Spring Tours agency (Ⓣ26950 43795, Ⓦwww.springtours.gr) can also arrange accommodation. The two *Stanis* **tavernas** have extensive menus of Greek and international dishes, although the beachside version is geared more to lunches and its sibling more to evening meals. A fine alternative is *Zepo's*, near the beach, and there are a number of places serving ethnic cuisine, though none stand out. **Nightlife** centres around bars like *Fire* and *Down Under* on the Laganás road, although the *Cave Club*, which lives up to its name, and upmarket *Byzantio* disco, both on the hillside above the village, are more atmospheric spots.

Kerí

The village of **Kerí** is hidden in a fold above the cliffs at the island's southernmost tip. The village retains a number of pre-quake Venetian buildings, including the church of the **Panayía Kerioú**; the Virgin is said to have saved the island from marauding pirates by hiding it in a sea mist. A rough path leaving the southern end of the village leads 1km on to the lighthouse, with spectacular views of the sea, rock arches and stacks and a taverna. En route a road branches off to **Límni Kerioú** at the southwestern end of Laganás Bay, which has

Loggerhead turtles

The Ionian islands harbour the Mediterranean's main concentration of **loggerhead sea turtles**, a sensitive species which is, unfortunately, under direct threat from the tourist industry. Easily frightened by noise and lights, these creatures lay their eggs at night on sandy coves and are therefore uneasy cohabitants with rough campers and late-night discos. Each year, many turtles fall prey to motorboat injuries, nests are destroyed by bikes and the newly hatched young die, entangled in deckchairs and umbrellas left out at night.

The Greek government has passed laws designed to protect the loggerheads, including restrictions on activities at some beaches, but local economic interests tend to prefer a beach full of bodies to a sea full of turtles. On Laganás, nesting grounds are concentrated around the fourteen-kilometre bay, and Greek marine zoologists have clashed angrily with those involved in the tourist industry. Other important locations include the turtles' nesting ground just west of Skála on Kefaloniá, although numbers have dwindled to around 800, half their former strength. Ultimately, as more efforts towards ecotourism are made, the turtles' best hope for survival may rest in their draw as a unique tourist attraction.

While capitalists and environmentalists are still at, well, loggerheads, the **World Wildlife Fund** has issued guidelines for visitors:

1. Don't use the beaches of Laganás and Yérakas between sunset and sunrise.
2. Don't stick umbrellas in the sand in the marked nesting zones.
3. Take your rubbish away with you – it can obstruct the turtles.
4. Don't use lights near the beach at night – they can disturb the turtles, sometimes with fatal consequences.
5. Don't take any vehicle onto the protected beaches.
6. Don't dig up turtle nests – it's illegal.
7. Don't pick up the hatchlings or carry them to the water, as it's vital to their development that they reach the sea on their own.
8. Don't use speedboats in Laganás Bay – a 9kph speed limit is in force for vessels in the bay.

developed into a laid-back and picturesque resort, home to the Turtle Beach Diving Centre (Ⓣ26950 48768, Ⓦwww.diving-center-turtle-beach.com). **Rooms** can be found at the friendly *Pansion Limni* (Ⓣ26950 48716, Ⓦwww.pansionlimni.com; ❸), now sporting a smart new block, or through the local Room Owners Association (Ⓣ & Ⓕ26950 45105). For **food** there is the *Poseidon* overlooking the bay from the far end and the *Keri* restaurant, which has good daily specials.

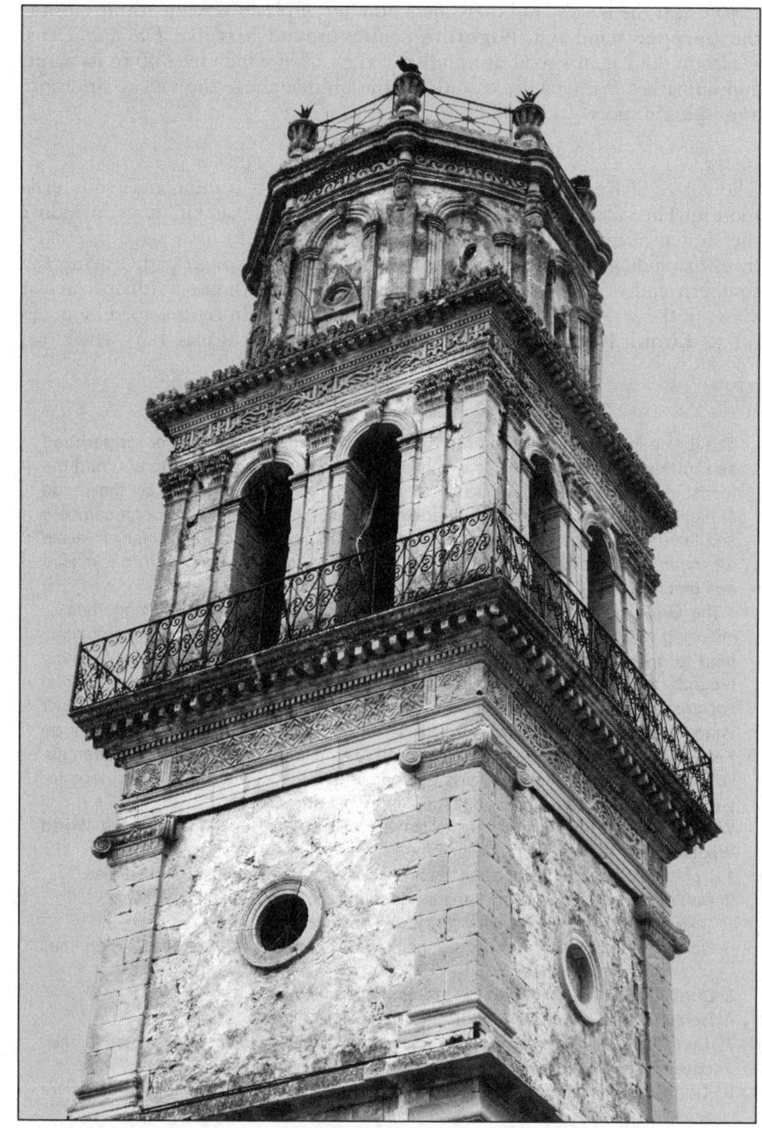

▲ Campanile, Áyios Nikólaos, Zákynthos

The west coast

The bus system does not reach the wild western side of the island, but a rental car or sturdy motorbike will get you there. **Maherádho** boasts impressive pre-earthquake architecture set in beautiful arable uplands, surrounded by olive and fruit groves. The church of **Ayía Mávra** has an impressive free-standing campanile and, inside, a splendid carved iconostasis and icons. It hosts the biggest festivals on the island on the first Sunday in June, the saint's day. Another venerable church, Panayía, commands breathtaking views over the central plain.

Kiliómeno is the best place to see surviving pre-earthquake domestic architecture, in the form of the island's traditional two-storey houses. The town was originally named after its church, **Áyios Nikólaos**, whose impressive campanile, begun over a hundred years ago, still lacks a capped roof. The *Alitzerini* **taverna** (evenings only) still occupies a cave-like house that dates from 1630 and dishes up superb traditional food. The road from Kiliómeno passes through the nondescript village of Áyios Léon, from where a loop road leads through fertile land to the impressive rocky coast at **Limniónas**, where there is a tiny bay and a taverna, and back again.

Further along the main road another turning leads to the tiny clifftop hamlet of **KAMBÍ**, popular with day-trippers, who come to catch the sunset over the sea; there are extraordinary views to be had of the 300-metre-high cliffs and western horizon from Kambí's three clifftop **tavernas**. The best of the three is named after the imposing concrete **cross** above the village, a memorial to islanders killed here during the 1940s, either by royalist soldiers or Nazis. The tiny village of **Mariés**, set in a wooded valley 5km to the north, has the only other coastal access on this side of Zákynthos; a seven-kilometre track leads down to the rocky inlet of **Stenítis Bay**, where there's a taverna and yacht dock, and another road to uninspiring **Vrómi Bay**, from where speedboats run trips to Shipwreck Bay (see p.889).

The north

A few kilometres north of the capital the contiguous resorts of **Tsiliví** and **Plános** are the touristic epicentre of this part of the island. Further north they give way to a series of tiny beaches, while picturesque villages punctuate the lush landscape inland. Beyond **Alykés**, as you approach the island's tip at **Cape Skinári**, the coast becomes more rugged, while the mountains inland hide the weaving centre of **Volímes**.

Tsiliví, Plános and around

North and inland from Zákynthos Town, the roads thread their way through luxuriantly fertile farmland, punctuated with tumulus-like hills. **TSILIVÍ**, 5km north of the capital, effectively merges with **PLÁNOS** to create the first beach resort here, matching Argási for development. There's a good, basic **campsite**, *Zante Camping* (Ⓣ26950 61710), beyond Plános, and, for a prime package-tour location, a surprising variety of **accommodation** – try the beachside *Anetis Hotel* (Ⓣ26950 28899, Ⓦanetishotel@yahoo.gr; ❸), which has air conditioning and TV in all rooms; *Gregory's* rooms (Ⓣ26950 61853; ❷); or contact Tsilivi Travel (Ⓣ26950 44194, Ⓦwww.tsilivi-travel.gr), on the inland road in from town. *The Olive Tree* **taverna** is the best place for Greek fare, while the *Passage to India* serves fairly authentic Chinese, as well as Indian. Drinking dens such as the *Mambo Club* and *Planet Pub* tend to be Brit-oriented.

The beaches further along this stretch of coast become progressively quieter and pleasanter, and they all have at least a smattering of accommodation and restaurants to choose from. Good choices include **Pahiá Ámmos**, the beach of Kypséli village, with the *Pension Petra* (Ⓣ26950 63593, Ⓦwww.zakynthos-petra.com; ③) and *Porto Roulis* fish taverna. Also recommended is **Dhrossiá**, where you can find the modern *Drosia* apartments (Ⓣ26950 62256, Ⓦwww.drosiaapartments.gr; ④) and eat at another popular fish taverna, *Andreas*.

Alykés and its bay

Órmos Alykón, 12km north of Tsiliví, is a large sandy bay with lively surf and two of the area's largest resorts. The first, **Alikanás**, is a small but expanding village, much of its accommodation being overseas villa rentals; the second, **ALYKÉS**, named after the salt pans behind the village, has the best beach north of the capital. There are **rooms** near the beach, most easily found through the local branch of Spring Tours (Ⓣ26950 83035, Ⓦwww.springtours.gr), and a number of **hotels** set back from it, but with sea views, such as the *Ionian Star* (Ⓣ26950 83416, Ⓦwww.ionian-star.gr; ④), although the best deal is inland from the crossroads at the chaotic *Eros Piccadilly* (Ⓣ26950 83606, Ⓦwww.erospiccadilly.com; ②). There are many **eating** joints, among the best the *Vineleaf*, which has unusual items such as jalapeño peppers stuffed with cream, and the more standard *Fantasia* and *Ponderosa* tavernas. Alykés is the last true resort on this coast, and the one where the bus service largely gives out. **Xygiá** beach, 4km north, has sulphur springs flowing into the sea – follow the smell – which provide the odd sensation of swimming in a mix of cool and warm water. The next small beach of **Makrýs Yialós**, which has the good *Pylarinos* taverna with a makeshift campsite, also makes for an extremely pleasant break on a tour of the north.

Áyios Nikólaos, 6km on, is a small working port serving daily ferries to and from Pessádha on Kefaloniá. Few visitors **stay** here, which perhaps explains why it hosts one of the most exclusive establishments in the Ionian, the classy stone *Nobelos* apartments (Ⓣ26950 31131, Ⓦwww.nobelos.gr; ⑧), as well as the more modest *Panorama* (Ⓣ26950 31013, Ⓔpanorama@altecnet.gr; ③). Pre-ferry meals can be had at *La Storia* fish restaurant or *Porto* taverna. Ignore scams claiming that this is the last chance to take a boat to the **Blue Caves**, which are some of the more realistically named of the many contenders in Greece. They're terrific for snorkelling, and when you go for a dip here your skin will appear bright blue. You can in fact approach them by the road that snakes up through a landscape of gorse bushes and dry-stone walls to the clifftop at **Cape Skinári**, where, from the lighthouse below three friendly brothers operate the cheapest **boat trips** to the caves (€7.50; €15 combined with Shipwreck Bay). Not far away, steps also lead down to a swimming jetty, near the caves, from behind the two unique rentable **windmills** of *Anemomilos* (Ⓣ26950 31241, Ⓦwww.potamitisbros.gr; ④), belonging to the same welcoming family; they also have more conventional rooms, and run the excellent *To Faros* **taverna**.

Katastári and Volímes

The northern towns and villages are best explored with a car or sturdy motorbike, although there are guided coach tours from the resorts and limited bus services. Two kilometres inland from Alykés, **Katastári** is the largest settlement after the capital. Precisely because it's not geared towards tourism, it's the best place to see Zakynthian life as it's lived away from the usual racket. Its most impressive edifice is the huge rectangular church of Yperáyia Theotókos, with a twin belfry and small new amphitheatre for festival performances. *To Kendro psistariá* does tasty grills at rock-bottom prices. A couple of kilometres south of Katastári, the tiny hamlet of **Pighadhákia** is the unlikely setting for the **Vertzagio Cultural Museum** (summer daily 9am–3pm & 5–7pm; €3), which houses an interesting array of agricultural and folk artefacts. There is also the diminuitive **Áyios Pandeléïmon** chapel, which has the unusual feature of a well, hidden beneath the altar. Just above it the *Kaki Rahi* taverna provides tasty local cuisine.

Volímes is the centre of the island's embroidery industry and numerous shops sell artefacts produced here. With your own transport, you could make it to the **Anafonítria monastery**, 3km south, thought to have been the cell of the island's patron saint, Dhionysios, whose festivals are celebrated on August 24 and December 17. A paved road leads on to the cliffs overlooking **Shipwreck Bay** (Naváyio), with hair-raising views down to the shipwreck – a cargo ship which ran aground in the Sixties.

Travel details

Buses

Corfu:
Corfu Town to: Athens (3 daily; 9–10hr); Thessaloníki (2 daily; 8–9hr).

Kefaloniá:
Argostóli to: Athens (4 daily; 7–8hr); Pátra (1 daily; 4–5hr).
Póros to: Athens (1 daily; 6–7hr).
Sámi to: Athens (2 daily; 6–7hr).

Lefkádha:
Lefkádha Town to: Athens (1 daily; 5hr 30min); Pátra (2 weekly; 3hr); Préveza (4 daily; 30min); Thessaloníki (2 weekly; 10–11hr).

Zákynthos:
Zákynthos Town to: Athens (5–6 daily; 5hr 30min); Pátra (4 daily; 3hr); Thessaloníki (3 weekly; 12–13hr).

Ferries

The following listings are based on summer schedules, which are often reduced drastically in winter; any services that stop altogether are marked as being summer only. Tourist craft and *kaïkia* are not included below.

Corfu:
Corfu Town to: Eríkoussa/Mathráki/Othoní (3 weekly; 2–4hr); Igoumenítsa (every 10–45min; 1hr 15min); Pátra (6–10 daily; 6–9hr).
Lefkími to: Igoumenítsa (6 daily; 40min).

Itháki:
Fríkes to: Fiskárdho (Kefaloniá; 1 daily; 1hr); Nydhrí or Vassilikí (Lefkádha; 1 daily; 1hr 30min).
Pisaetós to: Sámi (Kefaloniá; 2–3 daily; 45min).
Vathý to: Astakós (1 daily; 2hr 30min); Pátra (2 daily; 3hr 30min); Sámi (Kefaloniá; 1–2 daily; 1hr).

Kefaloniá:
Argostóli to: Kyllíni (1 daily; 2hr 15min); Lixoúri (every 30min; 20min).
Fiskárdho to: Fríkes (Itháki; 1 daily; 1hr); Nydhrí (Lefkádha; 1 daily; 2hr 15min); Vassilikí (Lefkádha; 2–3 daily; 1–2hr).
Pessádha to: Áyios Nikólaos (Zákynthos; 2 daily May–Sept; 1hr 30min).
Póros to: Kyllíni (3–5 daily; 1hr 15min).
Sámi to: Astakós (1 daily; 2hr 30min); Kérkyra Town (1–2 weekly; 5hr); Pátra (1–2 daily; 3hr 30min); Pisaetós (Itháki; 2–3 daily; 40min); Vathý (Itháki; 1–2 daily; 1hr).

Lefkádha:
Nydhrí to: Fiskárdho (Kefaloniá; 1 daily; 2hr 15min); Fríkes (Itháki; 1 daily; 1hr 30min); Meganíssi (7 daily; 20min).
Vassilikí to: Fiskárdho (Kefaloniá; 2–3 daily; 1hr); Fríkes (Itháki; 1 daily; 2hr).

Paxí:
Gáïos to: Igoumenítsa (1–2 daily; 1hr).

Zákynthos:
Zákynthos Town to: Kyllíni (5–7 daily; 1hr 30min).
Áyios Nikólaos to: Pessádha (Kefaloniá; 2 daily May–Sept; 1hr 30min).

International Ferries

Kérkyra Town is a main stop on many of the ferry routes to Italy from Pátra and a stopover can be added for free with many companies. The frequency and journey time to the various Italian ports is: Ancona (1–2 daily; 14hr); Bari (2–3 daily; 11hr); Brindisi (3–5 daily; 4–9hr); and Venice (2–3 weekly; 25hr).

Hydrofoils

Corfu Town to: Gáïos (Paxí; 1–3 daily; 50min).
Gáïos to: Corfu Town (1–3 daily; 50min).

Flights

All domestic flights listed below are on Olympic, Aegean or the Airsea Lines seaplane service. For international flights see "Basics" p.31.

Corfu to: Athens (4–6 daily; 1hr); Ioánnina (5 weekly; 40min); Lefkádha (6 weekly; 45min–1hr 15min); Kefaloniá (8 weekly; 1hr 15min–2hr 20min); Pátra (7 weekly; 1hr 10min–1hr 45min); Paxí (1–3 daily; 20min); Préveza (3 weekly; 25min); Zákynthos (3 weekly; 2hr).
Kefaloniá to: Athens (2 daily; 1hr); Corfu (8 weekly; 1hr–1hr 15min); Ioánnina (1 weekly; 5hr); Pátra (5 weekly; 40min); Paxí (5 weekly; 2hr 55min); Préveza (3 weekly; 25min); Zákynthos (3 weekly; 25min).
Zákynthos to: Athens (4 daily; 55min); Corfu (3 weekly; 1hr 55min); Kefaloniá (3 weekly; 25min); Préveza (3 weekly; 1hr 15min).

Contexts

Contexts

A history of Greece

The geographical position of Greece, on the Mediterranean and at the crossroads of Europe, Asia and Africa, has long presented it with unique opportunities and dangers. The Greeks are a people who have suffered calamities, yet they have also achieved the highest reaches of human accomplishment. In the areas of politics, philosophy, literature, science and art, Greece has influenced Western society more than any other nation in history.

Prehistoric Greece: to 2100 BC

Evidence of human habitation in Greece goes back half a million years, as demonstrated by the discovery in 1976 of the skeleton of a **Neanderthal** youth embedded in a stalagmite in the **Petralóna Cave**, 50km east of the northern city of Thessaloníki, along with the earliest known site of a man-made fire in Europe.

Only very much later, about **40,000 years ago**, did **Homo sapiens** make his first appearance in Greece after migrating out of Africa. At several sites in **Epirus** in northwest Greece, Homo sapiens used tools and weapons of bone, wood and stone to gather wild plants and hunt. Even between **20,000 and 16,000 years ago**, when the Ice Age was at its peak, **Stone Age man** continued to make a home in Greece, though only when the glaciers finally receded about **10,000 BC** did a considerably warmer climate set in, altering the Greek environment to something more like that of present times.

The Neolithic period

Agricultural communities first appeared in **Macedonia** around **6500 BC** and in **Thessaly** a thousand years later. Whether agriculture developed indigenously or was introduced by migrants from Asia Minor is much debated: what is certain, however, is its revolutionary effect.

An assured supply of food enabled the Stone Age inhabitants of Greece to settle in fixed spots, building mud brick houses on stone foundations. Though still reliant on stone implements, this new farming culture marked a significant break with the past, so a "new stone age" or **Neolithic Period** is said to have begun in Greece from 6500 BC. As the strong kind of flint needed for weapons and tools was rare in Greece, the mainlanders imported obsidian, the hard black glassy stone formed by rapidly cooling volcanic lava, found on the island of **Melos** (Mílos) in the southern Cyclades. The earliest **seaborne trade** known anywhere in the world, this clearly involved a mastery of building and handling boats.

Cycladic culture and the beginnings of the Greek Bronze Age

Around **3000 BC** a new people settled in the **Cyclades**, probably from Asia Minor, bringing with them the latest metallurgical techniques. While continuing the old trade in obsidian, they also developed a **trade in tin** and were making prodigious voyages westwards as far as Spain by 2500 BC. The mining of **gold and silver** in the Cyclades may have dated from this period, too. Long before Crete or the Greek mainland, these new islanders became specialists in

jewellery-making, **metalwork** and **stone-cutting**. From the abundant marble of the Cyclades, they sculpted statuettes, mostly of female figures. Slender, spare and geometric, these **Cycladic sculptures** are startlingly modern in appearance, and were exported widely, to Crete and mainland Greece, along with other ritual objects.

In about 3000 BC, the introduction of bronze technology to the mainland, also from the Cyclades, marked the start of the **Bronze Age** in Greece. By **2500 BC**, thanks to a well-established network of long-distance trade, the widespread use of bronze had transformed farming and fighting throughout the Eastern Mediterranean and the Middle East. Because **tin** (which when alloyed with copper creates bronze) came from so far afield – in the East it could be obtained only in isolated pockets of the Caucasus, Persia and Afghanistan, while in the West sources were confined to Cornwall, Brittany, northwest Spain and northern Italy – the Aegean became an important trade route. Hence the burst of development that now took place along the eastern coast of **central Greece** and the **Peloponnese**, and on the **Aegean islands** which linked the Greek mainland to Asia Minor and the Middle East.

It is uncertain what **language** was spoken at this time on the mainland and the islands, but one thing is clear: it was not yet Greek. Indeed, when **Greek-speaking people** did arrive on the mainland in about 2100 BC, their destructive impact paralysed its development for five hundred years, while the large and secure island of **Crete** – which they did not invade or settle – flourished and dominated the Aegean.

The coming of the Greeks

The destruction of numerous mainland sites in about **2100 BC**, followed by the appearance of a new style of pottery, has suggested to archeologists the violent arrival of a **new people**. They domesticated the horse, introduced the potter's wheel, and possessed considerable metallurgical skills. These newcomers replaced the old religion centred on female fertility figures with **hilltop shrines**, thought to have been dedicated to the worship of male sky gods like Zeus. And with them came a new language, an early form of **Greek**, though they were obliged to adopt existing native words for such things as olives, figs, vines, wheat and the sea, suggesting that these new migrants or invaders may have come from distant inland steppes where they had been pastoral highlanders, not farmers, fishermen or sailors.

The shock of domination was followed by five centuries of adjustment and intermingling. The population increased, new settlements grew up, and there were advances in metallurgy. Yet in comparison with the Cyclades and Crete, which the invaders had never reached, the Greek mainland seems to have remained backward. Only around **1600 BC**, and then under the influence of Crete, did progress on the mainland quicken – until within little over a hundred years **Crete** itself was conquered by the Greek-speaking mainlanders.

Minoan and Mycenaean civilizations: 2100–1100 BC

The history of the Aegean during the second millennium BC can be seen as a struggle between two cultures, the **Mycenaean culture** of the Greek mainland

and the **Minoan culture** of Crete. Situated halfway between mainland Greece and Asia Minor, Crete exploited the Bronze Age boom in trade, to become the dominant power in the Aegean by the start of the second millennium BC. Its distinctive civilization, called Minoan, and beneficial economic influence were felt throughout the islands and also on the mainland. The subsequent Greek-speaking mainland invaders were "Minoanized", gradually developing a culture known as Mycenaean (after Mycenae, a principal mainland Bronze Age site) that owed a lot to Crete.

Minoan Crete

Living on a large and fertile island with good natural harbours, the people of **Crete** raised sufficient crops and livestock on the coastal plains and highland pastures to export surplus quantities of oil and wool. Among their most impressive tools, literally at the cutting edge of new technology, was a four-foot-long bronze saw that readily converted the forest-clad mountains into an ample source of **timber for ships**. Some timber was probably also exported, most likely to treeless Egypt, while metalwork, jewellery and pottery of superb Cretan craftsmanship were shipped to the mainland and beyond. **Kamares ware**, as Cretan pottery of this period is known, was especially valued; it has been found all along the Cretans' 1400-mile-long maritime trade route to the East – on the Aegean islands of Rhodes and Sámos, on the coast of Asia Minor at Miletus, and in Syria and Egypt.

On Crete itself, Minoan power was concentrated on three vast **palace complexes** – at **Knossos**, **Phaestos** and **Malia**, all in the centre of the island. First built around 2000 BC, their similarity of plan and lack of defences suggest that some form of confederacy had replaced any regional rivalries on the island, while Minoan sea power induced a sense of security against foreign invasion. Not that prosperity was confined to the palace centres; the numerous remains of villas of the Minoan gentry, and of well-constructed villages, show that the wealth generated by the palaces was redistributed among the island's population.

The Trojan War

For the Greeks, the story of the **Trojan War** was the central event in their early history, and in their minds Homer's **Iliad** was not just a poem of heroic deeds sung at noble courts, but the epic of their first great national adventure.

Excavations in the late nineteenth century by Heinrich Schliemann uncovered many Troys of several periods, but the layer known as **Troy VIIa** clearly suffered violent destruction in about 1220 BC. The Mycenaeans are the likeliest perpetrators, though the abduction of a Greek beauty called **Helen** would not have been the only reason they launched a thousand ships against the Trojans. Mycenaean prosperity greatly depended on trade with the Eastern Mediterranean, where increasingly unsettled conditions made it imperative that the Mycenaeans secure their lines of **trade and supply**. Troy commanded a strategic position overlooking the Hellespont, the narrow waterway (today called the Dardanelles) dividing Europe and Asia and linking the Aegean to the Black Sea, where it controlled important trade routes.

The capture of Troy was the last great success of the Mycenaeans, and perhaps for that reason it was long remembered in poetry and song. It inspired later generations of Greeks to dream of overseas expansion, culminating in the fourth century BC when Alexander the Great carried a copy of the Iliad as he marched across Asia, founding Greek cities as he went, and stood with his army on the banks of the Indus River.

Following an **earthquake** around 1700 BC, the palaces at Knossos and Phaestos were rebuilt, and a more modest palace constructed at **Zakros** on the east coast. This activity coincided with an apparent centralization of power at Knossos, whose ruler installed a vassal at Phaestos and seems to have united the entire island into a single kingdom, giving rise to a **Minoan golden age**.

Mycenaean dominance

Suddenly, however, around **1500 BC**, the Mycenaeans gained control of the palace of Knossos and were soon in full possession of Crete. How this happened is unknown, but it probably marked the culmination of a growing rivalry between the Mycenaeans and the Minoans for control of the Aegean trade, which perhaps coincided with a **volcanic explosion** on the island of Thera (Thíra/Santoríni) and its consequent **tsunami**.

Greek now became the language of administration at Knossos and the other former Minoan palaces, as well as on the mainland – indeed this is the earliest moment that Greek language can definitely be identified, as the palace records on Crete are from now on written in a script known as **Linear B**, which when deciphered in 1953 was shown to be a form of Greek. Having wrested control of the Aegean trade from the Minoans, the **Mycenaeans** were dominant for another three hundred years. At the end of that period in about 1220 BC, they famously laid siege to, and destroyed, yet another rival, the city of **Troy**: those events form the basis of Homer's great poetic narrative, the **Iliad**.

Yet within a generation the Mycenaean world was overwhelmed by a vast **migration** of northerners from somewhere beyond the Black Sea. Probably victims of a catastrophic change in climate that brought drought and famine to their homelands, these **Sea Peoples**, as the ancients called them, swept down through Asia Minor and the Middle East and also crossed the Mediterranean to Libya and Egypt, disrupting trade routes and destroying empires as they went. With the palace-based Bronze Age economies destroyed, the humbler **village-based economies** that replaced them lacked the wealth and the technological means to make a mark in the world. Greece was plunged into a Dark Age, and knowledge of the Minoan and Mycenaean civilizations slipped into dim memory.

The Dark Age and the rise of the city-state: 1150–720 BC

The poverty and isolation that characterized Greece for the next five hundred years did have one lasting effect, **emigration**. Greeks spread to the Dodecanese islands, to Cilicia along the south coast of **Asia Minor**, and to **Cyprus**, which now became Greek-speaking. Later, around 1000 BC, they also settled in large numbers along the western coast of Asia Minor. Even in the Dark Age, too, there were a few glimmers of light: **Athens**, for example, escaped the destruction that accompanied the fall of Mycenaean civilization and maintained trading links abroad. It became the route through which the **Iron Age** was introduced to mainland Greece with the importation of iron weapons, implements and technological know-how around 1100 BC. A new cultural beginning was also made in the form of pottery painted in the **Geometric style**, a highly intricate and controlled design that would lie at the heart of later Greek architecture, sculpture and painting. But it was the **Phoenicians**, sailing from Sidon and Tyre in present-day Lebanon, who really re-established trading links between the Middle East and the Aegean world in the eighth century BC, and Greeks followed swiftly in their wake. With wealth flowing in again, Greek civilization developed with remarkable rapidity; no other people achieved so much over the next few centuries. The institution most responsible for this extraordinary achievement, the **city-state** or **polis**, came into being at a time of rapidly growing populations, greater competition for land and resources, increasing productivity and wealth, expanding trade and more complex relationships with neighbouring states. The birthplace of **democracy** and of equality before the law, the city-state became the Greek ideal, and by the early seventh century BC it had spread throughout Greece itself and wherever Greeks established colonies overseas.

Trade also acted as a cultural stimulus. Contact with other peoples made the Greeks aware of what they shared among themselves, and led to the development of a **national sentiment**, notably expressed and fostered by the **panhellenic sanctuaries** that arose during the eighth century BC, of **Hera** and **Zeus** at **Olympia**, where the first **Olympic Games** were held in 776 BC, and of **Apollo** and **Artemis** at **Delos**, as well as the **oracles** of **Zeus** at **Dodona** and of **Apollo** at **Delphi**.

From the Phoenicians the Greeks obtained the basics of the **alphabet**, which they adapted to their own tongue and developed into a sophisticated tool for recording laws, composing literature and chronicling events. **Greek art**, under Eastern influence, saw the Geometric style gradually give way to depicting animals, mythical and real. Finally around 750 BC, for the first time in four

Homer and the Iliad and the Odyssey

The **Iliad** and the **Odyssey**, the oldest and greatest works in Greek literature, were the brilliant summation of five centuries of poetic tradition, first developed by nameless bards whose recitations were accompanied by music. Completed by 725 BC, they are far older than the *Pentateuch*, the first five books of the Old Testament, which achieved their finished form only around 400 BC. The admiration of the whole Greek world for the Homeric epics was unique, and their influence upon the subsequent development of Greek literature, art and culture in general cannot be overstated. Few works, and probably none not used in worship, have had such a hold on a nation for so long.

But from time to time the old argument flares up again: did the blind poet **Homer** write the *Iliad* and the *Odyssey*? The best answer came from Mark Twain who said, "The *Iliad* and the *Odyssey* were written by the blind poet Homer or by another blind poet of the same name. In truth, virtually nothing is known of Homer beyond the tradition that he was blind and was born into the eighth-century BC world of the Asian Greeks, perhaps at Smyrna or opposite on the island of Híos.

The Iliad is the story of a few days' action in the tenth and final year of the Trojan War, which in its tales of heroic exploits recalls the golden age of the Mycenaeans. The Odyssey begins after the war and follows the adventures of Odysseus, who takes ten years to return to his island home of Ithaca on the western side of Greece, his voyages showing the new Greek interest in the area around the Black Sea and in Italy and Sicily to the west. Taken together, the epics recover the past and look forwards into the future. In this they are an Ionian achievement, for it was in Asia Minor that Greek civilization first and most shiningly emerged from the Dark Age. But they are also a celebration of an emerging panhellenic identity, of a national adventure encompassing both shores of the Aegean and beyond.

hundred years, **human figures** were introduced to vase decorations, most strikingly in group scenes with a story to tell.

Expansion and renaissance: 720–491 BC

The revival of seafaring and commerce early in the first millennium BC contributed to the rise of the city-state around 750 BC, which in turn had two dramatic results: the **colonization** of the Mediterranean and beyond, and radical **social and political change** at home.

Colonization

The Greeks began by founding **colonies** in the Western Mediterranean. Those in **Sicily** and **southern Italy** became known as **Greater Greece**, while a century later, around 650 BC, further colonies were established round the shores of the **Black Sea**. By the fifth century BC Greeks seemed to sit upon the shores of the entire world, in Plato's words like "frogs around a pond".

One impetus for colonization was competition between the Greeks and the Phoenicians over trade routes; but there was also rivalry between the Greek city-states themselves. **Chalkis**, **Eretria** and **Corinth** were the major colonizers in the West, while the **Ionian Greeks**, prevented from expanding into the interior of Asia Minor by Phrygia and Lydia, were the chief colonizers around the Black Sea. When the Spartans needed more land, they conquered neighbouring Messenia in 710 BC, but generally land shortage drove Greeks overseas. Thus colonists were sent from Thera (Thíra) to found Cyrene in North Africa, and were forbidden to return on pain of death. Whatever the reason for their foundation, however, most colonies kept up close relations with their mother cities.

Democracy, tyranny and slavery

Meanwhile, at home in the city-states, political tensions were building between the **aristocratic rulers** and the **people**. A large class of farmers, merchants and the like were excluded from political life but forced to pay heavy taxes. The pressure led to numerous reforms and a gradual move towards **democracy**. Ironically, the transition was often hastened by **tyrants**. Despite the name – which simply means they seized power by force – many tyrants were in fact champions of the people, creating work, redistributing wealth and patronizing the arts. **Peisistratos**, tyrant of Athens during the sixth century BC, is perhaps the archetype. Successful and well-liked by his people, his populist rule ensured Athenian prosperity by gaining control of the route into the Black Sea. He also ordered that Homer's works be set down in their definitive form and performed regularly, and encouraged the theatrical festivals of Dionysus where Greek drama would be born.

Ironically, at much the same time as they were founding the city-states that gave birth to democracy, Greeks turned to **slavery** on a commercial scale. Previously, household slaves, as found in Homer, were usually war captives; their numbers were not many, nor was Greek society dependent on them. But during the seventh century BC slavery became widespread, involving the import of large numbers from Thrace, Asia Minor and the Black Sea coasts in the face of a shortage of free men to support the development of trade and manufacturing.

Athens and the Golden Age: 490–431 BC

Democracy itself was a very long way from universal. The population of **Athens** and surrounding Attica amounted to not more than 400,000 people, of whom about 80,000 were slaves, 160,000 resident foreigners, and another 160,000 free-born Athenians. Out of this last category came the **citizens**, those who could vote and be elected to office, and their number amounted to no more than 45,000 adult men.

Yet if the powers of democracy were in the hands of the few, the energy, boldness and creative spirit that it released raised Athens to greatness. Throughout the **fifth century BC** the political, intellectual and artistic activity of the Greek world was centred on the city. In particular Athens was the patron of **drama**, both tragedy and comedy. Athenian tragedy always addressed the

The Olympian gods

A high proportion of the ancient sites still seen in Greece today were built as **shrines and temples to the gods**. They include spectacular sites such as Delphi and the Acropolis in Athens, but also many other sanctuaries, great and small, in market-places and by roadsides, in cities and on islands, on mountaintops and headlands – everywhere, in fact, because the gods themselves were everywhere.

There were many lesser and local gods like the Nymphs and Pan, but the great gods known to all were the **twelve** who lived on **Mount Olympus**. Ten were already recognized by Homer in the eighth century BC: **Zeus**, the lord of the heavens and supreme power on Olympus; **Hera**, his wife and sister, and goddess of fertility; **Athena** the goddess of wisdom, patron of crafts and fearless warrior; **Apollo** the god of music, of prophecy and the arts; his sister **Artemis**, the virgin huntress and goddess of childbirth; **Poseidon**, the god of the sea and the forces of nature; the beautiful **Aphrodite**, goddess of love and desire; **Hermes**, the messenger who leads the souls of the dead to the underworld, but also the protector of the home and the market; **Hephaestus**, the lame god of craftsmen and for a while the husband of Aphrodite; and **Ares**, the god of war, who in cuckolding Hephaestus was subdued by the goddess of love. In the fifth century BC these were joined by two deities with a certain mystical quality of rebirth: **Demeter**, the goddess of crops and female fertility; and **Dionysus**, the god of wine and intoxication.

Though limited in number, the Olympian deities could be made to play infinite roles in local cult calendars by the addition of epithets; thus Zeus became "Zeus of the city" or "Zeus of mountaintops", as well as "kindly" or "fulfilling" as place and occasion required. The gods had human form, and were born and had sexual relations among themselves and humankind, but they never ate human food nor did they age or die. But whereas the gods of most nations claim to have created the world, the Olympians never did so. All they did was to conquer it and then enjoy its fruits, not so unlike mankind itself.

Worshipped, feared and admired, these deities formed the basis for the ancient Greek religion until paganism was banned throughout the newly Christianized Roman Empire in AD 391.

great issues of life and death and the relationship of man to the gods. And the Athenians themselves seemed to be conscious of living out a high drama as they fought battles, argued policy, raised temples and wrote plays that have decided the course and sensibility of Western civilization.

The Persian Wars

The wars between Greece and Persia began with a revolt against Persian rule by Ionian Greeks in Asia Minor. Athens and Eretria gave them support, burning the city of Sardis in 498 BC. Provoked by their insolence **Darius**, the Persian king, launched a punitive expedition. The **Persians'** unexpected repulse at **Marathon** in 490 BC persuaded Darius to hurl his full military might against Greece, to ensure its subjection once and for all to the Persian Empire.

After Darius died in 486 BC, **Xerxes** took over. In 483 BC, he began preparations that lasted two years and were on a fabulous scale. Bridges of boats were built across the Hellespont for Persia's vast imperial army to parade into Europe, and a canal was cut through the peninsular finger, now occupied by the Mount Athos monasteries, so that the Persian fleet could avoid storms while rounding the headlands of the Halkidhikí. Though the Greek historian **Herodotus** claimed that Xerxes' army held one million eight hundred thousand soldiers, his figure is probably a tenfold exaggeration. Even so, it was a massive force, an army of 46 nations, combined with a fleet of eight hundred triremes carrying almost as many sailors as there were soldiers in the army.

Despite their numerical superiority, the might of Asia was routed both at sea off **Salamis** in 480 BC and on land at **Plataea** the following year. Within a few days of that second battle came another, near **Miletus**. Fearing a renewed uprising in Ionia, Xerxes left his army under the command of Mardonius and

The Battle of Marathon

For the Athenians, victory in the **Battle of Marathon** set the seal on their democracy and marked the start of a new self-confident era. And indeed, it was the most remarkable of victories.

Fearing that it would be fatal to attack the larger numbers of Persian infantry supported by cavalry and archers, the Athenian army kept to its position astride the mountain pass leading into the plain of Marathon and waited there for Spartan reinforcements. On the fifth day the Persians gave up hope of joining battle at Marathon and embarked their cavalry to advance on Athens by sea, sending their infantry forwards to cover the operation. With the Persian forces divided, **Miltiades** saw his opportunity, Spartan help or no, and sent his hoplites racing downhill to get quickly under the hail of Persian arrows and engage their infantry in close combat. The Athenian centre was kept weak while the wings were reinforced, so that when the Persians broke through the centre of the charging line, the momentum of the Greek wings soon engulfed them on either side and to the rear. The Persians panicked, fell into disorder, and were beaten into the marshes and the sea. Seven Phoenician ships were lost and 6400 Persians killed. The 192 Athenian dead were buried on the spot, and covered by a mound that can still be seen today.

The remainder of the Persian force now sailed round Cape Sounion to land within sight of the Acropolis at Phaleron, but Miltiades had brought the army back to Athens by forced march and stood ready to meet the enemy again. That astonishing burst of energy – 10,000 men marching 26 miles in full armour after fighting one battle to fight, if need be, another – overwhelmed the Persians' morale, and their expedition returned to Asia.

came to Sardis to take charge of his reserves. The Ionians had indeed sent to Greece for help, and now a Greek fleet sailed for **Mycale**, off Sámos, where the battle was won when Xerxes' subject Ionians went over to their fellow Hellenes. Xerxes could do no more than return to Susa, his capital deep in Persia, leaving the entire Aegean free.

Despite occasional reversals, this sudden shift in the balance of power between East and West endured for the next 1500 years. Within 150 years, Alexander the Great achieved in Asia what Xerxes had failed to achieve in Europe, and the Persian Empire succumbed to a Greek conqueror.

Themistocles

The greatest Athenian statesman, and architect of the victory over Persia, was **Themistocles**. Following the Ionian revolt he understood that a clash between Persia and Greece was inevitable, and he had the genius to recognize that Athens' security and potential lay in its command of the sea. He began his life's mission of promoting his naval policy as archon in 493–492 BC, by developing **Piraeus** (Pireás) as the harbour of Athens. Though his initial pretext was the hostility of the island of Aegina (Égina), his eyes were always on the more distant but far greater Persian danger.

When the Persians marched into Attica in the late summer of 480 BC, the oracle at Delphi told the Athenians to trust in their wooden wall. Many took that to mean the wooden wall around the citadel of the Athenian Acropolis, but Themistocles argued that it referred to the Athenian fleet. Determined to fight at sea, Themistocles warned his Peloponnesian allies against retreating to the Isthmus where they too had built a wall, threatening that if they did the entire citizenry of Athens would sail to new homes in southern Italy, leaving the rest of Greece to its fate. On the eve of the Battle of Salamis, as the Persians stormed the Acropolis, slaughtering its defenders and burning down its temples, the taunt came back from the Peloponnesians that Athens had no city anyway. Themistocles replied that so long as the Athenians had 200 ships they had a city and a country.

The Greek victory at Salamis cut the Persians' maritime lines of supply and contributed to their defeat at Plataea the following year. It gave Athens and its allies command of the sea, ensuring their eventual victory throughout the Aegean. For his pains the Athenians later drove Themistocles into exile.

The Rise of the Athenian Empire: 478–431 BC

The first consequence of the Greek victory against the Persians was not, as might have been expected, the aggrandisement of **Sparta**, the pre-eminent Greek military power, whose soldiers had obediently sacrificed themselves at Thermopylae and won the final mainland battle at Plataea. Instead, many Greek city-states voluntarily placed themselves under the leadership of Athens.

This Aegean confederation was named the **Delian League**, after the island of Delos where the allies kept their treasury. Its first task was to protect the Greeks of Asia Minor against a vengeful Xerxes. This was the opposite of the policy proposed by Sparta and its Peloponnesian allies, which called for the abandonment of Greek homes across the Aegean and the resettlement of Asian Greeks in northern Greece.

That typified the Spartan attitude throughout the Persian crisis, in which Sparta had shown no initiative and acted only at the last minute. Its policy was provincial, protecting its position in the Peloponnese rather than pursuing the wider interests

Aeschylus and Sophocles: The development of Greek tragedy

When tragedy was invented in Athens, late in the sixth century BC, peasants were settling in the city but remained in touch with such country traditions as the fertility ritual celebrating the life and death of Dionysus, the god of the vine, who shed his blood for mankind. Because goats were sacrificed in the worship of Dionysus, the ritual, in which a chorus danced and sang, was called *trag-odia*, a goat-song. Around 520 BC the story moved away from the Dionysus cycle, and an actor was introduced who came and went, changing costumes and playing different roles in successive episodes.

Aeschylus transformed matters by introducing a second actor and increasing the amount of dialogue, while correspondingly reducing the size and role of the chorus. Thus tragedy truly became drama, driven by exchanges of words and actions. That Aeschylus had fought at Marathon, and, probably, Salamis, may explain the urgency of his play, *The Persians*, the oldest surviving Greek tragedy. Although a religious man who believed in the overwhelming power of the gods, Aeschylus makes clear that it is man himself, through the free choices he makes, who steps into the appalling conflicts of the tragic situation.

By tradition four plays were submitted to Athens' annual Dionysian festival. Three were tragedies, the fourth a satyr play providing comic relief. Here too Aeschylus broke new ground, making his three tragedies successive phases of one story – famously in the late work of his maturity, the *Oresteia*, a great drama of revenge and expiation turning on Agamemnon's return home from the Trojan War and his murder. By now Aeschylus was using a third actor and also painted scenery, ideas taken from **Sophocles**, his younger rival.

Sophocles' innovation made it possible to present plots of considerable complexity. He was a man of orthodox piety, not in rebellion against the world, but his was a world of inescapable consequences – in his *Oedipus Rex*, for example, to be unseeing is not enough, while the *Antigone* presents the ultimate tragic conflict, between right and right.

The effect of the tragedies of Aeschylus and Sophocles was to leave their audiences with an enhanced sense of pity or of terror. The unspoken moral was "You are in this too", the cathartic experience leaving everyone stronger – as though Athens, democratic, confident and imperial, was preparing itself to meet the blows of destiny.

of Greece. Sparta persistently lacked vision, adventure and experience of the sea, believing that what could not be achieved by land was impossible. Thus over the coming decades Sparta lost prestige to Athens, which Themistocles had established as a maritime power and whose imperial potential was realized under Pericles.

This was the **Athenian golden age**, and in so far as Athens was also "the school of Hellas", as its leader **Pericles** said, it was a golden age for all Greece. The fifty years following Salamis and Plataea witnessed an extraordinary flowering in architecture, sculpture, literature and philosophy; men recognized the historical importance of their experience and gave it realization through the creative impulse. Just as **Herodotus**, the "father of history", made the contest between Europe and Asia the theme of his great work, so **Aeschylus**, who fought at Marathon, made Xerxes the tragic subject of *The Persians* and thereby brought the art of drama to life. Indeed in the intoxicating Athenian atmosphere the warriors who turned back the Persian tide seemed to have fought in the same cause as Homer's heroes at Troy. In thanksgiving and celebration the temples upon the Acropolis that the Persians had destroyed were rebuilt, the city ennobling itself as it ennobled the houses of its gods – most notably with the building of the **Parthenon**.

Yet Athens was still just one among numerous city-states, each ready to come together during a common danger but reasserting its sovereignty as the foreign threat receded. This was illustrated by the ten-year struggle from 461 BC onwards between Athens and various **Peloponnesian states**, itself a warning of a yet greater war to come between Athens and Sparta. Perhaps 451 BC marks the fatal moment when Athens passed up the opportunity to create an institution more generous, and more inclusive, than the city-state. Instead Pericles supported the parochial and populist demand that **Athenian citizenship** should not be extended to its allies, thereby stoking up the flames of envy and foregoing the chance of creating a genuine and enduring Greek confederacy.

Pericles and his times

In 461 BC, **Pericles** (ca.495 BC–429 BC) was first elected to Athens' most important elected position, of *strategos* (general). The ten *strategoi* proposed the legislation that was then voted on in the Assembly. Pericles was so brilliant at winning over audiences in a society where the people were sovereign, in reality he governed the state for around thirty years; with only two exceptions, he was annually re-elected until his death in 429 BC.

Among his early triumphs – in the face of conservative opposition – was to make **peace with Persia** in 449 BC, the better to turn his attention to **Sparta**. Pericles believed that Athenian power was not only Greece's best defence against Persia but also the best hope for the unification of Greece under enlightened rule. The visible expression of this cultural excellence could be seen atop the Acropolis, where Pericles was directly responsible for the construction of the Propylaea and the Parthenon, but it was true too in sculpture, painting, drama, poetry, history, teaching and philosophy, where Athenian influence is felt to this day. Politically, as both Pericles and his enemies understood, the advance of democracy in Greece depended on the success of that Athenian imperialism which grew out of the Delian League.

But whatever the excellence of Athens, whatever the ideals of its power, the jealousies of the Peloponnesians were excited all the more, and it is a testimony to Pericles that he was able to avoid war with Sparta for as long as he did. Thucydides, the historian of the Peloponnesian War, greatly admired Pericles for his integrity and also for the restraint he exercised over Athenian democracy.

The decline of the city-state: 431–338 BC

The **Peloponnesian War** that began in **431 BC** was really a continuation of earlier conflicts between Athens and its principal commercial rivals, Corinth and Aegina and their various allies in the Peloponnese. Sparta had earlier stood aside, but by 432 BC when Corinth again agitated for war, the **Spartans** had become fearful of growing Athenian power.

The Athenian empire was built on trade, and the city was a great sea power, with 300 triremes. The members of Sparta's **Peloponnesian League**, meanwhile, had powerful armies but no significant navy. Just as Themistocles had sought to fight the Persians by sea, so Pericles followed the same startegy against Sparta and its allies, avoiding major battles against superior land forces. Athens and Piraeus were protected by their walls, but the Peloponnesians and their allies were allowed to invade Attica with impunity nearly every year, and Thrace saw constant warfare. On the other hand the Peloponnesians lacked the seapower to carry the fighting into Asia Minor and the Aegean islands or to interfere with Athens' trade, while the Athenians used their maritime superiority to launch attacks against the coasts of the Peloponnese, the Ionian islands and the mouth of the Gulf of Corinth, hoping to detach members from the Peloponnesian League. So long as Athens remained in command of the sea, it had every reason to expect that it could wear down its enemies' resolve.

Pericles' death in 429 BC was an early blow to the Athenian cause. Although **Kleon**, his successor, is widely blamed for Athens' eventual defeat, after Pericles the city was in fact always divided into a peace party and a military one, unable to pursue a consistent policy. The final straw came in 415 BC, when a bold operation designed to win Sicily to the Athenian cause turned into a catastrophic debacle, thanks at least partly to political interference. Though not entirely defeated, Athens was never to be a major power again.

City-state rivalries

The Peloponnesian War left **Sparta** the supreme power in Greece, but those whom the Spartans had "liberated" swiftly realized that they had simply acquired a new and inferior master, one that entirely lacked the style, the ability and the intelligence of Athens. Meanwhile Athens had lost its empire but not its trade, so its mercantile rivals faced no less competition than before. During the first decade of the fourth century, Athens managed to restore much of its naval power in the Aegean.

Thucydides: the first systematic historian

The writing of history began among the Greeks, first with **Herodotus**, then with Thucydides. Whereas Herodotus gives the feeling that he prefers telling a good story, that he still inhabits Homer's world of epic poetry, with **Thucydides** the paramount concern is to analyze events. In that sense Thucydides is the first modern historian; wherever possible he seeks out primary sources, and his concern is always with objectivity, detail and chronology. Not that there is anything dry about his writing; its vividness and insight make reading him as powerful an experience as watching a Greek drama.

Thucydides began writing his history at the outset of the **Peloponnesian War**, intending to give an account of its whole duration, For reasons unknown, however, he abruptly stopped writing in the twentieth year, though he is thought to have survived the war by a few years, living until about 400 BC. Born into a wealthy, conservative Athenian family around 455 BC, he was a democrat and an admirer of Pericles; his reconstruction of Pericles' speeches presents the most eloquent expression of the Athenian cause. But when Thucydides was exiled from his city seven years into the war, this was the making of him as a historian. As he put it, "Associating with both sides, with the Peloponnesians quite as much as with the Athenians, because of my exile, I was thus enabled to watch quietly the course of events".

Thucydides was himself a military man, who understood war at first hand. Hence his concern for method in his research and analysis in his writing, for he intended his book to be useful to future generals and statesmen. For these reasons we have a better understanding of the Peloponnesian War than of any ancient conflict until Julius Caesar wrote his own first-hand accounts of his campaigns. And for these reasons too, Thucydides' history stands on a par with the greatest literature of ancient Greece.

Adding to the intrigues between Persia, Athens and Sparta were a bewildering and unstable variety of alliances involving other Greek states. The most important of these was **Thebes**, which had been an ally of Sparta during the Peloponnesian War but came round to the Athenian side, and then for a spectacular moment under its brilliant general **Epaminondas** became the greatest power in Greece, in the process dealing Sparta a blow from which it never recovered. Theban supremacy did not survive the death of Epaminondas, however, and Greece subsequently found itself free for the first time in centuries from the dictates of Persia or any overpowerful Greek city-state. Exhausted and impoverished by almost continuous war, it was an opportunity for Greece to peacefully unite. But the political and moral significance of the city-state had by now eroded, and with the **rise of Macedonia** came the concept of an all-embracing kingship.

The Macedonian Empire and Hellenistic Greece: 348–146 BC

Despite its large size and population, **Macedonia** played little role in early Greek affairs. Its weakness was due to the constitutional position of the king, whose status was subject to approval by a vote of the nobility. Rivalries among potential heirs and fears of usurpation limited royal power. Moreover, the Greeks did not consider the Macedonians to be properly Greek, not in speech, culture or political system. They did not live in city-states, which Aristotle said was the mark of a civilized human being, but as a tribal people were closer to the barbarians.

Philip II and the rise of Macedonia

Towards the middle of the fourth century, however, the power of Macedonia grew, as **Philip II** strengthened royal authority by building up the army on the basis of personal loyalty to himself, not to tribe or locality. Philip was also determined to Hellenize his country. Borrowing from Greek ways and institutions, he founded the city of **Pella** as his capital and lured teachers, artists and intellectuals to his court, among them **Aristotle** and **Euripides**. An admirer of Athens, Philip sought an alliance that would make them joint-masters of the Greek world. But the Athenians opposed him, and he took matters into his own hands.

In **338 BC** Philip brought about the unity of the mainland Greeks, defeating the Theban and Athenian forces at **Chaeronia** with one of the most formidable fighting units the world has ever seen, the **Macedonian phalanx**. Armed with the *sarissa*, an eighteen-foot pike tapering from butt to tip, its infantrymen were trained to move across a battlefield with all the discipline of a parade ground drill. Instead of relying on a headlong charge, its effectiveness lay in manipulating the enemy line – its purpose always to open a gap through which the cavalry could make its decisive strike.

Alexander's conquests

After Chaeronia, Philip summoned the Greek states to Corinth, and announced his plans for a panhellenic conquest of the Persian Empire. But Philip was

Big Ideas: Socrates, Plato and Aristotle

The Golden Age of Athens under Pericles, and the city-state rivalry after the Peloponnesian War, saw the **birth of Western philosophy** under the towering figures of Socrates, Plato and Aristotle.

Socrates (ca.470–399 BC)

Born the son of an Athenian sculptor, Socrates was for a time a sculptor himself. Though he fought bravely for Athens as a hoplite in the Peloponnesian War, much earlier, in his twenties, he had turned to philosophy, which he practiced in his own peculiar style. Promoting no philosophical position of his own, he asserted, ceaselessly, the supremacy of reason. Often this was done in the streets of Athens, buttonholing some self-regarding Athenian of the older generation, asking him questions, picking his answers to pieces, until he came up with a definition that held water or, more likely, the spluttering victim was reduced to confess his own ignorance before crowds of Socrates' mirthful young supporters.

By this "Socratic method" he asked for definitions of familiar concepts such as piety and justice; his technique was to expose the ignorance that hid behind people's use of such terms, while acknowledging his own similar ignorance. Indeed when the Delphic oracle proclaimed that no man was wiser than Socrates, he explained this by saying wisdom lies in knowing how little one really knows. Because he valued this question-and-answer process over settling on fixed conclusions, Socrates never wrote anything down. Yet his influence was pivotal; before his time philosophical inquiry concerned itself with speculations on how the natural world was formed and how it operates; afterwards it looked to the analysis of concepts and to ethics.

Socrates' method could be irritating, especially when he questioned conventional morality, and his friendships with people associated with oligarchy did not put him in good stead with a democratic Athens that had just lost an empire and a war. Probably many factors directed the city's anger, fear and frustration at Socrates, and Athenians wanted to see the back of him. Having tried him for impiety and corrupting the young, and sentenced him to death, they gave him the option of naming another penalty, probably expecting him to choose exile. Instead Socrates answered that if he was to get what he deserved, he should be maintained for life at public expense. At this the death penalty was confirmed, but even then it was not to be imposed for two months, with the tacit understanding that Socrates would escape. Instead Socrates argued that it was wrong for a citizen to disobey even an unjust law, and in the company of his friends he drank the cup of hemlock. "Such was the end", wrote Plato, describing the scene in *Phaedo*, "of our friend; of whom I may truly say, that of all the men of his time whom I have known, he was the wisest and justest and best."

Plato (ca.427–c.347 BC)

As a young man, Plato painted, composed music and wrote a tragedy, as well as being a student of Socrates. He intended a career in politics, where his connections would have ensured success; his father could claim descent from the last king of Athens, his mother from Solon, and the family had been close allies of Pericles. But Socrates' death made Plato decide that he could not serve a government that had committed such a crime, and instead his mission became to exalt the memory of his teacher. In Plato's writings, many of them dialogues, Socrates is frequently the leading participant, while at the Academy in Athens, which Plato founded, the Socratic question-and-answer method was the means of instruction.

Plato's philosophy is elusive; he never sets out a system of doctrines, nor does he tell us which of his ideas are most basic, nor rank them in hierarchical order, nor show how they interrelate. Nevertheless, certain themes recur. He believed that men possess immortal souls separate from their mortal bodies. Knowledge, he believed, was the recollection of what our souls already know; we do not gain knowledge from experience, rather by using our reasoning capacity to draw more closely to the realm of our souls. The true objects of knowledge are not the transient, material things of this world, which are only reflections of a higher essence that Plato called Forms or Ideas. Forms are objects of pure thinking, cut off from our experience; but also Forms motivate us to grasp them, so that the reasoning part of us is drawn to Forms as a kind of mystic communion.

Plato's notion of a mystic union with a higher essence would play an important role in later religious thought. But more immediately his teachings at the Academy concerned themselves with logic, mathematics, astronomy and above all political science, for its purpose was to train a new ruling class. Prominent families sent him their sons to learn the arts of government. Plato, an aristocrat born into a calamitous age marked by Athens' imperial defeat, responded by teaching that the best form of government was a constitutional monarchy, at its head a philosopher-king with that higher knowledge of Justice and the Good drawn from the realm of Forms. Though it was a utopian vision, Plato's political philosophy helped prepare the intellectual ground for the acceptance of an absolutist solution to the increasing uncertainties of fourth-century BC Greece.

Aristotle (384–322 BC)

Aristotle grew up in Pella, the capital of an increasingly powerful Macedonia, where his father had been appointed doctor to King Amyntas II; it is therefore not unlikely that Amyntas' son, the future Philip II, and Aristotle were boyhood friends. However, aged seventeen, Aristotle was sent to Plato's Academy at Athens to continue his education, and he remained there, first as a student, then as a teacher, a faithful follower of Plato's ideas. His independent philosophy matured later, during the years he spent, again at Pella, as tutor to Alexander the Great, and later still, after 335 BC, when he founded his own school, the Lyceum, in Athens.

Aristotle came to reject Plato's dualism. He did not believe that the soul was of a substance separate from the body, rather that it was an aspect of the body. Instead of Plato's inward looking view, Aristotle sought to explain the physical world and human society from the viewpoint of an outside observer. Essentially a scientist and a realist, he was bent on discovering the true rather than establishing the good, and he believed sense perception was the only means of human knowledge. His vast output covered many fields of knowledge – logic, metaphysics, ethics, politics, rhetoric, art, poetry, physiology, anatomy, biology, zoology, physics, astronomy and psychology. Everything could be measured, analyzed and described, and he was the first to classify organisms into genera and species. He is probably the only person ever to assimilate the whole body of existing knowledge on all subjects and bring it within a single focus.

The exactitude of Aristotle's writings does not make them easy reading, and Plato has always enjoyed a wider appeal owing to his literary skill. All the same, Aristotle's influence on Western intellectual and scientific tradition has been enormous.

murdered two years later and to his son **Alexander** fell his father's plans for an **Asian campaign** – throughout which, it is said, he slept with the *Iliad* under his pillow.

In the East too there was an assassination, and in 335 BC the Persian throne passed to **Darius III**, namesake of the first and doomed to be the last king of his line. Using essentially his father's tactics, Alexander led his army through a series of astonishing victories, usually against greater numbers, until he reached the heart of the Persian Empire. Alexander crossed the Hellespont in May of **334 BC**, with thirty thousand foot soldiers and five thousand horse. By autumn all the Aegean coast of **Asia Minor** was his; twelve months later he stood on the banks of the Orontes River in **Syria**; in the winter of 332 BC **Egypt** hailed him as pharaoh; and by the spring of 330 BC the great Persian cities of **Babylon**, **Susa**, **Persepolis** and **Pasargadae** had fallen to him in rapid succession until, at **Ecbatana**, he found Darius in the dust, murdered by his own supporters. Alexander wrapped the corpse in his Macedonian cloak, and assumed the lordship of Asia.

Hellenistic Greece

No sooner had **Alexander** died at Babylon in 323 BC, aged thirty-three, then Athens led an alliance of Greeks in a **war of liberation** against Macedonian rule. But the Macedonians had built up a formidable navy which inflicted heavy losses on the Athenian fleet. Unable to lift the Macedonian blockade of Piraeus, Athens surrendered and a pro-Macedonian government was installed. The episode marked the end of Athens as a sea power and left it permanently weakened.

Greece was now irrevocably part of a new dominion, one that entirely altered the scale and orientation of the Greek world. Alexander's strategic vision had been to see the Mediterranean and the East as two halves of a greater whole. Opened to Greek settlement and enterprise, and united by Greek learning, language and culture, if not always by a single power, this **Hellenistic Empire** enormously increased international trade, created unprecedented prosperity, and established an **ecumene**, the notion of one world, no longer divided by the walls of city-states but a universal concept shared by all civilized peoples.

Asked on his deathbed to whom he bequeathed his empire, Alexander replied "To the strongest". Forty years of warfare between his leading generals gave rise to three dynasties, the **Antigonid** in Macedonia, which ruled over mainland Greece, the **Seleucid** which ultimately centred on Syria and Asia Minor, and the **Ptolemaic** in Egypt, ruled from Alexandria, founded by Alexander himself, which in wealth and population, not to mention literature and science, soon outshone anything in Greece.

The emergence of Rome

Meanwhile, in the Western Mediterranean, **Rome** was a rising power. **Philip V** of Macedonia had agreed a treaty of mutual assistance against Rome with Hannibal. After Hannibal's defeat. Rome's legions marched eastwards, and routed Philip's army at **Cynoscephalae** in Thessaly in 197 BC.

Rome was initially well disposed towards Greece, which they regarded as the originator of much of their culture, and granted autonomy to the existing city-states. However, after a number of uprisings, the country was divided into **Roman provinces** from 146 BC. For good measure Corinth was razed, and its inhabitants sold off, to deter any future Greek resistance.

Roman Greece: 146 BC–330 AD

During the first century BC Rome was riven by civil wars, many of whose climactic battlefields were in Greece: in 49 BC **Julius Caesar** defeated his rival Pompey at **Pharsalus** in Thessaly; in 42 BC Caesar's assassins were beaten by **Mark Antony** and **Octavian** at **Philippi** in Macedonia; and in 31 BC **Antony** and his Ptolemaic ally **Cleopatra** were routed by **Octavian** in a sea battle off **Actium** in western Greece. The latter effectively marked the birth of the **Roman Empire** – an empire that in its eastern half continued to speak Greek.

By the first century AD Greece had become a **tourist destination** for well-to-do Romans (and a relatively comfortable place of exile for troublemakers). They went to Athens and Rhodes to study literature and philosophy, and toured the country to see the temples with their paintings and sculpture. They also visited the by now thoroughly professional **Olympic Games**. When the emperor **Nero** came to Greece in AD 67, he entered the Games as a contestant; the judges prudently declared him the victor in every competition, even the chariot race, in which he was thrown and failed to finish.

Roman rule saw much **new building** in **Athens** and elsewhere, notably by the emperor Hadrian. The centre of the Athenian Agora, which had long ceased to serve the purposes of a democracy, was filled with an odeon, a covered theatre seating a thousand people, the gift of Augustus' general Agrippa. Nearby Hadrian built his public library; he loved Athens and stayed there in 125 and 129 AD, completing the vast **Temple of Olympian Zeus** begun nearly six hundred years before by Peisistratos. **Herodes Atticus**, also a generous patron of the arts in Athens, built the odeon that bears his name at the foot of the Acropolis in the 160s.

Saint Paul and early Christianity

Greece had an early taste of **Christian teaching** when **Saint Paul** came to preach in 49–52 AD. Brought before the Court of the Areopagus in Athens, a powerful body that exercised authority over religious affairs, he was asked to defend his talk of the death and resurrection of his foreign god, and dismissed as a crank. Paul then spent eighteen months in **Corinth**; he made some converts, but as his subsequent Epistles to the Corinthians show, their idea of Christianity often amounted to celebrating their salvation with carousing and fornication. In the last decades of the century, **Saint John the Divine**, who was proselytizing at Ephesus, was exiled by the Romans to Patmos, where in a cave still shown to visitors today he is said to have written *Revelation*, the apocalyptic last book of the Bible.

Although the books of the New Testament were composed in Greek, their authors came from the Greek East, and Christianity seems to have made little headway among the inhabitants of Greece itself. Throughout all the **Roman persecutions** of the third and early fourth centuries, in which hundreds of thousands died in Egypt, the Middle East and Asia Minor, there are few recorded martyrs in Greece – probably, it is thought, because there were few Greek Christians.

Barbarian incursions

During the mid-third century the **Heruli**, a tribe from southern Russia, succeeded in passing through the Bosphorus and into the Aegean. Ravaging far and wide, they plundered and burned **Athens** in 267. New city walls were built with the marble rubble from the wreckage, but their circumference was now so small that the ancient Agora, littered with ruins, was left outside, while what remained of the city huddled round the base of the Acropolis. It was a familiar scene throughout Greece, as prosperity declined and population fell, except in the north along the **Via Egnatia**, the Roman road passing through their province of Macedonia, linking ports on the Adriatic with Thessaloníki on the Aegean.

Byzantine and Medieval Greece: 330–1460 AD

The **Byzantine Empire** was founded in May 330 when the **emperor Constantine** declared Nova Roma (as he called the city of Byzantium – known today as Istanbul) the new capital of the Roman Empire. Founded on the banks of the Bosphorus by Greek colonists in the seventh century BC, Byzantium occupied the one supremely defensible and commanding point from where the entire trade between the Black Sea and the Mediterranean could be controlled. **Constantinople**, the city of Constantine, as it became popularly known, was perfectly positioned for the supreme strategic task confronting the empire: the defence of the Danube and the Euphrates frontiers. Moreover, the new capital stood astride the flow of goods and culture from the East, that part of the empire richest in economic resources, most densely populated and rife with intellectual and religious activity.

The Christian empire

Constantine's other act with decisive consequences was to **legalize** and patronize the **Christian church**. Here again Constantinople was important, for while Rome's pagan traditions could not yet be disturbed, the new capital was consciously conceived as a Christian city. Within the century Christianity was established as the religion of state, with its liturgies (still in use in the Greek Orthodox Church), the Creed and the New Testament all in Greek.

In 391 the emperor **Theodosius I** issued an edict banning all expressions of **paganism** throughout the empire. In Greece the mysteries at Eleusis ceased to be celebrated the following year, and in 395 the Olympic Games were suppressed, their athletic nudity an offence to Christianity. Around this time too the Delphic oracle fell silent. The conversion of pagan buildings to Christian use began in the fifth century. Under an imperial law of 435 the Parthenon and the Erectheion on the Acropolis, the mausoleum of Galerius (the Rotunda) in Thessaloníki and other temples elsewhere became churches. Even this did not eradicate pagan teaching: philosophy and law continued to be taught at the Academy in Athens, founded by Plato in 385 BC, until prohibited by the emperor Justinian in 529.

In 395 the Roman Empire split into **Western and Eastern empires**, and in 476 **Rome fell** to the barbarians. As the Dark Ages settled on Western Europe, Byzantium inherited the sole mantle of the empire. Latin remained its official language, though after the reign of Justinian (527–565) the emperors joined the people in speaking and writing Greek.

Thessaloníki, the second city of the Byzantine Empire, was relatively close to Constantinople, yet even so the journey by land or sea took five or six days. The rest of Greece was that much farther and Attica and the Peloponnese grew decidedly provincial. Conditions worsened sharply in the late sixth century when Greece was devastated by **plague**. In Athens after 580 life came almost

Islam and the iconoclastic controversy

The advent of Islam in the mid-seventh century had its effect on Greece. The loss to the Arabs of the Christian provinces of Syria in 636, and Egypt in 642, was followed by an attack by an Arab fleet in 677 on Constantinople itself. In 717–718 a combined Arab naval and land force beleaguered the city again, while in 823 the Arabs occupied Crete.

The proximity and pressure of Islam helped fuel the great iconoclastic controversy that ignited passions and pervaded daily life throughout the Byzantine Empire for over a century. In 730 the emperor Leo III, who was born on the Syrian frontier and earned the epithet "Saracen-minded", proscribed images in the Orthodox Church, claiming they amounted to idolatry. His strongest support came from the farmer-soldiers of Asia Minor, that is those closest to the lands recently conquered by the Muslims, while his opponents, the iconodules, who favoured icons, were found in the monasteries and in Greece. Indeed, it was the empress Irene, an Athenian, who briefly restored the images in 780, though they were again proscribed by imperial decree from 815 to 843, with the effect that almost no representational Byzantine art survives in Greece from before the ninth century.

to an end, as the remaining inhabitants withdrew to the Acropolis, while at Corinth the population removed itself entirely to the island of Égina. Only Thessaloníki fully recovered.

The Crusades

In 1071 the **Byzantine army** was destroyed at **Manzikert**, a fortress town on the eastern frontier, by the **Seljuk Turks** who went on to occupy almost all Asia Minor. After the Byzantine emperor turned to the West for help, the Roman Catholic Pope replied by launching the **First Crusade** in 1095. Together, the Crusaders and the Byzantines won a series of victories over the Seljuks in Asia Minor, but the Byzantines, wary of possible Crusader designs on the empire itself, were content to see their Latin allies from the West advance alone on Jerusalem, which they captured in 1099.

The worst fears of the Byzantines were borne out in 1204 when the **Fourth Crusade** attacked and sacked **Constantinople** itself. Greece was shared out between Franks, Venetians and many others in a bewildering patchwork of feudal holdings. Amid endless infighting in the West, a new Turkish dynasty, the **Ottomans**, emerged in the late thirteenth century. By 1400 they had conquered all of Byzantine Greece except Thessaloníki and the Peloponnese. In 1452 they invaded the Peloponnese as a diversion to the main attack on **Constantinople**, which fell on May 23, 1453. In 1456 the Ottomans captured **Athens** from the Venetians and turned the Parthenon church into a mosque, and in 1460 they conquered the **Peloponnese**. **Trebizond** fell the following year, and the Byzantine empire was no more.

Greece under Turkish occupation: 1460–1821

Western possessions in Greece after 1460 amounted to **Rhodes** – held by the Knights of St John – and, under **Venetian rule**, the Peloponnesian ports of

Koróni, Methóni and **Monemvasiá**, and the islands of **Évvia**, **Crete**, **Corfu**, **Égina** and (later) **Cyprus**. In 1522 the Ottomans drove the Knights of St John from Rhodes, and within two more decades they had captured all the Venetian mainland colonies in Greece, leaving them only Cyprus and Crete.

Although the Greeks refer to the Turkish occupation as *sklavía* – "slavery" – in practice, in exchange for submitting to Muslim rule and paying tribute, the Greeks were free to pursue their religion and were left very much in charge of their own religious and civil affairs. The essence of the Turkish administration was **taxation**. Tax collection was often farmed out to the leaders of the Greek communities, and some local magistrates profited sufficiently to exercise a dominant role not only within their own region but also in the Ottoman Empire at large. Generally the Ottomans controlled the towns and the plains but left the mountains almost entirely to the Greeks.

The other important institution within Greece was the **Orthodox Church**. The Church was wealthy and powerful; Greeks preferred to give their lands to the monasteries than have them occupied by the Turks, while the Muslims found it easier to allow the Church to act in a judicial capacity than to invent a new administration. Though often corrupt and venal, the Church did at least preserve the traditional faith and keep alive the written form of the Greek language, and it became the focus of Greek nationalism.

Ottoman conquests and the eclipse of Venice

In 1570 Ottoman troops landed on **Cyprus**. Nicosia was swiftly captured, and 30,000 of its inhabitants slaughtered. Turkish brutality in Cyprus horrified Europe, and the **Holy League** was formed under the aegis of the Pope. Spain and Genoa joined Venice in assembling a fleet led by Don John of Austria, the bastard son of the Spanish king, its lofty aim not only to retake the island but in the spirit of a crusade to recapture all Christian lands taken by the Ottomans. In the event, it was utterly ineffectual; no serious attempt was made even to launch an expedition to relieve Cyprus. Yet out of it something new arose – the first stirrings of **Philhellenism**, a desire to liberate the Greeks whose ancient culture stood at the heart of Renaissance thought and education.

There was, too, the encouragement of a naval victory, when in 1571 Don John's fleet surprised and overwhelmingly defeated the much larger Ottoman fleet, at its winter quarters at **Lepanto** on the Gulf of Corinth in western Greece. Two hundred and sixty-six Ottoman vessels were sunk or captured, fifty thousand sailors died, and fifteen thousand Christian galley slaves were freed. Throughout Europe the news of Lepanto was received with extraordinary rejoicing; this was the first battle in which Europe had triumphed against the Ottomans, and its symbolic importance was profound. Militarily and politically, however, the Ottomans remained dominant. They finally took **Crete** in 1669, after twenty years of resistance, which marked the end of the last bastion of Byzantine culture.

Greek nationalist stirrings

Meanwhile during the eighteenth century the islanders of **Ýdhra** (Hydra), **Spétses** and **Psará** built up a Greek merchant fleet that traded throughout the Mediterranean, where thriving colonies of Greeks were established in many ports. Greek merchant families were also established in the sultan's provinces of **Moldavia** and **Wallachia**, the area of present-day Romania. The rulers of these provinces were exclusively Greeks, chosen by the sultan from wealthy **Phanariot families**, that is residents of the Phanar, the quarter along the

Golden Horn in Constantinople and site of the Greek Orthodox Patriarchate which itself enjoyed considerable privileges and was an integral part of the administration of the Ottoman Empire.

These wealthier and more educated Greeks enjoyed greater than ever opportunities for advancement within the Ottoman system, while the Greek peasantry, unlike the empire's Muslim inhabitants, did not have to bear the burden of military service. Nevertheless the Greeks had their grievances against the Ottoman government, which mostly concerned the arbitrary, unjust and oppressive system of taxation. But among the Greek peasantry it was primarily their religion that opposed them to their Muslim neighbours – as much as one fifth of the population – and to their Ottoman overlords. Muslim leaders had long preached hatred of the infidel, a view reciprocated by the priests and bishops of the Orthodox Church.

The War of Independence: 1821–32

The **ideology** behind the **War of Independence** came from the Greeks of the diaspora, particularly those merchant colonies in France, Italy, Austria and Russia who had absorbed new European ideas of nationalism and revolution. Around 1814, assorted such Greeks formed a secret society, **Philiki Etairia** (the Friendly Society). Their sophisticated political concepts went uncomprehended by the peasantry, who assumed the point of an uprising was to exterminate their religious adversaries. And so when war finally broke out in **spring 1821**, almost the entire settled **Muslim population of Greece** – farmers, merchants and officials – was **slaughtered** within weeks by roaming bands of Greek peasants armed with swords, guns, scythes and clubs. They were often led by Orthodox priests, and some of the earliest Greek revolutionary flags portrayed a cross over a severed Turkish head.

The war

While the Greeks fought to rid themselves of the Ottomans, their further aims differed widely. Assuming their role was to lead, landowners sought to reinforce their traditional privileges; the peasantry saw the struggle as a means towards land redistribution; and westernized Greeks were fighting for a modern nation-state. Remarkably, by the end of **1823** the Greeks appeared to have won their independence. Twice the sultan had sent armies into Greece; twice they had met with defeat. Greek guerrilla leaders, above all **Theodoros Kolokotronis** from the Peloponnese, had gained significant military victories early in the rebellion, which was joined by a thousand or so **European Philhellenes**, almost half of them German, though the most important was the English poet, **Lord Byron**.

But the situation was reversed in 1825, when the Peloponnese was invaded by formidable Egyptian forces loyal to the sultan. Thus far, aid for the Greek struggle had come neither from Orthodox Russia, nor from the Western powers of France and Britain, both wearied by the Napoleonic Wars and suspicious of a potentially anarchic new state. But the death of Lord Byron from a fever while training Greek forces at **Mesolóngi** in 1824 galvanized European public opinion in the **cause of Greece**. When Mesolóngi fell to the Ottomans in

1826, Britain, France and Russia finally agreed to seek autonomy for certain parts of Greece, and sent a combined fleet to put pressure on the sultan's army in the Peloponnese and the Turkish-Egyptian fleet harboured in Navaríno Bay. Events took over, and an accidental naval battle at **Navaríno** in October 1827 resulted in the destruction of almost the entire Ottoman fleet. The following spring, Russia itself declared war on the Ottomans, and Sultan Mahmud II was forced to accept the existence of an autonomous Greece.

At a series of conferences from 1830 to 1832, **Greek independence** was confirmed by the Western powers, and borders were drawn in 1832. These included just 800,000 of the six million Greeks living within the Ottoman Empire, and territories that were largely the poorest of the classical and Byzantine lands: **Attica**, the **Peloponnese** and the islands of the **Argo-Saronic**, the **Sporades** and the **Cyclades**. The rich agricultural belt of **Thessaly**, **Epirus** in the west and **Macedonia** in the north remained in Ottoman hands, as did the Dodecanese and Crete. Meanwhile after the Napoleonic wars the **Ionian islands** had passed to British control.

The emerging state: 1832–1939

Modern Greece began as a **republic**. **Ioannis Kapodistrias**, its first president, concentrated his efforts on building a viable central authority. Almost inevitably he was assassinated – by two chieftains from the ever-disruptive Mani – and perhaps equally inevitably the "Great Powers" – Britain, France and Germany – stepped in. They created a **monarchy**, setting a Bavarian prince, Otto (Otho), on the throne. By 1834, Greece also had its own national, state-controlled **Orthodox Church**, independent from the Patriarchate in Constantinople; however, at the same time, two-thirds of the monasteries and convents were closed down and their assets used to fund secular public education.

Despite the granting of a constitution in 1844, **King Otto** proved autocratic and insensitive, filling official posts with fellow Germans and ignoring all claims by the landless peasantry for redistribution of the old estates. When he was forced from the country by a popular revolt in 1862, the Europeans produced a new prince, this time from Denmark. The accession of **George I** (1863–1913) was marked by Britain's decision to hand over the **Ionian islands** to Greece. During his reign, Greece's first roads and railways were built, , its borders were extended, and land reform began in the Peloponnese.

The Great Idea and expansionist wars

From the start, Greek foreign policy was motivated by the **Megáli Idhéa** (Great Idea) of redeeming ethnically Greek populations outside the country and incorporating the old territories of Byzantium into the new kingdom. There was encouragement all around, as Ottoman control was suddenly under pressure across the Balkans. The year 1875 saw revolts by Serbs and Montenegrins, followed by attacks by Russia on Anatolia and Bulgaria. These culminated in the creation of an independent Serbia-Montenegro and autonomous Bulgaria at the 1878 Treaty of Berlin, which also sanctioned a British takenover of the administration of **Cyprus**.

In 1881, revolts broke out among the Greeks of **Crete**, **Thessaly** and **Epirus**, aided by guerrillas from Greece. Britain forced the Ottoman Empire to cede Thessaly and Arta to Greece, but Crete remained Ottoman. When Cretan

Greeks set up an independent government in 1897, declaring *enosis* (union) with Greece, the Ottomans responded by invading the mainland and came within days of reaching Athens. The Great Powers came to the rescue by warning off the Turks and placing Crete under an international protectorate. Only in 1913 did **Crete** unite with Greece.

It was from Crete, nonetheless, that the most distinguished modern Greek statesman emerged: **Eleftherios Venizelos**, having led a civilian campaign for his island's liberation, was elected as Greek prime minister in 1910. Two years later he organized an alliance of Balkan powers to fight the **Balkan Wars** (1912–13), campaigns that saw the Ottomans virtually driven from Europe, and the Bulgarian competition bested in the culmination of a bitter, four-decade campaign for the hearts and minds of the **Macedonian** population. With Greek borders extended to include the **northeast Aegean islands**, **northern Thessaly**, **central Epirus** and parts of **Macedonia**, the Megáli Idhéa was approaching reality. Venizelos also shrewdly manipulated domestic public opinion to revise the constitution and introduce liberal social reforms.

Division, however, appeared with the outbreak of the **First World War**. Although Venizelos urged Greek entry on the Allied side, hoping to liberate Greeks in Thrace and Asia Minor, the new king, **Constantine I**, who was married to the German Kaiser's sister, imposed neutrality. Eventually Venizelos set up a revolutionary government in Thessaloníki, polarizing the country into a state of **civil war** along Venezelist–Royalist lines. In 1917 Greek troops entered the war to join the French, British and Serbians in the Macedonian campaign against Bulgaria and Germany. Upon the capitulation of Bulgaria and the Ottoman Empire, the Greeks occupied **Thrace**, and Venizelos presented demands at Versailles for predominantly Greek **Smyrna**, on the Asia Minor coast, to become part of the Greek state.

The Catastrophe and its aftermath

The demand for Smyrna triggered one of the most disastrous episodes in modern Greek history, the so-called **Katastrofí** (Catastrophe). Venizelos was authorized to move forces into Smyrna in 1919, but a new Turkish nationalist movement was taking power under Mustafa Kemal, or **Atatürk**. After monarchist factions took over when Venizelos lost elections in 1920, the Allies withdrew support for the venture. Nevertheless the monarchists ordered Greek forces to advance upon Ankara, seeking to bring Atatürk to terms. The Greeks' **Anatolian campaign** ignominiously collapsed in summer 1922 when Turkish troops forced the Greeks back to the coast. As the Greek army hurriedly evacuated from **Smyrna**, the Turks moved in and **massacred** much of the **Armenian and Greek** population before burning most of the city to the ground.

For the Turks, this was the successful conclusion of what they call their War of Independence. The First World War had already cost the Ottoman sultan his empire, and in 1922 the sultan himself was deposed. The borders of modern Turkey, as they remain today, were established by the **1923 Treaty of Lausanne**, which also provided for the **exchange of religious minorities** in each country – in effect, the first large-scale regulated ethnic cleansing. Turkey was to accept 390,000 Muslims resident on Greek soil. Greece, mobilized almost continuously for the last decade and with a population of under five million, was faced with the resettlement of over **1,300,000 Christian refugees** from **Asia Minor.** Many of these had already read the writing on the wall after 1918 and arrived of their own accord; significant numbers were settled across Macedonia, western Thrace, Epirus and in Athens, as well as on Límnos, Lésvos, Híos, Sámos, Evvía and Crete.

The Katastrofí had intense and far-reaching consequences. The bulk of the agricultural estates of **Thessaly** were finally redistributed, both to Greek tenants and refugee farmers, and huge shanty towns grew into new quarters around **Athens**, **Pireás** and **Thessaloníki**, spurring the country's then almost non-existent industry. Politically, reaction was even swifter. By September 1922, a group of Venizelist army officers "invited" King Constantine to abdicate and executed six of his ministers held most responsible for the debacle. Democracy was nominally restored with the proclamation of a **republic**, but for much of the next decade changes in government were brought about by factions within the armed forces. Meanwhile, among the urban refugee population, unions were being formed and the **Greek Communist Party** (**KKE**) was established.

The End of Venizelos and the rise of Metaxas

Elections in 1928 **returned Venizelos to power**, but his freedom to manoeuvre was restricted by the Great Crash of the following year. Late 1932 saw a local crash and Venizelos forced from office. His supporters tried forcibly to reinstate him in March 1933, but their coup was put down and Venizelos fled to Paris, where he died three years later.

A 1935 plebiscite restored the king, **George II**, to the throne, and the next year he appointed **General John Metaxas** as prime minister. Metaxas had opposed the Anatolian campaign, but had little support in parliament, and when KKE-organized strikes broke out, the king dissolved parliament without setting a date for new elections. This blatantly unconstitutional move opened the way for five years of ruthless and at times absurd **dictatorship**. Metaxas proceeded to set up a state based on the fascist models of the era. Left-wing and trade-union opponents were imprisoned or forced into exile, a state youth movement and secret police were set up and rigid censorship, extending even to passages of Thucydides, was imposed. But it was at least a Greek dictatorship, and while Metaxas was sympathetic to fascist organizational methods and economics, he utterly opposed German or Italian domination.

World War II and the Civil War: 1939–1950

When World War II broke out, the most immediate threat to Greece was **Italy** which had invaded Albania in April. Even so, Metaxas hoped Greece could remain neutral, and when the Italians torpedoed the Greek cruiser *Elli* in Tinos harbour on August 15, 1940, they failed to provoke a response. **Mussolini**, however, was determined to have a war with Greece, and after accusing the Greeks of violating the Albanian frontier, he delivered an ultimatum on October 28, 1940, to which Metaxas famously if apocryphally answered "**ohi**" (no). Galvanized by the crisis, the Greeks not only drove the invading Italians out of Greece but managed to gain control over the long-coveted and predominantly Greek-populated area of northern Epirus in southern Albania. ("Ohi Day" is still celebrated as a national holiday.)

Mussolini's failure, however, only provoked Hitler into sending his own troops into Greece, while the British rushed an expeditionary force across the Mediterranean from Egypt where they were already hard-pressed by the Germans. Within days of the **German invasion**, on April 6, 1941, the German army was pouring into central Greece. Outmanoeuvered by the enemy's highly mechanized forces and at the mercy of the Luftwaffe, resistance was soon broken. When the Germans occupied Crete in May, King George and his ministers fled to Egypt and set up a government-in-exile. Metaxas himself had died before the German invasion.

Occupation and Resistance

The joint Italian-German-Bulgarian Axis **occupation of Greece** was among the bitterest experiences of the European war. Nearly half a million Greek civilians starved to death over the winter of 1941–42, as all food was requisitioned to feed the occupying armies. In addition, entire villages throughout the mainland, but especially on Crete, were burned at the least hint of resistance and nearly 130,000 civilians were slaughtered up to autumn 1944. In their northern sector, which included Thássos and Samothráki, the Bulgarians demolished ancient sites and churches to support any future bid to annex "Slavic" Macedonia. Meantime, the Germans supervisede, during the summer

Greek Jewry and World War II

Following the German invasion of Greece, Jews who lived in the Italian zone of occupation were initially no worse off than their fellow Greeks. But after Italy capitulated to the Allies in September 1943 and German troops took over from the Italian troops, the Jewish communities in Rhodes and Kos in the Dodecanese, as well as in Crete, Corfu, Vólos, Évvia and Zákynthos, were exposed to the full force of Nazi racial doctrine. The Germans applied their "final solution" in Greece during the spring and summer of 1944 with the deportation of virtually the entire Jewish population, about 80,000 in all, to extermination camps in Poland. Thessaloníki alone contained 57,000, the largest Jewish population of any Balkan city, and all the Greek mainland towns and many of the islands also held significant numbers.

Greek Christians often went to extraordinary lengths to protect their persecuted countrymen. Thus when the Germans demanded the names of the Jews of Zákynthos prior to a roundup, Archbishop Khrysostomos and Mayor Loukas Karrer presented them with a roster of just two names – their own – and secretly oversaw the smuggling of all the island's 275 Jews to remote farms. Their audacious behaviour paid off, as every Zakynthian Jew survived the war. In Athens, the police chief and the archbishop arranged for false identity cards and baptismal certificates to be issued, which again saved large numbers of Jews. Elsewhere, others were warned in good time of what fate the Germans had in store for them, and often took to the hills to join the partisans.

Too few survivors returned to Greece from the death camps for most provincial towns to experience a revival, so most preferred to move to Athens – home to about 3000 of today's 5000 Greek Jews – or emigrate to Israel rather than live with ghosts. Thessaloníki now holds fewer than a thousand Sephardim, while Lárissa retains about three hundred, many in the clothing trade. Small Romaniot communities of a hundred or less also continue to exist in Halkídha, Ioánnina, Corfu, Tríkala and Vólos. The Kos, Haniá and Rhodes congregations were effectively wiped out, and today only about thirty Jews – many from the mainland – live in Rhodes Town, where the Platia ton Evreon Martaron (Square of the Jewish Martyrs) commemorates over 1800 Jews of Kos and Rhodes deported and murdered by the Germans.

of 1944 the **deportation** to extermination camps of the entire **Jewish populations** of Kavála, Ioánnina and Thessaloníki.

No sooner had the Axis powers occupied Greece than a spontaneous resistance movement sprang up in the mountains. The National Popular Liberation Army, known by its initials **ELAS**, founded in September 1941, quickly grew to become the most effective resistance organization, working in tandem with **EAM**, the National Liberation Front. Communists formed the leadership of both organizations, but opposition to the occupation and disenchantment with the pre-war political order ensured they won the support of many non-communists. By 1943 ELAS/EAM controlled most areas of the country, working with the British SOE, Special Operations Executive, against the occupiers.

But the Allies were already eyeing the shape of postwar Europe, and British prime minister **Winston Churchill** was determined that Greece should not fall into the communist sphere. Ignoring advice from British agents in Greece that ELAS/EAM were the only effective resistance group, and that the king and his government-in-exile had little support within the country, Churchill ordered that only right-wing groups like **EDES**, the National Republican Greek Army, should receive British money, intelligence and arms. In August 1943 a resistance delegation asked the Greek king, George, in Cairo, for a postwar coalition government in which EAM would hold the ministries of the interior, justice and war, and requested that the king himself not return to Greece without popular consent expressed through a plebiscite. Backed by Churchill, King George flatly rejected their demands.

Liberation and Civil War

As the Germans began to withdraw from Greece in September 1944, most of the ELAS/EAM leadership agreed to join a British-sponsored interim government headed by the liberal anti-communist politician **George Papandreou**, and to place its forces under that government's control, which effectively meant under command of the British troops who landed in Greece that October. But many partisans felt they were losing their chance to impose a communist government and refused to lay down their arms. On December 3, 1944 the police fired on an EAM demonstration in Athens, killing at least sixteen. The following day, vicious **street fighting** broke out between members of the Greek Communist Party (KKE) and British troops which lasted throughout the month, until eleven thousand people were killed and large parts of Athens destroyed. In other large towns, ELAS rounded up its most influential and wealthy opponents and marched them out to rural areas in conditions that guaranteed their deaths.

After Papandreou resigned and the king agreed not to return without a plebiscite, a **ceasefire** was signed on February 12, 1945, and a new British-backed government agreed to institute democratic reforms. Many of these were not implemented, however. The army, police and civil service remained in right-wing hands, and while collaborators were often allowed to retain their positions, left-wing sympathizers, many of them merely Venizelist Republicans and not communists, were excluded. A KKE boycott of elections in March 1946 handed victory to the parties of the right, and a **rigged plebiscite** followed that brought the king back to Greece. Right-wing gangs now roamed the towns and countryside with impunity, and by the summer of 1946 eighty thousand leftists who had been associated with ELAS had taken to the mountains.

By 1947 guerrilla activity had again reached the scale of a **full civil war**, with ELAS reorganized into the Democratic Army of Greece(DSE). In the interim, King George had died and been succeeded by his brother Paul, while the Americans had taken over the British role and began implementing the **Truman Doctrine**, heralding the Cold War against Soviet intimidation and expansion, that involved giving massive economic and military aid to an amenable Greek government. In the mountains American military advisors trained the initially woeful Greek army for campaigns against the DSE, while the cities saw mass arrests, courtmartials and imprisonments. From their stronghold on the slopes of Mount Grámmos on the border of Greece and Albania, the partisans waged a losing guerrilla struggle. At the start of 1948 Stalin withdrew Soviet support, and in the autumn of 1949, after Tito closed the Yugoslav border, denying the partisans the last means of outside supplies, the remnants of the DSE retreated into Albania and the KKE admitted defeat by proclaiming a supposedly temporary suspension of the civil war.

Reconstruction and dictatorship: 1950–74

After a decade of war that had shattered much of Greece's infrastructure (it is said that not one bridge was left standing by 1948), and had killed twelve percent of the 1940 population, it was a demoralized, shattered country that emerged into the Western political orbit of the 1950s. Greece was perforce **American-dominated**, enlisted into the **Korean War** in 1950 and **NATO** the following year. The US embassy – still giving the orders – foisted an electoral system upon the Greeks that ensured victory for the Right for the next twelve years. Overt leftist activity was banned (though a "cover" party for communists was soon founded), and many of those who were not herded into political "re-education" camps or dispatched by firing squads, legal or vigilante, went into exile throughout Eastern Europe, to return only after 1974. The 1950s also saw the wholesale **depopulation of remote villages** as migrants sought work in Australia, America and Western Europe, or the larger Greek cities.

Constantine Karamanlis and Cyprus

The American-backed right-wing **Greek Rally** party, led by **General Papagos**, won the first decisive post-civil-war elections in 1952. After the general's death, the party's leadership was taken over – and to an extent liberalized – by **Constantine Karamanlis**. Under his rule, stability of a kind was established and some economic advances registered, particularly after the revival of Greece's traditional German markets.

The main ongoing crisis in foreign policy was **Cyprus**, where Greek Cypriots demanding *enosis* (union) with Greece waged a long terrorist campaign against the British. Turkey adamantly opposed *enosis* and said that if Britain left Cyprus it should revert to Turkish rule. A 1959 compromise granted independence to the island and protection for its Turkish Cypriot minority but ruled out any union with Greece.

By 1961, unemployment, the Cyprus issue and the presence of US nuclear bases on Greek soil were changing the political climate, and when Karamanlis was again elected there was strong suspicion of intimidation and fraud carried out by right-wing elements and the army. After eighteen months of strikes and protest demonstrations, Karamanlis resigned and went into voluntary exile in Paris.

George Papandreou and the Colonels

New elections in 1964 gave the **Centre Union Party**, headed by **George Papandreou**, an outright majority and a mandate for social and economic reform. The new government was the first to be controlled from outside the right since 1935, and in his first act as prime minister, Papandreou sought to heal the wounds of the civil war by **releasing political prisoners** and allowing exiles to return. When King Paul died in March and his son came to the throne as **Constantine II**, it seemed a new era had begun.

But soon **Cyprus** again took centre stage. Fighting between Turkish and Greek Cypriots broke out in 1963, and only the intervention of the United States in 1964 dissuaded Turkey from invading the island. In the mood of military confrontation between Greece and Turkey – both NATO members – Papandreou questioned Greece's role in the Western alliance, to the alarm of the Americans and the Greek right. The right was also opposed to Papandreou's economic policies. When he moved to purge the army of disloyal officers, the army, with the support of the king, resisted.

Amid growing tension, elections were set for May 1967. It was a foregone conclusion that George Papandreou's Centre Union Party would win but **King Constantine**, disturbed by the party's leftward shift, was said to have briefed senior generals for a coup. True or not, the king, like almost everyone else in Greece, was caught by surprise when a group of unknown **colonels** staged their own **coup** on April 21, 1967. In December the king staged a counter-coup against the colonels, and when it failed he went into exile.

The junta announced itself as the "**Revival of Greek Orthodoxy**" against corrupting Western influences, not least long hair and miniskirts, which hardly helped the tourist trade. All political activity was banned, independent trade unions were forbidden to recruit or meet, the press was so heavily censored that many papers stopped printing, and thousands of communists and others on the left were arrested, imprisoned and often tortured. Among these were both Papandreous, father and son, the composer Mikis Theodorakis and Amalia Fleming, the widow of the discoverer of penicillin, Alexander Fleming. Thousands were maimed physically and psychologically in the junta's torture chambers. The world-famous Greek actress Melina Mercouri was stripped of her citizenship in absentia, and thousands of prominent Greeks joined her in exile. Culturally, the colonels put an end to popular music and inflicted ludicrous censorship on literature and the theatre, including a ban on the production of classical tragedies. In 1973, chief colonel **Papadopoulos** abolished the monarchy and declared Greece a republic with himself as president.

Restoration of democracy

The colonels lasted for seven years. Whatever initial support they may have met among Greeks, after the first two years they were opposed by the vast majority, including a great many on the right. Opposition was voiced from the start by exiled Greeks in London, the US and Western Europe, but only in 1973 did demonstrations break out openly in Greece – the colonels' secret police had done too thorough a job of infiltrating domestic resistance groups and terrifying everyone else into docility. After students occupied the **Athens Polytechnic** on **November 17**, the ruling clique sent armoured vehicles to storm the gates. A still-undetermined number of students (estimates range from 34 to 300) were killed. Martial law was tightened and Colonel Papadopoulos was replaced by the even more noxious and reactionary **General Ioannides**, head of the secret police.

The end came within a year when the dictatorship embarked on a disastrous adventure in **Cyprus**. By attempting to topple the Makarios government, the junta provoked a **Turkish invasion** and occupation of forty percent of Cypriot territory. The army finally mutinied and **Constantine Karamanlis** was invited to return from Paris to resume office.

Karamanlis swiftly negotiated a ceasefire in Cyprus, and in November 1974 he and his **Néa Dhimokratía** (New Democracy) party were rewarded by a sizeable majority in elections. The chief opposition was the new Panhellenic Socialist Movement (PASOK), led by **Andreas Papandreou**, son of George.

Europe and a new Greece: 1974 to the present

To Karamanlis's enduring credit, his New Democracy party oversaw an effective return to **democratic stability**, even legalizing the KKE (the Greek Communist Party) for the first time. Karamanlis also held a **referendum on the monarchy**, in which seventy percent of Greeks rejected the return of Constantine II. So a largely symbolic presidency was instituted instead, occupied by Karamanlis from 1980 to 1985, and again from 1990 to 1995. In 1981, Greece joined the **European Community**.

"Change" and "Out with the Right" were the slogans of the election campaign that swept the socialist party, **PASOK**, and its leader Andreas Papandreou to power on October 18, 1981. The new era started with a bang as long-overdue **social reforms** were enacted. Peasant women were granted pensions for the first time; wages were indexed to the cost of living; civil marriage was introduced; family and property law was reformed in favour of wives and mothers; and equal rights legislation was passed. By the time PASOK was returned to power in 1985, it was apparent the promised economic bonanza was not happening: hit by low productivity, lack of investment (not helped by anti-capitalist rhetoric from the government) and world recession, unemployment rose, inflation hit 25 percent and the national debt soared.

In the event it was the European Community, once Papandreou's bête noire, which rescued him, with a huge loan on condition that an austerity programme was maintained. Forced to drop many of his populist policies, the increasingly autocratic Papandreou turned on his former left-wing allies. Combined with the collapse of Soviet rule in Eastern Europe, his own very public affair with an Olympic Airways hostess half his age, and a raft of economic scandals, PASOK's hold on power was not surprisingly weakened. Since 1989, when New Democracy was elected once more, the two parties have exchanged power in an increasingly stable political system, helped enormously by the growth and funding brought by European Union membership.

Nonetheless, the 1990s were not easy, with an economy still riven by unrest and division, and huge foreign policy headaches caused by the break-up of the former Yugoslavia and the ensuing wars on Greece's borders. Some problems

Immigration – and the Albanian influx

Greece may continue to occupy the EU's economic cellar with Portugal, but it's still infinitely wealthier (and more stable) than many of its neighbours, This has acted as a magnet for a permanent underclass of immigrants. Since 1990 they have arrived in numbers estimated at 800,000 to well over a million, a huge burden for a not especially rich country of just over ten million citizens. These days your waiter, hotel desk clerk or cleaning lady is most likely to be Albanian, Bulgarian or Romanian, to cite the three largest groups. There are also significant communities of Pakistanis, Egyptians, Poles, Bangladeshis, Syrians, Filipinos, Ukrainians, Russians, Equatorial Africans, Kurds and Georgians, not to mention ethnic Greeks from the Caucasus – a striking change in what had hitherto been a homogeneous and parochial culture.

The Greek response has been decidedly mixed. Albanians, who make up roughly half the influx, are almost universally detested, and blamed for all manner of social ills. For the first time, crime – especially burglaries – is a significant issue. The newcomers have also prompted the first significant anti-immigration measures in a country whose population is more used to being on the other side of such laws. A member of the Schengen visa scheme, Greece sees itself, as in past ages, as the first line of defence against the barbarian hordes from the East. The Aegean islands regularly receive boatloads of people from every country in Asia.

In June 2001, as an attempt to cope, legal residence was offered to the estimated half-million illegals who could demonstrate two years' presence in Greece, and pay a hefty amount for retroactive social security contributions. This and a subsequent amnesty legalized about 300,000 residents. Not that the other illegals are likely to be deported en masse, as they do the difficult, dirty and dangerous work that Greeks now disdain, especially farm labour, restaurant work and rubbish collection. From an employer's point of view, they are cheap and they are net contributors to the social welfare system, especially to pensions where Greece, like much of Europe, is seeing its population shrinking and aging. Albanians in particular are also buoying up the banking system by their phenomenal saving habits and wiring of funds home.

Though there is much that is positive about immigration, it must also be said that it is having the effect of making Greece less identifiably Greek and of making the native Greeks themselves less welcoming and more self-absorbed.

were largely self-inflicted: when one breakaway republic named itself **Macedonia**, the threatened Greeks fought tooth and nail against anyone recognizing the breakaway state, let alone its use of the name Macedonia. Ultimately, they failed miserably and were eventually forced to recognize the FYROM – the Former Yugoslav Republic of Macedonia – with just minor concessions. Meanwhile, alone among NATO members, Greece was conspicuous for its open support of **Serbia**, ostentatiously supplying trucks to Belgrade via Bulgaria.

By the end of the Nineties, the economy was stabilizing, with inflation consistently in single figures, and in 1997 national morale was further boosted with the award of the 2004 Olympic Games to Athens. Abroad, a dramatic and unexpected change in Greece's always distrustful **relations with Turkey** came when a severe **earthquake** struck northern Athens on September 7, 1999, killing scores and rendering almost 100,000 homeless. Coming less than a month after a devastating earthquake in northwest Turkey, it spurred a thaw between the two historical rivals. Greeks donated massive amounts of blood and foodstuffs to the Turkish victims, and were the earliest foreign rescue teams to reach Turkey; in turn they saw Turkish disaster-relief squads among the first on the scene in Athens. Soon afterwards, foreign minister George Papandreou (son of Andreas) announced that Greece had dropped its long-time opposition to EU financial aid to Turkey and that Greece would no longer oppose Turkish candidacy for the EU.

The 21st century

In March 2004, New Democracy took control of government again – PASOK having been in power for nineteen of the previous twenty-three years – and was re-elected more narrowly, in snap elections of September 2007. For an outsider one of the most striking aspects of modern Greek democracy is the clan-based nature of its leadership: Prime Minister **Kostas Karamanlis** is the nephew of former president Constantine, while PASOK is led by **George Papandreou**, son of Andreas, grandson of George.

With the **2004 Olympic Games** considered a triumph – which, despite a last-minute rush to complete the facilities, huge cost overruns and serious doubts over the long-term legacy, they probably were – Greek confidence is at an all time high. Joining the euro may have raised prices and industrial relations remain problematic, but economic growth continues strongly. Nearly a fifth of the world's merchant fleet is owned by Greek companies, while infrastructure improvement, thanks to the Olympics and EU funds, would seem to provide a secure foundation for future development.

Archeology in Greece

Until the second half of the nineteenth century, archeology was a very hit-and-miss, treasure-hunting affair. The early students of antiquity went to Greece to draw and make plaster casts of the great masterpieces of Classical sculpture. Unfortunately, a number soon found it more convenient or more profitable to remove objects wholesale, and might be better described as looters than scholars or archeologists.

Early excavations

The **British Society of Dilettanti** was one of the earliest promoters of Greek culture, financing expeditions to draw and publish antiquities. Founded in the 1730s as a club for young aristocrats who had completed the Grand Tour and fancied themselves arbiters of taste, the society's main qualification for membership (according to most critics) was habitual drunkenness. Its leading spirit was **Sir Francis Dashwood**, a notorious rake who founded the infamous Hellfire Club. Nevertheless, the society was the first body organized to sponsor systematic research into Greek antiquities, though it was initially most interested in Italy. Greece, then a backwater of the Ottoman Empire, was not a regular part of the Grand Tour and only the most intrepid adventurers undertook so hazardous a trip.

In the 1740s, two young artists, **James Stuart** and **Nicholas Revett**, formed a plan to produce a scholarly record of ancient Greek buildings. With the support of the society they spent three years in Greece, principally in and around Athens, drawing and measuring the antiquities. The first volume of *The Antiquities of Athens* appeared in 1762. The publication of their exquisite illustrations and the 1764 publication of **Johann Winckelmann**'s *History of Art*, in which the **Parthenon** and its sculptures were exalted as the eternal standard by which beauty should be measured, gave an enormous fillip to the study (and popularity) of Greek sculpture and architecture; many European Neoclassical town and country houses date from this period.

The Dilettanti financed a number of further expeditions to study Greek antiquities, including one to Asia Minor in 1812. The expedition was to be based in Smyrna, but while waiting in Athens for a ship to Turkey, the party employed themselves in excavations at **Eleusis**, where they uncovered the **Temple of Demeter**. It was the first archeological excavation made on behalf of the society, and one of the first in Greece. After extensive explorations in Asia Minor, the participants returned via Attica, where they excavated the **Temple of Nemesis** at **Rhamnous** and examined the **Temple of Poseidon** at **Soúnio**.

Several other antiquarians of the age were less interested in discoveries for their own sake. A French count, **Choiseul-Gouffier**, removed part of the **Parthenon frieze** in 1787 and his example prompted **Lord Elgin** to detach much of the rest in 1801. These were essentially acts of looting – "Bonaparte has not got such things from all his thefts in Italy", boasted Elgin – and their legality was suspect even at the time.

Other discoveries of the period were more ambiguous. In 1811, a party of English and German travellers, including the architect **C. R. Cockerell**, uncovered the **Temple of Aphaea** on **Égina** and shipped away the pediments. They auctioned off the marbles for £6000 to Prince Ludwig of Bavaria, and, inspired by this success, returned to Greece for further finds. This time they struck it lucky with 23 slabs from the **Temple of Apollo Epikourios** at **Bassae**, for which the British Museum laid out a further £15,000. These were huge sums for the time and highly profitable exercises, but they were also pioneering archeology for the period. Besides, removing the finds was hardly surprising: Greece, after all, was not yet a state and had no public museum; antiquities discovered were sold by their finders – if they recognized their value.

The new nation

The Greek War of Independence (1821–28) and the establishment of a modern Greek nation changed all this. As a result of the selection of Prince Otto of Bavaria as the first king of modern Greece in 1832, the **Germans**, whose education system stressed Classical learning, were in the forefront of archeological activity. One dominant Teutonic figure during the early years of the new state was **Ludwig Ross**, who in 1834 began supervising the excavation and restoration of the **Acropolis**. Dismantling the accretion of Byzantine, Frankish and Turkish fortifications, and reconstructing Classical originals, began the following year.

The Greeks themselves had begun to focus on their ancient past when the first stirrings of the independence movement were felt. In 1813 the **Philomuse Society** was formed, aiming to uncover and collect antiquities, publish books and assist students and foreign philhellenes. In 1829 an orphanage on the island of Égina became the first **Greek archeological museum**.

In 1837 the **Greek Archeological Society** was founded "for the discovery, recovery and restoration of antiquities in Greece". Its moving spirit was **Kyriakos Pittakis**, a remarkable figure who during the War of Independence had used his knowledge of ancient literature to discover the Klepsydra spring on the Acropolis – solving the problem of lack of water during the Turkish siege. In the first four years of its existence, the Archeological Society sponsored excavations in Athens at the **Theatre of Dionysos**, the **Tower of the Winds**, the **Propylaia** and the **Erechtheion**. Pittakis also played a major role in the attempt to convince Greeks of the importance of their heritage; antiquities were still being looted or burned for lime.

The great Germans: Curtius and Schliemann

Although King Otto was deposed in 1862 in favour of a Danish prince, Germans remained in the forefront of Greek archeology in the 1870s. Two men dominated the scene: Heinrich Schliemann and Ernst Curtius.

Ernst Curtius was a traditional Classical scholar. He had come to Athens originally as tutor to King Otto's family and in 1874 returned to Greece to secure permission to conduct excavations at **Olympia**. He set up a **German Archeological Institute** in Athens and negotiated the **Olympia Convention**, under the terms of which the Germans were to pay for and have total control of the dig; all finds were to remain in Greece, though the excavators could make copies and casts; and all finds were to be published simultaneously in Greek and German.

This was an enormously important agreement, which almost certainly prevented the treasures of Olympia and Mycenae following that of Troy to a German museum. But other Europeans were still in acquisitive mode: **French consuls**, for example, had been instructed to buy any "available" local antiquities in Greece and Asia Minor, and had picked up the Louvre's great treasures, the **Venus de Milo** and **Winged Victory of Samothrace**, in 1820 and 1863 respectively.

At **Olympia**, digging began in 1875 on a site buried beneath river mud, silt and sand. Only one corner of the **Temple of Zeus** was initially visible, but within months the excavators had turned up statues from the east pediment. Over forty magnificent sculptures, as well as terracottas, statue bases and a rich collection of bronzes, were uncovered, together with more than four hundred inscriptions. The laying bare of this huge complex was a triumph for official German archeology.

While Curtius was digging at Olympia, a man who represented everything that was anathema to orthodox Classical scholarship was standing archeology on its head. **Heinrich Schliemann** was the son of a drunken German pastor who left school at fourteen and spent the next five years as a grocer's assistant. En route to seeking his fortune in Venezuela, he was left for dead on the Dutch coast after a shipwreck; later, working as a book-keeper in Amsterdam, he began to study languages. His phenomenal memory enabled him to master four by the age of 21. Following a six-week study of Russian, Schliemann was sent to St Petersburg as a trading agent and had amassed a fortune by the time he was 30. In 1851 he visited California, opened a bank during the Gold Rush and made another fortune.

His financial position secure for life, Schliemann was almost ready to tackle his life's ambition – the **search for Troy** and the vindication of his lifelong belief in the truth of Homer's tales of prehistoric cities and heroes. Although most of the archeological establishment, led by Curtius, was unremittingly hostile, Schliemann sunk his first trench at the hill called Hisarlik, in northwest Turkey, in 1870; excavation proper began in 1871. In his haste to find Homer's city of Priam and Hector, and to convince the world of his success, Schliemann dug a huge trench straight through the mound, destroying a mass of important evidence, but he was able nevertheless to identify nine cities, superimposed in layers. In May 1873 he discovered the so-called **Treasure of Priam**, a stash of gold and precious jewellery and vessels. It convinced many that the German had indeed found **Troy**, although others contended that Schliemann, desperate for academic recognition, assembled it from other sources.

Three years later Schliemann turned his attentions to **Mycenae**, again inspired by Homer, and once more following a hunch. Alone among contemporary scholars, he sought and found the legendary graves of Mycenaean kings inside the existing Cyclopean wall of the citadel rather than outside it, unearthing in the process the magnificent treasures that today form the basis of the **Bronze Age collection** in the National Archeological Museum in Athens.

He dug again at Troy in 1882, assisted by a young architect, **Wilhelm Dörpfeld**, who was destined to become one of the great archeologists of the following century. In 1884 Schliemann returned to Greece to excavate another famous prehistoric citadel, this time at **Tiryns**.

Almost single-handedly, and in the face of continuing academic obstruction, Schliemann had revolutionized archeology and pushed back the knowledge of Greek history and civilization a thousand years. Although some of his results have been shown to have been deliberately falsified in the sacrifice of truth to beauty, his achievement remains enormous.

The last two decades of the nineteenth century saw the discovery of other important Classical sites. Excavation began at **Epidaurus** in 1881 under the Greek archeologist **Panayotis Kavvadias**, who made it his life's work. Meanwhile at **Delphi**, the **French** began digging at the **sanctuary of Apollo**. Their excavations continued nonstop from 1892 to 1903, revealing the extensive site visible today; work on the site has continued sporadically ever since.

Evans and Knossos

The early twentieth century saw the domination of Greek archeology by an Englishman, **Sir Arthur Evans**. An egotistical maverick like Schliemann, he too was independently wealthy, with a brilliantly successful career behind him when he started his great work and recovered another millennium for Greek history. Evans excavated what he called the "Palace of Minos" at **Knossos** on **Crete**, discovering one of the oldest and most sophisticated of Mediterranean societies, which he christened Minoan.

The son of a distinguished antiquarian and collector, Evans read history at Oxford, failed to get a fellowship and began to travel. His chief interest was in the Balkans, where he was special correspondent for the *Manchester Guardian* during the 1877 uprising in Bosnia. He took enormous risks in the war-torn country, filing brilliant dispatches and still finding time for exploration and excavation. In 1884, aged 33, Evans was appointed curator of the Ashmolean Museum in Oxford. He travelled whenever he could, and it was in 1893, while in Athens, that his attention was drawn to Crete. Evans, though very short-sighted, had almost microscopic close vision. In a vendor's stall he came upon some small drilled stones with tiny engravings in a hitherto unknown script; he was told they came from Crete. He had seen Schliemann's finds from Mycenae and had been fascinated by this prehistoric culture. Crete, the crossroads of the Mediterranean, seemed a good place to look for more.

Evans visited Crete in 1894 and headed for the legendary site of Knossos, which had earlier attracted the attention of Schliemann (who had been unable to agree a price with the Turkish owners of the land) and where a Cretan, appropriately called Minos, had already done some impromptu digging, revealing massive walls and a storeroom filled with jars. Evans succeeded in buying the site and in March 1900 began excavations. Within a few days, evidence of a great complex building was revealed, along with artefacts that indicated an astonishing cultural sophistication. The huge team of diggers unearthed elegant courtyards and verandahs, colourful wall-paintings, pottery, jewellery and sealstones – the wealth of a civilization which dominated the eastern Mediterranean 3500 years ago.

Evans continued to excavate at Knossos for the next thirty years, during which time he established, on the basis of changes in the pottery styles, the **system of dating** that remains in use today for classifying **Greek prehistory**: Early, Middle and Late Minoan (Mycenaean on the mainland). Like Schliemann, Evans attracted criticism and controversy for his methods – most notably his decision to speculatively reconstruct parts of the palace in concrete – and for many of his interpretations. Nevertheless, his discoveries and his dedication put him near the pinnacle of Greek archeology.

Into the twentieth century: the foreign institutes

In 1924 Evans gave to the **British School at Athens** the site of **Knossos** along with his on-site residence, the Villa Ariadne, and all other lands within his possession on Crete (it was only in 1952 that Knossos became the property of the Greek State). At the time the British School was one of several foreign archeological institutes in Greece; founded in 1886, it had been preceded by the **French School**, the **German Institute** and the **American School**.

Greek archeology owes much to the work and relative wealth of these foreign schools and others that would follow. They have been responsible for the excavation of many of the most famous sites in Greece: the **Heraion** on

Sámos (German); the sacred island of **Delos** (French); sites on **Kós** and in southern **Crete** (Italian); **Corinth**, **Samothráki** and the **Athenian Agora** (American), to name but a few. Life as a resident foreigner in Greece at the beginning of the twentieth century was not for the weak-spirited – one unfortunate member of the American School was shot and killed by bandits while in the Peloponnese – but there were compensations in unlimited access to antiquities in an unspoilt countryside.

The years between the two World Wars saw an expansion of excavation and scholarship, most markedly concerning the prehistoric civilizations. Having been shown by Schliemann and Evans what to look for, a new generation of archeologists was uncovering numerous **prehistoric sites** on the mainland and Crete, and its members were spending proportionately more time studying and interpreting their finds. Digs in the 1920s and 1930s had much smaller labour forces (there were just 55 workmen under Wace at Mycenae, as compared with hundreds in the early days of Schliemann's or Evans's excavations) and they were supervised by higher numbers of trained archeologists. Though perhaps not as spectacular as their predecessors, these scholars would prove just as pioneering as they established the history and clarified the chronology of the newly discovered civilizations.

One of the giants of this generation was **Alan Wace** who, while director of the British School at Athens from 1913 to 1923, conducted excavations at **Mycenae** and established a chronological sequence from the nine great tholos tombs on the site. This led Wace to propose a new chronology for prehistoric Greece, which put him in direct conflict with Arthur Evans. Evans believed that the mainland citadels had been ruled by Cretan overlords, whereas Wace was convinced of an independent Mycenaean cultural and political development. Evans was by now a powerful member of the British School's managing committee, and his published attacks on Wace's claims, combined with the younger archeologist's less than tactful reactions to Evans's dominating personality, resulted in the abrupt halt of the British excavations at Mycenae in 1923 and the no less sudden termination of Wace's job. Wace returned to Mycenae in 1950, nine years after Evans's death, and found examples of the "Minoan" **Linear B script**, which British architect **Michael Ventris** deciphered in 1952 as the earliest Greek language. This meant that the Mycenaean Greeks had conquered the Minoans in approximately 1450 BC, which vindicated Wace.

Classical archeology was not forgotten in the flush of excitement over the Mycenaeans and Minoans. The period between the wars saw the continuation of excavation at most established sites, and many new discoveries, among them the sanctuary of **Asklepios** and its elegant Roman buildings on **Kós**, excavated by the Italians from 1935 to 1943, and the Classical Greek city of **Olynthos**, in northern Greece, which was dug by the American School from 1928 to 1934. After the wholesale removal of houses and apartment blocks that had occupied the site, the American School also began excavations in the **Athenian Agora**, the ancient marketplace, in 1931, culminating in the complete restoration of the **Stoa of Attalos**.

More recent excavations

Archeological work was greatly restricted during and after World War II, and in the shadow of the Greek civil war. A few monuments and museums were restored and reopened but it was not until 1948 that excavations were resumed with a Greek clearance of the **Sanctuary of Artemis** at **Brauron** in Attica. In 1952 the American School resumed its activities with a dig at the Neolithic and Bronze Age site of **Lerna** in the Peloponnese, and **Carl Blegen** cleared **Nestor's Palace** at **Pylos** in Messenia. Greek archeologists began work at the Macedonian site of **Pella**, the capital of ancient Macedonia, and at the **Nekromanteion of Ephyra** in Epirus.

These and many other excavations – including renewed work on the major sites – were relatively minor operations in comparison to earlier digs. This reflected a modified approach to archeology, which laid less stress on discoveries and more on **documentation**. Instead of digging large tracts of a site, archeologists concentrated on small sections, establishing chronologies through meticulous analysis of data. Which is not to say that there were no spectacular finds. At **Mycenae**, in 1951, a second circle of graves was unearthed; at Pireás, a burst sewer in 1959 revealed four superb Classical bronzes; and a dig at the **Kerameikos** cemetery site in Athens in 1966 found four thousand potsherds used as ballots for ostracism. Important work has also been undertaken on restorations – in particular the **theatres** at the Acropolis in **Athens**, at **Dodona** and **Epidaurus**, which are now used in summer festivals.

A number of postwar excavations were as exciting as any in the past. In 1961 the fourth great **Minoan palace** (following the unearthing of Knossos, Phaestos and Malia) was uncovered by torrential rains at the extreme eastern tip of the island of Crete at **Káto Zákros** and cleared by Cretan archeologist **Nikolaos Platon**. Its harbour is now thought to have been the Minoans' main gateway port to and from southwest Asia and Africa, and many of the artefacts discovered in the palace storerooms – bronze ingots from Cyprus, elephants' tusks from Syria, stone vases from Egypt – seem to confirm this. Greek teams have found more Minoan palaces at **Arhánes**, **Haniá**, **Galatás** and **Petrás**, and a new generation of scholars believe that these were ceremonial buildings and not the seats of dynastic authority, as Evans proposed. American excavations at **Kommós**, in western Crete, have uncovered another gateway site, like Káto Zákros, of the Minoan and Mycenaean periods.

At **Akrotíri** on the island of **Thíra** (Santoríni), **Spyros Marinatos** revealed, in 1967, a Minoan-era site that had been buried by volcanic explosion in either 1650 or 1550 BC – the jury is still deliberating that one. Its buildings were two or three storeys high, and superbly frescoed. Marinatos was later tragically killed while at work on the site when he fell off a wall, and is now buried there.

A decade later came an even more dramatic find at **Vergina** – **ancient Aegae** – in northern Greece, the early capital of the Macedonian kingdom, which later became its necropolis. Here, **Manolis Andronikos** found a series of royal tombs dating from the fourth century BC. Unusually, these had escaped plundering by ancient grave robbers and contained an astonishing hoard of exquisite gold treasures. Piecing together clues – the haste of the tomb's construction, an ivory effigy head, gilded leg armour – Andronikos showed this to have been the **tomb of Philip II** of Macedon, father of Alexander the Great. Subsequent forensic examination of the body's remains supported historical accounts of Philip's limp and blindness.

At the beginning of this century the various foreign schools, recently joined by the Australian, Austrian, Belgian, Canadian, Danish, Dutch, Finnish, Georgian, Irish, Norwegian, Spanish, Swedish and Swiss, along with Greek universities and the 25 *ephorates*, or inspectorates, of Prehistoric and Classical Antiquities are still at work in the field, although the emphasis today is as concerned with the task of **conserving and protecting** what has been revealed as unearthing new finds. All too often newly discovered sites have been inadequately fenced off or protected, and a combination of the elements, greedy developers and malicious trespassers – sometimes all three – have caused much damage and deterioration.

Wild Greece

For anyone who has seen Greece at the height of summer with its brown parched hillsides and desert-like ambience, the richness of the wildlife – in particular the flora – may come as a surprise. As winter warms into spring, the countryside (and urban waste ground) transforms itself into a mosaic of coloured flowers, which attract a plethora of insect life, followed by birds. Isolated areas, whether islands or remote mountains such as Olympus, have had many thousands of years to develop their own individual species. Overall, Greece has around six thousand species of native flowering plants, nearly four times that of Britain but in the same land area. Many are unique to Greece, and make up about one-third of Europe's endemic plants.

Despite an often negative attitude to wildlife, Greece was probably the first place in the world where it was an object of study. **Theophrastos** (372-287 BC) from Lésvos was the first recorded botanist and a systematic collector of general information on plants, while his contemporary, **Aristotle**, studied the animal world. During the first century AD the distinguished physician **Dioscorides** compiled a herbal study that remained a standard work for over a thousand years.

Some background

In early antiquity Greece was thickly forested: pines and oaks grew in coastal regions, giving way to fir or black pine up in the hills and low mountains. But this **native woodland** contracted rapidly as human activities expanded. By Classical times, a pattern had been set of forest clearance, followed by agriculture, abandonment to scrub and then a resumption of cultivation or grazing. Huge quantities of timber were consumed in the production of charcoal, pottery and smelted metal, and for ships and construction work. Small patches of virgin woodland have remained, mostly in the north and northeast, but even these are under threat from loggers and arsonists.

Greek **farming** often lacks the rigid efficiency of northern European agriculture. Many peasant farmers still cultivate little patches of land, and even city-dwellers travel at weekends to collect food plants from the countryside. Wild greens under the generic term *hórta* are gathered to be cooked like spinach. The buds and young shoots of capers, and the fruit of wild figs, carobs, plums, strawberry trees, cherries and sweet chestnuts are harvested. Emergent snails and mushrooms are collected after wet weather. For many Greeks only those species that have practical uses are regarded as having any value. Nowadays, heavy earth-moving machinery means a farmer can sweep away an ancient meadow full of orchids in an easy morning's work – often to produce a field that is used for forage for a year or two and then abandoned to coarse thistles. Increasingly, the pale scars of dirt tracks crisscross once intact hill- and mountainsides, allowing short-termist agricultural destruction of previously undisturbed upland habitats.

During the 1950s the official policy of draining wetlands for conversion to agriculture meant important areas were lost to wildlife completely. Those lakes, lagoons and deltas that remain are, in theory, now protected for their fragile biodiversity and their environmental and scientific value – but industrial and sewage pollution, disturbance, and misuse are unchecked. Visit, for example, the Peloponnese's **Yiálova lagoon** reserve – one of Greece's most stunningly beautiful wetlands – to understand the problems of many protected areas. Four-wheel-drive vehicles and noisy motorbikes race through the dunes, destroying the surface stability and decimating the nesting chameleons; military aircraft fly low over flamingo flocks; rows of illegally overnighting camper vans disfigure the beaches; and locals drive here to dump unwanted televisions and fridges. On Lésvos, the **Kalloní salt-pans**, once beloved by rare birds and bird-watchers, are being poisoned by sewage. In the mainland interior, increasing demand for power brings huge **hydroelectric schemes** to remote rivers and gorges with little chance for opposition to be heard. Even the **Orthodox Church**, whose lands once often provided wildlife with a refuge from hunters, now looks to capitalize on their value for major tourist developments. In the north, the forests of sacred **Mount Áthos** are being surrendered to commercial logging. On the bright side, the **Kárla marsh-lake** near Vólos is being allowed to partially refill again, to the delight of migratory birds.

Since the 1970s, tourist developments have ribboned along **coastlines**, sweeping away both agricultural plots and wildlife havens as they do so. These expanding resorts increase local employment, often attracting inland workers to the coast; the generation that would once have herded sheep on remote hillsides now works in tourist bars and tavernas. Consequently, the pressure of domestic animal grazing, particularly in the larger islands, has been significantly reduced, allowing the regeneration of tree seedlings; Crete, for example, has more woodland now than at any time in the last five centuries. However, **forest fires** remain a threat everywhere. Since 1980 blazes have destroyed much of the tree cover in Thássos, southern Rhodes, Kárpathos, Híos, Sámos and parts of the Peloponnese; the trees may well regenerate eventually, but by then the complex shade-dependent ecology is irrecoverably lost.

Flowers

Whereas in temperate northern Europe plants flower from spring until autumn, the arid summers of Greece confine the main **flowering period** to the spring, a narrow climatic window when the days are bright, the temperatures not too high and the groundwater supply still adequate. **Spring** starts in the southeast, in Rhodes, in early March, and then travels progressively westwards and northwards. Rhodes, Kárpathos and eastern Crete are at their best in March, western Crete in early April, the Peloponnese and eastern Aegean mid- to late April, and the Ionian islands in early May, though a cold dry winter can cause several weeks' delay. In the high mountains the floral spring arrives in the chronological summer, with the alpine zones of central and western Crete in full flower in June, and mainland mountain blooms emerging in July.

The delicate flowers of early spring – orchids, fritillaries, anemones, cyclamen, tulips and small bulbs – are replaced as the season progresses by more robust shrubs, tall perennials and abundant annuals, but many of these close down completely for the fierce **summer**. A few tough plants, like shrubby thyme and savory, continue to flower through the heat and act as magnets for butterflies.

Once the worst heat is over, and the first showers of **autumn** arrive, so does a second "spring", on a much smaller scale but no less welcome after the brown drabness of summer. Squills, autumn cyclamen, crocus in varying shades, pink or lilac colchicum, yellow sternbergia and other small bulbs all come into bloom, while the seeds start to germinate for the following year's crop of annuals. By the new year, early-spring bulbs and orchids are flowering in the south.

Plants on the **beach** grow in a difficult environment: fresh water is scarce, salt is in excess, and dehydrating winds are often very strong. Feathery **tamarisk** trees are adept at surviving this habitat, and consequently are often planted to provide shade. On hot days or nights you may see or feel them sweating away surplus saltwater from their foliage. Sand dunes provide shelter for a variety of colourful small plants, while the sandy depressions or slacks behind the dunes – where they have not been illegally ploughed for short-term forage crops – can be home to a variety of plants. Open stretches of beach sand usually have fewer plants, particularly in resort areas where the bulldozed spring cleaning of the beach removes both the winter's rubbish and all the local flora.

Large areas of **freshwater** are naturally scarce, particularly in the warmer south. Many watercourses dry up completely in the hot season, and what seem to be dry river-beds are often simply flood channels which fill irregularly at times of torrential rain. However, species that survive periodic drying-out can flourish, such as the giant reed or **calamus**, a bamboo-like grass reaching up to 6m in height and often cut for use as canes. It frequently grows in company with the shrubby, pink- or white-flowered and highly poisonous **oleander**.

Arable fields can be rich with colourful weeds: scarlet poppies, blue bugloss, yellow or white daisies, wild peas, gladioli, tulips and grape hyacinths. Small, unploughed **meadows** may be equally colourful, with slower-growing plants such as orchids in extraordinary quantities.

The rocky earth makes cultivation on some **hillsides** difficult and impractical. Agriculture is often abandoned and areas regenerate to a rich mixture of shrubs and perennials – known as **garigue**. With time, a few good wet winters, and in the absence of grazing, some shrubs will develop into small trees, intermixed with tough climbers – the much denser **maquis** vegetation. The colour yellow often predominates in early spring, with brooms, gorse, Jerusalem sage and giant fennel followed by the blues, pinks and purples of bee-pollinated plants. An abundance of the pink and white of Cistus rockroses is usually indicative of an earlier fire, since they are primary recolonizers. A third vegetation type is **phrygana** – smaller, frequently aromatic or spiny shrubs, often with a narrow strip of bare ground between each hedgehog-like bush. Many aromatic herbs such as lavender, rosemary, savory, sage and thyme are native to these areas.

Nearly 190 species of **orchid** are believed to occur in Greece; their complexity blurs species' boundaries and keeps botanists in a state of taxonomic flux. In particular, the Ophrys bee and spider orchids have adapted themselves, through subtleties of lip colour and false scents, to seduce small male wasps. These insects mistake the flowers for a potential mate, and unintentionally assist the plant's pollination. Though all species are officially protected, many are still picked.

The **higher mountains** of Greece have winter snow cover, and cooler weather for much of the year, so flowering is consequently later than at lower altitudes. The **limestone peaks** of the mainland, and of islands such as Corfu, Kefaloniá, Crete, Rhodes, Sámos and Thássos, hold rich collections of attractive **rock plants**, flowers whose nearest relatives may be from the Balkan Alps or from the Turkish mountains. **Gorges** are another spectacular habitat, particularly rich in Crete. Their inaccessible cliffs act as refuges for plants that cannot survive the grazing, competition or more extreme climates of open areas. Many of Greece's endemic plants are confined to cliffs, gorges or mountains.

Much of the surviving **original woodland** is in mountain areas. In the south it includes cypress: native to the south and east Aegean, but, in its columnar form, planted everywhere with a Mediterranean climate. The cooler shade of woodland provides a haven for plants that cannot survive full exposure to the Greek summer, including peonies and numerous ferns.

With altitude, the forest thins out to scattered individual conifers and kermes oak, before finally reaching a limit at around 1500-2000m on the mainland – much lower on the islands. Above this treeline are **summer meadows**, and then bare rock. If not severely grazed, these habitats are home to many low-growing, gnarled, but often splendidly floriferous plants.

Birds

Migratory species that have wintered in East Africa move north, through the eastern Mediterranean, from around **mid-March to mid-May**. Some stop in Greece to breed; others move on into the rest of Europe. The southern islands are the first landfall after a long sea-crossing, and smaller birds recuperate for a few days before moving on. Larger birds such as storks and ibis often fly very high, and binoculars are needed to spot them as they pass over. In autumn birds return, but usually in more scattered numbers. Although some are shot, there is not the wholesale slaughter that takes place in some other Mediterranean countries.

At **night**, the tiny Scops owl has a very distinct, repeated single-note call, very like the sonar beep of a submarine; the equally diminutive Little owl, with a weird repertoire of cries, may be visible by day in ruined buildings. Near wooded streams, the most evocative nocturnal bird is the nightingale, most audible in the May mating season.

Larger raptors occur in remoter areas, preferring mountain gorges and cliffs. Buzzards are the most abundant, and often mistaken by optimistic birdwatchers for the rarer, shyer eagles. Griffon vultures, however, are unmistakable, soaring on broad, straight-edged wings, whereas the lammergeier is a state-of-the-art flying machine with narrow, swept wings, seen over mountain tops by the lucky few; the remaining nine or ten pairs in Crete are now the Balkans' largest breeding population.

In **lowland areas**, hoopoes are a startling combination of pink, black and white, obvious when they fly and the only natural predator of the processionary caterpillar, a major pest of pine forests. The shy golden oriole has an attractive song but is adept at hiding its brilliant colours among the olive trees. Multicoloured flocks of elegant bee-eaters fill the air with their soft calls as they hunt insects. Brightest of all is the kingfisher, more commonly seen sea-fishing here than in northern Europe.

In areas of **wetland** that remain undrained and undisturbed, such as saltmarshes, coastal lagoons, estuaries and freshwater ponds, ospreys, egrets, ibis, spoonbills, storks, pelicans and many waders can be seen feeding. Flamingoes sometimes occur, as lone individuals or small flocks, particularly in the eastern Aegean salt pans between December and May.

Mammals

Greece's small **mammal** population ranges from rodents and shrews to hedgehogs, hares and squirrels (including the dark-red Persian squirrel on Lésvos). Medium-sized mammals include badgers and foxes and the persecuted golden jackal, but the commonest is the ferret-like stone (or beech) marten, named for its habit of decorating stones with its droppings to mark territory.

In the mainland mountains, mostly in the north, are found the shy chamois and wild boar, with even shyer predators like lynx, wolves and brown bear. Occasionally seen running wild in Crete's White Mountains, but more often as a zoo attraction, is an endemic ibex, known to hunters as the *agrími* or *krí-krí*. Formerly in danger of extinction, a colony of them was established on the offshore islet of Dhía, where they thrived, exterminating the rare local flora.

Reptiles and amphibians

Reptiles flourish in the hot dry summers of Greece, the commonest being **lizards**. Most of these are small, agile and wary, rarely staying around for closer inspection. They're usually brown to grey, subtly spotted, striped or tessellated, though in adult males the undersides are sometimes brilliant orange, green or blue. The more robust green lizards, with long whip-like tails, can be 50cm or more in length, but are equally shy and fast-moving unless distracted by territorial disputes with each other.

Nocturnal **geckos** are large-eyed, short-tailed lizards. Their spreading toes have claws and ingenious adhesive pads, allowing them to cross house walls and ceilings in their search for insects, including mosquitoes. The rare **chameleon** is a slow-moving, swivel-eyed inhabitant of eastern Crete, Yiálova and some eastern Aegean islands such as Sámos. Essentially green, it has the ability to adjust its coloration to match the surroundings.

Once collected for the pet trade, **tortoises** can be found on much of the mainland, and some islands, though not Crete. Usually their noisy progress through hillside scrub vegetation is the first signal of their presence, as they spend their often long lives grazing the vegetation. Closely related **terrapins** are more streamlined, freshwater tortoises that love to bask on waterside mud by streams or ponds. Shy and nervous, omnivorous scavengers, usually only seen as they disappear under water, their numbers have recently declined steeply on many islands.

Sea turtles occur mostly in the Ionian Sea, but also in the Aegean. The least rare are the loggerhead turtles (*Caretta caretta*), which nest on Zákynthos and Kefaloniá, the Peloponnese, and occasionally in Crete. Their nesting grounds are disappearing under tourist resorts, although they are a protected endangered species (see the box on p.885).

Snakes are abundant in Greece and many islands; most are shy and non-venomous. Several species, including the Ottoman and nose-horned vipers, do have a poisonous bite, though they are not usually aggressive; they are adder-like and often have a very distinct, dark zigzag stripe down the back. Snakes are only likely to bite if a hand is put in the crevice of a wall or a rock-face where one of them is resting, or if they are molested. Unfortunately, the locals in some areas attempt to kill any snake they see, thereby greatly increasing the probability of their being bitten. Leave them alone, and they will do the same for you (but if bitten, see the advice on p.56). Most snakes are not only completely harmless to humans, but beneficial since they keep down populations of pests such as rats and mice.

Frogs and toads are the commonest and most obvious amphibians throughout much of Greece, particularly during the spring breeding season. Frogs prefer the wettest places, and the robust marsh frog revels in artificial water-storage ponds, whose concrete sides magnify their croaking impressively. Tree frogs are tiny emerald-green jewels, with huge and strident voices at night, sometimes found in quantity on the leaves of waterside oleanders.

Insects

Greece teems with insects: some pester, like flies and mosquitoes, but most are harmless to humans. **Grasshoppers** and **crickets** swarm through open areas of vegetation in summer, with larger species that are carnivorous and can bite if handled. Larger still are grey-brown locusts, flying noisily before crash-landing into trees and shrubs. The high-pitched, endlessly repeated chirp of house

Flora and fauna field guides

In case of difficulty obtaining titles listed below from conventional booksellers, try Summerfield Books (Ⓣ01768/484909; Ⓦwww.summerfieldbooks.com).

Flowers

Hellmut Baumann *Greek Wild Flowers and Plant Lore in Ancient Greece*. Crammed with fascinating ethnobotany, plus good colour photographs.

Marjorie Blamey and Christopher Grey-Wilson Mediterranean Wild Flowers. Comprehensive field guide, with coloured drawings; recent and taxonomically reasonably up to date.

Lance Chilton *Plant Check-Lists*. Small booklets that also include birds, reptiles and butterflies, for a number of Greek islands and resorts. Available direct at Ⓣ01485/532710, Ⓦwww.marengowalks.com).

Pierre Delforge *Orchids of Britain and Europe*. A comprehensive guide, with recent taxonomy.

John Fielding & Nicholas Turland *Flowers of Crete*. Large volume with 1900 coloured photos of the Cretan flora, much of which is also widespread in Greece.

Oleg Polunin *Flowers of Greece and the Balkans*. Classic, older field guide (reprinted 1997), with colour photographs and line drawings, plus good sections on regional geology, climate and habitats.

Kit Tan and Gregoris Iatrou *Endemic Plants of Greece – The Peloponnese*. Hardly pocket size but the first of three volumes planned to cover the entire endemic Greek flora; detailed text and excellent coloured drawings.

Birds

Richard Brooks *Birding on the Greek Island of Lesvos*. Superb guide, with colour photos and detailed maps, including a list of bird-watching sites and an annotated species-by-species bird list with much useful information. Revised 2002, yearly updates available. Contact the author directly at Ⓔemail@richard-brooks.co.uk.

George Handrinos and T. Akriotis *Birds of Greece*. A comprehensive guide that includes island birdlife.

Lars Jonsson *Birds of Europe with North Africa and the Middle East*. The ornithologist's choice for the best coverage of Greek birds, with excellent descriptions and illustrations.

Mammals

Corbet and Ovenden *Collins Guide to the Mammals of Europe*. The best field guide on its subject.

Reptiles

Arnold, Burton and Ovenden *Collins Guide to the Reptiles and Amphibians of Britain and Europe*. A useful guide, though it excludes the Dodecanese and east Aegean islands.

Insects

Michael Chinery *Collins Guide to the Insects of Britain and Western Europe*. Although Greece is outside the geographical scope of the guide, it will provide generic identifications for many insects seen.

Lionel Higgins and Norman Riley *A Field Guide to the Butterflies of Britain and Europe*. A thorough and detailed field guide that illustrates nearly all species seen in Greece.

Marine life

B. Luther and K. Fiedler *A Field Guide to the Mediterranean (o/p)*. Very thorough; includes most Greek shallow-water species.

crickets can drive one to distraction, as can the summer whirring of cicadas on the trunks of trees.

From spring through to autumn, Greece is full of **butterflies**. Swallowtail species are named for the drawn-out corners of the hind-wings, in shades of cream and yellow, with black and blue markings. The unrelated, robust brown-and-orange pasha is Europe's largest butterfly. In autumn, black-and-orange African monarchs may appear, sometimes in large quantities. However, the "butterflies" occurring in huge quantity in sheltered sites on islands such as Rhodes, Níssyros and Páros are in fact Tiger moths, with their black-and-white forewings and startling bright orange hindwings.

Other insects include the camouflaged **praying mantis**, holding their powerful forelegs in a position of supplication until another insect comes within reach. The females are notorious for eating the males during mating. Hemispherical **scarab beetles** collect balls of dung and push them around with their back legs.

Corfu and the Epirot mainland opposite are famous for its extraordinary **fireflies**, which flutter in quantities across meadows and marshes on May nights, speckling the darkness with bursts of cold light to attract partners; look carefully in nearby hedges, and you may spot the less flashy, more sedentary glow-worm.

Other non-vertebrates of interest include the **land crabs**, which are found in the south and east of Greece. They need water to breed, but can surprise when seen crawling across remote hillsides.

Greek popular music

Music is ubiquitous in modern Greek culture; even the most indifferent visitor will notice it in tavernas and other public spaces. Like so many aspects of the country, it amalgamates "native" and Anatolian styles, with occasional contributions from points west, and flourishes alongside and often in preference to Western pop. In fact, Western music made little impression in Greece until the 1960s, when disputes arose between adherents of indigenous styles and those spurning ethnic roots in favour of jazz, rock or symphonic idioms – reflecting broader modernizing-versus-traditionalism debates that preoccupied the country.

Many older songs in Eastern-flavoured minor scales (more correctly, modes) have direct antecedents in the forms and styles of both **Byzantine religious chant** and the popular music of the **Ottoman Empire**, though more nationalist-minded musicologists claim their original descent from the now-lost melodies of ancient Greece. Almost all native Greek instruments are near-duplicates of ones used throughout the Islamic world, though it's an open question as to whether the Byzantines, Arabs or Persians first constructed particular instruments. To this broadly Middle Eastern base neighbouring Slavs, Albanians and Italians have added their share, resulting in an extraordinarily varied repertoire.

Regional folk music

The best opportunities to hear live Greek folk music are the numerous summer **paniyíria** (saints' day festivals) or more tourist-oriented **cultural programmes**, when musicians based in Athens clubs during winter tour the islands and villages. All too often, alas, traditional instrumentation is replaced by rock instruments, with excess reverb and pick-ups tacked on to string instruments not designed for amplification. However, various high-quality revival groups are attempting to recapture the musicianship of the old-timers, fortunately well archived on CD.

Island music

The arc of southern Aegean islands comprising **Crete**, **Kássos**, **Kárpathos** and **Hálki** is one of the most promising areas to hear live music. The dominant instrument here is the **lýra**, a lap-fiddle related to the Turkish *kemençe*. It is played not on the shoulder but balanced on the thigh, with – in the Dodecanese – a loose bow that can touch all three gut strings (the middle one a drone) simultaneously, making double chords possible. The contemporary **Cretan lýra** is larger, tuned lower (like a Western violin), played with a much tauter bow, and lacks a drone. Outstanding Cretan composer-players include the late **Kostas Moundakis** and **Andonis Xylouris (Psarandonis)**.

Usually, the *lýra* is backed up by a **laoúto**, related to the Turkish/Arab *oud* but more closely resembling a mandolin, with a long fretted neck and four sets of double strings. Usually restricted in mediocre playing to percussive chords, these are rarely used to solo, but a virtuoso player will enter a true dialogue with the *lýra*, using well-chosen rhythms and melodic phrases in chime-like tones.

In parts of the southeastern Aegean, most notably **Kálymnos** and northern **Kárpathos**, you also find a simple, **droneless bagpipe** with a double chanter – the **askomandoúra** or *tsamboúna*. On most islands, though, this instrument is seen as fit for generating carnival noise only – played together with a two-headed, shoulder-strung drum called the *toumbáki*. Crete, Náxos, Sámos, Ikaría and Tínos each have just one elderly player apiece, with no younger disciples. Much the same goes for the **sandoúri** (hammer dulcimer) – which in Kazantzakis's classic novel, or its film, *Zorba the Greek*, was played by his Cretan hero. The instrument, which today tends to have a supporting role (at best), was introduced to most islands by Asia Minor refugees.

On most Aegean islands, particularly the **Cyclades**, the *lýra* is replaced by a more familiar-looking **violí**, essentially a Western violin. Accompaniment was provided until recently by *laoúto* or *sandoúri*, though these days you're most likely to be confronted by a bass guitar and rock drums. Among the better fiddle players, **Stathis Koukoularis** (from Náxos) and younger **Nikos Ikonomidhes** (Skhinoússa/Amorgós) or **Kyriakos Gouvendas** are well worth seeking out. Unlike on Crete, where you often catch music in special clubs or *kéndra*, Aegean island performances tend to be community-based events in village squares or monastery courtyards.

Island folk songs – **nisiótika** – feature melodies which, like much folk music the world over, rely heavily on the pentatonic scale. Lyrics, especially on smaller islands, touch on the perils of the sea, exile and (in a society where long separations and arranged marriages were the norm) thwarted love. The prolific and decidedly uneven **Konitopoulos** clan from Náxos has become synonymous with *nisiótika*, but older stars like **Anna and Emilia Hatzidhaki**, **Effi Sarri** and **Anna Karabesini** – all from the Dodecanese – offer a warmer, more innocent delivery.

Lésvos occupies a special place in terms of island music; before the turbulent decade of 1912–22, its "mainland" was Asia Minor not Greece, its urban poles Smyrna and Constantinople rather than Athens. Thus its music is more varied and sophisticated than the Aegean norm, having absorbed melodies and instrumentation from various nationalities of neighbouring Anatolia; it is the only island with a vital **brass band** tradition, and nearly every Greek dance rhythm is represented in local music.

By way of contrast, the **Ionian islands** (except Lefkádha) alone of all modern Greek territory never saw Turkish occupation and have a predominantly Western musical tradition. Their indigenous song-form is Italian both in name – **kantádhes** – and in instrumentation (guitar and mandolin) and vocalization (major scales, choral delivery); it's most often heard now on Lefkádha, Kefaloniá and Zákynthos.

Mainland music

In the **Peloponnese** and **central/western Greece**, many folk songs – known as **paliá dhimotiká** – hark back to the Ottoman occupation and the War of Independence; others, in a lighter tone, refer to aspects of pastoral life (sheep, elopements, fetching water from the well). Their essential instrument is the **klaríno** (clarinet), which reached Greece during the 1830s, introduced either by Gypsies or King Otto's Bavarian entourage. Backing was traditionally provided by a *koumpanía* consisting of *kythára* (guitar), *laoúto*, *laoutokythára* (a hybrid instrument) and *violí*, with *toumberléki* (lap drum) or *défi* (tambourine) for rhythm.

Many mainland melodies are **dances**, divided by rhythm into such categories as *kalamatianó* (a line dance), *tsámiko*, *hasaposérviko* or *syrtó*, the quintessential circle dance of Greece. Those that aren't danceable include the slow, stately *kléftiko*, similar to the *rizítiko* of western Crete, which relate, baldly or in metaphor, incidents or attitudes from the Ottoman era and the fight for freedom. Stalwart vocalists on old recordings include **Yiorgos Papasidheris** and **Yioryia Mittaki**, as well as **Sofia Kollitiri** and **Stathis Kavouras** from the 1960s to the 1980s. Among instrumentalists, violinist **Yiorgos Koros** and clarinetist **Vassilis Saleas** are especially remarkable.

The folk music of **Epirus (Ípiros)** shows strong resemblances to that of northern Epirus (now in neighbouring Albania) and the Former Yugoslav Republic of Macedonia, particularly in the **polyphonic pieces** sung by both men and women. The repertoire divides into three categories, also found further south: *mirolóyia* or laments; drinking songs or *tís távlas*; and various danceable melodies as noted above, common to the entire mainland and many islands also. Most notable of the Epirot **clarinettists** are the late **Vassilis Soukas** and **Tassos Halkias**, and the younger (distantly related) **Petro-Loukas Halkias** – all examples of the (mostly) **Gypsy** or Gypsy-descent musicians who dominate instrumental music on the mainland.

Macedonia and Thrace in the north remained Ottoman territory until the early 1900s, with a bewilderingly mixed population, so music here still sounds more generically Balkan. Worth special mention are the **brass bands** peculiar to western Macedonia, introduced during the nineteenth century by Ottoman military musicians. Owing to the huge, post-1923 influx of Anatolian refugees, these regions have been a treasure-trove for collectors and ethnomusicologists seeking to document the old music of Asia Minor. Noteworthy singers – both still alive and active – include **Xanthippi Karathanassi** and **Khronis Aïdhonidhis**.

Among Thracian instruments, the **kaváli** (end-blown pastoral flute) is identical to the Turkish and Bulgarian article, as is the local drone bagpipe or **gáïda**, made like its island counterpart from a goat-skin. The **zournás**, a screechy, double-reed oboe similar to the Islamic world's *shenai*, is an integral part of weddings or festivals, along with the deep-toned *daoúli* drum, as a typically Gypsy ensemble. Other percussion instruments like the *daïrés* or tambourine and the *darboúka* provide sharply demarcated dance rhythms such as the *zonarádhikos*. The *klaríno* is present here as well, as are two types of *lýras*, but the most characteristic melodic instrument of Thrace is the **oúti** (*oud*), whose popularity received a boost after refugee players arrived. **Nikos Saragoudas** is its acknowledged living master.

Rebétika

Rebétika began as the music of the Greek urban dispossessed – petty criminals, bar-girls, refugees, drug-users, defiers of social norms. It existed in some form in **Greece**, **Smyrna** and **Constantinople** since at least the very early 1900s – probably a few decades earlier. But it is as hard to define as American blues, with which half-useful comparisons are often made. Although rebétika shares marked similarities in spirit with that genre, there's little or none in its musical form. That said, the themes of the earlier songs – illicit or frustrated love, drug addiction, police oppression, disease and death; and their tone – resignation to the singer's lot, coupled with defiance of authority – will be familiar to old-time blues fans.

Even the word "rebétika" is of uncertain derivation, most likely from *harabati*, an old Turkish word meaning variously "a shanty town", "a privileged drunkard" and "unconventionally dressed bohemian" – all aspects of early rebétika culture. Accordingly, searches for its beginnings must be conducted in the Asia Minor of the Ottoman empire's last years as well as in Greece proper.

Origins: café-aman

Most people equate Greek music with the **bouzoúki**, a long-necked, fretted, three-stringed lute derived, like the Turkish *saz*, from the Byzantine *tambourás*. Early in the twentieth century, however, only a few Greek mainland musicians used it. At the same time, across the Aegean in Smyrna and Constantinople, musical cafés, owned or staffed almost entirely by Greeks, Jews, Armenians, Slavs and even a few Gypsies, were popular. They featured groups comprising a violinist, a *sandoúri* player and a (usually female) vocalist, who might also jingle castanets and dance. The metrically free, improvisational song-style became known as **café-aman** or **amanés**, after the frequent repetition of the exclamation *aman aman* (Turkish for "alas, alas"), used both for its sense and to fill time while performers searched for more articulate lyrics.

Despite sparse instrumentation, the *amanés* was an elegant, riveting style requiring considerable skill, similar to the *gazal* of central Asia. Among its greatest practitioners were **Andonis "Dalgas" Dhiamandidhis**, so nicknamed (Dalgas means "Wave") for his vocal undulations; **Roza Eskenazi**, a Greek Jew raised in Constantinople, whose voice inimitably combined innocence and sensuality; her contemporary rival **Rita Abatzi**, from Smyrna, with a huskier, more textured tone; **Marika Papagika**, from the island of Kós, who emigrated to America where she made her career; **Agapios Tomboulis**, a *tambur* and *oud* player of Armenian background; and **Dhimitris "Salonikiyé" Semsis**, a master fiddler from northern Macedonia who in the course of his career travelled across the Mediterranean. The spectrum of these performers' origins gives an idea of the cosmopolitan influences in the years immediately preceding the emergence of "real" rebétika.

The 1919–22 Greco-Turkish war and the subsequent **1923 exchange of populations** were key events for rebétika, resulting in the influx to Greece of over a million Asia Minor Greeks, many of whom settled in shanty towns around Athens, Pireás and Thessaloníki. The *café-aman* musicians, like many of the refugees, were far more sophisticated than the Greeks of the host country; most were highly educated, able to read and compose music. Such men included the Smyrniots **Vangelis Papazoglou**, a noted songwriter, and **Panayiotis Toundas**, another composer who later ran Columbia Records.

But less lucky refugees lived on the periphery of the new society: most had lost all they had in the hasty evacuation, and many, from inland Anatolia, initially spoke only Turkish. In their misery they sought relief in another Ottoman institution, the **tekés** or hashish den, whose habitués were known as *dervíses* (dervishes). This apparent burlesque of the Islamic mystical tradition was in fact not as flippant as it appears; the Turkish word *harabati*, noted above, is in turn derived from the Arabo-Persian *kharabat*, the Sufi musician's quarter in Afghan or Persian towns, "the place you go to be destroyed (and reborn)" by partaking in the rituals.

The tekédhes and Pireás-style rebétika

In the *tekédhes* of Pireás, Athens and Thessaloníki, a few men would sit around a charcoal brazier, toking from a *(n)argilés* (hookah) filled with hashish. One might improvise a tune on the *baglamás* or the *bouzoúki* and begin to sing. The words would be heavily laced with insiders' argot incorporating Turkish and Venetian words (plus a few Arabic or Albanian ones). As the *taxími* (long, studied introduction) was completed, a smoker might rise and begin to dance a **zeïbékiko**, named after the Zeybeks, a warrior caste of western Anatolia. Following an unusual metre (9/8), it would be a slow, intense performance, not for the benefit of others but for himself.

By the early 1930s, key (male) musicians had emerged from the *tekés* culture. Foremost among them was a Pireás-based quartet: the beguiling-voiced **Stratos Payioumtzis**; composer and lyricist **Anestis Delias** (aka **Artemis**), who died in the street of a drug overdose in 1943; *baglamá*-player Yiorgos Tsoros, better known as **Batis**, an indifferent musician but another excellent composer; and **Markos Vamvakaris**, a Catholic from Sýros who became the linchpin of the group. After a tough childhood, he'd stowed away aged fifteen on a boat for Pireás; within months of arrival, he had taught himself *bouzoúki* as a way out of a particularly grim job in a slaughterhouse, and a few years later was playing with the other three. Though a master instrumentalist, he initially considered that his voice, ruined perhaps from too much hash-smoking, wasn't fit for singing. But he soon bowed to the encouragement of record label Columbia, and his gravelly, unmistakable delivery set the standard for male rebétic vocals until the 1940s. His only close peer as an instrumentalist and composer was **Ioannis Papaïoannou**, with whom he played steadily from 1936 to 1939.

Songs about getting stoned – known as *mastoúriaka* or *hasiklídhika* – were a natural outgrowth of the *tekédhes*. A famous one, composed by Batis and first recorded in the mid-1930s with Stratos singing, commemorated the quartet's exploits:

On the sly I went out in a boat
And arrived at Dhrákou Cave
Where I saw three hash-heads
Stretched out on the sand.
It was Batis, and Artemis,
And Stratos the Lazy.
Hey you, Strato! Yeah you, Strato!
Fix us a terrific nargilé,
So old Batis can have a smoke...

Subsequent decades saw such lyrics bowdlerized, as made clear below; the most-heard version of this song from the 1950s substitutes "Play us a fine bit of *bouzoúki*" for "Fix us a fine *nargilé*", and so forth.

Persecution

This "Golden Age" of rebétika – as indeed it was, despite the unhappy lives of many performers, and a limited audience – was short-lived; the music's association with a drug-laced underworld would prove its undoing. During the strait-laced **Metaxas dictatorship** in 1936, musicians with uncompromising lyrics and lifestyles were blackballed by the recording industry; existing anti-hashish laws were systematically enforced, and police harassment of the *tekédhes* increased. In Athens, even possession of a *bouzoúki* or *baglamás* became a criminal offence – thus frequent lyrics about instruments being hidden under coats or smashed by the cops – and several performers did jail time. Others went to Thessaloníki, where police chief Vassilis Mouskoundis was a big fan of the music and allowed its practitioners to smoke in private.

For a while, such persecution – and the official encouragement of tangos and frothy Italianate love songs (which always had a much wider public) – failed to dim the enthusiasm of the *mánges* ("wide boys") who frequented the hash dens. Police beatings or prison terms were taken in their stride; time behind bars could be used, as it always had been, to make *skaptó* (hollowed-out) instruments. A *baglamás* could easily be fashioned from a gourd cut in half or even a tortoise shell (the sound box), any piece of wood (the neck), catgut (frets) and wire strings; the result would be small enough to hide from the guards. **Jail songs** were composed and became popular in the underworld. The lyrics below, with some literal translation from the 1930s argot, are from a much-recorded song, "Iy Lahanádhes" ("The Pickpockets," or literally "The Cabbage-Dealers") by Vangelis Papazoglou:

Down in Lemonádhika there was a ruckus
They caught two pickpockets who acted innocent
They took 'em to the slammer in handcuffs
They'll get a beating if they don't cough up the loot.
Don't beat us, Mr. Copper, you know very well
This is our job, and don't expect a cut.
We "eat cabbages" and pinch "slippers" so we can
Have a regular rest in jail.
Death don't scare us, it's only hunger we mind,
That's why we nick "cabbage" and get along fine.

The unfortunate rebétes incurred disapproval from the puritanical Left as well as the puritanical Right; the growing **Communist Party** of the 1930s considered the music and its habitués hopelessly decadent and politically unevolved. When Vamvakaris went to join the leftist resistance army ELAS in 1943, he was admonished not to sing his own material; the Left preferred **andártika** (Soviet-style revolutionary anthems), although **Sotiria Bellou**, a rebétissa (female rebétika musician) and active communist whose career began late in the 1940s, was a conspicuous exception. Despite this, rebétika was strangely popular amongst the rank-and-file on both sides of the 1946–49 civil war – perhaps the only taste uniting a fatally polarized country.

Rebétika goes mainstream, declines, then revives

Bellou was one of several important female vocalists to accompany **Vassilis Tsitsanis**, the most significant composer and *bouzoúki* player after Vamvakaris; the others were **Marika Ninou**, an Armenian refugee from the Caucasus, and **Ioanna Yiorgakopoulou**, the latter also a composer in her own right. From Tríkala in Thessaly, Tsitsanis abandoned law studies to cut his first record in 1936 for Odeon, directed by composer **Spyros Peristeris**. The war interrupted his – and everyone else's – recording career by closing the studios from late 1940 until late 1945, a period which Tsitsanis spent more comfortably than many, running a musical taverna in Thessaloníki.

When World War II, and the civil war that followed, ended, a huge backlog of songs composed during the interim finally went onto 78s. The traumatic decade between 1939 and 1949 had erased any lingering taste for *mastoúriaka*; the 1950s Greek public instead craved softer **quasi-Neapolitan melodies**, words about love and new heroes. Tsitsanis was happy to oblige on all three counts, and for the first time rebétika enjoyed a mass following. But his love lyrics were anything but insipid; the demoralization of the war years saw him also compose darker works, most famous of these "Synnefiasmeni Kyriaki" (written in the first days of the German occupation but only recorded much later):

Cloudy Sunday, you seem like my heart
Which is always overcast, Christ and Holy Virgin!
You're a day like the one I lost my joy.
Cloudy Sunday, you make my heart bleed.
When I see you rainy, I can't rest easy for a moment;
You blacken my life and I sigh deeply.

Although Tsitsanis performed almost up to his death in 1984 – his funeral in Athens was attended by nearly a quarter of a million people – 1953 effectively marked the end of the original rebetic style. In that year, **Manolis Hiotis** added a **fourth string** to the **bouzoúki**, allowing it to be tuned tonally rather than modally; electrical amplification to reach larger audiences, maudlin lyrics and over-orchestration were not long in following. Performances in huge, barnlike clubs, also called *bouzoúkia*, became vulgarized. Virtuoso *bouzoúki* players like Hiotis, **Yiorgos Mitsakis** and **Yiorgos Zambetas**, assisted by large-chested female vocalists of little distinction, became immensely rich – the so-called *arhondorebétes*. The clubs themselves were clip-joints where Athenians paid half a month's wage to break plates and watch dancers whose flashy steps and gyrations were a travesty of the simple dignity and precise, synchronized footwork of the old-time *zeïbékiko*.

Ironically, the original rebétika material was rescued from oblivion by the 1967–74 **colonels' junta**. Along with various other features of Greek culture, most rebétika verses were banned. The generation coming of age under the dictatorship took a closer look at the forbidden fruit and derived solace, and deeper meanings, from the nominally apolitical lyrics. When the junta fell in 1974 – even a little before – there was an outpouring of reissued recordings of the old masters.

Over the next decade-plus live rebétika also enjoyed a revival, beginning with a reunion of old-timers in 1973, and continuing with a clandestine 1978 club near Athens' old Fix brewery, its street cred validated by being raided and closed by the police. These smoky attempts to recapture pre-war atmosphere, and eventually larger venues, saw performances by revival groups such as the Athens-based **Ta Pedhia apo tin Patra**, **Iy Rebetiki Kompania** and **Iy Opisthodhromiki Kompania**, and from Thessaloníki, **Hondronakos** plus **Maryo** and **Agathonas (Iakovidhis)** with his **Rebetika Synkrotima Thessalonikis**. Both Maryo and Agathonas still perform, the latter in a quartet, **Rebetiki Tetras**, with Glykeria, Babis Goles and Babis Tsertos.

A feature film by Kostas Ferris, **Rembetiko** (1983), based loosely on the life of Marika Ninou, attempted to trace the music from Asia Minor of the 1920s to Greece of the 1950s, and garnered worldwide acclaim. Today, however, the rebétika fashion has long since peaked in Greece, and scarcely any clubs and bands remain from the dozens which existed between 1978 and 1986. Interestingly, rebétika has garnered a new lease of life overseas, with a keen following and revival groups in such unlikely countries as Sweden and Israel, but the music is now effectively retro and historic.

The éntekhno revolution

The "Westernization" of rebétika that began with Tsitsanis and was finished by the *arhondorebétes* preceded the rise of the **éntekhno music** that emerged during the late 1950s. *Éntekhno*, literally "artistic" or "sophisticated", was an orchestral genre where folk or rebétika instrumentation and melodies became part of a much larger symphonic fabric, but with a still recognizably Greek sound.

Its first and most famous exponents were **Manos Hatzidhakis** and **Mikis Theodhorakis**, both classically trained musicians and admirers of rebétika. Already in 1948, Hatzidhakis had defended rebétika in a public lecture, urging Greek composers to be inspired by it, rather than scorn it as low-rent. At a time when most Greek tunes imitated Western light popular music, he transcribed rebétika for piano and orchestra, keeping only the melody and nostalgic mood of the original. Theodhorakis, a disciple of Tsitsanis, included *zeïbékika* on his earliest albums, with **Grigoris Bithikotsis** on vocals and Manolis Hiotis as *bouzoúki* soloist.

The *éntekhno* of Theodhorakis and Hatzidhakis combined not only rebetic and Byzantine influences with orchestral arrangements, but also successfully used the country's rich **poetic tradition**. Among Theodhorakis's first albums was his 1958 *Epitafios/Epifaneia*, settings of poems by **Yiannis Ritsos** and **George Seferis** respectively, and its successor, *To Axion Esti*, a Byzantine-flavoured oratorio incorporating verses by **Odysseas Elytis**. Hatzidhakis countered with *Matomenos Gamos*, a version of Garcia Lorca's *Blood Wedding* translated by poet-lyricist **Nikos Gatsos**, and also tried his hand at rendering Elytis in song. These early works changed Greek perceptions of *bouzoúki*-based music, popularized Greek poetry for a mass audience and elevated lyricists like Gatsos and **Manos Eleftheriou** to the status of bards.

The down-side of increased sophistication was an inevitable distancing from indigenous roots, in particular the modal scale which had done yeoman service since antiquity. And with its catchy tunes, *éntekhno* fell prey to the demands of the local film industry – writing a soundtrack became a composer's obligatory rite of passage – and at its worst degenerated to muzak cover versions. Hatzidhakis composed **soundtracks** for various movies starring Melina Mercouri, most notably *Never on Sunday* (1960); Theodhorakis' international reputation subsequently became distorted by his overplayed and over-covered 1965 tunes for *Zorba the Greek*. Soon after he shunned Byzantine/folk/rebétic influence in favour of quasi-classical, overtly political symphonic works and film soundtracks dictated by his communist affiliation. Hatzidhakis (who died in 1994) steered clear of political statements; instead he launched, during the 1980s, his own record label, Seirios, to provide a forum for young, non-mainstream musicians.

Theodhorakis and Hatzidhakis paved the way for less classicizing and more folk-leaning successors such as **Stavros Xarhakos**, most famous for his soundtracks to the films *Ta Kokkina Fanaria* (The Red Lanterns), and *Rembetiko*; Xarkhakos's contemporary **Yiannis Markopoulos** also paid his soundtrack dues (*Who Pays the Ferryman*, 1978) but is arguably the most consistently Greek-sounding of these four composers to emerge from the 1960s. His best work dates from the early- to mid-1970s – the Indian summer of *éntekhno* – when golden-voiced Cretan **Nikos Xylouris** graced many of his (and Xarhakos') recordings.

Laïká: son of rebétika

Diametrically opposed to *éntekhno* was the **laïká** ("popular") music of the 1950s and 1960s, its gritty, tough style directly linked to rebétika, undiluted by Western influences. *Laïká* used not only *zeïbékiko* and *hasápiko* time signatures but also the *tsiftetéli*, another Asia Minor rhythm mistakenly known overseas as belly-dance music. Once again, "debased" oriental influences dominated, much to the chagrin of those who objected to the apolitical, decadent, escapist song content.

The most notable *laïká* performer was **Stelios Kazantzidhis** (1931–2001), whose volcanic, mournful style was never equalled. His work, often in duets with **Marinella** and **Yiota Lidhia**, immortalized the experiences of the Greek working class that emerged from the 1940s faced with a choice of life under restrictive regimes or emigration. "Stellaras" inspired fanatical devotion in his fans over a fifty-year career: truck-drivers emblazoned their cabs with a single word, "Yparho" (the name of his biggest hit). On the day he died nearly every CD player in the land played Kazantzidhis songs in tribute, and his funeral in industrial Elefsína was thronged by thousands.

Top *laïká* star of the next generation has indubitably been **Yiorgos (George) Dalaras**, a musical phenomenon in Greece since he made his 1968 vinyl debut with composer **Manos Loïzos**. Born in 1952, Dalaras has featured on well over a hundred recordings spanning all Greek genres – including those of Theodhorakis, Hatzidhakis and Markopoulos – and collaborated with flamenco guitarist Paco de Lucia and American jazz star Al Di Meola. Dalaras has also been a staunch supporter (through benefit concerts) of progressive causes, enough to forgive him his recent, forgettable symphonic extravaganzas.

Amongst notable *laïká* composers and lyricists, **Apostolos Kaldharas** was the most prolific during the 1950s and 1960s; he gave singer **Yiannis Parios** his start, and introduced *laïká* star **Haris Alexiou** with his landmark 1972 album *Mikra Asia*. **Khristos Nikolopoulos** was a 1970s *bouzoúki* virtuoso who composed for Kazantzídhis, and subsequently did mega-selling co-efforts with Dalaras and Alexiou. **Akis Panou** (1934–99) was less prolific and commercially successful – doubling up as a painter and copper-engraver – but he too produced noteworthy albums with Dalaras, Bithikotsis, Kazantzidhis and Stratos Dhionysiou.

The opposite poles of *laïká* and *éntekhno* sometimes met, with *éntekhno* composers – especially Markopoulos – often hiring *laïká* singers for dates, or trying their hand at writing in *laïká* style. These syntheses became rarer as Greek record labels tried to marginalize *laïká* – a trend accelerated under the junta, a disaster for many types of music. Not only was most *laïká* banned from radio as being too "oriental" and "defeatist", but folk music – already disparaged as old-fashioned by a generation coming of age with the Beatles – fell into further disrepute through its use for propaganda purposes. In these conditions, only *elafrolaïká* (literally "light popular songs") and *éntekhno*, with its minority audience and potential for coded messages within oblique lyrics, flourished. But the stage was set for the emergence of singer-songwriters – many from Thessaloníki – and folk-rockers, who together arrested the decline of Greek music.

Singer-songwriters and folk-rock

The first significant musician to break the *bouzoúki* mould was Thessalonian **Dhionysis Savvopoulos**, who emerged in 1966 with a maniacal, rasping voice and angst-ridden lyrics, his persona rounded out by shoulder-length hair and outsized glasses. Initially linked with the short-lived **néo kýma** movement – a blend of stripped-down *éntekhno* and French *chanson* performed in *boîtes* soon closed by the colonels – Savvopoulos's work soon became impossible to pigeonhole: perhaps equal parts twisted northern Greek folk,

Bob Dylan and Frank Zappa at his jazziest. Though briefly detained and tortured, he resumed performing, and became something of a touchstone for late 1960s Greek youth.

Out of Savvopoulos's **"Balkan rock"** experiments sprang a short-lived movement whose artists alternated electric versions of traditional songs with original material. The most significant of these were folk "updater" **Mariza Koch**, Gypsy guitarist-protest singer **Kostas Hatzis**, **Nikos Portokaloglu** and his group Fatme, and folk/*éntekhno* performer **Arletta**, all still active to various degrees.

Despite a modest discography, Savvopoulos had a considerable effect on younger artists. Credit (or blame) for much Greek rock and fusion-folk can be laid at his door; during his brief tenure as a record producer, Savvopoulos gave breaks to numerous younger artists, many of them also from northern Greece. Among his protegés were **Nikos Xydhakis** and **Manolis Rasoulis**, whose landmark 1978 pressing, *Iy Ekdhikisi tis Yiftias* (The Revenge of Gypsydom) actually embodied the backlash of *laïká* culture (*laïká*, in Greek, means "common" or "low-class" as well as "popular") against the pretentiousness of 1960s and 1970s *éntekhno* and other "politically correct" music. Its spirited, defiant lyrics – with Nikos Papazoglou on most vocals – and *tsifteteli* rhythms were both homage to and send-up of the music beloved by Greek truck-drivers, Gypsy or otherwise.

Real **Gypsies** have been disproportionately important in *laïká*, both as performers and composers, though many strenuously conceal the fact; however, for every assimilated personality there are others, such as **Eleni Vitali** and **Vassilis Païteris**, who make no bones about their identity.

Contemporary roots: the 1980s to the present

After an equally successful 1979 reprise (*Ta Dhithen*) with similar personnel, **Xydhakis** and **Papazoglou** pursued successful independent careers, Xydhakis in a notably orientalized style reflecting perhaps his Egyptian childhood. His most successful venture was the 1987 *Konda sti Dhoxa mia Stigmi* with rising vocal star **Eleftheria Arvanitaki** guesting. Arvanitaki, who began her career on a Savvopoulos album, and continued with rebétika revival group Opisthodhromiki Kompania, went on to dabble in various genres, and around the millennium was Greece's hottest vocalist. Nikos Papazoglou is a more varied, though less prolific, songwriter than Xydhakis; his material, also *laïká*- and folk-based, often has a harder electric-rock edge, though he can match Xydhakis for introspection and orientalism. Other performers emerging from the "Salonica Scene" after 1981 included **Himerini Kolymvites** led by Aryiris Bakirtzis, Papazoglou disciple **Sokratis Malamas** and his frequent collaborator **Melina Kana**. Later, Lárissa native **Thanassis Papakonstandinou** erupted with startling reworkings of folk material and original compositions, relying on Hendrix-like guitar licks, sampling, and dialogue.

Otherwise, Westernizing trends often prevailed, under the aegis of composers such as classically trained **Thanos Mikroutsikos**, briefly Minister of Culture after Melina Mercouri's death, who despite his high-brow leanings worked with Alexiou, Dalaras and top vocalist **Dhimitra Galani**. Lyricist **Lina Nikolakopoulou** also made a splash with some thoughtful, if often slick, albums stretching into the 1990s, exploring the boundaries between rock, jazz-cabaret and *éntekhno*.

A post-1970s offshoot of *éntekhno* involved combining folk and **Byzantine traditions**. Musicologist-arranger **Khristodhoulos Halaris** made the riveting *Dhrossoulites* – featuring Dhimitra Galani with **Khrysanthos**, a high-voiced male singer of Pontic descent, and lyrics by Nikos Gatsos – and a version of the medieval Cretan epic *Erotokritos*, showcasing Nikos Xylouris and **Tania Tsanaklidou**.

Ottoman rather than Byzantine Constantinople was the inspiration for **Bosphorus/Vosporos**, a 1986–92 Istanbul-based group co-ordinated by Nikiforos Metaxas to explore Ottoman classical, devotional and popular music. Since then, briefly rebaptized as **Fanari tis Anatolis**, they have mixed Greek folk material with Anatolian songs or mystical Alevî ballads. Most recently they collaborated with **Mode Plagal**, since 1995 Greece's most accomplished funky deconstructors of folk material.

English-born but Irish by background, **Ross Daly** frequently appears live in Greece or tours abroad, offering fusion interpretations of traditional pieces plus his own improvisations. He plays numerous traditional Greek instruments and has absorbed influences not just from Crete, where he was long resident, but from throughout the Near East. Two other exports from Crete are mandolinist **Loudhovikos ton Anoyeion**, originally one of Hatzidhakis's late-1980s Seirios artists, and the all-acoustic group **Haïnidhes**, last heard accompanying acrobats and shadow-puppet players in a major Athens club. To foreign ears either may be more accessible than orthodox, scholarly revivalists such as octogenarian **Domna Samiou**, the foremost living collector and interpreter of Greek folk material; since the 1960s, she has nurtured a generation-plus of young traditional musicians.

Various other, less durable groups have attempted to explore foreign influences on Greek music with mixed success. Often this eclecticism has gone too far, with bells, sitar, ney and synthesizer resulting in a bland, New Age-y sound not identifiably Greek. Individuals who have managed to avoid this trap include innovative young clarinettist **Manos Achalinotopoulos**; *oud* player **Haig Yagdjian**; the group **Notios Ihos**, led by Ahilleas Persidhis; singer **Savina Yiannatou**; and the **Greeks-and-Indians** fusion concerts and recordings coordinated by visionary Alexandhros Karsiotis of Saraswati Records.

Discography

The following CDs are among the best available for each of the genres detailed above: ✪ denotes a particularly strong recommendation, as does a mention in the preceding text (not repeated here). Unless otherwise specified, all are Greek pressings. For good Greek CD stores, see the Athens shopping section (p.155). Online, you'll find some of our choices at Amazon, but rather more at Thessaloníki-based Studio 52 (@www.studio52.gr), which operates a worldwide online order service.

Folk

Compilations

✪ **Lesvos Aiolis** *Tragoudhia ke Hori tis Lesvou/Songs & Dances of Lesvos* (2 CDs). Field recordings (1974–96) of this island's last traditional music, supervised by musicologist Nikos Dhionysopoulos. The quality and uniqueness of the pieces, and lavishly illustrated booklet, merit the expense.

Seryiani sta Nisia Mas, vol 1. Excellent retrospective of mostly 1950s *nisiótika* hits and artists; the easiest way to hear the vintage stars cited on p.938. A highlight is Emilia Hatzidhaki's rendering of "Bratsera".

Thalassa Thymisou: Tragoudhia ke Skopi apo tis Inousses. Superb result of Thessaloníki music school En Khordais' "field trip" to Inoússes, a small islet near Híos; live sessions in

Inoussan tavernas plus studio recordings.

Artists

Khronis Aïdhonidhis *T'Aïdhonia tis Anatolis: Songs of Thrace and Asia Minor.* Flawlessly produced 1990 session featuring the top singer of material from Thrace and western Asia Minor, plus an orchestra directed by Ross Daly, and guest Yiorgos Dalaras.

Petro-Loukas Halkias *Petro-Loukas Chalkias and Kompania* (World Network, Germany). Halkias and his *kompanía* (group) of *laoúto*, *violí*, guitar and percussion realize the true sense of the *kompanía*: tight coordination, yet clearly articulated instrumental voices.

Xanthippi Karathanasi *Tragoudhia ke Skopi tis Makedhonias/Songs and Tunes of Macedonia.* A native of Halkidhikí, Karathanasi is a foremost interpreter of north-mainland material – and her sidemen are so good they almost steal the show.

Andonis Xylouris (Psarandonis) *Palio Krasi In'iy Skepsi Mou* and *Idheon Antron.* Psarandonis – shunned by other Cretan musicians – has an idiosyncratically spare and percussive *lýra* style, but here unusual instruments are well integrated into a densely textured whole. Daughter Niki executes a gorgeous rendition of "Meraklidhiko Pouli" on *Idheon Antron.*

Rebétika

Compilations

Greek Archives. This 1990s series has skeletal English notes but well chosen track selections. From the 28 discs still in print, go for *Rembetiko Song in America vol 1, 1920–1940*; *Women of the Rembetiko Song*; *Anthology of Rebetiko Songs 1933–1940* and *Anthology of Smyrnean Songs 1920–1938 vol 1.*

Greek Orientale: Smyrneic-Rembetic Songs and Dances (Arhoolie-Polylyric, US). Superb collection spanning 1911 to 1937, with Roza, Rita, Marika Papagika and Dhimitris Semsis.

Lost Homelands: The Smyrneic Song in Greece 1928–35 (Interstate/Heritage, UK). Exceptional sound quality and literate liner notes give this collection the edge over rivals.

Rembetika: Songs of the Greek Underground 1925–1947 (Trikont, Germany). This crammed-full, 2-CD set makes an excellent starter collection, with classics such as Papaïoannou's "Pende Ellines ston Adhi" and Kaldaras' "Nykhtose Horis Fengari".

Rough Guide to Rebetika (World Music Network, UK). The best single introduction to the genre, with performers from its earliest recorded days to current revivalists.

Artists

Dhimitris Moustakydhis *16 Rebetika Paigmena se Kithara.* Thessalonian revivalist gem: 16 classics, mostly from the 1920s and 1930s, accompanied by guitar instead of *bouzoúki*.

Roza Eskenazi: Rembetissa (Rounder, US). Ace renditions of standards and rare gems with her usual sidemen Semsis, Tomboulis, and Lambros on *kanonáki*.

Marika Ninou *Stou Tzimi tou Hondrou/At Jimmy the Fat's.* Poor sound quality – it was a clandestine recording – but still a classic: one of the few documents of a live rebetic evening, with Ninou and Tsitsanis performing at their habitual club in 1955.

Rebetiki Kompania *Pos Tha Perasi Iy Vradhia* The easiest found offering from a group that spearheaded the late-1970s rebétika revival.

Tetras Iy Xakousti tou Pireos The gang of four – Vamvakaris, Batis, Anestis and Stratos – at the height of their form.

Vangelis Papazoglou 1897–1943 1920s/30s compositions sung by the era's top stars, including Stellakis Perpiniadhis, Roza Eskenazi, Kostas Roukounas and Rita Abatzi. Poor sound quality, but several versions of his classic "Iy Lahanadhes".

Vassilis Tsitsanis *Vassilis Tsitsanis 1936–1946* (Rounder, US). Mostly male singers, but includes several rare (for him) *mastoúriaka*. The 20 hits of *Ta Klidhia* – look for the ring of three keys (*klidhiá*) on the cover – pair him with such mid-1960s stars as Grigoris Bithikotsis, Kaity Grey and Poly Panou.

Markos Vamvakaris *Bouzoúki Pioneer 1932–1940* (Rounder, US). Excellent sound quality, good notes and unusual material.

Stavros Xarhakos *Rembetiko*. Soundtrack to the eponymous film, and virtually the only "original" rebétika composed in the last fifty years; lyrics by Nikos Gatsos.

Éntekhno

Manos Hatzidhakis *Matomenos Gamos: Paramythi horis Onoma* (Columbia). Nikos Gatsos lyrics, with Lakis Pappas singing.

Yannis Markopoulos *Rizitika*. "La Chante Profunde de Crète" – the French subtitle – says it all: stirring anthems like "Pote Tha Kamei Xasteria", which launched Xylouris' *éntekhno* career. *Thiteia*, with lyrics by Manos Eleftheriou, is also a sentimental favourite.

Mikis Theodhorakis *Epitafios/Epifaneia* with Bithikotsis and Hiotis, and *To Axion Esti* with Manos Katrakis, are among his most influential, reputation-justifying works, in white-boxed remasters of the original sessions.

Stavros Xarhakos *Syllogi*. More lyrics by Nikos Gatsos, Nikos Xylouris's crystalline voice and orchestra (including funky electric guitar licks) conducted by Khristodhoulos Halaris make this a 1973 landmark.

Nikos Xylouris *Itane mia Fora* (2 CDs). A thorough selection of Xylouris' best 1970s work, with Yiannis Markopoulos and others, making clear why he is still worshipped nearly three decades after his tragically early death. The title track is particularly loved and still frequently heard.

Laïká

Haris Alexiou Start with *Ta Tragoudhia tis Haroulas*, with lyrics by Manolis Rasoulis and Manos Loïzos, which established her as alto queen of 1980s *laïká*. *Ta Tsilika* has her rebétika interpretations; *Yirizondas ton Kosmo* is a more recent live *éntekhno*/pop disc.

Eleftheria Arvanitaki *Tragoudhia yia tous Mines* is upbeat and *laïká*-based; in *Ektos Programmatos* Eleftheria gets rootsily down in lively sessions at Athens and Thessaloníki clubs.

Yiorgos Dalaras *Latin*. A 1987 team-up with Al Di Meola, Glykeria, Alkistis Protopsalti and others, plus Latin rhythms and instrumentalists, resulted in nearly half a million copies sold.

Glykeria (Kotsoula) *Me ti Glykeria stin Omorfi Nhykhta*. Live recording showcases this versatile *laïká* singer and rebétika/*nisiótika* revivalist active since the 1980s.

Stelios Kazantzidhis *Iy Zoi Mou Oli* (2 CD). Retrospective of all the classic hits that made him a national institution.

Singer-songwriters

Himerini Kolymvites. Eponymous First and still best of their CDs, with often surreal lyrics plus richly textured, drunken melodies.

Sokratis Malamas *Ena*. A 2000 release that embodies his mature, confident style, with just voice and guitar; 1992's *Tis Meras ke tis Nykhtas*, with Melina Kana, was the big breakthrough for both.

Lina Nikolakopoulou and Stamatis Kraounakis *Kykloforo ke Oploforo*. First and best of their collaborations, featuring Alkistis Protopsalti. Protopsalti and Nikolakopoulou later linked up with Goran Bregovic for the rootsily Balkan *Paradekhtika*.

Thanassis Papakonstandinou He's not for everyone, but arguably among the most original musicians working in Greece. If you like his trend-setting *Vrahnos Profitis* (2000), carry on to *Agrypnia* (2002), where he reprises "Ayia Nostalgia", title track of his utterly different 1993 debut.

Nikos Papazoglou *Synerga*. A gentle, mystical album; 2005's *Ma'issa Selini* is rootsier and broke a long recording silence.

Dhionysis Savvopoulos *Trapezakia Exo* (Lyra MBI). The catchiest outing from the man who set off the folk-rock movement.

Nena Venetsanou This female singer has a deep, earthy voice lending itself to a number of genres. *Ikones* reworks everything from Hatzidhakis (including some premieres) to *nisiótika* to chanson; *Zeïbekika* is a suprisingly successful recasting of rebétika as "profane prayers", performed in French chapels.

Folk revival and fusion

Bosphorus (Fanari tis Anatolis) *Beyond the Bosphorus*. This tour de force, with guests Mode Plagal, revisits Constantinopolitan and Anataloian melodies, with Vassiliki Papayeoryiou on vocals.

Haïnidhes *Haïnidhes* (MBI) and *Kosmos ki Oneiro ine Ena* (MBI) are their first two, and arguably best, albums, with folk-influenced original compositions taking precedence over old standards.

Loudhovikos Ton Anoyion *O Erotas stin Kriti ine Melangolikos* helped rescue the Cretan mandolin from its rhythm-backing ghetto; *Pyli tis Ammou* exemplifies his evolution in a larger group, with guests Malamas, Papazoglou and Venetsanou.

Mode Plagal *Mode Plagal II*. The best of several solo albums; folk tunes meet funky guitar and saxophone licks à la Coltrane and Miles Davis improvisations/compositions.

Savina Yiannatou *Anixi sti Saloniki/Spring in Salonika*. Ladino Sephardic songs, with crisp backing from Kostas Vomvolos' orchestra; Savina's voice (and trademark vibrato) can take some getting used to, though.

Greeks & Indians (9 vols to date): This series (vol 3, *Ta Ipirotika*; vol 4, *Ta Pondiaka*; and vol 8, *Ta Laïka*) sees top performers of Greek regional music – including Petro-Loukas Halkias, Ross Daly, Nikos Saragoudhas, Sofia Papazogou, Yiorgos Amarantidis and Yiorgos Koros – joining forces with some of the best North Indian musicians around.

Books

The best books in this selection are marked by a ⭑ symbol; titles currently out of print are indicated as "o/p". Almost all of our recommendations are available online. Amazon is an obvious first stop; for out of print or secondhand books, consult sites such as ⓦwww.abebooks.com or ⓦwww.bookfinder.com. Two UK specialist Greek bookshops are Hellenic Bookservice (91 Fortess Rd, London NW5 1AG; ⓣ020/7267 9499; ⓦwww.hellenicbookservice.com), or Zeno's (57a Nether St, London N12 7NP; ⓣ020/8446 1985); in Canada, Kalamos Books (2020 Old Station Rd, Streetsville, Ontario L5M 2V1; ⓣ905/542-1877; ⓦwww.kalamosbooks.com) is excellent.

Travel/Impressions

⭑ **Kevin Andrews** *The Flight of Ikaros* (o/p). Intense, compelling account by a sensitive young archeologist wandering the backcountry during the civil war. Five decades on, still one of the best books on Greece as it was before "development".

James Theodore Bent *Aegean Islands: The Cyclades, or Life Among the Insular Greeks*. Originally published in 1881– re-released by Archaeopress – this remains an authoritative account of Greek island customs and folklore, gleaned from a year's Aegean travel.

Gillian Bouras *A Foreign Wife*; *A Fair Exchange*; *Aphrodite and the Others* (all o/p). This trilogy by a woman who married a Greek-Australian and moved to Messinía in 1980, is full of insights into Greek rural life, child-rearing and the migrant experience in both directions.

⭑ **Gerald Durrell** *My Family and Other Animals*. Durrell's 1930s childhood on Corfu, where his family settled, and where he developed a passion for the island's fauna while elder brother Lawrence entertained Henry Miller and others.

Lawrence Durrell *Prospero's Cell* and *Reflections on a Marine Venus*. The former constitutes Durrell's Corfu memoirs, from his time there as World War II loomed. *Marine Venus* recounts his 1945–47 colonial-administrator experiences of Rhodes and other Dodecanese islands.

⭑ **Patrick Leigh Fermor** *Roumeli* and *Mani*. Sir Patrick – knighted in 2004 for his writing and contribution to British-Greek relations – is an aficionado of rural Greece's vanishing minorities and customs. These two volumes, written in the late 1950s and early 1960s respectively, are scholarly travelogues interspersed with strange yarns. Despite self-indulgent passages, they remain among the best books on modern Greece.

Eleni Gage *North of Ithaka*. Eleni is the namesake and granddaughter of the Eleni whose murder her son Nicholas famously set out to avenge (see p.957). A New York journalist, she decided to spend most of 2002 in her grandmother's old Epirot village in Epirus, rebuilding the family house – and more. Her open-hearted account takes in village life and travels from Albania to Árta.

Roy Hounsell *The Papas and the Englishman: From Corfu to Zagoria*. Roy and wife Effie forsake the usual expat arenas and settle in Koukoúli under Mount Gamíla – year-round, a brave choice in this harsh climate – renovating an ancient, crumbled mansion.

Yorgos Ioannou *Refugee Capital*. Brilliant, wide-ranging essays on Thessaloníki by a native, touching on its political powerlessness, its vanished Jews, the grip of the Orthodox Church, flowering shade trees, and gay cruising at its old cinemas.

Sheelagh Kannelli *Earth and Water: A Marriage in Kalamata* (o/p). A foreign woman integrates successfully into provincial Greek society of the 1960s; rich in period detail of pre-earthquake Kalamáta.

Edward Lear *The Corfu Years* and *The Cretan Journal*; *Journals of a Landscape Painter in Greece and Albania* (o/p). Highly entertaining – the first two beautifully illustrated – journals from the 1840s and 1850s.

Peter Levi *The Hill of Kronos*. Finely observed landscapes, monuments, personalities and politics, as poet and classical scholar Levi describes his first journeys to Greece in the 1960s, before being drawn into resistance against the colonels' junta.

Sidney Loch *Athos, The Holy Mountain* (o/p). Resident in Ouranópoli tower on Mount Áthos from 1924 to 1954, Loch recounts the legends surrounding the various monasteries, gleaned from years of visiting the monastic republic.

Willard Manus *This Way to Paradise: Dancing on the Tables* (@www.lycabettus.com). American expat's memoir of nearly four decades in Líndhos, Rhodes, beginning long before its submersion in tourism. Wonderful period detail, including bohemian excesses and cameos from such as S.J. Perelman, Germaine Greer and Martha Gellhorn.

Christopher Merrill *Things of the Hidden God: Journey to the Holy Mountain*. Merrill, an accomplished poet and journalist, first came to Áthos in the wake of a traumatic time reporting on the breakup of Yugoslavia. This, with fine black-and-white photographs, is probably the best contemporary take on Áthos, and Orthodoxy, by an outsider.

Henry Miller *The Colossus of Maroussi*. Corfu, Crete, Athens and the soul of Greece in 1939, with Miller completely in his element; funny, sensual and transporting.

James Pettifer *The Greeks: The Land and People Since the War*. Useful, if patchily edited, introduction to contemporary Greece – and its recent past up to 2000. Pettifer charts, among other things, the nation's politics, family life, religion and tourism.

Dilys Powell *An Affair of the Heart* and *The Villa Ariadne*. Powell accompanied archeologist husband Humfry Payne on excavations at the Hereon of Perahóra, and after his sudden death in 1936 maintained strong links with the local villagers, described in *An Affair*.... The clearer-eyed, less sentimental *The Villa Ariadne* chronicles her 1950s travels to Crete.

Tim Salmon *The Unwritten Places* (@www.lycabettus.com). Salmon has spent half his life in Greece and here describes his bond with the Píndhos mountains and its Vlach communities, following the last clan and their flocks to undertake the autumn migration (*dhiáva*) to the flatlands on foot.

Leon Sciaky *Farewell to Salonica*. Memoir of a Belle Époque boyhood in a middle-class Sephardic Jewish family, before their 1915 emigration to the US. The Sciakys had close ties with Bulgarian peasants in Kukush (now Kilkís) – and Leon is far more sympathetic to Bulgaria than to the

Greek regime which assumed control of cosmopolitan Salonica in 1912.

Terence Spencer *Fair Greece, Sad Relic: Literary Philhellenism from Shakespeare to Byron*. How Classics-educated travellers and poets – culminating in Byron – fuelled European support for the 1821 Revolution, despite misgivings about the contemporary Greeks.

Tom Stone *The Summer of My Greek Taverna*. Enjoyable cautionary tale for those fantasizing about a new life in the Aegean sun. Moving to Pátmos in the early 1980s, Stone tries to mix friendship and business at a beach taverna, with predictable (for onlookers anyway) results.

Richard Stoneman, ed *A Literary Companion to Travel in Greece*. Ancient and medieval authors, plus Grand Tourists – an excellent selection.

Patricia Storace *Dinner with Persephone*. A New York poet, resident for a year in Athens (with forays to the provinces) puts the country's 1990s psyche on the couch. Storace has a sly humour and an interesting take on Greece's "imprisonment" in its imagined past.

John L. Tomkinson, ed *Travellers' Greece: Memories of an Enchanted Land* (Ⓦwww.anagnosis.gr). Seventeenth- to nineteenth-century (mostly English) travellers' impressions of islands and mainland, ranging from the enraptured to the appalled; ideal for dipping into.

Sofka Zinovieff *Eurydice Street*. An anthropologist and journalist by training, Zinovieff first came to Greece in the early 1980s, then returned in 2001 with her diplomat husband and two daughters to live in Athens. With sharp observations on nationalism, Orthodoxy, politics, November 17 and leisure (to cite just a few topics), this is the best single account of life in today's urban Greece.

Photo books

Yann Arthus-Bertrand; Janine Trotereau, text *Greece from the Air*. This veteran aerial photographer makes it look great, from the Parthenon to the most remote islands and ancient sites.

Chris Hellier *Monasteries of Greece* (o/p). Magnificently photographed survey of surviving, active monasteries and treasures, with insightful accompanying essays.

Constantine Manos *A Greek Portfolio*. The fruits of a gifted Greek-American photographer's three-year odyssey in the early 1960s through a country on the cusp of modernization; the quality and insight you'd expect from a member of the Magnum co-operative, in elegiac black and white.

Hugh Palmer; Mark Ottaway, text *The Most Beautiful Villages of Greece*. Not exhaustively inclusive, but a good survey of the mainland and islands in 285 images.

Clay Perry *Vanishing Greece*. Well-captioned photos depict threatened landscapes and relict ways of life in rural Greece.

Suzanne Slesin et al *Greek Style*. In print for over two decades, and rightly so: stunning – if sometimes designer-tweaked – interiors, from villas to simpler village houses, primarily on Rhodes, Corfu, Sérifos and Ýdhra.

Ancient history and politics

General

Timothy Boatswain and Colin Nicolson *A Traveller's History of Greece*. Well-written overview of crucial Greek periods and personalities, from earliest times to 2003.

A.R. Burn *Pelican/Penguin History of Greece*; **Paul Cartledge** *Cambridge Illustrated History of Ancient Greece*. The two best general introductions to ancient Greece; choose between brief paperback, or large illustrated tome.

Early Greece

M.I. Finley *The World of Odysseus*. Reprint of a 1954 warhorse, pioneering in its investigation of the historicity (or not) of the events and society related by Homer. Breezily readable and stimulating.

Oswyn Murray *Early Greece*. The story from the Mycenaeans and Minoans through to the beginning of the Classical period.

Robin Osborne *Greece in the Making 1200–479 BC*. Well-illustrated paperback on the rise of the city-state.

Classical era

Paul Cartledge *The Spartans: The World of the Warrior-Heroes of Ancient Greece*. Reassessment of this much-maligned city-state, secretive and a source of outsider speculation even in its own time.

John Kenyon Davies *Democracy and Classical Greece*. Established, accessible account of the Classical period and its political developments.

Simon Hornblower *The Greek World 479–323 BC*. An erudite survey of ancient Greece at its zenith, from the end of the Persian Wars to the death of Alexander.

Roger Ling *Classical Greece*. Covers the greatest period of Greek civilization, from the 5th to the 1st centuries BC, taking in the arts, military and political history, and surveying archeology of the period.

Hellenistic era

Paul Cartledge *Alexander the Great: The Hunt for a New Past*. An evocative, meticulous and accessible biography, stinting on neither the man's brutality nor his achievements.

Robin Lane Fox *Alexander the Great*. Another absorbing study, mixing historical scholarship with imaginative psychological detail.

F.W. Walbank *The Hellenistic World*. Greece under the sway of the Macedonian and Roman empires.

Ancient culture and religion

Walter Burkert *Greek Religion: Archaic and Classical*. Superb overview of deities and their attributes and antecedents, the protocol of sacrifice and the symbolism of festivals. Especially good on relating Greek worship to its predecessors in the Middle East.

James Davidson *Courtesans and Fishcakes*. Absorbing book on the politics, class characteristics and etiquette of consumption and

The classics

Many of the classics make excellent companions for a trip around Greece; reading Homer's Odyssey when battling the vagaries of island ferries puts your own plight into perspective. Most of these good beginners' choices are published in a range of paperback editions. Particularly outstanding translations are noted.

Mary Beard and John Henderson *The Classics: A Very Short Introduction*. Exactly as it promises: an excellent overview.

Herodotus *The Histories*. Revered as the father of narrative history – and anthropology – this fifth-century-BC Anatolian writer chronicled both the causes and campaigns of the Persian Wars, as well as the assorted tribes and nations inhabiting Asia Minor.

Homer *The Iliad and The Odyssey*. The first concerns itself, semi-factually, with the late Bronze Age war of the Achaeans against Troy in Asia Minor; the second recounts the hero Odysseus's long journey home, via seemingly every corner of the Mediterranean. The best prose translations are by Martin Hammond, and in verse Richmond Lattimore. For a stirring, if very loose verse *Iliad*, try also Christopher Logue's recent version, *War Music*.

Ovid *The Metamorphoses* (trans A.D. Melville). Collected by a first-century-AD Roman poet, this remains one of the most accessible renditions of the more piquant Greek myths, involving transformations as divine blessing or curse.

Pausanias *The Guide to Greece*. Effectively the first-ever guidebook, intended for Roman pilgrims to central mainland and Peloponnesian sanctuaries. Invaluable for later archeologists in assessing damage or change to temples over time, or (in some cases) locating them at all. The two-volume Penguin edition is usefully annotated with the later history and nomenclature of the sites.

Thucydides *History of the Peloponnesian War*. Bleak month-by-month account of the conflict, by a cashiered Athenian officer whose affiliation and dim view of human nature didn't usually obscure his objectivity.

Xenophon *The History of My Times*. Thucydides' account of the Peloponnesian War stops in 411 BC; this eyewitness account continues events until 362 BC.

consummation – with wine, women, boys and seafood – in Classical Athens.

Mary Lefkowitz *Greek Gods, Human Lives: What We Can Learn from Myths*. Rather than being frivolous, immoral or irrelevant, ancient religion and its myths, in their bleak indifference of the gods to human suffering, are shown as being more "grown up" than the later creeds of salvation and comfort.

Ancient archeology and art

Mary Beard *The Parthenon*. Compelling reassessment of the building, both in terms of its real purpose and the possible meaning of its relief sculptures, in light of the discoveries made during its ongoing reconstruction.

William R. Biers *Archeology of Greece: An Introduction*. A good survey of the subject, published in 1987.

John Boardman *Greek Art*. An evergreen study in the *World of Art* series, first published in 1964. For more detailed treatment, there are three period volumes entitled *Greek Sculpture*, subtitled in turn: *Archaic Period, Classical Period* and *The Late Classical Period*.

Reynold Higgins *Minoan and Mycenaean Art*. Concise, well-illustrated round-up of the culture of Mycenae, Crete and the Cyclades, again part of the *World of Art* series.

Colin Renfrew *The Cycladic Spirit*. Illustrated with the core of Athens' Goulandris Cycladic art museum, and convincing on the meaning and purpose of these artefacts.

R.R.R. Smith *Hellenistic Sculpture*. Recent reappraisal of the art of Greece under Alexander and his successors.

Byzantine and medieval Greece

Nicholas Cheetham *Medieval Greece* (o/p). A general survey of the period's infinite convolutions in Greece, with Frankish, Catalan, Venetian, Byzantine and Ottoman struggles for power.

John Julius Norwich *Byzantium: The Early Centuries*; *Byzantium: the Apogee* and *Byzantium: The Decline*. Perhaps the main surprise for first-time travellers to Greece is the fascination of its Byzantine monuments. This is an astonishingly detailed yet readable – often witty – trilogy of the empire that produced them. There's also an excellent, one-volume abridged version, *A Short History of Byzantium*.

Steven Runciman *The Fall of Constantinople, 1453*. Unsurpassed narrative of perhaps the key event of the Middle Ages, and its repercussions throughout Europe and the Islamic world.

Byzantine art and religion

John Beckwith *Early Christian and Byzantine Art*. Comprehensive illustrated study placing Byzantine art within a wider context.

Steven Runciman *Byzantine Style and Civilization* (o/p). Survey of the empire's art, culture and monuments; well worth tracking down.

Archbishop Kallistos (Timothy Ware) *The Orthodox Church*. Good introduction to what is still the established religion of Greece, by the UK's ranking Orthodox archbishop. Part One describes the history of Orthodoxy, Part Two its currently held beliefs.

Modern Greek history

Richard Clogg *A Concise History of Greece*. If you read only one title, this should be it: a remarkably clear account, from the decline of Byzantium to 2000, with numerous maps and feature captions to the well-chosen artwork.

John S. Koliopoulos and Thanos M. Veremis *Greece: The Modern Sequel, from 1831 to the Present*. Thematic rather than chronological study that pokes into corners rarely illuminated by conventional histories, with some tart debunkings; especially good on Macedonian issues, brigandage and the Communists. Best read after you've digested Clogg.

Mark Mazower *Salonica, City of Ghosts: Christians, Muslims and Jews 1450–1950*. Masterfully records how this multi-ethnic port, the most cosmopolitan European city under Ottoman rule, became homogeneously Greek Orthodox; the only flaw is scant coverage of the Slavs who populated much of the hinterland as well as the town itself.

David Brewer *The Flame of Freedom: The Greek War of Independence 1821–1833* (o/p). Best narrative on revolutionary events (with some black-and-white illustrations), strong both on the background of Ottoman Greece, as well as the progress of the war.

Michael Llewellyn Smith *Ionian Vision: Greece in Asia Minor, 1919–22*. Still the best work on the disastrous Anatolian campaign, which led to the population exchanges between Greece and Turkey. Llewellyn-Smith's account evinces considerable sympathy for the post-1920 royalist government pursuing an inherited, unwinnable war.

C.M. Woodhouse *Modern Greece: A Short History*. Woodhouse, long a Conservative MP, was a key liaison officer with the Greek Resistance during World War II. Writing from a more right-wing perspective than Clogg, his account – from the foundation of Constantinople to 1990 – is briefer and drier, but scrupulous with facts.

World War II and the civil war

David H. Close *The Origins of the Greek Civil War*. Excellent, readable and even-handed study that focuses on the social conditions in 1920s and 1930s Greece that made the country so ripe for conflict; draws on primary sources to overturn various received wisdoms.

Nicholas Gage *Eleni*. Controversial account by a Greek-born *New York Times* correspondent who returns to Epirus to avenge the death of his mother, condemned by an ELAS tribunal in 1948. Good descriptions of village life, but the book has its agenda and its political "history" is at best selective.

Iakovos Kambanellis, translated by Gail Holst-Warhaft *Mauthausen*. Kambanellis was active in the Resistance, caught, and sent to Mauthausen, a concentration camp for politicians or partisans who opposed the Nazis' rise to power. Harrowing atrocities in flashback there are aplenty, but the book dwells equally on post-liberation, as the initially idealist inmates realize that the "New World Order" will be scarcely different from the old. The basis of a play, and the eponymous Theodhorakis oratorio.

Mark Mazower *Inside Hitler's Greece: The Experience of Occupation 1941–44*. Eccentrically organized, but the scholarship is top-drawer and the photos alone justify purchase. Demonstrates how the utter demoralization of the country and incompetence of conventional politicians led to the rise of ELAS and the onset of civil war.

Eddie Myers *Greek Entanglement* (o/p). The inside story of sabotaging the Gorgopotamos viaduct by the British brigadier who led it, and lots else about co-ordinating the resistance from 1942 to 1944. Myers comes across as being under no illusions about the various Greek guerrillas he dealt with.

C.M. Woodhouse *The Struggle for Greece, 1941–49*. Masterly, well-illustrated account of the so-called "three rounds" of resistance and rebellion, and how Greece emerged without a communist government. Despite the 1990s opening of Soviet archives, never bettered.

Ethnography

John Kennedy Campbell *Honour, Family and Patronage*. Landmark 1960s study of a Sarakatsáni community on Mount Gamíla in Epirus, with much wider applicability to rural Greece.

Bruce Clark *Twice a Stranger: How Mass Expulsion Forged Modern Greece and Turkey*. The build-up to and execution of the 1923 population exchanges, and how both countries are still digesting the experience eight-plus decades on. Compassionate and readable, especially the encounters with elderly refugees.

Richard Clogg, ed. *The Greek Minorities*. Collection of articles on all the various Greek ethnic and religious minorities, as of the mid-1990s – despite its age, still authoritative.

Rae Dalven *The Jews of Ioannina* (www.lycabettus.com). History and culture of the thriving pre-Holocaust community, related by the poet-translator of Cavafy, herself an Epirot Jew.

Loring Danforth and Alexander Tsiaras *The Death Rituals of Rural Greece*. Many visitors and foreign residents find Greek funeral customs – the wailing, the open-casket vigils, the disinterment of bones after five years – disturbing; this book helps make sense of it all.

Renée Hirschon *Heirs of the Greek Catastrophe: the Social Life of Asia Minor Refugees in Piraeus*. Wherein a district in Kokkinia maintained a separate identity for three generations after 1923. It's inevitably nostalgic, as increasing wealth has largely dissolved the community, but helps explain why Athens is so higgledy-piggledy.

Gail Holst-Warhaft *Road to Rembetika: Music of a Greek Subculture*. The most intriguing Greek urban musical style of the past century, evocatively traced by a Cornell University professor and long-term observer of the Greek music scene; look out for the revised 2006 edition.

Anastasia Karakasidou *Fields of Wheat, Hills of Blood*. Excellent, controversial work establishing how Macedonia only became "Greek" politically and ethnically in the early twentieth century, through a deliberate, official Hellenization process. Sensationally declined for initial publication by Cambridge after ultra-nationalists' threats both in Greece and the diaspora.

John Cuthbert Lawson *Modern Greek Folklore and Ancient Greek Religion: A Study in Survivals*. Exactly as it says: a fascinating, thorough study still applicable a century after first publication.

John L. Tomkinson *Festive Greece: A Calendar of Tradition*. Copiously photographed gazetteer by date of all the still-observed rites of the Orthodox Church, with their pagan substrata erupting frequently and vividly at popular *paniyíria*.

Fiction

Greek writers in translation

Apostolos Doxiadis *Uncle Petros and Goldbach's Conjecture*. Uncle Petros is the disgraced family black sheep, living reclusively in outer Athens; his nephew discovers that Petros had staked everything to solve a theorem unsolved for centuries. Math-phobes take heart; it's more a meditation on how best to spend life, and what really constitutes success.

Eugenia Fakinou *The Seventh Garment*. Greece from the 1820s through the colonels' junta is viewed through the life stories (interspersed in counterpoint) of three generations of women.

Rhea Galanaki *Eleni, or Nobody*. Fine novelization of the life of Eleni Altamura, Greece's first, mid-nineteenth-century woman painter, who lived in Italy for some years disguised as a man.

Vangelis Hatziyannidis Hatziyannidis' abiding obsessions – confinement, blackmail, abrupt disappearances – get a workout in his creepy debut novel *Four Walls*, set on an unspecified east Aegean isle, where a reclusive landowner takes in a fugitive woman who convinces him to revive his father's honey trade – with unexpected consequences. His next novel, *Stolen Time*, revisits the same themes as an impoverished young student gets a tidy fee from a mysterious tribunal for agreeing to spend two weeks in the Hotel from Hell.

Panos Karnezis Karnezis has become the most accessible, and feted, Greek writer since the millennium. He grew up in Greece but now lives in London, writing in English; however, his concerns remain utterly Greek. *Little Infamies* is a collection of short stories set in his native Peloponnese during the late 1950s and early 1960s; *The Maze* is a darker-shaded, more successful novel concerning the Asia Minor Catastrophe. Both have a flair for old-fashioned plot twists – or a soupçon of magical realism, depending on your point of view. His 2007 *The Birthday Party* is based on events in the life of Aristotle Onassis and daughter Christina.

Nikos Kazantzakis *Zorba the Greek; The Last Temptation of Christ; Christ Recrucified/The Greek Passion; Freedom and Death; The Fratricides; Report to Greco.* Whether in intricate Greek or not-quite-adequate English, Kazantzakis can be hard going, yet the power of his writing shines through. *Zorba the Greek* is a dark, nihilistic work, worlds away from the two-dimensional film. By contrast, the movie version of *The Last Temptation of Christ* – specifically Jesus's vision, once crucified, of a normal life with Mary Magdalene – provoked riots amongst Orthodox fanatics in Athens in 1989. *Christ Recrucified* (*The Greek Passion*) resets the Easter drama against the backdrop of Christian/Muslim relations, while *Freedom and Death* chronicles the rebellions of nineteenth-century Crete. *The Fratricides* portrays a family riven by the civil war. *Report to Greco* – perhaps the most accessible work – is an autobiographical exploration of his Cretan-ness.

Artemis Leontis (ed) *Greece: A Traveller's Literary Companion.* A nice idea, brilliantly executed: various regions of the country as portrayed in (very) short fiction or essays by modern Greek writers.

Stratis Myrivilis, translated by Peter Bien *Life in the Tomb.* A harrowing and unorthodox war memoir, based on the author's 1917–18 experience on the Macedonian front.

Alexandros Papadiamantis *Tales from a Greek Island.* The island in question being Skiáthos, Papadiamantis' birthplace. These quasi-mythic tales of grim fate make him comparable to Hardy and Maupassant.

Nick Papandreou *Father Dancing* (UK)/*A Crowded Heart* (US). Autobiographical *roman à clef* by the late Andreas's younger son in which Papandreou Senior, not too surprisingly, comes across as a gasbag and petty domestic tyrant.

Dido Sotiriou *Farewell Anatolia* (Kedros, Greece). A perennial favourite since publication in 1962, this chronicles the traumatic end of Greek life in Asia Minor, from World War I to the 1922 catastrophe, as narrated by a fictionalized version of Sotiriou's father.

Stratis Tsirkas *Drifting Cities*. Set by turns in World War II Jerusalem, Cairo and Alexandria, this unflinchingly honest and humane epic of a Greek officer secretly working for the Leftist resistance got the author expelled from the Communist Party.

Vassilis Vassilikos *Z* (o/p). A novel based closely enough on events – the 1963 assassination of Grigoris Lambrakis in Thessaloníki – to be banned under the junta, and brilliantly filmed by Costa-Gavras in 1968.

Alki Zei *Achilles' Fiancée*. Friendships and intrigues amongst a collection of communist exiles floating between Athens, Rome, Moscow, Paris and Tashkent between the civil war and the colonels' junta. Semi-autobiographical, it often movingly captures their illusions, nostalgia and chronic party-line schisms. Her recent (2007) *Tina's Web* (translated by John Thornley) concerns a Greek girl raised in Germany, sent by her divorced parents to live with her grandmother in Greece, getting caught up in drug use.

Greece in foreign fiction

Louis de Bernières *Captain Corelli's Mandolin*. Set on Kefaloniá during the World War II occupation and aftermath, this accomplished 1994 tragi-comedy quickly acquired cult, then bestseller status in the UK and US. But in Greece it provoked a scandal, once islanders, Greek Left intellectuals and surviving Italian partisans woke up to its virulent disparaging of ELAS. It seems the novel was based on the experiences of Amos Pampaloni, an

Books for kids

The Greek myths and legends are perfect holiday reading for kids.

Ingri and Edgar Parin D'Aulaire *D'Aulaires' Book of Greek Myths*. An old-fashioned treatment from the late 1950s, but still sound, and marvellously illustrated.

Terry Deary *Gruesome Greeks* and *Greek Legends*. Even decently read adults will find themselves delving into these very funny, brilliantly conceived books for a refresher on ancient Greek history and myths.

Caroline Lawrence *The Roman Mysteries*. This six-part, authentically detailed series of Roman-era mystery books for 8- to 11-year-olds has children as the protagonists. The final two volumes, *The Colossus of Rhodes* and *Fugitive from Corinth*, are set in Greece.

Mary Renault *The King Must Die; The Last of the Wine; The Masks of Apollo; The Praise Singer*. Mary Renault's impeccably researched and tightly written reconstructions are great for all ages. The quartet above retell, respectively, the myth of Theseus, the life of a pupil of Socrates, that of a fourth-century-BC actor and the fortunes of poet Simonides at the court of Samian tyrant Polykrates. The life of Alexander the Great is told in *Fire from Heaven*, *The Persian Boy* and *Funeral Games*, available separately or as *The Alexander Trilogy*.

Franzcesca Simon *Helping Hercules*. Fans of *Horrid Henry* will enjoy this clever retelling of Greek myths by the same author, where young heroine Susan sorts out the not-so-heroic heroes.

artillery captain on Kefaloniá in 1942–44 who later joined ELAS, and who accused De Bernières (forced to eat humble pie in the UK press) of distorting the roles of both Italians and ELAS on the island. The Greek translation was abridged to avoid causing offence, and the movie, watered down to a feeble love story as a condition for filming Kefaloniá, sank without trace in 2001.

Oriana Fallaci *A Man* (o/p). Gripping tale of the junta years, based on the author's involvement with Alekos Panagoulis, the army officer who attempted to assassinate Colonel Papadopoulos in 1968 – and who himself died in mysterious circumstances in 1975.

John Fowles *The Magus*. Fowles' biggest and best tale of mystery and manipulation – plus Greek island life – based on his stay on Spétses as a teacher during the 1950s. A period piece that repays revisiting.

Victoria Hislop *The Island*. The former leper colony of Spinalonga forms the backdrop to this novel about a young woman discovering her Cretan roots. A potentially good story is marred by the cloying, derivative nature of its telling.

Olivia Manning *The Balkan Trilogy, Volume 3: Friends and Heroes*. Wonderfully observed tale, in which Guy and Harriet Pringle escape from Bucharest to Athens, in the last months before the 1941 invasion.

Steven Pressfield *The Virtues of War*. Alexander the Great tells his warrior's life to brother-in-law Itanes. And he does it well, for Pressfield informs his drama with impressive scholarship.

Evelyn Waugh *Officers and Gentleman*. This second volume of Waugh's brilliant, acerbic wartime trilogy includes an account of the Battle of Crete and subsequent evacuation.

Greek poetry

With two twentieth-century Nobel laureates – George Seferis and Odysseus Elytis – modern Greece has an intense and dynamic poetic tradition. Translations of all of the following are excellent.

Anthologies

Peter Bien, Peter Constantine, Edmund Keeley, Karen Van Dyck, eds *A Century of Greek Poetry, 1900–2000*. Well produced bilingual volume, with some lesser-known surprises alongside the big names.

Nanos Valaoritis and Thanasis Maskaleris, eds *An Anthology of Modern Greek Poetry*. English-only text, but excellent biographical info on the poets and good renditions by two native Greek speakers.

Individual poets

C.P. Cavafy, translated by Rae Dalwen *Complete Poems of Cavafy*. Perhaps the most accessible modern Greek poet, resident for most of his life in Alexandria.

Odysseus Elytis *Collected Poems*; *The Axion Esti*; and *Eros, Eros, Eros: Selected and Last Poems* pretty much covers his entire ouevre.

Yannis Kondos *Absurd Athlete*. One of the best of the latest generation of poets, well translated in a bilingual edition by David Connolloy.

Yannis Ritsos, translated by Edmund Keeley *Repetitions, Testimonies, Parentheses*. A fine volume of Greece's foremost Leftist poet, including work from 1946 to 1975.

George Seferis *Collected Poems, 1924–1955*. Virtually the complete works of the Nobel laureate, with Greek and English verses on facing pages; later editions are only in English.

Food and wine

Rosemary Barron *Flavours of Greece*. The leading Greek cookbook – among many contenders – by an internationally recognized authority. Contains over 250 recipes.

Andrew Dalby *Siren Feasts: A History of Food and Gastronomy in Greece*. Demonstrates just how little Greek cuisine has changed in three millennia; also excellent on the introduction and etymology of common vegetables and herbs.

Konstantinos Lazarakis *The Wines of Greece*. An excellent, up-to-2005 overview of what's happening in Greece's eleven recognized wine-producing regions.

Nikos Stavroulakis *Cookbook of the Jews of Greece* (®www.lycabettus.com). Tasty if often fiddly recipes interspersed with their relation to the Jewish liturgical year, plus potted histories of the communities that devised them.

Specific guides

See also the Wildlife guides detailed on p.935.

Archeology

A.R. and Mary Burn *The Living Past of Greece: A Time Traveller's Tour of Historic and Prehistoric Places* (o/p). This wide-ranging guide covers sites from Minoan through to Byzantine and Frankish, with good clear plans and lively text.

Paul Hetherington *Byzantine and Medieval Greece: Churches, Castles and Art of the Mainland and Peloponnese* (o/p). A gazetteer of all major mainland sites – readable, authoritative and with useful plans. His more recent *The Greek Islands: Guide to Byzantine and Medieval Buildings and their Art*, is equally good, with more illustrations, though there are some peculiar omissions of worthy monuments.

Hiking

Lance Chilton Various walking pamphlets (®www.marengowalks.com). Small but thorough guides to the best walks at various mainland and island resorts, accompanied by three-colour maps.

Marc Dubin *Trekking in Greece* (o/p). Though many sections are showing their 1988–92 research age, this volume is still useful for the smaller islands in particular.

Tim Salmon, with Michael Cullen *The Mountains of Greece: A Walker's Guide*. Updated in 2006, this volume sticks strictly to the mainland, covering mounts Pílio, Ólymbos, Áthos, the Peloponnese and the best of the Píndhos, from Delphi to Albania.

Loraine Wilson *The White Mountains of Crete*. Sixty walks and treks, from easy to gruelling, by the doyenne of foreign trekking guides in Crete; trustworthy directions and prudent warnings.

Sailing

Rod Heikell *Greek Waters Pilot*. Updated to 2007, and the standard reference for Greek yachters.

Regional guides

Rough Guides publishes regional guides to The Ionian Islands; The Dodecanese and East Aegean Islands; Crete; Corfu; and Athens. You might also want to get:

Anagnosis Guides (www.anagnosis.gr) Four well-illustrated guides to Athens and surroundings that highlight the quirky, obscure and overlooked from every era, with directions to mentioned sites.

Peter Greenhalgh and Edward Eliopoulos *Deep Into Mani* (o/p). A former member of the wartime Resistance revisits the Máni forty years after first hiding there, in the company of a British scholar. The result is a superb guide – with precise directions – and excellent armchair reading.

Oliver Rackham and Jennifer Moody *The Making of the Cretan Landscape*. It's hard to classify this impressive academic press product written for the casual visitor. It takes in geology, natural history, agricultural practices, place names, architecture and demography, all arranged by topic.

Lycabettus Press Guides (www.lycabettus.com). These cover some of the more popular islands and certain mainland highlights; despite long intervals between revisions, most pay their way in interest and usefulness – particularly those on Kós, Pátmos, Náfplio, Póros and the travels of Saint Paul.

Language

Language

Greek

So many Greeks have lived or worked abroad in North America, Australia, South Africa and Britain that you will find **English**-speakers in the tiniest island village. Add the thousands attending language schools or working in the tourist industry – English is the lingua franca of most resorts, with German second – and it's easy to see how so many visitors return home having learned only minimal restaurant vocabulary.

You can certainly get by this way, but it isn't very satisfying, and the willingness and ability to say even a few words will transform your status from that of dumb *turístas* to the more honourable one of *xénos/xéni*, which can mean foreigner, traveller and guest all combined.

Learning basic Greek

Greek is not an easy language for English-speakers – UK translators' unions rate it as harder than German, slightly less complex than Russian – but it is a very beautiful one, and even a brief acquaintance will give you an idea of the debt owed to it by Western European languages. Greek **grammar** is predictably complicated; **nouns** are divided into three genders, all with different case endings in the singular and in the plural, and all adjectives and articles have to agree with these in gender, number and case. To simplify life for beginners, all adjectives are arbitrarily cited in the neuter form in the lists on the following pages. **Verbs** are even more complex; they're in two conjugations, in both active and passive voices, with passively constructed verbs often having transitive sense. As a novice, it's best to simply say what you want the way you know it, and dispense with the niceties.

Teach-yourself Greek courses

Alison Kakoura and Karen Rich *Talk Greek* (book and 2 CDs). Probably the best in-print product for beginners' essentials, and for developing the confidence to try them.

Anne Farmakides *A Manual of Modern Greek, 1, for University Students*. If you have the discipline and motivation, this is among the best for learning proper, grammatical Greek.

Hara Garoufalia et al *Read & Speak Greek for Beginners* (book & CD). Unlike many quickie courses, this provides a good grammatical foundation; new in 2008.

David Holton et al *Greek: A Comprehensive Grammar of the Modern Language*. A bit technical, so not for rank beginners, but it covers almost every conceivable construction.

Aristarhos Matsukas *Teach Yourself Greek* (book and optional cassettes or CDs). Another complete course, touching on idiomatic expressions too.

Phrasebooks and dictionaries

Rough Guide Greek Phrasebook Current, accurate and pocket-sized, with phrases that you'll actually need. The English–Greek section is transliterated, though the Greek–English part requires mastery of the Greek alphabet.
The Pocket Oxford Greek Dictionary, by J. T. Pring. A bit bulky for travel, but generally considered the best Greek–English, English–Greek paperback dictionary.
Collins Pocket Greek Dictionary, by Harry T. Hionides. Very nearly as complete as the Pocket Oxford and probably better value for money. The inexpensive *Collins Gem Greek Dictionary* (UK only) is palm-sized but identical in contents – the best day-pack choice.
Oxford Greek–English, English–Greek Learner's Dictionary, by D. N. Stavropoulos. For a prolonged stay, this pricey, hardbound, two-volume set is unbeatable for usage and vocabulary.

Katharévoussa, dhimotikí and dialects

The intrinsic complexities of Greek have been aggravated by the fact that since the early 1800s there has been fierce competition between two versions of the language: **katharévoussa** and **dhimotikí**.

When Greece achieved independence in 1832, its people were mostly illiterate, and the spoken language – *dhimotikí*, "demotic" or "popular" Greek – had undergone enormous change since the Byzantine and Classical eras. The vocabulary had numerous loan-words from the languages of the various invaders and conquerors – especially Turks, Venetians and Slavs – and the grammar had been considerably streamlined since ancient times.

Funding and inspiration for the new Greek state, and some of its early leaders, came largely from the diaspora – Greeks who had been living in the sophisticated cities of central Europe, in Constantinople or in Russia. With their Enlightenment conception of Hellenism, based on Greece's past glory, they set about obliterating traces of foreign subjugation in every possible field. And where better to start than by purging the language of foreign accretions and reviving its Classical purity?

They accordingly created what was in effect a new language, *katharévoussa* (literally "cleansed" Greek). The complexities of Classical grammar and syntax were largely reinstated, and long-forgotten Classical words and phrases were reintroduced. *Katharévoussa* became the language of the schools and the prestigious professions, government, business, the law, newspapers and academia. Everyone aspiring to membership in the elite strove to master it, and to speak it – even though there was no consensus on how many words were pronounced.

The *katharévoussa/dhimotikí* debate remained contentious, even virulent, until the early 1980s. Most writers – from Solomos and Makriyiannis in the nineteenth century to Seferis, Kazantzakis and Ritsos in the twentieth – championed the demotic, or some approximation of it, in their literature, with advocacy of demoticism becoming increasingly linked to left-wing politics during the twentieth century. Meanwhile, right-wing governments forcibly (re)instated *katharévoussa* at every opportunity. Most recently, the **colonels' junta** (1967–74) reversed a decision of the previous government to use *dhimotikí* for instruction in schools, bringing back *katharévoussa*, even on sweet wrappers, as part of their ragbag of notions about racial purity and heroic ages.

Dhimotikí returned permanently after the fall of the colonels. Perhaps the final blow to the classicizers was the official 1981 decision to abolish breath marks (which in fact no longer signified anything) and the three different stress accents in favour of a **single accute accent** (though there are still plenty of pre-1981 road-signs in the older system). *Dhimotikí* is used in schools, on radio and TV, and in most newspapers. The only institutions which refuse to update themselves are the Church and the legal profession.

All this has reduced, but not eliminated, confusion. The Metaxas dictatorship of the 1930s, elaborating on attempts at the same by previous regimes, changed scores of village names from Slavic, Turkish or Albanian words to Greek ones – often reviving the name of the nearest ancient site. These official **place names** still hold sway on most road signs and maps – even though the local people may use the *dhimotikí* or non-Greek form. Thus you will see "Plomárion" or "Spétsai" written, while everyone actually says "Plomári" or "Spétses"; Pándhrossos on Sámos, and Ayía Paraskeví in Epirus, are still referred to by locals as Arvanítes and Kerásovo respectively.

Dialects and minority languages

Greece exhibits considerable linguistic diversity, both in its regional dialects and minority languages. Ancient **dialects** survive in many remote areas, some quite incomprehensible to outsiders. The dialect of Sfákia in Crete is one such; Tsakónika of the east-central Peloponnese is another, while the dialect of the Sarakatsáni shepherds is apparently the oldest, related to the language of the Dorian settlers.

The language of the Sarakatsáni's traditional rivals, the **Vlachs**, is not Greek at all, but derived from early Latin, with strong affinities to Romanian. In the regions bordering the FYROM and southwestern Bulgaria, you can still hear **Slavic Macedonian** spoken, while small numbers of Sephardic Jews in the north speak **Ladino**, a medieval form of Spanish. Until a few decades ago **Arvanítika** – a dialect of medieval Albanian – was the first language of many villages of inland Attica, southern Évvia, northern Ándhros, and much of the Argo-Saronic; lately the clock has been turned back, so to speak, as throngs of Albanian immigrants circulate in Athens and other parts of the country. In Thrace there is a substantial **Turkish-speaking** population, as well as some speakers of **Pomak** (a derivative of Bulgarian with a large Greco-Turkish vocabulary), while Gypsies countrywide speak Romany.

The Greek alphabet: transliteration and accentuation

Besides the usual difficulties of learning a new language, Greek has an entirely separate **alphabet**. Despite initial appearances, this is in practice fairly easily mastered – a skill that will help enormously in getting around independently. In addition, certain combinations of letters have unexpected results. This book's transliteration system should help you make intelligible noises, but remember that the correct **stress** (marked throughout the book with an acute accent or sometimes dieresis) is crucial. With the right sounds

but the wrong stress people will either fail to understand you, or else understand something quite different from what you intended. There are numerous word-pairs with the same spelling and phonemes, distinguished only by their stress.

The **dieresis** is used in Greek over the second of two adjacent vowels to change the pronunciation that you would expect from the table below; often in this book it can function as the primary stress. In the word *kaïki* (caique), the use of a dieresis changes the pronunciation from "cake-key" to "ka-ee-key" and additionally the middle "i" carries the primary stress. In the word *païdhákia* (lamb chops), the dieresis again changes the sound of the first syllable from "pay" to "pah-ee", but in this case the primary stress is on the third syllable. It is also, uniquely among Greek accents, used on capital letters in signs and personal-name spellings in Greece, and we have followed this practice on our maps.

Set out below is the Greek alphabet, the system of transliteration used in this book and a brief aid to pronunciation.

Greek	Transliteration	Pronounced
Α, α	a	a as in father
Β, β	v	v as in vet
Γ, γ	y/g	y as in yes except before consonants or a, o or ou when it's a breathy g, approximately as in gap
Δ, δ	dh	th as in then
Ε, ε	e	e as in get
Ζ, ζ	z	z sound
Η, η	i	i as in ski
Θ, θ	th	th as in theme
Ι, ι	i	i as in ski
Κ, κ	k	k sound
Λ, λ	l	l sound
Μ, μ	m	m sound
Ν, ν	n	n sound
Ξ, ξ	x	x sound, never z
Ο, ο	o	o as in toad
Π, π	p	p sound
Ρ, ρ	r	r sound
Σ, σ, ς	s	s sound, except z before m or g; single sigma has the same phonic value as double sigma
Τ, τ	t	t sound
Υ, υ	y	y as in barely
Φ, φ	f	f sound
Χ, χ	h before vowels, kh before consonants	harsh h sound, like ch in loch
Ψ, ψ	ps	ps as in lips
Ω, ω	o	o as in toad, indistinguishable from o

Combinations and diphthongs

ΑΙ, αι	e	e as in hey
ΑΥ, αυ	av/af	av or af depending on following consonant
ΕΙ, ει	i	long i, exactly like i or g

ΕΥ, ευ	ev/ef	ev or ef, depending on following consonant
ΟΙ, οι	i	long i, exactly like i or g
ΟΥ, ου	ou	ou as in tourist
ΓΓ, γγ	ng	ng as in angle; always medial
ΝΓ, νγ	g/ng	g as in goat at the start of a word, ng in the middle
ΜΠ, μπ	b/mb	b at start of a word, mb if medial
ΝΔ, νδ	d/nd	d at start of a word, nd if medial
ΤΣ, τσ	ts	ts as in hits
ΤΖ, τζ	tz	dg as in judge; j as in jam in some dialects

Greek words and phrases

Essentials

Né	Yes	**Ekí**	There
Málista	Certainly	**Aftó**	This one
Óhi	No	**Ekíno**	That one
Parakaló	Please	**Kaló**	Good
Endáxi	OK, agreed	**Kakó**	Bad
Efharistó (polý)	Thank you (very much)	**Megálo**	Big
(Dhén) Katalavéno	I (don't) understand	**Mikró**	Small
Miláte angliká?	Do you speak English?	**Perisótero**	More
Signómi	Sorry/excuse me	**Ligótero**	Less
Símera	Today	**Lígo**	A little
Ávrio	Tomorrow	**Polý**	A lot
Khthés	Yesterday	**Ftinó**	Cheap
Tóra	Now	**Akrivó**	Expensive
Argótera	Later	**Zestó**	Hot
Anikhtó	Open	**Krýo**	Cold
Klistó	Closed	**Mazí (mé)**	With (together)
Méra	Day	**Horís**	Without
Nýkhta	Night	**Grígora**	Quickly
Tó proï	In the morning	**Sigá**	Slowly
Tó apóyevma	In the afternoon	**Kýrios/Kyria**	Mr/Mrs
Tó vrádhi	In the evening	**Dhespinís**	Miss
Edhó	Here		

Other needs

Trógo/píno	To eat/drink	**Trápeza**	Bank
Foúrnos	Bakery	**Leftá/Khrímata**	Money
Farmakío	Pharmacy	**Toualéta**	Toilet
Tahydhromío	Post office	**Astynomía**	Police
Gramatósima	Stamps	**Yiatrós**	Doctor
Venzinádhiko	Petrol station	**Nosokomío**	Hospital

Requests and questions

To ask a question, it's simplest, though hardly elegant, to start with *parakaló*, then name the thing you want in an interrogative tone.

Parakaló, o foúrnos?	Where is the bakery?
Parakaló, ó dhrómos yiá . . . ?	Can you show me the road to . . . ?
Parakaló, éna dhomátio yiá dhýo átoma	We'd like a room for two
Parakaló, éna kiló portokália?	May I have a kilo of oranges?
Poú?	Where?
Pós?	How?
Póssi, pósses or póssa?	How many?
Póso?	How much?
Póte?	When?
Yiatí?	Why?
Tí óra . . . ?	At what time . . . ?
Tí íne/Pió íne . . . ?	What is/Which is . . . ?
Póso káni?	How much (does it cost)?
Tí óra aníyi?	What time does it open?
Tí óra klíni?	What time does it close?

Talking to people

Greek makes the distinction between the informal (*essý*) and formal (*essís*) second person, like the French "tu" and "vous". Young people and country people often use *essý* even with total strangers, though it's best to address everyone formally until/unless they start using the familiar at you, to avoid offence. By far the most common greeting, on meeting and parting, is *yiá sou/ yiá sas* (literally "health to you"). Incidentally, as across most of the Mediterranean, the approaching party utters the first greeting, not those seated at sidewalk *kafenío* tables or doorsteps – thus the silent staring as you enter a village.

Hérete	Hello
Kalí méra	Good morning
Kalí spéra	Good evening
Kalí níkhta	Good night
Adío	Goodbye
Tí kánis/Tí kánete?	How are you?
Kalá íme	I'm fine
Ké essís?	And you?
Pós se léne?	What's your name?
Mé léne . . .	My name is . . .
Parakaló, na milísate pió sigá	Speak slower, please
Pós léyete avtó stá Elliniká?	How do you say it in Greek?
Dhén xéro	I don't know
Thá sé dhó ávrio	See you tomorrow
Kalí andhámosi	See you soon
Páme	Let's go
Parakaló, ná mé voithíste	Please help me

Greek's Greek

There are numerous words and phrases which you will hear constantly, even if you don't have the chance to use them. These are a few of the most common.

Éla!	Come (literally) but also Speak to me! You don't say! etc.
Oríste!	Literally, Indicate!; in effect, What can I do for you?
Embrós!/Léyete!	Standard phone responses
Tí néa?	What's new?
Tí yínete?	What's going on (here)?
Étsi k'étsi	So-so
Ópa!	Whoops! Watch it!
Po-po-po!	Expression of dismay or concern, like French "O là là!"

Pedhí moú	My boy/girl, sonny, friend, etc.
Maláka(s)	Literally "wanker", but often used (don't try it!) as an informal term of address.
Sigá sigá	Take your time, slow down
Kaló taxídhi	Bon voyage

Accommodation

Xenodhohío	Hotel
Xenón(as)	Inn
Xenónas neótitos	Youth hostel
Éna dhomátio . . .	A room . . .
yiá éna/dhýo/ tría átoma	for one/two/three people
yiá mía/dhýo/ trís vradhiés	for one/two/three nights
mé dhipló kreváti	with a double bed
mé doús	with a shower
Zestó neró	Hot water
Krýo neró	Cold water
Klimatismós	Air conditioning
Anamistíra	Fan
Boró ná tó dhó?	Can I see it?
Boroúme na válоume ti skiní edhó?	Can we camp here?
Kámping/Kataskínosi	Campsite

On the move

Aeropláno	Aeroplane
Leoforío, púlman	Bus, coach
Aftokínito, amáxi	Car
Mihanáki, papáki	Motorbike, scooter
Taxí	Taxi
Plío/vapóri/karávi	Ship
Tahyplóö, katamarán	High-speed boat, catamaran
Dhelfíni	Hydrofoil
Tréno	Train
Sidhirodhromikós stathmós	Train station
Podhílato	Bicycle
Otostóp	Hitching
Mé tá pódhia	On foot
Monopáti	Trail
Praktorío leoforíon, KTEL	Bus station
Stássi	Bus stop
Limáni	Harbour
Ti óra févyi?	What time does it leave?
Ti óra fthháni?	What time does it arrive?
Póssa hiliómetra?	How many kilometres?
Pósses óres?	How many hours?
Poú pás?	Where are you going?
Páo stó . . .	I'm going to . . .
Thélo ná katévo stó . . .	I want to get off at . . .
O dhrómos yiá . . .	The road to . . .
Kondá	Near
Makriá	Far
Aristerá	Left
Dhexiá	Right
Katefthía, ísia	Straight ahead
Éna isitírio yiá . . .	A ticket to . . .
Éna isitírio aplí/mé epistrofí	A ticket one-way/ return
Paralía	Beach
Spiliá	Cave
Kéndro	Centre (of town)
Eklissía	Church
Thálassa	Sea
Horió	Village

Numbers

énas/éna/mía	1
dhýo	2
trís/tría	3
tésseris/tésseres/téssera	4

pénde	5
éxi	6
eftá	7
okhtó	8
ennéa (or, in slang, enyá)	9
dhéka	10
éndheka	11
dhódheka	12
dhekatrís	13
dhekatésseres	14
íkossi	20
íkossi éna (all compounds written separately thus)	21
triánda	30
saránda	40
penínda	50
exínda	60
evdhomínda	70
ogdhónda	80
enenínda	90
ekató	100
ekatón penínda	150
dhiakóssies/ dhiakóssia	200
pendakóssies/ pendakóssia	500
hílies/hília	1000
dhlo hiliádhes	2000
éna ekatomírio	1,000,000
próto	first
dhéftero	second
tríto	third

Days of the week and the time

Kyriakí	Sunday
Dheftéra	Monday
Tríti	Tuesday
Tetárti	Wednesday
Pémpti	Thursday
Paraskeví	Friday
Sávato	Saturday
Tí óra íne?	What time is it?
Mía íy óra/dhýo iy óra/trís íy óra	One/two/three o'clock
Tésseres pará íkossi	Twenty minutes to four
Eftá ké pénde	Five minutes past seven
Éndheka ké misí	Half past eleven
Sé misí óra	In half an hour
S'éna tétarto	In a quarter-hour
Sé dhlo óres	In two hours

Months and seasonal terms

NB: You may see *katharévoussa*, or hybrid, forms of the months written on schedules or street signs; these are the spoken demotic forms.

Yennáris	January
Fleváris	February
Mártis	March
Aprílis	April
Maïos	May
Ioúnios	June
Ioúlios	July
Ávgoustos	August
Septémvris	September
Októvrios	October
Noémvris	November
Dhekémvris	December
Therinó dhromolóyio	Summer schedule
Himerinó dhromolóyio	Winter schedule

A food and drink glossary

Basics

Aláti	Salt
Avgá	Eggs
(Horís) ládhi	(Without) oil
Hortofágos	Vegetarian
Katálogos, menoú	Menu
Kréas	Meat

Lahaniká	Vegetables
O logariasmós	The bill
Méli	Honey
Neró	Water
Psári(a)	Fish
Psomí....	Bread...
Olikís	Wholemeal
Sikalísio	Rye
Kalambokísio	Corn
Thalassiná	Seafood
Tyrí	Cheese
Yiaoúrti	Yoghurt
Záhari	Sugar

Cooking terms

Akhnistó	Steamed
Frikasé	Stew, either lamb, goat or pork, with celery
Iliókafto	Sun-dried
Kondosoúvli	Any spit-roasted beast, whole or in chunks
Kourkoúti	Egg-and-flour batter
Makaronádha	Any spaghetti/ pasta-based dish
Pastó	Fish marinated in salt
Petáli	Butterflied fish, eel, shrimp
Psitó	Roasted
Saganáki	Cheese-based red sauce; also fried cheese
Skáras	Grilled
Sti soúvla	Spit-roasted
Stó foúrno	Baked
Tiganitó	Pan-fried
Tís óras	Grilled/fried to order
Yakhní	Stewed in oil and tomato sauce
Yemistá	Stuffed (squid, vegetables, etc)

Soups and starters

Avgolémono	Egg and lemon soup
Bouréki, bourekákia	Courgette/zucchini, potato and cheese pie
Dolmádhes, yaprákia	Vine leaves stuffed with rice and mince; are vegetarian ones
Fasoládha	Bean soup
Fáva	Purée of yellow peas, served with onion and lemon
Féta psití	Baked feta cheese slabs with chilli
Galotýri	Curdled creamy dip
Hortópitta	Turnover or pie stuffed with wild greens
Kápari	Pickled caper leaves
Kopanistí, khtypití	Pungent, fermented cheese purée
Krítamo	Rock samphire
Lahanodolmádhes	Stuffed cabbage leaves
Mavromátika	Black-eyed peas
Melitzanosaláta	Aubergine/eggplant dip
Piperiá florínes	Marinated sweet Macedonian red peppers
Plevrótous	Oyster mushrooms
Rengosaláta	Herring salad
Revythokeftédhes	Chickpea/garbanzo patties
Skordhaliá	Garlic dip
Soúpa	Soup
Taramosaláta	Cod roe paté
Tiganópsomo	Toasted oiled bread
Trahanádhes	Crushed wheat and milk soup, sweet or savoury
Tyrokafterí	Cheese dip with chilli, different from **kopanistí**
Tzatzíki	Yoghurt and cucumber dip
Tzirosaláta	Cured mackerel dip

Vegetables

Ambelofásola	Crimp-pod runner beans
Angináres	Artichokes
Angoúri	Cucumber
Ánitho	Dill
Bámies	Okra, ladies' fingers
Boúkovo	Macedonian chilli flakes

LANGUAGE | Greek words and phrases

Briám, tourloú	Ratatouille of zucchini, potatoes, onions, tomato
Domátes	Tomatoes
Fakés	Lentils
Fasolákia	French (green) beans
Fasóles	Small white beans
Horiátiki (saláta)	Greek salad (with olives, feta, etc)
Hórta	Greens (usually wild), steamed
Kolokythákia	Courgette/zucchini
Koukiá	Broad fava beans
Maroúli	Lettuce
Melitzánes imám/ Imám baïldí	Aubergine/eggplant slices baked with onion, garlic and copious olive oil
Patátes	Potatoes
Piperiés	Peppers
Pligoúri, pinigoúri	Bulgur wheat
Radhíkia	Wild chicory – a common hórta
Rókka	Rocket, arugula
Rýzi/Piláfi	Rice (usually with **sáltsa** – sauce)
Saláta	Salad
Spanáki	Spinach
Vlíta	Notchweed – another common hórta
Yígandes	White haricot beans

Fish and seafood

Ahini	Sea urchins
Astakomakaronádha	Lobster flaked into pasta
Astakós	Aegean lobster
Atherína	Sand smelt
Bakaliáros	Cod or hake, usually latter
Barbóuni	Red mullet
Fangri	Common bream
Foúskes	*Uovo di mare* (Italian), *violet* (French); no English equivalent for this invertebrate.
Galéos	Dogfish, hound shark, tope
Garídhes	Shrimp, prawns
Gávros	Mild anchovy
Glóssa	Sole
Gónos, Gonákia	Any hatchling fish
Gópa	Bogue
Kalamarákia	Baby squid
Kalamária	Squid
Karavídhes	Crayfish
Karavidhópsyha	Crayfish nuggets
Kefalás	Axillary bream
Koliós	Chub mackerel
Koutsomoúra	Goatfish (small red mullet)
Kydhónia	Warty Venus
Lakérdha	Light-fleshed bonito, marinated
Marídhes	Picarel
Mayiátiko	Amberjack
Melanoúri	Saddled bream
Ménoula	Sprat
Mýdhia	Mussels
Okhtapódhi	Octopus
Pandelís	Corvina; aka **sykiós**
Petalídhes	Limpets
Platý	Skate, ray
Sardhélles	Sardines
Sargós	White bream
Seláhi	Skate, ray
Skáros	Parrotfish
Skathári	Black bream
Skoumbrí	Atlantic mackerel
Soupiá	Cuttlefish
Spiniálo, spinóalo	Marinated foúskes
Synagrídha	Dentex
Thrápsalo	Large, deep-water squid
Tsipoúra	Gilt-head bream
Xifías	Swordfish
Yermanós	Leatherback
Yialisterés	Smooth Venus; common ouzerí shellfish

Meat- and poultry-based dishes

Arní	Lamb
Bekrí mezé	Pork chunks in red sauce
Biftéki	Hamburger
Brizóla	Pork or beef chop

Hirinó	Pork
Keftédhes	Meatballs
Kokorétsi	Liver/offal roulade, spit-roasted
Kopsídha	(Lamb) shoulder chops
Kókoras krasáto	Coq au vin
Kotópoulo	Chicken
Kounélli	Rabbit
Loukánika	Spicy course-ground sausages
Manári	Spring lamb
Moskhári	Veal
Moussakás	Aubergine/eggplant, potato and lamb-mince casserole with béchamel topping
Païdhákia	Rib chops, lamb or goat
Papoutsákia	Stuffed aubergine/ eggplant "shoes" like *moussakás* without bechamel
Pastítsio	Macaroni "pie" baked with minced meat
Pastourmás	Cured, highly spiced meat; traditionally camel, nowadays beef
Patsás	Tripe soup
Provatína	Female mutton
Psaronéfri	Pork tenderloin medallions
Salingária	Garden snails
Soutzoukákia	Minced meat rissoles/ beef patties
Spetzofáï	Sausage and pepper stew
Stifádho	Meat stew with tomato and boiling onions
Sykóti	Liver
Tiganiá	Pork chunks fried with onions
Tziyéro sarmás	Lamb's liver in cabbage leaves
Yiouvétsi	Baked clay casserole of meat and **kritharáki** (short pasta)
Zygoúri	1-to-2-year-old lamb

Sweets and dessert

Baklavás	Honey and nut pastry
Bergamóndo	Bergamot
Bougátsa	Salt or sweet cream pie served warm with sugar and cinnamon
Galaktoboúriko	Custard pie
Glykó koutalioú	Spoon sweet (syrupy fruit preserve)
Halvás	Sesame-based sweet meat
Karydhópita	Walnut cake
Kréma	Custard
Loukoumádhes	Dough fritters in honey syrup and sesame seeds
Pagotó	Ice cream
Pastélli	Sesame and honey bar
Ravaní	Sponge cake, lightly syruped
Ryzógalo	Rice pudding
Simigdhalísios halvás	Semolina-based halva

Fruits

Akhládhia	Big pears
Aktinídha	Kiwis
Fistíkia	Pistachio nuts
Fráoules	Strawberries
Himoniátiko	Autumn (cassava) melon
Karpoúzi	Watermelon
Kerásia	Cherries
Krystália	Miniature pears
Kydhóni	Quince
Lemónia	Lemons
Míla	Apples
Pepóni	Melon
Portokália	Oranges
Rodhákina	Peaches
Sýka	Figs
Stafýlia	Grapes
Yiarmádhes	Autumn peaches

Cheese

Ayeladhinó	Cow's-milk cheese
Féta	Salty, creamy white cheese

(Kefalo)graviéra	(Extra-hard) Gruyère-type cheese
Katsikísio	Goat cheese
Kasséri	Medium-sharp cheese
Myzíthra	Sweet cream cheese
Próvio	Sheep cheese

Drinks

Alisfakiá	Island sage tea
Boukáli	Bottle
Býra	Beer
Gála	Milk
Galakakáo	Chocolate milk
Kafés	Coffee
Krasí	Wine
áspro	white
kokkinélli/rozé	rosé
kókkino	red
Limonádha	Lemonade
Metalikó neró	Mineral water
Portokaládha	Orangeade
Potíri	Glass
Stinyásas!	Cheers!
Tsáï	Tea
Tsáï vounoú	"Mountain" (mainland sage) tea

A glossary of words and terms

Acropolis Ancient, fortified hilltop.

Agora Market and meeting place of an ancient Greek city; also the "high street" of a modern village (**agorá** in modern Greek).

Amphora Tall, narrow-necked jar for oil or wine.

Áno Upper; common prefix of village names.

Apse Curved recess at the east end of a church nave.

Archaic period Late Iron Age period, from around 750 BC to the start of the Classical period in the fifth century BC.

Arhondikó A lordly stone mansion, eg in Kastoriá or Pílio, often restored as boutique accommodation.

Astykó (Intra) city, municipal, local; adjective applied to phone calls and bus services.

Ayíasma A sacred spring, usually flowing out of church foundations.

Áyios/Ayía/Áyii (m/f/plural). Saint or holy. Common place-name prefix (abbreviated Ag or Ay), often spelled **Agios** or **Aghios**.

Basilica Colonnaded, "hall-" or "barn-" type church adapted from Roman models, most common in northern Greece.

Bema Rostrum for a church oratory.

Bouleuterion Auditorium for meetings of an ancient town's deliberative council.

Capital The flared top, often ornamented, of a column.

Cavea Seating curve of an ancient theatre.

Cella Sacred room of a temple, housing the cult image.

Classical period From the end of the Persian Wars in 480 BC until the unification of Greece under Philip II of Macedon (338 BC).

Conch Concave semi-dome surmounting a church apse, often frescoed.

Corinthian Decorative columns, festooned with acanthus florettes; any temple built in this order.

Dhimarhío Town hall.

Dhomátia Rooms for rent in purpose-built block, without staffed reception.

Dorian Northern civilization that displaced and succeeded the Mycenaeans and Minoans through most of Greece around 1100 BC.

Doric Minimalist, unadorned columns, dating from the Dorian period; any temple built in this order.

Drum Cylindrical or faceted vertical section, usually pierced by an even number of narrow windows, upholding a church cupola.

Entablature The horizontal linking structure atop the columns of an ancient temple; same as **architrave**.

Eparhía Subdivision of a modern province, analogous to a county.

Exedra Display niche for statuary.

Exonarthex The outer vestibule or entrance hall of a church, when a true **narthex** is present.

Forum Market and meeting place of a Roman-era city.

Frieze Band of sculptures around a temple. Doric friezes consist of various tableaux of figures (**metopes**) interspersed with grooved panels (**triglyphs**); Ionic ones have continuous bands of figures.

Froúrio Medieval citadel; nowadays, can mean a modern military headquarters.

Garsoniéra/es Studio villa/s, self-catering apartment/s.

Geometric period Post-Mycenaean Iron Age era named for its pottery style; starts in the early eleventh century BC with the arrival of Dorian peoples. By the eighth century BC, with development of representational styles, the **Archaic period** begins.

Hamam Domed "Turkish" bath, found on Rhodes and certain northeast Aegean islands.

Hellenistic period The last and most unified "Greek empire", created in the wake of Alexander the Great's Macedonian empire and finally collapsing with the fall of Corinth to the Romans in 146 BC.

Heroön Shrine or sanctuary-tomb, usually of a demigod or mortal; war memorials in modern Greece.

Hóra Main town of an island or region; literally it means "the place". A hóra is often known by the same name as the island.

Ierón The sanctuary between the altar screen and the apse of a church, reserved for priestly activities.

Ikonostási Wood or masonry screen between the nave of a church and the altar, supporting at least three icons.

Ionic Elaborate, decorative development of the older **Doric** order; Ionic temple columns are slimmer, with deeper "fluted" edges, spiral-shaped capitals and ornamental bases.

Kafenío Coffee house or café.

Kaïki (plural **kaïkia**) Caique, or medium-sized boat, traditionally wooden and used for transporting cargo and passengers; now refers mainly to island excursion boats.

Kalderími A cobbled mule-track or footpath.

Kámbos Fertile agricultural plain, usually near a river mouth.

Kantína Shack, caravan or even a disused bus on the beach, serving drinks and perhaps sandwiches or quick snacks.

Kástro Any fortified hill, but most often the oldest, highest, walled-in part of an island hóra, intended to protect civilians.

Katholikón Central church of a monastery.

Káto Lower; common prefix of village names.

Kendrikí platía Central square.

Kouros Nude Archaic statue of an idealized young man, usually portrayed with one foot slightly in front of the other.

Megaron Principal hall or throne room of a Mycenaean palace.

Meltémi North wind that blows across the Aegean in summer, starting softly from near the mainland and hitting the Cyclades, the Dodecanese and Crete full on.

Metope see **Frieze**.

Minoan Crete's great Bronze Age civilization, which dominated the Aegean from about 2500 to 1400 BC.

Moní Formal term for a monastery or convent.

Moreas Medieval term for the Peloponnese; the peninsula's outline peninsula was likened to the leaf of a mulberry tree, mouriá in Greek.

Mycenaean Mainland civilization centred on Mycenae and the Argolid from about 1700 to 1100 BC.

Naos The inner sanctum of an ancient temple; also, the central area of an Orthodox Christian church.

Narthex Western vestibule of a church, reserved for catechumens and the unbaptized; typically frescoed with scenes of the Last Judgment.

Neolithic Earliest era of settlement in Greece; characterized by use of stone tools and weapons together with basic agriculture. Divided arbitrarily into Early (ca. 6000 BC), Middle (ca. 5000 BC) and Late (ca. 3000 BC).

Néos, Néa, Néo "New" – a common prefix to a town or village name.

Nomós Modern Greek province – there are more than fifty of them. Village bus services are organized according to their borders.

Odeion Small theatre, used for musical performances, minor dramatic productions or councils.

Orchestra Circular area in a theatre where the chorus would sing and dance.

Palaestra Gymnasium for athletics and wrestling practice.

Paleós, Paleá, Paleó "Old" – again a common prefix in town and village names.

Panayía Virgin Mary.

Pandokrátor Literally "The Almighty"; generally refers to the stern portrayal of Christ in Majesty frescoed or in mosaic in the dome of many Byzantine churches.

Paniyíri Festival or feast – the local celebration of a holy day.

Paralía Beach, or seafront promenade.

Pediment Triangular, sculpted gable below the roof of a temple.

Pendentive Triangular sections of vaulting with concave sides, positioned at a corner of a rectangular space to support a circular or polygonal dome; in churches, often adorned with frescoes of the four Evangelists.

Períptero Street kiosk.

Peristereónes Pigeon towers, in the Cyclades.

Peristyle Gallery of columns around a temple or other building.

Pinakothíki Picture gallery, ancient or modern.

Pithos (plural **pithoi**) Large ceramic jar for storing oil, grain, etc. Very common in Minoan palaces and used in almost identical form in modern Greek homes.

Platía Square, plaza.

Polygonal masonry Wall-building technique of Classical and Hellenistic periods, using unmortared, closely joined stones; often called "Lesvian polygonal" after the island where the method supposedly originated. The much-(ab)used term **Cyclopean** refers only to Bronze Age mainland sites such as Tiryns and Mycenae.

Propylaion Monumental columned gateway of an ancient building; often used in the plural, **propylaia**.

Pýrgos Tower or bastion; also tower-mansions found in the Máni or on Lésvos.

Skála The port of an inland island settlement, nowadays often larger and more important than its namesake, but always younger since built after the disappearance of piracy.

Squinch Small concavity across a corner of a column-less interior space, which supports a superstructure such as a dome.

Stele Upright stone slab or column, usually inscribed with an edict; also an ancient tombstone, with a relief scene.

Stoa Colonnaded walkway in Classical-to-Roman-era marketplaces.

Távli Backgammon; a favourite café pastime, especially among the young. There are two more difficult local variations (févga and plakotó) in addition to the standard international game (pórtes).

Témblon Wooden altar screen of an Orthodox church, usually ornately carved and painted and studded with icons; more or less interchangeable with **ikonostási**.

Temenos Sacred precinct of ancient temple, often used to refer to the sanctuary itself.

Theatral area Open area found in most of the Minoan palaces with seat-like steps around. Probably a type of theatre or ritual area.

Tholos Conical or beehive-shaped building, eg a Mycenaean tomb.

Triglyph see **Frieze**.

Tympanum The recessed space, flat or carved in relief, inside a pediment.

Votsalotó Mosaic of coloured pebbles, found in church or house courtyards of the Dodecanese and Spétses.

Yperastykó Long-distance – as in bus services.

Acronyms

ANEK Anónymi Navtiliakí Etería Krítis (Shipping Co of Crete, Ltd), which runs most ferries between Pireás and Crete, plus many to Italy.

EAM National Liberation Front, the political force behind ELAS.

ELAS Popular Liberation Army, the main Resistance group during World War II and predecessor of the Communist army during the civil war.

ELTA Postal service.

EOS Greek Mountaineering Federation, based in Athens.

EOT Ellinikós Organismós Tourismoú, National Tourist Organization.

FYROM Former Yugoslav Republic of Macedonia.

KKE Communist Party, unreconstructed.

KTEL National syndicate of bus companies; also refers to individual bus stations.

LANE Lasithiakí Anónymi Navtiliakí Etería (Lasithian Shipping Company Ltd), based in eastern Crete.

ND Conservative (Néa Dhimokratía) party.

NEL Navtiliakí Etería Lésvou (Lesvian Shipping Co).

OSE Railway corporation.

OTE Telecommunications company.

PASOK Socialist party (Pan-Hellenic Socialist Movement).

SEO Greek Mountaineering Club, based in Thessaloníki.

SYRIZA Synaspismós tis Rizospastikís Aristerás (Coalition of the Radical Left) – alternative, "Euro"-Socialist party.

Travel store

ROUGH GUIDES Complete Listing

UK & Ireland
Britain
Devon & Cornwall
Dublin **D**
Edinburgh **D**
England
Ireland
The Lake District
London
London **D**
London Mini Guide
Scotland
Scottish Highlands & Islands
Wales

Europe
Algarve **D**
Amsterdam
Amsterdam **D**
Andalucía
Athens **D**
Austria
Baltic States
Barcelona
Barcelona **D**
Belgium & Luxembourg
Berlin
Brittany & Normandy
Bruges **D**
Brussels
Budapest
Bulgaria
Copenhagen
Corfu
Corsica
Costa Brava **D**
Crete
Croatia
Cyprus
Czech & Slovak Republics
Denmark
Dodecanese & East Aegean Islands
Dordogne & The Lot
Europe
Florence & Siena
Florence **D**
France
Germany
Gran Canaria **D**
Greece
Greek Islands
Hungary
Ibiza & Formentera **D**
Iceland
Ionian Islands
Italy
The Italian Lakes
Languedoc & Roussillon
Lanzarote & Fuerteventura **D**
Lisbon **D**
The Loire Valley
Madeira **D**
Madrid **D**
Mallorca **D**
Mallorca & Menorca
Malta & Gozo **D**
Menorca
Moscow
The Netherlands
Norway
Paris
Paris **D**
Paris Mini Guide
Poland
Portugal
Prague
Prague **D**
Provence & the Côte D'Azur
Pyrenees
Romania
Rome
Rome **D**
Sardinia
Scandinavia
Sicily
Slovenia
Spain
St Petersburg
Sweden
Switzerland
Tenerife & La Gomera **D**
Turkey
Tuscany & Umbria
Venice & The Veneto
Venice **D**
Vienna

Asia
Bali & Lombok
Bangkok
Beijing
Cambodia
China
Goa
Hong Kong & Macau
Hong Kong & Macau **D**
India
Indonesia
Japan
Kerala
Laos
Malaysia, Singapore & Brunei
Nepal
The Philippines
Rajasthan, Dehli & Agra
Singapore
Singapore **D**
South India
Southeast Asia
Sri Lanka
Taiwan
Thailand
Thailand's Beaches & Islands
Tokyo
Vietnam

Australasia
Australia
Melbourne
New Zealand
Sydney

North America
Alaska
Baja California
Boston
California
Canada
Chicago
Colorado
Florida
The Grand Canyon
Hawaii
Honolulu **D**
Las Vegas **D**
Los Angeles
Maui **D**
Miami & South Florida
Montréal
New England
New Orleans **D**
New York City
New York City **D**
New York City Mini Guide
Orlando & Walt Disney World® **D**
Pacific Northwest
San Francisco
San Francisco **D**
Seattle
Southwest USA
Toronto
USA
Vancouver
Washington DC
Washington DC **D**
Yellowstone & The Grand Tetons
Yosemite

Caribbean & Latin America
Antigua & Barbuda **D**
Argentina
Bahamas
Barbados **D**
Belize
Bolivia
Brazil
Cancùn & Cozumel **D**
Caribbean
Central America
Chile
Costa Rica
Cuba
Dominican Republic
Dominican Republic **D**
Ecuador
Guatemala
Jamaica
Mexico
Peru
St Lucia **D**
South America
Trinidad & Tobago
Yúcatan

Africa & Middle East
Cape Town & the Garden Route
Dubai **D**
Egypt
Gambia
Jordan

D: Rough Guide **DIRECTIONS** for short breaks

Available from all good bookstores

ROUGH GUIDES Complete Listing

Kenya
Marrakesh **D**
Morocco
South Africa, Lesotho & Swaziland
Syria
Tanzania
Tunisia
West Africa
Zanzibar

Travel Specials
First-Time Africa
First-Time Around the World
First-Time Asia
First-Time Europe
First-Time Latin America
Travel Health
Travel Online
Travel Survival
Walks in London & SE England
Women Travel
World Party

Maps
Algarve
Amsterdam
Andalucia & Costa del Sol
Argentina
Athens
Australia
Barcelona
Berlin
Boston & Cambridge
Brittany
Brussels
California
Chicago
Chile
Corsica
Costa Rica & Panama
Crete
Croatia
Cuba
Cyprus
Czech Republic
Dominican Republic
Dubai & UAE
Dublin
Egypt
Florence & Siena
Florida
France
Frankfurt
Germany
Greece
Guatemala & Belize
Iceland
India
Ireland
Italy
Kenya & Northern Tanzania
Lisbon
London
Los Angeles
Madrid
Malaysia
Mallorca
Marrakesh
Mexico
Miami & Key West
Morocco
New England
New York City
New Zealand
Northern Spain
Paris
Peru
Portugal
Prague
Pyrenees & Andorra
Rome
San Francisco
Sicily
South Africa
South India
Spain & Portugal
Sri Lanka
Tenerife
Thailand
Toronto
Trinidad & Tobago
Tunisia
Turkey
Tuscany
Venice
Vietnam, Laos & Cambodia
Washington DC
Yucatán Peninsula

Dictionary Phrasebooks
Croatian
Czech
Dutch
Egyptian Arabic
French
German
Greek
Hindi & Urdu
Italian
Japanese
Latin American Spanish
Mandarin Chinese
Mexican Spanish
Polish
Portuguese
Russian
Spanish
Swahili
Thai
Turkish
Vietnamese

Computers
Blogging
eBay
iPhone
iPods, iTunes & music online
The Internet
Macs & OS X
MySpace
PCs and Windows
PlayStation Portable
Website Directory

Film & TV
American Independent Film
British Cult Comedy
Chick Flicks
Comedy Movies
Cult Movies
Film
Film Musicals
Film Noir
Gangster Movies
Horror Movies
Kids' Movies
Sci-Fi Movies
Westerns

Lifestyle
Babies
Ethical Living
Pregnancy & Birth
Running

Music Guides
The Beatles
Blues
Bob Dylan
Book of Playlists
Classical Music
Elvis
Frank Sinatra
Heavy Metal
Hip-Hop
Jazz
Led Zeppelin
Opera
Pink Floyd
Punk
Reggae
Rock
The Rolling Stones
Soul and R&B
Velvet Underground
World Music (2 vols)

Popular Culture
Books for Teenagers
Children's Books, 5-11
Conspiracy Theories
Crime Fiction
Cult Fiction
The Da Vinci Code
His Dark Materials
Lord of the Rings
Shakespeare
Superheroes
The Templars
Unexplained Phenomena

Science
The Brain
Climate Change
The Earth
Genes & Cloning
The Universe
Weather

ROUGH GUIDES

Small print and

Index

A Rough Guide to Rough Guides

Published in 1982, the first Rough Guide – to Greece – was a student scheme that became a publishing phenomenon. Mark Ellingham, a recent graduate in English from Bristol University, had been travelling in Greece the previous summer and couldn't find the right guidebook. With a small group of friends he wrote his own guide, combining a highly contemporary, journalistic style with a thoroughly practical approach to travellers' needs.

The immediate success of the book spawned a series that rapidly covered dozens of destinations. And, in addition to impecunious backpackers, Rough Guides soon acquired a much broader and older readership that relished the guides' wit and inquisitiveness as much as their enthusiastic, critical approach and value-for-money ethos.

These days, Rough Guides include recommendations from shoestring to luxury and cover more than 200 destinations around the globe, including almost every country in the Americas and Europe, more than half of Africa and most of Asia and Australasia. Our ever-growing team of authors and photographers is spread all over the world, particularly in Europe, the USA and Australia.

In the early 1990s, Rough Guides branched out of travel, with the publication of Rough Guides to World Music, Classical Music and the Internet. All three have become benchmark titles in their fields, spearheading the publication of a wide range of books under the Rough Guide name.

Including the travel series, Rough Guides now number more than 350 titles, covering: phrasebooks, waterproof maps, music guides from Opera to Heavy Metal, reference works as diverse as Conspiracy Theories and Shakespeare, and popular culture books from iPods to Poker. Rough Guides also produce a series of more than 120 World Music CDs in partnership with World Music Network.

Visit www.roughguides.com to see our latest publications.

Rough Guide travel images are available for commercial licensing at www.roughguidespictures.com

Rough Guide credits

Text editor: Natasha Foges, Samantha Cook and Anna Streiffert
Layout: Sachin Tanwar
Cartography: Amod Singh
Picture editor: Nicole Newman
Production: Rebecca Short
Proofreader: Anita Sach
Cover design: Chloë Roberts
Photographer: Michelle Grant, Geoff Garvey and John Fisher
Editorial: **London** Ruth Blackmore, Alison Murchie, Karoline Thomas, Andy Turner, Keith Drew, Edward Aves, Alice Park, Lucy White, Jo Kirby, James Smart, Róisín Cameron, Emma Traynor, Emma Gibbs, Kathryn Lane, Christina Valhouli, Monica Woods, James Rice, Mani Ramaswamy, Joe Staines, Peter Buckley, Matthew Milton, Tracy Hopkins, Ruth Tidball; **New York** Andrew Rosenberg, Steven Horak, Courteney Miller, Paula Neudorf, AnneLise Sorensen, April Isaacs, Ella Steim, Anna Owens, Sean Mahoney; **Delhi** Madhavi Singh, Karen D'Souza
Design & Pictures: **London** Scott Stickland, Dan May, Diana Jarvis, Mark Thomas, Chloë Roberts, Sarah Cummins, Emily Taylor **Delhi** Umesh Aggarwal, Ajay Verma, Jessica Subramanian, Ankur Guha, Pradeep Thapliyal, Anita Singh, Nikhil Agarwal
Production: Vicky Baldwin
Cartography: **London** Maxine Repath, Ed Wright, Katie Lloyd-Jones; **Delhi** Jai Prakash Mishra, Rajesh Chhibber, Ashutosh Bharti, Rajesh Mishra, Animesh Pathak, Jasbir Sandhu, Karobi Gogoi, Alakananda Bhattacharya, Swati Handoo
Online: Narender Kumar, Rakesh Kumar, Amit Verma, Rahul Kumar, Ganesh Sharma, Debojit Borah, Saurabh Sati
Marketing & Publicity: **London** Liz Statham, Niki Hanmer, Louise Maher, Jess Carter, Vanessa Godden, Vivienne Watton, Anna Paynton, Rachel Sprackett, Libby Jellie; **New York** Geoff Colquitt, Katy Ball; **Delhi** Ragini Govind
Manager India: Punita Singh
Reference Director: Andrew Lockett
Operations Manager: Helen Phillips
PA to Publishing Director: Nicola Henderson
Publishing Director: Martin Dunford
Commercial Manager: Gino Magnotta
Managing Director: John Duhigg

Publishing information

This twelfth edition published May 2008 by
Rough Guides Ltd,
80 Strand, London WC2R 0RL
345 Hudson St, 4th Floor,
New York, NY 10014, USA
14 Local Shopping Centre, Panchsheel Park,
New Delhi 110017, India
Distributed by the Penguin Group
Penguin Books Ltd,
80 Strand, London WC2R 0RL
Penguin Group (USA)
375 Hudson Street, NY 10014, USA
Penguin Group (Australia)
250 Camberwell Road, Camberwell,
Victoria 3124, Australia
Penguin Books Canada Ltd,
10 Alcorn Avenue, Toronto, Ontario,
Canada M4V 1E4
Penguin Group (NZ)
67 Apollo Drive, Mairangi Bay, Auckland 1310,
New Zealand
Cover concept by Peter Dyer.

Typeset in Bembo and Helvetica to an original design by Henry Iles.

Printed in Italy by Lego Print s.p.a.

1016pp includes index

A catalogue record for this book is available from the British Library

ISBN: 978-1-85828-155-1

3 5 7 9 8 6 4 2

Help us update

We've gone to a lot of effort to ensure that the twelfth edition of **The Rough Guide to Greece** is accurate and up to date. However, things change – places get "discovered", opening hours are notoriously fickle, restaurants and rooms raise prices or lower standards. If you feel we've got it wrong or left something out, we'd like to know, and if you can remember the address, the price, the hours, the phone number, so much the better.

Please send your comments with the subject line **"Rough Guide Greece Update"** to ⓔmail @roughguides.com. We'll credit all contributions and send a copy of the next edition (or any other Rough Guide if you prefer) for the very best emails.

Have your questions answered and tell others about your trip at ⓦcommunity.roughguides.com

Acknowledgements

Lance Chilton thanks wife Hilary; Julia Tzanidou-Zuberer of Porfyra Travel and Mrs Venardos in Kýthira; Chris & Dave Windell in Pyrgiótika; Ioannis Katranis in Spárti; Nicola Dyas of Doufexis Travel in Stoúpa; Mikhalis Kovaios, Vasilis Mavros, Evangelia Mavrou and Moschoula Symidala in Amorgós; Spyros Karelis in Ándhros; Lonie in Dhonoússa; the Marinakis family and the Folk Museum in Folégandros; Thomas Robinson & Ieuan Walker in Íos; Anna Koveos and Ralf in Iráklia; Maria Melanis in Kímolos, Katerina Prasinos and family in Koufoníssi; Papa Dimitrios and Andreas Mallis in Mílos; Dimitris Xenarios, Maria of the Terra Maria and Nicoletta of K' Group in Mýkonos; Nikolaos Karavias, Despina Kitini, Nikos Perrakis, and, in particular, Stavros Panagopoulos in Náxos; Mike Akalestos and Dimitri Sarris in Páros; Kostas Mindrinos in Santorini; Stou Stratou café in Sérifos; Iakovos Korakis and Mr Gerontopoulos in Sífnos; Irini Divoli and Mrs Manalis in Síkinos; Anna Vidou in Tínos; and Andy McCosh for extensive info on several islands.

Marc Dubin thanks: Khrysoula Papalexi in Galaxídhi, the Sakellaris brothers in Náfpaktos, Jill Sleeman in Moúressi, Roy and Effie Hounsell in Koukoúli, the Pappas family in Lyngiádhes, Thanassis and Toula Nakis in Kastráki, Panayiotis and Aphrodite Sotiriou on Límnos, Theo and Melinda Kosmetos in Mólyvos, Markos Kostalas and Theo and Güher Spordhilis on Híos, Alexis and Dhionysia Zikas on Kós, David and Lisa on Tílos, Kim Sjögren and his staff at Triton, Constance Rivemale, Efi and Spyros Dedes and Patrick on Rhodes, Gerald Brisch for updates of both Rhodes and Évvia, Denise Harvey in Límni, Alexandhros Karsiotis in Kapandhríti, Roger Jinkinson and the Yializis family on Kárpathos, Nikos, Wendy, Adriana and Nicholas on Sými, Andonis and Themelina Andonoglou on Kálymnos, the management of the hotels Porphyris (Níssyros), Australian (Astypálea), Crithoni's Paradise (Léros), and Irini (Tílos) for their support, Dudley der Partogh at Sunvil and Carol Coulter at Skycars for travel facilities, and once again to the Zdravets for keeping me company in Epirus, Thessaly and the northeast Aegean.

Nick Edwards would like to thank friends old and new in the Ionians and northern Greece for special assistance and/or hospitality: Mariana & Petros and Kostas V on Corfu (via Gosport); Maria in Nydhri; Panayis in Argostoli; the Potamitis family and Limni Keriou people on Zakynthos; Phil Simmonds for the Kassandra tour; Mik Smith for Sithonia details; Dimitra & Pandelis in Xanthi; Hotel Lena on Thassos; the Imaret in Kavala, Archondiko Varosi in Edessa and Pension Filoxenia in Kastoria. And thanks to Maria for waiting for me to come home again!

John Fisher would like to thank everyone who helped, especially, in Athens, Nick, James and Kate, Alexandra Rokou-Pikioni and Vangelis Lagoutaris, and in Crete to Iorgos Margaritakis, the Perrakis family, and above all Alex Stivanakis and family, who are in our thoughts; not forgetting the brilliant team at Rough Guides and, as ever, A & the two Js for love, support and disrupting the research.

Geoff Garvey would once again like to thank Nikos Karellis, editor of Stigmes magazine, Iráklion, for help and advice regarding all matters Cretan. A grateful "efharisto pára polí" also goes to Manolis Sergentakis in Kastélli Kissámou, Irene Michaelakis in Haniá, Yiannis and Katerina Hatzidakis in Sitía, Heracles Papadakis in Spili, Lambros Papoutsakis in Thrónos, Yiorgos Margaritakis in Iráklion, Froso Bora in Réthymnon and last but by no means least to Stelios Manousakas in Aryiroúpolis for his amity, altercations and avocados.

Readers' letters

Thanks to all those readers of the eleventh edition who took the trouble to write in with their amendments and suggestions. Apologies for any misspellings or omissions.

Ana Anastasijevic, Chuck Arthur, Giorgio Balzarro, Guy Bickel, Nis Brandt, Allan Brigham, Jennifer & Chris Britton, Penny and Richard Bunting, Candy Burns, Paul Burroughts, Oliver Carfrae, Richard Ciecierski, Kathy Darby, Peter Davies, Malcolm Elwell, Ann Farquharson, P Field & K Hagelund, Per Ivar Gaarder, Allan Gammons, Jenny Gisbertz & Klaas Halbesma, Alastair Graham, Alistair Grant, Mike & Ruth Hall, John Hardie, Christine Hathway, Peter Hodgson, Rod Ingham, Roger Jinkinson, Mike Keating, Annette Kelly, Nick Kelly, Linda Kirby, Ros & Fergus Macbeth, Bob & Denise Mark, Pauline Maynard, Andy McCosh, David McKee, Chris Moore, Anthony Nichols, Nick Nicolaides, Stephen Ollivier, Jim and Jane Panzer, David Reavey, Sarah Robinson, Ann Sacra, Bob & Rose Sandham, Will Sawyer, Anthony Schlesinger, Carola Scupham, Peter Serres, Brian Shepherd, Kate Spreadbury, Kate Sutton, Jamie Verinis, Dave & Rachel Ward, Randy Welch, Margaret Williamson, John P. Yannopapas.

Photo credits

All photos © Rough Guides except the following:

Title page

Taverna, Cyclades © Christos Drazos/digital railroad

Introduction

Old Town square at dusk, Rhodes Town © Anzenberger/eyevine/drr.net

Helmos Ski Centre, Peloponnese © IML Image Group Ltd/Alamy

Metéora monasteries © David Noton/naturepl.com

Roadside shrine to St George © Terry Harris/Alamy

Evil Eye amulet © Helene Rogers/Art Directors and TRIP

Things not to miss

01 Hozoviótissa monastery, Amorgós © photolibrary

02 View across Sámos © Christopher McGowan/Alamy

03 Mosaics, Ósios Loukás © Aliki Sapountzi/Alamy

04 Monemvasiá © photolibrary.com

05 Samariá Gorge © Loraine Wilson/Robert Harding

07 Yialós harbour © Walter Bibikow/JAI/Corbis

08 Beach, Mylopótamos, Pílio © Anestis Rekkas /Alamy

10 Lindos acropolis, Rhodes © Marco Simoni/Robert Harding

11 Mystra © Art Kowalsky/Alamy

12 Roussánou monastery in the Metéora © Rod Edwards/Alamy

14 Loggerhead sea turtle © CuboImages srl/Alamy

16 Tholos, Delphi © Russell Kord/Alamy

17 Mount Olympus © Getty Images/National Geographic Creative

18 Préspa lakes © IML Image Group Ltd/Alamy

19 Monastery of Ayíou Ioánnou Theológou, Pátmos © Marc Dubin

20 Stone walls of Acrocorinth © Getty Images/National Geographic

21 View of Skýros Town © Terry Harris/Alamy

23 Osíou Grigoríou monastery, Mount Athos © Nick Edwards

24 Náfplio, Peloponnese © photolibrary.com

26 Lion Gate, Mycenae © Getty Images/DeAgostini

27 Víkos Gorge, Epirus © Loraine Wilson/Robert Harding

28 Windsurfing, Vassilikì, Lefkádha © Doug McKinlay/Axiom

Colour Section: An Orthodox nation

Ía, Santorini © Macduff Everton/digital railroad

Easter icon procession © IML Image Group/drr.net

Easter in Kárpathos © Anzenberger/eyevine/drr.net

Woman carrying basket with bread decorated with red eggs © IML/drr.net

Good Friday candles © IML Image Group/drr.net

Priest, western Macedonia © IML Image Group/drr.ne

Colour Section: Wild Greece

Butterfly on Pyramidal Orchid © Bob Gibbons/Alamy

Aerial view of the Samariá Gorge © Marco Simoni/Robert Harding

Wildflowers, Lésvos © David Tipling/naturepl.com

Stork in nest © FLPA/Richard Brooks

Piyés Aöou reservoir, Píndhos mountains © FLPA/Jean Hall/Holt

View to Voïdokiliá bay, Peloponnese © Alamy

Mount Athos © Yann Arthus-Bertrand/Corbis

Walking near the Metéora © Frits Meyst/digital railroad

Black and whites

p.166 Olympia © Oliviero Olivieri/Robert Harding

p.209 View through a natural stone arch, Kýthira © DK images

p.223 Váthia village © Andia.fr/drr.net

p.252 The Boúrtzi, Methóni © Jon Arnold Images Ltd/Alamy

p.278 Náfpaktos © PCL/Alamy

p.322 Taverna tables, Tsangarádha, Pílio © Marc Dubin

p.347 Timíou Stavroú church © Marc Dubin

p.352 Ancient Kassope © photolibrary.com

p.379 Plakídha Bridge, near Kípi © Marc Dubin

p.408 Mount Olympus © PCL/Alamy

p.420 Áyios Dhimítrios church, Thessaloníki © JTB Photo/Alamy

p.440 Mosaic Floor at Pella © John Heseltine/Corbis

p.482 Temple of Aphaea, Égina © Marc Dubin

p.504 View from Áno Sýros © Alamy

p.521 Firopotamos, Mílos © Marco Simoni/Corbis

p.537 Café, Mýkonos © Hugh Sitton/Getty

p.579 Santoríni © Chris Chrisoforou

p.658 Thermal springs on the island of Kós © Sharky/Alamy

p.674 Old Town, Rhodes © Walter Bibikow/Corbis

p.703 Volcano, Níssyros © Hemis/Alamy

p.716 Astypálea Hóra © IML Image Group Ltd/Alamy

p.740 Byzantine Castle, Mýrina town © Malcolm Lee/Alamy

p.766 Old ladies in Pyrgí © Bob Gibbons/Alamy

p.785 Byzantine-Genoese castle, Mólyvos © photolibrary.com

p.808 Goat Festival, Skýros © Roger Cracknell/Alamy

p.817 Skópelos town, Sporades Islands© James Davis/Corbis

Index

Map entries are in colour.

INDEX

B

I

INDEX

I

INDEX

INDEX

INDEX

H

I

INDEX

L

I INDEX

M

INDEX

INDEX

X

Y

Z

Map symbols

maps are listed in the full index using coloured text

Chapter division boundary	Lighthouse
International boundary	Airport
Motorway	Metro station
Major paved road	Tram stop
Minor paved road	Bus/taxi stop
Unpaved road	Boat
Road under construction	Fuel station
Pedestrianized street	Point of interest
Steps	Internet access
Railway	Information office
Funicular railway	Post office
Tram route	Hospital
Footpath	Parking
Waterway	Accommodation
Ferry route	Campsite
Cable car	Refuge
Wall	Winery
Gate	Ski area
Bridge	Museum
Stone bridge	Castle
Cutting	Tower
Mountains	Archeological site
Peak	Statue/memorial
Mountain pass	Synagogue
Dam	Mosque
Steep slope	Monastery or convent
Crater	Church
Gorge	Stadium
Cave	Building
Waterfall	Church
Spring/spa	Christian cemetery
Marshland	Park
Viewpoint	Beach